# everyWORD
SCRIPTURE | OUTLINE | COMMENTARY

## THE GOSPEL ACCORDING TO JOHN

NEW TESTAMENT | ENGLISH STANDARD VERSION

**LEADERSHIP MINISTRIES WORLDWIDE**
CHATTANOOGA, TN

## everyWORD®—JOHN
## ENGLISH STANDARD VERSION

Copyright © 2019 by LEADERSHIP MINISTRIES WORLDWIDE.

All other Bible study aids, references, indexes, reference materials
Copyright © 1991 by Alpha-Omega Ministries, Inc.

**All rights reserved. No part of this publication may be reproduced, stored in a retrieval system, or transmitted in any form or by any means—electronic, mechanical, photo-copy, recording, or otherwise—without the prior permission of the copyright owners.**

Previous Editions of The Preacher's Outline & Sermon Bible®,
New International Version NT Copyright © 1998
King James Version NT Copyright © 1991, 1996, 2000
by Alpha-Omega Ministries, Inc.

This publication contains The Holy Bible, English Standard Version®, copyright © 2001 by Crossway, a publishing ministry of Good News Publishers. The ESV® text appearing in this publication is reproduced and published by cooperation between Good News Publishers and Leadership Ministries Worldwide and by permission of Good News Publishers. Unauthorized reproduction of this publication is prohibited.

The Holy Bible, English Standard Version (ESV) is adapted from the Revised Standard Version of the Bible, copyright Division of Christian Education of the National Council of the Churches of Christ in the U.S.A. All rights reserved.

English Standard Version USPTO Reg. No. 3026768. English Standard Version ®, ESV® and the ESV® logo are trademarks of Good News Publishers located in Wheaton, Illinois.
Used by permission.

Please address all requests for information or permission to:
Leadership Ministries Worldwide
1928 Central Avenue
Chattanooga, TN 37408
Ph.# (423) 855-2181 FAX (423) 855-8616 E-Mail info@lmw.org
http://www.lmw.org

ISBN Softbound Edition: 978-1-57407-450-5
ISBN Casebound Edition: 978-1-57407-453-6

**LEADERSHIP MINISTRIES WORLDWIDE**
Chattanooga, TN

Printed in the United States of America

# DEDICATED

To all the men and women of the world who preach and teach the Gospel of our Lord Jesus Christ and to the Mercy and Grace of God

&

- Demonstrated to us in Christ Jesus our Lord.

 "In him we have redemption through his blood, the forgiveness of our trespasses, according to the riches of his grace." (Ep.1:7)

- Out of the mercy and grace of God, His Word has flowed. Let every person know that God will have mercy upon him, forgiving and using him to fulfill His glorious plan of salvation.

 "For God so loved the world, that he gave his only Son, that whoever believes in him should not perish but have eternal life. For God did not send his Son into the world to condemn the world, but in order that the world might be saved through him." (Jn.3:16-17)

 "This is good, and it is pleasing in the sight of God our Savior; who desires all men to be saved and to come unto the knowledge of the truth." (1 Ti.2:3-4)

**everyWORD®**

is written for God's servants to use in their study, teaching, and preaching of God's Holy Word . . .

- to share the Word of God with the world.
- to help believers, both ministers and laypersons, in their understanding, preaching, and teaching of God's Word.
- to do everything we possibly can to lead men, women, boys, and girls to give their hearts and lives to Jesus Christ and to secure the eternal life that He offers.
- to do all we can to minister to the needy of the world.
- to give Jesus Christ His proper place, the place the Word gives Him. Therefore, no work of Leadership Ministries Worldwide—no Outline Bible Resources—will ever be personalized.

# CONTENTS

| | |
|---|---|
| Acknowledgments and Bibliography | viii |
| Abbreviations | xii |
| How to Use everyWord® | xiv |
| The Gospel According to John Introduction | 1 |
| Outline of John | 3 |
| Division I. The Witnesses to the Revelation of Jesus Christ, 1:1-51 | 7 |
|    A. Jesus the Living Word: The First Witness of John the Apostle, 1:1-5 | 7 |
|    B. Jesus the Light of the World: The Special Witness of John the Baptist, 1:6-8 | 14 |
|    C. Jesus the Light of the Human Race: The Second Witness of John the Apostle, 1:9-13 | 18 |
|    D. Jesus the Word Made Flesh: The Third Witness of John the Apostle, 1:14-18 | 24 |
|    E. Jesus the Messiah, the Lord: The Second Witness of John the Baptist, 1:19-28 | 31 |
|    F. Jesus the Lamb of God—the Son of God: The Third Witness of John the Baptist, 1:29-34 | 39 |
|    G. Jesus the Messiah, the Christ: The Witness of Andrew, 1:35-42 | 45 |
|    H. Jesus, the One Prophesied: The Witness of Philip, 1:43-45 | 51 |
|    I. Jesus the Son of God, the King of Israel: The Witness of Nathanael, 1:46-49 | 57 |
|    J. Jesus the Son of Man, God's Mediator: The Witness of Jesus Himself, 1:50-51 | 62 |
| Division II. The Revelation of Jesus, the Son of God, 2:1-3:21 | 65 |
|    A. Revelation 1: Jesus' Creative Power, 2:1-11 | 65 |
|    B. Revelation 2: Jesus' Supremacy Over God's House, 2:12-22 | 72 |
|    C. Revelation 3: Jesus Knows All People, 2:23-25 | 78 |
|    D. Revelation 4: The New Birth, 1 3:1-15 | 83 |
|    E. Revelation 5: God's Great Love, 3:16-17 | 92 |
|    F. Revelation 6: Humanity's Condemnation, 3:18-21 | 97 |
| Division III. The Revelation of Jesus, the New Master, 3:22-36 | 103 |
| Division IV. The Revelation of Jesus, the Living Water, 4:1-42 | 112 |
|    A. The Offer of Living Water, 4:1-14 | 112 |
|    B. The Subject of Sin, 4:15-18 | 118 |
|    C. The Subject of Worship, 4:19-24 | 121 |
|    D. The Subject of the Messiah, 4:25-30 | 131 |
|    E. The Subject of Labor for God, 4:31-42 | 135 |
| Division V. The Revelation of Jesus, the Object of Faith, 4:43-54 | 142 |
|    A. The Evidence of Faith, 4:43-45 | 142 |
|    B. The Stages of Faith, 4:46-54 | 147 |
| Division VI. The Revelation of Jesus, the Authority and Power Over Life, 5:1-47 | 153 |
|    A. The Essential Authority: Power to Meet the World's Desperate Needs, 5:1-16 | 153 |
|    B. The Astounding Authority: Equality with God, 5:17-30 | 163 |
|    C. The Five Witnesses to Jesus' Authority and Power, 5:31-39 | 172 |
|    D. The Rejection of Jesus' Claim: Why People Reject Him, 5:40-47 | 179 |
| Division VII. The Revelation of Jesus, the Bread of Life, 6:1-71 | 184 |
|    A. Jesus Feeds Five Thousand: The Kind of Faith Necessary to Meet Human Need, 6:1-15 | 184 |
|    B. Jesus Walks on Water: The Deliverance from Fear, 6:16-21 | 193 |
|    C. The Answer to People's Gnawing Hunger, Their Sense of Discontentment and Emptiness, 6:22-29 | 198 |
|    D. The Bread of Life: The Source of Lasting Fulfillment and Satisfaction, 6:30-36 | 203 |
|    E. The Assurance of the Believer, 6:37-40 | 209 |
|    F. The Way a Person Partakes of the Bread of Life, 6:41-51 | 214 |

| | |
|---|---|
| G. The Results of Partaking of the Bread of Life, 6:52-58 | 219 |
| H. The Reasons Some People Are Offended by Christ, the Bread of Life, 6:59-71 | 224 |

Division VIII. The Responses to the Revelation of Jesus, 7:1-53 — 230
- A. The Response of Jesus' Brothers: Mockery and Unbelief, 7:1-9 — 230
- B. The Response of the Jews: Seeking Yet Questioning, 7:10-19 — 235
- C. The Response of the People: A Charge of Insanity, Yet Still Questioning, 7:20-31 — 241
- D. The Response of the Rulers and Authorities: A Charge of Being a Rabble-Rouser, 7:32-36 — 247
- E. The Great Claim of Jesus and Divided Opinions About Him, 7:37-53 — 251

Division IX. The Revelation of Jesus, the Light of Life, 8:1-9:41 — 257
- A. Humanity's Dark Sinfulness and God's Great Forgiveness, 8:1-11 — 257
- B. Humanity's Need: The Light of the World, 8:12-20 — 263
- C. Humanity's Futile Search for Messiah: The Pursuit of Utopia, the Perfect World, 8:21-24 — 271
- D. Humanity's Tragic Failure to Understand the Light, 8:25-30 — 275
- E. Humanity's Freedom from Sin: Being Liberated Is Conditional, 8:31-32 — 280
- F. Humanity's Enslavement to Sin: Four Proofs 8:33-40 — 284
- G. Humanity's Depravity—Corrupt Birth, 8:41-47 — 290
- H. Humanity's Escape from Death, 8:48-59 — 296
- I. Humanity's Eyes Opened (Part 1): The Mission of Jesus, 9:1-7 — 302
- J. Humanity's Eyes Opened (Part II): The Stages of Spiritual Sight, 9:8-41 — 307

Division X. The Revelation of Jesus, the Shepherd of Life, 10:1-42 — 315
- A. The Shepherd and His Sheep: False vs. True Teachers, 10:1-6 — 315
- B. The Door of the Sheep: The Only Way to God, 10:7-10 — 321
- C. The Good Shepherd: Jesus, the True Savior of the World, 10:11-21 — 326
- D. The Great Shepherd's Claims, 10:22-42 — 333

Division XI. The Revelation of Jesus, the Resurrection and the Life, 11:1-12:11 — 341
- A. The Death of Lazarus and Its Purposes, 11:1-16 — 341
- B. Jesus and Martha: Growth in Faith, 11:17-27 — 348
- C. Jesus and Mary: The People's Real Needs, 11:28-37 — 355
- D. Jesus and Lazarus: Power Over Death, 11:38-46 — 362
- E. Jesus and the Religious Leaders: Unbelief and Opposition, 11:47-57 — 370
- F. Jesus and Reactions to His Revelation: He is the Resurrection and Life, 12:1-11 — 378

Division XII. The Revelation of Jesus, the Glorified Son of Man, 12:12-50 — 385
- A. Jesus Proclaimed as King: The Triumphal Entry, 12:12-19 — 385
- B. Jesus Approached As King: The Misunderstood Messiah, 12:20-36 — 392
- C. Jesus Rejected and Accepted as King, 12:37-50 — 405

Division XIII. The Revelation of Jesus, the Great Minister, and His Legacy, 13:1-16:33 — 415
- A. The Demonstration of Royal Service, 13:1-17 — 415
- B. The Prediction of the Betrayer: A Picture of Apostasy, 13:18-30 — 424
- C. The Departure of Jesus from This World, 13:31-38 — 431
- D. Jesus' Death Delivers Troubled Hearts, 14:1-3 — 438
- E. The Way to God Is Through Jesus Alone, 14:4-7 — 444
- F. The Embodiment of God Is Jesus Himself, 14:8-14 — 450
- G. The Holy Spirit: Who He Is, 14:15-26 — 458
- H. The Source of Peace, Joy, and Security, 14:27-31 — 466
- I. The Relationship of Jesus to the People of the World, 15:1-8 — 471
- J. The Relationship of Jesus to Believers, 15:9-11 — 479
- K. The Relationship of Believers to Believers, 15:12-17 — 484
- L. The Relationship of Believers to the World: Persecution (Part I), 15:18-27 — 489
- M. The Relationship of Believers to Religionists: Persecution (Part II), 16:1-6 — 495
- N. The Work of the Holy Spirit, 16:7-15 — 500
- O. The Resurrection and Its Effects Foretold, 16:16-33 — 507

| | |
|---|---:|
| Division XIV. The Revelation of Jesus, the Great Intercessor, 17:1-26 | 517 |
|     A. Jesus Prayed for Himself, 17:1-8 | 517 |
|     B. Jesus Prayed for His Disciples, 17:9-19 | 523 |
|     C. Jesus Prayed for Future Believers, 17:20-26 | 532 |
| Division XV. The Revelation of Jesus, the Suffering Savior, 18:1-19:42 | 540 |
|     A. The Arrest of Jesus: Absolute Surrender, 18:1-11 | 540 |
|     B. The Jews and Peter: The Cowardly Denial, 18:12-27 | 547 |
|     C. The Trial Before Pilate: Indecisive Compromise, 18:28-19:15 | 556 |
|     D. The Crucifixion: The Major Events at the Cross, 19:16-37 | 568 |
|     E. The Burial: The Conquest of Fear, 19:38-42 | 576 |
| Division XVI. The Revelation of Jesus, the Risen Lord, 20:1-21:25 | 582 |
|     A. Event 1: The Great Discovery—the Empty Tomb, 20:1-10 | 582 |
|     B. Event 2: The Great Recognition—Jesus Appears to Mary, 20:11-18 | 588 |
|     C. Event 3: The Great Charter of the Church—Jesus Appears to the Disciples, 20:19-23 | 594 |
|     D. Event 4: The Great Conviction—Thomas' Confession, 20:24-29 | 602 |
|     E. Event 5: The Great Purpose of the Signs (Wonderful Works) of Jesus, 20:30-31 | 609 |
|     F. Event 6: The Great Reality of Jesus' Resurrection Body, 21:1-14 | 611 |
|     G. Event 7: The Great Question About a Disciple's Love and Devotion, 21:15-17 | 619 |
|     H. Event 8: The Great Call to Total Commitment, 21:18-25 | 625 |
| Outline and Subject Index | 633 |

# ACKNOWLEDGMENTS AND BIBLIOGRAPHY

Every child of God is precious to the Lord and deeply loved. And every child, as a servant of the Lord, touches the lives of those who come in contact with them or their ministries. The writing ministries of the following servants have touched this work, and we are grateful that God brought their writings our way. We hereby acknowledge their ministry to us, being fully aware that there are so many others down through the years whose writings have touched our lives and who deserve mention, but whose names have faded from our memory. May our wonderful Lord continue to bless the ministries of these dear servants—and the ministries of us all—as we diligently labor to reach the world for Christ and to meet the desperate needs of those who suffer so much.

**THE GREEK SOURCES**

Balz, Horst and Schneider, Gerhard M. *Exegetical Dictionary of the New Testament.* Grand Rapids: Wm. B. Eerdmans Publishing Co., 2003. Via Wordsearch digital edition.

Black, David Alan. *Linguistics for Students of New Testament Greek.* Grand Rapids: Baker Publishing Group, 1988.

Burton, Ernest De Witt. *Syntax of the Moods and Tenses in New Testament Greek.* Grand Rapids: Kregel Publications, 1976. Via Wordsearch digital edition.

Cotterell, Peter and Turner, Max. *Linguistics and Biblical Interpretation.* Downers Grove, IL: InterVarsity Press, 1989.

Davis, William Hersey. *Beginner's Grammar of the Greek New Testament.* New York: Harper & Row, 1923.

*Expositor's Greek Testament,* Edited by W. Robertson Nicoll. Grand Rapids: Wm. B. Eerdmans Publishing Co., 1970.

Gilbrant, Thoralf and Harris, Ralph W. *The Complete Biblical Library Greek-English Dictionary.* Springfield, MO: World Library Press, Inc., 1989. Via Wordsearch digital edition.

Guthrie, George H. and Duval, J. Scott. *Biblical Greek Exegesis: A Graded Approach to Learning Intermediate and Advanced Greek.* Grand Rapids: Zondervan, 1998.

Harris, Murray J. *Exegetical Guide to the Greek New Testament: John.* Nashville: B & H Academic, 2015.

Kittel, Gerhard and Friedrich, Gerhard. *Theological Dictionary of the New Testament.* Grand Rapids: Wm. B. Eerdmans Publishing Co., 1977.

Kostenberger, Andreas J., Merkle, Benjamin L., and Plummer, Robert L. *Going Deeper with New Testament Greek: An Intermediate Study of the Grammar and Syntax of the New Testament.* Nashville: B & H Academic, 2016.

Kubo, Sakae. *A Reader's Greek-English Lexicon of the New Testament and a Beginner's Guide for the Translation of New Testament Greek.* Grand Rapids: Zondervan, 1975.

Moulton, Harold K., ed. *The Analytical Greek Lexicon Revised.* Grand Rapids: Zondervan, 1977.

*Practical Word Studies in the New Testament.* Chattanooga, TN: Leadership Ministries Worldwide, 1998. Via Wordsearch digital edition.

Robertson, A.T. *A Grammar of the Greek New Testament in the Light of Historical Research.* New York: George H. Doran Company, 1915.

_____. A.T. *A Short Grammar of the Greek New Testament.* New York: A.C. Armstrong & Son, 1909.

_____. A.T. *Word Pictures in the New Testament.* Nashville, TN: Broadman Press, 1930.

Staats, Gary. *Christological Greek Grammar.* Austin, TX: Wordsearch Bible Software, 2001.

Strong, James. *Strong's Greek and Hebrew Dictionary of the Bible.* Public Domain. Via Wordsearch digital edition.

Thayer, Joseph Henry. *Greek-English Lexicon of the New Testament.* New York: American Book Co, n.d.

Vincent, Marvin R. *Word Studies in the New Testament.* Grand Rapids: Wm. B. Eerdmans Publishing Co., 1969.

Vine, W.E. *Expository Dictionary of New Testament Words.* Old Tappan, NJ: Fleming H. Revell Co., n.d.

Wallace, Daniel B. *Greek Grammar Beyond the Basics: An Exegetical Syntax of New Testament with Scripture, Subject, and Greek Word Indexes.* Grand Rapids: Zondervan. 1997.

Wuest, Kenneth S. *Word Studies in the Greek New Testament.* Grand Rapids: Wm. B. Eerdmans Publishing Co., 1966.

Wallace, Daniel B. *Greek Grammar Beyond the Basics: An Exegetical Syntax of the New Testament*. Grand Rapids: Zondervan, 1996.

Young, Richard A. *Intermediate New Testament Greek: A Linguistic and Exegetical Approach*. Nashville: Broadman & Holman, 1994.

Zodhiates, Spiros. *The Complete Word Study Dictionary: New Testament*. Chattanooga, TN: AMG Publishers, 1992. Via Wordsearch digital edition.

## THE REFERENCE WORKS

Berkhof, Louis. *Principles of Biblical Interpretation*. Grand Rapids: Baker Book House, 1950.

Blomberg, Craig. *The Historical Reliability of the Gospels*. Downers Grove, IL: InterVarsity, 1987.

Bruce, F. F. *New Testament History*. New York: Doubleday, 1983. Via Wordsearch digital edition.

Bryant, T. Alton, ed. *The New Compact Bible Dictionary*. Grand Rapids: Zondervan Publishing House, 1967.

Butler, Trent C., ed. *Holman Bible Dictionary*. Nashville: Holman Bible Pub., 1991.

Carson, D. A. and Moo, Douglas. *An Introduction to the New Testament*. 2nd ed. Grand Rapids: Zondervan, 2005.

*Cruden's Complete Concordance of the Old & New Testament*. Philadelphia: The John C. Winston Co., 1930.

Easton, Matthew G. *Illustrated Bible Dictionary*. Public Domain. Via Wordsearch digital edition.

Edersheim, Alfred. *The Life and Times of Jesus the Messiah*. Peabody, MA: Hendrickson Publishers. 1993. Via Wordsearch digital edition.

Evans, Craig A. and Porter, Stanley E. *Dictionary of New Testament Background*. Downers Grove, IL: InterVarsity Press, 2000. Via Wordsearch digital edition.

Gromacki, Robert. *New Testament Survey*. Grand Rapids: Baker Book House, 1974.

Gundry, Robert. *Survey of the New Testament*. 4th ed. Grand Rapids: Zondervan, 2003.

Guthrie, Donald. *New Testament Introduction*. rev. ed. Downers Grove, IL: InterVarsity, 1981, 1064 pp.

Habermas, Gary R. *The Historical Jesus: Ancient Evidence for the Life of Christ*. Joplin, MO: College Press, 1996. Via Wordsearch digital edition.

Hiebert, D. Edmond. *An Introduction to the New Testament*. 3 vols. Chicago: Moody Press, 1975-77.

Jensen, Irving L. *Jensen's Survey of the New Testament*. Chicago: Moody Press, 1981.

*Josephus' Complete Works*. Grand Rapids: Kregel Publications, 1981.

Kaiser, Walter, Jr., and Silva, Moises. *An Introduction to Biblical Hermeneutics: The Search for Meaning*. Grand Rapids: Zondervan, 1994.

Klein, William W., Blomberg, Craig L., and Hubbard, Robert, Jr. *Introduction to Biblical Interpretation*. Nashville: W Publishing Group, 1993.

Larkin, Clarence. *Rightly Dividing the Word*. Philadelphia, PA: The Rev. Clarence Larkin Est., 1921.

Lockyer, Herbert. Series of books, including his books on *All the Men, Women, Miracles, and Parables of the Bible*. Grand Rapids: Zondervan Publishing House, 1958-1967.

Marshall, I. Howard. ed. *New Testament Interpretation*. Grand Rapids: Wm. B. Eerdmans Publishing Co., 1977, 406 pp.

Martin, Ralph. *New Testament Foundations*. 2 vols. Grand Rapids: Wm. B. Eerdmans Publishing Co., 1975-78.

McGarvey, John William. *Lands of the Bible: A Geographical and Topographical Description of Palestine*. Public Domain. Via Wordsearch digital edition.

Morris, Leon. *New Testament Theology*. Grand Rapids: Zondervan, 1996.

*Nave's Topical Bible*. Nashville, TN: The Southwestern Co., n.d.

Orr, James. *The International Standard Bible Encyclopedia*. Grand Rapids: Wm. B. Eerdmans Publishing Co., 1939. Via Wordsearch digital edition.

Ramm, Bernard. *Protestant Biblical Interpretation: A Textbook of Hermeneutics*. Grand Rapids: Baker Book House, 1970.

Tenney, Merrill C. *Genius of the Gospels*. Grand Rapids: Wm. B. Eerdmans Publishing Co., 1951, 124 pp.

_____. *New Testament Survey*. Grand Rapids: Wm. B. Eerdmans Publishing Co., 1961.

*The Amplified New Testament*. (Scripture Quotations are from the Amplified New Testament, Copyright 1954, 1958, 1987 by the Lockman Foundation. Used by permission.)

*The Four Translation New Testament*. (Including King James, New American Standard, Williams—New Testament in the Language of the People, Beck—New Testament in the Language of Today.) Minneapolis, MN: World Wide Publications.

*The New Thompson Chain Reference Bible*. Indianapolis: B.B. Kirkbride Bible Co., 1964.

Unger, Merrill F., Harrison R. K., (ed.). *The New Unger's Bible Dictionary*. Chicago: Moody Publishers, 2006. Via Wordsearch digital edition.

Water, Mark. *AMG's Encyclopedia of Jesus' Life & Time*. Chattanooga, TN: AMG Publishers, 2006. Via Wordsearch digital edition.

Willmington, Harold L. *Willmington's Bible Handbook*. Wheaton, IL: Tyndale House, 1997.

_____. *Willmington's Guide to the Bible*. Wheaton, IL: Tyndale House, 1981.

## THE COMMENTARIES

Barclay, William. *Daily Study Bible Series*. Philadelphia, PA: Westminster Press, Began in 1953.

Barnes, Albert. *Barnes' Notes on the New Testament*. Grand Rapids: Kregel Classics, 1962. Via Wordsearch digital edition.

Barton, Bruce, ed. *Life Application Bible Commentary*. Carol Stream, IL: Tyndale House Publishers, Inc., various dates. Via Wordsearch digital edition.

Baxter, J. Sidlow. *Explore the Book*. Grand Rapids: Zondervan, 1960.

Boice, James Montgomery. *Expositional Commentary* (27 volumes). Grand Rapids: Baker Publishing Group, various dates. Via Wordsearch digital edition.

Bruce, F.F. *The Gospel of John: Introduction, Exposition, Notes*. Grand Rapids: Wm. B. Eerdmans Publishing Co., 1994.

_____. *The Epistle to the Ephesians*. Westwood, NJ: Fleming H. Revell Co., 1968.

_____. *Epistle to the Hebrews*. Grand Rapids, MI: Wm. B. Eerdmans Publishing Co., 1964.

_____. *The Epistles of John*. Old Tappan, NJ: Fleming H. Revell Co., 1970.

Carson, D.A. *The Gospel According to John*. Grand Rapids: Wm. B. Eerdmans Publishing Co., 1991

Criswell, W.A. *Expository Sermons on Revelation*. Grand Rapids, MI: Zondervan Publishing House, 1962-66.

Dods, Marcus. *The Gospel of St. John*. London: Hodder & Stoughton, 1899.

Elwell, Walter A. *Baker Commentary on the Bible*. Grand Rapids: Baker Academic, 2001. Via Wordsearch digital edition.

Gaebelein, Arno. *The Gospel of John*. New York: Our Hope Publications, 1925.

Gilbrant, Thoralf and Harris, Ralph W. *The Complete Biblical Library New Testament Commentary*. Springfield, MO: World Library Press. 1992. Via Wordsearch digital edition.

Greene, Oliver. *The Epistles of John*. Greenville, SC: The Gospel Hour, Inc., 1966.

_____. *The Epistles of Paul the Apostle to the Hebrews*. Greenville, SC: The Gospel Hour, Inc., 1965.

_____. *The Epistles of Paul the Apostle to Timothy & Titus*. Greenville, SC: The Gospel Hour, Inc., 1964.

_____. *The Revelation Verse by Verse Study*. Greenville, SC: The Gospel Hour, Inc., 1963.

_____. *The Gospel According to John*. Greenville, SC: The Gospel Hour, 1966.

Harrison, Paul W. *The Light That Lighteth Every Man*. Grand Rapids: Wm. B. Eerdmans Publishing Co., 1960.

Hendriksen, William. *John*. Grand Rapids: Baker Publishing Group, 2002

Henry, Matthew. *Commentary on the Whole Bible*. Old Tappan, NJ: Fleming H. Revell Co.

Hodge, Charles. *Exposition on Romans & on Corinthians*. Grand Rapids: Wm. B. Eerdmans Publishing Co., 1972-1973.

Holman Bible editorial staff. *Holman New Testament Commentary*. Nashville: Holman Reference, 2001.

Hughes, R. Kent. *John: That You May Believe*. Wheaton, IL: Crossway Books, 1999.

Ironside, H.A. *Addresses on the Gospel of John*. New York: Loizeaux Brothers, 1942.

Jamieson, Robert; Fausset, A. R. and Brown, David. *Jamieson, Fausset & Brown's Commentary on the Whole Bible*. Public Domain. Via Wordsearch digital edition.

Kostenberger, Andreas J. *John*. Grand Rapids: Baker Academic, 2004.

Ladd, George Eldon. *A Commentary On the Revelation of John*. Grand Rapids: Wm. B. Eerdmans Publishing Co., 1972-1973.

Lenski, R.C.H. *Preaching on John*. Grand Rapids: Baker Book House, 1973.

Leupold, H.C. *Exposition of Daniel*. Grand Rapids: Baker Book House, 1969.

MacArthur, John. *The MacArthur New Testament Commentary* (34 volumes). Chicago: Moody Publishers, 2015 (box set edition). Via Wordsearch digital edition.

Macaulay, J.C. *Devotional Studies in St. John's Gospel*. Grand Rapids: Wm. B. Eerdmans Publishing Co., 1954.

MacDonald, William. *Believer's Bible Commentary*. Nashville: Thomas Nelson, 1995.

MacLaren, Alexander. *Expositions of the Holy Scriptures* (17 volumes). Grand Rapids: Baker Publishing Group, 1988.

McGee, J. Vernon. *Through the Bible* (5 volumes). Nashville: Thomas Nelson, 1990. Via Wordsearch digital edition.

Meyer, F.B. *The Gospel of John*. Grand Rapids: Zondervan Publishing House, 1950.

Morris, Leon. *The Gospel According to John*. Grand Rapids: Wm. B. Eerdmans Publishing Co., 1971.

Mounce, Robert. *The Expositor's Bible Commentary, Revised Edition, Volume 10: Luke-Acts*. Grand Rapids: Zondervan, 2007.

Murray, Andrew. *The True Vine*. Chicago: Moody Press, nd.

Newell, William R. *Hebrews, Verse by Verse*. Chicago: Moody Press, 1947.

Pfeiffer, Charles F and Harrison, Everett F., eds. *The New Testament & Wycliffe Bible Commentary*. New York: The Iverson Associates, 1971. Produced for *Moody Monthly*. Chicago: Moody Press, 1962.

Phillips, John. *Exploring the Gospel of John: An Expository Commentary*. Grand Rapids: Kregel, 1989.

Pink, Arthur W. *Exposition of the Gospel of John*. Grand Rapids: Zondervan, 1968. Via Wordsearch digital edition.

Poole, Matthew. *Matthew Poole's Commentary on the Holy Bible*. Peabody, MA: Hendrickson Publishers, 1985.

Rainsford, Marcus. *Our Lord Prays for His Own: Thoughts on John 17*. Chicago: Moody Press, 1950.

Rice, John R. *The Son of God: A Verse-by-Verse Commentary on the Gospel According to John*. Murfreesboro, TN: Sword of the Lord Publishers, 1976.

Strauss, Lehman. *Devotional Studies in Galatians & Ephesians*. Neptune, NJ: Loizeaux Brothers, 1957.

_____. *Devotional Studies in Philippians*. Neptune, NJ: Loizeaux Brothers, 1959.

_____. *James, Your Brother*. Neptune, NJ: Loizeaux Brothers, 1956.

_____. *The Book of the Revelation*. Neptune, NJ: Loizeaux Brothers, 1964.

Tasker, RVG. *The Gospel According to St. John* (Tyndale New Testament Commentaries). Grand Rapids: Wm. B. Eerdmans Publishing Co., 1960.

*The Pulpit Commentary*, Edited by H.D.M. Spence & Joseph S. Exell. Grand Rapids: Wm. B. Eerdmans Publishing Co., 1950.

Thomas, W.H. Griffith. *The Apostle John: Studies in His Life and Writing*. Grand Rapids: Wm. B. Eerdmans Publishing Co., 1946.

_____. *Hebrews, A Devotional Commentary*. Grand Rapids: Wm. B. Eerdmans Publishing Co., 1970.

_____. *Outline Studies in the Acts of the Apostles*. Grand Rapids: Wm. B. Eerdmans Publishing Co., 1956.

_____. *St. Paul's Epistle to the Romans*. Grand Rapids: Wm. B. Eerdmans Publishing Co., 1946.

_____. *Studies in Colossians & Philemon*. Grand Rapids: Baker Book House, 1973.

*Tyndale New Testament Commentaries*. Grand Rapids: Wm. B. Eerdmans Publishing Co., Began in 1958.

Various authors. *The IVP New Testament Commentary Series* (20 volumes). Downers Grove, IL: InterVarsity Press, 1991-2009. Via Wordsearch digital edition.

Various authors. *The New American Commentary* (43 volumes). Nashville: Broadman & Holman, various dates. Via Wordsearch digital edition.

Walker, Thomas. *Acts of the Apostles*. Chicago: Moody Press, 1965.

Walvoord, John. *The Thessalonian Epistles*. Grand Rapids: Zondervan Publishing House, 1973.

_____ and Roy B. Zuck, eds. *The Bible Knowledge Commentary New Testament: An Exposition of the Scriptures by Dallas Seminary Faculty*. Wheaton, IL: Victor Books. Via Wordsearch digital edition.

Witherington, Ben III. *John's Wisdom: A Commentary on the Fourth Gospel*. Louisville, KY: Westminster John Knox Press, 1995.

Wiersbe, Warren W. *The Bible Exposition Commentary*. Colorado Springs, CO: David C. Cook, 2004. Via Wordsearch digital edition.

# ABBREVIATIONS

| | | | | | |
|---:|:---:|:---|---:|:---:|:---|
| & | = | and | O.T. | = | Old Testament |
| bc. | = | because | p./pp. | = | page/pages |
| concl. | = | conclusion | pt. | = | point |
| cp. | = | compare | quest. | = | question |
| ct. | = | contrast | rel. | = | religion |
| e.g. | = | for example | rgt. | = | righteousness |
| f. | = | following | thru | = | through |
| illust. | = | illustration | v./vv. | = | verse/verses |
| N.T. | = | New Testament | vs. | = | versus |

## THE BOOKS OF THE OLD TESTAMENT

| Book | Abbreviation | Chapters | Book | Abbreviation | Chapters |
|---|---|---|---|---|---|
| GENESIS | Gen. or Ge. | 50 | Ecclesiastes | Eccl. or Ec. | 12 |
| Exodus | Ex. | 40 | The Song of Solomon | S. of Sol. or Song | 8 |
| Leviticus | Lev. or Le. | 27 | | | |
| Numbers | Num. or Nu. | 36 | Isaiah | Is. | 66 |
| Deuteronomy | Dt. or De. | 34 | Jeremiah | Jer. or Je. | 52 |
| Joshua | Josh. or Jos. | 24 | Lamentations | Lam. | 5 |
| Judges | Judg. or Jud. | 21 | Ezekiel | Ezk. or Eze. | 48 |
| Ruth | Ruth or Ru. | 4 | Daniel | Dan. or Da. | 12 |
| 1 Samuel | 1 Sam. or 1 S. | 31 | Hosea | Hos. or Ho. | 14 |
| 2 Samuel | 2 Sam. or 2 S. | 24 | Joel | Joel | 3 |
| 1 Kings | 1 Ki. or 1 K. | 22 | Amos | Amos or Am. | 9 |
| 2 Kings | 2 Ki. or 2 K. | 25 | Obadiah | Obad. or Ob. | 1 |
| 1 Chronicles | 1 Chron. or 1 Chr. | 29 | Jonah | Jon. or Jona. | 4 |
| 2 Chronicles | 2 Chron. or 2 Chr. | 36 | Micah | Mic. or Mi. | 7 |
| Ezra | Ezra or Ezr. | 10 | Nahum | Nah. or Na. | 3 |
| Nehemiah | Neh. or Ne. | 13 | Habakkuk | Hab. | 3 |
| Esther | Est. | 10 | Zephaniah | Zeph. or Zep. | 3 |
| Job | Job or Jb. | 42 | Haggai | Hag. | 2 |
| Psalms | Ps. | 150 | Zechariah | Zech. or Zec. | 14 |
| Proverbs | Pr. | 31 | Malachi | Mal. | 4 |

## THE BOOKS OF THE NEW TESTAMENT

| Book | Abbreviation | Chapters | Book | Abbreviation | Chapters |
|---|---|---|---|---|---|
| MATTHEW | Mt. | 28 | 1 Timothy | 1 Tim. or 1 Ti. | 6 |
| Mark | Mk. | 16 | 2 Timothy | 2 Tim. or 2 Ti. | 4 |
| Luke | Lk. or Lu. | 24 | Titus | Tit. | 3 |
| John | Jn. | 21 | Philemon | Phile. or Phm. | 1 |
| Acts | Acts or Ac. | 28 | Hebrews | Heb. or He. | 13 |
| Romans | Ro. | 16 | James | Jas. or Js. | 5 |
| 1 Corinthians | 1 Cor. or 1 Co. | 16 | 1 Peter | 1 Pt. or 1 Pe. | 5 |
| 2 Corinthians | 2 Cor. or 2 Co. | 13 | 2 Peter | 2 Pt. or 2 Pe. | 3 |
| Galatians | Gal. or Ga. | 6 | 1 John | 1 Jn. | 5 |
| Ephesians | Eph. or Ep. | 6 | 2 John | 2 Jn. | 1 |
| Philippians | Ph. | 4 | 3 John | 3 Jn. | 1 |
| Colossians | Col. | 4 | Jude | Jude | 1 |
| 1 Thessalonians | 1 Th. | 5 | Revelation | Rev. or Re. | 22 |
| 2 Thessalonians | 2 Th. | 3 | | | |

# HOW TO USE
## everyWORD®

❶ SUBJECT HEADING

❷ MAJOR POINTS

❸ SUBPOINTS & SCRIPTURE

❹ COMMENTARY

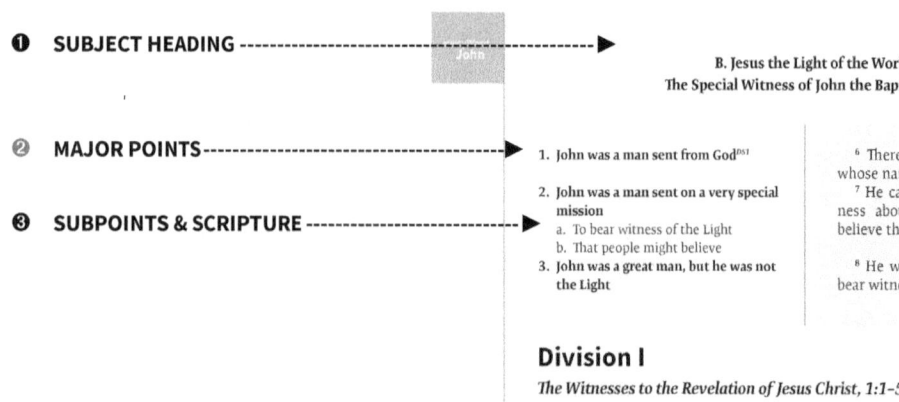

❶ Glance at the **Subject Heading**. Think about it for a moment.

❷ Glance at the **Subject Heading** again, and then the **Major Points** (1, 2, 3, etc.). Do this several times, reviewing them together while quickly grasping the overall subject.

❸ Glance at **both** the **Major Points** and **Subpoints** together while reading the **Scripture**. Do this slower than Step 2. Note how these points sit directly beside the related verse and simply restate what the Scripture is saying—in Outline form.

❹ Next read the **Commentary. Note** that the *Major Point Numbers* in the Outline match those in the Commentary. When applicable, a small raised number (**DS1, DS2, etc.**) at the end of a Subject Heading or Outline Point directs you to a related Deeper Study (shown on opposite page) in the Commentary.

❺ and ❻ Finally, read the **Thoughts** and **Support Scriptures** (shown on opposite page).

The **everyWORD®** series and study system contains everything you need for sermon preparation and Bible study:

1. The **Subject Heading** describes the overall theme of the passage and is located directly above the Outline and Scripture (keyed *alphabetically*).
2. **Major Points** are keyed with an outline *number* guiding you to related commentary.
3. **Subpoints** explain and clarify the Scripture as needed.
4. **Commentary** is fully researched and developed for every point.

xiv

John (Lk.1:13). The name *John* means *gracious*. John was a man sent forth with a name to match his message: *God's grace* is now to enter upon the scene of world history.

> John answered, "A person cannot receive even one thing unless it is given him from heaven." (Jn.3:27)
>
> What is man, that you make so much of him, and that you set your heart on him? (Jb.7:17)
>
> What is man that you are mindful of him, and the son of man that you care for him? (Ps.8:4)
>
> Do you not know? Do you not hear? Has it not been told you from the beginning? Have you not understood from the foundations of the earth? It is he [God] who sits above the circle of the earth, and its inhabitants are like grasshoppers; who stretches out the heavens like a curtain, and spreads them like a tent to dwell in. (Is.40:21-22)

**THOUGHT 1.** Like John, we too, as believers, are sent by God to bear witness of Jesus Christ. Note three significant points about the servants and messengers of God:

- First, the servants and messengers of God are not sent forth by another person, but by God. We are sent forth as the ambassadors of God.
- Second, God's messengers are sent forth *from* God, from the very side and heart of God.
- Third, as God's messengers, we have received the highest of all callings and missions, the calling of telling the world about Christ and the mission of bringing others into a saving relationship with Christ. This is an enormous responsibility, and we must never lose sight of the sobering fact that we are accountable to God Himself for our faithfulness to this holy task.

◄------- ❺ **THOUGHTS**

> "You did not choose me, but I chose you and appointed you that you should go and bear fruit and that your fruit should abide, so that whatever you ask the Father in my name, he may give it to you." (Jn.15:16)
>
> Not that we are sufficient in ourselves to claim anything as coming from us, but our sufficiency is from God, who has made us sufficient to be ministers of a new covenant, not of the letter but of the Spirit. For the letter kills, but the Spirit gives life. (2 Co.3:5-6)
>
> All this is from God, who through Christ reconciled us to himself and gave us the ministry of reconciliation; that is, in Christ God was reconciling the world to himself, not counting their trespasses against them, and entrusting to us the message of reconciliation. Therefore, we are ambassadors for Christ, God making his appeal through us. We implore you on behalf of Christ, be reconciled to God. (2 Co.5:18-20)
>
> Of this gospel I was made a minister according to the gift of God's grace, which was given me by the working of his power. (Ep.3:7)
>
> I thank him who has given me strength, Christ Jesus our Lord, because he judged me faithful, appointing me to his service. (1 Ti.1:12)

◄------- ❻ **SUPPORT SCRIPTURE**

**DEEPER STUDY # 1**

(1:6) **Sent—Apostle—Commission:** *Sent* (apestalmenos) means to send out; to commission as a representative, an ambassador, an envoy. Three things are true of the person sent from God.
1. He belongs to God, who has sent him out.
2. He is commissioned to be sent out.
3. He possesses all the authority and power of God, who has sent him out.

◄------- ❼ **DEEPER STUDY**

**2 John was a man sent on a very special mission.**

Two Old Testament prophets foretold John's special mission and purpose. Both Isaiah and Malachi prophesied that John would prepare the way of the Lord, who is the embodiment

1:7

⁷ He came as a witness, to bear witness about the light, that all might believe through him.

◄------- ❽ **SCRIPTURE CALLOUTS**

---

5. **Thoughts** help apply the Scripture to daily life.
6. **Support Scripture** provides one or more Bible verses that correspond to the Major Points and Subpoints.
7. **Deeper Studies** provide in-depth discussions of key words or phrases.
8. **Scripture Callouts** repeat segments of Scripture used in the Scripture and Outline sections below the Subject Headings

*"Woe to me, if I do not preach the gospel!"*
(1 Co.9:16)

# THE GOSPEL ACCORDING TO JOHN

## INTRODUCTION

**AUTHOR**: John, the Apostle, the son of Zebedee (see note—Mk.3:17. Also see Introductory Notes—1 John; Revelation for more discussion.)

Irenaeus, bishop of Lyons in A.D. 177, summarizes the testimony of the early church: "John the disciple of the Lord who reclined on his breast and himself issued the Gospel at Ephesus."[1] Tradition says that John spent the latter years in Ephesus preaching, teaching, and writing. At some point he was exiled to the Isle of Patmos during the reign of the Roman emperor, Domitian.

1. John was one of the very first disciples of Jesus (Jn.1:35, 39).
2. John and James were either partners with their father or worked for their father in a large fishing business (Lu.5:10).
3. John and James left everything to follow Christ (Mt.4:21-22).
4. John, along with Peter and James, comprised the inner circle of disciples, a group that was with Christ on very special occasions. (See the Transfiguration, Mt.17:1f; Gethsemane, Mt.26:36f. See Mk.5:37-43.)
5. John is called the "beloved disciple" because he seems to have been especially close to Christ and because he stresses love so much in his writings. He was a close companion of Peter (see Lu.5:10; Jn.19:26; 21:20, 23; Ac.4:13).
6. John was the disciple to whom Jesus committed the care of his mother (Jn.19:26-27).
7. John is said by Paul to be one of the three "pillars" of the church (Ga.2:9).

**DATE**: uncertain. Probably A.D. 80-95.

John lived at least until the reign of the Roman emperor Trajan, according to Irenaeus. Trajan's reign began in A.D. 98. Clement of Alexandria, who died in A.D. 212, said: "Last of all; John, perceiving that the external facts had been made plain in the Gospels, being urged by his friends and inspired by the Spirit, composed a spiritual Gospel." Fragments of the Gospel were discovered in Egypt in 1925. These fragments were dated in the first half of the second century. This would mean John wrote the Gospel in the first century.

This much is known. John was a young man when called by Jesus, and the early church fathers say that John's Gospel was the last Gospel written. All this points to a late date somewhere in the latter years of John's life; however, John's exact age would have had a bearing as to when it was written. He probably would have been unable to write beyond a certain age because of feebleness.

A moving picture is painted of John by Jerome's *Commentary on the Epistle to the Galatians*. "When he tarried at Ephesus to extreme old age, and could only with difficulty be carried to the church in the arms of his disciples, and was unable to give utterance to many words, he used to say no more at their several meetings than this, 'Little children, love one another.' At length the disciples and fathers who were there, wearied with hearing always the same words, said, 'Master, why dost thou always say this?' 'It is the Lord's command,' was his worthy reply, 'and if this alone be done, it is enough.'"[2]

**TO WHOM WRITTEN**: John writes to the lost (3:16), the unbelieving (20:31), the new believers (1:50-51; 15:11; 16:33), the philosopher (1:1), and the theologian (1:12-14).

**PURPOSE**: "These are written that you may believe that Jesus is the Christ, the Son of God, and that by believing, you may have life in His name" (Jn.20:31). This is John's clearly stated purpose for writing. However, there is a secondary purpose. The Gospel refutes almost any heresy that might arise in any generation.

---

1 RVG Tasker. *The Gospel According to St. John*. "Tyndale New Testament Commentaries." (Grand Rapids, MI: Wm. B. Eerdmans Publishing Co., 1960), p.17.

2 Tasker, p.18.

1. To those who deny Christ's deity, John argues: He is the Son of God, the very Word of God Himself (1:1-5; 7:1f; etc.)

2. To those who deny Jesus' humanity, John argues: He is the Word become flesh, the very flesh which must be experienced (1:14f; 6:31f; etc.)

3. To those who continue to look for a human messiah and an earthly utopia, John argues: He is the Messiah, the Savior of the world, the very One who had been promised by God from the beginning of time (1:1-51, etc.)

**SPECIAL FEATURES:**

1. *John is The Gospel of Simplicity.* John used the simplest language and the most pure Greek possible. The Gospel serves as a first reader for many Greek students.

2. *John is The Gospel of Revelation.* The stress and compulsion of John is to show that Jesus Christ is the very revelation of God Himself. A quick glance at the outline clearly shows this.

3. *John is The Gospel of the Messiah.* John shows time and again that the Old Testament prophecies find their fulfillment in Jesus. However, there is a unique point in this that differs somewhat from the Synoptic Gospels. John shows that the salvation brought by Jesus is the very climax of Jewish religion. Jesus Himself is the fulfillment of the blessings promised Israel, the substance and truth, the symbolic meaning of the great Jewish festivals.

Jesus claims the Messianic right to secure disciples (1:35-51); to cleanse the temple (2:13-22); to associate and converse with Samaritans (4:1f; esp.25-26); to work on the Sabbath, overriding the religious prohibitions (5:1-47; esp. 17f; 7:1-53); to feed the people even as Moses, and to claim that He Himself is the very Bread of Life (6:1-14, 22-71; esp., 31f); to forgive sins (8:1-11); and many, many other claims. He dramatically pictures His Messianic claim with the triumphal entry (12:12f).

4. *John is The Gospel of Redemption.* This redemption is centered in the cross and death of Jesus Christ. He is "the (sacrificial) Lamb of God, who takes away the sin of the world" (1:29). His passion is the hour toward which His whole life is moving (2:4; 7:7, 8, 30; 12:23; 17:1). His own flesh and blood is to be *eaten*, that is, *partaken of*, if men are to have life (6:33-53). He compares His death to a grain of wheat that must fall into the ground before it bears fruit (12:24). He is to lay down His life for His sheep (10:11). He draws all men to Himself—but it is only by being lifted up on the cross (12:32-33). He is to sacrifice Himself that others might be set apart unto God (17:19).

5. *John is The Gospel of Jesus' Humanity.* John shows Jesus weary and thirsty (4:6-8, 31); spitting on the ground (9:6); weeping at the death of a dear friend, Lazarus (11:35); troubled because He is to die (12:27); disgusted with His betrayer (13:21); burning with thirst while dying (19:28); and having normal blood and water flowing through His body (19:34). John stresses this point by proclaiming that Jesus is the Son of Man (1:51; 5:27; 6:53; 12:23; 13:31).

6. *John is The Gospel of the Word.* John shows Jesus to be the very Word of God. By this he means that Jesus is everything God ever wanted to say to man. God has done more than speak what He wanted to say; God has pictured what He wanted to say in the very life of Jesus. Jesus is the expression, the thought, the idea, the picture of what God wanted to say to man. The Word of God has become flesh. (See note—Jn.1:1.)

7. *John is The Gospel of 'I Am,'* of God Himself, of Yahweh, Jehovah. The words "I Am" are extremely important to Jewish history. It is the great name of God revealed to Moses at the burning bush (Ex.3:13-15). And John shows Jesus revealing Himself as the "I Am" at least ten times. (See note—Jn.6:20.)

8. *John is The Gospel of Signs.* John records eight miracles of Jesus, six of which are reported only in this Gospel. What John does is select representative examples that point and show that Jesus is the Son of God. The miracles, he says, were not done to amaze people. They were performed as signs of His deity and godly powers (see note—Jn.2:23). These signs are: the water turned into wine (2:1-11); the healing of the nobleman's son (4:46-54); the healing of the man at the pool (5:1-9); the healing of the man born blind (9:1-7); the raising of Lazarus (11:1f); and the second netting of fish (21:1-6).

9. *John is The Gospel of the Holy Spirit.* John gives the fullest teaching of Jesus on the Holy Spirit among the Gospel writers (14:16, 26; 15:26; 16:7-8, 13-15).

# OUTLINE OF JOHN

**everyWORD®** is *unique*. It differs from all other study Bibles and sermon resource materials in that every passage and subject is outlined right beside the Scripture. When you choose any subject below and turn to the reference, you have not only the Scripture, but also an outline of the Scripture and subject *already prepared for you—verse by verse*.

For a quick example, choose one of the subjects below and turn over to the Scripture. You should find this system to be a marvelous help for more organized and streamlined study.

In addition, every point of the Scripture and Outline is *fully developed in a* Commentary section with supporting Scripture at the end of each point. Again, this arrangement makes sermon or lesson preparation much simpler and more efficient.

Note something else: The subjects of *John* have titles that are both *biblical* and *practical*. The practical titles are often more appealing to people. This benefit is clearly seen for use on billboards, bulletins, church newsletters, and so forth.

A suggestion: For the *quickest* overview of *John*, first read all the Division titles (I, II, III, etc.), then come back and read all the individual outline titles.

## OUTLINE OF JOHN

I. **THE WITNESSES TO THE REVELATION OF JESUS CHRIST, 1:1–51**
   A. Jesus the Living Word: The First Witness of John the Apostle, 1:1-5
   B. Jesus the Light of the World: The Special Witness of John the Baptist, 1:6-8
   C. Jesus the Light of the Human Race: The Second Witness of John the Apostle, 1:9-13
   D. Jesus the Word Made Flesh: The Third Witness of John the Apostle, 1:14-18
   E. Jesus the Messiah, the Lord: The Second Witness of John the Baptist, 1:19-28
   F. Jesus the Lamb of God, the Son of God: The Third Witness of John the Baptist, 1:29-34
   G. Jesus the Messiah, the Christ: The Witness of Andrew, 1:35-42
   H. Jesus the One Prophesied: The Witness of Philip, 1:43-45
   I. Jesus the Son of God, the King of Israel: The Witness of Nathanael, 1:46-49
   J. Jesus the Son of Man, God's Mediator: The Witness of Jesus Himself, 1:50-51

II. **THE REVELATION OF JESUS, THE SON OF GOD, 2:1–3:21**
   A. Revelation 1: Jesus' Creative Power, 2:1-11
   B. Revelation 2: Jesus Is Supremacy Over God's House, 2:12-22 (Matthew 21:12-16; Mark 11:15-19; Luke 19:34-46)
   C. Revelation 3: Jesus Knows All People, 2:23-25
   D. Revelation 4: The New Birth, 3:1-15
   E. Revelation 5: God's Great Love, 3:16-17
   F. Revelation 6: Humanity's Condemnation, 3:18-21

III. **THE REVELATION OF JESUS, THE NEW MASTER, 3:22–36**

IV. **THE REVELATION OF JESUS, THE LIVING WATER, 4:1–42**
   A. The Offer of Living Water, 4:1-14
   B. The Subject of Sin, 4:15-18
   C. The Subject of Worship, 4:19-24
   D. The Subject of the Messiah, 4:25-30
   E. The Subject of Labor for God, 4:31-42

V. **THE REVELATION OF JESUS, THE OBJECT OF FAITH, 4:43–54**
   A. The Evidence of Faith, 4:43-45
   B. The Stages of Faith, 4:46-54

VI. **THE REVELATION OF JESUS, THE AUTHORITY AND POWER OVER LIFE, 5:1–47**
   A. The Essential Authority: Power to Meet the World's Desperate Needs, 5:1-16
   B. The Astounding Authority: Equality with God, 5:17-30

      C. The Five Witnesses to Jesus' Authority and Power, 5:31-39
      D. The Rejection of Jesus' Claim: Why People Reject Him, 5:40-47

**VII. THE REVELATION OF JESUS, THE BREAD OF LIFE, 6:1-71**
      A. Jesus Feeds Five Thousand: The Kind of Faith Necessary to Meet Human Need, 6:1-15
      B. Jesus Walks on Water: The Deliverance from Fear, 6:16-21
        (Matthew 14:22-33; Mark 6:45-52)
      C. The Answer to People's Gnawing Hunger, Their Sense of Discontentment and Emptiness, 6:22-29
      D. The Bread of Life: The Source of Lasting Fulfillment and Satisfaction, 6:30-36
      E. The Assurance of the Believer, 6:37-40
      F. The Way a Person Partakes of the Bread of Life, 6:41-51
      G. The Results of Partaking of the Bread of Life, 6:52-58
      H. The Reasons Some People Are Offended by Christ, the Bread of Life, 6:59-71

**VIII. THE RESPONSES TO THE REVELATION OF JESUS, 7:1-53**
      A. The Response of Jesus' Brothers: Mockery and Unbelief, 7:1-9
      B. The Response of the Jews: Seeking Yet Questioning, 7:10-19
      C. The Response of the People: A Charge of Insanity Yet Still Questioning, 7:20-31
      D. The Response of the Rulers and Authorities: A Charge of Being a Rabble-Rouser, 7:32-36
      E. The Great Claim of Jesus and Divided Opinions About Him, 7:37-53

**IX. THE REVELATION OF JESUS, THE LIGHT OF LIFE, 8:1-9:41**
      A. Humanity's Dark Sinfulness and God's Great Forgiveness, 8:1-11
      B. Humanity's Need: The Light of the World, 8:12-20
      C. Humanity's Futile Search for Messiah: The Pursuit of Utopia, the Perfect World, 8:21-24
      D. Humanity's Tragic Failure to Understand the Light, 8:25-30
      E. Humanity's Freedom from Sin Is Conditional, 8:31-32
      F. Humanity's Enslavement to Sin: Four Proofs, 8:33-40
      G. Humanity's Depravity—Corrupt Birth, 8:41-47
      H. Humanity's Escape from Death, 8:48-59
      I. Humanity's Eyes Opened (Part I): The Mission of Jesus, 9:1-7
      J. Humanity's Eyes Opened (Part II): The Stages of Spiritual Sight, 9:8-41

**X. THE REVELATION OF JESUS, THE SHEPHERD OF LIFE, 10:1-42**
      A. The Shepherd and His Sheep: False vs. True Teachers, 10:1-6
      B. The Door of the Sheep: The Only Way to God, 10:7-10
      C. The Good Shepherd: Jesus, the True Savior of the World, 10:11-21
      D. The Great Shepherd's Claims, 10:22-42

**XI. THE REVELATION OF JESUS, THE RESURRECTION AND THE LIFE, 11:1-12:11**
      A. The Death of Lazarus and Its Purposes, 11:1-16
      B. Jesus and Martha: Growth in Faith, 11:17-27
      C. Jesus and Mary: The People's Real Needs, 11:28-37
      D. Jesus and Lazarus: Power Over Death, 11:38-46
      E. Jesus and the Religious Leaders: Unbelief and Opposition, 11:47-57
      F. Jesus and Reactions to His Revelation: He Is the Resurrection and Life, 12:1-11
        (Matthew 26:6-13; Mark 14:3-9)

**XII. THE REVELATION OF JESUS, THE GLORIFIED SON OF MAN, 12:12-50**
      A. Jesus Proclaimed as King: The Triumphal Entry, 12:12-19
        (Matthew 21:1-11; Mark 11:1-11; Luke 19:28-40)
      B. Jesus Approached as King: The Misunderstood Messiah, 12:20-36
      C. Jesus Rejected and Accepted as King, 12:37-50

**XIII. THE REVELATION OF JESUS, THE GREAT MINISTER, AND HIS LEGACY, 13:1-16:33**
      A. The Demonstration of Royal Service, 13:1-17
        (Matthew 26:20-24; Mark 14:14-17; Luke 22:14, 21-23)
      B. The Prediction of the Betrayer: A Picture of Apostasy, 13:18-30
      C. The Departure of Jesus from This World, 13:31-38
        (Matthew 26:30-35; Mark 14:26-31; Luke 22:31-34)

      D. Jesus' Death Delivers Troubled Hearts, 14:1-3
      E. The Way to God Is Through Jesus Alone, 14:4-7
      F. The Embodiment of God Is Jesus Himself, 14:8-14
      G. The Holy Spirit: Who He Is, 14:15-26
      H. The Source of Peace, Joy, and Security, 14:27-31
      I. The Relationship of Jesus to the People of the World, 15:1-8
      J. The Relationship of Jesus to Believers, 15:9-11
      K. The Relationship of Believers to Believers, 15:12-17
      L. The Relationship of Believers to the World: Persecution (Part I), 15:18-27
      M. The Relationship of Believers to Religionists: Persecution (Part II), 16:1-6
      N. The Work of the Holy Spirit, 16:7-15
      O. The Resurrection and Its Effects Foretold, 16:16-33

**XIV. THE REVELATION OF JESUS, THE GREAT INTERCESSOR, 17:1-26**
      A. Jesus Prayed for Himself, 17:1-8
      B. Jesus Prayed for His Disciples, 17:9-19
      C. Jesus Prayed for Future Believers, 17:20-26

**XV. THE REVELATION OF JESUS, THE SUFFERING SAVIOR, 18:1-19:42**
      A. The Arrest of Jesus: Absolute Surrender, 18:1-11
         (Matthew 26:36-56; Mark 14:32-52; Luke 22:39-53)
      B. The Jews and Peter: The Cowardly Denial, 18:12-27
         (Matthew 26:69-75; Mark 14:53-72; Luke 22:54-62)
      C. The Trial Before Pilate: Indecisive Compromise, 18:28-19:15
         (Matthew 27:11-25; Mark 15:1-15; Luke 23:1-5, 13-25)
      D. The Crucifixion: The Major Events at the Cross, 19:16-37
         (Matthew 27:26-56; Mark 15:16-41; Luke 23:26-49)
      E. The Burial: The Conquest of Fear, 19:38-42
         (Matthew 27:57-66; Mark 15:42-47; Luke 23:50-56)

**XVI. THE REVELATION OF JESUS, THE RISEN LORD, 20:1-21:25**
      A. Event 1: The Great Discovery—the Empty Tomb, 20:1-10
      B. Event 2: The Great Recognition—Jesus Appears to Mary, 20:11-18
         (Matthew 28:1-15; Mark 16:1-11; Luke 24:1-49)
      C. Event 3: The Great Charter of the Church—Jesus Appears to the Disciples, 20:19-23
         (Mark 16:14; Luke 24:36-49)
      D. Event 4: The Great Conviction—Thomas' Confession, 20:24-29
      E. Event 5: The Great Purpose of the Signs (Wonderful Works) of Jesus, 20:30-31
      F. Event 6: The Great Reality of Jesus' Resurrection Body, 21:1-14
      G. Event 7: The Great Question About a Disciple's Love and Devotion, 21:15-17
      H. Event 8: The Great Call to Total Commitment, 21:18-25

# Chapter 1

## I. The Witnesses to the Revelation of Jesus Christ, 1:1-51

### A. Jesus the Living Word: The First Witness of John the Apostle,<sup>DS1</sup> 1:1-5

| | |
|---|---|
| In the beginning was the Word, and the Word was with God, and the Word was God. <sup>2</sup> He was in the beginning with God. | **1. Christ is eternal**<br>a. Preexistent—always existed<br>b. Coexistent—always with God<br>c. Self-existent—is God, possessing God's very nature, but is a distinct person |
| <sup>3</sup> All things were made through him, and without him was not any thing made that was made. | **2. Christ is the Creator**<br>a. He created all things<br>b. Nothing was created apart from Christ |
| <sup>4</sup> In him was life, and the life was the light of men.<br><sup>5</sup> The light shines in the darkness, and the darkness has not overcome it. | **3. Christ is life**<sup>DS2</sup><br>a. He is the source of light<br>b. He is the answer to darkness<br>  1) Shines in darkness<sup>DS3</sup><br>  2) Conquers darkness<sup>DS4</sup> |

# Division I

*The Witnesses to the Revelation of Jesus Christ, 1:1-51*

A. Jesus the Living Word: The First Witness of John the Apostle, 1:1-5

## 1:1-5
## Introduction

This marvelous passage is one of the summits of Scripture. In fact, it rises to the highest level of human thought. What is the most awe-inspiring thought that stands at the peak of human concepts? It is the life-giving declaration that Jesus Christ, the Son of God, is . . .

- the Word of God
- the Creator of life
- the very being and essence of life

We have to think deeply about these three truths in order to understand their meaning. A quick reading of this passage perhaps leaves us disinterested and likely far removed from understanding what God is revealing to us. However, it is crucial that we put forth the effort to understand these truths, for they lie at the very foundation of life. They cannot be overstated, for they determine every person's destiny. If Jesus Christ is the Word of God, then each of us must hear and understand that Word or else be lost forever in ignorance of God Himself. This is, *Jesus the Living Word: The First Witness of John the Apostle,* 1:1-5.

1. Christ is eternal (vv.1-2).
2. Christ is the Creator (v.3).
3. Christ is life (vv.4-5).

## 1 Christ is eternal.

**1:1-2**

Guided by the supernatural direction of God's Spirit, John made three profound statements about Jesus, the Living Word (see DEEPER STUDY #1). These statements declare that Jesus was, and is, more than a mere man. He is God: the Son of God, and God the Son.

In the beginning was the Word, and the Word was with God, and the Word was God. ² He was in the beginning with God.

### a. Christ is preexistent—He always existed (v.1a).

Jesus Christ existed before creation. He has always existed. *In the beginning* (Gk. en archei) does not mean *from the beginning*. When the heavens and earth were created, Jesus Christ was already there. He did not *become*; He was not created; He never had a beginning. In the beginning, Jesus existed along with God the Father (see Jn.17:5; 8:58).

*Was* (en) is the Greek imperfect tense of *eimi* which is the word so often used for God. It means *to be* or *I am*. *To be* means continuous existence, without beginning or origin (see DEEPER STUDY # 1—Jn.6:20 for discussion). The testimony of John was that Jesus Christ was the *Word*, the One who has always existed. He is the Son of the living God (see outline and notes—Ph.2:5-8 for more discussion).

> And now, Father, glorify me in your own presence with the glory that I had with you before the world existed. (Jn.17:5)

> [Christ Jesus] who, though he was in the form of God, did not count equality with God a thing to be grasped, but emptied himself, by taking the form of a servant, being born in the likeness of men. And being found in human form, he humbled himself by becoming obedient to the point of death, even death on a cross. (Ph.2:6-8; see also 2Co. 8:9)

> Ages ago I was set up, at the first, before the beginning of the earth. (Pr.8:23)

### b. Christ is coexistent—He was always with God (v.1b).

Jesus was and is face-to-face with God forever. *With* (pros) has the idea of both *being with* and *acting toward*. Jesus Christ (the Word) was both with God and acting with God. This means that He was by God's side, acting, living, and moving in the closest of relationships. Christ had the ideal and perfect relationship *with* God the Father. Their life together—their relationship, communion, fellowship, and connection—was a perfect eternal bond. This is what is meant by, "He was *in the beginning with God*" (v.2). The testimony of John was that Jesus Christ was the *Word*, the One who has always coexisted with God.

> That which was from the beginning, which we have heard, which we have seen with our eyes, which we looked upon and have touched with our hands, concerning the word of life—the life was made manifest, and we have seen it, and testify to it and proclaim to you the eternal life, which was with the Father and was made manifest to us. (1 Jn.1:1-2)

### c. Christ is self-existent—He is God, possessing God's very nature, but is a distinct person (v.1c-2).

John declared unmistakably that Jesus Christ is God. Note that he did not say that "the Word" was *the God* (ho Theos). He simply says "the Word" was *God* (Theos). He purposely omits the definite article *the*. By doing so, John was saying that "the Word," Jesus Christ . . .

- is of the very nature and character of God the Father, but He is not the identical person of God the Father
- is a distinct person from God the Father, but He is of the very being and essence (perfection) of God the Father

When a person sees Christ, a *distinct person* is seen. However, Christ is the *very substance and character* of God in all of His perfect being. Jesus Christ is God, but He is a unique, separate person from God the Father: He is the Son of the Living God.

To summarize, the inspired testimony of John was that Jesus Christ is the *Word*, self-existent and eternal, the Supreme Majesty of the universe who owes His existence to no one. Jesus Christ is the Son of the living God.

**THOUGHT 1.** Jesus Christ is the living, eternal Word. Grasp what this critical truth means to us:

➢ First, Christ reveals to us the most important Person in all the universe: God. He reveals all that God is and wants to say to us. Therefore, we need to diligently study Christ, all that He is and everything He says. Furthermore, we must believe and obey everything He says (Jn.5:24).

➢ Second, Christ reveals God perfectly. He is just like God the Father, identical to God the Father; therefore, when people look at Christ they see God (see DEEPER STUDY # 1, 2, 3—Jn.14:9 for discussion).

➢ Third, Christ reveals that God is the most wonderful Person who has ever existed. God is far, far beyond anyone we could have ever imagined. He is loving and caring, full of goodness and truth. He will not tolerate injustices such as murder, stealing, lying, cheating, and abuse, whether it be the abuse of a husband, wife, child, neighbor, brother, sister, or stranger. God loves us and is working and moving toward a perfect universe that will be filled with people who choose to love and worship and live and work for Him (Jn.5:24–29).

**Jesus said to him, "Have I been with you so long, and you still do not know me, Philip? Whoever has seen me has seen the Father. How can you say, 'Show us the Father'?" (Jn.14:9)**

**To them belong the patriarchs, and from their race, according to the flesh, is the Christ, who is God over all, blessed forever. Amen. (Ro.9:5)**

**He is the image of the invisible God, the firstborn of all creation. (Col.1:15)**

**For in him the whole fullness of deity dwells bodily. (Col.2:9)**

**Great indeed, we confess, is the mystery of godliness: He was manifested in the flesh, vindicated by the Spirit, seen by angels, proclaimed among the nations, believed on in the world, taken up in glory. (1 Ti.3:16)**

**He is the radiance of the glory of God and the exact imprint of his nature, and he upholds the universe by the word of his power. After making purification for sins, he sat down at the right hand of the Majesty on high. (He.1:3)**

**THOUGHT 2.** God has made us—all genuine believers in Jesus Christ—a wonderful promise: we are going to be like Christ (1 Jn.3:2). As Scripture says, we do not know everything we will be, but we do know that the very nature of Christ will be conveyed to us (2 Pe.1:4). The very nature of Christ is . . .

- to exist eternally
- to exist in a perfect state of being, knowing nothing but eternal perfection
- to exist in perfect communion and fellowship eternally (see 1 Jn.1:3)

Because the very nature of Christ will be transferred to us as believers, all three of these qualities will become our personal experience—a glorious thought!

**"In that day you will know that I am in my Father, and you in me, and I in you." (Jn.14:20)**

**For those whom he foreknew he also predestined to be conformed to the image of his Son, in order that he might be the firstborn among many brothers. (Ro.8:29)**

**And we all, with unveiled face, beholding the glory of the Lord, are being transformed into the same image from one degree of glory to another. For this comes from the Lord who is the Spirit. (2 Co.3:18)**

**Who will transform our lowly body to be like his glorious body, by the power that enables him even to subject all things to himself. (Ph.3:21)**

**By which he has granted to us his precious and very great promises, so that through them you may become partakers of the divine nature, having escaped from the corruption that is in the world because of sinful desire. (2 Pe.1:4)**

**Beloved, we are God's children now, and what we will be has not yet appeared; but we know that when he appears we shall be like him, because we shall see him as he is. (1 Jn.3:2)**

## Deeper Study # 1

(1:1-5) **The Word—Jesus Christ, Son of God**: the *Word* (Gr. logos) is Jesus Christ. John faced a serious problem in writing to the Gentiles, that is, the non-Jewish world. Most Gentiles had never heard of the Messiah or Savior who was expected by the Jews. The idea was foreign to them. However, the Messiah was the very center of Christianity. How was John going to present Christ so that a Gentile could understand?

The answer lay in the idea of the *Word*, for the *Word* was understood by both Gentile and Jew.

1. The Jews saw a word as something more than a mere sound. A word was something active and existing. It was power—it possessed the power to express something, to do something. This is seen in the many Old Testament references where *The Word of God* was seen as the creative power of God, the power that made the world and gave light and life to every human being (Ge.1:3, 6, 11; Ps.33:6; 107:20; 147:15; Is.55:11).
2. The Gentiles or Greeks saw the *Word* more philosophically.
   a. When they looked at the world of nature, they saw that things were not chaotic, but orderly. Everything had its place and moved or grew in an orderly fashion, including the stars above and the vegetation below. Therefore, the Greeks said that behind the world was a mind, a reason, a power that made and kept things in their proper place. This creative and sustaining mind, this supreme reason, this unlimited power was said to be the *Word*.
   b. The *Word* was also seen as the power that enabled people to think and reason. It was the power that brought light and understanding to the human mind, enabling people to express their confused thoughts in an orderly fashion.
   c. More importantly, the *Word* was the power by which people came into contact with God and expressed their feelings to God.
3. John utilized this common idea of the Jews and Gentiles to proclaim that Jesus Christ was the *Word*. John saw that a word is the expression of an idea, a thought, an image in the mind of a person. He saw that a word describes what is in the mind of a person. Thus, he proclaimed that in the life of Jesus Christ, God was speaking to the world, speaking and demonstrating just what He wanted to say to humanity. John said three things.
   a. God has given us much more than mere words in the Holy Scriptures. God has given us Jesus Christ, *The Word*. As *The Word*, Jesus Christ was the picture, the expression, the pattern, the very image of what God wished to say to the human race. The very image within God's mind of the *Ideal Man* was demonstrated in the life of Jesus Christ. Jesus Christ was the perfect expression of all that God wishes us to be. Jesus Christ was God's utterance, God's speech, *God's Word* to us. Jesus Christ was the *Word* of God who came down to earth in human flesh to bring us into a face-to-face relationship with God (see vv.1-2). Jesus was the *Word of God who came to earth to live out the written Word of God.*
   b. Jesus Christ is the Mind, the Reason, the Power that both made and keeps things in their proper order. He is the creative and sustaining Mind, the Supreme Reason, the unlimited Power (see v.3).
   c. Jesus Christ is the Light, the Illumination, the Power that penetrates the darkness of the world. He, the Life and Light of the world, is what makes sense of the world and enables us to understand the world (see vv.4-5).

## 2 Christ is the Creator.

John revealed a second profound truth about Jesus Christ: not only did He exist before all things were created, but He is the Creator of all things.

### a. Christ created all things (v.3a).

*All things* (panta) means every detail of creation—not creation as a whole, but every single detail. Each element and thing, each being and person—whether material or spiritual, angelic or human—has been brought into being by Christ (Col.1:16).

> ³ All things were made through him, and without him was not any thing made that was made.

The words *were made* (egeneto) mean *came into being* or *became*. Note what this is saying. Nothing was existing—no substance, no matter whatsoever. Matter is not eternal. God did not take something outside of Himself, something less than perfect (evil) and create the world. Christ, the Word, took nothing but His will and power; and He spoke *the Word* and created every single thing *out of nothing* (He.11:3).

Scripture clearly states that Christ was the One who created all things—one by one. Among the Godhead, He was the active Agent, the Person who made all things. Creation was His function and work (1 Co.8:6; Col.1:16; He.1:2).

### b. Nothing was created apart from Christ (v.3b).

Note that two statements of fact are made:
- The positive statement of fact: "All things were made through Him."
- The absolute statement of fact: "*Without Him* was not any thing made that was made."

Christ was actively involved in the creation of every single thing: "Without Him was not any thing made." The words "not any thing" (oude hen) mean not even *one* thing, not a single thing. Not even a detail was made apart from Him.

**THOUGHT 1.** The world is God's; He made it, every element of it, one by one. How does this fact apply to us?
(1) God is not off in some distant place far removed from the world, unconcerned and disinterested in what happens to the world. God cares about the world. He cares deeply, even about the most minute detail and smallest person. He cares about everything and every person in the world.
(2) The problems of the world are not due to God and His attitude. The problems of the world are due to sin, to the attitude and evil of the human heart.
(3) The answer to the world's problems is not human beings and their technical skills. The answer is Christ: for every one of us to turn to Christ, surrendering and giving our lives to know Christ in the most personal and intimate way possible. Then, and only then, can we set our lives and world in order as God intends.

> **Yet for us there is one God, the Father, from whom are all things and for whom we exist, and one Lord, Jesus Christ, through whom are all things and through whom we exist. (1 Co.8:6)**

> **For by him all things were created, in heaven and on earth, visible and invisible, whether thrones or dominions or rulers or authorities—all things were created through him and for him. (Col.1:16)**

> **But in these last days [God] has spoken to us by his Son, whom he appointed the heir of all things, through whom also he created the world. (He.1:2)**

## 3 Christ is life.

John concluded introducing Jesus to his readers by revealing that Christ is life (see DEEPER STUDY #2). The life that is in Jesus Christ sheds light on our sinful condition. Then, it points us to the abundant, eternal life that Christ came to bring us (Jn.10:10).

> ⁴ In him was life, and the life was the light of men.
> ⁵ The light shines in the darkness, and the darkness has not overcome it.

**a. Christ is the source of light (v.4).**

Note the statement: "The life [Christ] was the light of men." From the very beginning God intended for us to know *that life*, to know God personally and intimately. The knowledge of the life of Christ was to be the light of all people, the beam that gives real life to every person who believes, both abundant and eternal life. This light, the light we receive through the life of Christ, infuses energy and motivation into us so that we might walk and live as we should.

**b. Christ is the answer to darkness (v.5).**

Christ's life did shine in the darkness (see DEEPER STUDY # 2—8:12 for discussion). Very simply, since humans had brought darkness into the world (by sin), the life of Christ was the light of humanity, the *beam* that showed us the way, the truth and the life (see DEEPER STUDY # 3, 4; DEEPER STUDY # 2—8:12; DEEPER STUDY # 1, 2, 3—14:6 for discussion).

➤ Christ showed us the *way* God intended us to live.
➤ Christ showed us the *truth* of life, that is, the truth about God and humanity and the truth about the world in which we live.
➤ Christ showed us the *life*, that is, how to save our lives and avoid the things that can cause us to stumble.

Not only did Christ's life penetrate the darkness, but it also conquered darkness. The Greek word for *overcome* (katelaben) expresses the truth that the darkness of the world can neither overcome nor extinguish the light of Jesus Christ. But it also conveys another truth: the darkness of the world cannot understand or grasp that light, as expressed by the Bible versions which translate katelaben as *comprehend*.

> Again Jesus spoke to them, saying, "I am the light of the world. Whoever follows me will not walk in darkness, but will have the light of life." (Jn.8:12)

> "The thief comes only to steal and kill and destroy. I came that they may have life and have it abundantly." (Jn.10:10)

> So Jesus said to them, "The light is among you for a little while longer. Walk while you have the light, lest darkness overtake you. The one who walks in the darkness does not know where he is going." (Jn.12:35)

> "I have come into the world as light, so that whoever believes in me may not remain in darkness." (Jn. 12:46)

> For God, who said, "Let light shine out of darkness," has shone in our hearts to give the light of the knowledge of the glory of God in the face of Jesus Christ. (2 Co.4:6)

> At the same time, it is a new commandment that I am writing to you, which is true in him and in you, because the darkness is passing away and the true light is already shining. (1 Jn.2:8)

## DEEPER STUDY # 2

(1:4) **Life—Jesus Christ, Life:** the simple statement "in him was life" means at least three things.

1. Life is the quality and essence, the energy and power, the force and principle of being. Christ is life; He is . . .

- the very quality of life
- the very essence of life
- the very energy of life
- the very power of life
- the very force of life
- the very principle of life

Without Christ, there would be no life whatsoever. Life is in Him, within His very being. All things exist and have their being (life) in Him.

2. Life is purpose, meaning, and significance of being. Christ is life; He is . . .

- the very purpose of life
- the very meaning of life
- the very significance of life

3. Life is perfection. Life is all that a person must be and possess in order to live perfectly. This is what is meant by life. Life is completeness of being, absolute satisfaction, the fullness of all good, and the possession of all good things. Life is perfect love, joy, peace, long-suffering, gentleness, goodness, faith, meekness, and self-control (see Ga.5:22-23).

Whatever life is and all that life is, it is all in Jesus Christ. Even the legitimate human cravings that are sometimes entangled with evil—such as power, fame and wealth—are all included in the life given by Jesus Christ. Those who partake of His life will reign forever as kings and priests (see outline and notes—Lu.16:10-12 for more discussion). This is the very thing that is distinctive about life—it is eternal. It lasts forever and it is rewarding. It will eventually exalt the believer to the highest life and place and position. (see Re.21:1f).

Jesus Christ is the source of life: He is the way to life, and He is the truth of life. He is the very substance of life, its very being and energy (Jn.5:26; 1 Jn.1:2) (see Deeper Study # 1—Jn.10:10; Deeper Study # 1—17:2-3).

## Deeper Study # 3

(1:5) **Light**: light reveals, strips away (Jn.3:19-20), subdues the chaos (see Ge.1:2-3), and guides (Jn.12:36, 46). It shows the way, the truth, and the life (Jn.14:6).

## Deeper Study # 4

(1:5) **Darkness**: darkness does not understand the light, does not overcome the light, does not extinguish the light (see note—Jn.8:12).

## B. Jesus the Light of the World: The Special Witness of John the Baptist, 1:6-8

|  |  |
|---|---|
| 1. John was a man sent from God<sup>DS1</sup> | <sup>6</sup> There was a man sent from God, whose name was John. |
| 2. John was a man sent on a very special mission<br>  a. To bear witness of the Light<br>  b. That people might believe | <sup>7</sup> He came as a witness, to bear witness about the light, that all might believe through him. |
| 3. John was a great man, but he was not the Light | <sup>8</sup> He was not the light, but came to bear witness about the light. |

# Division I

### *The Witnesses to the Revelation of Jesus Christ, 1:1-51*

B. Jesus the Light of the World: The Special Witness of John the Baptist, 1:6-8

## 1:6-8

## Introduction

Of all the people who bore witness of Jesus, one individual stands out as unique. John the Baptist was a very special witness of Christ. In fact, John's sole purpose on earth was to witness and to bear testimony of the Light of the world. His purpose stands as a dynamic example for us. As believers, our purpose is to bear the same witness as John: Jesus Christ is the Light of the world. This is, *Jesus the Light of the World: The Special Witness of John the Baptist*, 1:6-8.

1. John was a man sent from God (v.6).
2. John was a man sent on a very special mission (v.7).
3. John was a great man, but he was not the Light (v.8).

### 1:6

<sup>6</sup> There was a man sent from God, whose name was John.

### 1 John was a man sent from God.

Scripture makes a strong contrast between what had been said about Christ and what is now being said about John. Christ "was in the beginning"; He was "with God," and He "was God" (vv.1-2). On the other hand, John was "a man" who had come into existence at birth, just like every other human who has ever lived. John had a biological mother and father, whereas Jesus Christ had no human father; He was the only begotten Son of God (v.14; Jn.3:16). John was not a divine being, not even an angel. He was a mere man.

This man, however, was *sent from God*; and he was sent on a very special mission. Two facts show this:

> - The meaning of the word *sent* (see Deeper Study # 1).
> - The phrase *from God* (Gk. para Theou), which literally means "from beside God." John was not only sent by God, he was sent from the very side and heart of God. John was only a man, but a man of high calling and mission, of enormous responsibility and accountability. He was a man sent uniquely by God, not by some other person.

Luke recorded a fascinating fact about this unusual man: his name was not chosen by his parents, but by God Himself. The angel whom God sent to Zacharias, instructed him to name his son

John (Lk.1:13). The name *John* means *gracious*. John was a man sent forth with a name to match his message: *God's grace* is now to enter upon the scene of world history.

> John answered, "A person cannot receive even one thing unless it is given him from heaven." (Jn.3:27)
>
> What is man, that you make so much of him, and that you set your heart on him? (Jb.7:17)
>
> What is man that you are mindful of him, and the son of man that you care for him? (Ps.8:4)
>
> Do you not know? Do you not hear? Has it not been told you from the beginning? Have you not understood from the foundations of the earth? It is he [God] who sits above the circle of the earth, and its inhabitants are like grasshoppers; who stretches out the heavens like a curtain, and spreads them like a tent to dwell in. (Is.40:21-22)

**THOUGHT 1.** Like John, we too, as believers, are sent by God to bear witness of Jesus Christ. Note three significant points about the servants and messengers of God:
- First, the servants and messengers of God are not sent forth by another person, but by God. We are sent forth as the ambassadors of God.
- Second, God's messengers are sent forth *from* God, from the very side and heart of God.
- Third, as God's messengers, we have received the highest of all callings and missions, the calling of telling the world about Christ and the mission of bringing others into a saving relationship with Christ. This is an enormous responsibility, and we must never lose sight of the sobering fact that we are accountable to God Himself for our faithfulness to this holy task.

> "You did not choose me, but I chose you and appointed you that you should go and bear fruit and that your fruit should abide, so that whatever you ask the Father in my name, he may give it to you." (Jn.15:16)
>
> Not that we are sufficient in ourselves to claim anything as coming from us, but our sufficiency is from God, who has made us sufficient to be ministers of a new covenant, not of the letter but of the Spirit. For the letter kills, but the Spirit gives life. (2 Co.3:5-6)
>
> All this is from God, who through Christ reconciled us to himself and gave us the ministry of reconciliation; that is, in Christ God was reconciling the world to himself, not counting their trespasses against them, and entrusting to us the message of reconciliation. Therefore, we are ambassadors for Christ, God making his appeal through us. We implore you on behalf of Christ, be reconciled to God. (2 Co.5:18-20)
>
> Of this gospel I was made a minister according to the gift of God's grace, which was given me by the working of his power. (Ep.3:7)
>
> I thank him who has given me strength, Christ Jesus our Lord, because he judged me faithful, appointing me to his service. (1 Ti.1:12)

### DEEPER STUDY # 1

(1:6) **Sent—Apostle—Commission**: *Sent* (apestalmenos) means to send out; to commission as a representative, an ambassador, an envoy. Three things are true of the person sent from God.
1. He belongs to God, who has sent him out.
2. He is commissioned to be sent out.
3. He possesses all the authority and power of God, who has sent him out.

## 2 John was a man sent on a very special mission.

Two Old Testament prophets foretold John's special mission and purpose. Both Isaiah and Malachi prophesied that John would prepare the way of the Lord, who is the embodiment

> [7] He came as a witness, to bear witness about the light, that all might believe through him.

of God's glorious grace (Is.40:3; Mal.3:1; Mt.3:3). John was sent to this world for the greatest of all human missions:

### a. To bear witness of the Light (v.7a).

John was sent with a very specific message: to proclaim the Light, Christ Himself (see DEEPER STUDY # 1—8:12; DEEPER STUDY # 5—12:35-36). This crucial message, the good news of salvation through Christ, must be declared to all people. In our natural state as unbelieving sinners, Satan has blinded our minds to the light of Christ. When we hear the message of Jesus, the light of Christ breaks through to us (1 Co.4:3-7). John was the first person sent to bear witness to the Light, Jesus Christ.

**THOUGHT 1.** Like John's message, our message is a *given* message. As God's servants, we are not left on our own to think up a message; we are not dependent upon our own reason, thoughts, and ideas. Our message is Christ, the Light of the world.

> For we are not, like so many, peddlers of God's word, but as men of sincerity, as commissioned by God, in the sight of God we speak in Christ. (2 Co.2:17)
>
> For what we proclaim is not ourselves, but Jesus Christ as Lord, with ourselves as your servants for Jesus' sake. (2 Co.4:5)
>
> And we also thank God constantly for this, that when you received the word of God, which you heard from us, you accepted it not as the word of men but as what it really is, the word of God, which is at work in you believers. (1 Th.2:13)
>
> You shall not add to the word that I command you, nor take from it, that you may keep the commandments of the LORD your God that I command you. (De.4:2)

### b. That people might believe (v.7b).

The purpose of John's witness is clearly stated: that all people, through Christ, might believe. His purpose was not . . .
- to start a movement for God
- to organize and administer
- to minister (note that John never healed, nor performed a miracle, nor built a ministry around the synagogue or temple, Jn.10:41)

John's purpose was *not even to preach*. His purpose was *to lead people to believe* in the Light. He witnessed and proclaimed the Light *so that* all might believe. John was sent to focus on people and to lead them to believe in Christ Jesus (see DEEPER STUDY # 2—Jn.2:24 for discussion of this point).

**THOUGHT 1.** God's messengers have *one primary purpose*: to lead others to believe in Christ Jesus, the Light of the world. As witnesses, our *purpose* is not to organize, to administer, to oversee, to manage, to teach, or to preach. Our purpose is as stated: to lead people to believe in Christ Jesus. Everything else has to do with methods, not purpose. Many of God's servants have too often confused methods with purpose. The result has been that teeming millions are still unreached, and countless believers are being deceived by confusing the methods of religion with the purpose of God: the salvation of humanity through belief in His Son.

> "For God so loved the world, that he gave his only Son, that whoever believes in him should not perish but have eternal life." (Jn.3:16)
>
> "Truly, truly, I say to you, whoever hears my word and believes him who sent me has eternal life. He does not come into judgment, but has passed from death to life." (Jn.5:24)

1:8

⁸ He was not the light, but came to bear witness about the light.

## 3 John was a great man, but he was not the Light.

John the Baptist was extraordinarily great. Jesus Himself said, that John was the greatest person to ever be born (Mt.11:11). *But*, he was not the Light. John's humility is striking. (Read Jn.1:19-23, 27 to see the example his humility sets for every servant of God along with its impact.) No matter how great a person's ministry may be in the eyes of others, John's greatness eclipses it. Yet John said that he was not worthy to untie the straps of Jesus' sandals (Jn.1:27)!

**THOUGHT 1.** Like John, we need to humble ourselves before the Lord, steadfastly resisting every temptation to exalt or glorify ourselves. John's humble spirit is summarized in his simple, yet utterly profound declaration, "He must increase, but I must decrease" (Jn.3:30). We would do well to adopt this statement as our daily prayer, asking God to help us to become small that Christ might be magnified before others. Our goal should ever be to "become less and less" in order that Christ may "become greater and greater" (Jn.3:30, NLT). When we seek to promote ourselves, we make ourselves worthless servants whom God cannot use and bless. But when we humble ourselves in order to exalt Christ, not only will we be fruitful for the Lord, but He will also exalt us.

> **Whoever exalts himself will be humbled, and whoever humbles himself will be exalted. (Mt.23:12)**
>
> **Do nothing from selfish ambition or conceit, but in humility count others more significant than yourselves. Let each of you look not only to his own interests, but also to the interests of others. (Ph.2:3-4; see Ro.12:3)**
>
> **Humble yourselves before the Lord, and he will exalt you. (Js.4:10)**
>
> **Likewise, you who are younger, be subject to the elders. Clothe yourselves, all of you, with humility toward one another, for "God opposes the proud but gives grace to the humble." (1 Pe.5:5)**

## C. Jesus the Light of the Human Race: The Second Witness of John the Apostle, 1:9-13

1. **Christ is the Light**
   a. The true Light<sup>DS1</sup>
   b. His mission: To give light to people
2. **Christ was tragically rejected by the world**
   a. He came to the world He made, but He was not recognized<sup>DS2</sup>
   b. He came to His own people, but they rejected Him
3. **Christ was wonderfully received by some**
   a. They believed in His name
   b. They became children of God
   c. They were born of God, given a new birth
      1) Is not a natural birth
      2) Is of God

⁹ The true light, which gives light to everyone, was coming into the world.

¹⁰ He was in the world, and the world was made through him, yet the world did not know him.

¹¹ He came to his own, and his own people did not receive him. ¹² But to all who did receive him, who believed in his name, he gave the right to become children of God,

¹³ who were born, not of blood nor of the will of the flesh nor of the will of man, but of God.

# Division I

## The Witnesses to the Revelation of Jesus Christ, 1:1-51

C. Jesus the Light of the Human Race: The Second Witness of John the Apostle, 1:9-13

## 1:9-13
## Introduction

Our world is in a desperate dilemma. It is full of darkness—the darkness of sin and despair, of sickness and death, of corruption and destruction. This crippling darkness looms over the entire world.

John 1:9-13 deals with this crucial problem, announcing that there is hope for a world eclipsed by sin. That hope—the world's *only* hope—is in Jesus Christ, for Christ is the *true Light*. Light drives away darkness, and the light of Jesus Christ eliminates the darkness of our sin-blackened world. This is, *Jesus the Light of the Human Race: The Second Witness of John the Apostle*, 1:9-13.

1. Christ is the Light (v.9).
2. Christ was tragically rejected by the world (vv.10-11).
3. Christ was wonderfully received by some (vv.12-13).

### 1:9

⁹ The true light, which gives light to everyone, was coming into the world.

### 1 Christ is the Light.

Christ is "the true Light." Others may claim to be *lights*; they may claim that they can lead people to the truth. Some may claim they can . . .
- reveal God to humanity
- show the nature, meaning, and destiny of the future and other things

- guide a person out of the darkness of sin, shame, doubt, despair, as well as the fear of death and hell
- do away with and eliminate the darkness entirely

However, such individuals are *false* lights. Their claims are only ideas in their minds, fictitious ideas, and counterfeit claims. Their thoughts and positions are defective, frail, and uncertain—just as imperfect as any other man-made position dealing with the truth. Note two glorious truths.

### a. The true Light (v.9a).

Jesus is the true Light (see Deeper Study # 1). What does this mean? It means that Jesus Christ is what other individuals are not. Others may claim to be the light of humanity, but their thoughts are only false imaginations. Christ alone is the true Light. Christ is to humanity what light is to the world, and Christ did for man what light does for our world.

- ➢ Light is clear, pure, clean, and good. So is Christ (Ep.5:8).
- ➢ Light penetrates. It cuts through and eliminates darkness. So does Christ.
- ➢ Light enlightens. It enlarges one's vision and knowledge. So does Christ.
- ➢ Light reveals. It opens up the truth of an area, a whole new world and life. It clears up the way to the truth and life. So does Christ (Jn.14:6).
- ➢ Light guides. It keeps us from groping and grasping about in the dark trying to find our way. It directs the way to go, leads along the right path. So does Christ (Jn.12:36, 46).
- ➢ Light exposes and strips away darkness. So does Christ (Jn.3:19-20).
- ➢ Light calms/conquers/ends the chaos. So does Christ (see Ge.1:2-3).
- ➢ Light discriminates between the right way and the wrong way. So does Christ (see note—Ep.5:10. see Ep.5:8-10).
- ➢ Light warns. It warns of dangers that lie ahead in our path. So does Christ.
- ➢ Light protects. It keeps us from tripping, stumbling, falling, and injuring ourselves and losing our life. So does Christ.

### b. His mission: To give light to people (v.9b).

The mission of Christ is to give light to people. Note that He gives light to every human being. How does He do this?

First, Christ gives light to people through natural revelation, the creation and order of the universe. Scripture declares that nature reveals the existence, power, and truth of God:

> Yet he did not leave himself without witness, for he did good by giving you rains from heaven and fruitful seasons, satisfying your hearts with food and gladness. (Ac.14:17)

> For his invisible attributes, namely, his eternal power and divine nature, have been clearly perceived, ever since the creation of the world, in the things that have been made. So they are without excuse. (Ro.1:20)

> The heavens declare the glory of God, and the sky above proclaims his handiwork. (Ps.19:1)

> The heavens proclaim his righteousness, and all the peoples see his glory. (Ps.97:6)

Second, Christ gives light by giving good gifts to us. Every good thing we receive comes from the Father above. God's goodness to us enlightens us to the truth that He loves us and cares about us.

> Every good gift and every perfect gift is from above, coming down from the Father of lights, with whom there is no variation or shadow due to change. (Js.1:17)

Third, Christ gives light through God's Word. The Lord has revealed Himself and His truth to us through Scripture, the inspired, inerrant written record He has given us by His Spirit.

> And we have the prophetic word more fully confirmed, to which you will do well to pay attention as to a lamp shining in a dark place, until the day dawns and the morning star rises in your hearts. (2 Pe.1:19)

> The precepts of the Lord are right, rejoicing the heart; the commandment of the Lord is pure, enlightening the eyes. (Ps.19:8)

> Your word is a lamp to my feet and a light to my path. (Ps.119:105)

> I have chosen the way of faithfulness; I set your rules before me. (Ps.119:30)

For the commandment is a lamp and the teaching a light, and the reproofs of discipline are the way of life. (Pr.6:23)

**THOUGHT 1.** Since Christ came into the world, humanity has more light from the Lord than ever before. In addition to the forms of lights mentioned above, Christ's coming to earth as a man brought:

1) The *light of Christ Himself*: He is the Savior who now stands before the world as "the Christ, the Son of God," who came into the world (Jn.11:27). Because of this, all people can now see the truth. They may reject it, but they can see it.

> "I have much to say about you and much to judge, but he who sent me is true, and I declare to the world what I have heard from him." (Jn.8:26)
>
> "For I have not spoken on my own authority, but the Father who sent me has himself given me a commandment—what to say and what to speak." (Jn.12:49)
>
> "For I have given them the words that you gave me, and they have received them and have come to know in truth that I came from you; and they have believed that you sent me." (Jn.17:8)
>
> "I will raise up for them a prophet like you from among their brothers. And I will put my words in his mouth, and he shall speak to them all that I command him." (De.18:18)

2) The *light of the gospel*: Because Christ came as a light into the world, all who believe on Him will no longer live in darkness (Jn.12:46). The truth is that every individual can now be delivered from the darkness of sin, despair, death, and hell.

> "And this is the judgment: the light has come into the world, and people loved the darkness rather than the light because their works were evil." (Jn.3:19)
>
> Again Jesus spoke to them, saying, "I am the light of the world. Whoever follows me will not walk in darkness, but will have the light of life." (Jn.8:12)
>
> And even if our gospel is veiled, it is veiled to those who are perishing. In their case the god of this world has blinded the minds of the unbelievers, to keep them from seeing the light of the gospel of the glory of Christ, who is the image of God. (2 Co.4:3-4)
>
> For anything that becomes visible is light. Therefore it says, "Awake, O sleeper, and arise from the dead, and Christ will shine on you." (Ep.5:14)

3) The *light of the Spirit*: both the guiding and the convicting power of the Spirit.

> "And when he comes, he will convict the world concerning sin and righteousness and judgment: concerning sin, because they do not believe in me; concerning righteousness, because I go to the Father, and you will see me no longer; concerning judgment, because the ruler of this world is judged." (Jn.16:8-11)
>
> "When the Spirit of truth comes, he will guide you into all the truth, for he will not speak on his own authority, but whatever he hears he will speak, and he will declare to you the things that are to come." (Jn.16:13)
>
> Now we have received not the spirit of the world, but the Spirit who is from God, that we might understand the things freely given us by God. (1 Co.2:12)

Grasp a crucial truth: all the light existing in the world is due to Christ, both the light from nature and from heaven, from the physical world and from the spiritual world. Christ is "the true Light" [the Life], and He gives light to every person in the world (v.9).

## DEEPER STUDY # 1

(1:9) **Truth**: the words true, truth, and real are taken from two Greek words very much alike. But each has a different shade of meaning (see DEEPER STUDY # 1—Jn.8:32; DEEPER STUDY # 2—14:6).

1. *Alethes* means true, the opposite of false.
2. *Alethinos* means the true, the genuine, the real. It is the *opposite* of the unreal, the fictitious, the counterfeit, the imaginary. It is also the opposite of the imperfect, defective, frail, uncertain.

Jesus Christ is seen as the true, the real, the genuine life which has come to give light to every person (see Deeper Study # 1—Jn.8:12).

## 2 Christ was tragically rejected by the world.

1:10-11

These verses convey the tragic truth of the world's response to Jesus Christ: He was in the world—a world created by Him—but the world did not know (recognize) Him. Because the world did not recognize who He truly was, they rejected Him as their Messiah, Savior, and Lord.

> ¹⁰ He was in the world, and the world was made through him, yet the world did not know him.
> ¹¹ He came to his own, and his own people did not receive him.

**a. He came to the world He made, but He was not recognized (v.10).**

Christ's presence and power were in the world long before He came to earth as a man. He—the Word and the Light—made the world, and He loved and cared deeply for it. Therefore, God's Son was actively working to help the world and its people from the very beginning of creation.

- ➢ Christ gave the *light of order and purpose and beauty* to the universe as a whole. The universe is lovingly supplied to take care of humanity's needs, and the world shows the glorious power and deity of God (Ro.1:19-20).
- ➢ Christ gave humanity the *glorious light* [privilege] *of living* in such a beautiful world. He gave each of us a soul, the very *light* of life by which we can learn and reason, love and care, work and serve—all for the purpose of building a better world, both for God and for ourselves.
- ➢ Christ gave a spirit to every person, the *light of knowing and worshiping* God and living forever with God.
- ➢ Christ gave messengers to humanity, *prophetic lights* to proclaim the truth and to encourage people to follow God and to be diligent in their work and service to the world.

But note what happened: the world did not *know* or *recognize* (Gk. egno) Him. Likewise, when Jesus came into the world as a man, people did not perceive or grasp who He was. The people of the world have always rejected Christ; they have closed their eyes and failed to see Him as who He truly is. (See Ro.1:19-32 for the tragic indictment against man's rejection of God's activity in the world.)

**b. He came to His own people, but they rejected Him (v.11).**

Christ (the Word and the Light) came to His own people, but they, too, rejected Him. The words *to His own* (eis ta idia) mean literally to *His own home, to His own people*. This phrase conveys two important thoughts:

First, the world is Christ's home, and all people are His by creation. He came to all the people of the world, but they did not receive Him. They rejected Him.

Second, the nation of Israel was His specific home, the people whom He had chosen to be the messengers of God to the world. They, of all people, should have recognized and embraced Christ because of the special privileges they had received, but they too rejected Him (see Deeper Study # 1—Jn.4:22).

**Thought 1.** What happened in ages gone by still happens today: the world still refuses to recognize Christ as who He truly is. Throughout the world, people today continue to reject Jesus as God, the Son of God, their Savior, and their Lord. Tragically, all who refuse to accept Christ will face His judgment. Because they did not believe on Him, they will spend eternity separated from Him and His glorious, joyous presence (Jn.3:15-18, 36; Re.20:15).

> **And behold, all the city came out to meet Jesus, and when they saw him, they begged him to leave their region. (Mt.8:34)**

"Is not this the carpenter, the son of Mary and brother of James and Joses and Judas and Simon? And are not his sisters here with us?" And they took offense at him. (Mk.6:3)

When they heard these things, all in the synagogue were filled with wrath. And they rose up and drove him out of the town and brought him to the brow of the hill on which their town was built, so that they could throw him down the cliff. (Lu.4:28-29)

But they all cried out together, "Away with this man, and release to us Barabbas." (Lu.23:18)

"I have come in my Father's name, and you do not receive me. If another comes in his own name, you will receive him." (Jn.5:43)

"The one who rejects me and does not receive my words has a judge; the word that I have spoken will judge him on the last day." (Jn.12:48)

### 1:12-13

¹² But to all who did receive him, who believed in his name, he gave the right to become children of God,
¹³ who were born, not of blood nor of the will of the flesh nor of the will of man, but of God.

### 3 Christ was wonderfully received by some.

When Jesus came to earth as a man, He was rejected by most of the people, but not all. Some received Him, both as the Messiah and Son of God, and ultimately as their Savior and Lord.

a. **They believed in His name (v.12a).**

Those who received Jesus did so by faith. They believed in Jesus' name—that He is the Word (v.1), the Life (v.4), and the Light (vv.4-8). Specifically, the name *Jesus* means *Jehovah is salvation*. *Christ* means the Anointed One, the Messiah. Those who received Him believed that He is the anointed Savior and Redeemer promised by the Lord. Their faith was more than a mental assent—a head knowledge, a belief of the facts about Jesus. Through their faith, they were fully committing their lives to Him (see Deeper Study # 2—Jn.2:24).

b. **They became children of God (v.12b).**

Those who received Jesus were presented with a wonderful gift: the right to become children of God. The word *right* in this verse (exousian) implies power or authority. In normal usage, it was a legal term referring to a right or privilege officially granted by a judge, a king, or a government. *To become* (genesthai) means to become something a person is not.

When we receive Christ, God, the Highest Power of all, gives us the privilege of becoming one of His dear children. This is the blessed, eternal result of receiving Christ. We are given the right to become something we are not—a child of God.

c. **They were born of God, given a new birth (v.13).**

A person who receives Christ by faith becomes a child of God through *birth*. He or she is born into God's family. Note two crucial facts:

First, this birth is not a natural birth: it is "not of blood," not a physical birth. It is something completely different from the process by which we are physically born into this world. We are not, by nature, the children of God. In addition, our physical heritage bears no weight on our becoming God's children. Being born of a particular family, race, nation or people is of no value in becoming a child of God. Blood is not what causes the new birth.

To further explain that this is not a physical birth, John states that it is not *of the will of the flesh* (ek thelematos sarkos): not the result of human passion (sexual desire) or a human decision. A person is not spiritually born again by *wanting* and *willing* to become a child of God in the way a person *wills* to have an earthly child.

Second, this birth is of God. It is not by *the will of man* (ek thelematos andros): the male or husband. In the culture of the day, the husband usually made the decision whether to have a child. The idea is that the man (the husband, the stronger partner, the one who is usually the leader) cannot bring about the spiritual birth of others. No man, no matter who he is—husband or world leader—can cause or make a person a child of God. It is entirely the will and work of God (see Deeper Study # 1—Jn.3:1-15 for discussion).

**THOUGHT 1.** What a wonderful concept: that we—sinful humans—can become the children of God! John will shortly present Jesus' thorough explanation of this glorious truth, the truth of the new birth (3:1-15). Here, he briefly introduces it, establishing the fact that we become the children of God "by grace . . . through faith" (Ep.2:8):

- God *gives* us the right to become His children (v.12a). Salvation is "by grace . . . it is the gift of God" (Ep.2:8).
- We become the children of God by believing in the name of Jesus—everything that He is (v.12b). It is through faith that we are saved, not by our works (Ep.2:8-9).

> "And there is salvation in no one else, for there is no other name under heaven given among men by which we must be saved." (Ac.4:12)
>
> For you did not receive the spirit of slavery to fall back into fear, but you have received the Spirit of adoption as sons, by whom we cry, "Abba! Father!" The Spirit himself bears witness with our spirit that we are children of God. (Ro.8:15-16)
>
> For in Christ Jesus you are all sons of God, through faith. (Gal.3:26)
>
> But when the fullness of time had come, God sent forth his Son, born of woman, born under the law, to redeem those who were under the law, so that we might receive adoption as sons. And because you are sons, God has sent the Spirit of his Son into our hearts, crying, "Abba! Father!" (Ga.4:4-6)

## D. Jesus the Word Made Flesh:
## The Third Witness of John the Apostle, 1:14–18

1. Proof 1: Christ dwelt visibly among us
   a. Christ became flesh<sup>DS1</sup>
   b. He & His glory were seen
   c. He was full of grace<sup>DS2</sup> & truth
2. Proof 2: John the Baptist bore witness of the superiority of Christ


3. Proof 3: We have received His grace & blessing upon blessing
   a. God's grace & blessing do not come by law
   b. God's grace & blessing come through Jesus Christ
5. Proof 4: God has revealed Himself through Christ

¹⁴ And the Word became flesh and dwelt among us, and we have seen his glory, glory as of the only Son from the Father, full of grace and truth.

¹⁵ (John bore witness about him, and cried out, "This was he of whom I said, 'He who comes after me ranks before me, because he was before me.'")

¹⁶ For from his fullness we have all received, grace upon grace.

¹⁷ For the law was given through Moses; grace and truth came through Jesus Christ.

¹⁸ No one has ever seen God; the only God, who is at the Father's side, he has made him known.

# Division I

## The Witnesses to the Revelation of Jesus Christ, 1:1-51

D. Jesus the Word Made Flesh: The Third Witness of John the Apostle, 1:14–18

## 1:14–18
## Introduction

Over two thousand years later, much of the world pauses every year on December 25 to recognize and celebrate the birth of Jesus Christ. While Matthew and Luke provided lengthy, detailed reports of Christ's birth, John summarized it in one wonder-filled statement:

> "*The Word became flesh and dwelt among us . . .*" *(Jn.1:14).*

"The Word became flesh"—God's Son, the Lord Jesus Christ, was made flesh and blood; He became a man. No greater message could ever be proclaimed to human ears and souls. This is, *Jesus, the Word Made Flesh: The Third Witness of John the Apostle,* 1:1-14.
1. Proof 1: Christ dwelt visibly among us (v.14).
2. Proof 2: John the Baptist bore witness of the superiority of Christ (v.15).
3. Proof 3: We have received His grace and blessing upon blessing (vv.16-17).
4. Proof 4: God has revealed Himself through Christ (v.18).

### 1:14

¹⁴ And the Word became flesh and dwelt among us, and we have seen his glory, glory as of the only Son from the Father, full of grace and truth.

## 1 Proof 1: Christ dwelt visibly among us, 1 Jn.1:1-3.

John described what we commonly refer to as the Incarnation of Christ. God's eternal Son, the Creator of the universe, came to earth as a man. He took on a human body and dwelt visibly among us. He became one of us.

a. **Christ became flesh (v.14a).**

John's clear statement leaves no room for doubt about its meaning: the Incarnation *did* take place. The Son of God was actually made flesh. He came to earth in the person of Jesus Christ. This is a staggering thought. Jesus Christ is God—fully God, yet He is man—fully man (see 1 Jn.4:2-3). Jesus Christ is beyond question God Himself who became human, who partook of the very same flesh as all other people. (See 1 Jn.1:1-4; see also Deeper Study # 1 for the meaning of "flesh" and why Jesus Christ had to become flesh. Also see Deeper Study # 1, *Flesh*—1 Co.3:1-4 for more discussion.)

b. **He and His glory were seen (v.14b).**

John went on to report that the people beheld Christ's glory. The word *have seen* or *beheld* (Gk. theasthai) means actually seeing with the human eye. Once again, John's meaning is clear. He left no room for anybody to say that God's becoming a man was merely a vision of some person's mind or imagination. John said that he and others actually *saw* the Word made flesh.

Specifically, John testified that the people saw God's glory with their own eyes. By the word *glory*, John was saying that Christ was the *Shekinah glory* of God. The word Shekinah means "that which dwells" or "dwelling." It refers to the *bright cloud* that God used to guide Israel out of Egypt and that rested upon the tabernacle and above the mercy seat in the Most Holy Place (Ex.40:34-38). The cloud symbolized God's presence, and that is just what John is saying: We actually saw the Shekinah glory, God's very presence dwelling among us.

Moreover, John also says that Christ is the very embodiment of God, all that God is and does. When they looked at Jesus, it was obvious that He was God. They saw that all that Jesus was in His person and being, character and behavior, was so enormously different from any another person. In person and behavior, work and ministry He was . . .

- the very embodiment of grace and truth
- the perfect embodiment of "love, joy, peace, patience, kindness, goodness, faithfulness, gentleness, and self-control" (Ga.5:22-23)
- the absolute embodiment of all that God is

The glory of all that God is stood right before them, right in their very presence. They saw Him with their very own eyes. Jesus Christ, the Man who dwelt among them, could be no other than the glory of God among humanity. It was clearly seen that He was the fullness of God in bodily form (Col.2:9). The glory of His being was the very glory God Himself possessed. It was the very glory God would give to His only begotten Son (just as any father would give the best of his glory and all he is to a son).

*Only Son* or *only begotten* (monogenous) speaks of Jesus' uniqueness as the one and only Son of God. As genuine believers, we are the spiritual children (tekna) of God (v.12). But in all of human history, Jesus alone was the physical Son of God. This occurred through the miracle of the Virgin Birth (Is.7:14; Lu.1:31, 34-35).

A striking fact is that James, who was the Lord's brother, even called Jesus "the Lord of glory." Just think: James was reared alongside Jesus from childhood to adulthood. If anyone ever had an opportunity to see and observe Jesus, it was James. He had every chance to witness some act of disobedience, some sin, something contrary to the nature of God. However, James described Jesus as the Lord of Glory, the One in whom the very presence of God dwelt (Js.2:1).

The references in John dealing with Christ's glory are as follows: Jn.2:11; 5:41; 7:18; 8:50, 54; 11:4; 12:41; 17:5, 22, 24.

c. **He was full of grace and truth (v.14c).**

John further describes Jesus Christ as full of grace and truth. He was and still is the very embodiment of grace. Through Him, God's kindness and unmerited favor were showered on every human being (see Deeper Study # 2). In addition, Jesus was the very embodiment of truth while He lived on this earth. Through His teaching and His sinless, perfect life, Jesus proclaimed and demonstrated God's truth to the world (see Deeper Study # 2, *Truth*—Jn.14:6; Deeper Study # 1—8:32).

> "And behold, you will conceive in your womb and bear a son, and you shall call his name Jesus." . . . And Mary said to the angel, "How will this be, since I am a virgin?" And the angel answered her,

"The Holy Spirit will come upon you, and the power of the Most High will overshadow you; therefore the child to be born will be called holy—the Son of God." (Lu.1:31, 34-35)

Concerning his Son, who was descended from David according to the flesh. (Ro.1:3)

But emptied himself, by taking the form of a servant, being born in the likeness of men. (Ph.2:7)

Great indeed, we confess, is the mystery of godliness: He was manifested in the flesh, vindicated by the Spirit, seen by angels, proclaimed among the nations, believed on in the world, taken up in glory. (1 Ti.3:16)

"Therefore the Lord himself will give you a sign. Behold, the virgin shall conceive and bear a son, and shall call his name Immanuel." (Is.7:14)

For to us a child is born, to us a son is given; and the government shall be upon his shoulder, and his name shall be called Wonderful Counselor, Mighty God, Everlasting Father, Prince of Peace. (Is.9:6)

## Deeper Study # 1

(1:14) **Flesh**: What does the Bible mean by "flesh"? And why did Jesus Christ have to become flesh? The best description of the flesh is probably found in 1 Co.15:42-44.

Note the following Scriptural points about our flesh and how Christ's becoming a man delivered us from it:

1. The flesh is corruptible.
   a. The flesh is tainted, debased, ruined and depraved by sinful desires or lust (2 Pe.1:4). There is a seed of corruption within human flesh; therefore, the flesh sins and thereby ages, dies, deteriorates and decays. It does not live beyond a few years on this earth.

      I tell you this, brothers: flesh and blood cannot inherit the kingdom of God, nor does the perishable inherit the imperishable. (1 Co.15:50)

      For the one who sows to his own flesh will from the flesh reap corruption, but the one who sows to the Spirit will from the Spirit reap eternal life. (Ga.6:8)

   b. Christ (the Word) delivered us from the corruption of our flesh.

      "For God so loved the world, that he gave his only Son, that whoever believes in him should not perish but have eternal life." (Jn.3:16)

      Knowing that you were ransomed from the futile ways inherited from your forefathers, not with perishable things such as silver or gold, but with the precious blood of Christ, like that of a lamb without blemish or spot.... since you have been born again, not of perishable seed but of imperishable, through the living and abiding word of God; for "All flesh is like grass and all its glory like the flower of grass. The grass withers, and the flower falls, but the word of the Lord remains forever." And this word is the good news that was preached to you. (1 Pe.1:18-19, 23-25)

      By which [Christ] has granted to us his precious and very great promises, so that through them you may become partakers of the divine nature, having escaped from the corruption that is in the world because of sinful desire. (2 Pe.1:4)

2. The flesh is dishonorable.
   a. The flesh is not what God created it to be. It does not hold the glory, the honor, nor the prestige it once did when God created it. It is disgraced and shamed, and it is reproached by sin and lust. It is held in the grip of sin and fear and subject to being held in bondage—even the bondage of death.

      And since they did not see fit to acknowledge God, God gave them up to a debased mind to do what ought not to be done. They were filled with all manner of unrighteousness, evil, covetousness, malice. They are full of envy, murder, strife, deceit, maliciousness. They are gossips, slanderers, haters of God, insolent, haughty, boastful, inventors of evil, disobedient to parents, foolish, faithless, heartless, ruthless. Though they know God's righteous decree that those who practice such things deserve to die, they not only do them but give approval to those who practice them. (Ro.1:28-32; see Ga.5:19-21)

      For I know that nothing good dwells in me, that is, in my flesh. For I have the desire to do what is right, but not the ability to carry it out. (Ro.7:18)

      For those who live according to the flesh set their minds on the things of the flesh.... For to set the mind on the flesh is death. (Ro.8:5-6)

b. Jesus Christ delivered us from the dishonor of our flesh.

   But God shows his love for us in that while we were still sinners, Christ died for us. Since, therefore, we have now been justified by his blood, much more shall we be saved by him from the wrath of God. For if while we were enemies we were reconciled to God by the death of his Son, much more, now that we are reconciled, shall we be saved by his life. (Ro.5:8-10)

   Since therefore the children share in flesh and blood, he himself likewise partook of the same things, that through death he might destroy the one who has the power of death, that is, the devil, and deliver all those who through fear of death were subject to lifelong slavery. (He.2:14-15; see 2:14-18)

3. The flesh is weak.
   a. The flesh is impotent, feeble, infirmed, and decrepit because of sin (lust). It has no strength to please God nor to save itself.

   "It is the Spirit who gives life; the flesh is no help at all. The words that I have spoken to you are spirit and life." (Jn.6:63)

   No human being will be justified in his sight. (Ro.3:20; Ga.2:16)

   Those who are in the flesh cannot please God. (Ro.8:8)

   b. Jesus Christ delivered us from the weakness of our flesh.

   For while we were still weak, at the right time Christ died for the ungodly. (Ro.5:6)

   For God has done what the law, weakened by the flesh, could not do. By sending his own Son in the likeness of sinful flesh and for sin, he condemned sin in the flesh. (Ro.8:3)

4. The flesh is a natural body.
   a. The flesh is of the earth and is part of the earth; it is made up of the chemicals and substances of the earth. It is physical, material, animal. It is the "earthly dwelling," the "tent," which houses the human soul and spirit (2 Co.5:1). It is neither spirit nor spiritual; therefore, it cannot live beyond the strength of the chemicals and substances that form its flesh. It cannot live beyond its *natural life*.

   "See my hands and my feet, that it is I myself. Touch me, and see. For a spirit does not have flesh and bones as you see that I have." (Lu.24:39)

   It is sown a natural body; it is raised a spiritual body. If there is a natural body, there is also a spiritual body. Just as we have borne the image of the man of dust, we shall also bear the image of the man of heaven. I tell you this, brothers: flesh and blood cannot inherit the kingdom of God, nor does the perishable inherit the imperishable. (1 Co.15:44, 49-50)

   b. Jesus Christ delivered us from the natural body of the flesh. He "became a life-giving spirit," the Savior who could make alive all those who would trust Him (1 Co.15:45).

   If the Spirit of him who raised Jesus from the dead dwells in you, he who raised Christ Jesus from the dead will also give life to your mortal bodies through his Spirit who dwells in you. (Ro.8:11)

   But God, being rich in mercy, because of the great love with which he loved us, even when we were dead in our trespasses, made us alive together with Christ—by grace you have been saved. (Ep.2:4-5)

   For Christ also suffered once for sins, the righteous for the unrighteous, that he might bring us to God, being put to death in the flesh but made alive in the spirit. (1 Pe.3:18)

## DEEPER STUDY # 2

(1:14) **Grace**: grace is one of the most meaningful words in the human vocabulary. The word *grace* (charis) means far more in the Bible than it does when people generally use it. To most people, the word grace means three things.

1. Grace is that quality within a thing that is beautiful or joyful. It may be the fragrance of a flower, the rich greenness of the grass, or the beauty of a lovely person.

2. Grace is anything that has loveliness. It may be a thought, an act, a word, a person.

3. Grace is a gift, a favor that someone might extend to a friend. The favor is always freely done, where the giver is expecting nothing in return. The favor is always done for a friend.

However, when the early Christians looked at what God had done for humanity, they had to add a deeper, much richer meaning to the word *grace*. God had saved sinners, those who had acted against Him. Therefore, grace became the favor of God showered upon sinful people—people who did not deserve His favor. Grace became the kindness and love that dwells within the very nature of God, the kindness and love that God freely gives to His *enemies*.

No other word expresses so adequately the depth and richness of the heart and mind of God. This is the distinctive difference between God's grace and human grace. Whereas people sometimes do favors for their friends and thereby can be said to be gracious, God has done a thing unheard of among humans: He has given His very own Son to die for His *enemies* (Ro.5:8-10). In this act He has done something that shows He is the perfect embodiment of grace, full . . .

- of beauty and joy
- of loveliness and goodness
- of favors freely given
- of kindness and love freely demonstrated

## 1:15

¹⁵ (John bore witness about him, and cried out, "This was he of whom I said, 'He who comes after me ranks before me, because he was before me.'")

## 2 Proof 2: John the Baptist bore witness of the superiority of Christ.

The second proof of the Incarnation is the testimony of John the Baptist. He, too, bore witness of the Word becoming flesh. John made three simple statements that, together, testify of the superiority of Christ:

First, John the Baptist said that Jesus came *after* him. Jesus was born after John (6 months after), and He appeared publicly after John.

Second, John stated that even though Jesus was younger and less experienced in ministry than he, Jesus *ranks* or was *preferred before [him]* (emprosthen mou gegonen: literally translated, *He before me has become*). This means that Jesus was more important in being, status, and dignity than John was.

Third, John declared strongly the reason Jesus was greater than he: "*because He was before me*" (hoti protos mou en). Literally, this statement means, *for He was first to me* or *first of me*. It refers both to time and importance. Jesus Christ was first in time, existing before John. He existed "in the beginning"—throughout all eternity (v.1). John proclaimed clearly, that, even though Jesus was born *after* he was born, He existed *before* him. Jesus had always existed; He was the First. As the Creator, He was the very cause for John's existence.

John also declared that Jesus was first in importance. He was first in superiority, being, and person. One of Jesus' names testifies to this truth. His very name is the First and the Last, the Alpha and the Omega, the Beginning and the End (Re 1:8, 11; 21:6; 22:13).

> And he is before all things, and in him all things hold together. (Col.1:17)
>
> "I am the Alpha and the Omega, the first and the last, the beginning and the end." (Re.22:13; see Re.1:8; 21:6; Is.44:6)
>
> Thus says the LORD, the King of Israel and his Redeemer, the LORD of hosts: "I am the first and I am the last; besides me there is no god." (Is.44:6)

## 1:16-17

¹⁶ For from his fullness we have all received, grace upon grace.
¹⁷ For the law was given through Moses; grace and truth came through Jesus Christ.

## 3 Proof 3: We have received His grace and blessing upon blessing.

The third proof of the Incarnation is the fullness and grace of Christ which was given to us. Genuine believers can testify to the reality of this gift.

*Fullness* (pleroma) means that which fills completely, the sum total, the totality. It is the sum total of all that is in God (Col.1:19). In Jesus dwelt all the wisdom, righteousness, sanctification, and redemption—all the abundance of God (1 Co.1:30). All that Christ is, the very fullness of His being, is given to believers—all His "love, joy, peace, patience, kindness, goodness, faithfulness, gentleness, self-control" (Ga.5:22-23). We are complete in Him.

> **For in him the whole fullness of deity dwells bodily, and you have been filled in him, who is the head of all rule and authority. (Col.2:9-10)**

The term "grace upon grace" or "grace for grace" means that He gives grace on top of grace, grace enough to meet all our needs, no matter the circumstances. It is one blessing leading to another blessing; new wonders dawning upon us every day; fresh expressions of His goodness constantly springing up into our lives.

In addition, *grace upon* or *for grace* means that there is a never-ending flow of grace from God to us. God's grace is unlimited and never depleted. Under the law, when the atoning sacrifice was offered annually, forgiveness was granted for another year. Under grace, the once-and-for-all sacrifice of Christ secured eternal, unlimited forgiveness (He.9:23-10:18). God's grace covers *all* of our sins—both past and future—with the blood of His dear Son (1 Jn.1:7-2:2). God's grace is more abundant than our sins (Ro.5:20).

A word of warning is due here: The granting of grace upon grace—unlimited, abundant grace—through Christ does not mean that we are free to continue in sin. In his first epistle, John assured us of God's unlimited forgiveness (1 Jn.1:7-2:2). John proceeded to offer a grave warning:

> **And by this we know that we have come to know him, if we keep his commandments. Whoever says "I know him" but does not keep his commandments is a liar, and the truth is not in him, but whoever keeps his word, in him truly the love of God is perfected. By this we may know that we are in him. (1 Jn.2:3-5)**

John's admonition is clear: those who profess to know Christ but continue carelessly in sin *do not know Him*. They are not genuine believers and have not been truly born again. The truth—Jesus Christ—is not in them.

### a. God's grace and blessing do not come by law (v.17a).

The fullness of God, His grace and truth, does not come by the law. It does not come . . .
- by being as good as we can
- by working to please God as much as we can
- by keeping the rules and commandments of the law

The law only points out our failure and condemns us for breaking the law. No person can keep God's law perfectly. Under the law, people were acceptable to God because they kept coming to God, offering sacrifices and begging for His forgiveness for breaking the law. God forgave them as they fulfilled the sacrificial requirements for violating His law. The law demonstrated God's righteousness and justice; but the *fullness* of God—His sacrificial love and grace—were never displayed in this system.

### b. God's grace and blessing come through Jesus Christ (v.17b).

However, when Christ came into the world, He came as the demonstration of God's grace. God gave His Son to the world as the eternal sacrifice for our sins. We cannot keep God's law, nor can we offer any sacrifices that will eternally atone for our sin. Out of His great love, mercy, and grace, God offered His Son so that we might have eternal salvation. Through this act—the greatest act of love and grace in world history—we received the fullness of God. God's righteousness and justice demanded a price for our sin. God's love, mercy, and grace offered His Son as that sacrifice.

Such is the grace, the undeserved favor, of God. God's grace comes by Jesus Christ, and we would not know the grace of God unless Jesus Christ had come to reveal it to us. The glorious fact that we do experience the fullness of God and His grace is proof of the Incarnation (that God did become flesh in the person of Jesus Christ).

> **"But we believe that we will be saved through the grace of the Lord Jesus, just as they will." (Ac.15:11)**

> **For all have sinned and fall short of the glory of God, and are justified by his grace as a gift, through the redemption that is in Christ Jesus. (Ro.3:23-24)**

For by grace you have been saved through faith. And this is not your own doing; it is the gift of God, not a result of works, so that no one may boast. (Ep.2:8-9)

For the grace of God has appeared, bringing salvation for all people. (Tit.2:11)

But when the goodness and loving kindness of God our Savior appeared, he saved us, not because of works done by us in righteousness, but according to his own mercy, by the washing of regeneration and renewal of the Holy Spirit, whom he poured out on us richly through Jesus Christ our Savior, so that being justified by his grace we might become heirs according to the hope of eternal life. (Tit.3:4-7)

## 1:18

¹⁸ No one has ever seen God; the only God, who is at the Father's side, he has made him known.

## 4 Proof 4: God has revealed Himself through Christ

The fourth proof of the Incarnation is Christ Himself—God's Son. God revealed Himself to humanity through Christ. John presents four facts concerning this revelation of God to humanity:

- ➢ No person had ever seen God at any time (Jn.5:37).
- ➢ Jesus Christ, the Word made flesh, is the one and only Son of God (v.14; 3:16).
- ➢ Jesus came from the *side* or *bosom* (kolpon) of the Father—the deepest part, the most intimate place, the most honorable place of fellowship. He alone had seen the Father (Jn.6:46).
- ➢ Jesus came to reveal and to proclaim the Father (see Deeper Study # 1, 2, 3—Jn.14:6; see note, Re.14:7).

Throughout His earthly ministry, Jesus Christ declared unequivocally that He had come from God (see outline and notes—Jn.3:31 for more discussion). Moreover, He stated specifically that anyone who saw Him was seeing the Father (Jn.14:7-9). This fact is proof of the Incarnation (that God became flesh).

**THOUGHT 1.** Every person either believes or does not believe that Jesus Christ is God in the flesh. Every person either believes or does not believe the grace and truth of God as revealed in Jesus Christ. The greatest question every individual must answer is the question Jesus asked the Pharisees:

[Jesus asked them], "What do you think about the Christ? Whose son is he?" They said to him, "The son of David." (Mt.22:42)

And the question Jesus asked His disciples:

He said to them, "But who do you say that I am?" (Mt.16:15)

Your eternal destiny hinges on your answer to this question. We can only be saved by believing that Jesus is the Son of God and God the Son, and that He is the only Savior—the way, the truth, and the life (Jn.14:6).

He said to them, "But who do you say that I am?" Simon Peter replied, "You are the Christ, the Son of the living God." And Jesus answered him, "Blessed are you, Simon Bar-Jonah! For flesh and blood has not revealed this to you, but my Father who is in heaven." (Mt.16:15-17)

"I and the Father are one." (Jn.10:30)

"If you had known me, you would have known my Father also. From now on you do know him and have seen him." Philip said to him, "Lord, show us the Father, and it is enough for us." Jesus said to him, "Have I been with you so long, and you still do not know me, Philip? Whoever has seen me has seen the Father. How can you say, 'Show us the Father'?" (Jn.14:7-9)

That is, in Christ God was reconciling the world to himself, not counting their trespasses against them, and entrusting to us the message of reconciliation. (2 Co.5:19)

For in him the whole fullness of deity dwells bodily. (Col.2:9)

# E. Jesus the Messiah, the Lord: The Second Witness of John the Baptist, 1:19–28

¹⁹ And this is the testimony of John, when the Jews sent priests and Levites from Jerusalem to ask him, "Who are you?"

²⁰ He confessed, and did not deny, but confessed, "I am not the Christ."

²¹ And they asked him, "What then? Are you Elijah?" He said, "I am not." "Are you the Prophet?" And he answered, "No."

²² So they said to him, "Who are you? We need to give an answer to those who sent us. What do you say about yourself?"

²³ He said, "I am the voice of one crying out in the wilderness, 'Make straight the way of the Lord,' as the prophet Isaiah said."

²⁴ (Now they had been sent from the Pharisees.)

²⁵ They asked him, "Then why are you baptizing, if you are neither the Christ, nor Elijah, nor the Prophet?"

²⁶ John answered them, "I baptize with water, but among you stands one you do not know,

²⁷ "even he who comes after me, the strap of whose sandal I am not worthy to untie."

²⁸ These things took place in Bethany across the Jordan, where John was baptizing.

1. John was questioned by religious leaders who were suspicious of him: They asked, "Who are you?"[DS1]

2. John was a man who knew who he was
   a. He was not the Christ[DS2]
   b. He was not Elijah
   c. He was not "the prophet"

3. John was only a voice—only a forerunner for the Lord
   a. His clear declaration: He was merely a man proclaiming the coming of the Lord
   b. His questioners: The Pharisees[DS3]

4. John was a baptizer

   a. He baptized with water
   b. He pointed to One whom they did not know: The Messiah

5. John was an unworthy servant of the One whom he proclaimed, the Messiah

6. John was a man who brought honor to the place where he ministered

# Division I

*The Witnesses to the Revelation of Jesus Christ, 1:1–51*

E. Jesus the Messiah, the Lord: The Second Witness of John the Baptist, 1:19–28

## 1:19–28
## Introduction

The witness of John the Baptist is a dynamic example for every servant of God. His response to those who questioned him teaches us what our role is as witnesses for Jesus Christ. This is, *Jesus the Messiah, the Lord: The Second Witness of John the Baptist,* 1:19–28.

1. John was questioned by religious leaders who were suspicious of him: They asked, "Who are you?" (v.19).
2. John was a man who knew who he was (vv.20-22).
3. John was only a voice—only a forerunner for the LORD (vv.23-24).
4. John was a baptizer (vv.25-26).
5. John was an unworthy servant of the One whom he proclaimed, the Messiah (v.27).
6. John was a man who brought honor to the place where he ministered (v.28).

### 1:19

<sup>19</sup> And this is the testimony of John, when the Jews sent priests and Levites from Jerusalem to ask him, "Who are you?"

### 1 John was questioned by religious leaders who were suspicious of him: They asked, "Who are you?"

The leaders of the Jews were very suspicious of John. Therefore, they sent a fact-finding commission made up of priests and Levites from Jerusalem, the headquarters of Jewish religion (see DEEPER STUDY #1).

The Jewish leaders' questioning of John was to be expected, for John's father, Zechariah, was a priest (Lu.1:5); and in the eyes of the authorities, all the sons of priests were automatically priests by descent. However, John was not a priest like other priests. He was most unusual, for the way he lived and preached was radically different (see Mt.3:1-12). He did not conform to Jewish rules and rituals, and the authorities had to find out why.

> **THOUGHT 1.** Too often institutional religions are suspicious and opposed to the unusual. If we are different or do things differently, we will most likely be questioned. Or, if we are unusually blessed or if miraculous things are happening in our lives and ministries, we can expect to be questioned.
>
> Like John, we need to respond to questions graciously and truthfully. We must never back down from our call, and we must never compromise the truth in order to appease those who may be suspicious of us or antagonistic toward us.
>
> > Rather, speaking the truth in love, we are to grow up in every way into him who is the head, into Christ. (Ep.4:15)
> >
> > But in your hearts honor Christ the Lord as holy, always being prepared to make a defense to anyone who asks you for a reason for the hope that is in you; yet do it with gentleness and respect. (1 Pe.3:15)

### DEEPER STUDY # 1

(1:19) **Levites**: these men were servants of the priests. They were descendants of Levi just as the descendants of Aaron were. However, only Aaron's descendants could serve as priests; all other Levites served under them.

## 2 John was a man who knew who he was.

While others had questions about John, John knew exactly who he was. He knew God personally; therefore, he knew God had sent him into the world for a specific ministry. He was from God, called and commissioned by God; therefore, He knew exactly who he was and what he was doing (see Deeper Study # 1—Jn.1:6; also see outline and notes—Jn.1:6-8 for more discussion).

> [20] He confessed, and did not deny, but confessed, "I am not the Christ."
>
> [21] And they asked him, "What then? Are you Elijah?" He said, "I am not." "Are you the Prophet?" And he answered, "No."
>
> [22] So they said to him, "Who are you? We need to give an answer to those who sent us. What do you say about yourself?"

### a. He was not the Christ (v.20).

John confessed that he was not the Christ, the promised Messiah of Israel (see Deeper Study # 2). He was not the One whom God would send to deliver the Jewish people and redeem humanity from sin.

### b. He was not Elijah (v.21a).

The Jewish people expected Elijah to return to proclaim the coming of the Messiah (Mal.4:5). They thought the great prophet would return supernaturally to do several significant things: to warn the people, to anoint the Messiah to His kingly office, to raise the dead, and to help select those who were to have a part in the Messiah's kingdom.

John clearly denied that he was Elijah in person. It should be noted that Jesus did later identify John with Elijah (Mk.9:11f). However, what Jesus meant was that John was like Elijah, both in spirit and power (Lk.1:17). But he was *not* Elijah.

### c. He was not "the prophet" (v.21b).

This prophet was thought to be another forerunner of the Messiah (Jn.7:40). Some persons thought he would be either Jeremiah or Isaiah. This belief was based on Moses' prediction that there would be a prophet like unto himself (De.18:15). However, today most Christians interpret the prophet predicted by Moses to be Christ Himself (Ac.3:22; 7:37).

**THOUGHT 1.** The lessons are clear. The servant (minister or layman) of God must not . . .

- claim to be the Christ nor any other great prophet
- pretend to be some great man or woman of God
- seek recognition
- assume some honor that does not belong to them
- allow God's power upon their lives and ministries to turn their heads toward pride, thinking more highly of themselves than they should

> But the centurion replied, "Lord, I am not worthy to have you come under my roof, but only say the word, and my servant will be healed." (Mt.8:8)
>
> For I am the least of the apostles, unworthy to be called an apostle, because I persecuted the church of God. (1 Co.15:9)
>
> Abraham answered and said, "Behold, I have undertaken to speak to the Lord, I who am but dust and ashes." (Ge.18:27)
>
> "I am not worthy of the least of all the deeds of steadfast love and all the faithfulness that you have shown to your servant, for with only my staff I crossed this Jordan, and now I have become two camps." (Ge.32:10)
>
> But Moses said to God, "Who am I that I should go to Pharaoh and bring the children of Israel out of Egypt?" (Ex.3:11)
>
> Then King David went in and sat before the Lord and said, "Who am I, O Lord God, and what is my house, that you have brought me thus far?" (2 S.7:18)

## Deeper Study # 2

(1:20) **Christ—Messiah**: the words *Christ* and *Messiah* are essentially the same title. Messiah comes from the Hebrew (Messias), while Christ comes from the Greek (Christos). Both words refer to the same person and mean the same thing: *the anointed one*. The Messiah is the anointed one of God. Matthew said Jesus "is called Christ" (Mt.1:16); that is, He is recognized as *the anointed one of God*, the Messiah Himself.

In the day of Jesus Christ, Jewish people fervently prayed and yearned for the coming of the long-promised Messiah. The weight of impoverished life for many was harsh and difficult. And Jews of all social statuses felt the burden of the Roman oppressors. Under the Romans, people felt that God could not wait much longer to fulfill His promise. Such longings for deliverance left the people gullible. Many arose who claimed to be the Messiah and led the gullible followers into rebellion against the Roman state. Barabbas, a revolutionary who was set free in the place of Jesus at Jesus' trial, is an example (Mk.15:6f). (See note—Mt.1:1; Deeper Study # 2—3:11; notes 11:1-6; 11:2-3; Deeper Study # 1—11:5; Deeper Study # 2—11:6; notes 12:16; notes 22:42; Lu.7:21-23.)

The Messiah was thought to be several things.

1. Nationally, He was to be the leader from David's line who would free the Jewish state and establish it as an independent nation, leading it to be the greatest nation the world had ever known.

2. Militarily, He was to be a great military leader who would lead Jewish armies victoriously over all the world.

3. Religiously, He was to be a supernatural figure straight from God who would bring righteousness over all the earth.

4. Personally, He was to be the One who would bring peace to the whole world.

Jesus Christ accepted the title of Messiah on three different occasions (Mt.16:17; Mk.14:61; Jn.4:26). The name *Jesus* shows Him to be man. The name *Christ* shows Him to be God's anointed, God's very own Son. *Christ* is Jesus' official title. It identifies Him officially as Prophet (De.18:15-19), Priest (Ps.110:4), and King (2 S.7:12-13). These officials were always anointed with oil, a symbol of the Holy Spirit who was to perfectly anoint the Christ, the Messiah (Mt.3:16; Mk.1:10-11; Lu.3:21-22; Jn.1:32-33).

> He first found his own brother Simon and said to him, "We have found the Messiah" (which means Christ). (Jn.1:41)
>
> Philip found Nathanael and said to him, "We have found him of whom Moses in the Law and also the prophets wrote, Jesus of Nazareth, the son of Joseph." (Jn.1:45)
>
> The woman said to him, "I know that Messiah is coming (he who is called Christ). When he comes, he will tell us all things." Jesus said to her, "I who speak to you am he." (Jn.4:25-26)
>
> "And we have believed, and have come to know, that you are the Holy One of God." (Jn.6:69)
>
> Jesus said to her, "I am the resurrection and the life. Whoever believes in me, though he die, yet shall he live, and everyone who lives and believes in me shall never die. Do you believe this?" She said to him, "Yes, Lord; I believe that you are the Christ, the Son of God, who is coming into the world." (Jn.11:25-27)

## 1:23-24

[23] He said, "I am the voice of one crying out in the wilderness, 'Make straight the way of the Lord,' as the prophet Isaiah said."

[24] (Now they had been sent from the Pharisees.)

### 3 John was only a voice—only a forerunner—for the Lord.

John identified himself as only a voice—a forerunner—for the Lord. By doing so, John established himself as the fulfillment of a specific prophecy concerning the Messiah: *he* was the special messenger whom Isaiah said God would send to announce the coming of His Son (Is.40:3).

a. **His clear declaration: he was merely a man proclaiming the coming of the Lord (v.23).**
In response to the direct question, "Who are you?" John made a clear declaration: He was merely a man proclaiming the coming of the Lord (v.23). Why was it necessary for the Messiah to have a forerunner? Why did John have to run ahead of Christ crying, "Prepare. Make straight the way of the Lord"? What kind of preparation needed to be done?

> *The people needed their concept of the Messiah straightened out.* Their concept had deteriorated through the years. Few had ever seen the seed or offspring promised to Adam and Abraham as referring to the Messiah (see Deeper Study # 1—Ga.3:8, 16; Deeper Study # 1—Ro.4:1-25). They interpreted this special descendant to be the nation of Israel; that is, all circumcised Jews. They would later tell Christ that *they* were the offspring of Abraham (Jn.8:33). They saw Christ as being a descendant of Abraham only in the sense that any ordinary Jew was. He was just an ordinary man born through Abraham's line. Few ever saw the Messiah as the One in whom all the promises made to Abraham were to be fulfilled.
>
> Furthermore, the Jews saw the Messiah primarily as the Son of David. David had liberated and led their nation to its highest peak, so they saw the Messiah as following in David's footsteps (see notes—Mt.1:1; Lu.3:24-31; Jn.1:45; Deeper Study # 1—1:18; Deeper Study # 2—3:11; notes—11:1-6; 11:2-3; 12:16; 22:42; Lu.7:21-23). At first, the Jews saw the Messiah as a liberator, One who was going to deliver them from all their enemies and restore their nation to its greatest glory. (Keep in mind how awful the Jews had been treated and persecuted throughout history.) However, as centuries rolled on and they suffered brutal violence after violence, their concept of the Messiah deteriorated into anger.
>
> The Jews saw themselves as the subjects of the Messiah's salvation (deliverance) and saw all other people (Gentiles) as the subjects of the Messiah's judgment. The Jews were the ones acceptable to God; all others were unacceptable. Therefore, the Messiah was to come and free Israel, elevating the nation to rule over all the nations of the earth. This, of course, led to two tragic faults. First, the Jews became blind to their own sinful condition and personal need for salvation. Second, they saw salvation as a matter of national heritage and personal rites (being circumcised) and rituals (religious observances). They believed that they were safe because they had been circumcised and their forefathers were godly people.
>
> The forerunner, John the Baptist, had to begin breaking through the barriers of these errors. Salvation was not a national thing, not an institutional thing, not even a religious thing. It was not a matter of heritage and rites. It was a personal matter, a spiritual matter of the heart and life. An individual had to personally want forgiveness of sins and then repent if he/she wished to be saved. This was to be the message of the Messiah. Therefore, because of the hardness of the people in understanding the personal need for salvation, God had to send a forerunner to begin penetrating through the barriers of self-righteousness which had become so cemented in the minds of the Jews. (Just how deeply rooted the false concept of the Messiah was can be seen in the enormous struggle the disciples had with it. See note—Mt 18:1-2.)

> *The people needed their religion straightened out.* They had allowed their religion to become formal and institutionalized, that is, just a form of godliness which denied the power thereof (2 Ti.3:5). So many were going through the motions of religion, its services and rites, yet living as they wished. Godly living was of little concern. The Messiah was to bring a new message, a message of God's love—a love so strong that it would proclaim the truth of humanity's condition: that every human being is sinful and perishing (Jn.3:16), and, consequently, must repent (Mk.2:17). This repentance was critical and could not be delayed because the Kingdom of Heaven was at hand (Mt.4:17).
>
> The message was to be so radical that some preparations were needed among the people before the Messiah appeared on the scene. Therefore, God sent the forerunner, John the Baptist.

➤ *The world needed to know about the Messiah.* As the Son of God, the Messiah would be so different—so pure, so holy, so truthful—that people would not tolerate His presence too long. His proclamation of the truth and salvation would be very, very short. His enemies would destroy Him. Therefore, people needed to be stirred to a high pitch of excitement when the Messiah arrived. They needed to be buzzing about with great anticipation and with the glorious news that the Messiah had finally come. People would need to sit up and take notice. They may not respond; they might even react violently, but they needed to be aware of the Messiah's historical coming and claims to be the Son of God. The forerunner was to stir the people to expect the Messiah immediately.

b. **His questioners: The Pharisees (v.24).**
Note that Scripture includes an important detail: John the Baptist's questioners were the Pharisees, who were disturbed that John was ministering outside of their authority (see Deeper Study #3, Pharisees—Ac.23:8 for more discussion). From the very beginning of the Messiah's coming, even before Jesus actually started His ministry, the Pharisees opposed Him.

**THOUGHT 1.** What was true of the people of John's day is true of many today. Many need their concept of the Messiah straightened out. Some have never seen that the *promised seed* is Christ. Some still think of themselves as being *special* to God. They are blind to their sin and need for personal salvation. Many others need their religion straightened out. Many simply need to hear about the Messiah: they have never heard that He has come.

**THOUGHT 2.** We are God's messengers of the good news that Jesus Christ has come, bringing salvation to every human being. As such, we need to always remember that we are only a voice, only a forerunner for the Lord. But we *are* a voice and a forerunner; therefore, we *must* speak up for the Lord.
(1) We must be a *clear voice* proclaiming a clear *message*.

> "For it is not you who speak, but the Spirit of your Father speaking through you." (Mt.10:20)
>
> And he said to them, "Go into all the world and proclaim the gospel to the whole creation." (Mk.16:15)
>
> And we impart this in words not taught by human wisdom but taught by the Spirit, interpreting spiritual truths to those who are spiritual. (1 Co.2:13)
>
> Whoever speaks, as one who speaks oracles of God; whoever serves, as one who serves by the strength that God supplies—in order that in everything God may be glorified through Jesus Christ. To him belong glory and dominion forever and ever. Amen. (1 Pe.4:11)

(2) We must be an *earnest voice* proclaiming the desperate need to prepare and repent.

> "Repent, for the kingdom of heaven is at hand." (Mt.3:2)
>
> "Repent therefore, and turn back, that your sins may be blotted out." (Ac.3:19)

1:25-26

²⁵ They asked him, "Then why are you baptizing, if you are neither the Christ, nor Elijah, nor the Prophet?"
²⁶ John answered them, "I baptize with water, but among you stands one you do not know,

## 4 John was a baptizer.

The messenger was a baptizer—a fact that incited and puzzled the religious leaders. This is why they wondered if he were the Christ (vv.19-20). They believed that when the Christ came He might institute the practice of baptism. When John stated that he was not the Christ, they wanted to know if John were a prophet. In theory a true prophet was said to have the right to institute new practices and to change some laws.

a. **He baptized with water (v.26a).**

John's practice of water baptism shocked the Jewish nation, for Jews had never been baptized before. Baptism was only for non-Jewish persons who were converts to the Jewish faith. The Jews considered all Gentiles unclean, so Gentiles had to be baptized when they became converts. (All males were also circumcised.) However, Jews were thought to be clean and acceptable to God no matter how they lived. Why? Because Jews were "of the seed of Abraham," of his heritage. They were his seed, the people promised to Abraham.

John's baptism was radical, most unusual, a shocking practice. It was a baptism of repentance *for* the forgiveness of sins (Lu.3:3). What does this mean? Simply this: when a person wanted God to forgive their sins, they made the decision to repent, to turn from their sins, and to change their life. Then they were immediately baptized, thereby proclaiming that they were becoming a follower of the Messiah whom John preached (see note—Lu.3:3 for detailed discussion).

The Old Testament prophets had cried for Israel to wash themselves and to be cleansed of their filthiness. John used water baptism to show that a person was turning from their sins and turning to God, seeking forgiveness of sins.

> "Wash yourselves; make yourselves clean; remove the evil of your deeds from before my eyes; cease to do evil." (Is.1:16)

> "I will sprinkle clean water on you, and you shall be clean from all your uncleannesses, and from all your idols I will cleanse you. And I will give you a new heart, and a new spirit I will put within you. And I will remove the heart of stone from your flesh and give you a heart of flesh." (Eze.36:25-26)

> "On that day there shall be a fountain opened for the house of David and the inhabitants of Jerusalem, to cleanse them from sin and uncleanness." (Zec.13:1)

b. **He pointed to One whom they did not know: The Messiah (v.26b).**

John directed his questioners' attention *away* from the act of baptism *to* the true subject of His message: the Messiah. His primary mission was not to baptize, but to prepare the people for the coming of the Messiah. Accordingly, John pointed the religious leaders to the Messiah, whom he revealed was standing among them.

**THOUGHT 1.** Baptism is critical. All believers are to be baptized, but they are to be baptized because they are truly repenting and sincerely turning to God. Like John, the servant of God is to be a baptizer, one who proclaims and practices baptism in its full meaning, as commanded by Christ (Mt.28:19). But our message is not the message of baptism; it is the message of Christ. We are to point people to Christ, just as John did the religious leaders. Then, once they have believed upon Christ, we are to direct them to be baptized, as Christ commanded.

> "Go therefore and make disciples of all nations, baptizing them in the name of the Father and of the Son and of the Holy Spirit." (Mt.28:19)

> And Peter said to them, "Repent and be baptized every one of you in the name of Jesus Christ for the forgiveness of your sins, and you will receive the gift of the Holy Spirit." (Ac.2:38)

> What shall we say then? Are we to continue in sin that grace may abound? By no means! How can we who died to sin still live in it? Do you not know that all of us who have been baptized into Christ Jesus were baptized into his death? We were buried therefore with him by baptism into death, in order that, just as Christ was raised from the dead by the glory of the Father, we too might walk in newness of life. (Ro.6:1-4)

## 5 John was an unworthy servant of the One whom he proclaimed, the Messiah.

[27] "even he who comes after me, the strap of whose sandal I am not worthy to untie."

The messenger of God was an unworthy servant. Two statements demonstrated this:

➢ John proclaimed and confessed that Jesus was preferred before him (see note—Jn.1:15).
➢ John proclaimed that he was not worthy even to unloose the straps of Jesus' sandals. He confessed the *nothingness of self*. Slaves were the ones who loosed the sandals of guests

and washed their feet. John said that he was *less* than a slave, unworthy to do even what a slave did.

**THOUGHT 1.** The same confession of unworthiness must be made by every servant of God.

> "But not so with you. Rather, let the greatest among you become as the youngest, and the leader as one who serves." (Lu.22:26)

> For by the grace given to me I say to everyone among you not to think of himself more highly than he ought to think, but to think with sober judgment, each according to the measure of faith that God has assigned. (Ro.12:3)

> Do nothing from selfish ambition or conceit, but in humility count others more significant than yourselves. Let each of you look not only to his own interests, but also to the interests of others. (Ph.2:3–4)

> He has told you, O man, what is good; and what does the LORD require of you but to do justice, and to love kindness, and to walk humbly with your God? (Mi.6:8)

## 1:28

²⁸ These things took place in Bethany across the Jordan, where John was baptizing.

### 6 John was a man who brought honor to the place where he ministered.

John was ministering in Bethany beyond or across the Jordan, which means it was a great distance from Jerusalem. John brought honor to this place. It would not be known apart from John, for nothing else is known about the city. Note that this is not the Bethany which was the home of Mary, Martha, and Lazarus. It was near Jerusalem. This is a different Bethany, a town which apparently no longer existed by AD 200.[1]

**THOUGHT 1.** Servants of God who are faithful in their witness and ministry (like John) will bring honor to a place. In God's eyes a place is honored because believers are there (see Ge.18:16f). The point is this: by bringing the message of Christ to a place, we can make a difference in that place. The gospel changes people, who then impact the community in which they live. This impact, an impact for righteousness, truth, and good works, brings honor to the community.

---

1 John F. Walvoord and Roy B. Zuck, eds., *The Bible Knowledge Commentary* (Wheaton, IL: Victor Books, 1983), Digital edition via Wordsearch Bible Software.

## F. Jesus the Lamb of God—the Son of God: The Third Witness of John the Baptist, 1:29-34

| | |
|---|---|
| ²⁹ The next day he saw Jesus coming toward him, and said, "Behold, the Lamb of God, who takes away the sin of the world! | **1. Jesus is the Lamb of God** |
| ³⁰ This is he of whom I said, 'After me comes a man who ranks before me, because he was before me.' | **2. Jesus is the Preeminent One**<br>a. He was before John: Pre-existent |
| ³¹ I myself did not know him, but for this purpose I came baptizing with water, that he might be revealed to Israel." | b. John did not know Him, only that He was to come |
| ³² And John bore witness: "I saw the Spirit descend from heaven like a dove, and it remained on him. | **3. Jesus is the Messiah, the One upon whom the Spirit of God remained** |
| ³³ I myself did not know him, but he who sent me to baptize with water said to me, 'He on whom you see the Spirit descend and remain, this is he who baptizes with the Holy Spirit.' | a. John did not know Jesus at first<br>b. John was, however, given a sign to identify Jesus |
| ³⁴ And I have seen and have borne witness that this is the Son of God." | **4. Jesus is the Son of God** |

# Division I

*The Witnesses to the Revelation of Jesus Christ, 1:1-51*

F. Jesus the Lamb of God, the Son of God: The Third Witness of John the Baptist, 1:29-34

## 1:29-34
## Introduction

John's witness about Jesus Christ is one of the greatest testimonies any person has ever given. When presented with the unique privilege and grave responsibility of introducing Jesus to the world, John unmistakably proclaimed the Lord Jesus Christ (Lu.4:18-19). He fulfilled this critical responsibility faithfully, identifying Christ simply, clearly, and powerfully. This is, *Jesus the Lamb of God, the Son of God: The Third Witness of John the Baptist,* 1:29-34.

1. Jesus is the Lamb of God (v.29).
2. Jesus is the Preeminent One (vv.30-31).
3. Jesus is the Messiah, the One upon whom the Spirit of God remained (vv.32-33).
4. Jesus is the Son of God (v.34).

## 1 Jesus is the Lamb of God.

Jesus Christ is the *Lamb of God*. Down through the centuries the Lamb of God has been one of the most cherished symbols of Jesus Christ held by believers. There are four reasons for this.

First, the Lamb is a picture of Christ our Passover who was sacrificed for us.

²⁹ The next day he saw Jesus coming toward him, and said, "Behold, the Lamb of God, who takes away the sin of the world!

**Cleanse out the old leaven that you may be a new lump, as you really are unleavened. For Christ, our Passover lamb, has been sacrificed. (1 Co.5:7)**

*Historically*, the Passover refers back to the time when God delivered Israel from Egyptian bondage (Ex.11:1f). God had pronounced judgment, the taking of the firstborn, upon the people of Egypt for their injustices. As He prepared to execute this final judgment, the faithful, those who believed God, were instructed to slay a pure lamb and sprinkle its blood over the door posts of their homes. The blood of the innocent lamb would then serve as a sign that the coming judgment had already been carried out. When seeing the blood, God would *pass over* that house. Those who believed God applied the blood to their homes and were saved, but those who did not believe did nothing, and their firstborn were destroyed.

*Symbolically*, the Passover pictured the coming of Jesus Christ as the Savior. The *lamb without blemish* pictured His sinless life (see Jn.1:29), and the *blood sprinkled on the door posts* pictured His blood shed for the believer. It was a sign that the life and blood of an innocent lamb had been substituted for the firstborn. The *eating of the lamb* pictured the need for spiritual nourishment gained by feeding on Christ, the Bread of Life. The unleavened bread (bread without yeast) pictured the need for putting evil out of one's life and household (see DEEPER STUDY # 1, *Feast of Unleavened Bread*—Mt.26:17).

Second, the Lamb is a picture of the precious blood of Christ which redeems us.

**Knowing that you were ransomed . . . not with perishable things such as silver or gold, but with the precious blood of Christ, like that of a lamb without blemish or spot. (1 Pe.1:18-19)**

Historically, two lambs were sacrificed every day, one in the morning, and the other . . . at twilight (Ex.29:38-39). The sacrifice of the two lambs, the shedding of their precious blood, became a substitute for the people. The people knew their sins had separated them from God and that their sins had to be removed before they could be reconciled to God. Thus, symbolically, the two animals, without blemish and without spot, had the sins of the people placed upon them; and symbolically, they bore the judgment of sin, which was death. The lambs were sacrificed for sin, and through their deaths, people were symbolically set free or redeemed from their sins. (But note a critical point. It was not the deed that caused God to remove the sins but the *faith* of the person in God's Word *that He would remove the sins*.)

This, of course, is a picture of Christ (see Is.53:6-7; Je.11:19; Ac.8:32; 1 Co.5:7; He.9:28; 1 Pe.2:22-24; Re.5:6; 6:1; 7:9; 12:11; 13:8; 14:1; 15:3; 17:14; 19:9; 21:22). Jesus Christ is . . .

- the perfect Lamb of God, without sin (blemish or spot) (see note, *Jesus Christ, Sinless*—Jn.8:45-47)
- the One upon whom the sins of the people were placed
- the One who bore the judgment for sin, which was death
- the One who was sacrificed for sin
- the One whose death sets people free by redeeming them
- the One whose blood is counted precious both by God and believers

Note that Christ *willingly* offered Himself as the sacrificial Lamb, as our substitute and sin-bearer, and God willingly accepted the offering and sacrifice of His Son for us (Jn.10:17-18). God is *satisfied* with the settlement for sin that Christ made. If any person really believes the blood of Christ to be precious—really believes that the blood of Christ covers their sins—God will take that person's belief and count it as righteousness (see DEEPER STUDY # 1, 2—Ro.4:22; notes—5:1; 1 Jn.2:1-2).

Third, the "Lamb of God" is not *of people*, but *of God* (Gk. tou Theou). The idea is that the Lamb belonged to God; that is, God gave, supplied, and provided the Lamb for sacrifice. (See Ge.22:8 where God provided the lamb for Abraham as a substitute for Isaac.)

This glorious truth speaks volumes on . . .
- the unbelievable love of God for humanity (Jn.3:16; Ro.5:1)
- the great sacrifice and humiliation Christ underwent for us (Ph.2:6-8; 1 Pe.2:24)
- the forgiveness of sins and salvation which came from God's grace and not from our resources or works (Ep.2:8-9; Tit.2:4-7)
- the deity of Christ, His being *of God*

Fourth, the "Lamb of God" takes away the sin of the world. The phrase *takes away* (airon) means to lift away, to carry off. It means to bear in behalf of one, as one's substitute. Jesus Christ is the sacrificial Lamb of God who bore our sins. He lifted our sins off of us and bore and carried them away.

> **So Christ, having been offered once to bear the sins of many, will appear a second time, not to deal with sin but to save those who are eagerly waiting for him. (He.9:28)**

> **He himself bore our sins in his body on the tree, that we might die to sin and live to righteousness. By his wounds you have been healed. (1 Pe.2:24)**

The word *sin* (harmartian) is singular, not plural. All the sins of the world are taken and placed into one package. The whole package of sin—all the sin of every person who has ever lived—was laid upon and borne by Christ.

> **But if we walk in the light, as he is in the light, we have fellowship with one another, and the blood of Jesus his Son cleanses us from all sin. (1 Jn.1:7)**

The world is looked at as a whole. Christ bore the sins of the whole world, not the sins of just some people. No matter the depth and ugliness of a person's sin, Christ bore the sins of the whole world.

> **My little children, I am writing these things to you so that you may not sin. But if anyone does sin, we have an advocate with the Father, Jesus Christ the righteous. He is the propitiation for our sins, and not for ours only but also for the sins of the whole world. (1 Jn.2:1-2)**

**THOUGHT 1.** The major point to note is this: it was the blood of the lamb that saved the people. The lamb was sacrificed; that is, its blood was shed as a substitute for the people. The lamb symbolized Christ our Passover who was sacrificed for us. If we believe and apply His blood to our hearts, He saves us. If we do not believe and do not apply the blood to our hearts, we are destroyed. It is the Lamb of God who was sacrificed for us; it is His blood which saves us.

> **"For this is my blood of the covenant, which is poured out for many for the forgiveness of sins." (Mt.26:28)**

> **In him we have redemption through his blood, the forgiveness of our trespasses, according to the riches of his grace. (Ep.1:7)**

> **And from Jesus Christ the faithful witness, the firstborn of the dead, and the ruler of kings on earth. To him who loves us and has freed us from our sins by his blood. (Re.1:5)**

## 2 Jesus is the Preeminent One.

Jesus Christ is the Preeminent One, the *One before all*. Note what John said.

<sup>30</sup> "This is he of whom I said, 'After me comes a man who ranks before me, because he was before me.'

<sup>31</sup> "I myself did not know him, but for this purpose I came baptizing with water, that he might be revealed to Israel."

### a. He was before John—Preexistent (v.30).

John said that Christ "was before me"; that is, He existed before me. He was the Preexistent One, the Eternal God (see note—Jn.1:15 for discussion).

### b. John did not know Him, only that He was to come (v.31).

Note that John knew Jesus personally; they were cousins (Lu.1:36). However, John did not know that his cousin, Jesus, was to be the Messiah. Note another fact: how faithful John was! He was a man of strong faith. Even before He knew Jesus was the Messiah, he went about his mission of preaching and baptizing. He acted on God's Word and on God's Word alone, believing that the Messiah would come.

**THOUGHT 1.** Christ is the Preeminent One, the Eternal God. We must follow the example of John and . . .
- declare that Christ is before all
- believe God's promise: the Messiah has come
- act and get about our mission of proclaiming Christ

> He first found his own brother Simon and said to him, "We have found the Messiah" (which means Christ). (Jn.1:41)
>
> So the woman left her water jar and went away into town and said to the people. (Jn.4:28)
>
> That which we have seen and heard we proclaim also to you, so that you too may have fellowship with us; and indeed our fellowship is with the Father and with his Son Jesus Christ. (1 Jn.1:3)

## 1:32-33

<sup>32</sup> And John bore witness: "I saw the Spirit descend from heaven like a dove, and it remained on him.
<sup>33</sup> "I myself did not know him, but he who sent me to baptize with water said to me, 'He on whom you see the Spirit descend and remain, this is he who baptizes with the Holy Spirit.'

### 3 Jesus is the Messiah, the One upon whom the Spirit of God remained.

God had spoken to John, instructing him as to how he would be able to identify the Messiah when He came. Note two facts.

**a. John did not know Jesus at first (v.33a).**

John bore witness of how he came to know—with certainty—that Jesus was the promised Messiah. John repeated that he did not know who the Messiah would be. But something happened that gave him proof positive that Jesus was the Lamb of God.

**b. John was, however, given a sign to identify Jesus (vv.32, 33b).**

God had told John previously that He would see the Spirit descend and remain on a specific individual. This would be a sign to identify that individual as the Messiah. When John saw the Spirit, in the form of a dove, descend and remain on Jesus, he knew without a doubt that his cousin was the Messiah.

The dove was a sacred bird to the Jews. It was a symbol of peace and gentleness, of purity and innocence; but even more significant, the dove was often identified with the Spirit of God. When the dove descended upon Christ, it symbolized the Spirit of God Himself, descending upon Christ. The dove identified Jesus as the Messiah and endued Him with the power of God (see outline and notes—Mk.1:9-10).

In the Old Testament, the Spirit of God came upon people only on special occasions. He never remained upon them. John went out of his way to point out that the Spirit's descent upon Christ was unique: He abode (v.32), and He remained upon Christ (v.32). The Holy Spirit entered the life of Christ once-for-all, permanently and powerfully, in His full manifestation and unlimited power.

**THOUGHT 1.** When a person is baptized by the Holy Spirit into Christ, the Holy Spirit enters the life of the believer, becoming a permanent experience of the believer. The person who receives the Spirit of God has the presence and care of God looking over their life (see notes—Jn.14:15-26; Jn.16:7-15; DEEPER STUDY #1—Ac.2:1-4; note—Ro.8:1-17).

> "You did not choose me, but I chose you and appointed you that you should go and bear fruit and that your fruit should abide, so that whatever you ask the Father in my name, he may give it to you. These things I command you, so that you will love one another." (Jn.15:16-17)
>
> "Nevertheless, I tell you the truth: it is to your advantage that I go away, for if I do not go away, the Helper will not come to you. But if I go, I will send him to you." (Jn.16:7)

You, however, are not in the flesh but in the Spirit, if in fact the Spirit of God dwells in you. Anyone who does not have the Spirit of Christ does not belong to him. But if Christ is in you, although the body is dead because of sin, the Spirit is life because of righteousness. (Ro.8:9-10)

For in one Spirit we were all baptized into one body—Jews or Greeks, slaves or free—and all were made to drink of one Spirit. (1 Co.12:13)

## 4 Jesus is the Son of God.

Jesus Christ is the Son of God (see notes—Jn.1:1-2; 10:30-33; Ph.2:6-7 for more discussion). What did John mean by "the Son of God"? Note the definite article. Christ is *the* Son, not *a* son of God. He is . . .

[34] "And I have seen and have borne witness that this is the Son of God."

- the *only* Son
- the only *begotten* Son
- the only begotten Son who came from the *Father's side* or *bosom*, that is from the deepest part, from the most intimate place, from the most honorable fellowship of God (v.18)

Note the following testimony of Scripture to the fact that Jesus Christ is the Son of God:

First, the gospel writers say that Jesus Christ is the Son of God.

| Matthew | Mark | Luke | John |
|---|---|---|---|
| 1:21 | 1:1 | 1:31-32 | 1:18, 34, 45 |
| 2:15 | 3:11 | 1:35 | 3:16-18, 35-36 |
| 3:17 | 13:32 | 3:38 | 5:19, 21-23, 25-26 |
| 4:3 | 14:61 | 4:3, 9 | 6:40, 42 |
| 8:29 | 15:39 | 4:41 | 8:35-36 |
| 11:27 | | 8:28 | 9:35 (see 19:7) |
| 14:33 | | 10:22 | 10:36 |
| 14:61 | | 22:70 | 11:4 |
| 16:16 | | | 14:13 |
| 17:5 | | | 17:1 |
| 26:63 | | | 19:17 |
| 27:30, 40, 43, 54 | | | 20:31 |

The gospel writers also say that Jesus Christ constantly claimed that God was His Father, that He was the Son of the Father in a unique sense.

| Matthew | Mark | Luke | John |
|---|---|---|---|
| 7:21 | 8:38 | 2:49 | 3:35 |
| 10:32-33 | 13:32 | 9:26 | 5:17, 19-23, 26, 30, 36-37, 43, 45 |
| 11:25-27 | 14:36 | 10:21-22 | |
| 12:50 | | 22:29, 42 | 6:27, 32, 37, 39, 42, 44-46, 57, 65 |
| 15:13 | | 23:34, 46 | |
| 16:17, 27 | | 24:49 | 8:16, 18-19, 27-29, 38, 49, 54 |
| 18:10, 19, 35 | | | |
| 20:23 | | | 10:15, 17 18, 25, 29 30, 32, 36 38 |
| 24:36 | | | |

| Matthew | Mark | Luke | John |
|---|---|---|---|
| 25:34 | | | 11:41 |
| 26:29, 39, 42, 53 | | | 12:26-28, 49-50 |
| 28:19 | | | 14:6-13, 16, 20-21, 26, 23-24, 28, 31 |
| | | | 15:1, 8-10, 15-16, 23-24, 26 |
| | | | 16:3, 10, 15-17, 25-28, 32 |
| | | | 17:1, 5, 11, 24-25 |
| | | | 18:11 |
| | | | 20:17, 21 |

Second, the book of *Acts* says that Jesus Christ is the Son of God:

*Acts*          3:13, 26; 8:37; 9:20

Third, Paul says that Jesus Christ is the Son of God:

| *Romans* | 1:4, 9; 5:10; 8:3, 29, 32 |
| *1 Corinthians* | 1:9; 15:58 |
| *2 Corinthians* | 1:19 |
| *Galatians* | 1:16; 2:20; 4:4, 6 |
| *Ephesians* | 4:13 |
| *Colossians* | 1:13 |
| *1 Thessalonians* | 1:10 |
| *Hebrews* | 1:2, 5, 8; 3:6; 4:14; 5:8; 6:6; 7:3, 28; 10:29; 11:17 |

Paul also says that God is the Father of our Lord Jesus Christ:

| *Romans* | 15:6 |
| *2 Corinthians* | 1:3; 11:31 |
| *Ephesians* | 1:3 |

Fourth, Peter says that God is the Father of our Lord Jesus Christ:

*1 Peter*       1:3

Fifth, John, in his Epistles and *Revelation*, says that Jesus Christ is the Son of God and that God is the Father of our Lord Jesus Christ:

| *1 John* | 1:3, 7; 2:22-24; 3:8, 23; 4:9-10, 14-15; 5:5, 9-13, 20 |
| *2 John* | 3, 9 |
| *Revelation* | 2:18, 27; 3:5 |

## G. Jesus the Messiah, the Christ: The Witness of Andrew, 1:35-42

**1. Andrew's experience**
   a. He stood in the midst of John's preaching
   b. He heard John proclaim that Jesus is the Lamb of God
   c. He followed Jesus

35 The next day again John was standing with two of his disciples,
36 and he looked at Jesus as he walked by and said, "Behold, the Lamb of God!"
37 The two disciples heard him say this, and they followed Jesus.

**2. Andrew's critical hour**
   a. Jesus turned: A symbol of initiative
   b. Jesus asked the basic question of life: What do you want? What do you seek?
   c. Jesus extended an invitation: Come

38 Jesus turned and saw them following and said to them, "What are you seeking?" And they said to him, "Rabbi" (which means Teacher), "where are you staying?"
39 He said to them, "Come and you will see." So they came and saw where he was staying, and they stayed with him that day, for it was about the tenth hour.

**3. Andrew's great decision: He accepted Jesus' invitation & remained with Jesus**[DS1]

40 One of the two who heard John speak and followed Jesus was Andrew, Simon Peter's brother.

**4. Andrew's first concern: His brother**
**5. Andrew's conviction: Jesus is the Messiah**
**6. Andrew's fruit: Simon was brought to Jesus**

41 He first found his own brother Simon and said to him, "We have found the Messiah" (which means Christ).
42 He brought him to Jesus. Jesus looked at him and said, "You are Simon the son of John. You shall be called Cephas" (which means Peter).

# Division I

*The Witnesses to the Revelation of Jesus Christ, 1:1-51*

G. Jesus the Messiah, the Christ: The Witness of Andrew, 1:35-42

## 1:35-42
## Introduction

Every time a person hears the gospel and believes on Christ, heaven rejoices (Lu.15:10). This jubilant passage records one such occasion: the salvation experience of Andrew. He discovered that Jesus was the Messiah, the Christ, and began to follow Him. Scripture also notes the very first thing Andrew did after he believed on Jesus: he found his brother and told him about Christ (see note, *Andrew*—Mk.3:18 for more discussion). This is *Jesus the Messiah, the Christ: The Witness of Andrew, 1:35-42*.

1. Andrew's experience (vv.35-37).
2. Andrew's critical hour (vv.38-39).
3. Andrew's great decision: He accepted Jesus' invitation and remained with Jesus (vv.39-40).
4. Andrew's first concern: His brother (v.41).

5. Andrew's conviction: Jesus is the Messiah (v.41).
6. Andrew's fruit: Simon was brought to Jesus (v.42).

## 1:35–37

³⁵ The next day again John was standing with two of his disciples,
³⁶ and he looked at Jesus as he walked by and said, "Behold, the Lamb of God!"
³⁷ The two disciples heard him say this, and they followed Jesus.

## 1 Andrew's experience.

Andrew's experience was simple, somewhat like the experience of many who come to Christ. The simplicity of Andrew's conversion testifies of how easy it is to be saved. We simply *hear* and *believe* (Ac.4:4; Ro.10:13–17; Ep.1:13).

### a. He stood in the midst of John's preaching (v.35).

Note the word *standing* or *stood*. John had been holding his campaign around the Jordan. Andrew, with a growing desire to learn more from the Word of God, had become interested in what was happening and had attended the meetings. At some point, he became a follower of this preacher of righteousness. The point to see is that Andrew hungered for righteousness; therefore, he availed himself of the opportunity to hear preaching. He "stood" right in the midst of preaching and was there to hear the Messiah proclaimed.

### b. He heard John proclaim that Jesus is the Lamb of God (vv.36–37a).

Andrew heard the preacher declare that Jesus is the Lamb of God. He was listening to the message, not allowing his mind to wander elsewhere. He was alert and awake; therefore, when the announcement of the Messiah came, he was ready. Note also the message: "Behold, the Lamb of God." It was the message of the Messiah's sacrificial death (see note—Jn.1:29).

Note three significant facts about John and his preaching:

First, his message was Christ, the Lamb of God, who takes away the sin of the world.

Second, his purpose was to point people, even his own followers, to Christ. He wanted people *to be* where they could receive and grow the most. (How different from so many ministers!)

Third, his spirit was filled with enormous humility. He was completely selfless. He pointed His own followers to Christ and encouraged them to follow Him.

### c. He followed Jesus (v.37b).

The Greek word translated *followed* (ekolouthesan) is in the aorist tense, meaning a once-for-all act. Andrew was turning to Jesus, *ready* to make a commitment to Him. He wanted to become a disciple of Jesus.

**THOUGHT 1.** The same three steps must be taken by each of us.
➢ We must *stand* where the Word, Christ Himself, is preached. We must have a hunger that drives us to hear the message, a hunger that drives us to stay alert and awake to hear the Word proclaimed.
➢ We must *hear* the Word, the announcement: the Lamb of God has come to take away the sin of the world.
➢ We must *follow* Jesus.

Two things will cause a person to miss Christ. First, not *standing* where Christ is preached: standing elsewhere in the world, in self, in the flesh; standing in the midst of those who do not care for Christ nor for the preaching of the Word. Second, not *hearing*: allowing your mind to wander, being sleepy-eyed, disinterested, distracted, inattentive.

> Again Jesus spoke to them, saying, "I am the light of the world. Whoever follows me will not walk in darkness, but will have the light of life." (Jn.8:12)

> "My sheep hear my voice, and I know them, and they follow me." (Jn.10:27)

> "If anyone serves me, he must follow me; and where I am, there will my servant be also. If anyone serves me, the Father will honor him." (Jn.12:26)

"Let us know; let us press on to know the Lord; his going out is sure as the dawn; he will come to us as the showers, as the spring rains that water the earth." (Ho.6:3)

## 2 Andrew's critical hour.

1:38-39

This is a most graphic picture: it shows the *great eagerness* of Jesus to reach people. Jesus longs for every one of us to come to Him, and He longs to reach out to help us in our coming. Note: Jesus was walking some distance away and Andrew and his friend were following behind Jesus. Jesus did three things that demonstrated His great eagerness.

> ³⁸ Jesus turned and saw them following and said to them, "What are you seeking?" And they said to him, "Rabbi" (which means Teacher), "where are you staying?"
>
> ³⁹ He said to them, "Come and you will see." So they came and saw where he was staying, and they stayed with him that day, for it was about the tenth hour.

a. **Jesus turned: A symbol of initiative (v.38a).**

"Jesus turned" to face them. This was a clear demonstration of His open arms, His willingness, and His eagerness for them to join Him. He knew their hearts had just been stirred to reach out to Him and to follow Him, so He immediately snapped around to face them and help them (see Lu.15:20).

b. **Jesus asked the basic question of life: What do you want? What do you seek (v.38b)?**

Note that Jesus did not ask, *Whom do you seek?* but "What do you seek?" What are you after? Are you seeking . . .

- meaning, purpose, and significance in life?
- a religion of self-improvement and human development?
- rules and regulations and laws of righteousness?
- fellowship and companionship?
- deliverance from trials and trouble and suffering?
- approval and acceptance of God?
- blessings from God, His care and provision and security?

Note also what Andrew and his friend asked: "Rabbi . . . where are you staying?" They had never met Jesus before, yet they called Him Master or Teacher, acknowledging His position as *their* Teacher. They were not asking for a simple conversation by the side of the road. They were asking to join Him in the quiet of His home, to open and pour out their hearts to Him and for Him to become their teacher. They wanted Jesus to meet the crying need of their hearts and to do such in the quiet confines of His dwelling.

> "That they should seek God, and perhaps feel their way toward him and find him. Yet he is actually not far from each one of us." (Ac.17:27)
>
> "But from there you will seek the Lord your God and you will find him, if you search after him with all your heart and with all your soul." (De.4:29)
>
> "Seek the Lord while he may be found; call upon him while he is near." (Is.55:6)
>
> "You will seek me and find me, when you seek me with all your heart." (Je.29:13)

c. **Jesus extended an invitation: Come (v.39a).**

Jesus extended the invitation, "Come and see." The invitation was immediate: it was while Andrew and his friend were drawn to Jesus. Jesus invited them while they sensed their need. He did not postpone their request nor leave them hanging.

**THOUGHT 1.** Whether witnessing personally or preaching to a congregation, we need to give people the opportunity to receive Christ *while* the Holy Spirit is speaking to their hearts. God's Word is powerful. It speaks to people's hearts and accomplishes what God sends it forth to accomplish (Is.55:11). If we share or preach the gospel, it will bring conviction to the listener's heart. It will bring the one convicted to the place of desiring to be saved. But if we do not encourage the listener to act, to repent and turn to Christ, to believe on Christ at once, Satan may snatch away the seed that was planted in that individual's heart (Mt.13:19). How critical it is that we do not give Satan time to work, that we encourage people to come to Christ immediately, that we give them the opportunity to receive Christ while His Word is fresh in their hearts and while the Holy Spirit is convicting them.

> "Come to me, all who labor and are heavy laden, and I will give you rest." (Mt.11:28)

> The Spirit and the Bride say, "Come." And let the one who hears say, "Come." And let the one who is thirsty come; let the one who desires take the water of life without price. (Re.22:17)

> "Come now, let us reason together, says the LORD: though your sins are like scarlet, they shall be as white as snow; though they are red like crimson, they shall become like wool." (Is.1:18)

> "Come, everyone who thirsts, come to the waters; and he who has no money, come, buy and eat! Come, buy wine and milk without money and without price." (Is.55:1)

## 1:39b–40

<sup>39</sup> He said to them, "Come and you will see." So they came and saw where he was staying, and they stayed with him that day, for it was about the tenth hour.
<sup>40</sup> One of the two who heard John speak and followed Jesus was Andrew, Simon Peter's brother.

## 3 Andrew's great decision: He accepted Jesus' invitation and remained with Jesus.

At that moment—on the spot—Andrew made a decision, the greatest decision any individual can make. He *came and saw* and *stayed* or *remained* with Jesus. Note three significant facts about Andrew's decision:

➢ Andrew "came" to Jesus. He accepted the invitation. He walked up to Jesus and walked along with Him *in order to* see just where Jesus lived.

➢ The word *see* (opsesthe) was a promise. When Jesus said, "Come and you will see," He was talking about much more than just seeing where He lived. He was talking about *seeing* the truth and learning of Him. Andrew was being assured, if he would come, that he would most definitely see and learn the truth of life. The Lord guaranteed it (see note, *See*—Jn.20:20).

> For God, who said, "Let light shine out of darkness," has shone in our hearts to give the light of the knowledge of the glory of God in the face of Jesus Christ. (2 Co.4:6)

> Having the eyes of your hearts enlightened, that you may know what is the hope to which he has called you, what are the riches of his glorious inheritance in the saints, and what is the immeasurable greatness of his power toward us who believe, according to the working of his great might. (Ep.1:18-19)

> But you are a chosen race, a royal priesthood, a holy nation, a people for his own possession, that you may proclaim the excellencies of him who called you out of darkness into his marvelous light. Once you were not a people, but now you are God's people; once you had not received mercy, but now you have received mercy. (1 Pe.2:9-10)

➢ Andrew and his friend stayed with Jesus, that is, by Jesus' side, in His presence. As Jesus taught and ministered to them, He met their needs. This confrontation with Jesus changed their lives forever. This fact is seen in that the very hour is still remembered fifty or more years later (see DEEPER STUDY # 1). Simply stated, Andrew and his friend committed their lives to Jesus.

> And he said to all, "If anyone would come after me, let him deny himself and take up his cross daily and follow me." (Lu.9:23)

> But to all who did receive him, who believed in his name, he gave the right to become children of God. (Jn.1:12)

> For "everyone who calls on the name of the Lord will be saved." (Ro.10:13)

**THOUGHT 1.** All who receive Christ must follow Andrew's example. They have to accept the invitation, and they have to be willing to *come* to Jesus and to *see* Him—to see the truth of who He is. They must make the great decision to receive Christ, believe on Him, and stay with Him—follow Him.

> For he says, "In a favorable time I listened to you, and in a day of salvation I have helped you." Behold, now is the favorable time; behold, now is the day of salvation. (2 Co.6:2)

But as for me, my prayer is to you, O LORD. At an acceptable time, O God, in the abundance of your steadfast love answer me in your saving faithfulness. (Ps.69:13)

### DEEPER STUDY # 1

(1:39) **John the Apostle—Confrontation—Conversion**: Is the hour known by John the Apostle because he was the other unnamed disciple with Andrew? Apparently so. Note how significant the experience with Jesus was. John still remembered the hour some fifty years later (see Jn.18:15; 20:3).

## 4 Andrew's first concern: His brother.

**1:41**

Andrew's first concern is for his brother Peter. The scene is striking. As quickly as he could after discovering Jesus for himself, Andrew rushed to find his own brother, Simon. Andrew had met Jesus personally, and Jesus had met the crying need of his heart. Andrew could not contain his peace and joy; he just had to tell his loved ones immediately. He wanted them also to experience the love and joy and peace of Jesus.

⁴¹ He first found his own brother Simon and said to him, "We have found the Messiah" (which means Christ).

> **THOUGHT 1.** Andrew was a great witness, a great personal worker for the Lord. He was always seen bringing someone to Jesus (see Jn.6:8; 12:22). What a marvelous example he sets for us, an example each of us should faithfully follow.
>
> And he said to them, "Follow me, and I will make you fishers of men." (Mt.4:19)
>
> "For the Son of Man came to seek and to save the lost." (Lu.19:10)
>
> Jesus said to them again, "Peace be with you. As the Father has sent me, even so I am sending you." (Jn.20:21)
>
> And have mercy on those who doubt; save others by snatching them out of the fire; to others show mercy with fear, hating even the garment stained by the flesh. (Jude 22-23)
>
> The fruit of the righteous is a tree of life, and whoever captures souls is wise. (Pr.11:30)
>
> "And those who are wise shall shine like the brightness of the sky above; and those who turn many to righteousness, like the stars forever and ever." (Da.12:3)

## 5 Andrew's conviction: Jesus is the Messiah.

What was it that compelled Andrew to immediately find his brother? It was his firm conviction that he had found the *Messiah*. (For the meaning of the word "Messiah," see DEEPER STUDY # 2, Christ—Jn.1:20.) How could he not share his excitement and this glorious news with his brother?

> **THOUGHT 1.** If we have come to the conviction of who Jesus is—the Messiah, the Son of God, the one and only Savior—how can we not share this glorious message with others, especially our loved ones?
>
> For if I preach the gospel, that gives me no ground for boasting. For necessity is laid upon me. Woe to me if I do not preach the gospel! (1 Co.9:16)
>
> All this is from God, who through Christ reconciled us to himself and gave us the ministry of reconciliation; that is, in Christ God was reconciling the world to himself, not counting their trespasses against them, and entrusting to us the message of reconciliation. Therefore, we are ambassadors for Christ, God making his appeal through us. We implore you on behalf of Christ, be reconciled to God. (2 Co.5:18-20)

## 6 Andrew's fruit: Simon was brought to Jesus.

Upon believing on Christ, Andrew immediately bore fruit for him: Simon was reached for Jesus. Andrew saw his brother Simon come to Jesus.

**42** He brought him to Jesus. Jesus looked at him and said, "You are Simon the son of John. You shall be called Cephas" (which means Peter).

Note the word *looked at* (Gk. emblepsas). It means to look upon with an intense, earnest look, to concentrate, to stare and gaze upon. Jesus looked into the innermost being of Peter.

Note also the words, "You shall be called." They refer to the future. Simon's name would be changed to Cephas. This was a prediction that he would be converted and changed from a self-centered, defensive, overbearing, and carnal man into a strong, solid, immovable, and unbreakable rock for God.

**THOUGHT 1.** Jesus' response to Simon demonstrates how He deals with each of us. First, Jesus *looks at* us: studies and knows us intimately. This is both a comfort and a warning, depending upon our response to Him. Second, Jesus sees the potential within each of us and longs to change us to make us everything we can become.

> "Nothing is covered up that will not be revealed, or hidden that will not be known." (Lu.12:2)

> And needed no one to bear witness about man, for he himself knew what was in man. (Jn.2:25)

> Therefore, if anyone is in Christ, he is a new creation. The old has passed away; behold, the new has come. (2 Co.5:17; see Ep.4:24)

> Since you have been born again, not of perishable seed but of imperishable, through the living and abiding word of God. (1 Pe.1:23)

> "And I will give you a new heart, and a new spirit I will put within you. And I will remove the heart of stone from your flesh and give you a heart of flesh." (Eze.36:26)

## H. Jesus, the One Prophesied: The Witness of Philip, 1:43-45

⁴³ The next day Jesus decided to go to Galilee. He found Philip and said to him, "Follow me."

⁴⁴ Now Philip was from Bethsaida, the city of Andrew and Peter.

⁴⁵ Philip found Nathanael and said to him, "We have found him of whom Moses in the Law and also the prophets wrote, Jesus of Nazareth, the son of Joseph."

1. **Philip's experience**
   a. He was sought by Jesus
   b. He was called by Jesus<sup>DS1</sup>
   c. The reason: Philip knew Andrew & Peter, who had apparently witnessed to him<sup>DS2</sup>
2. **Philip's first concern: To share with Nathanael**
3. **Philip's conviction: Jesus was the One prophesied**<sup>DS3</sup>

# Division I

## *The Witnesses to the Revelation of Jesus Christ, 1:1-51*

H. Jesus, the One Prophesied: The Witness of Philip, 1:43-45

## 1:43-45
## Introduction

Philip's recognition and witness of Jesus Christ was unmistakable. Jesus was the One prophesied in Scripture; He was the promised Messiah. This is, *Jesus the One Prophesied: The Witness of Philip*, 1:43-45.

1. Philip's experience (vv.43-44).
2. Philip's first concern: To share with Nathanael (v.45).
3. Philip's conviction: Jesus was the One prophesied (v.45).

### 1 Philip's experience.

1:43-44

Scripture clearly teaches that salvation is entirely of God. This includes its initiation. Our path to salvation does not begin with us seeking God, but, rather, God seeking us (Ro.3:11). Philip's experience illustrates this truth.

⁴³ The next day Jesus decided to go to Galilee. He found Philip and said to him, "Follow me."
⁴⁴ Now Philip was from Bethsaida, the city of Andrew and Peter.

#### a. He was sought by Jesus (v.43a).

Jesus Himself went forth and sought Philip—Philip was not seeking Jesus. The initiative came from Jesus entirely. Jesus made the move to find and save Philip and to enlist Philip in His mission.

Jesus traveled a long distance to find Philip. Galilee was a long distance away, and Jesus made this strenuous journey for one purpose: to find Philip. This demonstrates how far Christ will go to reach a soul. In order to reach an individual, Christ will go any distance . . .
- to any sin, no matter how terrible or awful. He will prick and prick at the mind and heart of a person.
- to any place, no matter how hidden or shameful. He will send a thought or memory or person of righteousness to remind and warn a person.

- to any condition, no matter how hopeless or helpless. He will see that the message of hope and help crosses a person's path.
- to any person, no matter how shameful or guilty. He will see that a person hears the word of salvation if they repent and hears the word of judgment if they do not repent.

Christ will go any distance to reach people. He will go to any place, to any condition, to any person. He will see that every person has some chance of turning to God. The word of deliverance can come from any number of sources: another person, a thought, a stirring of conscience, a memory, a writing, or just through seeing nature (Ro.1:20). Christ seeks every person, and He will go any distance to reach that individual, no matter the difficulty.

Jesus is seen fulfilling His mission in seeking and saving Philip. He came into the world for the very purpose of seeking and saving the lost.

> "For the Son of Man came to seek and to save the lost." (Lu.19:10)

> "The thief comes only to steal and kill and destroy. I came that they may have life and have it abundantly." (Jn.10:10)

> Then Pilate said to him, "So you are a king?" Jesus answered, "You say that I am a king. For this purpose I was born and for this purpose I have come into the world—to bear witness to the truth. Everyone who is of the truth listens to my voice." (Jn.18:37)

> The saying is trustworthy and deserving of full acceptance, that Christ Jesus came into the world to save sinners, of whom I am the foremost. (1 Ti.1:15)

b. **He was called by Jesus (v.43b).**
Just as Jesus personally sought Philip, He personally called Philip. Jesus *Himself* called Philip to follow Him (see Deeper Study # 1; Deeper Study # 1—Lu.9:23).

> And he said to all, "If anyone would come after me, let him deny himself and take up his cross daily and follow me." (Lu.9:23)

> "My sheep hear my voice, and I know them, and they follow me." (Jn.10:27)

> "If anyone serves me, he must follow me; and where I am, there will my servant be also. If anyone serves me, the Father will honor him." (Jn.12:26)

c. **The reason: Philip knew Andrew and Peter, who had apparently witnessed to him (v.44).**
The reason Jesus called Philip is apparently the reason verse 44 is mentioned. He was from Bethsaida, the same town as Andrew and Peter (see Deeper Study #2). Philip longed for deliverance; he yearned to see the Messiah (see "We have found Him," v.45). Therefore, he had sought the company of those who were like-minded. He wanted the fellowship of those who wanted godly deliverance. In his search for such people, he had met Andrew and Peter and had apparently been their friends for some time. Therefore, it was only natural for Andrew and Peter to suggest that Jesus seek out Philip to become a disciple. The point is this: Jesus called Philip because Philip . . .
- had taken action about the longing and aching for deliverance within his soul
- had sought the fellowship of those who were seeking God's salvation
- had placed himself where the message would reach him when it came

> "Blessed are those who hunger and thirst for righteousness, for they shall be satisfied." (Mt.5:6)

> "Blessed are you who are hungry now, for you shall be satisfied. Blessed are you who weep now, for you shall laugh." (Lu.6:21)

> On the last day of the feast, the great day, Jesus stood up and cried out, "If anyone thirsts, let him come to me and drink." (Jn.7:37)

> For he satisfies the longing soul, and the hungry soul he fills with good things. (Ps.107:9)

> "Come, everyone who thirsts, come to the waters; and he who has no money, come, buy and eat! Come, buy wine and milk without money and without price." (Is.55:1)

**THOUGHT 1.** Every person must heed Christ's *seeking* when His seeking or calling is sensed. We must respond immediately, for God's Spirit does not always strive with people. When we first feel the pull to make a decision for Christ, if we put the decision off for even an hour or two, the pull fades and eventually leaves us completely. God's Spirit does not continue to strive with us.

> Then the LORD said, "My Spirit shall not abide in man forever, for he is flesh: his days shall be 120 years." (Ge.6:3)
>
> He who is often reproved, yet stiffens his neck, will suddenly be broken beyond healing. (Pr.29:1)

**THOUGHT 2.** Every believer should be willing to go any distance to reach people, no matter how far or how deeply depraved individuals may be. Whether we acknowledge it or not, too many of us consider and treat others as *untouchables*: alcoholics, immoral, the poor, prisoners, those who are diseased, and so forth.

> "'For I was hungry and you gave me food, I was thirsty and you gave me drink, I was a stranger and you welcomed me, I was naked and you clothed me, I was sick and you visited me, I was in prison and you came to me.'" (Mt.25:35-36). (Remember that the person in *prison* is guilty of the most serious offenses and sins.)
>
> "But you will receive power when the Holy Spirit has come upon you, and you will be my witnesses in Jerusalem and in all Judea and Samaria, and to the end of the earth." (Ac.1:8)

## DEEPER STUDY # 1

(1:43) **Follow** (Gk. akolouthei): to become a close companion, a close follower, a disciple. Two significant ideas are in the word: union and likeness, or cleaving and conformity. To follow Christ means . . .
- to cleave, to be united to Him, to be in close union with Him
- to become like Him, to be conformed to Him

## DEEPER STUDY # 2

(1:44) **Bethsaida**: Jesus carried on a large ministry in Bethsaida, but the gospels tell us nothing about the city itself. The city was denounced by Jesus because of its rejection of Him (Mt.11:21; Lu.10:13). (See Mk.6:45; 8:22; Lu.9:10; Jn.12:21 for other references to the city.)

## 2 Philip's first concern: To share with Nathanael.

Philip's first concern was to reach his friend Nathanael. Jesus had challenged Philip to follow Him, to become just like Him, and Philip did. He went out and did exactly what Jesus had done for him. Jesus had sought and found him. Now, following the example of his Lord, he went out and found his friend Nathanael. Philip became a personal soul-winner just like his Lord.

⁴⁵ Philip found Nathanael and said to him, "We have found him of whom Moses in the Law and also the prophets wrote, Jesus of Nazareth, the son of Joseph."

**THOUGHT 1.** Our first concern as believers should be to reach our friends and loved ones with the gospel of Jesus Christ. Like Philip, we need to follow the example of our Lord and intentionally take Christ to others.

> Jesus said to them again, "Peace be with you. As the Father has sent me, even so I am sending you." (Jn.20:21)
>
> "For we cannot but speak of what we have seen and heard." (Ac.4:20)
>
> "'For you will be a witness for him to everyone of what you have seen and heard.'" (Ac.22:15)

## 3 Philip's conviction: Jesus was the One prophesied.

**1:45**

⁴⁵ Philip found Nathanael and said to him, "We have found him of whom Moses in the Law and also the prophets wrote, Jesus of Nazareth, the son of Joseph."

Philip was unmovable in his conviction that Jesus Christ is the prophesied Messiah. With excitement and without reservation, he testified to Nathanael that he and his friends had found the One of whom Moses and the prophets wrote. Jesus of Nazareth, the son of Joseph, is the prophesied One. Note four observations:

➤ Philip was extremely joyful. With unbridled enthusiasm, he proclaimed, "We have found Him!" Jubilation, excitement, and rejoicing beat in Philip's chest. Jesus had met the needs and craving of his heart.

> "These things I have spoken to you, that my joy may be in you, and that your joy may be full." (Jn.15:11)
>
> For the kingdom of God is not a matter of eating and drinking but of righteousness and peace and joy in the Holy Spirit. (Ro.14:17)
>
> You make known to me the path of life; in your presence there is fullness of joy; at your right hand are pleasures forevermore. (Ps.16:11)
>
> With joy you will draw water from the wells of salvation. (Is.12:3)

➤ God's eternal plan for the human race is recorded in Scripture. It is there for our direction.

> "You search the Scriptures because you think that in them you have eternal life; and it is they that bear witness about me." (Jn.5:39)
>
> And how from childhood you have been acquainted with the sacred writings, which are able to make you wise for salvation through faith in Christ Jesus. All Scripture is breathed out by God and profitable for teaching, for reproof, for correction, and for training in righteousness. (2 Ti.3:15–16)

➤ Philip and Nathanael knew the Scripture. They were familiar with the prophecies of the promised Messiah.

> Do your best to present yourself to God as one approved, a worker who has no need to be ashamed, rightly handling the word of truth. (2 Ti.2:15)
>
> Like newborn infants, long for the pure spiritual milk, that by it you may grow up into salvation— if indeed you have tasted that the Lord is good. (1 Pe.2:2-3)

➤ Jesus of Nazareth was definitely identified as the Messiah (see DEEPER STUDY # 3).

## DEEPER STUDY # 3

(1:45) **Scripture, Fulfilled—Prophecy, Fulfilled**:

OLD TESTAMENT PROPHECIES OF JESUS AND THEIR
FULFILLMENT IN THE NEW TESTAMENT

| OT Scripture | Prophecies | Fulfillment |
| --- | --- | --- |
| Ge.3:15 | The Promised Seed of a Woman | Ga.4:4; Lu.2:7; Re.12:5 |
| Ge.12:3; 18:18; 22:18 | The Promised Seed of Abraham | Ac.3:25; Ga.3:8 (Mt.1:1; Lu.3:34) |
| Ge.17:19; 22:16-17 | The Promised Seed of Isaac | Mt.1:2; Lu.1:55, 72-74 |
| Ge.28:14 (Nu.24:17) | The Promised Seed of Jacob | Lu.3:34 (Mt.1:2) |
| Ge.49:10[a] | Will Spring from the Royal Tribe of Judah | Lu.3:33; He.7:14 |
| De.18:15, 18 | Will Be a Prophet | Jn.6:14; Ac.3:22-23 |
| 2 S.7:13[b] (2 S.7:13; Is.9:1, 7; 11:1-5) | Will Be the Eternal Heir to David's Throne | Mt.1:1 (Mt.1:6; Lu.1:32-33) |

| OT Scripture | Prophecies | Fulfillment |
|---|---|---|
| 2 S.7:14a | Will Be God's Son | Mk.1:1 |
| Is.35:6; 61:1-2 (see Ps.72:2; 146:8; Zec.11:11) | Will Meet the Desperate Needs of Men | Mt.11:4-6 |
| Jb.17:3 | Will Ransom Men | Ep.1:7 (1 Jn.2:1-2) |
| Ps.2:1-2 | Will Be Rejected by the Nations | Lu.23:36a, 38 |
| Ps.2:7 | Is the Son of God | Ac.13:33; He.1:5; 5:5 |
| Ps.8:2 | Is to Be Praised | Mt.21:16 |
| Ps.16:8-11 | Will Be Resurrected | Ac.13:34-35; 2:25-28, 31 (Mt.28:1-2; Mk.16:6, 12, 14; Lu.24:1-53) |
| Ps.22:1 | Will Be Forsaken by God | Mt.27:46; Mk.15:34 |
| Ps.22:7 | People Will Wag Their Heads at the Cross | Mt.27:39 |
| Ps.22:18 | Clothes Gambled for | Mt.27:35; Mk.15:24; Lu.23:34; Jn.19:24 |
| Ps.22:22 | To Secure Many Brothers | He.2:12 |
| Ps.31:5 | Commends His Spirit to God | Lu.23:46 |
| Ps.40:6-8 | Fulfills God's Will | He.10:5-7 |
| Ps.41:9 | Is Betrayed by Judas | Jn.13:18; Ac.1:16 |
| Ps.45:6, 7 | Is Eternal and Preeminent | He.1:8, 9 |
| Ps.68:18 | Will Lead Captivity Captive | Ep.4:8-10 |
| Ps.69:21 | Was Offered Drugs on the Cross | Mt.27:48; Mk.15:36; Lu.23:36; Jn.19:28, 29 |
| Ps.69:25; 109:8 | Judas' Fate | Ac.1:20 |
| Ps.89:26-27 | Exaltation | Ph.2:9 (see Re.11:15) |
| Ps.95:7-11 | Hearts Hardened Against | He.3:7-11; 4:3, 5-7 |
| Ps.102:25-27 | Is Creator and Is Eternal | He.1:10-12 |
| Ps.110:1 | To Be Exalted | Mt.22:44; Mk.12:36; Lu.20:42; Ac.2:34, 35; He.1:13 |
| Ps.110:4 | The High Priest | He.5:6 |
| Ps.118:22, 23 | The Stone | Mt.21:42; Mk.12:10; Lu.20:17; Ac.4:11 |
| Ps.118:25, 26 | The Triumphal Entry | Mt.21:9; Mk.11:9; Jn.12:13 |
| Ps.132:11, 17 | The Son of David | Lu.1:69; Ac.2:30 |
| Is.7:14 | The Virgin Birth | Mt.1:23 |
| Is.9:1, 2 | A Light to Those in Darkness | Mt.4:15, 16 |
| Is.11:2 | The Spirit Rests Upon in a Special Way | Lu.4:18-21 (see Mt.12:18; Jn.3:34) |
| Is.11:10 | To Save the Gentiles | Ro.15:12 |
| Is.25:8 | To Conquer Death | 1 Co.15:54 |
| Is.28:16 | The Stone | Ro.9:33; 1 Pe.2:6 |
| Is.40:3-5 | To Have a Forerunner | Mt.3:3; Mk.1:3; Lu.3:4-6 |
| Is.42:1-4 | To Minister to the Gentiles | Mt.12:17-21 |

| OT Scripture | Prophecies | Fulfillment |
|---|---|---|
| Is.49:6 | A Light to the Gentiles | Lu.2:32; Ac.13:47, 48; 26:23 |
| Is.53:1 | Would Not Be Believed | Jn.12:38; Ro.10:16 |
| Is.53:3-6 | To Die and Arise | Ac.26:22, 23 |
| Is.53:4-6, 11 | To Die for Man's Sins | 1 Pe.2:24, 25 |
| Is.53:4 | To Heal and Bear Man's Sickness | Mt.8:17 |
| Is.53:9 | To Be Sinless | 1 Pe.2:22 |
| Is.53:12 | To Be Counted a Sinner | Mk.15:28; Lu.22:37 |
| Is.54:13 | To Teach As God | Jn.6:45 |
| Is.55:3 | To Be Raised | Ac.13:34 |
| Is.59:20, 21 | To Save Israel | Ro.11:26, 27 |
| Je.31:31-34 | To Make a New Covenant with Man | He.8:8-12; 10:16, 17 |
| Ho.1:10-11 | To Bring About the Restoration of Israel | Ro.11:1-36 |
| Ho.1:10 | The Conversion of the Gentiles | Ro.9:26 |
| Ho.2:23 | The Conversion of the Gentiles | Ro.9:25; 1 Pe.2:10 |
| Joel 2:28-32 | The Promise of the Spirit | Ac.2:16-21 |
| Amos 9:11, 12 | The Lord's Return and David's Kingdom Reestablished | Ac.15:16, 17 |
| Mi.5:2 | The Birthplace of Messiah | Mt.2:5, 6; Jn.7:42 |
| Hab.1:5 | The Jews' Unbelief | Ac.13:40, 41 |
| Hag.2:6 | The Return of Christ | He.12:26 |
| Zec.9:9 | The Triumphal Entry | Mt.21:4, 5; Jn.12:14, 15 |
| Zec.11:13 | Judas' Betrayal | Mt.27:9, 10 |
| Zec.12:10 | The Spear Pierced in Side | Jn.19:37 |
| Zec.13:7 | The Scattering of the Disciples at the Cross | Mt.26:31, 56; Mk.14:27, 50 |
| Mal.3:1 | The Forerunner, John the Baptist | Mt.11:10; Mk.1:2; Lu.7:27 |
| Mal.4:5, 6 | The Forerunner, John the Baptist | Mt.11:13, 14; 17:10-13; Mk.9:11-13; Lu.1:16, 17 |

## I. Jesus the Son of God, the King of Israel: The Witness of Nathanael,[DS1] 1:46-49

| | |
|---|---|
| ⁴⁶ Nathanael said to him, "Can anything good come out of Nazareth?" Philip said to him, "Come and see." | **1. Nathanael's experience**[DS2]<br>a. A man of despair & prejudice<br>b. A man invited to follow Jesus despite his prejudice |
| ⁴⁷ Jesus saw Nathanael coming toward him and said of him, "Behold, an Israelite indeed, in whom there is no deceit!"<br>⁴⁸ Nathanael said to him, "How do you know me?" Jesus answered him, "Before Philip called you, when you were under the fig tree, I saw you." | **2. Nathanael's confrontation with Jesus**<br><br>a. Jesus knew him: His beliefs & character<br>b. Jesus knew his innermost being—all things about him[DS3] |
| ⁴⁹ Nathanael answered him, "Rabbi, you are the Son of God! You are the King of Israel!" | **3. Nathanael's conviction: Jesus is the Son of God**[DS4] |

# Division I

### *The Witnesses to the Revelation of Jesus Christ, 1:1-51*

I. Jesus the Son of God, the King of Israel: The Witness of Nathanael, 1:46-49

## 1:46-49
## Introduction

After Philip realized that Jesus was the Messiah, he carried the news to his friend, Nathanael (see DEEPER STUDY #1; see outline and notes—Jn.1:45 for more discussion). Nathanael's confrontation with Jesus was dramatic. Nathanael was a man of prejudice and strong feelings, yet he knew despair and hopelessness; therefore, Philip had some difficulty leading him to Christ. Yet Philip refused to give up in witnessing to him. As a result, Nathanael was won to Christ. This is, *Jesus the Son of God, the King of Israel: The Witness of Nathanael*, 1:46-49.
1. Nathanael's experience (v.46).
2. Nathanael's confrontation with Jesus (vv.47-48).
3. Nathanael's conviction: Jesus is the Son of God (v.49).

### 1 Nathanael's experience.

1:46

Nathanael's salvation experience began with someone who cared enough about him to tell him about Christ. His close friend, Philip, shared the good news with him (cp. Jn.1:45). Philip loved Nathanael so much that he shared the most important experience of his life with Nathanael.

⁴⁶ Nathanael said to him, "Can anything good come out of Nazareth?" Philip said to him, "Come and see."

#### a. A man of despair and prejudice (v.46a).

Nathanael was a man gripped by despair and prejudice. His despair is seen in his response to Philip. Initially, he rejected Philip's testimony in a way that revealed his skeptical, reactionary spirit: "Can anything good come out of Nazareth?" He lashed out at what Philip had reported and not only questioned it; he showed no willingness to accept it or believe it. There was a sense of hopelessness, of despair and skepticism in his question. Apparently Nathanael was a man who had tried and followed so many voices in the world that he had just lost hope. Many in the world had promised so much, only to leave him still empty and searching. Why should he believe and follow another voice?

**THOUGHT 1.** So many voices in the world promise the path to fulfillment and joy and satisfaction in life. However, their claims are soon discovered to be false, while leaving people with empty hearts and endless wondering. A person caught up in despair wonders about the real purpose, meaning, and significance of life.

> Remember that you were at that time separated from Christ . . . having no hope and without God in the world. (Ep.2:12)
>
> But we do not want you to be uninformed, brothers, about those who are asleep, that you may not grieve as others do who have no hope. (1 Th.4:13)
>
> "I loathe my life; I will give free utterance to my complaint; I will speak in the bitterness of my soul." (Jb.10:1)
>
> For my life is spent with sorrow, and my years with sighing; my strength fails because of my iniquity, and my bones waste away. (Ps.31:10)
>
> But Zion said, "The Lord has forsaken me; my Lord has forgotten me." (Is.49:14)

Nathanael's prejudice is seen in his slur against Jesus because Jesus was from Nazareth (see Deeper Study # 2). Nathanael was apparently a crowd-follower. He had allowed himself to be influenced by the world's foolish prejudices.

**THOUGHT 1.** Prejudice has a great failing; it disregards the wrong within oneself and with one's own place (city, home, business, church); it overlooks one's own wrongs, shortcomings, weaknesses, and error.

> So Peter opened his mouth and said: "Truly I understand that God shows no partiality, but in every nation anyone who fears him and does what is right is acceptable to him." (Ac.10:34–35)
>
> For God shows no partiality. (Ro.2:11)
>
> For there is no distinction between Jew and Greek; for the same Lord is Lord of all, bestowing his riches on all who call on him. (Ro.10:12)

b. **A man invited to follow Jesus despite his prejudice (v.46b).**
Nathanael was still invited to follow Jesus. His sin, despair, and prejudice did not discourage nor keep Philip from inviting his friend and neighbor to "come and see" Jesus. Note also that Philip did not argue with Nathanael. He simply confronted him with Jesus.

**THOUGHT 1.** No matter what a person's sin is, we must still go and invite them to "come and see" Jesus. Because Philip went to Nathanael, his dear friend did come to Jesus, despite Nathanael's despair and prejudice. Think what Nathanael would have missed if he had let his prejudice against the people of Nazareth keep him from the One who was called Jesus the Nazarene. Or if he had let his wallowing around in despair keep him from coming to Jesus.

Moreover, think what Nathanael would have missed had Philip not been willing to invite him to Jesus, if Philip had let Nathanael's prejudice keep him from speaking to him about Christ. Like Philip, we must realize that those who are prejudiced—or guilty of any other detestable sin—need Christ the most.

Philip teaches us another important lesson: the way to lead a person to Christ is not by argument, but by confronting them with Christ. As we share Christ with others, some people will bring up all sorts of objections and attempt to argue with us about any number of topics. But we need to keep the focus on Christ and move the conversation back to the eternally-important subject of the salvation that is available only through Him.

> "For we cannot but speak of what we have seen and heard." (Ac.4:20)
>
> Declare these things; exhort and rebuke with all authority. Let no one disregard you. (Tit.2:15)
>
> Come and hear, all you who fear God, and I will tell what he has done for my soul. (Ps.66:16)

## DEEPER STUDY # 1

(1:46-49) **Nathanael:** John alone mentions Nathanael. However, the other three gospels mention a disciple that John does not, Bartholomew. These two names quite possibly refer to the same person. Nathanael may have been his first name, and Bartholomew could have been a second name or another name he went by.

## DEEPER STUDY # 2

(1:46) **Nazareth:** Nazareth was an obscure village in Galilee. Galilee bordered Gentile or heathen nations; therefore, it was sometimes called *Galilee of the Gentiles*. The Jews were so deeply prejudiced against the Gentiles that they considered anyone or anything touched by a Gentile to be unclean in the sight of God. Nazareth was despised by the Jews because it was on the border of Gentile country and was so commercially touched by Gentiles. It was despised by the Romans because its citizens were a conquered people (see note, pt.2—Mt.13:53-58 for more discussion).

## 2 Nathanael's confrontation with Jesus.

Upon meeting Jesus, Nathanael realized that He was not an ordinary man. There are two very significant items to note in Nathanael's confrontation with the Lord.

> ⁴⁷ Jesus saw Nathanael coming toward him and said of him, "Behold, an Israelite indeed, in whom there is no deceit!"
>
> ⁴⁸ Nathanael said to him, "How do you know me?" Jesus answered him, "Before Philip called you, when you were under the fig tree, I saw you."

### a. Jesus knew him, his beliefs and character (v.47).

Jesus knew Nathanael's beliefs. This is seen in Jesus' calling Nathanael an "Israelite indeed." He was the epitome of an Israelite, everything an Israelite should be. He *believed* the promises of God. He tried to live up to the covenant name, the standard God had set for Israel, and he was looking for that blessed hope and glorious appearing of the Messiah.

**THOUGHT 1.** Christ knows the beliefs of each individual, upon which that person has set their heart. He knows both the good and bad beliefs, both the godly and evil thoughts of the human heart.

> And needed no one to bear witness about man, for he himself knew what was in man. (Jn.2:25)
>
> For whenever our heart condemns us, God is greater than our heart, and he knows everything. (1 Jn.3:20)
>
> O God, you know my folly; the wrongs I have done are not hidden from you. (Ps.69:5)
>
> "I the LORD search the heart and test the mind, to give every man according to his ways, according to the fruit of his deeds." (Je.17:10)

In addition, Jesus knew Nathanael's character. He stated that Nathanael was a man without *deceit* or *guile* (Gk. dolos). This means he did not manipulate, bait, or mislead people. He did not hide what he thought; he said what he thought and acted what he felt. He was straightforward, open and honest, not deceptive nor hypocritical. This trait had just been demonstrated in his response to Philip. He would not hide his true thoughts (v.46).

**THOUGHT 1.** One of the great tragedies in a person's legacy is that they are full of deceit. Many manipulate, bait, and mislead others. Few are straightforward, open and honest, free of deception and hypocrisy.

> "Blessed are the pure in heart, for they shall see God." (Mt.5:8)

> Therefore, beloved, since you are waiting for these, be diligent to be found by him without spot or blemish, and at peace. (2 Pe.3:14)

> And in their mouth no lie was found, for they are blameless. (Re.14:5)

> Who shall ascend the hill of the Lord? And who shall stand in his holy place? He who has clean hands and a pure heart, who does not lift up his soul to what is false and does not swear deceitfully. (Ps.24:3–4)

> Blessed is the man against whom the Lord counts no iniquity, and in whose spirit there is no deceit. (Ps.32:2)

b. Jesus knew his innermost being, all things about him (v.48).

Nathanael was perplexed at Jesus' intimate knowledge of him, as he had never met Jesus before. Jesus answered that he had seen Nathanael previous to this encounter, when he was under the fig tree (see Deeper Study # 3). It was this knowledge—the knowledge of his innermost being—that sparked the realization in Nathanael's heart that Jesus was not just another man.

**THOUGHT 1.** Jesus knows everything about every human being. Nothing escapes His watchful eye, not even a single thought. The realization of this truth offers great hope to all who will cast themselves upon Christ. Christ can help you by meeting your need and giving purpose and direction to your life.

At the same time, this truth is a great warning to all who go their merry way, thinking their sin is hidden and will not be judged.

> "Nothing is covered up that will not be revealed, or hidden that will not be known." (Lu.12:2)

> Therefore do not pronounce judgment before the time, before the Lord comes, who will bring to light the things now hidden in darkness and will disclose the purposes of the heart. Then each one will receive his commendation from God. (1 Co.4:5)

> "For my eyes are on all their ways. They are not hidden from me, nor is their iniquity concealed from my eyes." (Je.16:17)

> But they do not consider that I remember all their evil. Now their deeds surround them; they are before my face. (Ho.7:2)

## Deeper Study # 3

(1:48) **Fig Tree—Worship**: in Palestine the fig tree stood for peace, security, rest, and worship (see 1 K.4:25; Mi.4:4). Very often a person would seek solitude and worship under his fig tree. Most likely, this is what Nathanael had been doing. When Jesus told Nathanael that He had seen him under his fig tree, He was telling Nathanael that He knew everything about him, even the deepest longings of his heart. Jesus knew Nathanael's despair and sense of hopelessness; He knew his longing for peace and release and freedom. That was enough to cause Nathanael to give his life to Jesus forever.

## 3 Nathanael's conviction: Jesus is the Son of God.

Upon realizing that Jesus knew everything about him, Nathanael readily confessed that Jesus is the Rabbi (Prophet), the Son of God, the King of Israel. Note how clearly Nathanael grasped who Jesus is:

➢ He is *Rabbi*, the great Teacher or Prophet promised to Israel (see note—Lu.3:38 for discussion).

➢ He is the Son of God (see notes—Jn.1:1-2; 1:34 for discussion).

➢ He is the King of Israel (see DEEPER STUDY # 4 for discussion).

⁴⁹ Nathanael answered him, "Rabbi, you are the Son of God! You are the King of Israel!"

**THOUGHT 1.** We can only be saved once we have come to the full conviction of who Jesus is. He is the Messiah, the Son of God, the only Savior of the world. The most critical question in all the world is, "What do you think about Christ?" (Mt.22:42).

> "So everyone who acknowledges me before men, I also will acknowledge before my Father who is in heaven." (Mt.10:32)
>
> Because, if you confess with your mouth that Jesus is Lord and believe in your heart that God raised him from the dead, you will be saved. (Ro.10:9)
>
> No one who denies the Son has the Father. Whoever confesses the Son has the Father also. (1 Jn.2:23)
>
> Whoever confesses that Jesus is the Son of God, God abides in him, and he in God. (1 Jn.4:15)

### DEEPER STUDY # 4

(1:49) **Jesus Christ, King of Israel:** Jesus was declared to be the Messianic King. God had given to David and his seed (the Messiah) the promise of eternal government (2 S.7:12; Ps.39:3f; 132:11).

Note how often Jesus was called the son of David (see Mt.12:23; 15:22; 20:30-31; 21:9, 15; Ac.2:29-36; Ro.1:3; 2 Ti.2:8; Re.22:16). It was the common title and popular concept of the Messiah. Generation after generation of Jews had pined and looked for the promised deliverer of Israel. The people expected Him to be a great general who would deliver and restore the nation to its greatness. In fact, they expected Him to make the nation the center of universal rule. He would, under God, conquer the world and center the glory and majesty of God Himself in Jerusalem; and from His throne, the throne of David, He would execute *the Messianic fire of judgment* upon the nations and peoples of the world. (See DEEPER STUDY # 2—Mt.1:18; DEEPER STUDY # 2—3:11; notes—11:1-6; 11:2-3; DEEPER STUDY # 1—11:5; DEEPER STUDY # 2—11:6; note—Lu.7:21. A review of these DEEPER STUDY notes will shed more light on the Jewish concept of the Messiah.) (See note, *Jesus, Davidic Heir*—Lu.3:24-31 for more discussion.)

**J. Jesus the Son of Man, God's Mediator: The Witness of Jesus Himself, 1:50–51**

1. Jesus is the revelation of God
   a. Jesus responds to Nathanael, (vv.46-49)
   b. Jesus is the One who reveals greater things
2. Jesus is the mediator: The One who opens the doors of heaven
3. Jesus is the Son of Man: The ideal pattern, the perfect representative of mankind

⁵⁰ Jesus answered him, "Because I said to you, 'I saw you under the fig tree,' do you believe? You will see greater things than these."

⁵¹ And he said to him, "Truly, truly, I say to you, you will see heaven opened, and the angels of God ascending and descending on the Son of Man."

# Division I

## *The Witnesses to the Revelation of Jesus Christ, 1:1–51*

J. Jesus the Son of Man, God's Mediator: The Witness of Jesus Himself, 1:50–51

## 1:50–51

## Introduction

After presenting a variety of witnesses to the deity of Jesus Christ, this first chapter of John's gospel concludes with the witness of Jesus Himself. In His response to Nathanael, Jesus bore witness to Himself. He clearly declared who He is. This is, *Jesus the Son of Man, God's Mediator: The Witness of Jesus Himself,* 1:50-51.

1. Jesus is the revelation of God (v.50).
2. Jesus is the mediator: The One who opens the doors of heaven (v.51a).
3. Jesus is the Son of Man: the ideal pattern, the perfect representative of mankind (v.51b).

**1:50**

⁵⁰ Jesus answered him, "Because I said to you, 'I saw you under the fig tree,' do you believe? You will see greater things than these."

### 1 Jesus is the Revelation of God.

Upon realizing that Jesus knew everything about him, even though He had never met him, Nathanael professed his faith in Jesus as the Messiah. His faith was rewarded with a confession from Jesus Himself: He is the revelation of God, the One who reveals greater things.

a. **Jesus responds to Nathanael (v.50a; see vv.46–49).**
   Jesus always responds to our faith. He responded to Nathanael's faith by making him a compelling promise: Nathanael would see *greater things* than he had already seen from Jesus. What he *would* see would be far more miraculous and glorious than what he had *already* seen. It was belief in Jesus that brought "greater things" into Nathanael's life. Nathanael believed Jesus; therefore, he could expect to receive greater things, to receive more.

   > He said to them, "Because of your little faith. For truly, I say to you, if you have faith like a grain of mustard seed, you will say to this mountain, 'Move from here to there,' and it will move, and nothing will be impossible for you." (Mt.17:20)

   > And Jesus said to him, "'If you can'! All things are possible for one who believes." (Mk.9:23)

   > But, as it is written, "What no eye has seen, nor ear heard, nor the heart of man imagined, what God has prepared for those who love him." (1 Co.2:9)

So that Christ may dwell in your hearts through faith—that you, being rooted and grounded in love, may have strength to comprehend with all the saints what is the breadth and length and height and depth, and to know the love of Christ that surpasses knowledge, that you may be filled with all the fullness of God. (Ep.3:17-19)

b. Jesus is the One who reveals greater things (v.50b).

It is Jesus Himself who is the revelation of God; therefore, it is Jesus who reveals the "greater things" of life (see note—Jn.14:6 for more discussion). Note what Scripture teaches about Jesus and revelation:

➢ Jesus Christ is the embodiment of revelation.

In the beginning was the Word, and the Word was with God, and the Word was God. He was in the beginning with God. (Jn.1:1-2)

Jesus said to him, "I am the way, and the truth, and the life. No one comes to the Father except through me." (Jn.14:6)

For in him the whole fullness of deity dwells bodily. (Col.2:9)

➢ Jesus Christ is the communicator of revelation.

In him was life, and the life was the light of men. (Jn.1:4; cp. Jn.1:1-3)

And the Word became flesh and dwelt among us, and we have seen his glory, glory as of the only Son from the Father, full of grace and truth. (Jn.1:14)

Jesus said to him, "Have I been with you so long, and you still do not know me, Philip? Whoever has seen me has seen the Father. How can you say, 'Show us the Father'? Do you not believe that I am in the Father and the Father is in me? The words that I say to you I do not speak on my own authority, but the Father who dwells in me does his works." (Jn.14:9-10)

➢ Jesus Christ is the liberator of revelation—the revelation He gives sets us free from the bondage of sin to enjoy the abundant life.

So Jesus said to the Jews who had believed him, "If you abide in my word, you are truly my disciples, and you will know the truth, and the truth will set you free." (Jn.8:31-32)

"The thief comes only to steal and kill and destroy. I came that they may have life and have it abundantly." (Jn.10:10)

## 2 Jesus Christ is the Mediator: The One who opens the doors of heaven.

Jesus Christ is the mediator between God and humanity. This truth is seen in the picture Jesus painted with His words, "You will see *heaven opened*, and the angels of God *ascending* and descending on the Son of man."

⁵¹ And he said to him, "Truly, truly, I say to you, you will see heaven opened, and the angels of God ascending and descending on the Son of Man."

Jesus' statement is a picture of Jacob's ladder (Ge. 28:10-22). It is a picture of open access into the very presence of God: the door of heaven is open, and the angels are *ascending from earth* to heaven. Jesus was saying...

- He is Jacob's ladder, the ladder is a symbol of Him. He is the One who opens heaven.
- He is the One who reaches *from earth* to heaven, the One by whom we have our communication carried up into heaven.

**THOUGHT 1.** This glorious statement from our Savior reveals three critical truths:

- First, we *can* approach God and enter heaven through Christ (Jn.14:6). The gulf, the loneliness, and the alienation which we all know have been bridged.
- Second, we have access to God *only* through Christ (Jn.14:6).
- Third, we can have *constant* communication with God. The picture is that of angels carrying messages from earth to heaven and back to earth again.

So Jesus again said to them, "Truly, truly, I say to you, I am the door of the sheep. All who came before me are thieves and robbers, but the sheep did not listen to them. I am the door. If anyone enters by me, he will be saved and will go in and out and find pasture." (Jn.10:7-9)

For there is one God, and there is one mediator between God and men, the man Christ Jesus. (1 Ti.2:5)

Since then we have a great high priest who has passed through the heavens, Jesus, the Son of God, let us hold fast our confession.... Let us then with confidence draw near to the throne of grace, that we may receive mercy and find grace to help in time of need. (He.4:14, 16)

## 1:51

⁵¹ And he said to him, "Truly, truly, I say to you, you will see heaven opened, and the angels of God ascending and descending on the Son of Man."

### 3  Jesus is the Son of Man: The ideal pattern, the perfect representative of mankind.

Jesus Christ is the Son of Man. This title is a testimony to the humanity of Christ, but it means far more than simply Jesus being born of a human being. It means that He is more than what an ordinary person is, more than just a son of some man. Jesus is what every person ought to be, *the Son of Man Himself*.

Jesus Christ is the Ideal Man: the *Representative Man*, the *Perfect Man*, the *Pattern*, the *embodiment* of everything a human being ought to be (see DEEPER STUDY # 3—Mt.1:16). Jesus Christ is the *perfect picture* of a man. Everything God wants a person to be is seen perfectly in Jesus Christ (cp. Jn.1:14; Col.2:9-10; He.1:3).

In addition, Jesus Christ is the Ideal Servant of humanity. The term *Ideal Servant* stresses Jesus' sympathy for the poor, the brokenhearted, the captives, the blind, the bruised, the outcasts, the bereaved (cp. Lu.4:18). Jesus is the pattern, the model, the perfect example of concern and caring. He served other people just like every one of us ought to serve other people.

Jesus called Himself "the Son of Man" about eighty times. It was His favorite title for Himself. The title *Son of Man* is probably based upon the Son of Man in Daniel 7:13-14. The apostle Paul also presents a picture of Jesus as the heavenly Son of Man contrasted with Adam as the earthly man (1 Co.15:45-47). Both references picture Jesus as *the Representative Man, the Ideal Man*, in God's plan for world history.

And Jesus said to him, "Foxes have holes, and birds of the air have nests, but the Son of Man has nowhere to lay his head." (Mt.8:20)

"But that you may know that the Son of Man has authority on earth to forgive sins"—he then said to the paralytic—"Rise, pick up your bed and go home." (Mt.9:6)

Now when Jesus came into the district of Caesarea Philippi, he asked his disciples, "Who do people say that the Son of Man is?" ... Simon Peter replied, "You are the Christ, the Son of the living God." (Mt.16:13, 16)

"Even as the Son of Man came not to be served but to serve, and to give his life as a ransom for many." (Mt.20:28)

"For as the lightning comes from the east and shines as far as the west, so will be the coming of the Son of Man." (Mt.24:27)

"For whoever is ashamed of me and of my words in this adulterous and sinful generation, of him will the Son of Man also be ashamed when he comes in the glory of his Father with the holy angels." (Mk.8:38)

"I tell you, he will give justice to them speedily. Nevertheless, when the Son of Man comes, will he find faith on earth?" (Lu.18:8)

"For the Son of Man came to seek and to save the lost." (Lu.19:10)

"For as the Father has life in himself, so he has granted the Son also to have life in himself. And he has given him authority to execute judgment, because he is the Son of Man." (Jn.5:26-27)

So Jesus said to them, "Truly, truly, I say to you, unless you eat the flesh of the Son of Man and drink his blood, you have no life in you." (Jn.6:53)

And Jesus answered them, "The hour has come for the Son of Man to be glorified." (Jn.12:23)

When he had gone out, Jesus said, "Now is the Son of Man glorified, and God is glorified in him. If God is glorified in him, God will also glorify him in himself, and glorify him at once." (Jn.13:31-32)

And he said, "Behold, I see the heavens opened, and the Son of Man standing at the right hand of God." (Ac.7:56)

Then I turned to see the voice that was speaking to me, and on turning I saw seven golden lampstands, and in the midst of the lampstands one like a son of man, clothed with a long robe and with a golden sash around his chest. (Re.1:12-13)

# Chapter 2

## II. The Revelation of Jesus, the Son of God, 2:1–3:21

### A. Revelation 1: Jesus' Creative Power, 2:1–11

On the third day there was a wedding at Cana in Galilee, and the mother of Jesus was there. ² Jesus also was invited to the wedding with his disciples. ³ When the wine ran out, the mother of Jesus said to him, "They have no wine." ⁴ And Jesus said to her, "Woman, what does this have to do with me? My hour has not yet come." ⁵ His mother said to the servants, "Do whatever he tells you." ⁶ Now there were six stone water jars there for the Jewish rites of purification, each holding twenty or thirty gallons.

⁷ Jesus said to the servants, "Fill the jars with water." And they filled them up to the brim. ⁸ And he said to them, "Now draw some out and take it to the master of the feast." So they took it. ⁹ When the master of the feast tasted the water now become wine, and did not know where it came from (though the servants who had drawn the water knew), the master of the feast called the bridegroom ¹⁰ and said to him, "Everyone serves the good wine first, and when people have drunk freely, then the poor wine. But you have kept the good wine until now." ¹¹ This, the first of his signs, Jesus did at Cana in Galilee, and manifested his glory. And his disciples believed in him.

1. The setting: A wedding in Cana, three days after Jesus entered Galilee[DS1, DS2]
   a. Mary attended
   b. Jesus & the disciples attended

2. The concern regarding Jesus' power
   a. Mary's social concern
   b. Jesus' deeper concern: To meet people's spiritual needs through the hour of His death
   c. Mary's confidence in her Son

3. The revelation of Jesus' power
   a. The materials: Water jars—used for cleaning & for carrying drinking water
   b. The command: Prepare
   c. The obedience: They drew water & experienced the creative power of Jesus

4. The results of Jesus' power
   a. The people's needs were met[DS3]
      1) The host did not know where the good wine had come from
      2) The host teased the bridegroom about holding out on the guests by keeping the best wine until last
   b. Christ's power & glory were revealed
   c. The disciples' faith was strengthened

# Division II

## The Revelation of Jesus, the Son of God, 2:1–3:21

### A. Revelation 1: Jesus' Creative Power, 2:1-11

## 2:1-11
## Introduction

This passage records the first miracle Jesus performed. It demonstrated His very purpose for coming to earth: to reveal the *creative power* of God. He had the power to *create* and *produce* what was needed to meet our need. This is, *Revelation 1: Jesus' Creative Power,* 2:1-11.

1. The setting: A wedding in Cana, three days after Jesus entered Galilee (vv.1-2).
2. The concern regarding Jesus' power (vv.3-5).
3. The revelation of Jesus' power (vv.6-8).
4. The results of Jesus' power (vv.9-11).

### 2:1-2

**O**n the third day there was a wedding at Cana in Galilee, and the mother of Jesus was there.
² Jesus also was invited to the wedding with his disciples.

### 1 The setting: A wedding in Cana, three days after Jesus entered Galilee.

The setting for Jesus' first miracle was a marriage in Cana of Galilee (see DEEPER STUDY # 1, # 2). The marriage took place on the third day after Jesus came into Galilee, or two days after Nathanael's encounter with Jesus.

**a. Mary attended (v.1).**

Mary, the mother of Jesus, was there. Note that Joseph is not mentioned. Most commentators believe that he had died years prior to this wedding, and that Jesus, being the older child, had stayed home to take care of the family until the other children were old enough to go out on their own.

**b. Jesus and the disciples attended (v.2).**

Jesus and His disciples attended the wedding. Marriages during that time were happy, festive occasions, and were among the largest social events in a community. Jesus' attendance tells us two things about Him.

First, in His earthly ministry, Jesus was a people person: He liked people, and people liked Him. He enjoyed socializing, and His ministry was focused on people, being with and helping them all He could (see Mt.11:19; Lu.7:34. See note—Mt.11:16-19).

Second, Jesus honored marriage. Here He demonstrates His approval and honor in two ways: by attending the marriage feast and by meeting the urgent need of the bridegroom.

**THOUGHT 1.** Note the extreme sufferings of Christ. He had come to bear all the trials of the world for the human race. He suffered . . .
- the death of a parent (see note, pt.3—Mt.13:53-58)
- being the child of a one-parent family
- having to go to work at an early age to provide for His mother and half-brothers and sisters

> For it was fitting that he, for whom and by whom all things exist, in bringing many sons to glory, should make the founder of their salvation perfect through suffering. (He.2:10)

> Although he was a son, he learned obedience through what he suffered. And being made perfect, he became the source of eternal salvation to all who obey him. (He.5:8-9)

> For to this you have been called, because Christ also suffered for you, leaving you an example, so that you might follow in his steps. (1 Pe.2:21)

**THOUGHT 2.** Humans are social beings. Jesus teaches us to not become so busy we end up anti-social. However, He expects us to balance our lives. A troubling truth about our day and time is that many people do not lead balanced lives. Many do not spend enough time alone. Many people are not working, producing, and making their God-called contribution to the world, or at least not as diligently as they should. Many have the problem of socializing too much, whether in recreation, partying, or on the job.

> And they devoted themselves to the apostles' teaching and the fellowship, to the breaking of bread and the prayers. (Ac.2:42)
>
> Contribute to the needs of the saints and seek to show hospitality. (Ro.12:13)
>
> But hospitable, a lover of good, self-controlled, upright, holy, and disciplined. (Tit.1:8)
>
> Show hospitality to one another without grumbling. (1 Pe.4:9)
>
> I am a companion of all who fear you, of those who keep your precepts. (Ps.119:63)

**THOUGHT 3.** Jesus graced and blessed the marriage at Cana because He was invited to the wedding. He has to be genuinely invited into a marriage before He will effectively bless it.

> But to all who did receive him, who believed in his name, he gave the right to become children of God. (Jn.1:12)
>
> "'Behold, I stand at the door and knock. If anyone hears my voice and opens the door, I will come in to him and eat with him, and he with me.'" (Re.3:20)
>
> For "everyone who calls on the name of the Lord will be saved." (Ro.10:13)

## DEEPER STUDY # 1

(2:1) **Wedding—Marriage, Jewish Ceremony**: a Jewish wedding ceremony included three major events (see DEEPER STUDY # 1—Mt.25:1-13 for more discussion).

1. A marriage feast and ceremony were held on the same evening.

2. The couple would be escorted through the streets to their home. The procession usually took place at night. Flaming torches were used, and the longest route to the home was taken to attract more attention and to allow the community to share in the joyful event.

3. Jewish weddings were followed by large "open house" celebrations that lasted for a week. These celebrations were known for their happy, festive spirit that swept through the community and surrounded the couple. All week long the couple would wear their wedding garments (gown and robe) and entertain guests. The whole community was expected to participate and celebrate with the couple in their new-found happiness.

## DEEPER STUDY # 2

(2:1) **Cana**: a small, remote, obscure country village. It is thought to have been in the highlands of Galilee, for a person traveled from Cana *down* to Capernaum. It was close to Nazareth, and according to the early church father, Jerome, the city could be seen from Nazareth. Little else is known about the village. Two miracles took place in Cana: this event of creative power where the water was turned into wine (Jn.2:1-11), and the healing of the nobleman's son (Jn.4:46-54). Cana is mentioned only one other time in Scripture (Jn.21:2), three times altogether, and only by John in his Gospel.

## 2 The concern regarding Jesus' power.

**2:3-5**

³ When the wine ran out, the mother of Jesus said to him, "They have no wine."
⁴ And Jesus said to her, "Woman, what does this have to do with me? My hour has not yet come."
⁵ His mother said to the servants, "Do whatever he tells you."

Early in this wedding ceremony, a great concern arose: the hosts had run out of wine. The story seems to indicate that Mary had a key role in the wedding. A steward had been overseeing the household affairs (v.9), but Mary was also apparently helping in some manner. She brought the concern to Jesus, and it presented an opportunity for Him to demonstrate His divine power.

### a. Mary's social concern (v.3).

The need was indeed serious, for the wine was already gone, and the celebration had just begun. A *whole* week of celebration was yet to come. The couple was to have *open house* and to provide the wine and refreshments for the week. What were they to do? The importance of wine in the Middle East must always be remembered. Good, germ-free water was scarce, and it was used only when necessary. Wine was used as a drinking substitute. There was a critical need, a predicament that was going to affect everyone involved. With no wine, the joyful spirit of the guests would be dampened. The couple would be shamed and humiliated, becoming the object of jokes among some. Mary, the mother of Jesus, probably one of the hostesses, would be embarrassed.

Mary, naturally, was concerned about the matter. However, Mary's concern was a *social concern*, a concern for seeing that the needs of a social group were met. She did what any single mother would have done. She brought the problem to her son.

### b. Jesus' deeper concern: to meet people's spiritual needs through the hour of His death (v.4).

Jesus had a deeper concern than just the social aspect of the problem. In Mary's concern, Jesus saw a unique opportunity to begin familiarizing His mother with the truth of who He was: the Son of God who had entered the world for a particular *hour* (the cross). Neither Mary nor anyone else understood Jesus' person, true mission, or Messiahship—not yet anyway (see note—Mk.3:31-32). Therefore, at the very beginning of His ministry, Jesus began to teach everyone, starting with the person who was so dear to His heart, His mother, about His divine purpose. He wanted to do all He could to prepare her and the others for the terrible pain that was to come during *His hour*. He was truly the Son of God; He had been born of God. He—His person and mission—had *to do with God and the things of the Spirit,* not with Mary and her social and material needs. To put it bluntly, He had nothing in common with her and her fleshly interests. *He was of God and of the Spirit.* She had to begin to see and understand this. The more she could hear the truth, the more she would see and understand, especially after *His hour* had come. Therefore, Jesus used every opportunity possible to familiarize all His loved ones with the term, "My hour." *His hour* was to become a constant symbol of His death (see Jn.7:6, 8, 30; 8:20; 12:23-24, 27, 33; 13:1; 17:1; Mt.26:18, 45; Mk.14:41).

The point Jesus makes is that *His hour* had not yet come . . .
- the hour when He would really meet humanity's needs.
- the hour when He must die for our salvation.

### c. Mary's confidence in her Son (v.5).

Night had fallen, and wine could no longer be purchased. Most likely, Mary was not asking Jesus to perform a miracle. So far as we know, He had performed no miracles yet. She most likely was seeking His help, asking Him to take care of the matter. Of course, He could attempt to get a merchant to reopen his shop and meet the need, or He could try to secure wine from some neighbors. Mary had utter confidence in Him. But, again, that is not the point. Jesus saw the *opportunity* to demonstrate His creative power, the kind of power needed to meet humanity's need for regeneration.

**THOUGHT 1.** Jesus was always focused on His purpose for coming to earth: to face *His hour*, to die for our salvation.

> Jesus said to them, "My food is to do the will of him who sent me and to accomplish his work." (Jn.4:34)
>
> "We must work the works of him who sent me while it is day; night is coming, when no one can work." (Jn.9:4)
>
> And Jesus answered them, "The hour has come for the Son of Man to be glorified. Truly, truly, I say to you, unless a grain of wheat falls into the earth and dies, it remains alone; but if it dies, it bears much fruit. . . . Now is my soul troubled. And what shall I say? 'Father, save me from this hour'? But for this purpose I have come to this hour. . . . And I, when I am lifted up from the earth, will draw all people to myself." He said this to show by what kind of death he was going to die. (Jn.12:23–24, 27, 32–33)
>
> Now before the Feast of the Passover, when Jesus knew that his hour had come to depart out of this world to the Father, having loved his own who were in the world, he loved them to the end. (Jn.13:1)

**THOUGHT 2.** Mary's concern pictures the social concern of humanity. People have many social needs. Society—whether social workers or communities of individuals—is concerned with . . .

- social health
- social comfort
- social plenty
- social housing
- social peace
- social justice

Christ met the social concern, the need, the predicament. He solved the problem. However, Christ did not stop there. Meeting the physical and material needs of society is not enough. Christ meets the deeper concerns of all people:

- life
- assurance
- happiness
- fulfillment
- love
- security
- satisfaction
- completeness

> "The thief comes only to steal and kill and destroy. I came that they may have life and have it abundantly." (Jn.10:10)
>
> "These things I have spoken to you, that my joy may be in you, and that your joy may be full." (Jn.15:11)

## 3 The revelation of Jesus' power.

2:6–8

Jesus revealed His creative power when the servants at the celebration obeyed His instructions. Note the spiritual lessons Jesus teaches through the miracle He performed.

### a. The materials: Water jars—used for cleaning and for carrying drinking water (v.6).

Water pots were used for both drinking water and for cleansing. Jewish practice of that time observed *ceremonial and religious cleansing* of hands and utensils. Whenever Jews saw water jars, they knew they were there both

⁶ Now there were six stone water jars there for the Jewish rites of purification, each holding twenty or thirty gallons.

⁷ Jesus said to the servants, "Fill the jars with water." And they filled them up to the brim.

⁸ And he said to them, "Now draw some out and take it to the master of the feast." So they took it.

for satisfying thirst and for religious cleansing. Jesus used the water pots to show that He had the power . . .
- to *purify, cleanse, and satisfy* every person
- to *create and produce* whatever was necessary to cleanse and satisfy every person

> Or do you not know that the unrighteous will not inherit the kingdom of God? Do not be deceived: neither the sexually immoral, nor idolaters, nor adulterers, nor men who practice homosexuality, nor thieves, nor the greedy, nor drunkards, nor revilers, nor swindlers will inherit the kingdom of God. And such were some of you. But you were washed, you were sanctified, you were justified in the name of the Lord Jesus Christ and by the Spirit of our God. (1 Co.6:9–11)

> He saved us, not because of works done by us in righteousness, but according to his own mercy, by the washing of regeneration and renewal of the Holy Spirit. (Tit.3:5)

> Draw near to God, and he will draw near to you. Cleanse your hands, you sinners, and purify your hearts, you double-minded. (Js.4:8)

> And from Jesus Christ the faithful witness, the firstborn of the dead, and the ruler of kings on earth. To him who loves us and has freed us from our sins by his blood (Re.1:5)

### b. The command: Prepare (v.7a).

Jesus commanded the servants to prepare for the miracle He was about to perform. He directed them to fill the large pots with water.

Our Lord had a deeper concern than just meeting the social need of the host. He had come to meet humanity's need for spiritual purification and inner cleansing, and He was to do it through *His hour* (the cross). Therefore, He seized the opportunity to reveal His creative power, His power to create us anew (see DEEPER STUDY # 1—Jn.3:1-15).

### c. The obedience: They drew water and experienced the creative power of Jesus (vv.7b-8).

Jesus simply instructed that preparations be made, and the servants obeyed Him. The result of their obedience blessed not only the hosts, but everyone who attended the celebration. They all experienced Christ's creative power and were fully satisfied.

**THOUGHT 1.** We either believe Christ is the Messiah, or we do not. We either believe He has the power to create anew, or we do not. We either believe that He demonstrates such power in this miracle, or we do not. The critical question—the question upon which all eternity hinges for you—is, do you believe these things?

> But these are written so that you may believe that Jesus is the Christ, the Son of God, and that by believing you may have life in his name. (Jn.20:31)

**THOUGHT 2.** We have to obey Christ's instructions if we wish to be cleansed and created spiritually. His instructions: that we genuinely repent of our sin and believe on Him, accepting His death on the cross as the payment for our sin.

> "Not everyone who says to me, 'Lord, Lord,' will enter the kingdom of heaven, but the one who does the will of my Father who is in heaven." (Mt.7:21)

> "Everyone then who hears these words of mine and does them will be like a wise man who built his house on the rock. And the rain fell, and the floods came, and the winds blew and beat on that house, but it did not fall, because it had been founded on the rock." (Mt.7:24–25)

> "Truly, truly, I say to you, whoever hears my word and believes him who sent me has eternal life. He does not come into judgment, but has passed from death to life." (Jn.5:24)

> Who through him are believers in God, who raised him from the dead and gave him glory, so that your faith and hope are in God. (1 Pe.1:21)

## 4 The results of Jesus' power.

2:1-11

The results of Jesus' power blessed everyone involved with the wedding celebration. His gracious miracle met their need, and it proved that He was far more than just another man.

2:9-11

a. **The people's needs were met (vv.9-10).**

The master or headwaiter of the feast did not know where the wine had come from, so he teased the bridegroom about holding out on the guests by keeping the best wine until last. But it was Jesus who had met his need. The master of the feast would have been held personally responsible for failing to purchase enough wine for the wedding celebration. Jesus' gracious miracle met his need and relieved him of the punishment he would have faced for not fulfilling his responsibility. In addition, Jesus met the need of the bridegroom, who would have been shamed and derided for not providing adequately for his guests. And He met the need of all who attended the celebration, providing refreshment for their thirst.

⁹ When the master of the feast tasted the water now become wine, and did not know where it came from (though the servants who had drawn the water knew), the master of the feast called the bridegroom

¹⁰ and said to him, "Everyone serves the good wine first, and when people have drunk freely, then the poor wine. But you have kept the good wine until now."

¹¹ This, the first of his signs, Jesus did at Cana in Galilee, and manifested his glory. And his disciples believed in him.

b. **Christ's power and glory were revealed (v.11a).**

Christ's power to create anew—to create something that did not previously exist—was demonstrated by this first of His many miracles. His incomparable glory was revealed publicly for the first time. His turning of water into wine was the first sign that He is more than a mere man: He is the only begotten Son of God.

c. **The disciples' faith was strengthened (v.11b).**

As a result of Jesus' miraculous display of His divine power, His disciples believed in Him even more than they had previously. The Lord had given evidence that He was the Messiah.

> **This man came to Jesus by night and said to him, "Rabbi, we know that you are a teacher come from God, for no one can do these signs that you do unless God is with him." (Jn.3:2)**
>
> **Yet many of the people believed in him. They said, "When the Christ appears, will he do more signs than this man has done?" (Jn.7:31)**
>
> **Jesus answered them, "I told you, and you do not believe. The works that I do in my Father's name bear witness about me." (Jn.10:25)**
>
> **"Do you say of him whom the Father consecrated and sent into the world, 'You are blaspheming,' because I said, 'I am the Son of God'? If I am not doing the works of my Father, then do not believe me; but if I do them, even though you do not believe me, believe the works, that you may know and understand that the Father is in me and I am in the Father." (Jn.10:36-38)**
>
> **Now Jesus did many other signs in the presence of the disciples, which are not written in this book; but these are written so that you may believe that Jesus is the Christ, the Son of God, and that by believing you may have life in his name. (Jn.20:30-31)**

# B. Revelation 2: Jesus' Supremacy Over God's House, 2:12-22

*Mt.21:12-16; Mk.11:15-19; Lu.19:45-46*

1. **Jesus' trip to Capernaum & then to Jerusalem: He wanted to attend the Passover**

2. **Jesus' discovery of evil in the temple**<sup>DS1</sup>

3. **Jesus' right to cleanse the temple**
   a. The whip: A symbol of His righteous anger

   b. His unique relationship to God: He called God "My Father"

   c. His consuming zeal for God's House

4. **Jesus' power to erect a new temple**
   a. His authority questioned
   b. His sign given: A new meeting place for God & all His people<sup>DS2</sup>

   c. His intent & ability challenged by the Jews

   d. His symbolic meaning explained: He spoke of His body—His death & resurrection

5. **Jesus' objective achieved: The disciples remembered this event & believed the Scripture & what Jesus had said**

¹² After this he went down to Capernaum, with his mother and his brothers and his disciples, and they stayed there for a few days.
¹³ The Passover of the Jews was at hand, and Jesus went up to Jerusalem.
¹⁴ In the temple he found those who were selling oxen and sheep and pigeons, and the money-changers sitting there.
¹⁵ And making a whip of cords, he drove them all out of the temple, with the sheep and oxen. And he poured out the coins of the money-changers and overturned their tables.
¹⁶ And he told those who sold the pigeons, "Take these things away; do not make my Father's house a house of trade."
¹⁷ His disciples remembered that it was written, "Zeal for your house will consume me."
¹⁸ So the Jews said to him, "What sign do you show us for doing these things?"
¹⁹ Jesus answered them, "Destroy this temple, and in three days I will raise it up."
²⁰ The Jews then said, "It has taken forty-six years to build this temple, and will you raise it up in three days?"
²¹ But he was speaking about the temple of his body.

²² When therefore he was raised from the dead, his disciples remembered that he had said this, and they believed the Scripture and the word that Jesus had spoken.

# Division II

*The Revelation of Jesus, the Son of God, 2:1–3:21*

B. Revelation 2: Jesus' Supremacy Over God's House, 2:12–22

*Mt.21:12-16; Mk.11:15-19; Lu.19:45-46*

## 2:12–22
## Introduction

This passage presents one of the most stunning episodes from the life of Christ: His radical cleansing of the temple. Its lesson is one forgotten all too often in present times, when much takes place in many churches that is surely as displeasing to the Lord as the evil deeds of the moneychangers and merchants in this story. That lesson is, Jesus Christ has supremacy over God's house, that is, over the temple or church. He alone has the right to rule and reign over God's house. This is, *Jesus' Supremacy Over God's House*, 2:12-22.

1. Jesus' trip to Capernaum & then to Jerusalem: He wanted to attend the Passover (vv.12-13).
2. Jesus' discovery of evil in the temple (v.14).
3. Jesus' right to cleanse the temple (vv.15-17).
4. Jesus' power to erect a new temple (vv.18-21).
5. Jesus' objective achieved: The disciples remembered this event and believed the Scripture and what Jesus had said (v.22).

## 1 Jesus' trip to Capernaum and then to Jerusalem: He wanted to attend the Passover.

2:12-13

¹² After this he went down to Capernaum, with his mother and his brothers and his disciples, and they stayed there for a few days.
¹³ The Passover of the Jews was at hand, and Jesus went up to Jerusalem.

Upon leaving Cana, Jesus went down to Capernaum and stayed there for just a brief time. Capernaum was His headquarters (see note—Mt.4:12). He then left for Jerusalem to attend the Passover Feast (see note, *Passover*—Mt.26:17-30).

## 2 Jesus' discovery of evil in the temple.

2:14

¹⁴ In the temple he found those who were selling oxen and sheep and pigeons, and the money-changers sitting there.

Upon arrival in the Holy City, Jesus went to the temple (see DEEPER STUDY # 1). There, He discovered evil practices and desecration being carried out. The Court of the Gentiles had become a hub of commercialism with regular market activity occurring within its walls. How did a marketplace ever get into the temple of God? Very simply, due to greed. Worshipers needed animals (oxen, sheep, doves), incense, meal, wine, oil, salt, and other items for their sacrifices and offerings. Pilgrims from foreign nations needed their currency exchanged. At some point in the history of this temple structure (the Second Temple, largely renovated by Herod the Great), the priests had decided to take advantage of the market themselves instead of letting retailers on the outside reap all the profits. Therefore, the priests began to set up booths within the Court of the Gentiles and to lease space to *outside retailers*. These merchants often turned out to be family members. Annas the High Priest apparently owned the booths or space. The outer courtyard of the temple, the very worship center for the Gentiles, had become filled with booth-like spaces where worshipers could find any kind of service or product they needed. The atmosphere was one of common retail traffic and commotion, not of worship and prayer.

Remembering the teeming thousands who attended the great feasts, we can imagine the loudest commercial commotion, and our picture would still come short of the actual scene.

Who can picture thousands of animals with their peculiar noises, wastes, and smells within the temple of God? And for what? What would cause people to so abuse the worship center of God? As said above, money—the greed of covetous individuals. It is no wonder Jesus did what He did. He could not do otherwise, for He was the Son of God, the Messiah sent into the world to bring about a true worship of God; and there was no hope of genuine worship taking place within the Court of the Gentiles under these circumstances.

> Saying to them, "It is written, 'My house shall be a house of prayer,' but you have made it a den of robbers." (Lu.19:46)

> A God greatly to be feared in the council of the holy ones, and awesome above all who are around him? (Ps.89:7)

> Guard your steps when you go to the house of God. To draw near to listen is better than to offer the sacrifice of fools, for they do not know that they are doing evil. (Ec.5:1)

## DEEPER STUDY # 1

(2:14) **Temple**: a person must understand the layout of the temple in order to see what was happening in this event. The temple mount area sat on top of Mt. Zion, and it is thought to have covered about thirty acres of land. The temple consisted of two parts, the temple building itself and the temple precincts or courtyards. The Greek language has two different words to distinguish which is meant.

1. *The temple building* (Gk. naos) was a small ornate structure which sat in the center of the temple property. It was called the Holy Place or Holy of Holies. Only the High Priest could enter its walls, and he could enter only once a year, on the Day of Atonement.
2. *The temple precincts* (hieron) were four courtyards that surrounded the temple building, each decreasing in importance to the Jewish mind. It is important to know that great walls separated the courts from each other.
   a. First, was the Court of the Priests. Only the priests were allowed to enter this court. Within this courtyard stood the great furnishings of worship: the Altar of Burnt Offering, the Brazen Laver, the Seven-Branched Lampstand, the Altar of Incense, and the Table of Showbread.
   b. Second, was the Court of the Israelites. This was a huge courtyard where Jewish worshipers met together for joint services on the great feast days. It was also where worshipers handed over their sacrifices to the priests.
   c. Third, was the Court of the Women. Women were usually limited to this area except for joint worship with men. They could, however, enter the Court of the Israelites when they came to make a sacrifice or worship in a joint assembly on a great feast day.
   d. Last, was the Court of the Gentiles. It covered a vast space, surrounding all the other courtyards and was the place of worship for all Gentile converts to Judaism.

Two facts need to be noted about the Court of the Gentiles.

1. It was the courtyard farthest removed from the center of worship, the Holy of Holies, which represented God's very presence (see note, pt.2—Ep.2:14-15).

2. A high wall separated the Court of the Gentiles from the other courts, disallowing any Gentile a closer approach into God's presence. In fact, there were tablets hanging all around the wall threatening death to any Gentile who went beyond their own courtyard or center of worship.

## 3 Jesus' right to cleanse the temple.

Jesus could not tolerate the evil taking place in the temple. He judged the greedy merchants on the spot by driving them out of the temple. He was well within His rights, for it was His Father's house they were desecrating.

**a. The whip: a symbol of His righteous anger (v.15).**

Jesus made a whip out of cords and drove the profiteers out of the temple. In so doing, He demonstrated His righteous anger, His right to be obeyed, and His right to enforce obedience within the temple. The whip was a symbol of the power and cleansing judgment of God—the kind of power and cleansing judgment that causes people to tremble before God (Ph.2:9-11).

> 15 And making a whip of cords, he drove them all out of the temple, with the sheep and oxen. And he poured out the coins of the money-changers and overturned their tables.
> 16 And he told those who sold the pigeons, "Take these things away; do not make my Father's house a house of trade."
> 17 His disciples remembered that it was written, "Zeal for your house will consume me."

Provoked by the desecration of His Father's house, Jesus chased out *all* who were buying and selling. He threw over the tables of the moneychangers as well as the chairs of the dove or pigeon dealers.

**b. His unique relationship to God: He called God "My Father" (v.16).**

Jesus naturally referred to God as His Father and to the temple as His Father's house. Note that Jesus continually called God, "My Father" (see notes—Jn.1:34; 10:30-33 for discussion). He was fully aware of who He was, and from the beginning of His public ministry, He emphasized His unique relationship to God.

**c. His consuming zeal for God's House (v.17).**

As Jesus' disciples observed His cleansing of the temple, they remembered a psalm that prophesied of the Messiah's zeal for God's House (Ps.69:9). They recognized the fact that Christ's zeal fulfilled Scripture and demonstrated that He was the Messiah. The Messiah was bound to be zealous for God's house and to react in anger at such corruption within the temple. Scripture had predicted the Lord's zeal; therefore, Jesus had the right to show *zeal and anger* against such desecration of the temple. He was the Messiah, and His quick action further assured the disciples of His identity.

> "You shall keep my Sabbaths and reverence my sanctuary: I am the LORD." (Le.19:30)
>
> A God greatly to be feared in the council of the holy ones, and awesome above all who are around him? (Ps.89:7)
>
> "But the LORD is in his holy temple; let all the earth keep silence before him." (Hab.2:20)

By calling the temple "My Father's house," Jesus is saying the temple belonged to God; therefore, it was to be a house of worship *for all people* (Is.56:17). This included the Gentiles as well as the Jews. All people should be able to worship in quietness and peace within God's temple. No one should be barred, separated, or discouraged from worshiping God here. All should be welcomed.

Note that the temple was to be a house of worship, not a house of sacrifice, offerings, teaching, prophecy, or preaching. Everything done within the House of God was to lead to the *worship* of the Father and *communion* with the Father.

**THOUGHT 1.** The temple—in our present age, the church—is the House of God, God's House of worship (1 Ti.3:15). It is not to be used as a place for buying and selling, marketing and retailing, stealing and cheating. It is not to be profaned. To the contrary, it is to be a place of sanctity, refined and purified by God Himself, a place of quietness and meditation, a place set aside for worship, not for financial gain.

The temple (church) can be abused by . . .
- forgetting what worship is all about
- misusing the facilities and buildings of God's house
- ignoring God's holiness and forgetting one's duty to reverence God
- allowing questionable, non-worshipful activities

And they worshiped him and returned to Jerusalem with great joy, and were continually in the temple blessing God. (Lu.24:52-53; see Jn.4:24)

If I delay, you may know how one ought to behave in the household of God, which is the church of the living God, a pillar and buttress of the truth. Great indeed, we confess, is the mystery of godliness: He was manifested in the flesh, vindicated by the Spirit, seen by angels, proclaimed among the nations, believed on in the world, taken up in glory. (1 Ti.3:15-16)

O LORD, I love the habitation of your house and the place where your glory dwells. (Ps.26:8; see Ps.23:6)

One thing have I asked of the LORD, that will I seek after: that I may dwell in the house of the LORD all the days of my life, to gaze upon the beauty of the LORD and to inquire in his temple. (Ps.27:4)

Blessed is the one you choose and bring near, to dwell in your courts! We shall be satisfied with the goodness of your house, the holiness of your temple! (Ps.65:4)

Guard your steps when you go to the house of God. To draw near to listen is better than to offer the sacrifice of fools, for they do not know that they are doing evil. (Ec.5:1)

## 2:18-21

[18] So the Jews said to him, "What sign do you show us for doing these things?"
[19] Jesus answered them, "Destroy this temple, and in three days I will raise it up."
[20] The Jews then said, "It has taken forty-six years to build this temple, and will you raise it up in three days?"
[21] But he was speaking about the temple of his body.

### 4 Jesus' power to erect a new temple.

As we might expect, Jesus' radical act was not well-received by the leaders of the temple. Once again, Jesus seized the opportunity to point His listeners to His mission, His ultimate reason for coming to earth as a man.

**a. His authority questioned (v.18).**

The Jewish leaders questioned Jesus' authority, challenging His right to do such a thing. Because Jesus had claimed that the temple was His *Father's*, they knew that He was claiming to be the Messiah. Therefore, they wanted proof that His claim was true. They wanted some spectacular sign.

**b. His sign given: A new meeting place for God and all His people (v.19).**

Jesus replied with a statement that stunned the Jews: "[You] destroy this temple and in three days I will raise it up" (see DEEPER STUDY # 2). He was telling them that His sign would be given in the future. He was going to build a new temple, a *new meeting place* for God and His people.

**c. His intent and ability challenged by the Jews (v.20).**

The Lord's puzzling statement was misunderstood by the Jewish leaders. They could not understand how He could possibly rebuild the temple in three days. The present temple had taken forty-six years to build. Their skeptical comment was a direct challenge to Jesus' intent and ability to do what He said He would do.

**d. His symbolic meaning explained: He spoke of His, body, His death and resurrection (v.21).**

Jesus answered the Jews by explaining what He meant. His puzzling statement about Him rebuilding the temple in three days had a *symbolic meaning.* Jesus was speaking of His body, of His death, and His resurrection.

The proof that He was the Son of God with authority over God's house would be given later. The sign was to be His body, His death, and resurrection. The resurrection would be the supreme proof of His Messiahship. They would destroy (kill) Him, but He would be raised from the dead after three days (see outline and notes—Lu.11:29-36).

And with great power the apostles were giving their testimony to the resurrection of the Lord Jesus, and great grace was upon them all. (Ac.4:33)

"And we are witnesses of all that he did both in the country of the Jews and in Jerusalem. They put him to death by hanging him on a tree, but God raised him on the third day and made him to appear, not to all the people but to us who had been chosen by God as witnesses, who ate and drank with him after he rose from the dead." (Ac.10:39-41)

And was declared to be the Son of God in power according to the Spirit of holiness by his resurrection from the dead, Jesus Christ our Lord. (Ro.1:4)

Jesus' death and resurrection would provide a new temple, a new meeting place for God and His people. It was to be *in Him* that people would thereafter meet God. The temple of His body was to become the temple whereby all who believe would worship and be reconciled to God (See note, *Mediator*—Jn.1:51 for discussion. Also see notes—1 Co.3:16; 6:19. See Jn.14:16-21.)

> Jesus said to him, "I am the way, and the truth, and the life. No one comes to the Father except through me." (Jn.14:6)

> For there is one God, and there is one mediator between God and men, the man Christ Jesus. (1 Ti.2:5)

### Deeper Study # 2

(2:19-20) **Jesus—Charges Against**: this is the statement used to charge Jesus with being an insurrectionist (a rebel against the government) at His trial (Mt.26:61; Mk.14:58). It was also used to taunt Jesus as He hung upon the cross (Mt.27:40). The Jews, showing their spiritual blindness and attachment to a materialistic world, understood Jesus to be saying that He would perform an architectural wonder.

## 5 Jesus' objective achieved: The disciples remembered this event and believed the Scripture and what Jesus had said.

²² When therefore he was raised from the dead, his disciples remembered that he had said this, and they believed the Scripture and the word that Jesus had spoken.

Even Jesus' disciples did not yet understand the meaning of His baffling statement. But approximately three years later, after Jesus was raised from the dead, they remembered this day and grasped the meaning of Jesus' prophetic words. Then they fully understood and believed the Scriptures that predicted the coming and resurrection of the Messiah along with what Jesus had said (see Deeper Study # 3—Jn.1:45; Mt.17:23).

> And he said to them, "O foolish ones, and slow of heart to believe all that the prophets have spoken! Was it not necessary that the Christ should suffer these things and enter into his glory?" And beginning with Moses and all the Prophets, he interpreted to them in all the Scriptures the things concerning himself. (Lk.24:25-27)

> For you will not abandon my soul to Sheol, or let your holy one see corruption. (Ps.16:10; see Ac.2:31; 13:35)

> Therefore I will divide him a portion with the many, and he shall divide the spoil with the strong, because he poured out his soul to death and was numbered with the transgressors; yet he bore the sin of many, and makes intercession for the transgressors. (Is.53:12)

## C. Revelation 3:
## Jesus Knows All People, 2:23-25

1. **Fact 1: Many believed in Jesus**
   a. Believed in His name
   b. Believed because of the miraculous signs<sup>DS1</sup>
2. **Fact 2: Jesus did not commit nor entrust Himself to any persons**<sup>DS2</sup>

   a. He knew people
   b. He knew what was in people's hearts

²³ Now when he was in Jerusalem at the Passover Feast, many believed in his name when they saw the signs that he was doing.
²⁴ But Jesus on his part did not entrust himself to them, because he knew all people
²⁵ and needed no one to bear witness about man, for he himself knew what was in man.

# Division II

## The Revelation of Jesus, the Son of God, 2:1–3:21

C. Revelation 3: Jesus Knows All People, 2:23–25

## 2:23–25
## Introduction

This brief passage is packed full of powerful truths. Its primary truth is one we should remember every day, every time we are tempted to sin in word, thought, or deed. It is a truth that we need to let penetrate us to the deepest part of our hearts: Jesus knows us and knows everything about us. This is, *Revelation 3: Jesus Knows All People*, 2:23-35.
1. Fact 1: Many believed in Jesus (v.23).
2. Fact 2: Jesus did not commit nor entrust Himself to any persons (vv.24-25).

**2:23**

²³ Now when he was in Jerusalem at the Passover Feast, many believed in his name when they saw the signs that he was doing.

### 1 Fact 1: Many believed in Jesus (v.23).

Jesus' radical cleansing of the temple was no doubt the talk of Jerusalem. The Jewish people who had gathered there for the Passover began to take notice of Him. Upon seeing the miracles He performed, many believed in Jesus.

**a. Believed in His name.**
Many believed in His name. *Believe* (Gk. episteusan) is in the Greek aorist tense, which means they believed *once-for-all*. Many more claimed belief in Christ. But some of these claims were not genuine. The fact that Jesus knew "all people" (all of those professing belief) and did not commit Himself to them shows the inadequacy of their faith (v.24).

**b. Believed because of the miraculous signs.**
They believed because of the *miracles* (semeia) they had witnessed Jesus perform (see DEEPER STUDY # 1). His ability to do supernatural deeds convinced them that He was not an ordinary man, but that He was indeed, God in human flesh.

# DEEPER STUDY # 1

(2:23) **Signs—Miracles—Power—Works—Sensationalism**: there are four words used in the Bible for miracles or signs. These words are used to describe the works of God, and they show why people believed in Jesus.

1. *Teras* is used to describe something spectacular, staggering, amazing, dazzling. Many believed in Jesus because of the spectacular signs He performed. However, such belief made a person only a spectator, not a participant in His life. The word *teras* can also describe something sensational; that is, something that appeals to the sensations of people. Many believed and followed Jesus because it made them feel good and comfortable and secure. In most cases, such belief is less than genuine. This word is never used by itself to initiate faith in the Lord Jesus. If people are to have genuine faith in the Lord Jesus, they must have some basis other than the spectacular *sign* (teras).

> "And some [seed] fell on the rock, and as it grew up, it withered away, because it had no moisture.... And the ones on the rock are those who, when they hear the word, receive it with joy. But these have no root; they believe for a while, and in time of testing fall away." (Lu.8:6, 13. See note, pt.2—Lu.8:11-15 for discussion of this person.)

> Jesus said to him, "No one who puts his hand to the plow and looks back is fit for the kingdom of God." (Lu.9:62)

> "But my righteous one shall live by faith, and if he shrinks back, my soul has no pleasure in him." (He.10:38)

2. *Dunamis* means power—unusual, extraordinary power; effective, explosive power. There were those who were attracted to Jesus because of the unusual power (dunamis) they witnessed. They believed because of the power. Such is a legitimate belief and leads to salvation for everyone who believes.

> And he could do no mighty work there, except that he laid his hands on a few sick people and healed them. And he marveled because of their unbelief. And he went about among the villages teaching. (Mk.6:5-6)

> For I am not ashamed of the gospel, for it is the power of God for salvation to everyone who believes, to the Jew first and also to the Greek. (Ro.1:16)

> But to those who are called, both Jews and Greeks, Christ the power of God and the wisdom of God. (1 Co.1:24)

3. *Ergon* means distinctive works, deeds, and miracles. Such works come from God (Jn.14:10) and bear witness to Christ. They point people to Christ (Jn.5:36; 10:25). Many individuals look at the very special works of Christ and believe because of the works (ergon).

> "If I am not doing the works of my Father, then do not believe me; but if I do them, even though you do not believe me, believe the works, that you may know and understand that the Father is in me and I am in the Father." (Jn.10:37-38)

> "Believe me that I am in the Father and the Father is in me, or else believe on account of the works themselves." (Jn.14:11)

4. *Semeion* refers to a sign that characterizes a person, his nature and character. A few throughout Jesus' ministry did believe because they saw *in the miracles* exactly who He was, the very Son of God.

> This, the first of his signs, Jesus did at Cana in Galilee, and manifested his glory. And his disciples believed in him. (Jn.2:11)

> Now Jesus did many other signs in the presence of the disciples, which are not written in this book; but these are written so that you may believe that Jesus is the Christ, the Son of God, and that by believing you may have life in his name. (Jn.20:30-31)

However, the word *semeion* is also used of those who believed the signs but *did not have* the highest or right kind of faith. Their faith was *not a faith that committed itself* (see DEEPER STUDY # 2).

a. It was a faith that arose only from . . .
- a mental conviction, a head knowledge, an intellectual belief
- a surface acceptance of the fact that Jesus was the Savior

> Now when he was in Jerusalem at the Passover Feast, many believed in his name when they saw the signs that he was doing. But Jesus on his part did not entrust himself to them, because he knew all people (Jn.2:23-24; believe and commit are the same words)

b. It was also a faith . . .
- that only sought Jesus for what a person could get out of Him
- that never gave any thought to what a person might do for Christ
- that was unaware of the cost of discipleship, unaware that people had to sacrifice themselves and give all they were and had to Christ in order to become a follower of His (see note—Lu.9:23)

> Jesus answered them, "Truly, truly, I say to you, you are seeking me, not because you saw signs, but because you ate your fill of the loaves." (Jn.6:26)

## 2:24-25

²⁴ But Jesus on his part did not entrust himself to them, because he knew all people
²⁵ and needed no one to bear witness about man, for he himself knew what was in man.

## 2 Fact 2: Jesus did not commit nor entrust Himself to any persons.

Jesus did not commit Himself to any people. The word *entrust* (or *commit*) and the word *believe* are translated from the same Greek word (v.23, see Deeper Study # 2). Jesus did not trust nor believe in the people; He did not commit Himself into their lives or hands. The Greek verb describes continuous action: Jesus kept on refusing to trust people, kept on refusing to commit Himself into their lives. Two reasons are given for this continuing attitude of Jesus.

a. **He knew people (v.24).**
Jesus knew all people. The idea is that He knew every single individual personally and thoroughly. Not a single person escaped His knowledge. The same is true today: Jesus knows every individual and every detail about them.

b. **He knew what was in people's hearts (v.25).**
Jesus knows what is in people. No one needs to tell Him about human beings. He knows our sinful human nature: its depravity, evil, deception, and fickleness. He knows the individuals He can trust and those He cannot trust. He knows every person who professes to believe, yet would . . .
- betray Him
- deny their faith under pressure
- forsake Him, turning back to the world
- slip and fall back into sin
- be weak and easily influenced, tossed to and fro
- prove untrustworthy
- lack zeal and genuine commitment
- lack courage to stand

Jesus knows all this about every single person. Nothing is hidden from Him. Therefore, just as when He walked the earth, He is not able to commit Himself and His blessings to some people despite the fact that they profess to believe,

**Thought 1.** Those who make false professions never receive the *indwelling presence of Christ*. Christ cannot commit Himself to them. Tragically, this means that He . . .
- cannot give the assurance of salvation: the confidence that a person is really saved

- cannot give the Holy Spirit to live within the heart of a person: the presence and knowledge of Him
- cannot give the fullness of life: the sense of completeness and the security of God's care and of being looked after
- cannot give the hope and certainty of eternal life
- cannot commit and entrust His mission into their hands

> "And we are witnesses to these things, and so is the Holy Spirit, whom God has given to those who obey him." (Ac.5:32)

> For those who live according to the flesh set their minds on the things of the flesh, but those who live according to the Spirit set their minds on the things of the Spirit. For to set the mind on the flesh is death, but to set the mind on the Spirit is life and peace. (Ro.8:5-6)

> For if you live according to the flesh you will die, but if by the Spirit you put to death the deeds of the body, you will live. (Ro.8:13)

> "Therefore go out from their midst, and be separate from them, says the Lord, and touch no unclean thing; then I will welcome you, and I will be a father to you, and you shall be sons and daughters to me, says the Lord Almighty." (2 Co.6:17-18)

**THOUGHT 2.** Christ knows everything about everyone. As this Scripture says: He knows "*all people*," and He knows what is "*in man*": all their thoughts and deeds—good or bad, done in the light or in the dark, in the open or behind closed doors, publicly or secretly.

> "Nothing is covered up that will not be revealed, or hidden that will not be known." (Lu.12:2)

> And again, "The Lord knows the thoughts of the wise, that they are futile." (1 Co.3:20)

> "For his eyes are on the ways of a man, and he sees all his steps." (Job 34:21)

> You have set our iniquities before you, our secret sins in the light of your presence. (Ps.90:8)

> You know when I sit down and when I rise up; you discern my thoughts from afar. You search out my path and my lying down and are acquainted with all my ways. (Ps.139:2-3)

> But they do not consider that I remember all their evil. Now their deeds surround them; they are before my face. (Ho.7:2)

## DEEPER STUDY # 2

(2:24) **Believe (episteusan)—Entrust or Commit (episteuen):** the word *entrust* or *commit* comes from the very same Greek word as *believe* (see Jn.2:23). This gives an excellent picture of *saving faith*, of what *genuine faith* is—of the kind of faith that really saves a person.

1. Saving faith is not head knowledge, not just a mental conviction and intellectual agreement. It is not just *believing the fact* that Jesus Christ is the Savior of the world. It is not just believing history, merely that Jesus Christ lived on earth as a man, similar to the way a person believes George Washington lived on earth as the first President of the United States. Saving faith is not just believing the *words* and *claims* of Jesus in the same way that a person would believe the *words* of George Washington.

2. Saving faith is believing in Jesus, *who* and *what* He is, that He is the *Savior* and *Lord* of life. It is giving and turning your life over to Jesus. It is casting yourself upon Jesus as Savior and Lord.

3. Saving faith is commitment—the commitment of your total being and life to Jesus Christ. It is the commitment of all you are and have to Jesus. It gives Jesus everything; therefore, it involves all your affairs. It is trusting Jesus to take care of your past (sins), your present (welfare), and your future (destiny). It is entrusting your whole life, being, and possessions into Jesus' hands. When you have genuine, saving faith, you lay yourself upon Jesus' keeping, confiding in Him about your daily necessities and acknowledging Him in all the ways of your life. You follow Jesus in every area and in every detail of life, seeking His instructions and leaving your welfare up to Him. It is simply commitment of your whole being, all you are and have, to Jesus (see notes—Jn.4:50; pt.4, He.5:5-10).

There are three steps involved in faith, steps that are clearly seen in this passage (see note—Ro.10:16-17 for more discussion).

1. The step of *seeing* (Jn.2:23) or *hearing* (Ro.10:16). You must be willing to listen to the message of Christ, the revelation of truth.

2. The step of *mental assent*. You must agree that the message is true, that the facts of the case are thus and so. But this is not enough. Mere agreement does not lead to action. Many people know that something is true, but they do not change their behavior to match their knowledge. For example, we know that eating too much harms our body, but we may continue to eat too much. We agree to the truth and know the truth, but we do nothing about it. A person may believe and know that Jesus Christ is the Savior of the world and yet do nothing about it, never make a decision to follow Christ. This individual still does not have faith, not the kind of faith that the Bible talks about.

3. The step of *commitment*. When the New Testament speaks of faith, it speaks of *commitment*, a *personal commitment to the truth*. You hear the truth and agree that it is true and do something about it. You commit and yield your life to the truth. The truth becomes a part of your very being, a part of your behavior and life.

# Chapter 3

## D. Revelation 4:
## The New Birth,[DS1] 3:1-15

| | |
|---|---|
| Now there was a man of the Pharisees named Nicodemus, a ruler of the Jews. ² This man came to Jesus by night and said to him, "Rabbi, we know that you are a teacher come from God, for no one can do these signs that you do unless God is with him." | 1. **The setting: Nicodemus approached Jesus**<br>  a. He came on behalf of some religious leaders: "We"<br>  b. He acknowledged Jesus as a teacher from God, but the miracles indicated Jesus was more: He seemed to be asking, "Are you the Messiah?" |
| ³ Jesus answered him, "Truly, truly, I say to you, unless one is born again he cannot see the kingdom of God." | 2. **The new birth is a necessity**<br>  a. The strong assertion<br>  b. The importance: You can never see God's kingdom unless you are born again |
| ⁴ Nicodemus said to him, "How can a man be born when he is old? Can he enter a second time into his mother's womb and be born?"<br>⁵ Jesus answered, "Truly, truly, I say to you, unless one is born of water and the Spirit, he cannot enter the kingdom of God.<br>⁶ That which is born of the flesh is flesh, and that which is born of the Spirit is spirit.<br>⁷ Do not marvel that I said to you, 'You must be born again.'<br>⁸ The wind blows where it wishes, and you hear its sound, but you do not know where it comes from or where it goes. So it is with everyone who is born of the Spirit." | 3. **The new birth is a spiritual event**<br>  a. Its source:<br>    1) It is not a natural birth<br>    2) It is being born of the Spirit[DS2]<br>  b. Its importance repeated: You cannot enter God's kingdom unless you are born again<br>  c. Its nature: Spiritual, not physical or material<br>  d. Its absolute necessity re-emphasized: You must be born again<br>  e. Its illustration: The wind |
| ⁹ Nicodemus said to him, "How can these things be?"<br>¹⁰ Jesus answered him, "Are you the teacher of Israel and yet you do not understand these things?<br>¹¹ Truly, truly, I say to you, we speak of what we know, and bear witness to what we have seen, but you do not receive our testimony.<br>¹² If I have told you earthly things and you do not believe, how can you believe if I tell you heavenly things?" | 4. **The new birth is a true experience**<br>  a. Nicodemus' heart touched<br><br>  b. Jesus' strong assertion: We know; we have seen<br>5. **The new birth is rejected**<br>  a. Some did not accept the testimony<br>  b. The reason: People's nature of unbelief |

6. **The new birth is revealed only by Jesus:** He alone is from (out of) heaven & He alone has been in heaven
7. **The new birth is secured by two acts**
   a. By Jesus' death
   b. By believing in Jesus

¹³ "No one has ascended into heaven except he who descended from heaven, the Son of Man.
¹⁴ And as Moses lifted up the serpent in the wilderness, so must the Son of Man be lifted up,
¹⁵ that whoever believes in him may have eternal life."

## Division II

*The Revelation of Jesus, the Son of God, 2:1–3:21*

D. Revelation 4: The New Birth, 3:1-15

# 3:1-15
# Introduction

The new birth, along with God's great love (vv.16-17), is the most important revelation ever made in all of human history. This passage records the revelation of this glorious truth. Jesus unveiled the new birth in a conversation with a curious Pharisee who came to visit Him late one night. God's Spirit preserved His teaching of this life-changing, destiny-determining truth through the hand of the apostle John.

All of Scripture is inspired, and all of Scripture is profitable, but some portions are especially important. When we journey through these critical chapters, we sense that we are truly on holy ground. John 3 is one such chapter. This is, *Revelation 4: The New Birth,* 3:1-15.

1. The setting: Nicodemus approached Jesus (vv.1-2).
2. The new birth is a necessity (v.3).
3. The new birth is a spiritual event (vv.4-8).
4. The new birth is a true experience (vv.9-11).
5. The new birth is rejected (vv.11-12).
6. The new birth is revealed only by Jesus: He alone is from (out of) heaven and He alone has been in heaven (v.13).
7. The new birth is secured by two acts (vv.14-15).

**3:1-2**

Now there was a man of the Pharisees named Nicodemus, a ruler of the Jews.
² This man came to Jesus by night and said to him, "Rabbi, we know that you are a teacher come from God, for no one can do these signs that you do unless God is with him."

## 1 The setting: Nicodemus approached Jesus.

John 3 begins by introducing us to Nicodemus, who secretly approached Jesus late one night. Nicodemus was a *ruler* (Gk. archon) of the Jews. This means he was a senator or a member of the Sanhedrin, the ruling body of the Jews (see DEEPER STUDY # 1—Mt.26.59). In addition, Scripture tells us the following about Nicodemus:

➢ He was a Pharisee (see DEEPER STUDY # 3—Ac.23:8).
➢ He was *the teacher of Israel* (v.10, ho didaskalos); the definite pronoun *the* (ho) indicates that he held some official position of the highest rank. He was either the *leading official* or the *leading teacher* of Israel who was either authorized or accepted as such by the public.
➢ He apparently was wealthy. He spent a great deal of money on the burial of Jesus (Jn.19:39).

> He was silent at the trial of Jesus, saying nothing to defend Jesus, but he boldly stepped forth after the Lord's death to publicly help in Jesus' burial (Jn.19:39-42).

a. **He came on behalf of some religious leaders: "We" (v.2a).**

Nicodemus said, "*We* know," indicating that he was asking questions of Jesus on behalf of others. Some of the Jewish leaders wondered if Jesus were the true Messiah, thinking that perhaps He was. Some eventually became believers (see Lu.13:31; Ac.6:7; 15:5; 18:8, 17). Jesus was claiming to be the Messiah and performing the spectacular works that were prophesied of the Messiah; therefore, He was the talk of everyone throughout the nation. The rulers were questioning and wondering: Is He really the Messiah (see notes—Mt.21:8-9; 21:23)? This was the question, the thing that Nicodemus felt compelled to find out (see DEEPER STUDY # 2—Mt.1:18). Note that Nicodemus came to Jesus at night. He apparently did this because he *feared* the other leaders who opposed Jesus. John seemed to be saying this at the burial of Jesus (see Jn.19:39).

b. **He acknowledged Jesus as a teacher from God, but the miracles indicated Jesus was more: He seemed to be asking, "Are you the Messiah?" (v.2b).**

Nicodemus acknowledged Jesus as a teacher from God. He and others saw the miracles Jesus did, and they knew that only a man from God could do such wonders. Yet, they were not convinced that Jesus was truly the Messiah.

In essence, Nicodemus was asking, "Who are you? The miracles show that God is *with you*, but you are claiming to be the Messiah, the Son of God. Are you—truthfully, in all honesty—the Messiah?"

Note that Jesus did not answer Nicodemus directly. He saw into his empty, searching heart and saw the honesty of his question. So, Jesus went right to the heart of the matter. Miracles and signs were not what was important. What was important was for Nicodemus to be changed: changed spiritually, changed within, and changed completely—to undergo such a spiritual change that it could only be described as being born again.

## DEEPER STUDY # 1

(3:1-15) **New Birth—Born Again—New Creation—Regeneration**: a spiritual birth, a rebirth of one's spirit, a new life, a renewed soul, a regenerated spirit. It is the regeneration and renewal of one's spirit and behavior (2 Co.5:17). It is the provision or infusion of a new life, of a godly nature (2 Pe.1:4). The new birth is so radical a change in a person's life that it can only be a spiritual birth, a birth beyond the grasp of human hands and efforts. It is so radical, so life-changing, and so wonderful that it can be wrought only by the love and power of God Himself.

The New Testament teaching on the new birth is rich and full.

1. The new birth is a necessity. A person will never see (Jn.3:3) nor ever enter (Jn.3:5) the Kingdom of God unless he or she is born again (Jn.3:7).
2. The new birth is a spiritual birth, the birth of a new power and spirit in life. It is not reformation of the old nature (Ro.6:6). It is the actual creation of a new birth within—spiritually (Jn.3:5-6; see Jn.1:12-13; 2 Co.5:17; Ep.2:10; 4:24; see notes—Ep.1:3; 4:17-19; DEEPER STUDY # 3—4:24). A person is spiritually born again:
   a. By water, even the Spirit (see DEEPER STUDY # 2).
   b. By the will of God (Js.1:18).
   c. By incorruptible seed, even by the Word of God (1 Pe.1:23).
   d. By God from above (1 Pe.1:3). The word *again* (ana) in the phrase "born again" also means *above* (see Jn.1:12-13).
   e. By Christ, who gives both the *power and right* to be born again (Jn.1:12-13).
3. The new birth is a definite experience, a real experience. A person experiences the new birth:
   a. By believing that Jesus is the Christ, the Son of God (1 Jn.5:1; see Jn.3:14-15).

> b. By the gospel as it is shared by believers (1 Co.4:15; Phm.10).
> c. By the Word of God (1 Pe.1:23) or by the Word of Truth (Js.1:18).
>
> 4. The new birth is a changed life, a totally new life. We prove that we are born again:
>    a. By doing righteous acts (1 Jn.2:29; see Ep.2:10; 4:24).
>    b. By not practicing sin (1 Jn.3:9; 5:18).
>    c. By loving other believers (1 Jn.4:7).
>    d. By overcoming the world (1 Jn.5:4).
>    e. By possessing the divine seed or nature (1 Pe.1:23; 2 Pe.1:4; 1 Jn.3:9; see Col.1:27).

**3:3**

³ Jesus answered him, "Truly, truly, I say to you, unless one is born again he cannot see the kingdom of God."

## 2 The new birth is a necessity.

Jesus' answer to Nicodemus addressed his greatest need, which is the greatest need of every human being. We *must* be born again. We *must* experience a new birth. The new birth is a necessity, an imperative.

> a. **The strong assertion (v.3a).**
>
> Jesus' statement to Nicodemus was strong and absolute: *unless one is born again*. The word *again* (anothen) has three different meanings in Greek. It means . . .
> - *From the first*: from the beginning or completely and fully (see Lu.1:3)
> - *Again*: a second time, a repeated act (v.4) (see Ga.4:9)
> - *From above*: from the top, which means from God (see Jn.19:11)
>
> It is critical that we grasp Jesus' point. A person must be "born *again*." We must be . . .
> - born completely and fully, undergoing a complete and full change
> - born all over *again*, in the sense of a second time
> - born *from above*, from God
>
> b. **The importance: You can never see God's kingdom unless you are born again (v.3b).**
>
> Again, Jesus' statement is clear, and there is no mistaking of what He meant: if we are not born again, we will never see God's kingdom. The words, "cannot see the kingdom of God" are critically important. We must be "born again" or else we will never "see" (v.3) nor "enter" (v.5) the Kingdom of God. It is an absolute imperative that a person be born again (3:7; see Deeper Study # 3—Mt.19:23-24).
>
>> "Whoever believes in him is not condemned, but whoever does not believe is condemned already, because he has not believed in the name of the only Son of God." (Jn.3:18)
>>
>> And Peter said to them, "Repent and be baptized every one of you in the name of Jesus Christ for the forgiveness of your sins, and you will receive the gift of the Holy Spirit." (Ac.2:38)
>>
>> For the wages of sin is death, but the free gift of God is eternal life in Christ Jesus our Lord. (Ro.6:23)
>>
>> "I call heaven and earth to witness against you today, that I have set before you life and death, blessing and curse. Therefore choose life, that you and your offspring may live." (De.30:19)

**3:4-8**

⁴ Nicodemus said to him, "How can a man be born when he is old? Can he enter a second time into his mother's womb and be born?"

⁵ Jesus answered, "Truly, truly, I say to you, unless one is born of water and the Spirit, he cannot enter the kingdom of God.

⁶ That which is born of the flesh is flesh, and that which is born of the Spirit is spirit.

⁷ Do not marvel that I said to you, 'You must be born again.'

⁸ The wind blows where it wishes, and you hear its sound, but you do not know where it comes from or where it goes. So it is with everyone who is born of the Spirit."

## 3 The new birth is a spiritual event.

Nicodemus was puzzled by the words "born again." He did not know what Jesus meant. He understood Jesus to be saying that a person must be born physically a second time. But Jesus wanted Nicodemus—and every individual—to understand clearly that the new birth is a *spiritual* birth (see note, pt.2—Jn.3:1-15). Therefore, He gave a thorough explanation of what it means to be born again.

a. **Its source (vv.4–5a).**

Jesus clearly identified the *source of the new birth* as the Holy Spirit. The new birth is being born of water, even of the Spirit (see Deeper Study # 2). The Holy Spirit is the One who brings about the spiritual birth of every individual who believes.

Just as there are two parents—a mother and a father—of every physical child born into this world, there are two parents for every spiritual birth. These two parents are the *Word of God* and the *Spirit of God*. Scripture specifically states that we are born again by the Word of God (1 Pe.1:23), and Jesus explains here that we are born of the Spirit. Saving faith begins with the hearing of God's Word, the hearing of the gospel (Ro.10:13-17). Then, when the Holy Spirit moves upon the Word we have heard, we fall under conviction of our sinful condition and see our need of salvation (Jn.16:8). The action of the Holy Spirit upon the Word of God produces genuine repentance and faith in our hearts, and we are born again—born spiritually, born into the family of God. Just as it is the action of the father's seed upon the mother's egg that brings about a new physical life, it is the action of the Holy Spirit on God's Word that brings about a new spiritual life.

b. **Its importance repeated: You cannot enter God's kingdom unless you are born again (v.5b).**

Jesus *repeated the importance* of being born again. After saying that a person can never *see* (grasp, understand, know, experience) the kingdom of God unless they are born again (v.3), Jesus repeated this absolute fact, stating that an individual can never *enter* (gain entrance to) the kingdom of God apart from being born of the Spirit.

c. **Its nature: Spiritual, not physical or material (v.6).**

Jesus explained the *nature* of the new birth. It is spiritual, not physical and material (see notes—Ep.1:3; 4:17-19; Deeper Study # 3—4:24). The flesh cannot bridge the gap between flesh and spirit. Flesh is only flesh; it has no power to be born again, to become spirit (see Deeper Study # 1—Jn.1:14).

d. **Its absolute necessity re-emphasized: You must be born again (v.7).**

Jesus re-emphasized the absolute necessity of the new birth. He said emphatically, "You *must* be born again." The word *must* (dei) means it is an absolute necessity, an imperative.

e. **Its illustration: The wind (v.8).**

Jesus illustrated the Spirit's work in the new birth by comparing it to the wind. The Spirit of God works just like the wind. We may not know how the wind works, but we can see and feel the effects. It is the same with the Spirit of God: we may not know *how* He works, but we can see the effects of His working.

> **But to all who did receive him, who believed in his name, he gave the right to become children of God, who were born, not of blood nor of the will of the flesh nor of the will of man, but of God. (Jn.1:12-13)**
>
> **He saved us, not because of works done by us in righteousness, but according to his own mercy, by the washing of regeneration and renewal of the Holy Spirit. (Tit.3:5)**
>
> **Blessed be the God and Father of our Lord Jesus Christ! According to his great mercy, he has caused us to be born again to a living hope through the resurrection of Jesus Christ from the dead. (1 Pe.1:3)**
>
> **Since you have been born again, not of perishable seed but of imperishable, through the living and abiding word of God. (1 Pe.1:23)**

## Deeper Study # 2

(3:5) **Water—Spirit**: the word "*and*" (kai) can also be translated "even." The way it is translated here is subject to the interpretation of the translator. In light of the rest of Scripture, it probably should be translated "even." This would mean that water with all of its cleansing power is a symbol of the Holy Spirit: "Unless one is born of water, *even* the Spirit, he cannot enter the kingdom of God." A strong argument for this is in the very next verse. The new birth is spiritual, apart from any natural phenomenon. It has nothing to do with any physical substance, including water. It is not of the flesh, not of any material thing. It is of the Spirit (see Ro.8:11; Ep.2:1).

Is it possible that *water* means "baptism" here? When John was writing this Gospel, he and the readers of his Gospel would have known what was meant by *Christian baptism*. However, when Jesus was speaking to Nicodemus, there was no such thing as Christian baptism. It is unlikely that Jesus would say something that Nicodemus could not grasp and understand. Jesus was not out to confuse him but to lead him to be born again. There was no way Nicodemus could be baptized in order to be born again, for Christian baptism had not yet been instituted. (Regardless of our position on baptism, honesty demands that we note this.)

3:9-11a

⁹ Nicodemus said to him, "How can these things be?"
¹⁰ Jesus answered him, "Are you the teacher of Israel and yet you do not understand these things?
¹¹ "Truly, truly, I say to you, we speak of what we know, and bear witness to what we have seen, but you do not receive our testimony."

## 4  The new birth is a true experience.

Jesus wanted Nicodemus to understand that the new birth is not some lofty concept, not some obscure, mysterious idea that cannot be truly grasped or personally known. The new birth is a true experience, a real experience, a definite experience (see Deeper Study # 1, pt.3).

### a.  Nicodemus' heart touched (vv.9-10).

Even after Jesus' thorough explanation of the new birth, Nicodemus still did not grasp its meaning. Clearly, his heart was touched by what Jesus was saying, and he genuinely longed to know what it means to be born again. He did not know, but he wanted to know. (Think how many do not even care to know.)

> The natural person does not accept the things of the Spirit of God, for they are folly to him, and he is not able to understand them because they are spiritually discerned. (1 Co.2:14)

Note the great tragedy of Nicodemus. He was *the* teacher of Israel, yet he did not know about spiritual things (v.10; see note, pt.1—Jn.3:1-2). Jesus told Nicodemus that the truth of the new birth should not be so difficult for him to grasp. As one who was deeply grounded in the Old Testament, Nicodemus "should have understood something about the new birth" (Is.44:3; Jer.31:31-33; Ezk.36:25-27).[1]

### b.  Jesus' strong assertion: We know; we have seen (v.11a).

For the third time in Jesus' conversation with Nicodemus, He prefaced a statement with the words *truly, truly* or *most assuredly* (vv.3, 5). Jesus' assertion of the truth of His teaching was strong. He affirmed the truth of the new birth without leaving any room for doubt. Furthermore, He affirmed its reality, the fact that it is a true, definite experience. He firmly declared that he *knew* what He was talking about, and He had personally *seen* its reality.

**Thought 1.** Jesus was implying that Nicodemus could have this experience: He *could* be born again, and he could *know* the powerful reality of the new birth in his own life. Our Savior's message is to every human being. We can be born again, and we can know the power of the new

---

1  Max Anders, ed., *Holman New Testament Commentary* (Nashville: Broadman and Holman Publishers), Digital edition via Wordsearch Bible Software.

birth—a new life, a spiritual life, eternal life—personally and experientially. Simply stated, we can have abundant, eternal life! We can have a relationship with God! We can be His children! How? By being born again, born spiritually, born into His family. We must declare this wonderful message to every man, woman, boy, and girl.

> **The Spirit himself bears witness with our spirit that we are children of God. (Ro.8:16)**
>
> **And because you are sons, God has sent the Spirit of his Son into our hearts, crying, "Abba! Father!" (Ga.4:6)**
>
> **Because our gospel came to you not only in word, but also in power and in the Holy Spirit and with full conviction. You know what kind of men we proved to be among you for your sake. (1 Th.1:5)**
>
> **Which is why I suffer as I do. But I am not ashamed, for I know whom I have believed, and I am convinced that he is able to guard until that day what has been entrusted to me. (2 Ti.1:12)**
>
> **Whoever keeps his commandments abides in God, and God in him. And by this we know that he abides in us, by the Spirit whom he has given us. (1 Jn.3:24)**
>
> **By this we know that we abide in him and he in us, because he has given us of his Spirit. (1 Jn.4:13)**

## 5 The new birth is rejected.

3:11b–12

Jesus made two statements that seem to indicate that Nicodemus did not believe and receive Jesus at this point in his life:

➤ You do not receive our testimony (v.11b)
➤ You do not believe (v.12)

¹¹ "Truly, truly, I say to you, we speak of what we know, and bear witness to what we have seen, but you do not receive our testimony.
¹² If I have told you earthly things and you do not believe, how can you believe if I tell you heavenly things?"

### a. Some did not accept the testimony (v.11b).

Nicodemus did what so many do: he rejected Jesus. The Lord pointed out Nicodemus' true problem: it was not that he did not understand what Jesus was teaching him, but, rather, he did not believe it.

When Jesus addressed Nicodemus as *you*, He was speaking not only of Nicodemus, but also of the other Jewish leaders who rejected Him and salvation through Him. Actually, Jesus was speaking of *all* who reject Christ as Lord and Savior. In Jesus' day, some did not accept the testimony of Jesus. Today, many still do not believe the truth about Jesus and salvation. They reject Him as their Lord and Savior, effectively rejecting the salvation and eternal life that is available only through Him.

### b. The reason: People's nature of unbelief (v.12).

Why do so many reject Christ? What is the reason? Jesus stated it directly: it is because of people's nature of unbelief. Jesus said that he had tried to help Nicodemus grasp the glorious truth of salvation using *earthly things*—the earthly illustrations of birth and the wind. Jesus had made salvation easy to understand by explaining it with these simple pictures, but Nicodemus still did not believe, not at that time. His unbelief ruled the day. Again, it was not that he did not understand, but that He refused to believe in Jesus.

**THOUGHT 1.** Nicodemus symbolizes every single person who rejects Christ. People spend eternity in hell because of their unbelief. Certainly, we are sinners, and we deserve eternal punishment because we are sinners. But God offers us full forgiveness of our sins through His Son, Jesus Christ. He solved the problem of our sin through His death on the cross. Those who suffer the punishment for their sins eternally in hell do so because of their unbelief. They refused to believe on Jesus Christ unto salvation.

> **He came to his own, and his own people did not receive him. (Jn.1:11)**
>
> **"Whoever believes in him is not condemned, but whoever does not believe is condemned already, because he has not believed in the name of the only Son of God." (Jn.3:18)**
>
> **Whoever believes in the Son has eternal life; whoever does not obey the Son shall not see life, but the wrath of God remains on him. (Jn.3:36)**

"I told you that you would die in your sins, for unless you believe that I am he you will die in your sins." (Jn.8:24)

"The one who rejects me and does not receive my words has a judge; the word that I have spoken will judge him on the last day." (Jn.12:48)

Whoever believes in the Son of God has the testimony in himself. Whoever does not believe God has made him a liar, because he has not believed in the testimony that God has borne concerning his Son. (1 Jn.5:10)

## 3:13

¹³ "No one has ascended into heaven except he who descended from heaven, the Son of Man."

### 6 The new birth is revealed only by Jesus: He alone is from (out of) heaven and He alone has been in heaven.

Only Jesus could reveal the new birth because only He is from heaven. No human being has ascended up into heaven; no human can penetrate the spiritual world. Flesh is flesh, that is, born of the earth; therefore, it is earthly (1 Co.15:47). However, Jesus Christ was different from all other humans. His origin was *out of* heaven, out of the spiritual world and dimension of being. Therefore, He alone could reveal *heavenly things* (v.12) to us (see DEEPER STUDY # 1—Jn.3:31; note—1:18; DEEPER STUDY # 1, 2, 3—14:6 for discussion).

"For the bread of God is he who comes down from heaven and gives life to the world. . . . For I have come down from heaven, not to do my own will but the will of him who sent me." (Jn.6:33, 38)

"This is the bread that comes down from heaven, so that one may eat of it and not die. I am the living bread that came down from heaven. If anyone eats of this bread, he will live forever. And the bread that I will give for the life of the world is my flesh." (Jn.6:50-51)

Jesus said to them, "If God were your Father, you would love me, for I came from God and I am here. I came not of my own accord, but he sent me." (Jn.8:42)

Jesus, knowing that the Father had given all things into his hands, and that he had come from God and was going back to God. (Jn.13:3)

## 3:14-15

¹⁴ "And as Moses lifted up the serpent in the wilderness, so must the Son of Man be lifted up,
¹⁵ that whoever believes in him may have eternal life."

### 7 The new birth is secured by two acts.

How is the new birth possible? What must be done in order for us to be saved? What must we do? Jesus explained that the new birth is secured by two acts.

#### a. By Jesus' death (v.15).

The first act is Jesus' death. Jesus illustrated His point by using the Old Testament story of Moses lifting up the bronze serpent in the wilderness (Nu.21:4-9). The children of Israel had begun to murmur and grumble about the trials of the wilderness, wishing they had never left Egypt. God disciplined them by sending fiery serpents to plague them. The discipline worked; the people repented and begged for mercy. God met the people's need by telling Moses to make a bronze image of a serpent and to hold it up upon a pole in the midst of the people. All who looked upon the *lifted up* serpent were healed.

Jesus said that He must be lifted up just as the serpent was lifted up. What did He mean? There are several pictures here.

➤ The people of Israel had a great need, for they were dying from the poison of the fiery serpents. People today are dying from the poison of the serpent, the deadly poison of sin.

➤ The serpent is a symbol of the evil one, Satan (Ge.3:1f; Re.12:9; 20:2). Jesus Christ destroyed the works of the devil by being lifted up (He.2:14-15); therefore, the serpent's hanging upon the pole symbolized the defeat of Satan. By looking upon the *defeated evil* (the serpent), Israel was healed. Today we are healed of our sinful condition by looking upon the Son of Man who has been lifted up upon the cross.

> "Now is the judgment of this world; now will the ruler of this world be cast out. And I, when I am lifted up from the earth, will draw all people to myself." (Jn.12:31-32)

> Since therefore the children share in flesh and blood, he himself likewise partook of the same things, that through death he might destroy the one who has the power of death, that is, the devil, and deliver all those who through fear of death were subject to lifelong slavery. (He.2:14-15)

➤ The serpent was a cursed creature from the very beginning (Ge.3:14-15). Jesus became a curse for mankind (Ga.3:13).

> Christ redeemed us from the curse of the law by becoming a curse for us—for it is written, "Cursed is everyone who is hanged on a tree." (Ga.3:13)

> He himself bore our sins in his body on the tree, that we might die to sin and live to righteousness. By his wounds you have been healed. (1 Pe.2:24)

b. **By believing in Jesus (v.15).**

The second act is our belief in Jesus. Everyone who believes in the Son of Man who was lifted up on the cross will not perish but will have eternal life (see Deeper Study # 2—Jn.3:16; Deeper Study # 2; Deeper Study # 1—10:10; Deeper Study # 1—17:2-3).

**THOUGHT 1.** In Numbers 21, if an Israelite believed God's message (the good news of healing), he or she looked upon the lifted up serpent and was healed. Those who did not believe God's message did not look, and they died. The same is true today: every person must believe the message of Christ in order to be healed, that is, be born again.

> "For God so loved the world, that he gave his only Son, that whoever believes in him should not perish but have eternal life." (Jn.3:16)

> "Truly, truly, I say to you, whoever hears my word and believes him who sent me has eternal life. He does not come into judgment, but has passed from death to life." (Jn.5:24)

> But he was pierced for our transgressions; he was crushed for our iniquities; upon him was the chastisement that brought us peace, and with his wounds we are healed. (Is.53:5)

# E. Revelation 5: God's Great Love, 3:16–17

1. The fact: God so loved<sup>DS1</sup>
2. The evidence: God gave His son
3. The purpose: To save us
   a. From perishing<sup>DS2</sup>
   b. To eternal life
   c. By believing
4. The proof: God sent His Son (the Incarnation)
   a. Not to condemn us
   b. To save the world
5. The means: Through Christ

<sup>16</sup> "For God so loved the world, that he gave his only Son, that whoever believes in him should not perish but have eternal life.

<sup>17</sup> "For God did not send his Son into the world to condemn the world, but in order that the world might be saved through him."

# Division II

## The Revelation of Jesus, the Son of God, 2:1–3:21

E. Revelation 5: God's Great Love, 3:16–17

## 3:16–17 Introduction

Often called "the Bible in a nutshell," John 3:16 is the world's best-known Scripture. Brief and to the point, Jesus told the story of salvation and summarized God's purpose for creating the human race in this single verse. This is, *Revelation 5: God's Great Love,* 3:16-17.

1. The fact: God so loved (v.16).
2. The evidence: God gave His Son (v.16).
3. The purpose: To save us (v.16).
4. The proof: God sent His Son (the Incarnation) (v.17).
5. The means: Through Christ (v.17).

### 3:16

<sup>16</sup> "For God so loved the world, that he gave his only Son, that whoever believes in him should not perish but have eternal life."

### 1 The fact: God so loved.

*God so loved the world*—the *whole* world (see DEEPER STUDY # 1). The idea that God loves the whole world was a new idea when Jesus revealed it, and it is a foreign concept to many today. The Jews believed God loved the religious (the true Jew) and hated the non-religious (the Gentiles). The same thoughts are held by many in every generation, especially by those who cling to religion. The fact that God truly loves *every* human being is shocking to many. Some wonder, and others question how God could possibly love the . . .

- vile person
- murderer
- immoral person
- wife beater
- child abuser
- prostitute
- thief
- alcoholic
- street person
- oppressor
- enslaver
- bitter, vengeful

The basis of God's love is His nature. God is love (1 Jn.4:8, 16); therefore, He loves. He acts, demonstrates, and shows His love because He *is* love.

> But God shows his love for us in that while we were still sinners, Christ died for us. (Ro.5:8)
>
> Anyone who does not love does not know God, because God is love. . . . So we have come to know and to believe the love that God has for us. God is love, and whoever abides in love abides in God, and God abides in him. (1 Jn.4:8, 16)

Love is far more than a mere emotion, far more than something we feel inside. Love is a driving force, a dynamic that compels us to act. Love acts; it expresses itself. It does not sit still, doing nothing. It is not dormant, complacent, inactive. If love actually exists, it has to act and express itself; it has to do something good for those loved. Love is *loving*; that is, love is always demonstrating love to others. Therefore, God's love acts and reveals Him to be love.

**THOUGHT 1.** God loves *every* individual, not just the religious and the good. He does not love only the people who love Him. He loves everyone, even the unlovely and the unloving, the unbelieving and the obstinate, the selfish and the greedy, the spiteful and the vengeful.

> "And I have other sheep that are not of this fold. I must bring them also, and they will listen to my voice. So there will be one flock, one shepherd." (Jn.10:16)
>
> For there is no distinction between Jew and Greek; for the same Lord is Lord of all, bestowing his riches on all who call on him. For "everyone who calls on the name of the Lord will be saved." (Ro.10:12-13)
>
> Who desires all people to be saved and to come to the knowledge of the truth. (1 Ti.2:4)
>
> The Lord is not slow to fulfill his promise as some count slowness, but is patient toward you, not wishing that any should perish, but that all should reach repentance. (2 Pe.3:9)

In addition, God wants every human being to know His love. He wants to reach everyone in the world with His love.

> By this we know love, that he laid down his life for us, and we ought to lay down our lives for the brothers. (1 Jn.3:16)
>
> In this the love of God was made manifest among us, that God sent his only Son into the world, so that we might live through him. (1 Jn.4:9)

## DEEPER STUDY # 1

(3:16) **God Loved**: past tense. It is a past, proven fact. An outline of the greatness of God's love is seen in this verse. (1) Height: God loved. (2) Depth: so loved. (3) Length: God gave. (4) Breadth: whosoever (see note—Jn.21:15-17).

## 2 The evidence: God gave His Son.

Although God has expressed His love for humanity in many ways, one act is more than enough to prove His love for every man, woman, boy, and girl. What is this supreme evidence of God's love? *He gave His only Son.*

> [16] "For God so loved the world, that he gave his only Son, that whoever believes in him should not perish but have eternal life."

God demonstrated His love in the *most perfect way* possible: He gave His only begotten Son to the world. As God, He is perfect, which means His love is perfect. Therefore, God not only loves, but He *so* loves. He loves to perfection, loves to the ultimate degree. Whatever the ultimate degree and the perfect act and expression of love is, God shows it. Without question, the greatest act of love is the sacrifice of one's own life; therefore, God sacrificed the life of His own Son to save mankind.

> "Greater love has no one than this, that someone lay down his life for his friends." (Jn.15:13)

*Gave* (Gk. edoken) has a twofold meaning: God gave His Son to the world, and He gave His Son to die. The idea of *sacrifice*, of great cost, is in both acts. It cost God dearly to give His Son *up to the world and up to the cross.*

First, God gave up His Son to be separated from Him, *allowing Jesus to leave His presence*, to leave the majesty and glory, worship and honor of heaven (see note—Mk.9:2-3). He gave up His Son to be separated from Him, *allowing Jesus to come to earth* . . .

*Into a world that was . . .*
- fallen
- depraved
- wicked
- rebellious
- revolting
- apostate

*Into a world full of . . .*
- darkness
- hostility
- bitterness
- wrath
- anger
- war

- selfishness
- greed
- immorality
- barriers
- sin
- shame

Second, God gave up His Son to be separated from Him, *allowing Jesus to die* for the sins of the human race (see Deeper Study # 2—Mt.26:37-38).

> **For while we were still weak, at the right time Christ died for the ungodly. (Ro.5:6)**
>
> **For I delivered to you as of first importance what I also received: that Christ died for our sins in accordance with the Scriptures. (1 Co.15:3)**
>
> **For our sake he made him to be sin who knew no sin, so that in him we might become the righteousness of God. (2 Co.5:21)**
>
> **He himself bore our sins in his body on the tree, that we might die to sin and live to righteousness. By his wounds you have been healed. (1 Pe.2:24)**
>
> **But he was pierced for our transgressions; he was crushed for our iniquities; upon him was the chastisement that brought us peace, and with his wounds we are healed. All we like sheep have gone astray; we have turned—every one—to his own way; and the Lord has laid on him the iniquity of us all. (Is.53:5-6)**

A most glorious evidence of God's love is that God took the *initiative* to save us. We did not seek to save ourselves; God sought to save us. God gave His Son so that we might be forgiven and saved. God is the *seeking Savior*. He is not angry, unloving, or unforgiving toward us. He does not hate any human being, and we do not have to do anything to make Him love us. Nor does He have to be convinced to forgive us. Salvation is entirely of God. Because He loves us, He made a way for us to be forgiven and saved. He stands ready to forgive anybody and everybody who comes to Him in genuine repentance and faith *because He loves us so*.

> **But God shows his love for us in that while we were still sinners, Christ died for us. (Ro.5:8)**
>
> **But God, being rich in mercy, because of the great love with which he loved us, even when we were dead in our trespasses, made us alive together with Christ—by grace you have been saved. (Ep.2:4-5)**
>
> **"The Lord appeared to him from far away. I have loved you with an everlasting love; therefore I have continued my faithfulness to you." (Je.31:3)**

The most glorious truth in all the world is that God gave His *only Son*. This is the most remarkable proof of God's love. It magnifies and shows how great His love really is. He was willing to give the thing most dear to His heart in order to save the world. Note this: God even planned to give His Son throughout eternity.

> **"This Jesus, delivered up according to the definite plan and foreknowledge of God, you crucified and killed by the hands of lawless men. God raised him up, loosing the pangs of death, because it was not possible for him to be held by it." (Ac.2:23-24)**
>
> **Knowing that you were ransomed from the futile ways inherited from your forefathers, not with perishable things such as silver or gold, but with the precious blood of Christ, like that of a lamb without blemish or spot. He was foreknown before the foundation of the world but was made manifest in the last times for the sake of you (1 Pe.1:18-20)**
>
> **And all who dwell on earth will worship it, everyone whose name has not been written before the foundation of the world in the book of life of the Lamb who was slain. (Re.13:8)**

## 3 The purpose: To save us.

The purpose of God's love is simple, yet profound. God's purpose in giving His Son was to *save us*.

### a. From perishing.

Through the gift of His Son, God saves us from perishing (see Deeper Study # 2). Why are we condemned to perish? Because we are sinners. Every single one of us, without exception is a sinner, and sin demands a penalty (Ro.3:10-12, 23; 6:23).

> ¹⁶ "For God so loved the world, that he gave his only Son, that whoever believes in him should not perish but have eternal life."

### b. To eternal life.

God not only saves us from perishing, He saves us to eternal life (see Deeper Study # 2—Jn.1:4; Deeper Study # 1—10:10; Deeper Study # 1—17:2-3). What a glorious truth, the ultimate expression of God's love for us! Just think about it. If God merely waived our penalty for sin, spared us from perishing—from spending eternity in hell—it would be an act of mercy far greater than we deserve. But God goes exceedingly beyond that. He gives us eternal life! His presence lives inside us the rest of our lives on this earth, and when this life is over, we spend eternity with Him!

### c. By believing.

How are we saved? Through believing (see Deeper Study # 2—Jn.2:24). We must believe in God's Son in order to be saved. This fact declares that salvation is conditional. Not everybody is saved. Not everybody automatically goes to heaven. Not everybody has eternal life. Only those who believe are spared from perishing and given eternal life.

This truth also declares that we do not have to earn salvation and eternal life. We do not have to work for it. It is a gift from a God who loves us so that He gave His only Son for us. We simply must accept this unimaginable gift by believing in Jesus Christ.

> **Thanks be to God for his inexpressible gift! (2 Co.9:15)**
>
> **For by grace you have been saved through faith. And this is not your own doing; it is the gift of God, not a result of works, so that no one may boast. For we are his workmanship, created in Christ Jesus for good works, which God prepared beforehand, that we should walk in them. (Ep.2:8-10)**
>
> **He saved us, not because of works done by us in righteousness, but according to his own mercy, by the washing of regeneration and renewal of the Holy Spirit, whom he poured out on us richly through Jesus Christ our Savior. (Tit.3:5-6)**

## Deeper Study # 2

(3:16) **Perish—Perishing** (apoletai): to be lost, to destroy utterly, to lose utterly, to lose eternal life, to be spiritually destitute, to be cut off.

1. Perishing means to be in a lost state in this world. It means to be . . .
   - aging, deteriorating, decaying, dying (see Deeper Study # 2—Mt.8:17; notes—1 Co.15:50; Col.2:13; Deeper Study # 1—2 Pe.1:4).
   - without life (purpose, meaning, significance; see Deeper Study # 2—Jn.1:4; Deeper Study # 1—10:10; Deeper Study # 1—17:2-3).
   - without peace (assurance, confidence, security in God's keeping; see note—Jn.14:27).
   - without hope (of living forever; see Deeper Study # 1—2 Ti.4:18).

2. Perishing means to be in a lost state in the world to come. It means . . .
   - having to die
   - facing judgment
   - being condemned
   - suffering separation from God and all loved ones
   - experiencing all that hell is

(See Deeper Study # 2—Mt.5:22; Deeper Study # 4—Lu.16:24; Deeper Study # 1—He.9:27.)

## 4 The proof: God sent His Son (the Incarnation).

The incarnation of Christ—God the Son becoming a man—is the proof of God's love. God actually sent His Son into the world (see notes—Jn.1:14).

**3:17a**

<sup>17</sup> "For God did not send his Son into the world to condemn the world, but in order that the world might be saved through him."

### a. Not to condemn us.

Christ was not sent to condemn or to judge the world. That was not His purpose. However, we, the world, deserve to be judged and condemned.

- ➢ We are guilty both of breaking God's law and of coming short of God's glory (Ro.3:23).
- ➢ We are convicted (Ro.3:9-18; see Ro.1:18-32).

### b. To save the world.

Christ was sent to save the world. His purpose was to save us from perishing and to save us to eternal life. By becoming a man, Jesus would be able to die in order that the penalty God demands for our sin could be paid and we could be pardoned (see Deeper Study #1—1 Co.1:18).

> "Even as the Son of Man came not to be served but to serve, and to give his life as a ransom for many." (Mt.20:28)

> "For unto you is born this day in the city of David a Savior, who is Christ the Lord." (Lu.2:11)

> "For the Son of Man came to seek and to save the lost." (Lu.19:10)

**3:17b**

## 5 The means: Through Christ.

The only means of salvation is *through Him* (Christ Jesus) and through Him alone. There is no other way we can be saved. The only path to heaven goes by the cross. The death of Jesus Christ is the only payment God accepts for our sins. Believing in Jesus Christ is the only thing we can do to receive forgiveness and eternal life.

> They said to the woman, "It is no longer because of what you said that we believe, for we have heard for ourselves, and we know that this is indeed the Savior of the world." (Jn.4:42)

> Jesus said to him, "I am the way, and the truth, and the life. No one comes to the Father except through me." (Jn.14:6)

> "And there is salvation in no one else, for there is no other name under heaven given among men by which we must be saved." (Ac.4:12)

> For there is one God, and there is one mediator between God and men, the man Christ Jesus. (1 Ti.2:5)

> Consequently, he is able to save to the uttermost those who draw near to God through him, since he always lives to make intercession for them. (He.7:25)

> And we have seen and testify that the Father has sent his Son to be the Savior of the world. (1 Jn.4:14)

## F. Revelation 6:
## Humanity's Condemnation, 3:18–21

¹⁸ "Whoever believes in him is not condemned, but whoever does not believe is condemned already, because he has not believed in the name of the only Son of God.

¹⁹ And this is the judgment: the light has come into the world, and people loved the darkness rather than the light because their works were evil. ²⁰ For everyone who does wicked things hates the light and does not come to the light, lest his works should be exposed. ²¹ But whoever does what is true comes to the light, so that it may be clearly seen that his works have been carried out in God."

1. **Who is condemned: Not believers but unbelievers**
2. **When are they condemned: Already**
3. **Why are they condemned**
   a. Because they have not believed in Christ, the Son of God
   b. Because light has come into the world
   c. Because they love darkness, love their evil & sin
   d. Because they fear exposure and do not come to the light
4. **Who escapes condemnation**
   a. Those who do what is right, who live out the truth
   b. Those who do what God wants

# Division II
*The Revelation of Jesus, the Son of God, 2:1–3:21*

F. Revelation 6: Humanity's Condemnation, 3:18–21

## 3:18–21
## Introduction

One of the most dangerous doctrines in the world today is the doctrine of universalism, which says that all people will ultimately be saved and reconciled to God, and nobody will spend eternity in hell. God sent His Son into the world to save the world, but this does not mean that everyone is automatically saved. In fact, many are condemned and doomed. Jesus reveals this sobering fact in this passage. This is, *Revelation 6: Humanity's Condemnation*, 3:18–21.

1. Who is condemned: Not believers, but unbelievers (v.18).
2. When are they condemned: Already (v.18).
3. Why are they condemned (vv.18–20)?
4. Who escapes condemnation (v.21)?

### 1 Who is condemned: Not believers, but unbelievers.

Jesus first identified who is condemned. He stated definitively that the believer is not condemned. The critical importance of belief cannot be overstressed. Belief stays, prevents, and stops judgment. All who *believe in Christ* . . .
- are acquitted as though they never sinned
- are released from the bondage of sin

3:18a

¹⁸ "Whoever believes in him is not condemned, but whoever does not believe is condemned already, because he has not believed in the name of the only Son of God."

- are not to be captured again (by guilt, fear, bondage, shame)
- are not to be condemned (judged)
- are not to be dealt with injustice

Why are believers not condemned? Because they are saved. They are as guilty as unbelievers, but there is one critical difference: they have believed in Jesus Christ and have committed their lives to Him. Believers are actively and diligently seeking Christ (He.11:6). God will save any person who will believe and seek and honor His Son (see Jn.12:26. See DEEPER STUDY # 2—Jn.2:24; note—3:17).

Again, believers are released from condemnation because they believe in Christ. They believe that Christ died for their sins, in their place, as their substitute, paying the penalty for their sins (which is death).

> "Truly, truly, I say to you, whoever hears my word and believes him who sent me has eternal life. He does not come into judgment, but has passed from death to life." (Jn.5:24)
>
> There is therefore now no condemnation for those who are in Christ Jesus. (Ro.8:1)
>
> Who is to condemn? Christ Jesus is the one who died—more than that, who was raised—who is at the right hand of God, who indeed is interceding for us. (Ro.8:34; see DEEPER STUDY # 1, 2—Ro.4:22; note—5:1)

However, all unbelievers are condemned. Jesus clearly identifies who are unbelievers. Unbelievers are those who have not believed in the name of God's only Son. God has *only one* begotten Son. The person who *has not* believed in God's Son is the unbeliever. It does not matter who they are or where they are; they are unbelievers if they *have not* believed in the only begotten Son of God.

## 3:18b-20

¹⁸ "Whoever believes in him is not condemned, but whoever does not believe is condemned already, because he has not believed in the name of the only Son of God.

¹⁹ And this is the judgment: the light has come into the world, and people loved the darkness rather than the light because their works were evil.

²⁰ For everyone who does wicked things hates the light and does not come to the light, lest his works should be exposed."

## 2 When are they condemned: Already.

When are unbelievers condemned? Already, right now. It is not that they *are* to be condemned; they are *condemned* or *judged already* (Gk. ede kekritai).

Condemnation is a sure fact. The judgment of unbelievers is sure; so sure it is as though they have already been condemned. Nothing can change or stop God's judgment from coming upon an unbeliever. Ignoring, denying, and struggling against the great day of judgment will not change one detail of the day. It is coming, and every single unbeliever will be judged.

Unbelievers are *already* under the present curse of sin. They are without Christ and alienated from the people of God. They are strangers to the promises of God, without hope and without God in the world (Ep.2:12; see DEEPER STUDY # 2, pt.1, *Perish*—Jn.3:16 for a description of what this means).

Unbelievers already stand guilty of all the sins they have ever committed; they are already condemned. The law of God already exists. Every time a person breaks the law of God, they immediately become guilty and are condemned. The judgment is already pronounced. Unbelievers must pay the penalty for every transgression of God's law. They are already *under the curse, the full force* of the law.

> For all who rely on works of the law are under a curse; for it is written, "Cursed be everyone who does not abide by all things written in the Book of the Law, and do them." (Ga.3:10)
>
> But the law is not of faith, rather "The one who does them shall live by them." (Ga.3:12)

## 3 Why are they condemned?

Out of His great love for every sinner, the Lord Jesus wants every person born into this world to understand clearly why he or she is already condemned. He gave four reasons why all sinners are doomed to God's righteous judgment.

a. **Because they have not believed in Christ, the Son of God (v.18c).**
   The unbeliever has not believed. The great sin of unbelief is that it neglects, ignores, denies, abuses, and rejects God's Son.
   ➢ The dignity of God's Son is ignored (see note—Jn.1:1-2).
   ➢ The truth of God's Son is not believed (see notes—Jn.1:14).
   ➢ The goodness of God's Son is not embraced (see notes—Jn.1:14).
   ➢ The dearest thing to God's heart is denied (see notes—Jn.3:16).
   ➢ The name that is above every name is abused and cursed (Ph.2:9).
   ➢ The only begotten Son of God is rejected (Jn.3:16-19).

   Christ is the great remedy for our sins. Therefore, unbelief—rejecting and refusing to believe in Him—is the great sin that condemns us to God's judgment.

   > Whoever believes in the Son has eternal life; whoever does not obey the Son shall not see life, but the wrath of God remains on him. (Jn.3:36)
   >
   > "I told you that you would die in your sins, for unless you believe that I am he you will die in your sins." (Jn.8:24)

b. **Because light has come into the world (v.19a).**
   The unbeliever is condemned because Light has come into the world. The Light came into the world to give us light, to enable us to walk out of the darkness of a sinful and perishing world. The Light came to show us the way, the truth, and the life (Jn.14:6):
   ➢ The Light shows us the way God intends for us to live.
   ➢ The Light shows us the truth of life, that is, the truth about God and about us and about the world that surrounds us.
   ➢ The Light shows us the life, that is, how to save our lives and avoid the things that cause us to stumble and lose our lives.

   The point is this: the life of Jesus Christ now stands in the world to give Light. All who do not turn and walk in the Light are naturally in the dark. They are condemned to the darkness and to all that happens to those who walk in the darkness (see Deeper Study # 1—1:9; Deeper Study # 1—8:12).

c. **Because they love darkness, love their evil and sin (v.19b).**
   All unbelievers are condemned because they love darkness. Why would they love darkness? Because their deeds are evil, and to turn and walk in the Light would expose their evil deeds for what they are: immoral, unrighteous, and disobedient to God. Why do unbelievers prefer to walk in darkness and prefer to hold on to their sins?

   First, because unbelievers love their sin and do not want to turn and face the conviction of the Light. If they turn to the Light, they will have to give up their sin. They are not willing to turn from—repent of—their sin because they love all the things which sin brings: the feeling, the stimulation, the pleasure, the comfort, the ease, the challenge, the recognition, the power, the fame, the possessions. They love it all too much to give it up.

   Second, because unbelievers are full of pride. They do not want to confess their sin, the fact that they are in darkness and fall short of what God demands. They deny that they are in darkness, refusing to turn to the Light (Christ).

   Third, because unbelievers are enslaved, in bondage to sin and gripped by the darkness. They been in darkness so long that they do not have the strength to break the enslavement.

   > But sexual immorality and all impurity or covetousness must not even be named among you, as is proper among saints. Let there be no filthiness nor foolish talk nor crude joking, which are out of place, but instead let there be thanksgiving. For you may be sure of this, that everyone who is sexually immoral or impure, or who is covetous (that is, an idolater), has no inheritance in the kingdom of Christ and God. Let no one deceive you with empty words, for because of these things the wrath of God comes upon the sons of disobedience. . . . Take no part in the unfruitful works of darkness, but instead expose them. (Ep.5:3-6, 11)

But you are not in darkness, brothers, for that day to surprise you like a thief. . . . So then let us not sleep, as others do, but let us keep awake and be sober. For those who sleep, sleep at night, and those who get drunk, are drunk at night. (1 Th.5:4, 6–7)

If we say we have fellowship with him while we walk in darkness, we lie and do not practice the truth. (1 Jn.1:6)

They have neither knowledge nor understanding, they walk about in darkness; all the foundations of the earth are shaken. (Ps.82:5)

The way of the wicked is like deep darkness; they do not know over what they stumble. (Pr.4:19)

### d. Because they fear exposure and do not come to the light (v.20).

Unbelievers are condemned because they do not come to the Light. They fear the shame, embarrassment, and consequence of their sin. In some cases they would like to confess their evil and correct it, but fear of being exposed keeps them from coming out and facing the Light (Christ). Whatever their reasons, unbelievers refuse to come to the Light; therefore, they are condemned.

"Let them alone; they are blind guides. And if the blind lead the blind, both will fall into a pit." (Mt.15:14)

The night is far gone; the day is at hand. So then let us cast off the works of darkness and put on the armor of light. (Ro.13:12)

"Therefore their way shall be to them like slippery paths in the darkness, into which they shall be driven and fall, for I will bring disaster upon them in the year of their punishment, declares the Lord." (Je.23:12)

**THOUGHT 1.** Unbelievers are uncomfortable in the Light. Therefore, they shun everything that presents the Light to them: the church, believers, the Bible, prayer, and spiritual conversation.

Note that unbelievers are said to hate the Light. They ignore, reject, deny, and fight the Light. They speak and write against it, ridicule and curse it, persecute and seek to stamp it out.

In him was life, and the life was the light of men. The light shines in the darkness, and the darkness has not overcome it. (Jn.1:4–5)

Again Jesus spoke to them, saying, "I am the light of the world. Whoever follows me will not walk in darkness, but will have the light of life." (Jn.8:12)

So Jesus said to them, "The light is among you for a little while longer. Walk while you have the light, lest darkness overtake you. The one who walks in the darkness does not know where he is going." (Jn.12:35)

"I have come into the world as light, so that whoever believes in me may not remain in darkness." (Jn.12:46)

For God, who said, "Let light shine out of darkness," has shone in our hearts to give the light of the knowledge of the glory of God in the face of Jesus Christ. (2 Co.4:6)

The people who walked in darkness have seen a great light; those who dwelt in a land of deep darkness, on them has light shone. (Is.9:2)

3:21

[11] "But whoever does what is true comes to the light, so that it may be clearly seen that his works have been carried out in God."

## 4 Who escapes condemnation?

By God's grace and mercy, people can escape the condemnation of our sins. Who escapes condemnation? *All who come to the light*—genuinely believe in Jesus Christ. Jesus describes genuine believers as the following.

### a. Those who do what is right, who live out the truth.

Those who practice truth and live righteously refers to believers: those who come to the light. They escape condemnation because they believe in Christ, and their changed lives prove that their faith is genuine (Js.2:17-18). They live in the light of Christ and of God's Word. Therefore, they know what is right and they do it. The verb is continuous action; it speaks of practicing the truth, continually and habitually.

This does not mean they live perfectly, without ever sinning. No one is or can be perfect. It means that genuine believers direct their life toward truth: diligently seek the truth and seek to be truthful. They may slip and sin, but they turn back to God, repenting and walking again in the light. Christ said that the one who does truth hears His voice (Jn.18:37; 1 Jn.1:6). Only the person who desires truth is saved, and everyone who comes to the truth is saved. Christ is truth.

> "And you will know the truth, and the truth will set you free." (Jn.8:32)
>
> Jesus said to him, "I am the way, and the truth, and the life. No one comes to the Father except through me." (Jn.14:6)
>
> If we say we have fellowship with him while we walk in darkness, we lie and do not practice the truth. But if we walk in the light, as he is in the light, we have fellowship with one another, and the blood of Jesus his Son cleanses us from all sin. (1 Jn.1:6-7)
>
> For I rejoiced greatly when the brothers came and testified to your truth, as indeed you are walking in the truth. (3 Jn.3)
>
> For your steadfast love is before my eyes, and I walk in your faithfulness. (Ps.26:3)
>
> Teach me your way, O LORD, that I may walk in your truth; unite my heart to fear your name. (Ps.86:11)

b. **Those who do what God wants.**

Those whose works are carried out in God escape condemnation. *Carried out* (eirgasmena) means to work, produce, perform, originate, manufacture, and fashion from something. The idea is that the believer *comes to Christ* (the Light) so that his/her works will be wrought, originated, and worked in and of God. Those who come to Christ live close to God. They walk and talk and listen to God (His Word), and they do what God says (see 2 Co.1:12). The point is reemphasized here: their works prove the genuineness of their faith. The fact that they do what God wants verifies that God has truly performed His work in their lives.

> "In the same way, let your light shine before others, so that they may see your good works and give glory to your Father who is in heaven." (Mt.5:16)
>
> "Whoever has my commandments and keeps them, he it is who loves me. And he who loves me will be loved by my Father, and I will love him and manifest myself to him." (Jn.14:21)
>
> So also faith by itself, if it does not have works, is dead. But someone will say, "You have faith and I have works." Show me your faith apart from your works, and I will show you my faith by my works. (Js.2:17-18)
>
> And by this we know that we have come to know him, if we keep his commandments. Whoever says "I know him" but does not keep his commandments is a liar, and the truth is not in him. (1 Jn.2:3-5)
>
> No one born of God makes a practice of sinning, for God's seed abides in him; and he cannot keep on sinning, because he has been born of God. (1 Jn.3:9)

## III. The Revelation of Jesus, the New Master, 3:22-36

1. The setting for the revelation
   a. Jesus & His disciples were baptizing in Judea
   b. John & his disciples were baptizing close by

   c. John's disciples asked him about what was occurring
      1) Who really purifies the human heart?
      2) Who is our supreme Master, the One we should follow?

2. Answer 1: Jesus alone is God's appointed Messiah
   a. God alone appoints people
   b. God had not appointed John as the Messiah but as the forerunner

²² After this Jesus and his disciples went into the Judean countryside, and he remained there with them and was baptizing. ²³ John also was baptizing at Aenon near Salim, because water was plentiful there, and people were coming and being baptized ²⁴ (for John had not yet been put in prison). ²⁵ Now a discussion arose between some of John's disciples and a Jew over purification.

²⁶ And they came to John and said to him, "Rabbi, he who was with you across the Jordan, to whom you bore witness—look, he is baptizing, and all are going to him." ²⁷ John answered, "A person cannot receive even one thing unless it is given him from heaven. ²⁸ You yourselves bear me witness, that I said, 'I am not the Christ, but I have been sent before him.'

# Division III

*The Revelation of Jesus, the New Master, 3:22-36*

## 3:22-36 Introduction

This next revelation of Jesus was given humbly and eloquently by John the Baptist. In response to his disciples' concern about people flocking to Jesus instead of John, John clearly taught that Jesus Christ is the New Master, the One whom God has set before humanity as the only Master worthy of serving. This is, *The Revelation of Jesus, the New Master,* 3:22-36.

1. The setting for the revelation (vv.22-26).
2. Answer 1: Jesus alone is God's appointed Messiah (vv.27-28).
3. Answer 2: Jesus alone is the Bridegroom (vv.29-30).
4. Answer 3: Jesus alone is *from above*—out of—heaven (v.31).
5. Answer 4: Jesus alone is God's spokesman (Messiah) (vv.32-34).
6. Answer 5: Jesus alone has the Spirit without limit (v.34).
7. Answer 6: Jesus alone determines our destiny (vv.35-36).

²⁹ The one who has the bride is the bridegroom. The friend of the bridegroom, who stands and hears him, rejoices greatly at the bridegroom's voice. Therefore this joy of mine is now complete.

³⁰ He must increase, but I must decrease."

³¹ He who comes from above is above all. He who is of the earth belongs to the earth and speaks in an earthly way. He who comes from heaven is above all.

³² He bears witness to what he has seen and heard, yet no one receives his testimony.

³³ Whoever receives his testimony sets his seal to this, that God is true.

³⁴ For he whom God has sent utters the words of God, for he gives the Spirit without measure.

³⁵ The Father loves the Son and has given all things into his hand.

³⁶ Whoever believes in the Son has eternal life; whoever does not obey the Son shall not see life, but the wrath of God remains on him.

3. **Answer 2: Jesus alone is the Bridegroom**
   a. He is the One by whom the friend stands
   b. He is the voice that is to be heard
   c. He is the cause of joy
   d. He is to be the only object of loyalty
4. **Answer 3: Jesus alone is *from above*—out of heaven**[DS1]
   a. He is not from the earthly world
   b. He is from the spiritual world of heaven & is above all
5. **Answer 4: Jesus alone is God's spokesman (Messiah)**
   a. He testifies to heaven's reality
   b. Most reject His testimony
   c. Some accept & seal, or verify, His testimony[DS2]
   d. Proof: He was sent from God & speaks God's Word[DS3]
6. **Answer 5: Jesus alone has the Spirit without limit**
7. **Answer 6: Jesus alone determines our destiny**
   a. To believe in Him brings eternal life
   b. Not to believe brings God's eternal wrath[DS4, DS5]

## 1 The setting for the revelation.

3:22–26

After His interview with Nicodemus, Jesus moved out into the country districts of Judaea. There, He found a multitude of people who realized their need for cleansing from their sin, leading to an extended period of fruitful ministry.

**a. Jesus and His disciples were baptizing in Judea (v.22).**

Jesus and His disciples *remained* or *spent time* (Gk. dietriben) in the Judean countryside. The Greek word has the idea of staying for a considerable period of time in sharing and ministering. Note the statement: He baptized. This is the only place in Scripture where Jesus is said to baptize, though strictly speaking, it was His disciples who actually did the baptizing (Jn.4:2). It was His baptizing that set the table for what was now to happen.

**b. John and his disciples were baptizing close by (vv.23–24).**

John and his disciples were also baptizing in Aenon, which was near to Salim. Nothing is known about either place beyond what is mentioned here.

²² After this Jesus and his disciples went into the Judean countryside, and he remained there with them and was baptizing.

²³ John also was baptizing at Aenon near Salim, because water was plentiful there, and people were coming and being baptized

²⁴ (for John had not yet been put in prison).

²⁵ Now a discussion arose between some of John's disciples and a Jew over purification.

²⁶ And they came to John and said to him, "Rabbi, he who was with you across the Jordan, to whom you bore witness—look, he is baptizing, and all are going to him."

c. **John's disciples asked him about what was occurring (vv.25–26).**

People began to flock from John to Jesus. This decline in John's popularity gave the religious leaders an opportunity to attack John. They attacked him by questioning his disciples about the purifying value of John's baptism (v.25). They thought he must be a sham, a false prophet. If John's baptisms were really cleansing the people's hearts and giving them a sense of cleanliness, why were the people now flocking to Jesus? If his baptisms were really meeting the people's needs, they would continue to come to him for cleansing. Instead, they were deserting him and flocking to Jesus.

This charge, of course, cut John's disciples to the core, so they asked John why people were now turning to Jesus instead of remaining with him (v.26).

Note how the question of purifying strikes at two of the basic questions of life:

➢ Who really purifies the human heart? Can the human heart really be cleansed? Can people's need for cleansing really be met (v.25)?

➢ Who is our supreme Master, the one we should follow? To whom should we turn for cleansing? To other people, such as religious leaders, or to Jesus Christ (v.26)?

**THOUGHT 1.** We all seek the cleansing of our hearts from someplace. We seek release from sensing wrong and failure; we look for some dissolving of guilt. However, few seek cleansing in Christ. They seem to search for cleansing everywhere except in Christ:
- in religion
- in attending church enough to salve their conscience and give a feeling of acceptance by God
- in giving to charities
- in doing some good deed for others
- in being loyal to some person's teaching or leadership

In addition, we all follow some master and give our allegiance to something, whether a person or thing (see Mt.6:24; Lu.16:13; Ro.6:16).

But the truth is, only Christ can purify our hearts and truly cleanse us from sin. The only solution for sin, the only thing that can cleanse us, is the blood of Jesus Christ. As the beloved hymn so clearly says:

> *What can wash away my sin?*
> *Nothing but the blood of Jesus.*
> *What can make me whole again?*
> *Nothing but the blood of Jesus.*

Because Jesus shed His blood and died for us, thereby purchasing our salvation, He is our supreme Master. True, He is God, and He is our Creator. But we should follow Him and be fully devoted to Him for an even greater reason: because He loved us and died for us.

The answer to the basic questions of life is Jesus Christ, and Him alone.

> **"Pay careful attention to yourselves and to all the flock, in which the Holy Spirit has made you overseers, to care for the church of God, which he obtained with his own blood." (Ac.20:28)**
>
> **You were bought with a price; do not become bondservants of men. (1 Co.7:23)**
>
> **In him we have redemption through his blood, the forgiveness of our trespasses, according to the riches of his grace. (Ep.1:7)**
>
> **Knowing that you were ransomed from the futile ways inherited from your forefathers, not with perishable things such as silver or gold, but with the precious blood of Christ, like that of a lamb without blemish or spot. (1 Pe.1:18-19)**
>
> **"On that day there shall be a fountain opened for the house of David and the inhabitants of Jerusalem, to cleanse them from sin and uncleanness." (Zec.13:1)**

## 2 Answer 1: Jesus alone is God's appointed Messiah.

John answered the questions by pointing clearly to Jesus Christ. He offered five answers—five reasons—why people should turn to Jesus instead of him for cleansing. First, Jesus alone was God's appointed Messiah. He alone was God's anointed One.

a. **God alone appoints people (v.27).**
We do not have the right nor the power to appoint ourselves to some place of service or leadership in God's kingdom. God and God alone decides where and how we will serve Him.
- ➤ He is God, so He has the right to appoint people.
- ➤ He calls people to be His servants.
- ➤ He appoints individuals to a particular service and equips them with gifts.

> ²⁷ John answered, "A person cannot receive even one thing unless it is given him from heaven.
> ²⁸ "You yourselves bear me witness, that I said, 'I am not the Christ, but I have been sent before him.'"

John taught us a critical truth that we should always keep before us: no person can receive a *true* appointment, a *true* service, or a *true* gift unless it is given from heaven, that is, from God Himself. All appointments and gifts that have not come from heaven *are false*.

> "To one he gave five talents, to another two, to another one, to each according to his ability. Then he went away." (Mt.25:15)
>
> Having gifts that differ according to the grace given to us, let us use them: if prophecy, in proportion to our faith. (Ro.12:6)
>
> For who sees anything different in you? What do you have that you did not receive? If then you received it, why do you boast as if you did not receive it? (1 Co.4:7)
>
> Now there are varieties of gifts, but the same Spirit. (1 Co.12:4)
>
> Every good gift and every perfect gift is from above, coming down from the Father of lights, with whom there is no variation or shadow due to change. (Js.1:17)

b. **God had not appointed John as the Messiah but as the forerunner (v.28).**
John's humility shone through his response to his disciples' question. He gave strong witness about Christ's being the Messiah. He was unquestionably clear about this. *He* was not the Messiah; Jesus Christ was. John clearly understood who he himself was and what his specific appointment and ministry were. He was the forerunner, the one whose calling was to point people to the Messiah, not to himself. His task was not to build a following for himself, but to direct people to follow Christ.

**THOUGHT 1.** Jesus Christ is the Messiah; He *alone* is the One appointed from heaven. This is the strong declaration of John.

> He said to them, "But who do you say that I am?" Simon Peter replied, "You are the Christ, the Son of the living God." And Jesus answered him, "Blessed are you, Simon Bar-Jonah! For flesh and blood has not revealed this to you, but my Father who is in heaven." (Mt.16:15-17)
>
> But Jesus remained silent. And the high priest said to him, "I adjure you by the living God, tell us if you are the Christ, the Son of God." Jesus said to him, "You have said so. But I tell you, from now on you will see the Son of Man seated at the right hand of Power and coming on the clouds of heaven." (Mt.26:63-64)
>
> And he said to them, "O foolish ones, and slow of heart to believe all that the prophets have spoken! Was it not necessary that the Christ should suffer these things and enter into his glory?" (Lu.24:25-26)
>
> The woman said to him, "I know that Messiah is coming (he who is called Christ). When he comes, he will tell us all things." Jesus said to her, "I who speak to you am he." (Jn.4:25-26)
>
> So Jesus said to them, "When you have lifted up the Son of Man, then you will know that I am he, and that I do nothing on my own authority, but speak just as the Father taught me. And he who sent me is with me. He has not left me alone, for I always do the things that are pleasing to him." (Jn.8:28-29)

**THOUGHT 2.** The true servants of God are appointed to their service and ministry by God. As God's appointed servants . . .
- we serve God and God alone.
- we can trust God to take care of us and our ministry.
- we should be humble. We should not envy others, for every servant's ministry is special to God and necessary to His plan of salvation. And we should be satisfied in our service and ministry, for we are there by God's appointment.

> "You did not choose me, but I chose you and appointed you that you should go and bear fruit and that your fruit should abide, so that whatever you ask the Father in my name, he may give it to you." (Jn.15:16)

> "Serving the Lord with all humility and with tears and with trials that happened to me through the plots of the Jews." (Ac.20:19)

> I appeal to you therefore, brothers, by the mercies of God, to present your bodies as a living sacrifice, holy and acceptable to God, which is your spiritual worship. (Ro.12:1)

> And he gave the apostles, the prophets, the evangelists, the shepherds and teachers, to equip the saints for the work of ministry, for building up the body of Christ. (Ep.4:11-12)

## 3:29-30

²⁹ "The one who has the bride is the bridegroom. The friend of the bridegroom, who stands and hears him, rejoices greatly at the bridegroom's voice. Therefore this joy of mine is now complete.
³⁰ "He must increase, but I must decrease."

## 3 Answer 2: Jesus alone is the Bridegroom.

John illustrated his role in comparison to Christ's with the picture of the bridegroom and the friend of the bridegroom. The *friend* of the bridegroom was his attendant or assistant. In some cultures today, this person is referred to as the best man. John declared that Jesus was the Bridegroom. The bridegroom is the One who has the bride (the church, the followers of Christ). Therefore, it was only right that people should come to Jesus instead of John. The friend is important, but he is not the bridegroom. John said four things about Jesus as the Bridegroom.

a. **He is the One by whom the friend stands (v.29a).**
It is true that the friend (God's servant) is important, for he takes care of matters for the bridegroom, and he has the privilege of bringing the bride to the bridegroom. But there is only one Bridegroom, and He is the focus of the friend's attention.

b. **He is the voice that is to be heard (v.29b).**
Christ's voice is the important voice. His will is the will to be done: serving Him and doing what He says are important.

c. **He is the cause of joy (v.29c).**
It is not the friend who brings joy to the bride or to the guests and community; it is the Bridegroom. Everyone's joy is found in seeing the Bridegroom's will done and in seeing Him pleased.

d. **He is to be the only object of loyalty (v.30).**
The Bridegroom (Christ) is the only object of loyalty. The words "He" and "I" are an *emphatic contrast* (v.30). That is to say, there is a *compulsion* to lift up the Person and the honor of the Bridegroom. In no sense nor in any place does the friend try to draw attention, praise, or honor toward himself.
  ➢ The servant draws back and shrinks from attention, decreasing himself in the eyes of all. He does nothing for himself but does *all for the Bridegroom,* for His honor and increase.
  ➢ The servant focuses attention upon the Bridegroom: pushes Him out front, increases His presence and stature before everyone.

As the friend and not the Bridegroom, John's ministry was for a specific purpose and for a limited time. That purpose was to prepare the world for the coming of Jesus and to identify

Jesus as the Messiah, the Lamb of God, when He arrived. Once Jesus arrived, John's ministry would die. Accordingly, John said that Jesus must *increase,* and he must *decrease.*

**THOUGHT 1.** We must never use our ministry to build a name or following for ourselves. We must never seek to become famous, popular, revered, or wealthy through our ministry. We must never seek the praise or devotion of others. To the contrary, our role is to build a following for Jesus, to make His name famous, to compel others to praise and give their full devotion to Him.

Tragically, many so-called ministers today use the gospel and the ministry to increase themselves. But the true servant of God makes John's humble and noble words his or her creed: *He must increase, but I must decrease.*

> **"That all may honor the Son, just as they honor the Father. Whoever does not honor the Son does not honor the Father who sent him." (Jn.5:23)**
>
> **For to this end Christ died and lived again, that he might be Lord both of the dead and of the living. (Ro.14:9)**
>
> **Have this mind among yourselves, which is yours in Christ Jesus, who, though he was in the form of God, did not count equality with God a thing to be grasped, but emptied himself, by taking the form of a servant, being born in the likeness of men. And being found in human form, he humbled himself by becoming obedient to the point of death, even death on a cross. Therefore God has highly exalted him and bestowed on him the name that is above every name. (Ph.2:5-9)**
>
> **And he is the head of the body, the church. He is the beginning, the firstborn from the dead, that in everything he might be preeminent. (Col.1:18)**
>
> **Ascribe to the LORD the glory due his name; worship the LORD in the splendor of holiness. (Ps.29:2)**
>
> **Let them extol him in the congregation of the people, and praise him in the assembly of the elders. (Ps.107:32)**

## 4 Answer 3: Jesus alone is from above—out of—heaven.

Third, Jesus alone was from above, that is, from heaven. The meaning of "from above" is significant (see DEEPER STUDY # 1). The phrase "above all" is mentioned twice; it is very important. It means superior and preeminent. Jesus, who came from heaven (out of the dimension of heaven), is the superior and preeminent One. He is above all.

> [31] He who comes from above is above all. He who is of the earth belongs to the earth and speaks in an earthly way. He who comes from heaven is above all.

### a. He is not from the earthly world.

Christ's origin was "from above." He is not from the earthly world. He was not of the earth, not earthly, as we are. We are born of the flesh, that is, we are born of a man and woman who both are of this world. Therefore, we are of the earth and are earthly. But not Jesus.

### b. He is from the spiritual world of heaven and is above all.

Jesus was "from heaven"—*out of* God Himself. His Father is God. He is from the spiritual world. Therefore, He *is above* all—superior and preeminent (see DEEPER STUDY # 1, pt.4—Jn.1:14).

A person of this world can only speak of the earth and of earthly things. He comes *only* out of the earth; therefore, he can know *only* earthly things. When he speaks of heavenly things, he only shares his *ideas* and *speculations*, for he has never been to heaven. Therefore, the only conceivable way for us to know anything about heaven was for Someone from heaven to come and tell us. John left no room for misunderstanding: Jesus—not John—was this Someone (see notes—Jn.1:18; 3:13; DEEPER STUDY # 1, 2, 3—14:6).

## DEEPER STUDY # 1

**(3:31) "From Above"—Jesus Christ:** Jesus came *out of* (Gk. ek) the spiritual world into the physical world, out of the heavenly dimension of being into the earthly dimension of being. Jesus came out of . . .
- the incorruptible world into the corruptible world
- the glorious world into the dishonorable world
- the powerful world into the weak world
- the spiritual world into the natural world (see 1 Co.15:42-44.)

"No one has ascended into heaven except he who descended from heaven, the Son of Man." (Jn.3:13)

"For the bread of God is he who comes down from heaven and gives life to the world. . . . For I have come down from heaven, not to do my own will but the will of him who sent me." (Jn.6:33, 38)

So the Jews grumbled about him, because he said, "I am the bread that came down from heaven." They said, "Is not this Jesus, the son of Joseph, whose father and mother we know? How does he now say, 'I have come down from heaven'?" (Jn.6:41-42)

"This is the bread that comes down from heaven, so that one may eat of it and not die. I am the living bread that came down from heaven. If anyone eats of this bread, he will live forever. And the bread that I will give for the life of the world is my flesh." (Jn.6:50-51)

"This is the bread that came down from heaven, not like the bread the fathers ate, and died. Whoever feeds on this bread will live forever." (Jn.6:58)

"Then what if you were to see the Son of Man ascending to where he was before?" (Jn.6:62)

He said to them, "You are from below; I am from above. You are of this world; I am not of this world." (Jn.8:23)

Jesus said to them, "If God were your Father, you would love me, for I came from God and I am here. I came not of my own accord, but he sent me." (Jn.8:42)

Jesus, knowing that the Father had given all things into his hands, and that he had come from God and was going back to God. (Jn.13:3)

"Now we know that you know all things and do not need anyone to question you; this is why we believe that you came from God." (Jn.16:30)

"And now, Father, glorify me in your own presence with the glory that I had with you before the world existed." (Jn.17:5)

The first man was from the earth, a man of dust; the second man is from heaven. (1 Co.15:47)

---

**3:32-34**

³² He bears witness to what he has seen and heard, yet no one receives his testimony.
³³ Whoever receives his testimony sets his seal to this, that God is true.
³⁴ For he whom God has sent utters the words of God, for he gives the Spirit without measure.

## 5 Answer 4: Jesus alone is God's spokesman (Messiah).

Fourth, Jesus alone was God's Spokesman. Jesus was "from above," *out of the dimension of heaven*; therefore, He had seen and heard the truth of heaven.

### a. He testifies to heaven's reality (v.32a).

Jesus testified, revealed, and proclaimed what He had seen and heard in heaven. He was the Spokesman of God who revealed heaven and the truth of it (see DEEPER STUDY # 3—Mt.19:23-24). He is the only One who could share heaven with the human race.

### b. Most reject His testimony (v.32b).

Note the words *no one*. This simply means the vast majority of people (see v.33 where some few do receive His words). So many people reject the Lord's words that it can be said that "mankind as a whole has rejected His message."[1]

---

1 Walvoord and Zuck, eds., *The Bible Knowledge Commentary* (Wheaton, IL, Victor Books), Digital edition via Wordsearch Bible Software.

c. **Some accept and seal, or verify, His testimony (v.33).**

Some do, however, receive or accept the Lord's testimony. Those who do will verify without reservation that what Jesus has said is true. *Sets his seal* or *has certified* speaks of the way a person legally verified a document, contract, or statement in Jesus' day (see DEEPER STUDY # 2). If they did so falsely, they were guilty of perjury and faced serious punishment. Those who have received the truth of Jesus Christ will stand by it, regardless of the cost.

d. **Proof: He was sent from God and speaks God's Word (v.34).**

The proof that Jesus was God's spokesman is clearly stated without any room for questions. Jesus was the One sent from God. He was the *Apostle of God*.

> "For I have come down from heaven, not to do my own will but the will of him who sent me." (Jn.6:38)

> "I know him, for I come from him, and he sent me." (Jn.7:29)

> Jesus said to them, "If God were your Father, you would love me, for I came from God and I am here. I came not of my own accord, but he sent me." (Jn.8:42)

> "That they may all be one, just as you, Father, are in me, and I in you, that they also may be in us, so that the world may believe that you have sent me." (Jn.17:21)

As the One sent from God, Jesus is the spokesman of God. He spoke the Words of God. Whatever He said was the Word of God. How can we be sure? Because God sent Him and gave His Spirit *without measure* to Him (see DEEPER STUDY # 3).

> And they were astonished at his teaching, for his word possessed authority. (Lu.4:32)

> "It is the Spirit who gives life; the flesh is no help at all. The words that I have spoken to you are spirit and life." (Jn.6:63)

> Simon Peter answered him, "Lord, to whom shall we go? You have the words of eternal life." (Jn.6:68)

> The officers answered, "No one ever spoke like this man!" (Jn.7:46)

> "Whoever does not love me does not keep my words. And the word that you hear is not mine but the Father's who sent me." (Jn.14:24)

> "For I have given them the words that you gave me, and they have received them and have come to know in truth that I came from you; and they have believed that you sent me." (Jn.17:8)

## DEEPER STUDY # 2

(3:33) **Seal**: a man's seal was affixed to a document to show he agreed with it. He reckoned it as legal, binding, valid, authentic. A seal guaranteed that the record was true and genuine. When someone receives the testimony of Jesus, they show that God is true. Conversely, the only way a person can show that God is true is to accept the testimony of Jesus (see Jn.6:27).

## DEEPER STUDY # 3

(3:34) **"God has Sent"—Jesus Christ, Origin**: Jesus is the Apostle of God. He is God's Ambassador, God's perfect Spokesman. It should be noted that God poured out His Spirit *without measure* upon Jesus—the only apostle upon whom this was ever done. See Jn.4:34; 5:23-24, 30, 36-37; 6:38-40, 44, 57; 7:16, 18; 8:16, 42; 9:4; 10:36; 11:42; 12:44-45, 49; 14:24; 15:21; 16:5; 17:3, 18, 21, 23, 25; 20:21.)

## 6 Jesus alone has the Spirit without limit.

Fifth, Jesus alone had the full measure of the Spirit. There was no limit to the Spirit's . . .

- presence
- call
- equipping
- blessings
- fullness
- appointment
- work

**3:34**

³⁴ For he whom God has sent utters the words of God, for he gives the Spirit without measure.

The Spirit was of the same being with Jesus, in perfect harmony, communion, and fellowship with Jesus. He was given to Jesus in a way far different than He was given to other people. There was no measure of His presence with Jesus because Jesus had the perfect and full measure of the Spirit. The purpose for the full measure was clearly stated by Jesus:

> "The Spirit of the Lord is upon me, because he has anointed me to proclaim good news to the poor. He has sent me to proclaim liberty to the captives and recovering of sight to the blind, to set at liberty those who are oppressed, to proclaim the year of the Lord's favor." (Lu.4:18-19)

> "How God anointed Jesus of Nazareth with the Holy Spirit and with power. He went about doing good and healing all who were oppressed by the devil, for God was with him." (Ac.10:38)

**3:35-36**

³⁵ The Father loves the Son and has given all things into his hand.
³⁶ Whoever believes in the Son has eternal life; whoever does not obey the Son shall not see life, but the wrath of God remains on him.

## 7 Answer 6: Jesus alone determines our destiny.

There has never been a more tender statement than, "the Father loves the Son" (v.35). God loves His Son beyond anything that could ever be understood. Why does God love His Son so much?

First, because Jesus is God's only Son, the Son in His very own bosom (see note—Jn.1:18).

Second, because Jesus is God's only begotten Son, the Son who willingly partook of flesh and came into the world to save mankind, thereby fulfilling the will of God perfectly (see notes—Jn.1:14).

Third, because Jesus gave Himself as an offering and a sacrifice to God Himself (see note—Ep.5:2).

Fourth, because Jesus willingly learned perfect obedience by the things which He suffered (see notes—Jn.13:31-32; He.5:5-10).

How much does God love Jesus? So much that He has given all things into the hands of His Son: all power, all authority, all rule, all reign, all supremacy, all dominion, all honor, all glory, all praise, all worship, all service. As clearly and as simply as can be said, all things have been given to God's only Son.

> [Jesus Christ] who has gone into heaven and is at the right hand of God, with angels, authorities, and powers having been subjected to him. (1 Pe.3:22)

Nothing exists that has not been given to Him. This includes our eternal destiny. Jesus alone determines our destiny, according to whether or not we believe in Him.

a. **To believe Him brings eternal life (v.36a).**

The person who believes in the Son has everlasting life (v.36a; see Deeper Study # 2—Jn.1:4; Deeper Study # 1—10:10; Deeper Study # 1—17:2-3). God will receive and honor anyone who receives and honors His Son whom He loves so much. It does not matter who the person is or what the person has done. If the person believes in God's only Son, God gives that individual everlasting life.

b. **Not to believe brings God's eternal wrath (v.36b; see Deeper Study # 4).**

The person who does not believe the Son will not see eternal life. All who refuse to believe perish eternally (see Deeper Study # 2—Jn.3:16) because the wrath of God remains or abides on them (see Deeper Study # 5).

## Deeper Study # 4

(3:36) **Does Not Obey, Does Not Believe (NKJV)** (ho apeithon): literally, "the one disobeying." If a person does not obey, he does not really believe. Conversely, if a person really believes, he obeys (see note and Deeper Study # 2—Jn.2:24; Deeper Study # 1—He.5:9).

## Deeper Study # 5

(3:36) **Wrath** (orge): anger, temper, indignation. It is not an uncontrolled, unthinking, violent reaction. It is deep, permanent, settled, thoughtful, controlled anger and temper.

There is another Greek word which is also translated *wrath* (thumos), and it is also used to describe God's wrath. *Thumos* is anger that arises more quickly, blazes forth, and just as quickly cools down. It is an anger that is more turbulent, more sudden, but the agitation lasts for only a short period of time. This simply means that God does not dodge His responsibility to execute justice and to punish injustice and sin (see Ro.1:22). His wrath is His . . .

- anger against sin
- reaction against unrighteousness
- opposition to the injustices of humanity
- punishment of evil and wicked people

The wrath or anger of God is kindled for four reasons

1. People do not believe on the Son of God. They allow their hearts to become hardened and impenitent (Ro.2:5). They spurn and wound God's love—rejecting, abusing, cursing and denying His Son, the dearest thing to His heart (Jn.3:36; 2 Th.1:7-9; see notes—Jn.3:18-20; 3:35-36).

2. People reject God's mercy, which is ever attempting to reach out and save them (Ro.2:3-6).

3. People transgress God's law (Ro.1:18f; Col.3:6).

4. People sin and come short of God's will, violating His holiness (Ep.5:6).

God's wrath is real and active. God is holy, righteous, and pure as well as loving, gracious, and merciful. He executes justice as well as love. He shows wrath and anger as well as compassion. His wrath is both present and future.

1. God's wrath is present and active in this life. His wrath abides upon people now. His wrath is manifested against all ungodliness and unrighteousness of men (Ro.1:18). God punishes sin in this life by giving people up . . .

- to uncleanness
- to vile affections
- to reprobate minds

2. God's wrath is future and it is to be actively executed in the next life (see Deeper Study # 2—Mt.5:22; Deeper Study # 4—Lu.16:24; Deeper Study # 1—He.9:27). God will punish sin by giving the unrighteous up . . .

- to everlasting fire (Mt.25:41; 25:46)
- to hell (Mt.5:22)
- to outer darkness (Mt.8:12)
- to weeping and gnashing of teeth (Mt.8:12)
- to the Lake of Fire (Re.20:15)

3. God's wrath will be especially manifested and active in the last days (see Re.6:16; 11:8; 14:10; 16:19; 19:15).

# Chapter 4

## IV. The Revelation of Jesus, the Living Water, 4:1–42

### A. The Offer of Living Water, 4:1–14

1. **Fact 1: Jesus left Judea** to share the good news of living water with others
   a. He left for John's sake, to keep from diminishing John's ministry
   b. He left for the sake of His mission: "He had to go"
   c. He left to confront a Samaritan woman
      1) He entered Sychar, Samaria[DS1,2]
      2) He was weary, sat by a well
      3) He requested drink from the Samaritan woman
      4) The disciples had gone for food
      5) The woman questioned Jesus
         • She was shocked that Jesus talked with her
         • She questioned Jesus because of racial prejudice
2. **Fact 2: There is both natural water & living water**
   a. Living water is "of God"
   b. Living water is "the gift" of God
   c. Living water is given by asking for it
3. **Fact 3: Living water is from One much greater than a religious leader or founder**

4. **Fact 4: Living water is the only water that will quench thirst fully & eternally**

Now when Jesus learned that the Pharisees had heard that Jesus was making and baptizing more disciples than John

² (although Jesus himself did not baptize, but only his disciples),

³ he left Judea and departed again for Galilee.

⁴ And he had to pass through Samaria.

⁵ So he came to a town of Samaria called Sychar, near the field that Jacob had given to his son Joseph.

⁶ Jacob's well was there; so Jesus, wearied as he was from his journey, was sitting beside the well. It was about the sixth hour.

⁷ A woman from Samaria came to draw water. Jesus said to her, "Give me a drink."

⁸ (For his disciples had gone away into the city to buy food.)

⁹ The Samaritan woman said to him, "How is it that you, a Jew, ask for a drink from me, a woman of Samaria?" (For Jews have no dealings with Samaritans.)

¹⁰ Jesus answered her, "If you knew the gift of God, and who it is that is saying to you, 'Give me a drink,' you would have asked him, and he would have given you living water."

¹¹ The woman said to him, "Sir, you have nothing to draw water with, and the well is deep. Where do you get that living water?

¹² Are you greater than our father Jacob? He gave us the well and drank from it himself, as did his sons and his livestock."

¹³ Jesus said to her, "Everyone who drinks of this water will be thirsty again,

¹⁴ but whoever drinks of the water that I will give him will never be thirsty again. The water that I will give him will become in him a spring of water welling up to eternal life."

# Division IV

*The Revelation of Jesus, the Living Water, 4:1-42*

A. The Offer of Living Water, 4:1-14

## 4:1-42
## DIVISION OVERVIEW: Salvation

Jesus offered the Samaritan woman living water, and she showed an intriguing interest. However, there were some matters with which she needed to be confronted before she could ever have the living water. There was the matter of sin in her life, of worship, of the Messiah, and of laboring for God. Therefore, Jesus began to discuss these subjects with her one by one.

## 4:1-14
## Introduction

Jesus' encounter with the woman at the well is one of the most heart-stirring stories from His earthly ministry. It reveals one of the most profound truths about Jesus: He is the Living Water, the only satisfaction for our spiritual thirst. The Savior made the woman—and every human being—a glorious promise: if we will drink this water, the living water of Christ supplied endlessly through His Holy Spirit, we will never thirst again. This is, *The Offer of Living Water*, 4:1-14.

1. Fact 1: Jesus left Judea to share the good news of living water with others (vv.1-9).
2. Fact 2: There is both natural water and living water (v.10).
3. Fact 3: Living water is from One much greater than a religious leader or founder (vv.11-12).
4. Fact 4: Living water is the only water that will quench thirst fully and eternally (vv.13-14).

## 1 Fact 1: Jesus left Judea to share the good news of living water with others.

4:1-9

Jesus lived every day of His life with purpose, and He took every step of every day to fulfill that purpose. When Jesus left Judaea, he departed for Galilee for a purpose. The primary purpose: to share the good news of living water with others, especially the woman at the well.

**a. He left for John's sake, to keep from diminishing John's ministry (vv.1-3).**

Jesus left Judea for another reason: He left for John's sake. The crowds were leaving John and coming to Jesus, and the religious leaders were using the fact to degrade John's ministry (see note—Jn.3:22-26). Jesus did not want to create a competitive scene that would damage John's ministry, so He left the area to return to Galilee.

**b. He left for the sake of His mission: "He had to" go (v.4).**

Scripture says that Jesus *had to* or *needed to* pass through Samaria. The words *had to* in verse 4 state it was a necessity, that He went out of compulsion, or according to destiny. Jesus was compelled to go through Samaria for the sake of His mission. Samaria needed the gospel as much as other areas. (The Greek word, edei, translated as *had to* or *needed to* or *must* is so often used in connection with Jesus' mission that it makes an excellent word study; see Jn.3:14; 9:4; 10:16; 12:34; 20:9.)

Now when Jesus learned that the Pharisees had heard that Jesus was making and baptizing more disciples than John

² (although Jesus himself did not baptize, but only his disciples),

³ he left Judea and departed again for Galilee.

⁴ And he had to pass through Samaria.

⁵ So he came to a town of Samaria called Sychar, near the field that Jacob had given to his son Joseph.

⁶ Jacob's well was there; so Jesus, wearied as he was from his journey, was sitting beside the well. It was about the sixth hour.

⁷ A woman from Samaria came to draw water. Jesus said to her, "Give me a drink."

⁸ (For his disciples had gone away into the city to buy food.)

⁹ The Samaritan woman said to him, "How is it that you, a Jew, ask for a drink from me, a woman of Samaria?" (For Jews have no dealings with Samaritans.)

**c. He left to confront a Samaritan woman (vv.5–9).**

Jesus left Judea to confront a Samaritan woman. He entered Sychar, a city of Samaria (v.5; see Deeper Study # 2). He then sat on the wall of a well, for He was both tired and thirsty from His journey (v.6). While sitting there, one of the events for which He had come into Samaria happened: He confronted a woman with the claims of the Messiah.

The woman came to draw water, and Jesus initiated a conversation by asking her for a drink of water (v.7). She was shocked, for the Jews had no dealings with the Samaritans (see Deeper Study # 1). She asked Jesus why He would ask her, a Samaritan, for a drink. It was this question, this subject of water, that Jesus used...

- to discuss one of the greatest truths of spiritual life, that of living water
- to present the claims of God upon a person's life

## Deeper Study # 1

(4:5) **Samaria—Samaritans**: Samaria was in the central part of Palestine. Palestine was a small area, stretching only 120 miles north to south. The region was divided into three sections:
- ➤ Judaea, the southern section.
- ➤ Galilee, the northern section.
- ➤ Samaria, the central section, lying between the two.

There was bitter hatred between the Jews and Samaritans. Two things in particular caused this hatred.

1. The Samaritans were biracial, half-Jews, *by birth*. Centuries before (about 720 B.C.), the King of Assyria had captured the ten tribes of Israel and deported a large number of the people, scattering them all throughout the Medio-Persian empire (see 2 Ki.17:6–41). He then took people from all over the Assyrian empire and transplanted them into Samaria to repopulate the land. The result was only natural. Intermarriage took place, and the people became a mixed race, including...
   - the transplanted people
   - the weak of the land who had been left behind
   - the outcast and irreligious who had intermarried with the original Samaritans

   The fact of a mixed race, infuriated the strict Jews who held to a pure race.

2. The Samaritans were biracial or half-Jews, *by religion*. The transplanted heathen, of course, brought their gods with them. Eventually the God of Israel won out, but the Samaritan religion never became pure Judaism. Three things happened to cause this.
   a. When Ezra led the Jews back from exile in Babylon, the first thing the Jews did was to start rebuilding their temple. The Samaritans offered to help them, but the Jews rejected their help, declaring that the Samaritans—through intermarriage and worship of false gods—had lost their purity and forfeited their right to worship the only true God. This severe denunciation embittered the Samaritans against the Jews in and around Jerusalem.
   b. The Samaritans built a rival temple on Mount Gerizim to stand in competition with the Jewish temple at Jerusalem.
   c. The Samaritans twisted both the Scripture and history to favor their own people and nation.
      - ➤ They twisted Scripture in that they accepted only five books of the Bible, the Pentateuch. (Just imagine! They missed all the richness and depth of the *Psalms* and prophets.)
      - ➤ They twisted history in that they claimed three great events took place on Mt. Gerizim that set it apart as a place of worship. They claimed it was the place where Abraham offered Isaac, where Melchizedek met Abraham, and where Moses built his first altar after leading Israel out from Egyptian bondage.

## Deeper Study # 2

(4:5) **Sychar**: little is known about the city; however, three significant biblical events happened there.
- ➢ Jacob bought a piece of land in the area (Ge.33:19).
- ➢ Jacob, as he was dying, willed the land to Joseph (Ge.48:22).
- ➢ Joseph's bones were buried there (Jos.24:32).

## 2 Fact 2: There is both natural water and living water.

4:10

Living water is truly alive. Living water was water that was always flowing and moving along, such as a creek fed by springs or a lake with both an inflow and an outflow. Dead water was stagnant water such as ponds or pools that were always sitting still with no inflow or outflow. However, when Jesus spoke of "living water," He meant much more than living streams and lakes.

> [10] Jesus answered her, "If you knew the gift of God, and who it is that is saying to you, 'Give me a drink,' you would have asked him, and he would have given you living water."

### a. Living water is "of God."

Living water comes from Him who is living, who always has and always will be living. The water that God gives is the most *alive* water there is. No other water, no matter how alive it may be considered, can compare with the living water that is of God.

> **For with you is the fountain of life; in your light do we see light. (Ps.36:9)**

### b. Living water is "the gift" of God.

*Gift* means it is freely given, is *not earned* and is *not deserved*. Nothing we can do—no good works or noble deeds—can qualify us to receive this indescribable gift. It is given entirely of grace.

> **For by grace you have been saved through faith. And this is not your own doing; it is the gift of God, not a result of works, so that no one may boast. (Ep.2:8-9)**

> **"Come, everyone who thirsts, come to the waters; and he who has no money, come, buy and eat! Come, buy wine and milk without money and without price." (Is.55:1)**

### c. Living water is given by asking for it.

Note what Jesus said: "If you knew . . . you would have asked." The woman had never received living water because she *had never known* about it and *had never asked* for it. It was now available simply by asking for it.

## 3 Fact 3: Living water is from One much greater than a religious leader or founder.

4:11-12

Living water is from a Person much greater than any religious leader. The woman saw clearly that Jesus was making an unusual claim. She did not yet understand what the claim was, but she knew He was alluding to something. She noticed He had no leather pouch with which to draw water, so she asked two significant questions:

> [11] The woman said to him, "Sir, you have nothing to draw water with, and the well is deep. Where do you get that living water?
> [12] Are you greater than our father Jacob? He gave us the well and drank from it himself, as did his sons and his livestock."

First, from where did He get this living water?

Second, was He *greater* than Jacob who was one of the great religious patriarchs of the Samaritans? Jacob had to dig this well centuries earlier in order to secure water for his family. Was Jesus greater, able to do more than Jacob did?

The point is, the woman recognized something most people do not. Jesus was claiming to be greater than one of the greatest religious fathers, Jacob himself. He was claiming to have access to a much better water for quenching the thirst of all people.

**THOUGHT 1.** Throughout Scripture Jesus claimed to be . . .
- greater than the temple (Mt.12:6)
- greater than Jonah (Mt.12:41)
- greater than Solomon (Mt.12:42; Lu.11:31)
- greater than Abraham, "before Abraham" (Jn.8:53, 58)
- greater than Jacob (Jn.4:11–12)
- worthy of more glory than Moses (Jn.5:45–47; He.3:3)

**He who comes from above is above all. He who is of the earth belongs to the earth and speaks in an earthly way. He who comes from heaven is above all. (Jn.3:31)**

**And he is the head of the body, the church. He is the beginning, the firstborn from the dead, that in everything he might be preeminent. (Col.1:18)**

**For Jesus has been counted worthy of more glory than Moses—as much more glory as the builder of a house has more honor than the house itself. (He.3:3)**

4:13–14

¹³ Jesus said to her, "Everyone who drinks of this water will be thirsty again,
¹⁴ but whoever drinks of the water that I will give him will never be thirsty again. The water that I will give him will become in him a spring of water welling up to eternal life."

## 4 Fact 4: Living water is the only water that will quench thirst fully and eternally.

Every human being has two types of thirst: a physical thirst and a spiritual thirst. The living water that Christ gives is the only water that will quench our spiritual thirst.

**As a deer pants for flowing streams, so pants my soul for you, O God. (Ps.42:1)**

**"On that day there shall be a fountain opened. . . . to cleanse them from sin and uncleanness." (Zec.13:1)**

We all know immediately how to quench our physical thirst, but our spiritual thirst is a different matter. Within our hearts each of us senses a thirst for . . .
- purpose
- meaning
- significance
- satisfaction
- fulfillment
- something that is missing
- something to fill the void, the emptiness and the loneliness
- deliverance from a sense of being lost
- freedom from undue anxiety, stress, and pressure

Most people have a problem, however. They usually misunderstand the concept of spiritual thirst and try to quench it with the stagnant waters of the flesh and of this world. The result is spiritual poisoning and death. The stagnant waters of the flesh are the things of this world that satisfy the cravings of our human nature, such things as lust, immorality, drunkenness, indulgence, and pride. Or they may be the love of money, cars, houses, lands, clothes, extravagant living, position, and power (1 Jn.2:16). The stagnant waters of the flesh and the world never quench our thirst. They are like salt water; they only make us crave for more and more (see DEEPER STUDY # 1—Js.4:1–3).

**"For my people have committed two evils: they have forsaken me, the fountain of living waters, and hewed out cisterns for themselves, broken cisterns that can hold no water." (Je.2:13)**

In contrast, living water satisfies our spiritual longing, like cool, bubbling spring water satisfies our physical thirst on a scorching summer day. Grasp what Jesus taught us about living water.

First, living water does not come from anything this world offers; it comes from Christ. He and He alone is its source.

> On the last day of the feast, the great day, Jesus stood up and cried out, "If anyone thirsts, let him come to me and drink." (Jn.7:37)

> And he said to me, "It is done! I am the Alpha and the Omega, the beginning and the end. To the thirsty I will give from the spring of the water of life without payment." (Re.21:6)

Second, living water keeps us from ever thirsting again. Our inner thirst is gone forever. It is quenched and fully satisfied.

> "And the LORD will guide you continually and satisfy your desire in scorched places and make your bones strong; and you shall be like a watered garden, like a spring of water, whose waters do not fail." (Is.58:11)

> "On that day there shall be a fountain opened. . . . to cleanse them from sin and uncleanness." (Zec.13:1)

Third, living water is a spring, fountain, or well placed *in* us. The well is not placed outside of us, not placed anywhere in the world, not in our homes, professions, or businesses. It is placed *in* us.

> "Whoever believes in me, as the Scripture has said, 'Out of his heart will flow rivers of living water.'" Now this he said about the Spirit, whom those who believed in him were to receive, for as yet the Spirit had not been given, because Jesus was not yet glorified. (Jn.7:38-39)

Fourth, living water springs up and continues to spring up and bubble, flowing on and on. It is ever in motion.

> With joy you will draw water from the wells of salvation. (Is.12:3)

Finally, living water springs up into eternal life. It will never end.

> "For the Lamb in the midst of the throne will be their shepherd, and he will guide them to springs of living water, and God will wipe away every tear from their eyes." (Re.7:17. See Eze.47:1-12, the river of life.)

> The Spirit and the Bride say, "Come." And let the one who hears say, "Come." And let the one who is thirsty come; let the one who desires take the water of life without price. (Re.22:17)

**THOUGHT 1.** Jesus interprets what He says in Jn.7:37-39. All five of the above facts are seen fulfilled in the Holy Spirit. When we genuinely repent and believe in Christ unto salvation, the Holy Spirit begins to live within us. It is the indwelling Spirit—God's presence with us—who is the spring of living water.

> On the last day of the feast, the great day, Jesus stood up and cried out, "If anyone thirsts, let him come to me and drink. Whoever believes in me, as the Scripture has said, 'Out of his heart will flow rivers of living water.'" Now this he said about the Spirit, whom those who believed in him were to receive, for as yet the Spirit had not been given, because Jesus was not yet glorified. (Jn.7:37-39)

> "And I will ask the Father, and he will give you another Helper, to be with you forever." (Jn.14:16)

> "But you will receive power when the Holy Spirit has come upon you, and you will be my witnesses in Jerusalem and in all Judea and Samaria, and to the end of the earth." (Ac.1:8)

> So that in Christ Jesus the blessing of Abraham might come to the Gentiles, so that we might receive the promised Spirit through faith. (Gal.3:14)

B. The Subject of Sin, 4:15-18

1. The request for living water
2. The first essential: Facing the truth, the fact of sin
   a. Jesus stirred conviction within the woman
   b. Jesus accepted no evasion from the woman
   c. Jesus knew all about her
   d. Jesus reproved the woman's sin

¹⁵ The woman said to him, "Sir, give me this water, so that I will not be thirsty or have to come here to draw water."
¹⁶ Jesus said to her, "Go, call your husband, and come here."
¹⁷ The woman answered him, "I have no husband." Jesus said to her, "You are right in saying, 'I have no husband';
¹⁸ for you have had five husbands, and the one you now have is not your husband. What you have said is true."

# Division IV

## The Revelation of Jesus, the Living Water, 4:1-42

B. The Subject of Sin, 4:15-18

## 4:15-18
## Introduction

Jesus promised the woman at the well the living water of spiritual rebirth. However, something had to be addressed before spiritual rebirth could be given to her: the subject of her sin. Jesus' message is clear: before we can be born again, before we can receive the living water, we must first acknowledge our sinful condition. This is, *The Subject of Sin*, 4:15-18.
  1. The request for living water (v.15).
  2. The first essential: Facing the truth, the fact of sin (vv.16-18).

**4:15**

¹⁵ The woman said to him, "Sir, give me this water, so that I will not be thirsty or have to come here to draw water."

### 1 The request for living water.

Jesus had just made a profound promise to the Samaritan woman. If she would drink of the water that He offered, she would never thirst again. The water Jesus offered her was the water of eternal life (v.14).

The woman responded that she wanted this water. She asked for it, but note the reasons why:

➢ That she would not be thirsty (physical thirst).
➢ That she would not have to come and draw water every day.

What did the woman truly mean by these statements? Many commentators think that she was jesting with Jesus. They hold that she certainly knew that Jesus did not have a well of water from which she could drink and never thirst again, water that would cause her to live forever, never having to die. Perhaps she thought that Jesus was jesting with her, so she played along, humoring Him. Others think she was sincere and just did not understand what Jesus was saying, but that she wanted a drink of these waters, whatever they were.

Whatever the case may be, the woman clearly was thinking in terms of the physical world, only of the physical benefits. She had grasped nothing of the spiritual meaning, nothing of the inner satisfaction that Jesus could give which would quench all the thirst of her heart.

**THOUGHT 1.** Every one of us does thirst, but our thirst is much deeper than physical thirst. Every human being has an inner, spiritual thirst (see note—Jn.4:13-14 for discussion of our thirst).

Christ alone can satisfy this thirst, the thirsting of our souls. If we drink of the water Christ gives, we are infused with purpose, meaning, significance, energy, and motivation. Once we drink of Christ, we do not mind drawing water; that is, we do not mind the work involved. In fact, the water of Christ stirs us to work and serve, helping others in every way possible. We want to help and to share the wonderful news of a saving God, a God who can save from the thirst of . . .

- emptiness
- loneliness
- lostness
- despair
- hopelessness

"Go therefore and make disciples of all nations, baptizing them in the name of the Father and of the Son and of the Holy Spirit." (Mt.28:19)

"But you will receive power when the Holy Spirit has come upon you, and you will be my witnesses in Jerusalem and in all Judea and Samaria, and to the end of the earth." (Ac.1:8)

Therefore, we are ambassadors for Christ, God making his appeal through us. We implore you on behalf of Christ, be reconciled to God. (2 Co.5:20)

## 2 The first essential: Facing the truth, the fact of sin.

4:16–18

The woman had requested living water, but before she could be given the living water of spiritual rebirth, she had to be convicted of her sin and repent of it. For this reason, Jesus gave her a puzzling command. He instructed her to go call her husband and then come back to the well (v.16).

¹⁶ Jesus said to her, "Go, call your husband, and come here."

¹⁷ The woman answered him, "I have no husband." Jesus said to her, "You are right in saying, 'I have no husband';

¹⁸ "for you have had five husbands, and the one you now have is not your husband. What you have said is true."

a. **Jesus stirred conviction within the woman (vv.16–17a).**

Jesus' command to the woman to call her husband stirred conviction and ultimately a confession of sin. Why was this necessary? Why did the woman have to face the truth of her sin before she could be spiritually reborn?

First, because she was weary and heavy laden, and her burden was caused by her sin. She had to know what her problem was in order to seek the cure. Sin had to be removed and renounced, forgiven and cleansed before *true rest* and *true relief* could come. Once she was freed from sin, rest and relief would come. She would no longer be weary and heavy laden under the load of sin and irresponsibility, guilt and shame. She would be set free and given a life of spiritual rest and security (see notes, *Rest*—Mt.11:28, 30; He.4:1 for more discussion).

Second, she had the symptoms of disease and did not know what the disease was; therefore, she was unable to cure her disease. She needed deliverance but did not know how to be delivered. The woman's disease was the same as the disease of all humans: sin. Sin had to be renounced before the living water of spiritual rebirth could be given.

> Therefore put away all filthiness and rampant wickedness and receive with meekness the implanted word, which is able to save your souls. (Js.1:21)

b. **Jesus accepted no evasion from the woman (v.17b).**

The woman tried to evade—avoid, bypass, sidestep—the fact of her sin. She told the truth, but she only told the partial truth. She did not have a husband. But she failed to tell Jesus the rest of her situation: she was living with a man just as if she were living with a husband. Jesus refused to let her get by with telling a half-truth. He would not accept her attempt to get around the subject of her sin.

c. **Jesus knew all about her (v.18a).**

Jesus knew all about the woman, that she had gone through five husbands. He knew the truth about her. Moreover, Jesus knew what she had done to fail in so many marriages. He knew whether she was guilty...
- of making ungodly, worldly choices
- of being argumentative and defensive
- of being a poor housekeeper, wife, and mother
- of being cold, distant, withdrawn, and indifferent
- of being unfaithful and immoral

Jesus knew the truth about her sin, and He knows the truth about every person's sin.

**And again, "The Lord knows the thoughts of the wise, that they are futile." (1 Co.3:20)**

**"For my eyes are on all their ways. They are not hidden from me, nor is their iniquity concealed from my eyes." (Je.16:17)**

**"He reveals deep and hidden things; he knows what is in the darkness, and the light dwells with him." (Da.2:22)**

d. **Jesus reproved the woman's sin (v.18b).**

Jesus confronted her sin directly and clearly. She had not only gone through five different husbands, but she was now living with a man who was not her husband. He forced her to face the truth of her sin.

**THOUGHT 1.** The point is clear: we cannot sidestep our sin. We have to face it and repent of it if we wish to receive the living water of spiritual rebirth.

We cannot hide our sin from the Lord. Christ not only knows all about our sin; He keeps an account of it. We are guilty of every act of disobedience to God we have committed. We stand guilty of every one of His righteous laws we have broken.

We have to face the truth, the fact of our sin, and renounce it if we wish to receive the living water of spiritual rebirth. We have to do what Christ is pointing out to the Samaritan woman: we have to repent of our sin. Once we have repented, we can then ask for the living water, and Christ will give it. But note: drinking the water of Christ is essential.

**"Repent therefore, and turn back, that your sins may be blotted out." (Ac.3:19)**

**"Being then God's offspring, we ought not to think that the divine being is like gold or silver or stone, an image formed by the art and imagination of man. The times of ignorance God overlooked, but now he commands all people everywhere to repent, because he has fixed a day on which he will judge the world in righteousness by a man whom he has appointed; and of this he has given assurance to all by raising him from the dead." (Ac.17:29-31)**

**For the wages of sin is death, but the free gift of God is eternal life in Christ Jesus our Lord. (Ro.6:23)**

**If we confess our sins, he is faithful and just to forgive us our sins and to cleanse us from all unrighteousness. (1 Jn.1:9)**

**Whoever conceals his transgressions will not prosper, but he who confesses and forsakes them will obtain mercy. (Pr.28:13)**

**"'Only acknowledge your guilt, that you rebelled against the LORD your God and scattered your favors among foreigners under every green tree, and that you have not obeyed my voice, declares the LORD.'" (Je.3:13)**

## C. The Subject of Worship, 4:19-24

| | |
|---|---|
| ¹⁹ The woman said to him, "Sir, I perceive that you are a prophet. | **1. Fact 1: A person must sense the need for help & for worship**<br>a. The woman sensed that Jesus was a prophet<br>b. The woman sensed her sin & the need for true worship, vv.15-18 |
| ²⁰ "Our fathers worshiped on this mountain, but you say that in Jerusalem is the place where people ought to worship." | |
| ²¹ Jesus said to her, "Woman, believe me, the hour is coming when neither on this mountain nor in Jerusalem will you worship the Father. | **2. Fact 2: The place of worship is not what is important** |
| ²² "You worship what you do not know; we worship what we know, for salvation is from the Jews. | **3. Fact 3: True worship & salvation are from the Jews (through the Messiah, Jesus Christ)**[DS1] |
| ²³ "But the hour is coming, and is now here, when the true worshipers will worship the Father in spirit and truth, for the Father is seeking such people to worship him. | **4. Fact 4: True worship is worshiping God in spirit & in truth**[DS2,3]<br>a. Because God seeks the kind of worshiper who approaches Him genuinely |
| ²⁴ "God is spirit, and those who worship him must worship in spirit and truth." | b. Because God Himself is Spirit & He seeks to commune with us on a deep spiritual level |

# Division IV

*The Revelation of Jesus, the Living Water, 4:1-42*

C. The Subject of Worship, 4:19-24

## 4:19-24
## Introduction

So many things changed with the coming of Jesus. In his encounter with the woman at the well, Jesus introduced an entirely new concept and approach to worship. Whether Jew, Gentile, or like this woman, half-Jew and half-Gentile, we all must come to God and worship Him the same way. This is, *The Subject of Worship,* 4:19-24.
1. Fact 1: A person must sense the need for help and for worship (vv.19-20).
2. Fact 2: The place of worship is not what is important (v.21).
3. Fact 3: True worship and salvation are from the Jews (through the Messiah, Jesus Christ). (v.22).
4. Fact 4: True worship is worshiping God in spirit and in truth (vv.23-24).

## 1 Fact 1: A person must sense the need for help and for worship.

The woman was troubled. Jesus had confronted her with her sin (vv.15-18), and she could either respond or react. She could have reacted by . . .

- being angry
- neglecting
- ignoring
- arguing
- counting it as foolishness

However, she did not react. Instead, she was stirred and convicted because of what she sensed about Jesus and about her need.

4:19-20

¹⁹ The woman said to him, "Sir, I perceive that you are a prophet.
²⁰ "Our fathers worshiped on this mountain, but you say that in Jerusalem is the place where people ought to worship."

a. **The woman sensed that Jesus was a prophet (v.19).**
When Jesus told her about her sin, the woman realized that Jesus was not an ordinary man. She sensed that Jesus was a prophet, a man who was in touch with God; therefore, Jesus was a man who could help her. Note that, at this point, she did not understand that Jesus is God's Son, but only that He was a prophet, one through whom God spoke in a special way.

b. **The woman sensed her sin and the need for true worship (v.20; see vv.15-18).**
The woman felt a deep awareness of her sin and the need to take care of her sin in order that she could truly worship God. But where was she to worship? There was a dispute about where God's presence really was, a dispute about where a person could truly meet God. The Samaritans said that God's presence was in Mount Gerizim; the Jews said He dwelled in Jerusalem (see note—Jn.4:5).

Standing before her was the prophet who wrought the piercing conviction in her that she was to worship. He was a prophet; therefore, He could help and direct her, so she asked Him where to worship. Where could she find help from God?

**THOUGHT 1.** The woman was under powerful conviction. She knew that she had to worship God, to make sacrifice for her sin. When we are stirred and convicted, we need to turn to God immediately. If we do not know how to turn to God, we need to ask a person who is in touch with God—seek help from someone who knows the Lord.

> "And when he comes, he will convict the world concerning sin and righteousness and judgment." (Jn.16:8)
>
> Now when they heard this they were cut to the heart, and said to Peter and the rest of the apostles, "Brothers, what shall we do?" (Ac.2:37)
>
> For I know my transgressions, and my sin is ever before me. (Ps.51:3)
>
> When my soul was embittered, when I was pricked in heart. (Ps.73:21)

4:21

²¹ Jesus said to her, "Woman, believe me, the hour is coming when neither on this mountain nor in Jerusalem will you worship the Father."

## 2 Fact 2: The place of worship is not what is important.

Jesus answered the woman's question by stating that the place of worship is not what is important. Some did worship in Mount Gerizim, and some worshiped in Jerusalem, but the place is not what is important.

Jesus said that *an hour* was coming that would change the whole nature of worship. The way people approached and worshiped God was going to be radically and completely transformed. Jesus was, of course, referring to His death and the coming of the Holy Spirit. The place of worship is no longer the temple or any other particular location on earth. God's presence now dwells in the hearts and lives of His people. His people worship Him wherever they are, and we can worship Him every day all day long.

> "And I will ask the Father, and he will give you another Helper, to be with you forever, even the Spirit of truth, whom the world cannot receive, because it neither sees him nor knows him. You know him, for he dwells with you and will be in you." (Jn.14:16-17)
>
> You, however, are not in the flesh but in the Spirit, if in fact the Spirit of God dwells in you. Anyone who does not have the Spirit of Christ does not belong to him. But if Christ is in you, although the body is dead because of sin, the Spirit is life because of righteousness. (Ro.8:9-10)
>
> Or do you not know that your body is a temple of the Holy Spirit within you, whom you have from God? You are not your own, for you were bought with a price. So glorify God in your body. (1 Co.6:19-20)
>
> "And I will put my Spirit within you, and cause you to walk in my statutes and be careful to obey my rules." (Eze.36:27)

What *is* important is *the object of worship*, being sure we are truly worshiping *the Father*, God Himself. A person may be in the temple worshiping, and yet not truly understand *whom* they are worshiping (v.22). Our whole being must be focused upon the only true and living God, the Father Himself, before we can be truly worshiping Him.

> That together you may with one voice glorify the God and Father of our Lord Jesus Christ. (Ro.15:6)
>
> Through him [Christ] then let us continually offer up a sacrifice of praise to God, that is, the fruit of lips that acknowledge his name. (He.13:15)
>
> But you are a chosen race, a royal priesthood, a holy nation, a people for his own possession, that you may proclaim the excellencies of him who called you out of darkness into his marvelous light. (1 Pe.2:9)
>
> "You are my witnesses," declares the LORD, "and my servant whom I have chosen, that you may know and believe me and understand that I am he. Before me no god was formed, nor shall there be any after me." (Is.43:10)

## 3 Fact 3: True worship and salvation are from the Jews (through the Messiah, Jesus Christ).

²² "You worship what you do not know; we worship what we know, for salvation is from the Jews."

Jesus stated—to this Samaritan woman—that worship and salvation are from the Jews. Before she could be cleansed of her sin and truly worship God, she needed to understand the truth. In the Greek text for this verse, a definite article is used for *salvation* (he soteria); literally, it reads *the salvation*. The salvation, the only true salvation, came to the human race through the Jews. This refers to the fact that the Messiah, who is the salvation of the human race, came through the Jews, not from any other source, not from any other nation or people group. There is only one salvation, one way to God, one way to heaven, and that salvation is through Jesus Christ, whom God gave to the earth through the Jews. All other worship is an expression of people's own ideas, no matter how rational and highly esteemed and followed. As Jesus stated, they do not know or perceive what they are worshiping (see DEEPER STUDY # 1).

Note also that Jesus uses the pronoun *we*, identifying Himself with the Jews. He was a full-blooded Jew, not of another nationality, nor was He a mixture of races.

> **THOUGHT 1.** Throughout our world, multitudes are ignorant of God Himself, of the only living and true God. And they are ignorant of Christ, the Son of God. They do not know that the only true and living God is the God who gave His Son for humanity's sin. Nor do they know that the only way to God, *the salvation*, is through His Son, Jesus Christ.
>
> We are under constant pressure to acknowledge the false concept that there is one God who is the same God of all religions and the false concept that there are many paths to God. But we must stand firm on the truth. We must cry out that the only true God is the Father of Jesus Christ, and the only way to Him is through His Son. We must boldly declare *the salvation*, for every other way leads to hell. The souls of men, women, boys, and girls across the globe depend on our firm adherence to and faithful proclamation of the truth.

"'For this people's heart has grown dull, and with their ears they can barely hear, and their eyes they have closed, lest they should see with their eyes and hear with their ears and understand with their heart and turn, and I would heal them.'" (Mt.13:15)

They said to him therefore, "Where is your Father?" Jesus answered, "You know neither me nor my Father. If you knew me, you would know my Father also." (Jn.8:19)

The man answered, "Why, this is an amazing thing! You do not know where he comes from, and yet he opened my eyes." (Jn.9:30)

Jesus said to him, "I am the way, and the truth, and the life. No one comes to the Father except through me." (Jn.14:6)

"And they will do these things [persecutions] because they have not known the Father, nor me." (Jn.16:3)

"And there is salvation in no one else, for there is no other name under heaven given among men by which we must be saved." (Ac.4:12)

"For as I passed along and observed the objects of your worship, I found also an altar with this inscription: 'To the unknown god.' What therefore you worship as unknown, this I proclaim to you." (Ac.17:23)

For, being ignorant of the righteousness of God, and seeking to establish their own, they did not submit to God's righteousness. (Ro.10:3)

They are darkened in their understanding, alienated from the life of God because of the ignorance that is in them, due to their hardness of heart. (Ep.4:18)

For there is one God, and there is one mediator between God and men, the man Christ Jesus, who gave himself as a ransom for all, which is the testimony given at the proper time. (1 Ti.2:5-6)

Always learning and never able to arrive at a knowledge of the truth. (2 Ti.3:7)

They bend their tongue like a bow; falsehood and not truth has grown strong in the land; for they proceed from evil to evil, and they do not know me, declares the Lord. (Je.9:3)

## DEEPER STUDY # 1

(4:22) **Israel—God's Plan—History—Jews**: why did Jesus Christ come to the Jewish nation and come to earth as a Jew? Very simply stated, the Jews were God's special people. They had been born by a special act of God. It all started long, long ago. God had wanted . . .

- a people who would love Him supremely and give Him their first loyalty (see Ge.17:7; Is.43:10).
- a people who would witness to all other nations that He and He alone was the one true and living God (see Ge.12:3; 22:18; Ac.13:26, 47).
- a people through whom He could send the promised Seed, the Savior and Messiah, Jesus Christ, to all people everywhere (see Ge.3:15; 17:7; 22:18; Jn.4:22; Ga.3:16).
- a people through whom He could send His written Word, the Holy Bible, and preserve it for all generations (see Ro.9:4-5; 1 Pe.2:10-12).

In searching the earth for such a people, God could find none (see Ro.1:18-32). God could do only one thing. He had to find one man and through him begin a new people, a new nation.

1. God found and chose Abraham and through him established the Jewish nation (Ge.12:1-5; 13:14-17; 15:1-7; 17:1-8, 15-19; 22:16-18; 26:2-5, 24; 28:13-15; 31:13; 35:9-12). God chose one man and challenged him to worship God supremely. If that man would worship God supremely, then God would cause a special people to be born of his seed. That man was Abraham. Abraham was the first Jew (see Ge.12:1-4; Ga.3:16). In the Old Testament the Jews and their land (Palestine) were continually pointed to as the very special people and land of God. The Jews were called . . .

- God's special people (De.7:6)
- God's peculiar people (De.14:2; 26:18)
- God's peculiar treasure (Ex.19:5; Ps.135:4)
- the Lord's portion (De.32:9)

- the Lord's land (Le.25:23; Je.2:7; 16:18; Ho.9:3)
- the holy land (Zec.2:12; see DEEPER STUDY # 1—Ro.4:1-25 for more discussion)

However, the Jewish nation failed to obey God supremely. The whole plot of the Old Testament centers around God's pleading and dealing with the Jews. Again and again, He gave the nation the opportunity to obey Him. He dealt with them in mercy and in judgment, but at every turn they refused to heed His pleading.

2. God chose the family of David (see DEEPER STUDY # 4—Jn.1:49). God made another move, choosing one faithful family within the Jewish nation and giving to that family one great promise. The family was that of King David, and the promise was that of the Messiah, God's great King, God's very own Son. God's Son was to come through the line of David and establish an eternal nation of people who would love God supremely. However, the Jewish nation again failed God. They misinterpreted God's Word—the prophecies of His coming.

a. The Jews misinterpreted God's Word by saying the seed of Abraham included only the Jewish nation. In their minds, God had no children except the children of the Jewish nation. The Bible says explicitly that the seed of Abraham is Christ, and the special people of God are those individuals within all nations who believe in Christ and worship God supremely (Ga.3:16).

b. The Jews misinterpreted God's Word by saying that the eternal kingdom promised to David was the Jewish nation and the Jewish nation only. They expected Israel to be established as an earthly nation forever and all other nations to be subservient to Israel. But again, God's promise was not that narrow, nor was it that prejudiced. The Bible says there is not, and never has been, any respect of persons with God (De.10:17; 2 Chr.19:7; Jb.34:19; Ac.10:34; Ro.2:11; Ga.2:6; Ep.6:9; Col.3:25; 1 Pe.1:17). God did say that Christ was to come from the Davidic line, but He also said that He was going to establish an *eternal nation* made up of people everywhere who would believe in Christ and love God supremely (Ro.2:28-29).

By misinterpreting God's promises, the Jews failed to be the missionaries to the world that God had chosen them to be. They became *earthly bound* and *materialistic*. They twisted the idea of the promised Messiah to fit their own schemes. They conceived of Him as One who was to establish an earthly kingdom for the Jewish nation alone. They failed to see that God was speaking . . .

- of an eternal kingdom of righteousness
- of a kingdom that is of another dimension entirely—the dimension of the spiritual
- of a new heaven and a new earth that would give each person an eternal life beyond just one earthly generation

3. God made a third move. He sent His own Son into the world through the Jewish nation. God sent Him so that the world through Him might be saved (Jn.3:16-19). However, the people rejected God's Son and crucified Him. This act—the killing of God's Son—was the final blow. When the only Son of God was slain, the whole world *was* involved. Both Jew and Gentile were represented symbolically in the Jewish religious leaders and the Roman authorities. They both actually did the plotting, sentencing, and execution. If the world were ever to be saved, it was now perfectly clear that God had to make every move Himself.

This He did once-for-all. In His eternal purpose and plan for our salvation, God took the sins of all people and laid them upon His Son while He was being slain upon the cross. He allowed His Son to bear the sins of the world (1 Pe.2:24). Then He raised His Son from the dead—never to die again. He did what the people had always failed to do: in His Son's resurrection God began to build a lasting kingdom of righteousness, a new nation that is presently being made up of people from all earthly nations who desire and are willing to follow Jesus Christ supremely. He is calling out and forming a new people who have genuinely been born again—spiritually. These new born people shall live eternally—beyond just one earthly generation. These people are identified as His church, as a body of people who genuinely believe and follow Him. They are destined to be the inhabitants of the new heavens and earth (see notes—pt.5, Lu.8:21; Ep.2:11-18; 4:17-19).

God, acting solely upon His own through the death and resurrection of His Son, has fulfilled His promises to both Abraham and David. All the people of the nations of the world now have the opportunity to become children of God, the special people of God.

## 4:23-24

23 "But the hour is coming, and is now here, when the true worshipers will worship the Father in spirit and truth, for the Father is seeking such people to worship him.
24 "God is spirit, and those who worship him must worship in spirit and truth."

### 4 Fact 4: True worship is worshiping God in spirit and in truth.

Jesus referred again to the coming change in worship (v.21), announcing that it had arrived. Christ changed worship. Before Christ, people worshiped God in special places, for example, in temples and before altars. Since Christ, place and locality mean nothing. We do not have to be in a particular place to worship God. Christ has opened the door into God's presence from anyplace in the universe (see note—Jn.4:21 for more discussion). What matters most now is *how* we worship God. True worship is worshiping God in spirit and in truth.

**a. Because God seeks the kind of worshiper who approaches Him genuinely (v.23).**

We are to worship God in spirit and in truth (see DEEPER STUDY # 2). What does this mean?

To worship God in spirit means to worship God with the *spiritual drive and ability* of our soul, seeking the most intimate communion and fellowship with Him. In addition, it means to worship with the *spiritual core* of our life and being, trusting and resting in God's acceptance and love and care,

To worship God in truth means to approach God in the right or true way. There is only one way we can approach God, through His Son Jesus Christ (see note—Jn.4:21; 14:6). And it means to worship God sincerely and truthfully, not coming half-heartedly with wandering mind and sleepy eyes, or with a heart that is not devoted fully to Him. It also means to worship God according to who He truly is, rather than according to our concept or perception of Him.

Why are we to worship? Because the Father seeks people to worship Him. God desires worship, for He created us to worship and fellowship with Him. Therefore, God seeks people who will worship Him, but only in spirit and truth.

> Even as he chose us in him before the foundation of the world, that we should be holy and blameless before him. In love he predestined us for adoption to himself as sons through Jesus Christ, according to the purpose of his will, to the praise of his glorious grace, with which he has blessed us in the Beloved. (Ep.1:4-6)

> But you are a chosen race, a royal priesthood, a holy nation, a people for his own possession, that you may proclaim the excellencies of him who called you out of darkness into his marvelous light. (1 Pe.2:9; see Ro.15:6; 1 Co.6:20)

> "Everyone who is called by my name, whom I created for my glory, whom I formed and made.... You are my witnesses," declares the LORD, "and my servant whom I have chosen, that you may know and believe me and understand that I am he. Before me no god was formed, nor shall there be any after me." (Is.43:7, 10)

**b. Because God Himself is Spirit and He seeks to commune with us on a deep spiritual level (v.24).**

There is a reason that we must worship God in spirit: because God Himself is Spirit (see DEEPER STUDY # 3). We must worship God according to who and what He is. While we often express our worship physically—for example, through speaking or singing, or through kneeling or raising our hands—our gestures are nothing more than meaningless motions if they do not come genuinely from our spirits. God is Spirit, and we must commune with him on a deep spiritual level. There is no other way. If we are going to worship God, we *must* worship Him in spirit and in truth.

Then Jesus said to him, "Be gone, Satan! For it is written, 'You shall worship the Lord your God and him only shall you serve.'" (Mt.4:10)

And they worshiped him and returned to Jerusalem with great joy. (Lu.24:52)

Not neglecting to meet together, as is the habit of some, but encouraging one another, and all the more as you see the Day drawing near. (He.10:25)

Ascribe to the Lord the glory due his name; bring an offering and come before him! Worship the Lord in the splendor of holiness. (1 Chr.16:29)

Oh come, let us worship and bow down; let us kneel before the Lord, our Maker! (Ps.95:6)

Worship the Lord in the splendor of holiness; tremble before him, all the earth! (Ps.96:9)

## DEEPER STUDY # 2

(4:23) **Man, Creation—Spirit—Worship**: we are to worship God in Spirit. Three points need to be looked at to fully understand what this means.

1. We have been created by God.

   **Then the Lord God formed the man of dust from the ground and breathed into his nostrils the breath of life, and the man became a living creature. (Ge.2:7)**

   The material used to form man was *dust*; or as Isaiah said, "clay" (Is.64:8); or as Luther translated, a lump of earth (Ger. erdenkloss). Our physical material or substance is of the earth; the forming of the body is like that of an earthen vessel (Jb.10:8-9; Ro.9:21); the food we eat is of the earth (Job 28:5); and the end of the body is to return to the earth (Ec.3:20).

   There is a sense in which the human being is a paradox. We were created with all the dignity and honor possible—created by the hand of God and given the very breath of God. Yet, we were also created out of the most base and lowly stuff of all—dirt. So, in one sense we have every reason to glory; in another sense we have every reason to be humble. What should our attitude be? What should our air—our demeanor—be? There is nothing wrong with glorying; there is nothing wrong with being humble. It is the reason or object for glorying and being humble that makes one right or wrong. We are to worship and glory in God—that God gave us life and the dignity and honor (privilege) of life. We are to walk humbly toward God and toward other people because we all come from the same material, the earth (Je.9:24; see Ro.11:36; 1 Co.1:31; 2 Co.10:17; Ga.1:5; 2 Ti.4:18; He.13:21; 1 Pe.5:11). Therefore, we are exhorted to present our bodies to God as "living sacrifices" and as "the temple of the Holy Spirit" (Ro.12:1; 1 Co.6:19-20).

   But note: humans are not only body and soul; we are also spirit (see Deeper Study # 3). This is our distinctive difference from all other creatures. As the psalmist says, we are *fearfully and wonderfully made* (Ps.139:14-15). What makes humans distinct?

   a. It is not just the breath of life that is given to humans. It is the very breath of God Himself. God's breath is life, eternal life; therefore, we are given the eternal life, the very Spirit of God Himself. Just think! God's very own breath, His Spirit, is within every person who is "renewed" (recreated) after the image of Him that created him.

      **And to put on the new self, created after the likeness of God in true righteousness and holiness. (Ep.4:24)**

      **And have put on the new self, which is being renewed in knowledge after the image of its creator. (Col.3:10)**

   b. God breathes His own breath or spirit into the nostrils of human beings. Just imagine the picture. The body of Adam was lying before God; it had just been formed by God's hands from the dust of the earth. Adam was lifeless—just a body—never having breathed. God then breathed into Adam's nostrils His own breath or Spirit, the life of His very own being (which is the life that goes on and on, never ending, that is eternal).

Now, here is the point. God made no other creature like this. God gave no other creature His own breath, nor did He use this method of creation with any other creature. These two facts make man's creation distinctive.

What a shame that so many people cleave to this earth and its worldliness when God has placed His own breath within us, when we have the capacity to know intimate communion with Him!

2. We have been created in *the image and likeness of God*.

> **Then God said, "Let us make man in our image, after our likeness." . . . So God created man in his own image. (Ge.1:26-27)**

Whatever *the image and likeness of God* means, it is that which distinguishes humans from all other life which God created. Nowhere else does God say He created a being in *His own image* and *after His own likeness*. Only humans are in the image and likeness of God. What is the *image and likeness* of God in us?

a. It is unlikely that it is the *soul*. The Bible says all living creatures are souls. They were created as *living souls*. This is clearly pointed out in the Hebrew language of Ge.1:20, which says, "Let the waters swarm with swarms of living creatures [Hb. nephesh]." All living creatures possess the breath of life (see Deeper Study # 5—Mt.22:37 for more discussion).

b. It is unlikely that it is the ability to reason. Even animals have the ability to reason and learn to varying degrees. They show ability to think when facing an enemy or difficulties in the innumerable experiences of life.

c. It is unlikely that it is the ability to be moral and just. Some animals (both individually and within family groups) have rules, practices, deeds, or acts that lead to moral and virtuous behavior among themselves and even toward others. There seems to be an exercise of right and wrong among some animals. However, it needs to be pointed out that just as humans are far superior to animals mentally, we are also far superior to animals morally. Humans are far superior to animals both as rational beings (beings that reason) and moral beings (beings that are just, relating to others as they should). (Note that being *spiritually* and *mentally renewed* in Christ affects the rational and moral powers of a person. We can be *created* in righteousness and *true* holiness. We can be delivered from the legalistic bondage and rules of a man-conceived righteousness and holiness; see Ep.4:24; Col.3:10.)

d. It is likely His spirit: His immortal breath, His life that lives forever just like God. God gave human beings His spirit. God went beyond what He had made when He created the animals of the earth (a soul, an earthly life, a temporal breath); God made man a spirit (an eternal life, an immortal breath) that is just like Himself, just like His own life. To be in the image and likeness of God means that we alone can worship Him *in spirit* and in truth (Jn.4:24). No animal is a spirit; animals are only souls. As living souls, they are enabled by varying degrees to breathe, to reason and to relate—but none of them have the inherent power to breathe eternally, nor the drive and ability to reason after God and to relate to God. We alone have that power, that drive, and that ability. *We are spirit, even as God is Spirit*. We are not only body and soul as the animals of creation. A human is not only a *living, breathing soul made for this earth; he/she is a spirit, an immortal being made to live with God eternally*.

3. In light of the above fact, there are at least two distinguishing marks of God's image in humans, two distinguishing marks of man as a spirit.

a. God's image in the human is the *spirit or power of immortality*. We will live beyond this earth, live eternally just like God. As mentioned above, according to the Bible, no animal is a spirit. Animals are only souls. As souls they are enabled to breathe and to live on this earth, but they do not have the inherent power to breathe eternally. However, we do have that power. We are spirit, even as God is Spirit. *A human is not* only a living, breathing soul and body like the animals made for this earth; the human is a spirit, an immortal being made both for this earth and for eternity.

b. God's image in the human is the *spirit or the drive and ability (choice) to worship*. We not only have the soulish ability to reason and to relate, but an unquenchable spiritual drive and ability to reason after God and to relate to God. Again, as mentioned above, no earthly animal has that spiritual drive and ability (freedom of choice). The Bible does ascribe to souls varying abilities, but no animal soul has the ability to reason *after God* or to *relate to God*. Worship is a spiritual drive and ability, an ability of spirit (of man) only. Just like animals, *we know and understand the things* of this earth; but we are created to know, believe, and understand God first and foremost (Is.43:10). We are to worship God. God is Spirit and He has created us as spirit; therefore, we are to worship God in spirit and in truth (Jn.4:24).

There are two very significant facts to be noted about the image of God in man or of man as a spirit.

1. The rebellion of the human race against God (humanity's fall) affected God's image within humanity. God had created humans as immortal beings. We were to live on this earth and to live with God forever. Once we exercised our ability or choice and turned against God, we lost both rights. We could no longer live on the earth forever, nor could we live with God forever. In our rebellion against God, we were saying that we preferred a different world other than God's world and we preferred a different god (our own will) other than God Himself. We thereby condemned ourselves to leave this earth (to die, Ge.2:17; 31f; 3:19) and to be separated from God eternally (Jn.3:18). Note that we were already created as immortal beings.

Therefore, humanity would continue on, would exist forever—but was (a) to be placed somewhere else other than this earth (we had chosen such); and (b) was to be separated from God forever. It was humanity's choice. The image of God—the power of immortality and the drive and ability to worship and live with God—was marred eternally.

2. The image of God within us can be renewed.

a. We can now put on *the new man,* the new self.

**And to put on the new self, created after the likeness of God in true righteousness and holiness. (Ep.4:24)**

**The new self . . . is being renewed . . . after the image of its creator [God]. (Col.3:10)**

b. We can be "born again" spiritually; we can be made alive to God just as humanity was in the beginning—never to perish. (3:3f; 1 Pe.1:23).

c. We can live and worship God forever (3:16; 2 Pe.1:4). We can now partake of God's divine nature and be assured of living forever in the new heavens and new earth (2 Pe.3:3-4, 8-18; Re.21:1-7).

d. We are renewed, reborn, recreated in Christ Jesus. He bore our sins on the cross in order that we might die to sin and live to righteousness. He has healed us of the disease of sin by His wounds (see 3:18; 5:17; 1 Pe.2:24; notes—Ro.5:1; 2 Co.5:1).

**Just as we have borne the image of the man of dust, we shall also bear the image of the man of heaven. (1 Co.15:49)**

**Then God said, "Let us make man in our image, after our likeness." . . . So God created man in his own image, in the image of God he created him; male and female he created them. (Ge.1:26-27)**

## Deeper Study # 3

(4:23-24) **Spirit—God, Spirit**: what is meant by "spirit"? At least three things are gleaned from Scripture.

1. Spirit is not flesh and bone. Spirit is not physical and material. Spirit is immaterial, non-physical. Spirit is of another dimension of being, another dimension entirely different from the physical and material dimension of being.

2. Spirit is the innermost part of being, the very core and heart of life. Spirit is the very *breath of God's life,* the very *breath of God's existence,* the very *being of God's life.* That is, spirit is *eternal existence and being.* It is permanent, unending existence. A spirit has the breath of life, of existence, of *being forever.*

> Then the LORD God formed the man of dust from the ground and breathed into his nostrils the breath of life, and the man became a living creature. (Ge.2:7)

3. God is Spirit. This means He is the very expression or personification of life eternal, of permanent, unending existence. His nature is not flesh and bone; for the physical ages, deteriorates, dies, and decays—it ends. But not Spirit, not God. God exists forever and ever. He is life, the very personification of life eternal. Whatever life is—in all of its perfection—*God is.* God is the perfect Person, Life, Intelligence, Being. The basic nature of God is Spirit: eternal being, eternal life, the Perfect Being, the Perfect Life.

> "And this is eternal life . . . the only true God." (Jn.17:3)

## D. The Subject of the Messiah, 4:25-30

| | |
|---|---|
| ²⁵ The woman said to him, "I know that Messiah is coming (he who is called Christ). When he comes, he will tell us all things." | 1. The women's sense that Jesus is the Messiah |
| ²⁶ Jesus said to her, "I who speak to you am he." | 2. The great claim of Jesus: He is the Messiah |
| ²⁷ Just then his disciples came back. They marveled that he was talking with a woman, but no one said, "What do you seek?" or, "Why are you talking with her?" | 3. The spirit contrary to the Messiah: A spirit of evil thought & pride |
| ²⁸ So the woman left her water jar and went away into town and said to the people, | 4. Her proclamation that Jesus is the Messiah |
| ²⁹ "Come, see a man who told me all that I ever did. Can this be the Christ?" | |
| ³⁰ They went out of the town and were coming to him. | 5. The response of searching for the Messiah |

# Division IV

*The Revelation of Jesus, the Living Water, 4:1-42*

D. The Subject of the Messiah, 4:25-30

## 4:25-30
## Introduction

In this passage, the account of Jesus' encounter with the sinful Samaritan woman reaches its conclusion. It is a vivid, dramatic picture of the convicting and convincing work of the Spirit, of the passion of God for all sinful people, and of the power of Christ to change lives. It is also an example for all who believe to follow: the woman discovered the Messiah, and she excitedly shared her discovery with everybody she could find. This is, *The Subject of the Messiah*, 4:25-30.

1. The woman's sense that Jesus is the Messiah (v.25).
2. The great claim of Jesus: He is the Messiah (v.26).
3. The spirit contrary to the Messiah: A spirit of evil thought and pride (v.27).
4. Her proclamation that Jesus is the Messiah (vv.28-29).
5. The response of searching for the Messiah (v.30).

### 1 The woman's sense that Jesus is the Messiah.

4:25

After Jesus had spoken with the Samaritan woman, she sensed that He is the Messiah. God had consumed her with an intense, flaming sense of His presence. The subject of her sin and of true worship was causing her heart to reach out for God. She sensed something very, very special about Jesus . . .

²⁵ The woman said to him, "I know that Messiah is coming (he who is called Christ). When he comes, he will tell us all things."

- that no man could speak as He had spoken unless He had a very special relationship with God
- that perhaps He was the Messiah Himself

Therefore, she brought up the subject of the Messiah, confessing two things that she believed.

First, she believed that the Messiah was *coming* (Gk. erchetai). The idea is that the Messiah was *coming soon*. His coming was at hand, imminent. Her belief was based upon such Scriptures as Genesis 3:15; 49:10; Numbers 24:17; and Deuteronomy 18:15.

Second, she believed that the Messiah would be the Supreme Authority. When He came, He would tell the people all things. This woman did not deny the Messiah; she believed in the coming and authority of the Messiah. However, her belief was not a saving belief, not a belief of commitment (see DEEPER STUDY # 2—Jn.2:24). It was only a mental or an intellectual belief, a belief of knowledge. But the fact that she believed the facts about the Messiah made her *open* to saving faith. She did not reject the witness of Jesus: she was not rude; she listened to Him. Therefore, God was able to give her a sense of His presence.

**THOUGHT 1.** The person who constantly rejects Jesus Christ or claims to be agnostic or atheistic is seldom reached for Christ. However, a person who listens to the Scripture and believes intellectually, mentally accepting the facts of God's promises, stands a much better chance of being reached by God. Mental or intellectual belief is more open; it is exposed to God's Word. Thereby it is more likely to become a saving belief, the belief of commitment.

However, a warning does need to be issued. People with only a mental belief can hear and reject so much that they become gospel-hardened, that is, so numb to the gospel that they never trust Jesus Christ as their Savior (see DEEPER STUDY # 1—Mt.13:4, 19 for more discussion).

> And the scribe said to him, "You are right, Teacher. You have truly said that he is one, and there is no other besides him. And to love him with all the heart and with all the understanding and with all the strength, and to love one's neighbor as oneself, is much more than all whole burnt offerings and sacrifices." And when Jesus saw that he answered wisely, he said to him, "You are not far from the kingdom of God." And after that no one dared to ask him any more questions. (Mk.12:32-34)

> An intelligent heart acquires knowledge, and the ear of the wise seeks knowledge. (Pr.18:15)

> The prudent sees danger and hides himself, but the simple go on and suffer for it. (Pr.22:3)

> For he is rightly instructed; his God teaches him. (Is.28:26)

> Whoever is wise, let him understand these things; whoever is discerning, let him know them; for the ways of the LORD are right, and the upright walk in them, but transgressors stumble in them. (Ho.14:9)

## 2 The great claim of Jesus: He is the Messiah.

4:26

²⁶ Jesus said to her, "I who speak to you am he."

Jesus responded to the woman with a bold, phenomenal claim. He unequivocally declared that He is the Messiah (see DEEPER STUDY # 2—Jn.1:20 for discussion). Moreover, He claimed to be the great *I Am* (Ego eimi), which is the basic name for God (see DEEPER STUDY # 1—Jn.6:20 for discussion). Most literally translated, Jesus said, *I am He*. In addition, Jesus claimed to be the Supreme One, the Supreme Authority who would tell her all things. He claimed . . .

- that what He told her about her sin was true
- that she must take care of her sin
- that the only way to take care of her sin was to worship God in spirit and in truth (see DEEPER STUDY # 2—Jn.4:23 for more discussion)

## 3 The spirit contrary to the Messiah: A spirit of evil thought and pride.

4:25–30

Just as Jesus was making His phenomenal claims, the disciples arrived. They *marveled*—were astonished, shocked, bewildered—because He was talking with the woman. Two reasons were behind their concern.

4:27

First, she was a woman. The rabbis of that day would not *talk* with women in public. They feared what people might think and say.

Second, she was a Samaritan. The Jews considered Samaritans despicable, below their social standing, unfit to be seen with in public.

> ²⁷ Just then his disciples came back. They marveled that he was talking with a woman, but no one said, "What do you seek?" or, "Why are you talking with her?"

Although the disciples controlled their tongues from questioning and gossiping, their spirit was contrary to the Messiah's spirit. Note how Christ tore down these barriers—the barriers of gender and race. He elevated both women and Samaritans to a place of societal equality and worthiness. Perhaps even more important, He showed that God views and loves all people equally. He does not see race, gender, nationality, or any other factor that provokes sinful humans to discriminate.

> **THOUGHT 1.** Prejudice, discrimination, and bigotry are sins. These attitudes are completely opposite the attitude of the Lord. When we display an attitude of prejudice—whether in thought, word, or deed—we not only sin against the people involved, but also against Christ.
>
>> So Peter opened his mouth and said: "Truly I understand that God shows no partiality, but in every nation anyone who fears him and does what is right is acceptable to him." (Ac.10:34-35)
>>
>> For there is no distinction between Jew and Greek; for the same Lord is Lord of all, bestowing his riches on all who call on him. (Ro.10:12)
>>
>> There is neither Jew nor Greek, there is neither slave nor free, there is no male and female, for you are all one in Christ Jesus. (Ga.3:28)

## 4 Her proclamation that Jesus is the Messiah.

4:28–29

Somewhere between verse 25 and verse 27, a glorious change occurs in the sinful woman's heart. She moves from believing *about* the Messiah to believing *in* Christ as the Messiah, the One sent from God to deliver us from our sins. Note the tender, yet meaningful statement *the woman left her water jar* or *waterpot*. She was so excited that she forgot her original purpose for coming to the well! The Messiah had confronted her; she had actually met Him, and He had met the need of her heart and life. She had to tell everyone about Him.

> ²⁸ So the woman left her water jar and went away into town and said to the people,
> ²⁹ "Come, see a man who told me all that I ever did. Can this be the Christ?"

Note also the strength of the woman's witness. She was an outcast from society, had no friends because of the immoral life she had lived. However, meeting the Messiah changed all that. He dealt with her sin and shame. She could now face everyone. They, too, must have the opportunity to meet the Messiah.

> **THOUGHT 1.** What a lesson for every believer! This joyful, grateful woman set an example for us all to follow. If we have truly been saved, truly been cleansed and forgiven, how can we not exuberantly proclaim the saving power of Christ?
>
>> And he did not permit him but said to him, "Go home to your friends and tell them how much the Lord has done for you, and how he has had mercy on you." (Mk.5:19)
>>
>> "For we cannot but speak of what we have seen and heard." (Ac.4:20)
>>
>> "'for you will be a witness for him to everyone of what you have seen and heard.'" (Ac.22:15)
>>
>> Come and hear, all you who fear God, and I will tell what he has done for my soul. (Ps.66:16)

I will recount the steadfast love of the Lord, the praises of the Lord, according to all that the Lord has granted us, and the great goodness to the house of Israel that he has granted them according to his compassion, according to the abundance of his steadfast love. (Is.63:7)

It has seemed good to me to show the signs and wonders that the Most High God has done for me. (Da.4:2)

**4:30**

<sup>30</sup> They went out of the town and were coming to him.

## 5  The response of searching for the Messiah.

This woman was of no social importance, not to the men of the city. In fact, she had often been misused, and was likely the very subject of gossip and jokes. But now something had happened to her: she had met the Messiah. The event had so changed her appearance, behavior, and attitude that people listened eagerly to what she said.

They responded to her witness—at least a good number did. The idea of the words *were coming* or *came to Him* is that of a long, streaming procession. The people "kept on coming to Him." It was her dynamic witness, the striking change seen in her life, that caused this enormous response. Because of her witness, many set out to find the Messiah for themselves.

Therefore, if anyone is in Christ, he is a new creation. The old has passed away; behold, the new has come. (2 Co.5:17)

But when the goodness and loving kindness of God our Savior appeared, he saved us, not because of works done by us in righteousness, but according to his own mercy, by the washing of regeneration and renewal of the Holy Spirit, whom he poured out on us richly through Jesus Christ our Savior, so that being justified by his grace we might become heirs according to the hope of eternal life. (Tit.3:4–7)

Of his own will he brought us forth by the word of truth, that we should be a kind of firstfruits of his creatures. (Js.1:18)

"And I will give you a new heart, and a new spirit I will put within you. And I will remove the heart of stone from your flesh and give you a heart of flesh." (Eze.36:26)

## E. The Subject of Labor for God, 4:31–42

31 Meanwhile the disciples were urging him, saying, "Rabbi, eat."
32 But he said to them, "I have food to eat that you do not know about."
33 So the disciples said to one another, "Has anyone brought him something to eat?"
34 Jesus said to them, "My food is to do the will of him who sent me and to accomplish his work.
35 Do you not say, 'There are yet four months, then comes the harvest'? Look, I tell you, lift up your eyes, and see that the fields are white for harvest.
36 Already the one who reaps is receiving wages and gathering fruit for eternal life, so that sower and reaper may rejoice together.

37 For here the saying holds true, 'One sows and another reaps.'
38 I sent you to reap that for which you did not labor. Others have labored, and you have entered into their labor."

39 Many Samaritans from that town believed in him because of the woman's testimony, "He told me all that I ever did."
40 So when the Samaritans came to him, they asked him to stay with them, and he stayed there two days.
41 And many more believed because of his word.
42 They said to the woman, "It is no longer because of what you said that we believe, for we have heard for ourselves, and we know that this is indeed the Savior of the world."

1. **Physical vs. spiritual concerns**
   a. The disciples' concern: Physical nourishment

   b. Jesus' concern: Spiritual food—to do the will & work of God

2. **Labor—for the harvest is ripe, the task is urgent**

3. **Labor—for there are rewards & great benefits**
   a. You receive wages
   b. You have an eternal impact
   c. You rejoice with other believers
   d. You receive the privilege of a specific part in God's great work
   e. You receive the privilege of being sent forth by Christ
   f. You receive the privilege of serving with other great servants of God

4. **Labor—for results follow**
   a. Many believed the woman's testimony

   b. Other opportunities were created

   c. Many more believed: "This man really is the Savior of the world"[DS1]

# Division IV

## The Revelation of Jesus, the Living Water, 4:1-42

### E. The Subject of Labor for God, 4:31-42

## 4:31-42
## Introduction

The sinful Samaritan woman's story has a glorious ending. As a result of her sharing her testimony, many others believed in Christ. She became a laborer for the Lord, setting a wonderful example for us to follow. Just as her life—from the day Jesus saved her—was focused on the Lord's work, our lives are to be focused on the will and work of God. Our purpose for being on earth is to serve God, to obey and work for Him. This is, *The Subject of Labor for God,* 4:31-42.

1. Physical vs. spiritual concerns (vv.31-34).
2. Labor—for the harvest is ripe, the task is urgent (v.35).
3. Labor—for there are rewards and great benefits (vv.36-38).
4. Labor—for results follow (vv.39-42).

### 4:31-35

<sup>31</sup> Meanwhile the disciples were urging him, saying, "Rabbi, eat."
<sup>32</sup> But he said to them, "I have food to eat that you do not know about."
<sup>33</sup> So the disciples said to one another, "Has anyone brought him something to eat?"
<sup>34</sup> Jesus said to them, "My food is to do the will of him who sent me and to accomplish his work.
<sup>35</sup> "Do you not say, 'There are yet four months, then comes the harvest'? Look, I tell you, lift up your eyes, and see that the fields are white for harvest."

## 1 Physical vs. spiritual concerns.

Having gone to town to buy food (v.8), the disciples returned to Jesus. Earlier, when they had arrived at the well on the outskirts of the city, Jesus had been tired and hungry. But now, as the disciples sat eating, they noticed Jesus made no effort to eat. They were concerned, so they suggested He eat (v.31).

### a. The disciples' concern: Physical nourishment (vv.31-33).
The concern of the disciples was for physical nourishment. Their minds were not on the woman to whom Jesus had just witnessed, not on her spiritual needs. They had no spiritual depth yet. Their minds were not . . .

- focused on Christ and His mission of salvation
- concentrating upon a world lost in sin and shame
- looking for every opportunity possible to reach and help people for God

They had not yet learned the great warfare being waged between the physical and spiritual concerns of life. Their minds were on the physical: on food, on not missing a meal, on satisfying a temporary craving of the body.

### b. Jesus' concern: Spiritual food—to do the will and work of God (v.34).
In contrast, Christ's concern was for spiritual food and nourishment, to do the will and work of God. This should be our primary concern as well. The *will* that must concern us is *God's will,* and the *work* that must concern us is *God's work.* Our first priority ought to be bringing people to God, leading them to the Living Water and helping them quench their inner thirst (vv.10, 14). No greater will or work exists or can be done. *God alone* is God. His will and work is supreme.

Christ's statement reveals His *esteem* for God: it is *God's will and work* that is to be done. And it reveals His *devotion* to God: God's will and work *must* be done.

Jesus reminded the disciples that God had sent Him for a particular purpose (see Deeper Study # 3—Jn.3:34). The words *sent me* are significant: Christ was not sent to do the will of men, but of God. His work was not the work of men, but of God. Christ had to finish the will and work of God. God expected it to be completed. God expected obedience, faithfulness, and perseverance until His will and work was done. Christ was faithful; He did complete God's mission (Jn.17:4; 19:30). He now challenges us, His followers, to labor for God—finish our tasks—and complete our purpose for being on earth.

**THOUGHT 1.** As believers, we too are sent by God. We are on earth primarily to do the will and work of God, even in our secular labor in the world. Like our Lord, we are to be single-minded. We must not allow our own personal goals and desires to keep us from doing God's will. Nor should we become so entangled with the business and affairs of the world that we do not have the time or energy to do the Lord's work. We have a God-given responsibility to finish the work that God sent us to do. If we are going to fulfill our sacred duty, we have to be disciplined and self-controlled. We have to conquer wandering thoughts and desires for worldly things. We cannot be given over to the world and the flesh, indulgence and license, money and material possessions, pleasures and worthless pursuits.

God *expects* us to be faithful, and He is going to hold us accountable for doing His will and work. Our lives will be evaluated at the Judgment Seat of Christ, where the Lord will reward us if we have been faithful. If we are unfaithful, we will suffer a great loss, the loss of the rewards we could have received. We will stand empty-handed before the One who loved us and gave Himself for us, with nothing to show for the life He redeemed.

> **Jesus said to them again, "Peace be with you. As the Father has sent me, even so I am sending you." (Jn.20:21)**
>
> **Each one's work will become manifest, for the Day will disclose it, because it will be revealed by fire, and the fire will test what sort of work each one has done. If the work that anyone has built on the foundation survives, he will receive a reward. If anyone's work is burned up, he will suffer loss, though he himself will be saved, but only as through fire. (1 Co.3:13-15)**
>
> **For we must all appear before the judgment seat of Christ, so that each one may receive what is due for what he has done in the body, whether good or evil. (2 Co.5:10)**
>
> **No soldier gets entangled in civilian pursuits, since his aim is to please the one who enlisted him. (2 Ti.2:4)**

## 2 Labor—for the harvest is ripe, the task is urgent.

4:35

Jesus stressed that there is a work that is waiting to be done, a harvest that is ripe. The task is urgent, for there is but a limited period of time to do the work.

> ³⁵ "Do you not say, 'There are yet four months, then comes the harvest'? Look, I tell you, lift up your eyes, and see that the fields are white for harvest."

Jesus ordered us to look on the *fields*—a symbol of the world and the people in the world. The heart of Jesus was set on the harvest of souls. We focus our hearts on a worldly harvest, the planting of seed and the reaping of grain, the investment of our energy, time, and money in a business, job, or profession, and the receiving of wages and gain. But the heart of Jesus was, and still is, upon people, upon the planting of the gospel seed and the reaping of souls for God.

The challenge from Jesus is to quit looking down upon the earth and upon the affairs of the world. Instead, He calls us to *look up* and observe the fields of people streaming across the world. John 4:35 reveals to us a very dramatic scene likely unfolding. The Samaritans in their long flowing white robes were probably streaming across the fields by the hundreds, if not the thousands. Jesus' heart and arms reached out in a burst of compassion and intense feeling; in so many words He cried, "Look, lift up your eyes and look at the fields of lost souls streaming toward you. Let the things of earth grow strangely dim."

Jesus pointed out a fact that invalidates every excuse we can invent for not winning souls: the fields of souls are white *already*; they are ready for harvesting *right now*. Since Christ has come to earth, God has put His Spirit into the world and supernaturally activated . . .

- a thirst for God
- a sense of sin, a conviction of coming short
- a deep loneliness and emptiness

- a lack of a sense of purpose
- the knowledge that Jesus Christ has come to earth claiming to be the Savior of the world, the very Son of God

It is absolutely necessary that as believers we lift up our eyes and look *now*. If not, the ripe harvest of souls and bodies will . . .
- remain in the fields of the earth
- ripen *beyond* being tasteful and useful (be too old, too far gone)
- rot and be lost forever—die and spend eternity in hell

**THOUGHT 1.** We need to grasp the practical truth of what Jesus said. First, we must lift up our eyes in order to look. We cannot see ahead or around us if we do not lift up our eyes to look. The things of the earth have to grow *strangely* dim *before* we can look and see.

Second, we must look where we are so that our eyes will see the reality of the harvest of souls around us upon which we are to focus our attention.

Note an important fact: we can look upon foreign fields through the challenge of others. Note another fact: the world is becoming more and more *one neighborhood*. Distance is becoming more and more insignificant. Modern technology has made the world smaller, so to speak. Technological advances have hastened the spread of the gospel, making it easier than ever before to take Christ to the world. Consequently, every believer is becoming more and more responsible for the souls in foreign fields.

> And he said to them, "Follow me, and I will make you fishers of men." (Mt.4:19)

> "But when the grain is ripe, at once he puts in the sickle, because the harvest has come." (Mk.4:29)

> And he said to them, "The harvest is plentiful, but the laborers are few. Therefore pray earnestly to the Lord of the harvest to send out laborers into his harvest." (Lu.10:2)

> "You did not choose me, but I chose you and appointed you that you should go and bear fruit and that your fruit [souls] should abide, so that whatever you ask the Father in my name, he may give it to you." (Jn.15:16)

> Do not be conformed to this world, but be transformed by the renewal of your mind, that by testing you may discern what is the will of God, what is good and acceptable and perfect. (Ro.12:2)

> For the one who sows to his own flesh will from the flesh reap corruption, but the one who sows to the Spirit will from the Spirit reap eternal life. And let us not grow weary of doing good, for in due season we will reap, if we do not give up. (Ga.6:8-9)

> Those who sow in tears shall reap with shouts of joy! He who goes out weeping, bearing the seed for sowing, shall come home with shouts of joy, bringing his sheaves with him. (Ps.126:5-6)

> The fruit of the righteous is a tree of life, and whoever captures souls is wise. (Pr.11:30)

## 4:36-38

<sup>36</sup> "Already the one who reaps is receiving wages and gathering fruit for eternal life, so that sower and reaper may rejoice together. <sup>37</sup> For here the saying holds true, 'One sows and another reaps.' <sup>38</sup> I sent you to reap that for which you did not labor. Others have labored, and you have entered into their labor."

## 3 Labor—for there are rewards and great benefits.

God is just and righteous. He promises us that we will not forget our labors for Him (He.6:10). He rewards us graciously and generously for our faithful service. Christ mentioned six particular rewards and benefits for laboring in God's fields.

### a. You receive wages (v.36a).

The laborer will receive wages. God is going to pay His faithful servants and pay them well. Note that the wages are *already* there, ready to be paid (see note, *Rewards*—Mt.20:8-16; Lu.16:10-12; see also Lu.10:7; 2 Ti.2:6).

> "And everyone who has left houses or brothers or sisters or father or mother or children or lands, for my name's sake, will receive a hundredfold and will inherit eternal life." (Mt.19:29)

> "His master said to him, 'Well done, good and faithful servant. You have been faithful over a little; I will set you over much. Enter into the joy of your master.'" (Mt.25:23)

> "And those who are wise shall shine like the brightness of the sky above; and those who turn many to righteousness, like the stars forever and ever." (Da.12:3)

b. **You have an eternal impact (v.36b).**

God's laborers gather fruit for *eternal life*. What we do is of supreme value. It is the greatest work imaginable. Our work is lasting; it endures forever. It affects people for eternity. Our work actually delivers people from *ever* perishing, and it leads to them receiving God's gift of abundant and eternal life.

> "For God so loved the world, that he gave his only Son, that whoever believes in him should not perish but have eternal life." (Jn.3:16)

> Whoever believes in the Son has eternal life; whoever does not obey the Son shall not see life, but the wrath of God remains on him. (Jn.3:36)

c. **You rejoice with other believers (v.36c).**

When we serve the Lord, we experience the overflowing joy of serving God with other devoted laborers (see note, *Joy*—Ph.1:4). Note that there is no envy or conflict between the two laborers. Both laborers—the sower and the reaper—work and rejoice together. (How different from so many!)

> "And when he comes home, he calls together his friends and his neighbors, saying to them, 'Rejoice with me, for I have found my sheep that was lost.' Just so, I tell you, there will be more joy in heaven over one sinner who repents than over ninety-nine righteous persons who need no repentance." (Lu.15:6-7)

> For what is our hope or joy or crown of boasting before our Lord Jesus at his coming? Is it not you? For you are our glory and joy. (1 Th.2:19-20)

> He who goes out weeping, bearing the seed for sowing, shall come home with shouts of joy, bringing his sheaves with him. (Ps.126:6)

d. **You receive the privilege of a specific part in God's great work (v.37).**

The laborer is given the privilege of having a specific part in God's great work. It may be sowing; it may be reaping. It does not matter. It is God's work, and it is an honor for us to have a part in it.

Note something else. Each individual has only a part. No one person does it all. One sows, and another reaps. The task is too great for one individual. All are needed. The task of every worker is critical to the work. If the sower fails to sow, the reaper cannot reap. Some soul is not fed enough to grow to maturity. If the reaper does not reap, the soul ripened by the sower passes its usefulness: it rots and falls to the ground and decays.

> I planted, Apollos watered, but God gave the growth. So neither he who plants nor he who waters is anything, but only God who gives the growth. He who plants and he who waters are one, and each will receive his wages according to his labor. (1 Co.3:6-8)

e. **You receive the privilege of being sent forth by Christ (v.38a).**

Jesus said, "*I* sent you." We have been chosen and sent by Christ, the Son of God Himself. What a privilege it is to be selected by Christ Himself and to serve Him!

> "You did not choose me, but I chose you and appointed you that you should go and bear fruit and that your fruit should abide, so that whatever you ask the Father in my name, he may give it to you." (Jn.15:16.)

f. **You receive the privilege of serving with other great servants of God (v.38b).**

We are given another glorious privilege: serving with other great servants of the Lord. Other devoted believers are laboring, and each servant enters into the labors of all others. (What a challenge to pray for all of God's servants and to get to the task of either sowing or reaping, whichever God has called us to do!)

> For we are God's fellow workers. You are God's field, God's building. According to the grace of God given to me, like a skilled master builder I laid a foundation, and someone else is building upon it. Let each one take care how he builds upon it. For no one can lay a foundation other than that which is laid, which is Jesus Christ. (1 Co.3:9-11)

## 4:39-42

³⁹ Many Samaritans from that town believed in him because of the woman's testimony, "He told me all that I ever did."
⁴⁰ So when the Samaritans came to him, they asked him to stay with them, and he stayed there two days.
⁴¹ And many more believed because of his word.
⁴² They said to the woman, "It is no longer because of what you said that we believe, for we have heard for ourselves, and we know that this is indeed the Savior of the world."

## 4 Labor—for results follow.

Scripture promises us again and again that our labors are not in vain. We *will* see fruit for our labor, for results do follow (see 1 Co.15:58; Ga.6:9; Ps.126:6). The results of the Samaritan woman's labors give a picture of exactly what Christ had been saying about laboring for God.

a. **Many believed the woman's testimony (v.39).**
Many believed in Christ because of the woman's testimony. The seed of salvation had been sown in the woman's heart by the prophets of old and through the first five books of Scripture (see vv.12, 19-20). Jesus reaped her soul. She in turn went and bore her testimony within the city. The result: many believed after she shared her story of what Jesus had done for her.

b. **Other opportunities were created (v.40).**
Other opportunities were created because of the woman's faithful witness; The new believers begged Christ to stay with them. They wanted to learn more, and they had friends who needed to hear Him as well.

> Since we have the same spirit of faith according to what has been written, "I believed, and so I spoke," we also believe, and so we also speak. (2 Co.4:13)

> Then those who feared the Lord spoke with one another. The Lord paid attention and heard them, and a book of remembrance was written before him of those who feared the Lord and esteemed his name. (Mal.3:16)

c. **Many more believed: "This man really is the Savior of the world" (vv.41-42).**
The fruit of the woman's testimony contained seed for even more fruit. Those she won to Christ led others to Christ. Many more believed that Jesus was the Christ, the Savior of the world (see Deeper Study # 1; Deeper Study # 2—Jn.1:20).

**Thought 1.** This is exactly how the Great Commission will be fulfilled. We are to share Christ with others, who share Christ with others, who share Christ with others . . . and it never stops. *Multiplication* is Christ's plan for taking the gospel to the ends of the earth. If each of us faithfully does our part, results will follow. The field—the world—will be harvested, and untold millions will believe and be rescued from hell.

> "You did not choose me, but I chose you and appointed you that you should go and bear fruit and that your fruit should abide, so that whatever you ask the Father in my name, he may give it to you." (Jn.15:16)

> "But you will receive power when the Holy Spirit has come upon you, and you will be my witnesses in Jerusalem and in all Judea and Samaria, and to the end of the earth." (Ac.1:8)

> Therefore, my beloved brothers, be steadfast, immovable, always abounding in the work of the Lord, knowing that in the Lord your labor is not in vain. (1 Co.15:58)

> And let us not grow weary of doing good, for in due season we will reap, if we do not give up. (Gal.6:9)

> He who goes out weeping, bearing the seed for sowing, shall come home with shouts of joy, bringing his sheaves with him. (Ps.126:6)

## Deeper Study # 1

(4:42) **Jesus Christ, Savior**: the word *Savior* (soter) means a Deliverer, a Preserver. It has the idea of a Deliverer, a Savior who snatches a person from some terrible disaster that leads to perishing (see Jn.3:16; also Deeper Study # 6—Mt.1:21 for more discussion).

1. Jesus Christ is said to be the Savior (Lu.2:11; Jn.4:42; Ac.5:31; 13:23; Ep.5:23; Ph.3:20; 2 Ti.1:10; Tit.1:4; 2:13; 3:6; 2 Pe.1:1, 11; 2:20; 3:2, 18; 1 Jn.4:14).

2. God is said to be the Savior (Lu.1:47; 1 Ti.1:1; 2:3; 4:10; Tit.1:3; 2:10; 3:4; Jude 25).

## V. The Revelation of Jesus, the Object of Faith, 4:43-54

### A. The Evidence of Faith, 4:43-45

1. The setting: Jesus entered Galilee[DS1]

2. The first evidence of faith: Honoring Jesus

3. The second evidence of faith: Welcoming & receiving Jesus

⁴³ After the two days he departed for Galilee. ⁴⁴ (For Jesus himself had testified that a prophet has no honor in his own hometown.) ⁴⁵ So when he came to Galilee, the Galileans welcomed him, having seen all that he had done in Jerusalem at the feast. For they too had gone to the feast.

## Division V

### The Revelation of Jesus, the Object of Faith, 4:43-54

A. The Evidence of Faith, 4:43-45

### 4:43-45 Introduction

One of the great lessons of the gospel is presented in this scene from the ministry of Christ. That lesson—simple, but ever so critical—is the evidence of faith. From the very beginning of our relationship with God, genuine faith has evidence. That evidence was displayed by the Galileans. This is, *The Evidence of Faith*, 4:43-45.

1. The setting: Jesus entered Galilee (v.43).
2. The first evidence of faith: Honoring Jesus (v.44).
3. The second evidence of faith: Welcoming and receiving Jesus (v.45).

**4:43**

⁴³ After the two days he departed for Galilee.

### 1 The setting: Jesus entered Galilee.

After spending two days with the Samaritans, Jesus entered Galilee. He had experienced great success in His brief ministry in Samaria; many had believed in Him. However, Galilee was the area especially prepared by God for the Lord's ministry, so Jesus returned to the area where most of His ministry was to be conducted (see DEEPER STUDY # 1).

#### DEEPER STUDY # 1

(4:43) **Galilee**: the district of Galilee was the northernmost part of Palestine. Palestine was divided into three districts: Judea in the far south, Samaria in the middle, and Galilee in the north. God had prepared Galilee down through history for His Son's eventual earthly ministry. Several facts show this (see Ga.4:4).

1. Throughout history Galilee had been invaded and repopulated again and again with different people and cultures from all over the world. Over the years such an influx of differing cultures had created an atmosphere susceptible to new personalities and ideas.

2. Galilee was strategically located. The world's leading roads passed right through its borders. Merchants from all over the world passed through and boarded in the inns of the cities.

3. Galilee was heavily populated. It was also surrounded by the Samaritans, Phoenicians, and Syrians, making it an open door for world evangelization. It was one of the most fertile lands in that part of the world. This fact, in addition to the region being a hub for business travelers, led scores of people to settle within its borders. The district held over two hundred cities with a population of fifteen thousand people or more,[1] resulting in multitudes for Jesus to reach.

4. Galilee was open to new and fresh ideas. Its people, having come from all over the world, were open-minded, always looking for new and fresh ideas to stimulate and challenge their thinking.

It was for these reasons that Jesus chose Galilee to begin His ministry. International commerce and a melting pot of cultures and ideas presented an open door for people to spread the news that the Messiah had come and that the kingdom of heaven was being ushered in.

## 2 The first evidence of faith: Honoring Jesus. 4:44

The first evidence of the Galileans' faith is seen in their honoring of Jesus. When Jesus went to Galilee, He stayed away from His hometown of Nazareth. His neighbors and fellow citizens had rejected Him and had attempted to kill Him (Lu.4:29). As a result, Jesus had declared that no prophet is accepted in his own country (Lu.4:24).

[44] (For Jesus himself had testified that a prophet has no honor in his own hometown.)

- Joseph was not honored by his brothers (Ge.37:23-36).
- David was not honored by his brother (1 S.17:28).
- Jeremiah was not honored in his hometown, Anathoth (Je.11:21; see Je.1:1).
- Paul was not honored by his countrymen (Ac.9:23-24; see note—2 Co.1:12-22).
- Jesus was not honored by His hometown (Mk.6:1-6).

Now, as Jesus returned to Galilee, bypassing the city of Nazareth, John referred to Jesus' statement that a prophet has no honor in His own homeland—the place where He grew up.

No doubt, Jesus' heart was broken over His hometown. They were a special people to Him: He had played with some of them as a child, grown up with them, lived as a friend with them; and had fellowshipped, worked, eaten, and moved among them day in and day out. The thought of their rejection and hostility toward Him often preyed upon His mind (see outline and notes—Mk.6:1-6 for discussion of their rejection).

Jesus' statement served to prepare the disciples for persecution. They were to be severely persecuted by their fellow countrymen. He discussed this fact time and again to drive it into their minds. He wanted them prepared and not caught off guard when persecution came.

A sharp contrast is being drawn between the refusal of Nazareth to honor Jesus and the receiving of Him by other Galileans. The first evidence that a person has faith is that he or she honors Jesus.

Jesus is due honor. He is due all the honor and glory in the universe. He is the Son of God who brought God's presence to the people of the world.

> "Behold, the virgin shall conceive and bear a son, and they shall call his name Immanuel" (which means, God with us). (Mt.1:23)
>
> And the Word became flesh and dwelt among us, and we have seen his glory, glory as of the only Son from the Father, full of grace and truth. (Jn.1:14)

---

1 Josephus. Quoted by William Barclay in *The Gospel of Matthew*, Vol.1. "The Daily Study Bible." (Philadelphia, PA: The Westminster Press, 1956), p.66.

He is the Savior of the world who came to save us from perishing and made it possible for us to live forever (see Deeper Study # 1—Jn.4:42).

> "For God so loved the world, that he gave his only Son, that whoever believes in him should not perish but have eternal life." (Jn.3:16)

> "The God of our fathers raised Jesus, whom you killed by hanging him on a tree. God exalted him at his right hand as Leader and Savior, to give repentance to Israel and forgiveness of sins." (Ac.5:30-31)

He is the Son of Man who came to earth to experience all the trials of life that He might feel and be touched by our infirmities and thereby become qualified to help us in all our suffering.

> "Even as the Son of Man came not to be served but to serve, and to give his life as a ransom for many." (Mt.20:28)

> For we do not have a high priest who is unable to sympathize with our weaknesses, but one who in every respect has been tempted as we are, yet without sin. Let us then with confidence draw near to the throne of grace, that we may receive mercy and find grace to help in time of need. (He.4:15-16)

People who believe in Jesus honor Him. Honoring Jesus is a clear evidence of faith. *Honor* (Gk. timen) means to value, esteem, respect. It has three ideas that are significant.

First, it conveys the idea of superior standing, exaltation, distinction, homage, reverence, and, of course, worship when referring to the Son of God.

> Therefore God has highly exalted him and bestowed on him the name that is above every name, so that at the name of Jesus every knee should bow, in heaven and on earth and under the earth, and every tongue confess that Jesus Christ is Lord, to the glory of God the Father. (Ph.2:9-11)

Second, there is the idea of a price paid or received, of credit due, of counting something of extreme value. Jesus is due the payment of our lives. True honor pays the price due to the Lord: those who honor the Lord give their lives to Him (see note, *Self-denial*—Lu.9:23).

> "Who, on finding one pearl of great value, went and sold all that he had and bought it." (Mt.13:46)

> Or do you not know that your body is a temple of the Holy Spirit within you, whom you have from God? You are not your own, for you were bought with a price. So glorify God in your body. (1 Co.6:19-20)

> To this end we always pray for you, that our God may make you worthy of his calling and may fulfill every resolve for good and every work of faith by his power, so that the name of our Lord Jesus may be glorified in you, and you in him, according to the grace of our God and the Lord Jesus Christ. (2 Th.1:11-12)

Third, the idea of preciousness is expressed. The Greek word for *precious* (timay) means *to be due honor, to be of precious value.*

> Indeed, I count everything as loss because of the surpassing worth of knowing Christ Jesus my Lord. For his sake I have suffered the loss of all things and count them as rubbish, in order that I may gain Christ (Ph.3:8)

> So the honor is for you who believe, but for those who do not believe, "The stone that the builders rejected has become the cornerstone." (1 Pe.2:7)

People who do not believe in Jesus do not honor Him. This is particularly seen in the dishonor of Jesus by His fellow citizens and the religious leaders (see outline and notes—Mk.6:1-6; Lu.4:16-30; Deeper Study # 2—Jn.5:15-16). Unbelievers . . .

- do not give Christ the worship, exaltation, or reverence due His name
- do not pay the price of surrendering their life to Christ as Lord
- do not count Christ as precious (due honor). Jesus' fellow citizens demonstrate this fact. He, the very Prophet of God Himself, had no honor in His own country

> "'For this people's heart has grown dull, and with their ears they can barely hear, and their eyes they have closed, lest they should see with their eyes and hear with their ears and understand with their heart and turn, and I would heal them.'" (Mt.13:15)

> "I have come in my Father's name, and you do not receive me. If another comes in his own name, you will receive him. How can you believe, when you receive glory from one another and do not seek the glory that comes from the only God?" (Jn.5:43-44)

> "The one who rejects me and does not receive my words has a judge; the word that I have spoken will judge him on the last day." (Jn.12:48)

## 3 The second evidence of faith: Welcoming and receiving Jesus.

The second evidence of faith is welcoming and receiving Jesus. The only way to be saved and to receive the benefits of Jesus' presence is to welcome and receive Him. Common sense tells us that a person who does not *have* the presence of Jesus Christ does not have the *blessings* of Jesus' presence. Jesus is simply not there to bless and care for that person. However, the Galileans were indeed experiencing the presence of Jesus. They were receiving the benefits of Jesus' life and ministry, and they were receiving His blessings for three very specific reasons.

> ⁴⁵ So when he came to Galilee, the Galileans welcomed him, having seen all that he had done in Jerusalem at the feast. For they too had gone to the feast.

First, they had heard the Lord preach and had seen His marvelous works in Jerusalem at the Passover Feast. The citizens of Jerusalem had been Jesus' focus there, not the Galileans. However, the Galileans had not felt slighted, not to the point that they shut Him out and refused to listen when He came to minister to them in their own territory. They were attracted to Him, for their souls were reaching out for God. Therefore, they attended His preaching and observed His ministry. They opened their hearts to what He was saying about repentance and receiving the kingdom of God (see note—Mk.1:14-15).

> **THOUGHT 1.** People can never be led to believe in Christ *until* they are receptive to Christ. In other words, they *must be willing* to listen to the message of Christ.
>
>> "But blessed are your eyes, for they see, and your ears, for they hear." (Mt.13:16)
>>
>> Now these Jews were more noble than those in Thessalonica; they received the word with all eagerness, examining the Scriptures daily to see if these things were so. (Ac.17:11)
>>
>> And we also thank God constantly for this, that when you received the word of God, which you heard from us, you accepted it not as the word of men but as what it really is, the word of God, which is at work in you believers. (1 Th.2:13)
>>
>> Know this, my beloved brothers: let every person be quick to hear, slow to speak, slow to anger. (Js.1:19)
>>
>> "Blessed is the one who listens to me, watching daily at my gates, waiting beside my doors." (Pr.8:34)
>>
>> Guard your steps when you go to the house of God. To draw near to listen is better than to offer the sacrifice of fools, for they do not know that they are doing evil. (Ec.5:1)

Second, they were a people seeking and worshiping God. Note why they had been to Jerusalem. They had gone to seek and worship God at the Passover, and it had cost them. The journey was long and difficult, for they lived in the northernmost part of Palestine, whereas the temple was in Jerusalem, much further south. Also, they had to take a circular route because Samaria lay between Galilee and Jerusalem, and the Samaritans considered them enemies, posing a threat to the Galileans' safety.

Obviously, these Galileans had a hunger for God; therefore, their hearts were better prepared and willing to receive Christ.

> **THOUGHT 1.** A person who *sincerely* seeks God is better prepared to receive Christ. For this reason, people should be constantly seeking after God. Seeking God and receiving Christ are evidences of true faith (He.11:6).
>
>> And without faith it is impossible to please him, for whoever would draw near to God must believe that he exists and that he rewards those who seek him. (He.11:6)
>>
>> "But from there you will seek the LORD your God and you will find him, if you search after him with all your heart and with all your soul." (De.4:29)
>>
>> "Seek the LORD while he may be found; call upon him while he is near." (Is.55:6)

Finally, the Galileans welcomed and received Christ. They wanted to experience Christ for themselves. They had seen Him preach and minister in Jerusalem, and they wanted the same experience for themselves and for the rest of their people. Of course, some Galileans did not receive Him into their lives and hearts. They deserted Him (see Jn.6:66). But all who received Him, all who believed in His name, became the children of God (see note —Jn.1:12–13.)

**THOUGHT 2.** Welcoming, receiving, and experiencing Christ for oneself is the greatest evidence of genuine faith.

> "As for that in the good soil, they are those who, hearing the word, hold it fast in an honest and good heart, and bear fruit with patience." (Lu.8:15)

> "'Behold, I stand at the door and knock. If anyone hears my voice and opens the door, I will come in to him and eat with him, and he with me.'" (Re.3:20)

## B. The Stages of Faith, 4:46-54

⁴⁶ So he came again to Cana in Galilee, where he had made the water wine. And at Capernaum there was an official whose son was ill.

⁴⁷ When this man heard that Jesus had come from Judea to Galilee, he went to him and asked him to come down and heal his son, for he was at the point of death.

⁴⁸ So Jesus said to him, "Unless you see signs and wonders you will not believe."

⁴⁹ The official said to him, "Sir, come down before my child dies."

⁵⁰ Jesus said to him, "Go; your son will live." The man believed the word that Jesus spoke to him and went on his way.

⁵¹ As he was going down, his servants met him and told him that his son was recovering.

⁵² So he asked them the hour when he began to get better, and they said to him, "Yesterday at the seventh hour the fever left him."

⁵³ The father knew that was the hour when Jesus had said to him, "Your son will live." And he himself believed, and all his household.

⁵⁴ This was now the second sign that Jesus did when he had come from Judea to Galilee.

1. **A beginning faith**
   a. He had a desperate need
   b. He heard about Jesus
   c. He came to Jesus
   d. He begged Jesus to help

2. **A persistent faith**
   a. A lesson in faith: What is essential is not miracles but believing in Jesus' word
   b. A desperate insistence: He believed that Jesus could help him

3. **A trusting, obedient, & working faith**
   a. The promise: Your need is met
   b. The result: He believed & obeyed Jesus' Word

4. **A confirmed faith**
   a. He was on the way home
   b. He received glorious news: His prayer was answered
   c. He confirmed that a supernatural miracle had happened & not a natural healing
   d. He believed & knew that Jesus had healed his son

5. **A witnessing faith: He shared his encounter with Christ with his household**

# Division V

## The Revelation of Jesus, the Object of Faith, 4:43-54

B. The Stages of Faith, 4:46-54

### 4:46-54
### Introduction

Many people do not truly understand what biblical faith is. They think it is something we feel, a mere emotion. But genuine faith is far more than a feeling. True faith compels us to act, to do something, to obey the Lord. Scripture states unequivocally that faith without works is dead (Js.2:17). This passage in John's Gospel tells us the story of a man who illustrates this truth. He was a government official who likely held some high position in Herod's court. His experience reveals the various stages of faith, the kind of growing faith that every person should experience. This is, *The Stages of Faith*, 4:46-54.

1. A beginning faith (vv.46-47).
2. A persistent faith (vv.48-49).
3. A trusting, obedient, and working faith (v.50).
4. A confirmed faith (vv.51-53).
5. A witnessing faith: He shared his encounter with Christ with his household (vv.53-54).

## 4:46-47

⁴⁶ So he came again to Cana in Galilee, where he had made the water wine. And at Capernaum there was an official whose son was ill.

⁴⁷ When this man heard that Jesus had come from Judea to Galilee, he went to him and asked him to come down and heal his son, for he was at the point of death.

## 1 A beginning faith.

The first stage of faith is a beginning faith. When Jesus entered the city of Cana, an *official* or *nobleman* (Gk. basilixos), a high-ranking officer of the king's royal court, approached Jesus. This man's actions demonstrate exactly what is involved in a beginning faith.

### a. He had a desperate need (v.46).

The royal official had a desperate need. His son was gravely ill, at the point of death.

**THOUGHT 1.** Needs confront every human being. Eventually the severe needs arising from accident, illness, disease, suffering, and death strike everyone. No one is exempt. One may be an official in government or even the king himself—it does not matter. The day eventually comes when each of us needs help. The severe disasters of life are beyond any person's control.

### b. He heard about Jesus (v.47a).

The desperate man heard about Jesus, and he heard that Jesus had come to Galilee. He listened attentively to what he heard. He did not . . .

- turn a deaf ear to the message
- think himself too important
- consider the message to be foolish
- mock the person sharing about Jesus

### c. He came to Jesus (v.47b).

Facing one of the severe disasters of life, the man came to Jesus. Jesus was the only person he had ever heard about that might be able to help. Going to Jesus required the man to pay a price. He had to make some sacrifices. First, he had had to leave the side of his dying son, knowing he would be gone for many hours. Imagine the anxiety and fear that his son might die while he was away. The man would literally have to tear himself away from his son. Such an act shows how strongly he believed that Jesus could help him.

The man also had to travel almost a day's journey to reach Jesus. Capernaum was about twenty miles from Cana. Imagine the concern and apprehension gripping the father's heart every foot of the way, wondering if he should have left his son's side. The fact that he *persevered* and kept his eyes on the hope of Jesus shows his genuine faith.

> Be strong, and let your heart take courage, all you who wait for the LORD! (Ps.31:24)
>
> Behold, the eye of the LORD is on those who fear him, on those who hope in his steadfast love. (Ps.33:18)
>
> "And now, O Lord, for what do I wait? My hope is in you." (Ps.39:7)
>
> "Blessed is the man who trusts in the LORD, whose trust is the LORD." (Je.17:7)

The man did not let his high position keep him from Jesus. He did not wrap himself in pride nor did he allow what others might say to keep him from Jesus. Swallowing his pride, he confessed his need in the face of all who ridiculed him, and he went to Jesus.

"When he calls to me, I will answer him; I will be with him in trouble; I will rescue him and honor him." (Ps.91:15)

"Then you shall call, and the LORD will answer; you shall cry, and he will say, 'Here I am.' If you take away the yoke from your midst, the pointing of the finger, and speaking wickedness." (Is.58:9)

"Call to me and I will answer you, and will tell you great and hidden things that you have not known." (Je.33:3)

**d. He begged Jesus to help (v.47c).**

The Greek word for *asked* (erota) indicates something far more intense than a simple request. The man literally *begged* Jesus to come and help his son. The tense of the word indicates continuous action: he kept on begging Jesus to meet his need.

## 2 A persistent faith.

The second stage of faith is a persistent faith. When Jesus did not at first grant the man's urgent request, he did not back down. He continued to beg Jesus to help his dying boy.

⁴⁸ So Jesus said to him, "Unless you see signs and wonders you will not believe."
⁴⁹ The official said to him, "Sir, come down before my child dies."

**a. A lesson in faith: What is essential is not miracles but believing in Jesus' word (v.48).**

The desperate father begged Jesus to come to Capernaum and heal his son (v.47). But Jesus had an important lesson to teach the man. Our omniscient Lord knew what was in the man's heart: if Jesus miraculously healed the official's son, he would believe. But Jesus wanted the man to realize that *His Word alone* was enough. *Belief in His Word* was what was going to assure an answer to the request. Christ's power was at the nobleman's disposal if he would just believe Him. Belief is to precede signs and wonders.

Note that the word "you" in verse 48 is plural. Jesus was addressing both the man and the crowd. He wanted the crowd to get the message as well (see DEEPER STUDY # 1—Jn.2:23; DEEPER STUDY # 2—2:24).

**b. A desperate insistence: He believed that Jesus could help him (v.49).**

The man was in no position to argue, not even to think through what Jesus had just said. He was desperate. A severe crisis had descended upon his family. He believed Jesus was the only One who could help him, and he was determined to secure Jesus' help. He cried out to Jesus to come to Capernaum immediately before his boy died.

Note the man's persistence. He did not allow Jesus' rebuke to deter him, and he continued to plead with Jesus until the Lord helped him.

**THOUGHT 1.** The lessons from these verses are crucial for us today. First, we need to grasp the truth that the Lord responds to our faith (He.11:6). Signs and wonders (the boy's healing) were not as important as *believing Jesus*. A man's eternal salvation was at stake, and the man had to believe to be saved.

Second, we need to persist in prayer until the Lord answers (Lk.11:8-9; 18:1-8). The man was helped because he persisted. Persistence was absolutely necessary in securing the Lord's help. Persistence shows that we really recognize and acknowledge our need, and that we truly believe God can and will help. If we cease to ask, we show that we do not believe God will answer. We give up on God, disbelieving Him. This man did not allow the Lord's hesitation to stop him.

> "I tell you, though he will not get up and give him anything because he is his friend, yet because of his impudence he will rise and give him whatever he needs. And I tell you, ask, and it will be given to you; seek, and you will find; knock, and it will be opened to you. For everyone who asks receives, and the one who seeks finds, and to the one who knocks it will be opened." (Lu.11:8-10)

> And he told them a parable to the effect that they ought always to pray and not lose heart. He said, "In a certain city there was a judge who neither feared God nor respected man. And there was a widow in that city who kept coming to him and saying, 'Give me justice against

my adversary.' For a while he refused, but afterward he said to himself, 'Though I neither fear God nor respect man, yet because this widow keeps bothering me, I will give her justice, so that she will not beat me down by her continual coming.'" And the Lord said, "Hear what the unrighteous judge says. And will not God give justice to his elect, who cry to him day and night? Will he delay long over them? I tell you, he will give justice to them speedily. Nevertheless, when the Son of Man comes, will he find faith on earth?" (Lu.18:1-8)

And without faith it is impossible to please him, for whoever would draw near to God must believe that he exists and that he rewards those who seek him. (He.11:6)

The LORD redeems the life of his servants; none of those who take refuge in him will be condemned. (Ps.34:22)

"Trust in the LORD forever, for the LORD GOD is an everlasting rock." (Is.26:4)

"You will seek me and find me, when you seek me with all your heart." (Je.29:13)

## 4:50

⁵⁰ Jesus said to him, "Go; your son will live." The man believed the word that Jesus spoke to him and went on his way.

### 3 A trusting, obedient, and working faith.

The third stage of faith is a trusting, obedient, working faith. When Jesus gave the official His word, the man believed Him, without actually seeing that his son had been healed. His faith was proven by his obedience to the Lord's command to go back to Capernaum.

a. **The promise: Your need is met.**

Jesus' response to the man's persistent faith was forceful. The Lord charged him to go back to Capernaum. Then, Christ made the desperate father a powerful, assuring promise: his son would live and not die.

b. **The result: He believed and obeyed Jesus' Word.**

The man believed Jesus' Word, and he obeyed the Lord's command to go on his way. His belief demonstrates *instantaneous* faith *and action*: he believed immediately and he turned immediately, heading home to his son. He *acted* on his faith. Note what he believed.

- The Lord's love, compassion, and concern: that Jesus cares for those who have a desperate need.
- The Lord's knowledge (omniscience): that Jesus knew his son was healed, although he was twenty miles away.
- The Lord's power (omnipotence): that Jesus had the power to heal his son, even from a great distance.
- The Lord's faithfulness to His Word: that Jesus will do what He promises.

Both faith and obedience were necessary to receive the promise and help of Jesus. The man would not have received Jesus' help if he had not *accepted and believed* the Word of the Lord or if he had rebelled and acted childishly. The man could have easily acted like so many when they bring their needs to God: "Your word is not good enough. My son is not healed. He is there in Capernaum and you are far away, *no place close* to him. How could he be helped with you so far away? Come, visit, *show yourself, stand before us*: help us." Such, of course, is pleading to God for help; but it is not crying to God in faith, not basing our request upon the Word and promise of Christ. It is asking God to help, but it is also dictating how God is to help. It is telling God how He is to act instead of *accepting and acting* upon His Word.

**THOUGHT 1.** There is no real faith apart from obedience and works (see DEEPER STUDY # 2—Jn.2:24; DEEPER STUDY # 1—He.5:9). Our faith is proved by our actions, not our words.

> But Jesus looked at them and said, "With man this is impossible, but with God all things are possible." (Mt.19:26)

> "Therefore I did not presume to come to you. But say the word, and let my servant be healed." (Lu.7:7)

When he saw them he said to them, "Go and show yourselves to the priests." And as they went they were cleansed. (Lu.17:14)

So also faith by itself, if it does not have works, is dead. But someone will say, "You have faith and I have works." Show me your faith apart from your works, and I will show you my faith by my works. (Js.2:17-18)

Trust in the LORD with all your heart, and do not lean on your own understanding. (Pr.3:5)

"You keep him in perfect peace whose mind is stayed on you, because he trusts in you. Trust in the LORD forever, for the LORD GOD is an everlasting rock." (Is.26:3-4)

## 4 A confirmed faith.

The fourth stage of faith is a confirmed faith. As the man was on his way home, his servants met him to tell him that his son was alive and well (v.51). He was in the act of *obeying Christ* when he received the glorious news that his prayer had been answered. Again, it was his believing the promise of Jesus and obeying Him that brought the blessing. Both belief and obedience were essential.

The ecstatic man confirmed that a supernatural miracle had occurred, and that his son's recovery was not a natural healing (v.52). He asked the exact hour the boy recovered. He wanted to be certain; he wanted absolute confirmation. He was reaching out for stronger faith in Jesus. He was so full of joy and thankfulness to Jesus that he wanted to believe in Him more and more. And when his servants told him the exact time of the boy's recovery, he believed fully in Christ and knew that Jesus had healed his son (v.53).

> ⁵¹ As he was going down, his servants met him and told him that his son was recovering.
> ⁵² So he asked them the hour when he began to get better, and they said to him, "Yesterday at the seventh hour the fever left him."
> ⁵³ The father knew that was the hour when Jesus had said to him, "Your son will live." And he himself believed, and all his household.

And Jesus answered them, "Have faith in God. Truly, I say to you, whoever says to this mountain, 'Be taken up and thrown into the sea,' and does not doubt in his heart, but believes that what he says will come to pass, it will be done for him. Therefore I tell you, whatever you ask in prayer, believe that you have received it, and it will be yours." (Mk.11:22-24)

"But even now I know that whatever you ask from God, God will give you." (Jn.11:22)

Consequently, he is able to save to the uttermost those who draw near to God through him, since he always lives to make intercession for them. (He.7:25)

Now faith is the assurance of things hoped for, the conviction of things not seen. (He.11:1)

"For I am the LORD; I will speak the word that I will speak, and it will be performed. It will no longer be delayed, but in your days, O rebellious house, I will speak the word and perform it, declares the Lord GOD." (Eze.12:25)

## 5 A witnessing faith: He shared his encounter with Christ with his household.

The fifth stage is a witnessing faith. The royal official's entire household—his family and servants—came to faith in Christ (v.53). Why? Because the grateful father told them about the experience, the word of promise and instructions Jesus had given. The man's *personal witness*—the witness of somebody they knew well and trusted—led them to salvation. They committed themselves fully to Jesus as the Messiah.

> ⁵³ The father knew that was the hour when Jesus had said to him, "Your son will live." And he himself believed, and all his household.
> ⁵⁴ This was now the second sign that Jesus did when he had come from Judea to Galilee.

Witnessing for Jesus was not easy for this man. He was a high official, moving about in the halls of a corrupt government and among immoral officials. He would definitely be facing ridicule and persecution, and perhaps loss of position and even loss of life. Regardless of the potential consequences, his faith was a witnessing faith. He loved Jesus for what Jesus had done for him, and he wanted others to know Jesus' glorious salvation.

**THOUGHT 1.** Each of us has relationships with people we love as well as with people we influence. We are to use our relationships with others to win them to the Lord. How can we *not* tell those we love—our family, friends, associates, neighbors—about Christ and His salvation? We should not expect preachers or churches to reach our loved ones. We should take personal responsibility for their souls, doing everything we can to rescue them from hell and reach them with the gospel.

> "In the same way, let your light shine before others, so that they may see your good works and give glory to your Father who is in heaven." (Mt.5:16)

> "Return to your home, and declare how much God has done for you." And he went away, proclaiming throughout the whole city how much Jesus had done for him. (Lu.8:39)

> Then he brought them out and said, "Sirs, what must I do to be saved?" And they said, "Believe in the Lord Jesus, and you will be saved, you and your household." (Ac.16:30–31)

> But in your hearts honor Christ the Lord as holy, always being prepared to make a defense to anyone who asks you for a reason for the hope that is in you; yet do it with gentleness and respect. (1 Pe.3:15)

# Chapter 5

## VI. The Revelation of Jesus, the Authority and Power Over Life, 5:1–47

### A. The Essential Authority: Power to Meet the World's Desperate Needs, 5:1–16

After this there was a feast of the Jews, and Jesus went up to Jerusalem. ² Now there is in Jerusalem by the Sheep Gate a pool, in Aramaic called Bethesda, which has five roofed colonnades. ³ In these lay a multitude of invalids—blind, lame, and paralyzed.

⁵ One man was there who had been an invalid for thirty-eight years. ⁶ When Jesus saw him lying there and knew that he had already been there a long time, he said to him, "Do you want to be healed?" ⁷ The sick man answered him, "Sir, I have no one to put me into the pool when the water is stirred up, and while I am going another steps down before me." ⁸ Jesus said to him, "Get up, take up your bed, and walk." ⁹ And at once the man was healed, and he took up his bed and walked. Now that day was the Sabbath.

¹⁰ So the Jews said to the man who had been healed, "It is the Sabbath, and it is not lawful for you to take up your bed." ¹¹ But he answered them, "The man who healed me, that man said to me, 'Take up your bed, and walk.'" ¹² They asked him, "Who is the man who said to you, 'Take up your bed and walk'?" ¹³ Now the man who had been healed did not know who it was, for Jesus had withdrawn, as there was a crowd in the place. ¹⁴ Afterward Jesus found him in the temple and said to him, "See, you are well! Sin no more, that nothing worse may happen to you."

1. Scene 1: Jesus & the Jewish feasts—a picture of reaching out to people
2. Scene 2: The diseased & the ill—a picture of the world's desperate need

   a. Humanity's desperate hope: Lying in a pool of water
   b. Humanity's desperate faith: Seeking for healing power in a worldly source, the pool of water

3. Scene 3: Jesus & the man—a picture of Jesus' power to meet the world's need

   a. The man's plight
   b. The Lord's compassion
      1) Saw his state
      2) Initiated a relationship
   c. The man's helplessness: He had no family & no friends to help him

   d. The Lord's power

   e. The sinister problem: Jesus healed the man on the Sabbath

4. Scene 4: The religious leaders & the man—a picture of dead religion trying to meet the world's need[DS1]

   a. A religion of legalism
   b. A religion ignorant of true authority, of the Messiah's true mission

   c. A religion blind to love & doing good

5. Scene 5: Jesus & the man after his healing—a picture of the believer's responsibility

   a. To worship in the temple
   b. To remember his healing
   c. To stop sinning
   d. To fear the judgment

6. **Scene 6: The religious leaders against Jesus—a picture of the world rejecting God's Son, the Savior**[DS2]
   a. The religious leaders heard of Jesus' work, v.15
   b. The religious leaders reacted & sought to kill Jesus

15 The man went away and told the Jews that it was Jesus who had healed him.

16 And this was why the Jews were persecuting Jesus, because he was doing these things on the Sabbath.

# Division VI

*The Revelation of Jesus, the Authority and Power Over Life, 5:1-47*

A. The Essential Authority: Power to Meet the World's Desperate Needs, 5:1-16

## 5:1-47
## DIVISION OVERVIEW

Chapter 5 reveals Jesus to be the Authority over all of life. He is due the same worship, obedience, and service as God; for He is equal with God, and He is God (Jn.5:17-18). As God possesses life within Himself, so Jesus possesses life within Himself (Jn.5:26). As God has authority over all of life, so Jesus has authority over all of life.

In revealing His authority, Jesus first demonstrated the truth of His authority. He healed a man who had been ill for thirty-eight years—and He healed him on the Sabbath. Both acts pictured the truth of His authority. The healing of the man revealed Jesus' authority over the physical world, and the breaking of the Jewish Sabbath law revealed His authority to determine the rules of worship. After demonstrating the truth of His equality with God, Jesus then began to teach the truth. This procedure, first demonstrating some truth and then teaching it, was to be followed time and again, as Jesus revealed who He was throughout the Gospel of John (see Chapters 6, 8).

## 5:1-16
## Introduction

Through this healing miracle, Jesus was claiming to have supreme authority over the Sabbath (see DEEPER STUDY # 1—Mt.12:1; see also Jn.5:9-10, 16, 18). However, there are other striking lessons: the Lord's compassion (vv.6-9), the problem of formal religion (vv.10-12), and the charge to a converted man (vv.13-14). This is, *The Essential Authority: Power to Meet the World's Desperate Needs*, 5:1-16.

1. Scene 1: Jesus and the Jewish feasts—a picture of reaching out to people (v.1).
2. Scene 2: The diseased and the ill—a picture of the world's desperate need (vv.2-4).
3. Scene 3: Jesus and the man—a picture of Jesus' power to meet the world's need (vv.5-9).
4. Scene 4: The religious leaders and the man—a picture of dead religion trying to meet the world's need (vv.10-12).
5. Scene 5: Jesus and the man after his healing—a picture of the believer's responsibility (vv.13-14).
6. Scene 6: The religious leaders against Jesus—a picture of the world rejecting God's Son, the Savior (vv.15-16).

# 1 Scene 1: Jesus and the Jewish feasts—a picture of reaching out to people.

Jesus attended a Jewish feast in Jerusalem. The feast is not named in Scripture, but it was probably one of the three Feasts of Obligation: the Passover, the Feast of Tabernacles, or Pentecost. These were called Feasts of Obligations because every male Jew who lived within twenty miles of Jerusalem was required by law to attend them. It is significant that Jesus was seen attending the feast.

> After this there was a feast of the Jews, and Jesus went up to Jerusalem.

5:1

Attending the feast gave Jesus an opportunity to reach a large number of people. Most of the people who attended the feast would be God-fearing people and have their minds upon God; therefore, they would be more prepared for the gospel. In addition, it gave Him an opportunity to teach people to be faithful to the worship of God. He, the Son of God Himself, was faithful, setting an example for others to follow.

> **THOUGHT 1.** If Jesus Himself, the Son of God, was faithful in worshiping God the Father, how much more should we be faithful in our worship of God?
>
> > And day by day, attending the temple together and breaking bread in their homes, they received their food with glad and generous hearts. (Ac.2:46)
> >
> > Not neglecting to meet together, as is the habit of some, but encouraging one another, and all the more as you see the Day drawing near. (He.10:25)
> >
> > "But you shall seek the place that the LORD your God will choose out of all your tribes to put his name and make his habitation there. There you shall go." (Dt.12:5)
> >
> > Ascribe to the LORD the glory due his name; bring an offering, and come into his courts! (Ps.96:8)

# 2 Scene 2: The diseased and the ill—a picture of the world's desperate need.

5:2-4

At Jerusalem, Jesus encountered a sad sight: a gathering of the diseased and the ill. The setting was a pool by a sheep gate. It may have been the entrance to a sheep market or sheep stall where the animals were kept. Whatever it was, there was a pool to provide water for the animals to drink and five porches to provide a resting area for the comfort of the people. This pool and a large number of disabled people lying around the pool were the focus of attention.

> ² Now there is in Jerusalem by the Sheep Gate a pool, in Aramaic called Bethesda, which has five roofed colonnades.
>
> ³ In these lay a multitude of invalids—blind, lame, and paralyzed.

a. Humanity's desperate hope: Lying in a pool of water (vv.2-3a).

Some of the sick people who gathered at the pool were blind. Others were lame or paralyzed. These handicapped people represent all in the world who live in desperate need, all who are blind, lame, or paralyzed spiritually.

> Remember that you were at that time separated from Christ . . . having no hope and without God in the world. (Ep.2:12)
>
> "I loathe my life; I will give free utterance to my complaint; I will speak in the bitterness of my soul." (Jb.10:1)
>
> For my life is spent with sorrow, and my years with sighing; my strength fails because of my iniquity, and my bones waste away. (Ps.31:10)
>
> And my God. My soul is cast down within me; therefore I remember you from the land of Jordan and of Hermon, from Mount Mizar. (Ps.42:6)

b. Humanity's desperate faith: Seeking for healing power in a worldly source, the pool of water (vv.3b-4).

The people believed that at certain times an angel came down and stirred up the water in the pool, and the first person who stepped into the water was healed. Some modern translations, including the English Standard Version (ESV), do not include these statements, as these statements do not appear in the earliest Greek manuscripts. However, the same translations do include verse 7, which refers back to the event related here.[1] It seems that there are three possible explanations for this description of the event:

➢ It is what actually happened and should be taken literally.
➢ It was the way that the people explained what caused the water to be stirred. If this is true, then there may have been a subterranean pocket of energy, either air or a stream underneath the pool that caused the pool to occasionally bubble up. The people of that day, grasping for something to help them in their daily lives, said that a supernatural occurrence was happening when the water bubbled. An angel was thought to be swimming around in the water.
➢ It was a superstitious tradition created by and perpetuated by hopeless, desperate people.

*The Bible Knowledge Commentary* states that, "the Bible nowhere teaches this kind of superstition, a situation which would be a most cruel contest for many ill people."[2] However, outstanding Bible teacher Warren Wiersbe reasons, "Why would anybody, especially a man sick for so many years, remain in one place if nothing special were occurring? . . . It seems wisest for us to accept the fact that something extraordinary kept all these handicapped people at this pool, hoping for a cure."[3]

Whatever the case, the gathering of disabled people at the pool reveals their desperate hope and faith. The hurting people were so desperate to be healed that they were willing to try anything. They were willing to spend their lives lying beside a pool with the hope that they *might* be healed.

**THOUGHT 1.** People are always grasping for something to help them in their daily lives. It may be some *supernatural or destined power* in a pool of water or in the astrology of stars above or in some magical person on earth. People never change, regardless of the generation. In their grasp for help in life, many continue to seek everywhere except in Christ, the Son of God Himself. They hope and put their faith in everything except Him.

There is a way that seems right to a man, but its end is the way to death. (Pr.14:12)

5:5–9

⁵ One man was there who had been an invalid for thirty-eight years.
⁶ When Jesus saw him lying there and knew that he had already been there a long time, he said to him, "Do you want to be healed?"
⁷ The sick man answered him, "Sir, I have no one to put me into the pool when the water is stirred up, and while I am going another steps down before me."
⁸ Jesus said to him, "Get up, take up your bed, and walk."
⁹ And at once the man was healed, and he took up his bed and walked. Now that day was the Sabbath.

## 3 Scene 3: Jesus and the man—a picture of Jesus' power to meet the world's need.

The One who has the power to meet the needs of the desperate passed by the pool. Scripture records Jesus' encounter with one man, a man with a heartbreaking plight (v.5). He was either paralyzed or lame, and he had been that way for thirty-eight *long* years.

Our merciful Savior had *compassion* on the pitiful man (v.6). Jesus' response was heart-warming, touching, and revealing—demonstrating how He wants to reach out to every person. He *saw* the man's state, saw him lying there and *knew* all about his desperate condition. A striking point in all this is that Jesus initiated a relationship with the man by approaching him and reaching out to help Him.

---

1 Stanley M. Horton, Ralph W. Harris, Thoralk Gilbrandt, eds., *The Complete Biblical Library Commentary, New Testament,* (Iowa Falls, IA: World Bible Publishers, 1992), Wordsearch digital edition.
2 Walvoord, Zuck, eds., *The Bible Knowledge Commentary,* Wordsearch digital edition.
3 Warren W. Wiersbe, *The Bible Exposition Commentary, Vol. 5, Matthew-Galatians* (Colorado Springs, CO: David C. Cook Publishers, 2002).

The man confessed his helplessness to Jesus. He had never made it into the water because he had no family or friends to help him (v.7). But Jesus did what nobody else could do for him: He deployed His unlimited power to heal the man, commanding him to get up and walk (v.8). The man obeyed the Lord's order, and he picked up his bed and walked (v.9a)!

Note a significant point: the man did not know he was healed until he obeyed the command of the Lord. Jesus did not pronounce a word of healing; He merely commanded the man to take action. Through this action the man would reveal his faith. If he believed, he would arise and walk; if he did not believe, he would simply lie there, continuing on just as he had always done (see Deeper Study # 2—Jn.2:24).

Jesus' miracle created a sinister problem: He had healed the man on the Sabbath (v.9b). By healing the man on the Sabbath, Jesus had violated the Jewish ceremonial law. Seemingly, he had committed a serious sin, violating a ritual and rule of religion. The rest of the man's story centers upon this fact.

**THOUGHT 1.** Jesus *sees* and *knows* every person's condition. He reaches out to every single one of us in compassion, offering help. He reaches out through . . .
- the message of the Word
- the witness of family or friends
- the beauty of nature
- the thoughts about God that penetrate every person's mind

> **Who shall separate us from the love [compassion] of Christ? Shall tribulation, or distress, or persecution, or famine, or nakedness, or danger, or sword? (Ro.8:35)**
>
> **For we do not have a high priest who is unable to sympathize with our weaknesses, but one who in every respect has been tempted as we are, yet without sin. (He.4:15)**
>
> **Casting all your anxieties on him, because he cares for you. (1 Pe.5:7)**
>
> **As a father shows compassion to his children, so the Lord shows compassion to those who fear him. (Ps.103:13)**
>
> **The steadfast love of the Lord never ceases; his mercies never come to an end. (Lam.3:22)**

**THOUGHT 2.** Nobody has to continue on and on through life just as they have always been, enslaved to the sin and corruption and desperate needs of the world. We can experience the healing power of Jesus Christ, the power to change our lives and make us into a new creation. All we have to do is one simple thing: believe the Word of Jesus Christ enough to obey, doing exactly what Jesus says. It is a clear fact: if we believe Him, we obey Him; if we do not believe Him, we do not obey Him. To be made whole and changed into a new creation—a new person who is freed from the sin and desperate needs of this corruptible world—we have to believe Him enough to obey Him (see note—Jn.4:50 for more verses of Scripture).

> **"For nothing will be impossible with God." (Lu.1:37)**
>
> **When he saw them he said to them, "Go and show yourselves to the priests." And as they went they were cleansed. (Lu.17:14)**
>
> **Therefore, if anyone is in Christ, he is a new creation. The old has passed away; behold, the new has come. (2 Co.5:17)**
>
> **And being made perfect, he became the source of eternal salvation to all who obey him. (He.5:9)**
>
> **So also faith by itself, if it does not have works, is dead. (Js.2:17)**

## 4 Scene 4: The religious leaders and the man—a picture of dead religion trying to meet the world's need.

Jewish authorities were outraged at Jesus' healing of the man on the Sabbath (see Deeper Study # 1). They interrogated the

¹⁰ So the Jews said to the man who had been healed, "It is the Sabbath, and it is not lawful for you to take up your bed."

¹¹ But he answered them, "The man who healed me, that man said to me, 'Take up your bed, and walk.'"

¹² They asked him, "Who is the man who said to you, 'Take up your bed and walk'?"

former cripple, seeking to find out who had violated their laws. The man and the miracle didn't matter; they cared only about their authority being challenged. This is a picture of dead religion trying to meet the world's desperate need.

### a. A religion of legalism (v.10).

Dead religion is a religion of legalism. The religious leaders were trying to meet the needs of people through rules and regulations, ceremony and rituals (see Deeper Study # 1—Lu.6:2; Deeper Study # 2—Jn.5:15-16). They were more concerned with the man who was violating the ritual of the Sabbath than with the man who was suffering in a pitiful condition.

### b. A religion ignorant of true authority, of the Messiah's true mission (v.11).

Dead religion is a religion ignorant of true authority. The Jewish leaders should have known that the power of God had healed the man, and they should have been eager to share Jesus with the man, since Jesus is where such power rested. But they cared little about the power of God and His messenger. They cared only that the status quo be maintained, that their religious practices continue as they were and not be violated. Their thoughts were upon their own religious position and security (see Deeper Study # 2—Jn.5:15-16).

### c. A religion blind to love and doing good (v.12).

Dead religion is a religion blind to love and good. Note the question of the religious leaders. It was not, "Who is the man who has healed and helped you so much?" but, "Who is the man that broke the religious law?" They did not see the good that had been done. They saw only that their position and security were threatened, that someone had more power and influence and was doing more good than they were.

**THOUGHT 1.** How many true messengers of God are criticized by powerless religious heads, criticized because they do things differently or do more good than others? Men fear the loss of their position and security, fear that people may begin to wonder about their lack of the true power that honestly helps other people.

> "And if you had known what this means, 'I desire mercy, and not sacrifice,' you would not have condemned the guiltless. For the Son of Man is lord of the Sabbath." (Mt.12:7-8)
>
> "And a second is like it: You shall love your neighbor as yourself." (Mt.22:39)
>
> And he said to them, "You have a fine way of rejecting the commandment of God in order to establish your tradition!" (Mk.7:9)
>
> Love does no wrong to a neighbor; therefore love is the fulfilling of the law. (Ro.13:10)
>
> They profess to know God, but they deny him by their works. They are detestable, disobedient, unfit for any good work. (Tit.1:16)
>
> By this we know love, that he laid down his life for us, and we ought to lay down our lives for the brothers. But if anyone has the world's goods and sees his brother in need, yet closes his heart against him, how does God's love abide in him? (1 Jn.3:16-17)

## Deeper Study # 1

(5:10) **Jews:** the Jews (Gk. Ioudaio) are spoken of some seventy times in the Gospels. They are always spoken of as the opposition to Jesus Christ—as those who set themselves against Him. They include some Pharisees, Sadducees, Scribes, priests, and secular leaders. They were the religious leaders who personally refused to believe Jesus Christ. They rejected both His claim to be the Son of God and His offer of salvation and eternal life (see Jn.1:10-11, 19; see also Deeper Study # 2; Subject Index).

# 5 Scene 5: Jesus and the man after his healing—a picture of the believer's responsibility.

Jesus left the man right after healing him because of the large crowd on the porches (v.13). For some unstated reason, Jesus did not want to attract a crowd at this time. But Jesus sought the man out again—a striking point! Remember, Jesus had reached out to save the man; now He was reaching out for another purpose. Upon finding this new believer, Jesus paints a picture of his new responsibility.

> [13] Now the man who had been healed did not know who it was, for Jesus had withdrawn, as there was a crowd in the place.
> [14] Afterward Jesus found him in the temple and said to him, "See, you are well! Sin no more, that nothing worse may happen to you."

### a. To worship in the temple (v.14a).

After being touched by Jesus, believers have a duty to worship. Jesus found the man in the temple worshiping and giving thanks to God.

> Not neglecting to meet together, as is the habit of some, but encouraging one another, and all the more as you see the Day drawing near. (He.10:25)

> Ascribe to the Lord the glory due his name; bring an offering and come before him! Worship the Lord in the splendor of holiness. (1 Chr.16:29)

> Blessed is the one you choose and bring near, to dwell in your courts! We shall be satisfied with the goodness of your house, the holiness of your temple! (Ps.65:4)

> Enter his gates with thanksgiving, and his courts with praise! Give thanks to him; bless his name! (Ps.100:4)

### b. To remember his healing (v.14b).

Jesus directed the man's attention to what He had done for him. We have a responsibility to remember what Christ has done for us, our salvation. The moment should never be forgotten or lost (see 2 Pe.1:9).

> Giving thanks always and for everything to God the Father in the name of our Lord Jesus Christ. (Ep.5:20)

> Giving thanks to the Father, who has qualified you to share in the inheritance of the saints in light. (Col.1:12)

> For whoever lacks these qualities is so nearsighted that he is blind, having forgotten that he was cleansed from his former sins. (2 Pe.1:9)

> "Only take care, and keep your soul diligently, lest you forget the things that your eyes have seen, and lest they depart from your heart all the days of your life. Make them known to your children and your children's children." (De.4:9)

### c. To stop sinning (v.14c).

Jesus charged the man to sin no more. It may be that the man had been lame or paralyzed because of some accident caused by sin. Upon saving us, Christ commands us to stop sinning. If we have truly repented, we will no longer desire to live in sin.

**THOUGHT 1.** How many are physically crippled or diseased because of some sin? Many suffer *crippling accidents and diseases* through poor choices related to drunkenness, immorality, disobeying laws, abusing our bodies, or a host of other self-harming sins.

> She said, "No one, Lord." And Jesus said, "Neither do I condemn you; go, and from now on sin no more." (Jn.8:11)

> Let not sin therefore reign in your mortal body, to make you obey its passions. (Ro.6:12)

> Wake up from your drunken stupor, as is right, and do not go on sinning. For some have no knowledge of God. I say this to your shame. (1 Co.15:34)

> "Wash yourselves; make yourselves clean; remove the evil of your deeds from before my eyes; cease to do evil." (Is.1:16)

### d. To fear the judgment (v.14d).

We should be gripped by the fear of God and his judgment. Jesus warned the man that if he did not turn from his sin, he would face a more terrible judgment than his crippling paralysis. Scripture warns believers of God's fatherly discipline, stating that some are sick and some even die prematurely because of their refusal to turn from sin.

> That is why many of you are weak and ill, and some have died. But if we judged ourselves truly, we would not be judged. But when we are judged by the Lord, we are disciplined so that we may not be condemned along with the world. (1 Co.11:30–32)

> And have you forgotten the exhortation that addresses you as sons? "My son, do not regard lightly the discipline of the Lord, nor be weary when reproved by him. For the Lord disciplines the one he loves, and chastises every son whom he receives." It is for discipline that you have to endure. God is treating you as sons. For what son is there whom his father does not discipline? If you are left without discipline, in which all have participated, then you are illegitimate children and not sons. Besides this, we have had earthly fathers who disciplined us and we respected them. Shall we not much more be subject to the Father of spirits and live? (He.12:5–9)

## 5:15-16

¹⁵ The man went away and told the Jews that it was Jesus who had healed him.
¹⁶ And this was why the Jews were persecuting Jesus, because he was doing these things on the Sabbath.

## 6 Scene 6: The religious leaders against Jesus—a picture of the work of God's Son, the Savior.

Upon learning that Jesus had healed the man on the Sabbath, the Jewish religious leaders began pursuing Jesus with a view to killing Him. This is a picture of the world rejecting God's Savior.

### a. The religious leaders heard of Jesus work (v.15).

The man told the Jewish authorities who had healed him. He did not do this to bring harm to Jesus. The religious leaders had asked him previously who had healed him on the Sabbath, and at that time, he did not know who Jesus was (vv.12-13). No doubt fearing retribution from the authorities, after the man realized who Jesus was, he went back to them with the answer to their question. In addition, he may have thought the religious leaders should know and would want to benefit from knowing Jesus personally.

### b. The religious leaders rejected and sought to kill Jesus (v.16).

The Jewish authorities responded to Jesus' healing on the Sabbath by persecuting Him. The reason they opposed Jesus so viciously needs to be studied closely (see DEEPER STUDY # 2; also see note—Jn.5:17-18 for discussion).

### DEEPER STUDY # 2

(5:15-16) **Religionist Rules and Regulations Opposed by Jesus:** breaking the Sabbath law was a serious matter to the Jew. Just how serious can be seen in the strict demands governing the Sabbath. Law after law was written to govern all activity on the Sabbath. A person could not travel, fast, cook, buy, sell, draw water, walk beyond a certain distance, lift anything, fight in a war, or heal on the Sabbath unless life was at stake. A person was not to contemplate any kind of work or activity. A good example of the legal restriction and the people's loyalty to it is seen in the women who witnessed Jesus' crucifixion. They would not even walk to His tomb to prepare the body for burial until the Sabbath was over (Mk.16:1f; Mt.28:1f).

It was a serious matter to break the Sabbath law. A person was condemned, and if the offense were serious enough, the person was put to death.

The leaders' conflict with Jesus over religious beliefs and rules is sometimes thought by modern people to be petty and harsh, or else such conflicts are just not understood. Three facts will help in understanding why the conflicts happened and were life-threatening, ending in the murder of Jesus Christ.

1. The Jewish nation had been held together by their religious beliefs. Through the centuries the Jewish people had been conquered by army after army, and by the millions they had been deported and scattered over the world. Even in the day of Jesus they were enslaved by Rome. Their religion was the *binding force* that kept Jews together, in particular...
- their belief that God had called them to be a distinctive people (who worshiped the only true and living God)
- their rules governing the Sabbath and the temple
- their laws governing intermarriage, worship, and cleansing
- their rules governing what foods they could and could not eat

Their religious beliefs and rules protected them from alien beliefs and from being swallowed up by other nationalities through intermarriage. Their religion was what maintained their distinctiveness as a people and as a nation. Jewish leaders knew this. They knew that *their religion was the binding force* that held their nation together. They therefore opposed anyone or anything that threatened or attempted to break the laws of their religion and nation.

2. Many of the religious leaders were men of deep, deep conviction, strong in their beliefs. Therefore, they became steeped in religious belief and practice, law and custom, tradition and ritual, ceremony and liturgy, rules and regulations. To break any law or rule governing any belief or practice was a serious offense, for it taught loose behavior. And loose behavior, once it had spread enough, would weaken their religion. Therefore, in their minds Jesus was committing a terrible offense by breaking their law. He was weakening their religion and threatening their nation.

3. The religious authorities were men who had profession, position, recognition, esteem, livelihood, and security. Anyone who went contrary to what they believed and taught was a threat to all they had. Some undoubtedly felt that Jesus was a threat to them. Every time Jesus broke their law, they felt He was undermining their very position and security (see notes—Mt.12:1-8; 16:1-12; 21:23; 22:15-22; 22:23-33; 22:34-40; 23:1-12).

The error of the Jewish religious leaders was fourfold.

1. They misinterpreted and corrupted God's Word (see notes—Mt.12:1-3; DEEPER STUDY # 1—Jn.4:22; cp. Ro.9:4).

2. They committed serious sin after sin in God's eyes (see notes—1 Th.2:15-16; see Ro.2:17-29).

3. They rejected God's way of righteousness, God's Messiah, who is Jesus Christ (see notes—Ro.11:28-29; 1 Th.2:15-16; see Ro.10:1-21, esp. 1-4, 19-21).

4. They allowed religion in its tradition and ritual, ceremony and rules to become more important than meeting the basic needs of human life: the need for God and the need for spiritual, mental, and physical health. Being the true Messiah, Jesus was bound to expose such error. Therefore, the battle lines were drawn.

The Messiah had to liberate people from such enslaving behavior. He had to liberate them so they could be saved and worship God in freedom of spirit.

The religious leaders had to oppose anyone who broke their law. They had to oppose Jesus because He was a threat to their nation and to their own personal position and security.

The religious leaders' attack took two forms.

1. First, they tried to discredit Jesus so the multitudes would stop following Him (see Mt.21:46).

> And a man was there with a withered hand. And they asked him, "Is it lawful to heal on the Sabbath?"—so that they might accuse him. (Mt.12:10)
>
> Then the Pharisees went and plotted how to entangle him in his words. And they sent their disciples to him, along with the Herodians, saying, "Teacher, we know that you are true and teach the way of God truthfully, and you do not care about anyone's opinion, for you are not swayed by appearances. Tell us, then, what you think. Is it lawful to pay taxes to Caesar, or not?" (Mt.22:15-17)

And the scribes and the Pharisees watched him, to see whether he would heal on the Sabbath, so that they might find a reason to accuse him. (Lu.6:7)

2. Second, failing to discredit Jesus, they sought some way to kill Him.

But the Pharisees went out and conspired against him, how to destroy him. (Mt.12:14; see Mt.26:3–4)

And the chief priests and the scribes were seeking how to put him to death, for they feared the people. (Lu.22:2)

This was why the Jews were seeking all the more to kill him, because not only was he breaking the Sabbath, but he was even calling God his own Father, making himself equal with God. (Jn.5:18; see Jn.7:1; 7:19–20, 25)

## B. The Astounding Authority: Equality with God, 5:17-30

ⁱ⁷ But Jesus answered them, "My Father is working until now, and I am working."
¹⁸ This was why the Jews were seeking all the more to kill him, because not only was he breaking the Sabbath, but he was even calling God his own Father, making himself equal with God.
¹⁹ So Jesus said to them, "Truly, truly, I say to you, the Son can do nothing of his own accord, but only what he sees the Father doing. For whatever the Father does, that the Son does likewise.
²⁰ "For the Father loves the Son and shows him all that he himself is doing. And greater works than these will he show him, so that you may marvel.
²¹ "For as the Father raises the dead and gives them life, so also the Son gives life to whom he will.
²² "For the Father judges no one, but has given all judgment to the Son,
²³ "that all may honor the Son, just as they honor the Father. Whoever does not honor the Son does not honor the Father who sent him.
²⁴ "Truly, truly, I say to you, whoever hears my word and believes him who sent me has eternal life. He does not come into judgment, but has passed from death to life.

²⁵ "Truly, truly, I say to you, an hour is coming, and is now here, when the dead will hear the voice of the Son of God, and those who hear will live.
²⁶ "For as the Father has life in himself, so he has granted the Son also to have life in himself.
²⁷ "And he has given him authority to execute judgment, because he is the Son of Man.

²⁸ "Do not marvel at this, for an hour is coming when all who are in the tombs will hear his voice

1. **Proof 1: Jesus claimed to be equal with God**
   a. His claim: Called God "My Father"
   b. His claim clearly understood by the Jewish leaders: They sought to kill Him

2. **Proof 2: Jesus' obedience**
   a. He did not act alone
   b. He did exactly what He saw the Father do

3. **Proof 3: Jesus' great works**
   a. God loves His Son
   b. God showed His Son what to do

4. **Proof 4: Jesus' power to quicken, to give life, to raise people from the dead**

5. **Proof 5: Jesus' control over the whole judicial process**
   a. The purpose: That all may honor the Son
   b. The fact: If Christ is not honored, God is not honored

6. **Proof 6: Jesus' power to save people from death**
   a. How people are saved
      1) Hearing His Word
      2) Believing that God sent His Son, Jesus
   b. The result: Eternal life
   c. The facts: The spiritually dead can hear the voice of God's Son & live—now

7. **Proof 7: Jesus' energy of life, His self-existence**

8. **Proof 8: Jesus' authority to execute judgment**

9. **Proof 9: Jesus' claim to be the Son of Man**

10. **Proof 10: Jesus' power to resurrect all people from the grave**
    a. People who have done good: Resurrected to life

b. People who have done evil: Resurrected to condemnation

c. The judgment: Will be a just judgment

²⁹ "and come out, those who have done good to the resurrection of life, and those who have done evil to the resurrection of judgment.

³⁰ "I can do nothing on my own. As I hear, I judge, and my judgment is just, because I seek not my own will but the will of him who sent me."

## Division VI

*The Revelation of Jesus, the Authority and Power Over Life, 5:1-47*

B. The Astounding Authority: Equality with God, 5:17-30

## 5:17-30
## Introduction

All people have to face the earth-shaking claim Christ made in this passage. He made the astounding claim that all authority belongs to Him. How could He make such an astounding claim? Because He proclaimed that He was equal with God and then He proceeded to give proof after proof which unequivocally verified His claim. This is, *The Astounding Authority: Equality with God, 5:17-30*.

1. Proof 1: Jesus claimed to be equal with God (vv.17-18).
2. Proof 2: Jesus' obedience (v.19).
3. Proof 3: Jesus' great works (v.20).
4. Proof 4: Jesus' power to quicken, to give life, to raise people from the dead (v.21).
5. Proof 5: Jesus' control over the whole judicial process (vv.22-23).
6. Proof 6: Jesus' power to save people from death (vv.24-25).
7. Proof 7: Jesus' energy of life, His self-existence (v.26).
8. Proof 8: Jesus' authority to execute judgment (v.27).
9. Proof 9: Jesus' claim to be the Son of Man (v.27).
10. Proof 10: Jesus' power to resurrect all people from the grave (vv.28-30).

### 5:17-18

¹⁷ But Jesus answered them, "My Father is working until now, and I am working."
¹⁸ This was why the Jews were seeking all the more to kill him, because not only was he breaking the Sabbath, but he was even calling God his own Father, making himself equal with God.

### 1 Proof 1: Jesus claimed to be equal with God.

The first proof that Jesus is equal with God is His own words: He clearly said that He is equal with God. Because of this startling claim, the Jewish leaders became more determined than ever to kill Him.

a. **His claim: Called God "My Father" (v.17).**

Jesus clearly said, "My Father," asserting that God is *His Father* and making Himself *equal* with God (v.18). He was clearly claiming that He is "*the* Son of God," "the only begotten Son of God" (see Jn.3:16). By calling God, "My Father" rather than "our Father," Jesus was claiming a unique relationship, a Father-Son union with God.

Jesus made an additional claim when He said, *"My Father is working until now"* (Gk. heos arti ergazetai). Translated more literally, Jesus said, "My Father keeps on working even until now." That is, God never ceases to work, even on the Sabbath. It is true that when God created the world, Scripture says He rested on the Sabbath day; but this means He rested from His creative work, not from His other work. His work of love and mercy, helping and caring (compassion), looking after and overseeing (sovereignty) continued. Jesus also said, "And I am working," meaning that He did good on the Sabbath as well. Again, He was claiming to be equal with God, claiming to have the same right to work even as God works: that is, to erase the wrong laws of men and to establish the just and compassionate laws of God.

b. **His claim clearly understood by the Jewish leaders: They sought to kill Him (v.18).**
Christ's claim was unquestionable. The shattering fact was *clearly understood* by the religious leaders. They knew exactly what He was claiming (see note—Jn.1:34 for more discussion). They understood clearly . . .
- that Jesus had said God was *His Father* (see "His *own* Son," Ro.8:32)
- that Jesus was making Himself equal with God (see "Equal to God," Ph.2:6)

Along with making this shocking claim, Jesus had broken the law against working on the Sabbath, claiming that He had the same authority as God, the authority to do good on the Sabbath. He had the authority to be compassionate by teaching and helping and caring for people. Scripture states that for these two reasons—claiming equality with God and breaking the Sabbath law—the Jewish religious leaders determined to kill Jesus.

**THOUGHT 1.** People either accept Jesus' claim to be equal with God, or they simply reject it. Regardless of what people do, Jesus' claim is unmistakably clear. The claim was clearly made. There is no longer a middle ground upon which people can stand. Every person decides whether to accept or reject the truth about Jesus. We cannot avoid this decision. Some say they have not decided whether or not they believe Jesus is God. But to *not* decide *is* to decide; it is to refuse to believe in Jesus, resulting in eternal death (Jn.3:18).

**THOUGHT 2.** Instead of the Sabbath (Saturday), most Christian believers observe Sunday as a day of rest and worship. Referred to as the Lord's Day, Sunday was the day Jesus rose from the dead. Some take the words and behavior of Jesus on the Sabbath as the approval for not setting aside a day for rest and worship. This is false reasoning. Jesus was neither violating nor erasing the need for a day of rest and worship. Just the opposite is true. He was saying that the day was to be used for compassion and mercy and good, helping people in their needs.

## 2 Proof 2: Jesus' Obedience.

The second proof that Jesus is equal with God is found in His obedience. In John 5:19, Jesus states two astounding facts regarding His work in relation to the Father.

[19] So Jesus said to them, "Truly, truly, I say to you, the Son can do nothing of his own accord, but only what he sees the Father doing. For whatever the Father does, that the Son does likewise."

a. **He did not act alone.**
Jesus made it clear that He did not act alone. He did not act independently of God (cp. Jn.5:30; 7:28; 8:28; 14:10). He was not disobedient to God. He did not . . .
- take His life into His own hands
- do His own thing
- act selfishly
- walk separately from God

Jesus stressed the crucial importance of this point. By saying, "Truly, truly," or, "Most assuredly," Jesus was calling His listeners to pay close attention to what He said.

### b. He did exactly what He saw the Father do.

Jesus did exactly what He had seen the Father do. There was no division whatsoever between the Father and Jesus.

- ➤ Jesus was in perfect, unbroken communion with God.
- ➤ Jesus was of the very same nature and person as God.
- ➤ Jesus acted as God because He was God: He did exactly what God did. *That* (tauta) means the very same things. *Likewise* (homoios) means in the very same manner. Jesus acted and behaved exactly as God acted and behaved.

Jesus Christ was perfectly obedient to His Father; He acted exactly in the nature of God. (What a lesson *on* obedience! A challenge *for* obedience!)

> "I know him, for I come from him, and he sent me." (Jn.7:29)

> "But you have not known him. I know him. If I were to say that I do not know him, I would be a liar like you, but I do know him and I keep his word." (Jn.8:55)

> "I and the Father are one." (Jn.10:30)

> "If I am not doing the works of my Father, then do not believe me; but if I do them, even though you do not believe me, believe the works, that you may know and understand that the Father is in me and I am in the Father." (Jn.10:37-38)

> "Do you not believe that I am in the Father and the Father is in me? The words that I say to you I do not speak on my own authority, but the Father who dwells in me does his works." (Jn.14:10)

> "And I am no longer in the world, but they are in the world, and I am coming to you. Holy Father, keep them in your name, which you have given me, that they may be one, even as we are one." (Jn.17:11)

## 5:20

[20] "For the Father loves the Son and shows him all that he himself is doing. And greater works than these will he show him, so that you may marvel."

## 3 Proof 3: Jesus' great works.

The third proof that Jesus is equal with God is His great works. In this verse, the Savior made two astounding statements (see note—Jn.5:36 for more discussion).

### a. God loves the Son.

The Greek verb for *love* (philei) indicates that the Father continues to love and never stops loving the Son. There is never a moment when the love diminishes. It is a perfect love that never ceases to give.

> He was still speaking when, behold, a bright cloud overshadowed them, and a voice from the cloud said, "This is my beloved Son, with whom I am well pleased; listen to him." (Mt.17:5)

> "For this reason the Father loves me, because I lay down my life that I may take it up again." (Jn.10:17)

> "As the Father has loved me, so have I loved you. Abide in my love." (Jn.15:9)

> "I in them and you in me, that they may become perfectly one, so that the world may know that you sent me and loved them even as you loved me." (Jn.17:23)

> "I made known to them your name, and I will continue to make it known, that the love with which you have loved me may be in them, and I in them." (Jn.17:26)

### b. God showed his Son what to do.

Because of the Father's great love for the Son, He showed Christ all that He was doing. All the things which Jesus did were the very things which the Father did.

Jesus said that the Father was going to show Him greater works to do, greater things than the healing of the paralyzed man (vv.8-9). Jesus would be . . .

- controlling the forces of nature (storms on the Sea of Galilee)
- multiplying food
- raising the dead and healing multitudes of people
- instituting a greater law, the law of the Son of Man (see note—Mt.5:17-18).
- instituting new ordinances
- creating people anew

"But the testimony that I have is greater than that of John. For the works that the Father has given me to accomplish, the very works that I am doing, bear witness about me that the Father has sent me." (Jn.5:36)

"We must work the works of him who sent me while it is day; night is coming, when no one can work." (Jn.9:4)

Jesus answered them, "I told you, and you do not believe. The works that I do in my Father's name bear witness about me." (Jn.10:25)

"If I am not doing the works of my Father, then do not believe me; but if I do them, even though you do not believe me, believe the works, that you may know and understand that the Father is in me and I am in the Father." (Jn.10:37-38)

"Do you not believe that I am in the Father and the Father is in me? The words that I say to you I do not speak on my own authority, but the Father who dwells in me does his works. Believe me that I am in the Father and the Father is in me, or else believe on account of the works themselves." (Jn.14:10-11)

## 4  Proof 4: Jesus' power to quicken, to give life, to raise people from the dead.

The fourth proof that Jesus is equal with God is His power to give life. God gives life, and *only* God can give life. Therefore, if He wishes to give life to a dead body, He can. In giving life and raising the dead, God is sovereign, acting fully as He alone wills. He is neither constrained nor restrained, but He has the power and authority to do exactly as He desires. In everything God does, He exercises perfect love, justice, and wisdom. He knows exactly what He is doing, and He does it perfectly.

²¹ "For as the Father raises the dead and gives them life, so also the Son gives life to whom he will."

Likewise, the Son, Jesus Christ, gives life to whom *He wills*. Just as God does, so Christ does. Christ is equal with God in giving life and raising the dead.

**THOUGHT 1.** Not only can Christ raise people who are dead *physically,* but He also gives *spiritual* life to those who are dead spiritually (Ep.2:1-9. He quickens and gives life to a person when that person believes on Him, and the life which He gives is both abundant and eternal (see note—Jn.3:16).

"But that you may know that the Son of Man has authority on earth to forgive sins"—he then said to the paralytic—"Rise, pick up your bed and go home." (Mt.9:6)

And Jesus came and said to them, "All authority in heaven and on earth has been given to me." (Mt.28:18)

"Since you have given him authority over all flesh, to give eternal life to all whom you have given him." (Jn.17:2)

If the Spirit of him who raised Jesus from the dead dwells in you, he who raised Christ Jesus from the dead will also give life to your mortal bodies through his Spirit who dwells in you. (Ro.8:11)

And you were dead in the trespasses and sins (Ep.2:1; see vv.2-3)

But God, being rich in mercy, because of the great love with which he loved us, even when we were dead in our trespasses, made us alive together with Christ—by grace you have been saved—and raised us up with him and seated us with him in the heavenly places in Christ Jesus, so that in the coming ages he might show the immeasurable riches of his grace in kindness toward us in Christ Jesus. For by grace you have been saved through faith. And this is not your own doing; it is the gift of God, not a result of works, so that no one may boast. (Ep.2:4-9)

And you, who were dead in your trespasses and the uncircumcision of your flesh, God made alive together with him, having forgiven us all our trespasses. (Col.2:13)

## 5 Proof 5: Jesus' control over the whole judicial process.

The fifth proof that Jesus is equal with God is seen in His control over the entire judicial process. Most people think that God (the Father) will judge the world in the day of judgment and that they will have to stand before Him on that day. But not so, Jesus says. He informs us that God will judge *no* one, but that He has given all judgment to the Son (v.22). The scene is the picture of a supreme court—not just the supreme court of a nation, but the supreme court of the universe presided over by Jesus Christ.

### 5:22-23

²² "For the Father judges no one, but has given all judgment to the Son,
²³ "that all may honor the Son, just as they honor the Father. Whoever does not honor the Son does not honor the Father who sent him."

> "Before him will be gathered all the nations, and he will separate people one from another as a shepherd separates the sheep from the goats." (Mt.25:32)

> "And he commanded us to preach to the people and to testify that he is the one appointed by God to be judge of the living and the dead." (Ac.10:42)

> "Because he has fixed a day on which he will judge the world in righteousness by a man whom he has appointed; and of this he has given assurance to all by raising him from the dead." (Ac.17:31)

> On that day when, according to my gospel, God judges the secrets of men by Christ Jesus. (Ro.2:16)

> I charge you in the presence of God and of Christ Jesus, who is to judge the living and the dead, and by his appearing and his kingdom. (2 Ti.4:1)

**a. The purpose: That all may honor the Son (v.23a).**

God has one purpose for committing all judgment to Christ: God has willed that all people honor the Son just as they honor Him. The idea is that God has determined that people will *keep on honoring the Son* with the very same honor and worship they give Him. (This is seen in the Greek tense which is present active subjective.)

**b. The fact: If Christ is not honored, God is not honored (v.23b).**

This is a truth that shatters many people, for it means that if a person does not honor Christ, they do not honor God. If they do not worship Christ, they do not worship God.

> "The one who hears you hears me, and the one who rejects you rejects me, and the one who rejects me rejects him who sent me." (Lu.10:16)

> "Whoever hates me hates my Father also." (Jn.15:23)

> No one who denies the Son has the Father. Whoever confesses the Son has the Father also. (1 Jn.2:23)

### 5:24-25

²⁴ "Truly, truly, I say to you, whoever hears my word and believes him who sent me has eternal life. He does not come into judgment, but has passed from death to life.
²⁵ "Truly, truly, I say to you, an hour is coming, and is now here, when the dead will hear the voice of the Son of God, and those who hear will live."

## 6 Proof 6: Jesus' power to save people from death.

The sixth proof that Jesus is equal with God is reflected in His power over people's destiny, the power to save people from death. Here, Jesus provided the critical information about salvation, simple answers to eternity's most important questions.

**a. How people are saved (v.24a).**

First, Jesus explains *how* people are saved. We are saved by hearing Jesus' Word. *Hearing* (akouon) is more than just listening with our ears. It is *commitment* and *obedience* to what is heard. In order to be saved, we must hear and follow Jesus' Word, doing exactly as He says. Then, we are saved by believing God, that is, by believing that God has sent His Son, Jesus Christ to save us.

> "For God so loved the world, that he gave his only Son, that whoever believes in him should not perish but have eternal life." (Jn.3:16)

> But God shows his love for us in that while we were still sinners, Christ died for us. (Ro.5:8)

b. The result: eternal life (v.24b).

Second, Jesus explains *what happens* when we are saved. We pass from the state of death into the state of life, from the state of condemnation into the state of justification. When we are truly saved, we are never condemned to judgment; we are declared righteous and given eternal life. Note the descriptive way of expressing it: "has *passed* from death to life." Note also that people are presently in a *state of death*; that is, in the process of dying. Every person *must die and will die.* We cannot stop the process (see Deeper Study # 1—He.9:27; see also Ep.2:1, 5; 5:14).

c. The facts: The spiritually dead can hear the voice of God's Son and live—now (v.25).

Third, Jesus explains *when* we can be saved. We can be saved now! The time is *now here.* The hour has come, and now is when the spiritually dead *can hear* the voice of the Son of God and *live*—have eternal life (see Deeper Study # 1)!

> Whoever believes in the Son has eternal life; whoever does not obey the Son shall not see life, but the wrath of God remains on him. (Jn.3:36)

> For he says, "In a favorable time I listened to you, and in a day of salvation I have helped you." Behold, now is the favorable time; behold, now is the day of salvation. (2 Co.6:2)

### Deeper Study # 1

(5:25) **Jesus Christ, Son of God**: there are three places in the Gospel of John where Jesus calls Himself the Son of God (Jn.5:25; 10:36; 11:4; see Jn.19:7). Note also the claim to be the Son (Jn.5:19-23, 26; 6:40; 8:35-36; 14:13; 19:1). John's stated purpose should also be noted at this point:

> But these are written so that you may believe that Jesus is the Christ, the Son of God, and that by believing you may have life in his name. (Jn.20:31)

## 7 Proof 7: Jesus' energy of life, His self existence.

The seventh proof that Jesus is equal with God is in His energy of life, His self-existence. God is the . . .

- Energy of life
- Power of life
- Being of life
- Possessor of life
- Source of life
- Essence of life
- Sovereign of life
- Self-existent life

> 26 "For as the Father has life in himself, so he has granted the Son also to have life in himself."

God has life within Himself, and He has given the very same energy of life to the Son. Jesus Christ possesses the very being of life, the power and energy of self-existence within Himself.

The implication of this truth is clear. Because Jesus Christ has life in Himself, He has the *power* to give everlasting life to those who hear Him and believe on God.

> In him was life, and the life was the light of men. (Jn.1:4)

> "The thief comes only to steal and kill and destroy. I came that they may have life and have it abundantly." (Jn.10:10)

> Jesus said to her, "I am the resurrection and the life. Whoever believes in me, though he die, yet shall he live." (Jn.11:25)

> Jesus said to him, "I am the way, and the truth, and the life. No one comes to the Father except through me." (Jn.14:6)

> And which now has been manifested through the appearing of our Savior Christ Jesus, who abolished death and brought life and immortality to light through the gospel. (2 Ti.1:10)

> Whoever has the Son has life; whoever does not have the Son of God does not have life. (1 Jn.5:12)

> For with you is the fountain of life; in your light do we see light. (Ps.36:9)

## 8  Proof 8: Jesus' authority to execute judgment.

The eighth proof that Jesus is equal with God is His authority to execute judgment. Jesus Christ is the Son of Man, having lived just as all human beings live. He walked through life as a human, bearing all the weight and pressure, trials and temptations, sufferings and death, joys and victories that people experience. He knows every facet and fiber of human life; therefore, He is able to execute perfect judgment. For this reason, God has given Him the right and the authority to judge all people (see note, *Son of Man*—Jn.1:51).

**5:27**

[27] "And he has given him authority to execute judgment, because he is the Son of Man."

## 9  Proof 9: Jesus' claim to be the Son of Man.

The ninth proof that Jesus is equal with God appears in His claim to be the Son of Man. This title emphasizes His incarnation—that as God, He became a man, that He was and is both God and man. This was Jesus' favorite description of Himself (see notes, *Son of Man*—Jn.1:51 for discussion; see also 3:13-14; 5:27; 6:27, 53, 62; 8:28; 9:35; 12:3-34; 13:31). Ponder this glorious truth: Jesus—the eternal God and our Creator—delighted in being one of us!

**5:28-30**

[28] "Do not marvel at this, for an hour is coming when all who are in the tombs will hear his voice
[29] and come out, those who have done good to the resurrection of life, and those who have done evil to the resurrection of judgment.
[30] I can do nothing on my own. As I hear, I judge, and my judgment is just, because I seek not my own will but the will of him who sent me."

## 10  Proof 10: Jesus' power to resurrect all people from the grave.

The tenth proof that Jesus is equal with God is found in His power to resurrect all people from the grave. Notice four facts (v.28):

➢ It is the *voice*—the Word, the power of Jesus—that will resurrect all that are in the graves.
➢ *All* who are in the tombs or graves will be resurrected. Not a single deceased person will be left in the earth. Everyone will come out of their grave (v.29).
➢ The *hour is coming* when all will be resurrected. The hour is set, fixed, already determined.
➢ We are *not* to *marvel* or be amazed at this. It is neither incredible nor ridiculous, for *God is*; He does exist, and He has a plan for the world. The world has not just happened. Life has not happened by chance, without purpose and meaning beyond a few brief years. Life is not doomed, without hope, destined to despair and dirt. There is meaning, purpose, and significance, both to life and to the world.

a. **People who have done good: Resurrected to life (v.29a).**
People who have done good will come out of their graves to the resurrection of life. How you live matters. The person who professes and lives for God will take part in the resurrection of life. Jesus is not teaching here that we receive eternal life by works. Rather, He is identifying those who are genuinely saved *by* their works. Remember, our works prove whether our faith is genuine (Jas.2:17-20; Ep.2:8-10).

b. **People who have done evil: Resurrected to condemnation (v.29b).**
In chilling contrast, those who have done evil will be raised to face judgment or condemnation (see Jn.3:17). A profession of faith in Christ is not enough to receive eternal life. It must be a profession of genuine faith, a faith that is proven by a change of life. How a person has lived will determine whether or not their faith is real. Have they lived righteously and godly in this present world—believing on Christ and serving Him? Believing on Christ means that a person has committed their life to follow Christ, to obey and serve Him (see note—Jn.2:2).

c. **The judgment: Will be a just judgment (v.30).**

The judgment of Christ will be a *just* judgment. He will judge precisely as He *hears*, exactly as *God wills*. Christ hears and does the will of God perfectly; therefore, He will hear God and execute God's judgment exactly as He wills.

> "For the Son of Man is going to come with his angels in the glory of his Father, and then he will repay each person according to what he has done." (Mt.16:27)
>
> He will render to each one according to his works. (Ro.2:6)
>
> For we must all appear before the judgment seat of Christ, so that each one may receive what is due for what he has done in the body, whether good or evil. (2 Co.5:10)
>
> And that to you, O Lord, belongs steadfast love. For you will render to a man according to his work. (Ps.62:12)
>
> "I the LORD search the heart and test the mind, to give every man according to his ways, according to the fruit of his deeds." (Je.17:10)

**THOUGHT 1.** Grasp the two critical facts about the resurrection:

(1) There will be a resurrection of all who have believed and obeyed the Lord Jesus Christ.

> "For this is the will of my Father, that everyone who looks on the Son and believes in him should have eternal life, and I will raise him up on the last day." (Jn.6:40)
>
> Jesus said to her, "I am the resurrection and the life. Whoever believes in me, though he die, yet shall he live." (Jn.11:25)
>
> For as in Adam all die, so also in Christ shall all be made alive. (1 Co.15:22)
>
> Knowing that he who raised the Lord Jesus will raise us also with Jesus and bring us with you into his presence. (2 Co.4:14)
>
> For the Lord himself will descend from heaven with a cry of command, with the voice of an archangel, and with the sound of the trumpet of God. And the dead in Christ will rise first. Then we who are alive, who are left, will be caught up together with them in the clouds to meet the Lord in the air, and so we will always be with the Lord. (1 Th.4:16-17)
>
> But God will ransom my soul from the power of Sheol, for he will receive me. Selah. (Ps.49:15)
>
> You who have made me see many troubles and calamities will revive me again; from the depths of the earth you will bring me up again. (Ps.71:20)
>
> I shall ransom them from the power of Sheol; I shall redeem them from Death. O Death, where are your plagues? O Sheol, where is your sting? Compassion is hidden from my eyes. (Ho.13:14)

(2) There will be a resurrection not only of believers but also of all those who have rejected and disobeyed the Lord Jesus Christ.

> "Having a hope in God, which these men themselves accept, that there will be a resurrection of both the just and the unjust." (Ac.24:15)
>
> Then I saw a great white throne and him who was seated on it. From his presence earth and sky fled away, and no place was found for them. And I saw the dead, great and small, standing before the throne, and books were opened. Then another book was opened, which is the book of life. And the dead were judged by what was written in the books, according to what they had done. And the sea gave up the dead who were in it, Death and Hades gave up the dead who were in them, and they were judged, each one of them, according to what they had done. Then Death and Hades were thrown into the lake of fire. This is the second death, the lake of fire. And if anyone's name was not found written in the book of life, he was thrown into the lake of fire. (Re.20:11-15)
>
> "And many of those who sleep in the dust of the earth shall awake, some to everlasting life, and some to shame and everlasting contempt." (Da.12:2)

## C. The Five Witnesses to Jesus' Authority and Power, 5:31–39

1. A basic law of society: A person's own testimony must be supported by other witnesses
2. The first witness to Jesus' authority: The Holy Spirit within Jesus
3. The second witness to Jesus' authority: John the Baptist
   a. Jesus did not need human witnesses, but He gave them so some might believe & be saved
   b. John's witness was like a shining light, clearly seen to be of God
4. The third witness to Jesus' authority: His miraculous works
5. The fourth witness to Jesus' authority: God Himself through all His works & His Word[DS1]
6. The fifth witness to Jesus' authority: The Scriptures

31 "If I alone bear witness about myself, my testimony is not true.

32 There is another who bears witness about me, and I know that the testimony that he bears about me is true.

33 You sent to John, and he has borne witness to the truth.

34 Not that the testimony that I receive is from man, but I say these things so that you may be saved.

35 He was a burning and shining lamp, and you were willing to rejoice for a while in his light.

36 But the testimony that I have is greater than that of John. For the works that the Father has given me to accomplish, the very works that I am doing, bear witness about me that the Father has sent me.

37 And the Father who sent me has himself borne witness about me. His voice you have never heard, his form you have never seen,

38 and you do not have his word abiding in you, for you do not believe the one whom he has sent.

39 You search the Scriptures because you think that in them you have eternal life; and it is they that bear witness about me,"

# Division VI

*The Revelation of Jesus, the Authority and Power Over Life, 5:1–47*

C. The Five Witnesses to Jesus' Authority and Power, 5:31–39

## 5:31–39
## Introduction

In this intense passage, Jesus stooped down to the human level. What He had claimed was true: He was the Son of God; He could not lie. He was precisely who He claimed to be, and that fact should have been known. People should have been searching and seeking after God so diligently that they could not miss the fact that He was the Son of God. He was so different and so Godly. However, to meet their need, Jesus would support His testimony by meeting and even exceeding the demands of justice. He would call forth five witnesses to prove His claim. This is, *The Five Witnesses to Jesus' Authority and Power, 5:31-39.*

1. A basic law of society: A person's own testimony must be supported by other witnesses (v.31).
2. The first witness to Jesus' authority: The Holy Spirit within Jesus (v.32).
3. The second witness to Jesus' authority: John the Baptist (vv.33-35).
4. The third witness to Jesus' authority: His miraculous works (v.36).
5. The fourth witness to Jesus' authority: God Himself, through all His works and His Word (vv.37-38).
6. The fifth witness to Jesus' authority: The Scriptures (v.39).

## 1 A basic law of society: A person's own testimony must be supported by other witnesses.

⁣³¹ "If I alone bear witness about myself, my testimony is not true."

Jesus pointed out a fact of life: in a just society, a person's own testimony is usually considered unacceptable in and of itself. That witness has to be supported by other witnesses, and at least two witnesses are usually required. This is one of the most fundamental laws of society throughout much of the world (see De.17:6; 19:15; Mt.18:16; 2 Co.13:1; 1 Ti.5:19).

**THOUGHT 1.** The fact that a person's word by itself is considered untrustworthy reflects our human nature and sinful tendencies. Our word, our honesty and integrity, without some corroboration, generally cannot be trusted and is even deemed insufficient in a court of law. This unfortunate fact is due to our nature of self-centeredness. Simply put, many people love themselves much more than truth, even when the good of society and its laws are threatened. Therefore, in a just society, none of us can be completely trusted.

> **They were filled with all manner of unrighteousness, evil, covetousness, malice. They are full of envy, murder, strife, deceit, maliciousness. They are gossips, slanderers, haters of God, insolent, haughty, boastful, inventors of evil, disobedient to parents, foolish, faithless, heartless, ruthless. Though they know God's righteous decree that those who practice such things deserve to die, they not only do them but give approval to those who practice them. (Ro.1:29-32)**

> **As it is written: "None is righteous, no, not one; no one understands; no one seeks for God. All have turned aside; together they have become worthless; no one does good, not even one." "Their throat is an open grave; they use their tongues to deceive." "The venom of asps is under their lips." "Their mouth is full of curses and bitterness." (Ro.3:10-14)**

> **The heart is deceitful above all things, and desperately sick; who can understand it? (Jer.17:9)**

**THOUGHT 2.** In this passage, Jesus demonstrates His immeasurable love for humanity. He is seeking after people, using every method He can to convince people of who He is so that they might be saved.

> **"Greater love has no one than this, that someone lay down his life for his friends." (Jn.15:13)**

> **And to know the love of Christ that surpasses knowledge, that you may be filled with all the fullness of God. (Ep.3:19)**

## 2 The first witness to Jesus' authority: The Holy Spirit within Jesus.

³² "There is another who bears witness about me, and I know that the testimony that he bears about me is true."

In John 5:32, Jesus *says* there is another who bears witness about Him. However, Christ does not identify who He means by *another* (Gk. allos; see also Jn.14:16). Most commentators believe Jesus is referring to the Holy Spirit, and there are three reasons why they believe this:

First, the Holy Spirit had already been given to Christ without measure (see note—Jn.3:34). Jesus was, of course, very conscious of the witness of the Spirit both within and without Him. The Spirit was empowering Him and doing the works of God through Him.

Second, the Holy Spirit is One of the witnesses that bears witness of Christ (see 1 Jn.5:6-12). When John the Apostle discusses the witness to Christ in one of his epistles, he mentions the Spirit. If John 5:32 is not referring to the Spirit, then the Spirit is not listed as one of the witnesses in the passage. This would be most unlikely, especially since the witness of the Father is covered in vv.37-38, and the ministry and witness of the Spirit is covered so thoroughly in this Gospel (see outline and notes—Jn.14:15-26; 16:7-15).

Third, Christ seems to be talking more about an inner witness, the witness of a Presence which He senses within His innermost being, a Power that works in and through Him. This of course could be God the Father, but again it could also be the Spirit, which would fit more naturally in the context.

Note that the Lord specifically says that He *knew* that the Spirit's testimony about Him is true. What does this mean?

> ➣ He knows the truth of the witness within His own heart and life. He has the consciousness, the sense, the awareness, the personal knowledge of the Spirit's witness within His own inner Being. The Spirit bears witness with Jesus' own Spirit that He is the Son of God.
>
> ➣ He knows that the witness and the work of the Holy Spirit, in and through Him, were true. The Spirit convicts people, works in hearts and lives, and convinces them of the claims of Christ (see outline and notes—Jn.16:7-15 for the Lord's discussion of the Spirit's work).

> For he whom God has sent utters the words of God, for he gives the Spirit without measure. (Jn.3:34)

> "It is the Spirit [Holy Spirit] who gives life; the flesh is no help at all. The words that I have spoken to you are spirit and life." (Jn.6:63)

> "How God anointed Jesus of Nazareth with the Holy Spirit and with power. He went about doing good and healing all who were oppressed by the devil, for God was with him." (Ac.10:38)

## 5:33-35

⁳³ "You sent to John, and he has borne witness to the truth.
³⁴ Not that the testimony that I receive is from man, but I say these things so that you may be saved.
³⁵ He was a burning and shining lamp, and you were willing to rejoice for a while in his light."

### 3 The second witness to Jesus' authority: John the Baptist.

Second, John the Baptist had testified of Jesus' authority. The religious leaders had sent some men to ask John about his witness, and John bore witness to *the truth*. The words *borne witness* (memartureken) speak of a permanent and continuing witness. John's message was not a fly-by-night witness that appeared on the scene and suddenly disappeared. His witness continued and still continues and will always continue. It was a trustworthy message, a witness to the truth (see Jn.1:19-27, 29-36).

> In those days John the Baptist came preaching in the wilderness of Judea, "Repent, for the kingdom of heaven is at hand.... Bear fruit in keeping with repentance." (Mt.3:1-2, 8)

> "Even now the axe is laid to the root of the trees. Every tree therefore that does not bear good fruit is cut down and thrown into the fire. I baptize you with water for repentance, but he who is coming after me is mightier than I, whose sandals I am not worthy to carry. He will baptize you with the Holy Spirit and fire." (Mt.3:10-11)

*The truth* not only refers to the truth of John's message but also to Christ Himself, who is *the Truth*, the very embodiment of truth (see Deeper Study # 2—Jn.14:6).

> Jesus said to him, "I am the way, and the truth, and the life. No one comes to the Father except through me." (Jn.14:6)

a. **Jesus did not need human witnesses, but He gave them so some might believe and be saved (v.34).**

Jesus does not need or plead the witness of a mere man. The implication for us is clear: people should not plead the witness of a mere man when dealing with eternal issues that determine their destiny. The testimony of God's Son should be counted the strongest of witnesses, yet tragically, people want the testimony of others just like themselves.

During His earthly ministry, Jesus did not receive the witness of men, for He knew what was in all people (see Jn.2:24-25). He also rebuked Nicodemus for not receiving His witness and letting it be enough (Jn.3:11).

Jesus reached out to people, giving them what they required, hoping to save some. He gave them the most dynamic human witness He could—John the Baptist. John's witness was as clear and pointed as it could be. He unmistakably identified Jesus as the Lamb of God who takes away the sin of the world (Jn.1:29).

b. **John's witness was like a shining light, clearly seen to be of God (v.35).**

The witness of John was that of a burning and shining lamp or light. His light was clearly seen to be of God, lit by God as the light of God. That John's message (witness) was of God could not be questioned by any reasonable and honest person. John definitely showed people the way to God, just as a light shows the way out of darkness.

The people rejoiced in John's light, but *only for a season*. They looked upon John as a sensation, a flash of excitement, listening and accepting only what they wished. Very simply, if John said anything that did not allow them to do as they desired, they rejected it.

## 4 The third witness to Jesus' authority: His miraculous works.

Jesus' miraculous works also bear witness of His authority. He says four significant things about His works (see notes—Jn.5:19; 5:20; Deeper Study # 2—Jn.10:25 for more discussion).

36 "But the testimony that I have is greater than that of John. For the works that the Father has given me to accomplish, the very works that I am doing, bear witness about me that the Father has sent me."

First, Jesus' works were a greater witness than the witness of John the Baptist.

Second, Jesus' works were given to Him by the Father. He was on a mission for God; therefore, what He did—all the works—were of God (see Jn.3:35). He was the One appointed by God *to carry out* the works of God; and He was the One empowered by God *to do* the works of God.

Third, Jesus' works were the Father's works. The Father was the Originator, the Planner, the Overseer of the works. He was the One who had given the works to be done and completed. Note that Jesus claimed to have completed the works perfectly (see Jn.17:4; 19:30).

Fourth, Jesus' works proved that the Father had sent Him. They were works which had never been, or ever would be, done by others (Jn.15:24). They were so unusual—so full of power and wisdom, love and care, glory and honor to God—that all who failed to see and believe were without excuse. Remember, He had just performed one of the Godly works, healing the paralyzed man.

> And coming to his hometown he taught them in their synagogue, so that they were astonished, and said, "Where did this man get this wisdom and these mighty works?" (Mt.13:54; see Mk.6:2, 14)
>
> "We must work the works of him who sent me while it is day; night is coming, when no one can work." (Jn.9:4)
>
> Jesus answered them, "I told you, and you do not believe. The works that I do in my Father's name bear witness about me." (Jn.10:25)
>
> "If I am not doing the works of my Father, then do not believe me; but if I do them, even though you do not believe me, believe the works, that you may know and understand that the Father is in me and I am in the Father." (Jn.10:37-38)

"Believe me that I am in the Father and the Father is in me, or else believe on account of the works themselves." (Jn.14:11)

"If I had not done among them the works that no one else did, they would not be guilty of sin, but now they have seen and hated both me and my Father." (Jn.15:24)

## 5:37–38

⁳⁷ "And the Father who sent me has himself borne witness about me. His voice you have never heard, his form you have never seen,
³⁸ and you do not have his word abiding in you, for you do not believe the one whom he has sent."

## 5 The fourth witness to Jesus' authority: God Himself through all His works and His Word.

The fourth witness was God Himself. God sent Christ into the world, so Christ naturally bore witness of God. That witness included all that God had ever revealed to humanity down through the centuries. Everything God did was to prepare the way for His Son, and every single act bore witness that God was sending His Son (see Deeper Study # 1—Jn.4:22).

> But when the fullness of time had come, God sent forth his Son, born of woman, born under the law, to redeem those who were under the law, so that we might receive adoption as sons. And because you are sons, God has sent the Spirit of his Son into our hearts, crying, "Abba! Father!" (Ga.4:4-6)

The point is striking: the way was being prepared for the coming of God's Son . . .
- every time God spoke
- every time God appeared (theophany, in whatever form or manner)
- every time God acted

Christ presented two charges against the religious authorities. The same charges can be made against the world today.

**a. You have never heard nor seen God (v.37).**

First, Jesus stated that they had never heard God's voice *at any* time, nor seen His form, what He looks like. Some people may think they have seen God the Father, but they have not. However, it is not because God has not spoken or shown what He is like. He has revealed the truth about Himself and the coming of His Son.

> No one has ever seen God; the only God, who is at the Father's side, he has made him known. (Jn.1:18)

> He [Jesus Christ] is the image of the invisible God, the firstborn of all creation. (Col.1:15)

> To the King of the ages, immortal, invisible, the only God, be honor and glory forever and ever. Amen. (1 Ti.1:17)

> [God] who alone has immortality, who dwells in unapproachable light, whom no one has ever seen or can see. To him be honor and eternal dominion. Amen. (1 Ti.6:16)

> No one has ever seen God; if we love one another, God abides in us and his love is perfected in us. (1 Jn.4:12)

> "But," he said, "you cannot see my face, for man shall not see me and live." (Ex.33:20)

> "Behold, he passes by me, and I see him not; he moves on, but I do not perceive him." (Jb.9:11)

**b. You do not allow His Word to dwell in you: Because you do not believe in Christ (v.38).**

The Jews had God's Word—the Old Testament Scriptures in their hands, but they did not have the Word of God *abiding* in their hearts and lives (see Deeper Study # 1). If God's Word was truly alive in their hearts, they would have believed in Christ, for God had spoken clearly about the coming of His Son in the Scriptures (v.39).

## Deeper Study #1

(5:38) **Word of God—Abiding**: the Word of God must abide in a person for a person to know God in a personal way. Two things are necessary for the Word of God to abide in a person.
1. The Word of God must be accepted as *God's* Word. The Word must be accepted as coming from God; it must be accepted as truth, as fact, as gospel. Where the Jewish authorities failed is seen in the next point (also see note—Jn.5:39).
2. The Word of God *must be abiding* in a person. This means two things.
a. The Word of God must be *"in* you" not just *among* you (v.38). A Jewish religious leader had the Word of God all around him: on his desk and table, in his home and church, on his tongue, and sounding upon his ears. However, he did not have the Word *in* his heart, and *unless something is within, it is not abiding* in a person.
b. The Word of God must be *abiding*. It must not only be allowed to come into a person's mind and heart, it must be grasped and clung to. It must stay within and remain and not be allowed to depart. *Abiding* means the Word of God is . . .
- living, moving, ruling, and reigning in a person's life and heart
- stirring, convicting, and challenging a person
- leading to confession, repentance, growth, and maturity
- teaching love, compassion, forgiveness, goodness, and just behavior
- causing one to believe and trust God's Son, Jesus Christ, as their Savior and Lord

**THOUGHT 1.** When God's word *truly abides* in a person, that person naturally *accepts what God says and lives as God says*, and that person believes God's Son. It would be impossible to accept God's Word and not accept what He says about His Son. To reject what God says about His Son is to reject God's Word. If a person does not believe God's Son, to whom God witnesses, then God's Word does not abide in that person.

> "The one who rejects me and does not receive my words has a judge; the word that I have spoken will judge him on the last day." (Jn.12:48)

> For the word of God is living and active, sharper than any two-edged sword, piercing to the division of soul and of spirit, of joints and of marrow, and discerning the thoughts and intentions of the heart. (He.4:12)

## 6 The fifth witness to Jesus' authority: The Scriptures.

5:39

<sup>39</sup> "You search the Scriptures because you think that in them you have eternal life; and it is they that bear witness about me,"

Finally, the Scriptures bear witness of Jesus. Jesus noted that the religious leaders searched the Scriptures. *You search* (eraunate) can be either a fact, that "you search the scriptures," or a command, "search the scriptures." It seems that the words *you think that in them* point toward the meaning being a statement of fact. The religious leaders did "search the scriptures," for they thought they had eternal life in their searching.

The Scriptures *proclaim* the message of eternal life and show us how to secure eternal life, but the Scriptures do not impart or give eternal life. Only Christ can give eternal life. People do not secure eternal life . . .
- by reading the Scriptures, no matter how much they read
- by knowing the Scriptures, no matter how much they know
- by being religious, no matter how religious they are
- by doing religious works, no matter how much good they do

A person receives eternal life only by believing and giving their heart and life to Jesus Christ (see DEEPER STUDY # 2—Jn.2:24).

> "For God so loved the world, that he gave his only Son, that whoever believes in him should not perish but have eternal life." (Jn.3:16)

**And this is the testimony, that God gave us eternal life, and this life is in his Son. Whoever has the Son has life; whoever does not have the Son of God does not have life. (1 Jn.5:11-12)**

The Jewish leaders felt that the source of eternal life—the Scriptures—held the secret to eternal life. But they refused to see that secret in the Scriptures. Jesus informed the religious leaders that the Scriptures testify of Him. They bear inspired witness to the truth that Jesus is Israel's Messiah, God's Son and our Savior.

**THOUGHT 1.** Many—if not most—believers read only the New Testament, and many preachers seldom preach from the Old Testament. Jesus' statement ought to ignite a fervent passion within us to study and understand the Old Testament. We ought to diligently and excitedly search the Old Testament Scriptures that we might learn more about Jesus and know Him better.

> **And beginning with Moses and all the Prophets, he interpreted to them in all the Scriptures the things concerning himself. . . . Then he said to them, "These are my words that I spoke to you while I was still with you, that everything written about me in the Law of Moses and the Prophets and the Psalms must be fulfilled." Then he opened their minds to understand the Scriptures. (Lu.24:27, 44-45)**

> **Concerning this salvation, the prophets who prophesied about the grace that was to be yours searched and inquired carefully, inquiring what person or time the Spirit of Christ in them was indicating when he predicted the sufferings of Christ and the subsequent glories. (1 Pe.1:10-11)**

### D. The Rejection of Jesus' Claim: Why People Reject Him, 5:40–47

| | |
|---|---|
| ⁴⁰ "yet you refuse to come to me that you may have life. | 1. People do not want the life He offers |
| ⁴¹ "I do not receive glory from people. | |
| ⁴² "But I know that you do not have the love of God within you. | 2. People do not genuinely love God |
| ⁴³ "I have come in my Father's name, and you do not receive me. If another comes in his own name, you will receive him. | 3. People can more easily accept a false messiah than someone coming in God's name |
| ⁴⁴ "How can you believe, when you receive glory from one another and do not seek the glory that comes from the only God? | 4. People seek approval & honor from other people instead of from God |
| ⁴⁵ "Do not think that I will accuse you to the Father. There is one who accuses you: Moses, on whom you have set your hope. | 5. People do not believe the Scripture—do not believe the prophecies of Moses' writings |
| ⁴⁶ "For if you believed Moses, you would believe me; for he wrote of me. | |
| ⁴⁷ "But if you do not believe his writings, how will you believe my words?" | 6. People will not believe the words of the true Messiah if they do not believe prophecy |

# Division VI

*The Revelation of Jesus, the Authority and Power Over Life, 5:1–47*

D. The Rejection of Jesus' Claim: Why People Reject Him, 5:40–47

## 5:40–47
## Introduction

When Jesus came, His own people, the Jews, rejected Him and ultimately participated in crucifying Him (Jn.1:11). Throughout John's Gospel, he traces the path of hatred and rejection of Christ that ended at the cross. In this chapter, John points out two of the early reasons the Jewish leaders persecuted Jesus: because He broke the Sabbath and because He claimed to be equal with God (Jn.5:18). Here, Jesus gave six reasons for people's rejection of Him. This is, *The Rejection of Jesus' Claim: Why People Reject Him,* 5:40–47.

1. People do not want the life He offers (vv.40–41).
2. People do not genuinely love God (v.42).
3. People can more easily accept a false messiah than someone coming in God's name (v.43).
4. People seek approval and honor from other people instead of from God (v.44).
5. People do not believe the Scripture—do not believe the prophecies of Moses' writings (vv.45–46).
6. People will not believe the words of the true Messiah if they do not believe prophecy (v.47).

## 1 People do not want the life He offers.

**5:40-41**

⁴⁰ "yet you refuse to come to me that you may have life.
⁴¹ "I do not receive glory from people."

Jesus emphasized the role of the human will in people's coming to Christ. They are not *willing* to accept Christ. They *refuse* to come to Him. People deliberately choose to reject Jesus Christ. They actually exercise the will not to come to Him for salvation. There is an obstinacy and a hardness within the human heart, a rebellion against God (see Mt.23:37; Jn.1:11).

> "You stiff-necked people, uncircumcised in heart and ears, you always resist the Holy Spirit. As your fathers did, so do you." (Ac.7:51)
>
> Yet he sent prophets among them to bring them back to the LORD. These testified against them, but they would not pay attention. (2 Chr.24:19)
>
> "They have turned to me their back and not their face. And though I have taught them persistently, they have not listened to receive instruction." (Je.32:33)
>
> "As for the word that you have spoken to us in the name of the LORD, we will not listen to you." (Je.44:16)

Jesus claimed that life was in Him (see DEEPER STUDY # 2—Jn.1:4; DEEPER STUDY # 1—10:10; DEEPER STUDY # 1—Jn.17:2-3).

> In him was life, and the life was the light of men. (Jn.1:4)
>
> "For as the Father has life in himself, so he has granted the Son also to have life in himself." (Jn.5:26)
>
> "The thief comes only to steal and kill and destroy. I came that they may have life and have it abundantly." (Jn.10:10)
>
> Jesus said to her, "I am the resurrection and the life. Whoever believes in me, though he die, yet shall he live." (Jn.11:25)
>
> Jesus said to him, "I am the way, and the truth, and the life. No one comes to the Father except through me." (Jn.14:6)

People receive life by coming to Jesus Christ. They keep from dying eternally by coming to Jesus Christ (see notes—Jn.5:21; 5:24-25; DEEPER STUDY # 1—He.9:27).

> "For as the Father raises the dead and gives them life, so also the Son gives life to whom he will." (Jn.5:21)
>
> "Truly, truly, I say to you, whoever hears my word and believes him who sent me has eternal life. He does not come into judgment, but has passed from death to life. Truly, truly, I say to you, an hour is coming, and is now here, when the dead will hear the voice of the Son of God, and those who hear will live." (Jn.5:24-25)

Jesus did not claim to be the Son of God in order to receive praise and glory from people (v.41). He proclaimed the truth because He loved people, and the fact of His deity is the truth. We must face up to this truth if we wish to be saved. Our rejection cuts deeply to the heart of Christ, and the hurt is seen in the tenderness and appeal of this verse. There is a pleading in His words, deep emotion in His voice when He says, "You refuse to come to me that you may have life."

> "'For this people's heart has grown dull, and with their ears they can barely hear, and their eyes they have closed; lest they should see with their eyes and hear with their ears and understand with their heart and turn, and I would heal them.'" (Ac.28:27)
>
> How shall we escape if we neglect such a great salvation? It was declared at first by the Lord, and it was attested to us by those who heard. (He.2:3)
>
> See that you do not refuse him who is speaking. For if they did not escape when they refused him who warned them on earth, much less will we escape if we reject him who warns from heaven. (He.12:25)

**5:42**

⁴² "But I know that you do not have the love of God within you."

## 2 People do not genuinely love God.

People choose to reject Christ, to reject the claim of Christ because they do not love God. The love of God is not in their hearts.

The people to whom Jesus spoke in John 5:40-47 professed to love God deeply. They . . .
- worshiped faithfully
- knew the Scriptures
- were always praying
- were unashamed to talk about Him

However, the love of God was not *in* them, not really. Their love for God was not *genuine* love, not the kind of love that honors and praises God, giving all that one is and has to love and help people.

> "'This people honors me with their lips, but their heart is far from me.'" (Mt.15:8)

> And hope does not put us to shame, because God's love has been poured into our hearts through the Holy Spirit who has been given to us. (Ro.5:5)

> Beloved, let us love one another, for love is from God, and whoever loves has been born of God and knows God. Anyone who does not love does not know God, because God is love. (1 Jn.4:7-8)

Jesus said, *I know*. He knows a person's heart, if a person's profession is true and genuine or false and counterfeit. Jesus sees right through our words, down deep into our heart.

> "For nothing is hidden that will not be made manifest, nor is anything secret that will not be known and come to light." (Lu.8:17)

> "For his eyes are on the ways of a man, and he sees all his steps." (Job 34:21)

> "'Great in counsel and mighty in deed, whose eyes are open to all the ways of the children of man, rewarding each one according to his ways and according to the fruit of his deeds.'" (Je.32:19)

> And the Spirit of the LORD fell upon me, and he said to me, "Say, Thus says the LORD: So you think, O house of Israel. For I know the things that come into your mind." (Eze.11:5)

**THOUGHT 1.** If people truly loved God, they would receive Christ. He is the beloved Son of the Father. To love God is to love His Son. Moreover, He is the only way to God. It is impossible to have a relationship with God apart from Jesus (Jn.14:6).

> Jesus said to him, "I am the way, and the truth, and the life. No one comes to the Father except through me." (Jn.14:6)

> In this the love of God was made manifest among us, that God sent his only Son into the world, so that we might live through him. In this is love, not that we have loved God but that he loved us and sent his Son to be the propitiation for our sins. . . . So we have come to know and to believe the love that God has for us. God is love, and whoever abides in love abides in God, and God abides in him. . . . We love because he first loved us. (1 Jn.4:9-10, 16, 19)

## 3 People can more easily accept a false messiah than someone coming in God's name.

⁴³ "I have come in my Father's name, and you do not receive me. If another comes in his own name, you will receive him."

Jesus stated plainly that He came in the name, that is, in the authority and truthfulness, of God. However, *another*—a false messiah, comes in his own authority and by his own word.

Jesus then pointed out a baffling fact: the people rejected God's Son, the true Messiah who came with the Father's authority, but they would receive a false messiah who came in his own name. Why?

Generally speaking, people want either to escape from the world or to get all they can from the world. Some want to escape the pressure, tension, immorality, selfishness, hatred, and injustices of the world. Others want either a reasonable amount of the world's prosperity, pleasure, power, recognition, or fame.

Jesus, being the Son of God, cannot lie. He has to tell the truth. The way to life is not by escaping the world nor by getting plenty of the world. The way to life is to do exactly as Jesus said:

> And he said to all, "If anyone would come after me, let him deny himself and take up his cross daily and follow me. For whoever would save his life will lose it, but whoever loses his life for my sake will save it. For what does it profit a man if he gains the whole world and loses or forfeits himself?" (Lu.9:23-25)

The false messiah—a false teacher or prophet or human deliverer—is not truthful. He is a mere mortal, full of all the human weaknesses and infirmities. A false messiah is a person born of mere man and woman; he is a person who will die as a mere man just as all other people die. The false messiah is a deceiving person with leadership qualities and charisma who has learned to promise what people crave: escapism and possessions. Therefore, he sets himself up, claiming that belief in his "name," that is, in his power and in what he says, will meet people's needs. Jesus says that many people will receive such a false messiah or deliverer (see Mt.24:23-26; see also Deeper Study # 2—Mt.1:18).

> For such men are false apostles, deceitful workmen, disguising themselves as apostles of Christ. And no wonder, for even Satan disguises himself as an angel of light. So it is no surprise if his servants, also, disguise themselves as servants of righteousness. Their end will correspond to their deeds. (2 Co.11:13-15)

> Desiring to be teachers of the law, without understanding either what they are saying or the things about which they make confident assertions. (1 Ti.1:7)

> For the time is coming when people will not endure sound teaching, but having itching ears they will accumulate for themselves teachers to suit their own passions, and will turn away from listening to the truth and wander off into myths. (2 Ti.4:3-4)

> But false prophets also arose among the people, just as there will be false teachers among you, who will secretly bring in destructive heresies, even denying the Master who bought them, bringing upon themselves swift destruction. (2 Pe.2:1)

> Who is the liar but he who denies that Jesus is the Christ? This is the antichrist, he who denies the Father and the Son. No one who denies the Son has the Father. Whoever confesses the Son has the Father also. (1 Jn.2:22-23)

**5:44**

⁴⁴ "How can you believe, when you receive glory from one another and do not seek the glory that comes from the only God?"

## 4 People seek approval and honor from others instead of from God.

When people seek the approval and honor of *mere* men—other people—they make two gross mistakes. First, they seek the acceptance and approval, the recognition and honor, of others, and such becomes the driving force of their lives. People seek . . .

- the right position in which to be seen
- the right place to live and work
- the right car to drive
- the right clothes to wear
- the right looks to attract
- the right gifts to secure honor
- the power and wealth to possess
- the recognition and fame to be known

In seeking approval and honor from others, they do not seek the acceptance and approval nor the recognition and honor of God.

Second, they measure themselves against other people, not against God. When people measure themselves by other people, they are seen to be good and acceptable. Seemingly, they do not come short often, if at all. When they are being praised and honored by others, they feel acceptable, complete, fulfilled. Therefore, they often sense no need for God.

Only when we measure ourselves against God do we see ourselves as we truly are: we fall far short of God's glory (Ro.3:23). Only then will people bow in humility and beg forgiveness and cast themselves upon the mercy of God. Note the question of Christ: "[In light of this,] how can you believe?"

> For if anyone thinks he is something, when he is nothing, he deceives himself. (Ga.6:3)

> If we say we have no sin, we deceive ourselves, and the truth is not in us. (1 Jn.1:8)

> "'For you say, I am rich, I have prospered, and I need nothing, not realizing that you are wretched, pitiable, poor, blind, and naked.'" (Re.3:17)

> Many a man proclaims his own steadfast love, but a faithful man who can find? (Pr.20:6)

> It is not good to eat much honey, nor is it glorious to seek one's own glory. (Pr.25:27)

## 5 People do not believe the Scripture—do not believe the prophecies of Moses' writings.

The fifth reason people reject Christ is that they do not believe Scripture. To His audience of Jewish religious authorities, Jesus specifically referred to the prophecies in Moses' writings, the sacred Torah.

Here Jesus pointedly says, "Moses wrote of me." All the prophecies in Genesis through Deuteronomy are the prophecies to which Jesus refers (see Deeper Study # 3—Jn.1:45 for the prophecies by Moses). Therefore, Jesus says that Moses—the revered lawgiver and spokesman of Jehovah—is the one who condemned their unbelief, not Him. The men standing before Jesus professed to believe Moses, but they did not—not really.

⁴⁵ "Do not think that I will accuse you to the Father. There is one who accuses you: Moses, on whom you have set your hope.
⁴⁶ "For if you believed Moses, you would believe me; for he wrote of me."

➢ They did not believe what Moses said about the promised Messiah.
➢ They did not live as Moses said to live.
➢ Their profession would be condemned by the very one whom they said they trusted, by Moses himself.

> And he said to them, "You have a fine way of rejecting the commandment of God in order to establish your tradition!" (Mk.7:9)
>
> "Thus making void the word of God by your tradition that you have handed down. And many such things you do." (Mk.7:13)
>
> And he said to them, "O foolish ones, and slow of heart to believe all that the prophets have spoken!" (Lu.24:25)
>
> "I told you that you would die in your sins, for unless you believe that I am he you will die in your sins." (Jn.8:24)
>
> Therefore, as the tongue of fire devours the stubble, and as dry grass sinks down in the flame, so their root will be as rottenness, and their blossom go up like dust; for they have rejected the law of the Lord of hosts, and have despised the word of the Holy One of Israel. (Is.5:24)
>
> For they are a rebellious people, lying children, children unwilling to hear the instruction of the Lord. (Is.30:9)

## 6 People will not believe the words of the true Messiah if they do not believe prophecy.

⁴⁷ "But if you do not believe his writings, how will you believe my words?"

The final reason Jesus cited for rejecting Him is that people refuse to believe His words, the words of the true Messiah. As Jesus establishes in previous verses, the Jewish religious authorities, the experts and enforcers of the law, did not truly believe the law—Moses' writings, the words of Scripture. How then could they believe the promises of the Messiah?

They did not believe the testimony of a man whom they professed was a great and honorable man. They honored Moses, calling him great and honorable; yet they treated him as a liar, a man whose testimony was unreliable. How then could they believe the words of Christ?

> **THOUGHT 1.** How many acknowledge Christ as a great and honorable man yet treat Him as a liar, a man whose testimony and claims are totally untrustworthy?
>
> > "Truly, truly, I say to you, if anyone keeps my word, he will never see death." (Jn.8:51)
> >
> > "The one who rejects me and does not receive my words has a judge; the word that I have spoken will judge him on the last day." (Jn.12:48)
> >
> > "Whoever does not love me does not keep my words. And the word that you hear is not mine but the Father's who sent me." (Jn.14:24)
> >
> > If anyone teaches a different doctrine and does not agree with the sound words of our Lord Jesus Christ and the teaching that accords with godliness, he is puffed up with conceit and understands nothing. He has an unhealthy craving for controversy and for quarrels about words, which produce envy, dissension, slander, evil suspicions. (1 Tl.6:3-4)

# Chapter 6

## VII. The Revelation of Jesus, the Bread of Life, 6:1–71

### A. Jesus Feeds Five Thousand: The Kind of Faith Necessary to Meet Human Need, 6:1–15

|  |  |
|---|---|
| 1. The setting: Jesus crossed over the Sea of Galilee<sup>DS1</sup><br>a. Jesus drew a huge crowd of followers | After this Jesus went away to the other side of the Sea of Galilee, which is the Sea of Tiberias. |
| | ² And a large crowd was following him, because they saw the signs that he was doing on the sick. |
| b. Jesus sought rest & relief because it was nearly time to attend the Passover Feast | ³ Jesus went up on the mountain, and there he sat down with his disciples.<br>⁴ Now the Passover, the feast of the Jews, was at hand. |
| c. Jesus had two concerns<sup>DS2</sup><br>1) Providing a meal for the multitude: Jesus wanted to meet every need | ⁵ Lifting up his eyes, then, and seeing that a large crowd was coming toward him, Jesus said to Philip, "Where are we to buy bread, so that these people may eat?" |
| 2) Testing & strengthening His disciples: Jesus wanted to teach the kinds of faith | ⁶ He said this to test him, for he himself knew what he would do. |
| 2. There is a pessimistic faith<sup>DS3</sup> | ⁷ Philip answered him, "Two hundred denarii worth of bread would not be enough for each of them to get a little." |
| 3. There is an optimistic but questioning faith<sup>DS4</sup> | ⁸ One of his disciples, Andrew, Simon Peter's brother, said to him, |

# Division VII

*The Revelation of Jesus, the Bread of Life, 6:1–71*

A. Jesus Feeds Five Thousand: The Kind of Faith Necessary to Meet Human Need, 6:1–15

## 6:1–71 DIVISION OVERVIEW

Chapter 6 reveals Jesus to be the Provision for every human and material need. Jesus first demonstrated the truth, then He began to preach and teach it. He showed that He was . . .

- concerned with every need in life (even a missed meal, Jn.6:1-15)
- concerned with every overpowering need (the calming of a storm, Jn.6:16-21)

⁹ "There is a boy here who has five barley loaves and two fish, but what are they for so many?"

¹⁰ Jesus said, "Have the people sit down." Now there was much grass in the place. So the men sat down, about five thousand in number.

¹¹ Jesus then took the loaves, and when he had given thanks, he distributed them to those who were seated. So also the fish, as much as they wanted.

¹² And when they had eaten their fill, he told his disciples, "Gather up the leftover fragments, that nothing may be lost."
¹³ So they gathered them up and filled twelve baskets with fragments from the five barley loaves left by those who had eaten.
¹⁴ When the people saw the sign that he had done, they said, "This is indeed the Prophet who is to come into the world!"

¹⁵ Perceiving then that they were about to come and take him by force to make him king, Jesus withdrew again to the mountain by himself.

  a. Andrew brought a young boy & his meal to Jesus
  b. Andrew questioned the sufficiency of the supply

**4. There is a positive, unswerving faith**

  a. Jesus' faith
    1) He took & gave thanks for what He had
    2) He gave what He had
    3) He used others to help Him
  b. God's answer & provision
    1) God met the people's need: He fed & filled them
    2) God gave an overabundance
    3) Jesus allowed no waste

**5. There is a materialistic faith that desires only earthly things & worldly satisfaction**
  a. The people's profession: Jesus is the Messiah
  b. The people's concept: Jesus is an earthly, materialistic, worldly-minded king

No matter how small the need or how stormy the problem, Jesus is the Provision, the Bread of Life, and the power to meet our every need. He can provide a single meal, and He can calm the stormiest problem.

## 6:1–15
## Introduction

Jesus Christ is the Bread of Life, the Provision for human and material needs (see outline and notes—Mt.6:25–34). Note two significant facts.

First, trying to meet human needs by any other source than Christ is doomed to failure and will not satisfy.

Second, believing and trusting are essential for God to meet human need. However, there are several levels of faith and trust, several different kinds of faith. This is the lesson we must learn in order to see that Christ is the Bread of Life, the Provision for every need. Then, we need to examine ourselves to be sure our faith is the right kind of faith. This is, *Jesus Feeds Five Thousand: The Kind of Faith Necessary to Meet Human Need,* 6:1–15.1.

1. The setting: Jesus crossed over the Sea of Galilee (vv.1-6).
2. There is a pessimistic faith (v.7).
3. There is an optimistic but questioning faith (vv.8-9).
4. There is a positive, unswerving faith (vv.10-13).
5. There is a materialistic faith that desires only earthly things and worldly satisfaction (vv.14-15).

## 6:1-6

After this Jesus went away to the other side of the Sea of Galilee, which is the Sea of Tiberias.

² And a large crowd was following him, because they saw the signs that he was doing on the sick.

³ Jesus went up on the mountain, and there he sat down with his disciples.

⁴ Now the Passover, the feast of the Jews, was at hand.

⁵ Lifting up his eyes, then, and seeing that a large crowd was coming toward him, Jesus said to Philip, "Where are we to buy bread, so that these people may eat?"

⁶ He said this to test him, for he himself knew what he would do.

## 1 The setting: Jesus crossed over the Sea of Galilee.

John notes that *after this* or *after these things* (see DEEPER STUDY # 1), Jesus crossed over the Sea or Lake of Galilee (see DEEPER STUDY # 1—Mk.1:16; note—Lu.8:22). The lake was about thirteen miles long and eight miles wide. The intense, surging crowds saw where He was heading, so they rushed around the lake by foot. The journey was about nine miles.

a. **Jesus drew a huge crowd of followers (v.2).**
Note the words *was following* or *followed* (eklouthei) and *saw* (etheoroun, v.2). The two Greek words used together along with the imperfect active tense, imply that the people *had been following* Jesus for a long time and *kept on following Him, observing the ministry* of His miracles upon people.

b. **Jesus sought rest and relief because it was nearly time to attend the Passover Feast (v.3).**
Tired and weary from the pressure of facing the crowd day after day, Jesus sought refuge across the lake on the top of some unknown mountain. He needed time to be alone with God and with His disciples. It was the Passover season, a time when thousands of pilgrims flooded Jerusalem and the surrounding suburbs.

The picture is that of Jesus sitting on the mountainside, lifting up His eyes from resting upon His knees and a huge crowd of thousands streaming across the fields and up the mountain toward Him (v.5). The great multitude included both those who had followed Him around the lake and pilgrims who were caught up in the excitement of hearing about Jesus, the proclaimed Messiah.

c. **Jesus had two concerns (vv.5-6).**
Jesus was concerned about providing a meal for the people who were following Him (v.5). Our Lord always cares about meeting our needs, even the most trivial need of missing a meal. There is no need that Jesus does not want to meet. The multitude that had been following Him for days had just made a nine-mile journey, having rushed (*followed*, Gk. eklouthei) to keep from losing Him. They were not only hungry and apparently out of food, but they were in mountainous country, an area without any possibility of purchasing food. The people were so desperate to find and keep up with Jesus that they simply did not eat. As usual, Jesus was filled with compassion for those who so desperately sought Him out. He used the occasion to teach the great lesson that He will meet even the smallest human need. He asked His disciples where they could buy bread so the people could eat.

In addition, Jesus was concerned about testing and strengthening His disciples (v.6). He knew what He was going to do, but He used the occasion to teach them a tremendous lesson on faith. They were as we are, full of needs; and their greatest need was the same as ours, to grow in faith. Therefore, He taught them about the different kinds of faith (see DEEPER STUDY # 2).

### Deeper Study # 1

(6:1) **"After This or After These Things"**: this is a reference to the closing days of the Galilean ministry, the events covered between Mt.4:12-14:12. These events are not covered by John. His focus is on the Judean ministry of Jesus; therefore, He simply moves over the Galilean events by using the words "after these things."

### Deeper Study # 2

(6:5-15) **Faith**: Jesus was showing that He was concerned with every little need in life (even a missed meal), and that He was able to provide for every need—if people would just believe Him. Therefore, He taught a necessary lesson: there are four ways to respond to needs (see note—Mk.11:22-23).

## 2 There is a pessimistic faith.

6:7

The first kind of faith we observe in this passage is a pessimistic faith. This is seen in Philip. Philip needed to see his faith for what it was—pessimistic. Philip was from Bethsaida, so it is no surprise that he questioned Jesus, for the city rejected Christ (see Deeper Study # 2—Jn.1:44 for more discussion). The disciples either had two hundred denarii in their treasury or else Philip was just pulling a figure out of the air stressing that even such a large amount would not feed the crowd (see Deeper Study # 3).

⁶ He said this to test him, for he himself knew what he would do.
⁷ Philip answered him, "Two hundred denarii worth of bread would not be enough for each of them to get a little."

A pessimistic faith sees money and human resources, and that is all. A pessimistic faith . . .
- sees only the available resources. It stresses the hopelessness
- stresses the impossibility of the situation
- despairs of such meager resources
- is swamped by the hopelessness of an answer (note the tone of Philip's answer, v.7)

Moreover, a pessimistic faith sees neither God nor God's power. A pessimistic faith *professes* God and *professes* Christ to be the Son of God. It professes the belief that Christ has the power to meet the needs of every person. It even witnesses the miraculous working of Christ in other instances. But when a problem arises, the immediate response of a pessimistic faith is to focus more on the *problem*, than on the *power* of God. It does not see the opportunity for the power of God to be demonstrated in conquering the problem and bearing a strong testimony to His name. In the crises of the problem, the power of God seems forgotten.

**THOUGHT 1.** Is your faith pessimistic? How can you tell if it is? The following are characteristics of a pessimistic faith:
➢ A pessimistic faith forgets God's glorious power in the past.

> But Jesus, aware of this, said, "O you of little faith, why are you discussing among yourselves the fact that you have no bread? Do you not yet perceive? Do you not remember the five loaves for the five thousand, and how many baskets you gathered?" (Mt.16:8-9)

> But he was in the stern, asleep on the cushion. And they woke him and said to him, "Teacher, do you not care that we are perishing?" And he awoke and rebuked the wind and said to the sea, "Peace! Be still!" And the wind ceased, and there was a great calm. He said to them, "Why are you so afraid? Have you still no faith?" (Mk.4:38-40)

➢ A pessimistic faith fails to think of God's power. Its mind is on earthly things, not on spiritual things. It is carnal, not spiritual.

For those who live according to the flesh set their minds on the things of the flesh, but those who live according to the Spirit set their minds on the things of the Spirit. For to set the mind on the flesh is death, but to set the mind on the Spirit is life and peace. (Ro.8:5-6)

- ➢ A pessimistic faith feels that the problem is too big for God's power or either too little for God to be interested in.

    "Again I tell you, it is easier for a camel to go through the eye of a needle than for a rich person to enter the kingdom of God." When the disciples heard this, they were greatly astonished, saying, "Who then can be saved?" But Jesus looked at them and said, "With man this is impossible, but with God all things are possible." (Mt.19:24-26)

- ➢ A pessimistic faith fears that God's power will fail and the person's faith will be weakened. Therefore, the person is safer to pray weakly, "Lord, if it is your will, handle this problem."

    But let him ask in faith, with no doubting, for the one who doubts is like a wave of the sea that is driven and tossed by the wind. For that person must not suppose that he will receive anything from the Lord; he is a double-minded man, unstable in all his ways. (Js.1:6-8)

- ➢ A pessimistic faith fails to see God's care and love, interest and concern, over every little thing that happens to a person.

    "Look at the birds of the air: they neither sow nor reap nor gather into barns, and yet your heavenly Father feeds them. Are you not of more value than they?" (Mt.6:26)

    "But even the hairs of your head are all numbered." (Mt.10:30)

- ➢ A pessimistic faith gives thanks and praise to God for what one has (health, money, things) but fails to trust God for the miraculous (healing and multiplication of resources so that one can better serve and help others).

    Then the disciples came to Jesus privately and said, "Why could we not cast it out?" He said to them, "Because of your little faith. For truly, I say to you, if you have faith like a grain of mustard seed, you will say to this mountain, 'Move from here to there,' and it will move, and nothing will be impossible for you." (Mt.17:19-20)

- ➢ A pessimistic faith looks to others for help instead of looking to God and depending on Him alone.

    Do not be anxious about anything, but in everything by prayer and supplication with thanksgiving let your requests be made known to God. And the peace of God, which surpasses all understanding, will guard your hearts and your minds in Christ Jesus. (Ph.4:6-7)

    Unless the LORD builds the house, those who build it labor in vain. Unless the LORD watches over the city, the watchman stays awake in vain. (Ps.127:1)

    Stop regarding man in whose nostrils is breath, for of what account is he? (Is.2:22)

    I know, O LORD, that the way of man is not in himself, that it is not in man who walks to direct his steps. (Je.10:23)

- ➢ A pessimistic faith fails to see that God is glorified when He provides and meets the need.

    I rejoiced in the Lord greatly that now at length you have revived your concern for me. You were indeed concerned for me, but you had no opportunity. (Ph.4:10)

    I have received full payment, and more. I am well supplied, having received from Epaphroditus the gifts you sent, a fragrant offering, a sacrifice acceptable and pleasing to God. And my God will supply every need of yours according to his riches in glory in Christ Jesus. To our God and Father be glory forever and ever. Amen. (Ph.4:18-20)

## DEEPER STUDY # 3

(6:7) **Denarii**: one denarii was the average pay for a day's work. The amount in any generation's currency would be equal to that generation's average daily wage.

## 3 There is an optimistic but questioning faith.

The optimistic, but questioning faith is illustrated in this passage by Andrew (see DEEPER STUDY # 4). Note how Andrew's actions teach us about this kind of faith.

### a. Andrew brought a young boy and his meal to Jesus (v.9a).

Having a questioning faith does not mean that a person does not love the Lord or is not committed to the Lord. Andrew's love and commitment to Christ are clear. He saw Christ's concern, so he went among the crowd to search for food. He found and gathered all the resources he could: one young boy and his meager meal.

> ⁸ One of his disciples, Andrew, Simon Peter's brother, said to him,
> ⁹ "There is a boy here who has five barley loaves and two fish, but what are they for so many?"

### b. Andrew questioned the sufficiency of the supply (v.9b).

An optimistic, questioning faith lays what it can find before the Lord. No matter how little the resources or how poor the quality, it is all laid before the Lord. The boy's loaves were barley bread—the bread of the poor, the very cheapest bread that could be made or bought. It was anything but a delicacy. The fact that the boy had two fish for his supper indicates that they were most likely small. Note the simple, optimistic faith of Andrew. He had searched and could find nothing but five small barley cakes and two small fish, but he offered what he had found—the *boy* and his *food*—to the Lord.

At the same time, an optimistic, questioning faith doubts whether what one has is enough. The questioning faith often deteriorates into . . .

- complaining about the problem
- being anxious about meager resources
- grumbling over the small provision
- griping over the poor quality

**THOUGHT 1.** Is your faith a questioning faith? A questioning faith looks at the need and then looks at the *meager resources*, both how little and how poor the quality of the resources are, and it questions God. It questions instead of believing God to take care of the problem. The need may be what it is in this event, the need for food; or it may be the need for health, money, deliverance, or a myriad of other human needs. Whatever the need may be, we ought to learn to trust Christ and not to question and doubt His love and care, wisdom and power.

> "Therefore I tell you, do not be anxious about your life, what you will eat or what you will drink, nor about your body, what you will put on. Is not life more than food, and the body more than clothing?" (Mt.6:25)

> "Therefore do not be anxious, saying, 'What shall we eat?' or 'What shall we drink?' or 'What shall we wear?' For the Gentiles seek after all these things, and your heavenly Father knows that you need them all." (Mt.6:31-32)

> But Martha was distracted with much serving. And she went up to him and said, "Lord, do you not care that my sister has left me to serve alone? Tell her then to help me." But the Lord answered her, "Martha, Martha, you are anxious and troubled about many things." (Lu.10:40-41)

> "And do not seek what you are to eat and what you are to drink, nor be worried." (Lu.12:29)

> Do not be anxious about anything, but in everything by prayer and supplication with thanksgiving let your requests be made known to God. (Ph.4:6)

> If any of you lacks wisdom, let him ask God, who gives generously to all without reproach, and it will be given him. But let him ask in faith, with no doubting, for the one who doubts is like a wave of the sea that is driven and tossed by the wind. (Js.1:5-6)

## Deeper Study # 4

(6:8-9) **Andrew**: little is said about Andrew in the New Testament, but what is said shows a faithful and humble follower of the Lord (also see Deeper Study # 7—Mk.3:18).

1. Andrew was a follower of John the Baptist (Jn.1:35-40).

2. Andrew willingly took "second place." He was one of the very first to follow Christ, and he was also one of the very first to bring another person to Christ (his own brother, Peter). However, Andrew was called to take a back seat and tended to operate under the shadow of Peter. Throughout the New Testament Peter is always mentioned first, but from all indications Andrew never resented his place. To be with Jesus and to do what Jesus wanted was enough for Andrew.

3. In John, Andrew is always seen bringing others to Jesus. He is the focus of attention only three times in the New Testament, and in all three cases he is seen bringing someone to Jesus: Peter (Jn.1:41), the small boy with the loaves and fish (Jn.6:8-9), and the Greeks (Jn.12:22).

4. Andrew was an approachable person. He was able to approach his brother Peter without difficulty, and the small boy with the loaves and fish felt comfortable enough with him to follow him to Jesus. The Greeks also felt comfortable enough to approach Andrew first in seeking an interview with Jesus.

6:10-13

¹⁰ Jesus said, "Have the people sit down." Now there was much grass in the place. So the men sat down, about five thousand in number.

¹¹ Jesus then took the loaves, and when he had given thanks, he distributed them to those who were seated. So also the fish, as much as they wanted.

¹² And when they had eaten their fill, he told his disciples, "Gather up the leftover fragments, that nothing may be lost."

¹³ So they gathered them up and filled twelve baskets with fragments from the five barley loaves left by those who had eaten.

### 4 There is a positive, unswerving faith.

The positive, unswerving faith is seen in Christ. The Lord Himself demonstrated for His disciples the kind of strong faith they were to have in God.

a. **Jesus' faith (v.11).**

Jesus took what He had and gave thanks to God the Father for it. He had only a meager supply of bread. In fact, He could hold all He had in the palm of His hand. But He did not stand there looking at the meagerness of what He had, questioning, being gripped with despair and hopelessness, wondering how the need was going to be met. Instead, He looked up and gave thanks to God. The small supply and poor quality did not matter. What mattered was that He had something; there was some provision. A gift, a sacrifice, a resource—small though it was—had been given and laid at His feet for Him to use as He willed. So, He took it, being ever so appreciative, and lifted it up to God, giving thanks to God and trusting Him to meet the need of the hour. Note how positive and unswerving the act of Christ was. He knew beyond any question that God would meet the need and multiply the resources.

Jesus teaches us an important lesson: He distributed what was in His hands and trusted God the Father to do the rest. He simply gave what He had, and God the Father did the rest.

➤ Christ received the offering of the resources, meager as they were.
➤ Christ trusted God the Father to multiply the resources.
➤ Christ then gave the supply to the disciples, not to consume but to distribute. This is critical to note.
➤ Christ used others to help Him in meeting the need. The disciples distributed the food and fed the people. They were a vital part of the Lord's plan. They were the ones made responsible for feeding the people.

b. **God's answer and provision (vv.12-13).**

God met the need *because* of the positive, unswerving faith of Jesus. God met the people's need and filled them. In fact, and this is extremely important, He gave an overabundance and *more* than met their need. There was provision *left over*. How much? Twelve baskets full. Why twelve baskets? There were twelve disciples, twelve servants who had so obediently and trustingly helped Christ. Each servant had a supply that would last him for days. God always provides abundantly for His true servants (Ph.4:19). Note: Jesus allowed no waste. Every ounce of provision was to be used at some future date.

**THOUGHT 1.** A positive, unswerving faith gives what we have, does what we can do, and trusts God to do the rest. All we can do is give what we have, what we hold in our hands. But we can do *that*, and that is all God expects us to do. If we will give it to God, He will do the rest. The need will be met.

The needs of the whole world can be met only if we will give what we hold. Because many are holding and grasping after more and more, the world is reeling in the desperation of hunger and disease, war and death, sin and evil, doomed to live apart from God eternally.

> And he answered them, "Whoever has two tunics is to share with him who has none, and whoever has food is to do likewise." (Lu.3:11)
>
> "In all things I have shown you that by working hard in this way we must help the weak and remember the words of the Lord Jesus, how he himself said, 'It is more blessed to give than to receive.'" (Ac.20:35)
>
> Contribute to the needs of the saints and seek to show hospitality. (Ro.12:13)
>
> So then, as we have opportunity [to give], let us do good to everyone, and especially to those who are of the household of faith. (Ga.6:10)
>
> . . . let him labor, doing honest work with his own hands, so that he may have something to share with anyone in need. (Ep.4:28)
>
> They are to do good, to be rich in good works, to be generous and ready to share. (1 Ti.6:18)
>
> Do not neglect to do good and to share what you have, for such sacrifices are pleasing to God. (He.13:16)

**THOUGHT 2.** As we are giving what we have, we must trust the power and provision of God.

> "But seek first the kingdom of God and his righteousness, and all these things will be added to you." (Mt.6:33)
>
> And my God will supply every need of yours according to his riches in glory in Christ Jesus. (Ph.4:19)
>
> Now faith is the assurance of things hoped for, the conviction of things not seen. (He.11:1)
>
> Commit your way to the LORD; trust in him, and he will act. (Ps.37:5)
>
> Trust in the LORD with all your heart, and do not lean on your own understanding. (Pr.3:5)
>
> "Bring the full tithe into the storehouse, that there may be food in my house. And thereby put me to the test, says the LORD of hosts, if I will not open the windows of heaven for you and pour down for you a blessing until there is no more need." (Mal.3:10)

## 5 There is a materialistic faith that desires only earthly things and worldly satisfaction.

Finally, this passage presents a materialistic faith. This kind of faith desires only earthly things and worldly satisfaction. It gives in order to get. It claims to believe but only for the purpose of receiving the things of this world from God.

> ¹⁴ When the people saw the sign that he had done, they said, "This is indeed the Prophet who is to come into the world!"
>
> ¹⁵ Perceiving then that they were about to come and take him by force to make him king, Jesus withdrew again to the mountain by himself.

a. **The people's profession: Jesus is the Messiah (v.14).**

After Jesus' performed such an amazing feat, the miracle of feeding thousands with but a handful of food, the people professed him as the Messiah. They acknowledged Him to be *the Prophet* foretold in the Old Testament.

b. **The people's concept: Jesus is an earthly, materialistic, worldly-minded king (v.15).**

However, the people wanted Jesus as their king for the wrong reason. They professed Jesus to be the Messiah, but they were thinking of an earthly, materialistic king, a Messiah who could meet both their personal and community or national needs (see Deeper Study # 2—Jn.1:20; note—1:23).

Jesus had fed and healed them. He had done what the people wanted, met their need for health and food. Therefore, they wanted to set Him up as the king of their lives. They did not want to ever hunger or be sick again, not as long as they lived. They saw in Jesus the possibility of an earthly, human Messiah, One who could provide . . .

- food for their hunger
- healing for their sicknesses
- deliverance from their trials
- comfort for their sorrows
- plenty for their wants
- peace through their disturbances
- victory over their enemies

**THOUGHT 1.** Jesus, of course, can help us through anything. But too many people have the same problem as this crowd: the desire for earthly and worldly satisfaction. They have a materialistic faith, a faith that thinks in terms of the physical and material, not the spiritual. Even when Christ meets physical and material needs, the physical and material are only temporary. They pass away. The Lord's concern is primarily spiritual—spiritual strength and spiritual blessings, the strength and blessings that last forever (see note—Ep.1:3). This is the reason so many people forsake Christ. He requires . . .

- the denial of self

    **And he said to all, "If anyone would come after me, let him deny himself and take up his cross daily and follow me." (Lu.9:23)**

- separation from the world

    **Jesus answered them, "Truly, truly, I say to you, you are seeking me, not because you saw signs, but because you ate your fill of the loaves. Do not work for the food that perishes, but for the food that endures to eternal life, which the Son of Man will give to you. For on him God the Father has set his seal." (Jn.6:26-27)**

    **I appeal to you therefore, brothers, by the mercies of God, to present your bodies as a living sacrifice, holy and acceptable to God, which is your spiritual worship. Do not be conformed to this world, but be transformed by the renewal of your mind, that by testing you may discern what is the will of God, what is good and acceptable and perfect. (Ro.12:1-2)**

    **"Therefore go out from their midst, and be separate from them, says the Lord, and touch no unclean thing; then I will welcome you, and I will be a father to you, and you shall be sons and daughters to me, says the Lord Almighty." (2 Co.6:17-18)**

    **Do not love the world or the things in the world. If anyone loves the world, the love of the Father is not in him. For all that is in the world—the desires of the flesh and the desires of the eyes and pride of life—is not from the Father but is from the world. (1 Jn.2:15-16)**

- the giving of what we have

    **Jesus said to him, "If you would be perfect, go, sell what you possess and give to the poor, and you will have treasure in heaven; and come, follow me." (Mt.19:21)**

## B. Jesus Walks on Water: The Deliverance from Fear, 6:16–21

*Mt.14:22-33; Mk.6: 45-52*

| | |
|---|---|
| ¹⁶ When evening came, his disciples went down to the sea, | 1. The setting: The disciples set sail to cross the lake |
| ¹⁷ got into a boat, and started across the sea to Capernaum. It was now dark, and Jesus had not yet come to them. | 2. The causes of fear<br>  a. Being in the dark<br>  b. Being without Jesus |
| ¹⁸ The sea became rough because a strong wind was blowing. |   c. Being caught in a storm |
| ¹⁹ When they had rowed about three or four miles, they saw Jesus walking on the sea and coming near the boat, and they were frightened. |   d. Being tired & gripped with a sense of horror, of impending death |
| ²⁰ But he said to them, "It is I; do not be afraid." | 3. The answer to fear<br>  a. The presence & Word of Jesus: "I Am" is here^DS1<br>  b. Receiving the presence of Jesus |
| ²¹ Then they were glad to take him into the boat, and immediately the boat was at the land to which they were going. |   c. The result: Deliverance through the storms of life |

# Division VII

### *The Revelation of Jesus, the Bread of Life, 6:1–71*

B. Jesus Walks on Water: The Deliverance from Fear, 6:16–21

*Mt.14:22-33; Mk.6:45-52*

## 6:16–21
## Introduction

At one time or another, we will all experience the fear of being caught in dangerous circumstances beyond our control. Life-threatening accidents, illnesses, weather events, and violent attacks are just a few examples of situations that can fill us with indescribable terror.

Jesus' disciples fell into fear's strangling grip when a storm suddenly arose as they were sailing across the Sea of Galilee. When it seemed that they would not escape, the Lord came to them and delivered them.

God's Spirit inspired John to record this episode from the disciples' lives to teach us a comforting truth: Jesus Christ is the great Deliverer from fear. He is definitely revealed as the great Deliverer in this experience. This is, *Jesus Walks on Water: The Deliverance from Fear, 6:16-21.*

1. The setting: The disciples set sail to cross the lake (v.16).
2. The causes of fear (vv.17-19).
3. The answer to fear (vv.20-21).

## 1 The setting: The disciples set sail to cross the lake.

The disciples set sail to cross the Sea of Galilee. The crowd was about to take Jesus by force and make Him a king (see outline and note—vv.14-15). Knowing that the disciples might be swept up in the *excitement of the temptation* to make Jesus king before His time, Jesus instructed them to set sail. They obeyed Jesus, did exactly what He said: they fled and escaped the temptation.

Note that Jesus had not yet come to join the disciples (v.17). Apparently, Jesus had told them to row out some distance and then to turn and pick Him up at some other point on the shore. However, they were not to wait for Him beyond a certain time. He was going to send the crowd away and withdraw to pray (see Mk.6:45-46). The violent storm caught the disciples by surprise and pulled them out to sea (v.18).

**6:16**

¹⁶ When evening came, his disciples went down to the sea,

**6:17-19**

¹⁷ got into a boat, and started across the sea to Capernaum. It was now dark, and Jesus had not yet come to them.
¹⁸ The sea became rough because a strong wind was blowing.
¹⁹ When they had rowed about three or four miles, they saw Jesus walking on the sea and coming near the boat, and they were frightened.

## 2 The causes of fear.

Fear can invade our lives through any number of circumstances. The disciples' threatening experience clearly illustrates four causes of fear.

**a. Being in the dark (v.17a).**

Many people fear being in the dark. Verse 17 tells us that darkness had fallen, and the disciples could not see, compounding the threat, danger, and emotional strain caused by the storm.

**THOUGHT 1.** The darkness the disciples faced reminds us of the spiritual darkness in which all who do not know Christ live. People in spiritual darkness cannot see. Their blindness is a great threat and emotional strain upon them.

(1) It is a great threat in that they do not know what lies ahead (trouble, sorrow, difficulty, loss, death).

> "But if your eye is bad, your whole body will be full of darkness. If then the light in you is darkness, how great is the darkness!" (Mt.6:23)

> "Let them alone; they are blind guides. And if the blind lead the blind, both will fall into a pit." (Mt.15:14)

> But whoever hates his brother is in the darkness and walks in the darkness, and does not know where he is going, because the darkness has blinded his eyes. (1 Jn.2:11)

(2) It is a great danger in that they will definitely face some difficult times. Being in darkness, they will be caught unprepared. They will be *in the dark* about God, about how to call on Him and to receive strength and help from Him.

> They are darkened in their understanding, alienated from the life of God because of the ignorance that is in them, due to their hardness of heart. (Ep.4:18)

> They have neither knowledge nor understanding, they walk about in darkness; all the foundations of the earth are shaken. (Ps.82:5)

> The way of the wicked is like deep darkness; they do not know over what they stumble. (Pr.4:19)

(3) It is a great emotional strain in that fear will overtake them, covering them with a sense of helplessness and hopelessness.

> "And you shall grope at noonday, as the blind grope in darkness, and you shall not prosper in your ways. And you shall be only oppressed and robbed continually, and there shall be no one to help you." (De.28:29)

> The way of peace they do not know, and there is no justice in their paths; they have made their roads crooked; no one who treads on them knows peace. Therefore justice is far from

us, and righteousness does not overtake us; we hope for light, and behold, darkness, and for brightness, but we walk in gloom. (Is.59:8-9)

"Therefore their way shall be to them like slippery paths in the darkness, into which they shall be driven and fall, for I will bring disaster upon them in the year of their punishment, declares the LORD." (Je.23:12)

b. **Being without Jesus (v.17b).**
Being without Jesus should cause fear in people's hearts. The disciples were afraid because they had to face the storm without the Lord. Jesus had not yet come to the disciples; therefore, they did not have His presence and help with them. They were left alone to fend for themselves, having only the help of each other. Their own strength and abilities had to save them—or else they were would perish. They had every reason to fear, for they were honest men: each one knew down deep within his heart that their strength was limited and would eventually fail.

**THOUGHT 1.** It is a fearful thing to walk through life without the Lord. All who have not received Christ as Savior and Lord do not have the promise of Christ's powerful, strengthening presence in their lives. They must face the storms of life alone, having only themselves and other people to lean on.

Remember that you were at that time separated from Christ, alienated from the commonwealth of Israel [God's people] and strangers to the covenants of promise, having no hope and without God in the world. (Ep.2:12)

"I also will choose harsh treatment for them and bring their fears upon them, because when I called, no one answered, when I spoke, they did not listen; but they did what was evil in my eyes and chose that in which I did not delight." (Is.66:4)

c. **Being caught in a storm (v.18).**
Strong, gale-like winds and a violent storm arose as the disciples crossed the sea. Note that when they had launched out, conditions were calm and peaceful; they thought their journey would be successful, that they would confront no trouble whatsoever. Although they never expected to encounter a violent storm, the winds and clouds *did come*. The terrible storm *did strike and did threaten* their lives.

**THOUGHT 1.** So it is with the violent storms of life. Trouble, trial, sickness, death, financial difficulties, and a host of other storms strike everyone. They strike unexpectedly, too often when we are least prepared. The result is great fear and emotional upheaval in our lives.

We are afflicted in every way, but not crushed; perplexed, but not driven to despair; persecuted, but not forsaken; struck down, but not destroyed. (2 Co.4:8-9)

For when we were with you, we kept telling you beforehand that we were to suffer affliction [trials], just as it has come to pass, and just as you know. (1 Th.3:4)

"But man is born to trouble as the sparks fly upward." (Jb.5:7)

"Man who is born of a woman is few of days and full of trouble." (Jb.14:1)

d. **Being tired and gripped with a sense of horror, of impending death (v.19).**
The disciples had been struggling against the storm for six to nine hours, and they had progressed only three or four miles. They were physically exhausted, and they knew that they could not prevail against the untamable forces of nature. As a result, they lost all hope of surviving. A sense of horror and impending death seized their weary souls.

Note what happened next (see Mk.6:47-49 for full explanation). The disciples saw Jesus walking toward them *on* the sea. This miraculous sight heightened their level of fear, which was already sky-high. Remember, they were physically exhausted and mentally drained from battling the storm. Their lives were at stake; they were struggling for survival.

Suddenly, a mysterious figure appeared out of nowhere. They thought it was a ghost walking on the water. And it was not just one of them who saw it; all on board saw this fear-striking figure. They were terrified, perhaps even to the point of going into shock, because they thought that the death angel or a premonition of their death was at hand.

**THOUGHT 1.** The point of this passage is forceful: the storms of life can cause a sense of horror, of impending death, and can strike an awful fear in our hearts.

> And deliver all those who through fear of death were subject to lifelong slavery. (He.2:15)

> "For I know that you will bring me to death and to the house appointed for all living." (Job 30:23)

> What man can live and never see death? Who can deliver his soul from the power of Sheol? Selah. (Ps.89:48)

> For there is a time and a way for everything, although man's trouble lies heavy on him. For he does not know what is to be, for who can tell him how it will be? No man has power to retain the spirit, or power over the day of death. There is no discharge from war, nor will wickedness deliver those who are given to it. (Ec.8:6–8)

> At evening time, behold, terror! Before morning, they are no more! This is the portion of those who loot us, and the lot of those who plunder us. (Is.17:14)

**6:20–21**

²⁰ But he said to them, "It is I; do not be afraid."
²¹ Then they were glad to take him into the boat, and immediately the boat was at the land to which they were going.

## 3 The answer to fear.

We do not have to be slaves to the spirit of fear. God has given us the answer to fear, and that answer is Jesus Himself. Note how the disciples were delivered from their intense fear.

**a. The presence and Word of Jesus: "I Am" is here (v.20).**

The disciples were set free from fear by the presence and Word of Jesus. The Word of Christ delivers us from fear. He proclaimed to his terror-stricken servants, "It is I; do not be afraid" (see Deeper Study # 1).

> And Jesus came and said to them, "All authority in heaven and on earth has been given to me." (Mt.28:18)

> "I have said these things to you, that in me you may have peace. In the world you will have tribulation. But take heart; I have overcome the world." (Jn.16:33)

> "Call to me and I will answer you, and will tell you great and hidden things that you have not known." (Je.33:3)

**b. Receiving the presence of Jesus (v.21).**

The disciples believed what Jesus said to them and willingly took Him into the boat. Note the powerful lesson: receiving the presence of Christ delivers from fear.

**THOUGHT 1.** It is critical that we grasp this lesson, for having Christ present and hearing His Word to not be afraid are not enough. We must willingly receive Christ into our lives. Just as deliverance came to the disciples only after they had received Jesus into the ship, we will only be delivered from fear when we receive the all-powerful presence of Christ in our lives.

> But to all who did receive him, who believed in his name, he gave the right to become children of God. (Jn.1:12)

> "Peace I leave with you; my peace I give to you. Not as the world gives do I give to you. Let not your hearts be troubled, neither let them be afraid." (Jn.14:27)

> "'Behold, I stand at the door and knock. If anyone hears my voice and opens the door, I will come in to him and eat with him, and he with me.'" (Re.3:20)

> Fear not, for I am with you; be not dismayed, for I am your God; I will strengthen you, I will help you, I will uphold you with my righteous right hand. (Is.41:10)

c. **The result: Deliverance through the storms of life (v.21).**
Receiving Christ into the ship made an immediate difference in the disciples' desperate situation. Christ's presence on the ship produced two powerful results: deliverance from fear and the calming of the storm.

**THOUGHT 1.** Jesus Christ gives us the strength to row through all the storms of life. He has the power to erase fear and calm any storm.

> So we do not lose heart. Though our outer self is wasting away, our inner self is being renewed day by day. For this light momentary affliction is preparing for us an eternal weight of glory beyond all comparison, as we look not to the things that are seen but to the things that are unseen. For the things that are seen are transient, but the things that are unseen are eternal. (2 Co.4:16-18)
>
> And deliver all those who through fear of death were subject to lifelong slavery. (He.2:15)
>
> So we can confidently say, "The Lord is my helper; I will not fear; what can man do to me?" (He.13:6)
>
> For he will deliver you from the snare of the fowler and from the deadly pestilence. (Ps.91:3)
>
> For you have delivered my soul from death, my eyes from tears, my feet from stumbling. (Ps.116:8)

## DEEPER STUDY # 1

(6:20) "**It is I**" (eimi): this is one word in the Greek, *eimi*, which is simply "I AM" (Jn.18:6). Jesus essentially said, *"I AM" has come—do not fear.* He was reminding the disciples who He was, the Son of God Himself. He possessed all power; therefore, there was no need to fear. This was the same message that God gave to Moses at the burning bush when He said, "I am who I am" (Ex.3:13-15, esp. 14). It was the same message that Jesus used as a defense against the religious leaders, saying, "Before Abraham was, I am" (Jn.8:58). It is the same message that Col.1:15-17 claims for Him, and it is the same message that is proclaimed by the book of Revelation, "Him who is and who was and who is to come" (Re.1:4, 8; 11:17; 16:5; also see note—Jn.1:1-2).

Note the ["I Ams"] claimed by Christ:
- I Am the Messiah (Jn.4:26).
- I Am (It is I); be not afraid (Jn.6:20).
- I Am the Bread of Life (Jn.6:35).
- I Am from Above (Jn.8:23).
- I Am the Light of the World (Jn.8:12; 9:5; 12:46).
- I Am before Abraham was; I am (eternal) (Jn.8:58).
- I Am the Door (Jn.10:7).
- I Am the Good Shepherd (Jn.10:14).
- I Am the Son of God (Jn.10:36).
- I Am the Resurrection and Life (Jn.11:25).
- I Am the Lord and Master (Jn.13:13).
- I Am the Way, the Truth, and the Life (Jn.14:6).
- I Am the True Vine (Jn.15:1).
- I Am Alpha and Omega (Re.1:8).
- I Am the First and the Last (Re.1:17).

## C. The Answer to People's Gnawing Hunger, Their Sense of Discontentment and Emptiness, 6:22-29

1. **Answer 1: Recognize that people have a gnawing hunger, a lack of contentment in their hearts**
   a. The people noted that Jesus was absent

   b. The people sought Jesus
      1) Some boats from Tiberias landed nearby
      2) The crowd took the boats & left to search for Jesus

   c. The people found Jesus & questioned His absence

2. **Answer 2: Acknowledge that people's motives are corrupt**
   a. They sought the Messiah for what they could get out of Him
   b. They sought what was worldly: Food, which would spoil

3. **Answer 3: Work for food that endures—that gives eternal life**
   a. Source: The Son of Man
   b. God guarantees

4. **Answer 4: Do the work of God—believe in Christ**

²² On the next day the crowd that remained on the other side of the sea saw that there had been only one boat there, and that Jesus had not entered the boat with his disciples, but that his disciples had gone away alone. ²³ Other boats from Tiberias came near the place where they had eaten the bread after the Lord had given thanks. ²⁴ So when the crowd saw that Jesus was not there, nor his disciples, they themselves got into the boats and went to Capernaum, seeking Jesus. ²⁵ When they found him on the other side of the sea, they said to him, "Rabbi, when did you come here?" ²⁶ Jesus answered them, "Truly, truly, I say to you, you are seeking me, not because you saw signs, but because you ate your fill of the loaves. ²⁷ "Do not work for the food that perishes, but for the food that endures to eternal life, which the Son of Man will give to you. For on him God the Father has set his seal." ²⁸ Then they said to him, "What must we do, to be doing the works of God?" ²⁹ Jesus answered them, "This is the work of God, that you believe in him whom he has sent."

# Division VII

## The Revelation of Jesus, the Bread of Life, 6:1-71

C. The Answer to People's Gnawing Hunger, Their Sense of Discontentment and Emptiness, 6:22-29

### 6:22-29
### Introduction

People have a gnawing hunger within for both the physical and the spiritual. We hunger for both food and material things and for God and spiritual things, things such as love and joy and peace. Therefore, most of our time and energy are spent in seeking to satisfy our hunger. Tragically, so many people seek satisfaction in things that can never satisfy their hunger, not permanently. This passage points us to that which brings complete, lasting satisfaction. This is, *The Answer to People's Gnawing Hunger, Their Sense of Discontentment and Emptiness, 6:22-29*.

1. Answer 1: Recognize that people have a gnawing hunger, a lack of contentment, in their hearts (vv.22-25).
2. Answer 2: Acknowledge that people's motives are corrupt (vv.26-27).
3. Answer 3: Work for food that endures—that gives eternal life (v.27).
4. Answer 4: Do the work of God—believe in Christ (vv.28-29).

## 1 Answer 1: Recognize that people have a gnawing hunger, a lack of contentment—in their hearts.

The first answer to our great hunger is to *recognize* the hunger. The people had been miraculously fed earlier. It was a common belief that the Messiah would give manna from heaven even as Moses had done; in fact, it was thought that the Messiah would give more than Moses had given. The people were convinced that Jesus was the Messiah, so they wanted to lay hold of Him and make Him king (vv.1-15).

The people acknowledged their need for the Messiah. They had need, and they knew it. Confessing their need was not a problem for them (see Deeper Study # 2—Jn.1:20).

> 22 On the next day the crowd that remained on the other side of the sea saw that there had been only one boat there, and that Jesus had not entered the boat with his disciples, but that his disciples had gone away alone.
> 23 Other boats from Tiberias came near the place where they had eaten the bread after the Lord had given thanks.
> 24 So when the crowd saw that Jesus was not there, nor his disciples, they themselves got into the boats and went to Capernaum, seeking Jesus.
> 25 When they found him on the other side of the sea, they said to him, "Rabbi, when did you come here?"

a. **The people noted that Jesus was absent (v.22).**

The people noted Jesus' absence. There had been only one boat docked at shore, and the disciples had taken it to cross the lake. However, Jesus had not accompanied them; He had stayed behind. The people thought He was over in another section of the crowd or else off somewhere by Himself. The fact that He was not close by did not dawn on them until the next day. The point is filled with lessons: the people, knowing they had need, wanted their need met. Jesus had proclaimed that He could meet their need, but He was gone; therefore, their need was going to go unmet unless they could find Him.

**THOUGHT 1.** We do have a great need for God's Son. Before our need can be met, we must acknowledge that need. Then, we must observe to see if Christ is present. If Christ is absent, then our need remains unmet.

b. **The people sought Jesus (vv.23-24).**

Believing that Jesus was the answer to their need, the people did what they should have done: they sought Him. Some other boats had landed nearby, probably seeking refuge from the storm. Therefore, the people immediately took passage on these boats and left to search for Jesus. They crossed over to Capernaum, hoping to find Him there. Note how diligent they were in seeking Him.

**THOUGHT 1.** We should search diligently to find Christ. We should seek and seek until the Lord is found.

> "And I tell you, ask, and it will be given to you; seek, and you will find; knock, and it will be opened to you. For everyone who asks receives, and the one who seeks finds, and to the one who knocks it will be opened." (Lu.11:9-10)

> And without faith it is impossible to please him, for whoever would draw near to God must believe that he exists and that he rewards those who seek him. (He.11:6)

> "Seek the Lord while he may be found; call upon him while he is near." (Is.55:6)

c. **The people found Jesus and questioned His absence (v.25).**

The people questioned Jesus' absence. In their minds the Messiah was to give manna from heaven to meet the needs of the people just as Moses had done, only more so. They could not understand why Jesus would leave them, especially if He were the true Messiah.

**THOUGHT 1.** People of every generation do wonder and question that if Jesus is really the Savior, why does He so often seem absent and far away, especially in times of trouble? Another way to word the same thought is: If there is a God and if Christ really is the Son of God, why is the world in so much trouble and why are so many people suffering? Why would Christ not place Himself right in the midst of the world and its problems? Why would He not go ahead and solve the problems, meeting people's needs immediately? The answer, of course, is what this passage is all about.

## 6:26–27

26 Jesus answered them, "Truly, truly, I say to you, you are seeking me, not because you saw signs, but because you ate your fill of the loaves.
27 Do not work for the food that perishes, but for the food that endures to eternal life, which the Son of Man will give to you. For on him God the Father has set his seal."

## 2 Answer 2: Acknowledge that people's motives are corrupt.

The second answer to humanity's great hunger is acknowledging that peoples' motives are corrupt. This point is critical to see. Jesus stressed it with a solemn attention getter, *truly, truly* (listen, listen). People's motive in seeking the Lord—in seeking the answer to their problems—is often corrupt. In the case of these people it was, and tragically, it is with so many in every generation.

a. **They sought the Messiah for what they could get out of Him (v.26).**
Many people seek a Savior, but not to worship and serve Him. They seek a Savior for what they can get out of Him. People are interested in getting their needs met, whether by someone human or divine. They are interested in themselves, not in acknowledging and honoring Jesus to be Lord and not in serving Him and making Him known to a lost world. The thoughts of the crowd were focused on how wonderful it was to be *saved from hunger* and to have their *needs met*. Here was a Savior (Messiah) who could meet all their needs, who could satisfy and give them a complete and full life. He could provide all things for them and deliver them from all their enslavements and enemies. He could bring a perfect society (the Kingdom of God) to earth. Every need could be filled and satisfied. Note that many people's thoughts are focused . . .
- on the earth
- on material things and personal possessions
- on the flesh and its satisfaction
- on the human and the carnal only

In striking contrast, people should be interested in the Savior for who He is and not for what they can get out of Him. Very simply, as with any person, the Lord wants to be sought and loved for who He is and not for what He can do for a person. The Lord is not a tool to be used; He is a person to be sought and loved. The crowd should have seen that such a miracle could have been done *only by the* Son *of God* Himself. Therefore, seeing and standing before the Son of God, they should have fallen down before Him in all humility. They should have humbled themselves . . .
- to recognize and acknowledge Him to be the Son of God
- to worship and praise Him for who He is
- to offer their lives to Him, all they were and had
- to see that all things belonged to Him and were due Him
- to see that He was not the One who should be giving to them but that they were the ones who should be giving to Him. He was the One who should be receiving, not them

b. **They sought what was worldly: Food, which would spoil (v.27).**
People seek food that perishes. They simply misplace their labor. Humanity centers and focuses their thoughts, energies, and efforts upon the moment, that is, upon their years on earth. People seek to *feed their souls* on . . .
- feelings and pleasures
- comfort and ease

- plenty and more
- recognition and honor
- position and power
- fame and self

Such self-seeking is foolish, for all things pass away, even people themselves. A day is not guaranteed, much less a year. Even if an individual has years left to live, they pass ever so rapidly, as any middle age or older adult knows.

**THOUGHT 1.** We all desperately need to heed two eternal truths:

First, the things of the earth with all their pleasures and feelings do not satisfy (Is.55:2). They still leave us empty, incomplete, unfulfilled, hungry, dissatisfied, seeking more and more.

> "Food is meant for the stomach and the stomach for food"—and God will destroy both one and the other. The body is not meant for sexual immorality, but for the Lord, and the Lord for the body. (1 Co.6:13)

> You desire and do not have, so you murder. You covet and cannot obtain, so you fight and quarrel. You do not have, because you do not ask. You ask and do not receive, because you ask wrongly, to spend it on your passions. You adulterous people! Do you not know that friendship with the world is enmity with God? Therefore whoever wishes to be a friend of the world makes himself an enemy of God. (Js.4:2-4)

> "He wanders abroad for bread, saying, 'Where is it?' He knows that a day of darkness is ready at his hand." (Jb.15:23)

> All the toil of man is for his mouth, yet his appetite is not satisfied. (Ec.6:7)

> "Why do you spend your money for that which is not bread, and your labor for that which does not satisfy? Listen diligently to me, and eat what is good, and delight yourselves in rich food." (Is.55:2)

Second, the earth and its things with all their pleasures and feelings pass away. They age, deteriorate, die, and decay (see notes—Mt.8:17; 1 Co.15:50; Col.2:13; 2 Pe.1:4; He.9:27).

> For those who live according to the flesh set their minds on the things of the flesh, but those who live according to the Spirit set their minds on the things of the Spirit. For to set the mind on the flesh is death, but to set the mind on the Spirit is life and peace. (Ro.8:5-6)

> I tell you this, brothers: flesh and blood cannot inherit the kingdom of God, nor does the perishable inherit the imperishable. (1 Co.15:50)

> For all that is in the world—the desires of the flesh and the desires of the eyes and pride of life—is not from the Father but is from the world. And the world is passing away along with its desires, but whoever does the will of God abides forever. (1 Jn.2:16-17)

## 3 Answer 3: Work for food that endures—that gives eternal life.

6:27

²⁷ "Do not work for the food that perishes, but for the food that endures to eternal life, which the Son of Man will give to you. For on him God the Father has set his seal."

The third answer to humanity's great hunger is to labor for food that endures, that gives or lasts *to eternal life* (eis zoen aionion). The basic hunger within every person is for an abundant life, a life that is complete and fulfilled, full of love, joy, peace and all the good things of life (see DEEPER STUDY # 1—Jn.10:10). It is for eternal life, a life that survives, that is not snatched away, but goes on forever and ever (see DEEPER STUDY # 1—Jn.17:2-3).

### a. Source: The Son of Man (v.27a).

Jesus said that the Son of Man is the One who can give food that lasts forever. He is the One who can give life that is both abundant and eternal (see note, *Son of Man*—Jn.1:51).

### b. God guarantees (v.27b).

Jesus said that the Son of Man is sealed, that is, guaranteed by God (see DEEPER STUDY # 2—Jn.3:33). God guarantees . . .

- Christ is the Messiah
- Christ is the One who can give food that is abundant and lasts forever

> "But whoever drinks of the water that I will give him will never be thirsty again. The water that I will give him will become in him a spring of water welling up to eternal life." (Jn.4:14; cp. Jn.7:37)

> "For the bread of God is he who comes down from heaven and gives life to the world." They said to him, "Sir, give us this bread always." Jesus said to them, "I am the bread of life; whoever comes to me shall not hunger, and whoever believes in me shall never thirst." (Jn.6:33-35)

6:28-29

²⁸ Then they said to him, "What must we do, to be doing the works of God?"
²⁹ Jesus answered them, "This is the work of God, that you believe in him whom he has sent."

## 4 Answer 4: Do the work of God—believe in Christ.

The fourth answer to people's great hunger is to do the work of God. Jesus explained what He meant by *the work of* God: it is to believe in Him.

The people thought in terms of works (plural). They thought that by *doing good works* they could win the approval and acceptance of God. If they did enough good and lived a life that was moral and just, God would save them and give them food that satisfied, food and life that was both abundant and eternal.

Jesus corrected the people's thoughts, their concept of salvation by works. Their works (plural) did not secure God's acceptance or favor. They received God's favor and acceptance because of a work, one work (singular). The work of God is only one: believe—believe in Christ whom God has sent (see Deeper Study # 2—Jn.2:24).

> **Thought 1.** Many view themselves and others in one of three categories:
> 1. There are *good people*, people who do plenty of good works. They live good, moral, and just lives; therefore, they are acceptable to God.
> 2. There are *bad people*, people who do mostly bad works. They live immoral and unjust lives; therefore, they are not acceptable to God. They are not saved.
> 3. There are *compromising people*, people who do both good and bad. They live both moral and immoral, just and unjust lives. They are close to securing God's approval, not quite, but close. By doing just a few more *good works* and living just a little more morally, God will accept them.
>
> However, in reality, the only people who are acceptable to God are those who have believed in Jesus Christ, who have realized their sinfulness, their helplessness, and their inability to do anything to pay the debt they owe God for their sins. Believing in Christ involves turning from sin and to Him, accepting His sacrifice on the cross as payment for your sin, and committing your life to Him. This is the only way to receive eternal life.
>
>> Now when he was in Jerusalem at the Passover Feast, many believed in his name when they saw the signs that he was doing. (Jn.2:23)
>>
>> Yet we know that a person is not justified by works of the law but through faith in Jesus Christ, so we also have believed in Christ Jesus, in order to be justified by faith in Christ and not by works of the law, because by works of the law no one will be justified. (Ga.2:16)
>>
>> For by grace you have been saved through faith. And this is not your own doing; it is the gift of God, not a result of works, so that no one may boast. (Ep.2:8-9)

### D. The Bread of Life: The Source of Lasting Fulfillment and Satisfaction, 6:30–36

30 So they said to him, "Then what sign do you do, that we may see and believe you? What work do you perform? 31 Our fathers ate the manna in the wilderness; as it is written, 'He gave them bread from heaven to eat.'"

32 Jesus then said to them, "Truly, truly, I say to you, it was not Moses who gave you the bread from heaven, but my Father gives you the true bread from heaven.

33 "For the bread of God is he who comes down from heaven and gives life to the world."

34 They said to him, "Sir, give us this bread always."

35 Jesus said to them, "I am the bread of life; whoever comes to me shall not hunger, and whoever believes in me shall never thirst."

36 But I said to you that you have seen me and yet do not believe."

1. **Christ is the true bread from heaven**
   a. The people demanded proof—a miraculous sign—before they would believe
   b. The people focused on material provisions: They wanted a similar miracle as the manna (bread) given to Israel
   c. No person—not even Moses—can provide true bread from heaven, that is, lasting fulfillment & satisfaction
   d. God alone gives us the true bread from heaven
2. **Christ is the Bread of God**
   a. He came from heaven
   b. He came to give life
3. **Christ is the Bread of Life**[DS1]
   a. The request for the Bread of God
   b. The phenomenal claim: He is the Bread of life
      1) Anyone who comes to Jesus will never hunger
      2) Anyone who believes, will never thirst
4. **Christ was seen but rejected**

# Division VII

*The Revelation of Jesus, the Bread of Life, 6:1–71*

D. The Bread of Life: The Source of Lasting Fulfillment and Satisfaction, 6:30–36

## 6:30–36
## Introduction

Jesus Christ is the source of spiritual satisfaction, of man's spiritual nourishment. He is the only bread that can feed humanity's great hunger, the hunger that gnaws and gnaws within every person's inner being. There is no other source upon which we can feed and be nourished. This is, *The Bread of Life: The Source of Lasting Fulfillment and Satisfaction,* 6:30–36.
1. Christ is the true bread from heaven (v.32).
2. Christ is the Bread of God (v.33).
3. Christ is the Bread of Life (vv.34–35).
4. Christ was seen but rejected (v.36).

## 1 Christ is the true bread from heaven.

Jesus had just made some phenomenal claims. He claimed to be . . .
- the Son of Man (v.27).
- the One who feeds the world, who gives people bread which issues forth eternal life (v.27).
- the One whom God had sealed (v.27).
- the One whom God had sent into the world (v.29).
- the One on whom people were to believe (v.29).

### 6:30-32

<sup>30</sup> So they said to him, "Then what sign do you do, that we may see and believe you? What work do you perform? <sup>31</sup> Our fathers ate the manna in the wilderness; as it is written, 'He gave them bread from heaven to eat.'" <sup>32</sup> Jesus then said to them, "Truly, truly, I say to you, it was not Moses who gave you the bread from heaven, but my Father gives you the true bread from heaven.

**a. The people demanded proof—a miraculous sign—before they would believe (v.30).**

The people demanded proof that Jesus was who He claimed to be. They asked for a sign, a miraculous work that would satisfy their demands.

**b. The people focused on material provisions: They wanted a similar miracle as the manna (bread) given to Israel (v.31).**

The people were focused on the physical and material (see notes—Jn.6:26-27). They ignored all the signs, even the miracles of God which already surrounded them. Christ had just miraculously fed the crowd, yet the crowd ignored the witness of that particular sign (Jn.6:1f). It was not enough. They were so attached to the earth, to its physical pleasures and material goods, that they wanted more and more. They implied that Jesus was inferior to Moses, who had fed Israel for forty years in the wilderness. But Christ had fed them only once. In addition, Moses had fed Israel with manna falling out of the sky from heaven. Christ had merely multiplied bread from a few loaves in His hands.

The complaining people reasoned that Christ had not fed them enough—not enough to prove that He was who He claimed to be. Moreover, Christ had not fed them in the right way, not given "them bread from heaven to eat."

**THOUGHT 1.** Unbelieving people never have enough. They crave more and more, never being fully satisfied. They experience a gnawing hunger, a restlessness, emptiness, loneliness, vacuum, and a lack of purpose, meaning, and significance. Even in dealing with God, they never have enough evidence or proof to believe—not within their human nature.

On top of their constant cravings and skepticism, such people always want to tell God how to act and deal with them and their lives. They want their needs met in certain ways. It is not enough for God to meet their needs; they want their needs met as they will and desire. They try to dictate how God is to act and behave toward them. So much human religion is nothing more than this, nothing more than humans trying to spell out how God is to act and behave toward them.

**THOUGHT 2.** Generally speaking, people demand that they first see, *then* they will believe. This is contrary to *true* faith. It is not the way faith works. We must first believe God, then we see (see DEEPER STUDY #1—He.11:6). However, we must remember that faith is not fate; it is a matter of the heart, a matter of how the heart must relate to others. God relates with us just as we relate to others. If a person does not believe in us, they do not see; that is, they may ask all they want, but it is unlikely that we will do what they ask. But if they believe and trust us, we usually do whatever they ask, and they see their desires and requests fulfilled by our hands. Repeating the above, we must first believe God, then we see. Faith must precede sight. Believe God, and He will fulfill the desires of your heart (Ps.37:4-5).

> Eight days later, his disciples were inside again, and Thomas was with them. Although the doors were locked, Jesus came and stood among them and said, "Peace be with you." (Jn.20:26)

> And without faith it is impossible to please him, for whoever would draw near to God must believe that he exists and that he rewards those who seek him. (He.11:6)

> Delight yourself in the Lord, and he will give you the desires of your heart. Commit your way to the Lord; trust in him, and he will act. (Ps.37:4-5)
>
> Trust in the Lord with all your heart, and do not lean on your own understanding. (Pr.3:5)

c. **No person—not even Moses—can provide true bread from heaven, that is, lasting fulfillment and satisfaction (v.32a).**

Jesus responded to the people's faithless remarks by correcting their thinking. He informed them Moses was not the one who gave Israel the manna from heaven; God was the One who gave the manna. However, the manna only satisfied their *physical* hunger. No human—not even Moses—can provide true bread, that is, true satisfaction. No human being can provide the true bread which satisfies the soul and spirit.

d. **God alone gives us the true bread from heaven (v.32b).**

God alone provides true bread, that is, provides true satisfaction. We must look both beyond other people and beyond the things of this world. People and things cannot meet the gnawing hunger of the human soul; they cannot provide true satisfaction, for they do not possess the *true* bread. We must look to God to have our hunger met, to be truly filled, to be completely satisfied. Only God can give us what we need to be content and at peace.

The bread God gives is *true* bread (see Deeper Study # 1—Jn.1:9). The *bread* or *manna* of God is not physical and material bread: it is spiritual. God promises to provide for the physical necessities of His followers (Mt.6:24-33), but physical and material bread is not what Christ was talking about in this passage. Physical and material bread lasts only for a short while. Once consumed, it is gone. Its satisfaction passes, and our gnawing hunger arises again. But the bread God gives is spiritual bread, that is, spiritual food for the soul (see note—Ep.1:3). It is the bread that every person really needs more than anything else on earth. It is the only bread that can feed and meet the need of our . . .

- gnawing hunger
- restlessness
- emptiness
- loneliness
- lack of purpose, meaning, and significance

> "This is the bread that comes down from heaven, so that one may eat of it and not die. I am the living bread that came down from heaven. If anyone eats of this bread, he will live forever. And the bread that I will give for the life of the world is my flesh." (Jn.6:50-51)
>
> So Jesus said to them, "Truly, truly, I say to you, unless you eat the flesh of the Son of Man and drink his blood, you have no life in you. Whoever feeds on my flesh and drinks my blood has eternal life, and I will raise him up on the last day." (Jn.6:53-54)
>
> "As the living Father sent me, and I live because of the Father, so whoever feeds on me, he also will live because of me. This is the bread that came down from heaven, not like the bread the fathers ate, and died. Whoever feeds on this bread will live forever." (Jn.6:57-58)

## 2 Christ is the Bread of God.

Christ is the true bread, the Bread of God. He was given by God to meet the hunger of the human soul and to give eternal life.

> [33] "For the bread of God is he who comes down from heaven and gives life to the world."

a. **He came from heaven (v.33a).**

The origin of the true bread is God Himself. It is bread which came *from* or *out of* (Gk. ek) heaven itself. This means several things.

First, the Bread of God is not bread which comes out of the clouds above earth. Rather, it is bread which comes *out of* (ek) heaven itself, out of the spiritual dimension of being, from the very presence of God Himself. It is bread which comes from the very household of God.

Second, the Bread of God is not physical bread. It is of the nature of God Himself, spiritual and eternal bread (see vv.50-51).

Third, the Bread of God is possessed by God; therefore, only He can give it, and people cannot have the Bread of God unless God gives it to them.

Fourth, the Bread of God is a person. As stated previously, it is not physical bread. Note the personal pronoun *"He"* and the word *"bread"* (ho artos) which is the masculine form of the Greek word, not the neuter form. Note that *"He,"* the Bread of God who feeds and nourishes humanity, came *down* or *out of* heaven. He was not born of the earth. He came from the very presence of God Himself.

> He who comes from above is above all. He who is of the earth belongs to the earth and speaks in an earthly way. He who comes from heaven is above all. (Jn.3:31)
>
> "For I have come down from heaven, not to do my own will but the will of him who sent me." (Jn.6:38)
>
> He said to them, "You are from below; I am from above. You are of this world; I am not of this world." (Jn.8:23)
>
> Jesus said to them, "If God were your Father, you would love me, for I came from God and I am here. I came not of my own accord, but he sent me." (Jn.8:42)
>
> "Now we know that you know all things and do not need anyone to question you; this is why we believe that you came from God." (Jn.16:30)
>
> The first man was from the earth, a man of dust; the second man is from heaven. (1 Co.15:47)

**b. He came to give life (v.33b).**

The Bread of God gives *life* to the world. The purpose of bread is to give life (see Deeper Study # 2—Jn.1:4; Deeper Study # 1—10:10; Deeper Study # 1—17:2-3).

Bread gives life by . . .
- nourishing and sustaining
- satisfying
- energizing
- creating desire (the need) for more (see note—Lu.4:3-4; see also Ne.9:15).
- being partaken on a regular basis

The Bread of God came from heaven to give life to the *whole* world. It is not just to one person or to one nation that Christ came. He came to the whole world (see 1 Jn.2:1-2). He came to sacrifice Himself, to feed and save a starving world.

Note that Christ's coming as the sacrificial Bread of God had been foreshadowed by the sacrifices of the Old Testament. They are said to be the Bread of God (Le.21:21-22; see also Jn.6:50-51.)

> On the last day of the feast, the great day, Jesus stood up and cried out, "If anyone thirsts, let him come to me and drink." (Jn.7:37)
>
> For there is no distinction between Jew and Greek; for the same Lord is Lord of all, bestowing his riches on all who call on him. (Ro.10:12)
>
> Who desires all people to be saved and to come to the knowledge of the truth. For there is one God, and there is one mediator between God and men, the man Christ Jesus, who gave himself as a ransom for all, which is the testimony given at the proper time. (1 Ti.2:4-6)
>
> "Come, everyone who thirsts, come to the waters; and he who has no money, come, buy and eat! Come, buy wine and milk without money and without price." (Is.55:1)

**THOUGHT 1.** Christ (and the Word of God) gives life to the believer by doing the same things spiritually that earthly bread does physically.

> In him was life, and the life was the light of men. (Jn.1:4)
>
> "The thief comes only to steal and kill and destroy. I came that they may have life and have it abundantly." (Jn.10:10)
>
> "Since you have given him authority over all flesh, to give eternal life to all whom you have given him. And this is eternal life, that they know you, the only true God, and Jesus Christ whom you have sent." (Jn.17:2-3)

## 3 Christ is the Bread of Life.

Christ is the Bread of Life (see Deeper Study # 1). He alone can satisfy the hunger and thirst of our souls. He is the One who gives abundant and eternal life.

### a. The request for the Bread of God (v.34).

The people requested the Bread of God. They called Jesus *Sir* or *Lord* (Kurios), but how much they understood of His deity is not known. Apparently, it was just an address of respect. However, the point is clear in the Bible. When a person asks for the Bread of God, they must call Jesus "Lord" and be ready to submit to Him as Lord, serving Jesus day by day (see Lu.9:23; Ro.10:13).

> 34 They said to him, "Sir, give us this bread always."
>
> 35 Jesus said to them, "I am the bread of life; whoever comes to me shall not hunger, and whoever believes in me shall never thirst."

Note that the people requested *give us this bread always* (pantote dos hemin ton arton touton). The Greek aorist tense tells us this was a *once-for-all* request. The people wanted this Bread of God once-for-all, so that they might have a *permanent provision*. The Bible is again clear on this point. Salvation, that is, partaking of the Bread of Life, is a permanent experience. It is a once-for-all experience.

### b. The phenomenal claim by Jesus: He is the Bread of life (v.35).

Jesus Christ made a phenomenal claim to the people, declaring, *I am the Bread of life* (see Deeper Study # 1—Jn.6:20; also see Deeper Study # 2—Jn.1:4; Deeper Study # 1—10:10; Deeper Study # 1—17:2-3.) He is the true Bread, the Bread of God, the Bread of life.

Jesus proceeded to make an extraordinary promise: anyone who comes to Him will never hunger. Every human being has a starving, craving need for life. We all crave a life that is full and satisfying, nourishing and sustaining, energizing and fulfilling.

If people come to Christ, the craving for life will be fully satisfied. They will never hunger again. Their souls and spirits will be forever satisfied.

Jesus said further that anyone who believes will never thirst. The symbolism is switched from hunger to thirst. Our need is more than met; not only is our hunger satisfied, but our thirst is quenched. Every need of life, of nourishment, and of growth is met. Nothing is left out or lacking. When a person comes to Christ and *believes* (continuous action, meaning continuing to believe), every need of their life and growth is met. Of course, this does not mean they will never hunger after righteousness. They will, but their hunger and thirst will never go unsatisfied. As Jesus promised, they will be filled (Mt.5:6).

Note the words *not* and *never*. They are strong, emphatic words: "shall not hunger . . . shall never thirst."

**THOUGHT 1.** Jesus clearly stated how a person is *saved* from hungering and thirsting after life. We are saved . . .
- by coming to Christ (vv.35, 37, 44–45, 65)
- by believing on Christ (see Deeper Study # 2—Jn.2:24)

"Blessed are those who hunger and thirst for righteousness, for they shall be satisfied." (Mt.5:6)

"But whoever drinks of the water that I will give him will never be thirsty again. The water that I will give him will become in him a spring of water welling up to eternal life." (Jn.4:14)

Jesus said to them, "I am the bread of life; whoever comes to me shall not hunger, and whoever believes in me shall never thirst." (Jn.6:35)

"Truly, truly, I say to you, whoever believes has eternal life. I am the bread of life." (Jn.6:47–48)

On the last day of the feast, the great day, Jesus stood up and cried out, "If anyone thirsts, let him come to me and drink." (Jn.7:37)

The Spirit and the Bride say, "Come." And let the one who hears say, "Come." And let the one who is thirsty come; let the one who desires take the water of life without price. (Re.22:17)

## Deeper Study # 1

(6:34-35) **Jesus—the Living Bread:** bread does at least four things. It nourishes or sustains life; it satisfies; it energizes; and it creates a desire (the need) for more and more (see note—Lu.4:3-4; see also Ne.9:15).

**6:36**

⁳⁶ "But I said to you that you have seen me and yet do not believe."

### 4 Christ was seen but rejected.

The people saw Christ, but they rejected Him. The point is that the people were without excuse. They had every opportunity in the world.

➢ The Bread of God had come down from heaven.
➢ The Bread of God had come to give life to the world.
➢ The Bread of God had been seen (see 1 Jn.1:1-3).
➢ The Bread of God was being seen and proclaimed that very moment.

Any of the people could have easily come to Christ. Yet sitting there and hearing the glorious news, they still did not believe—like so many today.

> He came to his own, and his own people did not receive him. (Jn.1:11)

> Whoever believes in the Son has eternal life; whoever does not obey the Son shall not see life, but the wrath of God remains on him. (Jn.3:36)

> "I told you that you would die in your sins, for unless you believe that I am he you will die in your sins." (Jn.8:24)

> "The one who rejects me and does not receive my words has a judge; the word that I have spoken will judge him on the last day." (Jn.12:48)

## E. The Assurance of the Believer, 6:37-40

| | |
|---|---|
| ³⁷ "All that the Father gives me will come to me, and whoever comes to me I will never cast out. | 1. Assurance 1: God's predestination<br>2. Assurance 2: Jesus' promise, His Word |
| ³⁸ For I have come down from heaven, not to do my own will but the will of him who sent me. | 3. Assurance 3: Jesus' purpose, to do God's will |
| ³⁹ And this is the will of him who sent me, that I should lose nothing of all that he has given me, but raise it up on the last day. | 4. Assurance 4: God's will for those whom He gives to Christ<br>  a. That Jesus will not lose a single believer<br>  b. That Jesus will resurrect every one of them |
| ⁴⁰ For this is the will of my Father, that everyone who looks on the Son and believes in him should have eternal life, and I will raise him up on the last day." | 5. Assurance 5: God's will for the believer<br>  a. Is eternal life<br>  b. Is for Jesus to raise him up at the last day |

# Division VII

*The Revelation of Jesus, the Bread of Life, 6:1-71*

E. The Assurance of the Believer, 6:37-40

## 6:37-40 Introduction

God wants us to *know* that we have eternal life. He does not want us to float through life with doubt and uncertainty, constantly fearing that we are going to sink into the bottomless sea of an eternity separated from Him. Nor does He want us to be filled with fear as we fight the storms of life. Instead, He wants us to be anchored in Him, trusting Him to be with us and to keep us, both now and for eternity. Throughout His Word, God has given the believer great assurance and security. Here, John the Apostle, by inspiration of the Holy Spirit, gave us the very words of Jesus Himself on the subject. This is, *The Assurance of the Believer*, 6:37-40.

1. Assurance 1: God's predestination (v.37).
2. Assurance 2: Jesus' promise, His Word (v.37).
3. Assurance 3: Jesus' purpose, to do God's will (v.38).
4. Assurance 4: God's will for those whom He gives to Christ (v.39).
5. Assurance 5: God's will for the believer (v.40).

## 1 Assurance 1: God's predestination.

6:37

The first assurance for the believer is God's predestination. The meaning of the verse is clear. It is those whom "the Father gives" that come to Christ. However, note a critical fact. The emphasis is not on God's giving of Christ's followers; it is on their assurance. They will never be cast out. Christ wants believers to take heart and to be assured of their salvation. It is God, Himself, who has drawn believers,

³⁷ "All that the Father gives me will come to me, and whoever comes to me I will never cast out."

who has moved upon and stirred them to *come to Christ* (see note, *Draw*—Jn.6:44-46 for explanation and more discussion). Something should be noted at this point. There is a predestination thread that runs throughout John's Gospel. Things are controlled and happen as God means them to happen. The purpose of God is being done. He is God; therefore, He rules and controls all things (see Jn.1:12-13; 6:37; 6:44-46; 10:26; 16:8).

> "My sheep hear my voice, and I know them, and they follow me. I give them eternal life, and they will never perish, and no one will snatch them out of my hand. My Father, who has given them to me, is greater than all, and no one is able to snatch them out of the Father's hand." (Jn.10:27-29)

> And we know that for those who love God all things work together for good, for those who are called according to his purpose. For those whom he foreknew he also predestined to be conformed to the image of his Son, in order that he might be the firstborn among many brothers. And those whom he predestined he also called, and those whom he called he also justified, and those whom he justified he also glorified. (Ro.8:28-30)

> Blessed be the God and Father of our Lord Jesus Christ! According to his great mercy, he has caused us to be born again to a living hope through the resurrection of Jesus Christ from the dead, to an inheritance that is imperishable, undefiled, and unfading, kept in heaven for you, who by God's power are being guarded through faith for a salvation ready to be revealed in the last time. (1 Pe.1:3-5)

## 6:37

³⁷ "All that the Father gives me will come to me, and whoever comes to me I will never cast out."

## 2 Assurance 2: Jesus' promise, His Word.

The second assurance for the believer is Jesus' Word. His statement gives enormous security to every genuine believer.

Jesus clearly said that any individual who comes to Him will *never, in no wise, by no means, certainly not* be cast out. This is a double negative, a strong, forceful promise: "Never, no never be cast out."

By making this statement, Jesus was claiming the authority to accept and reject people (see Mt.8:12; 22:13). He accepts the person who comes to Him, the person who turns from the world and the flesh to Him.

The point is simply this: Jesus gives His Word that whoever comes to Him, He will never, no never cast out. The believer's assurance and security are as good as Jesus' Word. If Jesus is who He claims to be, the Bread of Life, then every person who comes to Him for spiritual nourishment—salvation and eternal life—can rest assured that . . .

- Jesus will receive them into God's household
- Jesus will feed, nourish, satisfy, and fill them
- Jesus will not cast them out
- Jesus will keep His Word with every generation of people

> "For truly, I say to you, until heaven and earth pass away, not an iota, not a dot, will pass from the Law until all is accomplished." (Mt.5:18)

> "Heaven and earth will pass away, but my words will not pass away." (Lu.21:33)

> The works of his hands are faithful and just; all his precepts are trustworthy. (Ps.111:7)

> "For I am the Lord; I will speak the word that I will speak, and it will be performed. It will no longer be delayed, but in your days, O rebellious house, I will speak the word and perform it, declares the Lord God." (Eze.12:25)

## 6:38

³⁸ "For I have come down from heaven, not to do my own will but the will of him who sent me."

## 3 Assurance 3: Jesus' purpose, to do God's will.

The third assurance for the believer is Jesus' purpose. He came to do God's will. Jesus clearly declared His origin: He came down from or out of heaven (see Deeper Study # 1—Jn.3:31). And He declared His purpose for coming: Jesus came not to do His own will, but the will of God.

Jesus had a mind and a will distinct and separate from the Father's. He could will and act separately from His Father. In Gethsemane He prayed, "Not as I will, but as You will" (Mt.26:39). He actually willed something different from His Father. He willed the cup to be removed, for some way other than the cross to be chosen for our salvation. Jesus had a distinct, separate will from God the Father.

However, Christ subjected His will to His Father's will. He fought and struggled to control His mind and will, to do exactly as the Father willed, and He conquered His own will. He always succeeded. In every instance He subjected Himself totally to His Father. He always did what God the Father willed—perfectly.

> "But I do as the Father has commanded me, so that the world may know that I love the Father. Rise, let us go from here." (Jn.14:31)
>
> "If you keep my commandments, you will abide in my love, just as I have kept my Father's commandments and abide in his love." (Jn.15:10)
>
> For as by the one man's disobedience the many were made sinners, so by the one man's obedience the many will be made righteous. (Ro.5:19)
>
> Then he added, "Behold, I have come to do your will." He does away with the first in order to establish the second. (He.10:9)
>
> Knowing that you were ransomed from the futile ways inherited from your forefathers, not with perishable things such as silver or gold, but with the precious blood of Christ, like that of a lamb without blemish or spot. (1 Pe.1:18-19)

As believers, our assurance is Jesus' purpose. He set out to do His Father's will and He did it perfectly. We can rest assured that Jesus is the full revelation of God. Jesus revealed God perfectly. What Jesus did—everything He did—is a picture of the perfect will of God. Any individual can come to Jesus for spiritual food and nourishment and *know* that he or she is coming to God.

> "For I have not spoken on my own authority, but the Father who sent me has himself given me a commandment—what to say and what to speak." (Jn.12:49)
>
> Jesus said to him, "Have I been with you so long, and you still do not know me, Philip? Whoever has seen me has seen the Father. How can you say, 'Show us the Father'? Do you not believe that I am in the Father and the Father is in me? The words that I say to you I do not speak on my own authority, but the Father who dwells in me does his works." (Jn.14:9-10)
>
> "For I have given them the words that you gave me, and they have received them and have come to know in truth that I came from you; and they have believed that you sent me." (Jn.17:8)

## 4 Assurance 4: God's will for those whom He gives to Christ.

The fourth assurance is God's will for *those whom He gives* to Christ. Note: the fact that God sent Christ is stressed once again (v.38). Note also that Jesus calls God His *Father* (v.40). This stresses the love and care of God. God's will is like the will of a loving father for His children. He wills only good and loving things.

> 39 "And this is the will of him who sent me, that I should lose nothing of all that he has given me, but raise it up on the last day."

God wills to give followers to His Son: *All that He has given me*. This has to do with predestination, but in the sense covered before (v.37). God wills that His Son Jesus be the first, that is, the most preeminent person among many brothers and sisters. Jesus is to have many brothers and sisters (see note—Ro.8:29). The followers of Jesus can rest assured that they are chosen by God to follow Jesus; therefore, they will not be lost, not ever.

### a. That Jesus will not lose a single believer.

God wills that Jesus should *lose nothing*. The Greek words translated, *I should lose nothing* (me apoleso ex autou) stress that He will not lose anything, not even a fragment, not any part of what God has given to Him. No person, not a single one, will be lost.

This was true while Jesus was on earth: He lost none (Jn.17:12). It will also be true of every believer throughout history. Again and again in God's Word, this peace-giving promise is affirmed.

> "And I am no longer in the world, but they are in the world, and I am coming to you. Holy Father, keep them in your name, which you have given me, that they may be one, even as we are one." (Jn.17:11)

> And I am sure of this, that he who began a good work in you will bring it to completion at the day of Jesus Christ. (Ph.1:6)

> But the Lord is faithful. He will establish you and guard you against the evil one. (2 Th.3:3)

> Which is why I suffer as I do. But I am not ashamed, for I know whom I have believed, and I am convinced that he is able to guard until that day what has been entrusted to me. (2 Ti.1:12)

> The Lord will rescue me from every evil deed and bring me safely into his heavenly kingdom. To him be the glory forever and ever. Amen. (2 Ti.4:18)

> Now to him who is able to keep you from stumbling and to present you blameless before the presence of his glory with great joy. (Jude 24)

> "'Because you have kept my word about patient endurance, I will keep you from the hour of trial that is coming on the whole world, to try those who dwell on the earth.'" (Re.3:10)

> Love the LORD, all you his saints! The LORD preserves the faithful but abundantly repays the one who acts in pride. (Ps.31:23)

> For the LORD loves justice; he will not forsake his saints. They are preserved forever, but the children of the wicked shall be cut off. (Ps.37:28)

> Guarding the paths of justice and watching over the way of his saints. (Pr.2:8)

> Thus says the LORD: "In a time of favor I have answered you; in a day of salvation I have helped you; I will keep you and give you as a covenant to the people, to establish the land, to apportion the desolate heritages." (Is.49:8)

### b. That Jesus will resurrect every one of them.

God wills a most wonderful thing: Jesus will save every true believer through all, even up until the final hour of the very last day—the day of the resurrection. The Lord's salvation is complete, ultimate, and final. No matter the trials, the heartaches, the hurts, the attacks of the enemy and the evil persecutors, Christ will save His dear followers through all; and He will raise them up at the last day. The *genuine believer* is assured and secure in the will of God. God wills that His Son lose no one—that each one will be saved through all circumstances—saved right up to the point of being raised up at the last day.

## 5 Assurance 5: God's will for the believer.

**6:40**

⁴⁰ "For this is the will of my Father, that everyone who looks on the Son and believes in him should have eternal life, and I will raise him up on the last day."

The fifth assurance is God's will for *the believer*. This verse also concerns God's will, but it differs from the former point in that it centers on those who *see and believe* on Jesus. In the former verse, the stress is on *God choosing* those who come to Christ, whereas in this verse, the stress is on *people choosing* Christ. Both are necessary steps in salvation as already discussed (v.37; see note—Jn.6:44-46).

### a. Is eternal life.

God wills that a person who *sees and believes* Jesus should have eternal life (see DEEPER STUDY # 2—Jn.2:24; DEEPER STUDY # 1—10:10; DEEPER STUDY # 1—17:2-3). A person must *look* or *see* (Gk. theoron)—behold, grasp—and believe in Jesus. Greek scholar A.T. Robertson notes that it is seeing "with the eye of faith as in John 12:45."[1] It is believing from the heart . . .
- that God *sent* Jesus to spiritually feed and nourish humanity (to save and to give life).
- that He is *the Son*, the Savior of the world.

---

1  A.T. Robertson, *Word Pictures in the New Testament Concise Edition* (Nashville: Holman Reference, 1958), via Wordsearch digital edition.

b. **Is for Jesus to raise him up at the last day.**

The result of seeing and believing Jesus is being *raised up from the dead*. Jesus said very emphatically, "I will raise him up on the last day." "I" is emphatic. No one but Jesus can raise the dead, and He will take the person who sees and believes and raise him up. The believer is assured of three very significant promises.

First, we are assured of eternal life.

> "For God so loved the world, that he gave his only Son, that whoever believes in him should not perish but have eternal life." (Jn.3:16)

> "Truly, truly, I say to you, whoever hears my word and believes him who sent me has eternal life. He does not come into judgment, but has passed from death to life." (Jn.5:24)

Second, we are assured of victory over death.

> In a moment, in the twinkling of an eye, at the last trumpet. For the trumpet will sound, and the dead will be raised imperishable, and we shall be changed. For this perishable body must put on the imperishable, and this mortal body must put on immortality. When the perishable puts on the imperishable, and the mortal puts on immortality, then shall come to pass the saying that is written: "Death is swallowed up in victory." "O death, where is your victory? O death, where is your sting?" The sting of death is sin, and the power of sin is the law. But thanks be to God, who gives us the victory through our Lord Jesus Christ. (1 Co.15:52-57)

> Since therefore the children share in flesh and blood, he himself likewise partook of the same things, that through death he might destroy the one who has the power of death, that is, the devil, and deliver all those who through fear of death were subject to lifelong slavery. (He.2:14-15)

Third, we are assured of the resurrection.

> "Truly, truly, I say to you, an hour is coming, and is now here, when the dead will hear the voice of the Son of God, and those who hear will live. For as the Father has life in himself, so he has granted the Son also to have life in himself. And he has given him authority to execute judgment, because he is the Son of Man. Do not marvel at this, for an hour is coming when all who are in the tombs will hear his voice and come out, those who have done good to the resurrection of life, and those who have done evil to the resurrection of judgment." (Jn.5:25-29; see Jn.11:25)

> "[I, Paul] having a hope in God, which these men themselves accept, that there will be a resurrection of both the just and the unjust." (Ac.24:15)

> Knowing that he who raised the Lord Jesus will raise us also with Jesus and bring us with you into his presence. (2 Co.4:14)

> For the Lord himself will descend from heaven with a cry of command, with the voice of an archangel, and with the sound of the trumpet of God. And the dead in Christ will rise first. (1 Th.4:16)

## F. The Way a Person Partakes of the Bread of Life, 6:41-51

1. **A person must stop rebelling against the claims of Jesus, Jn.6:35**
   a. The religious leaders questioned Jesus' origin: Misunderstood the incarnation, that Jesus came "down from [out of] heaven"
   b. Jesus appealed to the religious leaders to stop grumbling & rebelling
2. **A person must be drawn to Christ, drawn by God**
   a. God's part in salvation
      1) To draw us to Christ
      2) To teach us
   b. Our part in salvation
      1) To listen to God & learn
      2) To come to Christ
         • Because no one has seen God
         • Because Christ alone is from God & has seen God
3. **A person must believe in Christ**
   a. Believe He is the Bread of Life
   b. Believe He is *out of* heaven—has come to deliver us from death
   c. Believe He is the living bread—the One who gives us life forever
   d. Believe He gave His flesh for the life of the world

⁴¹ So the Jews grumbled about him, because he said, "I am the bread that came down from heaven."
⁴² They said, "Is not this Jesus, the son of Joseph, whose father and mother we know? How does he now say, 'I have come down from heaven'?"
⁴³ Jesus answered them, "Do not grumble among yourselves.
⁴⁴ No one can come to me unless the Father who sent me draws him. And I will raise him up on the last day.
⁴⁵ It is written in the Prophets, 'And they will all be taught by God.' Everyone who has heard and learned from the Father comes to me—
⁴⁶ not that anyone has seen the Father except he who is from God; he has seen the Father.
⁴⁷ Truly, truly, I say to you, whoever believes has eternal life.
⁴⁸ I am the bread of life.
⁴⁹ Your fathers ate the manna in the wilderness, and they died.
⁵⁰ This is the bread that comes down from heaven, so that one may eat of it and not die.
⁵¹ I am the living bread that came down from heaven. If anyone eats of this bread, he will live forever. And the bread that I will give for the life of the world is my flesh."

# Division VII

## *The Revelation of Jesus, the Bread of Life, 6:1-71*

F. The Way a Person Partakes of the Bread of Life, 6:41-51

# 6:41–51
# Introduction

The most important question any person can ask is the question asked by the Philippian jailer, "What must I do to be saved?" (Ac.16:30). In His great teaching on the Bread of Life, Jesus answered this question. How people partake of the Bread of Life, that is, how we come to know Jesus personally and be saved, is the focus of this passage. This is, *The Way a Person Partakes of the Bread of Life*, 6:41-51.

1. A person must stop rebelling against the claims of Jesus, Jn.6:35 (vv.41-43).
2. A person must be drawn to Christ, drawn by God (vv.44-46).
3. A person must believe in Christ (vv.47-51).

## 1 A person must stop rebelling against the claims of Jesus.

6:41-43

Jesus had claimed to be the Bread of Life that had come down from heaven (vv.35-38). However, the Jewish religious leaders rebelled against this claim. They *grumbled* or *complained* (Gk. egogguzon) against Him. This word means to murmur or mutter. As Jesus spoke, a buzz of opposition arose from the upset crowd.

⁴¹ So the Jews grumbled about him, because he said, "I am the bread that came down from heaven."

⁴² They said, "Is not this Jesus, the son of Joseph, whose father and mother we know? How does he now say, 'I have come down from heaven'?"

⁴³ Jesus answered them, "Do not grumble among yourselves."

a. **The religious leaders questioned Jesus' origin: Misunderstood the incarnation that Jesus came "down from [out of] heaven" (vv.41-42).**

The Jewish authorities radically disagreed with Jesus' claim that He had come down from heaven. They questioned His origin. They knew Him personally; and they knew His father, Joseph, and His mother, Mary. They knew He was a mere man just as they were mere men, having been reared by human parents. How could He possibly claim to be "from heaven"? Their problem was twofold.

➤ They were ignorant of the incarnation (see Deeper Study # 3—Mt.1:16; Deeper Study # 8—1:23; Deeper Study # 2—Jn.1:10; 1:14-18).
➤ They were so fixed on Christ's origin, on where He had come from, that they lost sight of His mission, which was, as the Bread of life, to feed and nourish people spiritually (to save and to give life).

b. **Jesus appealed to the religious leaders to stop grumbling and rebelling (v.43).**

Jesus appealed to the crowd to stop murmuring. He loved and cared for them and longed for them to listen to the truth. As long as they murmured, they would never be willing to listen to the truth. What a lesson for us all: "Be still, and know that I am God" (Ps.45:15).

## 2 A person must be drawn to Christ, drawn by God.

6:44-46

A person must be drawn by God in order to be saved. These three verses have to do with predestination (see v.37). The truth of predestination in the Bible is not so much a statement of theology or philosophy as it is a message that speaks to the spiritual experience of the believer. If the pure logic of philosophy and theology is applied, then predestination says that God chooses some for heaven and others for a terrible hell. But this is simply not what God means in the passages dealing with predestination, and this fact needs to be given close attention by all who so interpret the Scriptures. What God wants believers to do is to take heart, for He has assured their salvation. This is what He means by predestination (see note—Ro.8:29).

⁴⁴ "No one can come to me unless the Father who sent me draws him. And I will raise him up on the last day.

⁴⁵ "It is written in the Prophets, 'And they will all be taught by God.' Everyone who has heard and learned from the Father comes to me—

⁴⁶ "not that anyone has seen the Father except he who is from God; he has seen the Father."

The person who comes to Christ is a person who has been *drawn by God*, a person who has experienced the *divine initiative*. A person does not act alone, coming to Christ by his/her own effort and energy, not by his/her own works, whether mental (thought or will, Jn.1:13) or physical labor (good deeds, Ep.2:8-9). Unbelievers have a dead spirit; therefore, they can do nothing spiritually just as a dead body can do nothing physically. The natural man prefers self and sin;

therefore, if a person with a dead spirit is to come to Christ, that person has to be acted upon and drawn by God. Both God and man have a part in salvation.

**a. God's part in salvation (vv.44–45a).**

God's part in salvation is to draw man. God has to draw because people resist the gospel. Man's resistance is seen in the word *draw*. The word "draw" has the idea of both initiative and rebellion, of constraint and resistance. For example, the pulling in of a net loaded with fish involves both actions of pulling and resistance (see Jn.21:6); a person being dragged to court encounters both actions of pulling and resistance (Ac.16:19).

How God draws a person is clearly stated. He teaches us the truth of gospel (v.45). The teaching may come from the voice of a preacher, the reading of Scripture or a myriad of other sources. But one thing is always common: the movement of God's Spirit upon the human heart, teaching the need for God and drawing the heart toward God for salvation. The Spirit of God teaches a person and moves on their heart.

➢ The Holy Spirit quickens the gospel to people's minds so that they *see it as never before*. They see, understand, grasp as never before that the Father has sent Christ as the Bread of life to feed and nourish us (to save and to give us life).

**Jesus answered him, "Truly, truly, I say to you, unless one is born again he cannot see the kingdom of God." (Jn.3:3)**

**"For as the Father raises the dead [spiritually dead] and gives them life, so also the Son gives life to whom he will." (Jn.5:21)**

**"It is the Spirit who gives life; the flesh is no help at all. The words that I have spoken to you are spirit and life." (Jn.6:63)**

**And you were dead in the trespasses and sins (Ep.2:1)**

**But God, being rich in mercy, because of the great love with which he loved us, even when we were dead in our trespasses, made us alive together with Christ—by grace you have been saved. (Ep.2:4–5)**

➢ The Holy Spirit convicts people of sin, of righteousness, and of judgment, that is their need to be fed and nourished (saved and given life).

**"And when he [the Holy Spirit] comes, he will convict the world concerning sin and righteousness and judgment." (Jn.16:8)**

➢ The Holy Spirit attracts people to the cross of Christ through its glorious provisions.

**For the word of the cross is folly to those who are perishing, but to us who are being saved it is the power of God. (1 Co.1:18)**

**But far be it from me to boast except in the cross of our Lord Jesus Christ, by which the world has been crucified to me, and I to the world. (Ga.6:14)**

**And might reconcile us both to God in one body through the cross, thereby killing the hostility. (Ep.2:16)**

**And through him to reconcile to himself all things, whether on earth or in heaven, making peace by the blood of his cross. (Col.1:20)**

➢ The Holy Spirit stirs a person to respond by coming to Christ.

**"Come to me, all who labor and are heavy laden, and I will give you rest." (Mt.11:28)**

**On the last day of the feast, the great day, Jesus stood up and cried out, "If anyone thirsts, let him come to me and drink." (Jn.7:37)**

**The Spirit and the Bride say, "Come." And let the one who hears say, "Come." And let the one who is thirsty come; let the one who desires take the water of life without price. (Re.22:17)**

**"Come, everyone who thirsts, come to the waters; and he who has no money, come, buy and eat! Come, buy wine and milk without money and without price. Why do you spend your money for that which is not bread, and your labor for that which does not satisfy? Listen diligently to me, and eat what is good, and delight yourselves in rich food. Incline your ear, and come to me; hear, that your soul may live; and I will make with you an everlasting covenant, my steadfast, sure love for David." (Is.55:1–3)**

b. **Our part in salvation (vv.45b–46).**

Even though it is God's will for all to be saved (1 Ti.2:4; 2 Pe.3:9), nobody is automatically saved. Nor does God force anybody to believe on His Son. We must respond when God draws us. First, we must listen to God and learn of Him (v.45b). We must hear the voice of God when God draws. When we feel the pull, tug, or movement of God's Spirit, we must listen to the conviction of the Spirit. Then, we must learn of God. However, we can learn of God only through Christ. If we wish to learn of God, we have to come to Christ. The reasons are clearly stated by Christ (v.46):

➣ No person has seen God.
➣ Christ alone is of God.
➣ Christ alone has seen God.

> So Jesus answered them, "My teaching is not mine, but his who sent me. If anyone's will is to do God's will, he will know whether the teaching is from God or whether I am speaking on my own authority." (Jn.7:16-17)

> So Jesus said to the Jews who had believed him, "If you abide in my word, you are truly my disciples, and you will know the truth, and the truth will set you free." (Jn.8:31-32)

> "And this is eternal life, that they know you, the only true God, and Jesus Christ whom you have sent." (Jn.17:3)

> "But let him who boasts boast in this, that he understands and knows me, that I am the LORD who practices steadfast love, justice, and righteousness in the earth. For in these things I delight, declares the LORD." (Je.9:24)

> "Let us know; let us press on to know the LORD; his going out is sure as the dawn; he will come to us as the showers, as the spring rains that water the earth." (Ho.6:3)

We must come to Christ: we must yield to the drawing power of God. God reveals, pulls, and tugs at our hearts to come to Christ. Why? Because the only way a person can *learn of God* is to come to Christ, and God wants every person to learn of Him, to know Him personally.

Being self-centered and rebellious, humans like to feel independent; consequently, most resist the quickening pull and drawing power of God. However, those who give in to the godly constraint (Jn.6:44) and who partake of Christ (Jn.6:47-51) learn of God and are accepted into His family.

## 3 A person must believe in Christ.

To be saved, a person must believe in Christ (see DEEPER STUDY # 2—Jn.2:24). The person who believes has eternal life (see DEEPER STUDY # 2—Jn.1:4; DEEPER STUDY # 1—10:10; DEEPER STUDY # 1—17:2-3). Christ calls for us to pay close attention, saying, "Truly, truly," that is, "listen, listen" (see vv.26, 32). What He now says is critical: a person must believe in order to receive eternal life.

a. **Believe He is the Bread of Life (vv.48-49).**

A person must believe that Christ is *the* Bread of Life: the Bread that feeds and nourishes mankind spiritually, that saves and gives us life (v.48; see notes—Jn.6:32; 6:33; 6:34-35). Note the Lord's claim: "I am the Bread of Life."

➣ Note how straightforward the claim is.
➣ Note how brief, clear-cut, straight to the point, and unmistakable the claim is.
➣ Note Christ's claim to deity: "I Am." There is no hesitation—no reservation—no holding back. He pulls no punches: "I Am" (see DEEPER STUDY # 1—Jn.6:20).
➣ Note how Christ refers to the manna again (see v.32). Eating physical food will only sustain us temporarily; we still die. The point is clear: our concern should not be physical food. If it is, we have only death to anticipate.

47 "Truly, truly, I say to you, whoever believes has eternal life.
48 I am the bread of life.
49 Your fathers ate the manna in the wilderness, and they died.
50 This is the bread that comes down from heaven, so that one may eat of it and not die.
51 I am the living bread that came down from heaven. If anyone eats of this bread, he will live forever. And the bread that I will give for the life of the world is my flesh."

Jesus said to them, "I am the bread of life; whoever comes to me shall not hunger, and whoever believes in me shall never thirst." (Jn.6:35)

### b. Believe He is *out of* heaven—has come to deliver us from death (v.50).

We must believe that Christ is *from* or out of heaven, that He has come to deliver us from death. Christ stated clearly that He came down from heaven, from God Himself (see note—Jn.3:31). If a person eats and partakes of Him, that person will not die, not spiritually or eternally (see DEEPER STUDY # 1—He.9:27). Note: *eat* (phagei) is in the Greek aorist tense. This means that a person eats and partakes (receives) of Christ *once-for-all*. It is a one-time experience.

> "For I have come down from heaven, not to do my own will but the will of him who sent me. And this is the will of him who sent me, that I should lose nothing of all that he has given me, but raise it up on the last day. For this is the will of my Father, that everyone who looks on the Son and believes in him should have eternal life, and I will raise him up on the last day." (Jn.6:38-40)

> "This is the bread that came down from heaven, not like the bread the fathers ate, and died. Whoever feeds on this bread will live forever." (Jn.6:58)

### c. Believe He is the living bread—the One who gives us life forever (v.51a).

We must believe that Christ is the living Bread, the One who gives us life forever. Grasp the details of Christ's teaching:

First, the Bread is living; it is alive (Jn.1:4; 5:26). The words are literally, "the Bread, the Living" (ho artos ho zon; see v.35, 41, 48).

Second, the Bread "came down from heaven." The phrase *came down* (katabas) is again in the aorist tense which means Christ *came once*. The incarnation had never taken place before, nor will it ever take place again. The miraculous entrance of the living Bread into the world is a *one-time-only event*.

Third, the Bread, the Lord Jesus Christ, came to provide spiritual food for humanity: spiritual and eternal life.

Fourth, the offer of eternal life is conditional: *If* we eat of this Bread, we will live forever.

> So Jesus said to them, "Truly, truly, I say to you, unless you eat the flesh of the Son of Man and drink his blood, you have no life in you. Whoever feeds on my flesh and drinks my blood has eternal life, and I will raise him up on the last day. For my flesh is true food, and my blood is true drink." (Jn.6:53-55)

> "Truly, truly, I say to you, if anyone keeps my word, he will never see death." (Jn.8:51)

> "And everyone who lives and believes in me shall never die. Do you believe this?" (Jn.11:26)

### d. Believe He gave His flesh for the life of the world (v.51b).

We must believe that Christ gave His flesh for the life of the world. Note that Christ identifies the Bread: it is His flesh which He gives for the life of the world. The great truth of Scripture and the greatest truth in the world is that Jesus Christ came in the flesh—He became a man—and He gave His flesh—His life—for the life of the world.

> For God has done what the law, weakened by the flesh, could not do. By sending his own Son in the likeness of sinful flesh and for sin, he condemned sin in the flesh. (Ro.8:3)

> Great indeed, we confess, is the mystery of godliness: He was manifested in the flesh, vindicated by the Spirit, seen by angels, proclaimed among the nations, believed on in the world, taken up in glory. (1 Ti.3:16)

> Since therefore the children share in flesh and blood, he himself likewise partook of the same things, that through death he might destroy the one who has the power of death, that is, the devil, and deliver all those who through fear of death were subject to lifelong slavery. (He.2:14-15)

> He himself bore our sins in his body on the tree, that we might die to sin and live to righteousness. By his wounds you have been healed. (1 Pe.2:24)

> For Christ also suffered once for sins, the righteous for the unrighteous, that he might bring us to God, being put to death in the flesh but made alive in the spirit. (1 Pe.3:18)

> By this you know the Spirit of God: every spirit that confesses that Jesus Christ has come in the flesh is from God, and every spirit that does not confess Jesus is not from God. This is the spirit of the antichrist, which you heard was coming and now is in the world already. (1 Jn.4:2-3)

## G. The Results of Partaking of the Bread of Life, 6:52-58

52 The Jews then disputed among themselves, saying, "How can this man give us his flesh to eat?"

53 So Jesus said to them, "Truly, truly, I say to you, unless you eat the flesh of the Son of Man and drink his blood, you have no life in you.

54 Whoever feeds on my flesh and drinks my blood has eternal life, and I will raise him up on the last day.

55 For my flesh is true food, and my blood is true drink.

56 Whoever feeds on my flesh and drinks my blood abides in me, and I in him.

57 As the living Father sent me, and I live because of the Father, so whoever feeds on me, he also will live because of me.

58 This is the bread that came down from heaven, not like the bread the fathers ate, and died. Whoever feeds on this bread will live forever."

1. **An abundant life—a life that is real & lasting, Jn.10:10**
   a. The religious leaders were perplexed
   b. Jesus proclaimed a much more shocking thing: Unless a person partakes of Him, the person does not have life (abundant, overflowing life)[DS1]
2. **Eternal life—a life that conquers death & is to be resurrected by the Lord**
3. **A satisfying life—a life that is genuinely fulfilling**
4. **An indwelt life—a life of companionship & permanent fellowship with the Lord, 1 Jn.1:3**
5. **A purposeful life—a life that is filled to the brim with meaning & significance**
6. **An empowering life—a life that receives & is forever energized by Christ Himself, the incorruptible food**

# Division VII

*The Revelation of Jesus, the Bread of Life, 6:1-71*

G. The Results of Partaking of the Bread of Life, 6:52-58

## 6:52-58
## Introduction

In order to be saved, to receive eternal life, we must receive and partake of the Bread of Life, Jesus Christ. When we do, we receive a wonderful gift from God: a quality of life that far surpasses anything we have ever known. Even more glorious, it is a life that never ends. Jesus concluded His discourse on the Bread of Life by teaching about the life He gives. This is, *The Results of Partaking of the Bread of Life*, 6:52-58.

1. An abundant life—a life that is real and lasting, Jn.10:10 (vv.52-53).
2. Eternal life—a life that conquers death and is to be resurrected by the Lord (v.54).
3. A satisfying life—a life that is genuinely fulfilling (v.55).
4. An indwelt life—a life of companionship & permanent fellowship with the Lord, 1 Jn.1:3 (v.56).
5. A purposeful life—a life that is filled to the brim with meaning and significance (v.57).
6. An empowering life—a life that receives and is forever energized by Christ Himself, the incorruptible food (v.58).

## 1 An abundant life—a life that is real and lasting, Jn.10:10.

**6:52-53**

Jesus had revealed that He is the Bread of Life who would give His flesh for the life of the world. All who eat of the Bread—His flesh—would have eternal life (v.51). This life is an abundant life—a life that is real and lasting (Jn.10:10). An abundant life is the first result of partaking of the Bread of Life.

⁵² The Jews then disputed among themselves, saying, "How can this man give us his flesh to eat?"

⁵³ So Jesus said to them, "Truly, truly, I say to you, unless you eat the flesh of the Son of Man and drink his blood, you have no life in you."

a. **The religious leaders were perplexed (v.52).**
The Jewish religious leaders began to argue with what Jesus had said:

> "I am the living bread that came down from heaven. If anyone eats of this bread, he will live forever. And the bread that I will give for the life of the world is my flesh." (Jn.6:51)

They disputed (quarreled—NKJV; argued—NASB, NIV, CSB) among themselves over what this statement meant. *Disputed* (Gk. emachonto) means to argue, fuss, debate. They were debating what Jesus meant.

➢ Some interpreted His words as a parable, in a figurative and symbolic way. They knew He often spoke in parables.
➢ Others had no idea what He meant, but they did see that He was claiming to be the most important person in the world, the very Savior of all people. This, of course, bothered them beyond reason. How could any man claim to be so important to the world? As materialists and humanists they asked, "How can this be? He is but a man. How can He give His flesh for the world and the world receive eternal life?"
➢ A few disciples, genuine followers of the Lord, perhaps understood.

The point is that the religious authorities were disturbed. The message had been going on for a long time, and Jesus had made claim after claim—all most unusual. Moreover, what He was saying was not clear, and some of it offended them. Therefore, they were angry and perplexed and began to argue among themselves about what He meant and how they should respond to Him.

b. **Jesus proclaimed a much more shocking thing: Unless a person partakes of Him, the person does not have life (abundant, overflowing life) (v.53).**
Jesus responded by making a much more shocking statement: unless a person partakes of Him—eats His flesh and drinks His blood—that person has no life dwelling within them. Jesus was speaking symbolically, painting a picture of partaking of the Bread of Life. He was talking about receiving Him, taking Him personally into your heart and life, accepting the sacrifice of His body and blood personally as the payment for your sin.

*Eat* and *drink* are in the Greek aorist tense which means a once-for-all act. Jesus was not speaking of partaking time and again. He was not speaking of feasting upon Him day by day through prayer and Bible study. He was speaking of a one-time event. A person is to eat and drink of Christ, that is, receive Him once for all (see DEEPER STUDY # 1).

**THOUGHT 1.** Unless people receive (eat and drink) Christ, they have no life within them. They are dead spiritually and eternally. They are walking around as dead people.

Physically, they are in the process of aging and dying, of living in the realm of death and being doomed to die.

Spiritually, they are already dead, having no life with God. They have no life, no real and true relationship with the *true and living God*. They are doomed to eternal death and separation from God.

Partaking, eating and drinking, of Christ is absolutely essential in order to truly live—in order to possess real life, the abundant, overflowing life that lasts now and forever.

> And you were dead in the trespasses and sins (Ep.2:1)

> For anything that becomes visible is light. Therefore it says, "Awake, O sleeper, and arise from the dead, and Christ will shine on you." (Ep.5:14)

> And you, who were dead in your trespasses and the uncircumcision of your flesh, God made alive together with him, having forgiven us all our trespasses. (Col.2:13)

**DEEPER STUDY # 1**

(6:53) **Eat—Drink—Salvation:** to receive, accept, partake, appropriate, assimilate, absorb, and to make part of oneself. A person can actually receive and partake of Christ in the most intimate and nourishing sense of his being (flesh and blood). The receiving and partaking can be just as intimate and nourishing as eating and drinking.

The point is, people must receive Christ into their heart, into their innermost being if they wish to live. In fact, they are dead spiritually and eternally unless they so receive Christ.

## 2 Eternal life—a life that conquers death and is to be resurrected by the Lord.

6:54

The second result of receiving Christ, the Bread of Life, is eternal life. In this verse, Jesus used a different word for *eat* (trogon) than He had used in the previous verses (phage). It means to eat eagerly, to grasp at chunks, to eat with pleasure. It is the picture of hungering after Christ and eagerly wanting to feed and feast on Him.

[54] "Whoever feeds on my flesh and drinks my blood has eternal life, and I will raise him up on the last day."

The tense is also different. It is present tense, which means continuous action. A person must continue to eat and to develop and grow into the habit of feasting upon Christ. Christian growth day by day is the picture.

Now note the point. A genuine believer, a person who really receives Christ, is a person who partakes of Him continually. Day by day the individual will feast upon Christ. It is this person—the genuine believer—who has the promise of eternal life.

> **THOUGHT 1.** Remember, eternal life includes three great things:
> ➢ An abundant and meaningful life that lasts forever (see DEEPER STUDY # 2—Jn.1:4; DEEPER STUDY # 1—10:10; DEEPER STUDY # 1—17:2–3).
> ➢ The conquest of death (see note—Jn.3:14–15).
> ➢ The resurrection (see note—Jn.5:28–30).
>
> **"For God so loved the world, that he gave his only Son, that whoever believes in him should not perish but have eternal life." (Jn.3:16)**
>
> **"Truly, truly, I say to you, whoever hears my word and believes him who sent me has eternal life. He does not come into judgment, but has passed from death to life." (Jn.5:24)**
>
> **"And this is eternal life, that they know you, the only true God, and Jesus Christ whom you have sent." (Jn.17:3)**

## 3 A satisfying life—a life that is genuinely fulfilling.

6:55

The third result of receiving Christ is true, not false, satisfaction. *True* or *indeed* (alethes) means true as opposed to false (see DEEPER STUDY # 1—Jn.1:9). The things of the world do not feed and fill us, not with a true satisfaction. Worldly pleasures and satisfactions are false, and false satisfaction does not last, not permanently, not with full assurance and confidence and security. Worldly pleasures and satisfactions always leave us somewhat empty, dissatisfied, craving, void, unassured and wondering if this world is all there is—wondering if there is not more to life than what this world and its possessions have to offer.

[55] "For my flesh is true food, and my blood is true drink."

True satisfaction comes from receiving Christ into our lives, and it comes only through Christ. This is the Lord's point in this verse. Just as real life on the earth comes from eating and drinking food, so real and abundant life comes from eating and drinking Christ. We must receive Christ in the closest and most intimate and nourishing sense in order to have true life, life that is abundant and full of . . .

- assurance
- strength
- meekness
- goodness
- love
- security
- decisiveness
- temperance
- patience
- joy
- confidence
- courage
- faith
- gentleness
- peace

"Blessed are those who hunger and thirst for righteousness, for they shall be satisfied." (Mt.5:6)

"But whoever drinks of the water that I will give him will never be thirsty again. The water that I will give him will become in him a spring of water welling up to eternal life." (Jn.4:14)

On the last day of the feast, the great day, Jesus stood up and cried out, "If anyone thirsts, let him come to me and drink." (Jn.7:37)

They feast on the abundance of your house, and you give them drink from the river of your delights. (Ps.36:8)

For he satisfies the longing soul, and the hungry soul he fills with good things. (Ps.107:9)

"Come, everyone who thirsts, come to the waters; and he who has no money, come, buy and eat! Come, buy wine and milk without money and without price." (Is.55:1)

6:56

⁵⁶ "Whoever feeds on my flesh and drinks my blood abides in me, and I in him."

## 4 An indwelt life—a life of companionship and permanent fellowship with the Lord.

The fourth result is supernatural companionship and fellowship, care and being looked after by the Lord. This is seen in the word *abides* or *remains* (menei). It means to continue, inhabit, rest in or upon. It is being fixed and set and remaining there, continuing on and on. Such is the state and condition and being of the person who receives Christ. We receive Christ into our being, and Christ enters our lives, abiding within us. We are also placed into Christ, that is, placed with all other believers into the spiritual body of Christ (see notes—1 Co.12:12-31; Ep.1:22-23; 2:11-22; also see Deeper Study # 1—Ac.2:1-4, the section on baptism for more discussion). We abide in Christ even as Christ abides in us. This, of course, means fellowship and companionship with Christ and the presence of His care and watchful eye in looking after us (see Deeper Study # 1—Jn.15:1-8; Deeper Study # 3—Ac.2:42 for more discussion).

"In that day you will know that I am in my Father, and you in me, and I in you." (Jn.14:20)

"Abide in me, and I in you. As the branch cannot bear fruit by itself, unless it abides in the vine, neither can you, unless you abide in me. I am the vine; you are the branches. Whoever abides in me and I in him, he it is that bears much fruit, for apart from me you can do nothing." (Jn.15:4-5)

I have been crucified with Christ. It is no longer I who live, but Christ who lives in me. And the life I now live in the flesh I live by faith in the Son of God, who loved me and gave himself for me. (Ga.2:20)

To them God chose to make known how great among the Gentiles are the riches of the glory of this mystery, which is Christ in you, the hope of glory. (Col.1:27)

Whoever keeps his commandments abides in God, and God in him. And by this we know that he abides in us, by the Spirit whom he has given us. (1 Jn.3:24)

"'Behold, I stand at the door and knock. If anyone hears my voice and opens the door, I will come in to him and eat with him, and he with me.'" (Re.3:20)

## 5 A purposeful life—a life that is filled to the brim with meaning and significance.

The fifth result of receiving Christ is a life that is full of purpose, meaning, and significance. The key to a meaningful life is living for a greater purpose than self. Jesus said, "I live because of the Father." This means at least two things:

First, He lived *because of* or *by* the Father, that is, on account of the Father. His life was due to the Father.

Second, He lived *for* the Father; that is, He lived to do the Father's will. The Father *sent* Him to live on earth for a specific purpose: to fulfill the Father's will and task.

When we receive Christ ("feeds on me"), we *live because of Christ*. We begin to live in all the purpose, meaning, and significance of life, for apart from Christ there is no life. Note: the tense is present, continuous action. We must *continue* to partake, eat, and feast upon Christ to keep our sense of purpose and meaning, to really live and live abundantly.

> 57 "As the living Father sent me, and I live because of the Father, so whoever feeds on me, he also will live because of me."

> **For we who live are always being given over to death for Jesus' sake, so that the life of Jesus also may be manifested in our mortal flesh. (2 Co.4:11)**
>
> **I have been crucified with Christ. It is no longer I who live, but Christ who lives in me. And the life I now live in the flesh I live by faith in the Son of God, who loved me and gave himself for me. (Ga.2:20)**
>
> **For to me to live is Christ, and to die is gain. (Ph.1:21)**

Note that Jesus called God "the living Father."

> **Simon Peter replied, "You are the Christ, the Son of the living God." (Mt.16:16)**
>
> **"For as the Father has life in himself, so he has granted the Son also to have life in himself." (Jn.5:26)**
>
> **What agreement has the temple of God with idols? For we are the temple of the living God; as God said, "I will make my dwelling among them and walk among them, and I will be their God, and they shall be my people." (2 Co.6:16)**

## 6 An empowering life—a life that receives and is forever energized by Christ Himself, the incorruptible food.

The sixth result of receiving Christ is incorruptible food within our hearts, living nourishment that energizes our lives forever. Christ made a strong, descriptive contrast between the manna (v.31) and the true Bread from heaven. The manna eaten by Israel in the Old Testament *did come* from the clouds above, but it did not give life to the people. They *all died*. But all who eat *this bread*—the Bread which came down from heaven, Christ Himself—will *live forever*.

> 58 "This is the bread that came down from heaven, not like the bread the fathers ate, and died. Whoever feeds on this bread will live forever."

The idea is striking: it is the Living Bread, Christ Himself, who energizes and quickens us to live forever. Christ has the quality, the power, the substance to energize us and give us eternal life. However, He and He alone has such energizing, life-giving power.

> **In him was life, and the life was the light of men. (Jn.1:4)**
>
> **"For as the Father has life in himself, so he has granted the Son also to have life in himself." (Jn.5:26)**
>
> **And which now has been manifested through the appearing of our Savior Christ Jesus, who abolished death and brought life and immortality to light through the gospel. (2 Ti.1:10)**

## H. The Reasons Some People Are Offended by Christ, the Bread of Life, 6:59–71

1. The disturbing message of Jesus to the synagogue crowd: Many disciples had difficulty accepting His message

2. The idea of eating Jesus' flesh & drinking His blood, 6:51–56

3. The ascension & exaltation of Christ

4. The teaching that the Spirit gives life & that human efforts (the flesh) count for nothing
   a. Some did not believe
   b. One (Judas) would betray Him

5. The fact that God saves us, that we do not save ourselves

6. The conclusion: There were three reactions
   a. Many disciples turned back, quit following Jesus

   b. One disciple believed Jesus was the Christ: He (Simon Peter) declared that other disciples believed the same

   c. One disciple would betray Christ: Judas Iscariot

⁵⁹ Jesus said these things in the synagogue, as he taught at Capernaum.

⁶⁰ When many of his disciples heard it, they said, "This is a hard saying; who can listen to it?"

⁶¹ But Jesus, knowing in himself that his disciples were grumbling about this, said to them, "Do you take offense at this?

⁶² "Then what if you were to see the Son of Man ascending to where he was before?

⁶³ "It is the Spirit who gives life; the flesh is no help at all. The words that I have spoken to you are spirit and life.

⁶⁴ "But there are some of you who do not believe." (For Jesus knew from the beginning who those were who did not believe, and who it was who would betray him.)

⁶⁵ And he said, "This is why I told you that no one can come to me unless it is granted him by the Father."

⁶⁶ After this many of his disciples turned back and no longer walked with him.

⁶⁷ So Jesus said to the twelve, "Do you want to go away as well?"

⁶⁸ Simon Peter answered him, "Lord, to whom shall we go? You have the words of eternal life,

⁶⁹ "and we have believed, and have come to know, that you are the Holy One of God."

⁷⁰ Jesus answered them, "Did I not choose you, the twelve? And yet one of you is a devil."

⁷¹ He spoke of Judas the son of Simon Iscariot, for he, one of the twelve, was going to betray him.

# Division VII

*The Revelation of Jesus, the Bread of Life, 6:1-71*

H. The Reasons Some People Are Offended by Christ, the Bread of Life, 6:59-71

## 6:59-71
## Introduction

Many people are offended by Christ, His teachings, and His message. This tragedy was no less true in Jesus' day than it is in ours. It is hard to imagine that those who actually met Jesus face to face, actually saw Him perform miracles, and actually heard Him teach, could not bring themselves to believe. After Jesus finished His teaching on the Bread of life, many who had been following Him became offended and forsook Him. This passage reveals four things that offended them that still offend people today. This is, *The Reasons Some People Are Offended by Christ, the Bread of Life,* 6:59-71.

1. The disturbing message of Jesus to the synagogue crowd: many disciples had difficulty accepting His message (vv.59-60).
2. The idea of eating Jesus' flesh and drinking His blood, 6:51-56 (v.61).
3. The ascension and exaltation of Christ (v.62).
4. The teaching that the Spirit gives life and that human efforts (the flesh) count for nothing (vv.63-64).
5. The fact that God saves us, that we do not save ourselves (v.65).
6. The conclusion: There were three reactions (vv.66-71).

## 1 The disturbing message of Jesus to the synagogue crowd: Many disciples had difficulty accepting His message.

**6:59-60**

⁵⁹ Jesus said these things in the synagogue, as he taught at Capernaum.
⁶⁰ When many of his disciples heard it, they said, "This is a hard saying; who can listen to it?"

Jesus' message was to the synagogue crowd in Capernaum. Many of His disciples and followers were present, but they had difficulty accepting what He had said, calling it a hard saying or hard teaching. *Hard saying* or *teaching* (Gk. skleros) means rough and harsh. What Jesus had said was *hard* and *difficult to accept*, but His words were clearly understood. The people's problem was not in their understanding, but in their hearts. Jesus knew this, so He revealed some reasons why people are offended by Him.

## 2 The idea of eating Jesus' flesh and drinking His blood, 6:51-56.

**6:61**

⁶¹ But Jesus, knowing in himself that his disciples were grumbling about this, said to them, "Do you take offense at this?"

People are offended by the claims of Christ and the idea of eating His flesh and drinking His blood (see vv.51-56). People including counterfeit disciples are offended and repulsed by what is sometimes called . . .

- a *grotesque god,* a god who came to earth to impregnate a young girl, becoming incarnated into human flesh, being born half-man and half-god
- a *bloody religion* or a religion viewed by some as a religion of cannibalism

How do we respond to these objections, the protests of faithless people who do not understand God's Word?

First, Jesus claimed to be God *incarnated* in human flesh, but not in a grotesque sense—not half-man, half-god. In very simple terms, He was man, fully man; that is, He had the nature of man, being made of the very same substance as all humans. However, there was one difference:

He was not born of a human father; He was born of God. God very simply *spoke the Word*, and a miracle took place, just as He spoke the Word and created the world. There is nothing grotesque about God's words nor about His willing something to be done and doing it. God did what He always does when He wills something. He simply spoke, and the event was set in motion. Very simply stated, Jesus Christ was born *by the Word of God and by human flesh*. He was fully Man, fully God. He came *from God's* Word; He became a Man *by God's Word*. Therefore, all humans owe their obedience to Christ (see note—Jn.6:62 for more discussion).

Second, the cross or the blood of Christ *is offensive and repulsive*, just as some people feel it is. It represents the awful shame of sin and the death of Jesus Christ, God's very own Son; therefore, it is bound to be repulsive. But it also represents salvation and deliverance from sin and its awful guilt. Therefore, the cross is also the most attractive symbol in all the world (see note, *Cross*—Mt.16:21-23).

> He himself bore our sins in his body on the tree, that we might die to sin and live to righteousness. By his wounds you have been healed. (1 Pe.2:24)

> For Christ also suffered once for sins, the righteous for the unrighteous, that he might bring us to God, being put to death in the flesh but made alive in the spirit. (1 Pe.3:18)

The words "take . . . eat" of Christ are in no way referring to cannibalism. The words simply mean that we are to spiritually receive Christ into our lives, into our whole being. Our deliverance from the bondage of sin and death is by *spiritually taking and eating* of Christ's body; that is, we must spiritually receive, partake, consume, absorb, and assimilate Christ into our lives. We must allow Christ to become the very nourishment, the innermost part and energy, the very consumption of our being.

> But to all who did receive him, who believed in his name, he gave the right to become children of God. (Jn.1:12)

> "'Behold, I stand at the door and knock. If anyone hears my voice and opens the door, I will come in to him and eat with him, and he with me.'" (Re.3:20)

## 6:62

⁶² "Then what if you were to see the Son of Man ascending to where he was before?"

## 3 The ascension and exaltation of Christ.

Jesus responded to His disciples' grumbling by asking them a searching question: would they still take offense at His teaching if they witnessed Him ascending back to heaven, an act that would prove that He came from heaven? Many people today are offended by the ascension and exaltation of Christ (see note, *Ascension*—Mk.16:19-20). Why? If a person accepts the ascension and exaltation of Christ, they have to accept that He is who He claims to be, accept that He is God and that He is Lord. Consequently, they have to surrender the control of their life to Christ. They can no longer control their own lives and believe what they want to believe or do the things they wish.

It is significant that Christ referred to himself here as the *Son of Man* (see note—Jn.1:51). The counterfeit disciple is unwilling to look at Jesus as the "Son of Man," that is, as the Ideal and Perfect Man, as the Pattern for all people to copy (see Deeper Study # 3—Mt.8:20). If a person accepted Christ as the Son of Man, they would have to pattern their life after Christ by doing their very best to live as Christ lived. They would have to diligently seek to be like Christ (see He.11:6). The counterfeit disciple is unwilling to submit to the control and dominion of Jesus. He/she is adamantly opposed to patterning his/her life after Jesus, even though God exalted Jesus as Lord and Master.

*Where He was before* points to the fact that Jesus is eternal. He was preexistent: God of very God. Therefore, we are to believe and surrender to Him as Lord.

> Therefore God has highly exalted him and bestowed on him the name that is above every name, so that at the name of Jesus every knee should bow, in heaven and on earth and under the earth, and every tongue confess that Jesus Christ is Lord, to the glory of God the Father. (Ph.2:9-11)

> Who has gone into heaven and is at the right hand of God, with angels, authorities, and powers having been subjected to him. (1 Pe.3:22)

## 4 The teaching that the Spirit gives life and that human efforts (the flesh) count for nothing.

Some are offended by the teaching that the Spirit gives life and the flesh can do nothing to help us. Accepting this truth concedes that we are totally incapable of helping or saving ourselves.

The flesh cannot give us life. The flesh cannot help us at all. To the contrary, the flesh is given life by God. People do not like to accept or think about the *zero value* of the flesh. Think of all the things people do to preserve their flesh. They do everything they can to preserve their youth, attractiveness, and stamina. They use cosmetics, clothing, and activities to appear young, attractive, and physically capable. But before too long, before they ever imagine, the flesh proves unprofitable; it ages, deteriorates, and surrenders to the process of decay. The *seed of corruption* within wins, and every person dies.

> ⁶³ "It is the Spirit who gives life; the flesh is no help at all. The words that I have spoken to you are spirit and life.
> ⁶⁴ "But there are some of you who do not believe." (For Jesus knew from the beginning who those were who did not believe, and who it was who would betray him.)

Just as the flesh cannot preserve its own life, it can do nothing to give us spiritual life. The flesh proves its *zero value* spiritually; it profits nothing, not spiritually, and not eternally.

Such a thought, such a teaching—despite its truthfulness—offends many people. They love the world and the flesh, its pleasures and feelings; therefore, they want the right to feed it. They want more and more good feelings, getting and keeping all the physical and material pleasures they can. They want the . . .

- worldly ego
- fleshy image
- human recognition
- institutional praise
- self-centered fame
- benevolent honor
- stimulating pleasures
- earthly wealth

Moreover, they want to believe they can save themselves by their own efforts, their own way, in their own power. They refuse to concede that they are spiritually bankrupt, helpless in their own merits and strength. They will not admit that they need a Savior.

Only the Spirit can give us life, give us abundant and eternal life. How? By receiving the Word of Christ. The words that Christ spoke were Spirit and life. When a person receives the words of Christ into their heart and life, they begin to live: they actually experience the Spirit of God entering their life and begin to experience real life.

> "The thief comes only to steal and kill and destroy. I came that they may have life and have it abundantly." (Jn.10:10)
>
> If the Spirit of him who raised Jesus from the dead dwells in you, he who raised Christ Jesus from the dead will also give life to your mortal bodies through his Spirit who dwells in you. (Ro.8:11)
>
> And you were dead in the trespasses and sins (Ep.2:1)
>
> But God, being rich in mercy, because of the great love with which he loved us, even when we were dead in our trespasses, made us alive together with Christ—by grace you have been saved. (Ep.2:4-5)

### a. Some did not believe (v.64a).

Jesus knew that some who were following Him did not truly believe, and He knew exactly who they were. They did not accept His Words; therefore, they did not have the Spirit of God abiding in them, nor did they have life. They were counterfeit believers, merely pretending to follow Jesus. Like every unbeliever, they were only existing, not living abundantly and eternally. They did not have the knowledge and *unswerving assurance* of living forever. They doubted and wondered, ever hoping, but they were not quite sure.

### b. One (Judas) would betray Him (v.64b).

Jesus also knew that one of those who professed to follow Him would betray Him. As John would reveal at the end of the chapter, this counterfeit disciple was Judas.

## 5 The fact that God saves us, that we do not save ourselves.

**6:65**

⁶⁵ And he said, "This is why I told you that no one can come to me unless it is granted him by the Father."

Because the flesh—human efforts—cannot save, salvation is entirely of God. Some are offended by this fact, the fact that God draws and saves people, that we cannot and do not save ourselves. Christ clearly said that no one can come to Him unless it is granted to him by the Father. Christ was saying:

➤ No person can come to Him unless God draws and stirs him or her to come.
➤ No person really belongs to God who has not come to Him.
➤ No person is saved unless they have come to Him.
➤ All people are lost unless they come to Him.

This fact disturbs people greatly, for most people feel they are good enough and have done enough good to be acceptable to God. Few people think they are lost and doomed to be separated from God; therefore, hearing the fact preached offends them. But note the critical point. The only saved person is a person who has been drawn to Christ by God and who has surrendered to God's pull and movement within their heart.

> "No one can come to me unless the Father who sent me draws him. And I will raise him up on the last day." (Jn.6:44)

> "And he who sent me is with me. He has not left me alone, for I always do the things that are pleasing to him." (Jn.8:29)

> Who saved us and called us to a holy calling, not because of our works but because of his own purpose and grace, which he gave us in Christ Jesus before the ages began. (2 Ti.1:9)

> According to the foreknowledge of God the Father, in the sanctification of the Spirit, for obedience to Jesus Christ and for sprinkling with his blood: May grace and peace be multiplied to you. (1 Pe.1:2)

**6:66-71**

⁶⁶ After this many of his disciples turned back and no longer walked with him.
⁶⁷ So Jesus said to the twelve, "Do you want to go away as well?"
⁶⁸ Simon Peter answered him, "Lord, to whom shall we go? You have the words of eternal life,
⁶⁹ and we have believed, and have come to know, that you are the Holy One of God."
⁷⁰ Jesus answered them, "Did I not choose you, the twelve? And yet one of you is a devil."
⁷¹ He spoke of Judas the son of Simon Iscariot, for he, one of the twelve, was going to betray him.

## 6 The conclusion: There were three reactions.

Every individual decides what they will do with Jesus, whether they believe or whether they will reject Him and His Words. John records that there were three responses to the Lord's message:

**a. Many disciples turned back, quit following Jesus (v.66).** Many professing disciples or followers turned back and quit following Jesus. They deserted the Lord. Why? Very simply, following Christ cost too much (see DEEPER STUDY # 1—Lk.9:23). It involved the cross, which meant complete denial of self. They could not accept Jesus' claims nor agree to what He demanded. Jesus was claiming to be Lord. He was demanding total allegiance. This meant that they had to give all they were and had to Christ. Jesus was claiming to be the very Son of God, to have come down *out of* heaven. Some just could not receive and accept the fact. His words were too difficult to believe, too hard to follow.

**b. One disciple believed Jesus was the Christ: He (Simon Peter) declared that other disciples believed the same (vv.67-69).** After many of Jesus' followers deserted Him, He asked the twelve if they wanted to turn back as well (v.67). As the apostles' leader and spokesman, Peter answered for all of them.

First, Peter called Jesus *Lord*, and he used the title in its fullest meaning (vv.68-69). He recognized Jesus to be the sovereign Lord of the universe, the One to whom all people owe their allegiance.

Second, Peter declared that Jesus' words are the words of eternal life. He declared that what Jesus had just proclaimed was true. (v.63; see Deeper Study # 2—Jn.1:4; Deeper Study # 1—10:10; Deeper Study # 1—17:2-3).

Third, Peter proclaimed that he and the apostles both *believed* and *knew* something: Jesus was...
- "the Christ, the Son of the living God" (KJV, NKJV; the latest Greek manuscripts read this)
- "the Holy One of God" (ESV, NASB, NIV, CSB; the oldest Greek manuscripts read this)

c. **One disciple would betray Christ; Judas Iscariot (vv.70–71).**
After Peter spoke up, professing the devotion of the twelve, Jesus revealed a chilling fact: one of them was a devil (v.70). John added the fact that time would ultimately tell: Jesus was referring to Judas Iscariot, who would betray Jesus. Jesus exposed three facts about this evil man:
- ➤ Judas was a "chosen" man, chosen not only to be saved, but to be a minister of Christ.
- ➤ Judas was called "a devil," a false accuser (2 Ti.3:3), an adversary, an enemy of Christ. In fact, he would be both influenced by the devil (Jn.13:2), and Satan would actually enter into him—possess him (Jn.13:27).
- ➤ Judas was a betrayer, a professed follower, but a hypocrite.

# Chapter 7

## VIII. The Responses to the Revelation of Jesus, 7:1–53

### A. The Response of Jesus' Brothers: Mockery and Unbelief, 7:1–9

1. The setting: Jesus was forced to withdraw & to minister in Galilee because the leaders plotted His death
2. The brothers' mockery & unbelief
   a. The Feast of Tabernacles was at hand
      1) That He leave & go to the feast
      2) That He could get more attention there & become a greater public figure
      3) That He in fact should show Himself to the whole world
   b. The brothers' unbelief
3. The reply by Jesus
   a. It is not time (the day) for His acclaim but for the acclaim of people
   b. It is time for the world's works to be proclaimed evil
   c. It is not time for His full revelation, that is, the revelation of His death, resurrection, & the world's salvation

After this Jesus went about in Galilee. He would not go about in Judea, because the Jews were seeking to kill him. ² Now the Jews' Feast of Booths was at hand. ³ So his brothers said to him, "Leave here and go to Judea, that your disciples also may see the works you are doing. ⁴ For no one works in secret if he seeks to be known openly. If you do these things, show yourself to the world." ⁵ For not even his brothers believed in him. ⁶ Jesus said to them, "My time has not yet come, but your time is always here. ⁷ The world cannot hate you, but it hates me because I testify about it that its works are evil. ⁸ You go up to the feast. I am not going up to this feast, for my time has not yet fully come." ⁹ After saying this, he remained in Galilee.

# Division VIII

*The Responses to the Revelation of Jesus, 7:1–53*

A. The Response of Jesus' Brothers: Mockery and Unbelief, 7:1–9

## 7:1–53
## DIVISION OVERVIEW

Chapter 7 is a brief pause in the revelation of who Jesus is. Chapter 7 shows the reactions of various groups to the revelations and claims of Jesus.

## 7:1–9
## Introduction

The first reaction or response to Jesus came from his half-brothers. Jesus' response to their scorn and faithlessness teaches us how to answer mockery, sarcasm, and unbelief toward Christ. We should keep it in mind when we answer similar reactions toward Jesus (point 3, vv.6-9). This is, *The Response of Jesus' Brothers: Mockery and Unbelief,* 7:1-9.

1. The setting: Jesus was forced to withdraw and to minister in Galilee because the leaders plotted His death (v.1).
2. The brother's mockery and unbelief (vv.2-5).
3. The reply by Jesus (vv.6-9).

## 1 The setting: Jesus was forced to withdraw and to minister in Galilee because the leaders plotted His death.

7:1

After this Jesus went about in Galilee. He would not go about in Judea, because the Jews were seeking to kill him.

Jesus was forced to withdraw from Judea and minister in Galilee. The reason was tragic: the Jewish religious leaders throughout Judea and Jerusalem had reacted so violently against Him that they sought to kill Him. The words, *were seeking* or *sought* convey continuous action; they were continually seeking to kill Jesus. They kept on seeking to kill Him.

Just how long Jesus was away from Judea and Jerusalem is not known. The opinions of scholars range from six months to one and a half years. On His last journey into Jerusalem, He was seen attending the Passover (Jn.6:4). Here in Chapter 7, He is seen attending the Feast of Tabernacles (v.10).

> **THOUGHT 1.** Note three applicable lessons.
> (1) Jesus withdrew from conflict and danger so that He might continue to minister.
> (2) Galilee was not as prominent as Judea. In fact, it was an obscure place, considered both insignificant and unimportant. But note: God chose for His Son to minister there. This should speak to the hearts of believers. No servant of God should feel embarrassed or less important to be placed in an obscure ministry by the Lord.
> (3) When Jesus was forced to withdraw, He did not withdraw from ministry. He did not become idle, sitting still and doing nothing. He ministered wherever He was. Ministering to people and meeting their needs and teaching and preaching the gospel were His life. To live was to minister.

## 2 The brothers' mockery and unbelief.

7:2-5

Jesus had four half-brothers whose names were James, Joses, Simon, and Judas. He also had some half-sisters who are not named in Scripture (Mt.13:55-56). Their attitude toward Jesus was one of extreme concern and embarrassment. His claim to be *the Son of God* embarrassed them immensely and led them to think He was mentally ill. On one occasion the rumor of Jesus' insanity caused so much pressure from neighbors and friends that His family actually traveled a great distance to find Him and bring Him home. (See note—Mk.3:31-32 for more discussion. This is an important note in grasping the background of the brothers' attitude of mockery toward Jesus.)

² Now the Jews' Feast of Booths was at hand.
³ So his brothers said to him, "Leave here and go to Judea, that your disciples also may see the works you are doing.
⁴ "For no one works in secret if he seeks to be known openly. If you do these things, show yourself to the world."
⁵ For not even his brothers believed in him.

Jesus, of course, did not heed the urgings of His family to cease making such phenomenal claims. He had to proclaim the truth: He was the Son of God, the very Bread of life, the only One who could fill and satisfy people and give them abundant and eternal life.

The embarrassment felt by Jesus' family was bound to be a heavy load, making them extremely self-conscious and stirring within them some sense of responsibility for Jesus' abnormal behavior. The brothers compensated for their embarrassment by mocking Jesus.

### a. The Feast of Tabernacles was at hand (v.2).

The time of the Feast of Tabernacles was near. This approaching assembly of the Jews in Jerusalem provided an opportunity for Jesus' unbelieving brothers to taunt Him.

### b. The brothers' suggestion and mockery (vv.3-4).

With a spirit of mockery, Jesus' brothers suggested that He leave and go up to Jerusalem to the Feast and do His marvelous miracles there. He could get more attention there and become a greater public figure. They implied that He was failing to help and to strengthen the disciples He left there when He withdrew to Galilee. If He really wanted to be acclaimed the Messiah, the Son of God, He needed to show Himself to the whole world, to prove Himself in the center of the nation, Jerusalem itself.

The brothers, of course, knew the rumors about the leaders seeking to kill Jesus. It was not likely that they really wanted Jesus to go and jeopardize His life, nor did they think He would. The whole scene was one of mockery (vv.3-4) and unbelief (v.5). They were tolerating Him through sarcasm, through a half-amused teasing. They entertained themselves by goading Him on and by treating Him with an amused disrespect. Unfortunately, their disrespect and teasing were open for all to see.

Naturally, Jesus was deeply hurt by His family's scorn. His heart was bound to be cut to the core by the family's mockery, embarrassment, and unbelief. He loved His family, and their rejection strained their relationship. But of even greater concern, their unbelief in Him—the Savior of the world—would lead to their eternal condemnation.

### b. The brothers' unbelief (v.5).

The embarrassment of Jesus' family, in particular His brothers, led to their unbelief. The Greek imperfect tense used in this verse expresses that the brothers' unbelief was a persistent, continuing attitude. Their initial struggles to believe are understandable in light of . . .
- Jesus' phenomenal claims
- Jesus' rejection by His hometown, Nazareth, which the family witnessed. His former neighbors and city had rejected Him on two occasions, once with so much hostility that they tried to kill Him (see Mt.13:53-58; Mk.6:1-6; Lu.4:16-30)
- Jesus' rejection by His neighbors and the leaders of the nation, both religious and civil. The neighbors thought Him insane, and the leaders thought Him demon-possessed (see Mt.12:46-50; Mk.3:20-35; Lu.8:19-21)

**THOUGHT 1.** Jesus Christ bore every imaginable suffering we might face, even the rejection of His own family. It is through His suffering—the very fact that He has borne all our sufferings—that He is able to strengthen us through any and all trials. He is with those who stand alone in the world in a special way, having been rejected by His own family.

> **For because he himself has suffered when tempted [trials], he is able to help those who are being tempted. (He.2:18; see He.4:15-16)**

## 7:6-9

⁶ Jesus said to them, "My time has not yet come, but your time is always here.
⁷ "The world cannot hate you, but it hates me because I testify about it that its works are evil.
⁸ You go up to the feast. I am not going up to this feast, for my time has not yet fully come."
⁹ After saying this, he remained in Galilee.

## 3 The reply by Jesus.

Jesus' patiently and lovingly replied to His brothers' ridicule, sarcasm, and unbelief. He did not respond to their taunting by doing what they pressured Him to do. Instead, He remained in Galilee for the time being (v.9).

### a. It is not time (the day) for His public acclaim but for the acclaim of people (v.6).

Jesus replied that the day of the Lord's acclaim had not yet come. It was not yet the time when many would proclaim Him the Savior, the King of kings and Lord of lords. Nor was it yet the time when many would bow, acknowledging that His claim to be the Messiah, the Son of God, was true.

However, that day was coming. There was a time appointed by God, a destined time (see note, *My Hour*—Jn.2:3-5). But it had not yet arrived.

Note that Jesus had turned the mockery into a teaching situation. He used the very point of the mockery against His claims and works to make the claim again. There would be a time, a day, when He would be recognized and acclaimed for who He truly is, but not then.

> **And Jesus answered them, "The hour has come for the Son of Man to be glorified. Truly, truly, I say to you, unless a grain of wheat falls into the earth and dies, it remains alone; but if it dies, it bears much fruit." (Jn.12:23-24)**

> **"Now is my soul troubled. And what shall I say? 'Father, save me from this hour'? But for this purpose I have come to this hour.... And I, when I am lifted up from the earth, will draw all people to myself." He said this to show by what kind of death he was going to die. (Jn.12:27, 32-33)**

> **Now before the Feast of the Passover, when Jesus knew that his hour had come to depart out of this world to the Father, having loved his own who were in the world, he loved them to the end. (Jn.13:1)**

Jesus further explained that this is the time for man's acclaim. Jesus in essence said to his brothers, *Your time—man's time, the world's time—is now*. It was and still is man's day, the day...
- for acceptance and acclaim
- for reception and recognition
- for honoring and receiving honor

It should be noted that some interpret *time* to mean "the opportune time." In this interpretation Jesus was simply saying it was not the best time for Him to attend the feast. His brothers could go anytime, but He could not. This interpretation is based on the word *time* (Gk. kairos, which stresses opportune time). It differs from the Greek word usually translated "hour" when describing *Jesus' hour* (hora, Jn.2:4). However, *kairos* is a frequently used word in the New Testament, and its meaning cannot be held exclusively to opportune time. Three things support the interpretation that *kairos* refers to "Jesus' hour" in this passage.
➢ The contrast Jesus makes between His time and His brothers' time.
➢ The context of verses 7-8.
➢ The emphasis given to Jesus' answer. If the reply means only that He was waiting for the opportune time to go to Jerusalem, then the reply seems trivial, almost meaningless; so does the contrast between His time and His brothers' time and the points of verses 7-8.

### b. It is time for the world's works to be proclaimed evil (v.7).

While it was not yet time for Jesus to be glorified by the world, *it was* time for Him to proclaim the world's works as evil. It was—and is—time for Christ to point out...
- the sin of the world, not to receive its acclaim
- the false religion of the world, not to proclaim its hypocritical goodness
- the depravity of the world, not to camouflage the truth
- the corruption within the world, not to paint a rosy picture
- the need of the world, not to praise it
- the destiny of the world, not to hide its fate

Because of this, the fact that He proclaimed the truth, the world hated Jesus and would not acknowledge and acclaim Him. It was time for the world's reaction against Him, not time for its acceptance.

It was—and still is—the time that the people of the world accept each other. His brothers were part of the world, and the world does not hate its own. The world does not reject and hate but instead receives those who love it, serve it, and participate in it. Worldly people embrace those who approve of their behavior and go along with it. Therefore, the world receives those who mock, ridicule, criticize, reject, and treat Christ sarcastically. The world does not hate, but welcomes, opposition to Jesus Christ.

**THOUGHT 1.** This is the time and the day when we must proclaim the works of the world to be evil. The truth must be preached and proclaimed by the ministers of God. The world cannot be saved unless the evil of the world is acknowledged and corrected. It is the task of God's people to proclaim the truth; however, it must be proclaimed as Jesus proclaimed it: in love, appealing to the desperate needs of sinful humanity.

> "If I had not come and spoken to them, they would not have been guilty of sin, but now they have no excuse for their sin." (Jn.15:22)

> For all have sinned and fall short of the glory of God. (Ro.3:23; see Is.53:6; 64:6)

> For the wages of sin is death, but the free gift of God is eternal life in Christ Jesus our Lord. (Ro.6:23)

> If we say we have no sin, we deceive ourselves, and the truth is not in us. (1 Jn.1:8)

> The LORD saw that the wickedness of man was great in the earth, and that every intention of the thoughts of his heart was only evil continually. (Ge.6:5)

> Whoever is steadfast in righteousness will live, but he who pursues evil will die. (Pr.11:19)

c. **It was not time for His full revelation, that is, the revelation of His death, resurrection, and the world's salvation (vv.8–9).**

Lastly, Jesus replied that it was not yet time for the full revelation of His purpose for coming into the world. That time had not yet *fully come* (peplerotai). Christ's predestined *hour to die* for the world had not yet arrived. It *would* come, but in God's time. And when it came, His claims and works would be validated and proven beyond question. Many would proclaim Him to be both Lord and Savior, the Bread of life who alone can fill and satisfy the desperate and starving needs of all people.

**THOUGHT 1.** Our answer to mockery, ridicule, sarcasm, and unbelief is the same as the answer proclaimed by Jesus.

(1) This is not the day for His acclaim, but for man's acclaim.

(2) It is time for the world's works to be proclaimed evil.

(3) It is not time for His full revelation, that is, for the climax of human history, the day when He will return in glory and majesty, dominion and power, the day when all will acknowledge Him as Lord. It is, however, the time for all to know that He died and rose again for the sins of the human race and that He alone is the Savior of the world.

> For it is written, "As I live, says the Lord, every knee shall bow to me, and every tongue shall confess to God." (Ro.14:11)

> Therefore God has highly exalted him and bestowed on him the name that is above every name, so that at the name of Jesus every knee should bow, in heaven and on earth and under the earth, and every tongue confess that Jesus Christ is Lord, to the glory of God the Father. (Ph.2:9–11)

> "Who will not fear, O Lord, and glorify your name? For you alone are holy. All nations will come and worship you, for your righteous acts have been revealed." (Re.15:4)

> All the ends of the earth shall remember and turn to the LORD, and all the families of the nations shall worship before you. For kingship belongs to the LORD, and he rules over the nations. (Ps.22:27–28)

> "Turn to me and be saved, all the ends of the earth! For I am God, and there is no other. By myself I have sworn; from my mouth has gone out in righteousness a word that shall not return: 'To me every knee shall bow, every tongue shall swear allegiance.'" (Is.45:22–23; see Is.66:23)

## B. The Response of the Jews: Seeking Yet Questioning, 7:10-19

1. The setting: Jesus went secretly to the Feast, after His brothers had left

<sup>10</sup> But after his brothers had gone up to the feast, then he also went up, not publicly but in private.

2. The crowds were watching for Him & asking questions about Him: Opinions differed
   a. Some said, He is a good man
   b. Others, He is a deceiver

<sup>11</sup> The Jews were looking for him at the feast, and saying, "Where is he?"
<sup>12</sup> And there was much muttering about him among the people. While some said, "He is a good man," others said, "No, he is leading the people astray."

   c. Most, He is not important enough to defend
   d. Many, He is unaccredited—so capable yet uneducated
      1) Jesus eventually went up to the Temple & taught
      2) People questioned Jesus' credentials

<sup>13</sup> Yet for fear of the Jews no one spoke openly of him.
<sup>14</sup> About the middle of the feast Jesus went up into the temple and began teaching.

<sup>15</sup> The Jews therefore marveled, saying, "How is it that this man has learning, when he has never studied?"
<sup>16</sup> So Jesus answered them, "My teaching is not mine, but his who sent me.

3. The reply by Jesus: My teaching is God's teaching—it comes from Him who sent Me
   a. Proven by the subjective test (the inward or moral test): A person knows the truth by doing it

<sup>17</sup> "If anyone's will is to do God's will, he will know whether the teaching is from God or whether I am speaking on my own authority.

   b. Proven by the objective test (the outward or visible test): Does a person speak for his own glory or for God's glory?

<sup>18</sup> "The one who speaks on his own authority seeks his own glory; but the one who seeks the glory of him who sent him is true, and in him there is no falsehood.

   c. Proven by the personal test: Are you keeping the law? Obeying God's commandments?

<sup>19</sup> "Has not Moses given you the law? Yet none of you keeps the law. Why do you seek to kill me?"

# Division VIII

*The Responses to the Revelation of Jesus, 7:1-53*

B. The Response of the Jews: Seeking Yet Questioning, 7:10-19

## 7:10-19
## Introduction

Nobody can intelligently deny that Jesus Christ lived and walked on the earth. Historical evidence of the life of Christ abounds, even from secular sources. But, as people did then, many deny that He was who He claimed to be: the Messiah, the Son of God, the Savior of mankind. In Jesus' day, as well as today, many think He was merely a good man. Others think He was a liar and deceiver. Some believe He is not important enough to defend, while others think He lacked the credentials to be who He claimed to be.

The second reaction or response to Jesus came from the Jewish crowds, including both religious leaders and the people who had traveled to Jerusalem for the Feast of Tabernacles. This passage gives the answer to false beliefs about Jesus. This is, *The Response of the Jews: Seeking Yet Questioning,* 7:10-19.

1. The setting: Jesus went secretly to the Feast, after His brothers had left (v.10).
2. The crowds were watching for Him and asking questions about Him: Opinions differed (vv.11-15).
3. The reply by Jesus: My teaching is God's teaching—it comes from Him who sent Me (vv.16-19).

## 7:10

¹⁰ But after his brothers had gone up to the feast, then he also went up, not publicly but in private.

### 1 The setting: Jesus went secretly to the Feast, after His brothers had left.

Jesus finally went up to Jerusalem to attend the Feast, but He did not go up with His brothers. They had left sometime before, probably in a large caravan. The caravans of that time were huge expeditions (see Lu.2:43-44); therefore, He went quietly, almost in secret, so as not to attract too much attention. He was going to step forward to teach publicly, but He needed to be inconspicuous until that moment came (v.14). If He had traveled to Jerusalem publicly, the people might have escorted Him into the city, proclaiming Him King and causing His arrest before His "hour" (Jn.7:6). The Triumphal Entry would have taken place too soon.

## 7:11-15

¹¹ The Jews were looking for him at the feast, and saying, "Where is he?"
¹² And there was much muttering about him among the people. While some said, "He is a good man," others said, "No, he is leading the people astray."
¹³ Yet for fear of the Jews no one spoke openly of him.
¹⁴ About the middle of the feast Jesus went up into the temple and began teaching.
¹⁵ The Jews therefore marveled, saying, "How is it that this man has learning, when he has never studied?"

### 2 The crowds were watching for Him and asking questions about Him: Opinions differed.

The Jews' response was that of seeking Jesus and of questioning and murmuring about Him. *Jews* in this instance probably refers to all Jews, both religious leaders and pilgrims. Everyone wanted to find Jesus for one reason or another. The Jewish authorities wanted to entrap and discredit Him before the people, for they wished to have Him arrested and sentenced to death. The common people wanted to find Him so they could hear His teaching and see His miracles for themselves.

The Jewish crowds are to be commended for having sought Christ, for He is to be sought. Every person should seek Christ until He is found. But the motives of the religious leaders were evil. They were not seeking Jesus to worship and learn of Him, but to harm Him. They wanted to discredit Him, lest they lose the loyalty of the people and their own security and position. In addition, the motives of the common people were corrupt. They were not seeking Jesus as Savior and Lord, the One to whom they owed their allegiance. They were seeking Him out of curiosity, to see Him perform spectacular miracles (see Deeper Study # 1—Jn.2:23).

The response of the Jewish crowds was that of murmuring and questioning. It was not a discontented murmuring, but that of whispering and buzzing about, excitedly so. People were quietly asking and discussing their opinions about Jesus in soft voices and off to the side, in the corners and away from strangers, lest they stirred the suspicion that they were followers of Jesus and endangered their own lives.

a. **Some said He is a good man (v.12a).**
Some thought Jesus was a good man: a man to be supported, listened to, and heeded. By *good* they meant at least the following: a man who was . . .
- loving and caring
- giving and unselfish
- true and honest
- just and moral
- believing and worshipful toward God

But note the inadequacy and weakness of this belief. It sees Jesus only as a man, a good man, yes; but still only as a man. It does not believe Jesus is the *Son of Man* (see note—Jn.1:51).

b. **Others, He is a deceiver (v.12b).**
Some thought Jesus was the exact opposite: a deceiver, a man who was deliberately deceiving and leading the people away from true religion. By *leading astray or deceiving* they meant that He was . . .
- misleading, deluding, beguiling, actually leading the people away from God
- boasting of Himself, His own ideas and position
- reveling in the admiration, adulation, and flattery of the people
- trying to be novel and creative, to be recognized as a man of new ideas
- trying to attract attention and secure a following

In reality, they said He was . . .
- not of God, but of Beelzebub (the devil; Mt.12:24; Mk.3:22; Lu.11:15)
- a drunkard and a glutton (Mt.11:19; Lu.7:34)
- an associate of sinners (Mt.9:11; Mk.2:16; Lu.5:30; 15:2)
- a criminal and a law-breaker (Mt.12:1-8, 10; 15:1-20; 16:1-12)

Now note: if all this were true, if Jesus were a deceiver, then He was the most evil and deceptive man the world has ever seen.

c. **Most, He is a man not important enough to defend (v.13).**
Most of the common people thought Jesus was a man not significant enough to defend. Even those who felt Jesus was a good man cowered in fear rather than daring to speak up for Jesus. They feared the religious authorities. They felt Jesus was not worth the bother, the cost, the risk of jeopardizing their own safety.

d. **Many, He is unaccredited—so capable, yet uneducated (vv.14-15).**
Some thought Jesus was a man unaccredited and without proper credentials. About the middle of the Feast, Jesus ended His seclusion and hiding. He went into the temple and began teaching. The people were astonished; they marveled at His knowledge of the Law. He demonstrated that He had a thorough knowledge and understanding of both the Bible of the Old Testament (the *Torah)* and the commentaries or Scribal Law expounding the Scriptures. He had never been a student in the Jewish schools or of a Rabbi, yet He knew the Scriptures well. Their question was asked in contempt: "How does this man know so much? Who is He claiming to be? What right does He have to teach? He has never learned or studied in our schools, under our teachers. He is a *mere carpenter*, uneducated, and unlearned. What right does He have to set Himself up as a great teacher, a person to be heard? He is neither accredited nor ordained by our schools and leaders."

**THOUGHT 1.** How often people are rejected, despite their call and gifts, simply because they are not accredited by the right schools or leaders or do not have the *proper* education.

## 3 The Reply by Jesus: My teaching is God's teaching—it comes from Him who sent Me (vv.16-19).

**7:16-19**

Jesus' reply was threefold. He answered all four charges, the charges that He was...
- only a good man
- a deceiver
- a man not significant enough to defend
- a man unaccredited

16 So Jesus answered them, "My teaching is not mine, but his who sent me.
17 If anyone's will is to do God's will, he will know whether the teaching is from God or whether I am speaking on my own authority.
18 The one who speaks on his own authority seeks his own glory; but the one who seeks the glory of him who sent him is true, and in him there is no falsehood.
19 Has not Moses given you the law? Yet none of you keeps the law. Why do you seek to kill me?"

Jesus replied by making a phenomenal claim: "My teaching is not mine, but God's." He did not claim to be the Source of His message. Instead, He claimed to be *sent* by God to be the Representative, the Ambassador of God. He claimed to have been in the most intimate relationship with God: in His presence, communion, and fellowship (see note—Jn.3:34). Consequently, *God* was the Source of His message.

> So Jesus said to them, "When you have lifted up the Son of Man, then you will know that I am he, and that I do nothing on my own authority, but speak just as the Father taught me." (Jn.8:28)

> "For I have given them the words that you gave me, and they have received them and have come to know in truth that I came from you; and they have believed that you sent me." (Jn.17:8)

> Everyone who goes on ahead and does not abide in the teaching of Christ, does not have God. Whoever abides in the teaching has both the Father and the Son. (2 Jn.9)

Jesus proceeded to offer three tests that establish the validity of His message, that prove that His message was God's message:

a. **Proven by the subjective test (the inward or moral test): A person knows the truth by doing it (v.17).**

First, there is the subjective test, the inward or moral test. How can a person know if Jesus' claim is true? He or she can know by doing God's will. If a person will do what God says, that person *will know* the truth. Jesus was saying...
- that God's teaching, God's Word, is not for storing up head knowledge, but for experiencing real life
- that the person who really knows God is not the person who has some thoughts about God, but the person who does and lives as God wills, the person who is holy even as God is holy
- that the only person who can know God is the person who thinks and lives as God lives. People who do not live as God lives do not *know* God; they only know *about* God

If any person truly desires to do God's will, Jesus said, God will give him or her a knowledge of the truth. Jesus challenged the people to obey God, to do what they already knew God wanted them to do, and to sincerely seek God for more light. In return, God would reveal to them that what Jesus said was the truth.

> "Whoever has my commandments and keeps them, he it is who loves me. And he who loves me will be loved by my Father, and I will love him and manifest myself to him." (Jn.14:21)

> Do not be conformed to this world, but be transformed by the renewal of your mind, that by testing you may discern what is the will of God, what is good and acceptable and perfect. (Ro.12:2)

> But as he who called you is holy, you also be holy in all your conduct, since it is written, "You shall be holy, for I am holy." (1 Pe.1:15-16)

b. **Proven by the objective test (the outward or visible test): Does a person speak for his own glory or for God's glory? (v.18).**

Second, there is the objective test, the outward or observation test. Jesus invited the people to examine His motives. Jesus did not exalt Himself. He did not undermine God and seek to establish His authority over God's. To the contrary, every word He said and every good deed He performed were for the purpose of glorifying God His Father.

A man who is *sent by another person* and ends up speaking for himself is not a true representative. He is seeking his own glory. Furthermore, a man who is *sent by another person* and speaks the message of that person *is* a true representative, for he is doing what he should do: representing the person who sent him. Jesus clearly passed this test. Any person can look at Christ and observe and see that He declared God's message.

Note three very significant facts. First, Jesus did not seek to glorify Himself, but God. Jesus sought to stir people to glorify God in their lives. Such an effort is the constant subject of Jesus' preaching and teaching. He claimed to be empty of personal ambition and glory.

> "Whatever you ask in my name, this I will do, that the Father may be glorified in the Son." (Jn.14:13)

> "I glorified you on earth, having accomplished the work that you gave me to do." (Jn.17:4)

Second, Jesus was not just claiming to tell the truth; He was claiming to be *the truth*.

> Jesus said to him, "I am the way, and the truth, and the life. No one comes to the Father except through me." (Jn.14:6)

> Then Pilate said to him, "So you are a king?" Jesus answered, "You say that I am a king. For this purpose I was born and for this purpose I have come into the world—to bear witness to the truth. Everyone who is of the truth listens to my voice." (Jn.18:37)

Third, Jesus claimed that there was no unrighteousness in Him.

> "Which one of you convicts me of sin? If I tell the truth, why do you not believe me?" (Jn.8:46)

> For our sake he made him to be sin who knew no sin, so that in him we might become the righteousness of God. (2 Co.5:21)

> For we do not have a high priest who is unable to sympathize with our weaknesses, but one who in every respect has been tempted as we are, yet without sin. (He.4:15)

> For it was indeed fitting that we should have such a high priest, holy, innocent, unstained, separated from sinners, and exalted above the heavens. (He.7:26)

> How much more will the blood of Christ, who through the eternal Spirit offered himself without blemish to God, purify our conscience from dead works to serve the living God. (He.9:14)

> But with the precious blood of Christ, like that of a lamb without blemish or spot. (1 Pe.1:19)

> He committed no sin, neither was deceit found in his mouth. (1 Pe.2:22)

c. **Proven by the personal test: Are you keeping the law? Obeying God's commandments (v.19).** Jesus' third response was directed to religious authorities, but common people could apply it as well. He charged them to examine themselves personally. They boasted of their deep knowledge of Moses' law, but they did not keep it. To prove His point, Jesus asked them a question that cut them to the very core of their being and challenged their authority in the people's eyes: Why do you seek to kill Me, when Moses' law so clearly forbids killing?

Note what Jesus basically says in this passage: "You are the recipients of the law. God has been very gracious to you in giving the law. But being a recipient is not enough—you must keep the law. However, you do not keep it. You go about opposing and standing against me, instead of surrendering to God's Son. You oppose me, even seek to kill me, God's Son."

**THOUGHT 1.** Every individual should apply the personal test to his or her own heart and life. People can use the law to tell if Christ is true. They can measure themselves by the law and clearly see that they do not keep it. They break the law; therefore, they stand in need of God's forgiveness. This was exactly what Christ was preaching and teaching. He cried out that God loved the world and had sent His Son to save the world.

> For, being ignorant of the righteousness of God, and seeking to establish their own, they did not submit to God's righteousness. (Ro.10:3)

> For all who rely on works of the law are under a curse; for it is written, "Cursed be everyone who does not abide by all things written in the Book of the Law, and do them." (Ga.3:10)

> But the law is not of faith, rather "The one who does them shall live by them." (Ga.3:12)

**THOUGHT 2.** The *Holman New Testament Commentary* offers an excellent observation on verse 17: "God does not show us his will just to satisfy our curiosity; when we are prepared to do God's will, then in God's good time we will know it. Furthermore, only those prepared to do God's will are prepared to discern the truth of Jesus' words and the truth of Scripture as well."[1]

> "For I have come down from heaven, not to do my own will but the will of him who sent me." (Jn.6:38)

> "I know him, for I come from him, and he sent me." (Jn.7:29)

> Jesus said to them, "If God were your Father, you would love me, for I came from God and I am here. I came not of my own accord, but he sent me." (Jn.8:42)

> "We must work the works of him who sent me while it is day; night is coming, when no one can work." (Jn.9:4)

> "Do you say of him whom the Father consecrated and sent into the world, 'You are blaspheming,' because I said, 'I am the Son of God'?" (Jn.10:36)

> "That they may all be one, just as you, Father, are in me, and I in you, that they also may be in us, so that the world may believe that you have sent me." (Jn.17:21)

---

1 Kenneth O. Gangel, *Holman New Testament Commentary—John* (Nashville: Holman Reference, 2000), via Wordsearch digital edition.

# C. The Response of the People: A Charge of Insanity, Yet Still Questioning, 7:20–31

20 The crowd answered, "You have a demon! Who is seeking to kill you?"

21 Jesus answered them, "I did one work, and you all marvel at it.
22 "Moses gave you circumcision (not that it is from Moses, but from the fathers), and you circumcise a man on the Sabbath.
23 "If on the Sabbath a man receives circumcision, so that the law of Moses may not be broken, are you angry with me because on the Sabbath I made a man's whole body well?
24 "Do not judge by appearances, but judge with right judgment."

25 Some of the people of Jerusalem therefore said, "Is not this the man whom they seek to kill?
26 "And here he is, speaking openly, and they say nothing to him! Can it be that the authorities really know that this is the Christ?
27 "But we know where this man comes from, and when the Christ appears, no one will know where he comes from."

28 So Jesus proclaimed, as he taught in the temple, "You know me, and you know where I come from. But I have not come of my own accord. He who sent me is true, and him you do not know.
29 "I know him, for I come from him, and he sent me."

30 So they were seeking to arrest him, but no one laid a hand on him, because his hour had not yet come.

31 Yet many of the people believed in him. They said, "When the Christ appears, will he do more signs than this man has done?"

1. **The pilgrims' response**
   a. Their response: Jesus was possessed by a demon, that is, insane
   b. Jesus' reply: He had done only good by healing the helpless man, 5:5-9
      1) Consider how circumcision is doing good: It meets a religious & ceremonial need for people

      2) Consider how healing is doing good even if it takes place on the Sabbath: It meets a person's desperate need

      3) A principle: Do not judge mere appearances, but think & consider

2. **The local residents' response**

   a. Their questioning & reasoning: Could He be the Messiah?

   b. Their conclusion: Unbelief—they knew His earthly origin, so He could not possibly be the Messiah

3. **Jesus' reply: A pivotal claim**
   a. He is a man: This fact they know, that He was born of Mary & lived in Nazareth
   b. He also came from God
   c. He knows God: He is from God—God sent Him

4. **The local people's reaction**
   a. Some did not believe & rejected Jesus

   b. Some believed Jesus[DS2]

# Division VIII

*The Responses to the Revelation of Jesus, 7:1-53*

C. The Response of the People: A Charge of Insanity, Yet Still Questioning, 7:20-31

## 7:20-31
## Introduction

This passage records a third response to Jesus. This response or reaction came from all the people—the pilgrims and the local residents of Jerusalem. Provoked by Jesus' accusation against the Jewish authorities, the agitated people responded emotionally. Their charges against Jesus ranged all the way from being demon-possessed to being a mere man. Jesus' answer to all charges against Him was penetrating and demanded a decision from every person present. This is, *The Response of the People: A Charge of Insanity, Yet Still Questioning, 7:20-31*.

1. The pilgrims' response (vv.20-24).
2. The local residents' response (vv.25-27).
3. Jesus' reply: A pivotal claim (vv.28-29).
4. The local people's reaction (vv.30-31).

## 7:20-24

<sup>20</sup> The crowd answered, "You have a demon! Who is seeking to kill you?"
<sup>21</sup> Jesus answered them, "I did one work, and you all marvel at it.
<sup>22</sup> Moses gave you circumcision (not that it is from Moses, but from the fathers), and you circumcise a man on the Sabbath.
<sup>23</sup> If on the Sabbath a man receives circumcision, so that the law of Moses may not be broken, are you angry with me because on the Sabbath I made a man's whole body well?
<sup>24</sup> Do not judge by appearances, but judge with right judgment."

## 1 The pilgrim's response.

Jesus had just accused the Jewish religious leaders of a deplorable violation of Moses' law: seeking to kill Him (v.19). The pilgrims reacted with shock and anger at Jesus' accusation of their leaders.

**a. Their response: Jesus was possessed by a demon, that is, insane (v.20).**

The people who had traveled to Jerusalem for the Feast cried out that Jesus was demon-possessed; he was insane. This charge was made primarily by the pilgrims, not by the local residents of Jerusalem. The local residents' response is reported in the next passage (vv.25-31). The pilgrims were the people who did not know Jesus very well. They had come from all over the world; therefore, they did not know as much about Jesus, which made it easier to charge Him with being demon-possessed and mad or insane. It appeared to them that He was opposing...

- the religious establishment
- the religious leaders
- the religion that had proven itself for generations
- the religion that contributed so much to society and the nation
- the religion that was founded by the forefathers, the most godly leaders of history

In their minds, only an evil man or a man filled with an evil spirit would have opposed such a religion; therefore, Jesus must have been crazy. His mind must have been deranged, running wild with the imagination that people were out to get Him. He must have been controlled by an evil spirit. The pilgrims thought their religious leaders could do little if any evil. They thought their religious leaders would never...

- harm anyone
- be so unjust and immoral
- be so undisciplined and out of control
- react against anyone

- be so corruptible
- do such an unholy thing

**THOUGHT 1.** Some people think religious leaders can do no wrong. However, religion and religious leaders can be wrong just as any establishment or anyone else can be wrong. Everyone can fail and fall, come short and sin, be misled and become corruptible. Christ came . . .
- to point out this misconception
- to correct this misconception
- to forgive this misconception
- to pass judgment on those who would not repent or receive God's forgiveness and be corrected

**THOUGHT 2.** A person's choice, their decision, must be made for Jesus Christ and not for religion and religious leaders. Christ is the Truth, not religion and its leaders. Religion and religious leaders are to follow Christ just as all other people are to follow Christ. Christ is the Lord and Master, not religion and its leaders.

b. **Jesus' reply: He had done only good by healing the helpless man (vv.21–24; see Jn.5:5–9).**
Jesus answered the pilgrims by appealing to the great work He had just done. He had healed the crippled man by the pool of Bethsaida. The man had been bedridden for thirty-eight years, and the people had marveled at the power of Jesus (Jn.5:1f). But there was a problem. They considered Jesus' healing of the man on the Sabbath to be work, and working on the Sabbath was strictly forbidden. It was a serious offense in the minds of the Jewish leaders, for in their eyes it taught the people to break the law. The civil and religious leaders could not allow this offense to go unjudged, for it was their religion that had held the nation together (see DEEPER STUDY # 2—Jn.5:15–16 for more discussion).

The point is this. Jesus said that He was not evil; He was not demon-possessed and crazy. Doing good proves whether a person is full of evil or full of good. Jesus' work, healing the crippled man, was a good work not an evil work. His healing did as much good as the religious leaders who circumcised on the Sabbath day. He pointed out three logical realities that the people could not reasonably deny.

First, Jesus charged them to consider how circumcision is doing good because it meets a religious and ceremonial need for people (v.22). The religious leaders condemned Jesus for healing the crippled man on the Sabbath, and it was for this work and other so called law-breaking deeds that they were opposing Him, some even plotting to kill Him. But they circumcised people on the Sabbath, thereby determining that some good deeds *could* be performed on the Sabbath.

Second, Jesus challenged them to consider how healing is doing good even if it takes place on the Sabbath, because it meets a person's desperate need (v.23). Jesus wanted all the people, even the religious leaders, to see the truth. He was not a law-breaker, not an evil man. He was not out to destroy people and nations. He was the Son of God who had come to save people and nations and to correct and set religion straight.

Third, Jesus appealed to the people to judge rightly, that is, by facts, not by appearance. He challenged them to think reasonably and consider what is truly right (v.24). When they circumcised a male on the Sabbath, they were not doing evil, but good. They were meeting a religious and ceremonial need. Therefore, they were correct in circumcising on the Sabbath, for God commanded circumcision on the eighth day of a baby boy's life, and sometimes the eighth day child's birth was bound to fall on the Sabbath (Le.12:3). By the same token, [healing a] man on the Sabbath, He was not doing evil, but good, perhaps even a greater [good by meeting] a personal and bodily need of a man, a need much more desperate than [a cerem]onial need.

Jesus told the people to judge not according to appearance, but to look at what He did; and to look realistically, honestly, and objectively. If they did, they would see that Jesus was not full of evil but full of good and righteousness. They would see that Jesus was the Son of God.

"Woe to you, scribes and Pharisees, hypocrites! For you are like whitewashed tombs, which outwardly appear beautiful, but within are full of dead people's bones and all uncleanness." (Mt.23:27)

"But the testimony that I have is greater than that of John. For the works that the Father has given me to accomplish, the very works that I am doing, bear witness about me that the Father has sent me." (Jn.5:36)

So the Jews gathered around him and said to him, "How long will you keep us in suspense? If you are the Christ, tell us plainly." Jesus answered them, "I told you, and you do not believe. The works that I do in my Father's name bear witness about me." (Jn.10:24–25)

"If I am not doing the works of my Father, then do not believe me; but if I do them, even though you do not believe me, believe the works, that you may know and understand that the Father is in me and I am in the Father." (Jn.10:37–38)

But the LORD said to Samuel, "Do not look on his appearance or on the height of his stature, because I have rejected him. For the LORD sees not as man sees: man looks on the outward appearance, but the LORD looks on the heart." (1 S.16:7)

"Justice, and only justice, you shall follow, that you may live and inherit the land that the LORD your God is giving you." (De.16:20)

## 7:25-27

²⁵ Some of the people of Jerusalem therefore said, "Is not this the man whom they seek to kill? ²⁶ And here he is, speaking openly, and they say nothing to him! Can it be that the authorities really know that this is the Christ? ²⁷ But we know where this man comes from, and when the Christ appears, no one will know where he comes from."

## 2 The local residents' response.

The local people had a different response than that of the pilgrims. Unlike the pilgrims, many of them were there when Jesus healed the paralyzed man, and they no doubt had shared their eyewitness accounts with their families, friends, and neighbors. Consequently, they considered the possibility that Jesus actually *was* the promised Messiah.

a. Their questioning and reasoning: Could He be the Messiah (v.26)?

The citizens of Jerusalem questioned among themselves: is this the One who is so opposed and feared? Is He the One whom they seek to kill? They also reasoned: He speaks so openly and boldly, and He is not stopped. Is He indeed the Messiah?

b. Their conclusion: Unbelief—they knew His earthly origin, so He could not possibly be the Messiah (v.27).

Nevertheless, the local residents came to a tragic conclusion: Jesus is not the Messiah. Why? Because they knew His origin. They knew all about His family and rearing; therefore, they concluded that He was a mere man, a carpenter from Nazareth. In their minds there was absolutely nothing unusual about His origin; therefore, He could not possibly be of God. He could not be the promised Messiah.

**THOUGHT 1.** Some people always have and always will question, reason, and draw the wrong conclusion about Jesus.
- Some will question: Is this He, the One promised by God, the One so needed by the world?
- Some will reason: this is the very Christ, the Messiah. He is bound to be, for He continues on. He is still proclaimed, forcibly so, despite being so threatened and persecuted with the intention of being wiped out.
- Some will conclude: this could not be the Son of God. It is impossible for a man to be born of God, to literally come from God. A man is a man, just flesh and blood like all other men. His origin has to be that of a man and a woman. Note: unbelief prevails when the mind is set only upon the earth and its physical law. If God is God, He must be allowed to act supernaturally, above natural law. This was the problem with the people in Jesus' day, and it is the problem with so many of every generation.

## 3 Jesus' reply: A pivotal claim.

Jesus' reply to those who questioned and refused to believe in Him is a critical point. His answer centered around His origin. Note that He was gripped with great emotion in answering this point. He *proclaimed* or *cried out* (Gk. ekrazen)—shouted passionately—three truths about Himself that He desperately longed for the people to see.

### 7:28-29

<sup>28</sup> So Jesus proclaimed, as he taught in the temple, "You know me, and you know where I come from. But I have not come of my own accord. He who sent me is true, and him you do not know.
<sup>29</sup> I know him, for I come from him, and he sent me."

### a. He is a man: This fact they know, that He was born of Mary and lived in Nazareth (v.28a).

Jesus exclaimed that He *is* a man, and people do know where He came from. He was born of Mary and did come from Nazareth, but that is not all. There is much, much more.

### b. He also came from God (v.28b).

Jesus explained that He had come *from God.* God sent Him. Note exactly what Jesus claimed.

First, He had not come of Himself or of His own accord. His mission and message were not His own. He did not dream it up, plan it or plot it. He was not out for self-glory or to build a movement and a following. What He did was not of Himself.

Second, "He who sent me is true." A real Person sent Jesus, and note: the Person is not only real, He is true. He is a Person who is the very embodiment of truth (see Deeper Study # 1—Jn.1:9; Deeper Study # 2—14:6). What Jesus was claiming and doing was exactly what He had been sent and commissioned to claim and to do.

Third, they did not know that Person who is truth. Jesus was saying, of course, that they did not truly know God. If they knew God, really knew Him, they would recognize and know that Jesus' mission and works were of God. They would know that only God's perfect love and power could speak and do as Jesus did.

> "But all these things they will do to you on account of my name, because they do not know him who sent me." (Jn.15:21)

> "And they will do these things because they have not known the Father, nor me." (Jn.16:3)

> "For my people are foolish; they know me not; they are stupid children; they have no understanding. They are 'wise'—in doing evil! But how to do good they know not." (Je.4:22)

### c. He knows God: He is from God—God sent Him (v.29).

Jesus declared plainly that *He,* however, *did* know God. He knew God because *He was from God* (see Deeper Study # 1—Jn.3:31 for verses of Scripture). He actually came from God's presence, from being face-to-face with Him. In addition, He knew God because *He was sent by God* (see Deeper Study # 3—Jn.3:34). While face-to-face with God, God commissioned Him and sent Him forth to proclaim and live the truth before all people (see Deeper Study # 2—Jn.14:6).

> "For I have come down from heaven, not to do my own will but the will of him who sent me." (Jn.6:38)

> "I know him, for I come from him, and he sent me." (Jn.7:29)

> Jesus said to them, "If God were your Father, you would love me, for I came from God and I am here. I came not of my own accord, but he sent me." (Jn.8:42)

> "Do you say of him whom the Father consecrated and sent into the world, 'You are blaspheming,' because I said, 'I am the Son of God'?" (Jn.10:36)

> "That they may all be one, just as you, Father, are in me, and I in you, that they also may be in us, so that the world may believe that you have sent me." (Jn.17:21)

## 4 The local people's reaction.

7:30-31

After everything that had taken place, the reaction of the local residents was twofold. Some believed, and some refused to believe.

³⁰ So they were seeking to arrest him, but no one laid a hand on him, because his hour had not yet come.

³¹ Yet many of the people believed in him. They said, "When the Christ appears, will he do more signs than this man has done?"

### a. Some did not believe and rejected Jesus (v.30).

Some still did not believe, and some even became His sworn enemies. They tried to seize Jesus, but they failed, for God stopped them. He overrode their opposition and plots. Jesus' "hour" had not yet come, so God would not allow them to stop Him (see note, *My Hour*—Jn.2:3-5).

### b. Some believed Jesus (v.31).

However, many of the people believed in Jesus (see DEEPER STUDY # 2—Jn.2:24). Not only did they see the logic in Jesus' arguments, but they had seen His miracles. The believers charged their unbelieving neighbors to consider Jesus' miracles as proof of His claims. They reasoned that, if Jesus were not the Messiah, would the one who was actually the Messiah perform more miracles than Jesus did? Their point was, Jesus' miracles were His credentials, the proof of His Messiahship. If they would not believe in *Jesus* as the Messiah, they would never believe in the Messiah at all.

**THOUGHT 1.** The different reactions of the citizens of Jerusalem to Jesus on that day reflect the reactions of people today. Some choose to believe in Jesus, while many choose to reject Him as God's only Son and the only Savior of the world. Because of their unbelief, they choose to remain condemned before God, doomed to eternal separation from God in hell.

> "Whoever believes in him is not condemned, but whoever does not believe is condemned already, because he has not believed in the name of the only Son of God." (Jn.3:18)

> Whoever believes in the Son has eternal life; whoever does not obey the Son shall not see life, but the wrath of God remains on him. (Jn.3:36)

### D. The Response of the Rulers and Authorities: A Charge of Being a Rabble-Rouser, 7:32-36

1. **The response of the rulers & authorities: They considered Jesus a threat, a rabble-rouser, & sought to arrest Him**

32 The Pharisees heard the crowd muttering these things about him, and the chief priests and Pharisees sent officers to arrest him.

2. **The reply by Jesus**
   a. He foretold His destiny: His death, resurrection, & ascension

33 Jesus then said, "I will be with you a little longer, and then I am going to him who sent me.

   b. He foretold some people's destiny: They will seek to find Him—but they cannot come where He is

34 "You will seek me and you will not find me. Where I am you cannot come."

3. **The reaction of the rulers & authorities: They were perplexed & questioned Jesus' reply**

35 The Jews said to one another, "Where does this man intend to go that we will not find him? Does he intend to go to the Dispersion among the Greeks and teach the Greeks?

36 "What does he mean by saying, 'You will seek me and you will not find me,' and, 'Where I am you cannot come'?"

## Division VIII

*The Responses to the Revelation of Jesus, 7:1-53*

D. The Response of the Rulers and Authorities: A Charge of Being a Rabble-Rouser, 7:32-36

### 7:32-36
### Introduction

The fourth reaction or response to Jesus is that of the authorities, both religious and civil. They paint a clear picture of people in every generation who reject and oppose Jesus. What Jesus says is both striking and tragic for all unbelievers. This is, *The Response of the Rulers and Authorities: A Charge of Being a Rabble-Rouser*, 7:32-36.
1. The response of the rulers and authorities (v.32).
2. The reply by Jesus (vv.33-34).
3. The reaction of the rulers and authorities: They were perplexed and questioned Jesus' reply (vv.35-36).

### 1 The response of the rulers and authorities: They considered Jesus a threat, a rabble-rouse, and sought to arrest Him.

7:32

32 The Pharisees heard the crowd muttering these things about him, and the chief priests and Pharisees sent officers to arrest him.

The Pharisees took the lead in opposing Jesus (See DEEPER STUDY # 3—Ac.23:8; DEEPER STUDY # 2—Jn.5:16. This last note discusses why the religious leaders opposed Jesus so vehemently.) They apparently approached the chief priests and persuaded them that Jesus was a threat and a rabble rouser. Therefore, they sought to arrest Him.

The chief priests were primarily leaders among the Sadducees who held most of the high offices of Jewish government under Roman rule (see Deeper Study # 2—Ac.23:8). When Rome became dissatisfied with a chief priest, he was removed, and another one was placed in authority. The removal from office was a common occurrence, so there were quite a few chief priests surviving. In the eyes of the people, they were still honored despite being removed. The Jewish people blamed Rome for their removal, not the chief priests.

In the four Gospels, when the Pharisees, chief priests, and Scribes are mentioned as standing together against Jesus, it means that the Sanhedrin, the ruling body of the Jewish nation, has taken action (see Deeper Study # 1—Mt.26:59). In the present situation, the Sanhedrin had apparently met and dispatched the palace or temple police to arrest Jesus. From what follows it seems that they were told to watch for an appropriate moment lest they cause a riot among His supporters.

What disturbed the Jewish authorities so much was the murmuring of the people, in particular the fact that so many were believing in Jesus (v.31). He was a threat to their security and position, esteem and authority, profession and livelihood (see Deeper Study # 2—Jn.5:15-16 for more discussion). They wanted nothing to do with Him and wanted things to be left alone. They wanted to get rid of Him as soon as possible.

> **THOUGHT 1.** People (leaders) often murmur against and oppose Jesus because Jesus is a threat to their way of life. Because they are unwilling to change their lives, Jesus is a threat to them and their security. Wanting absolutely nothing to do with Jesus, they try to dispose of Him and His influence the best way they can.
>
> > "For what will it profit a man if he gains the whole world and forfeits his soul? Or what shall a man give in return for his soul?" (Mt.16:26)
> >
> > But thanks be to God, that you who were once slaves of sin have become obedient from the heart to the standard of teaching to which you were committed, and, having been set free from sin, have become slaves of righteousness. (Ro.6:17-18)
> >
> > Training us to renounce ungodliness and worldly passions, and to live self-controlled, upright, and godly lives in the present age. (Tit.2:12)
> >
> > Do not love the world or the things in the world. If anyone loves the world, the love of the Father is not in him. For all that is in the world—the desires of the flesh and the desires of the eyes and pride of life—is not from the Father but is from the world. (1 Jn.2:15-16)
> >
> > They close their hearts to pity; with their mouths they speak arrogantly. (Ps.17:10)
> >
> > "Behold, this was the guilt of your sister Sodom: she and her daughters had pride, excess of food, and prosperous ease, but did not aid the poor and needy." (Eze.16:49)

## 7:33-34

³³ Jesus then said, "I will be with you a little longer, and then I am going to him who sent me. ³⁴ "You will seek me and you will not find me. Where I am you cannot come."

## 2 The reply of Jesus.

When the officers arrived to arrest Jesus, He replied in a way that surely seemed strange to all who heard Him. His prophetic statement was puzzling and tragic, both to the unbelievers of His day and to the unbelievers of today.

**a. He foretold His destiny: His death, resurrection, and ascension. (v.33).**

Jesus foretold His destiny:

➢ He foretold His death saying, that He would not be with them much longer.

> "Little children, yet a little while I am with you. You will seek me, and just as I said to the Jews, so now I also say to you, 'Where I am going you cannot come.'" (Jn.13:33)
>
> "You heard me say to you, 'I am going away, and I will come to you.' If you loved me, you would have rejoiced, because I am going to the Father, for the Father is greater than I." (Jn.14:28)
>
> "But now I am going to him who sent me, and none of you asks me, 'Where are you going?'" (Jn.16:5)

"And I am no longer in the world, but they are in the world, and I am coming to you. Holy Father, keep them in your name, which you have given me, that they may be one, even as we are one." (Jn.17:11)

> He foretold His resurrection and ascension: He would be returning to God in heaven (see Jn.8:14; 13:3; 14:2-3; 16:5, 10, 17).

Jesus answered, "Even if I do bear witness about myself, my testimony is true, for I know where I came from and where I am going, but you do not know where I come from or where I am going." (Jn.8:14)

Jesus, knowing that the Father had given all things into his hands, and that he had come from God and was going back to God. (Jn.13:3)

"In my Father's house are many rooms. If it were not so, would I have told you that I go to prepare a place for you? And if I go and prepare a place for you, I will come again and will take you to myself, that where I am you may be also." (Jn.14:2-3)

"Concerning righteousness, because I go to the Father, and you will see me no longer." (Jn.16:10)

So some of his disciples said to one another, "What is this that he says to us, 'A little while, and you will not see me, and again a little while, and you will see me'; and, 'because I am going to the Father'?" (Jn.16:17)

What did the death and resurrection have to do with those who opposed Jesus? Why did Jesus predict His destiny in answering those who wanted nothing to do with Him? First, He was saying that those who opposed Him would shortly get rid of Him. They could reject and have nothing to do with Him. They did not have to worry about getting rid of Him; they would be allowed to do that. He would go away.

He was also saying, however, that He would not cease to be; He would not be annihilated and cease to exist. His life would not be extinguished. He would be killed because men would try to stop Him from living as a man on earth. But He would arise and return to His Father who sent Him. He would experience glory and give great hope to all those who have believed and do believe in Him (see note—Mk.16:19-20).

b. **Jesus foretold some people's destiny. They will seek to find Him—but they cannot come where He is (v.34).**

Jesus foretold the tragic destiny of all who opposed Him and wanted nothing to do with Him. He said that the day is coming when they will seek Him, but they will not find Him. They will not be allowed to come to where He is—heaven, in God's presence.

What Jesus meant is *just what He said*. All who reject Christ will face the day when they will seek Christ.

In this life, God's Spirit does not always strive with people (Ge.6:3; Pr.29:1). When a person is in church or anywhere else and feels pulled to make a decision for Christ and puts the decision off for even an hour or two (a half-day or a day at most), the pull fades and eventually dies completely. God's Spirit does not continue to strive with that individual. At one time or another, most of us have experienced such movements and, by failing to respond, killed the Spirit's striving within us.

Then the LORD said, "My Spirit shall not abide in man forever, for he is flesh: his days shall be 120 years." (Ge.6:3)

Cast me not away from your presence, and take not your Holy Spirit from me. (Ps.51:11)

He who is often reproved, yet stiffens his neck, will suddenly be broken beyond healing. (Pr.29:1)

But in the next life, at the day of judgment, the unbeliever will seek Christ.

"Not everyone who says to me, 'Lord, Lord,' will enter the kingdom of heaven, but the one who does the will of my Father who is in heaven. On that day many will say to me, 'Lord, Lord, did we not prophesy in your name, and cast out demons in your name, and do many mighty works in your name?'" (Mt.7:21-22)

"And while they were going to buy, the bridegroom came, and those who were ready went in with him to the marriage feast, and the door was shut. Afterward the other virgins came also, saying, 'Lord, lord, open to us.'" (Mt.25:10-11)

However, the great tragedy is that the unbeliever will not find Christ. It will be too late (see Mt.25:31-46). Unbelievers have never known Christ or what it is to walk in the Lord's kingdom on earth; therefore, they will neither know Christ nor His kingdom in that day. As Christ and heaven are unknown to the unbeliever today, so will Christ and heaven be unknown to the unbeliever in that day. Unbelievers will not be allowed to come where He is, that is, live in God's presence eternally.

Note: *I* and *you* are a climactic contrast. Jesus said, "Where *I* am *you* cannot come" (v.36). "Where I am" means:

➤ The rest and life of Christ, which is love, joy, and peace (see note, *Rest*—Jn.4:16-18)
➤ The state of eternal life (see Deeper Study # 2—1:4; Deeper Study # 1—10:10; Deeper Study # 1—17:2-3. See Deeper Study # 3—Mt.19:23-24.)

> "For I tell you, unless your righteousness exceeds that of the scribes and Pharisees, you will never enter the kingdom of heaven." (Mt.5:20)

> "When once the master of the house has risen and shut the door, and you begin to stand outside and to knock at the door, saying, 'Lord, open to us,' then he will answer you, 'I do not know where you come from.' Then you will begin to say, 'We ate and drank in your presence, and you taught in our streets.' But he will say, 'I tell you, I do not know where you come from. Depart from me, all you workers of evil!' In that place there will be weeping and gnashing of teeth, when you see Abraham and Isaac and Jacob and all the prophets in the kingdom of God but you yourselves cast out." (Lu.13:25-28)

> Or do you not know that the unrighteous will not inherit the kingdom of God? Do not be deceived: neither the sexually immoral, nor idolaters, nor adulterers, nor men who practice homosexuality. (1 Co.6:9)

> I tell you this, brothers: flesh and blood cannot inherit the kingdom of God, nor does the perishable inherit the imperishable. (1 Co.15:50)

> But nothing unclean will ever enter it, nor anyone who does what is detestable or false, but only those who are written in the Lamb's book of life. (Re.21:27)

## 7:35-36

<sup>35</sup> The Jews said to one another, "Where does this man intend to go that we will not find him? Does he intend to go to the Dispersion among the Greeks and teach the Greeks?
<sup>36</sup> What does he mean by saying, 'You will seek me and you will not find me,' and, 'Where I am you cannot come'?"

### 3 The reaction of the rulers and authorities: They were perplexed and questioned Jesus' reply.

The Jewish authorities did not understand what Jesus was saying. Very simply, they were perplexed, questioning what Jesus meant. They wondered if He was intending to join the Dispersion. The *Dispersion* (Gk. diasporan) refers to the Jews who were scattered all over the world. It seems that the rulers thought Jesus was going to leave Israel and go to some foreign nation, preaching to the Jews there.

Tragically, those who opposed Jesus were blind to spiritual truth, blind to His purpose for coming. They were puzzled by His death and resurrection and ascension. It was difficult for them to grasp its meaning and to believe in Him. In fact, it was offensive to them. This was exactly what Jesus had said (see note—Jn.6:62).

**Thought 1.** All who oppose and reject Jesus today are just like the Jewish leaders of Jesus' day; they are blind to the truth. They face the horrific future of all unbelievers: eternity separated from God in hell. They will never be where Jesus and all true believers will be, in the Lord's presence in heaven.

> "But if your eye is bad, your whole body will be full of darkness. If then the light in you is darkness, how great is the darkness!" (Mt.6:23)

> In their case the god of this world has blinded the minds of the unbelievers, to keep them from seeing the light of the gospel of the glory of Christ, who is the image of God. (2 Co.4:4)

> They are darkened in their understanding, alienated from the life of God because of the ignorance that is in them, due to their hardness of heart. (Ep.4:18)

> But whoever hates his brother is in the darkness and walks in the darkness, and does not know where he is going, because the darkness has blinded his eyes. (1 Jn.2:11)

## E. The Great Claim of Jesus and Divided Opinions About Him, 7:37–53

37 On the last day of the feast, the great day, Jesus stood up and cried out, "If anyone thirsts, let him come to me and drink.

38 "Whoever believes in me, as the Scripture has said, 'Out of his heart will flow rivers of living water.'"

39 Now this he said about the Spirit, whom those who believed in him were to receive, for as yet the Spirit had not been given, because Jesus was not yet glorified.

40 When they heard these words, some of the people said, "This really is the Prophet."

41 Others said, "This is the Christ." But some said, "Is the Christ to come from Galilee?

42 "Has not the Scripture said that the Christ comes from the offspring of David, and comes from Bethlehem, the village where David was?"

43 So there was a division among the people over him.

44 Some of them wanted to arrest him, but no one laid hands on him.

45 The officers then came to the chief priests and Pharisees, who said to them, "Why did you not bring him?"

46 The officers answered, "No one ever spoke like this man!"

47 The Pharisees answered them, "Have you also been deceived?

48 "Have any of the authorities or the Pharisees believed in him?

49 "But this crowd that does not know the law is accursed."

50 Nicodemus, who had gone to him before, and who was one of them, said to them,

51 "Does our law judge a man without first giving him a hearing and learning what he does?"

52 They replied, "Are you from Galilee too? Search and see that no prophet arises from Galilee."

53 [[They went each to his own house,

1. The setting: The day of the Feast of Tabernacles, 7:2
2. The claims of Jesus
    a. I am the water of life, the very source of life[DS1]
    b. I am living water, the source of abundant, overflowing life
    c. I am the source of the Holy Spirit[DS2]

3. The people's divided response
    a. Many: Jesus is the prophet[DS3]
    b. Others: Jesus is the Christ
    c. Some questioned Jesus' birthplace & misinterpreted Scripture[DS4]

    d. Some would seize & do away with Jesus
4. The rulers' response to Jesus
    a. They wished to remove Jesus
        1) The officers were sent to arrest Him, v.32
        2) The officers' response: He is a great teacher
    b. They claimed Jesus was a deceiver
        1) They charged the people with being mistaken
        2) They also charged the people with being cursed by God
    c. They rejected Jesus
        1) Nicodemus spoke up for Him[DS5]

        2) They rejected Nicodemus' questions, misinterpreting Scripture

    d. They returned to their own homes & lived as always

# Division VIII

## The Responses to the Revelation of Jesus, 7:1-53

### E. The Great Claim of Jesus and Divided Opinions About Him, 7:37-53

## 7:37-53
## Introduction

The people of Jesus' day were divided in their opinions about Him, and people still are today. The Jews who believed in Jesus when He walked the earth went against their leaders in order to do so. Today, the leaders of some nations and some religions are sharply opposed to Jesus, just as the Jewish leaders were then. Every week in our world, some faithful believers pay a great price for staying true to the Savior. This passage reminds us that genuine believers will stand for Christ regardless of what others think, and it challenges every individual to search his/her own response to Jesus. This is, *The Great Claim of Jesus and Divided Opinions About Him, 7:37-53.*

1. The setting: The day of the Feast of Tabernacles, 7:2 (v.37).
2. The claims of Jesus (vv.37-39).
3. The people's divided response (vv.40-44).
4. The rulers' response to Jesus (vv.45-53).

### 7:37

**37** On the last day of the feast, the great day, Jesus stood up and cried out, "If anyone thirsts, let him come to me and drink."

### 1 The setting: The day of the Feast of Tabernacles (see 7:2).

The Feast of Tabernacles was the most popular feast among the Jews. For that reason, it was known simply as *The Feast* (1 K.8:20). It was also called *The Feast of Ingathering* (Ex.23:16) and *The Feast of the Lord* (Le.23:39). The people celebrated the Feast for seven days. Each Jewish family built a small stucco or tent-like structure in their yard or on some other property they owned or secured for the occasion. Then they moved out of their home into the structure for the seven-day period.

The Feast celebrated two significant events. Historically, it celebrated the day when Israel wandered about in the wilderness as strangers and pilgrims without a homeland. The purpose for moving into the stucco or tent-like structure was to keep before their minds the wilderness wanderings of their forefathers (Le.23:40-43). Secondly, the Feast was to be a period of thanksgiving for the completion of the harvest season and for the goodness of God in all of life (Ex.23:16; De.16:13, 16). The people were to give thanks for all that God had given them: all the fruit of the land that enriched life and made life possible.

The ceremony of the festival was most impressive and gave a dramatic picture of Christ's claims (Jn.7:37-39). On each of the seven days, the people came to the temple and brought some fruit as an offering along with a few palm and willow branches. The branches were used to form a roof over the altar. Then the priest took a golden pitcher and led the people in a processional down to the pool of Siloam where he filled the pitcher with water. During this march the people played the flute and sang the Hillel, which was Psalms 113-118.

On the return march a significant drama took place.
- As the pitcher of water passed through the Water Gate, the people repeated in unison: "With joy you will draw water from the wells of salvation" (Is.12:3).
- When the pitcher reached the altar, the water was poured out over the altar as an offering to God. While this was being done, the people waved palm branches and recited the words "Save us, we pray, O LORD! O LORD, we pray, give us success" (Ps.118:25).

The processional was a dramatic way to thank God for rain, as well as to offer prayer to God for more rain, and for a fruitful season in the coming year. It was a vivid way for the people to acknowledge their need and dependence on God for the rains, the water that gave them the fruit of the ground and the bounty of life. The last day of the Feast was moving in particular, for the people repeated the processional seven times.

Note a significant point: Scripture says the Feast of Tabernacles will be celebrated and fulfilled in the end time when our Lord returns. The Feast will apparently symbolize our joy, liberty, and victory through the wilderness experience of life and the glorious provision of God: the glorious provision of living eternally and worshiping and serving God throughout the universe (Zec.14:16).

## 2 The claims of Jesus.

The last day of the Feast was the most important day. That was the day when the people marched in the processional seven times. On that day, Jesus made a phenomenal claim. He stood up and loudly invited all who are thirsty to come to Him and drink (v.37). Some imagine Jesus shouting His claim just as the people finished saying, "Give us success" (Ps.118:25).

Imagine the scene: Jesus did two unusual things. He *stood* (a teacher always sat in that day), and He *cried out* (Gk. ekrazen)—shouted loudly. Both actions would shock the people to attention. Picture thousands of voices simultaneously praying to God for the living rains in the coming season, reciting, "Give us success," and then, piercing the air comes the thundering cry:

> ³⁷ On the last day of the feast, the great day, Jesus stood up and cried out, "If anyone thirsts, let him come to me and drink.
> ³⁸ Whoever believes in me, as the Scripture has said, 'Out of his heart will flow rivers of living water.'"
> ³⁹ Now this he said about the Spirit, whom those who believed in him were to receive, for as yet the Spirit had not been given, because Jesus was not yet glorified.

> **On the last day of the feast, the great day, Jesus stood up and cried out, "If anyone thirsts, let him come to me and drink. Whoever believes in me, as the Scripture has said, 'Out of his heart will flow rivers of living water.'" (Jn.7:37-38)**

Jesus made three phenomenal claims:

### a. I am the water of life, the very source of life (v.37).

Jesus Christ is the source of life: He is the One who can quench the real thirst of every person's being, who can meet our desperate need for success or prosperity, the real fruit and bounty of life.

People genuinely thirst. We thirst for physical water and for spiritual life (see note—Jn.4:13-14 for a discussion of this point).

Jesus Christ claims to be the source, that is, the Water that can quench our thirst and give the fruit and bounty we so desperately need in our lives. He claims that He can do spiritually what earthly water does physically (see DEEPER STUDY # 1).

### b. I am the living water, the source of abundant, overflowing life (v.38).

Jesus Christ is the source of abundant life. We can have rivers of *living water* flowing out of us! We can experience an abundant life (see DEEPER STUDY # 1—Jn.1:4; DEEPER STUDY # 1—10:10).

> **"Blessed are those who hunger and thirst for righteousness, for they shall be satisfied." (Mt.5:6)**

> **"But whoever drinks of the water that I will give him will never be thirsty again. The water that I will give him will become in him a spring of water welling up to eternal life." (Jn.4:14)**

> **"The thief comes only to steal and kill and destroy. I came that they may have life and have it abundantly." (Jn.10:10)**

> **"They shall hunger no more, neither thirst anymore; the sun shall not strike them, nor any scorching heat." (Re.7:16)**

> **The Spirit and the Bride say, "Come." And let the one who hears say, "Come." And let the one who is thirsty come; let the one who desires take the water of life without price. (Re.22:17)**

How is this possible? How can hopeless sinners experience an abundant life? The answer is, through the cross.

The death of Jesus Christ (His having been smitten for the sins of the world) is the source of the living water. Out of His death (because He died) He was able to arise, and by arising He was able to conquer sin and death and to bring forth eternal life in all of its abundance.

The Word of God to Moses was a picture of the living water that was to come from Christ after He was smitten.

> "Behold, I will stand before you there on the rock at Horeb, and you shall strike the rock, and water shall come out of it, and the people will drink." And Moses did so, in the sight of the elders of Israel. (Ex.17:6; see Nu.20:11)

Living water comes only through believing in Christ. When we place our faith in Him, turning from our sin and accepting His death personally as payment for our sin, He gives us this living water (see Deeper Study # 2–Jn.2:24).

> Jesus said to them, "I am the bread of life; whoever comes to me shall not hunger, and whoever believes in me shall never thirst." (Jn.6:35)

c. **I am the source of the Holy Spirit (v.39).**

Jesus Christ is the source of the Holy Spirit. Rivers of living water refer to the Holy Spirit (see Deeper Study # 2). This is a crucial verse, for it is the only place "living water" is defined. When Jesus spoke of giving "living water," He meant He would give us the Holy Spirit. The presence of the Holy Spirit, of course, is the basis of the experience of abundant and eternal life.

Note: we can only receive the Holy Spirit through believing in Christ. Belief in Him is essential. Christ is the Giver of the Spirit (see note–Jn.4:13-14 for more discussion).

> But the fruit of the Spirit is love, joy, peace, patience, kindness, goodness, faithfulness, gentleness, self-control; against such things there is no law. (Ga.5:22-23)

> (For the fruit of light is found in all that is good and right and true). (Ep.5:9)

## Deeper Study # 1

(7:37) **Jesus Christ—Living Water**: like water, Jesus, the Living Water, does at least three things.

- ➢ He cleanses and purifies.

    > In him we have redemption through his blood, the forgiveness of our trespasses, according to the riches of his grace. (Ep.1:7; see 1 Jn.1:9)

- ➢ He refreshes.

    > "Repent therefore, and turn back, that your sins may be blotted out." (Ac.3:19)

    > To whom he has said, "This is rest; give rest to the weary; and this is repose"; yet they would not hear. (Is.28:12)

- ➢ He revitalizes and energizes.

    > "Come to me, all who labor and are heavy laden, and I will give you rest." (Mt.11:28)

## Deeper Study # 2

(7:39) **Holy Spirit**: what does the statement mean, "as yet the Spirit had not been given"? It does not mean the Spirit was not active in the Old Testament. To the contrary, He was very active (Ge.1:2; 6:3; Jb.26:13; 33:4; Ps.51:11; 139:7; Eze.3:24, 27; Hag.2:5). It seems to mean that the Holy Spirit was not *fully present* until after the death and glorification of Christ. He was not present . . .

- in all His fullness
- in the lives of believers all the time, in indwelling believers
- in equipping believers with permanent spiritual gifts

These three things certainly happened after the glorification of Christ.

- ➢ He entered the world in all His fullness at Pentecost (see Deeper Study # 1–Ac.2:1-4 for more discussion).

- He entered the lives of believers at conversion, and their bodies became "a temple of the Holy Spirit" (1 Co.6:19).
- He equips believers with spiritual gifts that are permanent (1 Co.12:7f).

## 3 The people's divided response to Jesus.

a. Many said Jesus is the prophet (v.40).
b. Others said Jesus is the Christ (v.41a).
c. Some questioned Jesus' birthplace and misinterpreted Scripture (vv.41b-42).
d. Some would seize and do away with Jesus (vv.43-44).

7:40-44

⁴⁰ When they heard these words, some of the people said, "This really is the Prophet."
⁴¹ Others said, "This is the Christ." But some said, "Is the Christ to come from Galilee?
⁴² Has not the Scripture said that the Christ comes from the offspring of David, and comes from Bethlehem, the village where David was?"
⁴³ So there was a division among the people over him.
⁴⁴ Some of them wanted to arrest him, but no one laid hands on him.

The people's response to Jesus was very divided (v.43). Some said He was the Prophet (v.40; see Deeper Study # 3; Deeper Study # 2—Jn.1:20). Others said He is the Christ, the Anointed One sent from God, the Messiah (v.41a; see Deeper Study # 2—Jn.1:20). Some questioned Jesus' birthplace and misinterpreted Scripture (vv.41b-42; see Deeper Study # 4). They knew that He was from Galilee, and they knew the true Messiah was to come out of Bethlehem, the city of David. Therefore, they saw no possible way He could be the Messiah.

Still others wanted to seize or arrest Jesus and do away with Him (v.44). They wanted nothing to do with Him. He was a threat to their peace and security and to their desire to live as they wished (see note, pt.4—Jn.7:32 for more discussion and thought).

> "But watch yourselves lest your hearts be weighed down with dissipation and drunkenness and cares of this life, and that day come upon you suddenly like a trap." (Lu.21:34)
>
> You adulterous people! Do you not know that friendship with the world is enmity with God? Therefore whoever wishes to be a friend of the world makes himself an enemy of God. (Js.4:4)
>
> Do not love the world or the things in the world. If anyone loves the world, the love of the Father is not in him. (1 Jn.2:15)

**THOUGHT 1.** Note what happened immediately on the heels of the Lord's dramatic claim. People began to quarrel over Him, arguing whether He was indeed the real Messiah. What people need is to accept the fact: He is the Messiah, the Christ. There is too much evidence to deny it, too much evidence...

- within the human soul that senses the truth of God
- within the confirmed historical accounts of His life on earth
- within the lives of so many who bear clear testimony to His love and forgiveness, presence and assurance

> "Truly, truly, I say to you, we speak of what we know, and bear witness to what we have seen, but you do not receive our testimony." (Jn.3:11)
>
> So the Jews gathered around him and said to him, "How long will you keep us in suspense? If you are the Christ, tell us plainly." Jesus answered them, "I told you, and you do not believe. The works that I do in my Father's name bear witness about me." (Jn.10:24-25)
>
> Though he had done so many signs before them, they still did not believe in him. (Jn.12:37)

**THOUGHT 2.** Many do question the *Lord's origin* and continue in unbelief because of it. When they look at Jesus, they see a great man, but only a man. They see and believe that He was flesh and blood, but not God incarnate in human flesh. They do not believe Jesus is the Son of God—a great prophet, yes; but the Messiah, the very Son of God, no.

> He was in the world, and the world was made through him, yet the world did not know him. He came to his own, and his own people did not receive him. (Jn.1:10-11)
>
> And this is the testimony, that God gave us eternal life, and this life is in his Son. Whoever has the Son has life; whoever does not have the Son of God does not have life. (1 Jn.5:11-12)

## Deeper Study # 3

(7:40) **Prophetic Reference**: see De.18:15.

## Deeper Study # 4

(7:42) **Prophetic Reference**: see Mi.5:2.

## 7:45-53

⁴⁵ The officers then came to the chief priests and Pharisees, who said to them, "Why did you not bring him?"
⁴⁶ The officers answered, "No one ever spoke like this man!"
⁴⁷ The Pharisees answered them, "Have you also been deceived?
⁴⁸ Have any of the authorities or the Pharisees believed in him?
⁴⁹ But this crowd that does not know the law is accursed."
⁵⁰ Nicodemus, who had gone to him before, and who was one of them, said to them,
⁵¹ Does our law judge a man without first giving him a hearing and learning what he does?"
⁵² They replied, "Are you from Galilee too? Search and see that no prophet arises from Galilee."
⁵³ [[They went each to his own house,

## 4 The rulers' response to Jesus.

Although the people were divided in their response to Jesus, the Jewish rulers were united in their opinion. Their response should be carefully noted, for it speaks volumes to rulers and leaders of every generation.

**a. They wished to remove Jesus (vv.45-46).**

The leaders wished to be rid of Jesus. They opposed Him and wanted nothing to do with Him (see note, pts.3, 4—Jn.7:32 for more discussion and thought). They sent the officers to arrest Jesus (v.32), but they would not seize Him (v.44). Their reason: they were greatly impressed with the Lord's teaching, testifying that they had never heard anybody speak as He spoke. To them He was a great teacher.

**b. They claimed Jesus was a deceiver (vv.47-49).**

The leaders claimed that Jesus was a deceiver and that the people were mistaken and accursed because they followed Him (see note, pt.2—Jn.7:11-15). With a scowl of disgust, the Pharisees accused the officers of being deceived along with the people. They then demanded to know if any of the Jewish leaders were among those who believed in Jesus.

**c. They rejected Jesus (vv.50-52).**

The leaders rejected Jesus, strongly so. Nicodemus spoke up for Christ, charging the leaders with breaking the law themselves and suggesting that they all hear Christ and observe His works closely (see Deeper Study # 5). The leaders rejected Nicodemus' questions, misinterpreting Scripture. They used Scripture as their basis for rejecting Christ. They said that no Scripture pointed to a prophet coming out of Galilee. They were wrong of course, wrong on two counts:

➢ Jonah came from Galilee.
➢ God is able to raise up prophets from anywhere He chooses.

**d. They returned to their own homes and lived as always (v.53).**

The leaders went to their own houses unchanged and lived just as they had always lived. God does not force people to subject themselves to His Son. Every individual has the freedom to live as he or she wishes, either for God or for self. The leaders chose to live for self.

> Whoever believes in the Son has eternal life; whoever does not obey the Son shall not see life, but the wrath of God remains on him. (Jn.3:36)

> "I told you that you would die in your sins, for unless you believe that I am he you will die in your sins." (Jn.8:24)

## Deeper Study # 5

(7:50) **Nicodemus**: see Jn.3:1-15.

# Chapter 8

## IX. The Revelation of Jesus, the Light of Life, 8:1–9:41

### A. Humanity's Dark Sinfulness and God's Great Forgiveness, 8:1-11

1. **A picture of Jesus' life: A life of devotion, worship, ministry, & teaching**

but Jesus went to the Mount of Olives. ² Early in the morning he came again to the temple. All the people came to him, and he sat down and taught them.

2. **A picture of humanity's dark guilt**
   a. A woman & an unknown man were guilty of adultery

³ The scribes and the Pharisees brought a woman who had been caught in adultery, and placing her in the midst ⁴ they said to him, "Teacher, this woman has been caught in the act of adultery. ⁵ "Now in the Law, Moses commanded us to stone such women. So what do you say?"

   b. Some witnesses who were offended were guilty of vindictiveness & seeking revenge
   c. The religious leaders & the public were guilty
      1) Had a hard, self-righteous, & condemning spirit
      2) Had a deceptive purpose: Hoped to trap Jesus into saying something that would discredit Him
   d. Jesus refused to give them what they wanted

⁶ This they said to test him, that they might have some charge to bring against him. Jesus bent down and wrote with his finger on the ground.

3. **A picture of humanity's dark nature: Everyone is sinful—guilty of serious sin**
   a. The counter-charge by Jesus: If any person is without sin, then that person can condemn her

⁷ And as they continued to ask him, he stood up and said to them, "Let him who is without sin among you be the first to throw a stone at her." ⁸ And once more he bent down and wrote on the ground.

   b. The result: All were convicted & began to slip away one by one

⁹ But when they heard it, they went away one by one, beginning with the older ones, and Jesus was left alone with the woman standing before him.

4. **A picture of humanity's being set free from condemnation: Jesus alone has the right to condemn & forgive**
   a. He forgave the woman & gave her a second chance
   b. He challenged & warned the woman: Sin no more

¹⁰ Jesus stood up and said to her, "Woman, where are they? Has no one condemned you?" ¹¹ She said, "No one, Lord." And Jesus said, "Neither do I condemn you; go, and from now on sin no more."

# Division IX

*The Revelation of Jesus, the Light of Life, 8:1–9:41*

A. Humanity's Dark Sinfulness and God's Great Forgiveness, 8:1-11

## 8:1–9:41
## DIVISION OVERVIEW

In Chapter 8 Christ reveals Himself to be the Light of life. Humanity is seen as gripped by sin (illustrated by the woman taken in adultery and by hypocritical religious leaders). Through Jesus' treatment of the immoral woman, the human race (every single person) is pictured as adulterous—living a life of darkness, without purpose and meaning and significance. Through the religious leaders in this account, the human race is pictured as deceitful, critical, condemnatory, selfish, self-righteous, and loaded with guilt. Not a single religious leader is seen to be free from the darkness of serious sin. Jesus reveals Himself to be the Light of the World, the One who brings liberty, forgiveness, purpose, meaning, and significance to the life of all people.

## 8:1-11
## Introduction

In this passage, John relates one of the most striking scenes from the life of Christ: His forgiving of the adulterous woman. It is a scene teeming with tension and drama. Someone had brought the sinful woman to the religious leaders for judgment, and the law called for her to be executed. Seeking to trap Jesus, the religious leaders asked Him what *He* thought should be done. The statement Jesus made at the height of the drama is one of the most quoted statements in all of history. However, we must never permit the drama of the story to overshadow its critical truths. This is, *Humanity's Dark Sinfulness and God's Great Forgiveness*, 8:1-11.

1. A picture of Jesus' life: A life of devotion, worship, ministry, & teaching (vv.1-2).
2. A picture of humanity's dark guilt (vv.3-6).
3. A picture of humanity's dark nature: Everyone is sinful—guilty of serious sin (vv.7-9).
4. A picture of humanity's being set free from condemnation: Jesus alone has the right to condemn and forgive (vv.10-11).

### 8:1-2

**b**ut Jesus went to the Mount of Olives.
² Early in the morning he came again to the temple. All the people came to him, and he sat down and taught them.

### 1 A picture of Jesus' life: A life of devotion, worship, ministry, and teaching.

John 8 begins with a picture of Jesus' life. A real contrast of lives is presented here. Jesus' quiet and worshipful life is contrasted with the turbulent and judgmental lives of the religious leaders. Jesus is drawn within the turbulence to calm, settle, and bring peace to it. A picture can be drawn of the Christian life as quiet and worshipful contrasted with a turbulent world.

Note the secret to Jesus' calm and peace: He managed to get alone with God. He often went off into the Mount of Olives to spend quiet moments with God the Father (see note—Lu.21:37). It was a favorite spot of His, a place where He could be alone with God and His disciples, a place of quietness where God could meet with Him face-to-face, strengthen and encourage Him (Mt.26:30, 36f; see outline and notes—Lu.21:37-38 for more discussion of this point).

Note also that Jesus began His teaching early in the morning. The Greek words translated *came* and *taught* in verse 2 denote continuous action. The people *kept coming* to Him, and He *kept teaching* them. Christ's very mission in life demonstrated how all people should walk through life: worshiping God and teaching and ministering to people. Every person needs to be taught, and every individual needs the ministry of others during the trials of life.

## 2 A picture of humanity's dark guilt.

The guilt of every human being is portrayed in this passage. It is so easy for us to focus on the sins of others while overlooking our own sinfulness. All too often, while we are pointing out the sins of others, we expose our own.

8:3-6

a. **A woman and an unknown man were guilty of adultery (v.3a).**

The religious leaders brought a woman to Jesus. She was guilty of the serious sin of adultery, a sin that affects so many lives. Under Jewish law it was considered so serious that the parties were to be stoned to death (Le.20:10; De.22:13-24). Obviously, there was a man involved as well. But the Scribes and Pharisees brought only the woman to Jesus. Note how the sin represents the sin of every person.

> ³ The scribes and the Pharisees brought a woman who had been caught in adultery, and placing her in the midst
> ⁴ they said to him, "Teacher, this woman has been caught in the act of adultery.
> ⁵ Now in the Law, Moses commanded us to stone such women. So what do you say?"
> ⁶ This they said to test him, that they might have some charge to bring against him. Jesus bent down and wrote with his finger on the ground.

- ➢ The sin was a work of darkness. All sin is dark, and most sin is actually done under the cover of darkness or shrouded in secrecy. Attempts are often made to hide adulterous acts from loved ones and friends.
- ➢ The man and woman thought what we all often think—that their sin would never be discovered, that no one would ever find out. But they overlooked two facts that we all ignore: in the vast majority of cases, sin has been or will be discovered; and sin, the very act of it, is always seen by God.
- ➢ The sin took place at the time of the feast, where the atmosphere was party-like, and where men and women were brought together by drinking and dancing and the indulgence of the crowd (see Jn.7:37f). Such an atmosphere can corrupt even those with the best intentions and the highest morals.

b. **Some witnesses who were offended were guilty of vindictiveness and seeking revenge (v.3b).**

Some of the witnesses against the woman were guilty of a different type of sin. Offended by the woman in particular, they dragged her to the religious authorities to be judged. Jewish law required two witnesses to convict a person. It is most unlikely that the woman and her male companion were seen by the religious leaders themselves. The Pharisees and Scribes would not have been in such a defiled atmosphere; they were too strict in their rules and regulations. Some commentators do think, however, that the religious leaders had some scoundrels set a trap for the woman in order to drag her before Jesus to entrap Him. This seems most unlikely. Plotting a sin of the flesh does not fit in with the nature of the Pharisees and Scribes. Their sins were more of the spirit, much deeper, but less visible and less condemning to the public.

The point is, the witnesses who caught the woman in the act of adultery were *great sinners* as well. They were vindictive and revengeful. They wanted to strike out, to get back at her. Therefore, they exposed her publicly. She should have been held in custody in some private place until judgment was passed, but she was unmercifully dragged before the public to expose her sin and to shame and punish her. Why? Perhaps she had hurt her husband or some loved one so much that they struck back at her through public exposure. However, the man who committed adultery with her was not exposed. Why? He may have escaped or fled before they grabbed him. Or he may have been feared for some reason or managed to buy off his accusers. Or he may have been released because, as is the case in so many societies, misbehavior (sin) by men was more overlooked than by women.

c. **The religious leaders and the public were guilty (vv.4-6a).**

The religious leaders and the public had sinned as well. When the accusers dragged the woman to the Jewish authorities, people all along the way joined in, as so often happens. The religious leaders saw a chance to test Jesus, so they took the woman before Him, hoping to discredit

Him. If Jesus said the woman was not guilty, He would be breaking Jewish law and be leaving Himself open to the charge of being too lenient with sin. On the other hand, if Jesus said the woman was guilty and should be killed, He would be breaking Roman law which did not consider adultery a sin worthy of death. He would also be criticized as lacking mercy and love, compassion and forgiveness.

The dark nature of sinful humanity is portrayed in these religious leaders and in the crowd who joined in the public exposure. First, they had a hard, self-righteous, and condemning spirit (v.5), a spirit . . .

- of self-righteousness that lacked forgiveness
- of criticism that lacked love
- of judging that lacked compassion
- of censoring that lacked understanding
- of condemning that lacked sympathy
- of punishing that lacked restoration
- of savagery that lacked caring
- of destroying that lacked the second chance

In addition, they had a deceptive purpose. They hoped to trap Jesus into saying something that would discredit Him (v.6a). On top of this, they were hypocrites. They felt and claimed that they were religious, better than the woman, free from any sin serious enough to be exposed. They even used Scripture to condemn *her* sin and to support *their* right to condemn her.

However, in doing so, they exposed themselves as lawbreakers as well. They had violated God's command to love their neighbor as themselves:

> "You shall do no injustice in court. You shall not be partial to the poor or defer to the great, but in righteousness shall you judge your neighbor. You shall not go around as a slanderer among your people, and you shall not stand up against the life of your neighbor: I am the LORD. You shall not hate your brother in your heart, but you shall reason frankly with your neighbor, lest you incur sin because of him. You shall not take vengeance or bear a grudge against the sons of your own people, but you shall love your neighbor as yourself: I am the LORD." (Le.19:15-18)

They completely failed to give the woman what we all need sometimes, to be embraced and pulled out of the sin and hurt gripping us. And they completely failed to hush—be quiet, and say nothing, except to the one caught in sin—and to set about a ministry of restoration and reconciliation to God and those hurt by the sin.

**d. Jesus refused to give them what they wanted (v.6b).**

Jesus refused to give the deceptive religious leaders—and the judgmental people—what they wanted. He would not give in to their demand that He pass judgment on the sinful woman. Instead, He silently bent down and wrote in the dirt with His finger. We are not told why Jesus stooped in silence or what He wrote on the ground. Various commentators say it was . . .

- to allow Him to think through the situation
- to force the accusers to repeat the charges (v.7). By so doing, they and the public would begin to see and sense their lack of compassion.
- to write Scripture or some of the sins of those standing around, hoping to convict them (see Jb.13:26)

8:7-9

⁷ And as they continued to ask him, he stood up and said to them, "Let him who is without sin among you be the first to throw a stone at her."
⁸ And once more he bent down and wrote on the ground.
⁹ But when they heard it, they went away one by one, beginning with the older ones, and Jesus was left alone with the woman standing before him.

## 3 A picture of humanity's dark nature: Everyone is sinful—guilty of serious sin.

All people are sinful and, by default, guilty of serious sin. Regardless of each person's particular sins, we have all broken God's laws, and we all stand guilty before Him. Consequently, none of us is qualified to condemn others.

a. The counter-charge by Jesus: If any person is without sin, then that person can condemn her (vv.7–8).

The Scribes and Pharisees persisted in pressing Jesus for an answer. This woman was guilty of a very serious sin. The law said she was to be condemned to death. Her accusers and others were legally justified in their charge. If they were to be stopped from killing her, and even more, if they were to be corrected and rebuked, something phenomenal would have to happen. And it did, when Jesus at last spoke: *"Let him who is without sin among you be the first to throw a stone at her" (v.7).*

> "And this is the judgment: the light has come into the world, and people loved the darkness rather than the light because their works were evil." (Jn.3:19)

> As it is written: "None is righteous, no, not one." (Ro.3:10; see vv.9-18; 3:23)

b. The result: All were convicted and began to slip away one by one (v.9).

Jesus said that stones could be cast at the sinner. But He placed a limitation on casting stones. Only those who are without sin have the right to cast stones at another person. Therefore, only Christ can judge, for no person is without sin.

The right to judge others is not based on how much Scripture a person knows, nor on how great a person's calling and gifts are, nor on the position a person has. It is based on moral goodness and perfection, and *no human being* has achieved that. No person is without sin. Every one of the men standing there knew it, and every one of them was convicted within his conscience. They all left, leaving Jesus and the woman alone.

> "Why do you see the speck that is in your brother's eye, but do not notice the log that is in your own eye? Or how can you say to your brother, 'Let me take the speck out of your eye,' when there is the log in your own eye? You hypocrite, first take the log out of your own eye, and then you will see clearly to take the speck out of your brother's eye." (Mt.7:3-5; see Ro.14:4, 13; 1 Co.4:5; Js.4:12)

> What then? Are we Jews any better off? No, not at all. For we have already charged that all, both Jews and Greeks, are under sin, as it is written: "None is righteous, no, not one; no one understands; no one seeks for God. All have turned aside; together they have become worthless; no one does good, not even one." (Ro.3:9-12)

## 4 A picture of humanity's being set free from condemnation: Jesus alone has the right to condemn and forgive.

8:10-11

¹⁰ Jesus stood up and said to her, "Woman, where are they? Has no one condemned you?"
¹¹ She said, "No one, Lord." And Jesus said, "Neither do I condemn you; go, and from now on sin no more."

The great revelation of this incident is that Jesus alone has the right to condemn and forgive. The picture of the woman is the picture of every person. When it comes to sin and judgment, every person stands alone before Christ—stands naked and stripped of all righteousness, for no person possesses righteousness. There are no accusers, not among men. No human being can condemn the woman nor anyone else. The only righteousness and the only perfection, the only One who is not guilty of sin, is Christ and Christ alone. He alone is worthy to stand in judgment. But instead of condemning the guilty woman, He announced the most glorious news in all of human history.

a. He forgave her and gave her a second chance (v.11a).

Jesus did not condemn the adulterous woman. Instead, He forgave her and gave her a *second chance*.

> Then Peter came up and said to him, "Lord, how often will my brother sin against me, and I forgive him? As many as seven times?" Jesus said to him, "I do not say to you seven times, but seventy-seven times." (Mt.18:21-22)

> "And if he sins against you seven times in the day, and turns to you seven times, saying, 'I repent,' you must forgive him." (Lu.17:4)

> My little children, I am writing these things to you so that you may not sin. But if anyone does sin, we have an advocate with the Father, Jesus Christ the righteous. He is the propitiation for our sins, and not for ours only but also for the sins of the whole world. (1 Jn.2:1–2)

### b. He challenged and warned her: Sin no more (v.11b).

Jesus wished to forgive and did forgive. He did not condemn the woman:

> Who is to condemn? Christ Jesus is the one who died—more than that, who was raised—who is at the right hand of God, who indeed is interceding for us. (Ro.8:34)

> In him we have redemption through his blood, the forgiveness of our trespasses, according to the riches of his grace. (Ep.1:7)

> If we confess our sins, he is faithful and just to forgive us our sins and to cleanse us from all unrighteousness. (1 Jn.1:9)

However, He did not give the woman a free pass to continue in her sin. To the contrary, He commanded her to repent, to turn away from her sin. Jesus essentially said, "Stop your sinning—make a clean break—do it no more." The warning is clear: repentance is essential for forgiveness.

> "And that repentance for the forgiveness of sins should be proclaimed in his name to all nations, beginning from Jerusalem." (Lu.24:47)

> Afterward Jesus found him in the temple and said to him, "See, you are well! Sin no more, that nothing worse may happen to you." (Jn.5:14)

> And Peter said to them, "Repent and be baptized every one of you in the name of Jesus Christ for the forgiveness of your sins, and you will receive the gift of the Holy Spirit." (Ac.2:38)

> Let not sin therefore reign in your mortal body, to make you obey its passions. (Ro.6:12)

> Wake up from your drunken stupor, as is right, and do not go on sinning. For some have no knowledge of God. I say this to your shame. (1 Co.15:34)

## B. Humanity's Need:
## The Light of the World, 8:12-20

¹² Again Jesus spoke to them, saying, "I am the light of the world. Whoever follows me will not walk in darkness, but will have the light of life."

¹³ So the Pharisees said to him, "You are bearing witness about yourself; your testimony is not true."

¹⁴ Jesus answered, "Even if I do bear witness about myself, my testimony is true, for I know where I came from and where I am going, but you do not know where I come from or where I am going.

¹⁵ "You judge according to the flesh; I judge no one.

¹⁶ "Yet even if I do judge, my judgment is true, for it is not I alone who judge, but I and the Father who sent me.

¹⁷ "In your Law it is written that the testimony of two people is true.

¹⁸ "I am the one who bears witness about myself, and the Father who sent me bears witness about me."

¹⁹ They said to him therefore, "Where is your Father?" Jesus answered, "You know neither me nor my Father. If you knew me, you would know my Father also."

²⁰ These words he spoke in the treasury, as he taught in the temple; but no one arrested him, because his hour had not yet come.

1. **Jesus made a great claim & promise**
   a. The claim: He is the Light of the world$^{DS1}$
   b. The promise: Follow Him &....$^{DS2}$
   c. The Pharisees objection: Questioned the validity of His claim

2. **Proof 1: Jesus' great knowledge of His origin & destiny**

3. **Proof 2: Humanity's incompetence & inability to know Christ's origin & destiny**
   a. The fact stated
   b. The reason: People judge by worldly standards

4. **Proof 3: Jesus' stand—His oneness—with the Father**
   a. Means what He says
   b. Means God sent Him

5. **Proof 4: The law's testimony**
   a. Jesus knew the legal requirements
   b. Jesus had two witnesses: Himself & God who sent Him

6. **Proof 5: The Father's presence within**
   a. Jesus was mocked
   b. Jesus' response: Declared they did not know Him or His Father

7. **The tragic conclusion: Jesus was rejected in the temple**

# Division IX

### *The Revelation of Jesus, the Light of Life, 8:1-9:41*

B. Humanity's Need: The Light of the World, 8:12-20

## 8:12-20
## Introduction

We human beings have great needs. We are ever aware of our physical needs—food, clothing, shelter, transportation, medical treatment—but not many of us are aware of our spiritual needs. Nevertheless, the need is still there. Every single one of us is in spiritual darkness.

➢ We cannot see into the future nor into the next world.

- We cannot see God, who He is and what He is like.
- We cannot see the real meaning, significance, and purpose in life.
- We cannot grasp perfect knowledge nor assurance of eternal life.

Therefore, our great need is to see "the Light of the world." In this passage, Jesus addresses this, our most urgent need. This is, *Humanity's Need: The Light of the World*, 8:12-20.

1. Jesus made a great claim and promise (vv.12-13).
2. Proof 1: Jesus' great knowledge of His origin and destiny (v.14).
3. Proof 2: Humanity's incompetence and inability to know Christ's origin and destiny (vv.14-15).
4. Proof 3: Jesus' stand—His oneness—with the Father (v.16).
5. Proof 4: The law's testimony (vv.17-18).
6. Proof 5: The Father's presence within (v.19).
7. The tragic conclusion: Jesus was rejected in the temple (v.20).

## 8:12-13

¹² Again Jesus spoke to them, saying, "I am the light of the world. Whoever follows me will not walk in darkness, but will have the light of life."

¹³ So the Pharisees said to him, "You are bearing witness about yourself; your testimony is not true."

## 1 Jesus made a great claim and promise.

Jesus made a great claim and promise. He claimed to be the Light of the world, and He promised the light of life to all who would follow Him.

### a. The claim: He is the Light of the world (v.12a).

Christ's great claim was, "I am the Light of the world" (see Deeper Study # 1. Also see note—Mt.5:14). In this statement, Jesus makes an even greater claim of deity: *I Am*. The Lord's claim to deity was emphatic. It was the very first thing He said in this passage (see Deeper Study # 1—Jn.6:20).

### b. The great promise: Follow Him and . . . (v.12b).

Jesus proceeded to make a great twofold promise: all who follow Him will not walk in darkness (see Deeper Study # 2), and they will have the light of life. None of us possess light, not within ourselves, not by nature. By nature, we are in darkness. We are delivered out of darkness by following Jesus Christ. The Greek word for *follows* (akolouthone) denotes continuous action. We must continue to follow Christ in order to receive light.

### c. The Pharisees' objection: Questioned the validity of His claim (v.13).

The religious leaders (Pharisees) objected to the claim of Jesus. They knew exactly what He was claiming: that He was the Messiah and that He alone could give light to the world. In their minds only God could give light to the world. Therefore, they charged Jesus with making a false claim. He alone was bearing witness to His claim. He had no other witnesses; therefore, His claim was false. (See note—Jn.5:31 for more discussion of the witnesses required to prove a person's testimony. Jesus gave five witnesses in Jn.5:31-39.)

**Thought 1.** Jesus used the term "*light of life*." We all exist in darkness until we follow Christ. The meaning, purpose, and significance of life cannot be seen and known apart from following Christ. It is Christ who throws light upon life, revealing what life really is.

> "As he spoke by the mouth of his holy prophets from of old." (Lk.1:70)

> "I have come into the world as light, so that whoever believes in me may not remain in darkness." (Jn.12:46)

> For God, who said, "Let light shine out of darkness," has shone in our hearts to give the light of the knowledge of the glory of God in the face of Jesus Christ. (2 Co.4:6)

> The people who walked in darkness have seen a great light; those who dwelt in a land of deep darkness, on them has light shone. (Is.9:2)

## DEEPER STUDY # 1

(8:12) **Light**: Jesus is said to be the *Light of men* (Jn.1:4) and the *Light of the world* (Jn.8:12; 9:5; 12:46). It is possible for the Light, Jesus Himself, to be *in people* (Jn.11:10; see Col.1:27) and for people to become children of Light (see notes—Jn.12:34-36).

Apparently, Jesus used the word *light* often. John uses the word about twenty-one times. What is meant by calling Jesus the Light?

1. Jesus, the Light, is light by nature. Light is what He is within Himself, within His being, His nature, His essence, His character. Scripture says . . .
   - that "God is Light" (1 Jn.1:5)
   - that Jesus is "the image of the invisible God" (Col.1:15)
   - therefore, "Jesus is Light." He is "the Light of the world"

2. Jesus, the Light, tells us that He is holy, righteous, and pure. Light is the symbol of purity and holiness. Light means the absence of darkness and blindness; it has neither spots of darkness or blackness, nor of sin and shame.

3. Jesus, the Light, reveals. His light shows clearly the nature, the meaning, and the destiny of all things. His light shines in, spots, opens up, identifies, illuminates, and shows things as they really are. The light of Jesus Christ shows the truth about the world and humanity and God. The light of Jesus Christ reveals that He loves and cares for us and wants us to love and care for Him.

4. Jesus, the Light, guides. His light allows us to walk out of darkness. We no longer have to grope, grasp, and stumble about trying to find our way through life. The path of life can now be clearly seen.

5. Jesus, the Light, does away with darkness and with chaos. His light routs, wipes out, strips away, and erases the darkness. The empty chaos of creation was routed by the light given by God (Ge.1:3). Jesus Christ is the Light that can save us from chaos (Jn.12:46; 14:1, 17; 16:33).

Jesus proclaimed Himself to be the Light of the world at the great Feast of Tabernacles (Jn.7:2). The very first ceremony of the Feast holds great significance for Jesus' claim. It was called "The Illumination of the Temple" and was held in the Court of the Women. The center of the Court was surrounded by large sections of stadium-like seats. In the open space of the Court sat four huge candelabra. When darkness fell, the candelabra were lit, and the elders danced and led the people in singing psalms before the LORD all night. The brilliance and glow from the burning flames of the huge candelabra were said to be so bright that the light could be seen throughout the whole city. It was against this background that Jesus cried out, "I am the Light of the world."

## DEEPER STUDY # 2

(8:12) **Darkness** (Gk. skotia): the word is used in Scripture to describe both the state and the works of sinful humanity. Darkness is very real in Scripture.

1. The darkness refers to the world of those who do not know Jesus Christ (Jn.8:12). By nature, we walk in ignorance . . .
   - of Jesus Christ
   - of God as revealed by Jesus Christ
   - of the real purpose and destiny of life as shown by Jesus Christ

Our sinful nature causes us to stumble and grope about in this world. We know nothing other than the things of this world as we see them. Our only hope is the hope of living a long life before death overtakes us. We walk in darkness, ignorant of real life now and hereafter (see Jn.12:35, 46).

2. The darkness symbolizes unpreparedness and unwatchfulness. It symbolizes the time when evil occurs (1 Th.5:4-8).

3. The darkness is loved by sinful humanity. Sinful people do their evil deeds under the cover of darkness. They therefore hate the light because the light uncovers their evil behavior (Jn.3:19-20).

4. The darkness is hostile to light (see DEEPER STUDY # 4—Jn.1:5).

### 8:14a

¹⁴ Jesus answered, "Even if I do bear witness about myself, my testimony is true, for I know where I came from and where I am going, but you do not know where I come from or where I am going."

## 2 Proof 1: Jesus' great knowledge of His origin and destiny.

The first proof of Jesus' claim is His great knowledge. He knew His origin and destiny. He declared, "I am the Light of the world," and He declared that His witness was enough. He simply said that His testimony or witness was *true* (alethes).

➢ It was not false.
➢ It was not a lie.
➢ It was not a deceptive claim.
➢ It was not the claim of an egomaniac setting Himself up as a *god*.
➢ It was not the claim of a man who is out to shatter people's dreams.
➢ It was not the claim of a man who is set on destroying other people.

The witness of Jesus Christ was true, and His witness was sufficient evidence for a very strong reason. Jesus knew His origin and destiny, where He had come from and where He was going. He was *out of* heaven, *out of* the spiritual dimension of being, and He was to return to heaven.

### 8:14b-15

¹⁴ Jesus answered, "Even if I do bear witness about myself, my testimony is true, for I know where I came from and where I am going, but you do not know where I come from or where I am going. ¹⁵ You judge according to the flesh; I judge no one.

## 3 Proof 2: Humanity's incompetence and inability to know Christ's origin and destiny.

The second proof of Jesus' claim is humanity's inability to know Christ's origin and destiny. This is because of the difference between the physical and spiritual worlds or dimensions of being.

a. **The fact stated (v.14b).**

The people could not tell where Jesus had come from nor where He was going. Why? For a very simple reason: humans cannot penetrate nor see the spiritual world. Physical eyes are blind to the world of the Spirit (see Jn.1:18). If there is to be communication with the *spiritual* dimension, the spiritual world must come into this world, into the *physical* dimension. This is exactly what had happened; this is just what Jesus is saying. He had come from heaven, from the spiritual dimension of being. He had been an eyewitness of heaven. He had been in the very presence of God Himself, and God had sent Him from heaven into this world to declare the glorious message of salvation.

> "Truly, truly, I say to you, we speak of what we know, and bear witness to what we have seen, but you do not receive our testimony." (Jn.3:11; see Jn.3:32)
>
> Again Jesus spoke to them, saying, "I am the light of the world. Whoever follows me will not walk in darkness, but will have the light of life." (Jn.8:12)
>
> Jesus answered, "Even if I do bear witness about myself, my testimony is true, for I know where I came from and where I am going, but you do not know where I come from or where I am going." (Jn.8:14)
>
> Then Pilate said to him, "So you are a king?" Jesus answered, "You say that I am a king. For this purpose I was born and for this purpose I have come into the world—to bear witness to the truth. Everyone who is of the truth listens to my voice." (Jn.18:37)
>
> And from Jesus Christ the faithful witness, the firstborn of the dead, and the ruler of kings on earth. To him who loves us and has freed us from our sins by his blood (Re.1:5)

**b. The reason: People judge by worldly standards (v.15).**

Jesus explained that people judge according to the flesh, that is, by appearance. They judge by what they see and know. The only evidence they have is what they see in their world, the world of the physical. However, if people are to judge Jesus' claim, they cannot do it on the basis of physical evidence. Why? Because Jesus is not of this world. People have to judge Him by faith. They either accept His testimony or reject it.

> "Do not judge by appearances, but judge with right judgment." (Jn.7:24)

## 4 Proof 3: Jesus' stand—His oneness—with the Father.

8:16

Jesus' judgment was true. He judged not after the flesh—not by appearance—but by God's presence. This was a phenomenal claim. Jesus is saying that He is not alone. He did not speak nor act alone. The Father was *with Him*, and the Father *sent Him*; therefore, what He claimed and did is of the Father. What did Jesus mean by these statements?

<sup>16</sup> "Yet even if I do judge, my judgment is true, for it is not I alone who judge, but I and the Father who sent me."

**a. Means what He says.**

Jesus said again that what He claimed was *true* (alethes, see discussion at v.14). He meant every word He said. Nothing He said was intended to be taken any way but literally.

**b. Means God sent Him.**

Jesus called God *Father* and referred to His mission: "the Father who *sent* me." He had a Father-Son relationship with God and knew God in a very personal and intimate way as His Father. He *had come* from the presence and the household of His Father, that is, from heaven or from the spiritual world and dimension of being. Therefore, He *alone* could know all the facts of that world. He had come, being *sent* of the Father to proclaim the glorious message of salvation.

> "I and the Father are one." (Jn.10:30)

> "If I am not doing the works of my Father, then do not believe me; but if I do them, even though you do not believe me, believe the works, that you may know and understand that the Father is in me and I am in the Father." (Jn.10:37–38)

> "Do you not believe that I am in the Father and the Father is in me? The words that I say to you I do not speak on my own authority, but the Father who dwells in me does his works." (Jn.14:10)

> "And I am no longer in the world, but they are in the world, and I am coming to you. Holy Father, keep them in your name, which you have given me, that they may be one, even as we are one." (Jn.17:11; see Jn.17:22)

## 5 Proof 4: The law's testimony.

8:17–18

The third proof of Jesus' claim is the law's testimony. Jesus appealed to the Pharisees' law, the law given by Moses, which required two witnesses to validate a claim (De.19:15).

<sup>17</sup> "In your Law it is written that the testimony of two people is true.
<sup>18</sup> "I am the one who bears witness about myself, and the Father who sent me bears witness about me."

**a. Jesus met the legal requirements (v.17).**

Jesus knew what the law required. If two witnesses verified any matter, their testimony was legally accepted as the truth.

**b. Jesus had two witnesses: Himself and God who sent Him (v.18).**

Jesus met the requirements of the law. He had two witnesses. He was the first witness, and His witness was true. It is perfectly clear that He spoke and acted only for God. Everything He said and did was to glorify God and to lead people to God: to worship and praise and to honor and serve God. It is also clear that He spoke and acted only for the good of people. Everything He said and did was to save people, to awaken them, and to show them compassion and mercy, meeting their desperate needs.

Very simply, everything Jesus said and did bore witness that His claim was true, that He was *of God* and *sent from God* to be "the Light of the world."

> For he whom God has sent utters the words of God, for he gives the Spirit without measure. (Jn.3:34; see Jn.7:29)

> Jesus said to them, "If God were your Father, you would love me, for I came from God and I am here. I came not of my own accord, but he sent me." (Jn.8:42)

> "Whoever does not love me does not keep my words. And the word that you hear is not mine but the Father's who sent me." (Jn.14:24)

> "For I have given them the words that you gave me, and they have received them and have come to know in truth that I came from you; and they have believed that you sent me." (Jn.17:8)

Jesus' second witness was the Father who had sent Him, and God's witness was true. It is perfectly clear that God acted in and through Jesus. The life, the words, and the works of Jesus demonstrated God's presence and power. The presence and power of God was in and upon Christ "without measure" (Jn.3:34). There is no other sensible explanation. The Father who sent Him bore clear, indisputable witness that Jesus is "the Light of the world."

> And behold, a voice from heaven said, "This is my beloved Son, with whom I am well pleased." (Mt.3:17)

> He was still speaking when, behold, a bright cloud overshadowed them, and a voice from the cloud said, "This is my beloved Son, with whom I am well pleased; listen to him." (Mt.17:5)

> "There is another who bears witness about me, and I know that the testimony that he bears about me is true." (Jn.5:32)

> "And the Father who sent me has himself borne witness about me. His voice you have never heard, his form you have never seen." (Jn.5:37)

> If we receive the testimony of men, the testimony of God is greater, for this is the testimony of God that he has borne concerning his Son. Whoever believes in the Son of God has the testimony in himself. Whoever does not believe God has made him a liar, because he has not believed in the testimony that God has borne concerning his Son. (1 Jn.5:9-10)

## 8:19

¹⁹ They said to him therefore, "Where is your Father?" Jesus answered, "You know neither me nor my Father. If you knew me, you would know my Father also."

## 6 Proof 5: The Father's presence within.

The fifth proof of Jesus' claim was the Father's presence *within Him*. The Pharisees demanded to see Christ's Father. But the Father was present right before them—in Jesus.

### a. Jesus was mocked.

The religious leaders mocked Jesus. They told Him to present His Father, to go get Him and bring Him to them, so He could bear witness of Christ's claims. Note how they proved Jesus' words: they judged by the flesh, by sight and appearance. They wanted physical evidence. They wanted to *see* Jesus' Father. (Of course, they had physical evidence in Christ Himself and in the working of God's power through Him, but obstinate unbelief blinded them.)

### b. Jesus' response: Declared they did not know Him or His Father.

Jesus declared the tragic fact that they did not know Him or His Father. The unbeliever *does not know Him*. He was Man standing before them, and they could see and know Him as Man, but He was also the Son of God. If they rejected His claim and refused to accept Him as LORD, they naturally did not know Him. The only way to know Jesus is to follow Him as LORD, as "the Light of the world." (Note: no person knows any other person until one spends time with that individual—getting to know them, associating with them, and learning all about them.)

> Jesus answered her, "If you knew the gift of God, and who it is that is saying to you, 'Give me a drink,' you would have asked him, and he would have given you living water." (Jn.4:10)

They said to him therefore, "Where is your Father?" Jesus answered, "You know neither me nor my Father. If you knew me, you would know my Father also." (Jn.8:19)

The man answered, "Why, this is an amazing thing! You do not know where he comes from, and yet he opened my eyes." (Jn.9:30)

Jesus said to him, "Have I been with you so long, and you still do not know me, Philip? Whoever has seen me has seen the Father. How can you say, 'Show us the Father'?" (Jn.14:9)

"For those who live in Jerusalem and their rulers, because they did not recognize him nor understand the utterances of the prophets, which are read every Sabbath, fulfilled them by condemning him." (Ac.13:27)

Jesus continued to explain that if they knew Him, they would know the Father. They would not need to see the Father, as they demanded, because the Father was *in* Jesus. The unbeliever *does not know God*. Nobody has seen God at any time (Jn.1:18). The only conceivable way a person can ever know God is for God to *reveal* Himself: God must come from the heavenly world, the spiritual dimension of being, and enter this world, revealing the truth about Himself to humanity. But note: *if God does come* and a person does not accept and believe Him, then that individual will never get to know God. This was the case with the Pharisees.

No one has ever seen God; the only God, who is at the Father's side, he has made him known. (Jn.1:18)

"And the Father who sent me has himself borne witness about me. His voice you have never heard, his form you have never seen." (Jn.5:37)

"And they will do these things because they have not known the Father, nor me." (Jn.16:3)

He [Jesus Christ] is the image of the invisible God, the firstborn of all creation. (Col.1:15)

Who alone has immortality, who dwells in unapproachable light, whom no one has ever seen or can see. To him be honor and eternal dominion. Amen. (1 Ti.6:16)

"For my people are foolish; they know me not; they are stupid children; they have no understanding. They are 'wise'—in doing evil! But how to do good they know not." (Je.4:22)

God was in Christ (2 Co.5:19). If a person knows Christ, he or she knows the Father *also*. This is a phenomenal claim.

Christ said that He was the revelation of God; He was God incarnate, in human flesh. He was the "image of the invisible God" (Col.1:15). Therefore, the only way to know God is to know Christ (see note—Jn.14:6). And He is the One who instructs people in the truth of God (see note—Jn.3:32-34 for verses of Scripture).

Jesus said to him, "I am the way, and the truth, and the life. No one comes to the Father except through me." (Jn.14:6)

[The gospel] which has come to you, as indeed in the whole world it is bearing fruit and increasing—as it also does among you, since the day you heard it and understood the grace of God in truth. (Col.1:6)

For in him the whole fullness of deity dwells bodily. (Col.2:9)

# 7 The tragic conclusion—Jesus was rejected in the temple.

Tragically, Jesus was rejected in the temple. The truth that He revealed to the religious leaders had no effect on them. They wanted nothing to do with Jesus. They rejected and opposed Him, desiring to get rid of Him. But even though they rejected Jesus, they dared not arrest Him. They could not destroy Him, for *His hour* had not yet come. God protected Him.

[20] These words he spoke in the treasury, as he taught in the temple; but no one arrested him, because his hour had not yet come.

**THOUGHT 1.** How often this scene of unbelief among the Jewish authorities is repeated in the church. Down through the centuries many religious leaders have wanted nothing to do with Christ, choosing self over Him.

"Not everyone who says to me, 'Lord, Lord,' will enter the kingdom of heaven, but the one who does the will of my Father who is in heaven." (Mt.7:21)

And he said to them, "Well did Isaiah prophesy of you hypocrites, as it is written, 'This people honors me with their lips, but their heart is far from me.'" (Mk.7:6)

Having the appearance of godliness, but denying its power. Avoid such people. (2 Ti.3:5)

They profess to know God, but they deny him by their works. They are detestable, disobedient, unfit for any good work. (Tit.1:16)

## C. Humanity's Futile Search for Messiah: The Pursuit of Utopia, the Perfect World, 8:21-24

21 So he said to them again, "I am going away, and you will seek me, and you will die in your sin. Where I am going, you cannot come."

22 So the Jews said, "Will he kill himself, since he says, 'Where I am going, you cannot come'?"

23 He said to them, "You are from below; I am from above. You are of this world; I am not of this world.

24 "I told you that you would die in your sins, for unless you believe that I am he you will die in your sins."

1. **People search for a great deliverer for the earth**[DS1]
   a. They fail in their search & die in their sin
   b. They face a tragic end: Exclusion from heaven
   c. They mock the idea of Jesus' Messiahship

2. **People's futility & failure**
   a. Reason 1: They have a different origin & being than Christ[DS2]
   b. Reason 2: They sin & die in their sins because they do not believe in Christ

# Division IX

### *The Revelation of Jesus, the Light of Life, 8:1-9:41*

C. Humanity's Futile Search for Messiah: The Pursuit of Utopia, the Perfect World, 8:21-24

## 8:21-24
## Introduction

This discussion of Christ is brief, but it is also earthshaking. It is the message that desperately needs to be proclaimed to the world. People seek a great deliverer upon earth. They are looking for someone who can lead them to utopia and light and heaven. Their search is tragic, because the great Deliverer (Messiah) has already come and brought the presence of utopia to humanity (see DEEPER STUDY # 1). Therefore, their search for an earthly deliverer (Messiah), that is, for utopia, the perfect world, is futile. This is, *Humanity's Futile Search for Messiah: The Pursuit of Utopia, the Perfect World,* 8:21-24.

1. People search for a great deliverer for the earth (vv.21-22).
2. People's futility and failure (vv.23-24).

### 1 People search for a great deliverer for the earth.

8:21-22

The Jewish people were seeking the Messiah, their deliverer. Their Messiah—and the great deliverer of the earth—had come, but they rejected Him. Jesus announced that He was going away (v.21a). He meant He would be leaving the world through dying and returning to the Father. Then He announced the terrible fate of so many people, a fate so horrific it is the *tragedy of tragedies*.

21 So he said to them again, "I am going away, and you will seek me, and you will die in your sin. Where I am going, you cannot come."

22 So the Jews said, "Will he kill himself, since he says, 'Where I am going, you cannot come'?"

a. **They fail in their search and die in their sin (v.21b).**

Jesus warned the people: because they refused to believe in Him, they would fail in their search and die in their sin. People fail to find the only Savior, and consequently die in their sin. In the Greek, the word *sin* (hamartiai) is singular. It is speaking of the greatest sin, the sin that sends people to hell, the terrible sin of unbelief. So long as people continue to reject Jesus, they are in a state or position of unbelief. Eventually, they die in a state of unbelief. When they die, they go directly into eternity still in *sin*, still in the state, position, and condition of an unbeliever (see note—Ro.5:12-21).

> "Whoever believes in him is not condemned, but whoever does not believe is condemned already, because he has not believed in the name of the only Son of God." (Jn.3:18)
>
> For the wages of sin is death, but the free gift of God is eternal life in Christ Jesus our Lord. (Ro.6:23)
>
> And just as it is appointed for man to die once, and after that comes judgment. (He.9:27)
>
> "But as for the cowardly, the faithless, the detestable, as for murderers, the sexually immoral, sorcerers, idolaters, and all liars, their portion will be in the lake that burns with fire and sulfur, which is the second death." (Re.21:8.)

b. **They face a tragic end: Exclusion from heaven (v.21c).**

All who reject Christ as Savior face a tragic end. That tragic end is separation from where Christ is. Christ stated clearly that they cannot go to where He was going and where He is today: in heaven, at the Father's side. Since Christ is . . .

- the Light of the world, the unbeliever cannot enter the Light
- the Son of God, the unbeliever cannot enter the presence of God
- the Lord of heaven, the unbeliever cannot enter heaven

Every unbeliever is separated forever from the presence of God and Christ (see DEEPER STUDY # 1—He.9:27).

> "For I tell you, unless your righteousness exceeds that of the scribes and Pharisees, you will never enter the kingdom of heaven." (Mt.5:20)
>
> "And while they were going to buy, the bridegroom came, and those who were ready went in with him to the marriage feast, and the door was shut. Afterward the other virgins came also, saying, 'Lord, lord, open to us.' But he answered, 'Truly, I say to you, I do not know you.'" (Mt.25:10-12)
>
> "Truly, I say to you, whoever does not receive the kingdom of God like a child shall not enter it." (Mk.10:15)
>
> Or do you not know that the unrighteous will not inherit the kingdom of God? Do not be deceived: neither the sexually immoral, nor idolaters, nor adulterers, nor men who practice homosexuality. (1 Co.6:9)
>
> Now the works of the flesh are evident: sexual immorality, impurity, sensuality, idolatry, sorcery, enmity, strife, jealousy, fits of anger, rivalries, dissensions, divisions, envy, drunkenness, orgies, and things like these. I warn you, as I warned you before, that those who do such things will not inherit the kingdom of God. (Ga.5:19-21)
>
> For you may be sure of this, that everyone who is sexually immoral or impure, or who is covetous (that is, an idolater), has no inheritance in the kingdom of Christ and God. (Ep.5:5)

c. **They mock the idea of Jesus' Messiahship (v.22).**

The Jews mocked the idea of Jesus' Messiahship, questioning sarcastically if He was planning to commit suicide. Still today, people mock the idea of Jesus as Lord and Savior. They still think in terms of the physical world and the dimension of sight only. The Jews understood perfectly that Jesus was referring to death. They mocked Him: "You say you are going to kill yourself. We do not care to follow you."

**THOUGHT 1.** Just as they always have, multitudes fail to accept the truth that Jesus is the One sent from God, the only Savior of the world. They do not care to follow Christ in His death. They are unwilling to take up the cross and follow Him (see DEEPER STUDY # 1—Lu.9:23). They want the world and the things it has to offer, so they continue to seek for an earthly deliverer and the utopia and heaven that only Christ can give.

## Deeper Study #1

(8:21) **Utopia—Messiah—Heaven**: utopia would be the ideal world, a world of perfection, provision, possessions, comfort, protection, peace, and security. Utopia would be four things: freedom from all negative circumstances, freedom from sin and its bondages, freedom from death, and freedom from hell (see note—Ro.10:6-7). Humanity uses all the scientific technology and human wisdom available to relieve and escape the reality of all these and their results. They look everywhere for an escape except the one place where it is found: in Jesus Christ, God's Son.

## 2 People's futility and failure.

Any search for a deliverer that does not end with Jesus is futile and a failure. Jesus pointed out three reasons why people fail to find Him—the true Savior—and utopia.

> [23] He said to them, "You are from below; I am from above. You are of this world; I am not of this world.
> [24] I told you that you would die in your sins, for unless you believe that I am he you will die in your sins."

### a. Reason 1: They have a different origin and being than Christ (v.23).

People fail to believe in Christ because they have a different origin and being than Christ (See Deeper Study # 2). He is from heaven, but people are of this world. Consequently, people see things from an earthly perspective, and they desire the things of this world as opposed to heaven. In short, we are sinners.

> Since therefore the children share in flesh and blood, he himself likewise partook of the same things, that through death he might destroy the one who has the power of death, that is, the devil, and deliver all those who through fear of death were subject to lifelong slavery. (He.2:14-15)
>
> Therefore, just as sin came into the world through one man, and death through sin, and so death spread to all men because all sinned. (Ro.5:12)
>
> The first man [Adam] was from the earth, a man of dust; the second man is from heaven. As was the man of dust, so also are those who are of the dust, and as is the man of heaven, so also are those who are of heaven. (1 Co.15:47-48)
>
> For "All flesh is like grass and all its glory like the flower of grass. The grass withers, and the flower falls." (1 Pe.1:24)
>
> We have all become like one who is unclean, and all our righteous deeds are like a polluted garment. We all fade like a leaf, and our iniquities, like the wind, take us away. (Is.64:6)

### b. Reason 2: They sin and die in their sins because they do not believe in Christ (v.24).

People fail to find their deliverer because they refuse to believe in Christ. They do not believe that Jesus is God, the great *I Am* (see Deeper Study # 1—Jn.6:20; Deeper Study # 2—Jn.2:24). They will not believe that Jesus is the Son of God who came to earth, became a man, and died for the world's sin. Consequently, they die in their sins. Here, *sins* (hamartiais) is plural; that is, it refers to the various *acts of sin*. They die with their sins unforgiven; therefore, they must pay the penalty for their sins throughout eternity (Re.21:8).

> "Whoever believes in him is not condemned, but whoever does not believe is condemned already, because he has not believed in the name of the only Son of God." (Jn.3:18)
>
> Whoever believes in the Son has eternal life; whoever does not obey the Son shall not see life, but the wrath of God remains on him. (Jn.3:36)
>
> "I told you that you would die in your sins, for unless you believe that I am he you will die in your sins." (Jn.8:24)
>
> "But as for the cowardly, the faithless, the detestable, as for murderers, the sexually immoral, sorcerers, idolaters, and all liars, their portion will be in the lake that burns with fire and sulfur, which is the second death." (Re.21:8)

## DEEPER STUDY # 2

(8:23) **Jesus—Incarnation**: Jesus was born from above or from heaven; that is, He was born of God, as well as of Mary. Therefore, Jesus is not only Man, but He is also God. He is the God-Man. Think of it this way. A human is born of the earth, from beneath: he is born of his father and his mother. Both are of this earth, of human flesh only. Therefore, a man is only a man; he is only human flesh and blood just like his mother and father.

However, this is not true with Jesus. Jesus is Man, but He is also God. He is Man through the flesh of His mother, and He is the eternal Son of God by the miraculous act of the Holy Spirit through Mary. God incarnated His Son in human flesh and sent Him into the world through Mary (see Jn.8:12-59, esp. 14, 23, 42, 57-58; see also DEEPER STUDY # 3—Mt.1:16.)

This means something critical. The only messiah and utopia that people can find is of this world, of the physical dimension. Therefore, their messiah and utopia fail; they waste away, deteriorate, decay, and die. But not Christ and His utopia. He is "from heaven," from the spiritual world and eternal dimension. Therefore, He and His utopia last forever (see notes, *Corruption*—Mt.6:19-20; DEEPER STUDY # 2—8:17; DEEPER STUDY # 1—2 Pe.1:4).

### D. Humanity's Tragic Failure to Understand the Light, 8:25-30

25 So they said to him, "Who are you?" Jesus said to them, "Just what I have been telling you from the beginning.
26 "I have much to say about you and much to judge, but he who sent me is true, and I declare to the world what I have heard from him."
27 They did not understand that he had been speaking to them about the Father.
28 So Jesus said to them, "When you have lifted up the Son of Man, then you will know that I am he, and that I do nothing on my own authority, but speak just as the Father taught me.
29 "And he who sent me is with me. He has not left me alone, for I always do the things that are pleasing to him."

30 As he was saying these things, many believed in him.

1. People ask a very basic question: Who is Jesus?
2. People do not grasp that Jesus is God's Spokesman & Judge—the One who brought the message of the true God to the world

3. People do not grasp that Jesus is the Son of Man—the One who was to be lifted up
4. People do not grasp that Jesus is the great "I Am"—the Son of God Himself
5. People do not grasp that Jesus is the One whom God never left alone
   a. God sent & was with Jesus
   b. Jesus pleased God—always
6. The wonderful result of Jesus' message: Many believed

# Division IX

*The Revelation of Jesus, the Light of Life, 8:1-9:41*

D. Humanity's Tragic Failure to Understand the Light, 8:25-30

## 8:25-30
## Introduction

The eternal destiny of every person hinges on his or her understanding of who Jesus is. In John 8, our Lord is teaching us that He is the light of the world. Tragically, many in Jesus' day misunderstood who He is, as do so many still today. This is, *Humanity's Tragic Failure to Understand the Light*, 8:25-30.

1. People ask a very basic question: Who is Jesus? (v.25).
2. People do not grasp that Jesus is God's Spokesman and Judge—the One who brought the message of the true God to the world (vv.26-27).
3. People do not grasp that Jesus is the Son of Man—the One who was to be lifted up (v.28).
4. People do not grasp that Jesus is the great "I Am"—the Son of God Himself (v.28).
5. People do not grasp that Jesus is the One whom God never left alone (v.29).
6. The wonderful result of Jesus' message: Many believed (v.30).

## 1 People ask a very basic question: Who is Jesus?

Jesus had just made a phenomenal claim: "I am the Light of the world" (v.12). His claim and His explanation of the claim shocked the people. The reason is clear, for Jesus had declared . . .

**8:25**

$^{25}$ So they said to him, "Who are you?" Jesus said to them, "Just what I have been telling you from the beginning."

- that all who follow Him will not walk in darkness (v.12)
- that the Father worked with Him and sent Him (v.16)
- that they did not know Him or His Father (v.19)
- that He was from above, but they were of this world (v.23)
- that they would die in their sins if they did not believe (v.24)

People of every generation blurt out, just as the people of Jesus' generation did, "Who are you?" Jesus proclaimed the wonderful truth that He was who, what, and all He had claimed to be from the very beginning.

The Greek text of Jesus' words in this verse is quite difficult to translate into English. A glance at various translations and commentaries will give insight into other possible meanings.

**8:26-27**

$^{26}$ "I have much to say about you and much to judge, but he who sent me is true, and I declare to the world what I have heard from him."
$^{27}$ They did not understand that he had been speaking to them about the Father.

## 2 People do not grasp that Jesus is God's Spokesman and Judge— the One who brought the message of the true God to the world.

People do not grasp that Jesus is God's Spokesman and Judge. Jesus was the One who brought the message of God to the world. Jesus claimed to be God's Spokesman to the world, saying that the words He spoke were what He had *heard from God*. His message, His words were given Him by God the Father.

> "It is the Spirit who gives life; the flesh is no help at all. The words that I have spoken to you are spirit and life." (Jn.6:63)

> So Jesus answered them, "My teaching is not mine, but his who sent me. If anyone's will is to do God's will, he will know whether the teaching is from God or whether I am speaking on my own authority." (Jn.7:16-17)

> So Jesus said to them, "When you have lifted up the Son of Man, then you will know that I am he, and that I do nothing on my own authority, but speak just as the Father taught me." (Jn.8:28)

> "I speak of what I have seen with my Father, and you do what you have heard from your father." (Jn.8:38)

> "For I have not spoken on my own authority, but the Father who sent me has himself given me a commandment—what to say and what to speak. And I know that his commandment is eternal life. What I say, therefore, I say as the Father has told me." (Jn.12:49-50)

> "Do you not believe that I am in the Father and the Father is in me? The words that I say to you I do not speak on my own authority, but the Father who dwells in me does his works." (Jn.14:10)

Jesus was *sent* by God to speak the words of God. He was on earth for the very special mission of proclaiming the message of God. Jesus came from the very presence of God, from an intimate relationship with Him. It was God the Father Himself who appointed and sent His Son, Jesus into the world. Jesus assured us that God's message is *true*. It is not false nor evil, not a lie nor a deception. We can trust and depend upon it.

Jesus was sent to the *world*. His message is for the whole world, and His message is the only message for the world.

> For he whom God has sent utters the words of God, for he gives the Spirit without measure. (Jn.3:34)

> Simon Peter answered him, "Lord, to whom shall we go? You have the words of eternal life." (Jn.6:68)

> "Whoever does not love me does not keep my words. And the word that you hear is not mine but the Father's who sent me." (Jn.14:24)

> "For I have given them the words that you gave me, and they have received them and have come to know in truth that I came from you; and they have believed that you sent me." (Jn.17:8)

In addition, Jesus claimed to be the Judge of the world. As the Spokesman of God, He had the duty not only to say many things but also to judge many things. His function as Spokesman included judgment.

Jesus' first mission to earth was to proclaim the message of salvation. His second mission to earth will be to judge all people. The people did not understand this truth when Jesus taught it, and people still do not understand it today.

> "For the Father judges no one, but has given all judgment to the Son." (Jn.5:22)

> "And he commanded us to preach to the people and to testify that he is the one appointed by God to be judge of the living and the dead." (Ac.10:42)

> "Because he has fixed a day on which he will judge the world in righteousness by a man whom he has appointed; and of this he has given assurance to all by raising him from the dead." (Ac.17:31)

> On that day when, according to my gospel, God judges the secrets of men by Christ Jesus. (Ro.2:16)

## 3 People do not grasp that Jesus is the Son of Man—the One who was to be lifted up.

People do not grasp that Jesus is the Son of Man. He referred to Himself by this title when saying that He would be *lifted up*. This is a definite reference to the cross and exaltation of Christ. The people would lift Jesus up on the cross, but in the end, God would lift Him up as Lord of all. It is as the Son of Man, as the Perfect and Ideal Man, that Jesus was able to die for humanity (see notes—Jn.1:51; Jn.12:31-33 for discussion of this point).

> 28 So Jesus said to them, "When you have lifted up the Son of Man, then you will know that I am he, and that I do nothing on my own authority, but speak just as the Father taught me."

## 4 People do not grasp that Jesus is the great "I Am"—the Son of God Himself.

In addition, people do not grasp that Jesus is the great "I Am," the Son of God Himself (see DEEPER STUDY # 1 —Jn.6:20). Jesus said specifically that it was His being lifted up—the cross and the resurrection and the ascension—that would convince people that He is the great "I Am." It is the message of the cross that awakens people to the glorious love and salvation of God.

> "For God so loved the world, that he gave his only Son, that whoever believes in him should not perish but have eternal life." (Jn.3:16)

> But God shows his love for us in that while we were still sinners, Christ died for us. (Ro.5:8)

> For the love of Christ controls us, because we have concluded this: that one has died for all, therefore all have died; and he died for all, that those who live might no longer live for themselves but for him who for their sake died and was raised. (2 Co.5:14-15)

The cross proves that Jesus . . .
- is the great *"I Am"*: deity, God Himself incarnate in human flesh (see DEEPER STUDY # 1—Jn.6:20; notes—8:12-13; 8:54-59)
- is *One with God*: does not act alone—does nothing of Himself (see note—Jn.8:15-16 for discussion and verses of Scripture)
- is *the Spokesman of God*: speaks only as His Father taught Him (see note—Jn.3:32-34 for discussion and verses of Scripture)

The resurrection declares Jesus to be the Son of God with power.

> And was declared to be the Son of God in power according to the Spirit of holiness by his resurrection from the dead, Jesus Christ our Lord. (Ro.1:4)

The ascension allowed the Holy Spirit to replace Christ on earth. It brought about the *pouring out* of the Spirit and His convicting power.

> On the last day of the feast, the great day, Jesus stood up and cried out, "If anyone thirsts, let him come to me and drink. Whoever believes in me, as the Scripture has said, 'Out of his heart will flow rivers of living water.'" Now this he said about the Spirit, whom those who believed in him were to receive, for as yet the Spirit had not been given, because Jesus was not yet glorified. (Jn.7:37-39)

> "Nevertheless, I tell you the truth: it is to your advantage that I go away, for if I do not go away, the Helper will not come to you. But if I go, I will send him to you. And when he comes, he will convict the world concerning sin and righteousness and judgment: concerning sin, because they do not believe in me; concerning righteousness, because I go to the Father, and you will see me no longer; concerning judgment, because the ruler of this world is judged." (Jn.16:7-11)

## 8:29

²⁹ "And he who sent me is with me. He has not left me alone, for I always do the things that are pleasing to him."

### 5 People do not grasp that Jesus is the One whom God never left alone.

People do not grasp that Jesus is the One whom God never left alone. This is a critical truth. In revealing it, Jesus made two powerful claims.

**a. God sent and was with Jesus.**

Jesus claimed that His Father had sent Him (see DEEPER STUDY # 3—Jn.3:34 for discussion and verses of Scripture). Along with this claim, He claimed that His Father was with Him and had never left Him alone. The idea and claim is that His Father had never abandoned Him; therefore, what Jesus said and did was always the message of God to humanity.

> "If I am not doing the works of my Father, then do not believe me; but if I do them, even though you do not believe me, believe the works, that you may know and understand that the Father is in me and I am in the Father." (Jn.10:37-38)

> Jesus said to him, "Have I been with you so long, and you still do not know me, Philip? Whoever has seen me has seen the Father. How can you say, 'Show us the Father'? Do you not believe that I am in the Father and the Father is in me? The words that I say to you I do not speak on my own authority, but the Father who dwells in me does his works. Believe me that I am in the Father and the Father is in me, or else believe on account of the works themselves." (Jn.14:9-11)

**b. Jesus pleased God—always.**

Jesus proceeded to claim that He had not failed. He always did the things God said; He obeyed God perfectly and completely, never sinning. People could trust and depend on Him.

> For our sake he made him to be sin who knew no sin, so that in him we might become the righteousness of God. (2 Co.5:21)

> For it was fitting that he, for whom and by whom all things exist, in bringing many sons to glory, should make the founder of their salvation perfect through suffering. (He.2:10)

> Although he was a son, he learned obedience through what he suffered. And being made perfect, he became the source of eternal salvation to all who obey him. (He.5:8-9)

## 8:30

³⁰ As he was saying these things, many believed in him.

### 6 The wonderful result of Jesus' message: Many believed.

The glorious result of Jesus' powerful teaching was that many believed (see DEEPER STUDY # 2—Jn.2:24). They became convinced that Jesus was all He claimed to be:
- ➢ the Light of the world
- ➢ the Spokesman and Judge of God
- ➢ the Son of Man
- ➢ the "I Am," the Son of God Himself
- ➢ the One whom God never left alone

"For God so loved the world, that he gave his only Son, that whoever believes in him should not perish but have eternal life." (Jn.3:16)

"Truly, truly, I say to you, whoever hears my word and believes him who sent me has eternal life. He does not come into judgment, but has passed from death to life." (Jn.5:24)

But these are written so that you may believe that Jesus is the Christ, the Son of God, and that by believing you may have life in his name. (Jn.20:31)

Because, if you confess with your mouth that Jesus is Lord and believe in your heart that God raised him from the dead, you will be saved. For with the heart one believes and is justified, and with the mouth one confesses and is saved. (Ro.10:9-10)

## E. Humanity's Freedom from Sin: Being Liberated Is Conditional, 8:31-32

1. The conditions: Believing & abiding

2. The results
   a. Will know the truth[DS1]
   b. Will be set free

<sup>31</sup> So Jesus said to the Jews who had believed him, "If you abide in my word, you are truly my disciples,
<sup>32</sup> and you will know the truth, and the truth will set you free."

# Division IX
## The Revelation of Jesus, the Light of Life, 8:1–9:41

E. Humanity's Freedom from Sin: Being Liberated Is Conditional, 8:31-32

### 8:31-32
### Introduction

Every human being is enslaved by sin and all its consequences. People cannot keep from sinning; therefore, they bear the consequences of sin: guilt, shame, hurt, pain, sorrow, suffering, destruction, devastation, brokenness, death, and judgment. We need to be freed from sin, set loose and delivered from its enslaving tentacles. We can be freed, but our freedom from sin depends on our meeting God's conditions. This is, *Humanity's Freedom from Sin: Being Liberated Is Conditional*, 8:31-32.
1. The conditions: Believing and abiding (v.31).
2. The results (v.32).

**8:31**

<sup>31</sup> So Jesus said to the Jews who had believed him, "If you abide in my word, you are truly my disciples,"

### 1 The conditions: Believing and abiding.

Christ presented two conditions for being delivered from sin. The first condition is belief. The people to whom Jesus spoke had believed in Him. As the gospel was proclaimed, they listened. They did not slumber, nor sleep, nor allow their minds to wander. They allowed no distraction whatsoever. They heard and believed in Christ; therefore, their hearts were stirred. As a result they sensed . . .
- a need, a lack, an emptiness
- a hunger, a thirst, a desire
- a darkness, a sin, a pollution
- a guilt, a shame, an ugliness
- an hope, a tug, a pull

Their hearts reached out for Jesus, and they experienced the *beginning* and the *infancy* of faith. They were as lambs or as newborn infants in Christ (see Jn.3:3; 1 Pe.2:2-3).

The point is this: the *very first* condition of deliverance from sin is belief. It is by believing in Christ that we are saved (see Deeper Study # 2—Jn.2:24).

"That whoever believes in him may have eternal life. For God so loved the world, that he gave his only Son, that whoever believes in him should not perish but have eternal life." (Jn.3:15-16)

"Truly, truly, I say to you, whoever hears my word and believes him who sent me has eternal life. He does not come into judgment, but has passed from death to life." (Jn.5:24)

> But these are written so that you may believe that Jesus is the Christ, the Son of God, and that by believing you may have life in his name. (Jn.20:31)
>
> "To him all the prophets bear witness that everyone who believes in him receives forgiveness of sins through his name." (Ac.10:43)
>
> And they said, "Believe in the Lord Jesus, and you will be saved, you and your household." (Ac.16:31)
>
> Everyone who believes that Jesus is the Christ has been born of God, and everyone who loves the Father loves whoever has been born of him. (1 Jn.5:1)

However, there is a second condition—a condition that effectively completes the experience of deliverance. It is that of *abiding* or *continuing* (Gk. meinete) in the Lord's Word. The idea is that of *dwelling*, just as a person dwells at home. The Word of the Lord is the believers' dwelling place. They continue to *abide* in God's Word.

Practically speaking, it is the Word of God that washes sin out of our lives:

> "Already you are clean because of the word that I have spoken to you." (Jn.15:3)
>
> "Sanctify them in the truth; your word is truth." (Jn.17:17)
>
> That he might sanctify her, having cleansed her by the washing of water with the word. (Ep.5:26)
>
> How can a young man keep his way pure? By guarding it according to your word. (Ps.119:9)

A believer who does not abide in the Word will never gain victory over sin, not in their daily lives. A believer who does not *continue* to abide in the Word will eventually fall back into sin. In either case, if a person is a genuine believer—has been truly born again, he or she will be unfruitful and will be chastened or disciplined by God (Jn.15:6).

> "Abide in me, and I in you. As the branch cannot bear fruit by itself, unless it abides in the vine, neither can you, unless you abide in me. I am the vine; you are the branches. Whoever abides in me and I in him, he it is that bears much fruit, for apart from me you can do nothing. If anyone does not abide in me he is thrown away like a branch and withers; and the branches are gathered, thrown into the fire, and burned." (Jn.15:4-6)
>
> "If you keep my commandments, you will abide in my love, just as I have kept my Father's commandments and abide in his love." (Jn.15:10)
>
> You therefore, beloved, knowing this beforehand, take care that you are not carried away with the error of lawless people and lose your own stability. (2 Pe.3:17)
>
> Whoever says he abides in him ought to walk in the same way in which he walked. (1 Jn.2:6)
>
> And now, little children, abide in him, so that when he appears we may have confidence and not shrink from him in shame at his coming. (1 Jn.2:28)

(See note, *Abiding*—Jn.6:56 for more discussion; also see outline and notes—Jn.15:1-8 for more discussion.)

## 2 The results.

> 32 "and you will know the truth, and the truth will set you free."

There are two results of abiding in the Word. These results assure the believer's complete deliverance from sin, that you are delivered not only from sin's penalty but also from its daily power in your life.

### a. Will know the truth.

The first result is that the true believer will know the truth (see Deeper Study # 1; see also Deeper Study # 1—Jn.1:9; Deeper Study # 2—14:6 for discussion). You must know the truth—what God says—about sin. We live in a world that does not know the truth and denies the truth of God's Word regarding sin. Our godless society calls evil good and good evil (Is.5:20). The world refuses to admit that some acts are actually sins. Tragically, even some denominations and churches are guilty of this. But the fact remains: you cannot be delivered from sin in your life until you know the truth about sin. God's Word teaches us this truth.

### b. Will be set free.

The second result is that the believer will be set free from sin's power over their life (see DEEPER STUDY # 1; notes—2 Co.3:17-18; Ep.2:8, pt.4g for discussion). Again, it is the truth that sets us free. The truth of God's Word performs its powerful cleansing work in our lives, delivering us completely from the sin that has held us in bondage.

**THOUGHT 1.** The truth of Christ is the answer to setting humanity and its world free, free from all the...

- prejudice and hate
- division and isolation
- hatred and bitterness
- hostility and war
- assault and killing
- hunger and sickness
- crime and injustice enslavements and abuses
- emptiness and loneliness
- fear and death
- selfishness and hoarding

### DEEPER STUDY # 1

(8:32) **Truth** (aletheia): moral truth, saving truth, working truth, living truth. Truth is not simply something to be *known*; it is something to be *done* (Jn.8:31), the knowledge and the experience of true reality as opposed to false reality. It is truth in "the inward parts" or the "inward being" (see Ps.51:6; Ep.5:9). Truth is diametrically opposed to sham and hypocrisy and permits no compromise with evil. It even abstains from the appearance of evil (1 Th.5:22). It is a regard for truth in every respect: believing it, reverencing it, speaking it, acting it, hoping in it, and rejoicing in it. Such truthful behavior frees a person from all the bondages and impediments of life (see DEEPER STUDY # 1—Jn.1:9; DEEPER STUDY # 2—14:6).

> So Jesus answered them, "My teaching is not mine, but his who sent me. If anyone's will is to do God's will, he will know whether the teaching is from God or whether I am speaking on my own authority." (Jn.7:16-17)
>
> So Jesus said to the Jews who had believed him, "If you abide in my word, you are truly my disciples, and you will know the truth, and the truth will set you free." (Jn.8:31-32)
>
> That I may know him and the power of his resurrection, and may share his sufferings, becoming like him in his death. (Ph.3:10)
>
> So as to walk in a manner worthy of the Lord, fully pleasing to him: bearing fruit in every good work and increasing in the knowledge of God. (Col.1:10)
>
> "Let us know; let us press on to know the LORD; his going out is sure as the dawn; he will come to us as the showers, as the spring rains that water the earth." (Ho.6:3)

God's Word is said to be the Truth (Jn.17:17), and Jesus Christ Himself claimed to be the Truth (Jn.14:6). To distinguish between the two, God's Word is sometimes said to be the *Written Truth*, and Jesus Christ is sometimes said to be the *Living Truth*.

1. The truth sets us free from the shadow of doubt and despair. We no longer have to grasp and grope about to know the truth, whether it be the truth of God or of the world. Jesus Christ has revealed the truth: the nature, the meaning, and the destiny of all things.

> The true light, which gives light to everyone, was coming into the world.... And the Word became flesh and dwelt among us, and we have seen his glory, glory as of the only Son from the Father, full of grace and truth. (Jn.1:9, 14)
>
> Now the Lord is the Spirit, and where the Spirit of the Lord is, there is freedom. (2 Co.3:17)

2. The truth sets us free from the bondages of sin. We no longer have to grasp after the power to overcome; nor do we have to struggle against the weight of guilt. The search for deliverance and for the power to conquer, to overcome, to attain, and to live is now over. It is all found in Jesus Christ (see Ro.6:1f. See note—Ro.8:28-39).

> But to all who did receive him, who believed in his name, he gave the right to become children of God. (Jn.1:12)

> Jesus said to him, "I am the way, and the truth, and the life. No one comes to the Father except through me." (Jn.14:6)

> But I see in my members another law waging war against the law of my mind and making me captive to the law of sin that dwells in my members. Wretched man that I am! Who will deliver me from this body of death? Thanks be to God through Jesus Christ our Lord! So then, I myself serve the law of God with my mind, but with my flesh I serve the law of sin. (Ro.7:23-25)

> For to set the mind on the flesh is death, but to set the mind on the Spirit is life and peace.... For you did not receive the spirit of slavery to fall back into fear, but you have received the Spirit of adoption as sons, by whom we cry, "Abba! Father!" (Ro.8:6, 15)

3. The truth sets us free from the bondage of death. We no longer have to be subjected to the fear of death. Jesus Christ—by His death and resurrection—has already conquered death (He.2:14-15). In His death and resurrection we now have the most glorious of hopes: we can now live eternally.

> "Truly, truly, I say to you, whoever hears my word and believes him who sent me has eternal life. He does not come into judgment, but has passed from death to life. Truly, truly, I say to you, an hour is coming, and is now here, when the dead will hear the voice of the Son of God, and those who hear will live. For as the Father has life in himself, so he has granted the Son also to have life in himself. And he has given him authority to execute judgment, because he is the Son of Man. Do not marvel at this, for an hour is coming when all who are in the tombs will hear his voice and come out, those who have done good to the resurrection of life, and those who have done evil to the resurrection of judgment." (Jn.5:24-29)

> For the law of the Spirit of life has set you free in Christ Jesus from the law of sin and death. (Ro.8:2)

> Since therefore the children share in flesh and blood, he himself likewise partook of the same things, that through death he might destroy the one who has the power of death, that is, the devil, and deliver all those who through fear of death were subject to lifelong slavery. (He.2:14-15)

4. The truth sets us free from the bondage of judgment and hell. The darkness of an unknown future and the apprehension of an impending judgment constantly face sinful people. At best, they can only hope for annihilation, and they shudder at the thought. At worst, they can expect torture by whatever gods they believe in, and they tremble at the possibility. But Jesus Christ has revealed the truth. He Himself has borne the judgment and the punishment of judgment for sinful humanity.

> "For God so loved the world, that he gave his only Son, that whoever believes in him should not perish but have eternal life." (Jn.3:16)

> For while we were still weak, at the right time Christ died for the ungodly.... But God shows his love for us in that while we were still sinners, Christ died for us. Since, therefore, we have now been justified by his blood, much more shall we be saved by him from the wrath of God. (Ro.5:6, 8-9)

> He himself bore our sins in his body on the tree, that we might die to sin and live to righteousness. By his wounds you have been healed. (1 Pe.2:24)

> For Christ also suffered once for sins, the righteous for the unrighteous, that he might bring us to God, being put to death in the flesh but made alive in the spirit. (1 Pe.3:18)

5. The truth sets people free to be saved to the uttermost. Existence, love, joy, peace, satisfaction, pleasure, hope—nothing has to be incomplete any longer. No good thing ever again has to be denied from us. Jesus Christ, the Truth, is able to save us to the uttermost—completely, perfectly, finally, and eternally. All we have to do is to come to Christ for salvation, for Christ lives forever to intercede for every person.

> But the fruit of the Spirit is love, joy, peace, patience, kindness, goodness, faithfulness, gentleness, self-control; against such things there is no law. (Ga.5:22-23)

> For in him the whole fullness of deity dwells bodily, and you have been filled in him, who is the head of all rule and authority. (Col.2:9-10)

> Consequently, he is able to save to the uttermost those who draw near to God through him, since he always lives to make intercession for them. (He.7:25)

## F. Humanity's Enslavement to Sin: Four Proofs 8:33-40

1. **People's denial: They claim a godly heritage & deny that they are enslaved or loyal to anyone other than God**

2. **Jesus' first proof: You are enslaved to sin**
   a. The proof: You sin often
   b. The warning: You—a slave to sin—are not guaranteed a place in the family (of God)
      1) The son, however, is

      2) The Son (Christ) can set you free from sin

3. **Jesus' second proof: People oppose & make no room in their hearts for the Lord's Word**

4. **Jesus' third proof: People follow the wrong father, the devil**[DS1]

5. **Jesus' fourth proof: People fail to do the works of Abraham**

   a. Abraham did not seek to kill the messengers of truth
   b. Abraham did the opposite: He believed the truth

<sup></sup>33 They answered him, "We are offspring of Abraham and have never been enslaved to anyone. How is it that you say, 'You will become free'?"
34 Jesus answered them, "Truly, truly, I say to you, everyone who practices sin is a slave to sin.
35 The slave does not remain in the house forever; the son remains forever.
36 So if the Son sets you free, you will be free indeed.
37 I know that you are offspring of Abraham; yet you seek to kill me because my word finds no place in you.
38 I speak of what I have seen with my Father, and you do what you have heard from your father."
39 They answered him, "Abraham is our father." Jesus said to them, "If you were Abraham's children, you would be doing the works Abraham did,
40 but now you seek to kill me, a man who has told you the truth that I heard from God. This is not what Abraham did."

# Division IX

*The Revelation of Jesus, the Light of Life, 8:1–9:41*

F. Humanity's Enslavement to Sin: Four Proofs, 8:33–40

## 8:33–40
## Introduction

Every human being is enslaved by sin. Many deny it, but it does not change the fact that they are. Personal experience, greed, lust, selfish behavior, and world history bear evidence. Any honest person can clearly see the evidence. This is, *Humanity's Enslavement to Sin, Four Proofs*, 8:33–40.

1. People's denial: They claim a godly heritage & deny that they are enslaved or loyal to anyone other than God (v.33).
2. Jesus' first proof: You are enslaved to sin (vv.34–36).
3. Jesus' second proof: People oppose and make no room in their hearts for the Lord's Word (v.37).
4. Jesus' third proof: People follow the wrong father, the devil (v.38).
5. Jesus' fourth proof: People fail to do the works of Abraham (vv.39–40).

## 1 People's denial: they claim a godly heritage and deny that they are enslaved or loyal to anyone other than God.

People deny that they are enslaved by sin. The Jews misunderstood Jesus in regard to this truth. They thought He was referring to being conquered and enslaved by a foreign nation. They denied such. They had, of course, been conquered by many nations and were in fact being ruled by the Romans at that very time. What they meant by not ever being enslaved is that they had never surrendered their will to any ruler. They had always given their allegiance to God, not to men, no matter how powerful the men were.

> ³³ They answered him, "We are offspring of Abraham and have never been enslaved to anyone. How is it that you say, 'You will become free'?"

8:33

However, Jesus meant something entirely different. Jesus meant that the Jews and all other people groups were enslaved by sin. They could not help sinning no matter how much they tried not to sin.

Like the Jews, many people deny being enslaved by sin. They claim a godly heritage and believe it makes them acceptable to God. The Jews claimed they were the *offspring* or *descendants* of Abraham, the children of one of the godliest men who ever lived. They felt, therefore, that Abraham's godliness and the godliness of those who followed him made their nation and its people very special to God. They felt they were acceptable to God no matter how they lived. They believed that every true Jew was covered by the godliness of their forefathers (see DEEPER STUDY # 1—Jn.4:22).

Many people believe the same thing today. They deny being so enslaved by sin that they are unacceptable to God. They believe that God will accept them, that they have enough *good heritage* to receive God's approval. They feel they have not done enough bad to be enslaved to sin nor to be rejected by God. In their minds, their heritage—their parents, their family, their friends, their good works, something in their lives—is good enough to keep them from being enslaved and doomed.

> **"Bear fruits in keeping with repentance. And do not begin to say to yourselves, 'We have Abraham as our father.' For I tell you, God is able from these stones to raise up children for Abraham." (Lu.3:8)**
>
> **And they reviled him, saying, "You are his disciple, but we are disciples of Moses." (Jn.9:28)**
>
> **And if you are sure that you yourself are a guide to the blind, a light to those who are in darkness. (Ro.2:19)**
>
> **Many a man proclaims his own steadfast love, but a faithful man who can find? (Pr.20:6)**
>
> **Every way of a man is right in his own eyes, but the LORD weighs the heart. (Pr.21:2)**
>
> **There are those who are clean in their own eyes but are not washed of their filth. (Pr.30:12)**

## 2 Jesus' first proof: You are enslaved to sin.

8:34–36

The first proof that we are enslaved to sin is undeniable—we commit sin on a regular basis. We are slaves to sin.

> ³⁴ Jesus answered them, "Truly, truly, I say to you, everyone who practices sin is a slave to sin.
> ³⁵ The slave does not remain in the house forever; the son remains forever.
> ³⁶ So if the Son sets you free, you will be free indeed."

a. The proof: You sin often (v.34).

The word *practices* or *commits* (Gk. poion) is continuous action. We continue to commit sin. It is our natural habit, our practice, to sin. Humans cannot keep from sinning; therefore, they are slaves to sin. The word *slave* (doulos) speaks of the bond-slave (see note—Ro.1:1). The bond-slave was purchased and bound to the person who bought him. The idea is that sinful humanity is *bought* by sin. When people sin, they are giving themselves over to sin. They become enslaved to sin; they are sinners forever: in a *condition*, a *state*, a *being of sin*. Very simply, they are unable to keep from sinning, no matter how hard they try.

b. The warning: You—a slave to sin—are not guaranteed a place in the family (of God) (vv.35-36).

Jesus warned His audience. A slave is not a permanent member of a family, but the Son is (v.35). The slave has no rights and no claims to privileges within the family. He is a slave and can be rejected and cast out of the house anytime, but not the Son. The Son is always the Son. He has all the rights and privileges to the house. However, there is a way the slave can become a member of the house. The Son can free the slave and ask the Father to adopt him, and if the Son makes the slave free, the slave is free indeed (v.36).

In these verses, Jesus makes four significant claims:

➢ He, Jesus Christ, is the Son of God.

> "For God so loved the world, that he gave his only Son, that whoever believes in him should not perish but have eternal life." (Jn.3:16; see vv.17-18)

> Jesus heard that they had cast him out, and having found him he said, "Do you believe in the Son of Man?" He answered, "And who is he, sir, that I may believe in him?" Jesus said to him, "You have seen him, and it is he who is speaking to you." (Jn.9:35-37)

> "Do you say of him whom the Father consecrated and sent into the world, 'You are blaspheming,' because I said, 'I am the Son of God'?" (Jn.10:36)

➢ We are all in slavery to sin.

> Jesus answered them, "Truly, truly, I say to you, everyone who practices sin is a slave to sin." (Jn.8:34)

> For all have sinned and fall short of the glory of God. (Ro.3:23)

> Do you not know that if you present yourselves to anyone as obedient slaves, you are slaves of the one whom you obey, either of sin, which leads to death, or of obedience, which leads to righteousness? (Ro.6:16)

> For we know that the law is spiritual, but I am of the flesh, sold under sin. (Ro.7:14)

> But I see in my members another law waging war against the law of my mind and making me captive to the law of sin that dwells in my members. (Ro.7:23)

➢ He, Jesus Christ, can free us.

> "And you will know the truth [Jesus Christ], and the truth will set you free." (Jn.8:32; see Jn.14:6)

> And, having been set free from sin, have become slaves of righteousness. (Ro.6:18)

> For the law of the Spirit of life has set you free in Christ Jesus from the law of sin and death. (Ro.8:2)

> Now the Lord is the Spirit, and where the Spirit of the Lord is, there is freedom. (2 Co.3:17)

> For freedom Christ has set us free; stand firm therefore, and do not submit again to a yoke of slavery. (Ga.5:1)

➢ We can be adopted into God's family.

> But to all who did receive him [Jesus Christ], who believed in his name, he gave the right to become children of God. (Jn.1:12)

> For all who are led by the Spirit of God are sons of God. (Ro.8:14)

> "Therefore go out from their midst, and be separate from them, says the Lord, and touch no unclean thing; then I will welcome you, and I will be a father to you, and you shall be sons and daughters to me, says the Lord Almighty." (2 Co.6:17-18)

> But when the fullness of time had come, God sent forth his Son, born of woman, born under the law, to redeem those who were under the law, so that we might receive adoption as sons. And because you are sons, God has sent the Spirit of his Son into our hearts, crying, "Abba! Father!" (Ga.4:4-6)

8:37

⁳⁷ "I know that you are offspring of Abraham; yet you seek to kill me because my word finds no place in you."

## 3 Jesus' second proof: People oppose and make no room in their hearts for the Lord's Word.

The second proof that humanity is enslaved by sin is that people oppose and make no room in their hearts for Jesus' Word. People reject and oppose Christ. They reject the claims of Christ upon their lives; they refuse to deny themselves and take up the cross as Christ demanded (see Deeper Study # 1—Lu.9:23). They do not want the claims of Christ to control their lives; they want to do their own thing and to live as they please. Therefore, they reject Christ and go about fulfilling their own desires, securing or taking whatever they want. Whenever possible, they ridicule and speak against Christ and those who follow Christ. Very simply, sinful humanity wants little if anything to do with Christ; they want Christ to have little if any authority in their lives. Therefore, they make no room in their heart for Jesus' Word (see note, pt.2—Jn.8:31 for discussion).

> "Thus making void the word of God by your tradition that you have handed down. And many such things you do." (Mk.7:13)
>
> "The one who rejects me and does not receive my words has a judge; the word that I have spoken will judge him on the last day." (Jn.12:48)
>
> "Whoever does not love me does not keep my words. And the word that you hear is not mine but the Father's who sent me." (Jn.14:24)
>
> Therefore, as the tongue of fire devours the stubble, and as dry grass sinks down in the flame, so their root will be as rottenness, and their blossom go up like dust; for they have rejected the law of the LORD of hosts, and have despised the word of the Holy One of Israel. (Is.5:24)
>
> To whom shall I speak and give warning, that they may hear? Behold, their ears are uncircumcised, they cannot listen; behold, the word of the LORD is to them an object of scorn; they take no pleasure in it. (Je.6:10)
>
> They made their hearts diamond-hard lest they should hear the law and the words that the LORD of hosts had sent by his Spirit through the former prophets. Therefore great anger came from the LORD of hosts. (Zec.7:12)

## 4 Jesus' third proof: People follow the wrong father, the devil.

38 "I speak of what I have seen with my Father, and you do what you have heard from your father."

The third proof that humanity is enslaved by sin is that they follow the wrong father, the devil (see v.44). Jesus makes a strong contrast here between the Father of Christ and the father of mankind, the devil (see DEEPER STUDY # 1—Re.12:9).

What Christ speaks is what He has seen *with* or *in the presence of* His Father. *With* (para) means by the side of. What Christ saw came from the very side of the Father. Christ was from the very presence of God, so what He spoke was God's Word. His message was the Word of God Himself. What was His message?

- ➢ We must believe in Him (v.31).
- ➢ We must abide in His Word (v.31).
- ➢ We are enslaved by sin (v.34).
- ➢ We can be freed and adopted as God's children by the eternal Son (vv.35-36).

In sharp contrast to Christ, we do what we see and hear with our father (see DEEPER STUDY # 1). Christ identifies the father of humanity as the devil (v.44). Humans, walking in sin, are by the very side of the devil (by the side of the devil's place, domain, rule, and reign). So much of what we naturally do is, therefore, of the devil. What are the deeds of the devil that people do? Both people and their father (the devil) . . .

- lust (see Ro.12:1-2; 2 Co.6:17-18;1 Jn.2:15-16)
- murder (see Mt.5:21-22)
- fail to abide in the truth (See DEEPER STUDY # 1—Jn.8:32.)
- believe, live, and speak a lie. As a whole, humanity lives and talks about a life that is a lie, that is not permanent and lasting nor sure and secure

No individual is free of these deeds of the devil. We are all enslaved by sin, desperately needing to be set free. (Just think! If sinful humanity were freed of these devilish deeds, what a different world this would be!)

## Deeper Study #1

**(8:38) Unbelievers**: all people who practice unrighteousness have not been born of God. They are said to be children of Satan (1 Jn.3:8-10).

> "The field is the world, and the good seed is the sons of the kingdom. The weeds are the sons of the evil one." (Mt.13:38)

> "You are of your father the devil, and your will is to do your father's desires. He was a murderer from the beginning, and does not stand in the truth, because there is no truth in him. When he lies, he speaks out of his own character, for he is a liar and the father of lies." (Jn.8:44)

> And said, "You son of the devil, you enemy of all righteousness, full of all deceit and villainy, will you not stop making crooked the straight paths of the Lord?" (Ac.13:10)

> In which you once walked, following the course of this world, following the prince of the power of the air [the devil], the spirit that is now at work in the sons of disobedience. (Ep.2:2)

> By this it is evident who are the children of God, and who are the children of the devil: whoever does not practice righteousness is not of God, nor is the one who does not love his brother. (1 Jn.3:10)

### 8:39-40

<sup>39</sup> They answered him, "Abraham is our father." Jesus said to them, "If you were Abraham's children, you would be doing the works Abraham did,
<sup>40</sup> but now you seek to kill me, a man who has told you the truth that I heard from God. This is not what Abraham did."

## 5 Jesus' fourth proof: People fail to do the works of Abraham.

The fourth proof that humanity is enslaved by sin is that we fail to do the works of Abraham. It is critical that we grasp the meaning of Christ's statement in verse 39.

To paraphrase a portion of verse 39, the Jews cried out, " 'Abraham is our father' (v.39a). Our father was a good man, a man of great goodness. And our people have done *enough good* through the years for us to claim God as our Father. Our father is certainly God, not someone else."

Few people would ever say the devil is their father. To most people such an idea is preposterous, even repulsive. It stirs emotions ranging from mild amusement to anger. Many feel that too much good is done upon earth for the devil to be called the father of the world or of humanity.

Jesus' reply to the Jews was simply logical. "If you were Abraham's children," Jesus reasoned, "you would do the same works Abraham did" (v.39b). The Lord proceeded to mention two specific works:

a. **Abraham did not seek to kill the messengers of truth (v.40a).**

The Jewish leaders were seeking to kill Jesus because He spoke the truth. In contrast, Abraham did not attempt to kill the messengers of truth. He did not oppose the messengers of the truth, but received and accepted the truth whenever a messenger crossed his path. However, many of the people were set on getting rid of Jesus.

b. **Abraham did the opposite: He believed the truth (v.40b).**

Abraham believed God and the truth of God (see outlines and Deeper Study # 1—Ro.4:1-25). Abraham would have recognized Jesus as the Messiah, and He would have believed that what He spoke was the truth.

Grasp the point Jesus was making: a person cannot claim the goodness of others for themselves. If a person is truly a child of Abraham's faith, that is, of God . . .

- they will do the works of Abraham (believe and diligently seek God, continuing in the truth; see note—Jn.8:31)
- they will not do the works of the devil (see Jn.8:44)

**Thought 1.** The true children of God are people who do the works of the Lord.
(1) They hear and receive the truth.

And the Word became flesh and dwelt among us, and we have seen his glory, glory as of the only Son from the Father, full of grace and truth. (Jn.1:14)

Jesus said to him, "I am the way, and the truth, and the life. No one comes to the Father except through me." (Jn.14:6)

Then Pilate said to him, "So you are a king?" Jesus answered, "You say that I am a king. For this purpose I was born and for this purpose I have come into the world—to bear witness to the truth. Everyone who is of the truth listens to my voice." (Jn.18:37)

By this it is evident who are the children of God, and who are the children of the devil: whoever does not practice righteousness is not of God, nor is the one who does not love his brother. For this is the message that you have heard from the beginning, that we should love one another. (1 Jn.3:10-11)

(2) They do not try to kill and eliminate the greatest truth God has given to this earth, the truth of His own Son.

But they were filled with fury and discussed with one another what they might do to Jesus. (Lu.6:11)

"But his citizens hated him and sent a delegation after him, saying, 'We do not want this man to reign over us.'" (Lu.19:14)

"The world cannot hate you, but it hates me because I testify about it that its works are evil." (Jn.7:7)

When the chief priests and the officers saw him, they cried out, "Crucify him, crucify him!" Pilate said to them, "Take him yourselves and crucify him, for I find no guilt in him." (Jn.19:6)

Do not love the world or the things in the world. If anyone loves the world, the love of the Father is not in him. For all that is in the world—the desires of the flesh and the desires of the eyes and pride of life—is not from the Father but is from the world. (1 Jn.2:15-16)

By this it is evident who are the children of God, and who are the children of the devil: whoever does not practice righteousness is not of God, nor is the one who does not love his brother. For this is the message that you have heard from the beginning, that we should love one another. (1 Jn.3:10-11)

## G. Humanity's Depravity—
## Corrupt Birth, 8:41-47

1. **Proof 1: People sin because they have the nature of their sinful father**
   a. They deny the fact
   b. They claim God as Father
2. **Proof 2: People do not love Christ**
   a. Fact 1: Christ came from God & was sent by God
   b. Fact 2: People do not understand the words & claims of Christ
3. **Proof 3: People show by their works that their father is the devil**
   a. Satan & people lust<sup>DS1</sup>
   b. Satan & people murder
   c. Satan & people do not follow the truth
   d. Satan & people lie
4. **Proof 4: Christ is sinless—He is of God**
   a. People still do not believe
   b. The reason: People are not of God—they are sinful, but they will not confess it
      1) Because they do not hear God's words
      2) Because they do not belong to God

⁴¹ "You are doing the works your father did." They said to him, "We were not born of sexual immorality. We have one Father—even God."
⁴² Jesus said to them, "If God were your Father, you would love me, for I came from God and I am here. I came not of my own accord, but he sent me.
⁴³ "Why do you not understand what I say? It is because you cannot bear to hear my word.
⁴⁴ "You are of your father the devil, and your will is to do your father's desires. He was a murderer from the beginning, and does not stand in the truth, because there is no truth in him. When he lies, he speaks out of his own character, for he is a liar and the father of lies.
⁴⁵ "But because I tell the truth, you do not believe me.
⁴⁶ "Which one of you convicts me of sin? If I tell the truth, why do you not believe me?
⁴⁷ "Whoever is of God hears the words of God. The reason why you do not hear them is that you are not of God."

# Division IX

*The Revelation of Jesus, the Light of Life, 8:1–9:41*

G. Humanity's Depravity—Corrupt Birth, 8:41–47

## 8:41–47
## Introduction

This passage shatters humanity's concept of itself. Nevertheless, it is a passage that must be studied very carefully, for it is one of the shocking truths revealed by Christ. Our destiny hangs upon what He revealed.

Every human being is a sinner and falls short of God's glory. We all sin because we are depraved, that is, totally corrupt. Depravity means that we are *always short* of God's glory, are *always coming short* of God, and are *always failing* to measure up to God. Very simply, we are *not holy* as God is holy; we are *not perfect* as God is perfect. Why? Because every single person is born with a corrupt, sinful, and depraved nature. We are born with a nature that sins, a nature that is imperfect and as radically different from God's perfect nature as it can be (see outline and notes—1 Jn.3:4-9 for more discussion). This is, *Humanity's Depravity—Corrupt Birth,* 8:41-47.

1. Proof 1: People sin because they have the nature of their sinful father (v.41).
2. Proof 2: People do not love Christ (vv.42-43).

3. Proof 3: People show by their works that their father is the devil (v.44).
4. Proof 4: Christ is sinless—He is of God (vv.45-47).

## 1 Proof 1: People sin because they have the nature of their sinful father.

This fact is stated most emphatically. People sin by doing the deeds of a father other than God.

> 41 "You are doing the works your father did." They said to him, "We were not born of sexual immorality. We have one Father—even God."

- ➤ Sin is not of God.
- ➤ Evil deeds are not of the Father in heaven.
- ➤ Therefore, they must be of another father.

A person who sins and does evil is following another father, an evil father. Sinful human beings have a depraved nature, a nature that cannot keep from sinning no matter how hard it tries (see notes—Ro.3:9-20; 3:9). That nature is the nature of some father who stands diametrically opposed to the Father in heaven.

### a. They deny the fact (v.41a).

Human sin and evil are due to the nature of an evil spiritual father—the devil. People sin because they are in the family likeness of that father (by nature). However, many deny that fact. The Pharisees, the strongest religious devotees who have ever lived (representing all mankind), knew exactly what Jesus was saying. They knew that Jesus was speaking spiritually and that He was charging them with being sinful and depraved, of always coming short of what God demands. They understood clearly that Jesus was saying that they follow some father other than the Father of heaven.

### b. They claim God as Father (v.41b).

The Jewish religious leaders (as most people) denied that they had an idolatrous father. In their minds God was their Father and they were children of God, and there was no question about it. They claimed that . . .

- they believed in and professed the God of the Bible
- they worshiped the true God
- they followed the true God
- they did enough good to be accepted by God
- they had not done enough evil deeds to be rejected by God
- they had done the best they could to please God
- they had enough righteousness to be acceptable to God
- they had enough godly heritage (parents, family, friends, works) to be accepted by God

**THOUGHT 1.** The tragic fact is, the vast majority of people make the very same claim, refusing to accept the truth. However, their claim is a false profession. What Christ was doing was trying to get people to see the truth. People desperately need to turn away from their evil deeds to God, to genuinely believe and diligently seek God (He.11:6).

> "Not everyone who says to me, 'Lord, Lord,' will enter the kingdom of heaven, but the one who does the will of my Father who is in heaven." (Mt.7:21)

> And he said to them, "Well did Isaiah prophesy of you hypocrites, as it is written, 'This people honors me with their lips, but their heart is far from me.'" (Mk.7:6)

> They profess to know God, but they deny him by their works. They are detestable, disobedient, unfit for any good work. (Tit.1:16)

> And without faith it is impossible to please him, for whoever would draw near to God must believe that he exists and that he rewards those who seek him. (He.11:6)

> See what kind of love the Father has given to us, that we should be called children of God; and so we are. The reason why the world does not know us is that it did not know him. (1 Jn.3:1)

## 2 Proof 2: People do not love Christ.

The second proof of humanity's depravity is that people do not love Jesus. Corrupt humans are not naturally inclined to love Jesus. We only truly love Him after we grasp His sacrificial love for us and believe on Him (1 Jn.4:19). The people of Jesus' day clearly illustrate this truth. Picture the scene Jesus described: God sent His Son into the world and the people did not embrace Him, His words, or His works. Their rejection of Jesus proved that God was not their Father.

**8:42–43**

⁴² Jesus said to them, "If God were your Father, you would love me, for I came from God and I am here. I came not of my own accord, but he sent me.
⁴³ Why do you not understand what I say? It is because you cannot bear to hear my word."

### a. Fact 1: Christ came from God and was sent by God (v.42).

If humans were of God, that is, of the same spiritual world and dimension as Jesus, they would recognize Jesus and recognize His words and works. It would be impossible not to recognize Him. This is what Jesus is saying. He came from God, that is, from the spiritual world and dimension of heaven itself. He was sent to this earth by God. Anyone who is of God is bound to recognize Him. Any person who is truly of God will love and welcome Him, not reject and oppose Him. Those who want nothing to do with Jesus are not of the family of God; they are not children of God. They are children of some father other than the Father of Jesus.

### b. Fact 2: People do not understand the words and claims of Christ (v.43).

No person could possibly be of God who does not understand the teaching of Christ and who does not *hear*—open their heart to—the word of Christ. Those who have the same Father as Jesus Christ will understand His teaching and hear His Word and open their hearts to *what* Christ teaches. When a person shuts their heart to the teaching of Christ, that individual shows that they have a father different than Christ's Father.

> **Jesus said to them, "If God were your Father, you would love me, for I came from God and I am here. I came not of my own accord, but he sent me." (Jn.8:42)**

> **"If you had known me, you would have known my Father also. From now on you do know him and have seen him." Philip said to him, "Lord, show us the Father, and it is enough for us." Jesus said to him, "Have I been with you so long, and you still do not know me, Philip? Whoever has seen me has seen the Father. How can you say, 'Show us the Father'? Do you not believe that I am in the Father and the Father is in me? The words that I say to you I do not speak on my own authority, but the Father who dwells in me does his works." (Jn.14:7–10)**

> **"For the Father himself loves you, because you have loved me and have believed that I came from God." (Jn.16:27)**

> **"Now we know that you know all things and do not need anyone to question you; this is why we believe that you came from God." (Jn.16:30)**

Note the word *cannot* in verse 43. It is strong. They *could have understood and heard* His Word, but they *would not*; that is, they refused His Word, for it offended them. They rejected it, deliberately willed to turn from it.

> **"'For this people's heart has grown dull, and with their ears they can barely hear, and their eyes they have closed; lest they should see with their eyes and hear with their ears and understand with their heart and turn, and I would heal them.'" (Ac.28:27)**

> **"No one understands; no one seeks for God." (Ro.3:11)**

> **Always learning and never able to arrive at a knowledge of the truth. (2 Ti.3:7)**

**8:44**

⁴⁴ "You are of your father the devil, and your will is to do your father's desires. He was a murderer from the beginning, and does not stand in the truth, because there is no truth in him. When he lies, he speaks out of his own character, for he is a liar and the father of lies."

## 3 Proof 3: People show by their works that their father is the devil.

The third proof of humanity's depravity is that people demonstrate that their father is the devil. It is *people's works* that reveal their true father. Many object and deny this fact rather strongly, sometimes angrily. Many think the idea is repulsive and horrible, a terrible thing to say. And it is. This is just what Jesus wants us to recognize. The fact has to be faced; it has to be considered so repulsive and horrible that a person will do something about it. It is shocking for some people to learn that Jesus would even say such a thing.

The point is, people's sinful behavior and evil works prove that their father is not the Father of Jesus. Sinful behavior and evil deeds are not of the Father in heaven; they are of the father in hell. The sins and evil mentioned by Jesus show this.

a. **Satan and people lust (v.44a).**
Satan and people *lust* (see DEEPER STUDY # 1; DEEPER STUDY # 1—Js.4:1-3; note—Js.4:2 for discussion). Both have evil desires. Both crave sinful things, things the Father in heaven forbids.

b. **Satan and people murder (v.44b).**
Both Satan and humans murder. Satan is a murderer in three senses:
First, he was behind the first murder, Cain's killing his brother, Abel (Ge.4:8).
Second, he was behind the sin of Adam, which brought death to the entire human race. He is the murderer, the one who caused the death of all people

> **Therefore, just as sin came into the world through one man, and death through sin, and so death spread to all men because all sinned. (Ro.5:12)**

Third, he is behind the murder of human life and behind the loss of people experiencing real life here on earth. The devil destroys life and all abundant living when he can—all love, joy, peace, patience, gentleness, goodness, faith, meekness, discipline.

> **"When anyone hears the word of the kingdom and does not understand it, the evil one comes and snatches away what has been sown in his heart. This is what was sown along the path." (Mt.13:19)**

> **Be sober-minded; be watchful. Your adversary the devil prowls around like a roaring lion, seeking someone to devour. (1 Pe.5:8)**

> **Then Satan answered the LORD and said, "Does Job fear God for no reason? Have you not put a hedge around him and his house and all that he has, on every side? You have blessed the work of his hands, and his possessions have increased in the land. But stretch out your hand and touch all that he has, and he will curse you to your face." (Jb.1:9-11)**

Jesus was saying that one thing is certain: God is not the father of murder—the devil is. They who commit murder are children of the devil. But note the real meaning of murder revealed by Jesus (see note 2—Mt.5:22 for discussion). Murder is . . .
- anger
- bitterness
- enmity
- an uncontrolled spirit
- desiring a person's ruin
- striking out at a person
- slandering, maligning, speaking ill about a person and destroying a person's image (who is created in God's image)
- envying and killing a person's happiness

c. **Satan and people do not follow the truth (v.44c).**
Both Satan and people do not stand in the truth. Both reject the truth (see DEEPER STUDY # 1—Jn.8:32).

> **"You are of your father the devil, and your will is to do your father's desires. He was a murderer from the beginning, and does not stand in the truth, because there is no truth in him. When he lies, he speaks out of his own character, for he is a liar and the father of lies." (Jn.8:44)**

> **Whoever makes a practice of sinning is of the devil, for the devil has been sinning from the beginning. The reason the Son of God appeared was to destroy the works of the devil. (1 Jn.3:8)**

d. **Satan and people lie (v.44d).**
Both Satan and people lie and deceive. It is their nature to lie and to protect and to look after themselves. They speak out of their own character or nature; that is, they are at ease and

comfortable in lying. Lying comes naturally. You do not have to teach somebody to lie. It is human nature to lie; we lie out of our own being. Saying this hurts the people's pride, but it is human nature to look out for ourselves even if we have to lie (or cheat, steal, maneuver, whatever) to get what we want. It is human nature to protect ourselves by misleading, deceiving, and twisting the truth.

> **And even if our gospel is veiled, it is veiled to those who are perishing. In their case the god of this world has blinded the minds of the unbelievers, to keep them from seeing the light of the gospel of the glory of Christ, who is the image of God. (2 Co.4:3-4)**

> **For such men are false apostles, deceitful workmen, disguising themselves as apostles of Christ. And no wonder, for even Satan disguises himself as an angel of light. So it is no surprise if his servants, also, disguise themselves as servants of righteousness. Their end will correspond to their deeds. (2 Co.11:13-15)**

Note: anything that is not true is false—whether a lie, thoughts, ideas, words, or actions. Lying is of the devil and exposes a person to be a child of the devil. A person is certainly not of God if they are lying. Their father is not the Father of Jesus.

> **I write to you, not because you do not know the truth, but because you know it, and because no lie is of the truth. Who is the liar but he who denies that Jesus is the Christ? This is the antichrist, he who denies the Father and the Son. No one who denies the Son has the Father. Whoever confesses the Son has the Father also. (1 Jn.2:21-23)**

Note also that Jesus is telling people the truth, but they refuse to accept it (v.45). It is tough to accept the truth that one follows and actually behaves as a child of the devil. However, people must accept the truth if they are going to change and see their world changed and become children of God's, the Father of the Lord Jesus Christ.

## DEEPER STUDY # 1

(8:44) **Lusts** (epithumia): a strong desire, a yearning passion for. The word is used in a positive sense three different times in Scripture (Lu.22:15; Ph.1:23; 1 Th.2:17). People are to turn their strong desires toward righteousness and godliness; however, they have to struggle to turn away from the desire to *please* themselves. People's natural tendency is the desire or lust to satisfy self before others, in particular when survival and comfort are at stake.

1. The very nature of humans is lust, the lust of the flesh and of the mind (Ep.2:2-3). Sinful and evil lust show that people are *by nature* . . .
   - the children of wrath
   - the children of disobedience
   - the children of the spirit who is the prince and power of the air, that is, the devil

   > **In which you once walked, following the course of this world, following the prince of the power of the air, the spirit that is now at work in the sons of disobedience. (Ep.2:2)**

2. The very nature of humans and of the world is lust, a tendency both *to be* and *to get*.

   > **Do not love the world or the things in the world. If anyone loves the world, the love of the Father is not in him. For all that is in the world—the desires of the flesh and the desires of the eyes and pride of life—is not from the Father but is from the world. And the world is passing away along with its desires, but whoever does the will of God abides forever. (1 Jn.2:15-17; see also Ro.13:14; Ga.5:16, 24; Col.3:5; 1 Th.4:5, 1 Ti.6:9; 2 Ti.3:6; 4:3; Ht.2:12; 3:3; 1 Pe.1:14; 2:11; 3:3; 4:2; 2 Pe.2:1, 8, 10, 18; Jude 18; Re.18:14)**

What people discover is that their cravings are never satisfied, and these cravings have to be controlled. There is something within our innermost being that craves for more and more; and as more and more is taken, the lust does not diminish, it grows. It craves for still more and more. Our sinful cravings are never satisfied; our only answer is to control them (see note, *Lust*—Js.4:2 for a discussion of the Spirit of God's control; see also Ga.5:22-23).

## 4 Proof 4: Christ is sinless—He is of God.

The fourth proof of humanity's depravity is the sinlessness of Jesus. Jesus made the most staggering claim: no man could prove Him to be a sinner. No person could prove a single sin in Him. He was sinless and perfect. He was in the closest imaginable relationship with God, of the very same nature as God: sinless, holy, righteous, pure—perfectly so. Jesus claimed to be the Perfect Man.

> For our sake he made him to be sin who knew no sin, so that in him we might become the righteousness of God. (2 Co.5:21)
>
> For we do not have a high priest who is unable to sympathize with our weaknesses, but one who in every respect has been tempted as we are, yet without sin. (He.4:15)
>
> For it was indeed fitting that we should have such a high priest, holy, innocent, unstained, separated from sinners, and exalted above the heavens. (He.7:26)
>
> He committed no sin, neither was deceit found in his mouth. (1 Pe.2:22)
>
> You know that he appeared in order to take away sins, and in him there is no sin. (1 Jn.3:5)

> 45 "But because I tell the truth, you do not believe me.
> 46 Which one of you convicts me of sin? If I tell the truth, why do you not believe me?
> 47 Whoever is of God hears the words of God. The reason why you do not hear them is that you are not of God."

a. **People still do not believe (v.46).**

Jesus raised the all-important question: Since He was sinless, why do people not believe Him? He was telling the truth. Therefore, people should believe Him. But very often they do not.

b. **The reason: People are not of God—they are sinful, but they will not confess it (v.47).**

Jesus answered His own question. People still do not believe because they do not hear God's words. All who are *of God* hear the words of God. Therefore, those who do not believe Jesus *are not of God*. They do not belong to God. This proves Jesus' point: they are the children of the father of lies, the devil.

> "'For this people's heart has grown dull, and with their ears they can barely hear, and their eyes they have closed, lest they should see with their eyes and hear with their ears and understand with their heart and turn, and I would heal them.'" (Mt.13:15)
>
> And will turn away from listening to the truth and wander off into myths. (2 Ti.4:4)
>
> But they refused to pay attention and turned a stubborn shoulder and stopped their ears that they might not hear. (Zec.7:11)

## H. Humanity's Escape from Death, 8:48–59

1. **The harsh insult: Jesus is a Samaritan & demon-possessed**
   a. Jesus' strong denial
   b. Jesus' purpose: To honor God
   c. Jesus' honor is God's concern

2. **The great revelation: People can escape death**<sup>DS1</sup>
   a. The condition: If a person obeys
   b. The reaction to Jesus' promise: A charge that He was demon-possessed
      1) The charge: All godly people have died
      2) The question: Are you greater than godly Abraham & the prophets?

3. **The great authority of Jesus to promise deliverance from death**
   a. He was honored by God
      1) The God often professed by people
      2) The God unknown by so many people
   b. He personally knew God, obeyed His Word
   c. He was the One whom Abraham hoped for & actually saw: The Messiah
   d. He & His claims were misunderstood by the Jews
   e. He is the great "I Am"<sup>DS2</sup>
      1) The fact: He was before Abraham
      2) The reaction: They rejected Him & sought to kill Him

⁴⁸ The Jews answered him, "Are we not right in saying that you are a Samaritan and have a demon?"
⁴⁹ Jesus answered, "I do not have a demon, but I honor my Father, and you dishonor me.
⁵⁰ "Yet I do not seek my own glory; there is One who seeks it, and he is the judge.
⁵¹ "Truly, truly, I say to you, if anyone keeps my word, he will never see death."

⁵² The Jews said to him, "Now we know that you have a demon! Abraham died, as did the prophets, yet you say, 'If anyone keeps my word, he will never taste death.'
⁵³ "Are you greater than our father Abraham, who died? And the prophets died! Who do you make yourself out to be?"
⁵⁴ Jesus answered, "If I glorify myself, my glory is nothing. It is my Father who glorifies me, of whom you say, 'He is our God.'
⁵⁵ "But you have not known him. I know him. If I were to say that I do not know him, I would be a liar like you, but I do know him and I keep his word.
⁵⁶ "Your father Abraham rejoiced that he would see my day. He saw it and was glad."
⁵⁷ So the Jews said to him, "You are not yet fifty years old, and have you seen Abraham?"
⁵⁸ Jesus said to them, "Truly, truly, I say to you, before Abraham was, I am."
⁵⁹ So they picked up stones to throw at him, but Jesus hid himself and went out of the temple.

# Division IX
*The Revelation of Jesus, the Light of Life, 8:1–9:41*

H. Humanity's Escape from Death, 8:48–59

## 8:48–59
## Introduction

Death is the fierce enemy of every person. In all of human history, we know of only two people who escaped it: Enoch and Elijah, both of whom were caught up into heaven without dying. Every other person who has walked the earth has succumbed to death. In this passage, Jesus makes an astonishing claim—a person does not have to die (v.51). What does He mean? This is, *Humanity's Escape from Death*, 8:48–59.

1. The harsh insult: Jesus is a Samaritan and demon-possessed (vv.48-50).
2. The great revelation: People can escape death (vv.51-53).
3. The great authority of Jesus to promise deliverance from death (vv.54-59).

### 1 The harsh insult: Jesus is a Samaritan and demon possessed.

8:48–50

The Jewish religious authorities cast a harsh insult against Jesus. They called Him a Samaritan and accused Him of being demon-possessed.

Being a Samaritan was a charge that implied He was full of heresy, not worshiping the true God, but following and building up the false religion of the Samaritans (see Deeper Study # 1—Jn.4:5). The Jews despised the Samaritans.

Being devil-possessed was a charge that He was empowered by an evil spirit, a spirit that was out to destroy others and the true religion of God and its people (see notes—Jn.7:20-24; 7:32; Deeper Study # 4—Mt.12:24).

> ⁴⁸ The Jews answered him, "Are we not right in saying that you are a Samaritan and have a demon?"
> ⁴⁹ Jesus answered, "I do not have a demon, but I honor my Father, and you dishonor me.
> ⁵⁰ "Yet I do not seek my own glory; there is One who seeks it, and he is the judge."

#### a. Jesus' strong denial (v.49a).
Jesus answered the Jewish leaders' charges but said absolutely nothing about the racial slur. (A racial slur was not worthy of comment by Him.) However, He strongly denied their charge that He was demon-possessed. He was not insane and was perfectly conscious of His actions. He knew exactly what He was saying and doing.

#### b. Jesus' purpose: To honor God (v.49b).
Jesus defended Himself by stating His purpose. He did not have an evil spirit within Him to destroy others and the worship of God. To the contrary, His very purpose was *to honor God* and *to turn people to God*. Note: He even called God "His Father."

Jesus stated boldly that the religious leaders were the ones who did evil to God. While Jesus honored God the Father, they tried to dishonor Jesus. In dishonoring Jesus, they were dishonoring God. It was the love of God that had sent Him into the world to offer salvation (vv.31-32). The real spirit of evil was seen in those who dishonored Him while He offered God's salvation to the world.

#### c. Jesus' honor is God's concern (v.50).
Jesus did not seek His own glory; instead, He sought to glorify God by leading people to God. However, there was One who sought the glory of Jesus, that is, God Himself. God will reward those who truly glorify Christ, and He will condemn all who dishonor Him. He will reveal what Christ did to glorify God the Father and what the religious leaders did to dishonor God. One (Christ) shall be proven and accepted, and the other (the religious leaders) disproven and condemned.

## 2 The great revelation: People can escape death.

8:51-53

Death is the just wages of sin, and, consequently, the deserved destiny of every human being (Ro.5:12, 6:23). Jesus revealed a glorious truth and promise: a person can escape death (v.51; see Deeper Study # 1).

⁵¹ "Truly, truly, I say to you, if anyone keeps my word, he will never see death."
⁵² The Jews said to him, "Now we know that you have a demon! Abraham died, as did the prophets, yet you say, 'If anyone keeps my word, he will never taste death.'
⁵³ "Are you greater than our father Abraham, who died? And the prophets died! Who do you make yourself out to be?"

a. **The condition: If a person obeys (v.51).**

The promise to escape death is conditional. Jesus said that a person must keep or obey His word in order to be spared from death. Jesus was referring to the controversial message He had been teaching: that He is the Bread of life, the Son of God sent from the Father in heaven to give eternal life to the world.

b. **The reaction to Jesus' promise: A charge that He was demon-possessed (vv.52-53).**

The Jews' reaction to Jesus' phenomenal claim was radical: they were sure that Jesus was under a demon's spell, that He was insane. He was bound to be demon-possessed, for everyone knows that every human being dies. Even the godliest men such as Abraham and the prophets died. Who did Jesus think He was? Did He think He was greater than Abraham and the prophets? Who was He claiming to be? Disgusted and enraged, they asked Jesus a biting question. To paraphrase, they asked, "Are you greater than godly Abraham and the prophets, who all died? Who do you think you are?" (v.53).

### Deeper Study # 1

(8:51) **Jesus' Deliverance from Death:** this is one of the great promises of Scripture. "If anyone keeps my word, he will never see death" (v.51).

1. Note the eye-catching words "Truly, truly" or "Most assuredly." Jesus is stating that what He was about to say next was of critical importance. In other words, "Listen—listen."
2. Note how the sentence effectively stresses the glorious truth.
   - The word "death" is emphatic in the Greek: it begins the sentence. Literally, Jesus said, "Death in no wise will he ever see."
   - A double negative is used (ou me): "Death *in no wise*, and *by no means* will he ever see."

3. Note the phrases *see death* (theorese thanaton) and *taste death* (geusetai thanatou, v.52). The meaning is that a genuine follower of Christ will . . .
   - never experience death nor see death
   - never know death nor partake of death
   - never face the condemnation of death
   - never experience the terror, the hurt, the pain, and the suffering of death
   - never experience the anguish of being separated from God and from the glory, beauty, perfection, and life of heaven

In a flash, quicker than lightning or the blinking of an eye, the followers of Christ pass from this world into the next. They never cease to experience life and never lose consciousness. One moment they are in this world, the next moment they are in the presence of God Himself.

Note the reason why the believer will never *see death* (v.51) or *taste death* (v.52): it is because Jesus came by the grace of God to taste death for everyone (He.2:9).

4. There is a condition for escaping death: a person must keep Jesus' *word* (logon). *Keep* (terese) means to watch over, to obey with diligence. It means to fix and set one's heart upon the Word of Christ and keep it with all diligence. If a person genuinely obeys Christ's

word—His message of salvation—he or she will never see death (see note—Jn.8:31 for discussion and verses of Scripture. See DEEPER STUDY # 1—He.9:27).

5. Note the glorious truth of this claim.

| *All People Do . . .* | *But the Follower of Christ . . .* |
|---|---|
| • pass through physical death | • never *sees* death |
| • have their body decay | • never *tastes* death |
| • face the judgment of God | • lives now and forever |

"For God so loved the world, that he gave his only Son, that whoever believes in him should not perish but have eternal life." (Jn.3:16)

"Do not work for the food that perishes, but for the food that endures to eternal life, which the Son of Man will give to you. For on him God the Father has set his seal." (Jn.6:27)

"My sheep hear my voice, and I know them, and they follow me. I give them eternal life, and they will never perish, and no one will snatch them out of my hand." (Jn.10:27-28)

"And everyone who lives and believes in me shall never die. Do you believe this?" (Jn.11:26)

"Since you have given him [Jesus Christ] authority over all flesh, to give eternal life to all whom you have given him. And this is eternal life, that they know you, the only true God, and Jesus Christ whom you have sent." (Jn.17:2-3)

And this is the promise that he made to us—eternal life. (1 Jn.2:25)

## 3 The great authority of Jesus to promise deliverance from death.

8:54-59

Jesus claimed He had the authority to make such a glorious promise, the promise of deliverance from death. He defended His authority by making four unique claims (subpoints a, b, c, and e).

### a. He was honored by God (v.54-55a).

First, Jesus claimed that He was honored by God. He was not out to honor Himself. If He sought His own honor, His honor would amount to nothing. When a man is seen honoring and praising himself, it is considered false honor. Self-honor is discounted and considered distasteful and usually turns people away. It certainly does not attract people.

However, there is One who does honor Christ: His Father honors Him.

54 Jesus answered, "If I glorify myself, my glory is nothing. It is my Father who glorifies me, of whom you say, 'He is our God.'
55 But you have not known him. I know him. If I were to say that I do not know him, I would be a liar like you, but I do know him and I keep his word.
56 Your father Abraham rejoiced that he would see my day. He saw it and was glad."
57 So the Jews said to him, "You are not yet fifty years old, and have you seen Abraham?"
58 Jesus said to them, "Truly, truly, I say to you, before Abraham was, I am."
59 So they picked up stones to throw at him, but Jesus hid himself and went out of the temple.

And behold, a voice from heaven said, "This is my beloved Son, with whom I am well pleased." (Mt.3:17)

"There is another who bears witness about me, and I know that the testimony that he bears about me is true." (Jn.5:32)

"And the Father who sent me has himself borne witness about me. His voice you have never heard, his form you have never seen, and you do not have his word abiding in you, for you do not believe the one whom he has sent." (Jn.5:37-38)

"I am the one who bears witness about myself, and the Father who sent me bears witness about me." (Jn.8:18)

If we receive the testimony of men, the testimony of God is greater, for this is the testimony of God that he has borne concerning his Son. Whoever believes in the Son of God has the testimony in himself. Whoever does not believe God has made him a liar, because he has not believed in the testimony that God has borne concerning his Son. And this is the testimony, that God gave us eternal life, and this life is in his Son. Whoever has the Son has life; whoever does not have the Son of God does not have life. (1 Jn.5:9-12)

Now, note an extraordinary claim. Who is Jesus' Father? According to Christ, "He is [your] God" (v.54). He is the God whom the Jews professed as their God. Likewise, many other people so often profess Him as *their God*. But He is the God whom many people do not really know. A lot of people say they know Him, professing . . .

- God to be the creator and sustainer of all
- to worship and follow Him
- to be looked after and cared for by Him

But such claims are often only imaginations, only ideas in people's minds. Jesus tells the religious leaders that they do not really know God, not the only true and living God—not really—not personally (v.55a). Apart from Christ, nobody can personally know God.

> "Not everyone who says to me, 'Lord, Lord,' will enter the kingdom of heaven, but the one who does the will of my Father who is in heaven." (Mt.7:21)

> And he said to them, "Well did Isaiah prophesy of you hypocrites, as it is written, 'This people honors me with their lips, but their heart is far from me.'" (Mk.7:6)

> "Why do you call me 'Lord, Lord,' and not do what I tell you?" (Lu.6:46)

> They profess to know God, but they deny him by their works. They are detestable, disobedient, unfit for any good work. (Tit.1:16)

> Little children, let us not love in word or talk but in deed and in truth. (1 Jn.3:18)

b. **He personally knew God, obeyed His Word (v.55b).**

Jesus claimed that He personally knew God, His Father, and obeyed His Word. He had a unique and very special knowledge of God the Father. Jesus knew God as no one else had ever known Him.

> "All things have been handed over to me by my Father, and no one knows the Son except the Father, and no one knows the Father except the Son and anyone to whom the Son chooses to reveal him." (Mt.11:27)

> "I know him, for I come from him, and he sent me." (Jn.7:29)

> "Just as the Father knows me and I know the Father; and I lay down my life for the sheep." (Jn.10:15)

> "O righteous Father, even though the world does not know you, I know you, and these know that you have sent me." (Jn.17:25)

Note that Jesus refused to lie. Most people lie when they claim to know God, but He would not lie like they did (v.55). He knew God, His Father, and He would neither lower nor retract His claim, although He knew this claim would result in His death. Note also that Jesus kept God's Word. This meant He had to tell the truth. He did know God personally, and He must proclaim the glorious Word of God to the world. He had to do what His Father said. He had to keep God's Word and fulfill God's purpose so that people might be saved. (Note that Jesus was claiming to be sinless, to keep God's Word perfectly.)

> "But I do as the Father has commanded me, so that the world may know that I love the Father. Rise, let us go from here." (Jn.14:31)

> For as by the one man's disobedience the many were made sinners, so by the one man's obedience the many will be made righteous. (Ro.5:19)

c. **He was the One whom Abraham hoped for and actually saw: The Messiah (v.56).**

Jesus claimed that He was the One whom Abraham hoped for and actually saw. As founder of the Jewish nation, Abraham held a unique position among the people. He was the man whom God had challenged to be a witness to the other nations of the world—a witness to the only true and living God. Therefore, God appeared to Abraham and challenged him to leave his home, his friends, his employment, and his country. God promised Abraham that if he would follow God unquestionably, he would become the father of a new nation and of a great host of people, and God would cause all nations to be blessed by his seed (Ge.13:14-17; 15:1-7; 17:1-8, 15-19; 22:15-18; 26:2-5, 24; 28:13-15; 35:9-12; see also Deeper Study # 1—Jn.4:22).

Scripture says that Abraham did as God requested. He went out not knowing where he went (He.11:8). He completely and unquestionably trusted God and took God at His word. The

Messiah would come from his seed. Abraham rejoiced to see the Messiah's day, the day when the promised Seed was sent into the world.

When Abraham lived on earth, he saw the Messiah's day—His coming to bring salvation—by faith. He was hopeful, and he rejoiced as much as any Old Testament saint.

> These all died in faith, not having received the things promised, but having seen them and greeted them from afar, and having acknowledged that they were strangers and exiles on the earth. (He.11:13)

When Jesus was born, Abraham was alive in paradise (see note, pt.3—Mt.22:31-32). He saw the Messiah's coming to earth and rejoiced with all who had died in faith. Salvation, the vindication of faith, was now to be secured by the Son of God Himself.

### d. He and His claims were misunderstood by the Jews (v.57).

The Jews misinterpreted Jesus' words, as people often do. They saw Jesus as a mere man, a man who lived on earth only for a few years. How could He possibly see Abraham, a man who had died hundreds and hundreds of years before?

> In their case the god of this world has blinded the minds of the unbelievers, to keep them from seeing the light of the gospel of the glory of Christ, who is the image of God. (2 Co.4:4)

> They [unbelievers] are darkened in their understanding, alienated from the life of God because of the ignorance that is in them, due to their hardness of heart. (Ep.4:18)

### e. He is the great "I Am" (vv.58-59).

Jesus claimed that He is the great "I Am" (v.58; see DEEPER STUDY # 2). This was the climactic claim—the claim . . .

- to be preexistent, always existing, to have been living when Abraham was born (Greek aorist tense, "came into being")
- to be above and beyond time
- to be eternal

The point is striking. Jesus was there when Abraham was born. He is God Himself, the great "I Am" standing on earth and in a human body. But why? The question is not *how*. God can do anything, even stand on earth in a human body if He wills. Therefore, the question is never *how*, but *why*. Why would God come to earth as a Man? The answer is clearly stated: to bring the message of God to the world, the glorious gospel (Jn.8:31-32).

However, note the reaction of the Jews to God's presence right before them. They were furious (v.59). They rejected and opposed Jesus and tried to get rid of Him. They wanted nothing to do with Him, lest His claims lay hold of their lives and they be forced to change the way they lived.

> But they were filled with fury and discussed with one another what they might do to Jesus. (Lu.6:11)

> "But his citizens hated him and sent a delegation after him, saying, 'We do not want this man to reign over us.'" (Lu.19:14)

> "The world cannot hate you, but it hates me because I testify about it that its works are evil." (Jn.7:7)

## DEEPER STUDY # 2

(8:58) **Jesus Christ, Deity—"I Am"**: see DEEPER STUDY # 1—Jn.6:20.

# Chapter 9

## I. Humanity's Eyes Opened (Part 1): The Mission of Jesus,[DS1] 9:1-7

| | |
|---|---|
| 1. Jesus came to teach the truth<br>   a. He saw a blind man<br>   b. He was questioned about the man's suffering & sin<br><br>   c. He replied that the man's suffering was not due to sin but was to demonstrate the work—the mighty power—of God in him<br>2. Jesus came to do the works of God<br><br><br>3. Jesus came to be the Light of the world<br><br>4. Jesus came to give sight to people<br>   a. Jesus' act: He made contact with the man<br><br>   b. Man's act: He had to obey to receive his sight | As he passed by, he saw a man blind from birth. ² And his disciples asked him, "Rabbi, who sinned, this man or his parents, that he was born blind?" ³ Jesus answered, "It was not that this man sinned, or his parents, but that the works of God might be displayed in him. ⁴ We must work the works of him who sent me while it is day; night is coming, when no one can work. ⁵ As long as I am in the world, I am the light of the world." ⁶ Having said these things, he spit on the ground and made mud with the saliva. Then he anointed the man's eyes with the mud ⁷ and said to him, "Go, wash in the pool of Siloam" (which means Sent). So he went and washed and came back seeing. |

# Division IX

*The Revelation of Jesus, the Light of Life, 8:1–9:41*

I. Humanity's Eyes Opened (Part I): The Mission of Jesus, 9:1-7

## 9:1-7 Introduction

Blindness is a horrible disability, and we have great compassion for those who suffer it. Jesus used an encounter with a blind man to teach us that we are all blind, spiritually speaking. Just as those who cannot see so desperately need sight, each of us needs our eyes to be opened spiritually. The mission of Jesus is to open our spiritual eyes that we might see the Light of eternal life. This is, *Humanity's Eyes Opened (Part I): The Mission of Jesus, 9:1-7*.

1. Jesus came to teach the truth (vv.1-3).
2. Jesus came to do the works of God (v.4).
3. Jesus came to be the Light of the world (v.5).
4. Jesus came to give sight to people (vv.6-7).

## DEEPER STUDY #1

(9:1-41) **Spiritual Sight**: this passage is a continuation of the subject *Humanity's Sinfulness*. Jesus took a man's physical blindness and demonstrated the stages of spiritual insight and sight (Jn.9:8-41). It should be noted that *spiritual insight* has to do with seeing Jesus and Jesus alone. Jesus is the very theme of God's revelation. He alone is the perfect revelation of God, and our spiritual eyes can be opened to see God only through Him. Apart from Jesus, no one will ever see God.

> Jesus said to him, "I am the way, and the truth, and the life. No one comes to the Father except through me." (Jn.14:6)

## 1 Jesus came to teach the truth.

9:1-3

Jesus passed by, but exactly where is not stated. The location is insignificant, for the spiritual lesson Jesus would teach is for people in all places.

As he passed by, he saw a man blind from birth. ² And his disciples asked him, "Rabbi, who sinned, this man or his parents, that he was born blind?" ³ Jesus answered, "It was not that this man sinned, or his parents, but that the works of God might be displayed in him."

**a. He saw a blind man (v.1).**

As Jesus passed by, He encountered a man who had been blind since birth. Something about the man attracted the attention of both Jesus and the disciples. Jesus *saw* him, which indicates interest, care, concern, and compassion. The disciples apparently felt the same interest and concern for the man, for they began to wonder why he had been doomed to suffer so terribly throughout his life.

**b. He was questioned about the man's suffering and sin (v.2).**

It was a common belief that a person suffered because of sin, either their own sin or their parents' sin. The disciples were concerned about the man and wondered about him. Was he suffering because of some great sin committed by his parents or because God had foreseen that the man would be a great sinner before he was born?

The question is often asked: How can a man who is not yet born be punished for sin he has not yet committed? Apparently, Jewish belief was that God foresaw a person's sin; therefore, the person was "born in sin" and thereby punished (see v.34).

**c. He replied that the man's suffering was not due to sin but was to demonstrate the work—the mighty power—of God in him (v.3).**

Jesus said that the man's suffering was not due to sin but that he suffered so that the works of God could be demonstrated in his life. Our Lord's statement gives insight to the age-old question of why good people suffer . . .

| *So that God can . . .* | *So that people can . . .* |
|---|---|
| • have an opportunity to work | • give God an opportunity to show what He can do in a life |
| • show His compassion | |
| • prove His power | • learn to trust God more and more |
| • demonstrate that He does care and look after people | • demonstrate a special strength and endurance |
| • lead unbelievers to trust Him | • set forth a dynamic example of God's care and power to a lost world |
| | • better learn and know that they live in a sinful, corruptible world and desperately need deliverance |

**THOUGHT 1.** Those who suffer have a very special opportunity to showcase the works of God in their lives. Sufferers can allow the Spirit of God to demonstrate Himself and show that the grace and power of God are sufficient in a greater way than a healthy person can. Very often a person suffers not because of sin but because God desires a unique opportunity to demonstrate His works through their life (see outline and notes—Lu.13:1-9; also see notes—Lu.5:18-20; Js.5:14-15 for more discussion).

## 9:4

⁴ "We must work the works of him who sent me while it is day; night is coming, when no one can work."

### 2 Jesus came to do the works of God.

Jesus carried the discussion beyond the man's blindness. The disciples were perplexed over this man's situation, wondering and asking questions about the problem of suffering and sin. How could a man such as this be punished from birth? Jesus picked up the question, moving it to His worldwide mission as the Light of the world (v.5). He dealt with the problem of suffering and sin throughout the whole world. His very mission on earth was to do the works of God.

Jesus emphasized that God had *sent* Him. God sent Jesus. Jesus had come into the world on God's mission. He was *of God*, from God's very presence, from the closest possible relationship with God (see notes—Jn.3:32-34; Deeper Study # 3—3:34 for verses of Scripture).

God sent Jesus for a purpose: to do the works of God. It was God's works that had to be done. Four works are stressed in this passage. Remember that the blind man represents the *spiritual blindness* of every human being.

➤ *The work of seeking people.* God seeks people. Jesus took the initiative with this man, reaching out to help him. It was not the man who reached out for help. In fact, the man was blind; he did not even know that help was available. If Jesus had not reached out for him, he would have remained blind and been in darkness forever.

"For the Son of Man came to seek and to save the lost." (Lu.19:10)

➤ *The work of caring for people.* God cares about people and their blindness.

"Even as the Son of Man came not to be served but to serve, and to give his life as a ransom for many." (Mt.20:28)

Casting all your anxieties on him, because he cares for you. (1 Pe.5:7)

➤ *The work of loving and having compassion.* God loves and has compassion for people in their blindness and darkness.

For we do not have a high priest who is unable to sympathize with our weaknesses, but one who in every respect has been tempted as we are, yet without sin. Let us then with confidence draw near to the throne of grace, that we may receive mercy and find grace to help in time of need. (He.4:15-16)

In all their affliction he was afflicted, and the angel of his presence saved them; in his love and in his pity he redeemed them; he lifted them up and carried them all the days of old. (Is.63:9)

➤ The work of delivering from darkness and giving sight.

He has delivered us from the domain of darkness and transferred us to the kingdom of his beloved Son. (Col.1:13)

Jesus stressed the urgency of His mission. *Must* (Gk. dei) speaks of compulsion and necessity. There are no questions, no suggestions, no urgings about the matter. The works of God *must* be done. Why? Because the time for working is limited. Christ and His followers did not have forever to do the work. It had to be done *then* or the opportunity would be lost.

Some texts read *us* or *we* (emas) instead of "I" (eme, v.4): "It is necessary for *us* to work" or "*We* must work the works of God." If this is accurate, then a wonderful truth is stated. Jesus ties us to His mission from the Father. We, too, are in the world to do the works of God. Our very purpose for being on earth is to proclaim and display the works of God.

Jesus said to them again, "Peace be with you. As the Father has sent me, even so I am sending you." (Jn.20:21)

"For we cannot but speak of what we have seen and heard." (Ac.4:20)

For if I preach the gospel, that gives me no ground for boasting. For necessity is laid upon me. Woe to me if I do not preach the gospel! (1 Co.9:16)

**THOUGHT 1.** We have only been given a limited amount of time to do the Lord's work. Whatever is to be done must be done today, while there is still some daylight left. Night is coming, the time when nobody can work. Time will end, and the opportunity will be gone forever.

Jesus said to them, "My food is to do the will of him who sent me and to accomplish his work." (Jn.4:34)

This is what I mean, brothers: the appointed time has grown very short. From now on, let those who have wives live as though they had none, and those who mourn as though they were not mourning, and those who rejoice as though they were not rejoicing, and those who buy as though they had no goods. (1 Co.7:29-30)

Making the best use of the time, because the days are evil. (Ep.5:16)

Walk in wisdom toward outsiders, making the best use of the time. (Col.4:5)

For this reason I remind you to fan into flame the gift of God, which is in you through the laying on of my hands. (2 Ti.1:6)

## 3  Jesus came to be the Light of the world.

9:5

Jesus used the man's infirmity to teach a spiritual lesson. He alone is the Light of the world (see DEEPER STUDY # 1—Jn.8:12 for discussion). If people wish to be delivered from darkness, they must come to Christ. Christ is the only One who gives spiritual sight to us and to our world.

⁵ "As long as I am in the world, I am the light of the world."

In him was life, and the life was the light of men. (Jn.1:4)

Again Jesus spoke to them, saying, "I am the light of the world. Whoever follows me will not walk in darkness, but will have the light of life." (Jn.8:12)

For God, who said, "Let light shine out of darkness," has shone in our hearts to give the light of the knowledge of the glory of God in the face of Jesus Christ. (2 Co.4:6)

For anything that becomes visible is light. Therefore it says, "Awake, O sleeper, and arise from the dead, and Christ will shine on you." (Ep.5:14)

## 4  Jesus came to give sight to people.

9:6-7

Jesus came to demonstrate the power to give sight. Note that Jesus did not just speak the *word of healing* to the man. His Word alone was the method He often used in healing, but this was not the case with this man. He did much more, and by His act He demonstrated two things to the world:

⁶ Having said these things, he spit on the ground and made mud with the saliva. Then he anointed the man's eyes with the mud ⁷ and said to him, "Go, wash in the pool of Siloam" (which means Sent). So he went and washed and came back seeing.

➢ First, He will do everything He can to give sight to and deliver a person from darkness.
➢ Second, He has the power to deliver people and to give them sight.

a. **Jesus' act: He made contact with the man (v.6).**

The blind man's faith needed to be awakened and stirred. Jesus used two things to activate the man's faith. He used a point of contact, the touch of His hands on the man's eyes. Note that He used clay made moist by saliva. People of that day believed saliva had some curing qualities, and perhaps Jesus used saliva because of this. The man's faith would certainly be helped by thinking of its healing qualities. However, Jesus would not want the man thinking that it was saliva that cured him. The man needed to know beyond question that Jesus was the One who healed him. Commentators offer a variety of insights as to why Jesus used the clay moistened with His saliva as a part of the man's healing, but His purpose is not clear. It is interesting to note that the Lord used His saliva in performing two other miraculous healings (Mk.7:32-33; 8:23).

b. **Man's act: He had to obey Jesus to receive his sight (v.7).**

Jesus sent the man to wash in the pool of Siloam. Scripture explains that *Siloam* means *Sent* for a significant reason: Jesus was using the pool as a symbol of the Messiah who was sent by God to give sight to the world. The blind man, by obeying Jesus and going to the pool, would receive his sight. His obedience would demonstrate to the spiritually blind that they, too, could receive their sight by coming to Jesus and obeying Him.

The man washed and *came back seeing*! He received his sight, because He did exactly what Jesus said.

**THOUGHT 1.** Our eyes can be opened; and we can be delivered from the darkness of sin and shame, death and corruption, hell and destruction by coming to Jesus Christ and by obeying Him.

> "So take heart, men, for I have faith in God that it will be exactly as I have been told." (Ac.27:25)
>
> No unbelief made him waver concerning the promise of God, but he grew strong in his faith as he gave glory to God, fully convinced that God was able to do what he had promised. That is why his faith was "counted to him as righteousness." (Ro.4:20-22)
>
> Oh, how abundant is your goodness, which you have stored up for those who fear you and worked for those who take refuge in you, in the sight of the children of mankind! (Ps.31:19)
>
> Commit your way to the LORD; trust in him, and he will act. (Ps.37:5)
>
> Who among you fears the LORD and obeys the voice of his servant? Let him who walks in darkness and has no light trust in the name of the LORD and rely on his God. (Is.50:10)

# J. Humanity's Eyes Opened (Part II): The Stages of Spiritual Sight, 9:8–41

1. **Stage 1: Seeing Jesus as a man**
   a. The blind man's neighbors were amazed & questioned his deliverance

⁸ The neighbors and those who had seen him before as a beggar were saying, "Is this not the man who used to sit and beg?"

⁹ Some said, "It is he." Others said, "No, but he is like him." He kept saying, "I am the man."

¹⁰ So they said to him, "Then how were your eyes opened?"

   b. The man testified: A man called Jesus gave me sight

¹¹ He answered, "The man called Jesus made mud and anointed my eyes and said to me, 'Go to Siloam and wash.' So I went and washed and received my sight."

¹² They said to him, "Where is he?" He said, "I do not know."

¹³ They brought to the Pharisees the man who had formerly been blind.

2. **Stage 2: Seeing Jesus as a helper or a healer**
   a. Jesus healed the man on the Sabbath: It was against the law to work on the Sabbath

¹⁴ Now it was a Sabbath day when Jesus made the mud and opened his eyes.

   b. The Pharisees questioned how the man could now see

¹⁵ So the Pharisees again asked him how he had received his sight. And he said to them, "He put mud on my eyes, and I washed, and I see."

   c. The man explained & testified: Jesus healed me

3. **Stage 3: Seeing Jesus as a prophet**
   a. The Pharisees were divided

¹⁶ Some of the Pharisees said, "This man is not from God, for he does not keep the Sabbath." But others said, "How can a man who is a sinner do such signs?" And there was a division among them.

   b. The Pharisees questioned the man again
   c. The man testified: Jesus is a prophet

¹⁷ So they said again to the blind man, "What do you say about him, since he has opened your eyes?" He said, "He is a prophet."

4. **Stage 4: Seeing Jesus as the Savior**
   a. The Pharisees' unbelief
   b. The Pharisees called & questioned the man's parents

¹⁸ The Jews did not believe that he had been blind and had received his sight, until they called the parents of the man who had received his sight

¹⁹ and asked them, "Is this your son, who you say was born blind? How then does he now see?"

   c. The parents' testimony
      1) They identified their son

²⁰ His parents answered, "We know that this is our son and that he was born blind.

      2) They denied being eyewitnesses

²¹ But how he now sees we do not know, nor do we know who opened his eyes. Ask him; he is of age. He will speak for himself."

3) They feared prejudgment & excommunication: Feared being banished from the synagogue

d. The Pharisees' summoned the healed man again & demanded that he deny Jesus

e. The man's testimony
1) I was blind, but now I see (Jesus saved me & gave me sight)

2) The clear evidence had been presented but rejected, doubted

5. **Stage 5: Seeing Jesus as being from God**
a. The Pharisees' case
1) Accused the man of being Jesus' disciple
2) Questioned Jesus' origin

b. The man's testimony
1) A marvelous thing has happened

²² (His parents said these things because they feared the Jews, for the Jews had already agreed that if anyone should confess Jesus to be Christ, he was to be put out of the synagogue.) ²³ Therefore his parents said, "He is of age; ask him."
²⁴ So for the second time they called the man who had been blind and said to him, "Give glory to God. We know that this man is a sinner." ²⁵ He answered, "Whether he is a sinner I do not know. One thing I do know, that though I was blind, now I see." ²⁶ They said to him, "What did he do to you? How did he open your eyes?" ²⁷ He answered them, "I have told you already, and you would not listen. Why do you want to hear it again? Do you also want to become his disciples?" ²⁸ And they reviled him, saying, "You are his disciple, but we are disciples of Moses.

²⁹ "We know that God has spoken to Moses, but as for this man, we do not know where he comes from." ³⁰ The man answered, "Why, this is an amazing thing! You do not know where he comes from, and yet he opened my eyes.

# Division IX

## *The Revelation of Jesus, the Light of Life, 8:1–9:41*

J. Humanity's Eyes Opened (Part II): The Stages of Spiritual Sight, 9:8–41

## 9:8–41
## Introduction

The blind man had been delivered from darkness and given sight by the compassion and power of the Lord Jesus. In this passage the delivered man is confronted by his neighbors (vv.8-12), by the Pharisees (vv.13-34), and by Jesus (vv.35-41).

The scene flows rapidly, and the man's growing knowledge of Jesus is easily seen and grasped. The outline should be adequate in carrying one through this passage. Therefore, the commentary will not discuss each subpoint, but rather concentrate on Jesus as seen by the man, that is, on the stages of spiritual sight. The message of this passage is seeing Jesus, and that message, rather than

³¹ "We know that God does not listen to sinners, but if anyone is a worshiper of God and does his will, God listens to him.

³² "Never since the world began has it been heard that anyone opened the eyes of a man born blind.

³³ "If this man were not from God, he could do nothing."

³⁴ They answered him, "You were born in utter sin, and would you teach us?" And they cast him out.

³⁵ Jesus heard that they had cast him out, and having found him he said, "Do you believe in the Son of Man?"

³⁶ He answered, "And who is he, sir, that I may believe in him?"

³⁷ Jesus said to him, "You have seen him, and it is he who is speaking to you."

³⁸ He said, "Lord, I believe," and he worshiped him.

³⁹ Jesus said, "For judgment I came into this world, that those who do not see may see, and those who see may become blind."

⁴⁰ Some of the Pharisees near him heard these things, and said to him, "Are we also blind?"

⁴¹ Jesus said to them, "If you were blind, you would have no guilt; but now that you say, 'We see,' your guilt remains."

2) We know that God does not hear sinners' (unbelievers') prayers but does hear those of His true followers

3) My experience proves that Jesus is *from God*

c. The Pharisees' denial of the man's experience & proof: They threw the man out

6. **Stage 6: Seeing Jesus as who He truly is**
   a. Jesus sought the man
   b. Jesus asked & invited the man to believe in Him
   c. The man requested to know the Son of Man
   d. Jesus identified Himself as the Son of Man, v.35
   e. The man believed & worshiped Jesus

7. **Stage 7: Seeing the lesson in Jesus' revelation**
   a. Jesus' mission: To bring judgment

   b. The religious leaders' expectation: To be exempt from judgment

   c. Jesus' declaration: He sought to convict them of their hypocrisy, their sin

---

the details of the passage, is the focus of the commentary. This is, *Humanity's Eyes Opened (Part II): The Stages of Spiritual Sight*, 9:8-41.

1. Stage 1: Seeing Jesus as a man (vv.8-12).
2. Stage 2: Seeing Jesus as a helper or a healer (vv.13-15).
3. Stage 3: Seeing Jesus as a prophet (vv.16-17).
4. Stage 4: Seeing Jesus as the Savior (vv.18-27).
5. Stage 5: Seeing Jesus as being *from God* (vv.28-34).
6. Stage 6: Seeing Jesus as who He truly is (vv.35-38).
7. Stage 7: Seeing the lesson in Jesus' revelation (vv. 39-41).

## 1 Stage 1: Seeing Jesus as a man.

The first stage of spiritual sight is *seeing Jesus as a man* (v.11). Note: all the healed man knew was that *a man* named Jesus had commanded him to do certain things, and he did them and received his sight.

9:8-12

⁸ The neighbors and those who had seen him before as a beggar were saying, "Is this not the man who used to sit and beg?"

⁹ Some said, "It is he." Others said, "No, but he is like him." He kept saying, "I am the man."

¹⁰ So they said to him, "Then how were your eyes opened?"

¹¹ He answered, "The man called Jesus made mud and anointed my eyes and said to me, 'Go to Siloam and wash.' So I went and washed and received my sight."

¹² They said to him, "Where is he?" He said, "I do not know."

Note what happened to the blind man:
- ➤ He was confronted by Jesus.
- ➤ He was commanded to do some specific things.
- ➤ He obeyed the commands of Jesus.
- ➤ He was delivered from darkness and given sight.

The blind man was blessed by Jesus despite an inadequate understanding of who Christ was. But note the crucial point: his heart was right toward Jesus. It was tender and willing to do what Jesus said.

The first stage in a person's spiritual journey is to *learn about Jesus*. We must learn *about* Jesus before we can ever learn *of* Jesus, before we can ever come to know Jesus personally. But once a person has learned *about* Jesus, it is imperative that they move on and come to know Jesus personally. The blind man could have stopped at any stage and failed in his spiritual journey.

> **THOUGHT 1.** Many people are like the blind man. They know *about* Jesus, but they do not *know* Jesus, not personally. They know His name, but little else. They have little understanding of His...
> - teaching and claims
> - presence and strength
> - love and care
> - power and promises
>
> **"Come to me, all who labor and are heavy laden, and I will give you rest. Take my yoke upon you, and learn from me, for I am gentle and lowly in heart, and you will find rest for your souls." (Mt.11:28–29)**
>
> **Indeed, I count everything as loss because of the surpassing worth of knowing Christ Jesus my Lord. For his sake I have suffered the loss of all things and count them as rubbish, in order that I may gain Christ (Ph.3:8)**
>
> **But grow in the grace and knowledge of our Lord and Savior Jesus Christ. To him be the glory both now and to the day of eternity. Amen. (2 Pe.3:18)**

## 2 Stage 2: Seeing Jesus as a helper or a healer.

9:13–15

¹³ They brought to the Pharisees the man who had formerly been blind.
¹⁴ Now it was a Sabbath day when Jesus made the mud and opened his eyes.
¹⁵ So the Pharisees again asked him how he had received his sight. And he said to them, "He put mud on my eyes, and I washed, and I see."

The second stage of spiritual sight is seeing Jesus as a helper or a healer (v.15). The delivered man was brought before the religious authorities (we are not told by whom) because the Sabbath law had been broken. This was a serious offense to the Jews (see DEEPER STUDY # 2—Jn.5:15-16).

Note the man's answer to the religious leaders' question about how he had received his sight. To paraphrase, he said that "He [the man, Jesus] put mud on my eyes, and I washed and received my sight." He still saw Jesus only as a man, but as a man who had done a great thing by helping him and healing him. He saw Jesus as a great *helper* and a great *healer*. This is a confession; the man was giving an answer to some questioners. He was confessing Jesus to be a great *helper* and *healer*.

> **THOUGHT 1.** Many confess Jesus just as the man confessed Him. They confess that He is a *great man*, a great...
> - teacher
> - moralist
> - martyr
> - healer
> - preacher
> - helper
> - law-giver
> - example

But this concept still comes far short of the truth. The delivered man did not yet know Jesus personally. He had not reached the stage of belief, of true salvation and worship (see vv.35-38).

And all spoke well of him and marveled at the gracious words that were coming from his mouth. And they said, "Is not this Joseph's son?" (Lu.4:22)

And they were astonished at his teaching, for his word possessed authority. (Lu.4:32)

"What does he mean by saying, 'You will seek me and you will not find me,' and, 'Where I am you cannot come'?" (Jn.7:36)

## 3 Stage 3: Seeing Jesus as a prophet.

The third stage of spiritual sight is seeing Jesus as a prophet (v.17). The man really progressed in his view of Jesus at this point. The people saw a prophet as the highest office a man could hold, the most authoritative voice among the people.

A prophet was a man chosen by God . . .
- to walk close to God
- to represent God among the people
- to proclaim the message of God (see Amos 3:7)
- to demonstrate the power of God
- to help people by demonstrating God before them and by guiding and warning and ministering to them

16 Some of the Pharisees said, "This man is not from God, for he does not keep the Sabbath." But others said, "How can a man who is a sinner do such signs?" And there was a division among them.

17 So they said again to the blind man, "What do you say about him, since he has opened your eyes?" He said, "He is a prophet."

But again, the healed man still saw Jesus only as a man, a godly man yes, but only a man. Such a concept was still short of what was needed for being delivered from spiritual blindness. The blind man's concept was still inadequate. He had not yet reached the stage of belief and worship (vv.35-38).

Now when Jesus came into the district of Caesarea Philippi, he asked his disciples, "Who do people say that the Son of Man is?" And they said, "Some say John the Baptist, others say Elijah, and others Jeremiah or one of the prophets." (Mt.16:13-14)

And when he entered Jerusalem, the whole city was stirred up, saying, "Who is this?" And crowds said, "This is the prophet Jesus, from Nazareth of Galilee." (Mt.21:10-11)

And although they were seeking to arrest him, they feared the crowds, because they held him to be a prophet. (Mt.21:46)

## 4 Stage 4: Seeing Jesus as the Savior.

The fourth stage of spiritual sight is seeing Jesus as the Savior (v.25). The man now confessed the immortal words, "One thing I do know, that though I was blind, now I see" (v.25).

The man underwent the most severe questioning and attack imaginable from the Pharisees. He should have been gripped with intense fear, but instead he gave one of the strongest confessions possible—his own personal experience with Jesus. He was blind, but now he could see. He saw the hand of God . . .
- in his own life
- in the touch of Jesus
- in the feelings within his heart
- in the beauty of nature, which he had never seen before

He was confessing his personal experience: he was blind, but now he could see. He could not answer the theological question: Is Jesus a mere man as all other men, or is He of God? But he could answer one thing: his own personal experience, what Jesus had done for him.

18 The Jews did not believe that he had been blind and had received his sight, until they called the parents of the man who had received his sight

19 and asked them, "Is this your son, who you say was born blind? How then does he now see?"

20 His parents answered, "We know that this is our son and that he was born blind.

21 But how he now sees we do not know, nor do we know who opened his eyes. Ask him; he is of age. He will speak for himself."

22 (His parents said these things because they feared the Jews, for the Jews had already agreed that if anyone should confess Jesus to be Christ, he was to be put out of the synagogue.)

23 Therefore his parents said, "He is of age; ask him."

24 So for the second time they called the man who had been blind and said to him, "Give glory to God. We know that this man is a sinner."

25 He answered, "Whether he is a sinner I do not know. One thing I do know, that though I was blind, now I see."

26 They said to him, "What did he do to you? How did he open your eyes?"

27 He answered them, "I have told you already, and you would not listen. Why do you want to hear it again? Do you also want to become his disciples?"

See how he had progressed in his view of Jesus. He saw that Jesus may be more than a mere man, but he could not say for sure. Just like a child, he did not know the theological terms nor how to express the nature of Jesus, but he did know one thing: Jesus had delivered and saved him from blindness. Jesus was his Savior and Deliverer from blindness to sight.

> "For the Son of Man came to seek and to save the lost." (Lu.19:10)

> "For God did not send his Son into the world to condemn the world, but in order that the world might be saved through him." (Jn.3:17)

> The saying is trustworthy and deserving of full acceptance, that Christ Jesus came into the world to save sinners, of whom I am the foremost. (1 Ti.1:15)

## 9:28-34

²⁸ And they reviled him, saying, "You are his disciple, but we are disciples of Moses. ²⁹ We know that God has spoken to Moses, but as for this man, we do not know where he comes from."
³⁰ The man answered, "Why, this is an amazing thing! You do not know where he comes from, and yet he opened my eyes. ³¹ We know that God does not listen to sinners, but if anyone is a worshiper of God and does his will, God listens to him. ³² Never since the world began has it been heard that anyone opened the eyes of a man born blind. ³³ If this man were not from God, he could do nothing."
³⁴ They answered him, "You were born in utter sin, and would you teach us?" And they cast him out.

## 5 Stage 5: Seeing Jesus as being from God.

The fifth stage of spiritual sight is seeing Jesus as being *from God* (vv.32-33). This was the man's final answer to those who questioned his confession of Jesus. He confessed that Jesus was *from God*. He reasoned that...

- helping and delivering a blind man was God's will
- Jesus delivered him. God heard Jesus' prayer for him and empowered Jesus to heal him.
- Jesus was bound to be *from God*

The man knew that the works of Jesus were proof that He was from God. Therefore, Jesus was not a liar and a deceiver; Jesus was not an evil man. He was bound to be who He claimed to be; He was bound to be *from God* (see note—Jn.7:25-31).

> "For I have come down from heaven, not to do my own will but the will of him who sent me." (Jn.6:38)

> So Jesus proclaimed, as he taught in the temple, "You know me, and you know where I come from. But I have not come of my own accord. He who sent me is true, and him you do not know. I know him, for I come from him, and he sent me." (Jn.7:28-29)

> Jesus said to them, "If God were your Father, you would love me, for I came from God and I am here. I came not of my own accord, but he sent me." (Jn.8:42)

## 9:35-38

³⁵ Jesus heard that they had cast him out, and having found him he said, "Do you believe in the Son of Man?"
³⁶ He answered, "And who is he, sir, that I may believe in him?"
³⁷ Jesus said to him, "You have seen him, and it is he who is speaking to you."
³⁸ He said, "Lord, I believe," and he worshiped him.

## 6 Stage 6: Seeing Jesus as who He truly is.

The sixth stage of spiritual sight is seeing Jesus as who He truly is, the Messiah, God's Son who came to earth as a man to be the Savior of the world. The blind man's answer about Jesus so infuriated the Pharisees that they threw him out of the synagogue. When Jesus heard about this, He found the man again. Note that the man did not seek Jesus; Jesus sought the man. Jesus was the One who did the seeking. He sought the man who had been cast out.

**THOUGHT 1.** Anyone can cast a person out—a business, a church, a family, neighbors, friends. But Jesus seeks the person who is cast out and rejected. He always does, no matter who the person is or what the person has done.

The climactic stage of spiritual sight is clearly demonstrated by the man's experience. Jesus invited the man to believe in Him (v.35). In answer to the man's question as to who the Messiah is, Jesus declared that He is (vv.36-37). The man believed in Jesus and worshiped Him (v.38). The climactic stage of spiritual sight is seeing Jesus as who He truly and uniquely is: God's Son who came to earth as a Man to be the Savior of the world.

> And those in the boat worshiped him, saying, "Truly you are the Son of God." (Mt.14:33)
>
> The beginning of the gospel of Jesus Christ, the Son of God. (Mk.1:1)
>
> "And I [John the Baptist] have seen and have borne witness that this is the Son of God." (Jn.1:34)
>
> "For God so loved the world, that he gave his only Son, that whoever believes in him should not perish but have eternal life. For God did not send his Son into the world to condemn the world, but in order that the world might be saved through him. Whoever believes in him is not condemned, but whoever does not believe is condemned already, because he has not believed in the name of the only Son of God." (Jn.3:16-18)
>
> "Do you say of him whom the Father consecrated and sent into the world, 'You are blaspheming,' because I said, 'I am the Son of God'?" (Jn.10:36)
>
> She said to him, "Yes, Lord; I believe that you are the Christ, the Son of God, who is coming into the world." (Jn.11:27)
>
> How much worse punishment, do you think, will be deserved by the one who has trampled underfoot the Son of God, and has profaned the blood of the covenant by which he was sanctified, and has outraged the Spirit of grace? (He.10:29)
>
> Whoever confesses that Jesus is the Son of God, God abides in him, and he in God. (1 Jn.4:15)

It is believing Jesus to be the Son of God and worshiping Him (see DEEPER STUDY # 2—Jn.2:24).

> "That whoever believes in him may have eternal life. For God so loved the world, that he gave his only Son, that whoever believes in him should not perish but have eternal life." (Jn.3:15-16)
>
> "Truly, truly, I say to you, whoever hears my word and believes him who sent me has eternal life. He does not come into judgment, but has passed from death to life." (Jn.5:24)
>
> Because, if you confess with your mouth that Jesus is Lord and believe in your heart that God raised him from the dead, you will be saved. For with the heart one believes and is justified, and with the mouth one confesses and is saved. (Ro.10:9-10)

## 7 Stage 7: Seeing the lesson in Jesus' revelation.

The final stage of spiritual sight is to see the lesson in Jesus' revelation. Once we receive spiritual sight by believing in Jesus, we need to see that His mission is now our mission.

### a. Jesus' mission: To bring judgment (v.39).

Jesus stated that His mission on earth was to bring judgment. Jesus judges every person—all generations of people. By *judgment*, Jesus meant that His mission was to pronounce all people guilty before God. The purpose behind this judgment was to make people understand their lost condition, their spiritual blindness; to cause them to recognize that they are condemned before God.

Christ judges or deals with the person who knows he/she is spiritually blind and wants to see. He takes those who are spiritually blind and gives them sight—if they really desire to see.

> ³⁹ Jesus said, "For judgment I came into this world, that those who do not see may see, and those who see may become blind."
>
> ⁴⁰ Some of the Pharisees near him heard these things, and said to him, "Are we also blind?"
>
> ⁴¹ Jesus said to them, "If you were blind, you would have no guilt; but now that you say, 'We see,' your guilt remains."

> Again Jesus spoke to them, saying, "I am the light of the world. Whoever follows me will not walk in darkness, but will have the light of life." (Jn.8:12)
>
> "I have come into the world as light, so that whoever believes in me may not remain in darkness." (Jn.12:46)
>
> For anything that becomes visible is light. Therefore it says, "Awake, O sleeper, and arise from the dead, and Christ will shine on you." (Ep.5:14)

In addition, He judges those who claim to have spiritual sight apart from Him, like the Pharisees. The person who claims to see spiritually and claims to know God apart from Christ is judged to be blind (see Jn.14:6-9).

> "But if your eye is bad, your whole body will be full of darkness. If then the light in you is darkness, how great is the darkness!" (Mt.6:23)

> The light shines in the darkness, and the darkness has not overcome it. (Jn.1:5)
>
> "And this is the judgment: the light has come into the world, and people loved the darkness rather than the light because their works were evil." (Jn.3:19)

### b. The religious leaders' expectation: To be exempt from judgment (v.40).

The Pharisees expected exemption from judgment. They were opposing Jesus, so they expected Him to say they were blind, but He shocked them with His response.

### c. Jesus' declaration: He sought to convict them of their hypocrisy, their sin (v.41).

Jesus said that the Pharisees' blindness was an excuse. If they had been blind, they would have been excused; for they would have been acting in ignorance, not knowing what they were doing (see Ro.5:13). But they . . .
- knew the law of God
- knew about spiritual things
- claimed to see
- did not recognize God's Son

They were, therefore, guilty and were judged blind and were to be condemned. In fact, they were even more guilty than those who have no knowledge of God and His Word.

> "But I tell you, it will be more bearable on the day of judgment for Tyre and Sidon than for you." (Mt.11:22)
>
> "And this is the judgment: the light has come into the world, and people loved the darkness rather than the light because their works were evil." (Jn.3:19)
>
> For God shows no partiality. For all who have sinned without the law will also perish without the law, and all who have sinned under the law will be judged by the law. (Ro.2:11-12)

**THOUGHT 1.** The lesson of Jesus' revelation is this: His mission was to help all people see that they are spiritually blind in order that they would believe in Him and receive spiritual sight. Like the Pharisees, many do not recognize their own spiritual blindness. Nevertheless, they are guilty before God.

Our mission is the same. Jesus has committed this mission to us. We are to take the gospel to every person so that they may be healed of their spiritual blindness and receive spiritual sight through believing in Christ.

> "But I tell you, it will be more bearable on the day of judgment for Tyre and Sidon than for you." (Mt.11:22)
>
> And Jesus came and said to them, "All authority in heaven and on earth has been given to me. Go therefore and make disciples of all nations, baptizing them in the name of the Father and of the Son and of the Holy Spirit." (Mt.28:18-19)
>
> And he said to them, "Go into all the world and proclaim the gospel to the whole creation." (Mk.16:15)
>
> And even if our gospel is veiled, it is veiled to those who are perishing. In their case the god of this world has blinded the minds of the unbelievers, to keep them from seeing the light of the gospel of the glory of Christ, who is the image of God. (2 Co.4:3-4)
>
> Hear, you deaf, and look, you blind, that you may see! (Is.42:18)

# Chapter 10

## X. The Revelation of Jesus, the Shepherd of Life, 10:1-42

### A. The Shepherd and His Sheep: False vs. True Teachers, 10:1-6

"Truly, truly, I say to you, he who does not enter the sheepfold by the door but climbs in by another way, that man is a thief and a robber.

² But he who enters by the door is the shepherd of the sheep.

³ To him the gatekeeper opens. The sheep hear his voice, and he calls his own sheep by name and leads them out.

⁴ When he has brought out all his own, he goes before them, and the sheep follow him, for they know his voice.

⁵ A stranger they will not follow, but they will flee from him, for they do not know the voice of strangers."

⁶ This figure of speech Jesus used with them, but they did not understand what he was saying to them.

1. The sheep pen: A place of safety & security
2. The false shepherd
   a. Enters the sheep pen the wrong way
   b. Is a thief & a robber
3. The true Shepherd
   a. Enters the appointed door
   b. Is known by the gatekeeper (God)
   c. Knows the sheep by name
   d. Leads & shepherds the sheep
4. The sheep
   a. Know the Shepherd's voice
   b. Follow the Shepherd who goes before them
   c. Flee from strange voices
5. The illustration: Was not understood

# Division X

## *The Revelation of Jesus, the Shepherd of Life, 10:1-42*

A. The Shepherd and His Sheep: False vs. True Teachers, 10:1-6

## 10:1-6
## Introduction

Jesus' revelation of Himself as the Good Shepherd presents one of the most beautiful images in all His teachings. It is an image that has inspired many artists, poets, and songwriters throughout the centuries. This passage begins the great revelation of Jesus as the Shepherd of Life. Jesus is pictured as the only true Shepherd of the sheep. This is, *The Shepherd and His Sheep: False vs. True Teachers,* 10:1-6.

1. The sheep pen: A place of safety and security (v.1).
2. The false shepherd (v.1).
3. The true Shepherd (vv.2-3).
4. The sheep (vv.4-5).
5. The illustration: Was not understood (v.6).

## 1 The sheep pen: A place of safety and security.

In order to gain the full attention of His audience, Jesus began this teaching with the solemn preface, *truly, truly* or *most assuredly*. What He had to say was of critical importance.

**10:1a**

"Truly, truly, I say to you, he who does not enter the sheepfold by the door but climbs in by another way, that man is a thief and a robber."

Jesus illustrated the relationship between God and people as that of a shepherd and his sheep, a familiar image from the Old Testament (Ps.23; Is.53:6). Jesus mentions a sheepfold, a pen where all the sheep are kept. The sheepfold pictures the place of acceptance by God, or the place of safety and security in God's presence (see DEEPER STUDY # 3—Mt.19:23-24). It is the *position* of salvation, of spiritual sight that comes by believing Jesus to be Son of God (Jn.9:36-38). It is the *position* of being accepted by God because a person approaches God through His Son, Jesus Christ. The sheepfold symbolizes the place where the sheep (believers) are kept. The sheep are kept...

- in the church
- in heaven
- in salvation
- in spiritual sight
- in the place of acceptance
- in the Kingdom of God
- in eternal life
- in spiritual deliverance from darkness
- in the position of faith

**10:1**

## 2 The false shepherd.

This entire discourse contrasts a false shepherd from the true shepherd. Both go after the sheep. The true shepherd, of course, is Christ, while the false shepherds are those who oppose Christ, including the religious leaders—the false teachers—who so blindly stood against His claim to be "the Light of the world" (8:12; 9:5; see 9:40). Today, all who teach any doctrine but the true doctrine of God's Holy Word—whether from some other world religion or under the name of Christianity—are false shepherds.

### a. Enters the sheep pen the wrong way (v.1b).

The sheepfold can be entered. There is a door into the sheepfold—an entrance, a way to get in—and the door is the only *acceptable* way to enter. The false shepherd does not enter the sheepfold through the door; he enters the wrong way.

### b. Is a thief and robber (v.1c).

False shepherds climb into the sheepfold from *another* or *some other way* (Gk. allachothen). This word is important, as it indicates origin. The false shepherd *comes from* and *originates from*...

- some other direction
- some other place
- some other position
- some other source
- some other road

Note also the terms *thief* (kleptes) and *robber* (leistes). The very same words were used to describe Judas (a thief) and Barabbas (a robber). It is an awful thing for a person to be put into the same class as Judas and Barabbas, two who were as opposite from Christ as any people could be.

The false shepherd is...
- a thief: a seducer and a deceiver, a crafty and dishonest person, a person who will use any means to get into the sheepfold to steal the sheep
- a robber: a plunderer; a person who will use violence and cruelty and will destroy and devour, if necessary, to get into the sheepfold

God has much to say to false shepherds (see outlines and notes—1 Ti.6:3-5; Tit.1:10-16; 2 Pe.2:1-22; Jude 1:3-16).

**All you beasts [false shepherds] of the field, come to devour—all you beasts in the forest. His watchmen are blind; they are all without knowledge; they are all silent dogs; they cannot bark,**

dreaming, lying down, loving to slumber. The dogs have a mighty appetite; they never have enough. But they are shepherds who have no understanding; they have all turned to their own way, each to his own gain, one and all. "Come," they say, "let me get wine; let us fill ourselves with strong drink; and tomorrow will be like this day, great beyond measure." (Is.56:9-12)

"Woe to the shepherds who destroy and scatter the sheep of my pasture!" declares the LORD. Therefore thus says the LORD, the God of Israel, concerning the shepherds who care for my people: "You have scattered my flock and have driven them away, and you have not attended to them. Behold, I will attend to you for your evil deeds, declares the LORD." (Je.23:1-2; see Je.25:34-38)

"My people have been lost sheep. Their shepherds have led them astray, turning them away on the mountains. From mountain to hill they have gone. They have forgotten their fold." (Je.50:6)

The word of the LORD came to me: "Son of man, prophesy against the shepherds of Israel; prophesy, and say to them, even to the shepherds, Thus says the Lord GOD: Ah, shepherds of Israel who have been feeding yourselves! Should not shepherds feed the sheep? You eat the fat, you clothe yourselves with the wool, you slaughter the fat ones, but you do not feed the sheep. The weak you have not strengthened, the sick you have not healed, the injured you have not bound up, the strayed you have not brought back, the lost you have not sought, and with force and harshness you have ruled them. So they were scattered, because there was no shepherd, and they became food for all the wild beasts. My sheep were scattered; they wandered over all the mountains and on every high hill. My sheep were scattered over all the face of the earth, with none to search or seek for them." (Eze.34:1-6; see Eze.34:7-31)

## 3 The True Shepherd.

The true shepherd stands in clear contrast to the false shepherd. Jesus pointed out four distinctives of the true shepherd.

² "But he who enters by the door is the shepherd of the sheep.
³ To him the gatekeeper opens. The sheep hear his voice, and he calls his own sheep by name and leads them out."

### a. Enters the appointed door (v.2).

The shepherd who enters the appointed door is the true shepherd (Jesus Christ). He knows where the door is and the way into the sheepfold. Therefore, He uses the door. There is no reason for Him not to use it, no reason for Him to climb in any other way.

➢ His purpose is not to steal some sheep from the Owner (God) and start a flock of His own. Such a thought is the farthest thing from His mind. His thoughts are focused on the sheep and the Owner's will.
➢ His purpose is to be the Shepherd of the Owner (God), to serve Him and to do His will.

The Shepherd enters the sheepfold by the door. The door was made for Him and the sheep to enter; therefore, He uses it.

### b. Is known by the gatekeeper (God) (v.3a).

The Shepherd is known by the gatekeeper (God or the Holy Spirit). This point is critical. The Holy Spirit is the One who opens the door into the sheepfold. The One who comes to the door is known by the gatekeeper; He is known to be the Shepherd. Therefore, the Shepherd is not afraid to face the gatekeeper. He has been appointed to use the door and has the authority to enter the sheepfold.

"Just as the Father knows me and I know the Father; and I lay down my life for the sheep." (Jn.10:15)

### c. Knows the sheep by name (v.3b).

The Shepherd knows the sheep; He knows each one by name. This is said to have been a common trait among shepherds in Jesus' day—they actually knew each sheep individually, even in large herds. This is certainly true with Christ and His sheep. The words *His own* (sidia) tell us He calls His own, not as a whole, not as a herd, but as individuals. The Shepherd, the Lord Jesus Christ, knows each of His sheep by name.

"I am the good shepherd. I know my own and my own know me." (Jn.10:14)

But if anyone loves God, he is known by God. (1 Co.8:3)

But God's firm foundation stands, bearing this seal: "The Lord knows those who are his," and, "Let everyone who names the name of the Lord depart from iniquity." (2 Ti.2:19)

But now thus says the LORD, he who created you, O Jacob, he who formed you, O Israel: "Fear not, for I have redeemed you; I have called you by name, you are mine." (Is.43:1)

### d. Leads and shepherds the sheep (v.3c).

The Shepherd leads and shepherds the sheep. He loves them as His own; therefore He must lead them to green pastures and still waters. He needs to see that they are nourished and protected and given the very best care possible (see note—Mk.6:34 for more discussion, what happens to sheep without a Shepherd).

> ➢ He feeds the sheep even if He has to gather them in His arms and carry them to the feasting pasture.

He will tend his flock like a shepherd; he will gather the lambs in his arms; he will carry them in his bosom, and gently lead those that are with young. (Is.40:11)

> ➢ He guides the sheep to the pasture and away from the rough places and dangerous cliffs.

The LORD is my shepherd; I shall not want. He makes me lie down in green pastures. He leads me beside still waters. He restores my soul. He leads me in paths of righteousness for his name's sake. Even though I walk through the valley of the shadow of death, I will fear no evil, for you are with me; your rod and your staff, they comfort me. (Ps.23:1-4)

> ➢ He seeks and saves the sheep who get lost.

"What do you think? If a man has a hundred sheep, and one of them has gone astray, does he not leave the ninety-nine on the mountains and go in search of the one that went astray?" (Mt.18:11-12)

"I will seek the lost, and I will bring back the strayed, and I will bind up the injured, and I will strengthen the weak, and the fat and the strong I will destroy. I will feed them in justice." (Eze.34:16)

> ➢ He protects the sheep. He even sacrifices His life for the sheep.

"I am the good shepherd. The good shepherd lays down his life for the sheep." (Jn.10:11)

Now may the God of peace who brought again from the dead our Lord Jesus, the great shepherd of the sheep, by the blood of the eternal covenant. (He.13:20)

> ➢ He restores the sheep who go astray and returns them to the sheepfold.

For you were straying like sheep, but have now returned to the Shepherd and Overseer of your souls. (1 Pe.2:25)

> ➢ He rewards the sheep for obedience and faithfulness.

And when the chief Shepherd appears, you will receive the unfading crown of glory. (1 Pe.5:4)

> ➢ He will keep the sheep separate from the goats.

"Before him will be gathered all the nations, and he will separate people one from another as a shepherd separates the sheep from the goats. And he will place the sheep on his right, but the goats on the left." (Mt.25:32-33)

10:4-5

⁴ "When he has brought out all his own, he goes before them, and the sheep follow him, for they know his voice.
⁵ A stranger they will not follow, but they will flee from him, for they do not know the voice of strangers."

## 4 The sheep.

The sheep in this illustration are disciples or believers of the Lord. Jesus pointed out three distinctives of those who are truly the Lord's sheep, who have genuinely been born again. Sheep:

### a. Know the Shepherd's voice (v.4).

The sheep know the Shepherd's voice. They know both His sound and His words. The sound of His voice is not uncertain and unclear, not weak and frail, not quivering and indecisive. It is clear, strong, sure, and decisive. The words of His voice are words of care and tenderness, of warning and safety, of truth and security.

**THOUGHT 1.** Believers trust the voice, the Word of Christ, because they know His voice.

> For he whom God has sent utters the words of God, for he gives the Spirit without measure. (Jn.3:34)
>
> "It is the Spirit who gives life; the flesh is no help at all. The words that I have spoken to you are spirit and life." (Jn.6:63)
>
> Simon Peter answered him, "Lord, to whom shall we go? You have the words of eternal life." (Jn.6:68)
>
> Then Pilate said to him, "So you are a king?" Jesus answered, "You say that I am a king. For this purpose I was born and for this purpose I have come into the world—to bear witness to the truth. Everyone who is of the truth listens to my voice." (Jn.18:37)
>
> And we also thank God constantly for this, that when you received the word of God, which you heard from us, you accepted it not as the word of men but as what it really is, the word of God, which is at work in you believers. (1 Th.2:13)
>
> Like newborn infants, long for the pure spiritual milk, that by it you may grow up into salvation—if indeed you have tasted that the Lord is good. (1 Pe.2:2-3)

b. **Follow the Shepherd who goes before them (v.4).**

The sheep follow the Shepherd. Note that He goes before them to lead the way. He does not drive them like cattle. He leads in order to pick out the safe and secure way to the pasture. He leads to show the sheep that the road is clear and safe. The sheep know this, so they follow the Shepherd, knowing they are perfectly safe and secure following the path He has laid out before them (see Jn.14:6).

➤ They follow Him because He saves them and gives them life.

> "Just as the Father knows me and I know the Father; and I lay down my life for the sheep." (Jn.10:15)
>
> "My sheep hear my voice, and I know them, and they follow me. I give them eternal life, and they will never perish, and no one will snatch them out of my hand." (Jn.10:27-28)
>
> On that day the LORD their God will save them, as the flock of his people; for like the jewels of a crown they shall shine on his land. (Zec.9:16)

➤ They follow Him because they are the sheep of His pasture.

> Know that the LORD, he is God! It is he who made us, and we are his; we are his people, and the sheep of his pasture. (Ps.100:3)

➤ They follow Him because they wish to give Him praise forever.

> But I will declare it forever; I will sing praises to the God of Jacob. (Ps.75:9)

➤ They follow Him because they are sheep in the midst of wolves.

> "I know that after my departure fierce wolves will come in among you, not sparing the flock." (Ac.20:29)

➤ They follow Him because He assures them and delivers them from fear.

> "Fear not, little flock, for it is your Father's good pleasure to give you the kingdom." (Lu.12:32)

➤ They follow Him because they have learned that without Him they are scattered and lost.

> And Jesus said to them, "You will all fall away, for it is written, 'I will strike the shepherd, and the sheep will be scattered.'" (Mk.14:27; see Mt.26:31)

➤ They follow Him because He takes care of all their wants.

> The LORD is my shepherd; I shall not want. (Ps.23:1)

c. **Flee from strange voices (v.5).**

The sheep flee from strange voices. They are puzzled and fearful of a stranger's voice. A stranger's sound and words are different. Therefore, they *will not* (ou me) follow a stranger. This is a double negative. They will not, in any case, never no never, follow a stranger. Instead, they run away from the strange voice, the way a person flees from danger.

**THOUGHT 1.** The strange voice can be the voice of . . .

- false religion
- false science
- false psychology
- false philosophy (humanism)
- materialism
- worldliness
- fame

10:6

⁶ This figure of speech Jesus used with them, but they did not understand what he was saying to them.

### 5 The illustration: Was not understood.

This *figure of speech* or *illustration* (paroimian) was not understood by Jesus' audience. The spiritual truth was beyond the Jewish religious leaders, the false teachers. They could not grasp the truth with their natural minds. They could not see themselves as false shepherds, and they could not see Jesus as the true Shepherd. Sinful human nature rebels against being called *false* and against Christ's being the *only Shepherd* of the sheep.

"'For this people's heart has grown dull, and with their ears they can barely hear, and their eyes they have closed; lest they should see with their eyes and hear with their ears and understand with their heart and turn, and I would heal them.'" (Ac.28:27)

Always learning and never able to arrive at a knowledge of the truth. (2 Ti.3:7)

### B. The Door of the Sheep: The Only Way to God, 10:7–10

⁷ So Jesus again said to them, "Truly, truly, I say to you, I am the door of the sheep.

⁸ All who came before me are thieves and robbers, but the sheep did not listen to them.

⁹ I am the door. If anyone enters by me, he will be saved and will go in and out and find pasture.

¹⁰ The thief comes only to steal and kill and destroy. I came that they may have life and have it abundantly."

1. **Jesus is the only gate for the sheep, the only way to God**
   a. All others are thieves & robbers, false messiahs
   b. Proof: The sheep did not listen to them, their teaching
2. **Jesus is the only gate that leads to salvation**
   a. He gives peace & security
   b. He gives abundant provision (pasture)
3. **Jesus is the only gate that leads to abundant life**
   a. All others come to steal, kill, & destroy
   b. Jesus comes to give a full life[DS1]

# Division X

*The Revelation of Jesus, the Shepherd of Life, 10:1–42*

B. The Door of the Sheep: The Only Way to God, 10:7–10

## 10:7–10
## Introduction

Jesus is the Door of the sheep. Jesus is probably referring to the door of a community sheepfold or a community pasture which housed all the flocks of an area. There is, however, another descriptive picture of Jesus as the door. When the sheep were kept out in the hill country overnight, they were contained in ravines surrounded by several rocky walls. Naturally, the opening into these ravines had no door at all. The shepherd himself literally became the door, for during the night he would simply lie across the opening. The sheep could get out only by going over him, and the enemies of the sheep could get in to the sheep only by going through him. Access in or out was only through the shepherd.

In this passage, Jesus teaches us that salvation is only through Him, the true Shepherd, and we must be diligent to recognize anybody who preaches any other message as a false shepherd. This is, *The Door of the Sheep: The Only Way to God*, 10:7-10.

1. Jesus is the only gate for the sheep, the only way to God (vv.7-8).
2. Jesus is the only gate that leads to salvation (v.9).
3. Jesus is the only gate that leads to abundant life (v.10).

### 10:7–8

### 1 Jesus is the only gate for the sheep, the only way to God.

Jesus is the *only* Door of the sheep. Once again, Jesus introduced His statement with *truly, truly* or *most assuredly* to

⁷ So Jesus again said to them, "Truly, truly, I say to you, I am the door of the sheep.
⁸ All who came before me are thieves and robbers, but the sheep did not listen to them."

stress the critical importance of what He was about to say. By *door* Jesus meant that He is the way or entrance into the sheepfold. Jesus Christ is the way...

- into God's presence
- into God's acceptance
- into salvation
- into the true church
- into heaven
- into the kingdom of God
- into eternal life

Therefore, if we wish to enter where God is, we must enter through the Door of Christ. A person enters God's sheepfold only through the Door of Christ, for Christ is the *only* Door into God's presence.

> **Jesus said to him, "I am the way, and the truth, and the life. No one comes to the Father except through me." (Jn.14:6)**
>
> **For through him we both have access in one Spirit to the Father. (Ep.2:18)**
>
> **For there is one God, and there is one mediator between God and men, the man Christ Jesus. (1 Ti.2:5)**
>
> **But as it is, Christ has obtained a ministry that is as much more excellent than the old as the covenant he mediates is better, since it is enacted on better promises. (He.8:6; see He.12:24)**
>
> **By the new and living way that he [Christ] opened for us through the curtain, that is, through his flesh. (He.10:20)**

Note that Jesus used the clear claim to deity: *I Am*. This gives additional emphasis to His claim to be the *only* Door to God.

### a. All others are thieves and robbers, false messiahs (v.8a).

All others who claim to be the door are thieves and robbers. There are some who claim to be the door and to have the way to God. They claim to know the right way and to have the newest and best ideas and teaching, the greatest religion, works, maturity, philosophy, psychology, ideas, and the most innovative concepts. They claim to be the door that opens into God's presence. But Jesus says that they are thieves and robbers. They are out to steal the sheep, both their wool (possessions) and their lives (loyalty). They want both their wool and their lives, for if they have both they have the sheep's *permanent loyalty* (see note, False Shepherd—Jn.10:1 for more discussion and verses).

> **Some indeed preach Christ from envy and rivalry, but others from good will. (Ph.1:15)**
>
> **"For from the least to the greatest of them, everyone is greedy for unjust gain; and from prophet to priest, everyone deals falsely." (Je.6:13)**
>
> **"I will set shepherds over them who will care for them, and they shall fear no more, nor be dismayed, neither shall any be missing, declares the LORD." (Je.23:4)**
>
> **Its heads give judgment for a bribe; its priests teach for a price; its prophets practice divination for money; yet they lean on the LORD and say, "Is not the LORD in the midst of us? No disaster shall come upon us." (Mi.3:11)**

### b. Proof: The sheep did not listen to them, their teaching (v.8b).

The sheep themselves are proof that Jesus is the only door and that all others are false doors. The sheep *do not listen* to the voices of false *doors*, not if they are the real sheep of the Shepherd. The real sheep of God know the Shepherd's voice and have the ability to discern it. If they hear the voice of a false shepherd, they know that he and his sheepfold are false. His voice and message are not the voice and message of the true Door, the Son of God Himself.

> **"I am the good shepherd. I know my own and my own know me." (Jn.10:14)**
>
> **"My sheep hear my voice, and I know them, and they follow me. I give them eternal life, and they will never perish, and no one will snatch them out of my hand." (Jn.10:27-28)**
>
> **Now we have received not the spirit of the world, but the Spirit who is from God, that we might understand the things freely given us by God.... The natural person does not accept the things of the Spirit of God, for they are folly to him, and he is not able to understand them because they are spiritually discerned. (1 Co.2:12, 14)**

## 2 Jesus is the only gate that leads to salvation.

Jesus is the only door that leads to salvation. He is the only way to a relationship with God, the only way to heaven, the only way to eternal life and all that it possesses for God's followers.

> "For God so loved the world, that he gave his only Son, that whoever believes in him should not perish but have eternal life. For God did not send his Son into the world to condemn the world, but in order that the world might be saved through him." (Jn.3:16-17)
>
> "And there is salvation in no one else, for there is no other name under heaven given among men by which we must be saved." (Ac.4:12)
>
> "But we believe that we will be saved through the grace of the Lord Jesus, just as they will." (Ac.15:11)
>
> And being made perfect, he became the source of eternal salvation to all who obey him. (He.5:9)

> 9 "I am the door. If anyone enters by me, he will be saved and will go in and out and find pasture."

### a. He gives peace and security.

Jesus is the only door that opens to peace and security. He is the only door that allows the sheep to *go in and out*. This was a common Jewish phrase and concept. If people can go in and out without difficulty or danger, it means they are safe and secure. Jesus brings to the believer safety and security, peace and tranquility.

When we enter through the door of Jesus, we have peace *with* God (Ro.8:1), and we can have the peace *of* God reigning in our hearts during times that make us anxious (Ph.4:6-7). As Jesus will state later in this chapter, we are safe and secure in His hand, and He is safe and secure in the Father's hand (Jn.10:28-29). Neither any person nor any thing can snatch us out of His hand, and we are shielded there from God's wrath.

> "I have said these things to you, that in me you may have peace. In the world you will have tribulation. But take heart; I have overcome the world." (Jn.16:33)
>
> Since, therefore, we have now been justified by his blood, much more shall we be saved by him from the wrath of God. (Ro.5:9)
>
> There is therefore now no condemnation for those who are in Christ Jesus. (Ro.8:1)
>
> Do not be anxious about anything, but in everything by prayer and supplication with thanksgiving let your requests be made known to God. And the peace of God, which surpasses all understanding, will guard your hearts and your minds in Christ Jesus. (Ph.4:6-7)
>
> For God has not destined us for wrath, but to obtain salvation through our Lord Jesus Christ. (1 Th.5:9)
>
> But the Lord is faithful. He will establish you and guard you against the evil one. (2 Th.3:3)
>
> Which is why I suffer as I do. But I am not ashamed, for I know whom I have believed, and I am convinced that he is able to guard until that day what has been entrusted to me. (2 Ti.1:12)
>
> The Lord will rescue me from every evil deed and bring me safely into his heavenly kingdom. To him be the glory forever and ever. Amen. (2 Ti.4:18)
>
> Who by God's power are being guarded through faith for a salvation ready to be revealed in the last time. (1 Pe.1:5)
>
> Now to him who is able to keep you from stumbling and to present you blameless before the presence of his glory with great joy. (Jude 24)
>
> "Behold, I am with you and will keep you wherever you go, and will bring you back to this land. For I will not leave you until I have done what I have promised you." (Ge.28:15)
>
> "The eternal God is your dwelling place, and underneath are the everlasting arms. And he thrust out the enemy before you and said, 'Destroy.'" (De.33:27)
>
> Behold, he who keeps Israel [His people] will neither slumber nor sleep. (Ps.121:4)
>
> Fear not, for I am with you; be not dismayed, for I am your God; I will strengthen you, I will help you, I will uphold you with my righteous right hand. (Is.41:10)

b. **He gives abundant provision (pasture).**

When we believe in Jesus, He provides for us abundantly. Jesus is the only door that opens to healthy and lasting nourishment. He is the only door that leads to the true pasture, the pasture that has the living stream flowing through it and the pasture that has the living food in it.

➤ His pasture alone can satisfy the soul.

**For he satisfies the longing soul, and the hungry soul he fills with good things. (Ps.107:9)**

**"And the Lord will guide you continually and satisfy your desire in scorched places and make your bones strong; and you shall be like a watered garden, like a spring of water, whose waters do not fail." (Is.58:11)**

➤ His pasture alone can restore the soul.

**He makes me lie down in green pastures. He leads me beside still waters. He restores my soul. He leads me in paths of righteousness for his name's sake. (Ps.23:2-3)**

➤ His pasture alone can give life and give it forever.

**"I am the living bread that came down from heaven. If anyone eats of this bread, he will live forever. And the bread that I will give for the life of the world is my flesh." (Jn.6:51)**

➤ His pasture alone can feed with knowledge and understanding.

**"And I will give you shepherds after my own heart, who will feed you with knowledge and understanding." (Je.3:15)**

## 10:10

¹⁰ "The thief comes only to steal and kill and destroy. I came that they may have life and have it abundantly."

## 3 Jesus is the only gate that leads to abundant life.

Jesus is the only door that leads to abundant life. This is a sharp contrast between the thief and Christ.

a. **All others come to steal, kill, and destroy.**

Any person who says there is another door is a thief and a robber who steals and kills and destroys the sheep. The thief misleads and deceives the sheep, leading them through a door that leads to destruction.

There are some who definitely want the wool and benefits of the sheep (false and liberal religions and false philosophies). That is, they want what the sheep can offer them—their money, possessions, time, devotion, service. They want the sheep to follow them and their position, so they do all they can to secure the sheep's . . .

- loyalty
- allegiance
- possessions
- time
- effort
- energy
- recognition
- praise
- honor

By leading the sheep away from the *protections offered exclusively* by Christ, the false teacher becomes a thief—a thief in that he steals the soul of the sheep from God, leading it into a sheepfold that will be destroyed. It causes the sheep never to know the true Shepherd.

b. **Jesus comes to give a full life.**

Jesus came not to steal life, but to give abundant life (see Deeper Study # 1). The difference between Christ and every false shepherd—every thieving, destroying false teacher—is clear: the false shepherds are concerned about themselves while Christ is concerned about the sheep. They *take from* the sheep, but Jesus *gives to* the sheep.

## Deeper Study # 1

(10:10) **Jesus Christ, Purpose—Life**: life is one of the great words of the Scriptures. The noun *life* (Gk. zoe) and the verb *to live* or *to have life* (zen) have a depth of meaning (see Deeper Study # 2—Jn.1:4; Deeper Study # 1—17:2-3).

1. Life is the energy, the force, the power of being.

2. Life is the opposite of perishing. It is deliverance from condemnation and death. It is the stopping or cessation of deterioration, decay, and corruption (Jn.3:16; 5:24, 29; 10:28).

3. Life is *eternal* (aionios). It is forever. It is the very life of God Himself (Jn.17:3). However, eternal life does not refer just to duration. Living forever would be a curse for some persons. The idea of eternal life is also quality of life, a certain kind of life, a life that consistently knows love, joy, peace, power, and responsibility (Jn.10:10).

4. Life is satisfaction (Jn.6:35).

5. Life is security and enjoyment (Jn.10:10).

6. Life is found only in God. God is the source and author of life, and it is God who has appointed Jesus Christ to bring life to all people. Jesus Christ gives the very life of God Himself (Jn.5:26; 6:27, 40; 10:28; 17:23).

7. Life has now been revealed. It has been unveiled and is clearly seen in Jesus Christ. Jesus Christ shows humanity what true life is (Jn.1:4-5; 5:26; 1 Jn.1:2).

8. Life only comes to people by believing in Jesus Christ. All who are outside of Jesus Christ merely exist; they go about their day-to-day existence without true purpose. Real life is found only in God, for God is the creator of life. As the creator of life, He alone knows what life really is and what it is supposed to be (Jn.3:36; 5:24; 6:47). This is the reason He sent His Son, the Lord Jesus Christ, into the world: to show us what life is. When we look at Jesus Christ, we see exactly what life is, exactly what it involves (see Ga.5:22-23):

- love
- joy
- peace
- longsuffering
- gentleness
- goodness
- faith
- meekness
- temperance or control and power

## C. The Good Shepherd: Jesus, the True Savior of the World,[DS1] 10:11–21

1. **The meaning of "Good Shepherd"**
   a. He is one who sacrificed His life[DS2]

   b. He is not a hired or employed shepherd
      1) Not one who sees danger & acts cowardly or flees
      2) Not one who causes the sheep to be caught by a wolf (false teacher)
      3) Not one who lacks genuine care

2. **The proof that Jesus is the Good Shepherd**
   a. He knows His sheep
   b. He knows His Father—the Owner
   c. He will die for His sheep

   d. He works to increase the number of sheep

3. **The final proof of Jesus' claim: His death & resurrection**
   a. Jesus is loved by God for His great sacrifice
   b. Jesus' death was the supreme act of obedience
      1) Was voluntary
      2) Was a command

4. **The reaction to Jesus' claim**

   a. Some reject: Call Jesus demon-possessed & mad

   b. Some question: Perhaps Jesus is who He claims

¹¹ "I am the good shepherd. The good shepherd lays down his life for the sheep.
¹² He who is a hired hand and not a shepherd, who does not own the sheep, sees the wolf coming and leaves the sheep and flees, and the wolf snatches them and scatters them.
¹³ He flees because he is a hired hand and cares nothing for the sheep.
¹⁴ I am the good shepherd. I know my own and my own know me,
¹⁵ just as the Father knows me and I know the Father; and I lay down my life for the sheep.
¹⁶ And I have other sheep that are not of this fold. I must bring them also, and they will listen to my voice. So there will be one flock, one shepherd.
¹⁷ For this reason the Father loves me, because I lay down my life that I may take it up again.
¹⁸ No one takes it from me, but I lay it down of my own accord. I have authority to lay it down, and I have authority to take it up again. This charge I have received from my Father."
¹⁹ There was again a division among the Jews because of these words.
²⁰ Many of them said, "He has a demon, and is insane; why listen to him?"
²¹ Others said, "These are not the words of one who is oppressed by a demon. Can a demon open the eyes of the blind?"

# Division X

## The Revelation of Jesus, the Shepherd of Life, 10:1-42

### C. The Good Shepherd: Jesus, the True Savior of the World, 10:11-21

**10:11-21**
## Introduction

Jesus continued to present Himself as the true Shepherd (see DEEPER STUDY # 1), and He continued to contrast Himself and false shepherds—false teachers and religious leaders. Revealing Himself to be "the Good Shepherd," Jesus spoke some of the most beautiful, heart-reaching words recorded in all of Scripture:

> "I am the good shepherd. The good shepherd lays down His life for the sheep" (v.11)

This is, *The Good Shepherd: Jesus, the True Savior of the World,* 10:11-21.
1. The meaning of "Good Shepherd" (vv.11-13).
2. The proof that Jesus is the Good Shepherd (vv.14-16).
3. The final proof of Jesus' claim: His death and resurrection (vv.17-18).
4. The reaction to Jesus' claim (vv.19-21).

### DEEPER STUDY # 1

(10:11-21) **Jesus, The Shepherd:** God foretold that He would send a Shepherd to save and to take care of His people.

> Behold, the Lord GOD comes with might, and his arm rules for him; behold, his reward is with him, and his recompense before him. He will tend his flock like a shepherd; he will gather the lambs in his arms; he will carry them in his bosom, and gently lead those that are with young. (Is.40:10-11)

> "I will rescue my flock; they shall no longer be a prey. And I will judge between sheep and sheep. And I will set up over them one shepherd, my servant David [the Messiah], and he shall feed them: he shall feed them and be their shepherd." (Eze.34:22-23)

> "They shall not defile themselves anymore with their idols and their detestable things, or with any of their transgressions. But I will save them from all the backslidings in which they have sinned, and will cleanse them; and they shall be my people, and I will be their God. My servant David shall be king over them, and they shall all have one shepherd. They shall walk in my rules and be careful to obey my statutes." (Eze.37:23-24)

> On that day the LORD their God will save them, as the flock of his people; for like the jewels of a crown they shall shine on his land. (Zec.9:16)

Jesus' work as the Shepherd is fourfold.

1. Jesus Christ is the *Good Shepherd*. He is called "good" because He risks and sacrifices His life for the sheep (Jn.10:11, 15; see Ps.22).

2. Jesus Christ is the *Great Shepherd*. He is called "great" because He arose from the dead and He perfects the sheep (He.13:20-21).

3. Jesus Christ is the *Shepherd and Overseer* of our souls. He is called the "shepherd and overseer" because He welcomes those who wandered off and went astray (1 Pe.2:25).

4. Jesus Christ is the *Chief Shepherd*. He is called "chief" because He is to return to earth with great glory to reward the faithful (1 Pe.5:4).

Note: God also is called a Shepherd in Scripture (Ge.48:15; Ps.23:1; 77:20; 80:1; Is.40:11; Eze.34:11-31).

## 1 The meaning of "Good Shepherd."

10:11-13

The contrast between the true Shepherd and false shepherds continues. This time, it is presented through contrasting the Good Shepherd with a bad shepherd, a mere hireling. The hireling flees when danger arises, but the true Shepherd gives His life for His sheep.

11 "I am the good shepherd. The good shepherd lays down his life for the sheep.
12 He who is a hired hand and not a shepherd, who does not own the sheep, sees the wolf coming and leaves the sheep and flees, and the wolf snatches them and scatters them.
13 He flees because he is a hired hand and cares nothing for the sheep."

### a. He is one who sacrificed His life (v.11).

Jesus is called the "Good Shepherd" because He gave and sacrificed His life *for the sheep* (see Deeper Study # 2). The image is of a shepherd fighting lions, wolves, bears or some other ravenous animal in order to save the lives of his sheep. Jesus took on our mortal enemy, the devil, and gloriously defeated him. But it cost our Shepherd His life.

### b. He is not a hired or employed shepherd (vv.12-13).

Jesus is called the "Good Shepherd" because He is not a hired or employed shepherd. Jesus is the Shepherd by birth. He was born to be the Shepherd with all the Shepherd's rights. The sheep are His, and He, the sheep's. The hired shepherd is not the true, permanent shepherd; he is just a man passing through, hired to provide temporary help to look after the sheep until the real shepherd came along. In the context of verses 12 and 13, the hired shepherd is a false, unfaithful, and irresponsible shepherd, who has little if any sense of responsibility for the sheep. He seeks to benefit himself, not the sheep.

> He is a shepherd for what he can get out of it, not to serve and care for the sheep.
> His primary interest is not the sheep but job security: wages and benefits, position and prestige, money and comfort.
> He values himself much more than the sheep.
> He seeks his own things and not the things of others (1 Co.10:24; Ph.2:3-4).
> He has no *natural* care for the state of the sheep (Ph.2:20).
> He has no interest in seeking the lost sheep, lest his life be threatened "in the wilderness" (see Lu.15:4).

The Good Shepherd is nothing like the hired shepherd. First, the Good Shepherd is not one who sees danger and acts cowardly or flees (v.12a). The irresponsible shepherd flees when he sees danger (the wolf). He seeks to save himself and to protect his own security and position, even if it means forsaking the sheep and leaving them exposed to the danger.

Second, the Good Shepherd is not one who causes the sheep to be caught by a wolf (v.12b). The wolf represents anything or any power that seeks to destroy the sheep, such as worldliness, false teaching, and carnal people. The irresponsible shepherd causes the sheep to be caught in the danger. Some of the sheep are ravaged and eaten by the dangerous wolf. The remaining sheep are scattered throughout the wilderness of the world and lost to the Owner (God).

Third, the Good Shepherd is not one who lacks genuine care for the sheep (v.13). The irresponsible hired shepherd does not care about the sheep. He is not involved and concerned with the fate and eternal welfare of the sheep (see note, *False Shepherds*—Jn.10:1 for verses of Scripture).

### Deeper Study # 2

(10:11) **Jesus Christ, Death**: the word *for* (huper) is a simple word with profound meaning when used with the death of Christ. It proclaims the most wonderful truth known to humanity. Note this striking truth: it does *not mean* that Christ died only as an example for us, showing us how we should be willing to die for the truth or for some great cause. What it means is that Christ died *in our place, in our stead, in our room, as our substitute*. This meaning is unquestionably clear (see note—Ep.5:2; Deeper Study # 1—1 Pe.2:21-25 for more discussion).

1. The idea of sacrifice to the Jewish and pagan mind of that day was the idea of a life given in another's place. It was *a substitutionary sacrifice*.

2. The idea of sacrifice is often in the very context of the words, "Christ gave Himself *for us*" (Ep.5:2).

> "I am the living bread that came down from heaven. If anyone eats of this bread, he will live forever. And the bread that I will give for the life of the world is my flesh." (Jn.6:51)
>
> "I am the good shepherd. The good shepherd lays down his life for the sheep." (Jn.10:11)
>
> "Just as the Father knows me and I know the Father; and I lay down my life for the sheep." (Jn.10:15)
>
> He did not say this of his own accord, but being high priest that year he prophesied that Jesus would die for the nation. (Jn.11:51)
>
> "Greater love has no one than this, that someone lay down his life for his friends." (Jn.15:13)
>
> "And for their sake I consecrate myself, that they also may be sanctified in truth." (Jn.17:19)

(See Ro.8:32; Ga.1:4; 2:20; Ep.5:2; 1 Ti.2:6; Tit.2:14.)

## 2 The proof that Jesus is the Good Shepherd.

What distinguishes the Good Shepherd from the hireling? Jesus offers four proofs that identify the Good Shepherd.

### a. He knows His sheep (v.14).

Jesus knows His sheep, and they know Him. There is an intimate knowledge between Jesus and His sheep. He knows them, their lives, their being, their all. He knows them...

- by name, individually and personally
- in all their joy and blessings
- in all their trials and sorrows
- in all their wanderings and stumblings
- in all their need and lack

Jesus' sheep are always on His mind. He is constantly looking after them through His Spirit and caring for them through intercession as well as by companionship. This is proof that He is the "Good Shepherd" of the sheep.

> "To him the gatekeeper opens. The sheep hear his voice, and he calls his own sheep by name and leads them out." (Jn.10:3)
>
> But if anyone loves God, he is known by God. (1 Co.8:3)
>
> But God's firm foundation stands, bearing this seal: "The Lord knows those who are his," and, "Let everyone who names the name of the Lord depart from iniquity." (2 Ti.2:19)

Jesus' sheep know Him as well, His life, His being, His all. They know Him, believing and trusting...

- His love and care
- His mind and Word
- His companionship and leadership
- His experience and knowledge
- His destiny and pasture (heaven)

The fact that the sheep know Him so well is clear proof that Jesus is the "Good Shepherd" of their lives.

> They said to the woman, "It is no longer because of what you said that we believe, for we have heard for ourselves, and we know that this is indeed the Savior of the world." (Jn.4:42)

<sup>14</sup> "I am the good shepherd. I know my own and my own know me,
<sup>15</sup> "just as the Father knows me and I know the Father; and I lay down my life for the sheep.
<sup>16</sup> "And I have other sheep that are not of this fold. I must bring them also, and they will listen to my voice. So there will be one flock, one shepherd."

> "When he has brought out all his own, he goes before them, and the sheep follow him, for they know his voice." (Jn.10:4)
>
> "My sheep hear my voice, and I know them, and they follow me." (Jn.10:27)
>
> "And this is eternal life, that they know you, the only true God, and Jesus Christ whom you have sent." (Jn.17:3)
>
> But whatever gain I had, I counted as loss for the sake of Christ. Indeed, I count everything as loss because of the surpassing worth of knowing Christ Jesus my Lord. For his sake I have suffered the loss of all things and count them as rubbish, in order that I may gain Christ (Ph.3:7-8)
>
> Which is why I suffer as I do. But I am not ashamed, for I know whom I have believed, and I am convinced that he is able to guard until that day what has been entrusted to me. (2 Ti.1:12)

### b. He knows His Father—the Owner (v.15a).

Jesus knows the Father, the Owner of the sheep. The question naturally arises, how well does Jesus know Him? One thing is of critical importance. When Jesus claims to know the Father, He does not mean that He knows God in the same sense as other people know Him. Note His exact words:

> "As the Father knows me and [even so] I know the Father" (Jn.10:15)

How well does God know any person? However well God the Father knows Jesus, that is how well Jesus knows God. That is what Jesus is claiming. God, of course, knows every individual perfectly, knows everything there is to know about a person. Therefore, Jesus knows the Father perfectly, just as the Father knows everything about Him. Jesus and the Father are one (v.30). There is a perfect, intimate knowledge and relationship between them.

This is exactly what Jesus is claiming. He is claiming to be *"the Good Shepherd,"* the very One sent by God to be the Good Shepherd of the sheep. The proof is that He knows the Father even (as well) as the Father knows Him.

> "All things have been handed over to me by my Father, and no one knows the Son except the Father, and no one knows the Father except the Son and anyone to whom the Son chooses to reveal him." (Mt.11:27)
>
> "I know him, for I come from him, and he sent me." (Jn.7:29)
>
> "But you have not known him. I know him. If I were to say that I do not know him, I would be a liar like you, but I do know him and I keep his word." (Jn.8:55)
>
> "O righteous Father, even though the world does not know you, I know you, and these know that you have sent me." (Jn.17:25)

### c. He will die for His sheep (v.15b).

Jesus will die for the sheep. He is the "Good Shepherd," not a bad shepherd; therefore, He stands ready to face His sheep's enemies. He would not flee from His calling and purpose. He would stand and fight the enemy as the Good Shepherd was sent to do. Note two striking facts:

First, Jesus does not say that He would fight and protect the sheep. He says He would *die* for the sheep—definitely die. He knew that death awaited Him, that His purpose was to die for them.

Second, Jesus drops the imagery of the shepherd in this statement and speaks directly of Himself. He no longer says, "the good shepherd lays down His life" (v.11); He now says, "*I* lay down my life" (see Deeper Study # 2).

### d. He works to increase the number of sheep (v.16).

Jesus works to enlarge the fold, saying that He has other sheep. The term, *other sheep* is a reference to worldwide evangelism, the salvation of the Gentiles. It refers to all believers who were not standing there with Him. It includes all countries and generations. The statement foresees every believer of all time.

> For there is no distinction between Jew and Greek; for the same Lord is Lord of all, bestowing his riches on all who call on him. (Ro.10:12)

*I have other sheep* speaks of a close, intimate relationship. The closest bond and fellowship imaginable, a Spirit-filled and supernatural relationship would exist between Christ and these future sheep (see DEEPER STUDY # 3—Ac.2:42 for discussion).

Jesus says that He *must* bring these other sheep into the fold. *Must* (dei) speaks of necessity, constraint. Jesus is compelled to reach the other sheep.

> Jesus said to them, "My food is to do the will of him who sent me and to accomplish his work." (Jn.4:34)

> "We must work the works of him who sent me while it is day; night is coming, when no one can work." (Jn.9:4)

Future sheep become Christ's sheep by listening to His voice (see note—Jn.10:4-5 for discussion). There would be one flock, not two flocks. In other words, there would not be *Jews and Gentiles* (Ep.2:11-22; 3:6). Every believer is a part of *one flock,* the Good Shepherd's flock.

There are not several shepherds and several flocks. There are not even two shepherds and two flocks. There is only one shepherd and one flock. All believers, regardless of race, nationality, gender, or any other factor, are a part of one flock and are all led by the same Shepherd: the Good Shepherd, Jesus Christ, who gave His life for them all.

> Who desires all people to be saved and to come to the knowledge of the truth. For there is one God, and there is one mediator between God and men, the man Christ Jesus, who gave himself as a ransom for all, which is the testimony given at the proper time. (1 Ti.2:4-6)

The very fact that Jesus enlarges the fold is proof that He is the Good Shepherd. He is the Good Shepherd in that He works and labors for both the Owner and the sheep. He works to keep the sheep healthy so that they will reproduce and increase the flock. An enlarged and healthy flock, of course, means a pleased Owner (the Father).

## 3 The final proof of Jesus' claim: His death and resurrection.

10:17-18

The final proof that Jesus is the "Good Shepherd" is His sacrificial death and resurrection. A shepherd could do no greater "good" than to give his life for his sheep. A shepherd who died for his sheep was beyond question a good shepherd. But there is something else here as well. The owner is pleased, deeply appreciative that the shepherd gave his life for the flock. The owner *deems* the shepherd to be a "good" shepherd.

> [17] "For this reason the Father loves me, because I lay down my life that I may take it up again.
> [18] No one takes it from me, but I lay it down of my own accord. I have authority to lay it down, and I have authority to take it up again. This charge I have received from my Father."

### a. Jesus is loved by God for His great sacrifice (v.17).

Christ's sacrificial death is the very reason God loves His Son so much. Of course, this does not mean that God does not love His Son just because of who He is. God naturally loves His Son just as any person loves their child. But God loves Jesus *even more*, in a much more special way, because Jesus was willing to pay such a price to bring people to God.

Note the teaching about the resurrection here. Jesus died so that He might arise from the dead. He took our sin upon Himself to free us from sin (that is, to provide righteousness for us, positionally; see note—Jn.1:51 for more discussion).

> He himself bore our sins in his body on the tree, that we might die to sin and live to righteousness. By his wounds you have been healed. (1 Pe.2:24)

> You know that he appeared in order to take away sins, and in him there is no sin. (1 Jn.3:5)

Then He arose from the dead to free us from death (that is, to provide eternal life for us).

> It [righteousness] will be counted to us who believe in him who raised from the dead Jesus our Lord, who was delivered up for our trespasses and raised for our justification. (Ro.4:24-25)

> We were buried therefore with him by baptism into death, in order that, just as Christ was raised from the dead by the glory of the Father, we too might walk in newness of life. For if we have been united with him in a death like his, we shall certainly be united with him in a resurrection like his. (Ro.6:4-5)

b. **Jesus' death was the supreme act of obedience (v.18).**

Our Lord's death was the supreme act of obedience. *He laid down His life of His own accord*. It was voluntary; He willingly died. Nobody took His life; He sacrificed it Himself. The power to take it was His and His alone.

Note the critical point: this *charge* or *command* to die was from God. This fact gives a higher meaning to the death of Jesus than just meeting humanity's need. It means that Jesus did not just die because of sin but because He wished, above all else, to show His love and adoration for God by honoring Him through death.

This aspect of Jesus' death—an aspect that rises far above the mere meeting of our need—is often overlooked. For in giving Himself as an offering to God, Christ was looking beyond our need to the majestic responsibility of glorifying God. This means that His *first purpose* was the glory of God. He was concerned primarily with doing the will of God, with obeying God. God had been terribly dishonored by the first human, Adam, and by all humans who followed after him. Jesus Christ wished to honor God by showing that at least one human thought more of God's glory than of anything else. Jesus wished to show that God's will meant more to Him than any personal desire or ambition He might have. He wanted to demonstrate His love for the Father. Shortly before He went to the cross, Jesus stated this fact directly and clearly (14:31; see Lu.22:42; Jn.5:30; see also Deeper Study # 2).

## 4 The reaction to Jesus' claim.

10:19-21

¹⁹ There was again a division among the Jews because of these words.
²⁰ Many of them said, "He has a demon, and is insane; why listen to him?"
²¹ Others said, "These are not the words of one who is oppressed by a demon. Can a demon open the eyes of the blind?"

Once again, the reaction to Jesus' claim was mixed (v.19). Some rejected Jesus, saying that He was demon-possessed and insane (v.20; see Jn.7:20; 8:48, 52). Others, however, questioned that He just might be who He claimed to be, the Messiah (v.21; see Jn.7:12, 40-44). The beautiful power of Jesus' words and the message He taught could not have been inspired by a demon, they reasoned. Moreover, a demon would have never healed the darkened eyes of a blind man.

"But the testimony that I have is greater than that of John. For the works that the Father has given me to accomplish, the very works that I am doing, bear witness about me that the Father has sent me. And the Father who sent me has himself borne witness about me. His voice you have never heard, his form you have never seen, and you do not have his word abiding in you, for you do not believe the one whom he has sent." (Jn.5:36-38)

## D. The Great Shepherd's Claims, 10:22-42

²² At that time the Feast of Dedication took place at Jerusalem. It was winter,
²³ and Jesus was walking in the temple, in the colonnade of Solomon.
²⁴ So the Jews gathered around him and said to him, "How long will you keep us in suspense? If you are the Christ, tell us plainly."
²⁵ Jesus answered them, "I told you, and you do not believe. The works that I do in my Father's name bear witness about me,
²⁶ but you do not believe because you are not among my sheep.
²⁷ My sheep hear my voice, and I know them, and they follow me.

²⁸ I give them eternal life, and they will never perish, and no one will snatch them out of my hand.

²⁹ My Father, who has given them to me, is greater than all, and no one is able to snatch them out of the Father's hand.
³⁰ I and the Father are one."

³¹ The Jews picked up stones again to stone him.
³² Jesus answered them, "I have shown you many good works from the Father; for which of them are you going to stone me?"
³³ The Jews answered him, "It is not for a good work that we are going to stone you but for blasphemy, because you, being a man, make yourself God."
³⁴ Jesus answered them, "Is it not written in your Law, 'I said, you are gods'?
³⁵ If he called them gods to whom the word of God came—and Scripture cannot be broken—
³⁶ do you say of him whom the Father consecrated and sent into the world, 'You are blaspheming,' because I said, 'I am the Son of God'?"

1. **The setting: Jesus was in Jerusalem attending the Feast of Dedication**[DS1]
   a. He was walking in Solomon's colonnade
   b. The religionists approached & questioned Him

2. **Claim 1: He is the Messiah**[DS2]
   a. Religionists did not believe
      1) His claim: It was clear
      2) His work: It was proof
      3) Reason: The religionists were not His sheep
   b. His sheep believe[DS3]
      1) Are receptive
      2) Are known
      3) Are followers, v.27
      4) Are given life
      5) Are kept from perishing
      6) Are secure
      7) Are assured a double security in God Himself

3. **Claim 2: He is one with God, that is, He is God Himself**
   a. The religionists reacted

   b. Jesus questioned their reaction


   c. The religionists admitted that His works were good
   d. The religionists understood His claim, but they rejected Him

4. **Claim 3: He is the Son of God**
   a. Jesus showed man's inconsistency



   b. Jesus' claim
      1) The Father consecrated Him, set Him apart
      2) The Father sent Him
      3) He is the Son of God

5. Claim 4: God is in Him & He is in God—absolutely
   a. His works are proof

   b. He was still rejected

6. Conclusion: Jesus retreated
   a. Jesus went to the area where John had baptized
   b. John's crowds began to follow Jesus

   c. Many believed in Jesus

³⁷ "If I am not doing the works of my Father, then do not believe me; ³⁸ but if I do them, even though you do not believe me, believe the works, that you may know and understand that the Father is in me and I am in the Father." ³⁹ Again they sought to arrest him, but he escaped from their hands.
⁴⁰ He went away again across the Jordan to the place where John had been baptizing at first, and there he remained. ⁴¹ And many came to him. And they said, "John did no sign, but everything that John said about this man was true." ⁴² And many believed in him there.

## Division X

*The Revelation of Jesus, the Shepherd of Life, 10:1-42*

D. The Great Shepherd's Claims, 10:22-42

## 10:22-42
## Introduction

Jesus Christ is the *Good* Shepherd because He laid down His life for the sheep. But He is also the *Great* Shepherd—great because of who He is. He revealed His unique greatness through the phenomenal claims He made. These claims infuriated some people, but they led others to believe—just as they do today. This is, *The Great Shepherd's Claims,* 10:22-24.

1. The setting: Jesus was in Jerusalem attending the Feast of Dedication (vv.22-24).
2. Claim 1: He is the Messiah (vv.25-29).
3. Claim 2: He is one with God, that is, He is God Himself (vv.30-33).
4. Claim 3: He is the Son of God (vv.34-36).
5. Claim 4: God is in Him and He is in God—absolutely (vv.37-39).
6. Conclusion: Jesus retreated (vv.40-42).

10:22-24

²² At that time the Feast of Dedication took place at Jerusalem. It was winter, ²³ and Jesus was walking in the temple, in the colonnade of Solomon. ²⁴ So the Jews gathered around him and said to him, "How long will you keep us in suspense? If you are the Christ, tell us plainly."

## 1 The setting: Jesus was in Jerusalem during the winter attending the Feast of Dedication.

a. He was walking in Solomon's colonnade (v.23).
b. The religionists approached and questioned Him (v.24). During the winter, Jesus was in Jerusalem at the Feast of Dedication (see DEEPER STUDY # 1). He was walking in Solomon's Porch (see note—Mk.11:27). The Jews approached and encircled Him, for they were determined to get a straight answer from Him as to who He was. They wanted Jesus to tell them plainly whether or not He was the Messiah.

## Deeper Study # 1

(10:22) **Feast of Dedication:** this feast was founded to celebrate the freedom of Israel from Syria in 164 BC. What had happened prior to Israel gaining this freedom was terrible. Antiochus Epiphanes, the King of Syria from 175 to 164 BC, loved Greek society and wanted to turn his part of the world into a model Greek society. William Barclay points out that he ran into trouble when he tried to transform the Jews into full-fledged Greeks, both in custom and religion. At first he tried peacefully, and some of the Jews adopted Greek ideas; but as history has shown throughout centuries, most Jews were not going to surrender their beliefs. In order to be successful, Antiochus knew that he had to destroy Jewish religion. He attacked Jerusalem, slaughtering 80,000 Jews by the most horrible means imaginable and enslaving another 80,000. He then desecrated the Jewish temple by . . .

- turning the great altar of the burnt offering into an altar to the Greek god, Zeus
- sacrificing swine flesh upon the altar
- setting up a trade of prostitution in the temple chambers

Such abhorrent acts caused some Jews to go underground and to take up the struggle against Antiochus. Judas Maccabaeus and his brothers soon came to the forefront as the leaders of the revolt against Syria. In 165 BC, they were successful, and one of their first acts was to cleanse, restore, and rededicate the temple. It was for the purpose of celebrating the rededication of the temple to the worship of God that the *Feast of Dedication* was founded.

The feast has also been called the Festival of Lights. Its Jewish name is Hanukkah, and it is still celebrated today. The Festival lasted eight days and was characterized by the burning of lights in every Jewish home throughout the city and countryside and in every corner of the temple. Every place throughout the land was lit up to celebrate the great day of deliverance. The lights symbolized the light of freedom that had been newly won for the nation. Note: the feast took place in the winter; its festivities were similar to the Feast of Tabernacles (2 Macc.1:9; 10:6). This is the only time the feast is mentioned in the Gospels.[1]

## 2 Claim 1: He is the Messiah.

Jesus gave the demanding Jewish leaders a clear, thorough answer to their question. The Lord's first claim was that He is the Messiah. There is a contrast in these verses (vv.24-29), a contrast between the religionists (religious leaders) and the Lord's sheep, between not believing and believing.

### a. Religionists did not believe (vv.25-26).

Jesus had clearly claimed to be the Messiah previous to this occasion (v.25a; see DEEPER STUDY # 2). Note His words, "I told you." He had told them time and again. In addition, Jesus' works proved that He was who He claimed to be (v.25b; see notes—Jn.5:19; 5:20; 5:36).

But the religious leaders did not believe Jesus' claims (v.26). Why? Because they were not His sheep. Note an important fact: Jesus does not say they were not His sheep *because* they did not believe; He says they did not believe *because* they were not His sheep. Essentially He says they did not believe because they were not His followers. This is the thread of predestination that John stresses throughout His gospel (see notes—Jn.6:44-46; 6:37

[25] Jesus answered them, "I told you, and you do not believe. The works that I do in my Father's name bear witness about me,

[26] "but you do not believe because you are not among my sheep.

[27] "My sheep hear my voice, and I know them, and they follow me.

[28] "I give them eternal life, and they will never perish, and no one will snatch them out of my hand.

[29] "My Father, who has given them to me, is greater than all, and no one is able to snatch them out of the Father's hand."

---

1 William Barclay. *The Gospel of John*, Vol.2., "The Daily Study Bible," (Philadelphia, PA: The Westminster Press, 1956), p.81f.

for discussion.) The religionists did not belong to God. They claimed to be His followers, but their claim was only a verbal profession. Their hearts and lives were far from God; therefore, what Jesus claimed, they rejected. They were not the sheep of Jesus; therefore, they rejected His claims and Words.

b. **His sheep believe (vv.27–29).**

In contrast, Jesus' sheep believe. They believe in the Shepherd. Jesus proceeded to list four attributes of His sheep and four promises He makes to them (see Deeper Study # 3).

### Deeper Study # 2

(10:25) **Jesus Christ, Claims—Deity:** Jesus was asked, "If you are the Christ, tell us plainly." Over the last few days, the people had heard Him proclaim the truth as forcefully as He could. The problem was not a lack of clarity on Christ's part in His proclamation; the problem was the people's unbelief. Christ's proclamation was clear, but the people pretended not to understand. They understood, but they refused to believe. This is, of course, the problem with most people. In unmistakable terms, Jesus proclaims . . .

- that His teaching is not His, but God's (see note—Jn.7:16-19)

**So Jesus answered them, "My teaching is not mine, but his who sent me." (Jn.7:16)**

- that He knows God intimately and was sent from God (see notes—Jn.7:25-31; 8:54-59; 10:14-16)

**"I know him, for I come from him, and he sent me." (Jn.7:29)**

- that He is the Source of life and the One who gives the Holy Spirit to people (see note—Jn.7:37-39)

**On the last day of the feast, the great day, Jesus stood up and cried out, "If anyone thirsts, let him come to me and drink." . . . Now this he said about the Spirit, whom those who believed in him were to receive, for as yet the Spirit had not been given, because Jesus was not yet glorified. (Jn.7:37, 39)**

- that He is the Light of the world (see Deeper Study # 1—Jn.8:12; note—Jn.9:5)

**Again Jesus spoke to them, saying, "I am the light of the world. Whoever follows me will not walk in darkness, but will have the light of life." (Jn.8:12; see 9:5)**

- that He is the Revelation of God (see note—Jn.8:19)

**They said to him therefore, "Where is your Father?" Jesus answered, "You know neither me nor my Father. If you knew me, you would know my Father also." (Jn.8:19)**

- that He has a different origin from other humans (see Deeper Study # 2—Jn.8:23)

**He said to them, "You are from below; I am from above. You are of this world; I am not of this world." (Jn.8:23)**

- that if a person does not believe in Him, that person will die in their sins (see note—Jn.8:23-24)

**"I told you that you would die in your sins, for unless you believe that I am he you will die in your sins." (Jn.8:24)**

- that He is the Spokesman for God (see note—Jn.8:26)

**"I have much to say about you and much to judge, but he who sent me is true, and I declare to the world what I have heard from him." (Jn.8:26)**

- that He is the Son of Man who was to be lifted up on the cross (see note Jn.8:28)

**So Jesus said to them, "When you have lifted up the Son of Man, then you will know that I am he, and that I do nothing on my own authority, but speak just as the Father taught me." (Jn.8:28)**

- that God never left Him alone; that He never sinned; that He never failed to please God (see note—Jn.8:29)

"And he who sent me is with me. He has not left me alone, for I always do the things that are pleasing to him." (Jn.8:29)

- that He came from God (see note—Jn.8:42-43)

Jesus said to them, "If God were your Father, you would love me, for I came from God and I am here. I came not of my own accord, but he sent me." (Jn.8:42)

- that He is sinless (see note—Jn.8:45-47; see notes—Jn.8:29; 8:54-59)

"But because I tell the truth, you do not believe me. Which one of you convicts me of sin? If I tell the truth, why do you not believe me?" (Jn.8:45-46)

- that He is the Savior or Deliverer from death; that a person who keeps His Word will never see death (see notes—Jn.8:51; 8:51-53)

"Truly, truly, I say to you, if anyone keeps my word, he will never see death." (Jn.8:51)

- that He is the great "I Am" (see note—Jn.8:54-59)

Jesus said to them, "Truly, truly, I say to you, before Abraham was, I am." (Jn.8:58)

- that He is the Son of God (see note—Jn.9:35-38)

Jesus heard that they had cast him out, and having found him he said, "Do you believe in the Son of Man?" He answered, "And who is he, sir, that I may believe in him?" Jesus said to him, "You have seen him, and it is he who is speaking to you." (Jn.9:35-37)

- that He is the Door of the sheep (see note—Jn.10:7-10)

So Jesus again said to them, "Truly, truly, I say to you, I am the door of the sheep. All who came before me are thieves and robbers, but the sheep did not listen to them. I am the door. If anyone enters by me, he will be saved and will go in and out and find pasture." (Jn.10:7, 9)

- that He is the Good Shepherd (see note—Jn.10:11-13; DEEPER STUDY # 2—10:11)

"I am the good shepherd. The good shepherd lays down his life for the sheep.... I am the good shepherd. I know my own and my own know me." (Jn.10:11, 14)

## DEEPER STUDY # 3

(10:27-29) **Sheep**: the sheep of the Shepherd believe in the Shepherd. Others may not, but the sheep do. This is what Jesus is saying. The following list presents four attributes of Christ's sheep and four promises He makes to them. Note how He uses the traits of sheep to describe His followers (believers).

1. Sheep are *receptive* to the voice of the Shepherd (v.27a). They know His voice and respond to it. When He calls them, they come and do what He says. Note also that they recognize the voice of false shepherds (see note—Jn.10:4-5).

2. Sheep are *known* by the Shepherd, and this knowledge leads them to trust Him implicitly (v.27b). The Shepherd responds to the sheep and to their faith and trust in Him. He cares for them deeply, leading and looking after them. He even knows them individually, calling them by name (see note—Jn.10:2-3). The fact that He responds to them with such care and attention gives them even greater faith and trust. They trust their Shepherd without question.

3. Sheep *follow* the shepherd (v.27c). They obey Him, knowing He goes *before* them in order to remove all obstacles and dangers (see notes—Jn.10:4-5).

4. Sheep are *communal* (v.27c). Due to space, this fact is not presented in the outline. Note the sheep follow in a group. They form a commune or a fellowship of sheep. They are a body who follow the Shepherd (see DEEPER STUDY # 3—Ac.2:42).

5. Sheep are given *eternal life* (v.28). And note: eternal life includes an abundant life while on this earth, which begins the moment the sheep become followers of the shepherd (see DEEPER STUDY # 1—Jn.10:10).

6. Sheep are *kept from perishing* (v.28b; see DEEPER STUDY # 2—Jn.3:16).

7. Sheep are *secure* (v.28c). No one can pluck them out of the Shepherd's hand. The person who is truly in the Shepherd's hand will not be lost. The Shepherd promises this time

and again (see Jn.6:37-39). Note exactly what Jesus said. The sheep are saved from someone *trying to snatch* them away, and they are saved no matter how great the *attempt* may be. (They are secure, kept from the evil one, the devil himself.)

8. Sheep possess a *double security* in the Owner, that is, God Himself (v.29). They are secure not only because they are in the hands of the Shepherd but because they belong to the Owner. The Owner is God, and God is greater than all. Therefore, being the greatest, no one, not even the devil, is now able nor ever will be able to pluck the sheep out of God's hand (see Ro.8:38-39).

## 10:30-33

³⁰ "I and the Father are one."
³¹ The Jews picked up stones again to stone him.
³² Jesus answered them, "I have shown you many good works from the Father; for which of them are you going to stone me?"
³³ The Jews answered him, "It is not for a good work that we are going to stone you but for blasphemy, because you, being a man, make yourself God."

### 3 Claim 2: He is one with God, that is, He is God Himself.

Jesus' second claim was that He is One with God, that is, He is God Himself. But note: Jesus was not claiming to be the same person as God. He was claiming to have the same *nature* of God, to be One with God . . .

- in nature
- in substance
- in essence
- in being
- in power
- in glory

This truth is seen in the word "one." When the Greek text speaks of God's person, masculine nouns and adjectives are used. Here, however, the adjective "one" is neuter, not masculine. It means *thing*, not *person*. Jesus is of the very same thing, of the very same substance as God.

There is no question that this is exactly what Jesus was claiming. His claim was perfectly understood by those standing around Him. The Scripture and outline clearly show this.

a. **The religionists reacted (v.31).**

The religious leaders were infuriated by Jesus' claim. They picked up rocks and prepared to stone Him.

b. **Jesus questioned their reaction (v.32).**

Jesus pointed out the fact that He had done nothing wrong, nothing against another person that called for execution according to the law. He had only done good for others, so He asked the Jewish leaders for which of His good works they were going to stone Him.

c. **The religionists admitted that His works were good (v.33).**

The religious leaders acknowledged that Jesus had done only good deeds. They made their accusation clear: they were stoning Him for blasphemy, for claiming to be God.

d. **The religionists understood His claim, but they rejected Him (v.33).**

The response of the Jewish religious authorities testified that they understood fully whom Jesus claimed to be. There was no further question about it. He was claiming to be the Messiah, the Son of God and God the Son. They picked up stones to execute Jesus because they rejected Him. They refused to accept the truth that He was—and is—the One sent by God to be Israel's king and the Savior of the world.

> In the beginning was the Word, and the Word was with God, and the Word was God. He was in the beginning with God. (Jn.1:1-2)

> "And whoever sees me sees him who sent me." (Jn.12:45)

> "If you had known me, you would have known my Father also. From now on you do know him and have seen him." Philip said to him, "Lord, show us the Father, and it is enough for us." Jesus said

to him, "Have I been with you so long, and you still do not know me, Philip? Whoever has seen me has seen the Father. How can you say, 'Show us the Father'?" (Jn.14:7-9)

"All that the Father has is mine; therefore I said that he will take what is mine and declare it to you." (Jn.16:15)

To them belong the patriarchs, and from their race, according to the flesh, is the Christ, who is God over all, blessed forever. Amen. (Ro.9:5)

For in him the whole fullness of deity dwells bodily. (Col.2:9)

Great indeed, we confess, is the mystery of godliness: He was manifested in the flesh, vindicated by the Spirit, seen by angels, proclaimed among the nations, believed on in the world, taken up in glory. (1 Ti.3:16)

## 4 Claim 3: He is the Son of God.

10:34-36

Jesus' third claim was that He is the Son of God. Those who rejected Jesus had stones in their hands, and they were ready to kill Him. But Jesus spoke up.

34 Jesus answered them, "Is it not written in your Law, 'I said, you are gods'?
35 If he called them gods to whom the word of God came—and Scripture cannot be broken—
36 do you say of him whom the Father consecrated and sent into the world, 'You are blaspheming,' because I said, 'I am the Son of God'?"

### a. Jesus showed man's inconsistency (vv.34-35).

Jesus pointed out the religious leaders' inconsistency. He referred them to their history when they called their rulers or judges "gods." Their ancestors had used the word "gods" to mean that their judges were rulers of people—rulers who had been appointed by God to represent God among the people (Ex.22:28; Ps.82:6). Jesus simply asked, if some rulers of Israel were called "gods," why was He being accused of blasphemy for claiming to be the Son of God?

### b. Jesus' claim (v.36).

Jesus made a threefold claim; however, note one critical point. Jesus was not saying, "Rulers were called gods, so I am to be called a 'god' as they were." He was claiming to be distinct from all other human beings. He claimed that He was . . .
- the One "whom the Father had *consecrated* or *sanctified* or *set apart*" (see Deeper Study # 1—1 Pe.1:15-16)
- the One whom the Father sent into the world (see Deeper Study # 3—Jn.3:34)
- the Son of God (see notes—Jn.1:1-2; 1:34)

How could they reject Him? Their rulers were mere human beings, yet they were called "gods." Jesus was much, much more—the very One sanctified and sent by God, the very Son of God Himself. How could they accuse Him of blasphemy when they so readily received rulers of the past as "gods" and those rulers were mere men?

"For God so loved the world, that he gave his only Son, that whoever believes in him should not perish but have eternal life." (Jn.3:16; see vv.17-18)

Jesus heard that they had cast him out, and having found him he said, "Do you believe in the Son of Man?" He answered, "And who is he, sir, that I may believe in him?" Jesus said to him, "You have seen him, and it is he who is speaking to you." (Jn.9:35-37)

Jesus said to her, "I am the resurrection and the life. Whoever believes in me, though he die, yet shall he live, and everyone who lives and believes in me shall never die. Do you believe this?" She said to him, "Yes, Lord; I believe that you are the Christ, the Son of God, who is coming into the world." (Jn.11:25-27)

## 5 Claim 4: God is in Him and He is in God—absolutely.

The fourth claim of Jesus was that God is in Him and He is in God (see note—Jn.14:10). This is the indwelling presence of

10:37-39

37 "If I am not doing the works of my Father, then do not believe me;
38 but if I do them, even though you do not believe me, believe the works, that you may know and understand that the Father is in me and I am in the Father."
39 Again they sought to arrest him, but he escaped from their hands.

each in the other. Jesus is One with the Father, and the Father is One with Him. They are of one mind and spirit, one being and nature, one purpose and work.

> For in him the whole fullness of deity dwells bodily. (Col.2:9)

### a. His works are proof (v.38).

It is absolutely essential for a person to know and believe this truth. Jesus performed miracles to prove it. Unquestionably, Jesus performed His miraculous works for the purpose of helping the afflicted. But His miracles had another purpose: they were to prove that He was God. Jesus pled with the unbelievers to recognize this fact, to see His miraculous works and believe that He is One with the Father.

### b. He was still rejected (v.39).

Although Jesus' works prove the indwelling presence of God in Him and Him in God, the Jewish leaders still rejected His claim. They sought again to arrest Jesus, but He escaped.

> "I and the Father are one." (Jn.10:30)

> "Do you not believe that I am in the Father and the Father is in me? The words that I say to you I do not speak on my own authority, but the Father who dwells in me does his works." (Jn.14:10)

> "And I am no longer in the world, but they are in the world, and I am coming to you. Holy Father, keep them in your name, which you have given me, that they may be one, even as we are one." (Jn.17:11)

> "The glory that you have given me I have given to them, that they may be one even as we are one." (Jn.17:22)

## 10:40–42

⁴⁰ He went away again across the Jordan to the place where John had been baptizing at first, and there he remained.
⁴¹ And many came to him. And they said, "John did no sign, but everything that John said about this man was true."
⁴² And many believed in him there.

## 6 Conclusion: Jesus retreated.

### a. Jesus went to the area where John had baptized (v.40).
### b. John's crowds began to follow Jesus (v.41).
### c. Many believed in Jesus (v.42).

Jesus retired to the area where John had first baptized, and many of John's followers began to follow Jesus. They recognized the truth that Jesus had so strongly tried to impress on the religious leaders: His miracles were a sign of His deity. Consequently, many believed on Jesus. John's faithfulness in the ministry throughout this area reaped great fruit.

> "That whoever believes in him may have eternal life." (Jn.3:15)

# Chapter 11

## XI. The Revelation of Jesus, the Resurrection and the Life, 11:1–12:11

### A. The Death of Lazarus and Its Purposes, 11:1–16

Now a certain man was ill, Lazarus of Bethany, the village of Mary and her sister Martha.

² It was Mary who anointed the Lord with ointment and wiped his feet with her hair, whose brother Lazarus was ill.

³ So the sisters sent to him, saying, "Lord, he whom you love is ill."

⁴ But when Jesus heard it he said, "This illness does not lead to death. It is for the glory of God, so that the Son of God may be glorified through it."

⁵ Now Jesus loved Martha and her sister and Lazarus.

⁶ So, when he heard that Lazarus was ill, he stayed two days longer in the place where he was.

⁷ Then after this he said to the disciples, "Let us go to Judea again."

⁸ The disciples said to him, "Rabbi, the Jews were just now seeking to stone you, and are you going there again?"

⁹ Jesus answered, "Are there not twelve hours in the day? If anyone walks in the day, he does not stumble, because he sees the light of this world.

¹⁰ But if anyone walks in the night, he stumbles, because the light is not in him."

¹¹ After saying these things, he said to them, "Our friend Lazarus has fallen asleep, but I go to awaken him."

¹² The disciples said to him, "Lord, if he has fallen asleep, he will recover."

¹³ Now Jesus had spoken of his death, but they thought that he meant taking rest in sleep.

¹⁴ Then Jesus told them plainly, "Lazarus has died,

¹⁵ and for your sake I am glad that I was not there, so that you may believe. But let us go to him."

¹⁶ So Thomas, called the Twin, said to his fellow disciples, "Let us also go, that we may die with him."

1. The setting: Lazarus was sick
   a. His home was Bethany
   b. His sisters were Mary & Martha




   c. His sisters sent the news of Lazarus' sickness to Jesus
2. Purpose 1: To glorify God & to proclaim that Jesus is the Son of God



3. Purpose 2: To show Jesus' great love

4. Purpose 3: To show the necessity for waiting on God in great crises

5. Purpose 4: To teach the need to grasp opportunity
   a. The disciples protested Jesus' return to Jerusalem: Because of the threat to His life
   b. Jesus reply: There is a duty to work—to do what is right, to grasp the opportunity—regardless of the danger


6. Purpose 5: To show Jesus' power over death
   a. Jesus called Lazarus "our friend"
   b. Jesus predicted Lazarus would be raised
   c. The disciples misunderstood

   d. Jesus said that death is as "sleep"^DS1




7. Purpose 6: To help strengthen the disciples' belief

8. Purpose 7: To stir the disciples' courage & loyalty

# Division XI

## The Revelation of Jesus, the Resurrection and the Life, 11:1-12:11

A. The Death of Lazarus and Its Purposes, 11:1-16

## 11:1-16
## Introduction

When some tragedy strikes—a severe illness, an accident or catastrophe, the death of a loved one—we cannot help but to wonder *why* God allowed it. What was His purpose, His reason? What good can possibly come from it?

This passage records the death of Lazarus, a man much loved by his family and by Jesus. Lazarus' sister wondered why Jesus allowed her brother to die. The death of Lazarus gave Jesus the opportunity to reveal Himself as the resurrection and the life. But there were other purposes for Lazarus' death, as revealed in this passage (each purpose is also applicable to the death of the believer). This is, *The Death of Lazarus and Its Purposes,* 11:1-16.

1. The setting: Lazarus was sick (vv.1-3).
2. Purpose 1: To glorify God and to proclaim that Jesus is the Son of God (v.4).
3. Purpose 2: To show Jesus' great love (v.5).
4. Purpose 3: To show the necessity for *waiting on God* in great crises (v.6).
5. Purpose 4: To teach the need to grasp opportunity (vv.7-10).
6. Purpose 5: To show Jesus' power over death (vv.11-14).
7. Purpose 6: To help strengthen the disciples' belief (v.15).
8. Purpose 7: To stir the disciples' courage and loyalty (v.16).

### 11:1-3

Now a certain man was ill, Lazarus of Bethany, the village of Mary and her sister Martha.

² It was Mary who anointed the Lord with ointment and wiped his feet with her hair, whose brother Lazarus was ill.

³ So the sisters sent to him, saying, "Lord, he whom you love is ill."

### 1 The setting. Lazarus was sick.

a. His home was Bethany (v.1a).
b. His sisters were Mary and Martha (v.1b-2).
c. His sisters sent the news of Lazarus' sickness to Jesus (v.3).

Lazarus was sick. At this particular time Jesus was being rejected by almost everyone. Apparently, He was an unwelcome guest in most homes (Mt.8:20; Lu.9:58). He was walking about, preaching and proclaiming that He was One with God, the Son of God Himself (see outline and notes—Jn.10:22-42). Just imagine a man making such a claim. He was thought to be insane and devil-possessed (Mk.3:20-21; Lu.4:25). His own family was even having difficulty with Him. They were apparently so embarrassed by His claims and the rumors of His insanity that on one occasion they traveled a great distance to bring Him home lest He be harmed (see outline and notes—Mt.12:46-50).

However, one family always opened their home to Jesus when He was in and around Jerusalem—the family of Lazarus, Martha, and Mary, who were brother and sisters. They lived in Bethany, a suburb about two miles outside Jerusalem (v.1). When Lazarus became gravely ill, his sisters sent the news of his sickness to Jesus (v.3). Their closeness to Jesus is the reason the sisters felt so free to interrupt His evangelistic tour with the request to help their sick brother. Jesus' great love for this family should be noted throughout this passage.

### 11:4

⁴ But when Jesus heard it he said, "This illness does not lead to death. It is for the glory of God, so that the Son of God may be glorified through it."

### 2 Purpose 1: To glorify God and to proclaim that Jesus is the Son of God.

The first purpose of Lazarus' sickness was to glorify God and to proclaim that Jesus is the Son of God. The purpose of

Lazarus' sickness was not his death. He was to die *for* the glory of God and Christ. He was sick, and he was to die so that the glory of God could be demonstrated. Lazarus died so that . . .

| *God could be glorified . . .* | *Christ could be glorified . . .* |
|---|---|
| • by showing His desire for people to have life | • by having the opportunity to do the work of God |
| • by proving His power to give life | • by demonstrating God's power |
| • by showing His approval of Christ by which He proved that He really did love the world enough to send His Son to save the world | • by showing compassion |
| | • by strengthening the faith of believers |
| | • by leading unbelievers to believe |

In dealing with the blind man in John 9, both Jesus and His Father were glorified as the *Light* of the world (9:3, 5; see note—Jn.9:5 for more discussion). Now, in raising Lazarus from the dead, both were glorified as the *Life* of the world.

> **"That all may honor the Son, just as they honor the Father. Whoever does not honor the Son does not honor the Father who sent him." (Jn.5:23)**
>
> **Ascribe to the LORD the glory due his name; worship the LORD in the splendor of holiness. (Ps.29:2)**
>
> **Oh, magnify the LORD with me, and let us exalt his name together! (Ps.34:3)**
>
> **My mouth is filled with your praise, and with your glory all the day. (Ps.71:8)**
>
> **On the glorious splendor of your majesty, and on your wondrous works, I will meditate. (Ps.145:5)**
>
> **O LORD, you are my God; I will exalt you; I will praise your name, for you have done wonderful things, plans formed of old, faithful and sure. (Is.25:1)**

## 3 Purpose 2: To show Jesus' great love.

11:5

The second purpose of Lazarus' sickness was to show Jesus' great love. Jesus dearly loved Martha, Mary, and Lazarus. Note that each member of the family is mentioned personally. He loved this family, but He also loved each member individually. This is a fact noted in Scripture that needs to be emphasized, for each family member had a need, and each member needed and received the help of Jesus. Lazarus' death gave Christ the opportunity to demonstrate His great love, not only for the families of the world but also for each individual.

⁵ Now Jesus loved Martha and her sister and Lazarus.

> **"To him the gatekeeper opens. The sheep hear his voice, and he calls his own sheep by name and leads them out." (Jn.10:3)**
>
> **Now before the Feast of the Passover, when Jesus knew that his hour had come to depart out of this world to the Father, having loved his own who were in the world, he loved them to the end. (Jn.13:1)**
>
> **"As the Father has loved me, so have I loved you. Abide in my love." (Jn.15:9)**
>
> **Who shall separate us from the love of Christ? Shall tribulation, or distress, or persecution, or famine, or nakedness, or danger, or sword? (Ro.8:35)**
>
> **I have been crucified with Christ. It is no longer I who live, but Christ who lives in me. And the life I now live in the flesh I live by faith in the Son of God, who loved me and gave himself for me. (Ga.2:20)**
>
> **By this we know love, that he laid down his life for us, and we ought to lay down our lives for the brothers. (1 Jn.3:16)**

## 4 Purpose 3: To show the necessity for waiting on God in great crises.

11:6

The third purpose of Lazarus' sickness was to show the necessity of *waiting on God* in great crises. When Jesus heard of Lazarus' sickness, He did a puzzling thing: He waited two

⁶ So, when he heard that Lazarus was ill, he stayed two days longer in the place where he was.

days before going to Bethany. Jesus was not waiting two days so that Lazarus would die and He could perform a great miracle. Jesus knew that Lazarus was either already dead or that Lazarus was going to die on the very day the person brought word of Lazarus' illness. We know this because Lazarus had already been buried four days when Jesus arrived in Bethany (vv.17, 39). Jewish burial immediately followed death. The four days would be counted from . . .

- the day of travel by the messengers in bringing word to Jesus (v.3)
- the two days needed for Jesus to complete His ministry (v.6)
- the day or two needed by Jesus to travel to Bethany (v.17) (Remember huge crowds thronged Jesus, which prevented Him from traveling rapidly. It is possible He completed His ministry in one day and allowed Himself two days for traveling to Bethany.)

The point is, Martha and Mary were learning to wait on God throughout the whole experience. In facing severe illness or death, we can do nothing except pray and wait on God. We have to remember that Jesus knows when to act. He knows the exact moment, the best time for us to bear the trial and to stand in faith. He knows precisely the moment when we will need help and how He will help us learn the most from the trying experience. He knows how much time needs to go by before we can bear testimony of God's power and strength.

Whenever that moment arrives, the Lord arises to meet our need. In the meantime, what we must do is what Martha and Mary had to do: learn to *wait on God*. The Lord will act at the right moment.

> **THOUGHT 1.** We cannot dictate to God when to act or how to act. Note two examples:
> (1) Mary, Jesus' own mother—at the marriage feast, she wanted Him to go and secure more wine (Jn.2:3-4). He rebuked her for interfering with His work, the work of God. He has His own way and time, the very best way and time for meeting the need.
> (2) Jesus' own brothers—they tried to ridicule Him into going by caravan with them to the feast in Jerusalem (Jn.7:2-4). Jesus rebuked them for the same reason He had rebuked Mary. He, the Son of God, knew how to conduct His ministry and when to go about doing it. He knew what was best.
>
> Lead me in your truth and teach me, for you are the God of my salvation; for you I wait all the day long. (Ps.25:5)
>
> Wait for the LORD; be strong, and let your heart take courage; wait for the LORD! (Ps.27:14)
>
> For God alone, O my soul, wait in silence, for my hope is from him. (Ps.62:5)
>
> Do not say, "I will repay evil"; wait for the LORD, and he will deliver you. (Pr.20:22)
>
> But they who wait for the LORD shall renew their strength; they shall mount up with wings like eagles; they shall run and not be weary; they shall walk and not faint. (Is.40:31)
>
> "So you, by the help of your God, return, hold fast to love and justice, and wait continually for your God." (Ho.12:6)

## 11:7-10

⁷ Then after this he said to the disciples, "Let us go to Judea again."
⁸ The disciples said to him, "Rabbi, the Jews were just now seeking to stone you, and are you going there again?"
⁹ Jesus answered, "Are there not twelve hours in the day? If anyone walks in the day, he does not stumble, because he sees the light of this world.
¹⁰ But if anyone walks in the night, he stumbles, because the light is not in him."

## 5 Purpose 4: To teach the need to grasp opportunity.

The fourth purpose of Lazarus' sickness was to teach the need to grasp opportunity. It had been three days since Jesus had received word of Lazarus' illness. Jesus now said it was time to go into Judea, for Bethany was in the district of Judea.

a. **The disciples protested Jesus' return to Jerusalem: Because of the threat to His life (v.8).**

The disciples protested, for it was the Judean leaders who had stood so opposed to Jesus and had threatened to kill Him (Jn.10:31). The disciples could not believe their ears. Why would Jesus jeopardize their lives?

b. **Jesus' reply: There is a duty to work—to do what is right, to grasp the opportunity—regardless of the danger (vv.9-10).**

Jesus' answer was forceful, and it stands as a great lesson for all of us. Jesus said there are only twelve hours in a day. He had to walk in the day, that is . . .
- go and do His work while it is day
- go and do what is right, regardless of the danger
- go and do what is right lest the day pass and the opportunity be lost (see Jn.9:4)

If Jesus had walked in the dark, failing to work and failing to do what He knew to be right, He would have stumbled. He would have shown that there is no light in Him. The idea is, of course, that there is light in Him. He knew the work to be done and the right thing to do, so He had to go into Judea.

Note the term, "the light of this world." Jesus is the Light of this world. A person has roughly twelve hours in a day, only a limited amount of time to see "the light of this world." Once the night comes, the opportunity is lost. Note also the statement, "The light is not in him [a person]." People have no light within. All they can do is walk as they see, or as other people see, or as the world sees.

The problem with such a walk is that nobody can see beyond the physical and material world, and at the end of this life in this world is fear—the fear and trembling brought about by bondage and death (note the fear of the disciples above, v.8.) The end of life in this world is not life. Life comes only from Jesus, the Light of this world (see Deeper Study # 1—Jn.8:12). We must look to Jesus—see the Light—while it is yet day; that is, while there is yet time.

> In him was life, and the life was the light [Jesus Christ] of men. (Jn.1:4)

> "And this is the judgment: the light has come into the world, and people loved the darkness rather than the light because their works were evil." (Jn.3:19)

> Again Jesus spoke to them, saying, "I am the light of the world. Whoever follows me will not walk in darkness, but will have the light of life." (Jn.8:12)

> So Jesus said to them, "The light is among you for a little while longer. Walk while you have the light, lest darkness overtake you. The one who walks in the darkness does not know where he is going." (Jn.12:35)

> "I have come into the world as light, so that whoever believes in me may not remain in darkness." (Jn.12:46)

**THOUGHT 1.** Our time is limited, as represented by the twelve hours of daylight. Like Jesus, we must walk, that is, work and do what is right, grasping the opportunity while it is day, while we have the opportunity. If we walk in the night, we will stumble. When the night comes, it is too late to walk. Works cannot be done in the night without stumbling about. The opportunity is lost.

> Jesus said to them, "My food is to do the will of him who sent me and to accomplish his work." (Jn.4:34)

> "We must work the works of him who sent me while it is day; night is coming, when no one can work." (Jn.9:4)

> Besides this you know the time, that the hour has come for you to wake from sleep. For salvation is nearer to us now than when we first believed. The night is far gone; the day is at hand. So then let us cast off the works of darkness and put on the armor of light. (Ro.13:11-12)

> Making the best use of the time, because the days are evil. (Ep.5:16)

> Walk in wisdom toward outsiders, making the best use of the time. (Col.4:5)

## 6 Purpose 5: To show Jesus' power over death.

The fifth purpose of Lazarus' sickness was to show Jesus' great power over death. Jesus stated very plainly what He was going to do. Lazarus was asleep; therefore, He would go and awaken Lazarus out of his sleep.

**11:11-14**

¹¹ After saying these things, he said to them, "Our friend Lazarus has fallen asleep, but I go to awaken him."
¹² The disciples said to him, "Lord, if he has fallen asleep, he will recover."
¹³ Now Jesus had spoken of his death, but they thought that he meant taking rest in sleep.
¹⁴ Then Jesus told them plainly, "Lazarus has died,"

### a. Jesus called Lazarus "our friend" (v.11a).

Jesus called Lazarus "our friend." He was dead, but he was still "our friend." This is a hint that Lazarus is still a friend despite being dead, that he is still living, still alive in another world. Note the strong feelings Jesus had for this believer, Lazarus.

**THOUGHT 1.** Jesus' love reaches out for every believer just as much as it did for Lazarus. Jesus calls every believer His friend. And note the words "*our* friend." Every believer is to be the friend of all other believers. There is to be a sweet fellowship between all believers.

### b. Jesus predicted Lazarus would be raised (v.11b).

Jesus predicted that He would raise Lazarus from the dead. He would awaken and resurrect him. This is a picture of the resurrection of all believers (see vv.23-26).

> "Do not marvel at this, for an hour is coming when all who are in the tombs will hear his voice and come out, those who have done good to the resurrection of life, and those who have done evil to the resurrection of judgment." (Jn.5:28-29)

> Jesus said to her, "I am the resurrection and the life. Whoever believes in me, though he die, yet shall he live." (Jn.11:25)

### c. The disciples misunderstood (v.12).

The disciples misunderstood what Jesus was saying. In saying that Lazarus had *fallen asleep* or *sleeps* (Gk. kekoimētai), Jesus meant that he was dead, but the disciples thought He meant that Lazarus was resting in sleep. Like the disciples, many still do not understand the nature of death and the truth of the resurrection.

### d. Jesus said that death is as "sleep" (vv.13-14).

Jesus then gave His meaning of sleep, saying plainly that Lazarus had died (v.14). He wanted the disciples—and us—to understand the truth that, for the believer, death is as sleep. Our bodies rest from a lifetime of labor, but they will rise again (see DEEPER STUDY # 1).

---

### DEEPER STUDY # 1

(11:13) **Sleep—Death**: death is sometimes spoken of as sleep when referring to believers (see DEEPER STUDY # 1—Lu.8:50 for more discussion; see also Mt.27:52; Ac.7:60; 13:36; 1 Co.15:18, 20, 51; 1 Th.4:13-15; 2 Pe.3:4.)
- ➢ Jesus said that Jairus' daughter was asleep (Mt.9:24).
- ➢ When Stephen was martyred, he is said to have fallen asleep (Ac.7:60).
- ➢ Some of the five hundred witnesses to Jesus' ascension are said to have "fallen asleep" (1 Co.15:6).
- ➢ Believers already in heaven are said to be asleep in Jesus (1 Th.4:13).

Death is called "sleep" in order to picture the idea that the believer is . . .
- resting in the presence and comfort of God
- resting from the labor of service on earth

- resting and refreshing oneself for a greater service for God
- resting temporarily, to rise again for a new day

Many within the world picture death as annihilation, as ceasing to exist. Scripture says it is not. Believers continue to exist, resting in the life and comfort of God. The body lays down and, so to speak, sleeps; but not the soul. The soul of the believer is alive in the presence of the Lord.

> Yes, we are of good courage, and we would rather be away from the body and at home with the Lord. (2 Co.5:8; see Ph.1:23)

## 7  Purpose 6: To help strengthen the disciples' belief.

11:15

The sixth purpose of Lazarus' sickness was to help strengthen the disciples' belief. Jesus made an astonishing statement: He was glad that He was not in Bethany when Lazarus was sick. Why? Jesus rejoiced over what was about to happen. Lazarus was to be raised from the dead, which meant that every thoughtful believer, both then and in succeeding generations, would experience a great leap in faith. They would know that Jesus has the power to raise the dead.

> ¹⁵ "and for your sake I am glad that I was not there, so that you may believe. But let us go to him."

**THOUGHT 1.** The glorious event of Lazarus' resurrection stirs the heart of sincere seekers, for it pictures the most glorious hope of life possible. Jesus Christ has the power to give life and to raise the dead (Jn.5:24-29; 1 Co.15:1-58; 1 Th.4:13f). All followers of Christ who truly experience the scene of Lazarus' resurrection are bound . . .
- to take a great leap in faith
- to have their faith stirred to new heights
- to see their faith grow progressively

> Now Jesus did many other signs in the presence of the disciples, which are not written in this book; but these are written so that you may believe that Jesus is the Christ, the Son of God, and that by believing you may have life in his name. (Jn.20:30-31)

## 8  Purpose 7: To stir the disciples' courage and loyalty.

11:16

The seventh purpose of Lazarus' sickness was to stir the disciples' courage and loyalty. Fearing that the Jewish leaders would kill them, the disciples did not want Jesus to go back to Judea (v.8). Nevertheless, they were willing to go with Him, even if it cost them their lives.

> ¹⁶ So Thomas, called the Twin, said to his fellow disciples, "Let us also go, that we may die with him."

Note that Thomas took the lead here. He showed great courage and loyalty to Christ, a dynamic example for every believer. He demonstrated . . .
- a deep love for Christ, a love that was ready to die for Him
- a willingness to stand and to die with his fellow believers in the Lord's work
- a knowledge that to die for Christ is better than to live without Him

> "For the Father himself loves you, because you have loved me and have believed that I came from God." (Jn.16:27)

> But rejoice insofar as you share Christ's sufferings, that you may also rejoice and be glad when his glory is revealed. . . . Yet if anyone suffers as a Christian, let him not be ashamed, but let him glorify God in that name. (1 Pe.4:13, 16)

> "'Do not fear what you are about to suffer. Behold, the devil is about to throw some of you into prison, that you may be tested, and for ten days you will have tribulation. Be faithful unto death, and I will give you the crown of life.'" (Rev.2:10)

> "And they have conquered him by the blood of the Lamb and by the word of their testimony, for they loved not their lives even unto death." (Rev.12:11)

## B. Jesus and Martha: Growth in Faith, 11:17–27

1. **The scene: Bethany, a suburb of Jerusalem**
   a. Lazarus had been in the tomb for four days
   b. Friends comforted the family
   c. Martha went out to meet Jesus
   d. Mary stayed at home
2. **Martha's complaining, limited faith**
   a. Her complaint: That Lazarus died bc. Jesus was absent
   b. Her limited belief: That Jesus' power was less than God's power
3. **Martha's fundamental faith**
   a. Jesus' declaration
   b. Martha's expression of faith in the future resurrection
4. **Martha's declared faith**
   a. Jesus' great claim
   b. Jesus' promise: Believe . . .
      1) Anyone who believes will live & dies, even after death
      2) Anyone who lives & believes will never die; never perish
   c. Martha's declaration
      1) He is the Christ
      2) He is the Son of God
      3) He is sent by God

<sup>17</sup> Now when Jesus came, he found that Lazarus had already been in the tomb four days. <sup>18</sup> Bethany was near Jerusalem, about two miles off, <sup>19</sup> and many of the Jews had come to Martha and Mary to console them concerning their brother. <sup>20</sup> So when Martha heard that Jesus was coming, she went and met him, but Mary remained seated in the house. <sup>21</sup> Martha said to Jesus, "Lord, if you had been here, my brother would not have died. <sup>22</sup> But even now I know that whatever you ask from God, God will give you." <sup>23</sup> Jesus said to her, "Your brother will rise again." <sup>24</sup> Martha said to him, "I know that he will rise again in the resurrection on the last day." <sup>25</sup> Jesus said to her, "I am the resurrection and the life. Whoever believes in me, though he die, yet shall he live, <sup>26</sup> and everyone who lives and believes in me shall never die. Do you believe this?" <sup>27</sup> She said to him, "Yes, Lord; I believe that you are the Christ, the Son of God, who is coming into the world."

# Division XI

*The Revelation of Jesus, the Resurrection and the Life, 11:1–12:11*

B. Jesus and Martha: Growth in Faith, 11:17–27

## 11:17–27
### Introduction

Our faith grows through being tried. God uses trials to strengthen and mature our faith. Note what Scripture teaches us about this truth:

> Therefore, since we have been justified by faith, we have peace with God through our Lord Jesus Christ. Through him we have also obtained access by faith into this grace in which we stand, and we rejoice in hope of the glory of God. Not only that, but we rejoice in our sufferings, knowing that suffering produces endurance, and endurance produces character, and character produces hope, and hope does not put us to shame, because God's love has been poured into our hearts through the Holy Spirit who has been given to us. (Ro.5:1-5)
>
> Count it all joy, my brothers, when you meet trials of various kinds, for you know that the testing of your faith produces steadfastness. And let steadfastness have its full effect, that you may be perfect and complete, lacking in nothing. (Jas.1:2-4)

The death of a loved one is the most difficult and painful trial we face. This passage is a dynamic conversation between Jesus and Martha about her brother's death. What happened caused a great growth in Martha's faith. A seeking heart and a study of the conversation will cause any believer's faith to grow significantly. This is, *Jesus and Martha: Growth in Faith*, 11:17-27.

1. The scene: Bethany, a suburb of Jerusalem (vv.17-20).
2. Martha's complaining, limited faith (vv.21-22).
3. Martha's fundamental faith (vv.23-24).
4. Martha's declared faith (vv.25-27).

## 1 The scene: Bethany, a suburb of Jerusalem.

> 17 Now when Jesus came, he found that Lazarus had already been in the tomb four days.
> 18 Bethany was near Jerusalem, about two miles off,
> 19 and many of the Jews had come to Martha and Mary to console them concerning their brother.
> 20 So when Martha heard that Jesus was coming, she went and met him, but Mary remained seated in the house.

The scene was Bethany, a suburb of Jerusalem about two miles away. John recorded what happened when Jesus arrived on the scene.

### a. Lazarus had been in the tomb for four days (v.17).

As Jesus approached Bethany, someone told Him that Lazarus had already been buried for four days (see note—Jn.11:6). This information is significant to the miracle Jesus was about to perform. "The general belief [of the Jews] was that the spirit of the deceased hovered around the body for three days in anticipation of some possible means of reentry into the body. But on the third day it was believed that the body lost its color and the spirit was locked out."[1] There could be no question about it, no other explanation for Lazarus' return to life. The superstitious belief of the Jews could not be a possibility. He had been dead and buried four days.

### b. Friends comforted the family (v.19).

Interestingly, Jesus did not actually enter the city of Bethany. He apparently stayed on the outskirts of the city (v.30). Scripture does not record the reason why. Perhaps the multitude following Him was too large to crowd into the city, or perhaps He was simply avoiding those in Bethany who were so bitterly opposed to Him. An enormous number of mourners had come to comfort the family, and some of those were opposed to Jesus (v.46).

### c. Martha went out to meet Jesus (v.20a).

Whatever the reason for remaining on the outskirts of the city, Jesus apparently sent a messenger to tell Martha that He had arrived (see v.28). As soon as she heard, she quietly left the house and ran out to meet Him (see v.28 for what apparently happened with Martha as well as Mary).

### d. Mary stayed at home (v.20b).

Mary, however, remained at home. Note the striking contrast between Martha and Mary, a contrast that is ever so characteristic. Martha was the woman of action and energy, the one brimming with initiative; therefore, she was the one who went out to meet Jesus. Mary was

---

1 Gerald L. Borchert, *The New American Commentary (John 1-11): An Exegetical and Theological Exposition of Holy Scripture* (Nashville: Holman Reference, 1996), via Wordsearch digital edition.

the contemplative and meditative one; therefore, she remained at home to receive the mourners (see Lu.10:38-42).

## 11:21-22

²¹ Martha said to Jesus, "Lord, if you had been here, my brother would not have died.
²² But even now I know that whatever you ask from God, God will give you."

### 2 Martha's complaining, limited faith.

Martha believed in Jesus, but her faith was immature. Her first words to Jesus upon His arrival reveal that she had a complaining, limited faith.

a. **Her complaint: That Lazarus died because Jesus was absent (v.21).**

Martha had enough faith in Jesus to believe that He could have healed Lazarus and kept him from dying. But Jesus had not come immediately when He was called; and now her brother was dead. Why did Jesus not come when He was called? Why did He not heal Lazarus when she and the family loved Jesus so much and had done so much for Him? Why did He let Lazarus die?

The point is, Martha did believe in Jesus, but her faith was a complaining faith. She did not believe to the point of *resting* in faith. She did not believe with an *unlimited and resting faith*. She simply was not entrusting the matter completely into the Lord's hands, and she was not yet convinced that what had happened was for the best. She trusted Jesus as her Savior, but she questioned what had happened. She complained and expressed her disappointment to Jesus. However, Martha immediately became convicted over what she had said to the Lord, as her next statement reveals.

b. **Her limited belief: That Jesus' power was less than God's power (v.22).**

Martha tried to make amends for her complaint by confessing her faith in Jesus. But even here, her *limited faith* showed itself. She did not say, "Lord, I know that you can do anything you will." She said, "I know that God will give you whatever you ask." She was still *limiting* Jesus to some level below God. She was not grasping that Jesus Himself was the Resurrection and the Life. She had a complaining, limited faith in Jesus.

**THOUGHT 1.** A complaining, questioning faith is a *limited faith*. It blames the Lord for our troubles. It says to Jesus, "If You had been here, if You had acted differently, if You had done this or that, then this trial would not have happened." It is a faith that questions Jesus' Lordship . . .
- that questions if Jesus has done what is best
- that questions if Jesus knows what is best

> And he said to them, "Why are you afraid, O you of little faith?" Then he rose and rebuked the winds and the sea, and there was a great calm. (Mt.8:26)

> Jesus immediately reached out his hand and took hold of him [Peter], saying to him, "O you of little faith, why did you doubt?" And when they got into the boat, the wind ceased. (Mt.14:31-32)

> But Jesus, aware of this, said, "O you of little faith, why are you discussing among yourselves the fact that you have no bread? Do you not yet perceive? Do you not remember the five loaves for the five thousand, and how many baskets you gathered?" (Mt.16:8-9)

> "Do you not believe that I am in the Father and the Father is in me? The words that I say to you I do not speak on my own authority, but the Father who dwells in me does his works." (Jn.14:10)

## 11:23-24

²³ Jesus said to her, "Your brother will rise again."
²⁴ Martha said to him, "I know that he will rise again in the resurrection on the last day."

### 3 Martha's fundamental faith.

Martha's faith was a fundamental faith. She believed in the resurrection, one of the basic teachings of the faith. She believed what Jesus had taught, and He had been drilling the resurrection into His followers (see Jn.5:28-29; 6:39, 40, 44, 54; 12:48).

### a. Jesus' declaration (v.23).

Jesus made a striking declaration, promising Martha that her brother would rise again. He could have said it no clearer. Lazarus was to arise from the dead.

### b. Martha's expression of faith in the future resurrection (v.24).

Martha understood Jesus' declaration in light of her fundamental faith. She thought Jesus meant that Lazarus would arise in the resurrection *at the last day*. This glorious truth did not soothe her disappointment. The promise of a future resurrection and reunion is not always a comfort. Her loved one was gone. There was now no contact and no relationship with him, not on this earth. Everything about her life was now completely changed. Her household was radically different. She believed in the resurrection and believed in all the truths of the faith, but the resurrection was so far in the future that it was of little comfort to her then.

> **THOUGHT 1.** A *fundamental faith* is essential. A person must believe in the truths of the faith, but a fundamental faith is not all there is to faith and to our life in Christ. It is not a *living faith*, not a faith that lives in the presence of Christ. And what we so desperately need is what was needed by Martha: a living faith, a faith that is alive and vibrant, dynamic and moving, conscious and acting, communicating and fellowshipping. What we need is the knowledge that Jesus, the very One who stands before us, *is* "the resurrection and the life."
>
> "You search the Scriptures because you think that in them you have eternal life; and it is they that bear witness about me." (Jn.5:39)
>
> "Not everyone who says to me, 'Lord, Lord,' will enter the kingdom of heaven, but the one who does the will of my Father who is in heaven." (Mt.7:21)
>
> And he said to them, "Well did Isaiah prophesy of you hypocrites, as it is written, 'This people honors me with their lips, but their heart is far from me.'" (Mk.7:6)
>
> Having the appearance of godliness, but denying its power. Avoid such people. (2 Ti.3:5)

## 4 Martha's declared faith.

In response to Martha's statement of fundamental faith, Jesus gave her a comforting assurance. He assured her, first, that He is the Source of all life. Second, He assured her that, even though Lazarus' body was dead, her brother was fully alive in another world, the spiritual dimension. Martha responded by declaring her faith in Jesus.

> ²⁵ Jesus said to her, "I am the resurrection and the life. Whoever believes in me, though he die, yet shall he live,
> ²⁶ and everyone who lives and believes in me shall never die. Do you believe this?"
> ²⁷ She said to him, "Yes, Lord; I believe that you are the Christ, the Son of God, who is coming into the world."

### a. Jesus' great claim (v.25a).

Jesus responds to Martha's statement with a great claim, a claim only God could make: "I Am the resurrection and the life." Here is a critical fact: Jesus does not say that He *gives* the resurrection and life to people, but He *is* the Resurrection and the Life. Jesus, of course, does give resurrection and life to believers; but His point here is far more important. Jesus declares that He is the very being and essence, the very power and energy, of life. Therefore, He can . . .

- give and sustain life as He wills
- resurrect and restore life as He wills

This is an extraordinary claim. It means that human beings—in fact all of life—exists only by the will and power of Jesus. Being the power and energy of life, Jesus is the Source of all life. Nothing exists apart from His will; therefore, if a dead person wishes to live, only Jesus can give him life. And if a living person does not wish to die, only Jesus can keep him from dying.

> In him was life, and the life was the light of men. (Jn.1:4)
>
> "For as the Father has life in himself, so he has granted the Son also to have life in himself." (Jn.5:26)
>
> "The thief comes only to steal and kill and destroy. I came that they may have life and have it abundantly." (Jn.10:10)

Jesus said to him, "I am the way, and the truth, and the life. No one comes to the Father except through me." (Jn.14:6)

And which now has been manifested through the appearing of our Savior Christ Jesus, who abolished death and brought life and immortality to light through the gospel. (2 Ti.1:10)

Whoever has the Son has life; whoever does not have the Son of God does not have life. (1 Jn.5:12)

**b. Jesus' promise: Believe . . . (vv.25b–26).**

Jesus followed His great claim with a great promise: anyone who believes in Him will live, even after death (v.25b). Upon dying, believers live in another world: in heaven, in the spiritual dimension of being, in the very presence of God Himself. The believer who has passed from this world is not some place . . .

- in a semi-conscious state
- in a deep sleep, locked up in a compartment someplace
- in space moving about and floating around on a fluffy cloud

The believer is fully alive, living in heaven, in the very presence of God Himself. Another world exists, just as this world exists. It is not a world that lies out in the future; it is a world that exists now—a spiritual world—a spiritual dimension—a world that the Bible calls heaven. It is the spiritual world and dimension where God and Christ and angels and all believers who have gone on before now live.

What glorious news! When people who have believed in Jesus die, they go to live in heaven, in the spiritual world where God and Christ and the heavenly hosts live. *Hallelujah!* is perhaps the most fitting word that can express the hope and joy that fills the soul of the true believer because of this truth.

And behold, two men were talking with him, Moses and Elijah, who appeared in glory and spoke of his departure, which he was about to accomplish at Jerusalem. (Lu.9:30-31)

And he said to him, "Truly, I say to you, today you will be with me in paradise." (Lu.23:43)

"If anyone serves me, he must follow me; and where I am, there will my servant be also. If anyone serves me, the Father will honor him." (Jn.12:26)

"Father, I desire that they also, whom you have given me, may be with me where I am, to see my glory that you have given me because you loved me before the foundation of the world." (Jn.17:24)

Yes, we are of good courage, and we would rather be away from the body and at home with the Lord. (2 Co.5:8)

I am hard pressed between the two. My desire is to depart and be with Christ, for that is far better. (Ph.1:23)

Jesus made a second promise: anyone who lives and believes in Him will never die (v.26). The idea is that the believer will never taste death, that is, never experience death. Quicker than the blink of an eye, the believer passes from this world into the next world. He or she is transported and transferred instantly into heaven. Believers never lose a single moment of consciousness. One moment they are conscious and living in this world; the next moment they are conscious and present in the next world. There is only one difference. They are immediately made perfect: transformed, made much more conscious and aware, more knowledgeable and alive than ever before (see Deeper Study # 1—2 Ti.4:18 for more discussion; also see Deeper Study # 2—Jn.1:4; Deeper Study # 1—10:10; Deeper Study # 1—17:2-3).

"That whoever believes in him may have eternal life." (Jn.3:15)

"Truly, truly, I say to you, whoever hears my word and believes him who sent me has eternal life. He does not come into judgment, but has passed from death to life." (Jn.5:24)

"Truly, truly, I say to you, if anyone keeps my word, he will never see death." (Jn.8:51)

For the one who sows to his own flesh will from the flesh reap corruption, but the one who sows to the Spirit will from the Spirit reap eternal life. (Ga.6:8)

A number of scholars believe Jesus was speaking here of physical life rather than spiritual life, of the future resurrection of the body. They believe Jesus was alluding to a future event known as "the Rapture," a mystery that would later be fully revealed by Paul:

> Behold! I tell you a mystery. We shall not all sleep, but we shall all be changed, in a moment, in the twinkling of an eye, at the last trumpet. For the trumpet will sound, and the dead will be raised imperishable, and we shall be changed. For this perishable body must put on the imperishable, and this mortal body must put on immortality. (1 Co.15:51-53)

> But we do not want you to be uninformed, brothers, about those who are asleep, that you may not grieve as others do who have no hope. For since we believe that Jesus died and rose again, even so, through Jesus, God will bring with him those who have fallen asleep. For this we declare to you by a word from the Lord, that we who are alive, who are left until the coming of the Lord, will not precede those who have fallen asleep. For the Lord himself will descend from heaven with a cry of command, with the voice of an archangel, and with the sound of the trumpet of God. And the dead in Christ will rise first. Then we who are alive, who are left, will be caught up together with them in the clouds to meet the Lord in the air, and so we will always be with the Lord. (1 Th.4:13-17)

The bodies of those who die believing in Jesus will live again (v.25). They will be raised as incorruptible, immortal bodies when Jesus comes again. However, those who are living when Jesus returns will never die (v.26). Their bodies will be instantly transformed into incorruptible, immortal bodies. Glory to God!

The most critical word in all that Jesus says here is the word *believes*. Receiving eternal life is conditional: a person must believe. It is the one who believes that lives after death. It is the one who believes that lives and never dies. It is as Jesus asked Martha: "Do you believe this?" If we believe Jesus, we will never die, not spiritually; we will live forever.

c. **Martha's declaration (v.27).**

Martha believed, and she confessed and called Jesus "Lord" (see DEEPER STUDY # 2—Jn.2:24). She declared that she believed three things:

➤ That Jesus is the Christ, the Messiah (see note—Jn.1:35-42).

> The woman said to him, "I know that Messiah is coming (he who is called Christ). When he comes, he will tell us all things." Jesus said to her, "I who speak to you am he." (Jn.4:25-26)

> "I know him [God], for I come from him, and he sent me." (Jn.7:29)

➤ That Jesus is the Son of God (see note—Jn.1:34; see John the Baptist, Jn.1:34; Peter, Mt.16:16; Jesus, Jn.11:41; 26:63f; John the Apostle, Jn.20:31).

> "For God so loved the world, that he gave his only Son, that whoever believes in him should not perish but have eternal life." (Jn.3:16)

> "And whoever sees me sees him who sent me." (Jn.12:45)

➤ That Jesus is the One who was to be sent into the world by God (see DEEPER STUDY # 1—Jn.3:31).

> "And he who sent me is with me. He has not left me alone, for I always do the things that are pleasing to him." (Jn.8:29)

> Jesus said to them, "If God were your Father, you would love me, for I came from God and I am here. I came not of my own accord, but he sent me." (Jn.8:42)

**THOUGHT 1.** Knowing that Jesus is the Resurrection and the Life means three things.

First, it means that Jesus is alive, living right before us in the person of the Holy Spirit. He is both *in us* and *all around us*. Our faith is living and alive and in constant communion and fellowship with Him.

Second, it means that our believing loved ones are present with Jesus when they die, no longer imperfect in mind and body, but perfect: more conscious, more aware, more alive than they were on earth. How do we know this? Jesus is alive in heaven, and when our souls and spirits depart from our bodies through death, we go immediately into the presence of the Lord (2 Co.5:8).

Third, it means that Jesus is alive, so the resurrection of our glorified bodies is assured (1 Co.15:1-58).

> For as in Adam all die, so also in Christ shall all be made alive. (1 Co.15:22)

Who will transform our lowly body to be like his glorious body, by the power that enables him even to subject all things to himself. (Ph.3:21)

And which now has been manifested through the appearing of our Savior Christ Jesus, who abolished death and brought life and immortality to light through the gospel. (2 Ti.1:10)

"And after my skin has been thus destroyed, yet in my flesh I shall see God." (Jb.19:26)

But God will ransom my soul from the power of Sheol, for he will receive me. Selah. (Ps.49:15)

## C. Jesus and Mary: The People's Real Needs, 11:28-37

1. **Need 1: To hear the glorious message of Christ**
   a. He is the Teacher[DS1]
   b. The Teacher is here
   c. The Teacher asks for you

28 When she had said this, she went and called her sister Mary, saying in private, "The Teacher is here and is calling for you."

2. **Need 2: To respond confidently—arise quickly & come to Christ**

29 And when she heard it, she rose quickly and went to him.
30 Now Jesus had not yet come into the village, but was still in the place where Martha had met him.

3. **Need 3: To reach out to help other people**

31 When the Jews who were with her in the house, consoling her, saw Mary rise quickly and go out, they followed her, supposing that she was going to the tomb to weep there.

4. **Need 4: To confess your faith (even if it is limited & weak)**
   a. The confession: Jesus is Lord
   b. The, limited faith: Failed to fully trust the Lord

32 Now when Mary came to where Jesus was and saw him, she fell at his feet, saying to him, "Lord, if you had been here, my brother would not have died."

5. **Need 5: To acknowledge Jesus' understanding & compassion**
   a. He was deeply moved
      1) Over death
      2) Over the people's pain
   b. He asked where the dead man was

33 When Jesus saw her weeping, and the Jews who had come with her also weeping, he was deeply moved in his spirit and greatly troubled.
34 And he said, "Where have you laid him?" They said to him, "Lord, come and see."
35 Jesus wept.

   c. He wept in love: Over death & the people's pain

36 So the Jews said, "See how he loved him!"

6. **Need 6: To wait on the Lord, not question His timing, His love, & His power**

37 But some of them said, "Could not he who opened the eyes of the blind man also have kept this man from dying?"

# Division XI

*The Revelation of Jesus, the Resurrection and the Life, 11:1–12:11*

C. Jesus and Mary: The People's Real Needs, 11:28-37

## 11:28-37

## Introduction

How assuring and comforting it is to know that Jesus genuinely cares about our needs! Scripture assures us that absolutely nothing can separate us from His love (Ro.8:35-39). In our darkest hours, He always shows up, filling us with His strengthening presence and grace.

Our Lord cares about all of our needs. He uses our trials to meet needs we may not even realize we have. Six of these needs are seen in Mary's experience with Jesus. This is, *Jesus and Mary: The Real Needs of People,* 11:28-37.

1. Need 1: To hear the glorious message of Christ (v.28).
2. Need 2: To respond confidently—arise quickly and come to Christ (vv.29-30).
3. Need 3: To reach out to help other people (v.31).
4. Need 4: To confess your faith (even if it is limited and weak) (v.32).
5. Need 5: To acknowledge Jesus' understanding and compassion (vv.33-36).
6. Need 6: To wait on the Lord, not question His timing, His love, and His power (v.37).

## 11:28

<sup>28</sup> When she had said this, she went and called her sister Mary, saying in private, "The Teacher is here and is calling for you."

## 1 Need 1: To hear the glorious message of Christ.

Our first great need is to hear the glorious message of Christ. Martha had made a strong confession of faith, testifying wholeheartedly that Jesus is the Christ, the Son of God who had come into the world (v.27). This great confession apparently struck some kind of hope within Martha. She may not have even known exactly what she was expecting, but she felt a spark of hope. Her Lord, the Son of God Himself, was now with her. Whatever could be done would be done; whatever help was available would be given. Her faith and trust were in Him. Only one thing was missing: her dear sister, Mary. So, she hastened to share the glorious news with her. Note that she shared three facts.

a. **He is the Teacher.**

Martha referred to Jesus as *the Teacher* (see Deeper Study # 1). As *the* Teacher, Jesus stands alone, above all other teachers, in a class by Himself, unique and unparalleled.

b. **The Teacher is here.**

Martha said, "The Teacher is here," or, "The Teacher has come." The answer that we so desperately need is now available. The One who can give us the help we need has now come: the Teacher who can teach us how to meet all of our . . .

- needs and necessities
- troubles and trials
- sorrow and hurt
- loneliness and emptiness

> "Even as the Son of Man came not to be served but to serve, and to give his life as a ransom for many." (Mt.20:28)

> "The Spirit of the Lord is upon me, because he has anointed me to proclaim good news to the poor. He has sent me to proclaim liberty to the captives and recovering of sight to the blind, to set at liberty those who are oppressed, to proclaim the year of the Lord's favor." (Lu.4:18-19)

> "The thief comes only to steal and kill and destroy. I came that they may have life and have it abundantly." (Jn.10:10)

> Consequently, he is able to save to the uttermost those who draw near to God through him, since he always lives to make intercession for them. (He.7:25)

c. **The Teacher asks for you.**

Martha said to Mary, "The Teacher is calling for you." The Teacher has come *for you.* Jesus calls and asks for you. He wonders where you are and why you have not come to Him. He wants you now.

> "Come to me, all who labor and are heavy laden, and I will give you rest. Take my yoke upon you, and learn from me, for I am gentle and lowly in heart, and you will find rest for your souls." (Mt.11:28-29)

> "Come, everyone who thirsts, come to the waters; and he who has no money, come, buy and eat! Come, buy wine and milk without money and without price." (Is.55:1)

## Deeper Study #1

(11:28) **The Teacher** (Gk. ho didaskalos): The definite article *the* is important. Jesus is not just another teacher like all other teachers. He is *the* Teacher, the teaching Master. This means at least two things.

1. Jesus is the Supreme Teacher, the very best teacher who has ever lived. He is known for being the greatest of teachers. No one even comes close to comparing with Him. He stands alone as *the Teacher*.

2. Jesus is the Master, the Lord, the Teacher of all people. In calling Jesus *the* Teacher, there is the idea of His Lordship and deity. Note that in conjunction with this title, Jesus claimed deity for Himself, saying that as the Teacher, He was *the Lord* (ho kurios; Jn.13:13). His being *the Teacher* is tied closely with His being *the Lord*. In fact, logic alone would tell us that *the Lord* would be *the greatest Teacher* among all people.

> "Let all the house of Israel therefore know for certain that God has made him both Lord and Christ, this Jesus whom you crucified." (Ac.2:36)

> "God exalted him at his right hand as Leader and Savior, to give repentance to Israel and forgiveness of sins." (Ac.5:31)

> Because, if you confess with your mouth that Jesus is Lord and believe in your heart that God raised him from the dead, you will be saved. (Ro.10:9)

> Yet for us there is one God, the Father, from whom are all things and for whom we exist, and one Lord, Jesus Christ, through whom are all things and through whom we exist. (1 Co.8:6)

> Therefore I want you to understand that no one speaking in the Spirit of God ever says "Jesus is accursed!" and no one can say "Jesus is Lord" except in the Holy Spirit. (1 Co.12:3)

## 2 Need 2: To respond confidently—arise quickly and come to Christ.

11:29-30

Our second great need is to make the right response to Christ. We need to arise quickly and run to Him.

The message of Christ was enough to stir Mary. It is enough to stir action within the heart of any person who honestly seeks the answer to the riddle and trials of life and death.

²⁹ And when she heard it, she rose quickly and went to him.

³⁰ Now Jesus had not yet come into the village, but was still in the place where Martha had met him.

When Mary heard that Jesus was calling for her, she responded quickly (v.29). The idea is that she jumped up (arose quickly) and ran to meet Jesus. Hope and expectation were stirred in her heart. Note that the message had come to her in a very quiet manner: in private, secretly, in a whisper, without anyone else knowing it (v.28).

Mary acted on her own and made her own decision.

➢ She did not consult with friends and neighbors, not even with those who were closest to her. She got up and went to Jesus, leaving both friends and neighbors behind.

➢ She did not consult with religious leaders. Religion was important to her. The local religious leaders were even present, visiting and comforting her in her sorrow and sharing the comfort that their religion offered. But it helped her so little. When she heard the message that the Lord *was calling for her*, she went to Him, saying nothing to the religious leaders.

➢ She did not consider appearance or decorum. Think about the situation. The house was full of friends and neighbors. Who was going to greet them, receive their sympathies, express appreciation, and handle their presence? None of that mattered to Mary, not now. The Lord was *calling for her*. She must respond and go to Him immediately.

➢ She did not consider the distance. Jesus had not yet entered town, so Mary had to walk a considerable distance to reach Him. She had to make the decision to break away from those back in the house despite what they might think and feel. She had to move forward and travel to Him in order to respond to His call.

**THOUGHT 1.** No matter how quietly the message is proclaimed, we should respond by arising quickly and running to meet Jesus. We should let nothing stand in our way. Nothing is more important than answering the call of Jesus.

> He said, "Come." So Peter got out of the boat and walked on the water and came to Jesus. (Mt.14:29)

> "And I tell you, ask, and it will be given to you; seek, and you will find; knock, and it will be opened to you. For everyone who asks receives, and the one who seeks finds, and to the one who knocks it will be opened." (Lu.11:9-10)

> For he says, "In a favorable time I listened to you, and in a day of salvation I have helped you." Behold, now is the favorable time; behold, now is the day of salvation. (2 Co.6:2)

> The Spirit and the Bride say, "Come." And let the one who hears say, "Come." And let the one who is thirsty come; let the one who desires take the water of life without price. (Re.22:17)

> "I call heaven and earth to witness against you today, that I have set before you life and death, blessing and curse. Therefore choose life, that you and your offspring may live." (De.30:19)

## 11:31

<sup>31</sup> When the Jews who were with her in the house, consoling her, saw Mary rise quickly and go out, they followed her, supposing that she was going to the tomb to weep there.

### 3  Need 3: To reach out to help other people.

Our third need is to reach out to help each other. This is a touching picture. When the neighbors and friends saw Mary leave quickly, they thought she was going to the tomb to mourn over Lazarus. They were with her for one reason: to *console* or *comfort* her. Naturally, they followed her, thinking she needed help in bearing up under her loss. By being concerned about Mary, they were blessed tremendously and unexpectedly: they, too, were brought face-to-face with Jesus. Because they were set on comforting Mary, they were to share in Mary's experience with Christ.

In addition, they, too, were given the opportunity to trust Christ. In fact, many did believe in Him (v.45).

**THOUGHT 1.** Mary's friends and neighbors set a clear example of helping others. The world needs more and more neighbors such as these. Note the result of sincere help. It does not go unnoticed by Christ. Many are brought to Christ when they help those who already know Christ.

> "In all things I have shown you that by working hard in this way we must help the weak and remember the words of the Lord Jesus, how he himself said, 'It is more blessed to give than to receive.'" (Ac.20:35)

> We who are strong have an obligation to bear with the failings of the weak, and not to please ourselves. (Ro.15:1)

> Bear one another's burdens, and so fulfill the law of Christ. (Ga.6:2)

> Remember those who are in prison, as though in prison with them, and those who are mistreated, since you also are in the body. (He.13:3)

> Religion that is pure and undefiled before God the Father is this: to visit orphans and widows in their affliction, and to keep oneself unstained from the world. (Js.1:27)

## 11:32

<sup>32</sup> Now when Mary came to where Jesus was and saw him, she fell at his feet, saying to him, "Lord, if you had been here, my brother would not have died."

### 4  Need 4: To confess your faith (even if it is limited and weak).

Our fourth great need is to confess our faith, even if our faith is limited and weak. As soon as Mary saw Jesus, she fell at His feet in worship and made a confession of faith in Him.

a. **The confession: Jesus is Lord.**
Mary called Jesus Lord (see Deeper Study # 1; Deeper Study # 1—Ph.2:11). To her, Jesus was not just a teacher. He was her Lord.

b. **The limited faith: Failed to fully trust the Lord.**
Mary expressed, however, the same complaining, limited faith that Martha did (see note—11:21-22 for discussion). She too was hurt that Jesus did not come immediately and prevent Lazarus' death.

> **THOUGHT 1.** The need of every individual is to make a genuine confession of faith. Even if a person's belief and confession are weak, they will grow as they walk with Jesus day by day.
>
> "So everyone who acknowledges me before men, I also will acknowledge before my Father who is in heaven." (Mt.10:32)
>
> Because, if you confess with your mouth that Jesus is Lord and believe in your heart that God raised him from the dead, you will be saved. For with the heart one believes and is justified, and with the mouth one confesses and is saved. (Ro.10:9-10)
>
> And every tongue confess that Jesus Christ is Lord, to the glory of God the Father. (Ph.2:11)
>
> Whoever confesses that Jesus is the Son of God, God abides in him, and he in God. (1 Jn.4:15)

## 5 To acknowledge Jesus' understanding and compassion.

11:33-36

Our fifth great need is the understanding, feelings, and compassion of Jesus. John recorded Jesus' compassion for His dear friends in one simple sentence, the briefest—and perhaps the most touching—in the New Testament: *Jesus wept* (v.35).

> 33 When Jesus saw her weeping, and the Jews who had come with her also weeping, he was deeply moved in his spirit and greatly troubled.
> 34 And he said, "Where have you laid him?" They said to him, "Lord, come and see."
> 35 Jesus wept.
> 36 So the Jews said, "See how he loved him!"

a. **He was deeply moved (v.33).**
Our Lord was deeply moved with compassion for the people out of their concerns over death itself and specifically over the grief and pain they felt due to Lazarus' death.
*Deeply moved* or *groaned* (enebrimesato) is often interpreted to mean a stern reaction, displeasure, or anger (because of its use in other places). Some interpreters feel that Jesus was angry with the friends and neighbors because of their loud wailing and moaning, feeling that they were being hypocritical and insincere in their sorrow. This interpretation is difficult to accept. Unquestionably, Mary was sincere in her sorrow, and Jesus was definitely touched by her need. In addition, the Jewish friends and neighbors (which were "many," v.19) were sincere in comforting her (v.31), and many were open to trusting the Lord (v.45). Jesus was certainly touched by those as well.

In light of the whole scene, it seems best to interpret Jesus' grief as His being gripped with intense emotion. He was deeply moved . . .
- by Mary, who was so broken in sorrow
- by Martha, who was gripped by pain and hurt
- by those who were genuinely affected by the death of Lazarus and the sorrow of the family
- by the tragedy of death and the pain it causes
- by the terrible price He was soon to pay conquering death (This was certainly glimpsed by Jesus in such a scene as He was now experiencing.)

We need to know that the spirit of Jesus *is* troubled by our hurting hearts. He is deeply moved with understanding and feeling and compassion for all who are hurting and suffering. The word *troubled* (etaraxen heauton) is more literally stated as *troubled within Himself*. It means agitated, moved deeply, disturbed within. Jesus was actually feeling the misery and pain of all the people present. His spirit was disturbed and agitated, deeply moved by the whole scene of sorrow and death.

b. **He asked where the dead man was (v.34).**

Jesus asked where Lazarus was. Jesus knew where the grave was, but He asked where it was for two reasons:

➤ If He had gone straight to the tomb, some may have accused Him and Lazarus of being in collusion and tricking the people.

➤ He needed to distract the people from their deep wailing and stir their expectation for something unusual that was about to happen.

Note also that Jesus demonstrated His concern over the dead. He wishes to know where every dead person is, both those who are *spiritually dead* and those who are *physically dead*. He wants to point our attention to the fact that all people lie in the grave, spiritually speaking. All must look to Him if they wish to escape death (see DEEPER STUDY # 1—He.9:27. See Jn.3:16; 5:24.)

c. **He wept in love: Over death and the people's pain (vv.35-36).**

*Jesus wept* along with those who mourned Lazarus. Why? He wept over death, over pain, sorrow, suffering, and fate. Humans were never made for sin and death; we were created for righteousness and life. Sin and death . . .

- deceive and lie
- hurt and maim
- separate and alienate
- misuse and defeat
- destroy and corrupt
- condemn and doom eternally

**THOUGHT 1.** The tears of Jesus tell us just how much our Savior loves us. His heart is broken over our sorrow and pain. And it was broken over our common destiny, death and the grave, broken so much that He came to earth as a Man in order to die in our place. Through His atoning death and victorious resurrection, He destroyed our great enemy—death (1 Co.15:25, 54-57)

> Who shall separate us from the love of Christ? Shall tribulation, or distress, or persecution, or famine, or nakedness, or danger, or sword? (Ro.8:35)

> For we do not have a high priest who is unable to sympathize with our weaknesses, but one who in every respect has been tempted as we are, yet without sin. (He.4:15)

> He remembered that they were but flesh, a wind that passes and comes not again. (Ps.78:39)

> As a father shows compassion to his children, so the LORD shows compassion to those who fear him. (Ps.103:13)

> But the steadfast love of the LORD is from everlasting to everlasting on those who fear him, and his righteousness to children's children. (Ps.103:17)

> In all their affliction he was afflicted, and the angel of his presence saved them; in his love and in his pity he redeemed them; he lifted them up and carried them all the days of old. (Is.63:9)

**11:37**

³⁷ But some of them said, "Could not he who opened the eyes of the blind man also have kept this man from dying?"

## 6 Need 6: To wait on the Lord, not question His timing, His love, and His power.

Our sixth great need is to learn to wait on the Lord instead of questioning His timing, love, and power. The people asked the same question that is so often asked by people of every generation: How could Jesus love so much and let this happen? The problem, of course, is not Jesus. People just do not understand . . .

- that the nature of the world is decay and corruption, trial and trouble, suffering and pain, death and hell—all because of selfishness and sin
- that trials and sickness can be an opportunity for God to do a great work (see note—Jn.11:4)

**THOUGHT 1.** We need to learn to trust Christ, to not question Him about the things we do not understand. We have to remember that the Lord is not the cause of our painful problems, that the painful things we experience are the result of sin. Even when we cannot see how, we have to believe that God will bring good out of evil and will work all things together for our good. When we suffer, His grace will be sufficient to carry us through. He has made these promises to us, and He will never fail to keep His Word.

> **And we know that for those who love God all things work together for good, for those who are called according to his purpose. (Ro.8:28)**

> **For all the promises of God find their Yes in him. That is why it is through him that we utter our Amen to God for his glory. (2 Co.1:20)**

> **But he said to me, "My grace is sufficient for you, for my power is made perfect in weakness." Therefore I will boast all the more gladly of my weaknesses, so that the power of Christ may rest upon me. (2 Co.12:9)**

> **"As for you, you meant evil against me, but God meant it for good, to bring it about that many people should be kept alive, as they are today." (Ge.50:20)**

> **"Though he slay me, I will hope in him; yet I will argue my ways to his face." (Jb.13:15)**

> **"For I know the plans I have for you, declares the Lord, plans for welfare and not for evil, to give you a future and a hope." (Je.29:11)**

## D. Jesus and Lazarus: Power Over Death, 11:38–46

1. The great confrontation of Jesus with the dead
   a. He was deeply moved
   b. He was confronted by a believer's (Martha's) objection

2. The great promise of unlimited faith[DS1]

3. The great prayer of purpose
   a. Addressed God as "Father"
   b. Made a silent request
   c. Offered thanksgiving
   d. Expressed perfect confidence
   e. Bore testimony to those standing by

4. The great shout of power over death
   a. The power was within Christ
   b. The shout was personal: Called Lazarus by name
   c. The result of Christ's power
      1) Lazarus arose
      2) Lazarus received Jesus' personal attention[DS2]

5. The reaction to Jesus' great power
   a. Some believed & put their faith in Him
   b. Some disbelieved & caused trouble

38 Then Jesus, deeply moved again, came to the tomb. It was a cave, and a stone lay against it.
39 Jesus said, "Take away the stone." Martha, the sister of the dead man, said to him, "Lord, by this time there will be an odor, for he has been dead four days."
40 Jesus said to her, "Did I not tell you that if you believed you would see the glory of God?"
41 So they took away the stone. And Jesus lifted up his eyes and said, "Father, I thank you that you have heard me.

42 I knew that you always hear me, but I said this on account of the people standing around, that they may believe that you sent me."
43 When he had said these things, he cried out with a loud voice, "Lazarus, come out."
44 The man who had died came out, his hands and feet bound with linen strips, and his face wrapped with a cloth. Jesus said to them, "Unbind him, and let him go."
45 Many of the Jews therefore, who had come with Mary and had seen what he did, believed in him,
46 but some of them went to the Pharisees and told them what Jesus had done.

# Division XI

## *The Revelation of Jesus, the Resurrection and the Life, 11:1–12:11*

D. Jesus and Lazarus: Power Over Death, 11:38–46

## 11:38–46
## Introduction

How wonderful it is to not have to fear death, to be able to face death with confidence and hope! And how wonderful it is to know that, when our loved ones die trusting Jesus, they are immediately in His glorious presence and we will see them again! We have this hope because Jesus was victorious over death.

In this passage, Jesus confronts death and demonstrates His great power over death. In conquering the tomb of Lazarus, He demonstrates that the believer's hope is not in vain. As with Lazarus, all believers will be raised from the dead, resurrected by the great shout of the Lord's power. This is, *Jesus and Lazarus: Power Over Death,* 11:38-46.

1. The great confrontation of Jesus with the dead (vv.38-39).
2. The great promise of unlimited faith (v.40).
3. The great prayer of purpose (vv.41-42).
4. The great shout of power over death (vv.43-44).
5. The reaction to Jesus' great power (vv.45-46).

## 1 The great confrontation of Jesus with the dead.

The faithless statement of some of the people present at Lazarus' grave pierced the heart of Jesus (v.37). Deeply moved again (v.33), the Lord of Life walked over to Lazarus' grave and boldly confronted death.

> ³⁸ Then Jesus, deeply moved again, came to the tomb. It was a cave, and a stone lay against it.
>
> ³⁹ Jesus said, "Take away the stone." Martha, the sister of the dead man, said to him, "Lord, by this time there will be an odor, for he has been dead four days."

### a. He was deeply moved (v.38).

Once again, we see Jesus deeply moved within. Again, He saw the pain of Mary and Martha and their dear friends. He sensed afresh the terrible dread and bondage that death held over His close friend Lazarus and over the entire human race. In addition, He was keenly conscious of His own terrible death that was now only a few days away.

Jesus felt both compassion and anger, sympathy and indignation. He groaned from deep within, sensing an intense love for all who suffer and a holy anger against death (see note—11:33-36). With all these emotions brewing in His spirit, the Son of God stood face-to-face with the grave.

### b. He was confronted by a believer's (Martha's) objection (v.39).

When Jesus commanded the stone be rolled away from Lazarus' tomb, He was confronted with an objection from a believer. In fact, the objection came from Martha, the dead man's sister who had been disappointed in Jesus because He did not keep Lazarus from dying. She was shocked at Jesus' request, for the body would have started to decompose after four days.

We should emphasize that it was a believer who objected to Jesus' handling of the situation. Martha's objection was rooted in distrust and uneasiness—a lack of faith. Uneasy about what Jesus was doing and asking, she was not sure that His action was wise or for the best. Satisfied with things as they were, with Lazarus laid to rest as he was, she did not want the situation disturbed or made worse. What she wanted was to be comforted, not distressed beyond what she was already feeling.

Note the emphasis on the fact that Lazarus was truly dead. An unbeliever might question if Lazarus were indeed dead. Lazarus was in a real tomb, a tomb of the wealthy. Martha's wealth was also indicated by her having owned a house large enough to lodge Jesus and His disciples. If by any chance Lazarus had only been mistaken for dead before, he was certainly dead now. It had been four days since he had been placed in an enclosed tomb. Four days without food, water, and adequate air in such circumstances would kill any weak and critically ill person. Jesus ordered the stone rolled away so everyone present could see—and smell—that Lazarus was unquestionably dead.

**THOUGHT 1.** Many believers want things left alone, being happy with things as they are. They want only enough of Christ to give them comfort and security and ease. They want little if anything to do with His demands and confrontation with the sin and death of the world (see DEEPER STUDY #1—Lu.9:23).

And he did not do many mighty works there, because of their unbelief. (Mt.13:58)

Though he had done so many signs before them, they still did not believe in him. (Jn.12:37)

That is true. They were broken off because of their unbelief, but you stand fast through faith. So do not become proud, but fear. (Ro.11:20)

Take care, brothers, lest there be in any of you an evil, unbelieving heart, leading you to fall away from the living God. But exhort one another every day, as long as it is called "today," that none of you may be hardened by the deceitfulness of sin. For we have come to share in Christ, if indeed we hold our original confidence firm to the end. (He.3:12-14)

Let us therefore strive to enter that rest, so that no one may fall by the same sort of disobedience. (He.4:11)

Now I want to remind you, although you once fully knew it, that Jesus, who saved a people out of the land of Egypt, afterward destroyed those who did not believe. (Jude 5)

## 11:40

⁴⁰ Jesus said to her, "Did I not tell you that if you believed you would see the glory of God?"

## 2 The great promise of unlimited faith.

Jesus challenged Martha to take an enormous leap of faith. He wanted her to conquer her complaining and to set aside her objections (see note—Jn.11:21-22). He wanted her to trust Him, to quit questioning what He did. He wanted her to trust...
- His judgment and will
- His knowledge and understanding
- His Word and instructions

Very simply, Jesus wanted Martha to *rest* in Him, to place an unlimited, resting faith in Him (see DEEPER STUDY # 1). With that purpose in mind, Jesus made a compelling promise to Martha (and to all): if she would believe and simply rest in Him, she would see the glory of God. By glory, Jesus meant His mercy and power, love and care on this earth. However, the promise applies to the next world as well. The person who will step back and let God act as He wills—the person who truly rests in God—will see the glory of God in the next world as well.

### DEEPER STUDY # 1

(11:40) **Faith, Unlimited; Resting**: there is a rest for the believer. It is called *the believer's rest* or *God's rest*. The believer enters *God's rest* by what may be called a *resting faith* or an *unlimited faith*. An unlimited, resting faith is the summit, the highest level or stage of faith. It is the level of faith God desires for every believer. He longs for every child of His to enter the rest of God. A resting (unlimited) faith is a faith that rests in at least four things.

1. A resting faith is a rest of *deliverance and salvation*. It is to rest in God's Word, to know beyond all question...
- that you are truly saved and delivered from sin and shame, death and hell
- that you are freed from the guilt and nagging of conscience
- that you have open access into God's presence through prayer

"Come to me, all who labor and are heavy laden, and I will give you rest." (Mt.11:28)

Therefore, since we have been justified by faith, we have peace with God through our Lord Jesus Christ. (Ro.5:1)

For we who have believed enter that rest, as he has said, "As I swore in my wrath, 'They shall not enter my rest,'" although his works were finished from the foundation of the world. (He.4:3)

To whom he has said, "This is rest; give rest to the weary; and this is repose"; yet they would not hear. (Is.28:12)

For thus said the Lord GOD, the Holy One of Israel, "In returning and rest you shall be saved; in quietness and in trust shall be your strength." But you were unwilling. (Is.30:15)

2. A resting faith is a rest of *service and ministry*. It is not inactivity, not a life that does nothing for God and the world. It is a rest that comes from committing your life to the call and purpose of Jesus Christ, a rest that is . . .
- filled with purpose, meaning, and significance
- committed to sharing Christ with a world lost, full of desperate needs
- surrendered to God's call for personal involvement and service
- filled with God's Spirit and equipped with His gifts for service
- pleased with God's call and gifts, with your lot in life and place of service
- complete, fulfilled, satisfied, and unashamed in your life

"Take my yoke upon you, and learn from me, for I am gentle and lowly in heart, and you will find rest for your souls." (Mt.11:29)

All this is from God, who through Christ reconciled us to himself and gave us the ministry of reconciliation; that is, in Christ God was reconciling the world to himself, not counting their trespasses against them, and entrusting to us the message of reconciliation. Therefore, we are ambassadors for Christ, God making his appeal through us. We implore you on behalf of Christ, be reconciled to God. (2 Co.5:18-20)

Let us therefore strive to enter that rest, so that no one may fall by the same sort of disobedience. (He.4:11)

"Agree with God, and be at peace; thereby good will come to you." (Jb.22:21)

3. A resting faith is a rest of *assurance and confidence* in the future. It is a rest of peace about the future. It is . . .
- the knowledge that all the enslavements and bondages of this life have been conquered in Christ, even death
- the knowledge and experience of God's daily care through all of life; the knowledge that God will take care of His people no matter what may come or fall
- the knowledge and very real presence of hope: the hope of eternal life, of heaven, of the *eternal and perfect rest* for the people of God

"Peace I leave with you; my peace I give to you. Not as the world gives do I give to you. Let not your hearts be troubled, neither let them be afraid." (Jn.14:27)

"I have said these things to you, that in me you may have peace. In the world you will have tribulation. But take heart; I have overcome the world." (Jn.16:33)

And I heard a voice from heaven saying, "Write this: Blessed are the dead who die in the Lord from now on." "Blessed indeed," says the Spirit, "that they may rest from their labors, for their deeds follow them!" (Re.14:13)

When the LORD has given you rest from your pain and turmoil and the hard service with which you were made to serve. (Is.14:3)

"You keep him in perfect peace whose mind is stayed on you, because he trusts in you." (Is.26:3)

4. A resting faith is a rest of *courage and knowledge*. It is a faith that neither questions nor complains. It is a faith that truly believes, trusts, and rests in God, that actually . . .
- takes God at His Word and does exactly what He says
- knows that God's presence and blessing are upon your life
- puts everything into God's hands and launches out as He says
- knows that what happens is under God's control
- knows that all things, no matter how terrible, will be worked out for good to those who love God (Ro.8:28)
- experiences God's presence and care day by day
- knows victory over all: being filled with all confidence, assurance, hope, and peace

And we know that for those who love God all things work together for good, for those who are called according to his purpose. (Ro.8:28)

Do not be anxious about anything, but in everything by prayer and supplication with thanksgiving let your requests be made known to God. And the peace of God, which surpasses all understanding, will guard your hearts and your minds in Christ Jesus. (Ph.4:6-7)

Return, O my soul, to your rest; for the LORD has dealt bountifully with you. (Ps.116:7)

Great peace have those who love your law; nothing can make them stumble. (Ps.119:165)

## 3 The great prayer of purpose.

**11:41-42**

⁴¹ So they took away the stone. And Jesus lifted up his eyes and said, "Father, I thank you that you have heard me.

⁴² "I knew that you always hear me, but I said this on account of the people standing around, that they may believe that you sent me."

When they rolled the stone away from Lazarus' tomb, Jesus looked up toward heaven and prayed. He prayed for a specific purpose, and in so doing He demonstrated the purpose and the power of prayer. Note the wording of this point: *prayer of purpose*. When we truly pray with purpose, we receive the answer to our prayer and witness the power of prayer. Every prayer is to be a prayer of purpose. This is Jesus' point.

a. **Addressed God as "Father" (v.41a).**

Jesus addressed God as "Father." Jesus had an intimate and continuous relationship with God: a Father-Son relationship. He knew God as His Father, and God knew Jesus as His Son (see note—Jn.10:14-16; esp. see v.15).

**THOUGHT 1.** Believers are hereby taught to call on God as "Father" and to approach God as a child would: intimately and boldly, yet respectfully and reverently.

b. **Made a silent request (v.41b).**

Jesus requested that His Father do something. This fact is revealed by His thanking the Father for hearing Him. What Jesus asked was not stated, but we know from the context that it has to do with . . .
- the power to conquer death
- the strengthening of believers standing around and watching Him
- the stirring of others to believe and trust Him

c. **Offered thanksgiving (v.41c).**

Jesus offered thanksgiving to the Father, praising the Father for the glorious privilege of prayer and of being heard and having His prayers answered. This is a striking lesson for believers. God is to be praised for prayer, for the open access He allows into His presence and for the glorious fact that He hears and answers us (see Jn.16:23-24, 26-27).

d. **Expressed perfect confidence (v.42a).**

Jesus expressed a perfect and confident knowledge in God; He *knew* that God always heard His prayers. There is no hesitancy, doubt, or questioning on Jesus' part. He knew perfectly that God heard His prayers—*always*.

e. **Bore testimony to those standing by (v.42b).**

Jesus bore testimony to the bystanders through His prayer. He prayed to show them the close personal relationship between Himself and God, and to stir belief that He was the *Sent One* of God (see DEEPER STUDY # 3—Jn.3:34; 4:31-35).

**THOUGHT 1.** The above points could be stated as the fivefold purposes for prayer:
(1) To honor and worship God as "Father."

> For you did not receive the spirit of slavery to fall back into fear, but you have received the Spirit of adoption as sons, by whom we cry, "Abba! Father!" The Spirit himself bears witness with our spirit that we are children of God. (Ro.8:15-16)

> But when the fullness of time had come, God sent forth his Son, born of woman, born under the law, to redeem those who were under the law, so that we might receive adoption as sons. And because you are sons, God has sent the Spirit of his Son into our hearts, crying, "Abba! Father!" (Ga.4:4-6)

(2) To secure whatever is needed to live righteously and to minister.

> "And whatever you ask in prayer, you will receive, if you have faith." (Mt.21:22)

"And I tell you, ask, and it will be given to you; seek, and you will find; knock, and it will be opened to you." (Lu.11:9)

"If you ask me anything in my name, I will do it." (Jn.14:14)

"If you abide in me, and my words abide in you, ask whatever you wish, and it will be done for you." (Jn.15:7)

(3) To praise and thank God.

That together you may with one voice glorify the God and Father of our Lord Jesus Christ. (Ro.15:6)

Ascribe to the Lord the glory due his name; worship the Lord in the splendor of holiness. (Ps.29:2)

My mouth is filled with your praise, and with your glory all the day. (Ps.71:8)

Let them extol him in the congregation of the people, and praise him in the assembly of the elders. (Ps.107:32)

On the glorious splendor of your majesty, and on your wondrous works, I will meditate. (Ps.145:5)

O Lord, you are my God; I will exalt you; I will praise your name, for you have done wonderful things, plans formed of old, faithful and sure. (Is.25:1)

(4) To prove and demonstrate our confidence in God.

And whatever we ask we receive from him, because we keep his commandments and do what pleases him. (1 Jn.3:22)

And this is the confidence that we have toward him, that if we ask anything according to his will he hears us. And if we know that he hears us in whatever we ask, we know that we have the requests that we have asked of him. (1 Jn.5:14–15)

(5) To bear testimony and proclaim that Jesus is the One sent by God.

"For I have come down from heaven, not to do my own will but the will of him who sent me." (Jn.6:38)

Jesus said to them, "If God were your Father, you would love me, for I came from God and I am here. I came not of my own accord, but he sent me." (Jn.8:42)

"For I have given them the words that you gave me, and they have received them and have come to know in truth that I came from you; and they have believed that you sent me." (Jn.17:8)

**THOUGHT 2.** Jesus always prayed with purpose; therefore, He always received the answer to His prayer and bore testimony to the power of prayer. So it is with every true believer. When we pray with purpose, God answers our prayer, and by so doing He proclaims . . .

- that Christ is the Son of the living God
- that Christ is the One sent into the world to open the door (secure access) into God's presence
- that Christ is the One who has the power over death

"Ask, and it will be given to you; seek, and you will find; knock, and it will be opened to you. For everyone who asks receives, and the one who seeks finds, and to the one who knocks it will be opened. Or which one of you, if his son asks him for bread, will give him a stone? Or if he asks for a fish, will give him a serpent? If you then, who are evil, know how to give good gifts to your children, how much more will your Father who is in heaven give good things to those who ask him!" (Mt.7:7–11)

And being in agony he prayed more earnestly; and his sweat became like great drops of blood falling down to the ground. (Lk.22:44)

Therefore, confess your sins to one another and pray for one another, that you may be healed. The prayer of a righteous person has great power as it is working. Elijah was a man with a nature like ours, and he prayed fervently that it might not rain, and for three years and six months it did not rain on the earth. (Jn.5:26)

## 4 The great shout of power over death.

**11:43-44**

⁴³ When he had said these things, he cried out with a loud voice, "Lazarus, come out."

⁴⁴ The man who had died came out, his hands and feet bound with linen strips, and his face wrapped with a cloth. Jesus said to them, "Unbind him, and let him go."

In one of the most dramatic, thrilling scenes of the New Testament, Jesus shouted loudly for the dead man to come out of his grave. Still bound in his grave clothes, Lazarus marched out of the grave at Christ's command! The Lord had demonstrated His power over death. The resurrection of Lazarus pictures the coming resurrection of all believers (see 1 Co.15:12-58).

### a. The power was within Christ (v.43).

The power over death comes from Jesus alone. Few prophets have ever raised a dead person except Jesus. Jesus alone has the power to raise the dead. He simply spoke three words, "Lazarus, come out (forth)"; but He shouted them out with a loud voice. Why?

First, a shout matched the enormity of the miracle. It stressed the enormous power required to raise the dead.

Second, a shout stressed that the power within Jesus is the power of God Himself. With just a shout Jesus can call forth the enormous power of God, call forth the greatest power imaginable, the power to raise a person from the dead.

> "For as the Father has life in himself, so he has granted the Son also to have life in himself." (Jn.5:26)
>
> Since therefore the children share in flesh and blood, he himself likewise partook of the same things, that through death he might destroy the one who has the power of death, that is, the devil, and deliver all those who through fear of death were subject to lifelong slavery. (He.2:14-15)

### b. The shout was personal: Called Lazarus by name (v.43).

Jesus shouted Lazarus' name. He did not just shout, "Come out"; He shouted "*Lazarus*, come out." Jesus knows every believer by name, and He is personally concerned over the death of everyone. The day is coming when He will shout "Come out," and only the ones personally known by Him will respond.

> "To him the gatekeeper opens. The sheep hear his voice, and he calls his own sheep by name and leads them out." (Jn.10:3)
>
> "I am the good shepherd. I know my own and my own know me." (Jn.10:14)
>
> "My sheep hear my voice, and I know them, and they follow me." (Jn.10:27)
>
> "In my Father's house are many rooms. If it were not so, would I have told you that I go to prepare a place for you? And if I go and prepare a place for you, I will come again and will take you to myself, that where I am you may be also." (Jn.14:2-3)

### c. The result of Christ's power (v.44).

Christ's death-defying, death-defeating power produced two results. First, the dead person came forth. The Son of God spoke and called him forth. There was no way he could remain in the grave, no power that could hold him there. He came out of the grave . . .

- unquestionably
- immediately
- obediently
- perfectly
- visibly
- just as he was

Second, the person who was resurrected received the personal attention of Jesus. The attention and the thoughtfulness of Jesus is displayed in His command to unbind Lazarus and let him go. The wonder of the miracle did not detract our Lord from continuing to minister and to help wherever He could. It was not enough to share in the wonder of the miracle. Service to God was, and always will be, the call of our Lord Jesus to every person, even in eternity

> "His master said to him, 'Well done, good and faithful servant. You have been faithful over a little; I will set you over much. Enter into the joy of your master.'" (Mt.25:23)
>
> And night will be no more. They will need no light of lamp or sun, for the Lord God will be their light, and they will reign forever and ever. (Re.22:5)

## Deeper Study # 2

(11:44) **Grave Clothes**: note there was a *kerchief* or *cloth* (soudario) wrapped around the face of Lazarus. This detail is important for two reasons.

1. Jesus had a napkin wrapped around His face when He was buried. It was folded either by Him or an angel and laid to the side after His resurrection. The folded napkin was the immediate thing that convinced John of the Lord's resurrection (see note—Jn.20:7-10).

2. The facecloth showed that the grave clothes of Jesus' day included at least two pieces of clothing. There was a separate cloth or kerchief wrapped around the face. It is mentioned two times in the New Testament (Jn.11:44; 20:7. See Lu.19:20; Ac.19:12 for two other uses of the same Greek word, soudario.)

## 5 The reaction to Jesus' great power.

11:45-46

a. Some believed and put their faith in Him (v.45).
b. Some disbelieved and caused trouble (v.46).

Even though Jesus raised a man from the dead, the reaction to His great power was divided. Some believed in Him (see Deeper Study # 2—Jn.2:24). Others were gripped with obstinate unbelief and caused trouble. They refused to accept Jesus as the Son of God despite the most powerful evidence. They ignored the evidence and evaded the issue of His demand for belief. Therefore, they lost their opportunity "to see the glory of God" (vv.40, 46).

⁴⁵ Many of the Jews therefore, who had come with Mary and had seen what he did, believed in him,

⁴⁶ but some of them went to the Pharisees and told them what Jesus had done.

> Whoever believes in the Son has eternal life; whoever does not obey the Son shall not see life, but the wrath of God remains on him. (Jn.3:36)

> "I told you that you would die in your sins, for unless you believe that I am he you will die in your sins." (Jn.8:24)

## E. Jesus and the Religious Leaders: Unbelief and Opposition, 11:47–57

1. The meeting of the Sanhedrin to discuss Jesus[DS1]
2. The causes of unbelief & opposition
   a. The fear of losing their recognition, esteem, & following
   b. The fear of losing their position, influence, & authority
   c. The fear of losing their nation
3. The outcome of unbelief & opposition
   a. The suggestion: By the chief religious leader himself, the High Priest[DS2]
   b. The conclusion: To sacrifice Jesus for the people

   c. The mysterious reason for the conclusion
      1) He was predicting that Jesus was to die for the Jews
      2) He was predicting that Jesus was to die for the world

   d. The decision was made: Do away with Jesus—kill Him
4. The response of Jesus to unbelief & opposition
   a. He withdrew from those who rejected Him
   b. He concentrated on grounding His disciples in the faith
5. The providence of God in moving events despite unbelief & opposition
   a. God controlled the time: The Passover

   b. God stirred the people's interest: Caused them to seek for Jesus

   c. God controlled everyone's devilish plots: Kept the people from helping & contributing to the evil

⁴⁷ So the chief priests and the Pharisees gathered the council and said, "What are we to do? For this man performs many signs."
⁴⁸ If we let him go on like this, everyone will believe in him, and the Romans will come and take away both our place and our nation."
⁴⁹ But one of them, Caiaphas, who was high priest that year, said to them, "You know nothing at all.
⁵⁰ Nor do you understand that it is better for you that one man should die for the people, not that the whole nation should perish."
⁵¹ He did not say this of his own accord, but being high priest that year he prophesied that Jesus would die for the nation,
⁵² and not for the nation only, but also to gather into one the children of God who are scattered abroad.
⁵³ So from that day on they made plans to put him to death.
⁵⁴ Jesus therefore no longer walked openly among the Jews, but went from there to the region near the wilderness, to a town called Ephraim, and there he stayed with the disciples.
⁵⁵ Now the Passover of the Jews was at hand, and many went up from the country to Jerusalem before the Passover to purify themselves.
⁵⁶ They were looking for Jesus and saying to one another as they stood in the temple, "What do you think? That he will not come to the feast at all?"
⁵⁷ Now the chief priests and the Pharisees had given orders that if anyone knew where he was, he should let them know, so that they might arrest him.

# Division XI

*The Revelation of Jesus, the Resurrection and the Life, 11:1–12:11*

E. Jesus and the Religious Leaders: Unbelief and Opposition, 11:47–57

## 11:47–57
## Introduction

How is it possible that so many people—most of the world—reject Jesus in spite of all the evidence that He is God's Son and the Savior of mankind? Yet, most of those who actually saw Jesus—those who heard Him teach with their ears and who saw Him perform miracles with their eyes—refused to believe in Him.

This passage gives an excellent lesson on unbelief and opposition to Jesus Christ, a lesson that needs to be studied by every individual. This is, *Jesus and the Religious Leaders: Unbelief and Opposition*, 11:47–57.

1. The meeting of the Sanhedrin to discuss Jesus (v.47).
2. The causes of unbelief and opposition (vv.47–48).
3. The conclusion of unbelief and opposition (vv.49–53).
4. The response of Jesus to unbelief and opposition (v.54).
5. The providence of God in moving events despite unbelief and opposition (vv.55–57).

## 1 The meeting of the Sanhedrin to discuss Jesus.

11:47

⁴⁷ So the chief priests and the Pharisees gathered the council and said, "What are we to do? For this man performs many signs."

The Sanhedrin met to discuss Jesus and to decide what to do about Him. This was an official meeting of the nation's leaders, including religious leaders (see DEEPER STUDY # 1). These were the very ones who should have been leading the people to God and giving moral and spiritual direction to the nation. Yet, here they were determining what to do about Jesus. The scene was pathetic and ironic.

Jesus, the Son of God, was standing right before them, having come to reveal God to all people everywhere. His *many signs* (miracles) proved that He was truly the Son of God.

The Jewish leaders were the very ones who should have been rejoicing and receiving Him. They recognized and acknowledged His many miracles and His great teaching—so great that all the people were about to follow Him (v.48). Yet, they were the ones taking the lead in rejecting and opposing Him.

> **THOUGHT 1.** The scene is repeated every time a person deliberately rejects and opposes Christ. A person who hears and sees the works of Christ should . . .
> - rejoice and receive Him
> - recognize and acknowledge His work
> - not reject and oppose Him and His salvation

### DEEPER STUDY # 1

(11:47) **Sanhedrin:** the ruling body, both the governing council and supreme court of the Jews. It had seventy-one members and was presided over by the High Priest. However, it took a quorum of only twenty-three members to pass the laws of the nation. Its membership was made up of Pharisees, Sadducees, Scribes or lawyers, and elders who were lay leaders from among the people. The legal power of the Sanhedrin to pass the death sentence was restricted about twenty years before the trial of Jesus. However, they did retain the right of excommunication (see Jn.9:22). To secure Jesus' death, they were forced by law to appeal to the Romans for the death sentence.

## 11:47-48

⁴⁷ So the chief priests and the Pharisees gathered the council and said, "What are we to do? For this man performs many signs. ⁴⁸ If we let him go on like this, everyone will believe in him, and the Romans will come and take away both our place and our nation."

## 2 The causes of unbelief and opposition.

The basic reason for unbelief and opposition is *selfish fear*. Self-centered fear, the fear of losing something, causes people to reject and oppose others. This type of fear caused the leaders to fear Jesus.

a. The fear of losing their recognition, esteem, and following (v.48a).

The Jewish leaders feared losing their esteem, recognition, and following. If *everyone* believed in Jesus, the leaders would have lost the same as any person who loses their circle of attention (friends, fellow-workers, neighbors, whomever). They would have lost:

- acceptance
- recognition
- loyalty
- following
- prestige
- esteem
- image
- friends

b. The fear of losing their position, influence, and authority (v.48b).

If the people made Jesus their leader and followed Him, the Roman authorities would remove the Jewish authorities from power for being unable to control the people. Consequently, the Jewish leaders would lose their *place,* position, influence, and authority. If they lost their place, they would have again lost their . . .

- jobs
- professions
- livelihood
- security
- comfort
- authority
- power
- wealth

c. The fear of losing their nation (v.48c).

The Jewish leaders were also afraid of losing their *nation*. If the Roman government ousted them, the identity of the Jewish nation might be lost, just as it had been during previous captivities (see DEEPER STUDY # 1—Mt.12:10 for discussion).

**THOUGHT 1.** It is selfishness that causes people to cling both to themselves and to their possessions. People want . . .

- to control all they are and have
- to do their own thing as they will and desire
- to have no interference in their life and desires, or as little as possible

"But the cares of the world and the deceitfulness of riches and the desires for other things enter in and choke the word, and it proves unfruitful." (Mk.4:19)

And he said to them, "Take care, and be on your guard against all covetousness, for one's life does not consist in the abundance of his possessions." (Lu.12:15)

But those who desire to be rich fall into temptation, into a snare, into many senseless and harmful desires that plunge people into ruin and destruction. For the love of money is a root of all kinds of evils. It is through this craving that some have wandered away from the faith and pierced themselves with many pangs. (1 Ti.6:9-10)

But understand this, that in the last days there will come times of difficulty. For people will be lovers of self, lovers of money, proud, arrogant, abusive, disobedient to their parents, ungrateful, unholy. (2 Ti.3:1-2)

"For from the least to the greatest of them, everyone is greedy for unjust gain; and from prophet to priest, everyone deals falsely." (Je.6:13)

Israel is a luxuriant vine that yields its fruit. The more his fruit increased, the more altars he built; as his country improved, he improved his pillars. (Ho.10:1)

"'And when you eat and when you drink, do you not eat for yourselves and drink for yourselves?'" (Zec.7:6)

Many people reject and oppose Jesus for demanding that we change by denying ourselves and giving all we are and have to meet the desperate needs of a lost and starving world. Most are unwilling to deny themselves, unwilling to live a life that is totally sacrificial (see DEEPER STUDY # 1—Lu.9:23; see notes—Mt.19:21-23 for more discussion, in particular dealing with possessions).

And he said to all, "If anyone would come after me, let him deny himself and take up his cross daily and follow me. For whoever would save his life will lose it, but whoever loses his life for my sake will save it. For what does it profit a man if he gains the whole world and loses or forfeits himself?" (Lu.9:23-25)

"Sell your possessions, and give to the needy. Provide yourselves with moneybags that do not grow old, with a treasure in the heavens that does not fail, where no thief approaches and no moth destroys. For where your treasure is, there will your heart be also." (Lu.12:33-34)

## 3 The outcome of unbelief and opposition.

Caiaphas, the High Priest, came to a conclusion. His conclusion—to sacrifice Jesus—was the instinctive outcome of unbelief and opposition.

**a. The suggestion: By the chief religious leader himself, the High Priest (v.49).**

The decision to oppose Jesus was made by the High Priest himself, Caiaphas, the highest religious leader in the nation. The very person who should have been leading others to Jesus was suggesting that everyone reject and oppose Him (see DEEPER STUDY # 2).

**THOUGHT 1.** How tragic it is . . .
- that sometimes religious positions become political
- that people reject Christ for the things of this world
- that people exchange eternity for a few short years

But false prophets also arose among the people, just as there will be false teachers among you, who will secretly bring in destructive heresies, even denying the Master who bought them, bringing upon themselves swift destruction. (2 Pe.2:1)

For many deceivers have gone out into the world, those who do not confess the coming of Jesus Christ in the flesh. Such a one is the deceiver and the antichrist. (2 Jn.7)

His watchmen are blind; they are all without knowledge; they are all silent dogs; they cannot bark, dreaming, lying down, loving to slumber. The dogs have a mighty appetite; they never have enough. But they are shepherds who have no understanding; they have all turned to their own way, each to his own gain, one and all. (Is.56:10-11)

"Son of man, prophesy against the shepherds of Israel; prophesy, and say to them, even to the shepherds, Thus says the Lord GOD: Ah, shepherds of Israel who have been feeding yourselves! Should not shepherds feed the sheep? You eat the fat, you clothe yourselves with the wool, you slaughter the fat ones, but you do not feed the sheep." (Eze.34:2-3)

**b. The conclusion: To sacrifice Jesus for the people (v.50).**

The High Priest reached a startling conclusion: Jesus should be sacrificed for the good of the people. The people were following Jesus in such numbers that the leaders feared the Romans might conclude that Jesus was inciting the people to riot. The Romans would, therefore, move

---

⁴⁹ But one of them, Caiaphas, who was high priest that year, said to them, "You know nothing at all.

⁵⁰ Nor do you understand that it is better for you that one man should die for the people, not that the whole nation should perish."

⁵¹ He did not say this of his own accord, but being high priest that year he prophesied that Jesus would die for the nation,

⁵² and not for the nation only, but also to gather into one the children of God who are scattered abroad.

⁵³ So from that day on they made plans to put him to death.

in and disperse the people, taking away what little liberty they had as a conquered nation. Moreover, the Romans might blame them, the present leadership, and remove them from power. Therefore, the High Priest reasoned that it was better for Jesus to die than for the people to perish. Jesus should be sacrificed and killed in order to save the people.

c. **The mysterious reason for the conclusion (vv.51–53).**

The mystery of the High Priest's conclusion is astounding. What is so remarkable is that he was being used as a spokesman by God: he did not say this on his own, of his own authority, initiative, or accord. God was using him to prophesy the death of Jesus Christ (v.51). Caiaphas proclaimed that Jesus should die *for* the people and be sacrificed in order to save the people. Through him, God revealed two significant truths about the death of Christ:

➢ Jesus would die as a *substitute* for the people. The idea of *substitution* is seen in the suggestion that Jesus would die *for* the nation (v.51).

> "I am the good shepherd. The good shepherd lays down his life for the sheep." (Jn.10:11)
>
> "Greater love has no one than this, that someone lay down his life for his friends." (Jn.15:13)
>
> For while we were still weak, at the right time Christ died for the ungodly. (Ro.5:6)
>
> For I delivered to you as of first importance what I also received: that Christ died for our sins in accordance with the Scriptures. (1 Co.15:3)
>
> Who gave himself for our sins to deliver us from the present evil age, according to the will of our God and Father. (Ga.1:4)
>
> Who gave himself for us to redeem us from all lawlessness and to purify for himself a people for his own possession who are zealous for good works. (Tit.2:14)

➢ Jesus would die to save both Jews and Gentiles, all the children of God who were scattered abroad (v.52; see Ac.2:5; 10:2; 17:4).

> In him [Christ] we have redemption through his blood, the forgiveness of our trespasses, according to the riches of his grace. . . . As a plan for the fullness of time, to unite all things in him, things in heaven and things on earth. (Ep.1:7, 10)
>
> But now in Christ Jesus you who once were far off have been brought near by the blood of Christ. For he himself is our peace, who has made us both one [Jew and Gentile] and has broken down in his flesh the dividing wall of hostility (Ep.2:13-14)

d. **The decision was made: Do away with Jesus—kill Him (v.53).**

The leaders of Israel reached a decision to kill Jesus; effectively and officially rejecting Jesus as Lord and Messiah. They wanted nothing to do with Him. Note the words "from that day on." The idea is that from that very moment on, they were set on doing away with Him.

**THOUGHT 1.** How tragic the decision . . .
- to reject Christ
- to have nothing to do with Him
- to push Him off to the side, out of the way, as unimportant
- to do away with Him
- to oppose Him

> He came to his own, and his own people did not receive him. (Jn.1:11)
>
> Whoever believes in the Son has eternal life; whoever does not obey the Son shall not see life, but the wrath of God remains on him. (Jn.3:36)
>
> "I told you that you would die in your sins, for unless you believe that I am he you will die in your sins." (Jn.8:24)
>
> "The one who rejects me and does not receive my words has a judge; the word that I have spoken will judge him on the last day." (Jn.12:48)

## Deeper Study # 2

(11:49) **High Priest—Caiaphas**: the office of High Priest began with Aaron and his sons (Ex.28:1). The office was hereditary and was for life; however, when the Romans conquered Palestine, they made the office political. They chose their own man, a man who would cooperate with the Roman government. Finding such a man was often difficult. For example, between 37 BC and AD 67 there were at least twenty-eight High Priests. These men were greatly respected and highly honored throughout life. Even when they were removed from power by the Romans, they were still consulted by other Jewish leaders. The ex-High Priest, Annas, is a prime example. He still wielded unusual power (see Jn.18:13; Ac.4:6). He and the other men who had served as High Priests or else held the top positions of leadership were also called "chief priests."

The term of office for a High Priest was determined solely by the Romans. The Romans let a High Priest reign as long as he pleased them. The reign of each of the twenty-eight priests averaged only about three years, except for Caiaphas. Caiaphas was High Priest for eighteen years (AD 18 to AD 36). Apparently, he was a master of intrigue and compromise. This throws great light on his fearing an uproar (Mt.26:5) and wishing to wait until the feast was over to arrest Jesus. There was the danger that the people might rally to the support of Jesus if they saw Him arrested. So many believed Him to be a great prophet that a serious uprising was a real possibility. Caiaphas knew the Romans would hold him responsible and remove him from office. If they did, He would lose everything he had. His shrewdness is seen in the strategy he put into motion. They were to arrest Jesus quietly, after the masses had left the feast.

## 4 The response of Jesus to unbelief and opposition.

Jesus was aware of the Jewish leaders' plan to execute Him. He was also aware of God's plan and timing for His death. Although His *hour* was drawing near, it had not yet come (Jn.7:30; 8:20).

⁵⁴ Jesus therefore no longer walked openly among the Jews, but went from there to the region near the wilderness, to a town called Ephraim, and there he stayed with the disciples.

### a. He withdrew from those who rejected Him (v.54a).

Jesus withdrew from those who rejected Him. He . . .

- went away
- pleaded no more with them
- walked no more among them
- gave them up to their own desires (see note—Ro.1:24-32)

The Lord's Spirit does not always strive with people (see note—Jn.7:33-34). Jesus even told His disciples to turn their backs on rejecters (see Mt.10:14; Mk.6:11; Lu.9:5).

> Or do you presume on the riches of his kindness and forbearance and patience, not knowing that God's kindness is meant to lead you to repentance? But because of your hard and impenitent heart you are storing up wrath for yourself on the day of wrath when God's righteous judgment will be revealed. (Ro.2:4-5)
>
> Then the LORD said, "My Spirit shall not abide in man forever, for he is flesh: his days shall be 120 years." (Ge.6:3)
>
> Blessed is the one who fears the LORD always, but whoever hardens his heart will fall into calamity. (Pr.28:14)
>
> He who is often reproved, yet stiffens his neck, will suddenly be broken beyond healing. (Pr.29:1)

### b. He concentrated on grounding His disciples in the faith (v.54b).

Upon leaving Bethany, Jesus retreated to Ephraim, a village about fifteen miles north of Jerusalem at the edge of the wilderness. There, Jesus concentrated on grounding His disciples in the faith, and He strengthened His relationship with them.

"For where two or three are gathered in my name, there am I among them." (Mt.18:20)

While they were talking and discussing together, Jesus himself drew near and went with them. (Lu.24:15)

Now when they saw the boldness of Peter and John, and perceived that they were uneducated, common men, they were astonished. And they recognized that they had been with Jesus. (Ac.4:13)

That which we have seen and heard we proclaim also to you, so that you too may have fellowship with us; and indeed our fellowship is with the Father and with his Son Jesus Christ. (1 Jn.1:3)

## 11:55-57

⁵⁵ Now the Passover of the Jews was at hand, and many went up from the country to Jerusalem before the Passover to purify themselves.

⁵⁶ They were looking for Jesus and saying to one another as they stood in the temple, "What do you think? That he will not come to the feast at all?"

⁵⁷ Now the chief priests and the Pharisees had given orders that if anyone knew where he was, he should let them know, so that they might arrest him.

## 5 The providence of God in moving events despite unbelief and opposition.

Scripture says that the Lamb of God was appointed to be slain from the foundation or creation of the world (Re.13:8). What a soul-gripping thought, a thought that conveys the immeasurable love of God for the human race! The plan of salvation was conceived in the heart of God before He even created man. He created us knowing that our sin would cost the life of His Son.

The fullness of time was quickly approaching that the dear Savior would lay down His life to redeem us (Ga.4:4-5). God was working providentially according to *His* schedule and *His* plan. He was moving events despite unbelief and opposition.

a. **God controlled the time: The Passover (v.55).**

God controlled the timing of all these events. The fact that it was the Passover season is significant. The Feast symbolized the removal of sins. How ironic it is that, while the Jewish people were celebrating the Passover Feast, the leaders were seeking to commit the most heinous crime: the murder of the very Son of God Himself (see Deeper Study # 1—Lu.22:7).

b. **God stirred the people's interest. Caused them to seek for Jesus (v.56).**

Pilgrims flooded into Jerusalem by the hundreds of thousands during the Passover season. The picture is that of people buzzing about wondering and asking if Jesus would come to the Feast. Note that the people were actually looking for Jesus (v.56). God took even the rejection of evil men and worked it out to cause others to seek His Son.

**Thought 1.** God takes rejection and opposition and uses it to stir interest in His Son. Throughout history some of the greatest movements and revivals of Christianity have been the result of persecution and attempts to stamp out the name of Christ. One person's rejection is often used by God to stir salvation in others.

> "And you will be hated by all for my name's sake. But the one who endures to the end will be saved." (Mt.10:22)
>
> And we know that for those who love God all things work together for good, for those who are called according to his purpose. (Ro.8:28)
>
> For we who live are always being given over to death for Jesus' sake, so that the life of Jesus also may be manifested in our mortal flesh. (2 Co.4:11)
>
> I want you to know, brothers, that what has happened to me has really served to advance the gospel, so that it has become known throughout the whole imperial guard and to all the rest that my imprisonment is for Christ. And most of the brothers, having become confident in the Lord by my imprisonment, are much more bold to speak the word without fear. (Ph.1:12-14)
>
> For it has been granted to you that for the sake of Christ you should not only believe in him but also suffer for his sake. (Ph.1:29)
>
> As an example of suffering and patience, brothers, take the prophets who spoke in the name of the Lord. (Js.5:10)

c. **God controlled everyone's devilish plots: Kept the people from helping and contributing to the evil (v.57).**

The Jewish authorities had publicly ordered anyone who saw Jesus to report the sighting so they could arrest Him. But God controlled their devilish plots. He kept the people from cooperating with the leaders and betraying His Son.

Nobody can move against the name of Christ or against the followers of Christ until God is ready. Although the world is corrupt and evil, God controls the times of His Son and His Son's followers. Not a hair of their heads can be touched until God is ready to use the trial and persecution for His good purpose.

> "And do not fear those who kill the body but cannot kill the soul. Rather fear him who can destroy both soul and body in hell. Are not two sparrows sold for a penny? And not one of them will fall to the ground apart from your Father. But even the hairs of your head are all numbered. Fear not, therefore; you are of more value than many sparrows. So everyone who acknowledges me before men, I also will acknowledge before my Father who is in heaven, but whoever denies me before men, I also will deny before my Father who is in heaven." (Mt.10:28-33)

# Chapter 12

## F. Jesus and Reactions to His Revelation: He is the Resurrection and Life, 12:1–11

*Mt.26:6-13; Mk.14:3-9*

1. **The setting: Jesus dined in a home in Bethany**
   a. Six days before the Passover
   b. Martha served
   c. Lazarus was present

2. **The supreme believer**
   a. A repentant love
   b. A sacrificial & costly love
   c. A believing love: Jesus is the Christ, the Anointed One of God

3. **The hypocritical, unbelieving disciple**
   a. He followed Jesus, but he criticized believers
   b. He expressed concern for the ministry, but he had an ulterior motive
   c. He worked for Jesus, but he did not love Jesus

4. **The half-sincere seekers**
   a. They came to see Jesus
   b. They came to see the spectacular
   c. They came for socializing

5. **The fearful, self-seeking religious leaders**
   a. They plotted to destroy Lazarus
   b. They feared personal loss: Because so many people were deserting them & following Jesus

Six days before the Passover, Jesus therefore came to Bethany, where Lazarus was, whom Jesus had raised from the dead. ² So they gave a dinner for him there. Martha served, and Lazarus was one of those reclining with him at table. ³ Mary therefore took a pound of expensive ointment made from pure nard, and anointed the feet of Jesus and wiped his feet with her hair. The house was filled with the fragrance of the perfume. ⁴ But Judas Iscariot, one of his disciples (he who was about to betray him), said, ⁵ "Why was this ointment not sold for three hundred denarii and given to the poor?" ⁶ He said this, not because he cared about the poor, but because he was a thief, and having charge of the moneybag he used to help himself to what was put into it. ⁷ Jesus said, "Leave her alone, so that she may keep it for the day of my burial. ⁸ For the poor you always have with you, but you do not always have me."

⁹ When the large crowd of the Jews learned that Jesus was there, they came, not only on account of him but also to see Lazarus, whom he had raised from the dead. ¹⁰ So the chief priests made plans to put Lazarus to death as well,

¹¹ because on account of him many of the Jews were going away and believing in Jesus.

# Division XI

*The Revelation of Jesus, the Resurrection and the Life, 11:1-12:11*

F. Jesus and Reactions to His Revelation: He Is the Resurrection and Life, 12:1-11

*Mt.26:6-13; Mk.14:3-9*

## 12:1-11
## Introduction

Of all Jesus' miracles, the raising of Lazarus from the dead drew the most attention. With our modern means of communication, imagine the coverage such an occurrence would attract today. When performing this miracle, Jesus Christ revealed Himself to be the Resurrection and the Life. The miracle proved His claim. In this passage, John gives four reactions to that revelation. This is, *Jesus and Reactions to His Revelation: He Is the Resurrection and Life,* 12:1-11.

1. The setting: Jesus dined in a home in Bethany (vv.1-2).
2. The supreme believer (v.3).
3. The hypocritical, unbelieving disciple (vv.4-8).
4. The half-sincere seekers (v.9).
5. The fearful, self-seeking religious leaders (vv.10-11).

## 1 The setting: Jesus dined in a home in Bethany.

The setting for this story is a home in Bethany, where a special dinner in honor of Jesus was served. Both Matthew and Mark also record the beautiful act that was performed to honor Jesus, the anointing of His feet by Mary.

> Six days before the Passover, Jesus therefore came to Bethany, where Lazarus was, whom Jesus had raised from the dead.
> ² So they gave a dinner for him there. Martha served, and Lazarus was one of those reclining with him at table.

### a. Six days before the Passover (v.1).

John notes that Jesus came back to Bethany six days before the Passover. Matthew's placement of this event in his Gospel differs from John's. Matthew arranged his account of Christ's life by subjects, so he placed this event in the midst of discussing Jesus' death. Jesus knew the Passover was fast-approaching. He was only six days away from becoming the Passover Lamb who would take away the sins of the world.

### b. Martha served (v.2a).

Matthew and Mark say that Jesus was in the house of Simon the Leper, and John mentions that Martha served (Mt.26:6; Mk.14:3). While Scripture does not specify what it was, there must have been some kind of close relationship between Martha and Simon the Leper for Martha to have served in his home (see DEEPER STUDY # 1—Mt.26:6 for more discussion). Most likely, Jesus had healed Simon of his leprosy, as he was not separated from society. It may be that Simon and the family of Lazarus joined together to host this dinner for Jesus to show their mutual gratitude for what He had done for them.

### c. Lazarus was present (v.2b).

Lazarus was there, and his presence drew a crowd of curious gawkers who wanted to see the man who had been raised from the dead (v.9). John notes that he sat at the table with Jesus. The fellowship between Jesus and the man whom He had given life points to the fellowship we will share with Jesus throughout eternity.

## 2 The supreme believer.

The first reaction in this story is the reaction of the supreme believer. The supreme believer is a person like Mary who *loves* the Lord with their whole being, sacrificing all that they are and have. Mary gave of herself out of a heart of pure love for the Lord.

³ Mary therefore took a pound of expensive ointment made from pure nard, and anointed the feet of Jesus and wiped his feet with her hair. The house was filled with the fragrance of the perfume.

### a. A repentant love.

The supreme believer expresses a repentant love. Mary had criticized and accused Jesus of neglecting her family when He had not come sooner to the aid of her brother, Lazarus (see Jn.11:32). Her beautiful act described here reveals that she had repented of her sin. Unquestionably, Mary's generous gift was rooted in her gratitude, but it may also have been given out of contrition (see outline notes 2, 4—Jn.21:15-17; Deeper Study # 1—Ac.17:29-30).

"Blessed are those who mourn, for they shall be comforted." (Mt.5:4)

"Repent, therefore, of this wickedness of yours, and pray to the Lord that, if possible, the intent of your heart may be forgiven you." (Ac.8:22)

"If my people who are called by my name humble themselves, and pray and seek my face and turn from their wicked ways, then I will hear from heaven and will forgive their sin and heal their land." (2 Chr.7:14)

"Let the wicked forsake his way, and the unrighteous man his thoughts; let him return to the Lord, that he may have compassion on him, and to our God, for he will abundantly pardon." (Is.55:7)

"Yet even now," declares the Lord, "return to me with all your heart, with fasting, with weeping, and with mourning." (Joel 2:12)

### b. A sacrificial and costly love.

The supreme believer expresses a sacrificial and costly love. The *ointment* (Gk., murou) Mary poured out on Jesus was a perfume or oil, and it was very expensive. Greedy Judas remarked that it could be sold for three hundred denarii, which equaled a year's wage (one denarii was the average pay for one day's labor). Just imagine the scene: a bottle of perfume worth a whole year's wage being poured on the feet of Jesus! Think of the costly sacrifice being made. Perfume was the most precious thing to Eastern women. Mary was taking her most precious possession and giving it to her Lord.

### c. A believing love: Jesus is the Christ, the Anointed One of God.

The supreme believer expresses a believing love. Mary's anointing was an act of love and faith in the Lord Jesus. Very simply stated, Mary anointed Jesus to show how deeply she loved Him and believed Him to be the true Messiah, the anointed One of God (see notes—Mt.26:6-13; see Mt.1:18). He was her Savior, Lord, and King. He had done so much for her and her family that she wanted Him to know how much she appreciated and loved Him.

Something else needs to be noted here. Mary sensed something within Jesus: a foreboding, a preoccupation of mind, a heaviness of heart, a weight of tremendous pressure. Her heart reached out to Him and wanted to encourage and help Him. Being a young woman in the presence of so many men, she was usually not allowed to vocally express herself. Such a privilege was not allowed women of that day, so she did all that she could. She acted by arising and going after the most precious gift she could think of—a very costly bottle of perfume. She gave it to Jesus in such a way that He would know that at least one person truly loved Him and believed Him to be the Messiah. Her hope was that such worship and love would boost His spirit (see note—Mt.26:6-13 for a descriptive picture of what Mary sensed).

**THOUGHT 1.** What do we do to show our love and faith to Christ? Imagine how difficult it was for Mary to do what she did in the presence of so many men. She set aside pride and embarrassment in order to demonstrate her love and faith in Jesus. How far are we willing to go in order to show our love and faith?

**THOUGHT 2.** Notice how Mary demonstrated her love and faith.

(1) Mary gave the most precious possession she had to the Lord.

> "But lay up for yourselves treasures in heaven, where neither moth nor rust destroys and where thieves do not break in and steal." (Mt.6:20)
>
> "Sell your possessions, and give to the needy. Provide yourselves with moneybags that do not grow old, with a treasure in the heavens that does not fail, where no thief approaches and no moth destroys." (Lu.12:33)
>
> Indeed, I count everything as loss because of the surpassing worth of knowing Christ Jesus my Lord. For his sake I have suffered the loss of all things and count them as rubbish, in order that I may gain Christ (Ph.3:8)

(2) Mary publicly demonstrated her love and faith in Christ for all to witness.

> "So everyone who acknowledges me before men, I also will acknowledge before my Father who is in heaven." (Mt.10:32)
>
> "And whoever does not take his cross and follow me is not worthy of me. Whoever finds his life will lose it, and whoever loses his life for my sake will find it." (Mt.10:38-39)
>
> Because I hear of your love and of the faith that you have toward the Lord Jesus and for all the saints. (Phm.5)
>
> Though you have not seen him [Jesus Christ], you love him. Though you do not now see him, you believe in him and rejoice with joy that is inexpressible and filled with glory. (1 Pe.1:8)
>
> "You shall love the LORD your God with all your heart and with all your soul and with all your might." (De.6:5)
>
> Love the LORD, all you his saints! The LORD preserves the faithful but abundantly repays the one who acts in pride. (Ps.31:23)

## 3 The hypocritical, unbelieving disciple.

12:4-8

The second reaction in the story is the reaction of the hypocritical, unbelieving disciple—Judas. A study of Judas' character in these verses reveals what it is that often causes a disciple to become hypocritical and unbelieving.

⁴ But Judas Iscariot, one of his disciples (he who was about to betray him), said,
⁵ "Why was this ointment not sold for three hundred denarii and given to the poor?"
⁶ He said this, not because he cared about the poor, but because he was a thief, and having charge of the moneybag he used to help himself to what was put into it.
⁷ Jesus said, "Leave her alone, so that she may keep it for the day of my burial.
⁸ For the poor you always have with you, but you do not always have me."

### a. He followed Jesus, but he criticized believers (v.4).

Judas followed Jesus, but he criticized other believers. He was a professing believer, but when he disagreed with others, he criticized them. His criticism of Mary shows that he criticized even . . .

- those who had great devotion and love for the Lord
- those who repented to the point of making great sacrificial gifts

Mark points out that Judas was especially harsh in his criticism. He says that Judas was indignant, growling, rebuking, and scolding (see note—Mk.14:4-5).

**THOUGHT 1.** Criticism is a sign of hypocrisy, for all stand in need of repentance and devotion, and all could give more to the Lord. When we come so short ourselves, how can we possibly criticize what we consider to be the mistakes of others?

> "Why do you see the speck that is in your brother's eye, but do not notice the log that is in your own eye?" (Mt.7:3; see vv.1-5)
>
> Who are you to pass judgment on the servant of another? It is before his own master that he stands or falls. And he will be upheld, for the Lord is able to make him stand. (Ro.14:4)
>
> Therefore let us not pass judgment on one another any longer, but rather decide never to put a stumbling block or hindrance in the way of a brother. (Ro.14:13)

Therefore do not pronounce judgment before the time, before the Lord comes, who will bring to light the things now hidden in darkness and will disclose the purposes of the heart. Then each one will receive his commendation from God. (1 Co.4:5)

### b. He expressed concern for the ministry, but he had an ulterior motive (vv.5–6).

Judas expressed concern for the ministry and other's needs, but he had an ulterior motive. Again, imagine the scene. A bottle of perfume worth a whole year's wage was being poured over the feet of Jesus. Common sense would seem to say, "Sell it. Use the money for the poor, the hungry and the homeless." This is exactly what Judas did say. He questioned the act, what he considered a waste. After all, if Mary wished to anoint Jesus, she could have used a less expensive perfume.

While Judas' intentions appear to be noble, his motive was impure. Judas was the treasurer of the small band of Jesus' disciples (v.6). However, he was a thief; he had been swindling some of the money. A gift of three hundred denarii would have allowed him the chance to steal quite a sum without being noticed. Deep within he was angry at the lost chance to enrich himself; he was angry at Mary, but he was angrier at Jesus for allowing what he deemed to be wastefulness.

**THOUGHT 1.** How many express concern for the ministry or others but do so in order to gain from it? Their concern is shown by joining a church and making some contribution, or by showing interest in some venture or need. However, their motive is . . .

- to be socially acceptable
- to be recognized and honored
- to please some family member
- to gain some credit with God
- to get a tax write-off from the government

> "Woe to you, scribes and Pharisees, hypocrites! For you clean the outside of the cup and the plate, but inside they are full of greed and self-indulgence." (Mt.23:25)
>
> "So you also outwardly appear righteous to others, but within you are full of hypocrisy and lawlessness." (Mt.23:28)
>
> For the love of money is a root of all kinds of evils. It is through this craving that some have wandered away from the faith and pierced themselves with many pangs. (1 Ti.6:10)
>
> Your gold and silver have corroded, and their corrosion will be evidence against you and will eat your flesh like fire. You have laid up treasure in the last days. (Js.5:3)
>
> The getting of treasures by a lying tongue is a fleeting vapor and a snare of death. (Pr.21:6)
>
> He who loves money will not be satisfied with money, nor he who loves wealth with his income; this also is vanity. (Ec.5:10)

### c. He worked for Jesus, but he did not love Jesus (vv.6–8).

Judas worked for Jesus, but he did not love Jesus. Jesus spoke strongly to Judas, ordering him to leave Mary alone (v.7a). The reason for this sharp rebuke was that Judas did not understand what Mary had done, and the reason he did not understand was because he did not love Jesus. Just because someone works for Jesus does not mean that he or she loves Jesus.

Jesus said that Mary's anointing pointed toward His burial, that is, His death (v.7b). Some commentators think that Mary knew what she was doing, that she understood what Jesus had been saying when He predicted His death. They feel that Mary grasped the fact when others did not. But this is unlikely. The atmosphere surrounding the whole scene was that the kingdom of God was about to be set up, and Israel was about to be freed from Roman domination and set up as the center of God's rule on earth. Whether Mary knew what she was doing or not, Jesus took her act and applied it to His death. He said that her love and faith, the anointing of His body, pointed toward His death. In simple terms, Mary's love and faith and her gift and anointing *were a witness of anticipation*. She was witnessing to the Lord's death by looking ahead to it.

Today our love and faith along with our gift and anointing are *a witness of fact*. As believers, we are to witness to the Lord's death by looking back to it. It is a fact: He did die for the sins of the world.

> **And he said to them, "Go into all the world and proclaim the gospel to the whole creation." (Mk.16:15)**
>
> **For I delivered to you as of first importance what I also received: that Christ died for our sins in accordance with the Scriptures, that he was buried, that he was raised on the third day in accordance with the Scriptures. (1 Co.15:3-4)**
>
> **My little children, I am writing these things to you so that you may not sin. But if anyone does sin, we have an advocate with the Father, Jesus Christ the righteous. He is the propitiation for our sins, and not for ours only but also for the sins of the whole world. (1 Jn.2:1-2)**

Judas lost the opportune time; Mary grasped it. Mary *loved* Jesus, while Judas did not. Jesus made a significant point that is often missed: opportunities come and go, and once they are gone, they are gone forever (v.8). Mary demonstrated the difference. The poor would always be present for believers to help, but the privilege of ministering to Jesus would not always be available. Therefore, if Jesus' disciples were to minister to Him, they had to grasp the opportunity while He was with them.

**THOUGHT 1.** What a lesson for believers! The presence of Jesus—a sense of His presence and of His Word—is not always pounding away at our minds and hearts. Like Mary, we must grasp the opportunity to show our love and sacrifice for Christ when it presents itself. The opportunity will soon pass. In fact, life, which is an opportunity and a privilege within itself, will pass and pass soon. The servant of the Lord must love and act while it is still day. The night will come when no person can work.

> **Besides this you know the time, that the hour has come for you to wake from sleep. For salvation is nearer to us now than when we first believed. The night is far gone; the day is at hand. So then let us cast off the works of darkness and put on the armor of light. (Ro.13:11-12)**
>
> **Making the best use of the time, because the days are evil. (Ep.5:16)**
>
> **Walk in wisdom toward outsiders, making the best use of the time. (Col.4:5)**

## 4 The half-sincere seekers.

The third reaction is the reaction of the half-sincere seekers. A person who is only half-sincere has three clear traits. These are seen in the crowd thronging the dinner which Jesus attended.

> ⁹ When the large crowd of the Jews learned that Jesus was there, they came, not only on account of him but also to see Lazarus, whom he had raised from the dead.

a. **They came to see Jesus (v.9a).**

The crowd came to see Jesus. Jesus was the central figure; He had raised a man from the dead. He was the Person being proclaimed by some to be the Messiah and being talked about so much by all. Everyone was wondering and questioning and had some desire to see Him and to find out for themselves. At the least, they wanted to find out what was going on and causing so much conversation across the country. The half-sincere person has some interest in Jesus.

b. **They came to see the spectacular (v.9b).**

The crowd came to see the spectacular, that is, to see Lazarus, the man rumored to have been raised from the dead. They were curious to see one who had experienced such a phenomenal event and to see if a resurrected man was any different (see note—Jn.2:23; Lu.4:9-12). The half-sincere person is interested in the spectacular.

c. **They came for socializing (v.9c).**

The large crowd came to a social occasion, a festive atmosphere. Wherever Jesus was, things were happening. It was where everyone was gathering. Think of the teeming thousands flooding into the area for the Passover and the atmosphere that surrounds such a convention-like crowd. There was bound to be a worldly, carnival-like atmosphere despite the religious observances. Half-sincere seekers always add to the carnality of a worldly atmosphere, no matter the focus of an event, because they are there to socialize.

**THOUGHT 1.** How many sitting in the presence of the Lord and His church are only half-sincere? How many come to church just because it is the thing to do, the place to be, the place where everyone else is? How many seek only the spectacular signs?

> Then some of the scribes and Pharisees answered him, saying, "Teacher, we wish to see a sign from you." (Mt.12:38)

> "So you also outwardly appear righteous to others, but within you are full of hypocrisy and lawlessness." (Mt.23:28)

> And he said to them, "Well did Isaiah prophesy of you hypocrites, as it is written, 'This people honors me with their lips, but their heart is far from me.'" (Mk.7:6)

> So they said to him, "Then what sign do you do, that we may see and believe you? What work do you perform?" (Jn.6:30)

> For Jews demand signs and Greeks seek wisdom, but we preach Christ crucified, a stumbling block to Jews and folly to Gentiles. (1 Co.1:22-23)

> They profess to know God, but they deny him by their works. They are detestable, disobedient, unfit for any good work. (Tit.1:16)

## 12:10-11

¹⁰ So the chief priests made plans to put Lazarus to death as well, ¹¹ because on account of him many of the Jews were going away and believing in Jesus.

### 5  The fearful, self-seeking religious leaders.

The fourth reaction is the reaction of the fearful, self-seeking religious leaders (see outline above and notes—Jn.11:47-48; 11:49-53 for discussion of this point). Jesus' raising of Lazarus had increased His popularity, resulting in Him being a greater threat than ever to the Jewish authorities. Now, Lazarus was a threat to them as well.

a. **They plotted to destroy Lazarus (v.10).**
The leaders now sought to destroy Lazarus. They may have thought Lazarus and Jesus were collaborating to deceive the people. Regardless, the miracle was having a tremendous impact. So many people were affected by the miracle that the authorities felt they had to kill Lazarus in order to prove that Jesus could not raise the dead.

> "But now you seek to kill me, a man who has told you the truth that I heard from God. This is not what Abraham did. You are doing the works your father did." They said to him, "We were not born of sexual immorality. We have one Father—even God." . . . [Jesus said] "You are of your father the devil, and your will is to do your father's desires. He was a murderer from the beginning, and does not stand in the truth, because there is no truth in him. When he lies, he speaks out of his own character, for he is a liar and the father of lies. But because I tell the truth, you do not believe me." (Jn.8:40-41, 44-45)

b. **They feared personal loss: Because so many people were deserting them and following Jesus (v.11).**
"Many" of the Jews, those who had formerly opposed Jesus, were now beginning to believe in Jesus. This fact is significant. It shows that the impact on the nation was enormous, affecting even the religious leaders.

> "That whoever believes in him may have eternal life." (Jn.3:15)

> "Truly, truly, I say to you, whoever hears my word and believes him who sent me has eternal life. He does not come into judgment, but has passed from death to life." (Jn.5:24)

> Jesus said to her, "I am the resurrection and the life. Whoever believes in me, though he die, yet shall he live." (Jn.11:25)

> "I have come into the world as light, so that whoever believes in me may not remain in darkness." (Jn.12:46)

# XII. The Revelation of Jesus, the Glorified Son of Man, 12:12-50

## A. Jesus Proclaimed as King: The Triumphal Entry, 12:12-19

*Mt.21:1-11; Mk.11:1-11; Lu.19:28-40*

¹² The next day the large crowd that had come to the feast heard that Jesus was coming to Jerusalem.

¹³ So they took branches of palm trees and went out to meet him, crying out, "Hosanna! Blessed is he who comes in the name of the Lord, even the King of Israel!"

¹⁴ And Jesus found a young donkey and sat on it, just as it is written,

¹⁵ "Fear not, daughter of Zion; behold, your king is coming, sitting on a donkey's colt!"

¹⁶ His disciples did not understand these things at first, but when Jesus was glorified, then they remembered that these things had been written about him and had been done to him.

¹⁷ The crowd that had been with him when he called Lazarus out of the tomb and raised him from the dead continued to bear witness.

¹⁸ The reason why the crowd went to meet him was that they heard he had done this sign.

¹⁹ So the Pharisees said to one another, "You see that you are gaining nothing. Look, the world has gone after him."

1. The setting: Crowds gathered for the Passover
2. The false concept of Christ: Was held by many people
   a. They went out to meet Him
   b. They took palm branches^DS1
   c. They cried Hosanna (save)
   d. They thought He was a political Messiah
3. The true concept of Christ
   a. The symbol of peace: A young donkey
   b. The prophecy: The King comes in peace
4. The disciples' reaction
   a. The bewilderment: They did not grasp the significance
   b. The symbol: They grasped the meaning only after His resurrection
5. The people's reaction
   a. The eyewitnesses to Lazarus' resurrection: They spread the news
   b. The people who heard about the miracle: They sought Jesus, sought for the sensational
6. The religious leaders' reaction: Despair & rage

# Division XII

*The Revelation of Jesus, the Glorified Son of Man, 12:12-50*

A. Jesus Proclaimed as King: The Triumphal Entry, 12:12-19

*Mt.21:1-11; Mk.11:1-11; Lu.19:28-40*

## 12:12-19
## Introduction

So many people—most of the world—have a false concept of Jesus. When Jesus came the first time to Jerusalem, the people did not understand who He truly was. They had a false concept of their King, even though He clearly presented the true concept of His mission and His coming. Their reaction is a picture of how people have seen Jesus down through the centuries. But make no mistake about it: when Jesus comes the second time, all people of the earth will see Him as He truly is (1 Jn.3:2; Re.1:7-8). This is, *Jesus Proclaimed as King: The Triumphal Entry*, 12:12-19.

1. The setting: Crowds gathered for the Passover (v.12).
2. The false concept of Christ: Was held by many people (vv.12-13).
3. The true concept of Christ (vv.14-15).
4. The disciples' reaction (v.16).
5. The people's reaction (vv.17-18).
6. The religious leaders' reaction: Despair and rage (v.19).

## 12:12

¹² The next day the large crowd that had come to the feast heard that Jesus was coming to Jerusalem.

## 1 The setting: Crowds gathered for the Passover.

A large crowd was swarming into Jerusalem for the Passover. Josephus, the notable Jewish historian of that day, estimated that over two million people were involved in the great Passover Feast. It is known that 256,500 lambs were slain at one Passover and that each lamb represented at least ten worshipers. This, of course, puts the number of people at well over two million.[1] The mass of people and the necessary housing and food arrangements to handle such an influx of people can hardly be imagined. An excitable vacation and carnival-like atmosphere was bound to prevail over such a mob of people. Such was the scene as the people gathered for the great Feast.

## 12:12-13

¹² The next day the large crowd that had come to the feast heard that Jesus was coming to Jerusalem.
¹³ So they took branches of palm trees and went out to meet him, crying out, "Hosanna! Blessed is he who comes in the name of the Lord, even the King of Israel!"

## 2 The false concept of Christ: Was held by many people.

The rumored attendance of Christ at the Passover Feast only added to the chaos. The people excitedly prepared to welcome Jesus as their Messiah when He arrived in Jerusalem.

However, the crowd had a false concept of Christ. They did not understand *who* Jesus truly was and *why* He had come. They saw Jesus as an *earthly* Savior, One who had come to bring a perfect earth for the people of God. This false concept sees Jesus . . .

- as the *Conqueror*, the One who is to straighten out the problems of this earth by overcoming all the enemies of mankind including evil people, hunger, disease, and poverty.
- as the *Provider*, the One who is to feed, house, and give health, plenty, and success to all people; the One who is to be sought to bless people in all the good things of life.
- as the *Indulgent, Passive Lord*, the One who accepts people no matter what they do, just as long as they are somewhat religious; the One who allows people to live as they desire, doing their own thing despite the sin and injustices and immorality of their behavior.

The false concept fails to see two truths critical to understanding the Messiahship of Jesus, who Jesus really is. First, it fails to see the demand of Christ, the demand to serve by reaching out to a world that is lost and reeling in needs so desperate that the thoughtful mind staggers at the reality of it. It fails to see the demand of Christ for self-denial, a denial that demands the giving of all one is and has to meet the needs of the world.

Second, the false concept of Christ fails to see the *spiritual* concern of Christ: His concern with bringing peace between humanity and God—with saving people and being mindful that all people need to live *with* God and not separate *from* God; His concern with our understanding that God is holy, righteous, and pure; His concern with our living a life of faith and diligently

---

1 William Barclay. *The Gospel of John*, Vol.2, p.134f.

seeking God; His concern with our living a holy, righteous, and pure life in order to be acceptable to God.

The actions of the crowd in Jerusalem clearly show the false concept of Christ held by so many, both in Jesus' day and down through the centuries.

### a. They went out to meet Him (vv.12–13a).

The people *went out* to welcome Jesus. They were not just sitting and waiting for Him to come; when they *heard* about Him, they actually went out to meet Him. A large crowd was involved in welcoming Jesus in the triumphal scene. Many, many people held the false concept of Jesus as the *earthly* king and savior, as the One who was to be sought in order to secure all the good things of this earth.

### b. They took palm branches (v.13b).

The people took palm branches to wave and lay before Christ (see Deeper Study # 1). The palm branches symbolized their false concept of Jesus.

### c. They cried Hosanna (v.13c).

The people cried "Hosanna," which means *save now*, or *save, we pray*. People desire to be free, but their main concern is to be free on this earth so they can do as they please. They think little if any about being free from the bondages of this sinful world. They love the things of this world and want all of it they can get: houses, lands, clothes, food, sex, and recreation. People think little about being held in bondage by such things; they think little about sin and death. They think little of being set free from the power of this earth and its possessions so they can live eternally. They think little of *spiritual* freedom.

### d. They thought He was a political Messiah (v.13d).

The people received Jesus as the political king and Messiah (see note—Jn.1:23). Their joyful chants were a quotation from a Messianic psalm (Ps.118:25-26). However, they welcomed Jesus as their *political* Savior or Deliverer, not as the One who would save them their sins.

**THOUGHT 1.** The crowd that welcomed Jesus is much like many people today. The false concept of Christ that sees Him as the One who gives us *material blessings* is proclaimed, and people rush "out to Him" (see note—Ep.1:3). What so many people fail to understand is that they must come to Jesus because they love Him, not because they can get something out of Him. They must come because of who He is, not because He blesses them with earthly possessions.

> And with many other words he bore witness and continued to exhort them, saying, "Save yourselves from this crooked generation." (Ac.2:40)
>
> And those who deal with the world as though they had no dealings with it. For the present form of this world is passing away. (1 Co.7:31)
>
> "Therefore go out from their midst, and be separate from them, says the Lord, and touch no unclean thing; then I will welcome you, and I will be a father to you, and you shall be sons and daughters to me, says the Lord Almighty." (2 Co.6:17-18)
>
> But far be it from me to boast except in the cross of our Lord Jesus Christ, by which the world has been crucified to me, and I to the world. (Ga.6:14)
>
> Do not love the world or the things in the world. If anyone loves the world, the love of the Father is not in him. For all that is in the world—the desires of the flesh and the desires of the eyes and pride of life—is not from the Father but is from the world. (1 Jn.2:15-16)

## Deeper Study # 1

**(12:13) Palm Branches**: these were a symbol of victory and triumph. They were waved triumphantly as a conqueror rode victoriously through the city streets. The people were welcoming Jesus as the great Conqueror and mighty Deliverer, the One who would deliver them from Roman rule. But Jesus had come in peace, not as the judge or conqueror of the Romans nor of anyone else—not right then and not right now. Presently He is the Savior of all people; later when He returns, He will come as King.

**12:14-15**

¹⁴ And Jesus found a young donkey and sat on it, just as it is written,
¹⁵ "Fear not, daughter of Zion; behold, your king is coming, sitting on a donkey's colt!"

### 3 The true concept of Christ.

When Jesus entered Jerusalem, He rode in on a young donkey. This act was a clear symbol of the true concept of Christ. The colt symbolized sacredness. This particular colt had never been ridden before, and this fact had a sacred meaning (Mk.11:2). Animals and things used for religious purposes had to be animals and things that had never been used before (Nu.19:2; De.21:3; 1 S.6:7). This detail points to the very sacredness of the event. It pictures for everyone that Jesus was deliberately taking every precaution to proclaim that *He was the sacred hope*, the promised Messiah of the people.

> "For I have come down from heaven, not to do my own will but the will of him who sent me." (Jn.6:38)

> So Jesus said to them, "When you have lifted up the Son of Man, then you will know that I am he, and that I do nothing on my own authority, but speak just as the Father taught me. And he who sent me is with me. He has not left me alone, for I always do the things that are pleasing to him." (Jn.8:28-29)

> Jesus said to her, "I am the resurrection and the life. Whoever believes in me, though he die, yet shall he live, and everyone who lives and believes in me shall never die. Do you believe this?" She said to him, "Yes, Lord; I believe that you are the Christ, the Son of God, who is coming into the world." (Jn.11:25-27)

a. **The symbol of peace: A young donkey (v.14).**

When a king entered a city as a conqueror, he rode a stallion. Jesus, in dramatic contrast, rode a donkey. In ancient days the young donkey was a noble animal. It was used as a service animal to carry people's burdens, but more significantly, it was used by kings and their representatives. When they entered a city in peace, they rode a donkey's colt to symbolize their peaceful intentions (cp. the judges of Israel and the chieftains throughout the land, Judges 5:10; 10:4).

> Therefore, since we have been justified by faith, we have peace with God through our Lord Jesus Christ. (Ro.5:1)

> But now in Christ Jesus you who once were far off have been brought near by the blood of Christ. For he himself is our peace, who has made us both one and has broken down in his flesh the dividing wall of hostility (Ep.2:13-14)

> And through him to reconcile to himself all things, whether on earth or in heaven, making peace by the blood of his cross. (Col.1:20)

b. **The prophecy: The King comes in peace (v.15).**

The prophet Zechariah had foretold that when Israel's coming King at last arrived, He would come on the scene humbly, riding a donkey's colt. Zechariah's prophecy intentionally "contrasted Jesus' coming (Zech.9:9) with the coming of [the political conqueror] Alexander the Great (Zech.9:1-8)."[2] Alexander came to conquer by force; Jesus came in peace.

---

2 Walvoord and Zuck, eds., *The Bible Knowledge Commentary (Old Testament)*, (Wheaton, IL: Victor Books), via Wordsearch digital edition.

Jesus' riding a young donkey into Jerusalem was a dramatic demonstration for the people. First, He was demonstrating that He was unquestionably the promised King, the Savior of the people; and second, that He was not coming as the conquering King. His mission was not to come as a worldly monarch, in pomp and ceremony, not to be the leader of an army to kill, injure and maim. Consequently, the people had to change their concept of the Messiah. The Messiah was coming as the Savior of Peace who had been sent to save all people. He was coming to serve people and to bear their burdens for them. He was coming to show humanity that God is the God of love and reconciliation.

> "Even as the Son of Man came not to be served but to serve, and to give his life as a ransom for many." (Mt.20:28)

> But emptied himself, by taking the form of a servant, being born in the likeness of men. And being found in human form, he humbled himself by becoming obedient to the point of death, even death on a cross. (Ph.2:7-8)

> Since therefore the children share in flesh and blood, he himself likewise partook of the same things, that through death he might destroy the one who has the power of death, that is, the devil, and deliver all those who through fear of death were subject to lifelong slavery. (He.2:14-15)

> Therefore he had to be made like his brothers in every respect, so that he might become a merciful and faithful high priest in the service of God, to make propitiation for the sins of the people. For because he himself has suffered when tempted, he is able to help those who are being tempted. (He.2:17-18)

## 4 The disciples' reaction.

The disciples were puzzled by Jesus' riding into Jerusalem on a donkey rather than a stallion. Even after walking so closely with Jesus, they did not fully understand His mission and purpose.

> [16] His disciples did not understand these things at first, but when Jesus was glorified, then they remembered that these things had been written about him and had been done to him.

### a. The bewilderment: They did not grasp the significance (v.16a).

Jesus' disciples did not grasp the meaning and significance of what was happening. They were as guilty as the people in misunderstanding Scripture. They misunderstood Jesus' Messiahship and kingship, thinking that He was to be a worldly king and earthly Messiah.

### b. The symbol: They grasped the meaning only after His resurrection (v.16b).

The truth of Scripture—its prediction of these things and how Jesus fulfilled them—became clear to the disciples after Jesus was glorified—after His resurrection and ascension. The task of revealing the truth to the people's hearts would be assigned to the Holy Spirit (Jn.14:26). When the Holy Spirit came, He made the truth come alive in the disciples' minds (Jn.16:12-14), and the disciples saw clearly how Jesus had fulfilled the Scripture in His triumphal entry.

**THOUGHT 1.** Scripture is unfathomable; its depth cannot be measured. It contains a world of truth, an eternity of insight. The Holy Spirit activates the believer's mind and heart to grasp the Scripture.

- ➢ To the person who seeks after the Word, the Spirit unfolds the Word of God and reveals the glorious truths of God.
- ➢ To the person who hungers after the Word, the Spirit fills their soul with the good things of God's Word.
- ➢ To the person who thirsts after the Word, the Spirit pours the living waters of the Word into their being.

> "For the Holy Spirit will teach you in that very hour what you ought to say." (Lu.12:12)

> "But the Helper, the Holy Spirit, whom the Father will send in my name, he will teach you all things and bring to your remembrance all that I have said to you." (Jn.14:26)

And we impart this in words not taught by human wisdom but taught by the Spirit, interpreting spiritual truths to those who are spiritual. (1 Co.2:13)

But the anointing that you received from him abides in you, and you have no need that anyone should teach you. But as his anointing teaches you about everything, and is true, and is no lie—just as it has taught you, abide in him. (1 Jn.2:27)

**THOUGHT 2.** Since Jesus has risen and been glorified, no person has an excuse for not understanding the mission of Jesus. Jesus came as the Prince of Peace and as the Savior of the world. He did not come to fulfill the lustful cravings and ambitions of worldly people. People are to be saved by Him and to surrender their lives to Him as the Lord of glory who now sits at the right hand of God the Father.

"Repent, for the kingdom of heaven is at hand." (Mt.3:2)

"No, I tell you; but unless you repent, you will all likewise perish." (Lu.13:3)

And Peter said to them, "Repent and be baptized every one of you in the name of Jesus Christ for the forgiveness of your sins, and you will receive the gift of the Holy Spirit." (Ac.2:38)

"Repent therefore, and turn back, that your sins may be blotted out." (Ac.3:19)

"Repent, therefore, of this wickedness of yours, and pray to the Lord that, if possible, the intent of your heart may be forgiven you." (Ac.8:22)

For you were bought with a price. So glorify God in your body. (1 Co.6:20)

**THOUGHT 3.** If we genuinely desire to understand Scripture, we must depend on the Holy Spirit. We *cannot understand Scripture* apart from the Spirit of God. As believers, we must...

- be the Lord's in the truest sense
- hunger and thirst after righteousness
- come to the Word, the Bible
- seek the Spirit for understanding
- seek exactly what the Word says (not what people say)
- seek what the Word says to our own heart (application)
- be prayerful, open-minded, depending on the Spirit for illumination (eliminating all preconceived notions)
- study, rightly dividing the Word, letting the Word interpret the Word
- study, *seeking the approval of God*, not of other people

"You search the Scriptures because you think that in them you have eternal life; and it is they that bear witness about me." (Jn.5:39)

Now these Jews were more noble than those in Thessalonica; they received the word with all eagerness, examining the Scriptures daily to see if these things were so. (Ac.17:11)

"And now I commend you to God and to the word of his grace, which is able to build you up and to give you the inheritance among all those who are sanctified." (Ac.20:32)

The natural person does not accept the things of the Spirit of God, for they are folly to him, and he is not able to understand them because they are spiritually discerned. (1 Co.2:14; cp. vv.9–15)

Let the word of Christ dwell in you richly, teaching and admonishing one another in all wisdom, singing psalms and hymns and spiritual songs, with thankfulness in your hearts to God. (Col.3:16)

Do your best to present yourself to God as one approved, a worker who has no need to be ashamed, rightly handling the word of truth. (2 Ti.2:15)

All Scripture is breathed out by God and profitable for teaching, for reproof, for correction, and for training in righteousness. (2 Ti.3:16)

Like newborn infants, long for the pure spiritual milk, that by it you may grow up into salvation—if indeed you have tasted that the Lord is good. (1 Pe.2:2–3)

## 5 The people's reaction.

As always, the people's reaction to Jesus was divided. Many were sincere in their belief, but the praise of many others was merely superficial.

### a. The eyewitnesses to Lazarus' resurrection: They spread the news (v.17).

Many of the people were sincere; they genuinely believed in Jesus and spread the news that He was the Messiah (Jn.11:45). These genuine believers were the people who had witnessed Jesus raise Lazarus from the dead.

**12:17-18**

> ¹⁷ The crowd that had been with him when he called Lazarus out of the tomb and raised him from the dead continued to bear witness.
> ¹⁸ The reason why the crowd went to meet him was that they heard he had done this sign.

### b. The people who heard about the miracle: They sought Jesus, sought for the sensational (v.18).

On the other hand, many others were as so many are in a crowd—simply sightseers, wanting to be where the people were and where the action was. They were after the excitement, the sensational, the spectacular (see DEEPER STUDY # 1—Jn.2:23; note—12:9 for more discussion and application).

> Then some of the scribes and Pharisees answered him, saying, "Teacher, we wish to see a sign from you." (Mt.12:38)

> And he said to them, "Well did Isaiah prophesy of you hypocrites, as it is written, 'This people honors me with their lips, but their heart is far from me.'" (Mk.7:6)

> So they said to him, "Then what sign do you do, that we may see and believe you? What work do you perform?" (Jn.6:30)

> They profess to know God, but they deny him by their works. They are detestable, disobedient, unfit for any good work. (Tit.1:16)

## 6 The religious leaders' reaction: Despair and rage.

**12:19**

The religious leaders were becoming more desperate by the moment. Standing there, they witnessed the whole scene of surging thousands thronging the roadway and welcoming Jesus as the Messiah. They became so enraged and full of despair that they began to accuse and blame each other for the failure of their plots against Jesus.

> ¹⁹ So the Pharisees said to one another, "You see that you are gaining nothing. Look, the world has gone after him."

> Whoever believes in the Son has eternal life; whoever does not obey the Son shall not see life, but the wrath of God remains on him. (Jn.3:36)

> "I told you that you would die in your sins, for unless you believe that I am he you will die in your sins." (Jn.8:24)

> Take care, brothers, lest there be in any of you an evil, unbelieving heart, leading you to fall away from the living God. (He.3:12)

Note the undeniable truth they exclaimed: "The world has gone after Him!" John pictures a most dramatic scene: even the enemies of Jesus saw Jesus conquering the world. Practically every pilgrim in the city must have been caught up in the excitement. Teeming thousands upon thousands were swarming the roadway between Bethany and Jerusalem, crying for their Savior.

> **THOUGHT 1.** What a picture of how the world should be crying for the Lord's deliverance! People by the thousands should be lining the roadways, crying for His salvation.
>
>> "That they should seek God, and perhaps feel their way toward him and find him. Yet he is actually not far from each one of us." (Ac.17:27)
>>
>> "But from there you will seek the LORD your God and you will find him, if you search after him with all your heart and with all your soul." (De.4:29)
>>
>> "Seek the LORD while he may be found; call upon him while he is near." (Is.55:6)
>>
>> "You will seek me and find me, when you seek me with all your heart." (Je.29:13)
>>
>> For thus says the LORD to the house of Israel: "Seek me and live." (Am.5:4)

## B. Jesus Approached As King:
## The Misunderstood Messiah, 12:20-36

1. **Some Greeks, representing the world, sought Jesus (see 12:19)**
   a. Jesus was accepted as king, 12:12f
   b. Some Greeks requested to see the king

2. **Misunderstanding 1: Jesus' glory**
   a. His hour had come[DS1]
      1) He had to die before being glorified
      2) He could then bear fruit & produce many seeds
   b. Humanity's hour had also come
      1) We must lose our lives to bear eternal life
      2) We must serve & follow Jesus to be assured of Jesus' presence & God's honor

3. **Misunderstanding 2: Jesus' cause**
   a. His troubled heart
   b. His great cause: To die for our sin

[20] Now among those who went up to worship at the feast were some Greeks. [21] So these came to Philip, who was from Bethsaida in Galilee, and asked him, "Sir, we wish to see Jesus." [22] Philip went and told Andrew; Andrew and Philip went and told Jesus. [23] And Jesus answered them, "The hour has come for the Son of Man to be glorified. [24] Truly, truly, I say to you, unless a grain of wheat falls into the earth and dies, it remains alone; but if it dies, it bears much fruit. [25] Whoever loves his life loses it, and whoever hates his life in this world will keep it for eternal life. [26] If anyone serves me, he must follow me; and where I am, there will my servant be also. If anyone serves me, the Father will honor him.

[27] Now is my soul troubled. And what shall I say? 'Father, save me from this hour'? But for this purpose I have come to this hour.

# Division XII

*The Revelation of Jesus, the Glorified Son of Man, 12:12-50*

B. Jesus Approached as King: The Misunderstood Messiah, 12:20-36

## 12:20-36
## Introduction

So many people do not understand the truth about Jesus. As Calvary drew near, many who welcomed Jesus to Jerusalem as their King did not understand the truth about Him. Tragically, in just a few days, these same people would be calling for Him to be crucified. In this passage, Jesus attempted to clear up their misunderstandings. This is, *Jesus Approached as King: The Misunderstood Messiah,* 12:20-36.

1. Some Greeks, representing the world, sought Jesus (see 12:19) (vv.20-22).
2. Misunderstanding 1: Jesus' glory (vv.23-26).
3. Misunderstanding 2: Jesus' cause (vv.27-30).
4. Misunderstanding 3: The world (vv.31-33).
5. Misunderstanding 4: The Messiah (the Light of the world) (vv.34-36).

²⁸ "Father, glorify your name." Then a voice came from heaven: "I have glorified it, and I will glorify it again."

²⁹ The crowd that stood there and heard it said that it had thundered. Others said, "An angel has spoken to him."

³⁰ Jesus answered, "This voice has come for your sake, not mine."

³¹ Now is the judgment of this world; now will the ruler of this world be cast out.

³² And I, when I am lifted up from the earth, will draw all people to myself."

³³ He said this to show by what kind of death he was going to die.

³⁴ So the crowd answered him, "We have heard from the Law that the Christ remains forever. How can you say that the Son of Man must be lifted up? Who is this Son of Man?"

³⁵ So Jesus said to them, "The light is among you for a little while longer. Walk while you have the light, lest darkness overtake you. The one who walks in the darkness does not know where he is going.

³⁶ While you have the light, believe in the light, that you may become sons of light."

    c. His prayer for God's glory
    d. God's audible approval

    e. The people's confusion

    f. God's purpose: To show His approval of Christ
4. **Misunderstanding 3: The world**
    a. It has to be judged$^{DS2}$
    b. It is ruled by an alien prince$^{DS3}$
    c. It is conquered by the cross$^{DS4}$

5. **Misunderstanding 4: The Messiah (the Light of the world)**
    a. The people misunderstood the Messiah

    b. The claim: He is the Light (the Messiah), but the light is to be extinguished$^{DS5}$
    c. The need for everyone
       1) To walk in the light

       2) To believe in the light

(12:20-36) **Another Outline**: The Glory and Power of the Cross.
1. Some Greeks, representing the world, sought Jesus (vv.20-22).
2. The cross is the glory of the Messiah (v.23).
3. The cross brings forth fruit (v.24).
4. The cross demands death to self (vv.25-26).
    a. We must lose our life to bear eternal life.
    b. We must serve and follow Jesus to be assured of Jesus' presence and God's honor.
5. The cross fulfills Jesus' cause (v.27).
6. The cross glorifies God's name (vv.28-30).
7. The cross judges the world—the prince of the world (v.31).
8. The cross draws all people (vv.32-33).
9. The cross reveals the true Messiah (vv.34-36).

(12:20-36) **Another Outline:** Seven pictures are presented here. **1.)** A grain of wheat (v.24). **2.)** A life lost (v.25). **3.)** A servant (v.26). **4.)** A troubled soul (vv.27-30). **5.)** A prince cast out (v.31). **6.)** The cross (vv.32-33). **7.)** A light extinguished (vv.34-36).

## 1 Some Greeks, representing the world, sought Jesus.

12:20-22

Watching the crowd thronging Jesus as He entered Jerusalem, the Pharisees had desperately exclaimed, "Look, the world has gone after Him" (v.19). It was not only Jews who celebrated the arrival of Jesus; pilgrims from other nations—including some Greeks—were there as well.

20 Now among those who went up to worship at the feast were some Greeks.
21 So these came to Philip, who was from Bethsaida in Galilee, and asked him, "Sir, we wish to see Jesus."
22 Philip went and told Andrew; Andrew and Philip went and told Jesus.

### a. Jesus was accepted as king, 12:12f.

Jesus had just been hailed as the coming king and Messiah by thousands and thousands of people. As He rode into Jerusalem on a young donkey, they had lined the road, waving palm branches and welcoming Him as Israel's king.

### b. Some Greeks requested to see the king (v.21).

Some Greek pilgrims who had come to attend the Passover Feast wished to see this Jesus who was being proclaimed king. In the author's mind, these Greeks represented the Gentile world, all the God-fearing people of the world who would see Jesus, if given the opportunity.

12:23-26

23 And Jesus answered them, "The hour has come for the Son of Man to be glorified.
24 Truly, truly, I say to you, unless a grain of wheat falls into the earth and dies, it remains alone; but if it dies, it bears much fruit.
25 Whoever loves his life loses it, and whoever hates his life in this world will keep it for eternal life.
26 If anyone serves me, he must follow me; and where I am, there will my servant be also. If anyone serves me, the Father will honor him."

## 2 Misunderstanding 1: Jesus' glory.

The Greeks had just seen Jesus *glorified* as Messiah by teeming thousands. It was as if the world were following after Him. They wanted to be part of the movement, so they requested an interview with Him. What Jesus did was try to correct the misunderstood idea of the Messiah held by the world. He wanted to prepare both Greeks and others standing around (representing the whole world) for His death. He wanted to teach that the way to glory is not through triumph and praise, not through domination and subjection. The way to glory is through death to self and through service to God and humanity. With that in mind, Jesus attempted to correct their misunderstanding of His glory by revealing His purpose for coming to Jerusalem.

### a. His hour had come (vv.23-24).

Jesus said that His hour had come: the Son of Man was now to be glorified. His hour, of course, referred to His death, as the next verse clearly states and this whole passage shows (see Deeper Study # 1; note—Jn.2:3-5). He had to die before He would be glorified.

Jesus revealed His death by using the picture of a grain of wheat (v.24). As stated, Jesus said that He would now be glorified, but His glory was not to be the glory of an earthly ruler. His glory was to be the glory of the cross. It would be through His death that He would gain the people's allegiance and be exalted as King of Kings.

➤ God would exalt Him as king because He had done exactly what God wished: He died for the sins of the whole world (see note—Jn.10:17-18 for important discussion of this fact).
➤ People would become His subjects because He had died for them and given them an eternal inheritance with God the Father.

The picture of the grain of wheat can be simply stated: before the glory—before a seed can be productive—death is a necessity. Once Jesus had died, He could then bear fruit and produce many seeds. Jesus had to die before He could be enthroned as king and bear the fruit of subjects and a kingdom (see note—Jn.13:31-32 for more discussion).

**THOUGHT 1.** The glory of Christ is the glory of the cross.

(1) It is the cross that stirs God to exalt His dear Son above every name that is named.

> For to this end Christ died and lived again, that he might be Lord both of the dead and of the living. (Ro.14:9)

> And being found in human form, he humbled himself by becoming obedient to the point of death, even death on a cross. Therefore God has highly exalted him and bestowed on him the name that is above every name, so that at the name of Jesus every knee should bow, in heaven and on earth and under the earth, and every tongue confess that Jesus Christ is Lord, to the glory of God the Father. (Ph.2:8–11)

> In whom we have redemption, the forgiveness of sins.... And he is the head of the body, the church. He is the beginning, the firstborn from the dead, that in everything he might be preeminent. (Col.1:14, 18)

> But of the Son he says, "Your throne, O God, is forever and ever, the scepter of uprightness is the scepter of your kingdom. You have loved righteousness and hated wickedness; therefore God, your God, has anointed you with the oil of gladness beyond your companions." (He.1:8–9)

> But we see him who for a little while was made lower than the angels, namely Jesus, crowned with glory and honor because of the suffering of death, so that by the grace of God he might taste death for everyone. (He.2:9)

> He himself bore our sins in his body on the tree, that we might die to sin and live to righteousness. By his wounds you have been healed. For you were straying like sheep, but have now returned to the Shepherd and Overseer of your souls. (1 Pe.2:24–25)

> For Christ also suffered once for sins, the righteous for the unrighteous, that he might bring us to God, being put to death in the flesh but made alive in the spirit.... Who has gone into heaven and is at the right hand of God, with angels, authorities, and powers having been subjected to him. (1 Pe.3:18, 22)

> Therefore I will divide him a portion with the many, and he shall divide the spoil with the strong, because he poured out his soul to death and was numbered with the transgressors; yet he bore the sin of many, and makes intercession for the transgressors. (Is.53:12)

(2) It is the cross that stirs people to offer themselves as living sacrifices to God's dear Son (in appreciation and love for saving them).

> For the death he died he died to sin, once for all, but the life he lives he lives to God. So you also must consider yourselves dead to sin and alive to God in Christ Jesus. (Ro.6:10–11)

> For if we live, we live to the Lord, and if we die, we die to the Lord. So then, whether we live or whether we die, we are the Lord's. For to this end Christ died and lived again, that he might be Lord both of the dead and of the living. (Ro.14:8–9)

> For you were bought with a price. So glorify God in your body. (1 Co.6:20)

> For the love of Christ controls us, because we have concluded this: that one has died for all, therefore all have died; and he died for all, that those who live might no longer live for themselves but for him who for their sake died and was raised. (2 Co.5:14–15)

> I have been crucified with Christ. It is no longer I who live, but Christ who lives in me. And the life I now live in the flesh I live by faith in the Son of God, who loved me and gave himself for me. (Ga.2:20)

> Who gave himself for us to redeem us from all lawlessness and to purify for himself a people for his own possession who are zealous for good works. (Tit.2:14)

b. **Humanity's hour had also come (vv.25–26).**

Jesus said that humanity's hour had also come. People must do the same as He did. We must lose our lives to keep them for eternal life (v.25). What did Jesus mean by this unusual statement? Very simply, those who *abandon* this life and world, who *sacrifice and give* all that they are and have for Christ, will keep their lives. But those who selfishly *love* and hold onto their lives and what they have and *seek* more and more of this life, will lose their lives completely and eternally.

The people who *love* their lives . . .

- who deny Christ—will lose their lives eternally

- who seek to make their lives more and more comfortable and easy and secure (beyond what is necessary) and neglect Christ—will lose their lives eternally
- who seek to gain wealth and power and fame by compromising Christ—will lose their lives eternally
- who seek the excitement and stimulation of this world and ignore Christ—will lose their lives eternally

As said above, the people who lose their lives for Christ and sacrifice all they have and are for Christ keep their lives and keep them eternally. The people who use their earthly lives and possessions for themselves will have nothing to show for their lives in eternity. They will have spent their lives on that which is of this world rather than on that which lasts throughout eternity (1 Co.3:12-16). The call of Christ is just what He says—a life of denial that takes up the cross and follows in His steps.

> "For what does it profit a man to gain the whole world and forfeit his soul?" (Mk.8:36)
>
> "But the one who hears and does not do them is like a man who built a house on the ground without a foundation. When the stream broke against it, immediately it fell, and the ruin of that house was great." (Lu.6:49)
>
> And he said to all, "If anyone would come after me, let him deny himself and take up his cross daily and follow me." (Lu.9:23)
>
> For if you live according to the flesh you will die, but if by the Spirit you put to death the deeds of the body, you will live. (Ro.8:13)
>
> And those who belong to Christ Jesus have crucified the flesh with its passions and desires. (Ga.5:24)
>
> "Your iniquities have turned these away, and your sins have kept good from you." (Je.5:25)

In addition, Jesus said that if we desire to serve Him, we must follow Him (v.26). He assured those who serve and follow Him that they will be where He is. They will live eternally in His presence. And He assured them of the Father's (God's) honor. The Father will honor any person who honors His Son—His only Son whom He loves with His whole Being.

> Then Peter said in reply, "See, we have left everything and followed you. What then will we have?" Jesus said to them, "Truly, I say to you, in the new world, when the Son of Man will sit on his glorious throne, you who have followed me will also sit on twelve thrones, judging the twelve tribes of Israel. And everyone who has left houses or brothers or sisters or father or mother or children or lands, for my name's sake, will receive a hundredfold and will inherit eternal life." (Mt.19:27-29)
>
> "But it shall not be so among you. But whoever would be great among you must be your servant, and whoever would be first among you must be slave of all." (Mk.10:43-44)
>
> Again Jesus spoke to them, saying, "I am the light of the world. Whoever follows me will not walk in darkness, but will have the light of life." (Jn.8:12)
>
> "You shall serve the LORD your God, and he will bless your bread and your water, and I will take sickness away from among you." (Ex.23:25)
>
> "When he calls to me, I will answer him; I will be with him in trouble; I will rescue him and honor him." (Ps.91:15)

## DEEPER STUDY # 1

(12:23-24) **Hour of Jesus Christ**: the phrase "the hour" or "my hour" is a constant symbol of Jesus' death. "The hour" refers to all the events of the cross and all the trouble and sufferings surrounding the cross. Note two facts.

1. "The hour" is a set, fixed time in the purpose of God.
   ➢ Jesus said, "The hour has come" (Jn.12:23-24, 27; 13:1; 17:1; Mt.26:18, 45; Mk.14:41).
   ➢ He had said some time before, "My hour has not yet come" (Jn.2:4; see 7:6, 8, 30; 8:20).

The hour of Jesus was inevitable: a definite period of time, a set of events, a number of experiences that He had to face and go through. As He said, He must die in order to bring forth fruit (v.24).

2. The hour was to have a definite beginning. There was a set time for the trouble to begin (v.27), a set time for Him to begin suffering for the sins of the world. There was a fixed hour when He was to begin suffering the pain and anguish, the agitation and disturbance, the pressure and weight, the strain and stress of having to be separated from God in behalf of sinful humanity (see notes—Mt.20:18; 27:46-49).

## 3 Misunderstanding 2: Jesus' cause.

Jesus wanted to clear up the misunderstandings about His cause or purpose for coming to Jerusalem. He came to Jerusalem to fulfill His purpose for coming into the world: to die for humanity's sin.

### a. His troubled heart (v.27a).

Jesus was experiencing a "troubled" soul. *Troubled* (Gk., tetaraktai) means agitated, pressured, heavy, weighed down, strained, stressed, disturbed.

### b. His great cause: To die for our sin (v.27b).

The reason our Lord's soul was so troubled was that He was about to face the great cause for which He had come into the world. His hour was at hand, staring Him in the face; the terrible sufferings were now beginning.

Christ's supreme purpose was to face the hour God had set for Him: He was to die. He had come to die.

Jesus demonstrated His supreme obedience to His purpose; that is, God's purpose for Him. Imagine the terrible sufferings of the hour, the pain He was experiencing in His mind and heart. He revealed His inward struggle, the desire to pray, "Father save me from this hour." But He could not pray this way, for He had come to die. He had to obey God, and to obey God was the supreme act of His life (see note—Jn.10:17-18).

### c. His prayer for God's glory (v.28a).

Instead of praying to be spared the cross, Jesus prayed for the glory of God. He prayed for the Father to glorify His own name. This is significant. It shows a complete selflessness on the part of Jesus. It shows that Jesus' primary concern was to complete His purpose and cause on earth, which was to glorify God by doing exactly what God wanted. How was God glorified? By Jesus' obedience. God was glorified in the same way a superior is honored and respected. His Word was carried out and obeyed.

"Glorify" is translated from the Greek aorist tense, which points to a single act or event which would glorify God. The single act concerned the cross. Jesus was asking His Father to glorify His own name through the cross. God would be glorified in the cross by the supreme act of obedience on the part of Jesus. It was God's will for Jesus to die for our sins. By dying, Jesus would show that God is the Supreme Being of the universe. God is the One who is to be honored and respected and obeyed. He would thereby be glorified.

> **And going a little farther he fell on his face and prayed, saying, "My Father, if it be possible, let this cup [death] pass from me; nevertheless, not as I will, but as you will." (Mt.26:39)**
>
> **"For this reason the Father loves me, because I lay down my life that I may take it up again. No one takes it from me, but I lay it down of my own accord. I have authority to lay it down, and I have authority to take it up again. This charge I have received from my Father." (Jn.10:17-18)**
>
> **"This Jesus, delivered up according to the definite plan and foreknowledge of God, you crucified and killed by the hands of lawless men." (Ac.2:23)**

---

27 "Now is my soul troubled. And what shall I say? 'Father, save me from this hour'? But for this purpose I have come to this hour.

28 "Father, glorify your name." Then a voice came from heaven: "I have glorified it, and I will glorify it again."

29 The crowd that stood there and heard it said that it had thundered. Others said, "An angel has spoken to him."

30 Jesus answered, "This voice has come for your sake, not mine."

> And walk in love, as Christ loved us and gave himself up for us, a fragrant offering and sacrifice to God. (Ep.5:2)

> Consequently, when Christ came into the world, he said, "Sacrifices and offerings you have not desired, but a body have you prepared for me; in burnt offerings and sin offerings you have taken no pleasure. Then I said, 'Behold, I have come to do your will, O God, as it is written of me in the scroll of the book.'" . . . And by that will we have been sanctified through the offering of the body of Jesus Christ once for all. (He.10:5-7, 10)

In addition, God would be glorified in the cross by *people seeing God's love* in the cross. God gave His only Son to die *for* us that we might not perish but have everlasting life. Some people would see and believe this glorious truth; therefore, they would bow down, surrendering their whole beings to God. They would begin to follow and obey His will, honoring and praising Him for all He had done and was doing for them. The name of God would thereby be glorified by the cross (see note, pt.1—Jn.12:23-26).

### d. God's audible approval (v.28b).

God accepted and approved Jesus' prayer in an unusual way: He spoke audibly from heaven. God actually spoke from heaven, saying that He had glorified His name and that He would glorify it again. What does this mean?

First, Jesus had prayed according to God's will, for God to glorify [honor] His name (see Mt.6:9). Therefore, God answered His prayer. God promises to answer any prayer that is according to His will (1 Jn.5:14-15). This truth stresses the importance of knowing God's will. Studying God's Word is the only way to know the will of God.

Second, God accepted Jesus' prayer. This means He accepted Jesus' death in behalf of sinful humanity. We can rest assured that we are delivered from death if we believe in Jesus (see Jn.5:24).

Third, God will glorify His name in the future. He will keep His Word and fulfill all His promises. We can rest assured of the promises of God.

### e. The people's confusion (v.29).

When God spoke audibly from heaven, the people standing around were confused about what they had heard. Some thought the voice was merely thunder; others thought that an angel had spoken to Jesus.

### f. God's purpose: To show His approval of Christ (v.30).

Jesus plainly told the people that the voice had spoken for a distinct purpose. God had spoken for their sakes in order to help them believe that Jesus was the Son of God.

By the thousands, people had just welcomed Jesus in the triumphal entry. But they welcomed Him as their earthly king and Messiah, the One who was to bring heaven and utopia to earth (see outline and notes—Jn.8:21-24). Jesus had to correct the misunderstanding of His cause. He had come not to rule as an earthly king for humanity; He had come to die for humanity. God's voice testified to this. God's concern was not just for the years of a person's earthly life; God's concern was to save people eternally.

> "For God so loved the world, that he gave his only Son, that whoever believes in him should not perish but have eternal life. For God did not send his Son into the world to condemn the world, but in order that the world might be saved through him." (Jn.3:16-17)

> "The thief comes only to steal and kill and destroy. I came that they may have life and have it abundantly." (Jn.10:10)

> "Just as the Father knows me and I know the Father; and I lay down my life for the sheep." (Jn.10:15)

> He himself bore our sins in his body on the tree, that we might die to sin and live to righteousness. By his wounds you have been healed. (1 Pe.2:24)

> For Christ also suffered once for sins, the righteous for the unrighteous, that he might bring us to God, being put to death in the flesh but made alive in the spirit. (1 Pe.3:18)

## 4 Misunderstanding 3: The world.

The third misunderstanding concerns the world. The world is not what it should be. It is not what it was created to be: perfect and permanent. The world was perfect in its distant past: it was created perfectly, just as it should be. However, people misunderstand the world. They ignore and neglect *the fact that the world* . . .

- is not perfect; is not in its original state or even close to it; is not what it should be; is not in the condition for which it was meant.
- is not permanent as it is; will not always be here; was not always here.
- is to be changed and recreated into a new heavens and earth just as God intended.

12:20-36

12:31-33

[31] "Now is the judgment of this world; now will the ruler of this world be cast out.
[32] And I, when I am lifted up from the earth, will draw all people to myself."
[33] He said this to show by what kind of death he was going to die.

The people had welcomed Jesus in the triumphal entry, thinking He was going to set up a kingdom on this *present earth*. They thought in terms of the physical earth, in terms of worldly kingdoms and material wealth and power. Jesus had to correct their misconception. He had to show them that God's concern was not for the human race and their world to exist for just a brief span of time, but for eternity.

What Jesus said to them was an alarming revelation. Note the phenomenal claim in the word "now." He said to them, *"Now,"* it is I—my being lifted up, my cross and my death—that would cause these things to happen.

a. **It has to be judged (v.31a).**

   Jesus said that this world has to be judged (see Deeper Study # 2). God is holy and just. He must judge everything and everybody that is sinful.

b. **It is ruled by an alien prince (v.31b).**

   Jesus said that this world—this world system and all associated with it—is ruled by an alien power. That power is Satan. Satan is the *ruler* or *prince* of this world (see Deeper Study # 3).

c. **It is conquered by the cross (v.31c-32).**

   Jesus said that both the world and Satan would be conquered by the cross, by His death (see Deeper Study # 4). When Jesus spoke of being lifted up from the earth, He was referring to His death on the cross, the six dark hours when He would hang suspended between heaven and earth.

### Deeper Study # 2

(12:31) **World, Judgment of:** the world has to be judged . . .
- judged as being imperfect
- judged as being in some state other than what it should be
- judged as being short of God's glory and of God's will

If the world is ever to be perfected, it has to be judged as imperfect. God has to judge the world as less than what He wills. Once the world is judged as defective and imperfect . . .
- then it can be condemned and destroyed
- then it can be recreated in a perfect form and state of being

This is exactly what Scripture teaches. Scripture says three things about the world having to be judged and recreated in order to be perfected.

1. The earth itself and the heavenly bodies above have to be judged. Why? Because they are imperfect; they have the seed of corruption within. The earth and the world are *running down*, wasting away, failing, and dying. Eventually, even if the world were allowed to run long enough, the earth could not sustain life. The Bible says the earth . .

- has to be judged because it is not perfect.
- has to be made perfect by being recreated and put into a permanent state (see 2 Pe.2:3-4, 8-13 for discussion).

2. Nature itself, the animal and vegetation life of the earth, has to be judged. (Note: this fact is closely aligned to point 1 above. It is separated only in an attempt to simplify the discussion and to help in understanding the teaching of Scripture.) Nature is imperfect; it has the seed of corruption within. Nature is often beautiful in its sunsets, green pastures, and animal life. But nature is also destructive in its storms, earthquakes, fires, and struggle for survival. The beautiful mockingbird sitting in a tree can be singing its song, and in a moment's time turn into a savage by attacking the worm. Nature is not perfect, not what it should be. It is short of God's glory and short of what God wills it to be. God's will is for *a nature* in which the lion lies down with the lamb, a nature in which all things are at peace and without corruption. In its present condition, nature...

- despite its beauty, can be savage
- despite its peace, can be stormy
- despite its producing good, can produce bad
- despite its being right, can be evil
- despite its enticements, can destroy
- despite its nourishment, can starve

The Bible says that nature has to be judged because it is not perfect. It has to be made perfect, that is, recreated and put into a permanent and perfect state.

> For the creation waits with eager longing for the revealing of the sons of God. For the creation was subjected to futility, not willingly, but because of him who subjected it, in hope that the creation itself will be set free from its bondage to corruption and obtain the freedom of the glory of the children of God. For we know that the whole creation has been groaning together in the pains of childbirth until now. (Ro.8:19-22)

3. The human race (and it's world system) has to be judged. Humans are imperfect; they have the seed of corruption within. People lie, steal, cheat, and kill. Every person has many good moments—every individual, no matter who they are—but every person also has many bad moments. Moods, feelings, thoughts, weaknesses of both body and mind—so much causes us to come ever so short. In addition, we all age; we waste away and die—and nothing can stop the process. We fall short of God's glory; we are not perfect; therefore, we must be judged. We have to be recreated and made into perfect creatures; we have to be given perfect and permanent bodies.

> So is it with the resurrection of the dead. What is sown is perishable; what is raised is imperishable. It is sown in dishonor; it is raised in glory. It is sown in weakness; it is raised in power. It is sown a natural body; it is raised a spiritual body. If there is a natural body, there is also a spiritual body. (1 Co.15:42-44)

> Just as we have borne the image of the man of dust, we shall also bear the image of the man of heaven. I tell you this, brothers: flesh and blood cannot inherit the kingdom of God, nor does the perishable inherit the imperishable. Behold! I tell you a mystery. We shall not all sleep, but we shall all be changed, in a moment, in the twinkling of an eye, at the last trumpet. For the trumpet will sound, and the dead will be raised imperishable, and we shall be changed. For this perishable body must put on the imperishable, and this mortal body must put on immortality. When the perishable puts on the imperishable, and the mortal puts on immortality, then shall come to pass the saying that is written: "Death is swallowed up in victory." (1 Co.15:49-54)

It is important to note why the seed of corruption is in the world. The world was not corrupted by its own will or act. It was corrupted because of sin (see Ro.8:20). The sin of man brought corruption into the world. As soon as man sinned...

- the world was no longer perfect. It was contaminated, polluted, dirtied, corrupted.
- the seed of corruption, of wasting away, deteriorating, decaying and dying was planted in the world.
- the results of sin fell upon the world as well as falling upon man.

The world had been made for man, for man's dwelling place and enjoyment (see Ge.1:1-3:24). And God gave man a choice: if man chose perfection, his world would remain perfect just as God had created it; but if man chose sin and evil and death, his world would become imperfect, full of sin and evil and death. Therefore, when man sinned and became corrupted, he plunged the world into corruption. All creation became as man, just as man had chosen.

As stated, the world and its physical dimension of being were made for man; therefore, it was bound to suffer the very same fate as man. God had so ordained it. Therefore, when man is saved and delivered from sin and corruption, his world will also share the deliverance of man. The world will be saved and delivered from sin and corruption. There is to be a glorious day of redemption, a redemption both for humanity and their world. God will give all believers a redeemed and perfected world in which to live. As God declares, "Behold, I am making all things new" (Re.21:5).

> Knowing this first of all, that scoffers will come in the last days with scoffing, following their own sinful desires. They will say, "Where is the promise of his coming? For ever since the fathers fell asleep, all things are continuing as they were from the beginning of creation." ... But do not overlook this one fact, beloved, that with the Lord one day is as a thousand years, and a thousand years as one day. The Lord is not slow to fulfill his promise as some count slowness, but is patient toward you, not wishing that any should perish, but that all should reach repentance. But the day of the Lord will come like a thief, and then the heavens will pass away with a roar, and the heavenly bodies will be burned up and dissolved, and the earth and the works that are done on it will be exposed. Since all these things are thus to be dissolved, what sort of people ought you to be in lives of holiness and godliness, waiting for and hastening the coming of the day of God, because of which the heavens will be set on fire and dissolved, and the heavenly bodies will melt as they burn! But according to his promise we are waiting for new heavens and a new earth in which righteousness dwells. (2 Pe.3:3-4, 8-13)

## DEEPER STUDY # 3

(12:31) **Satan:** Jesus said the world is ruled by an alien prince. The world is not ruled by God; it is ruled by Satan. The Bible says three significant things.

1. Satan is the ruler and the prince, that is, the power of the world in all its evil and corruption (Jn.12:31; 14:30; 16:11; 2 Co.4:4; Ep.2:2; see DEEPER STUDY # 1—Re.12:9 for more discussion.)

2. The sin and evil of the world prove the world is ruled by an alien prince. God is not the author of sin, nor *does He* tempt people with evil (Js.1:13). God is not the Father of sin and evil, of destruction and devastation. God does not do such things. The father of such corruption is the devil (see DEEPER STUDY # 1—8:38; note—8:41-47; DEEPER STUDY # 1 and note—8:44 for discussion).

3. Satan is now "cast out" by the cross of Christ. Note the words *cast out* (Gk., ekblethesetai exo, future passive of ekballo which means a sure fact *that will definitely happen in the future*). The words mean to cast out of, to cast from or forth, to cast *completely out* (exo) of a place. Satan in all his power, rule, and reign is cast out by the death of Christ. His power, rule, and reign over lives is now broken.

   a. Satan's power *to charge people with sin* is now "cast out." People now have the power to escape the penalty of sin. Christ took the sins of humanity upon Himself and paid the penalty for our sin. He died for the sins of the world.

   > Who shall bring any charge against God's elect? It is God who justifies. (Ro.8:33)

   > He himself bore our sins in his body on the tree, that we might die to sin and live to righteousness. By his wounds you have been healed. (1 Pe.2:24)

   b. Satan's power *to cause death* is now "cast out." People no longer have to die. Christ died *for all people*, became humanity's substitute in death.

> Since therefore the children share in flesh and blood, he himself likewise partook of the same things, that through death he might destroy the one who has the power of death, that is, the devil, and deliver all those who through fear of death were subject to lifelong slavery. (He.2:14-15)

c. Satan's power *to cause people to be separated from God* is now cast out. People no longer have to go to hell. Christ was separated from God *for people* (see note—Mt.27:46-49). We can now live forever with God.

> If the Spirit of him who raised Jesus from the dead dwells in you, he who raised Christ Jesus from the dead will also give life to your mortal bodies through his Spirit who dwells in you. (Ro.8:11)

> For Christ also suffered once for sins, the righteous for the unrighteous, that he might bring us to God, being put to death in the flesh but made alive in the spirit. (1 Pe.3:18)

d. Satan's power *to enslave people* with the habits of sin and shame is now "cast out." By His death, Christ made it possible for us to be freed from sin. The believer, cleansed by the blood of Christ, becomes a holy temple unto God, a temple fit for the presence and power of God's Spirit. We can now conquer the enslaving habits of sin by the power of God's Spirit.

> Or do you not know that your body is a temple of the Holy Spirit within you, whom you have from God? You are not your own, for you were bought with a price. So glorify God in your body. (1 Co.6:19-20)

> Little children, you are from God and have overcome them, for he who is in you is greater than he who is in the world. (1 Jn.4:4)

**THOUGHT 1.** Jesus Christ has destroyed and triumphed over the power of Satan (see DEEPER STUDY # 4—for discussion of how the cross delivers and gives us so much.)

> "I will no longer talk much with you, for the ruler of this world is coming. He has no claim on me." (Jn.14:30)

> He has delivered us from the domain of darkness and transferred us to the kingdom of his beloved Son, in whom we have redemption, the forgiveness of sins. (Col.1:13-14)

> He disarmed the rulers and authorities and put them to open shame, by triumphing over them in him. (Col.2:15)

> Whoever makes a practice of sinning is of the devil, for the devil has been sinning from the beginning. The reason the Son of God appeared was to destroy the works of the devil. (1 Jn.3:8)

## DEEPER STUDY # 4

(12:32) **Cross of Christ:** the words "lifted up" refer to the cross of Christ, to His death on the cross. Jesus said that once He is "lifted up," He will draw all people to Himself. Note two points.

1. Note why the cross of Christ attracts people. It was the cross...
   - that delivered humanity from sin, death, and hell
   - that made it possible for people to live abundantly and eternally
   - that gave to people the presence and power of God's Spirit to guide and care for us day by day

2. Note how the cross of Christ gives so much to humanity. Very simply stated, Jesus died *for all people* on the cross. When a person believes that Jesus died *for him or her*, God takes that person's belief and *counts* it as righteousness. God simply *counts* the individual as perfect. The person is *not* righteous, nowhere close to perfect. The individual, God, and everyone else knows he/she is not perfect. But the person honors God's Son by believing in Him; therefore, God honors the person.

The point to see is that God will do anything for the person who truly honors His Son. God loves His Son so much that He is willing to do anything for anyone who honors Jesus.

If a person honors Jesus by believing and following Him, God will take that individual's faith and . . .
- count their faith as righteousness
- deliver them from sin and from death
- give them both abundant and eternal life (Jn.10:10)
- place the Holy Spirit and His power within them to help them live day by day (see 1 Co.6:19-20; Ro.8:1-39; Ga.5:22-23)

The point is, it is the cross of Christ that breaks the power of Satan in the world. It is the cross of Christ that "casts out" Satan: his power, his rule, and his reign. All people, by believing that Christ died for them, can now be counted righteous and delivered from the power of Satan, from the evil power that entices us to sin and that causes us to die and face the judgment of God. We can now know the power of God, the power that freely forgives us and gives us life forever. We can now experience the marvelous grace of God (see DEEPER STUDY # 1—Tit.2:11-15; see notes, Justification—Ro.4:22; 5:1).

## 5 Misunderstanding 4: The Messiah (the Light of the world).

The fourth misunderstanding concerns the Messiah (the Light). The people clearly understood that Jesus was speaking of His death, but it was this that confused them.

**a. The people misunderstood the Messiah (v.34).**

The people had just acknowledged Jesus to be the Messiah, and they had always understood the Messiah was to live forever (see Ps.89:36; 110:4; Is.9:7; Dan.7:14). If Jesus was going to die, how could He be the Messiah? Was Jesus really the Messiah? Could they be mistaken? Was the Son of Man someone else?

34 So the crowd answered him, "We have heard from the Law that the Christ remains forever. How can you say that the Son of Man must be lifted up? Who is this Son of Man?"
35 So Jesus said to them, "The light is among you for a little while longer. Walk while you have the light, lest darkness overtake you. The one who walks in the darkness does not know where he is going.
36 "While you have the light, believe in the light, that you may become sons of light."

**b. The claim: He is the Light (the Messiah), but the Light is to be extinguished (v.35a).**

Jesus claimed to be the Messiah, *the Light of the world* (see DEEPER STUDY # 5; DEEPER STUDY # 1—8:12). But He stressed a critical point. The Light was to be with them for only a little while longer; the Light was to be extinguished. The Messiah would lay down His life.

**c. The need for everyone (vv.35b-36).**

Jesus pointed out the need of all people. First, they needed to walk in the Light *while* they had light (v.35b). If the Light was to be extinguished, it would not always be present for them to see. And once they lost the Light, darkness would overtake and overcome them. They would not know where they were going. They would be groping and stumbling, falling and dooming themselves to an eternity of darkness.

Second, they needed to believe in the Light (v.36). If they believed, something significant would happen. They would become *sons* or *children* (huioi) of the Light. *Believe* (pisteuete) is continuous action. *Become* (genesthe) is a once-for-all act, a personal experience that happens all at once. A person who truly sees Jesus Christ as the Light of the world believes and continues to believe. And the very moment their heart leaps toward Christ in belief, they become a child of the Light, a child of God Himself. That individual sees the Light and begins to walk in the Light, living the kind of life they should.

> In him was life, and the life was the light of men. (Jn.1:4)
>
> Again Jesus spoke to them, saying, "I am the light of the world. Whoever follows me will not walk in darkness, but will have the light of life." (Jn.8:12)
>
> For anything that becomes visible is light. Therefore it says, "Awake, O sleeper, and arise from the dead, and Christ will shine on you." (Ep.5:14)

## Deeper Study # 5

(12:35-36) **Light—Believers:** light is one of the great words of Scripture (see Deeper Study # 1—Jn.8:12).

1. God is light, and in Him is no darkness at all (1 Jn.1:5).
2. Jesus Christ is the Light of the world—the very embodiment of the heavenly light (Jn.8:12; 9:5).
3. The light of the knowledge of God is seen in the face of Jesus Christ (2 Co.4:6).
4. Jesus Christ gives light to everyone who comes into the world (Jn.1:9).
5. Believers are said to become "children of light" through belief in the Light, Jesus Christ Himself (Jn.12:36).
6. Believers have been transferred from the dominion of darkness into the Kingdom of Christ, the inheritance of light (Col.1:13).
7. Before they come to Christ, believers are not only in darkness but are an embodiment of darkness. But when they come to Christ, believers are placed in the Light and become an embodiment of the Light itself (Ep.5:8).
8. Believers are the light of the world (Mt.5:14-16).
9. Believers are to set their light on a candlestick—to make their light conspicuous (Mt.5:15).
10. Evildoers shun the light (Jn.3:20f).
11. The creation of light is a picture of the expulsion of spiritual darkness (Ge.1:2f).

## C. Jesus Rejected and Accepted as King, 12:37–50

37 Though he had done so many signs before them, they still did not believe in him, 38 so that the word spoken by the prophet Isaiah might be fulfilled: "Lord, who has believed what he heard from us, and to whom has the arm of the Lord been revealed?" 39 Therefore they could not believe. For again Isaiah said, 40 "He has blinded their eyes and hardened their heart, lest they see with their eyes, and understand with their heart, and turn, and I would heal them."

41 Isaiah said these things because he saw his glory and spoke of him. 42 Nevertheless, many even of the authorities believed in him, but for fear of the Pharisees they did not confess it, so that they would not be put out of the synagogue; 43 for they loved the glory that comes from man more than the glory that comes from God. 44 And Jesus cried out and said, "Whoever believes in me, believes not in me but in him who sent me. 45 "And whoever sees me sees him who sent me. 46 "I have come into the world as light, so that whoever believes in me may not remain in darkness. 47 "If anyone hears my words and does not keep them, I do not judge him; for I did not come to judge the world but to save the world. 48 "The one who rejects me and does not receive my words has a judge; the word that I have spoken will judge him on the last day. 49 "For I have not spoken on my own authority, but the Father who sent me has himself given me a commandment—what to say and what to speak. 50 "And I know that his commandment is eternal life. What I say, therefore, I say as the Father has told me."

1. **The unbelievers**
   a. They acted illogically
      1) They rejected miraculous signs
      2) They rejected revelation, the prophecy of God's Word
      3) They rejected the powerful arm of the Lord
   b. The results of unbelief: A just rejection by God[DS1]
      1) Unbelievers are blinded
      2) Unbelievers have hard, dead hearts
      3) Unbelievers are condemned to be lost
      4) Unbelievers are condemned to remain unhealed
      5) Unbelievers never see the glory of the Lord

2. **The silent believers**
   a. They failed to confess Jesus
   b. They failed, fearing personal loss
   c. They failed, loving the praise of people more than the approval & praise of God

3. **The true believers**
   a. They believe in God—through Jesus the Mediator[DS2]
   b. They see God—through Jesus the Mediator
   c. They are delivered from darkness—through Jesus the Light

4. **The judgment upon unbelievers**
   a. They are not judged by Jesus: He came to save, not to judge
   b. They are judged for rejecting the words of salvation: The words will stand as a witness against them
      1) Because Jesus' words are God's commandment
      2) Because God's Word is eternal, leads to eternal life
      3) Because the words of Jesus are the truth

# Division XII

## The Revelation of Jesus, the Glorified Son of Man, 12:12-50

### C. Jesus Rejected and Accepted as King, 12:37-50

## 12:37-50
## Introduction

There are only two possible responses to Jesus Christ: to accept Him and believe, or to reject Him and not believe. There is no middle ground. Those who say they have not decided, *have* decided. They have not accepted Jesus; therefore, they have effectively rejected Him.

In this passage, some rejected Jesus as Savior and King, while some accepted Him. It is a clear picture of Jesus' being rejected or accepted today. This is, *Jesus Rejected and Accepted as King*, 12:37-50.

1. The unbelievers (vv.37-41).
2. The silent believers (vv.42-43).
3. The true believers (vv.44-46).
4. The judgment upon unbelievers (vv.47-50).

### 12:37-41

<sup>37</sup> Though he had done so many signs before them, they still did not believe in him,
<sup>38</sup> so that the word spoken by the prophet Isaiah might be fulfilled: "Lord, who has believed what he heard from us, and to whom has the arm of the Lord been revealed?"
<sup>39</sup> Therefore they could not believe. For again Isaiah said,
<sup>40</sup> "He has blinded their eyes and hardened their heart, lest they see with their eyes, and understand with their heart, and turn, and I would heal them."
<sup>41</sup> Isaiah said these things because he saw his glory and spoke of him.

### 1 The unbelievers.

In spite of all Jesus had said and done, most of the people refused to believe in Him. As John noted, their unbelief was a fulfillment of prophecy.

#### a. They acted illogically (vv.37-38).

Many unbelievers act illogically. Their unbelief makes no sense, for God has done all He can to help people believe, yet they reject Him and refuse to believe. This was the case with those who refused to believe in Jesus. They had witnessed Jesus perform miracles, amazing feats only God could do, but they would not accept these miracles as a sign that Jesus was the Messiah (v.37). Even though it is highly illogical, unbelief rejects miracles.

Note the words "so many signs." Jesus was deeply touched by people's sufferings. He reached out in moving and loving compassion. He helped and ministered to everyone He could possibly reach—an innumerable number. In fact, John said Christ performed so many works and miracles that, if they should all be written, the world itself could not contain the books (Jn.21:25).

Jesus worked . . .

- miracle after miracle
- compassion after compassion
- help after help
- sign after sign
- healing after healing

Jesus' miracles arose from the heart of God Himself. They were miracles of compassion and help. They were miracles arising from a sincere motive, a heart that had been touched by suffering humanity. They were pure miracles, strong miracles—miracles that God's power alone could do.

John carefully noted that Jesus performed these miracles *before them*. Jesus did not do His works out in a desert, that is, far off in a corner in some obscure place out of the sight of people. Jesus did His miracles in front of people, where people could easily see them and where the miracles would demonstrate His deity and help the people to believe.

Still, though they witnessed these miracles with their own eyes, *they did not believe in Him*. The Greek tense here indicates continuous action: their unbelief continued even while He was ministering and demonstrating such enormous compassion and power. Their hearts were shut, closed to the clear and undeniable evidence that Jesus is truly the Son of God. They were in a *state of unbelief*. Their unbelief was illogical, making no sense whatsoever.

> **And he did not do many mighty works there, because of their unbelief. (Mt.13:58)**
>
> **Jesus answered them, "I told you, and you do not believe. The works that I do in my Father's name bear witness about me." (Jn.10:25)**
>
> **"If I am not doing the works of my Father, then do not believe me; but if I do them, even though you do not believe me, believe the works, that you may know and understand that the Father is in me and I am in the Father." (Jn.10:37-38)**
>
> **"Believe me that I am in the Father and the Father is in me, or else believe on account of the works themselves." (Jn.14:11)**
>
> **"If I had not done among them the works that no one else did, they would not be guilty of sin, but now they have seen and hated both me and my Father." (Jn.15:24)**

In addition to rejecting Jesus' miracles, the obstinate people rejected the prophecy of God's Word (v.38a). Unbelief rejects revelation. Ironically, the people's rejection of Jesus is a fulfillment of prophecy (Is.53:1). Isaiah had proclaimed the report or the message of God, yet the people did not believe. They rejected and acted illogically. Their unbelief cut deeply and broke Isaiah's heart. Filled with compassion and hurt for the people, Isaiah cried out to God about the people's rejection of his message. The cry was the beginning of one of the greatest prophecies ever made about Jesus.

The *report* or *message* (Gk. akoe; *what he heard from us* [ESV]) was from God Himself, His message and revelation to the world. The *report* was both the words and deeds of Jesus. All that Jesus did through preaching and teaching revealed the truth; however, the *report* was more than words and deeds. Jesus Himself was the *report*, the revelation of God to the world. God gave humanity more than just words, more than just ink and paper, more than just the sounds of a voice. God gave people a Life to live out the words. He gave humanity a *Person* . . .

- not only to speak the truth, but to live the truth
- not only to speak the works, but to do the works
- not only to preach God's will, but to demonstrate God's will
- not only to teach people, but to show them how to live

The Person, of course, was God's own Son, Jesus Christ. Yet despite the fact that God sent His own Son into the world to proclaim His report or His revelation, people still do not believe. They reject Jesus Christ, denying the report. They act illogically, making no sense whatsoever.

> **"Truly, truly, I say to you, we speak of what we know, and bear witness to what we have seen, but you do not receive our testimony." (Jn.3:11)**
>
> **"It is the Spirit who gives life; the flesh is no help at all. The words that I have spoken to you are spirit and life. But there are some of you who do not believe." (For Jesus knew from the beginning who those were who did not believe, and who it was who would betray him.) (Jn.6:63-64)**
>
> **Again Jesus spoke to them, saying, "I am the light of the world. Whoever follows me will not walk in darkness, but will have the light of life." So the Pharisees said to him, "You are bearing witness about yourself; your testimony is not true." Jesus answered, "Even if I do bear witness about myself, my testimony is true, for I know where I came from and where I am going, but you do not know where I come from or where I am going. You judge according to the flesh; I judge no one. Yet even if I do judge, my judgment is true, for it is not I alone who judge, but I and the Father who sent me. In your Law it is written that the testimony of two people is true. I am the one who bears witness about myself, and the Father who sent me bears witness about me." They said to him therefore, "Where is your Father?" Jesus answered, "You know neither me nor my Father. If you knew me, you would know my Father also." (Jn.8:12-19)**

The unbelieving people also rejected the powerful arm of the Lord (v.38b). Unbelief rejects the power of God. This, too, is a fulfillment of the same prophecy (Is.53:1). The *arm of the Lord* means the strength of God, His power to save and to deliver and to give life. It can also refer to the Savior and Deliverer Himself. The *Arm* that saves and gives life is Jesus Christ. When it comes to God's strength to save and deliver . . .

- who knows it?
- who has experienced it?

- to whom has it been revealed?
- who has humbled himself so that God could reveal it?
- who has diligently sought enough so that God could reveal it?

Unbelief rejects the arm and salvation of the Lord. This too is illogical, making no sense whatsoever.

> "If you are the Christ, tell us." But he said to them, "If I tell you, you will not believe." (Lu.22:67)

> Whoever believes in the Son has eternal life; whoever does not obey the Son shall not see life, but the wrath of God remains on him. (Jn.3:36)

> Jesus said to them, "I am the bread of life; whoever comes to me shall not hunger, and whoever believes in me shall never thirst. But I said to you that you have seen me and yet do not believe." (Jn.6:35-36)

> "I told you that you would die in your sins, for unless you believe that I am he you will die in your sins." (Jn.8:24)

> "'For this people's heart has grown dull, and with their ears they can barely hear, and their eyes they have closed; lest they should see with their eyes and hear with their ears and understand with their heart and turn, and I would heal them.'" (Ac.28:27)

> Take care, brothers, lest there be in any of you an evil, unbelieving heart, leading you to fall away from the living God. (He.3:12)

**b. The results of unbelief: A just rejection by God (vv.39-41).**

Many people take their unbelief lightly, thinking they will have plenty of time or plenty of future opportunities to receive Christ. However, they are tragically deceived. Note four simple words that should strike terror in the heart of every unbeliever: *they could not believe* (v.39). These people had reached a point where they were so stiff-necked, so calloused, that they could not believe. Unbelief results in some serious consequences (see DEEPER STUDY # 1). Five of these consequences are specified in this passage:

➢ Unbelievers are blinded (v.40a).
➢ Unbelievers have hard, dead hearts (v.40b).
➢ Unbelievers are condemned to be lost (v.40c).
➢ Unbelievers are condemned to remain unhealed (v.40d).
➢ Unbelievers never see the glory of the Lord (v.41).

## DEEPER STUDY # 1

(12:39-41) **Unbelief—Judicial Judgment**: this passage says that God blinds and hardens people. A person cannot reject Jesus Christ and expect matters to stay as they are. No matter how mild a person's rejection is, the matter is serious to God. A person may reject Jesus in thought only, never saying a word or committing a public (visible) sin against Him. But no matter how mild the rejection, God still cannot overlook the rejection of His Son. He loves His Son too much, and His Son has done too much for the human race. His Son has taken the sin of all people upon Himself and borne their punishment. His Son died for all people. Jesus has done too much for God to bypass people's unbelief and rejection. When an individual has the chance to see and open their heart to Christ but chooses not to look and closes their heart, that person suffers the consequences.

Another way to say the same thing is this: when God has loved the world and done so much for humanity, people cannot deny God's Son and expect to suffer no consequences. The consequences and results of unbelief are clearly spelled out, and they are terrible consequences, an awful fate for a person to suffer (vv.40-41).

An important question: Does this mean that God causes the unbelief of a person and condemns that person to be lost before he or she is ever born? No! Scripture shouts in a thousand ways, "No!" People are not lost apart from their will or against their own will.

People are lost only because they choose to have nothing to do with God and to be lost. What Scripture teaches is that God has set certain laws in the universe, laws both within humans and within nature. These laws go into motion and take effect when a person acts. If an individual does something, certain things will happen. If a person does something else, then something else will happen. Scripture teaches that unbelief is governed by these laws.

- *The law of sowing and reaping*: If a person sows unbelief, they reap unbelief.

    **Do not be deceived: God is not mocked, for whatever one sows, that will he also reap. For the one who sows to his own flesh will from the flesh reap corruption, but the one who sows to the Spirit will from the Spirit reap eternal life. (Ga.6:7-8)**

- *The law of measure*: If a person measures unbelief, they are measured by unbelief. Whatever a person measures, they receive.

    **"For with the judgment you pronounce you will be judged, and with the measure you use it will be measured to you." (Mt.7:2)**

- *The law of seeking*: If a person seeks, they find. The harder they seek, the more they find.

    **"Ask, and it will be given to you; seek, and you will find; knock, and it will be opened to you." (Mt.7:7)**

- *The law of willful hardness and impenitence*: The more people harden themselves and refuse to repent, the harder and more impenitent they become. In fact, people can become so hardened that they never repent, never even think about repenting. Such people store up wrath against themselves.

    **But because of your hard and impenitent heart you are storing up wrath for yourself on the day of wrath when God's righteous judgment will be revealed. He will render to each one according to his works. (Ro.2:5-6)**

- *The law of being prepared for destruction*: The more people refuse to believe, the more they are prepared and conditioned for destruction. Note that individuals through their unbelief prepare and condition themselves.

    **What if God, desiring to show his wrath and to make known his power, has endured with much patience vessels of wrath prepared for destruction. (Ro.9:22)**

- *The law of God's patience*: It is not God's will for anybody to perish; He wants all people to repent and be saved. Therefore, God allows the world to continue, allowing more and more people to be saved. He endures with patience the unbelievers who harden themselves and store up wrath against themselves in order that some might be saved and given the privilege of knowing the riches of His grace (Ro.2:5; see Ro.9:22-23).

    **Knowing this first of all, that scoffers will come in the last days with scoffing, following their own sinful desires. They will say, "Where is the promise of his coming? For ever since the fathers fell asleep, all things are continuing as they were from the beginning of creation." . . . But do not overlook this one fact, beloved, that with the Lord one day is as a thousand years, and a thousand years as one day. The Lord is not slow to fulfill his promise as some count slowness, but is patient toward you, not wishing that any should perish, but that all should reach repentance. (2 Pe.3:3-4, 8-9)**

- *The law of God's supreme purpose*: God's supreme purpose is that His Son "be the firstborn among many brothers" (Ro.8:29). God wants Jesus to have many siblings—brothers and sisters who will be conformed to His image and count Him as the Elder Brother: as the first and most honored, as the One who is to be worshiped and served eternally.

    **And we know that for those who love God all things work together for good, for those who are called according to his purpose. For those whom he foreknew he also predestined to be conformed to the image of his Son, in order that he might be the firstborn among many brothers. (Ro.8:28-29)**

In order for Christ to gain more and more brothers and sisters who will honor Him, God is willing for unbelievers to continue on in their unbelief, ever hardening themselves under the just and judicial laws He has established. People are allowed to go on in their unbelief, condemning themselves under the just and judicial laws of the universe.

These laws are what people call *the law of conditioning*. People would simply say that the more a person does anything, the more he conditions himself to do that thing. The more he does it, the more it becomes a habit (smoking, eating, or anything else.) This is what the Bible is saying: if people harden their minds and hearts to the truth, they become conditioned more and more against the truth. Their openness and sensitivity to Jesus Christ dwindles more and more, and it can dwindle so much that it is gone forever. Therefore, the more people reject Christ, the more they decrease their sensitivity and chance of ever accepting Christ.

What Scripture teaches can be summarized under what might be called *the law of judicial blindness and rejection*. This simply means that the person who rejects God's Son chooses to be blind and to harden their hearts. Therefore, they are given over to a *just punishment*. They are justly blinded and hardened (conditioned) more and more. A person is led to a judicial blindness and rejection by God through . . .

- obstinate unbelief
- constant sin
- continued rejection

God's Word plainly says that there are conditioning laws within humanity and nature, and it is a fact that unbelievers have to live under these laws the same as believers. God cannot play favorites; He cannot snatch unbelievers out from under the just and judicial laws of the universe and force them to believe, taking away their wills. God has to allow all people to live under the same laws and to make the choices of life day by day. Believers have made the choice to follow God's Son. Unbelievers have made the choice not to follow God's Son. There can be no violation of their wills: unbelievers have to be allowed to go on in their unbelief, ever hardening themselves under the just laws of God's will established in the universe. As Jesus Christ clearly said, the words of judgment are already spoken: they are set up as God's law and will within the universe. It is the law and will of God that Jesus Christ proclaimed, and it will be His words that will judge every person in the end time (Jn.12:48).

In addition to the above laws, compare the following verses.

> Therefore God gave them up in the lusts of their hearts to impurity. . . . For this reason God gave them up to dishonorable passions. . . . And since they did not see fit to acknowledge God, God gave them up to a debased mind to do what ought not to be done. (Ro.1:24, 26, 28. See outline and notes—Ro.1:24-32.)

> Then the LORD said, "My Spirit shall not abide in man forever, for he is flesh: his days shall be 120 years." (Ge.6:3)

> "But my people did not listen to my voice; Israel would not submit to me. So I gave them over to their stubborn hearts, to follow their own counsels." (Ps.81:11-12)

> He who is often reproved, yet stiffens his neck, will suddenly be broken beyond healing. (Pr.29:1)

> "For I will not contend forever, nor will I always be angry; for the spirit would grow faint before me, and the breath of life that I made." (Is.57:16)

> Ephraim is joined to idols; leave him alone. (Ho.4:17)

(See note—Jn.6:44-46 for a discussion of God's part in *drawing* men to salvation.)

## 2 The silent believers.

Not all who encountered Jesus were unbelievers. Some believed in Him but remained silent about their faith. These were the chief rulers and leaders among the people, and they were many. They believed in Jesus, realizing that He was who He claimed to be—the true Messiah. But they had one serious flaw. They were silent; therefore, they failed in three critical areas.

> 42 Nevertheless, many even of the authorities believed in him, but for fear of the Pharisees they did not confess it, so that they would not be put out of the synagogue;
> 43 for they loved the glory that comes from man more than the glory that comes from God.

### a. They failed to confess Jesus (v.42a).

These timid believers failed to confess Christ. They *would not* confess Him.

> "So everyone who acknowledges me before men, I also will acknowledge before my Father who is in heaven, but whoever denies me before men, I also will deny before my Father who is in heaven." (Mt.10:32-33)

> For I am not ashamed of the gospel, for it is the power of God for salvation to everyone who believes, to the Jew first and also to the Greek. (Ro.1:16)

### b. They failed, fearing personal loss (v.42b).

These silent believers failed because they feared the consequences of believing in Christ. They feared they would be excommunicated, put out of the synagogue. They feared they would lose their . . .

- positions
- jobs
- security
- professions
- livelihood
- authority
- recognition
- esteem
- honor

> "For what will it profit a man if he gains the whole world and forfeits his soul? Or what shall a man give in return for his soul?" (Mt.16:26)

> Yet for fear of the Jews no one spoke openly of him. (Jn.7:13)

> Set your minds on things that are above, not on things that are on earth. (Col.3:2)

> If we endure, we will also reign with him; if we deny him, he also will deny us. (2 Ti.2:12)

> You adulterous people! Do you not know that friendship with the world is enmity with God? Therefore whoever wishes to be a friend of the world makes himself an enemy of God. (Js.4:4)

### c. They failed, loving the praise of people more than the approval and praise of God (v.43).

The silent believers failed because they loved the praise of other people more than the praise of God. They loved what people gave them because of their position:

- acceptance
- esteem
- favor
- recognition
- prestige
- commendation
- honor
- image
- glory

They would rather be accepted and approved by other people than by God.

> "How can you believe, when you receive glory from one another and do not seek the glory that comes from the only God?" (Jn.5:44)

> Their graves are their homes forever, their dwelling places to all generations, though they called lands by their own names. Man in his pomp will not remain; he is like the beasts that perish. This is the path of those who have foolish confidence; yet after them people approve of their boasts. Selah. (Ps.49:11-13)

> "I, I am he who comforts you; who are you that you are afraid of man who dies, of the son of man who is made like grass." (Is.51:12)

## 3 The true believers.

**12:44-46**

Jesus declared the distinctives of all who truly believe in Him. The emphasis of these verses is Jesus Christ, the Mediator (see Deeper Study # 2). It is easier to see the meaning of the verses by switching the clauses as the outline does.

⁴⁴ And Jesus cried out and said, "Whoever believes in me, believes not in me but in him who sent me.

⁴⁵ And whoever sees me sees him who sent me.

⁴⁶ I have come into the world as light, so that whoever believes in me may not remain in darkness."

a. **They believe in God—through Jesus the Mediator (v.44).**
People believe in God—truly believe in God—only when they believe in Jesus Christ. Christ is the Mediator, the bridge builder between God and mankind. If people wish to approach God, the only living and true God, they can do so only by believing in Christ first. When people claim to believe in God apart from Christ, they are believing in a god of imagination, a god of their own making (see Jn.14:6; 1 Ti.2:5).

Note also that when people believe in Christ, their faith is placed in God, the Sovereign Majesty who sent Christ to save the world.

> "Truly, truly, I say to you, whoever hears my word and believes him who sent me has eternal life. He does not come into judgment, but has passed from death to life." (Jn.5:24)

> Then they said to him, "What must we do, to be doing the works of God?" Jesus answered them, "This is the work of God, that you believe in him whom he has sent." (Jn.6:28-29)

> Jesus said to him, "I am the way, and the truth, and the life. No one comes to the Father except through me." (Jn.14:6)

> "For I have given them the words that you gave me, and they have received them and have come to know in truth that I came from you; and they have believed that you sent me." (Jn.17:8)

> "That they may all be one, just as you, Father, are in me, and I in you, that they also may be in us, so that the world may believe that you have sent me." (Jn.17:21)

> This is good, and it is pleasing in the sight of God our Savior, who desires all people to be saved and to come to the knowledge of the truth. For there is one God, and there is one mediator between God and men, the man Christ Jesus, who gave himself as a ransom for all, which is the testimony given at the proper time. (1 Ti.2:3-6)

b. **They see God—through Jesus the Mediator (v.45).**
A person sees God only through seeing Jesus Christ. Christ claimed that those who have seen Him have seen the Father (Jn.14:9). When a person looks at Christ, they see the very nature of God—the very acts and words of God Himself. Christ is the revelation of God who came to earth to reveal God (see Deeper Study # 1, 2, 3—Jn.14:6).

> "I and the Father are one." (Jn.10:30)

> "If I am not doing the works of my Father, then do not believe me; but if I do them, even though you do not believe me, believe the works, that you may know and understand that the Father is in me and I am in the Father." (Jn.10:37-38)

> "And whoever sees me sees him who sent me." (Jn.12:45)

> "If you had known me, you would have known my Father also. From now on you do know him and have seen him." Philip said to him, "Lord, show us the Father, and it is enough for us." Jesus said to him, "Have I been with you so long, and you still do not know me, Philip? Whoever has seen me has seen the Father. How can you say, 'Show us the Father'? Do you not believe that I am in the Father and the Father is in me? The words that I say to you I do not speak on my own authority, but the Father who dwells in me does his works." (Jn.14:7-10)

c. **They are delivered from darkness—through Jesus the Light (v.46).**
A person is delivered from darkness only through Jesus Christ, the Light. Christ is the Light of the world (see note—Jn.8:12). He came to be the Light of the world in order to bring light and salvation to people. His very purpose on earth was to save and to give light. Christ came as a light into the world so that we would not have to live in a state of darkness. People who believe in Christ are given light, the light to see and learn the truth of God themselves, of the world and of others, of the future and of eternity.

"But if your eye is bad, your whole body will be full of darkness. If then the light in you is darkness, how great is the darkness!" (Mt.6:23)

In him was life, and the life was the light of men. The light shines in the darkness, and the darkness has not overcome it. (Jn.1:4-5)

"And this is the judgment: the light has come into the world, and people loved the darkness rather than the light because their works were evil." (Jn.3:19)

Again Jesus spoke to them, saying, "I am the light of the world. Whoever follows me will not walk in darkness, but will have the light of life." (Jn.8:12)

The night is far gone; the day is at hand. So then let us cast off the works of darkness and put on the armor of light. (Ro.13:12)

If we say we have fellowship with him while we walk in darkness, we lie and do not practice the truth. (1 Jn.1:6)

## Deeper Study # 2

(12:44) **Jesus the Mediator**: represents God before people and people before God. In Latin, the word for mediator is *pontifex*. It means bridge builder (see note—Jn.19:23-24).

## 4 The judgment upon unbelievers.

12:47-50

All who will not believe in Jesus face judgment. They will be judged by their own response to Christ and the gospel.

**a. They are not judged by Jesus: He came to save, not to judge (v.47).**

Jesus declared that it was not He who would judge the people who rejected Him. He would stand as a witness against those who would not believe. He came to save the world not to judge it.

**b. They are judged for rejecting the words of salvation: The words will stand as a witness against them (v.48).**

Unbelievers are judged by the words of salvation. The very words that people reject will stand as a witness

⁴⁷ "If anyone hears my words and does not keep them, I do not judge him; for I did not come to judge the world but to save the world.
⁴⁸ "The one who rejects me and does not receive my words has a judge; the word that I have spoken will judge him on the last day.
⁴⁹ "For I have not spoken on my own authority, but the Father who sent me has himself given me a commandment—what to say and what to speak.
⁵⁰ "And I know that his commandment is eternal life. What I say, therefore, I say as the Father has told me."

against them. Unbelievers reject the words of salvation—the message of the gospel. Therefore, these words, this message, will be their judge. Note that unbelievers condemn themselves, for the words of salvation have now been brought to earth by Jesus Christ. The full message of salvation is now available. No one is keeping people away from the words; no person is hiding the words from them. All people have to do is accept them and carry them to others. If people reject the words of salvation, they condemn and judge themselves. Why? Because in the last days, when all people stand before God, the words of salvation will not be found in them. The words will be *outside* the unbelievers, standing there to judge them.

There are three reasons why the words of Christ will judge unbelievers:

➢ Because Jesus' words are God's commandment (v.49).

And this is his commandment, that we believe in the name of his Son Jesus Christ and love one another, just as he has commanded us. (1 Jn.3:23)

➢ Because God's Word is eternal, leads to life eternal (v.50a).

"It is the Spirit who gives life; the flesh is no help at all. The words that I have spoken to you are spirit and life." (Jn.6:63)

Simon Peter answered him, "Lord, to whom shall we go? You have the words of eternal life." (Jn.6:68)

"Truly, truly, I say to you, if anyone keeps my word, he will never see death." (Jn.8:51)

➢ Because the words of Jesus are the truth, the very words God told Him to say (v.50b).

For he whom God has sent utters the words of God, for he gives the Spirit without measure. (Jn.3:34)

"Whoever does not love me does not keep my words. And the word that you hear is not mine but the Father's who sent me." (Jn.14:24)

"For I have given them the words that you gave me, and they have received them and have come to know in truth that I came from you; and they have believed that you sent me." (Jn.17:8)

# Chapter 13

## XIII. The Revelation of Jesus, the Great Minister, and His Legacy, 13:1–16:33

### A. The Demonstration of Royal Service, 13:1–17

*Mt.26:20-24; Mk.14:14-17; Lu.22:14, 21-23*

---

Now before the Feast of the Passover, when Jesus knew that his hour had come to depart out of this world to the Father, having loved his own who were in the world, he loved them to the end.

² During supper, when the devil had already put it into the heart of Judas Iscariot, Simon's son, to betray him,

³ Jesus, knowing that the Father had given all things into his hands, and that he had come from God and was going back to God,

⁴ rose from supper. He laid aside his outer garments, and taking a towel, tied it around his waist.

⁵ Then he poured water into a basin and began to wash the disciples' feet and to wipe them with the towel that was wrapped around him.

⁶ He came to Simon Peter, who said to him, "Lord, do you wash my feet?"

⁷ Jesus answered him, "What I am doing you do not understand now, but afterward you will understand."

⁸ Peter said to him, "You shall never wash my feet." Jesus answered him, "If I do not wash you, you have no share with me."

⁹ Simon Peter said to him, "Lord, not my feet only but also my hands and my head!"

¹⁰ Jesus said to him, "The one who has bathed does not need to wash, except for his feet, but is completely clean. And you are clean, but not every one of you."

¹¹ For he knew who was to betray him; that was why he said, "Not all of you are clean."

---

1. The setting: In the upper room right before the Passover
2. The motivation for royal service
    a. Jesus' death: His time or hour had come
    b. Jesus' love for His followers
    c. Jesus' knowledge of the devil's work in Judas' heart

3. The extreme demonstration of royal service
    a. Jesus knew who He was & that His mission was to serve
    b. Jesus laid aside His outer clothing[DS1]

    c. Jesus washed the disciples' feet

4. The prerequisite for royal service: Being washed & cleansed
    a. Being washed was misunderstood
    b. Being washed has a deeper meaning: Spiritual cleansing

    c. Being washed was requested

    d. Being washed was thorough & permanent

    e. Being washed was not automatic nor did it come by associating with the cleansed

5. The meaning of royal service

   a. To serve Jesus as Teacher & Lord

   b. To serve other believers royally, sacrificially: Leading them to be washed & cleansed

6. The reasons for royal service
   a. Because of Jesus' example

   b. Because believers are not as great as the Lord

   c. Because of the result: Joy, satisfaction

¹² When he had washed their feet and put on his outer garments and resumed his place, he said to them, "Do you understand what I have done to you? ¹³ You call me Teacher and Lord, and you are right, for so I am. ¹⁴ If I then, your Lord and Teacher, have washed your feet, you also ought to wash one another's feet. ¹⁵ For I have given you an example, that you also should do just as I have done to you. ¹⁶ Truly, truly, I say to you, a servant is not greater than his master, nor is a messenger greater than the one who sent him. ¹⁷ "If you know these things, blessed are you if you do them."

# Division XIII

*The Revelation of Jesus, the Great Minister, and His Legacy, 13:1–16:33*

A. The Demonstration of Royal Service, 13:1-17

*Mt.26:20-24; Mk.14:14-17; Lu.22:14, 21-23*

## 13:1-17
## Introduction

The disciples had been arguing over who would hold the leading positions in the government they thought Jesus was about to set up (see Lu.22:24; Mk.10:35-45, esp. v.41). The discussion was heated. They were caught up in the ambition for position and power and authority. How the heart of Jesus must have been cut! He had so little time left for them to learn that the way to glory is through service and not through position and authority. How could He get the message across forcibly enough so that they would never forget the truth? It was this concern that led Jesus to wash the disciples' feet and to demonstrate what true royalty is: serving others. This is, *The Demonstration of Royal Service*, 13:1-7.

1. The setting: In the upper room right before the Passover (v.1).
2. The motivation for royal service (vv.1-2).
3. The extreme demonstration of royal service (vv.3-5).
4. The prerequisite for royal service: Being washed and cleansed (vv.6-11).
5. The meaning of royal service (vv.12-14).
6. The reasons for royal service (vv.15-17).

### 13:1

Now before the Feast of the Passover, when Jesus knew that his hour had come to depart out of this world to the Father, having loved his own who were in the world, he loved them to the end.

### 1 The setting: In the upper room right before the Passover.

This demonstration of royal service took place in the upper room where so many significant events occurred. It happened right before the Passover.

## 2 The motivation for royal service.

What would compel Jesus, the Son of God and Lord of all, to wash the disciples' feet and to demonstrate the royalty of service and ministry? Scripture reveals three motivations.

a. Jesus' death: His time or hour had come (v.1a).

Jesus knew "His hour" had come (see Deeper Study # 1—Jn.12:23-24). He was to die soon, and His time in earthly ministry was running out. Whatever He hoped to teach His disciples had to be taught now, for there would soon be no more time.

> Now before the Feast of the Passover, when Jesus knew that his hour had come to depart out of this world to the Father, having loved his own who were in the world, he loved them to the end. ² During supper, when the devil had already put it into the heart of Judas Iscariot, Simon's son, to betray him,

b. Jesus' love for His followers (v.1b).

Jesus loved His own, that is, His earthly followers, those for whom He was responsible. *His own* includes *both* the heavenly host and all believers who have gone on to heaven. He is Lord, the Son of the living God to whom all has been given; therefore, His own includes all those in both heaven and earth who are His followers. And He loves them all. Here, however, the emphasis is on His own who were *in the world*. Therefore, He was compelled to zero in on them and to do whatever was necessary to help them, no matter the cost. He was compelled by love to wash their feet, no matter the humiliation associated with doing so.

c. Jesus' knowledge of the devil's work in Judas' heart (v.2).

Jesus knew His enemy, and He knew the enemy was about to strike and betray Him. He had to act before the enemy struck. The disciples had to be strengthened and fortified, shown and taught immediately. Once the enemy struck, it would be too late.

**THOUGHT 1.** The same three motivations should *drive* every believer to serve and to serve now:

(1) Knowing the hour has come, the time is ever so short.

> **Jesus said to them, "My food is to do the will of him who sent me and to accomplish his work." (Jn.4:34)**

> **"We must work the works of him who sent me while it is day; night is coming, when no one can work." (Jn.9:4)**

> **Besides this you know the time, that the hour has come for you to wake from sleep. For salvation is nearer to us now than when we first believed. The night is far gone; the day is at hand. So then let us cast off the works of darkness and put on the armor of light. (Ro.13:11-12)**

> **Making the best use of the time, because the days are evil. (Ep.5:16)**

> **Walk in wisdom toward outsiders, making the best use of the time. (Col.4:5)**

(2) Loving "his own," those for whom the believer is responsible.

> **"As the Father has loved me, so have I loved you. Abide in my love." (Jn.15:9)**

> **"Greater love has no one than this, that someone lay down his life for his friends." (Jn.15:13)**

> **For the love of Christ controls us, because we have concluded this: that one has died for all, therefore all have died; and he died for all, that those who live might no longer live for themselves but for him who for their sake died and was raised. (2 Co.5:14-15)**

> **By this we know love, that he laid down his life for us, and we ought to lay down our lives for the brothers. (1 Jn.3:16)**

(3) Knowing the enemy, that he is going to strike immediately and with all the force he can.

> **"When anyone hears the word of the kingdom and does not understand it, the evil one comes and snatches away what has been sown in his heart. This is what was sown along the path." (Mt.13:19)**

> **Finally, be strong in the Lord and in the strength of his might. Put on the whole armor of God, that you may be able to stand against the schemes of the devil. (Ep.6:10-11)**

Submit yourselves therefore to God. Resist the devil, and he will flee from you. (Js.4:7)

Be sober-minded; be watchful. Your adversary the devil prowls around like a roaring lion, seeking someone to devour. Resist him, firm in your faith, knowing that the same kinds of suffering are being experienced by your brotherhood throughout the world. (1 Pe.5:8-9)

These same facts should drive us to be faithful in our service, laboring all the time, persisting and persevering.

Therefore, my beloved brothers, be steadfast, immovable, always abounding in the work of the Lord, knowing that in the Lord your labor is not in vain. (1 Co.15:58)

## 13:3-5

³ Jesus, knowing that the Father had given all things into his hands, and that he had come from God and was going back to God,
⁴ rose from supper. He laid aside his outer garments, and taking a towel, tied it around his waist.
⁵ Then he poured water into a basin and began to wash the disciples' feet and to wipe them with the towel that was wrapped around him.

### 3 The extreme demonstration of royal service.

Jesus went to the extreme to demonstrate what royal service essentially is. What makes this service *royal*? Why do we refer to it as such? The answer is, because it was being performed by Jesus Christ, the Son of God Himself. He and He alone is Lord of lords and King of kings.

**a. Jesus knew who He was and that His mission was to serve (v.3).**

As mentioned above, both the heavenly host and believers, whether on earth or in heaven, are Christ's. God has given all things into His hands, put all things under His authority. The emphasis of this point is, Jesus knew who He was. He knew His glorious Person, yet He humbled Himself to perform a task that was far beneath Him.

Note exactly what Scripture says in this verse. Jesus knew that the Father had given all things into His hands: all power and authority and glory and honor—all beings both in heaven and earth—all administration (ministry) and rule—all judgment and responsibility for saving the universe. Jesus knew that He had come from God. He knew the exalted position from which He had come and the great gulf He had spanned in coming to earth as a man. Furthermore, Jesus knew the splendor and brilliance and glory of His Person. And He knew that He was going to be returning to God to assume His former position of glory, honor, and rule. He knew that He was to take His place at the right hand of God very soon.

**b. Jesus laid aside His outer clothing (v.4).**

Yet, He who was King of kings and Lord of lords, who was God Himself, took off His outer clothing and laid it aside to serve His disciples. This selfless act is a picture of the greatest act of humility performed by our Savior: he took off His glory—set His deity aside—to become a man so that He could serve us by dying on the cross for our sin.

Have this mind among yourselves, which is yours in Christ Jesus, who, though he was in the form of God, did not count equality with God a thing to be grasped, but emptied himself, by taking the form of a servant, being born in the likeness of men. And being found in human form, he humbled himself by becoming obedient to the point of death, even death on a cross. (Ph.2:5-8)

**c. Jesus washed the disciples' feet (v.5).**

Jesus, the Son of God and God the Son, proceeded to wash the feet of lowly men. He who was . . .
- Master became the slave
- the Lord took on the ministry of humiliation
- the Highest took the place of the lowest
- the Sovereign became the subject

Jesus knew who He was, yet He still gave the most extreme demonstration of service possible. He chose the most extreme act possible—the lowliest task of the lowest servant in a household—to demonstrate that there is royalty in service and ministry (see DEEPER STUDY # 1).

"Even as the Son of Man came not to be served but to serve, and to give his life as a ransom for many." (Mt.20:28)

"But not so with you. Rather, let the greatest among you become as the youngest, and the leader as one who serves. For who is the greater, one who reclines at table or one who serves? Is it not the one who reclines at table? But I am among you as the one who serves." (Lu.22:26-27)

For by the grace given to me I say to everyone among you not to think of himself more highly than he ought to think, but to think with sober judgment, each according to the measure of faith that God has assigned. (Ro.12:3)

Do nothing from selfish ambition or conceit, but in humility count others more significant than yourselves. Let each of you look not only to his own interests, but also to the interests of others. (Ph.2:3-4)

Humble yourselves before the Lord, and he will exalt you. (Js.4:10)

Likewise, you who are younger, be subject to the elders. Clothe yourselves, all of you, with humility toward one another, for "God opposes the proud but gives grace to the humble." (1 Pe.5:5)

## DEEPER STUDY # 1

(13:4-5) **Service—Greatness:** in the hot, dusty region of Palestine, most people wore sandals, and their feet became extremely dirty. A water basin sat at the entrance of most Jewish homes. Upon entering a person's home, the poor would wash their own feet, and the rich would have a servant available to handle this demeaning task.

Jesus was assuming the place of a *servant* or of a *slave* (doulos) who had no rights whatsoever (see note—Ro.1:1). He was demonstrating...
- the way to royalty is service
- the way to greatness is ministry
- the way to power is humility
- the way to position is serving
- the way to rule is giving

Luke tells us that the disciples were arguing over who was to assume the leading positions in Jesus' government once He took over the kingdom (Lu.22:24; see Mk.10:35-45). The disciples were probably so caught up in their thirst for power and authority that they were beyond considering anything rationally. What Jesus did was demonstrate for them the way of true royalty, the walk of a true statesman. There is a royalty to service—a kingly air to ministry—a real dignity in humbling oneself to meet the needs of others. There is such a thing as royal service.

## 4 The prerequisite for royal service: Being washed and cleansed.

13:6-11

Understanding the scene that follows is critical for every person who claims to be a follower and a servant of the Lord. The crucial point is this statement:

> Peter said to him, "You shall never wash my feet." Jesus answered him, "If I do not wash you, you have no share [part] with me." (Jn.13:8)

Jesus' washing of the disciples' feet holds a deeper meaning, a spiritual meaning. We have to be washed and cleansed by Jesus before we can become a part of Him and before we can serve Him.

To say it another way, before we can ever serve Christ, we must be a part of Christ. However, before we can become a part of Christ, there is a *critical prerequisite*, an absolute essential: we must be washed and cleansed by Christ.

Note what happened:

6 He came to Simon Peter, who said to him, "Lord, do you wash my feet?"

7 Jesus answered him, "What I am doing you do not understand now, but afterward you will understand."

8 Peter said to him, "You shall never wash my feet." Jesus answered him, "If I do not wash you, you have no share with me."

9 Simon Peter said to him, "Lord, not my feet only but also my hands and my head!"

10 Jesus said to him, "The one who has bathed does not need to wash, except for his feet, but is completely clean. And you are clean, but not every one of you."

11 For he knew who was to betray him; that was why he said, "Not all of you are clean."

### a. Being washed was misunderstood (v.6).

Washing and cleansing are often misunderstood. Jesus approached Peter to wash Peter's feet, that is, to clean the dirt and pollution from the lowliest part of his body. Peter saw Jesus washing him and the others (a picture of mankind) and counted it too humiliating a thing for his Lord to do. Therefore, Peter drew his feet back in objection. Never would the Lord of the universe be allowed to do such a lowly thing.

However, Peter saw only the human and physical act of Jesus in serving him and the others (mankind). He did not understand the true meaning of what Jesus was doing.

**THOUGHT 1.** Most people misunderstand and object to the cleansing act of Jesus...
- to the humiliation and demeaning nature of "His hour" (the cross, v.1)
- to the cleansing blood of the Lamb, the Lord Himself

Most people misunderstand Christ's mission and service...
- that He came to wash and cleanse us from our sin and death, from condemnation and hell
- that He came to cleanse us in His blood that we might be acceptable to God eternally
- that He came to cleanse us that we might be qualified to serve God, both now and forever

### b. Being washed has a deeper meaning: Spiritual cleansing (vv.7–8).

Jesus' washing of His disciples' feet had a deeper meaning, a spiritual meaning: we must be washed in the blood of Christ before we can be a part of Him. Jesus' ultimate act of service was His laying down His life so we can be cleansed (see the earlier part of this point for explanation). Peter did not understand this at first, but he did after Jesus' death and resurrection (see 1 Pe.2:24; 3:18).

**THOUGHT 1.** Today there is no excuse for not understanding what Jesus was doing.

> For we ourselves were once foolish, disobedient, led astray, slaves to various passions and pleasures, passing our days in malice and envy, hated by others and hating one another. But when the goodness and loving kindness of God our Savior appeared, he saved us, not because of works done by us in righteousness, but according to his own mercy, by the washing of regeneration and renewal of the Holy Spirit. (Tit.3:3-5)

> How much more will the blood of Christ, who through the eternal Spirit offered himself without blemish to God, purify our conscience from dead works to serve the living God. (He.9:14)

> But if we walk in the light, as he is in the light, we have fellowship with one another, and the blood of Jesus his Son cleanses us from all sin. (1 Jn.1:7)

### c. Being washed was requested (v.9).

Although Peter still did not understand the full meaning of what Jesus was saying, Peter knew one thing: he wanted to have a share or part with Jesus. Without further reservation, he asked Christ to wash and cleanse him. Every individual should cry out as Peter did: "Lord, not my feet only, but also my hands and my head." Note that Peter cried for a complete cleansing. He craved to be washed all over, through and through.

**THOUGHT 1.** There is no such thing as holding back a part of our body or behavior for ourselves, to do as we please. There is no such thing as a partial cleansing. The tongue, the eyes, the hands—what we say, look at, touch—must all be washed and cleansed by Christ, or we have no part with Him.

> Who can discern his errors? Declare me innocent from hidden faults. (Ps.19:12)

> Wash me thoroughly from my iniquity, and cleanse me from my sin! (Ps.51:2)

> Purge me with hyssop, and I shall be clean; wash me, and I shall be whiter than snow. (Ps.51:7)

> Help us, O God of our salvation, for the glory of your name; deliver us, and atone for our sins, for your name's sake! (Ps.79:9)

d. **Being washed was thorough and permanent (v.10).**

When we are washed in the blood of Christ, it is thorough and permanent. Peter had just cried for a complete and thorough cleansing. Christ responded by revealing one of the most glorious truths in all of Scripture:

> **Jesus said to him, "The one who has bathed does not need to wash, except for his feet, but is completely clean. And you are clean, but not every one of you." (Jn.13:10)**

Once we are washed, we are already cleansed. Peter had already been cleansed; therefore, he did not need another bath (experience of being saved and cleansed). But note what was needed: his feet needed to be cleansed. As he walked through the dirt of the world, he needed to ask Jesus to cleanse him from the pollution which he had picked up. He needed a localized cleansing, a cleansing of the body parts that had become dirty.

This is a clear picture of confessing our sins. When we get dirty—when we sin—we do not need another bath. That is, we do not need to be saved all over again. We need to confess our sins, agreeing with God about them and then turning from them and asking His forgiveness. As we confess our sins, the blood of Christ cleanses us from those sins (1 Jn.1:7-9).

> **Since we have these promises, beloved, let us cleanse ourselves from every defilement of body and spirit, bringing holiness to completion in the fear of God. (2 Co.7:1)**
>
> **Therefore, if anyone cleanses himself from what is dishonorable, he will be a vessel for honorable use, set apart as holy, useful to the master of the house, ready for every good work. So flee youthful passions and pursue righteousness, faith, love, and peace, along with those who call on the Lord from a pure heart. (2 Ti.2:21-22)**
>
> **If we confess our sins, he is faithful and just to forgive us our sins and to cleanse us from all unrighteousness. (1 Jn.1:9)**
>
> **Beloved, we are God's children now, and what we will be has not yet appeared; but we know that when he appears we shall be like him, because we shall see him as he is. And everyone who thus hopes in him purifies himself as he is pure. (1 Jn.3:2-3)**

e. **Being washed was not automatic, nor did it come by associating with the cleansed (v.11).**

Washing and cleansing are not automatic, nor do they come by association. This is clearly seen in Judas. Judas had been with Jesus, working by His side day in and day out. He was a professed follower and servant of the Lord, and, so far as could be seen, had no glaring public sin or corrupt habits. Yet, he never allowed Jesus to wash and cleanse him.

> **"And now why do you wait? Rise and be baptized and wash away your sins, calling on his name." (Ac.22:16)**
>
> **Your boasting is not good. Do you not know that a little leaven leavens the whole lump? Cleanse out the old leaven that you may be a new lump, as you really are unleavened. For Christ, our Passover lamb, has been sacrificed. (1 Co.5:6-7)**
>
> **And such were some of you. But you were washed, you were sanctified, you were justified in the name of the Lord Jesus Christ and by the Spirit of our God. (1 Co.6:11; see vv.9-10)**
>
> **Draw near to God, and he will draw near to you. Cleanse your hands, you sinners, and purify your hearts, you double-minded. (Js.4:8)**
>
> **"Wash yourselves; make yourselves clean; remove the evil of your deeds from before my eyes; cease to do evil." (Is.1:16)**
>
> **O Jerusalem, wash your heart from evil, that you may be saved. How long shall your wicked thoughts lodge within you? (Je.4:14)**

## 5 The meaning of royal service.

Jesus asked His disciples pointedly if they understood the meaning of what He had done (v.12). He wanted to be sure they grasped the full meaning of royal service. When we truly understand the meaning of Jesus' beautiful act, we will humbly serve Him and others.

¹² When he had washed their feet and put on his outer garments and resumed his place, he said to them, "Do you understand what I have done to you?
¹³ "You call me Teacher and Lord, and you are right, for so I am.
¹⁴ "If I then, your Lord and Teacher, have washed your feet, you also ought to wash one another's feet."

a. **To serve Jesus as Teacher and Lord (v.13).**
Royal service is *serving Jesus as Teacher and Lord*. Note Jesus' claim: *"I Am your Teacher and Lord."* The servants of the Lord Jesus are not just followers of Jesus. They are *servants*, *slaves* (Gk. doulos) with no rights of their own whatsoever. They are at the beck and call of Jesus. They do not act on their own, nor as they please. They do not seek the things of the world: its positions, wealth, power, recognition, honor. They do not exist to *secure* these things; they exist to serve Jesus and to serve Him alone (see note, *Slave*—Ro.1:1).

> "If anyone serves me, he must follow me; and where I am, there will my servant be also. If anyone serves me, the Father will honor him." (Jn.12:26)

> "Let all the house of Israel therefore know for certain that God has made him both Lord and Christ, this Jesus whom you crucified." (Ac.2:36)

> For to this end Christ died and lived again, that he might be Lord both of the dead and of the living. (Ro.14:9)

> Not by the way of eye-service, as people-pleasers, but as bondservants of Christ, doing the will of God from the heart, rendering service with a good will as to the Lord and not to man. (Ep.6:6-7)

> And he is the head of the body, the church. He is the beginning, the firstborn from the dead, that in everything he might be preeminent. (Col.1:18)

> Whatever you do, work heartily, as for the Lord and not for men, knowing that from the Lord you will receive the inheritance as your reward. You are serving the Lord Christ. (Col.3:23-24)

b. **To serve others royally, sacrificially: Leading them to be washed and cleansed (v.14).**
As Jesus' served others royally and sacrificially, we are to do likewise, leading people to walk in open confession and to be washed and cleansed from the dirt of the world.

➤ The servant of Jesus is to serve others just as Jesus did by ministering to the human needs of others in all humility.

> "And whoever gives one of these little ones even a cup of cold water because he is a disciple, truly, I say to you, he will by no means lose his reward." (Mt.10:42)

> "But it shall not be so among you. But whoever would be great among you must be your servant, and whoever would be first among you must be slave of all." (Mk.10:43-44)

> "Which of these three, do you think, proved to be a neighbor to the man who fell among the robbers?" He said, "The one who showed him mercy." And Jesus said to him, "You go, and do likewise." (Lu.10:36-37)

> For you were called to freedom, brothers. Only do not use your freedom as an opportunity for the flesh, but through love serve one another. (Ga.5:13)

> So then, as we have opportunity, let us do good to everyone, and especially to those who are of the household of faith. (Ga.6:10)

➤ The servant of Jesus is to minister to the spiritual needs of others by leading them to Christ for washing and cleansing from the dirt of the world.

> "Even as the Son of Man came not to be served but to serve, and to give his life as a ransom for many." (Mt.20:28)

> Jesus said to them again, "Peace be with you. As the Father has sent me, even so I am sending you." (Jn.20:21)

> He said to him a second time, "Simon, son of John, do you love me?" He said to him, "Yes, Lord; you know that I love you." He said to him, "Tend my sheep." (Jn.21:16)

> "Come now, let us reason together, says the Lord: though your sins are like scarlet, they shall be as white as snow; though they are red like crimson, they shall become like wool." (Is.1:18)

## 6 The reasons for royal service.

Why should we put on the apron and pick up the towel of royal service (vv.4-5)? Jesus taught us three reasons:

### a. Because of Jesus' example (v.15).

First, we are to serve because of Jesus' example. It would be easy to wash Jesus' feet, but to wash others' feet is where the difficulty lies. When we encounter somebody whom we do not want to serve, whose feet we are unwilling to wash, we need to remember Jesus' example: our Lord washed even Judas' feet, knowing that he was going to betray Him.

> 15 "For I have given you an example, that you also should do just as I have done to you.
>
> 16 "Truly, truly, I say to you, a servant is not greater than his master, nor is a messenger greater than the one who sent him.
>
> 17 "If you know these things, blessed are you if you do them."

> Then Jesus told his disciples, "If anyone would come after me, let him deny himself and take up his cross and follow me." (Mt.16:24)
>
> May the God of endurance and encouragement grant you to live in such harmony with one another, in accord with Christ Jesus. (Ro.15:5)
>
> Therefore be imitators of God, as beloved children. And walk in love, as Christ loved us and gave himself up for us, a fragrant offering and sacrifice to God. (Ep.5:1-2)
>
> Have this mind among yourselves, which is yours in Christ Jesus. (Ph.2:5)
>
> Put on then, as God's chosen ones, holy and beloved, compassionate hearts, kindness, humility, meekness, and patience, bearing with one another and, if one has a complaint against another, forgiving each other; as the Lord has forgiven you, so you also must forgive. (Col.3:12-13)

### b. Because believers are not as great as the Lord (v.16).

Second, we are to serve because, as believers, we are not as great as the Lord. We are less than Jesus Christ in person and position, as well as in mission and work. To say it in this way is a gross understatement; there are no words to truly convey how superior Christ is to us. If He was a servant, then we ought to be servants.

(The same saying is found in Mt.10:24; Lu.6:40; Jn.15:20. See also Lu.22:26-27 for a picture of this truth.)

### c. Because of the result: Joy, satisfaction (v.17).

Finally, we ought to serve because of the resulting joy. The Greek tense is continuous; literally, it is, "Blessed are you if you *keep on doing* them [these things, serving]." Jesus emphasized that just knowing this truth is not enough. We must do the truth and keep on doing the truth. When we do, we are filled with indescribable joy, a joy that can be obtained no other way but through humble service (see Jn.15:11).

> "Take my yoke upon you, and learn from me, for I am gentle and lowly in heart, and you will find rest for your souls." (Mt.11:29)
>
> "But now I am coming to you, and these things I speak in the world, that they may have my joy fulfilled in themselves." (Jn.17:13)
>
> For the kingdom of God is not a matter of eating and drinking but of righteousness and peace and joy in the Holy Spirit. (Ro.14:17)
>
> Though you have not seen him, you love him. Though you do not now see him, you believe in him and rejoice with joy that is inexpressible and filled with glory. (1 Pe.1:8)
>
> I will greatly rejoice in the LORD; my soul shall exult in my God, for he has clothed me with the garments of salvation; he has covered me with the robe of righteousness, as a bridegroom decks himself like a priest with a beautiful headdress, and as a bride adorns herself with her jewels. (Is.61:10)
>
> Your words were found, and I ate them, and your words became to me a joy and the delight of my heart, for I am called by your name, O LORD, God of hosts. (Je.15:16)

## B. The Prediction of the Betrayer: A Picture of Apostasy, 13:18–30

1. **The heartbreak of betrayal**
   a. Judas was not chosen
   b. Judas was of the basest sort: Ate with Christ yet turned away
2. **The prediction of betrayal**
   a. To assure the disciples that Jesus is the Messiah
   b. To strengthen the dignity of the Lord's call
   c. To give assurance of God's indwelling presence
3. **The last chance given to the betrayer**
   a. The distress conveyed by Jesus
   b. The betrayer's presence exposed
   c. The disciples' perplexity, nervousness, & self-consciousness

   d. The gesture by Peter for John to inquire further
   e. The inquiry by John
   f. The indirect & merciful identification by Christ: The giving of a last chance

4. **The warning against betrayal**
   a. The evil, satanic possession of the betrayer
   b. The charge by Jesus: Act now
   c. The deceiving of the disciples by the betrayer

   d. The judgment: Seen in the betrayer's being immediately separated

¹⁸ "I am not speaking of all of you; I know whom I have chosen. But the Scripture will be fulfilled, 'He who ate my bread has lifted his heel against me.' ¹⁹ I am telling you this now, before it takes place, that when it does take place you may believe that I am he. ²⁰ Truly, truly, I say to you, whoever receives the one I send receives me, and whoever receives me receives the one who sent me."

²¹ After saying these things, Jesus was troubled in his spirit, and testified, "Truly, truly, I say to you, one of you will betray me." ²² The disciples looked at one another, uncertain of whom he spoke. ²³ One of his disciples, whom Jesus loved, was reclining at table at Jesus' side, ²⁴ so Simon Peter motioned to him to ask Jesus of whom he was speaking. ²⁵ So that disciple, leaning back against Jesus, said to him, "Lord, who is it?" ²⁶ Jesus answered, "It is he to whom I will give this morsel of bread when I have dipped it." So when he had dipped the morsel, he gave it to Judas, the son of Simon Iscariot. ²⁷ Then after he had taken the morsel, Satan entered into him. Jesus said to him, "What you are going to do, do quickly." ²⁸ Now no one at the table knew why he said this to him. ²⁹ Some thought that, because Judas had the moneybag, Jesus was telling him, "Buy what we need for the feast," or that he should give something to the poor. ³⁰ So, after receiving the morsel of bread, he immediately went out. And it was night.

# Division XIII

*The Revelation of Jesus, the Great Minister, and His Legacy, 13:1-16:33*

B. The Prediction of the Betrayer: A Picture of Apostasy, 13:18-30

## 13:18-30
## Introduction

God's Word is clear: not everyone who claims to be a follower of Christ is a genuine believer (Mt.7:21-23). Some who claim to know Christ turn against Him and away from Him, proving that their faith was never genuine (1 Ti.4:1; He.3:12; 1 Jn.2:18-19).

Judas is a clear picture of such a person, of a person who turns away from Christ to the world. His example stands as a strong warning to every one of us who *professes* to follow Christ. This is, *The Prediction of the Betrayer: A Picture of Apostasy*, 13:18-30.
1. The heartbreak of betrayal (v.18).
2. The prediction of betrayal (vv.19-20).
3. The last chance given to the betrayer (vv.21-26).
4. The warning against betrayal (vv.27-30).

## 1 The heartbreak of betrayal.

13:18

When Judas betrayed the Lord, the Lord's heart was cut to the core. The Lord feels the same grief when any other person betrays Him, for a soul is being lost. Two facts in particular cut deeply.

<sup>18</sup> "I am not speaking of all of you; I know whom I have chosen. But the Scripture will be fulfilled, 'He who ate my bread has lifted his heel against me.'"

### a. Judas was not chosen (v.18a).

Betrayers are not chosen by Christ. They cannot be, for they have rejected Christ; therefore, Christ has to reject them (Mt.10:32-33). Christ did draw Judas; He did move upon Judas' heart to awaken his mind. He did stir Judas to understand that He, Jesus, *was* the Messiah, the very Son of God Himself. But Judas rebelled against the *drawing power* of Christ and rejected Christ's *life-giving power*.

When a person is so drawn and quickened by God's Spirit, he or she must respond then and there. God says that His Spirit will not always strive with people (Ge.6:3). At some point in their lives, most people experience a tugging and pulling within to decide for God. However, when the tugging and the drawing power are rejected, that tugging feeling within soon leaves; and the person ceases to think much about the matter.

> Then the LORD said, "My Spirit shall not abide in man forever, for he is flesh: his days shall be 120 years." (Ge.6:3)

> He who is often reproved, yet stiffens his neck, will suddenly be broken beyond healing. (Pr.29:1)

When people who profess to know Christ betray Him and return to a life of sin, they show that they did not truly respond to *the movement* of God's Spirit within their hearts. They expose their true unregenerate nature: they are not genuine believers. This breaks the heart of Christ, for He wants every individual to pay attention to the call of the Spirit, to respond to His offer of eternal salvation. He wants everyone to become a true follower of His. He wants no one to be lost.

> "For many are called, but few are chosen." (Mt.22:14. See notes—Jn.6:44-46; DEEPER STUDY # 1—12:39-41 for more discussion.)

> The Lord is not slow to fulfill his promise as some count slowness, but is patient toward you, not wishing that any should perish, but that all should reach repentance. (2 Pe.3:9)

b. **Judas was of the basest sort: Ate with Christ yet turned away (v.18b).**

Betrayers are of the basest sort; that is, they are totally corrupt. They eat with Christ (proclaim Him and identify with Him), yet they turn against Christ. Judas literally ate bread with Jesus. Judas was a friend of Jesus, not an enemy. He did not hate Jesus; he seemed to care for Him. He often walked into the house of God with Jesus and had close fellowship with Him. Judas was Christ's follower, a disciple, yet Judas lifted up his heel against Jesus. John noted that this act was a fulfillment of prophecy (see DEEPER STUDY # 1). The very wording of the prophecy shows the heartrending tragedy of the situation. *Lifted his heel* pictures a horse lifting up his hoof to kick. Judas *kicked* Jesus. He struck Him with the fatal blow . . .

- of disloyalty: he forsook Christ.
- of contempt: he rejected Christ.
- of betrayal: he spurned the love of Christ, turning his back upon Him.

The whole scene is one of deplorable and heartbreaking tragedy. One who professed Christ was not a true follower of Christ. He was in fact a betrayer, an enemy, a person who chose and stood for the things of the world (money, recognition, power; see note—Jn.12:4-8.)

> For you may be sure of this, that everyone who is sexually immoral or impure, or who is covetous (that is, an idolater), has no inheritance in the kingdom of Christ and God. Let no one deceive you with empty words, for because of these things the wrath of God comes upon the sons of disobedience. (Ep.5:5-6)

> For since the message declared by angels proved to be reliable, and every transgression or disobedience received a just retribution, how shall we escape if we neglect such a great salvation? It was declared at first by the Lord, and it was attested to us by those who heard. (He.2:2-3)

## DEEPER STUDY # 1

(13:18) **Prophetic Reference:** see Ps.41:9.

### 13:19-20

¹⁹ "I am telling you this now, before it takes place, that when it does take place you may believe that I am he.
²⁰ Truly, truly, I say to you, whoever receives the one I send receives me, and whoever receives me receives the one who sent me."

## 2 The prediction of betrayal.

Jesus predicted that one of His own followers would betray Him. He knew He would be betrayed, and He knew who would betray Him. Christ predicted His betrayal to strengthen and assure the disciples.

a. **To assure the disciples that Jesus is the Messiah (v.19).**

Christ wanted His disciples to be strong in their belief in Him as the Messiah. Once the prophecy came to pass, they would know He was omniscient (that He knew all things). And only God knows all things. Therefore, they would know that He was exactly who He claimed to be, the Son of God, the One who has the very nature of God Himself. Their faith in Him would be strongly strengthened.

b. **To strengthen the dignity of the Lord's call (v.20a).**

Christ wanted His disciples to be assured of the dignity of their call as servants of God. Judas had betrayed that call, and his betrayal had left a bad image in people's minds and reflected a poor image of the ministry. It could affect some people, causing them to question the power of Christ, even causing others to actually withdraw and turn away from the ministry. The betrayal could also cause true disciples to become discouraged, feeling that God's call and ministry did not have the dignity Christ claimed.

> We ask you, brothers, to respect those who labor among you and are over you in the Lord and admonish you, and to esteem them very highly in love because of their work. Be at peace among yourselves. (1 Th.5:12-13)

> Let the elders who rule well be considered worthy of double honor, especially those who labor in preaching and teaching. (1 Ti.5:17)

> Remember your leaders, those who spoke to you the word of God. Consider the outcome of their way of life, and imitate their faith. (He.13:7)

Christ was clear. A person may be dirty and unclean; he may even be a betrayer, but the call and ministry are not touched. The office of His servant and follower cannot be affected. Nothing can affect the relationship between Christ and His true disciple, nor the relationship between the Father and His disciple. People will still continue to be saved. Nothing can change this. People out in the world . . .

- who receive the Lord's messenger receive the Lord
- who receive the Lord receive God

> For "everyone who calls on the name of the Lord will be saved." (Ro.10:13)

> "'Behold, I stand at the door and knock. If anyone hears my voice and opens the door, I will come in to him and eat with him, and he with me.'" (Re.3:20)

c. **To give assurance of God's indwelling presence (v.20b).**

Christ wanted His disciples to be assured of God's indwelling presence. Note that Christ put Himself on the same level as God. To receive Christ is to receive God, and to receive Christ's indwelling presence is to have God's indwelling presence. What a glorious promise to the believer! Our bodies are the temple of God (cp. 1 Co.6:19-20; see DEEPER STUDY # 4—Jn.20:22; 2 Co.4:7 for more discussion).

> "That they may all be one, just as you, Father, are in me, and I in you, that they also may be in us, so that the world may believe that you have sent me." (Jn.17:21; cp. Jn.10:37-38; 14:10)

> "I in them and you in me, that they may become perfectly one, so that the world may know that you sent me and loved them even as you loved me." (Jn.17:23)

> Or do you not know that your body is a temple of the Holy Spirit within you, whom you have from God? You are not your own, for you were bought with a price. So glorify God in your body. (1 Co.6:19-20)

**THOUGHT 1.** God knows every person's heart. Even a person's inner thoughts are known to God, as well as what a person does. No one can hide what they do from God, not even a thought. God knows if a person is betraying His Son. He even knows if a person is thinking about sinning and turning his back on Jesus. The more a person thinks about sinning, the more likely they are to turn back. Their betrayal can be predicted.

> "For nothing is hidden that will not be made manifest, nor is anything secret that will not be known and come to light." (Lu.8:17)

> "But there are some of you who do not believe." (For Jesus knew from the beginning who those were who did not believe, and who it was who would betray him.) (Jn.6:64)

> "For his eyes are on the ways of a man, and he sees all his steps." (Job 34:21)

> "For my eyes are on all their ways. They are not hidden from me, nor is their iniquity concealed from my eyes." (Je.16:17)

> And the Spirit of the LORD fell upon me, and he said to me, "Say, Thus says the LORD: So you think, O house of Israel. For I know the things that come into your mind." (Eze.11:5)

**THOUGHT 1.** The fulfillment of prophecy is strong evidence for both the deity of Christ and the inspiration of the Bible.

> "For truly, I say to you, until heaven and earth pass away, not an iota, not a dot, will pass from the Law until all is accomplished." (Mt.5:18)

> So Jesus said to them, "When you have lifted up the Son of Man, then you will know that I am he, and that I do nothing on my own authority, but speak just as the Father taught me. And he who sent me is with me. He has not left me alone, for I always do the things that are pleasing to him." (Jn.8:28-29)

> "For I am the LORD; I will speak the word that I will speak, and it will be performed. It will no longer be delayed, but in your days, O rebellious house, I will speak the word and perform it, declares the Lord GOD." (Eze.12:25)

## 3 The last chance given to the betrayer.

This scene is most descriptive. Jesus exposed Judas, but He did it quietly, and He did it to give Judas a last chance to turn from his evil.

> ²¹ After saying these things, Jesus was troubled in his spirit, and testified, "Truly, truly, I say to you, one of you will betray me."
> ²² The disciples looked at one another, uncertain of whom he spoke.
> ²³ One of his disciples, whom Jesus loved, was reclining at table at Jesus' side,
> ²⁴ so Simon Peter motioned to him to ask Jesus of whom he was speaking.
> ²⁵ So that disciple, leaning back against Jesus, said to him, "Lord, who is it?"
> ²⁶ Jesus answered, "It is he to whom I will give this morsel of bread when I have dipped it." So when he had dipped the morsel, he gave it to Judas, the son of Simon Iscariot.

a. **The distress conveyed by Jesus (v.21a).**

Jesus was *troubled in spirit*; distressed, moved, disturbed over the desertion of this false believer and servant—this betrayer who was turning back to the sin of the world. He began His statement with the solemn attention getter *truly, truly* or *most assuredly*. In addition, Scripture says He *testified*—gave a strong, solemn witness. All of these things speak of Jesus' distress at the extreme seriousness of betrayal.

b. **The betrayer's presence exposed (v.21b).**

Jesus made the shocking announcement that His betrayer would be one of His closest followers. His distress and grief were surely portrayed in His voice as He spoke these heart-breaking words.

c. **The disciples' perplexity, nervousness, and self-consciousness (v.22).**

The disciples were perplexed and became nervous and self-conscious over Jesus' exposure of a betrayer. The disciples had no idea; they were totally unaware of a deserter. They looked at one another wondering just who it might be. Note two important details regarding this scene:

- Judas was a counterfeit disciple, an exceptional deceiver. In public he was ideal: moral, decent, upright. No one ever suspected him—not at all. It was what Judas did in secret that doomed him, not what he did in public. He was a deserter, a man of the world behind the scenes.
- The tenderness of Jesus toward His betrayer is seen in the wording of His statement. He did not reveal the betrayer by name. Jesus was making Judas aware that He knew about his desertion, and He was hoping that the two-faced man would begin to fear and turn from his evil deed.

d. **The gesture by Peter for John to inquire further (vv.23–24).**

The disciples wanted to know who the traitor was. One of the disciples who was leaning next to Jesus, apparently John himself (out of humility he did not give his name), was beckoned by Peter to ask Jesus for the name of the betrayer.[1] Most likely, Peter prodded John to ask because, of all the disciples, John had the closest relationship with Jesus.

e. **The inquiry by John (v.25).**

John complied with Peter's urging. He asked Jesus bluntly, "Lord, who is it?"

f. **The indirect and merciful identification by Christ: The giving of a last chance (v.26).**

Jesus identified His betrayer, but with tenderness and an appeal: His love still reached out to Judas. Jesus did not name Judas as the traitor, not vocally. Judas still had a chance.

Apparently, Judas was sitting near Jesus' side. He was close enough that Jesus could reach him and hand the piece of bread to him. Jesus wanted Judas to consider the seriousness of what he was doing. He gave the piece of bread to Judas—a sign of special attention and affection. This act of affection may have actually turned suspicion away from Judas, for Jesus seemed to be saying "Judas means something special to me." This act also gave Judas a chance to repent.

---

1 Throughout John's Gospel, he refers to himself as the "disciple whom Jesus loved" (19:26; 20:2; 21:7, 20).

The disciples did not grasp what was happening. They did not understand what Jesus meant (vv.28-29). Remember, the disciples had no idea that Jesus was about to be murdered. The giving of the morsel of bread, because it was usually a sign of affection, also threw suspicion away from Judas.

The whole scene, in all its descriptive drama and tragedy, is a picture of strong appeal—the appeal of the Lord to a man who was about to sell his soul for the goods of the world. It is an example of a last chance being given to a betrayer.

**THOUGHT 1.** If people are living in sin, God will have them listening. He wants them to consider the seriousness of their sin. God will place them in a position where they have to consider the seriousness of what they are doing.

Note that this is the last chance Judas would ever have to repent. There would be no more opportunities. The Lord was appealing and doing all He could. The decision was the deserter's. He would either turn to Christ or to the world. There would be no more chances. Likewise, God gives all sinners an opportunity to repent. But when that opportunity has passed, it is then too late.

> "Repent therefore, and turn back, that your sins may be blotted out." (Ac.3:19)

> "Repent, therefore, of this wickedness of yours, and pray to the Lord that, if possible, the intent of your heart may be forgiven you." (Ac.8:22)

## 4 The warning against betrayal.

This whole scene is a warning to every person who claims to be a follower of Christ. We need to examine ourselves, to be sure that we have truly repented and been born again (2 Co.13:5). Remember, Judas was a disciple, a man who ate with Jesus and appeared to be a close friend of Jesus. But he was a false believer, a pretender.

27 Then after he had taken the morsel, Satan entered into him. Jesus said to him, "What you are going to do, do quickly."
28 Now no one at the table knew why he said this to him.
29 Some thought that, because Judas had the moneybag, Jesus was telling him, "Buy what we need for the feast," or that he should give something to the poor.
30 So, after receiving the morsel of bread, he immediately went out. And it was night.

### a. The evil, satanic possession of the betrayer (v.27a).

Evil possessed Judas, as Satan had entered him. This was a critical moment. Sitting there, Judas stiffened and refused to listen. He hardened his heart and made the decision . . .

- to give himself over to evil and to do the work of Satan
- to be filled with the thoughts of wrong and of Satan
- to act for sin and for Satan
- to be controlled by evil and controlled by Satan

Judas made the firm decision to do as he had planned. By doing so, he gave himself over to evil. He opened himself up to be possessed and used by Satan.

**THOUGHT 1.** The warning is clear. A genuine believer will not betray Jesus as Judas did. Genuine believers will not give themselves over to Satan and evil.

### b. The charge by Jesus: Act now (v.27b).

Jesus charged Judas to act quickly, to go ahead and do what he was planning to do. Once a person has made the decision to desert Jesus, Jesus wants the traitor and counterfeit disciple out from among His fellowship.

### c. The deceiving of the disciples by the betrayer (vv.28-29).

Judas had hidden his sin well. The other disciples had no idea what was happening. Judas had deceived them so successfully that they did not grasp the message Jesus had given them.

**THOUGHT 1.** Being able to hide and keep sin a secret...
- is not a cute trick
- is not a reason for feeling smarter or more capable than others
- is not a reason for feeling that one's ego is boosted

Hiding and keeping sin a secret is building one's life upon a false foundation that will result in a collapsed life. The very fact that true disciples are unaware of a person's sin is a warning to the sinner. They are building a life of deception and lies that will crumble every worthwhile relationship they have.

> "And everyone who hears these words of mine and does not do them will be like a foolish man who built his house on the sand. And the rain fell, and the floods came, and the winds blew and beat against that house, and it fell, and great was the fall of it." (Mt.7:26-27)

> "The one who rejects me and does not receive my words has a judge; the word that I have spoken will judge him on the last day." (Jn.12:48)

> For the wages of sin is death, but the free gift of God is eternal life in Christ Jesus our Lord. (Ro.6:23)

> How shall we escape if we neglect such a great salvation? It was declared at first by the Lord, and it was attested to us by those who heard. (He.2:3)

> "Behold, all souls are mine; the soul of the father as well as the soul of the son is mine: the soul who sins shall die." (Eze.18:4)

d. **The judgment: Seen in the betrayer's being immediately separated (v.30).**

Judas' judgment is clear and descriptive. Jesus had commanded Judas to leave the upper room and to go perform the evil act he was plotting (v.27). The betrayer was separated immediately from Jesus' followers. He went out into the night and into the darkness (see note—Jn.3:18-20; Deeper Study # 2—8:12).

**THOUGHT 1.** Judas' judgment is a picture of the judgment coming on all false believers. Jesus will separate the sheep from the goats, the true believers from the false believers. The true believers will be with Jesus in His kingdom, but the false believers will be cast out from His presence.

> "Not everyone who says to me, 'Lord, Lord,' will enter the kingdom of heaven, but the one who does the will of my Father who is in heaven. On that day many will say to me, 'Lord, Lord, did we not prophesy in your name, and cast out demons in your name, and do many mighty works in your name?' And then will I declare to them, 'I never knew you; depart from me, you workers of lawlessness.'" (Mt.7:21-23)

> "When the Son of Man comes in his glory, and all the angels with him, then he will sit on his glorious throne. Before him will be gathered all the nations, and he will separate people one from another as a shepherd separates the sheep from the goats. And he will place the sheep on his right, but the goats on the left. Then the King will say to those on his right, 'Come, you who are blessed by my Father, inherit the kingdom prepared for you from the foundation of the world.' ... Then he will say to those on his left, 'Depart from me, you cursed, into the eternal fire prepared for the devil and his angels.' And these will go away into eternal punishment, but the righteous into eternal life." (Mt.25:31-34, 41, 46)

## C. The Departure of Jesus from This World, 13:31–38

*Mt.26:30-35; Mk.14:26-31; Lu.22:31-34*

31 When he had gone out, Jesus said, "Now is the Son of Man glorified, and God is glorified in him.
32 If God is glorified in him, God will also glorify him in himself, and glorify him at once."
33 Little children, yet a little while I am with you. You will seek me, and just as I said to the Jews, so now I also say to you, 'Where I am going you cannot come.'
34 A new commandment I give to you, that you love one another: just as I have loved you, you also are to love one another.
35 By this all people will know that you are my disciples, if you have love for one another."
36 Simon Peter said to him, "Lord, where are you going?" Jesus answered him, "Where I am going you cannot follow me now, but you will follow afterward."
37 Peter said to him, "Lord, why can I not follow you now? I will lay down my life for you."
38 Jesus answered, "Will you lay down your life for me? Truly, truly, I say to you, the rooster will not crow till you have denied me three times."

1. **Jesus' death brought a threefold glory**
   a. The Son of Man's glory: The cross
   b. God's glory: Jesus' obedience
   c. Jesus' glory: The resurrection

2. **Jesus' death demanded a new commandment**
   a. The reason: His departure from the earth
   b. The new commandment: To love as Jesus loved

   c. The mark of a true disciple: Love

3. **Jesus' death revealed stumbling loyalty**
   a. Cause 1: Misunderstanding Jesus' death

   b. Cause 2: Carnal commitment

# Division XIII

*The Revelation of Jesus, the Great Minister, and His Legacy, 13:1-16:33*

C. The Departure of Jesus from This World, 13:31-38

*Mt.26:30-35; Mk.14:26-31; Lu.22:31-34*

## 13:31-38
## Introduction

We all realize that, if the Lord delays His coming, we are going to die. If we are wise, we make preparations for our death. Among other things, we draft wills, purchase life insurance, and make plans for our responsibilities. Many people go as far as to pre-arrange and pre-pay for their funerals. If we have a terminal illness or otherwise know death is near, we prepare our family and friends for our imminent departure from this life and this world.

In this conversation with His disciples (through Jn.16:33), Jesus was preparing His closest followers for His approaching death and departure from this world. This passage is the beginning of that conversation. This is, *The Departure of Jesus from This World*, 13:31-38.
1. Jesus' death brought a threefold glory (vv.31-32).
2. Jesus' death demanded a new commandment (vv.33-35).
3. Jesus' death revealed stumbling loyalty (vv.36-38).

## 13:31-32

³¹ When he had gone out, Jesus said, "Now is the Son of Man glorified, and God is glorified in him.
³² If God is glorified in him, God will also glorify him in himself, and glorify him at once."

### 1 Jesus' death brought a threefold glory.

After Judas fled from the upper room, Jesus made a strange statement about His death. He said that it was time for Him to be glorified and for God to be glorified in Him. He proceeded to explain how His death would bring a threefold glory.

a. The Son of Man's glory: The cross (v.31).

The Son of Man would be glorified through His death.

The glory of Jesus was the cross (see note—Jn.12:23-26 for more discussion). Why is the cross a symbol of glory rather than of shame, of triumph rather than of tragedy, of victory rather than of defeat?

First, on the cross, Jesus would secure an eternal righteousness for humanity. As Jesus approached the cross, He was now ready to take the final step as the Son of Man . . .
- as the One who was the Servant of all people
- as the One who was to secure perfect righteousness by dying as God willed
- as the One who was to pay the supreme price in obeying God (to die)
- as the One who was ready to die in obedience to God's will so that God could save the fallen human race

Jesus became the perfect and ideal man because He was perfectly obedient to God the Father, even in dying. As the ideal man, His righteousness and death could stand for every person's righteousness and death. We must simply believe the fact that Jesus' death covers us personally. There was glory in being the Son of Man: in being every person's ideal righteousness and death. The cross glorifies Jesus as the Son of Man (see notes, *Son of Man*—Jn.1:51; DEEPER STUDY # 1, 2—Ro.4:22; note—5:1 for more discussion).

> "And as Moses lifted up the serpent in the wilderness, so must the Son of Man be lifted up, that whoever believes in him may have eternal life." (Jn.3:14-15)

> For our sake he made him to be sin who knew no sin, so that in him we might become the righteousness of God. (2 Co.5:21)

Second, on the cross, Jesus would make the final sacrifice for humanity. He was ready to pay the supreme price to bring about the greatest cause in all history: the salvation of the human race. The cross attracts and stirs people to give themselves to Jesus and to honor and praise Him. It is in what Christ did on the cross that we find our salvation; therefore, the cross is the glory of Jesus.

Third, on the cross, Jesus would triumph over Satan by breaking Satan's power over death and over people's souls (see DEEPER STUDY # 1—Mt.8:28-34; DEEPER STUDY # 2—Jn.12:31 for more discussion).

➢ Jesus spoiled principalities and power, triumphing over them in the cross.

> And you, who were dead in your trespasses and the uncircumcision of your flesh, God made alive together with him, having forgiven us all our trespasses. (Col.2:13)

➢ Jesus destroyed the works of the devil.

> Whoever makes a practice of sinning is of the devil, for the devil has been sinning from the beginning. The reason the Son of God appeared was to destroy the works of the devil. (1 Jn.3:8)

➢ Jesus broke the power and fear of Satan over lives and death.

> Since therefore the children share in flesh and blood, he himself likewise partook of the same things, that through death he might destroy the one who has the power of death, that

is, the devil, and deliver all those who through fear of death were subject to lifelong slavery. (He.2:14-15)

There is glory in Christ's triumph and victory over Satan, especially over a being so powerful and influential as Satan. The cross is the glory of Christ.

> "Now is the judgment of this world; now will the ruler of this world be cast out. And I, when I am lifted up from the earth, will draw all people to myself." (Jn.12:31-32)

Fourth, Jesus demonstrated what perfect sacrifice and self-denial, courage and strength, love and compassion, really are when He died on the cross. There is great glory in every one of these qualities. The cross is the glory of Christ.

### b. God's glory: Jesus' obedience (v.32a).

God would be glorified through Jesus' death, for in His submitting to the cross, Jesus would display perfect obedience to the Father. God was glorified by the supreme obedience of Jesus dying on the cross (see note, pt.3—Jn.12:27-30 for discussion).

> "For this reason the Father loves me, because I lay down my life that I may take it up again. No one takes it from me, but I lay it down of my own accord. I have authority to lay it down, and I have authority to take it up again. This charge I have received from my Father." (Jn.10:17-18)

> And walk in love, as Christ loved us and gave himself up for us, a fragrant offering and sacrifice to God. (Ep.5:2)

> Although he was a son, he learned obedience through what he suffered. (He.5:8)

God's justice was perfectly satisfied on the cross. His honor was restored by the cross, for the evil done against Him was justly punished on the cross.

> Whom God put forward as a propitiation by his blood, to be received by faith. This was to show God's righteousness, because in his divine forbearance he had passed over former sins. (Ro.3:25)

> He himself bore our sins in his body on the tree, that we might die to sin and live to righteousness. By his wounds you have been healed. (1 Pe.2:24)

> He is the propitiation for our sins, and not for ours only but also for the sins of the whole world. (1 Jn.2:2)

In addition, God's love was perfectly demonstrated on the cross. He gave His *only* Son to pay the supreme price *for* us: to sacrifice His life *for* us. For these reasons, the cross glorifies God.

> But God shows his love for us in that while we were still sinners, Christ died for us. (Ro.5:8)

### c. Jesus' glory: The resurrection (v.32b).

Jesus said that God would glorify Him at once or immediately "in Himself." This glorification would come through Christ's resurrection, ascension, and exaltation (Ph.2:8-11).

What is meant by "in Himself"? There are two possible answers:

➤ Jesus was asking to be glorified in God Himself: with God's own Person, with His very special presence and power and glory. This, of course, was done when Christ was set upon the throne of God Himself (Re.3:21).

➤ Jesus was asking to be glorified *in His own Person*: to be infused with a manifestation of God's presence and power and glory. This was done in the resurrection, ascension, and exaltation of Christ.

> And Jesus answered them, "The hour has come for the Son of Man to be glorified. Truly, truly, I say to you, unless a grain of wheat falls into the earth and dies, it remains alone; but if it dies, it bears much fruit." (Jn.12:23-24)

> When Jesus had spoken these words, he lifted up his eyes to heaven, and said, "Father, the hour has come; glorify your Son that the Son may glorify you. . . . I glorified you on earth, having accomplished the work that you gave me to do. And now, Father, glorify me in your own presence with the glory that I had with you before the world existed." (Jn.17:1, 4-5)

## 2 Jesus' death demanded a new commandment.

The greatest act of love ever performed in the history of the world is the voluntary death of Jesus Christ on the cross. Such a sacrifice demanded a new commandment, a commandment that would be the distinguishing mark of Jesus' true followers.

**13:33–35**

³³ "Little children, yet a little while I am with you. You will seek me, and just as I said to the Jews, so now I also say to you, 'Where I am going you cannot come.'
³⁴ A new commandment I give to you, that you love one another: just as I have loved you, you also are to love one another.
³⁵ By this all people will know that you are my disciples, if you have love for one another."

### a. The reason: His departure from the earth (v.33).

Jesus said that He was departing, that He would be with the disciples for only a little while longer. This was *the reason* Jesus had to give His disciples a new commandment. He was leaving. There were three reasons the new commandment on love was needed by every generation of believers.

First, there are times when believers differ. There is always the danger of becoming critical, judgmental, fault-finding, and divisive. Remember, the disciples had just been arguing over who should receive the highest positions of authority in Jesus' new government (see note—Lu.22:24–30). They had been struggling against each other and were highly critical and judgmental of each other. They had been deeply divided. The need for a new commandment and a new supernatural love existed then, even as it does today.

Second, there are times when believers feel a keen need for Jesus' physical presence. Jesus knew this. That is the reason He said that the disciples would seek His presence. True believers have the Holy Spirit, and the Spirit is the all-sufficient Comforter and the abiding Presence of God Himself. But being human, believers need another human presence with them. They need a brother or a sister in Christ, a genuine believer who loves them with the supernatural love of Jesus Himself. Jesus knew this, so He commanded believers to love each other. Believers are to meet each others' needs for companionship and fellowship and for care and concern.

Third, there is the need for some supernatural force to hold the disciples together. Jesus' physical presence had been the cohesive force that had held the disciples together when He was on earth. But once He had gone, His followers would need something else to hold them together. They must stay and serve together in one spirit and purpose. But how? The new commandment is the answer.

### b. The new commandment: To love as Jesus loved (v.34).

The new commandment is to *love* (Gk. agapate) *as Christ loved*. We are to exhibit and practice the same kind of love that Christ displayed for us: a selfless, sacrificial love.

This is not merely a restatement of the old commandment to love your neighbor as yourself. It is not a human, neighborly love that is being commanded. This *new commandment* was given to *disciples only*. It is the spiritual love that is to exist between believers as brothers and sisters and as servants of God who minister together.

The love being commanded is the love of Jesus Himself, which is the love of God Himself—the love that can be shed abroad in our hearts only by the Holy Spirit (see Ro.5:5). It is not the normal emotional love among human neighbors which is being commanded by God but is a spiritual love that is brought about only by the Spirit of God.

The distinctiveness of this love is that it is the love of Jesus Himself that dwells in the believer's heart. Only the Spirit of God can put the love of Jesus within the heart of the believer. The Holy Spirit can create within the believer the love of Jesus Himself, the very same love which Jesus had while here on earth. The love of Jesus is . . .

- the love of *spiritual being*: the love that causes us to hunger after union with God and God's people
- the love of *spiritual life*: the love that shares the same life with all believers, both abundant and eternal life
- the love of *spiritual union*: the love that binds and ties believers together in life and purpose
- the love of *spiritual attachment or fellowship*: the love that shares needs and blessings and joys and sorrows and gifts together

The Holy Spirit can create within the believer a love that can melt and mold our heart to the hearts of other believers. But note: it is a commandment; therefore, it is conditional. The Holy Spirit *can* create such a love, but we *have to receive it*. When the love of Jesus dwells in the believer's heart, several things happen. We have a love that *causes* us . . .
- to bind our life to the lives of other believers
- to tie our life to the same purpose as other believers
- to surrender our will and to be of the same mind as other believers
- to understand and empathize with other believers
- to forgive other believers—always
- to sacrifice ourselves for other believers—always
- to seek the welfare of other believers before our own
- to deny self completely

c. **The mark of a true disciple: Love (v.35).**

The new commandment is the mark of a true disciple. The distinguishing mark of a true believer is not the normal *human* love of neighbors, not even the love of brothers and sisters or of husband and wife. It is the *spiritual* and *supernatural* love of Jesus Himself that dwells within the believer. By this love all people will know that a person is a *true* disciple of the Lord.

> "This is my commandment, that you love one another as I have loved you." (Jn.15:12)
>
> Having purified your souls by your obedience to the truth for a sincere brotherly love, love one another earnestly from a pure heart. (1 Pe.1:22)
>
> By this we know love, that he laid down his life for us, and we ought to lay down our lives for the brothers. (1 Jn.3:16)
>
> Beloved, let us love one another, for love is from God, and whoever loves has been born of God and knows God. Anyone who does not love does not know God, because God is love. (1 Jn.4:7-8)

## 3 Jesus' death revealed stumbling loyalty.

Jesus' death revealed stumbling and faltering loyalty. Note that Peter no attention to the new commandment Jesus had just given. His Lord had just said that He was going away and leaving them. It was this statement that had gripped Peter's heart. He had to know what Jesus was talking about: if Jesus were talking about some spiritual truth and using symbolic terms or if He were really going to be leaving them.

Now note how Jesus responded. He still used the same language: He was leaving, and they could not follow Him to where He was going, not now. But they would follow Him later.

³⁶ Simon Peter said to him, "Lord, where are you going?" Jesus answered him, "Where I am going you cannot follow me now, but you will follow afterward."

³⁷ Peter said to him, "Lord, why can I not follow you now? I will lay down my life for you."

³⁸ Jesus answered, "Will you lay down your life for me? Truly, truly, I say to you, the rooster will not crow till you have denied me three times."

Peter was delving into things he could not yet understand. Jesus was returning to heaven and going back to the Father from whom He had come. He could not say it any clearer than what He had said. The disciples could not and would not understand this fact until after the resurrection and ascension.

> **THOUGHT 1.** How often our curiosity is stirred by the hints of Scripture about future events, the details of which are kept secret—all because it is not yet time for us to fully understand. Just think! If all were revealed, how could we walk by faith and prove our faith? If we walked by sight (seeing and understanding all), there would be nothing to believe.
>
> > Jesus said to him, "Have you believed because you have seen me? Blessed are those who have not seen and yet have believed." (Jn.20:29)
> >
> > Now faith is the assurance of things hoped for, the conviction of things not seen. (He.11:1)

**THOUGHT 2.** Peter became distracted and paid no attention to the greatest commandment Jesus had ever given His followers (Jn.13:34-35). It was the future event of Jesus' return to heaven that stirred his curiosity. It distracted his attention from where it should have been.

Jesus used the occasion to reveal Peter's stumbling and faltering faith. Peter stumbled for two reasons.

a. **Cause 1: Misunderstanding Jesus' death (vv.36-37).**
Peter misunderstood Jesus' death. Jesus was going to die and arise from the dead and then return to the Father. He had drilled this fact into the disciples for some months now, using words as clear and simple as possible (see note—Mt.16:21-28). Yet, they refused to accept His prediction. They thought of God's kingdom in terms of a physical kingdom and government set upon this earth. They saw the Messiah ruling over all the nations of the earth with Israel as the central capital of the world. They thought in terms of earthly freedom, position, power, fame, wealth, possessions, comfort, pleasure, and satisfaction. They saw the *physical* and were blind to the *spiritual*. They did not see . . .
- God's concern with eternity and the need for the cross
- that sinful people had to be created spiritually: created anew with the very same nature as God in order to live with God
- that the cross was God's way for people to be saved: created anew, forgiven and made clean and acceptable before God (see 1 Pe.2:24; 3:18)

Very simply stated, it was the idea of Jesus hanging on the cross that was going to cause Peter to deny Jesus. Jesus had told Peter about the cross, but Peter had refused to believe it (see Mt.12:22; 18:1). The fact that human flesh was so depraved that God's Son would have to be crucified in order to save sinful people was just too much to grasp (see outline and DEEPER STUDY # 1—Lu.9:23; DEEPER STUDY # 2—Ro.6:3-5; notes—Ro.6:6-7; Ga.2:19-21; 5:24; pt.1, Ga.6:14-17; see also Ro.6:2; Col.3:3).

**THOUGHT 1.** How many make the same mistake about the cross? Misunderstanding the cross and Jesus as the exalted Lord (as opposed to His being just a great teacher) causes stumbling and faltering faith.

> For the word of the cross is folly to those who are perishing, but to us who are being saved it is the power of God. (1 Co.1:18)
>
> But we preach Christ crucified, a stumbling block to Jews and folly to Gentiles. (1 Co.1:23)
>
> And even if our gospel is veiled, it is veiled to those who are perishing. In their case the god of this world has blinded the minds of the unbelievers, to keep them from seeing the light of the gospel of the glory of Christ, who is the image of God. For what we proclaim is not ourselves, but Jesus Christ as Lord, with ourselves as your servants for Jesus' sake. (2 Co.4:3-5)

b. **Cause 2: Carnal commitment (vv.37b-38).**
Peter pledged to lay down his life for Christ, if it became necessary. However, Peter's commitment was a carnal, fleshly commitment. It was caused by not knowing himself—his own personal weaknesses or the weaknesses of his human flesh. Peter's self-image was strong. He saw himself as being above serious sin and failure. He asserted with all the confidence in the world that he would die for Jesus before denying Him.

Peter was a strong believer, one of the strongest. But he failed to understand self and the flesh. The one sin that a believer should not commit is to deny Jesus. To die for Jesus rather than to deny Him is the one thing a genuine believer would be expected to do. Peter believed strongly that he (his flesh) was above such a serious sin (see Ro.3:9f; 7:8, 14-18; Ga.5:19f).

In the end, however, Peter failed to live up to his commitment. In fact, Peter failed not once, but three times, and all three failures were on the same night with Jesus right off to his side (Lu.22:61). Why did he fail? Because his commitment was rooted in his flesh, in his own strength, rather than in the power of Christ.

If anyone imagines that he knows something, he does not yet know as he ought to know. (1 Co.8:2)
Therefore let anyone who thinks that he stands take heed lest he fall. (1 Co.10:12)
For if anyone thinks he is something, when he is nothing, he deceives himself. (Ga.6:3)
Do you see a man who is wise in his own eyes? There is more hope for a fool than for him. (Pr.26:12)
Whoever trusts in his own mind is a fool, but he who walks in wisdom will be delivered. (Pr.28:26)

# Chapter 14

### D. Jesus' Death Delivers Troubled Hearts, 14:1-3

1. Delivers through trust in God & in Christ
2. Delivers through Christ's promise of a future home with God, in heaven's many mansions
3. Delivers through Christ's preparation on our behalf
4. Delivers through Christ's assurance of His return[DS1]
5. Delivers through the great hope of living with Christ eternally

"Let not your hearts be troubled. Believe in God; believe also in me.

² In my Father's house are many rooms. If it were not so, would I have told you that I go to prepare a place for you?

³ And if I go and prepare a place for you, I will come again and will take you to myself, that where I am you may be also."

## Division XIII

*The Revelation of Jesus, the Great Minister, and His Legacy, 13:1-16:33*

D. Jesus' Death Delivers Troubled Hearts, 14:1-3

## 14:1-3 Introduction

As Calvary drew near, Jesus' disciples had a number of reasons to be troubled. Several things had just happened that would disturb any group of people:

- ➤ *Divisiveness* had set in among them (see note—Lu.22:24-30).
- ➤ *Desertion and betrayal* by one of them was now known (Jn.13:18f).
- ➤ *Separation from the Lord* had been the topic of discussion (Jn.13:33).
- ➤ *Denying Jesus* had just been talked about (Jn.13:38).

The scene in the upper room needs to be clearly viewed, even felt in order to grasp the impact of what Jesus was about to say. The disciples were greatly *troubled* (tarassestho): disturbed, agitated, perplexed, worried, tossed about, confused, distressed. In the midst of their turmoil, they needed to be settled down and given some sense of peace. They needed encouragement and hope.

At times, we are just like the troubled disciples. How often we are afflicted with trouble and need the same words of encouragement and hope—the same deliverance from a troubled heart that they needed. This deliverance is available to us through what our Lord accomplished on the cross. This is, *Jesus' Death Delivers Troubled Hearts*, 14:1-3.

1. Delivers through trust in God and in Christ (v.1).
2. Delivers through Christ's promise of a future home with God, in heaven's many mansions (v.2).
3. Delivers through Christ's preparation in our behalf (v.2).
4. Delivers through Christ's assurance of His return (v.3).
5. Delivers through the great hope of living with Christ eternally (v.3).

(14:1-3) **Another Outline**: Jesus' Death Delivers Troubled Hearts.
1. His commandment: believe in me (v.1).
2. His assurance: God has a house (v.2).
3. His departure: to prepare (v.2).

4. His great promise: to return (v.3).
5. His great purpose: an eternal reunion (v.3).

## 1 Delivers through trust in God and in Christ.

Deliverance from troubled hearts comes through belief in Jesus Christ as well as in God. Jesus exhorted us to believe in Him as strongly as we believe in God the Father. He is the revelation of God, the Son of God Himself. We can trust Him the same as we can trust the Father. Believing in Him, that He is the Son of God, will deliver us from trouble (see notes—Jn.14:6; 14:27 for discussion).

"Let not your hearts be troubled. Believe in God; believe also in me."

In the Greek text, *believe* (pisteuete) is a verb that expresses continuous action. Continuing to believe even while you are in the midst of trouble will carry you through (see DEEPER STUDY # 2—Jn.2:24 for discussion).

> Then they said to him, "What must we do, to be doing the works of God?" Jesus answered them, "This is the work of God, that you believe in him whom he has sent." (Jn.6:28-29)

> Jesus said to her, "I am the resurrection and the life. Whoever believes in me, though he die, yet shall he live." (Jn.11:25)

> But these are written so that you may believe that Jesus is the Christ, the Son of God, and that by believing you may have life in his name. (Jn.20:31)

> And this is his commandment, that we believe in the name of his Son Jesus Christ and love one another, just as he has commanded us. (1 Jn.3:23)

## 2 Delivers through Christ's promise of a future home with God, in heaven's many mansions.

Deliverance from a troubled heart comes through the hope of heaven. Believing what Jesus told us about His Father's house delivers us from the cares of this life.

² "In my Father's house are many rooms. If it were not so, would I have told you that I go to prepare a place for you?"

Jesus called God *"My Father."* He knew His Father just as any son knows his father. He knew the truth: His Father *is*, really does exist and live (see He.11:6). Note the claim to deity Jesus makes in this verse (see note—Jn.1:51).

In addition, Jesus knew *His Father's house*, the truth and reality of it. God's house is real; it does exist. It is a real world that exists in another dimension of being, *the spiritual dimension*. It is named heaven, for it is His Father's house. This world—the physical and material world—is the property of God, but it is not His house. This earth is not the eternal and permanent dwelling place of God. Heaven is the spiritual world or dimension of being, the *home* of God where the mansions for believers exist.

The word *rooms* or *mansions* (monai) means abiding places. It means residences, dwellings, areas, spaces for living. What a glorious hope! How much clearer could Jesus be? There is *a place in the Father's house* for every one of us—a place for every believer to dwell and live. Just as we have dwellings and homes here on earth, so Jesus promises us dwellings and homes in heaven.

And note: there is no shortage of space. There are *many* rooms or mansions. (In the other Gospels, Jesus talks a great deal about believers inheriting huge areas or places, even whole realms and kingdoms, which may refer to the heavenly bodies all throughout the universe that will be recreated in the new heavens and earth; 2 Pe.3:10-13; Re.21:1; see notes—Mt.19:28; 24:45-47; 25:20-23.)

In this verse, Jesus stresses the truth and reality of God's house and its many rooms or mansions. He states explicitly that if it were not true, He would not have told us about it. Jesus does not lie. He tells only the truth.

Note a vital truth: one thing is essential to gain a place in the Father's house. That one thing is belief in Christ (v.1).

For we know that if the tent that is our earthly home is destroyed, we have a building from God, a house not made with hands, eternal in the heavens. (2 Co.5:1)

But when Christ appeared as a high priest of the good things that have come, then through the greater and more perfect tent (not made with hands, that is, not of this creation) (He.9:11)

For he was looking forward to the city that has foundations, whose designer and builder is God. (He.11:10)

These all died in faith, not having received the things promised, but having seen them and greeted them from afar, and having acknowledged that they were strangers and exiles on the earth. For people who speak thus make it clear that they are seeking a homeland. (He.11:13-14)

For here we have no lasting city, but we seek the city that is to come. (He.13:14)

Blessed be the God and Father of our Lord Jesus Christ! According to his great mercy, he has caused us to be born again to a living hope through the resurrection of Jesus Christ from the dead, to an inheritance that is imperishable, undefiled, and unfading, kept in heaven for you. (1 Pe.1:3-4)

## 14:2

² "In my Father's house are many rooms. If it were not so, would I have told you that I go to prepare a place for you?"

## 3 Delivers through Christ's preparation on our behalf.

Jesus reveals a comforting and thrilling fact: He was going to prepare a place for us! Deliverance from a troubled heart comes through Jesus' preparation on our behalf. Picture Jesus seated in the upper room surrounded by His disciples. He said, "I go to prepare a place for you." Where was He going?

First, Jesus was going to the cross: to prepare redemption for us, even the forgiveness of sins.

"Even as the Son of Man came not to be served but to serve, and to give his life as a ransom for many." (Mt.20:28)

In him we have redemption through his blood, the forgiveness of our trespasses, according to the riches of his grace. (Ep.1:7)

For there is one God, and there is one mediator between God and men, the man Christ Jesus, who gave himself as a ransom for all, which is the testimony given at the proper time. (1 Ti.2:5-6)

Knowing that you were ransomed from the futile ways inherited from your forefathers, not with perishable things such as silver or gold, but with the precious blood of Christ, like that of a lamb without blemish or spot. (1 Pe.1:18-19)

He himself bore our sins in his body on the tree, that we might die to sin and live to righteousness. By his wounds you have been healed. (1 Pe.2:24)

For Christ also suffered once for sins, the righteous for the unrighteous, that he might bring us to God, being put to death in the flesh but made alive in the spirit. (1 Pe.3:18.)

Second, Jesus was going to be raised from the dead: to prepare the conquest of death and a new life and power for us.

We were buried therefore with him by baptism into death, in order that, just as Christ was raised from the dead by the glory of the Father, we too might walk in newness of life. (Ro.6:4)

And God raised the Lord and will also raise us up by his power. (1 Co.6:14)

For he was crucified in weakness, but lives by the power of God. For we also are weak in him, but in dealing with you we will live with him by the power of God. (2 Co.13:4)

Having the eyes of your hearts enlightened, that you may know what is the hope to which he has called you, what are the riches of his glorious inheritance in the saints, and what is the immeasurable greatness of his power toward us who believe, according to the working of his great might (Ep.1:18-19)

Having been buried with him in baptism, in which you were also raised with him through faith in the powerful working of God, who raised him from the dead. (Col.2:12)

Third, Jesus was going to ascend into heaven and be exalted: to prepare an access into the presence of God and an eternal home for us.

Through him [Christ] we have also obtained access by faith into this grace in which we stand, and we rejoice in hope of the glory of God. (Ro.5:2)

Even when we were dead in our trespasses, [God] made us alive together with Christ—by grace you have been saved—and raised us up with him and seated us with him in the heavenly places in Christ Jesus. (Ep.2:5-6)

If then you have been raised with Christ, seek the things that are above, where Christ is, seated at the right hand of God. (Col.3:1)

The saying is trustworthy, for: If we have died with him, we will also live with him. (2 Ti.2:11)

Such a magnificent work on our behalf is bound to deliver us from trouble. But remember that Jesus began by stating a condition: "Believe in *God, believe* also in me" (v.1).

## 4 Delivers through Christ's assurance of His return.

Deliverance from a troubled heart comes through the hope of Jesus' return. He is coming again for a specific purpose: to receive us unto Himself. Jesus comes for every believer in one of two ways:

> ³ "And if I go and prepare a place for you, I will come again and will take you to myself, that where I am you may be also."

➢ Through the passing of the believer into heaven.
Death is a private escort or a private presentation to the Lord (2 Co.5:8). It is not the triumphant entrance and glorious march of victory which is promised when Jesus returns (see DEEPER STUDY # 1).

Yes, we are of good courage, and we would rather be away from the body and at home with the Lord. (2 Co.5:8)

➢ Through the return of Jesus Himself to gather all His dear followers unto Himself. It is this return to which He is referring in this passage.

As believers, we are going to be glorified with the Father and Jesus. Such a glorious hope—meditating on and grasping it—will carry our troubled souls through any trial, even the trial of martyrdom. But note again: believing in God and in His Son Jesus is the only way we can take part in His return (see outline and notes—1 Th.4:13-5:3; see also Jn.5:28-29; Tit.2:12-13; 2 Pe.3:3-4, 8-16 for more discussion).

"Truly, truly, I say to you, an hour is coming, and is now here, when the dead will hear the voice of the Son of God, and those who hear will live." (Jn.5:25)

"Do not marvel at this, for an hour is coming when all who are in the tombs will hear his voice and come out, those who have done good to the resurrection of life, and those who have done evil to the resurrection of judgment." (Jn.5:28-29)

For the Lord himself will descend from heaven with a cry of command, with the voice of an archangel, and with the sound of the trumpet of God. And the dead in Christ will rise first. Then we who are alive, who are left, will be caught up together with them in the clouds to meet the Lord in the air, and so we will always be with the Lord. (1 Th.4:16-17)

Training us to renounce ungodliness and worldly passions, and to live self-controlled, upright, and godly lives in the present age, waiting for our blessed hope, the appearing of the glory of our great God and Savior Jesus Christ. (Tit.2:12-13)

### DEEPER STUDY # 1

(14:3) **Jesus Christ, Return—Death:** The Bible distinguishes between the believer's meeting Jesus in death and meeting Jesus in the air at His return.

1. Believers meet Jesus at death. We pass immediately from this world into the next world, into heaven itself, *never tasting the pain of death* (see note—Jn.8:51). We pass quicker than the blinking of an eye, never losing a moment's consciousness. One moment we are in this world; the next moment we are in the presence of the Lord. This is the believer's personal presentation to the Lord. It is the very first sight we will have of our Lord.

➢ Stephen, while being stoned to death, anticipated going immediately to be with the Lord (Ac.7:59).

- Stephen even "saw the glory of God, and Jesus standing at the right hand of God" (Ac.7:55).
- Paul actually said that being absent or away from the body is to be at home or present with the Lord (2 Co.5:8).
- Paul even said that he desired to depart, and to be with Christ, which is far better (Ph.1:23).
- Jesus promised the thief on the cross, "Today you will be with me in Paradise" (Lu.23:43).
- The believers of Thessalonica who had already died are said to sleep in Jesus (1 Th.4:14). "Sleep" means that they are resting in the presence of the Lord (see note—Jn.11:13).

> And he said to him, "Truly, I say to you, today you will be with me in paradise." (Lu.23:43)

> "Father, I desire that they also, whom you have given me, may be with me where I am, to see my glory that you have given me because you loved me before the foundation of the world." (Jn.17:24)

> Yes, we are of good courage, and we would rather be away from the body and at home with the Lord. (2 Co.5:8)

> I am hard pressed between the two. My desire is to depart and be with Christ, for that is far better. (Ph.1:23)

2. The believer's body does arise and meet Jesus in the air when He returns. The deceased bodies of believers will arise from wherever and however many places they lie on earth. And the believers who are still living on earth will arise in their bodies to meet the Lord in the air. It will be as quick as the blinking of an eye, and it will definitely happen. All believers, both in heaven and on earth, will arise and receive glorified bodies—dramatically and instantaneously. Jesus promised that He would come again, and He will. We must never forget: God promised that His Son would come the first time, and He came; so He will come again despite the unbelief of the vast majority of people.

Jesus Christ is coming again to give both Himself and His people a glorious reunion and march of triumph over sin, death, and hell . . .

- A reunion and march so glorious it explosively exceeds all that we can think or dream.
- A reunion and march of indescribable perfection and joy, a march when all of the dear followers of Christ will be gathered together before Him for the very first time. Each will experience the presence and joy of all the saints, the dear, dear saints who have gone before and who have come after—including Paul, Peter, Augustine, Luther, Calvin, Wesley, Moody, and all the other well-known servants of God; the multitudes who have been unknown to people, but are well-known to God—known to be first because they labored in the insignificant corners of the world as God directed and were ever so faithful.

There, before the Lord Jesus Christ, we will all stand for the very first time, every believer who has ever lived.

> "Blessed are those servants whom the master finds awake when he comes. Truly, I say to you, he will dress himself for service and have them recline at table, and he will come and serve them." (Lu.12:37)

> But our citizenship is in heaven, and from it we await a Savior, the Lord Jesus Christ, who will transform our lowly body to be like his glorious body, by the power that enables him even to subject all things to himself. (Ph.3:20-21)

> When Christ who is your life appears, then you also will appear with him in glory. (Col.3:4)

> So that he may establish your hearts blameless in holiness before our God and Father, at the coming of our Lord Jesus with all his saints. (1 Th.3:13)

> For the Lord himself will descend from heaven with a cry of command, with the voice of an archangel, and with the sound of the trumpet of God. And the dead in Christ will rise first. Then

> we who are alive, who are left, will be caught up together with them in the clouds to meet the Lord in the air, and so we will always be with the Lord. (1 Th.4:16–17)
>
> Beloved, we are God's children now, and what we will be has not yet appeared; but we know that when he appears we shall be like him, because we shall see him as he is. (1 Jn.3:2)

## 5 Delivers through the great hope of living with Christ eternally.

Finally, deliverance from a troubled heart comes through the glorious hope of living forever with Jesus. Note the very reason Jesus will return to earth: "That where I am, there you may be also." Where is Jesus? Wherever He is, the very place He is, is exactly where we will be. We will be with Him—with our precious Lord forever—with Him who has saved us—with Him who has forgiven our sins despite their awfulness—with Him who has delivered us from the bondage of sin, death, and hell—with Him who has cared for us and guided us day by day—with Him who has shared and given us His presence. Again, we will be with our wonderful Lord forever and ever. This is the very longing of His heart, the very thing for which He prayed so intensely:

³ "And if I go and prepare a place for you, I will come again and will take you to myself, that where I am you may be also."

> "Father, I desire that they also, whom you have given me, may be with me where I am, to see my glory that you have given me because you loved me before the foundation of the world." (Jn.17:24)

## E. The Way to God Is Through Jesus Alone, 14:4-7

1. The declaration of Jesus: He was going to God
   a. The way to God is known
   b. The contradiction & skepticism of Thomas

2. The way to God is through Jesus Christ Himself[DS1,2,3]
3. The *only* way to God is through Jesus Christ
4. The only way to God is now unmistakably revealed: To know Christ is to know God

⁴ "And you know the way to where I am going."

⁵ Thomas said to him, "Lord, we do not know where you are going. How can we know the way?"

⁶ Jesus said to him, "I am the way, and the truth, and the life. No one comes to the Father except through me.

⁷ "If you had known me, you would have known my Father also. From now on you do know him and have seen him."

## Division XIII

*The Revelation of Jesus, the Great Minister, and His Legacy, 13:1-16:33*

E. The Way to God Is Through Jesus Alone, 14:4-7

### 14:4-7
### Introduction

This passage continues Jesus' discussion of His impending death and subsequent departure from this world. It is outlined separately because it is spurred on by another question, this one by Thomas (see Jn.13:36 for the first question by Peter).

This is a critical passage—one of the most critical in all of Scripture. Jesus declared in unmistakable terms how a person gets to God, and He makes it clear: *He* is the only way to God. This is, *The Way to God Is Through Jesus Alone*, 14:4-7.

1. The declaration of Jesus: He was going to God (vv.4-5).
2. The way to God is through Jesus Christ Himself (v.6).
3. The *only* way to God is through Jesus Christ (v.6).
4. The only way to God is now unmistakably revealed: To know Christ is to know God (v.7).

### 14:4-5

⁴ "And you know the way to where I am going."
⁵ Thomas said to him, "Lord, we do not know where you are going. How can we know the way?"

### 1 The declaration of Jesus: He was going to God.

In these verses, Jesus discusses His destination. He had unnerved the disciples badly, explaining at length the fact that He was leaving them. This is, of course, a forewarning of His death and ascension (Jn.13:33, 36, 14:3, 4).

a. The way to God is known (v.4).
   Jesus told the disciples that they knew where He was going, and they knew the way to get there. And they did, for He had told them time and time again. He was going back to the Father from whom He had come, back to heaven.

Jesus, knowing that the Father had given all things into his hands, and that he had come from God and was going back to God. (Jn.13:3)

"In my Father's house are many rooms. If it were not so, would I have told you that I go to prepare a place for you?" (Jn.14:2)

"But now I am going to him who sent me, and none of you asks me, 'Where are you going?' . . . I go to the Father, and you will see me no longer." . . . So some of his disciples said to one another, "What is this that he says to us, 'A little while, and you will not see me, and again a little while, and you will see me'; and, 'because I am going to the Father'?" (Jn.16:5, 10, 17)

The way to heaven is *through Him*.

"For God so loved the world, that he gave his only Son, that whoever believes in him should not perish but have eternal life." (Jn.3:16)

"Truly, truly, I say to you, whoever hears my word and believes him who sent me has eternal life. He does not come into judgment, but has passed from death to life." (Jn.5:24)

Jesus said to her, "I am the resurrection and the life. Whoever believes in me, though he die, yet shall he live, and everyone who lives and believes in me shall never die. Do you believe this?" (Jn.11:25-26)

b. **The contradiction and skepticism of Thomas (v.5).**

Thomas contradicted Jesus and spoke with skepticism. He bluntly stated, "We do not know where you are going," and then asked, "How can we know the way?"

Here sat the disciples, thinking that Jesus was about to lead them to set up the kingdom of God on earth, freeing Israel and establishing it as the greatest nation on the planet. Then all of a sudden Jesus began to talk about going someplace; in addition, He insisted they could not follow Him.

The disciples were, of course, thinking in terms of an *earthly* and *temporal* government, of worldly positions and power, of wealth and possessions, of pomp and ceremony. This was their problem. Jesus had told them where He was going in simple and clear terms. He had said frequently that He was . . .

- to die and rise again (see notes—Jn.7:33-34; Mt.16:21-28; 17:1-13; 17:22; 17:24-27)
- to go to the Father (see note—Jn.7:33-34; see also Jn.8:14; 13:3; 14:2-3; 16:5, 10, 17)

However, the disciples refused to accept the fact. The result was inevitable. They misunderstood what Jesus was saying and, consequently, were doomed to fail in their allegiance to Him.

**THOUGHT 1.** The world today is just like Thomas, full of contradiction and skepticism. The world proclaims: "We do not know where God is, not really. Even if He exists, we can only seek Him the best we can, trying to find out just where He is. Every person must find and discover their own way and hope they have found it."

> They said to him therefore, "Where is your Father?" Jesus answered, "You know neither me nor my Father. If you knew me, you would know my Father also." (Jn.8:19)
>
> "And they will do these things because they have not known the Father, nor me," (Jn.16:3)
>
> "For as I passed along and observed the objects of your worship, I found also an altar with this inscription: 'To the unknown god.' What therefore you worship as unknown, this I proclaim to you." (Ac.17:23)
>
> "'For this people's heart has grown dull, and with their ears they can barely hear, and their eyes they have closed; lest they should see with their eyes and hear with their ears and understand with their heart and turn, and I would heal them.'" (Ac.28:27)
>
> They [men] are darkened in their understanding, alienated from the life of God because of the ignorance that is in them, due to their hardness of heart. (Ep.4:18)

**THOUGHT 2.** The person who thinks in worldly terms and lives for the earth (position, power, wealth, honor, possessions) will never know where Christ has gone nor how they can get there. As Christ told Nicodemus, unless we are *born again*, we will neither see nor enter the kingdom of God.

Jesus answered him, "Truly, truly, I say to you, unless one is born again he cannot see the kingdom of God." . . . Jesus answered, "Truly, truly, I say to you, unless one is born of water and the Spirit, he cannot enter the kingdom of God." (Jn.3:3, 5)

The natural person does not accept the things of the Spirit of God, for they are folly to him, and he is not able to understand them because they are spiritually discerned. (1 Co.2:14)

## 14:6

⁶ Jesus said to him, "I am the way, and the truth, and the life. No one comes to the Father except through me."

## 2 The way to God is through Jesus Christ Himself.

This is a critical verse, for here Jesus says that no person can reach God unless they approach God through Jesus Himself. Note Jesus' claim to deity: "I Am" (see note—Jn.6:20). Jesus made three phenomenal claims:

➢ I Am the Way (see DEEPER STUDY # 1).
➢ I Am the Truth (see DEEPER STUDY # 2).
➢ I Am the Life (see DEEPER STUDY # 3).

### DEEPER STUDY # 1

(14:6) **Jesus the Way**: there is a difference between pointing the way to a particular place and taking someone by the hand to lead them there. The person who guides someone to their destination literally becomes the way to the desired location. Jesus Christ not only points out how to walk through life and how to reach God, He personally shows the person the way. Therefore, He Himself is the Way. Note the repetition of the word "way" (vv.4, 5, 6).

> Therefore, brothers, since we have confidence to enter the holy places [God's presence] by the blood of Jesus, by the new and living way that he opened for us through the curtain, that is, through his flesh. (He.10:19-20)

### DEEPER STUDY # 2

(14:6) **Jesus the Truth**: there is a difference between telling someone about the truth and living the truth before them. The one who lives the truth literally becomes the truth.

1. Jesus Christ is the *Embodiment* of truth (Jn.14:6). He is the picture of truth. God not only talks to humanity about Himself, God shows us what He is like in the person of Jesus Christ. We can look at Jesus Christ and see a perfect picture of the truth of God.

> "I and the Father are one." (Jn.10:30)

> "If I am not doing the works of my Father, then do not believe me; but if I do them, even though you do not believe me, believe the works, that you may know and understand that the Father is in me and I am in the Father." (Jn.10:37-38)

> "Do you not believe that I am in the Father and the Father is in me? The words that I say to you I do not speak on my own authority, but the Father who dwells in me does his works." (Jn.14:10)

> "And I am no longer in the world, but they are in the world, and I am coming to you. Holy Father, keep them in your name, which you have given me, that they may be one, even as we are one." (Jn.17:11)

2. Jesus Christ is the *Communicator* of truth. He Himself—His Person and His Life—makes things perfectly clear. He reveals the ultimate source and meaning and end of all things. He reveals the truth about us and about the world in which we live. He shows us the right way to the truth, and He enables us to choose the right way.

> "It is the Spirit who gives life; the flesh is no help at all. The words that I have spoken to you are spirit and life." (Jn.6:63)

> Simon Peter answered him, "Lord, to whom shall we go? You have the words of eternal life." (Jn.6:68)

Jesus answered, "Even if I do bear witness about myself, my testimony is true, for I know where I came from and where I am going, but you do not know where I come from or where I am going." (Jn.8:14)

"For I have given them the words that you gave me, and they have received them and have come to know in truth that I came from you; and they have believed that you sent me." (Jn.17:8)

Then Pilate said to him, "So you are a king?" Jesus answered, "You say that I am a king. For this purpose I was born and for this purpose I have come into the world—to bear witness to the truth. Everyone who is of the truth listens to my voice." (Jn.18:37)

And from Jesus Christ the faithful witness, the firstborn of the dead, and the ruler of kings on earth. To him who loves us and has freed us from our sins by his blood (Re.1:5)

3. Jesus Christ is the *Liberator* of truth (Jn.8:32; 15:3). He sets us free from the great gulf (estrangement) which exists between us and God, between us and our world, and between us and other people. He sets us free from the frustrations we constantly experience, frees us from the fears and weaknesses and defects that plague us. Jesus Christ is the only lasting liberator on earth (see Deeper Study # 1—Jn.1:9; Deeper Study # 2—8:23).

"And you will know the truth, and the truth will set you free.... So if the Son sets you free, you will be free indeed." (Jn.8:32, 36)

## Deeper Study # 3

(14:6) **Jesus the Life**: there is a difference between telling someone about life and actually living life. The one who lives is the one who possesses life, and the more perfectly one lives, the more life one possesses. Jesus Christ lived perfectly; therefore, He possessed life perfectly. He is the Life: the very embodiment, energy, force, and source of life itself (see notes—Jn.1:4; 10:10; 17:2-3).

In him was life, and the life was the light of men. (Jn.1:4)

"The thief comes only to steal and kill and destroy. I came that they may have life and have it abundantly." (Jn.10:10)

Jesus said to her, "I am the resurrection and the life. Whoever believes in me, though he die, yet shall he live." (Jn.11:25)

So that, as sin reigned in death, grace also might reign through righteousness leading to eternal life through Jesus Christ our Lord. (Ro.5:21)

And [salvation] which now has been manifested through the appearing of our Savior Christ Jesus, who abolished death and brought life and immortality to light through the gospel. (2 Ti.1:10)

## 3 The *only* way to God is through Jesus Christ.

⁶ Jesus said to him, "I am the way, and the truth, and the life. No one comes to the Father except through me."

There is but one way to God, and that way is through Jesus Christ (see outline and notes—Jn.10:7-10 for discussion). Note that the ultimate destination is God. Again, Jesus clearly said where He was going. He was going to "the Father." He was not going to remain dead. He was going to arise and ascend to the Father. This was a picture of both Jesus' resurrection and ascension.

Jesus had just said He was going to His "Father's *house*." Now He said that He was going to "the *Father*" of the house. His destination was not so much the house, as glorious as the house is, but the Father Himself. The house without the Father would not be *home*; it would not be heaven.

This detail says something of vital importance to the believer. Our primary objective should be to go to the Father Himself, not to heaven, not to a place. Our great longing should be to live in the *Father's presence* forever.

We should long to know and ever learn of the Father *personally* . . .

- to know the Father face-to-face as our Father: as the One who created us, both physically and spiritually; as the One who loves the world so much that He would give His only Son to save mankind and provide so glorious a salvation
- to know the Father face-to-face as the Creator and Sustainer of all things: of all life and all worlds, of all universes and in all dimensions of being
- to know the Father face-to-face as the glorious Person who dwells in Light so brilliant and full of splendor that no person can approach Him
- to know the Father face-to-face as the supreme majesty of the universe: the supreme majesty both of this world and of the world to come; the King of kings and Lord of lords who is and forever shall be above all, before all, over all

We should yearn to honor and worship the Father face-to-face: to praise the Father for Himself and for the wonderful privilege of life; to join in the praise of the universe which is to be given Him who is worthy of all praise, honor, glory, and worship forever and ever. In addition, we should long to serve the Father face-to-face: to serve in perfection, without the blemishes and weaknesses so common in our life and ministry here on earth.

> **THOUGHT 1.** The destination of Jesus was "the Father" Himself. Believers have the same destination: our destination is "the Father," the One who so willingly and graciously adopted us into His family. The only way to reach this destination is through Jesus.
>
> > "And there is salvation in no one else, for there is no other name under heaven given among men by which we must be saved." (Ac.4:12)
> >
> > For you did not receive the spirit of slavery to fall back into fear, but you have received the Spirit of adoption as sons, by whom we cry, "Abba! Father!" The Spirit himself bears witness with our spirit that we are children of God, and if children, then heirs—heirs of God and fellow heirs with Christ, provided we suffer with him in order that we may also be glorified with him. (Ro.8:15–17)
> >
> > But when the fullness of time had come, God sent forth his Son, born of woman, born under the law, to redeem those who were under the law, so that we might receive adoption as sons. And because you are sons, God has sent the Spirit of his Son into our hearts, crying, "Abba! Father!" So you are no longer a slave, but a son, and if a son, then an heir through God. (Ga.4:4–7)
> >
> > For there is one God, and there is one mediator between God and men, the man Christ Jesus, who gave himself as a ransom for all, which is the testimony given at the proper time. (1 Ti.2:5–6)
> >
> > My little children, I am writing these things to you so that you may not sin. But if anyone does sin, we have an advocate with the Father, Jesus Christ the righteous. (1 Jn.2:1)

## 14:7

⁷ "If you had known me, you would have known my Father also. From now on you do know him and have seen him."

## 4 The only way to God is now unmistakably revealed: to know Christ is to know God.

The only way to God is now revealed, and it is revealed unmistakably. Jesus Christ Himself is the perfect revelation of God. If people wish to see exactly who God is and what God is like, they must look at Jesus Christ. The supreme revelation of Jesus Christ is that God is love (Jn.3:16). And a God of love is bound to reveal the way, the truth, and the life in the most perfect picture possible. A God of love would never leave humanity in the dark, ever seeking, and never able to find and to know (see notes—Jn.1:18; 3:13; DEEPER STUDY # 1—3:31 for more discussion; also see outlines and notes—Jn.1:1-2; 1:14; 1:18).

➢ A God of love is bound (by absolute love) to show humanity THE WAY to Himself. As love, He would never leave people in the dark, feeling about and stumbling after the Way. Jesus Christ is THE WAY—the perfect picture of the Way.

➢ A God of love is bound (by absolute love) to show humanity THE TRUTH about Himself. As love, He would never leave people in the dark, searching and grasping after the Truth. Jesus Christ is THE TRUTH—the perfect picture of truth.

> A God of love is bound (by absolute love) to show humanity *THE LIFE* of Himself. As love, He would never leave people in the dark, wandering aimlessly about and being hopeless in seeking after the Life. Jesus Christ is *THE LIFE*, the perfect picture of life.

**"And whoever sees me sees him who sent me." (Jn.12:45)**

**"Do you not believe that I am in the Father and the Father is in me? The words that I say to you I do not speak on my own authority, but the Father who dwells in me does his works." (Jn.14:10)**

**"All that the Father has is mine; therefore I said that he will take what is mine and declare it to you." (Jn.16:15)**

**He is the radiance of the glory of God and the exact imprint of his nature, and he upholds the universe by the word of his power. After making purification for sins, he sat down at the right hand of the Majesty on high. (He.1:3)**

## F. The Embodiment of God Is Jesus Himself, 14:8-14

1. The request by Philip: Show us the Father, some spectacular sight
2. The revelation: Jesus is the full embodiment of God




3. The clear evidence
   a. The presence of God in Jesus Christ
   b. The words of Jesus Christ
   c. The works of Jesus Christ

4. The straightforward challenge: Believe the claim of Jesus Christ[DS1]

5. The conditional promises: Are only to the person who believes in Jesus Christ

   a. The person will receive the power to do great works[DS2]
   b. The person will receive the answer to all prayers[DS3], to anything if asked in Jesus' name

⁸ Philip said to him, "Lord, show us the Father, and it is enough for us."

⁹ Jesus said to him, "Have I been with you so long, and you still do not know me, Philip? Whoever has seen me has seen the Father. How can you say, 'Show us the Father'?"

¹⁰ Do you not believe that I am in the Father and the Father is in me? The words that I say to you I do not speak on my own authority, but the Father who dwells in me does his works.

¹¹ Believe me that I am in the Father and the Father is in me, or else believe on account of the works themselves.

¹² Truly, truly, I say to you, whoever believes in me will also do the works that I do; and greater works than these will he do, because I am going to the Father.

¹³ Whatever you ask in my name, this I will do, that the Father may be glorified in the Son.

¹⁴ If you ask me anything in my name, I will do it."

# Division XIII

*The Revelation of Jesus, the Great Minister, and His Legacy, 13:1–16:33*

F. The Embodiment of God Is Jesus Himself, 14:8-14

## 14:8-14

## Introduction

The disciples were struggling with what Jesus had revealed to them: His approaching death and departure from this world. He had assured them of where He was ultimately going—back to heaven—and that they knew the way to heaven. In spite of all they had heard and seen from Jesus, their faith was still weak. Jesus' word alone was not enough for them; they wanted to *see* the Father with their eyes. Jesus responded with one of the most astounding claims ever made—He is the very embodiment of God Himself. This is, *The Embodiment of God Is Jesus Himself,* 14:8-14.

1. The request by Philip: Show us the Father, some spectacular sight (v.8).
2. The revelation: Jesus is the full embodiment of God (v.9).
3. The clear evidence (v.10).
4. The straightforward challenge: Believe the claim of Jesus Christ (v.11).
5. The conditional promises: Are only to the person who believes in Jesus Christ (vv.12-14).

# 1 The request by Philip: Show us the Father, some spectacular sight.

Philip's asked Jesus to show the disciples the Father—a visible and tangible yet spectacular revelation of God. Jesus had been discussing the fact that He was returning to the Father and that the disciples could not go with Him, not now (Jn.13:33-14:7). Philip's request shows how the disciples interpreted His words. They thought Jesus meant that He was going to a mountaintop or some other quiet place to meet God face-to-face just as great men of God had done in the past, men such as . . .

⁸ Philip said to him, "Lord, show us the Father, and it is enough for us."

- Jacob (Ge.28:12f; 32:24f)
- Moses (Ex.3:1f; 24:9-11; 33:14-23; 34:5-9)
- Joshua (Jos.5:13f)
- Gideon (Jdg.6:21f)
- Elijah (1 K.19:4f)
- Isaiah (Is.6:1f)
- Ezekiel (Eze.1:1f; 10:1f)

Philip wanted to go with Jesus to see the Father as well. Why did he desire this experience?

First, Philip felt that a dramatic experience with God—that seeing God—would calm the disciples' troubled hearts and solve their problems . . .

- of strife and division (see notes—Jn.14:1-3; Lu.22:24-30)
- of betrayal and desertion (Jn.13:18f)
- of denial (Jn.13:38)
- of ignorance and misunderstanding (Jn.1:36; 14:5)

**THOUGHT 1.** Note the emphasis on the dramatic experience: on seeking the spectacular and the dazzling, the physical and visible evidence—some sign that God *is*—that He actually exists. How many ask for the dramatic experience and the spectacular sign? They think that once they have had a dazzling sight of God, then their peace will come. If they can only see God, their problems will be solved. They will believe and serve God. They will change and do what is right.

Second, Philip was not satisfied with what he saw in Jesus, nor with what He had received in Jesus. Walking by faith was not enough. Philip wanted to see some astounding and spectacular Person who appeared in dazzling form. Jesus, although the Son of God, appeared before Philip as a mere man in bodily form. He was not appearing in the dazzling, glorious being of a heavenly Person. He was not in a spectacular form or vision as men of old had seen and as people usually think of God, the Supreme Universal Being. Jesus was appearing and communicating and living as a mere human being. Philip wanted more than what Jesus was.

**THOUGHT 1.** What an indictment against unbelieving people! People often say, "Jesus is not enough. More is needed. Jesus was a mere man; He could not be *the Son* of God. Perhaps He was *a son* of God in the sense that He was the best man who ever lived, but no more." Such people walk through life being blind to the great love of God.

> "For God so loved the world, that he gave his only Son, that whoever believes in him should not perish but have eternal life." (Jn.3:16)
>
> But God shows his love for us in that while we were still sinners, Christ died for us. (Ro.5:8)
>
> In their case the god of this world has blinded the minds of the unbelievers, to keep them from seeing the light of the gospel of the glory of Christ, who is the image of God. (2 Co.4:4)
>
> They [men] are darkened in their understanding, alienated from the life of God because of the ignorance that is in them, due to their hardness of heart. (Ep.4:18)

## 2 The revelation: Jesus is the full embodiment of God.

Jesus responded to Philip's request with an astounding revelation—He is the full embodiment of God. Jesus stated plainly that whoever has seen Him *has* seen the Father. When people see Jesus, they see a Person . . .

**14:9**

⁹ Jesus said to him, "Have I been with you so long, and you still do not know me, Philip? Whoever has seen me has seen the Father. How can you say, 'Show us the Father'?"

- who is the very nature of God
- who is the very character of God
- who is the very substance of God
- who is the very perfection of God
- who is God in all of His perfect being

Jesus Christ is not the same Person as God the Father, but He has the same perfect nature. Jesus Christ is God the Son. Therefore, the person who has seen Jesus Christ has seen the Father in all the fulness of the Father's nature—that person has seen in Jesus the very embodiment of perfection, the perfect embodiment of Being, both perfect love and perfect righteousness.

"And whoever sees me sees him who sent me." (Jn.12:45)

"If you had known me, you would have known my Father also. From now on you do know him and have seen him." (Jn.14:7)

"All that the Father has is mine; therefore I said that he will take what is mine and declare it to you." (Jn.16:15)

For in him the whole fullness of deity dwells bodily. (Col.2:9)

Great indeed, we confess, is the mystery of godliness: He was manifested in the flesh, vindicated by the Spirit, seen by angels, proclaimed among the nations, believed on in the world, taken up in glory. (1 Ti.3:16)

He [Christ] is the radiance of the glory of God and the exact imprint of his nature, and he upholds the universe by the word of his power. After making purification for sins, he sat down at the right hand of the Majesty on high. (He.1:3)

(See notes—Jn.14:6; 14:7. Also see notes—Jn.1:1-2; 1:14; 1:18 for more discussion.)

**THOUGHT 1.** Note the emphasis is on God *as Father*. Just as an earthly father, God is not distant and far off. He has not created and wound up the world and left it to run on its own, being unconcerned and uncaring. As Father, God is exactly as Jesus showed us . . .

- loving and just
- giving and helpful
- full of goodness and truth
- responsible and accountable
- directing and correcting
- forgiving and caring

"If you then, who are evil, know how to give good gifts to your children, how much more will your Father who is in heaven give good things to those who ask him!" (Mt.7:11)

"For God so loved the world, that he gave his only Son, that whoever believes in him should not perish but have eternal life. For God did not send his Son into the world to condemn the world, but in order that the world might be saved through him." (Jn.3:16-17)

"For the Father himself loves you, because you have loved me and have believed that I came from God." (Jn.16:27)

For you did not receive the spirit of slavery to fall back into fear, but you have received the Spirit of adoption as sons, by whom we cry, "Abba! Father!" The Spirit himself bears witness with our spirit that we are children of God, and if children, then heirs—heirs of God and fellow heirs with Christ, provided we suffer with him in order that we may also be glorified with him. (Ro.8:15-17)

See what kind of love the Father has given to us, that we should be called children of God; and so we are. The reason why the world does not know us is that it did not know him. (1 Jn.3:1)

## 3 The clear evidence.

Jesus knew the disciples' questions were not so much due to a lack of understanding, but to a lack of faith. He directly challenged them, asking, "Do you not believe?" He proceeded to lay out clear evidence that He is the embodiment of God.

### a. The presence of God in Jesus Christ.

God's presence was proof that Jesus is the embodiment of God. God is *in* Jesus, and Jesus is *in* God. This can be called the *mutual indwelling presence* of God and Christ, each dwelling in the other. This simply means that each has the nature and being, the spirit and mind, of the other. Each has the presence, the very being and spirit, of the other dwelling within Him—*perfectly*.

¹⁰ "Do you not believe that I am in the Father and the Father is in me? The words that I say to you I do not speak on my own authority, but the Father who dwells in me does his works."

Note the point Jesus makes. The proof that He is the embodiment of God, that He is the One who came to earth to reveal God, is clear: God's presence is not only *with* Him; God's presence is *in* Him. He Himself *is* God. He Himself—His person, His being, His nature, His character, His love, His care, His just dealings, all that He is—revealed exactly what God is.

> "I and the Father are one." (Jn.10:30)

> "If I am not doing the works of my Father, then do not believe me; but if I do them, even though you do not believe me, believe the works, that you may know and understand that the Father is in me and I am in the Father." (Jn.10:37-38)

> "In that day you will know that I am in my Father, and you in me, and I in you." (Jn.14:20)

> "And I am no longer in the world, but they are in the world, and I am coming to you. Holy Father, keep them in your name, which you have given me, that they may be one, even as we are one." (Jn.17:11)

> "That they may all be one, just as you, Father, are in me, and I in you, that they also may be in us, so that the world may believe that you have sent me. The glory that you have given me I have given to them, that they may be one even as we are one." (Jn.17:21-22)

### b. The words of Jesus Christ.

Jesus' words were proof that He is the embodiment of God. His words were the very Words of God which God Himself wanted to say to humanity. When Jesus spoke, it was the Father who was speaking through Him. Look at His words, His teaching, and His doctrine, and know that He is who He claimed to be: the Son of God Himself, the very embodiment of God (see note—Jn.7:16-19 for more discussion).

> "Heaven and earth will pass away, but my words will not pass away." (Mk.13:31)

> And all spoke well of him and marveled at the gracious words that were coming from his mouth. And they said, "Is not this Joseph's son?" (Lu.4:22)

> And they were astonished at his teaching, for his word possessed authority. (Lu.4:32)

> For he whom God has sent utters the words of God, for he gives the Spirit without measure. (Jn.3:34)

> Simon Peter answered him, "Lord, to whom shall we go? You have the words of eternal life." (Jn.6:68)

> The officers answered, "No one ever spoke like this man!" (Jn.7:46)

### c. The works of Jesus Christ.

Jesus' works were proof that He is the embodiment of God (see notes—Jn.5:19-20, 36; DEEPER STUDY # 2—10:25 for discussion). Who but God could turn water into wine, open the eyes of the blind, and make the lame to walk again? Who but God could raise the dead? Who but God would dare to run the greedy merchants out of the temple? Jesus' works were the works of God; they were the works of the Father who embodies Him.

## 4 The straightforward challenge: Believe the claim of Jesus Christ.

Jesus issued a forceful challenge to His doubting disciples: *Believe Me.* They needed to believe Him, have faith in Him and His word, His claim. He is the embodiment of God. He is *in* the Father, and the Father is *in* Him—perfectly. Jesus is the One whom God the Father sent into the world to show people who God is and what He is like. Jesus Christ is the revelation of God to humanity, who came to the world to show us that God is "the Father," the Father who loves and cares, forgives and executes justice. The challenge is to believe Jesus . . .

**14:11**

¹¹ "Believe me that I am in the Father and the Father is in me, or else believe on account of the works themselves."

- believe in Him as a Person, as the Son of God Himself
- believe in His claim, that His testimony and witness to Himself is absolutely true

Jesus told the disciples that if they did not believe Him, they should believe on account of the mighty works He had done (see Deeper Study # 1). What a sad indictment of those who were closest to Jesus, of those who knew Him best! Nevertheless, our Lord's point remains: if people have difficulty believing His claim, then they should believe Him because of His phenomenal works—do whatever is needed to secure the evidence—but first believe and accept His claim (see Deeper Study # 2—Jn.2:24).

> "But the testimony that I have is greater than that of John. For the works that the Father has given me to accomplish, the very works that I am doing, bear witness about me that the Father has sent me." (Jn.5:36)

> Jesus answered them, "I told you, and you do not believe. The works that I do in my Father's name bear witness about me." (Jn.10:25)

> "But if I do them, even though you do not believe me, believe the works, that you may know and understand that the Father is in me and I am in the Father." (Jn.10:38)

> "If I had not done among them the works that no one else did, they would not be guilty of sin, but now they have seen and hated both me and my Father." (Jn.15:24)

> "Men of Israel, hear these words: Jesus of Nazareth, a man attested to you by God with mighty works and wonders and signs that God did through him in your midst, as you yourselves know." (Ac.2:22)

### Deeper Study # 1

(14:11) **Jesus Christ, Works**: note the purpose for the Lord's works—to stir the belief that He is the Son of God (Jn.10:38; 14:11; Ac.2:22).

**14:12-14**

¹² "Truly, truly, I say to you, whoever believes in me will also do the works that I do; and greater works than these will he do, because I am going to the Father.
¹³ "Whatever you ask in my name, this I will do, that the Father may be glorified in the Son.
¹⁴ "If you ask me anything in my name, I will do it."

## 5 The conditional promises: Are only to the person who believes in Jesus Christ.

Jesus made two clear promises to all who believe in Him. He prefaced these promises with *truly, truly* or *most assuredly*—words that call a person to wake up and listen closely. What was about to be said was of tremendous importance.

### a. The person will receive the power to do great works (v.12).

Jesus' first promise to the believer is the power to do great works. We have been given the power to do the very same works that Jesus did (see Deeper Study # 2).

**b. The person will receive the answer to all prayers, to anything if asked in Jesus' name (vv.13-14).**

Jesus promised believers an answer to all our prayers (see Deeper Study # 3). He pledged to do all that we ask in His name for the glory of the Father (v.13).

Jesus said that we are to pray to Him as well as to God (v.14). Jesus is claiming to be God, to have the wisdom and knowledge, the power and ability, the love and care, and the desire and willingness to do anything. A phenomenal claim! Yet it is a reasonable claim for the Son of God.

> "Do you not believe that I am in the Father and the Father is in me? The words that I say to you I do not speak on my own authority, but the Father who dwells in me does his works." (Jn.14:10)

> "And whatever you ask in prayer, you will receive, if you have faith." (Mt.21:22)

> "If you abide in me, and my words abide in you, ask whatever you wish, and it will be done for you." (Jn.15:7)

> And this is the confidence that we have toward him, that if we ask anything according to his will he hears us. And if we know that he hears us in whatever we ask, we know that we have the requests that we have asked of him. (1 Jn.5:14-15)

## Deeper Study # 2

(14:12) **Works**: John 14:12 contains a surprising statement that serves as a great promise: the believer will do the very same works and even greater works than Jesus did. Note three facts.

1. Genuine believers will do the same *kind* of work that Jesus did, work that is characterized...
   - by loving and caring
   - by ministering and healing
   - by proclaiming and teaching by witnessing and testifying
   - by sharing and discipling
   - by helping and performing miracles

Believers will work, doing all they can to demonstrate the love of God in order to lead people to a saving knowledge of His Son, Jesus Christ.

> "Even as the Son of Man came not to be served but to serve, and to give his life as a ransom for many." (Mt.20:28)

> "For the Son of Man came to seek and to save the lost." (Lu.19:10)

> Jesus said to them again, "Peace be with you. As the Father has sent me, even so I am sending you." (Jn.20:21)

2. Genuine believers will work hard for the very same purpose as Jesus did. They will work...
   - to show people the love and justice of God
   - to help people in all their need
   - to lead people to believe on the Son of God that they might be saved and delivered from sin, death, and hell

> "Go therefore and make disciples of all nations, baptizing them in the name of the Father and of the Son and of the Holy Spirit, teaching them to observe all that I have commanded you. And behold, I am with you always, to the end of the age." (Mt.28:19-20)

> And he said to them, "Go into all the world and proclaim the gospel to the whole creation." (Mk.16:15)

> And what you have heard from me in the presence of many witnesses entrust to faithful men, who will be able to teach others also. Share in suffering as a good soldier of Christ Jesus. (2 Ti.2:2-3)

3. Genuine believers will do even greater works than Jesus did. This means that the true servant of God will *reach more* people and have *broader results* than Jesus did. The whole

world would eventually hear, and an impact would be made on many societies and nations as a whole. But note the crucial point: Greater works are possible only through Jesus, only because He has gone to His Father and is sitting at the right hand of the Father. From there—from the throne of power—He equips and enables the believer to do the works. The believer is able to do great works only through the presence and power of Jesus who is with the Father (see note, Mt.28:19-20).

> "But you will receive power when the Holy Spirit has come upon you, and you will be my witnesses in Jerusalem and in all Judea and Samaria, and to the end of the earth." (Ac.1:8)
>
> And with great power the apostles were giving their testimony to the resurrection of the Lord Jesus, and great grace was upon them all. (Ac.4:33)
>
> Now to him who is able to do far more abundantly than all that we ask or think, according to the power at work within us. (Ep.3:20)
>
> Because our gospel came to you not only in word, but also in power and in the Holy Spirit and with full conviction. You know what kind of men we proved to be among you for your sake. (1 Th.1:5)

## DEEPER STUDY # 3

(14:13-14) **Praying in the name of Jesus:** these verses contain one of the most wonderful promises in all the Bible. God hears the prayers of the dear believer. Note two points.
1. The only prayers heard and answered are those asked "in Jesus' name." What does it mean to pray "in Jesus' name"? It means two things.
    a. The believer prays knowing that . . .
        - the only acceptance to God is *in Jesus;* God hears us only because Jesus is acceptable to Him and we come in the name of Jesus
        - the only mediator between God and us is Jesus; therefore, we approach God in the name of Jesus
        - the only intercessor before God, the only person asking God to accept us is Jesus
        - the only person, the only name that is perfect enough to approach God, is Jesus; therefore, we pray in the name of Jesus

        (See notes—Jn.12:44-46; DEEPER STUDY # 2—12:44; notes—16:23-24; 16:25-27 for more discussion.)
    b. The believer seeks to glorify the name of Jesus only. To pray "in His name" means that we ask only those things that will . . .
        - honor His name
        - praise His name
        - bring glory to His name
        - lead to His name being lifted up

        It means that we will ask nothing that would detract, lower, or lead away from His holy name.

> "You did not choose me, but I chose you and appointed you that you should go and bear fruit and that your fruit should abide, so that whatever you ask the Father in my name, he may give it to you." (Jn.15:16)
>
> "In that day you will ask nothing of me. Truly, truly, I say to you, whatever you ask of the Father in my name, he will give it to you. Until now you have asked nothing in my name. Ask, and you will receive, that your joy may be full." (Jn.16:23-24)

2. Note why Jesus answers the believer's prayers. Christ's purpose is to glorify God. When Jesus answers prayer, not only is the Father glorified, but so is Jesus. The power and wisdom, love and care shown in answered prayer are of God through the name of Jesus. Therefore, when we pray and receive what we asked for . . .
    - our attention is on both the Father and the Son
    - our praise and thanksgiving are heaped on both the Father and the Son

- our loyalty and surrender to both the Father and the Son are deeper and more mature

**Giving thanks to the Father, who has qualified you to share in the inheritance of the saints in light. He has delivered us from the domain of darkness and transferred us to the kingdom of his beloved Son, in whom we have redemption, the forgiveness of sins. (Col.1:12-14)**

**Give thanks in all circumstances; for this is the will of God in Christ Jesus for you. (1 Th.5:18)**

**Through him then let us continually offer up a sacrifice of praise to God, that is, the fruit of lips that acknowledge his name. (He.13:15)**

**But you are a chosen race, a royal priesthood, a holy nation, a people for his own possession, that you may proclaim the excellencies of him who called you out of darkness into his marvelous light. (1 Pe.2:9)**

**Ascribe to the Lord the glory due his name; worship the Lord in the splendor of holiness. (Ps.29:2)**

**Enter his gates with thanksgiving, and his courts with praise! Give thanks to him; bless his name! (Ps.100:4)**

## G. The Holy Spirit: Who He Is, 14:15–26

1. **He is the Helper, the Counselor, the Comforter**<sup>DS1</sup>
   a. His presence is conditional: Must love Jesus
   b. His presence is given forever
2. **He is the Spirit of truth**
   a. The world cannot receive Him
   b. The believer receives Him & knows Him
3. **He is the personal presence of Christ**
   a. A spiritual presence, not a physical presence
   b. A living, eternal presence
   c. A living union between God, Christ, & the believer[DS2]
4. **He is the very special manifestation of Christ within the believer**[DS3]
   a. The special presence is conditional: Must obey & love Christ
   b. The special presence is questioned
5. **He is the abiding presence of the Trinity**
   a. Is conditional: Must love & obey Jesus[DS4]
   b. Is the love & presence of God & Christ
   c. Is not given to those who do not love & obey Christ
   d. Is assured by God Himself
6. **He is the Teacher**
   a. The facts
      1) He is promised
      2) He is given by the Father in the name of Jesus
   b. His purpose: To teach the believer

15 "If you love me, you will keep my commandments.
16 And I will ask the Father, and he will give you another Helper, to be with you forever,
17 even the Spirit of truth, whom the world cannot receive, because it neither sees him nor knows him. You know him, for he dwells with you and will be in you.
18 I will not leave you as orphans; I will come to you.
19 Yet a little while and the world will see me no more, but you will see me. Because I live, you also will live.
20 In that day you will know that I am in my Father, and you in me, and I in you.
21 Whoever has my commandments and keeps them, he it is who loves me. And he who loves me will be loved by my Father, and I will love him and manifest myself to him."
22 Judas (not Iscariot) said to him, "Lord, how is it that you will manifest yourself to us, and not to the world?"
23 Jesus answered him, "If anyone loves me, he will keep my word, and my Father will love him, and we will come to him and make our home with him.

24 Whoever does not love me does not keep my words. And the word that you hear is not mine but the Father's who sent me.
25 These things I have spoken to you while I am still with you.
26 But the Helper, the Holy Spirit, whom the Father will send in my name, he will teach you all things and bring to your remembrance all that I have said to you."

# Division XIII

*The Revelation of Jesus, the Great Minister, and His Legacy, 13:1–16:33*

G. The Holy Spirit: Who He Is, 14:15-26

## 14:15-26
## Introduction

Three great Scriptures deal with the doctrine of the Holy Spirit at length:
- John 14:15-26—the Identity of the Holy Spirit or who He is.
- John 16:7-15—the Work of the Holy Spirit.
- Romans 8:1-17—the Power of the Holy Spirit.

Two of these passages involve a discussion by the Lord Himself. Jesus is in the upper room, spending the last hours He will ever have with His disciples while on earth. He is covering the major subjects they need to grasp before His death, revealing and filling them with the glorious truths that will *help* them through the upcoming trials they are to face.

The greatest help believers are to receive is the very presence of God Himself in the person of the Holy Spirit. It is this truth that Jesus now reveals. He reveals the Holy Spirit, His identity, who He is. This is, *The Holy Spirit: Who He Is*, 14:15-26.

1. He is the Helper, the Counselor, the Comforter (vv.15-16).
2. He is the Spirit of truth (v.17).
3. He is the personal presence of Christ (vv.18-20).
4. He is the very special manifestation of Christ within the believer (vv.21-22).
5. He is the abiding presence of the Trinity (vv.23-24).
6. He is the Teacher (vv.25-26).

## 1 He is the Helper, the Counselor, the Comforter.

14:15-16

The disciples were still reeling from the Lord's announcement that He would be leaving them. Jesus assured them that they would not be alone after He departed. The Father would give them another Helper, One who would never leave them.

¹⁵ "If you love me, you will keep my commandments.
¹⁶ And I will ask the Father, and he will give you another Helper, to be with you forever,"

### a. His presence is conditional: Must love Jesus (vv.15-16a).

The gift of the Holy Spirit is conditional. God gives the Spirit to those who love Jesus.

In this passage, Jesus begins His discussion about the Spirit by stating an obvious fact: if we love Jesus, we *will* keep His commandments. Obedience is not optional for believers. Jesus presents a simple fact that we need to understand: "If you love me you *will keep* [Gk. teresete] my commandments." This is the correct translation. Jesus is not giving an *optional commandment*, "If you love me, [you have the option to] keep my commandments." He is saying that the person who truly loves Him *will* keep His commandments. To the believer, there is no option. We love Jesus; therefore, we keep His commandments. This does not mean that we are claiming *to live* perfectly, but we are claiming *to love* Jesus and *to believe* with all our hearts that Jesus is the Son of God. As a byproduct of our love and belief, we diligently seek Jesus and seek to please Him in all that we do (He.11:6).

We need to clearly understand what it means to love Jesus. To love Jesus is not an emotional thing. It involves emotions, but it is *not based* on emotions. It is not *feelings*: not feeling good today and loving Jesus then feeling bad tomorrow and not loving Jesus. Loving Jesus is not a fluctuating experience, not an up and down emotion. It is not an *emotional love* that changes with feelings.

Furthermore, to love Jesus is not a rational or mental commitment. Of course it involves the mind, but it goes beyond deciding or acknowledging that Jesus is the Son of God and then adopting His teachings and morality as your standard in life. It is more than just living by His teachings and doing the best you can. It is not a matter of the mind alone, not a matter of disciplining yourself to keep the law and its rules and regulations.

To love Jesus is a matter of the heart and of the spirit: a matter of your innermost being, all that you are. The heart is the *seat* of a person's affections and will (devotion). The heart attaches and focuses our affections and will and devotion to an object or a person. The heart causes us to give ourselves either to good or bad. To love Jesus means that we focus our heart and affections and will (devotion) on God by giving and receiving the love of God. It means that we give our *affection* and *will* (devotion), all we are and have, to Jesus Christ. It means we . . .

- freely accept Jesus
- cherish and attach ourselves to Jesus
- sacrificially give all we are and have to Jesus
- commit all we are and have to serve Jesus and His cause

(See outlines and notes—Mt.22:37-40; Jn.13:33-35; 21:15-17 for more discussion.)

> "If you keep my commandments, you will abide in my love, just as I have kept my Father's commandments and abide in his love. . . . You are my friends if you do what I command you." (Jn.15:10, 14)

> And by this we know that we have come to know him, if we keep his commandments. (1 Jn.2:3)

Those who love Jesus keep His commandments, proving that they are genuine believers. Keeping the Lord's commandments is an evidence of salvation (see 1 Jn.2:3 above). Jesus promised the disciples that He would pray to God, His Father, and ask Him to send another *Helper* or *Counselor* to believers (see Deeper Study # 1). This Helper is the Holy Spirit.

Again, the receiving of the Holy Spirit is conditional. Note the conjunction "and" (v.16). The Holy Spirit is given only to those who genuinely love Jesus—genuine believers. Note also that the Spirit is given because Jesus prayed for the Father to give us the Spirit. Jesus is our *Intercessor*, the One who pleads our case. It is not that God is unwilling to give the Holy Spirit. That is not the point. The point is that Jesus Christ is our mediator—our intercessor—the one who makes it possible for us to receive the Spirit (see 1 Jn.2:1-2). If a person truly loves Jesus, is a genuine believer, that person is given the Holy Spirit.

The source of the Holy Spirit is "the Father." It is the Father who gave the Son, and it is the Father who gives the Holy Spirit. The picture is touching in that God is seen longing ever so deeply . . .

- to give the Holy Spirit to those who love His *only* Son
- to do everything He can for those who love His Son (Of course, the greatest thing God can do is to put His Spirit into a person.)

> "If you then, who are evil, know how to give good gifts to your children, how much more will the heavenly Father give the Holy Spirit to those who ask him!" (Lu.11:13)

### b. His presence is given forever (v.16b).

The Holy Spirit abides with the believer forever. His presence continues and never ends. God never withdraws His presence from us.

## Deeper Study # 1

(14:16) **Helper, Counselor, or Comforter** (paracletos): one called in, one called to the side of another. The purpose is to help in any way possible. (1) Picture a friend called in to help a person who is troubled or distressed or confused. (2) Or picture a commander called in to help a discouraged and dispirited army. (3) Finally, picture a lawyer, an advocate, called in to help a defendant who needs his case pleaded. No one word can adequately translate *paracletos*. The word that probably comes closest is simply *Helper*.

## 2 He is the Spirit of truth.

The Holy Spirit is the Spirit of truth, the very same truth that Christ is. He is the Embodiment, the Communicator, and the Liberator of truth, just as Jesus is (see DEEPER STUDY # 2, *Jesus the Truth*—Jn.14:6).

> [17] "even the Spirit of truth, whom the world cannot receive, because it neither sees him nor knows him. You know him, for he dwells with you and will be in you."

### a. The world cannot receive Him.

The world cannot receive the Holy Spirit. Note the word "cannot" or the words "is unable to." It is impossible for the world to receive the Holy Spirit. Why? Because the world of unbelievers does not "see" or "know" the Holy Spirit. The world lives only for what it can *see* and *know*, only for the physical and material, only for what it can touch and feel, taste and consume, think and use.

The point is, unbelievers simply reject Jesus. They do not love Him, and they care little if anything about Him. They are not interested in seeing or knowing Jesus. The result is natural:

- They do not see the spiritual world or know it; therefore, they do not see or know the Spirit of that world.
- They are unaware of the spiritual world; therefore, they are unaware of the Spirit of that world.
- They do not know and love Jesus; therefore, they do not know the Spirit of Christ.

Note this contrast between the "spirit of the world" and the "Spirit of God."

> Now we have received not the spirit of the world, but the Spirit who is from God, that we might understand the things freely given us by God. And we impart this in words not taught by human wisdom but taught by the Spirit, interpreting spiritual truths to those who are spiritual. The natural person does not accept the things of the Spirit of God, for they are folly to him, and he is not able to understand them because they are spiritually discerned. (1 Co.2:12-14)

### b. The believer receives Him and knows Him.

The believer definitely knows the Holy Spirit. We know the Spirit both by experience and by His presence. The Holy Spirit *dwells with* us, giving assurance, looking after, caring, guiding, and teaching us. He is *in* us, communing, fellowshipping, sharing, and conforming us to the image of Christ.

> You, however, are not in the flesh but in the Spirit, if in fact the Spirit of God dwells in you. Anyone who does not have the Spirit of Christ does not belong to him. (Ro.8:9)

> The Spirit himself bears witness with our spirit that we are children of God. (Ro.8:16)

> Now we have received not the spirit of the world, but the Spirit who is from God, that we might understand the things freely given us by God. (1 Co.2:12)

> Do you not know that you are God's temple and that God's Spirit dwells in you? (1 Co.3:16)

> And because you are sons, God has sent the Spirit of his Son into our hearts, crying, "Abba! Father!" (Ga.4:6)

> Whoever keeps his commandments abides in God, and God in him. And by this we know that he abides in us, by the Spirit whom he has given us. (1 Jn.3:24)

> "And I will put my Spirit within you, and cause you to walk in my statutes and be careful to obey my rules." (Eze.36:27)

## 3 He is the personal presence of Christ.

The Holy Spirit is the personal presence of Christ dwelling in the believer. Jesus said, "I will come to you" (v.18.) He meant that He would return to His disciples after He had gone away to heaven. He would come back to give believers His personal presence. He would not leave us *as orphans*

> [18] "I will not leave you as orphans; I will come to you.
> [19] Yet a little while and the world will see me no more, but you will see me. Because I live, you also will live.
> [20] In that day you will know that I am in my Father, and you in me, and I in you."

(orphanous): without parental help, helpless. Jesus would not leave us to struggle through the trials of life alone.

a. **A spiritual presence, not a physical presence (v.19a).**

Jesus' presence with His followers began with His resurrection and with the coming of the Holy Spirit. Jesus is saying that He would come to the believer in the person of the Holy Spirit.

The world lost its opportunity to see Jesus after He ascended to heaven. He said that He would be present for only a short time longer, then the world would see Him *"no more."* (The next time the world sees Him, He will be coming in judgment.) Although Jesus would no longer be seen *physically* until He returns, believers would see Him *spiritually*. He would be with His followers through His Spirit. His presence with them would be a spiritual presence, a presence they would know, feel, and experience in a real way.

b. **A living, eternal presence (v.19b).**

The presence of Jesus within believers is a living, eternal presence. He died, but He did not stay dead. He arose and conquered death. He arose to live forever. This fact leads to a logical truth: if Jesus Christ is living forever and dwells within the believer, then the believer lives eternally. Christ the Eternal Presence lives *within* believers; therefore, believers become eternal. We never die (see Deeper Study # 1—Jn.8:51). Believers live eternally through the eternal presence of Christ *within* us. Because He lives, we also will live.

In fact, when Jesus says "I live," He means He lives abundantly and eternally: He lives life in all of its full meaning. Therefore, by living *within* the believer, Christ imparts the same kind of life to the believer, a life that is both abundant and eternal (see Deeper Study # 2—Jn.1:4; Deeper Study # 1—10:10; Deeper Study # 1—17:2-3).

c. **A living union between God, Christ, and the believer (v.20).**

The presence of Christ is a living union, a *mutual indwelling* between God, Christ, and the believer. *In that day* refers to Jesus' resurrection and the coming of the Holy Spirit.

When Jesus arose from the dead, believers knew something. They knew His claim of resurrection was absolutely true. Jesus really was "in" God. God is eternal, so by being "in" God, Jesus was bound to live forever; He was bound to arise from the dead.

When the Spirit came, believers knew that all Jesus had said was true. He was placing all believers *"in"* Himself and Himself *"in"* them; or to say it another way, when the Holy Spirit came, believers were placed "in" His Spirit and His Spirit "in" them (see Deeper Study # 2; Deeper Study # 1—Ac.2:1-4 for more discussion).

## Deeper Study # 2

(14:20) **Christ in You:** this is the first time the glorious truth of *Christ in you* is revealed to the disciples. Paul later gave the full explanation of the indwelling Christ (see Deeper Study # 4—Jn.20:22; notes—1 Co.3:16; 6:19; Ep.3:6; Col.1:26-27; see also Jn.14:17-18, 20, 23; Ro.8:9; 1 Co.2:11-12; 3:16; 6:19; 2 Ti.1:14; 1 Jn.2:27; Eze.36:27).

> "I in them and you in me, that they may become perfectly one, so that the world may know that you sent me and loved them even as you loved me." (Jn.17:23)

> You, however, are not in the flesh but in the Spirit, if in fact the Spirit of God dwells in you. Anyone who does not have the Spirit of Christ does not belong to him. (Ro.8:9)

> I have been crucified with Christ. It is no longer I who live, but Christ who lives in me. And the life I now live in the flesh I live by faith in the Son of God, who loved me and gave himself for me. (Ga.2:20)

> So that Christ may dwell in your hearts through faith—that you, being rooted and grounded in love. (Ep.3:17)

> To them God chose to make known how great among the Gentiles are the riches of the glory of this mystery, which is Christ in you, the hope of glory. (Col.1:27)

## 4 He is the very special manifestation of Christ within the believer.

Christ promised to manifest or reveal Himself to those who obey Him. The Holy Spirit is the very special manifestation of Christ within the believer. Apparently, this refers to very special manifestations of the Lord to the heart of the believer, those very special times when there is a deep consciousness of love between the Lord and His dear follower (see DEEPER STUDY # 3). This is surely what Christ means, for He has already spoken about His personal presence within the believer (vv.18-20). When believers go through terrible trials and experience severe crises, God knows and He loves and cares; so He moves to meet the need of His dear children. He moves within the believer's heart, manifesting His presence and giving a deep sense of His love and care, helping and giving confidence, forgiveness, and assurance—giving whatever the believer needs. The depth of the experience and the intensity and emotion of the *special manifestation* depends on the need of the believer. God knows and loves His dear child perfectly, so He gives whatever experience and depth of emotion are needed to meet the need of His child. We must always remember that God loves each one of us so much He will do whatever is needed to lift us up, to strengthen us, and to conform us to the image of His dear Son, the Lord Jesus Christ.

> 14:21-22
>
> [21] "Whoever has my commandments and keeps them, he it is who loves me. And he who loves me will be loved by my Father, and I will love him and manifest myself to him."
> [22] Judas (not Iscariot) said to him, "Lord, how is it that you will manifest yourself to us, and not to the world?"

### a. The special presence is conditional: Must obey and love Christ (v.21).

The *special manifestations* of the Lord's presence are given only to the believer who does two things:

> ➢ The believer who *has* Jesus' commandments receives the special manifestations of the Holy Spirit. To have His commandments means that we have searched and possess the commandments of Jesus Christ. We have them in our hearts, know them, have made them our own (see Ps.119:11).
>
> ➢ The believer who *keeps* the commandments of Jesus receives the special manifestations of the Holy Spirit.

Those who do these two things show that they *truly* love the Lord Jesus—that they are genuine believers (see vv.14-15). The Father loves them, and the Lord Jesus will love them as well. In fact, the Lord will *manifest* Himself to the believers who hide His commandments in their heart.

### b. The special presence is questioned (v.22).

Judas questioned this special manifestation of the Lord's presence. Judas asked the question for the first time, but the special manifestation of Christ's presence has been questioned and doubted by thousands ever since. Judas was thinking like many people think—in terms of a physical manifestation, a visible appearance.

### DEEPER STUDY # 3

(14:21) **Manifestation** (emphanizo): when used in the sense of an unveiling or revelation, it suggests that a new thing has come to light; that something never known by humanity before is made known. Some mystery has now been revealed. It is something that cannot be discovered by human reason or wisdom. It is a mystery that is hidden from people and beyond our grasp. Here in Jn.14:21-22, it means that Jesus' presence is revealed (brought to light), illuminated, manifested, quickened in the life of the believer. It means that He *manifests* Himself to His disciples in a very special way. He discloses His person, His nature, His goodness. Jesus illuminates Himself *within* their hearts and lives. He gives a very special consciousness within their souls (see notes—Jn.14:21-22; DEEPER STUDY # 1—Ac.2:1-4).

"Whoever believes in me, as the Scripture has said, 'Out of his heart will flow rivers of living water.'" Now this he said about the Spirit, whom those who believed in him were to receive, for as yet the Spirit had not been given, because Jesus was not yet glorified. (Jn.7:38-39)

And they were all filled with the Holy Spirit and began to speak in other tongues as the Spirit gave them utterance. (Ac.2:4)

And when they had prayed, the place in which they were gathered together was shaken, and they were all filled with the Holy Spirit and continued to speak the word of God with boldness. (Ac.4:31)

And the disciples were filled with joy and with the Holy Spirit. (Ac.13:52)

And do not get drunk with wine, for that is debauchery, but be filled with the Spirit. (Ep.5:18)

## 14:23-24

²³ Jesus answered him, "If anyone loves me, he will keep my word, and my Father will love him, and we will come to him and make our home with him.
²⁴ Whoever does not love me does not keep my words. And the word that you hear is not mine but the Father's who sent me."

## 5 He is the abiding presence of the Trinity.

The Holy Spirit is the abiding presence of the Trinity. Note the words, "My Father . . . *we* will come . . . and make *our* home with him [the believer]." Both the Father and Christ come to abide in the believer in the person of the Holy Spirit (vv.16-17, 26). All three dwell within the believer. Note four simple but profound truths about the presence of the Trinity in the believer.

a. **Is conditional: Must love and obey Jesus (v.23a).**

The abiding presence of the Trinity is conditional: we must obey Christ, that is, love and keep His words (see DEEPER STUDY # 4).

b. **Is the love and presence of God and Christ (v.23b).**

The abiding presence of the Trinity is the *love* and *presence* of God and Christ and the Holy Spirit. All three dwell within the life of the believer.

c. **Is not given to those who do not love and obey Christ (v.24a).**

Those who do not obey Christ do not love Him; they are not genuine believers. Therefore, the abiding presence of the Trinity is not *in* the person who does not love and obey Jesus.

d. **Is assured by God Himself (v.24b).**

The abiding presence of the Trinity is assured by God Himself. Note what Jesus said: His words are the words of the Father who sent Him (see note, pt.2—Jn.14:10).

"And I am no longer in the world, but they are in the world, and I am coming to you. Holy Father, keep them in your name, which you have given me, that they may be one, even as we are one." (Jn.17:11)

"The glory that you have given me I have given to them, that they may be one even as we are one, I in them and you in me, that they may become perfectly one, so that the world may know that you sent me and loved them even as you loved me." (Jn.17:22-23)

### DEEPER STUDY # 4

(14:23) **Love—Commandments**: the person who really loves Jesus will want to do what He asks. Therefore, love and obedience are tied together so tightly that a person cannot love and not obey. Our love is proven and clearly seen in our obedience (see 1 Jn.2:9-11; 3:10-17; 4:7-21).

## 6 He is the Teacher.

The Holy Spirit is *the Teacher* who teaches "all things." *All things* means all the things which Jesus taught, including the presence of the Helper (Holy Spirit) given to help the believer through the trials of life along with the indwelling presence and love of the Father and Son.

²⁵ "These things I have spoken to you while I am still with you.
²⁶ "But the Helper, the Holy Spirit, whom the Father will send in my name, he will teach you all things and bring to your remembrance all that I have said to you."

a. **The facts (v.26a).**

In teaching His disciples of the coming of the Spirit, Jesus focused on two facts:
- ➤ *The Spirit is promised to believers.* The disciples needed to remember and cling to this promise until the day that the Spirit was actually given.
- ➤ *The Spirit is given by the Father in the name of Jesus.* Jesus emphasizes a crucial point: the Helper comes only from the Father. In calling God "the Father," Jesus emphasizes a Father-child relationship. A person must become a child of God, that is, of the Father, in order to be given the Father's Helper. The Spirit is given *in Jesus' name,* for He alone is acceptable to God (see Deeper Study # 3—Jn.14:13-14 for discussion).

b. **His purpose: To teach the believer (v.26b).**

The Holy Spirit has a clear purpose: He teaches us all things. *All things* speaks of both the words and the life of Christ, both the Truth and the Life, both the Word and how to live the Word, both the theory and the practice, both the principles and the conduct, both the morality and the behavior.

The Spirit also helps us remember all that we have been taught in the Word of God, especially in the moments of trial or temptation when we need God's truth. In a moment of trial or temptation the Holy Spirit either infuses us with the strength to endure or flashes across our mind the way to escape (see 1 Co.10:13).

> "For the Holy Spirit will teach you in that very hour what you ought to say." (Lu.12:12)

> "When the Spirit of truth comes, he will guide you into all the truth, for he will not speak on his own authority, but whatever he hears he will speak, and he will declare to you the things that are to come." (Jn.16:13)

> And we impart this in words not taught by human wisdom but taught by the Spirit, interpreting spiritual truths to those who are spiritual. (1 Co.2:13)

> But the anointing that you received from him abides in you, and you have no need that anyone should teach you. But as his anointing teaches you about everything, and is true, and is no lie—just as it has taught you, abide in him. (1 Jn.2:27)

## H. The Source of Peace, Joy, and Security, 14:27-31

1. The source of peace
   a. The peace of the world
   b. The peace of Christ
   c. The source: Jesus Christ
2. The source of joy
   a. The return of Jesus to the Father (His death, resurrection, & ascension) stirs joy
   b. The Father's greatness stirs joy
   c. The believer's faith being confirmed stirs joy

3. The source of security
   a. The victory of Jesus Christ over the prince of the world (Satan, the devil)
   b. The obedience of Jesus Christ to the Father

27 "Peace I leave with you; my peace I give to you. Not as the world gives do I give to you. Let not your hearts be troubled, neither let them be afraid.

28 You heard me say to you, 'I am going away, and I will come to you.' If you loved me, you would have rejoiced, because I am going to the Father, for the Father is greater than I.

29 And now I have told you before it takes place, so that when it does take place you may believe.

30 I will no longer talk much with you, for the ruler of this world is coming. He has no claim on me,

31 but I do as the Father has commanded me, so that the world may know that I love the Father. Rise, let us go from here."

# Division XIII

*The Revelation of Jesus, the Great Minister, and His Legacy, 13:1-16:33*

H. The Source of Peace, Joy, and Security, 14:27-31

## 14:27-31
## Introduction

Of all human needs, peace, joy, and security are three of the greatest. This passage speaks ever so warmly yet powerfully to these critical needs. It tells us where peace, joy, and security may be found. This is, *The Source of Peace, Joy, and Security,* 14:27-31.

1. The source of peace (v.27).
2. The source of joy (vv.28-29).
3. The source of security (vv.30-31).

### 14:27

27 "Peace I leave with you; my peace I give to you. Not as the world gives do I give to you. Let not your hearts be troubled, neither let them be afraid."

### 1 The source of peace.

The Greek word for *peace* (eirene) means to bind together, to join, to weave together. It means that a person is bound, woven, and joined together with himself and with God and others.

The Hebrew word is *shalom*. It means freedom from trouble and much more. It means experiencing the highest good, enjoying the very best, possessing all the inner good possible. It means wholeness and soundness. It means prosperity in the widest sense, especially prosperity in the spiritual sense of having a soul that blossoms and flourishes.

The idea of peace is a wonderful concept, but how can we have it? Where does it come from? What is its source?

a. **The peace of the world.**
   Jesus said that there is a peace that the world gives. This peace is one of escapism, of avoiding trouble, of refusing to face things, of unreality. It is a peace that is sought through pleasure, satisfaction, contentment, absence of trouble, positive thinking, or denial of problems.

b. **The peace of Christ.**
   The peace that Christ gives is totally different from the peace of the world. First, it is a *peace of heart,* a peace deep within. It is a tranquility of mind, a composure, a peace that is calm in the face of bad circumstances and situations. It is more than feelings—even more than attitude and thought.

   Second, it is a *peace of conquest,* a peace that overcomes trouble and adversity (see Jn.16:33). It is the peace independent of conditions and environment; the peace which no sorrow, no danger, no suffering, no experience can take away.

   > "I have said these things to you, that in me you may have peace. In the world you will have tribulation. But take heart; I have overcome the world." (Jn.16:33)

   Third, it is the *peace of assurance* (see Ro.8:28). It is the peace of unquestionable confidence; the peace with a sure knowledge that our life is in the hands of God and that all things will work out for good if we love God and are called according to His purpose.

   > And we know that for those who love God all things work together for good, for those who are called according to his purpose. (Ro.8:28)

   Fourth, it is the *peace of intimacy with God* (see Ph.4:6-7), the peace of the highest good. It is the peace that settles the mind, strengthens the will, and establishes the heart.

c. **The source: Jesus Christ.**
   The source of this wonderful peace is Jesus Christ. Only through Him can we know true peace. Peace is always born out of reconciliation. Its source is found only in the reconciliation brought about by Jesus Christ. Peace always has to do with personal relationships: a person's relationship to self, to God, and to other people. To truly know peace, we must be bound, woven, and joined together with ourselves, with God, and with others.

   > But now in Christ Jesus you who once were far off have been brought near by the blood of Christ. For he himself is our peace, who has made us both one and has broken down in his flesh the dividing wall of hostility. (Ep.2:13-14)

   > And through him to reconcile to himself all things, whether on earth or in heaven, making peace by the blood of his cross. And you, who once were alienated and hostile in mind, doing evil deeds. (Col.1:20-21)

   We secure this peace in the following ways:
   - By justification.

     > Therefore, since we have been justified by faith, we have peace with God through our Lord Jesus Christ. (Ro.5:1)

   - By loving God's Word.

     > "I have said these things to you, that in me you may have peace. In the world you will have tribulation. But take heart; I have overcome the world." (Jn.16:33)

     > Great peace have those who love your law; nothing can make them stumble. (Ps.119:165)

   - By praying about everything.

     > Do not be anxious about anything, but in everything by prayer and supplication with thanksgiving let your requests be made known to God. And the peace of God, which surpasses all understanding, will guard your hearts and your minds in Christ Jesus. (Ph.4:6-7)

   - By being spiritually minded.

     > For to set the mind on the flesh is death, but to set the mind on the Spirit is life and peace. (Ro.8:6)

> By keeping our minds on God.

**Finally, brothers, whatever is true, whatever is honorable, whatever is just, whatever is pure, whatever is lovely, whatever is commendable, if there is any excellence, if there is anything worthy of praise, think about these things. (Ph.4:8)**

"You keep him in perfect peace whose mind is stayed on you, because he trusts in you." (Is.26:3)

> By keeping God's commandments.

**What you have learned and received and heard and seen in me—practice these things, and the God of peace will be with you. (Ph.4:9)**

"Oh that you had paid attention to my commandments! Then your peace would have been like a river, and your righteousness like the waves of the sea." (Is.48:18)

The subject of peace is often divided into peace *with* God, which is received through salvation (Ro.5:1; Ep.2:14-17); the peace *of* God, which is the very peace of God Himself and which points to God as the Source of peace (Lu.7:50; Ph.4:6-7); the peace *from* God, which God gives to dwell in the heart of believers as we walk day by day in the Lord (Ro.1:7; 1 Co.1:3).

## 14:28-29

28 "You heard me say to you, 'I am going away, and I will come to you.' If you loved me, you would have rejoiced, because I am going to the Father, for the Father is greater than I.

29 And now I have told you before it takes place, so that when it does take place you may believe."

## 2 The source of joy.

The words *joy* (chara) and *rejoicing* (echarete, the same root word as joy) speak of an inner gladness and a deep-seated pleasure. It is a depth of assurance and confidence that ignites a cheerful heart. It is a cheerful heart that leads to cheerful behavior. How can we have joy? Where does it come from? What is its source (see DEEPER STUDY # 1—Jn.15:11 for more discussion)?

**a. The return of Jesus to the Father (His death, resurrection, and ascension) stirs joy (v.28a).**

The return of Jesus to the Father causes believers to rejoice and experience joy. When Jesus said, "I am going away," He was referring to His death, resurrection, and ascension.

The death or cross of Christ attracts people and causes them to experience joy and rejoice. The cross is the source of our deliverance from sin, death, and hell (see note—Jn.12:32).

"And I, when I am lifted up from the earth, will draw all people to myself." (Jn.12:32)

But far be it from me to boast except in the cross of our Lord Jesus Christ, by which the world has been crucified to me, and I to the world. (Ga.6:14)

The resurrection and ascension of Christ also attract people and cause them to have joy and rejoice. The resurrection and ascension are the sources of our new life and hope for eternity (see notes, *Resurrection*—Jn.14:6; 7:33-34; Mk.16:19-20).

Therefore, since we have been justified by faith, we have peace with God through our Lord Jesus Christ. Through him we have also obtained access by faith into this grace in which we stand, and we rejoice in hope of the glory of God. (Ro.5:1-2)

You make known to me the path of life; in your presence there is fullness of joy; at your right hand are pleasures forevermore. (Ps.16:11)

And the ransomed of the LORD shall return and come to Zion with singing; everlasting joy shall be upon their heads; they shall obtain gladness and joy, and sorrow and sighing shall flee away. (Is.35:10)

**b. The Father's greatness stirs joy (v.28b).**

The Father's greatness causes believers to experience joy and rejoice. The Father demonstrated His great love and power by releasing Jesus . . .
- from the flesh: in all its limitations and weaknesses
- from the world: in all its trials and tensions
- from the devil: in all his oppressions and attacks
- from the pressure of people: in all their needful demands and in some cases terrible threats and attacks

The Father took Jesus home, back from where He had come; and He restored Jesus to His seat of glory, exalting Jesus above every name that is named (Ph.2:9-11). The believer expresses joy and rejoices in the phenomenal power of the Father's greatness.

> "Until now you have asked nothing in my name. Ask, and you will receive, that your joy may be full." (Jn.16:24)

> For the kingdom of God is not a matter of eating and drinking but of righteousness and peace and joy in the Holy Spirit. (Ro.14:17)

> Rejoice in the Lord always; again I will say, rejoice. (Ph.4:4)

> Though you have not seen him, you love him. Though you do not now see him, you believe in him and rejoice with joy that is inexpressible and filled with glory, obtaining the outcome of your faith, the salvation of your souls. (1 Pe.1:8-9)

**THOUGHT 1.** The implication of the Father's power for the believer is phenomenal. The believer will also be released from the flesh, the world, the devil, and the pressure of other people, just as Jesus was.

> "These things I have spoken to you, that my joy may be in you, and that your joy may be full." (Jn.15:11)

c. **The believer's faith being confirmed stirs joy (v.29).**

A confirmed faith also causes believers to experience joy and rejoice. The claims of Jesus have been proven and verified. Just as He told His disciples, all that He predicted has come to pass:

➢ He did leave (die).
➢ He did return (the resurrection).
➢ He did go to His Father (the ascension).
➢ He did send the Holy Spirit.

By foretelling these things, Jesus strengthened the faith of believers enormously. (In fact, think about it: He could have chosen no better way to strengthen our faith.)

> "These things I have spoken to you, that my joy may be in you, and that your joy may be full." (Jn.15:11)

> "But now I am coming to you, and these things I speak in the world, that they may have my joy fulfilled in themselves." (Jn.17:13)

> Your words were found, and I ate them, and your words became to me a joy and the delight of my heart, for I am called by your name, O LORD, God of hosts. (Je.15:16)

## 3 The source of security.

Our Lord does not want us to have troubled hearts. He does not want us to be strangled in the grip of fear (v.27). Instead, He wants us to rest secure in Him. How can we have this security? Where does it come from? What is its source?

> ³⁰ "I will no longer talk much with you, for the ruler of this world is coming. He has no claim on me,
> ³¹ but I do as the Father has commanded me, so that the world may know that I love the Father. Rise, let us go from here."

a. **The victory of Jesus Christ over the prince of the world (Satan, the devil; v.30).**

Security comes from Jesus' victory over Satan (see DEEPER STUDY # 3—Jn.12:31; DEEPER STUDY # 4—12:32 for discussion). When Jesus said that Satan was "coming," He was speaking of the devil's use of men (Judas and the religious leaders) to make a last ditch effort to destroy Jesus. But Satan had nothing on Jesus, no claim on Him, no power over Him. There was nothing which he could use to attract Jesus to sin. There was no lust, no greed, no selfishness—nothing in Jesus that Satan could use to destroy Him.

> "Which one of you convicts me of sin? If I tell the truth, why do you not believe me?" (Jn.8:46)

> For our sake he made him to be sin who knew no sin, so that in him we might become the righteousness of God. (2 Co.5:21)

> For we do not have a high priest who is unable to sympathize with our weaknesses, but one who in every respect has been tempted as we are, yet without sin. (He.4:15)
>
> For it was indeed fitting that we should have such a high priest, holy, innocent, unstained, separated from sinners, and exalted above the heavens. (He.7:26)
>
> But with the precious blood of Christ, like that of a lamb without blemish or spot. (1 Pe.1:19)

Here Jesus predicts His complete victory and triumph over Satan. Satan would not succeed in bringing Him down. Instead, Jesus would bring Satan down through His death on the cross.

> "Now is the judgment of this world; now will the ruler of this world be cast out." (Jn.12:31)
>
> He disarmed the rulers and authorities and put them to open shame, by triumphing over them [upon the cross] in him. (Col.2:15)
>
> Since therefore the children share in flesh and blood, he himself likewise partook of the same things, that through death he might destroy the one who has the power of death, that is, the devil, and deliver all those who through fear of death were subject to lifelong slavery. (He.2:14-15)
>
> Whoever makes a practice of sinning is of the devil, for the devil has been sinning from the beginning. The reason the Son of God appeared was to destroy the works of the devil. (1 Jn.3:8)

b. **The obedience of Jesus Christ to the Father (v.31).**

Security comes from Jesus' obedience to the Father. The Father's great commandment was for Jesus to die for the sins of the world. His death was the supreme act of obedience (see note—Jn.12:27-30). By submitting to dying on the cross, Jesus displayed His love for the Father.

> "For this reason the Father loves me, because I lay down my life that I may take it up again. No one takes it from me, but I lay it down of my own accord. I have authority to lay it down, and I have authority to take it up again. This charge I have received from my Father." (Jn.10:17-18)
>
> "Now is my soul troubled. And what shall I say? 'Father, save me from this hour'? But for this purpose I have come to this hour. Father, glorify your name." Then a voice came from heaven: "I have glorified it, and I will glorify it again." (Jn.12:27-28)
>
> And walk in love, as Christ loved us and gave himself up for us, a fragrant offering and sacrifice to God. (Ep.5:2)

# Chapter 15

## I. The Relationship of Jesus to the People of the World, 15:1–8

"I am the true vine, and my Father is the vinedresser.

² Every branch in me that does not bear fruit he takes away, and every branch that does bear fruit he prunes, that it may bear more fruit.

³ Already you are clean because of the word that I have spoken to you.

⁴ Abide in me, and I in you. As the branch cannot bear fruit by itself, unless it abides in the vine, neither can you, unless you abide in me.

⁵ I am the vine; you are the branches. Whoever abides in me and I in him, he it is that bears much fruit, for apart from me you can do nothing.

⁶ If anyone does not abide in me he is thrown away like a branch and withers; and the branches are gathered, thrown into the fire, and burned.

⁷ If you abide in me, and my words abide in you, ask whatever you wish, and it will be done for you.

⁸ "By this my Father is glorified, that you bear much fruit and so prove to be my disciples."

1. **Jesus, the Vine; God, the Gardener; man, the branch**
2. **Unfruitful branches: Are taken away**
3. **Fruitful branches: Are pruned**
   a. The purpose for pruning: To bear more fruit[DS1]
   b. How branches are pruned
      1) By the Word
      2) By abiding, remaining in Christ[DS2]
4. **Unattached branches**
   a. Are by themselves: Not attached, connected, or abiding
   b. Cannot bear fruit
   c. Do not understand the nature of bearing fruit
      1) Must abide in Christ to bear fruit
      2) Can do nothing apart from Christ
   d. Are doomed: Gathered, thrown away, burned
5. **Attached branches: The results & promises**
   a. Receive nourishment—answered prayers
   b. Glorify God
   c. Prove their attachment—their discipleship—by bearing fruit

# Division XIII

*The Revelation of Jesus, the Great Minister, and His Legacy, 13:1–16:33*

I. The Relationship of Jesus to the People of the World, 15:1–8

## 15:1–8
## Introduction

Jesus was facing the most terrible scene in all human history. The Son of God was about to be murdered at the hands of hate-filled, bloodthirsty people. All that He had to face was weighing ever so heavily upon His mind, in particular the reaction of everyone to Him and their fate. He had come to save them all, and few were responding in a genuine way. He was even facing the collapse of His own inner circle. Most tragically, they were falling away.

➢ One disciple was in the very process of betraying Him (Judas).

> The leader of the disciples would deny Him three times, even by cursing (Peter).
> The other disciples would flee and desert Him.

And then, there was the world of people who were rejecting Him: the religious leaders who strongly professed to know and live for God, and the non-religious who had no attachment to God and professed none.

Jesus had come to save them all, and not one was standing with Him in His hour of greatest need. As the thought of it all raced through His mind, He recalled the vine of God so often described in the Old Testament (Ps.80:8-16; Is.5:1-7; Je.2:21; Eze.15:1-8; 19:10; Ho.10:1). In it He saw a graphic lesson that the disciples needed to learn, the great lesson of "The Vine and the Branches"—His relationship to different groups of people. This is, *The Relationship of Jesus to the People of the World,* 15:1-8.

1. Jesus, the Vine; God, the Gardener; man, the branch (vv.1-2).
2. Unfruitful branches: Are taken away (v.2).
3. Fruitful branches: Are pruned (vv.2-4).
4. Unattached branches (vv.4-6).
5. Attached branches: The results and promises (vv.7-8).

## 15:1

"I am the true vine, and my Father is the vinedresser."

### 1 Jesus, the Vine; God, the Gardener; man, the branch.

Jesus used the familiar image of the vineyard—the vine, the branches, and the gardener who tends the vineyard—to illustrate His relationship to the people of the world. He began by identifying who each of these represents.

The vine is Jesus (v.1a). Jesus is the *true* Vine. He is the genuine vine, not a false, counterfeit vine. In fact, He is opposed to the counterfeit, the sham, the deceitful, the *pretender* (see DEEPER STUDY # 1—Jn.1:9).

The vinedresser or gardener is God (v.1b). He is the One who carefully planted the Vine (Christ) and waters and feeds the Vine. He is the One who cares for, looks after, and watches over the Vine and the branches. He is the One who prunes and purges, cleans and protects the Vine and its branches.

The branches are mankind (v.2a). People are branches. And note, we are all judged on the basis of how we relate to the *True* Vine. We are . . .

- either *unfruitful* (v.2) or *fruitful* branches of the true Vine (vv.2-3)
- either *unattached* (v.4-6) or *attached* branches of the true Vine (vv.7-8)

## 15:2a

² "Every branch in me that does not bear fruit he takes away, and every branch that does bear fruit he prunes, that it may bear more fruit."

### 2 Unfruitful branches: Are taken away.

Many branches are unfruitful. Consequently, they are taken away. Note that these are *attached branches*. They differ from the unattached branches (vv.4-6). Jesus said that they are "in Me," but they have a critical problem: they bear no fruit.

The unfruitful branches *did become* attached to Christ. They did have some *organic* relationship to Him. There was a time, a point, when they began to bud and sprout. They even grew into branches. They . . .

- listened to Jesus and the gospel
- opened their ears
- made a profession
- were baptized
- seemed capable of bearing fruit
- appeared to be fruitful branches

However, these branches are unfruitful. They are "in" the Vine, a part of it, but they simply bear no fruit. What does this mean? (See outline and notes, *Judas*—Jn.13:18-30; *The Sower and the Seed*—Mt.13:1-9.)

First, unfruitful branches do *not relate enough* to Christ; they do not draw enough nourishment from Him to sustain life, to bear fruit, and to continue in the Vine (see Mt.24:13; 13:13).

Second, unfruitful branches are *not genuine enough* to bear fruit. Their profession is . . .
- more *profession* than *possession*
- more *pretending* then *being*
- more *deception* than *truth*
- more *counterfeit* than *real*

Third, unfruitful branches become apostate and deserters—men and women who abandon the faith (see 1 Jn.2:19).

> "As for what was sown among thorns, this is the one who hears the word, but the cares of the world and the deceitfulness of riches choke the word, and it proves unfruitful." (Mt.13:22)

> And he told this parable: "A man had a fig tree planted in his vineyard, and he came seeking fruit on it and found none." (Lu.13:6)

> They profess to know God, but they deny him by their works. They are detestable, disobedient, unfit for any good work. (Tit.1:16)

> Take care, brothers, lest there be in any of you an evil, unbelieving heart, leading you to fall away from the living God. (He.3:12)

> Suffering wrong as the wage for their wrongdoing. They count it pleasure to revel in the daytime. They are blots and blemishes, reveling in their deceptions, while they feast with you. They have eyes full of adultery, insatiable for sin. They entice unsteady souls. They have hearts trained in greed. Accursed children! (2 Pe.2:13-14)

God *takes away* (airei) the unfruitful branches. In relation to the vine, the branch is removed and taken away. This is a severe warning to every branch "in" the vine, to make sure their profession is genuine enough to bear fruit.

Some branches are unfruitful because of ongoing sin in their lives. Scripture says that the judgment of unfruitful branches is severe. The unfruitful branches that sin are taken away and removed from the Vine. They are taken away from the area where the Gardener—God the Father—works.

> "Even now the axe is laid to the root of the trees. Every tree therefore that does not bear good fruit is cut down and thrown into the fire." (Mt.3:10)

> "Take care then how you hear, for to the one who has, more will be given, and from the one who has not, even what he thinks that he has will be taken away." (Lu.8:18)

> But if it bears thorns and thistles, it is worthless and near to being cursed, and its end is to be burned. (He.6:8)

> They went out from us, but they were not of us; for if they had been of us, they would have continued with us. But they went out, that it might become plain that they all are not of us. (1 Jn.2:19)

The unfruitful branches that continue in sin are chastened and disciplined by being taken away and removed through death (see note—1 Jn.5:16). The Bible warns professing believers of severe chastening, the chastening of sinful behavior that . . .
- causes loss of all reward by fire—a loss so great a person is stripped as much as a burned-out building. It is the loss of all except the person's salvation (1 Co.3:11-15, esp. 15)
- destroys the flesh so that the Spirit may be saved (1 Co.5:5)
- causes death (1 Co.11:29-30; 1 Jn.5:16)
- merits no escape (He.2:1-3; 12:25f)
- prohibits a person from ever repenting again (He.6:4f)
- causes a person to miss God's rest (He.4:1f)
- prohibits any future sacrifice for sins and merits terrible punishment (He.10:26f; see Deeper Study # 1—1 Jn.5:16 for more discussion)

The point must be heeded, for Scripture gives severe warnings to believers, that is, to the branches "in" the Vine. The branches must make sure they are bearing fruit or else face severe judgment (again, see Deeper Study # 1—1 Jn.5:16 for more discussion).

## 3 Fruitful branches: Are pruned.

The branches that bear fruit are pruned by the Vinedresser (v.2b). All bad spots, useless buds, misdirected shoots, and discolored leaves are pruned off. Even fruitful believers have spots, buds, shoots, and leaves that are bad, useless, misdirected, and discolored. Believers have areas and things that must be cleaned away and cleared up, areas of . . .

**15:2b–4**

² "Every branch in me that does not bear fruit he takes away, and every branch that does bear fruit he prunes, that it may bear more fruit.
³ Already you are clean because of the word that I have spoken to you.
⁴ Abide in me, and I in you. As the branch cannot bear fruit by itself, unless it abides in the vine, neither can you, unless you abide in me."

- thought
- attitude
- commitment
- behavior
- relationships
- service
- passion
- motives
- willingness

a. **The purpose for pruning: To bear more fruit (v.2c).**
The fruitful branches are pruned for one productive purpose: to prepare the branch to bear more fruit. The purpose is not to punish, not to hurt and damage the branch. Note two things about fruit-bearing.

➣ The fruit a believer is to bear (see Deeper Study # 1).
➣ The different stages of fruit-bearing. All believers are not 100 percent fruit-bearers. Some bear 60 percent, others only 30 percent. There are degrees of fruit-bearing, of commitment and dedication to Christ (see Deeper Study # 1; Mt.13:8, 23).

"Other seeds fell on good soil and produced grain, some a hundredfold, some sixty, some thirty." (Mt.13:8)

"For the Son of Man is going to come with his angels in the glory of his Father, and then he will repay each person according to what he has done." (Mt.16:27)

"His master said to him, 'Well done, good and faithful servant. You have been faithful over a little; I will set you over much. Enter into the joy of your master.'" (Mt.25:23)

Now in a great house there are not only vessels of gold and silver but also of wood and clay, some for honorable use, some for dishonorable. (2 Ti.2:20)

b. **How branches are pruned (vv.3–4a).**
There are three ways the fruitful branches are *pruned* (katharoi) or purged and cleansed. First, branches are cleansed by the words which Jesus has given to us, by the Word of the Lord Himself (v.3). The Word of God refines us by purging away all the dross and contamination, pollution and dirt that clings to us. When we approach the Word of God sincerely, the Word of God shows . . .

- what we are doing and what we are not doing
- where we fail and how we fail
- the sins of commission and of omission

"Sanctify them in the truth; your word is truth." (Jn.17:17)

"And for their sake I consecrate myself, that they also may be sanctified in truth." (Jn.17:19)

That he might sanctify her, having cleansed her by the washing of water with the word. (Ep.5:26)

Having purified your souls by your obedience to the truth for a sincere brotherly love, love one another earnestly from a pure heart. (1 Pe.1:22)

How can a young man keep his way pure? By guarding it according to your word. (Ps.119:9)

I have stored up your word in my heart, that I might not sin against you. (Ps.119:11)

Second, branches are cleansed by the mirror of the Word of God (v.3). God's Word is like a mirror (Js.1:23-24). When we look into the Word of God, we see a reflection both of ourselves and our shortcomings and of Christ in His perfection. The Word of God forces us to measure ourselves against Christ.

All Scripture is breathed out by God and profitable for teaching, for reproof, for correction, and for training in righteousness. (2 Ti.3:16)

> For if anyone is a hearer of the word and not a doer, he is like a man who looks intently at his natural face in a mirror. For he looks at himself and goes away and at once forgets what he was like. (Js.1:23-24)

(See Deeper Study # 1—He.4:12 for more discussion.)

Third, branches are cleansed by "abiding" in Jesus (v.4a; see Deeper Study # 2). Note exactly what Jesus said: "Abide or remain in me, and I in you." This can mean at least two things:

➤ It can mean a promise: "Abide in me and I will abide in you." We are thereby cleansed by our position or by being in Christ (see note, pt.4—Jn.13:6-11).

➤ It can mean a command: "See to it that you abide in me, and I in you." We are cleansed by continuing in Christ and remaining faithful.

## Deeper Study # 1

(15:1-8) **Fruit-bearing—Abide:** Four stages of fruit-bearing are given: (1) no fruit (v.2), (2) fruit (v.2), (3) more fruit (v.2), and (4) much fruit (vs.5, 8).

What does it mean to say a Christian is to bear fruit? It means to bear converts (Ro.1:13), to bear righteousness (Ro.6:21-23), to bear Christian character or the fruit of the Spirit (see notes—Ga.5:22-23). Note also the conditions for bearing fruit in life: cleansing (v.3), abiding in Christ (v.5), and obedience (vv.10, 12). John said that to abide in Christ means eight things (see Deeper Study # 2).

1. It is to walk in open confession before God. It is to walk through life opening up your life to God; You confess all known sin. You do not walk in sin, and you do not allow any sin to go unconfessed (1 Jn.1:6-10).

2. It is to walk in fellowship with Christ. It is to live and move and have your being with Christ. You commune and live in a consciousness of God's presence, and from God's presence, you learn of God and draw the strength and authority to live victoriously day by day (1 Jn.2:6; 2:27; see Ps.16:11; Pr.3:5-6).

3. It is to continue in the church; you have not gone out from the church (1 Jn.2:19).

4. It is to possess confidence, an unashamedness in life, that prepares you for eternity (1 Jn.2:28).

5. It is to not walk in continuous sin (1 Jn.3:6). You experience ongoing victory over sin.

6. It is to actively surrender yourself to obey God's commandments (1 Jn.3:24).

7. It is to experience the indwelling presence and witness of the Spirit (1 Jn.4:12-13).

8. It is to dwell in love and unity and fellowship with all other believers (Jn.17:21-23; 1 Jn.4:16; see 1 Jn.4:20).

## Deeper Study # 2

(15:4) **Abide—Abiding:** to abide, dwell, continue, stay, sojourn, rest in or upon. It is being set and fixed and remaining there, continuing on and on in a fixed state, condition, or being (see Deeper Study # 1; 6:56). It should be noted that the more a branch abides in the vine, that is, the closer the branch abides to the heart of the vine, the more nourishment a branch draws from the vine and the more fruit it bears.

> "Whoever feeds on my flesh and drinks my blood abides in me, and I in him." (Jn.6:56)

> "And I will ask the Father, and he will give you another Helper, to be with you forever, even the Spirit of truth, whom the world cannot receive, because it neither sees him nor knows him. You know him, for he dwells with you and will be in you." (Jn.14:16-17)

> "If you keep my commandments, you will abide in my love, just as I have kept my Father's commandments and abide in his love." (Jn.15:10)

> Whoever says he abides in him ought to walk in the same way in which he walked. (1 Jn.2:6)

> And now, little children, abide in him, so that when he appears we may have confidence and not shrink from him in shame at his coming. (1 Jn.2:28)

> No one who abides in him keeps on sinning; no one who keeps on sinning has either seen him or known him. (1 Jn.3:6)
>
> Whoever keeps his commandments abides in God, and God in him. And by this we know that he abides in us, by the Spirit whom he has given us. (1 Jn.3:24)
>
> By this we know that we abide in him and he in us, because he has given us of his Spirit. (1 Jn.4:13)
>
> Whoever confesses that Jesus is the Son of God, God abides in him, and he in God. So we have come to know and to believe the love that God has for us. God is love, and whoever abides in love abides in God, and God abides in him. (1 Jn.4:15-16)

## 15:4-6

⁴ "Abide in me, and I in you. As the branch cannot bear fruit by itself, unless it abides in the vine, neither can you, unless you abide in me.

⁵ I am the vine; you are the branches. Whoever abides in me and I in him, he it is that bears much fruit, for apart from me you can do nothing.

⁶ If anyone does not abide in me he is thrown away like a branch and withers; and the branches are gathered, thrown into the fire, and burned."

### 4 Unattached branches.

Jesus proceeded to speak of unattached branches. Who are the unattached branches? What does it mean to be unattached to Christ? What happens to those who are unattached?

**a. Are by themselves: Not attached, connected, or abiding (v.4b).**

The unattached branch is outside of Christ and off by itself; it is not abiding in the Vine and not attached. Note the words "by or of itself" (v.4), off by itself. To say that a branch must be attached and abide in the vine may sound redundant at first. But the truth is pointed: there is no life and no fruit in life apart from Christ. Just as a branch suspended out in mid-air or lying on the ground without any attachment to the vine is lifeless and meaningless, so a person on the earth without attachment to Christ is lifeless and meaningless.

Those who seek life and meaning someplace other than in Christ are doomed to failure. The unattached and suspended branch is of and by itself—all alone on this earth—and it is doomed to be by itself forever.

**b. Cannot bear fruit (v.4c).**

The unattached branch cannot bear fruit, not real and permanent fruit that is *acceptable or pleasing* to God. It cannot bear . . .

- any good or righteousness that is acceptable to God (Ro.6:21-23)
- character that is acceptable to God (Ga.5:22-23)
- converts to the saving grace of God (Ro.1:13; Tit.2:11-15)

**c. Do not understand the nature of bearing fruit (v.5).**

The unattached branch does not understand the nature of bearing fruit in life: the fact that we can do nothing—cannot live and produce life—apart from Christ. We must abide in Christ to bear fruit. No one bears fruit apart from Christ. No one lives or experiences life (see Deeper Study # 2—Jn.1:4; Deeper Study # 1—10:10; Deeper Study # 1—17:2-3 for more discussion). Apart from Christ, a person is helpless to find the meaning, purpose, and significance to life.

**d. Are doomed: Gathered, thrown away, burned (v.6).**

The unattached branches are doomed. They are thrown away to wither and to be gathered and cast into the fire and burned. *Thrown away* or *aside*, or *cast out* (eblethe exo) means to be discarded, disposed of. The unattached branch chooses to be unattached, so God lets it. It is *given over* and *given up* to be unattached. God abandons it. It is cast out of the way and left to itself to do as it chooses (see outline and notes—Ro.1:24-32).

*Withers* or *withered* (exeranthe) means to be dried up, wrinkled, peeled; to become sapless and bare; to lose energy and strength. The unattached branch experiences everything withering away—its . . .

- gifts and abilities
- life and body
- family and friends
- fate and destiny
- hopes and dreams
- confidence and assurance
- purpose and meaning

The unattached branches are *gathered* (sunagousin): the day of judgment arrives. The Greek text does not specify who it is that gathers. The Greek simply says, "they are gathered." This is probably God having His angels gather up all the unattached branches, all who sin against God and continue to live in violation of His laws (see Mt.13:41).

Upon being gathered, the unattached branches are thrown into the fire and *burned* (kaietai). This is a picture of unbelievers being cast into hell (see DEEPER STUDY # 2—Mt.5:22; note—8:12; DEEPER STUDY # 4—Lu.16:24; see also Mt.13:42, 50; Re.20:15; 21:8).

> "'Let both grow together until the harvest, and at harvest time I will tell the reapers, "Gather the weeds first and bind them in bundles to be burned, but gather the wheat into my barn."'" (Mt.13:30)

> "So it will be at the end of the age. The angels will come out and separate the evil from the righteous and throw them into the fiery furnace. In that place there will be weeping and gnashing of teeth." (Mt.13:49-50)

> "And these will go away into eternal punishment, but the righteous into eternal life." (Mt.25:46)

> But for those who are self-seeking and do not obey the truth, but obey unrighteousness, there will be wrath and fury. There will be tribulation and distress for every human being who does evil, the Jew first and also the Greek. (Ro.2:8-9)

> And if anyone's name was not found written in the book of life, he was thrown into the lake of fire. (Re.20:15)

## 5 Attached branches: The results and promises.

The attached branches are the same as the fruitful branches mentioned earlier (vv.2-3). Jesus had already covered the pruning or the disciplining of the branches, so here He covers the promises made to them and the results of their "abiding" in Him. Note that these promises and results are conditional: "If you abide (remain) in me. . . ." Note also that the words of Christ must abide in the believer. The thought is that believers must take the words of Christ and . . .

- study and learn them
- have their thoughts and desires controlled by them
- be motivated and controlled by them

7 "If you abide in me, and my words abide in you, ask whatever you wish, and it will be done for you.
8 By this my Father is glorified, that you bear much fruit and so prove to be my disciples."

> Do your best to present yourself to God as one approved, a worker who has no need to be ashamed, rightly handling the word of truth. (2 Ti.2:15; see Jn.14:15, 21, 24; 15:10, 14)

The branches that are attached to the Vine are greatly blessed. Christ spoke of three promises and results of abiding in Him.

### a. Receive nourishment—answered prayers (v.7).

The attached branch receives nourishment, that is, answered prayers (see DEEPER STUDY # 3—Jn.14:13-14 for more discussion). It abides in the vine: dwells and lives and never faces a moment when it is not attached to the vine. So it is with genuine believers. They are attached to Christ: they abide, dwell, live, and walk in the very presence of Christ, never facing a moment when they are not attached to Christ.

The vine is always nourishing the branch, always sending its life-giving food and drink to the branch. So it is with Christ. Christ is always sharing His life-giving nourishment with abiding believers, always answering their prayers and meeting their needs.

> "And whatever you ask in prayer, you will receive, if you have faith." (Mt.21:22)

"Until now you have asked nothing in my name. Ask, and you will receive, that your joy may be full." (Jn.16:24)

And this is the confidence that we have toward him, that if we ask anything according to his will he hears us. And if we know that he hears us in whatever we ask, we know that we have the requests that we have asked of him. (1 Jn.5:14-15)

### b. Glorify God (v.8a).

The attached branch glorifies God by bearing much fruit. Remember what the fruit is. It is . . .
- righteousness

    But now that you have been set free from sin and have become slaves of God, the fruit you get leads to sanctification and its end, eternal life. (Ro.6:22)

    Filled with the fruit of righteousness that comes through Jesus Christ, to the glory and praise of God. (Ph.1:11)

    So as to walk in a manner worthy of the Lord, fully pleasing to him: bearing fruit in every good work and increasing in the knowledge of God. (Col.1:10)

- godly character

    But the fruit of the Spirit is love, joy, peace, patience, kindness, goodness, faithfulness, gentleness, self-control; against such things there is no law. (Ga.5:22-23)

- converts

    I do not want you to be unaware, brothers, that I have often intended to come to you (but thus far have been prevented), in order that I may reap some harvest among you as well as among the rest of the Gentiles. (Ro.1:13)

When people see fruit in the believer's life, it can move them to . . .
- turn their mind to God
- acknowledge that only God's power could do such
- desire God to save them
- begin asking God for help
- accept God or to close their mind and reject God

God is glorified by the fruit born in the life of a believer, glorified by *some people* beginning to think about God and calling on Him.

### c. Prove their attachment—their discipleship—by bearing fruit (v.8b).

Attached branches prove they are Christ's disciples by bearing fruit. There are ways to tell if people really are attached to Christ:
- ➢ Do they bear fruit?
- ➢ Do they live righteously or do shameful things (Ro.6:21-23)?
- ➢ Do they bear "love, joy, peace, patience or longsuffering, kindness, goodness, faithfulness, gentleness, self-control" (Ga.5:22-23)?
- ➢ Do they lead the lost to Christ (Ro.1:13)?

    "A new commandment I give to you, that you love one another: just as I have loved you, you also are to love one another. By this all people will know that you are my disciples, if you have love for one another." (Jn.13:34-35)

### J. The Relationship of Jesus to Believers, 15:9-11

⁹ "As the Father has loved me, so have I loved you. Abide in my love.

¹⁰ "If you keep my commandments, you will abide in my love, just as I have kept my Father's commandments and abide in his love.

¹¹ "These things I have spoken to you, that my joy may be in you, and that your joy may be full."

1. Jesus loves believers
2. Jesus charges believers to abide or remain in His love
   a. Abiding is conditional: If you obey
   b. Abiding has a standard: The obedience of Jesus
3. Jesus desires that believers be filled with His joy & that their joy<sup>DS1</sup> would be complete

# Division XIII

*The Revelation of Jesus, the Great Minister, and His Legacy, 13:1-16:33*

J. The Relationship of Jesus to Believers, 15:9-11

## 15:9-11
## Introduction

The abundant life Jesus came to bring us springs from our relationship with Him (Jn.10:10). Jesus has a very special relationship with believers. He loved us so much that He died for us; He laid down His life so He could have a relationship with us. In these three verses, our Savior expresses the deepest desire of His heart: that we abide in the fullness of His love, that we maintain a close relationship with Him. When we do, we will experience a dynamic relationship that delivers us from an existence that is barren, empty, lonely, unmeaningful, and sad. We will know a life of complete joy. This is, *The Relationship of Jesus to Believers*, 15:9-11.

1. Jesus loves believers (v.9).
2. Jesus charges believers to abide or remain in His love (vv.9-10).
3. Jesus desires that believers be filled with His joy and that their joy would be complete (v.11).

## 1 Jesus loves believers.

15:9a

Christ has loved believers. He has loved us with a very special love, the very same love with which God has loved Him. Two profound points are being discussed here:

⁹ "As the Father has loved me, so have I loved you. Abide in my love."

➢ The Father's love for His Son, Jesus Christ.
➢ Christ's love for believers.

There are three significant reasons why the Father loves Christ with such a special love. First, God loves Christ because of a *natural love*. Christ is His Son, His *only* Son. God naturally loves His Son just as most fathers naturally love their children.

> "For God so loved the world, that he gave his only Son, that whoever believes in him should not perish but have eternal life." (Jn.3:16)
>
> He [God] has delivered us from the domain of darkness and transferred us to the kingdom of his beloved Son. (Col.1:13)
>
> So also Christ did not exalt himself to be made a high priest, but was appointed by him who said to him, "You are my Son, today I have begotten you." (He.5:5)

Second, God loves His Son because of Christ's obedience. God is perfect, which means He is perfect love. Therefore, being perfect love, God is bound to love His Son. But this means much more than an ordinary love. Christ Himself is Perfect—the Perfect Son of God. Therefore, God loves Christ with a very special love. Imagine how much a parent would love a perfect child, a child who was always obedient: never being disrespectful, rebellious, haughty, selfish; and never causing hurt, pain, or doubt. Most parents love their children, but it is in special moments of obedience and caring that love swells up in the hearts of parents for their children. God's love for Christ is a perfect love, but it is a very special love based on the perfect obedience of Christ.

> "But I do as the Father has commanded me, so that the world may know that I love the Father. Rise, let us go from here." (Jn.14:31)
>
> "If you keep my commandments, you will abide in my love, just as I have kept my Father's commandments and abide in his love." (Jn.15:10)
>
> "Then I said, 'Behold, I have come to do your will, O God, as it is written of me in the scroll of the book.'" (He.10:7)

Third, God loves His Son because of Christ's sacrifice. Christ paid the *supreme* price of obedience. He died and sacrificed Himself in obedience to God's will. Therefore, God's love for His Son is very, very special in that it is a supreme love (see notes—Jn.10:17-18; 12:27-30 for discussion).

> "For this reason the Father loves me, because I lay down my life. . . . This charge I have received from my Father." (Jn.10:17-18)
>
> "But I do as the Father has commanded me, so that the world may know that I love the Father. Rise, let us go from here." (Jn.14:31)
>
> And walk in love, as Christ loved us and gave himself up for us, a fragrant offering and sacrifice to God. (Ep.5:2)

Christ said that He loves believers with the same *kind* of love, the very *same* love that God has for Him. This means that Christ loves us with a natural love.

➢ Christ loves us because we are God's children.

> For you did not receive the spirit of slavery to fall back into fear, but you have received the Spirit of adoption as sons, by whom we cry, "Abba! Father!" The Spirit himself bears witness with our spirit that we are children of God, and if children, then heirs—heirs of God and fellow heirs with Christ, provided we suffer with him in order that we may also be glorified with him. (Ro.8:15-17)
>
> "And in the very place where it was said to them, 'You are not my people,' there they will be called 'sons of the living God.'" (Ro.9:26)
>
> But when the fullness of time had come, God sent forth his Son, born of woman, born under the law, to redeem those who were under the law, so that we might receive adoption as sons. And because you are sons, God has sent the Spirit of his Son into our hearts, crying, "Abba! Father!" (Ga.4:4-6)
>
> See what kind of love the Father has given to us, that we should be called children of God; and so we are. The reason why the world does not know us is that it did not know him. Beloved, we are God's children now, and what we will be has not yet appeared; but we know that when he appears we shall be like him, because we shall see him as he is. (1 Jn.3:1-2)

➢ Christ loves us because we are His brothers and sisters.

> "For whoever does the will of my Father in heaven is my brother and sister and mother." (Mt.12:50)
>
> For those whom he foreknew he also predestined to be conformed to the image of his Son, in order that he might be the firstborn among many brothers. (Ro.8:29)
>
> For he who sanctifies and those who are sanctified all have one source. That is why he is not ashamed to call them brothers. (He.2:11)

➢ Christ loves us because we are the household and family of God.

> "Therefore go out from their midst, and be separate from them, says the Lord, and touch no unclean thing; then I will welcome you, and I will be a father to you, and you shall be sons and daughters to me, says the Lord Almighty." (2 Co.6:17-18)
>
> So then you are no longer strangers and aliens, but you are fellow citizens with the saints and members of the household of God. (Ep.2:19)

- In addition, Christ loves us with the love of obedience.
- He loves us because we believe God.

    "Truly, truly, I say to you, whoever hears my word and believes him who sent me has eternal life. He does not come into judgment, but has passed from death to life." (Jn.5:24)

- He loves us because we diligently seek God.

    And without faith it is impossible to please him, for whoever would draw near to God must believe that he exists and that he rewards those who seek him. (He.11:6)

- He loves us because we obey His commandments.

    "Whoever has my commandments and keeps them, he it is who loves me. And he who loves me will be loved by my Father, and I will love him and manifest myself to him." (Jn.14:21)

    "If you keep my commandments, you will abide in my love, just as I have kept my Father's commandments and abide in his love. . . . You are my friends if you do what I command you." (Jn.15:10, 14)

Christ also loves us with a supreme love. He loves us because we pay the *supreme* price of obedience: we deny self, take up our cross, and die daily in order to follow Him (see DEEPER STUDY # 1—Lu.9:23 for discussion).

And he said to all, "If anyone would come after me, let him deny himself and take up his cross daily and follow me." (Lu.9:23)

By this we know love, that he laid down his life for us, and we ought to lay down our lives for the brothers. (1 Jn.3:16)

## 2 Jesus charges believers to abide or remain in His love.

15:9b-10

Because our Lord loves us with such a special love, we should desire to live in the fullness of that love every day. However, the devil, the world, and our sinful flesh will constantly try to pull us away from Christ and His immeasurable love. Therefore, Christ charged us to abide or remain in His love.

⁹ "As the Father has loved me, so have I loved you. Abide in my love.
¹⁰ "If you keep my commandments, you will abide in my love, just as I have kept my Father's commandments and abide in his love."

### a. Abiding is conditional: If you obey (v.10a).

Abiding or remaining is conditional. Believers can . . .
- break fellowship with Christ
- cease to keep their thoughts centered on Christ
- turn back to the world and to their old worldly ways and companions (2 Co.6:17-18)
- give themselves back over to the lust of the flesh, the lust of the eyes, and the pride of life (1 Jn.2:15-16)

Jesus said that it is up to the believer to abide in His love. How? By doing what any person does when they want someone to love them. The individual draws near to the person they love: they try to please the person. So it is with the believer. The believer continues in the love of Christ by drawing near and doing good and seeking to please Him—very simply, by obeying His commandments (see Jn.14:21; 15:10, 14).

Now note a critical point. Christ always loves; His love is *always* there. But it is up to *us* to walk *in* that love. We can never know and experience the Lord's love unless we walk *in* it.

"Whoever has my commandments and keeps them, he it is who loves me. And he who loves me will be loved by my Father, and I will love him and manifest myself to him." (Jn.14:21)

"If you keep my commandments, you will abide in my love, just as I have kept my Father's commandments and abide in his love. . . . You are my friends if you do what I command you." (Jn.15:10, 14)

Therefore, as you received Christ Jesus the Lord, so walk in him. (Col.2:6)

Whoever says he abides in him ought to walk in the same way in which he walked. (1 Jn.2:6)

### b. Abiding has standard: The obedience of Jesus Christ (v.10b).

The supreme example of abiding in Christ's love is Christ Himself. He was perfectly obedient to God; therefore, He continued in the Father's love. We are to look at His obedience as our prime example (again, see note—Jn.10:17-18).

Note another critical point: we must do something if we are going to follow Jesus' example and keep Jesus' commandments. We must study and learn and abide in the Word of God, in the commandments and life of Christ. We cannot keep a commandment unless we know the commandment.

> "Abide in me, and I in you. As the branch cannot bear fruit by itself, unless it abides in the vine, neither can you, unless you abide in me. I am the vine; you are the branches. Whoever abides in me and I in him, he it is that bears much fruit, for apart from me you can do nothing." (Jn.15:4-5)

> Now these Jews were more noble than those in Thessalonica; they received the word with all eagerness, examining the Scriptures daily to see if these things were so. (Ac.17:11)

> Do your best to present yourself to God as one approved, a worker who has no need to be ashamed, rightly handling the word of truth. (2 Ti.2:15)

> Like newborn infants, long for the pure spiritual milk, that by it you may grow up into salvation—if indeed you have tasted that the Lord is good. (1 Pe.2:2-3)

> And now, little children, abide in him, so that when he appears we may have confidence and not shrink from him in shame at his coming. (1 Jn.2:28)

> No one who abides in him keeps on sinning; no one who keeps on sinning has either seen him or known him. (1 Jn.3:6)

## 15:11

¹¹ "These things I have spoken to you, that my joy may be in you, and that your joy may be full."

### 3 Jesus desires that believers be filled with His joy and that their joy would be complete.

Abiding in the deep, deep love of Jesus brings a joy that nothing else in this life can bring. Our Lord wants us to be filled with His joy, to experience the complete joy that can only be found in Him. Note what Christ teaches us about this indescribable joy.

First, it is the joy of Christ. Jesus called it, "My joy." His joy and glory were doing the will of God and looking ahead to the joy and glory of eternity with His Father and His followers (see notes—Jn.12:23-26; 14:28-29).

> Looking to Jesus, the founder and perfecter of our faith, who for the joy that was set before him endured the cross, despising the shame, and is seated at the right hand of the throne of God. (He.12:2)

Second, it is the joy of Christ Himself reigning within our hearts (see DEEPER STUDY # 1).

> Through him we have also obtained access by faith into this grace in which we stand, and we rejoice in hope of the glory of God. (Ro.5:2)

> Though you have not seen him, you love him. Though you do not now see him, you believe in him and rejoice with joy that is inexpressible and filled with glory. (1 Pe.1:8)

Finally, our joy of believers is *full* or *complete* as we study His Word, the promises and commandments which He made (see DEEPER STUDY # 1; notes—Jn.14:28-29).

> "These things I have spoken to you, that my joy may be in you, and that your joy may be full." (Jn.15:11)

> "But now I am coming to you, and these things I speak in the world, that they may have my joy fulfilled in themselves." (Jn.17:13)

> Your words were found, and I ate them, and your words became to me a joy and the delight of my heart, for I am called by your name, O LORD, God of hosts. (Je.15:16)

## Deeper Study # 1

(15:11) **Joy** (chara): an inner gladness; a deep-seated pleasure. It is a depth of assurance and confidence that ignites a cheerful heart, leading to cheerful behavior.

Several things need to be said about the believer's joy.

1. Joy is divine. It is possessed and given only by God. Its roots are not in earthly or material things or cheap triumphs. It is the joy of the Holy Spirit, a joy based in the Lord. It is His very own joy (Jn.15:11; Ac.13:52; Ro.14:17; Ga.5:22; 1 Th.1:6).

2. Joy does not depend on circumstances or happiness. Happiness depends on happenings, but the joy that God implants in the believer's heart overrides all, even the most troublesome matters of life and death (Ps.5:11; 2 Co.6:10; 7:4).

3. Joy springs from faith (Ro.15:13; Ph.1:25; 2 Ti.1:4; see also Mt.2:10).

4. Joy of future reward makes and keeps one faithful (Mt.25:21, 23; Ac.20:24; He.12:2).

The believer's joy springs from several sources.

1. The fellowship of the Father and His Son brings joy (1 Jn.1:3-4; Ps.16:11).

2. Victory over sin, death, and hell brings joy (Jn.14:28; 16:20-22; Is.12:3; 61:10).

3. Repentance brings joy (Lu.15:7, 10).

4. The hope of glory brings joy (Ro.14:17; He.12:2; 1 Pe.4:13).

5. The Lord's Word, the revelations, commandments, and promises which He made bring joy (Jn.15:11).

6. The commandments of Christ and the will of God bring joy. Obeying and pleasing the Lord stirs joy within the believer's heart (Jn.15:11, 32; 17:13; Ac.13:52; Je.15:16).

7. Prayer brings joy (Jn.16:24).

8. The presence and fellowship of other believers bring joy (1 Jn.1:3-4).

9. Winning people to Christ brings joy (Lu.15:5; Ph.4:1; 1 Th.2:19-20; Ps.126:5).

10. Hearing that others walk in the truth brings joy (3 Jn.1:4).

11. Giving brings joy (2 Co.8:2; He.10:34).

## K. The Relationship of Believers to Believers, 15:12–17

1. The supreme command to believers: Love one another

2. The supreme standard for believers: The love of Jesus

3. The supreme bond of believers: Friends of Jesus
   a. Is conditional: If you obey
   b. Is based upon revelation: The words of the Father made known by Christ

4. The supreme purpose of believers: Chosen & appointed . . .
   a. To go
   b. To bear fruit
   c. To receive the answer to their prayers

5. The supreme command of believers repeated

¹² "This is my commandment, that you love one another as I have loved you.
¹³ Greater love has no one than this, that someone lay down his life for his friends.
¹⁴ You are my friends if you do what I command you.
¹⁵ No longer do I call you servants, for the servant does not know what his master is doing; but I have called you friends, for all that I have heard from my Father I have made known to you.
¹⁶ You did not choose me, but I chose you and appointed you that you should go and bear fruit and that your fruit should abide, so that whatever you ask the Father in my name, he may give it to you.
¹⁷ These things I command you, so that you will love one another."

# Division XIII

### The Revelation of Jesus, the Great Minister, and His Legacy, 13:1–16:33

K. The Relationship of Believers to Believers, 15:12–17

## 15:12–17
## Introduction

How we relate to other believers is of critical importance. Division will destroy a body of people quicker than any other single thing. Division can destroy . . .
- the body of Christ
- a fellowship of believers
- the witness of believers
- a human soul seeking God

Too many are known more for their complaining, murmuring, and divisiveness than for anything else. Nothing cuts the heart of Jesus more than such self-centered and divisive behavior.

In this passage, Christ addresses our relationship with other believers. His command is simple, but we must overcome our selfish nature in order to obey it. This is, *The Relationship of Believers to Believers*, 15:12–17.

1. The supreme command to believers: Love one another (v.12).
2. The supreme standard for believers: The love of Jesus (vv.12–13).
3. The supreme bond of believers: Friends of Jesus (vv.14–15).
4. The supreme purpose of believers: Chosen and appointed to go (v.16).
5. The supreme command to believers repeated (v.17).

## 1 The supreme command to believers: Love one another.

Jesus restated His supreme command to believers: We are to love one another (see notes—Jn.13:33-35 for discussion). Our love for one another is the trait that distinguishes us as followers of Christ. The world is to identify us as His disciples by our love.

> "A new commandment I give to you, that you love one another: just as I have loved you, you also are to love one another. By this all people will know that you are my disciples, if you have love for one another." (Jn.13:34-35)
>
> Let love be genuine. Abhor what is evil; hold fast to what is good. (Ro.12:9)
>
> Having purified your souls by your obedience to the truth for a sincere brotherly love, love one another earnestly from a pure heart. (1 Pe.1:22)
>
> And this is his commandment, that we believe in the name of his Son Jesus Christ and love one another, just as he has commanded us. (1 Jn.3:23)

> 12 "This is my commandment, that you love one another as I have loved you."

## 2 The supreme standard for believers: The love of Jesus.

The *supreme standard* by which we are to love one another is the love of Jesus Christ Himself. We are to love other believers just as Jesus has loved us.

Jesus is clear about what He means. He is talking about a sacrificial love. He loved us so much that He paid the ultimate price: He died and sacrificed His life for us (see notes—Jn.10:17-18; 12:27-30; 13:31-32). In like manner, we are to put others ahead of ourselves. We are to spend our lives in the service of others (Ph.2:3-8; 1 Jn.3:16).

> 12 "This is my commandment, that you love one another as I have loved you.
> 13 Greater love has no one than this, that someone lay down his life for his friends."

> Now before the Feast of the Passover, when Jesus knew that his hour had come to depart out of this world to the Father, having loved his own who were in the world, he loved them to the end [death]. (Jn.13:1)
>
> Who shall separate us from the love of Christ? Shall tribulation, or distress, or persecution, or famine, or nakedness, or danger, or sword? (Ro.8:35)
>
> I have been crucified with Christ. It is no longer I who live, but Christ who lives in me. And the life I now live in the flesh I live by faith in the Son of God, who loved me and gave himself for me. (Ga.2:20)
>
> And walk in love, as Christ loved us and gave himself up for us, a fragrant offering and sacrifice to God. (Ep.5:2)
>
> By this we know love, that he laid down his life for us, and we ought to lay down our lives for the brothers. (1 Jn.3:16)

## 3 The supreme bond of believers: Friends of Jesus.

The *supreme bond* of believers is the bond of "friends." We are the friends of Jesus. Believers form a bond of "friends," a spiritual bond founded by Christ Himself. Our fellowship with one another is centered around our mutual friendship with Christ (1 Jn.1:1-7).

The great message of these verses is that Jesus treats us as friends rather than as servants. We rightly present ourselves to Him as His servants, for He is our Lord, our Master and King. But He longs for an intimate relationship with us, the relationship between friends. When we willingly obey Him, He draws us into this close, personal relationship.

> 14 "You are my friends if you do what I command you.
> 15 No longer do I call you servants, for the servant does not know what his master is doing; but I have called you friends, for all that I have heard from my Father I have made known to you."

a. **Is conditional: If you obey (v.14).**

Being a friend of Jesus is conditional. We are His friends if we *know* and *do* His commandments. We have to diligently seek to learn His Word and to do what He says in order to know Him and to become His friend. The implication is clear: there is no way to be Christ's friend apart from *knowing what He says*. A friendship is a relationship. Friends relate and commune with each other, *share* and *respond* to what each other says, rejoicing when the word or conversation is that of joy, and helping when the word or request is that of need.

> "For whoever does the will [Word] of my Father in heaven is my brother and sister and mother." (Mt.12:50)

> "If anyone's will is to do God's will, he will know whether the teaching is from God or whether I am speaking on my own authority." (Jn.7:17)

> "Whoever has my commandments and keeps them, he it is who loves me. And he who loves me will be loved by my Father, and I will love him and manifest myself to him." (Jn.14:21)

> Jesus answered him, "If anyone loves me, he will keep my word, and my Father will love him, and we will come to him and make our home with him. Whoever does not love me does not keep my words. And the word that you hear is not mine but the Father's who sent me." (Jn.14:23-24)

> And by this we know that we have come to know him, if we keep his commandments. (1 Jn.2:3)

> Let what you heard from the beginning abide in you. If what you heard from the beginning abides in you, then you too will abide in the Son and in the Father. (1 Jn.2:24)

b. **Is based upon revelation: The words of the Father made known by Christ.**

The bond of "friends" is based upon revelation, that is, upon Jesus Christ Himself. Jesus Christ revealed and made known exactly what God told Him. It is *the Word of God* that gives birth and structure to the bond of "friends." The friends of Christ are built upon and centered around *the Word of God* (see notes—Jn.14:10; 7:16-19; Deeper Study # 2—Ac.2:42 for discussion).

> "For I have not spoken on my own authority, but the Father who sent me has himself given me a commandment—what to say and what to speak. And I know that his commandment is eternal life. What I say, therefore, I say as the Father has told me." (Jn.12:49-50)

> "For I have given them the words that you gave me, and they have received them and have come to know in truth that I came from you; and they have believed that you sent me." (Jn.17:8)

> But, as it is written, "What no eye has seen, nor ear heard, nor the heart of man imagined, what God has prepared for those who love him"—these things God has revealed to us through the Spirit. For the Spirit searches everything, even the depths of God. (1 Co.2:9-10)

> Making known to us the mystery of his will, according to his purpose, which he set forth in Christ as a plan for the fullness of time, to unite all things in him, things in heaven and things on earth. (Ep.1:9-10)

> The mystery hidden for ages and generations but now revealed to his saints. To them God chose to make known how great among the Gentiles are the riches of the glory of this mystery, which is Christ in you, the hope of glory. (Col.1:26-27)

> For he who sanctifies and those who are sanctified all have one source. That is why he is not ashamed to call them brothers. (He.2:11)

## 15:16

16 "You did not choose me, but I chose you and appointed you that you should go and bear fruit and that your fruit should abide, so that whatever you ask the Father in my name, he may give it to you."

## 4 The supreme purpose of believers: Chosen and appointed...

This is one of the great verses of Scripture, for it expresses the *supreme purpose* of believers: to go into all the world and bear fruit. We are chosen and ordained by Jesus for this very purpose. We do not choose Him, nor do we ordain and send ourselves out to serve Him. It is God who approaches and draws us (see notes—Jn.6:44-46. Also see note—Jn.6:37), and it is God who appoints us to serve Him.

> There was a man sent from God, whose name was John. (Jn.1:6)

But the Lord said to him, "Go, for he is a chosen instrument of mine to carry my name before the Gentiles and kings and the children of Israel." (Ac.9:15)

"Pay careful attention to yourselves and to all the flock, in which the Holy Spirit has made you overseers, to care for the church of God, which he obtained with his own blood." (Ac.20:28)

But God chose what is foolish in the world to shame the wise; God chose what is weak in the world to shame the strong; God chose what is low and despised in the world, even things that are not, to bring to nothing things that are, so that no human being might boast in the presence of God. (1 Co.1:27-29)

And God has appointed in the church first apostles, second prophets, third teachers, then miracles, then gifts of healing, helping, administrating, and various kinds of tongues. (1 Co.12:28)

I thank him who has given me strength, Christ Jesus our Lord, because he judged me faithful, appointing me to his service. (1 Ti.1:12)

a. **To go.**

We are to go forth as ambassadors for Christ, proclaiming the glorious message of the great God and our Savior. Believers are not called to be an exclusive club of people who have it made and who can go about doing what they want, knowing they are eternally secure. Believers are the ambassadors of Christ in the world. Once we have been saved, our duty—our sole reason for being *appointed* and *left* in this world—is to deliver the message of our King.

"Go therefore and make disciples of all nations, baptizing them in the name of the Father and of the Son and of the Holy Spirit, teaching them to observe all that I have commanded you. And behold, I am with you always, to the end of the age." (Mt.28:19-20)

And he said to them, "Go into all the world and proclaim the gospel to the whole creation." (Mk.16:15)

Jesus said to them again, "Peace be with you. As the Father has sent me, even so I am sending you." (Jn.20:21)

"But you will receive power when the Holy Spirit has come upon you, and you will be my witnesses in Jerusalem and in all Judea and Samaria, and to the end of the earth." (Ac.1:8)

That is, in Christ God was reconciling the world to himself, not counting their trespasses against them, and entrusting to us the message of reconciliation. Therefore, we are ambassadors for Christ, God making his appeal through us. We implore you on behalf of Christ, be reconciled to God. (2 Co.5:19-20)

b. **To bear fruit.**

We are to go and bear fruit (see Deeper Study # 1—Jn.15:1-8 for discussion). The New Testament mentions different types of fruit we are to bear as Christians, but the natural fruit of the believer is another believer. This seems to be the fruit in view here, as implied by the connection of *bearing fruit* with *going* (Mt.28:19-20; Mk.16:15). We are to bear fruit that is lasting—that *abides* or *remains*. This seems to speak of discipleship. We are to not just win others to Christ, but to teach them to become faithful, fully devoted followers of Christ (Mt.28:19).

"Truly, truly, I say to you, unless a grain of wheat falls into the earth and dies, it remains alone; but if it dies, it bears much fruit." (Jn.12:24)

"Every branch in me that does not bear fruit he takes away, and every branch that does bear fruit he prunes, that it may bear more fruit." (Jn.15:2)

"I am the vine; you are the branches. Whoever abides in me and I in him, he it is that bears much fruit, for apart from me you can do nothing." (Jn.15:5)

Likewise, my brothers, you also have died to the law through the body of Christ, so that you may belong to another, to him who has been raised from the dead, in order that we may bear fruit for God. (Ro.7:4)

Filled with the fruit of righteousness that comes through Jesus Christ, to the glory and praise of God. (Ph.1:11; see vv.9-10)

So as to walk in a manner worthy of the Lord, fully pleasing to him: bearing fruit in every good work and increasing in the knowledge of God. (Col.1:10)

c. **To receive the answer to their prayers.**

Jesus assured fruitbearing believers that they would receive the answer to their prayers. If we are the friends of Christ, we know and understand His heart. Therefore, we ask only for those things He would want us to have. The promise of answered prayers is only for what we can genuinely ask in Jesus' name (see Deeper Study # 3—Jn.14:13-14; note—15:7-8 for discussion).

When viewed in the context (setting) of this verse, the answered prayers that Jesus mentions seem to involve God providing us with resources needed to accomplish what He has chosen and appointed us to do. As we go forth to sow the precious seed of the gospel, we can expect God to provide everything we need, everything we can appropriately ask for in Jesus' name.

> "And whatever you ask in prayer, you will receive, if you have faith." (Mt.21:22)

> "And I tell you, ask, and it will be given to you; seek, and you will find; knock, and it will be opened to you. For everyone who asks receives, and the one who seeks finds, and to the one who knocks it will be opened." (Lu.11:9-10)

> "Whatever you ask in my name, this I will do, that the Father may be glorified in the Son. If you ask me anything in my name, I will do it." (Jn.14:13-14)

> "If you abide in me, and my words abide in you, ask whatever you wish, and it will be done for you. By this my Father is glorified, that you bear much fruit and so prove to be my disciples." (Jn.15:7-8)

> And whatever we ask we receive from him, because we keep his commandments and do what pleases him. (1 Jn.3:22)

> And this is the confidence that we have toward him, that if we ask anything according to his will he hears us. And if we know that he hears us in whatever we ask, we know that we have the requests that we have asked of him. (1 Jn.5:14-15)

## 15:17

**5 The supreme command to believers repeated.**

17 "These things I command you, so that you will love one another."

Jesus concluded by repeating His command to love one another. As "bookends" to this message, this forceful command holds together everything Jesus said in between. We are to love one another as Christ loved us, sacrificing for and serving one another. Our bond of mutual friendship with Jesus—a bond based on obedience to Him and on His Word—should be stronger than whatever differences might tempt us to divide. We have all been chosen and appointed for the same purpose: to go and bear fruit for our Lord. Therefore, our love for one another should triumph over everything else. It should be the ruling force in our relationship with other believers.

> The one who exhorts, in his exhortation; the one who contributes, in generosity; the one who leads, with zeal; the one who does acts of mercy, with cheerfulness. Let love be genuine. Abhor what is evil; hold fast to what is good. Love one another with brotherly affection. Outdo one another in showing honor. (Ro.12:8-10)

> And this is his commandment, that we believe in the name of his Son Jesus Christ and love one another, just as he has commanded us. (1 Jn.3:23)

## L. The Relationship of Believers to the World: Persecution (Part I), 15:18-27

1. The chilling reality: The world will hate you

18 "If the world hates you, know that it has hated me before it hated you.

2. The unjustified reasons for the world's hatred
   a. Because believers are a new creation, 2 Co.5:17; 6:17-18

19 If you were of the world, the world would love you as its own; but because you are not of the world, but I chose you out of the world, therefore the world hates you.

   b. Because believers are identified with Christ

20 Remember the word that I said to you: 'A servant is not greater than his master.' If they persecuted me, they will also persecute you. If they kept my word, they will also keep yours.

   c. Because the world does not really know God

21 But all these things they will do to you on account of my name, because they do not know him who sent me.

   d. Because the world is convicted of sin
      1) The Lord's message convicts people

22 If I had not come and spoken to them, they would not have been guilty of sin, but now they have no excuse for their sin.
23 Whoever hates me hates my Father also.

      2) The Lord's life & works convict people

24 If I had not done among them the works that no one else did, they would not be guilty of sin, but now they have seen and hated both me and my Father.

3. The terrible guilt of the world: People hated Jesus without cause

25 But the word that is written in their Law must be fulfilled: 'They hated me without a cause.'

4. The promise of victory over the world
   a. Victory through the Holy Spirit: He is the Helper or Counselor—the Spirit of Truth who bears witness to Christ

26 But when the Helper comes, whom I will send to you from the Father, the Spirit of truth, who proceeds from the Father, he will bear witness about me.

   b. Victory through your own witness & fellowship with Christ

27 And you also will bear witness, because you have been with me from the beginning."

# Division XIII

*The Revelation of Jesus, the Great Minister, and His Legacy, 13:1-16:33*

L. The Relationship of Believers to the World (Part I): Persecution, 15:18-27

## 15:18-27
## Introduction

The relationship of true believers to the world is a bleak picture. The world hates true believers. The world and its people shun, isolate, talk about, ridicule, mock, bypass, overlook, consider strange, and joke about genuine believers. The persecution often goes even farther, involving abuse and murder within the workplace and community, depending on the society and the laws under which the believer lives. Jesus wanted believers to be informed and to know what their relationship with the world is. This is, *The Relationship of Believers to the World (Part I): Persecution,* 15:18-27.

1. The chilling reality: The world will hate you (v.18).
2. The unjustified reasons for the world's hatred (vv.19-24).
3. The terrible guilt of the world: People hated Jesus without cause (v.25).
4. The promise of victory over the world (vv.26-27).

## 15:18

¹⁸ "If the world hates you, know that it has hated me before it hated you."

## 1 The chilling reality: The world will hate you.

Jesus warned His followers of a chilling reality: the world will hate believers. *If* (ei) is better translated *since*. Literally, it is *you are*. It "assumes the fact as existing: if the world hate you *as it does.*"[1] It may be accurately stated as "since the world hates you": there is no question about the world hating believers. It *will* hate them.

> "Blessed are you when others revile you and persecute you and utter all kinds of evil against you falsely on my account." (Mt.5:11)

> "And you will be hated by all for my name's sake. But the one who endures to the end will be saved." (Mt.10:22)

> For it has been granted to you that for the sake of Christ you should not only believe in him but also suffer for his sake. (Ph.1:29)

> Indeed, all who desire to live a godly life in Christ Jesus will be persecuted. (2 Ti.3:12)

The *world* refers to unbelievers: the unredeemed, the lost, those who have never trusted Jesus Christ as Lord and Savior. The "world" stands for every person whose thoughts and lives are centered on...

- the lust of the flesh, the cravings of the sinful nature (food, clothes, money, immorality; see Ga.5:16-21)
- the lust of the eyes (evil and immoral thoughts, coveting, seeing and desiring people and things)
- the pride of life (position, boasting, honor, fame, highmindedness, self-centeredness; see 2 Ti.3:1-5)

> Do not love the world or the things in the world. If anyone loves the world, the love of the Father is not in him. For all that is in the world—the desires of the flesh and the desires of the eyes and pride of life—is not from the Father but is from the world. (1 Jn.2:15-16)

When we encounter hatred from the world, our Lord wants us to *know*—understand, be aware of, keep in mind—that the world hated Him *first*. We must not think some strange thing is happening to us; we should not be surprised; we should not become discouraged.

> Whoever speaks, as one who speaks oracles of God; whoever serves, as one who serves by the strength that God supplies—in order that in everything God may be glorified through Jesus Christ. To him belong glory and dominion forever and ever. Amen. Beloved, do not be surprised at the fiery trial when it comes upon you to test you, as though something strange were happening to you. (1 Pe.4:11-12)

> Do not be surprised, brothers, that the world hates you. (1 Jn.3:13)

Instead, we should take heart, for Christ was victorious over the world's hatred. He was triumphant even over the bitterness of death. He arose and ascended to the Father.

> For it was fitting that he, for whom and by whom all things exist, in bringing many sons to glory, should make the founder of their salvation perfect through suffering. (He.2:10)

---

1  Marvin R. Vincent, *Vincent's Word Studies in the New Testament,* (Peabody, MA: Hendrickson Publishers), via Wordsearch digital edition.

For Christ also suffered once for sins, the righteous for the unrighteous, that he might bring us to God, being put to death in the flesh but made alive in the spirit. (1 Pe.3:18)

But he was pierced for our transgressions; he was crushed for our iniquities; upon him was the chastisement that brought us peace, and with his wounds we are healed. (Is.53:5)

## 2 The unjustified reasons for the world's hatred.

The world hates believers for some specific reasons. These reasons are not justified, but they are real nonetheless.

### a. Because believers are a new creation, 2 Co.5:17; 6:17–18 (v.19).

The world hates believers because we are not of the world: we are new creations (2 Co.5:17; 6:17-18). Our Lord has *called us out* from the world. Believers are *in* the world, but we are not *of* the world. We are separated from the world, from its . . .

- spirit
- thoughts
- conversation
- pleasures
- friends
- comfort
- religion
- prejudices
- hoarding
- carnality
- passions
- covetousness

19 "If you were of the world, the world would love you as its own; but because you are not of the world, but I chose you out of the world, therefore the world hates you.
20 Remember the word that I said to you: 'A servant is not greater than his master.' If they persecuted me, they will also persecute you. If they kept my word, they will also keep yours.
21 But all these things they will do to you on account of my name, because they do not know him who sent me.
22 If I had not come and spoken to them, they would not have been guilty of sin, but now they have no excuse for their sin.
23 Whoever hates me hates my Father also.
24 If I had not done among them the works that no one else did, they would not be guilty of sin, but now they have seen and hated both me and my Father."

Because of our separation, the world does not love us. We are no longer of the world; therefore, it rejects and hates us.

"They are not of the world, just as I am not of the world." (Jn.17:16)

Therefore, if anyone is in Christ, he is a new creation. The old has passed away; behold, the new has come. (2 Co.5:17)

"Therefore go out from their midst, and be separate from them, says the Lord, and touch no unclean thing; then I will welcome you, and I will be a father to you, and you shall be sons and daughters to me, says the Lord Almighty." (2 Co.6:17-18)

### b. Because believers are identified with Christ (v.20).

The world hates believers because we are identified with Christ. We are *Christ's* servants, not the world's. As servants, we are not above our Lord. The Lord suffered persecution; therefore, we will suffer persecution. We should expect it and be ready for it.

**THOUGHT 1.** It is impossible for true disciples to be above their Master or for servants to be above their Lord. If our Master and Lord suffered persecution, so will we. Why? He is our Master and Lord; that is, we are His. What He stands for is what we stand for. Whatever there was about Him that caused people to persecute Him, the same is *in us*. They will persecute us for *the same thing* and for *the same reason*. If we are true followers of Christ, we will sacrifice ourselves, *all we are and have*, to the Lord; therefore, persecution is inevitable.

"I have given them your word, and the world has hated them because they are not of the world, just as I am not of the world." (Jn.17:14)

I appeal to you therefore, brothers, by the mercies of God, to present your bodies as a living sacrifice, holy and acceptable to God, which is your spiritual worship. Do not be conformed to this world, but be transformed by the renewal of your mind, that by testing you may discern what is the will of God, what is good and acceptable and perfect. (Ro.12:1-2)

Persecuted, but not forsaken; struck down, but not destroyed; always carrying in the body the death of Jesus, so that the life of Jesus may also be manifested in our bodies. For we who live are always being given over to death for Jesus' sake, so that the life of Jesus also may be manifested in our mortal flesh. (2 Co.4:9-11)

### c. Because the world does not really know God (v.21).

The world hates believers because it does not really know God. The world is deceived in its concept and belief of God. The world conceives God to be the One who fulfills their earthly desires and lusts (Jn.6:2, 26). Many people's idea of God is that of a Supreme Grandfather who protects and provides and gives no matter what a person's behavior is, just so the behavior is not too far out. The world believes that the Supreme Grandfather will accept and work all things out in the final analysis. However, the true believer knows better and understands and proclaims that God is both loving and just. God does love us, but He demands righteousness of us. The world, of course, rebels against this concept of God.

> "They will put you out of the synagogues. Indeed, the hour is coming when whoever kills you will think he is offering service to God. And they will do these things because they have not known the Father, nor me." (Jn.16:2-3)

> "For as I passed along and observed the objects of your worship, I found also an altar with this inscription: 'To the unknown god.' What therefore you worship as unknown, this I proclaim to you." (Ac.17:23)

> They are darkened in their understanding, alienated from the life of God because of the ignorance that is in them, due to their hardness of heart. (Ep.4:18)

### d. Because the world is convicted of sin (vv.22-24).

The world hates believers because it is convicted of sin. Christ's message convicts the world; it strips away the world's excuses for their sin (v.22). Christ preaches and teaches righteousness; therefore, His message exposes people's sin and establishes their guilt.

> "For if you believed Moses, you would believe me; for he wrote of me. But if you do not believe his writings, how will you believe my words?" (Jn.5:46-47)

> He said to them, "You are from below; I am from above. You are of this world; I am not of this world. I told you that you would die in your sins, for unless you believe that I am he you will die in your sins." (Jn.8:23-24)

> Jesus answered them, "Truly, truly, I say to you, everyone who practices sin is a slave to sin." (Jn.8:34)

> "You are of your father the devil, and your will is to do your father's desires. He was a murderer from the beginning, and does not stand in the truth, because there is no truth in him. When he lies, he speaks out of his own character, for he is a liar and the father of lies. But because I tell the truth, you do not believe me." (Jn.8:44-45)

In addition, Jesus' life and works convict the world of sin (v.24; see notes—Jn.5:19-20, 36; DEEPER STUDY # 2—10:25 for discussion.) Note the words, "they would not have been guilty of sin" (ESV), "they would have no sin" (NKJV) or "they would not have sin" (NASB, CSB). This does not mean that people would be innocent of sin if Jesus had not come. What it means is that since He has come, people have seen exactly who God is. God has been revealed to humanity; therefore, the human race stands guilty of the most terrible sin of all: rejecting God and His Son. If He had not come, they would not be guilty of *this particular* sin.

Jesus said that to hate Him is to hate the Father also (v.23). By making this statement, Jesus claimed to be the revelation of God—to be equal with Him.

> They said to him therefore, "Where is your Father?" Jesus answered, "You know neither me nor my Father. If you knew me, you would know my Father also." (Jn.8:19)

> So Jesus said to them, "When you have lifted up the Son of Man, then you will know that I am he, and that I do nothing on my own authority, but speak just as the Father taught me. And he who sent me is with me. He has not left me alone, for I always do the things that are pleasing to him." (Jn.8:28-29)

> Jesus said to them, "If God were your Father, you would love me, for I came from God and I am here. I came not of my own accord, but he sent me." (Jn.8:42)

> "But you have not known him. I know him. If I were to say that I do not know him, I would be a liar like you, but I do know him and I keep his word." (Jn.8:55)

"If I am not doing the works of my Father, then do not believe me; but if I do them, even though you do not believe me, believe the works, that you may know and understand that the Father is in me and I am in the Father." (Jn.10:37-38)

## 3 The terrible guilt of the world: People hated Jesus without cause.

15:25

The world is without excuse for its hatred of Christ (Ps.35:19). There is no justifiable cause for its hatred of Jesus. The world's hatred is not understandable; it makes no sense whatsoever. Think about it. The world hates and opposes the one Person . . .

- who lived and spoke for righteousness more than anyone else ever has
- who cared and ministered more than anyone else ever has
- who worked for true love and justice and the salvation of the world more than anyone else ever has

²⁵ "But the word that is written in their Law must be fulfilled: 'They hated me without a cause.'"

How deceived is the world and its people! To rush onward in madness for nothing but to return to dust and ashes. To seek life for, on average, some seventy years (if that long).

The world's hatred for Jesus Christ reveals that the true nature of the world is *evil*. The world is without excuse.

> For his invisible attributes, namely, his eternal power and divine nature, have been clearly perceived, ever since the creation of the world, in the things that have been made. So they are without excuse. (Ro.1:20)

> They repay me evil for good; my soul is bereft. (Ps.35:12)

> So they reward me evil for good, and hatred for my love. (Ps.109:5)

## 4 The promise of victory over the world.

15:26-27

Jesus would soon assure His followers that He has overcome the world (Jn.16:33). John would later write that our faith in Christ gives us the promise of victory. Jesus taught us that this victory comes from two sources.

²⁶ "But when the Helper comes, whom I will send to you from the Father, the Spirit of truth, who proceeds from the Father, he will bear witness about me.

²⁷ And you also will bear witness, because you have been with me from the beginning."

a. **Victory through the Holy Spirit: He is the Helper or Counselor—the Spirit of Truth who bears witness to Christ (v.26).**

We can be victorious over the world through the Holy Spirit. He is our *Helper* or *Counselor* through persecution (see Deeper Study # 1—Jn.14:16). He is the Spirit of Truth; therefore, the truth will prevail through our persecution (see note—Jn.14:17.)

In addition, the Spirit will testify to the world, convicting people even while they are hating Christ. Note: the Holy Spirit is sent "from the Father," and He *proceeds from the Father* (para tou patros ekporeuetai), that is, "from the side of the Father." He is said to be a *distinct Person* from the Father and Son; He is said to be a *Divine Person*, coming "from the very side of the Father."

> "When they deliver you over, do not be anxious how you are to speak or what you are to say, for what you are to say will be given to you in that hour." (Mt.10:19)

> "And when they bring you before the synagogues and the rulers and the authorities, do not be anxious about how you should defend yourself or what you should say, for the Holy Spirit will teach you in that very hour what you ought to say." (Lu.12:11-12)

> "For I will give you a mouth and wisdom, which none of your adversaries will be able to withstand or contradict." (Lu.21:15)

> And we impart this in words not taught by human wisdom but taught by the Spirit, interpreting spiritual truths to those who are spiritual. (1 Co.2:13)

b. **Victory through your own witness and fellowship with Christ (v.27).**

Our victory also comes through our own witness and fellowship with Christ. From the time we are saved, we walk and fellowship with the Lord. We see and hear with the eyes and ears of our heart, and we learn of Christ. Therefore, we declare the glorious message of Christ so that this world, even its persecutors, may have fellowship with believers and with the Father and His Son (1 Jn.1:3).

Note another fact: believers bear witness because they really know Christ. It is practically impossible to know the true Messiah, the Savior of the world—to know that nobody has to die—and not proclaim the message. Genuine believers are people of conviction, people who cannot keep quiet if they know and experience the truth themselves.

> Now when they saw the boldness of Peter and John, and perceived that they were uneducated, common men, they were astonished. And they recognized that they had been with Jesus. (Ac.4:13)
>
> And what you have heard from me in the presence of many witnesses entrust to faithful men, who will be able to teach others also. (2 Ti.2:2)
>
> That which we have seen and heard we proclaim also to you, so that you too may have fellowship with us; and indeed our fellowship is with the Father and with his Son Jesus Christ. (1 Jn.1:3)
>
> "You are my witnesses," declares the Lord, "and my servant whom I have chosen, that you may know and believe me and understand that I am he. Before me no god was formed, nor shall there be any after me." (Isa 43:10)

## CHAPTER 16

### M. The Relationship of Believers to Religionists: Persecution (Part II), 16:1-6

"I have said all these things to you to keep you from falling away.

² They will put you out of the synagogues. Indeed, the hour is coming when whoever kills you will think he is offering service to God.

³ And they will do these things because they have not known the Father, nor me.

⁴ But I have said these things to you, that when their hour comes you may remember that I told them to you.

⁵ But now I am going to him who sent me, and none of you asks me, 'Where are you going?'

⁶ But because I have said these things to you, sorrow has filled your heart."

1. The warning: Religionists will persecute believers
2. The persecution: Worship will be forbidden & believers will be killed

3. The reason for the persecution: The religionists do not know God or His Son

4. The preparation for persecution
   a. Believers must expect persecution & not be caught off guard
   b. Believers must know that God truly exists & that Jesus reigns with Him
   c. Believers must keep their minds on their destiny
   d. Believers must call upon the Holy Spirit, v.7

# Division XIII

*The Revelation of Jesus, the Great Minister, and His Legacy, 13:1-16:33*

M. The Relationship of Believers to Religionists: Persecution (Part II), 16:1-6

## 16:1-6
## Introduction

Believers live in a world of religion and religionists—leaders or strict followers of a religion. The world even looks upon believers as religionists, but we are not. Believers are ambassadors of the living Lord, ambassadors who have been left on earth to deliver the message of eternal hope and life to a hopeless and dying world. In this fact alone we face a tremendous problem. There is only One God and He has only One Son, whom He loves beyond anything people could ever dream. To demonstrate that love, God has set His Son up as the only way to approach Him. All people must approach God *in the name* of His Son. The world feels this is narrow—much, much too narrow. Therefore, the world rejects God's Son and sets up its own ways to approach God. The end result is a world full of religions and religious approaches to God (see outline and notes—Jn.10:7-10 for more discussion).

As we draw ever nearer to the return of Christ, we are seeing the fanatical followers of certain false religions or philosophies striking furiously against Christ-followers throughout the world. Jesus' words in this passage are just as relevant to believers today as they were to the disciples to whom He originally spoke them. This is, *The Relationship of Believers to Religionists: Persecution (Part II), 16:1-6*.

1. The warning: Religionists will persecute believers (v.1).

2. The persecution: Worship will be forbidden and believers will be killed (v.2).
3. The reason for the persecution: The religionists do not know God or His Son (v.3).
4. The preparation for persecution (vv.4-6).

## 16:1

"I have said all these things to you to keep you from falling away."

### 1 The warning: Religionists will persecute believers.

Jesus warned believers that religionists would persecute His followers. He issued this warning because He wants to prevent us from slipping away. The word *falling away or stumbling* (Gk. skandalisthete) means to trip and fall. Persecution can be a stumbling block to the believer; it can cause us to fall away from following Christ faithfully. We are living in a world that is hostile to Christ. Consequently, we can find ourselves being...

- questioned
- ridiculed
- passed over
- rejected
- mocked
- attacked
- criticized
- isolated and cut off
- tortured

We can easily stumble and fall over persecution. Persecution can cause us to question our beliefs or even to weaken or return to the way of false religion. It can silence us and our witness, and it can compel some very weak believers to even deny Jesus.

> **Therefore let us not pass judgment on one another any longer, but rather decide never to put a stumbling block or hindrance in the way of a brother. (Ro.14:13)**

## 16:2

² "They will put you out of the synagogues. Indeed, the hour is coming when whoever kills you will think he is offering service to God."

### 2 The persecution: Worship will be forbidden and believers will be killed.

Jesus warned His disciples that the persecution they would face would be severe, and it would be religious in nature. In their case, it would be the leaders of the Jewish religion who would persecute them. They would forbid Christ's disciples to worship Him. Some would face the ultimate persecution: they would be put out of the synagogues and killed.

Today, believers in many places face the same threats. They are forbidden to worship Christ, and some are being dragged out of their churches and killed.

In many cases, such persecution is religious in nature; it is carried out by those who think they truly know God and are doing exactly what God wants. They think they are purifying the world and cleansing it of false teaching, a teaching that is narrow, a teaching that is prejudiced against other religions and beliefs and other approaches to God.

**THOUGHT 1.** False religionists do not see how there can be only one way to God. They conclude that Christ is wrong, that He is not the only Way, the only Truth, the only Life. They conclude...

- that the way to God is by being good and doing good, the best one can
- that the particular religion does not really matter, what is important is that religion *inspires* one to be good and caring and to be a better person

False religionists have always rejected and abused true believers and prophets. And they have often been relentless in their opposition and mistreatment. Nothing can be any more tragic than religious persecution. It can involve such things as...

- having one's faith, position, and ministry questioned
- being accused, abused, talked about, and plotted against
- being denied rights

- being silenced, not allowed to worship or serve
- being removed from service
- being tried and imprisoned, tortured and killed

(See Saul of Tarsus, Ac.8:1-3; see Ac.26:9; Ga.1:13.)

> As an example of suffering and patience, brothers, take the prophets who spoke in the name of the Lord. (Js.5:10)

Persecution can even occur *within* the church. This happens all too frequently. It is a sad fact that God's house is filled with many people who have not genuinely committed their lives to God. They do not know God personally—not in a real and intimate way. Therefore, the believer who truly takes a stand for God and His righteousness is sometimes opposed and persecuted by those within the church. Because these persecutors do not understand God or His righteousness, they can become two-faced—slandering, reviling, and insulting faithful followers of Christ behind their backs. They can also scold, mock, and attack their targets face-to-face. They can even go so far as trying to destroy the faithful believer's reputation and life, depending on the society in which they live. It is a tragedy when persecution takes place within the walls of God's house.

> "Blessed are you when others revile you and persecute you and utter all kinds of evil against you falsely on my account. Rejoice and be glad, for your reward is great in heaven, for so they persecuted the prophets who were before you." (Mt.5:11-12)

> "Beware of men, for they will deliver you over to courts and flog you in their synagogues." (Mt.10:17)

> "Then they will deliver you up to tribulation and put you to death, and you will be hated by all nations for my name's sake. And then many will fall away and betray one another and hate one another." (Mt.24:9-10)

> "But before all this they will lay their hands on you and persecute you, delivering you up to the synagogues and prisons, and you will be brought before kings and governors for my name's sake." (Lu.21:12)

> Who are you to pass judgment on the servant of another? It is before his own master that he stands or falls. And he will be upheld, for the Lord is able to make him stand. (Ro.14:4)

> Indeed, all who desire to live a godly life in Christ Jesus will be persecuted, while evil people and impostors will go on from bad to worse, deceiving and being deceived. (2 Ti.3:12-13)

## 3 The reason for the persecution: The religionists do not know God or His Son.

³ "And they will do these things because they have not known the Father, nor me."

Jesus gives one reason that underlies all other reasons for persecution: false religionists do not know God or His Son, Jesus Christ. This is a staggering statement made by Jesus, for religionists *think* they know God. But Jesus says they do not, not really. They have their own idea of God, but it is only...

- their idea
- their imagination
- their reasoning
- their image
- their idol
- their devices

Religionists are deceived in their concept of God and in their understanding of Christ. They reject Christ, rejecting His claim to be the Son of God and the One who has existed *by the side of God* throughout all eternity. They look upon Christ only as a man: a good man, yes, but only a man. Therefore, they reject Him as the revelation and picture of God. The problem is that they want no God; they want no Lord that demands total self-denial and allegiance—no God other than themselves and their own imaginations. They want the right and freedom to seek their own desires instead of the demands of some supreme Lord (see Deeper Study # 2—Jn.5:15-16; notes—7:32; 11:47-57 for more discussion).

> "But all these things they will do to you on account of my name, because they do not know him who sent me." (Jn.15:21)

"And they will do these things because they have not known the Father, nor me." (Jn.16:3)

"For those who live in Jerusalem and their rulers, because they did not recognize him nor understand the utterances of the prophets, which are read every Sabbath, fulfilled them by condemning him." (Ac.13:27)

For, being ignorant of the righteousness of God, and seeking to establish their own, they did not submit to God's righteousness. (Ro.10:3)

They are darkened in their understanding, alienated from the life of God because of the ignorance that is in them, due to their hardness of heart. (Ep.4:18)

## 16:4-6

⁴ "But I have said these things to you, that when their hour comes you may remember that I told them to you.

⁵ But now I am going to him who sent me, and none of you asks me, 'Where are you going?'

⁶ But because I have said these things to you, sorrow has filled your heart."

## 4 The preparation for persecution.

Our gracious Lord does not want us to face persecution unprepared. He has told us everything we need to know and equipped us with everything we need to endure even the fiercest wrath of those who hate Christ. In these verses, our Lord told us four critical things we need to do to prepare for persecution.

### a. Believers must expect persecution and not be caught off guard (v.4).

Believers must expect persecution. We must remember that Jesus foretold that we would be persecuted. Remembering what Jesus said keeps us from being caught off guard and stumbling. We need to *prepare* for persecution by *thinking through* what we will do when we are . . .

- ridiculed
- criticized
- opposed
- questioned
- attacked
- slandered
- tortured
- imprisoned

The point is this: being forewarned, we know persecution is coming. Therefore, we are to prepare ourselves for it.

> "Remember the word that I said to you: 'A servant is not greater than his master.' If they persecuted me, they will also persecute you. If they kept my word, they will also keep yours." (Jn.15:20)

> "But I have said these things to you, that when their hour comes you may remember that I told them to you. I did not say these things to you from the beginning, because I was with you." (Jn.16:4)

### b. Believers must know that God truly exists and that Jesus reigns with Him (v.5a).

Jesus had told the disciples that they would face trouble and persecution in the world. Now, as He prepared to leave this world, He was revealing more to them and giving them a fuller revelation (see Jn.15:26-27; 16:7f as well as the whole teaching of Jn.15:18-27; 16:1-6). He reinforced the foundational truths that we must anchor ourselves to when we are persecuted:

➤ We must know that God *is* (exists): that our Lord has definitely gone to the Father who sent Him.

> "You heard me say to you, 'I am going away, and I will come to you.' If you loved me, you would have rejoiced, because I am going to the Father, for the Father is greater than I." (Jn.14:28)

> "But now I am going to him who sent me, and none of you asks me, 'Where are you going?'" (Jn.16:5)

> "Concerning righteousness, because I go to the Father, and you will see me no longer." (Jn.16:10)

> "I came from the Father and have come into the world, and now I am leaving the world and going to the Father." (Jn.16:28)

> "And I am no longer in the world, but they are in the world, and I am coming to you. Holy Father, keep them in your name, which you have given me, that they may be one, even as we are one." (Jn.17:11)

And without faith it is impossible to please him, for whoever would draw near to God must believe that he exists and that he rewards those who seek him. (He.11:6)

➢ We must know that our Lord truly reigns.

That he worked in Christ when he raised him from the dead and seated him at his right hand in the heavenly places. (Ep.1:20)

Therefore God has highly exalted him and bestowed on him the name that is above every name. (Ph.2:9)

But we see him who for a little while was made lower than the angels, namely Jesus, crowned with glory and honor because of the suffering of death, so that by the grace of God he might taste death for everyone. (He.2:9)

Saying with a loud voice, "Worthy is the Lamb who was slain, to receive power and wealth and wisdom and might and honor and glory and blessing!" (Re.5:12)

Knowing these two great facts will help believers of all generations to prepare for persecution.

### c. Believers must keep their minds on their destiny (v.5b-6).

Jesus emphasized that we need to know where He went when He departed this world. The disciples' hearts were filled with sorrow because they were not focused on where Jesus was going—heaven, their destiny and ours. We need to keep our minds focused on our destiny. Jesus has gone to the Father who sent Him. He has returned to heaven; therefore, the Father and heaven are the believer's destiny. If persecutors kill us, we gain; we do not lose. We gain something far better than this life, the presence of God Himself (see note, *Resurrection*—Jn.14:6; see also note—Lu.21:18-19; see also Ph.1:23.)

With this in mind, we must not wallow around in self-pity and sorrow, moaning over being persecuted. Our mind and thoughts are to be on God and heaven.

"If anyone serves me, he must follow me; and where I am, there will my servant be also. If anyone serves me, the Father will honor him." (Jn.12:26)

"And if I go and prepare a place for you, I will come again and will take you to myself, that where I am you may be also." (Jn.14:3)

"Peace I leave with you; my peace I give to you. Not as the world gives do I give to you. Let not your hearts be troubled, neither let them be afraid." (Jn.14:27)

"I have said these things to you, that in me you may have peace. In the world you will have tribulation. But take heart; I have overcome the world." (Jn.16:33)

"Father, I desire that they also, whom you have given me, may be with me where I am, to see my glory that you have given me because you loved me before the foundation of the world." (Jn.17:24)

Yes, we are of good courage, and we would rather be away from the body and at home with the Lord. (2 Co.5:8)

I am hard pressed between the two. My desire is to depart and be with Christ, for that is far better. (Ph.1:23)

"You keep him in perfect peace whose mind is stayed on you, because he trusts in you. Trust in the LORD forever, for the LORD GOD is an everlasting rock." (Is.26:3-4)

### d. Believers must call upon the Holy Spirit, v.7 (v.6).

We need to call upon our Helper, the Holy Spirit, when we are persecuted. This point is covered in the next few verses and outline (vv.7-15). The Holy Spirit is given by God to be the believer's constant companion, to help and comfort us as we endure persecution (see outline and notes—Jn.16:7-15).

"And I will ask the Father, and he will give you another Helper, to be with you forever, even the Spirit of truth, whom the world cannot receive, because it neither sees him nor knows him. You know him, for he dwells with you and will be in you." (Jn.14:16-17)

"But the Helper, the Holy Spirit, whom the Father will send in my name, he will teach you all things and bring to your remembrance all that I have said to you." (Jn.14:26)

"Nevertheless, I tell you the truth: it is to your advantage that I go away, for if I do not go away, the Helper will not come to you. But if I go, I will send him to you." (Jn.16:7)

## N. The Work of the Holy Spirit, 16:7-15

|  |  |
|---|---|
| 1. He helps believers by replacing Christ's presence: He works for the believer's good | ⁷ "Nevertheless, I tell you the truth: it is to your advantage that I go away, for if I do not go away, the Helper will not come to you. But if I go, I will send him to you. |
| 2. He convicts the world of sin, righteousness, & judgment | ⁸ And when he comes, he will convict the world concerning sin and righteousness and judgment: |
|    a. Of sin: Because people do not believe in Jesus | ⁹ concerning sin, because they do not believe in me; |
|    b. Of righteousness: Because Jesus' righteousness is proven—He is ascended as Lord[DS1] | ¹⁰ concerning righteousness, because I go to the Father, and you will see me no longer; |
|    c. Of judgment: Because Jesus condemned Satan (He.2:14-15) | ¹¹ concerning judgment, because the ruler of this world is judged. |
| | ¹² I still have many things to say to you, but you cannot bear them now. |
| 3. He guides true believers | ¹³ When the Spirit of truth comes, he will guide you into all the truth, for he will not speak on his own authority, but whatever he hears he will speak, and he will declare to you the things that are to come. |
|    a. By guiding them into all truth | |
|    b. By speaking the truth | |
|    c. By showing them things to come | |
| 4. He glorifies Jesus Christ: He shows the things of Christ to believers | ¹⁴ He will glorify me, for he will take what is mine and declare it to you. |
|    a. This includes the things of the Father | ¹⁵ All that the Father has is mine; therefore I said that he will take what is mine and declare it to you." |
|    b. This includes what Christ wants revealed | |

# Division XIII

*The Revelation of Jesus, the Great Minister, and His Legacy, 13:1–16:33*

N. The Work of the Holy Spirit, 16:7–15

## 16:7-15
## Introduction

God gives every genuine believer an indescribably wonderful gift, the gift of His Spirit. The Holy Spirit—the very presence of God—lives within us. God has given us the Spirit to help us throughout life. Yet, many believers never understand fully *how* the Holy Spirit helps us, exactly *what* He does for us. As a result, they never walk in the fullness of the Spirit's power.

The clearest revelation of the Holy Spirit is given by our Lord Himself. He had already revealed who the Holy Spirit is (Jn.14:15-26). Now, He reveals what the Holy Spirit does. This is, *The Work of the Holy Spirit*, 16:7-15.

1. He helps believers by replacing Christ's presence: He works for the believer's good (v.7).
2. He convicts the world of sin, righteousness, and judgment (vv.8-11).
3. He guides true believers (vv.12-13).
4. He glorifies Jesus Christ: He shows the things of Christ to believers (vv.14-15).

## 1 He helps believers by replacing Christ's presence: He works for the believer's good.

Surprisingly, Jesus said that His going away was to our advantage. It was for our benefit that Jesus would leave the world. Note the additional weight and emphasis Jesus gave to the fact: "I tell you the truth." It may be difficult for a person to see and understand, for it seems that we would be much better off if Jesus were here physically and bodily. Some people even cry out for His presence, for some sight, some vision, some dream of Him. But Jesus said that it was best that He leave and not be physically present. Why? There is one supreme reason: if He had not left, the Holy Spirit would not have come. We are *better off* with the presence of the Holy Spirit than we would be with the presence of Jesus.

> ⁷ "Nevertheless, I tell you the truth: it is to your advantage that I go away, for if I do not go away, the Helper will not come to you. But if I go, I will send him to you."

How can such a statement be made? How can the believer be better off with the Holy Spirit than with the physical, bodily presence of Jesus?

First, since Jesus departed, we now have a *glorified and exalted Lord*. We have a Lord who rules and reigns and controls all: who is able to fulfill all His promises and meet our desperate need for life—life that is both abundant and eternal.

> **And [that you may know] what is the immeasurable greatness of his power toward us who believe, according to the working of his great might that he worked in Christ when he raised him from the dead and seated him at his right hand in the heavenly places. (Ep.1:19-20)**

Second, since Jesus departed, we now have an *Intercessor* before the very throne of God. We have a Person who sympathizes with our weaknesses, because He was tempted in every way just as we are.

> **Since then we have a great high priest who has passed through the heavens, Jesus, the Son of God, let us hold fast our confession. For we do not have a high priest who is unable to sympathize with our weaknesses, but one who in every respect has been tempted as we are, yet without sin. Let us then with confidence draw near to the throne of grace, that we may receive mercy and find grace to help in time of need. (He.4:14-16)**

Third, since Jesus departed, we now have the *presence of the Holy Spirit* with us at all times. Jesus in His human body could be only in one place at a time; but the Holy Spirit, who is Spirit, is able to be with all believers at the same time no matter where we are.

> **"And I will ask the Father, and he will give you another Helper, to be with you forever." (Jn.14:16)**

Fourth, since Jesus departed, we now have *a real gospel* to proclaim, the gospel of the risen and exalted Lord who is able to give eternal life to every person who calls on Him.

> **But what does it say? "The word is near you, in your mouth and in your heart" (that is, the word of faith that we proclaim); because, if you confess with your mouth that Jesus is Lord and believe in your heart that God raised him from the dead, you will be saved. For with the heart one believes and is justified, and with the mouth one confesses and is saved. . . . For "everyone who calls on the name of the Lord will be saved." (Ro.10:8-10, 13)**

Fifth, since Jesus departed, we now have the *worldwide work of the Holy Spirit*, His work of . . .

- convicting and convincing the world (Jn.16:8-11)
- helping and guiding believers (Jn.16:12-13)
- glorifying Christ (Jn.16:14-15)

## 2 He convicts the world of sin, righteousness, and judgment.

The Holy Spirit convicts and convinces the world. The word *convict* (Gk. elegxei) means both *to convict* and *to convince* a person.

> ⁸ "And when he comes, he will convict the world concerning sin and righteousness and judgment:
> ⁹ concerning sin, because they do not believe in me;
> ¹⁰ concerning righteousness, because I go to the Father, and you will see me no longer;
> ¹¹ concerning judgment, because the ruler of this world is judged."

- Convict means to prick people's hearts until they sense and know they are guilty, that they have done wrong or failed to do right.
- Convince means to hammer and drive at people's hearts until they know the fact is true.

The Holy Spirit convicts and convinces the world of three sobering truths: sin, righteousness, and judgment.

**a. Of sin: Because people do not believe in Jesus (v.9).**

The Holy Spirit *convicts* the world of its sin, that the human race is sinful. The Holy Spirit convicts people that they . . .

- miss the mark, that is, fall short of the glory of God

   **For all have sinned and fall short of the glory of God. (Ro.3:23)**

- trespass, that is, wander off the right path

   **And you were dead in the trespasses and sins (Ep.2:1)**

- transgress, that is, break the law of God

   **For since the message declared by angels proved to be reliable, and every transgression or disobedience received a just retribution, how shall we escape if we neglect such a great salvation? It was declared at first by the Lord, and it was attested to us by those who heard. (He.2:2-3)**

In addition, The Holy Spirit *convinces* the world that their unbelief is wrong. The Holy Spirit convinces the world that Jesus really did die for sin. He takes people who do not believe in Jesus and convinces them that Jesus is the Savior—that their sins are really forgiven when they *believe* in Jesus.

**"I told you that you would die in your sins, for unless you believe that I am he you will die in your sins." (Jn.8:24)**

**My little children, I am writing these things to you so that you may not sin. But if anyone does sin, we have an advocate with the Father, Jesus Christ the righteous. He is the propitiation for our sins, and not for ours only but also for the sins of the whole world. (1 Jn.2:1-2)**

**b. Of righteousness: Because Jesus' righteousness is proven—He is ascended as Lord (v.10).**

The Holy Spirit *convicts* the world of its lack of righteousness, that people have no righteousness whatsoever that is acceptable to God. The Holy Spirit convicts people that their righteousness . . .

- is self-righteousness only
- is human righteousness only
- is the righteousness of works that are only human and therefore have an end
- is the righteousness of human goodness and therefore passes away when they die
- is inadequate, insufficient, and unacceptable to God

   **Now it is evident that no one is justified before God by the law, for "The righteous shall live by faith." (Ga.3:11; see Ga.2:16)**

   **We have all become like one who is unclean, and all our righteous deeds are like a polluted garment. We all fade like a leaf, and our iniquities, like the wind, take us away. There is no one who calls upon your name, who rouses himself to take hold of you; for you have hidden your face from us, and have made us melt in the hand of our iniquities. (Is.64:6-7; see vv.9-12)**

The Holy Spirit also *convinces* the world that Jesus' righteousness is acceptable to God. The Holy Spirit convinces people . . .

- that Jesus really was received up into heaven by the Father because He was righteous
- that Jesus has secured righteousness for every human being
- that we can approach God through the righteousness of Jesus
- that Jesus is the ideal and perfect man, the very Son of Man Himself (see note—Jn.1:51)

   **It [righteousness] will be counted to us who believe in him who raised from the dead Jesus our Lord, who was delivered up for our trespasses and raised for our justification. (Ro.4:24-25)**

   **For our sake he made him to be sin who knew no sin, so that in him we might become the righteousness of God. (2 Co.5:21)**

c. **Of judgment: Because Jesus condemned Satan (v.11).**

The Holy Spirit *convicts* the world that judgment is coming, that every individual must face the personal judgment of God. The Holy Spirit convicts people . . .
- that they are both responsible and accountable to God and mankind
- that there is to be a real day of judgment sometime out in the future
- that they must stand face-to-face with God and be judged
- that they will be judged for sin and lack of righteousness, for what they have done and not done

   **So then each of us will give an account of himself to God. (Ro.14:12)**

   **And just as it is appointed for man to die once, and after that comes judgment. (He.9:27)**

In addition, the Holy Spirit *convinces* the world that Jesus has borne the judgment of sin and death for every person. The Holy Spirit convinces people . . .
- that Jesus died bearing the penalty and judgment of sin for them

   **He himself bore our sins in his body on the tree, that we might die to sin and live to righteousness. By his wounds you have been healed. (1 Pe.2:24)**

   **For Christ also suffered once for sins, the righteous for the unrighteous, that he might bring us to God, being put to death in the flesh but made alive in the spirit. (1 Pe.3:18)**

- that Jesus, by His death, destroyed the power of Satan over sin and death (see DEEPER STUDY # 1)

   **"Now is the judgment of this world; now will the ruler of this world be cast out." (Jn.12:31)**

   **Since therefore the children share in flesh and blood, he himself likewise partook of the same things, that through death he might destroy the one who has the power of death, that is, the devil, and deliver all those who through fear of death were subject to lifelong slavery. (He.2:14-15)**

- that they can be freed from sin and death, that they can be forgiven for their sin and given eternal life through the death of Jesus.

   **"For God so loved the world, that he gave his only Son, that whoever believes in him should not perish but have eternal life." (Jn.3:16)**

   **In him we have redemption through his blood, the forgiveness of our trespasses, according to the riches of his grace. (Ep.1:7)**

   (See DEEPER STUDY # 2, 3—Jn.12:31; notes—12:31-33; 14:30-31 for more discussion.)

## DEEPER STUDY # 1

(16:11) **Satan:** this passage concerns the judgment of Satan. The judgment of Satan was executed by Christ upon the cross. It was upon the cross that Jesus Christ judged and condemned the devil in all his authority and power. How? There were two ways.
1. Satan is judged and condemned by the obedience of Christ on the cross. God is perfectly pleased with Christ, for Christ did exactly what God wanted: *He obeyed God perfectly.* Therefore, God is bound to be perfectly pleased.

   The point is this: what God wanted most of all was for Christ to die *for the human race.* Christ Himself said that He did exactly what the Father commanded. The ultimate commandment that would show perfect obedience was for Him . . .
   - to die for humanity's sin
   - to receive the judgment of (physical and spiritual) death for humanity's sin
   - to suffer separation from God for humanity

   It was upon the cross that Christ obeyed God in the supreme, ultimate, and absolute sense. It was because he died—because He obeyed God perfectly—that God . . .
   - has highly exalted Him (see Ph.2:9-11)
   - has given Him a name above every name
   - has destined that every knee will bow before Him, of things *in heaven,* and things *on earth,* and things *under the earth*

- has destined that every tongue will confess that Jesus Christ is Lord
- has judged the world and ordained that it will be recreated and made into a new heavens and earth (2 Pe.3:10-13)
- has cast out Satan and enthroned Christ, giving Him the loyalty of humans and the kingdoms of the whole world (Jn.12:31-32)
- has assured the return of Christ and His rule and reign (Tit.2:12-13)
- has promised that Christ will rule and reign over a new heavens and earth, over all throughout the universe (2 Pe.3:4-5, 8-13)

2. Satan is judged and condemned by the people's belief in the cross, in the death of Christ (see DEEPER STUDY # 4—Jn.12:32 for discussion).

The cross judged and condemned Satan in all his authority and power. The judgment can be summed up in three areas.

a. The cross judges and breaks the power of Satan over the world (Jn.12:31). Satan is the ruler, the prince, the power of the world. This is taught by the Bible (Jn.12:31; 14:30; 16:11; 2 Co.4:4; Ep.2:2). The one example of his dominion familiar to most is the temptation of Christ. Satan offered the kingdoms of the world to Christ if Christ would worship him (Lu.4:6). He possessed the kingdoms to offer. But Christ refused to yield to the temptation. Instead He chose to obey God, to secure the authority over the kingdoms of the world by way of the cross. In this particular passage, Christ proclaimed the coming triumph of the cross. The cross broke forever the power of the devil over the kingdoms of the world, and it assures the return of Christ to rule and reign throughout the universe forever.

"Now is the judgment of this world; now will the ruler of this world be cast out." (Jn.12:31)

Then comes the end, when he delivers the kingdom to God the Father after destroying every rule and every authority and power. For he must reign until he has put all his enemies under his feet. (1 Co.15:24-25)

And being found in human form, he humbled himself by becoming obedient to the point of death, even death on a cross. Therefore God has highly exalted him and bestowed on him the name that is above every name, so that at the name of Jesus every knee should bow, in heaven and on earth and under the earth, and every tongue confess that Jesus Christ is Lord, to the glory of God the Father. (Ph.2:8-11; see Re.21:1f)

He [God] has delivered us from the domain of darkness and transferred us to the kingdom of his beloved Son. (Col.1:13)

He disarmed the rulers and authorities and put them to open shame, by triumphing over them [upon the cross] in him. (Col.2:15)

b. The cross judges and breaks the authority and power of Satan over death (Jn.12:31). Satan holds the power of death. It is his selfish and sinful influence that has brought corruption, decay, and death to the earth. But Christ has broken the devil's grip over death forever. The cross delivers people from the fear and bondage of death and assures Christ the authority over life and death.

For he must reign until he has put all his enemies under his feet. The last enemy to be destroyed is death.... "O death, where is your victory? O death, where is your sting?" The sting of death is sin, and the power of sin is the law. But thanks be to God, who gives us the victory through our Lord Jesus Christ. (1 Co.15:25-26, 55-57)

Since therefore the children share in flesh and blood, he himself likewise partook of the same things, that through death he might destroy the one who has the power of death, that is, the devil, and deliver all those who through fear of death were subject to lifelong slavery. (He.2:14-15)

c. The cross judges and breaks the authority and power of Satan to corrupt people through worldliness and sin (Jn.12:32). Satan uses the world—its pleasures and desire for power and wealth and fame—to attract and enslave people, and enslavement inevitably leads to destruction. But the cross brings power to people, spiritual power...

- to break their habits and bondages
- to keep them from damaging and destroying their body and spirit

The cross and its power to deliver and to give life have become the focal attraction of time and eternity. The cross liberates and frees people forever.

> "I will no longer talk much with you, for the ruler of this world is coming. He has no claim on me [to which he can appeal]." (Jn.14:30)

> No temptation has overtaken you that is not common to man. God is faithful, and he will not let you be tempted beyond your ability, but with the temptation he will also provide the way of escape, that you may be able to endure it. (1 Co.10:13)

> Whoever makes a practice of sinning is of the devil, for the devil has been sinning from the beginning. The reason the Son of God appeared was to destroy the works of the devil. (1 Jn.3:8)

> Little children, you are from God and have overcome them, for he who is in you is greater than he who is in the world. (1 Jn.4:4)

## 3 He guides true believers.   16:12-13

God wants every believer to have a firm grasp on the truth. He desires that we have a "working knowledge" of His Word, that we know how to apply it effectively to our lives. This is one of the strongest reasons He has given us His Spirit. The Holy Spirit is our guide as we study the Scriptures; He guides us into the truth, leading us to understand what God has said.

> ¹² "I still have many things to say to you, but you cannot bear them now.
> ¹³ "When the Spirit of truth comes, he will guide you into all the truth, for he will not speak on his own authority, but whatever he hears he will speak, and he will declare to you the things that are to come."

### a. By guiding them into all truth (v.13a).

The Holy Spirit guides us into all truth. Christ said that
He had many things to say to the apostles, but they were not able to bear (handle, grasp) them, not yet (v.12). He would share them later through the Holy Spirit. Christ tells the Spirit what to say and how to guide believers. Christ, of course, is the One who knows our infirmities and needs. He knows by personal experience (He.4:15-16). Therefore, He is the One who is appointed by God to instruct the Spirit in His *guiding* ministry. This should cause our hearts to leap with great joy and confidence, for the Lord knows exactly what we face—knows by experience.

> For all who are led by the Spirit of God are sons of God. (Ro.8:14)

> That this is God, our God forever and ever. He will guide us forever. (Ps.48:14)

> You guide me with your counsel, and afterward you will receive me to glory. (Ps.73:24)

> And your ears shall hear a word behind you, saying, "This is the way, walk in it," when you turn to the right or when you turn to the left. (Is.30:21)

> And I will lead the blind in a way that they do not know, in paths that they have not known I will guide them. I will turn the darkness before them into light, the rough places into level ground. These are the things I do, and I do not forsake them. (Is.42:16)

> Thus says the Lord, your Redeemer, the Holy One of Israel: "I am the Lord your God, who teaches you to profit, who leads you in the way you should go." (Is.48:17)

### b. By speaking the truth (v.13b).

The Holy Spirit guides by speaking the truth. The Holy Spirit is called "the Spirit of Truth." He speaks only the truth and guides us into "all the truth." The truth, of course, is Jesus Christ Himself. The Spirit leads us to Christ, the Truth, and teaches us "all the truth" about Christ (see Deeper Study # 2—Jn.14:6; note—15:26-27 for more discussion).

> "But when the Helper comes, whom I will send to you from the Father, the Spirit of truth, who proceeds from the Father, he will bear witness about me." (Jn.15:26)

> We are from God. Whoever knows God listens to us; whoever is not from God does not listen to us. By this we know the Spirit of truth and the spirit of error. (1 Jn.4:6)

**c. By showing them things to come (v.13c).**

The Holy Spirit guides by declaring (announcing, showing) things to come. After Jesus arose, the Holy Spirit was the One who led the apostles to write the New Testament and to foresee the things revealed in its pages. Since that day, the Holy Spirit is the One who takes the things revealed in the Word and declares them to our hearts.

> But, as it is written, "What no eye has seen, nor ear heard, nor the heart of man imagined, what God has prepared for those who love him"—these things God has revealed to us through the Spirit. For the Spirit searches everything, even the depths of God. . . . Now we have received not the spirit of the world, but the Spirit who is from God, that we might understand the things freely given us by God. (1 Co.2:9-10, 12)

**THOUGHT 1.** We need to be dependent on the Holy Spirit's leadership in learning the truth. We can only grow in grace and in the knowledge of Christ and His Word with the Holy Spirit's help. This growth is progressive, coming only from the Holy Spirit's opening up the Word to us.

> And we impart this in words not taught by human wisdom but taught by the Spirit, interpreting spiritual truths to those who are spiritual. (1 Co.2:13)

> But the anointing that you received from him abides in you, and you have no need that anyone should teach you. But as his anointing teaches you about everything, and is true, and is no lie—just as it has taught you, abide in him. (1 Jn.2:27)

### 16:14-15

¹⁴ "He will glorify me, for he will take what is mine and declare it to you. ¹⁵ All that the Father has is mine; therefore I said that he will take what is mine and declare it to you."

## 4 He glorifies Jesus Christ: He shows the things of Christ to believers.

The Holy Spirit glorifies Christ and *only* Christ. Note that the Spirit *takes* what is Christ's and *declares* (Gk. anangelei)—makes known, announces, reports—it to believers. This means that He takes and declares . . .
- only what Christ is
- only what Christ did
- only what Christ said

**a. This includes the things of the Father (v.15a).**

Note the phenomenal claim of Jesus: all that the Father has is His. He is the Son of God, the Son of the Father (see note—Jn.1:34 for more discussion). Christ is declaring that there is *perfect unity* in the Godhead. All things of the Father . . .
- are the things of the Son, of Jesus Christ Himself
- are the things shown and declared by the Holy Spirit

> "I and the Father are one." (Jn.10:30)

> "If I am not doing the works of my Father, then do not believe me; but if I do them, even though you do not believe me, believe the works, that you may know and understand that the Father is in me and I am in the Father." (Jn.10:37-38)

> "Do you not believe that I am in the Father and the Father is in me? The words that I say to you I do not speak on my own authority, but the Father who dwells in me does his works." (Jn.14:10)

> "The glory that you have given me I have given to them, that they may be one even as we are one." (Jn.17:22)

**b. This includes what Christ wants revealed (v.15b).**

The Holy Spirit was sent *in Jesus' name* to proclaim Jesus alone. He does not promote Himself. He, the Spirit of Truth, leads believers to Christ, who alone is the Truth. He did not come to proclaim a movement and message of His own but to proclaim the movement and message of Christ. He takes what is Jesus' and declares it to us.

> "But the Helper, the Holy Spirit, whom the Father will send in my name, he will teach you all things and bring to your remembrance all that I have said to you." (Jn.14:26)

## O. The Resurrection and Its Effects Foretold, 16:16-33

16 "A little while, and you will see me no longer; and again a little while, and you will see me."

17 So some of his disciples said to one another, "What is this that he says to us, 'A little while, and you will not see me, and again a little while, and you will see me'; and, 'because I am going to the Father'?"

18 So they were saying, "What does he mean by 'a little while'? We do not know what he is talking about."

19 Jesus knew that they wanted to ask him, so he said to them, "Is this what you are asking yourselves, what I meant by saying, 'A little while and you will not see me, and again a little while and you will see me'?

20 Truly, truly, I say to you, you will weep and lament, but the world will rejoice. You will be sorrowful, but your sorrow will turn into joy.

21 When a woman is giving birth, she has sorrow because her hour has come, but when she has delivered the baby, she no longer remembers the anguish, for joy that a human being has been born into the world.

22 So also you have sorrow now, but I will see you again, and your hearts will rejoice, and no one will take your joy from you."

23 In that day you will ask nothing of me. Truly, truly, I say to you, whatever you ask of the Father in my name, he will give it to you.

24 Until now you have asked nothing in my name. Ask, and you will receive, that your joy may be full.

25 I have said these things to you in figures of speech. The hour is coming when I will no longer speak to you in figures of speech but will tell you plainly about the Father.

26 In that day you will ask in my name, and I do not say to you that I will ask the Father on your behalf;"

1. **The resurrection perplexes people**
   a. The death & resurrection of Jesus was predicted
   b. The resurrection was puzzling
      1) The disciples were perplexed

      2) Jesus knew the disciples' perplexity & wished to help them understand

2. **The resurrection brings joy—irrepressible joy**
   a. Grief gripped the apostles after Jesus' death
   b. Grief turned to joy after Jesus' resurrection
   c. An illustration conveyed the point well: A woman in labor experiences pain, but the pain is soon followed by great joy

   d. Irrepressible joy followed sorrow
      1) Because of the resurrection
      2) Because no one could take the joy away

3. **The resurrection gives open access into God's presence**
   a. The glorious promise

   b. The institution of prayer "in Jesus' name"

4. **The resurrection reveals all about the Father**
   a. The resurrection clearly declares the Father

   b. The resurrection shows that the approach to God is "in Jesus' name"

|   |   |
|---|---|
| c. The resurrection shows that the Father Himself loves the believer | ²⁷ "for the Father himself loves you, because you have loved me and have believed that I came from God. |
| 5. The resurrection validates the Messiahship of Jesus | ²⁸ I came from the Father and have come into the world, and now I am leaving the world and going to the Father." |
| 6. The resurrection exposes weak faith | ²⁹ His disciples said, "Ah, now you are speaking plainly and not using figurative speech! |
| a. The disciples declared their faith | ³⁰ "Now we know that you know all things and do not need anyone to question you; this is why we believe that you came from God." |
| b. Jesus questioned the disciples' weak profession | ³¹ Jesus answered them, "Do you now believe? |
| c. The cross would test & expose the disciples' weak profession | ³² Behold, the hour is coming, indeed it has come, when you will be scattered, each to his own home, and will leave me alone. Yet I am not alone, for the Father is with me. |
| 7. The resurrection makes true peace available—a peace that endures through all trouble<br>a. The world's peace: Trouble<br>b. The peace of Christ: Triumphant | ³³ I have said these things to you, that in me you may have peace. In the world you will have tribulation. But take heart; I have overcome the world." |

# Division XIII

*The Revelation of Jesus, the Great Minister, and His Legacy, 13:1–16:33*

O. The Resurrection and Its Effects Foretold, 16:16–33

## 16:16–33
## Introduction

The Apostle Paul made an extraordinary statement about the resurrection of Christ. He said that he counted everything in his life as rubbish in comparison to knowing Christ and the power of His resurrection (Ph.1:8-11). Paul's challenging statement emphasizes how important it is that we understand Christ's resurrection and how it impacts our lives.

In this passage, Jesus teaches us about the effects of His resurrection. It is one of the greatest passages on the resurrection of Jesus Christ, and it is one of the most glorious passages in all of Scripture. It is one of those passages that lays out more than we could ever imagine. This is, *The Resurrection and Its Effects Foretold, 16:16-33.*

1. The resurrection perplexes people (vv.16-19).
2. The resurrection brings joy—irrepressible joy (vv.20-22).
3. The resurrection gives open access into God's presence (vv.23-24).
4. The resurrection reveals all about the Father (vv.25-27).
5. The resurrection validates the Messiahship of Jesus (v.28).
6. The resurrection exposes weak faith (vv.29-32).
7. The resurrection makes true peace available—a peace that endures through all trouble (v.33).

## 1 The resurrection perplexes people.

The truth of the resurrection is beyond the logical laws of nature. Indeed, it is only possible through the miraculous power of the Lord of life and death. For this reason, our natural minds cannot understand it, and many people are perplexed by it. This should not surprise us, for even Jesus' disciples—those who knew Him best and had seen Him raise a dead man—were puzzled by the truth of His resurrection.

### a. The death and resurrection of Jesus was predicted (v.16).

Jesus told His disciples of His impending death and resurrection (v.16). When He said they would not see Him for a little while, He was speaking of His death. When He said that, after a little while, they would see Him again, He was predicting His resurrection.

### b. The resurrection was puzzling (vv.17–19).

This prediction of Jesus' death and resurrection perplexed the disciples, and they began to ask among themselves what Jesus meant. Jesus had also referred to His ascension, saying that He was going to the Father (vv.17–18). The Lord knew that they were puzzled and asked them about their perplexity, wishing to help them understand (v.19).

16:16-33

16:16–19

¹⁶ "A little while, and you will see me no longer; and again a little while, and you will see me."
¹⁷ So some of his disciples said to one another, "What is this that he says to us, 'A little while, and you will not see me, and again a little while, and you will see me'; and, 'because I am going to the Father'?"
¹⁸ So they were saying, "What does he mean by 'a little while'? We do not know what he is talking about."
¹⁹ Jesus knew that they wanted to ask him, so he said to them, "Is this what you are asking yourselves, what I meant by saying, 'A little while and you will not see me, and again a little while and you will see me'?

**THOUGHT 1.** The resurrection does puzzle and perplex people; it always has and always will. People are puzzled by both the resurrection of Jesus and the coming resurrection of all people at the end of the world. Accordingly, they try to explain it away.

(1) Some deny the resurrection outright, saying such is beyond human experience and could not possibly happen (an atheistic position).
(2) Some say the resurrection may have occurred, but it also may not have occurred. People have never known anything about it other than what Christians and a few others say about Jesus. They reason, "But that happened so long ago that it cannot be scientifically proven; therefore, there is no way to know if it is true" (an agnostic position).
(3) Some say that the resurrection is possible and that Jesus probably did arise but that it is a meaningless puzzle for *today*: "I will worry about its meaning tomorrow. I have no time to get involved and wrapped up in what it means, not now. Perhaps I will need to sit down and find out its meaning later, but right now other things are pressing and more important."

> For, being ignorant of the righteousness of God, and seeking to establish their own, they did not submit to God's righteousness. (Ro.10:3)
>
> They [men] are darkened in their understanding, alienated from the life of God because of the ignorance that is in them, due to their hardness of heart. (Ep.4:18)
>
> Therefore, preparing your minds for action, and being sober-minded, set your hope fully on the grace that will be brought to you at the revelation of Jesus Christ. As obedient children, do not be conformed to the passions of your former ignorance, but as he who called you is holy, you also be holy in all your conduct. (1 Pe.1:13-15)

## 2 The resurrection brings joy—irrepressible joy.

Jesus would be going away from the disciples by sacrificing Himself for the world, leaving His followers in deep sorrow.

16:20–22

²⁰ "Truly, truly, I say to you, you will weep and lament, but the world will rejoice. You will be sorrowful, but your sorrow will turn into joy.
²¹ "When a woman is giving birth, she has sorrow because her hour has come, but when she has delivered the baby, she no longer remembers the anguish, for joy that a human being has been born into the world.
²² "So also you have sorrow now, but I will see you again, and your hearts will rejoice, and no one will take your joy from you."

But their sorrow would not last long. When Jesus rose from the grave, their sorrow would be replaced with irrepressible joy.

a. **Grief gripped the apostles after Jesus' death (v.20a).**

Jesus said His disciples would be gripped with grief after His death. They would weep and mourn and experience deep despair. Their hopes would seem to be dashed on the rocks of humanity's ultimate enemy: death.

> And my God. My soul is cast down within me; therefore I remember you from the land of Jordan and of Hermon, from Mount Mizar. (Ps.42:6)
>
> I sink in deep mire, where there is no foothold; I have come into deep waters, and the flood sweeps over me. (Ps.69:2)
>
> But as for me, my feet had almost stumbled, my steps had nearly slipped. (Ps.73:2)
>
> But when I thought how to understand this, it seemed to me a wearisome task. (Ps.73:16)
>
> But Zion said, "The Lord has forsaken me; my Lord has forgotten me." (Is.49:14)

Jesus proceeded to say the world would rejoice at His death. Why? Because in the eyes of many, death would prove that He was not the Son of God; that He was only a self-proclaimed savior who was now dead. To many, Christ's death would prove Him false. And according to these misguided souls, if He were dead, His demands would be nonbinding—essentially meaningless. Therefore, people would not have to do what He said: deny themselves and give all they were and had to Him. They would not have to go and give all they had to meet the desperate needs of a lost world. If Christ's death were permanent, the belief that Jesus was a sham, that His life and teaching were meaningless, would be one hundred percent accurate.

> "But his citizens [of the world] hated him and sent a delegation after him, saying, 'We do not want this man to reign over us.'" (Lu.19:14)
>
> "Whoever loves his life loses it, and whoever hates his life in this world will keep it for eternal life." (Jn.12:25)

b. **Grief turned to joy after Jesus' resurrection (v.20b).**

The grief of those who loved Jesus would be only temporary. Jesus said that He would arise, and His resurrection would cause His followers to burst forth with joy.

Christ's resurrection meant that death was conquered. People no longer had to die, no longer had to be condemned for sin. They could be delivered from sin and death by following Jesus (see Deeper Study # 2—Jn.12:31; Deeper Study # 4—12:32; Deeper Study # 1—16:11 for discussion).

**THOUGHT 1.** This joy is the answer to the weeping and lamenting over death. The great source of joy is the glorious news of the resurrection, the absolute knowledge and certainty that Jesus Christ is risen.

> And if Christ has not been raised, your faith is futile and you are still in your sins. Then those also who have fallen asleep in Christ have perished. If in Christ we have hope in this life only, we are of all people most to be pitied. But in fact Christ has been raised from the dead, the firstfruits of those who have fallen asleep. (1 Co.15:17-20)
>
> But we do not want you to be uninformed, brothers, about those who are asleep, that you may not grieve as others do who have no hope. For since we believe that Jesus died and rose again, even so, through Jesus, God will bring with him those who have fallen asleep. (1 Th.4:13-14)

c. **An illustration conveyed the point well: A woman in labor experiences pain, but the pain is soon followed by great joy (v.21).**

In verse 21, Jesus offers a brilliant illustration of the immense contrast between the sorrow over death and the joy of the resurrection. He describes a woman's pain in giving birth. She suffers so much that she literally groans and grasps in desperation for the new life to begin. Once the child is born, the sorrow and pain are all forgotten, for a new life has emerged.

### d. Irrepressible joy followed sorrow (v.22).

The disciples would experience deep sorrow, but when they saw Jesus alive, their hearts would rejoice with a joy that no person could take from them. The resurrection brings irrepressible joy, just as a newborn baby brings joy to a woman in labor. Jesus explains this uncontainable joy:

First, the resurrection and presence of Jesus Himself brings indescribable joy. Seeing Jesus again would cause them to rejoice. Just think: Jesus is not dead. His body has not decayed in a grave: He has risen! He emerged from the grave and ascended to the Father. There is victory over the grave, triumph over death. We can now live forever! No truth could fill a person with any more joy and rejoicing than *really knowing* that death has been conquered in the resurrection of Jesus Christ.

> **For Christ also suffered once for sins, the righteous for the unrighteous, that he might bring us to God, being put to death in the flesh but made alive [resurrected] in the spirit. (1 Pe.3:18)**

Second, the believer's joy of *really knowing* the resurrection of Jesus Christ cannot be taken away by any person. The fact is there: Jesus did die for our sins and arise again to give us a new life—a life that is both abundant and eternal. The believer knows it. Our joy is permanent, deep-seated, and unmovable. When the trials and sorrows of earth come upon us, we still ...

- know the joy of the Lord's presence and care

> **"And I will ask the Father, and he will give you another Helper, to be with you forever, even the Spirit of truth, whom the world cannot receive, because it neither sees him nor knows him. You know him, for he dwells with you and will be in you. I will not leave you as orphans; I will come to you." (Jn.14:16-18)**

> **"Nevertheless, I tell you the truth: it is to your advantage that I go away, for if I do not go away, the Helper will not come to you. But if I go, I will send him to you." (Jn.16:7)**

- know that Christ will escort us into the Father's presence eternally

> **"And if I go and prepare a place for you, I will come again and will take you to myself, that where I am you may be also." (Jn.14:3)**

> **Yes, we are of good courage, and we would rather be away from the body and at home with the Lord. (2 Co.5:8)**

> **I am hard pressed between the two. My desire is to depart and be with Christ, for that is far better. (Ph.1:23)**

> **The Lord will rescue me from every evil deed and bring me safely into his heavenly kingdom. To him be the glory forever and ever. Amen. (2 Ti.4:18)**

- know that we will be a child of the new heavens and earth to be created for the Father's family

> **The Spirit himself bears witness with our spirit that we are children of God, and if children, then heirs—heirs of God and fellow heirs with Christ, provided we suffer with him in order that we may also be glorified with him. (Ro.8:16-17)**

> **But according to his promise we are waiting for new heavens and a new earth in which righteousness dwells. (2 Pe.3:13)**

> **Then I saw a new heaven and a new earth, for the first heaven and the first earth had passed away, and the sea was no more. (Re.21:1)**

## 3 The resurrection gives open access into God's presence.

After Christ's resurrection, the way His followers pray would be different. We have open access into God's presence. Therefore, we can ask the Father directly for whatever we need in Jesus' name.

> 23 "In that day you will ask nothing of me. Truly, truly, I say to you, whatever you ask of the Father in my name, he will give it to you.
> 24 Until now you have asked nothing in my name. Ask, and you will receive, that your joy may be full."

### a. The glorious promise (v.23).

Jesus made His followers a glorious promise: an *open door* into God's presence. Jesus said "in that day," after His resurrection, there will be no need to ask Him anything. (This does not mean, of course, that we cannot ask Him, only that we do not *have to* ask Him.) The believer can walk right into the Father's presence. There is an *open door* into His presence. Whatever we ask the Father in Jesus' name, He will give it to us. This is the most glorious of promises, that we can approach God as our Heavenly Father, just as children approach their earthly father.

**b. The institution of prayer "in Jesus' name" (v.24).**

Jesus instituted a new way of praying: our approach to God, our communion with Him, is to be *in Jesus' name*. This is the crucial point. Our approach to the Father, our prayer, must be *in Jesus' name* (see Deeper Study # 3—Jn.14:13-14). Before Jesus, people had always asked God for things directly, but no more. The resurrection instituted a new and living way into God's presence. We must now approach God through Jesus Christ . . .

- believing that the righteousness of Jesus covers us
- asking God to accept our faith *in* Jesus as righteousness
- thanking God for Jesus, His great love and sacrifice for us

> "Whatever you ask in my name, this I will do, that the Father may be glorified in the Son." (Jn.14:13)
>
> "You did not choose me, but I chose you and appointed you that you should go and bear fruit and that your fruit should abide, so that whatever you ask the Father in my name, he may give it to you." (Jn.15:16)
>
> For our sake he made him to be sin who knew no sin, so that in him we might become the righteousness of God. (2 Co.5:21)
>
> Therefore, brothers, since we have confidence to enter the holy places by the blood of Jesus, by the new and living way that he opened for us through the curtain, that is, through his flesh, and since we have a great priest over the house of God, let us draw near with a true heart in full assurance of faith, with our hearts sprinkled clean from an evil conscience and our bodies washed with pure water. (He.10:19-22)

Note two tremendous promises to those who ask *in Jesus' name*:

➢ They will receive what they ask.

> "If you abide in me, and my words abide in you, ask whatever you wish, and it will be done for you." (Jn.15:7)

➢ Their joy is full and complete (see Deeper Study # 1—Jn.15:11 for discussion).

> "These things I have spoken to you, that my joy may be in you, and that your joy may be full." (Jn.15:11)
>
> For the kingdom of God is not a matter of eating and drinking but of righteousness and peace and joy in the Holy Spirit. (Ro.14:17)
>
> Though you have not seen him, you love him. Though you do not now see him, you believe in him and rejoice with joy that is inexpressible and filled with glory. (1 Pe.1:8)

## 16:25-27

²⁵ "I have said these things to you in figures of speech. The hour is coming when I will no longer speak to you in figures of speech but will tell you plainly about the Father.
²⁶ In that day you will ask in my name, and I do not say to you that I will ask the Father on your behalf;
²⁷ for the Father himself loves you, because you have loved me and have believed that I came from God."

## 4 The resurrection reveals all about the Father.

Jesus explained that, to this point, He had taught His disciples using figurative language. But after His resurrection, He would tell them plainly about the Father, for the resurrection would reveal all about Him.

**a. The resurrection clearly declares the Father (v.25).**

Jesus said that the resurrection would declare the Father plainly. It reveals and declares God's nature . . .

- of *compassion*: of caring for the welfare of those gripped by sin and death
- of *salvation*: of delivering people from the fear and bondage of sin and death

- of *power*: of omnipotence, of being able to plan and carry out the plan of salvation by overruling all and by raising the dead
- of *life*: possessing life itself and being able to infuse life into the dead
- of *justice*: not allowing One who was sinless and perfect to be held by death
- of *omniscience*: knowing all, knowing the terrible injustice done to the innocent Son of God and knowing how to solve and work the whole scene out for the good of salvation

> **Blessed be the God and Father of our Lord Jesus Christ! According to his great mercy, he has caused us to be born again to a living hope through the resurrection of Jesus Christ from the dead, to an inheritance that is imperishable, undefiled, and unfading, kept in heaven for you. (1 Pe.1:3-4)**

b. **The resurrection shows that the approach to God is "in Jesus' name" (v.26).**
The resurrection shows that we must approach God—pray—in the name of Jesus (see Deeper Study # 3—Jn.14:13-14 for discussion; also see note, pt.2—Jn.16:23-24 of this outline). Our access to God is possible only through the atoning death of Jesus Christ. His death and redeeming blood tore down the veil that stood between us and the Father (Mt.27:50-51).

c. **The resurrection shows that the Father Himself loves the believer (v.27).**
The resurrection reveals the Father's love for those who believe in His Son. Jesus said that He would not have to beg the Father to receive and hear the believer. We do not need an intercessor to pray to the Father. The Father Himself loves us and receives us into His presence. We can come directly to God's throne in Jesus' name. However, there is a crucial point to note. The Father *loves* the believer for a reason: because we . . .
- love Jesus (see notes—Jn.14:15; 14:23)
- believe that Jesus "came from God" (see Deeper Study # 1—Jn.3:31; Deeper Study # 3—3:34; notes—7:16-19; 7:25-31)

**THOUGHT 1.** It is because of Jesus that the Father receives and hears us. This picture of God as Father differs radically from the normal picture . . .
- that God is angry and has to be begged by Jesus to receive and hear us
- that God is far off someplace out in space—almost too far to be reached
- that maybe God exists and maybe He does not, but one needs to go ahead and pray just in case

> **"For God so loved the world, that he gave his only Son, that whoever believes in him should not perish but have eternal life." (Jn.3:16)**

> **But God shows his love for us in that while we were still sinners, Christ died for us. (Ro.5:8)**

> **But God, being rich in mercy, because of the great love with which he loved us, even when we were dead in our trespasses, made us alive together with Christ—by grace you have been saved. (Ep.2:4-5)**

> **See what kind of love the Father has given to us, that we should be called children of God; and so we are. The reason why the world does not know us is that it did not know him. (1 Jn.3:1)**

## 5 The resurrection validates the Messiahship of Jesus.

The resurrection proves Jesus' claim to be the Messiah (Ro.1:4). In one brief statement Jesus summarized His mission:

> "I came from the Father and have come into the world" (see Deeper Study # 3—Jn.3:34; notes—7:16-19; 7:25-31).

28 "I came from the Father and have come into the world, and now I am leaving the world and going to the Father."

> **"I know him, for I come from him, and he sent me." (Jn.7:29)**

> **Jesus said to them, "If God were your Father, you would love me, for I came from God and I am here. I came not of my own accord, but he sent me." (Jn.8:42)**

"Do you say of him whom the Father consecrated and sent into the world, 'You are blaspheming,' because I said, 'I am the Son of God'?" (Jn.10:36)

"That they may all be one, just as you, Father, are in me, and I in you, that they also may be in us, so that the world may believe that you have sent me." (Jn.17:21)

➢ "I am leaving the world and going to the Father" (see note, *Resurrection*—Jn.14:6).

"You heard me say to you, 'I am going away, and I will come to you.' If you loved me, you would have rejoiced, because I am going to the Father, for the Father is greater than I." (Jn.14:28)

"A little while, and you will see me no longer; and again a little while, and you will see me." (Jn.16:16)

"And I am no longer in the world, but they are in the world, and I am coming to you. Holy Father, keep them in your name, which you have given me, that they may be one, even as we are one." (Jn.17:11)

Note Jesus' phenomenal claim. He came from "the Father" and is returning to "the Father."

> And was declared to be the Son of God in power according to the Spirit of holiness by his resurrection from the dead, Jesus Christ our Lord. (Ro.1:4)

## 16:29-32

²⁹ His disciples said, "Ah, now you are speaking plainly and not using figurative speech!
³⁰ Now we know that you know all things and do not need anyone to question you; this is why we believe that you came from God."
³¹ Jesus answered them, "Do you now believe?
³² Behold, the hour is coming, indeed it has come, when you will be scattered, each to his own home, and will leave me alone. Yet I am not alone, for the Father is with me."

## 6 The resurrection exposes weak faith.

The disciples claimed to believe, but their faith was not as strong as they thought it was. As Jesus revealed His resurrection, He exposed their weak faith.

a. **The disciples declared their faith (vv.29-30).**

Something Jesus said struck the disciples' hearts. It may have been His promise to show them the Father (explain all that He was saying) or the fact that the Father loves them. Whatever it was, it opened the disciples' understanding and caused them to make a great declaration of faith:

➢ "We know that you know all things."
➢ "We believe that you came from God."

**THOUGHT 1.** Note that the disciples confessed their faith in the *Incarnation*, God Himself in the person of His Son coming to earth. It is a critical confession that must be made by every person.

> By this you know the Spirit of God: every spirit that confesses that Jesus Christ has come in the flesh is from God, and every spirit that does not confess Jesus is not from God. This is the spirit of the antichrist, which you heard was coming and now is in the world already. (1 Jn.4:2-3)

b. **Jesus questioned the disciples' weak profession (v.31).**

Jesus questioned the disciples' belief. His question challenged them to examine their faith, to search themselves and discern just how strongly they believed in Him.

c. **The cross would test and expose the disciples' weak profession (v.32).**

Knowing all things, Jesus predicted that the disciples would desert Him. The cross would prove the weakness of their profession. In the end, they would not stand by Jesus, not when the world turned against Him.

This statement reveals several clear facts about Jesus, facts that are a great encouragement to the believer:

First, Jesus was never alone, even when His closest followers did not stand with Him. The Father was with Him through every situation, no matter how terrible. Even when He did not have the support of His disciples, He had God and His support.

> "I and the Father are one." (Jn.10:30)

"But if I do them, even though you do not believe me, believe the works, that you may know and understand that the Father is in me and I am in the Father." (Jn.10:38)

"Do you not believe that I am in the Father and the Father is in me? The words that I say to you I do not speak on my own authority, but the Father who dwells in me does his works." (Jn.14:10)

Second, Jesus was forgiving. He forgave every one of the men, even for deserting Him. He did not hold their sin and failure against them. (How His arms reach out for every deserter, to forgive and to receive back!)

Who was delivered up for our trespasses and raised for our justification [forgiveness and acceptance]. (Ro.4:25)

Because, if you confess with your mouth that Jesus is Lord and believe in your heart that God raised him from the dead, you will be saved. For with the heart one believes and is justified, and with the mouth one confesses and is saved. (Ro.10:9-10)

If we confess our sins, he is faithful and just to forgive us our sins and to cleanse us from all unrighteousness. (1 Jn.1:9)

Third, Jesus knew all. Even when He chose these men, He knew they would fail and desert Him, yet He went ahead and chose them. He knew they were trustworthy and would eventually prove faithful.

"You did not choose me, but I chose you and appointed you that you should go and bear fruit and that your fruit should abide, so that whatever you ask the Father in my name, he may give it to you." (Jn.15:16)

I thank him who has given me strength, Christ Jesus our Lord, because he judged me faithful, appointing me to his service. (1 Ti.1:12)

## 7 The resurrection makes true peace available—a peace that endures through all trouble.

Because of the resurrection, we can have true peace, triumphant peace (see note, *Peace*—Jn.14:27 for discussion). This peace is greater than anything the world may throw at us. It is a peace that endures through all trouble.

33 "I have said these things to you, that in me you may have peace. In the world you will have tribulation. But take heart; I have overcome the world."

### a. The world's peace: Trouble.

The world can give no lasting peace, only trials and tribulation. No matter who the person is, the trials and tribulations come. Such is the way of the world, and nobody can avoid it. Therefore, whatever peace comes through this world is transient, passing ever so quickly.

### b. The peace of Christ: Triumphant.

The peace of Jesus Christ—the peace that is *in Him*—is lasting. It is an *overcoming* peace, a peace that overcomes the trials and tribulations of the world, no matter what they are, even the terrible trials of sin and death. But this *overcoming peace* . . .
- is only *in Jesus*
- is only *in His Word*, in the things which He spoke

Note: the peace of God comes only through the resurrection of Jesus Christ, only through His conquest and victory over sin and death.

"God raised him up, loosing the pangs of death, because it was not possible for him to be held by it." (Ac.2:24)

For I delivered to you as of first importance what I also received: that Christ died for our sins in accordance with the Scriptures, that he was buried, that he was raised on the third day in accordance with the Scriptures. (1 Co.15:3-4; see vv.5-58)

And [that you may know] what is the immeasurable greatness of his power toward us who believe, according to the working of his great might that he worked in Christ when he raised him from the dead and seated him at his right hand in the heavenly places. (Ep.1:19-20)

But we do not want you to be uninformed, brothers, about those who are asleep, that you may not grieve as others do who have no hope. For since we believe that Jesus died and rose again, even so, through Jesus, God will bring with him those who have fallen asleep. (1 Th.4:13-14)

Blessed be the God and Father of our Lord Jesus Christ! According to his great mercy, he has caused us to be born again to a living hope through the resurrection of Jesus Christ from the dead, to an inheritance that is imperishable, undefiled, and unfading, kept in heaven for you. (1 Pe.1:3-4)

# Chapter 17

## XIV. The Revelation of Jesus, the Great Intercessor, 17:1–26

### A. Jesus Prayed for Himself, 17:1–8

When Jesus had spoken these words, he lifted up his eyes to heaven, and said, "Father, the hour has come; glorify your Son that the Son may glorify you,

² since you have given him authority over all flesh, to give eternal life to all whom you have given him.

³ And this is eternal life, that they know you, the only true God, and Jesus Christ whom you have sent.

⁴ I glorified you on earth, having accomplished the work that you gave me to do.

⁵ And now, Father, glorify me in your own presence with the glory that I had with you before the world existed.

⁶ I have manifested your name to the people whom you gave me out of the world. Yours they were, and you gave them to me, and they have kept your word.

⁷ Now they know that everything that you have given me is from you.

⁸ For I have given them the words that you gave me, and they have received them and have come to know in truth that I came from you; and they have believed that you sent me."

1. **Request 1: Glorify your Son—that He may glorify the Father**
   a. When: Now, because His time had come, that is, His death
   b. How: By giving Him authority over all people
   c. Purpose: That He may give eternal life
      1) Eternal life is knowing God
      2) Eternal life is knowing Christ
   d. Reason: Christ completed, finished God's work

2. **Request 2: Restore your Son to His former glory—to His preexistent exaltation**
   a. Because He has revealed the Father's name to His followers

   b. Because his followers now know that He is God's Son, the revelation of God Himself
      1) They now accept His Word
      2) They now know His origin
      3) They now believe God sent Him, that He is the Son of God Himself

# Division XIV

### The Revelation of Jesus, the Great Intercessor, 17:1–26

A. Jesus Prayed for Himself, 17:1–8

## 17:1–8
## Introduction

The prayer life of Jesus was so powerful that His disciples asked Him to teach them to pray as He prayed. In response, Jesus gave them what we call "The Lord's Prayer" (Mt.6:9-13; Lk.11:1-4). As many have noted, a more accurate title for that prayer would be "The Disciples' Prayer," for Jesus gave it to His followers as a pattern to follow. Jesus' prayer in John 17 is truly The Lord's

Prayer, for it is the prayer Jesus prayed Himself as He anticipated His impending death and return to heaven.

This particular passage begins the High Priestly Prayer of Jesus (Jn.17:1-26). In this chapter, Jesus is revealed to be *the great Intercessor*. He reached the summit of prayer: He prayed for Himself (vv.1-8), for His immediate disciples (vv.9-19), and for future believers (vv.20-26). This is, *Jesus Prayed for Himself,* 17:1-8.

1. Request 1: Glorify your Son—that He may glorify the Father (vv.1-4).
2. Request 2: Restore your Son to His former glory—to His preexistent exaltation (vv.5-8).

(17:1-8) **Another Outline**: The Hour Has Come.
1. The hour of glory (v.1).
2. The hour of power (v.2).
3. The hour of eternal life (vv.2-3).
4. The hour of a finished work (v.4).
5. The hour of restored glory (v.5).
6. The hour of revelation (v.6).
7. The hour of a mission accomplished, or the hour of belief (vv.7-8).

## 17:1-4

When Jesus had spoken these words, he lifted up his eyes to heaven, and said, "Father, the hour has come; glorify your Son that the Son may glorify you,

² "since you have given him authority over all flesh, to give eternal life to all whom you have given him.

³ "And this is eternal life, that they know you, the only true God, and Jesus Christ whom you have sent.

⁴ "I glorified you on earth, having accomplished the work that you gave me to do."

## 1 Request 1: Glorify your Son—that He may glorify the Father.

Jesus began His prayer by lifting up His eyes to heaven and calling God "Father." Once again, He was claiming to know God intimately, to be the very Son of God. As Jesus prayed, He made only two requests for Himself (vv.1, 5). First, He asked to glorify Him, that he may glorify the Father.

The whole purpose for God's sending Jesus to earth was to give eternal life to the human race; so in asking the two questions, "How is God glorified?" and "How is Jesus glorified?" the answer is simply, by people's receiving eternal life. Both God's glory and Jesus' glory are found in the completion of the great work of salvation. There is . . .

- the glory of righteousness which Jesus secured by a perfect life
- the glory of the cross itself
- the glory of Jesus' resurrection which vindicates His Messiahship beyond question
- the glory of Christ's ascension and exaltation

All is summed up in the glory of humanity's salvation, in people's receiving eternal life (see notes, *Jesus Christ, Glory of*—Jn.12:23-26; *God, Glory of*—Jn.12:27-30 for discussion; also see Deeper Study # 4—Mt.6:9; Deeper Study # 6—Mt.6:10 for more discussion). The death of Christ was necessary for people to be saved—for both the Son and the Father to be glorified.

a. **When: Now, because His time had come, that is, His death (v.1).**
Jesus acknowledged that His hour had come. "The hour" refers to His death (see notes—Jn.2:3-5; 12:23-24). The time had come for Him to offer His life as the sacrifice for humanity's sin.

b. **How: By giving Him authority over all people (v.2a).**
How is Jesus glorified? By God's giving Him the power and authority over all flesh, that is, over all people. (See note—Jn.13:31-32 for discussion. Also see note—Jn.12:23-26 for more discussion. These are important notes in seeing this point.)

> "Truly, truly, I say to you, whoever hears my word and believes him who sent me has eternal life. He does not come into judgment, but has passed from death to life. Truly, truly, I say to you, an hour is coming, and is now here, when the dead [spiritually dead] will hear the voice of the Son of God, and those who hear will live. For as the Father has life in himself, so he has granted the Son

also to have life in himself. And he has given him authority to execute judgment, because he is the Son of Man." (Jn.5:24-27)

c. **Purpose: That He may give eternal life (vv.2b-3).**
God has given Jesus authority over all people for a specific purpose, a selfless purpose. There is one reason Jesus was exalted to be the sovereign majesty of the universe, and it is the most wonderful news in all the universe. Jesus was glorified so that He could give people eternal life (see Jn.3:35-36; 10:28). Note exactly what Jesus said:

➤ He gives eternal life (see Deeper Study # 1; Deeper Study # 2—Jn.1:4; Deeper Study # 1—10:10).
➤ God gives Jesus the persons who are to receive eternal life. A person must be moved upon by the drawing power of God (Holy Spirit) in order to receive eternal life (see notes—Jn.6:44-46).

> "No one can come to me unless the Father who sent me draws him. And I will raise him up on the last day." (Jn.6:44)

What is eternal life? Jesus proceeded to give His definition of eternal life (v.3). First, eternal life is knowing God. Second, eternal life is knowing Christ. Simply and briefly stated, eternal life is a personal, intimate relationship with God and His Son, Jesus Christ.

d. **Reason: Christ completed, finished God's work (v.4).**
The reason Jesus was now ready to be glorified is clearly stated: He had finished the work God had given Him to do. In doing the work God had given Him to do, He had glorified God on earth.

**THOUGHT 1.** The only way a person can glorify God on earth is to do what God says. If we truly desire to glorify God, we will obey God (see note, *God, Glory of*—Jn.12:27-30 for more discussion).

> "Not everyone who says to me, 'Lord, Lord,' will enter the kingdom of heaven, but the one who does the will of my Father who is in heaven." (Mt.7:21)

> "By this my Father is glorified, that you bear much fruit and so prove to be my disciples." (Jn.15:8)

> And this is his commandment, that we believe in the name of his Son Jesus Christ and love one another, just as he has commanded us. (1 Jn.3:23)

## Deeper Study # 1

(17:2-3) **Eternal Life** (Gk. ainios): life, real life. It is the very life of God Himself. It is the very energy, force, being, essence, principle, and power of life. It has more to do with quality and with what life really is than with duration. To live forever in the present world is not necessarily a good thing. The world and our bodies need changing. Our lives need changing. That changed life is found only in eternal life. The only being who can be said to be eternal is God. Therefore, life—supreme life—is found only in God. To possess eternal life is to know God. Once people know God and Jesus Christ whom He has sent, they have eternal life—they will live forever. But more essential, the person has the supreme quality of life, the very life of God Himself (see Deeper Study # 2—Jn.1:4; Deeper Study # 1—10:10).

> Whoever believes in the Son has eternal life; whoever does not obey the Son shall not see life, but the wrath of God remains on him. (Jn.3:36)

> "Truly, truly, I say to you, whoever hears my word and believes him who sent me has eternal life. He does not come into judgment, but has passed from death to life." (Jn.5:24)

> "For this is the will of my Father, that everyone who looks on the Son and believes in him should have eternal life, and I will raise him up on the last day." (Jn.6:40)

> So that, as sin reigned in death, grace also might reign through righteousness leading to eternal life through Jesus Christ our Lord. (Ro.5:21)

And which now has been manifested through the appearing of our Savior Christ Jesus, who abolished death and brought life and immortality to light through the gospel. (2 Ti.1:10)

And this is the testimony, that God gave us eternal life, and this life is in his Son. Whoever has the Son has life; whoever does not have the Son of God does not have life. (1 Jn.5:11-12)

## 2 Request 2: Restore your Son to His former glory—to His preexistent exaltation.

Jesus' second request was for Himself to be restored to His former glory, to His preexistent exaltation (see notes—Jn.1:1-2; 13:31-32, pt.3 for discussion). Note what this says:

➢ Jesus *dwelt* in a preexistent, eternal state and glory with God.

> Jesus said to them, "Truly, truly, I say to you, before Abraham was, I am." (Jn.8:58)
>
> "I came from the Father and have come into the world, and now I am leaving the world and going to the Father." (Jn.16:28)
>
> He is the radiance of the glory of God and the exact imprint of his nature, and he upholds the universe by the word of his power. After making purification for sins, he sat down at the right hand of the Majesty on high. (He.1:3)
>
> But of the Son he says, "Your throne, O God, is forever and ever, the scepter of uprightness is the scepter of your kingdom." (He.1:8)

➢ Jesus set His glory aside when he came to earth as Man (see note—Ph.2:7).

> For you know the grace of our Lord Jesus Christ, that though he was rich, yet for your sake he became poor, so that you by his poverty might become rich. (2 Co.8:9)
>
> But emptied himself, by taking the form of a servant, being born in the likeness of men. (Ph.2:7)

➢ Jesus knew that He would return to the Father and be restored to His former glory.

> Jesus then said, "I will be with you a little longer, and then I am going to him who sent me." (Jn.7:33)
>
> "You heard me say to you, 'I am going away, and I will come to you.' If you loved me, you would have rejoiced, because I am going to the Father, for the Father is greater than I." (Jn.14:28)
>
> "And I am no longer in the world, but they are in the world, and I am coming to you. Holy Father, keep them in your name, which you have given me, that they may be one, even as we are one." (Jn.17:11)
>
> For to this end Christ died and lived again, that he might be Lord both of the dead and of the living. (Ro.14:9)
>
> And being found in human form, he humbled himself by becoming obedient to the point of death, even death on a cross. Therefore God has highly exalted him and bestowed on him the name that is above every name, so that at the name of Jesus every knee should bow, in heaven and on earth and under the earth, and every tongue confess that Jesus Christ is Lord, to the glory of God the Father. (Ph.2:8-11)

By asking God to restore Him to His former glory, Jesus acknowledged that He had completed the work God had sent Him to earth to do (v.4). He spoke of two specific aspects of that work, two bases for His request.

⁵ "And now, Father, glorify me in your own presence with the glory that I had with you before the world existed.
⁶ I have manifested your name to the people whom you gave me out of the world. Yours they were, and you gave them to me, and they have kept your word.
⁷ Now they know that everything that you have given me is from you.
⁸ For I have given them the words that you gave me, and they have received them and have come to know in truth that I came from you; and they have believed that you sent me."

### a. Because He has revealed the Father's name to His followers (v.6).

Jesus had revealed God's name. The word "name" expresses the whole character and nature of God—all that God is. This is a phenomenal claim, for Jesus was claiming to be the very revelation of God, the One who reveals God to people (see outline and notes—Jn.14:6; 14:8-11). Note exactly what Jesus said in this verse.

First, Jesus revealed God (the full revelation of God) to the people whom God had given Him. He shared the message of

God, but He did not scatter the seed among the unthankful and unreceptive. He had even told His followers not to waste time on the unreceptive.

> "And if any place will not receive you and they will not listen to you, when you leave, shake off the dust that is on your feet as a testimony against them." (Mk.6:11)

Second, God is the One who gave Jesus believers to be shown and taught all about the Father. God is Sovereign, so He led both Jesus and the disciples together. God stirred and led these people, the first believers, out of the world to follow Jesus and to receive and to be shown the revelation of God. They learned of God—of His person and nature, of His love and salvation—because God drew them to His dear Son (see note—Jn.6:44-46).

> "No one can come to me unless the Father who sent me draws him. And I will raise him up on the last day. It is written in the Prophets, 'And they will all be taught by God.' Everyone who has heard and learned from the Father comes to me." (Jn.6:44-45)

> "My Father, who has given them to me, is greater than all, and no one is able to snatch them out of the Father's hand." (Jn.10:29)

Third, the first believers belonged to God. They were His because He drew them to His Son through His sovereignty, power, and foreknowledge. He knew that they would believe on Jesus.

> For those whom he foreknew he also predestined to be conformed to the image of his Son, in order that he might be the firstborn among many brothers. (Ro.8:29)

Fourth, these people kept God's Word. They obeyed and did exactly what Jesus commanded (see note—Jn.15:9-10).

> Jesus answered him, "If anyone loves me, he will keep my word, and my Father will love him, and we will come to him and make our home with him." (Jn.14:23)

> "If you keep my commandments, you will abide in my love, just as I have kept my Father's commandments and abide in his love." (Jn.15:10)

b. **Because His followers now know that He is God's Son, the revelation of God Himself (vv.7-8).** These people now knew that Jesus was the Son of God, the very revelation of God Himself. They knew *that everything He had was given by God* (v.7). They knew that He was the very embodiment and revelation of God. (Note: Jesus was looking ahead beyond the resurrection in saying this. It would be the resurrection that would confirm all He had been revealing to them.)

➤ They now accepted Jesus' words as the very words of God (see notes—Jn.7:16-19; 12:47-50; 14:10).

> "It is the Spirit who gives life; the flesh is no help at all. The words that I have spoken to you are spirit and life." (Jn.6:63)

> Simon Peter answered him, "Lord, to whom shall we go? You have the words of eternal life." (Jn.6:68)

> So Jesus answered them, "My teaching is not mine, but his who sent me. If anyone's will is to do God's will, he will know whether the teaching is from God or whether I am speaking on my own authority." (Jn.7:16-17)

> "The one who rejects me and does not receive my words has a judge; the word that I have spoken will judge him on the last day." (Jn.12:48)

> "Whoever does not love me does not keep my words. And the word that you hear is not mine but the Father's who sent me." (Jn.14:24)

➤ They now knew Jesus' origin: He had come *from God* (see Deeper Study # 1—Jn.3:31; Deeper Study # 3—3:34; notes—7:16-19; 7:25-31).

> "No one has ascended into heaven except he who descended from heaven, the Son of Man." (Jn.3:13)

> "For the bread of God is he who comes down from heaven and gives life to the world. . . . For I have come down from heaven, not to do my own will but the will of him who sent me." (Jn.6:33, 38)

> He said to them, "You are from below; I am from above. You are of this world; I am not of this world." (Jn.8:23)

Jesus said to them, "If God were your Father, you would love me, for I came from God and I am here. I came not of my own accord, but he sent me." (Jn.8:42)

"Now we know that you know all things and do not need anyone to question you; this is why we believe that you came from God." (Jn.16:30)

➢ They now believed that God *had* sent Jesus, that He is the Son of God Himself who had come to earth as the ambassador of God to proclaim and reveal the salvation of God (see note—Jn.3:32-34; DEEPER STUDY # 3—3:34).

"For I have come down from heaven, not to do my own will but the will of him who sent me." (Jn.6:38)

"I know him, for I come from him, and he sent me." (Jn.7:29)

"That they may all be one, just as you, Father, are in me, and I in you, that they also may be in us, so that the world may believe that you have sent me." (Jn.17:21)

## B. Jesus Prayed for His Disciples, 17:9–19

⁹ "I am praying for them. I am not praying for the world but for those whom you have given me, for they are yours.

¹⁰ All mine are yours, and yours are mine, and I am glorified in them.

¹¹ And I am no longer in the world, but they are in the world, and I am coming to you. Holy Father, keep them in your name, which you have given me, that they may be one, even as we are one.

¹² While I was with them, I kept them in your name, which you have given me. I have guarded them, and not one of them has been lost except the son of destruction, that the Scripture might be fulfilled.

¹³ But now I am coming to you, and these things I speak in the world, that they may have my joy fulfilled in themselves.

¹⁴ I have given them your word, and the world has hated them because they are not of the world, just as I am not of the world.

¹⁵ I do not ask that you take them out of the world, but that you keep them from the evil one.

¹⁶ They are not of the world, just as I am not of the world.

¹⁷ Sanctify them in the truth; your word is truth.

¹⁸ As you sent me into the world, so I have sent them into the world.

¹⁹ And for their sake I consecrate myself, that they also may be sanctified in truth."

1. **Request 1: That God know the focus of His prayer—His disciples, not the world**
   a. Because God had given them to Him
   b. Because they belonged to both God & Jesus[DS1]
   c. Because they brought glory to Jesus
   d. Because Jesus was leaving the world
2. **Request 2: That God would protect His disciples & keep them together as one[DS2]**
   a. Because they were in a very divisive world
   b. Because He had kept them safe & had lost none[DS3]

3. **Request 3: That His disciples might have His joy in all its fullness**

4. **Request 4: That God would keep His disciples from the evil one, from Satan**
   a. Because the world hated them
   b. Because they were needed in the world
   c. Because they were now of the same nature as Jesus
5. **Request 5: That God would sanctify His disciples**
   a. Because they were sent into the world
   b. Because sanctification (being set apart to God) is the way of salvation

# Division XIV

## The Revelation of Jesus, the Great Intercessor, 17:1-26

B. Jesus Prayed for His Disciples, 17:9-19

## 17:9-19

### Introduction

As Jesus neared Calvary, His mind was not only on Himself. He was deeply burdened for His disciples. He loved each of them dearly. They had been with Him throughout His public ministry, and He was trusting them to carry out His mission after He returned to heaven. He knew the path that lay ahead of them would not be easy. They would pay a steep price for following Him: their faith would cost them their lives. And so, as His hour approached, Jesus prayed for His disciples. What He prayed is striking and full of meaning for believers of every generation. This is, *Jesus Prayed for His Disciples,* 17:9-19.

1. Request 1: That God know the focus of His prayer—His disciples, not the world (vv.9-11).
2. Request 2: That God would protect His disciples and keep them together as one (vv.11-12).
3. Request 3: That His disciples might have His joy in all its fullness (v.13).
4. Request 4: That God would keep His disciples from the evil one, from Satan (vv.14-16).
5. Request 4: That God would sanctify His disciples (vv.17-19).

### 17:9-11

⁹ "I am praying for them. I am not praying for the world but for those whom you have given me, for they are yours.
¹⁰ All mine are yours, and yours are mine, and I am glorified in them.
¹¹ And I am no longer in the world, but they are in the world, and I am coming to you. Holy Father, keep them in your name, which you have given me, that they may be one, even as we are one."

### 1 Request 1: That God know the focus of His prayer—His disciples, not the world.

Just hours away from His appointment with the cross, Jesus prayed for His disciples. He said specifically that He was not praying for the world, not now. Why?

➢ It was not because He and the Father do not love the world. They do; they love the world deeply (Jn.3:16). The world was the very reason Jesus had come to earth: to save the world and keep it from perishing.

➢ It was not because the world did not need prayer. It did, and He prayed for the forgiveness and conversion of the people in the world (Lu.23:34).

Jesus was praying only for His disciples for four reasons. These reasons are part of His prayer.

a. **Because God had given them to Him (v.9).**

Jesus' disciples had been given to Him *by His Father* (v.9). They belonged to His Father, but they had been *entrusted into His hands*. He was responsible for them and their welfare. Therefore, He had to pray for them, that His Father would give them special strength in the coming days.

> Even as he [God] chose us in him [Christ] before the foundation of the world, that we should be holy and blameless before him... (Ep.1:4)

> According to the foreknowledge of God the Father, in the sanctification of the Spirit, for obedience to Jesus Christ and for sprinkling with his blood: May grace and peace be multiplied to you. (1 Pe.1:2)

b. **Because they belonged to both God and Jesus (v.10a).**

Jesus' disciples belonged to both Him and the Father (v.10; see Deeper Study # 1). All the disciples were God's; they belonged to God. But all the disciples of God belonged to Jesus as well. Both Jesus and His Father have mutual possession of all believers. Both are deeply concerned over the welfare of believers. God the Father is as concerned over believers as His Son is; therefore, Jesus can count on God's hearing and answering His prayer.

"My Father, who has given them to me, is greater than all, and no one is able to snatch them out of the Father's hand." (Jn.10:29)

"I in them and you in me, that they may become perfectly one, so that the world may know that you sent me and loved them even as you loved me." (Jn.17:23)

For those whom he foreknew he also predestined to be conformed to the image of his Son, in order that he might be the firstborn among many brothers. (Ro.8:29)

c. **Because they brought glory to Jesus (v.10b).**

Jesus' disciples glorified Jesus; their lives brought glory to Him. They lived for Him by obeying His Word and working for Him and showing allegiance. They lifted Him up to the world and proclaimed Him to be the Savior of the world and the Lord of the universe. Jesus was thereby glorified, honored, and praised; therefore, He prayed for His disciples—that they might become strong in their lives and bold in their witness for Him.

So that the name of our Lord Jesus may be glorified in you, and you in him, according to the grace of our God and the Lord Jesus Christ. (2 Th.1:12)

But you are a chosen race, a royal priesthood, a holy nation, a people for his own possession, that you may proclaim the excellencies of him who called you out of darkness into his marvelous light. (1 Pe.2:9)

d. **Because Jesus was leaving the world (v.11a).**

Jesus was about to leave the world and return to heaven and the Father. The whole mission of preaching the gospel to the world would soon rest on the shoulders of His disciples. They were the ones who were to go out into the world as His ambassadors to proclaim His Word. As they went, they needed to be strengthened and equipped by God to stand against sinister forces (see Ep.6:12). His followers were the ones who needed special prayer. Christ's whole mission of reaching the world for God depended on their endurance and faithfulness. In these last hours before He returned to heaven, Jesus had to pray for them with power and intensity, asking great things of God.

"Go therefore and make disciples of all nations, baptizing them in the name of the Father and of the Son and of the Holy Spirit, teaching them to observe all that I have commanded you. And behold, I am with you always, to the end of the age." (Mt.28:19-20)

Jesus said to them again, "Peace be with you. As the Father has sent me, even so I am sending you." (Jn.20:21)

## Deeper Study # 1

(17:10) **Jesus—Deity:** when Jesus taught that all that was His was God's, and all that was God's was His, He made a phenomenal claim. A person can say that all they are and have *belongs to God,* but no one can say that all God is and has *belongs to them.* In Jesus' very prayer He was claiming deity—oneness with God (see note—Jn.14:10; see Jn.10:30).

"I and the Father are one." (Jn.10:30)

"If I am not doing the works of my Father, then do not believe me; but if I do them, even though you do not believe me, believe the works, that you may know and understand that the Father is in me and I am in the Father." (Jn.10:37-38)

"Do you not believe that I am in the Father and the Father is in me? The words that I say to you I do not speak on my own authority, but the Father who dwells in me does his works." (Jn.14:10)

"And I am no longer in the world, but they are in the world, and I am coming to you. Holy Father, keep them in your name, which you have given me, that they may be one, even as we are one." (Jn.17:11)

"The glory that you have given me I have given to them, that they may be one even as we are one." (Jn.17:22)

## 2 Request 2: That God would protect His disciples and keep them together as one.

Jesus prayed that God would keep His disciples—keep them together as one. Here, Jesus was praying for the disciples to be kept from the *divisiveness* of the world, not that they would be kept from evil. He dealt with the evil of the world later (vv.14-15).

**17:11-12**

¹¹ "And I am no longer in the world, but they are in the world, and I am coming to you. Holy Father, keep them in your name, which you have given me, that they may be one, even as we are one.
¹² "While I was with them, I kept them in your name, which you have given me. I have guarded them, and not one of them has been lost except the son of destruction, that the Scripture might be fulfilled."

a. **Because they were in a very divisive world (v.11b).**
The disciples would be ministering in an extremely divisive world (see Deeper Study # 2). It is a world governed by Satan, and one of Satan's chief strategies is to divide and conquer. They could only accomplish their mission if they were *one*—in unity. Satan would no doubt attempt to thwart their mission by coming between them, by tempting them with division.

b. **Because He had kept them safe and had lost none (v.12).**
Jesus protected the disciples while He was in the world. He lost none except Judas, and Judas' betrayal was to fulfill Scripture (see outline and notes—Jn.13:1-30 for discussion of Judas). Jesus was faithful *to God's name*, faithful in revealing God and lifting up His name to the disciples. Now Jesus was leaving the world, so it was now up to God to keep them, and He would. *Keep* (Gk. tereson) means to watch carefully, to guard, to keep one's eyes on (see Deeper Study # 3). God the Father would protect the disciples as well as His Son did, for God is both faithful and able.

### Deeper Study # 2

(17:11) **Unity:** believers are to be one just as Jesus and the Father are one. The unity between believers is to be as strong as the unity between Jesus and His Father. This is a remarkable truth, a truth that consumed the Lord's thoughts. It was the very theme of Jesus' prayer (vv.11, 21, 22, 23). Believers must be one.

Believers are in an extremely divisive world, a world full of . . .

- prejudice
- competition
- lust
- selfishness
- egotism
- hurt
- angry spirits
- possessiveness
- pride
- self-praise
- hate
- war

The list is unlimited, for divisiveness comes from the depraved nature of man, the nature that Christ came to change and to convert to love. The divisive world was a threat to the early disciples. Being in the world, they could have been influenced and led astray in ways of divisiveness. Jesus had to pray on their behalf, for God to keep them together as one.

Jesus' request is an eye-opener, an astounding request: "That they may be one, *as we are one*." Believers are to be as unified as God and Christ are. What does this mean? It means that we are to have the *same kind* of unity that Jesus and the Father have. We are to be one in *nature, character, and purpose.*

a. Believers are to be one in nature. The believer is a person who . . .
- has been "born again" (see Deeper Study # 1—Jn.3:1-15; see also Jn.1:13; Tit.3:5; 1 Jn.2:29; 4:7)

> Since you have been born again, not of perishable seed but of imperishable, through the living and abiding word of God. (1 Pe.1:23)

**Everyone who believes that Jesus is the Christ has been born of God, and everyone who loves the Father loves whoever has been born of him. (1 Jn.5:1)**

- has been made into a "new creation," become a new person (see Ga.6:15; Ep.4:24; Col.3:10)

  **Therefore, if anyone is in Christ, he is a new creation. The old has passed away; behold, the new has come. (2 Co.5:17)**

- has become a partaker of the "divine nature"

  **By which he has granted to us his precious and very great promises, so that through them you may become partakers of the divine nature, having escaped from the corruption that is in the world because of sinful desire. (2 Pe.1:4)**

However, the nature of believers includes more than just a personal rebirth of one's spirit. When a person becomes a believer, their new nature makes them a member of God's . . .

- new body of people

  **And might reconcile us both to God in one body through the cross, thereby killing the hostility. (Ep.2:16)**

- new nation

  **So then you are no longer strangers and aliens, but you are fellow citizens with the saints and members of the household of God. (Ep.2:19)**

- new temple

  **In whom the whole structure, being joined together, grows into a holy temple in the Lord. (Ep.2:21)**

- new family

  **So then you are no longer strangers and aliens, but you are fellow citizens with the saints and members of the household of God. (Ep.2:19)**

- new fellowship or church

  **In him you also are being built together into a dwelling place for God by the Spirit. (Ep.2:22)**

- new building

  **Built on the foundation of the apostles and prophets, Christ Jesus himself being the cornerstone, in whom the whole structure, being joined together, grows into a holy temple in the Lord. In him you also are being built together into a dwelling place for God by the Spirit. (Ep.2:20-22)**

- new race (see note—Ep.4:17-19)

  **Now this I say and testify in the Lord, that you must no longer walk as the Gentiles do, in the futility of their minds. (Ep.4:17. The believer is a new creation, a new race distinct from the Gentiles. He is no longer to walk as the Gentiles walk.)**

This, of course, means that a believer is to live and walk in unity with other believers. We are not to allow the divisive spirit of the world to infiltrate our lives through complaining, criticizing, envying, gossiping, opposing, overlooking, ignoring, or isolating (see notes—Ep.2:11-22; pt.4, 2:14-15; 1 Co.3:16 for more discussion).

  b. Believers are to be one in character. We are . . .
  - to be godly and holy, denying the works of the flesh and living pure lives even as Jesus and His Father are one in their holy being and life (see "Holy Father," v.11).

    **Now the works of the flesh are evident: sexual immorality, impurity, sensuality, idolatry, sorcery, enmity, strife, jealousy, fits of anger, rivalries, dissensions, divisions, envy, drunkenness, orgies, and things like these. I warn you, as I warned you before, that those who do such things will not inherit the kingdom of God. (Ga.5:19-21)**

Training us to renounce ungodliness and worldly passions, and to live self-controlled, upright, and godly lives in the present age, waiting for our blessed hope, the appearing of the glory of our great God and Savior Jesus Christ. (Tit.2:12-13)

But as he who called you is holy, you also be holy in all your conduct, since it is written, "You shall be holy, for I am holy." (1 Pe.1:15-16)

For this very reason, make every effort to supplement your faith with virtue, and virtue with knowledge, and knowledge with self-control, and self-control with steadfastness, and steadfastness with godliness, and godliness with brotherly affection, and brotherly affection with love. (2 Pe.1:5-7)

Then the Lord knows how to rescue the godly from trials, and to keep the unrighteous under punishment until the day of judgment. (2 Pe.2:9)

- to bear the fruit of the Spirit

    But the fruit of the Spirit is love, joy, peace, patience, kindness, goodness, faithfulness, gentleness, self-control; against such things there is no law. (Ga.5:22-23)

c. Believers are to be one in purpose. We are to surrender and give all we are and have to minister and proclaim the message of salvation to a lost and dying world, a world reeling in desperate need. Believers are to give all for the salvation of the world just as Jesus and the Father gave all for the salvation of the world.

(See note, *Church, Unity*—Ep.4:4-6 for more discussion of the unity upon which believers are built. Also see note—Lu.8:21 for more discussion.)

"Even as the Son of Man came not to be served but to serve, and to give his life as a ransom for many." (Mt.20:28)

Jesus said to them again, "Peace be with you. As the Father has sent me, even so I am sending you." (Jn.20:21)

Therefore, we are ambassadors for Christ, God making his appeal through us. We implore you on behalf of Christ, be reconciled to God. (2 Co.5:20)

## DEEPER STUDY # 3

(17:11-12) **Security—Assurance:** the *protecting power* of God does not mean that God delivers believers *from* the trials of this world, but He delivers us *through* the trials. It means that He gives a victorious life. As believers, we are guaranteed victorious lives if we will just follow Christ. There are two reasons for this guaranteed security. First, God is bound to answer the prayer of His Son; and second, God the Father has given all Christian believers to Christ. This fact is acknowledged six times in this chapter alone (Jn.17:2, 6, 9, 11, 12, 24). God will allow absolutely nothing to separate genuine believers from His Son.

"My sheep hear my voice, and I know them, and they follow me. I give them eternal life, and they will never perish, and no one will snatch them out of my hand. My Father, who has given them to me, is greater than all, and no one is able to snatch them out of the Father's hand." (Jn.10:27-29)

Who shall separate us from the love of Christ? Shall tribulation, or distress, or persecution, or famine, or nakedness, or danger, or sword? (Ro.8:35.)

But the Lord is faithful. He will establish you and guard you against the evil one. (2 Th.3:3)

Which is why I suffer as I do. But I am not ashamed, for I know whom I have believed, and I am convinced that he is able to guard until that day what has been entrusted to me. (2 Ti.1:12)

Who by God's power are being guarded through faith for a salvation ready to be revealed in the last time. (1 Pe.1:5)

Now to him who is able to keep you from stumbling and to present you blameless before the presence of his glory with great joy. (Jude 24)

## 3  Request 3: That His disciples might have His joy in all its fullness.

Jesus prayed that the disciples would have His joy in all its fullness (see note 3 and Deeper Study # 1—Jn.15:11; note—14:28-29 for discussion). Jesus lived with joy, and, as strange as it may seem, He died with joy. He endured the cross by focusing on the joy that lay before Him, all the glorious blessings His sacrificial death would bring (He.12:2). The disciples' lives would become indescribably hard; and, as time would ultimately tell, they would lay down their lives for Jesus. Even so, Jesus wanted them to be filled with joy every step of the way, just as He had been filled with joy throughout His earthly ministry.

**17:13**

¹³ "But now I am coming to you, and these things I speak in the world, that they may have my joy fulfilled in themselves."

## 4  Request 4: That God would keep His disciples from the evil one, from Satan.

Jesus prayed that God would keep the disciples from the world and from Satan. Both the world and Satan are evil, and stand opposed to all that Jesus and His disciples proclaimed.

> - The world and Satan stand against the love of God. Why? Because God's love is not the *grandfatherly love of indulgence*. God's love is the true love of obedience, an obedience that gives all one *is* and *has* to meet the needs of a desperate world lost in sin and death. True love loves so much that it gives every-

thing and does all it can to help any who are in desperate need. Most people in the world are unwilling to give anything other than a mere token, and, even then, recognition is desired for what little is given.

> - The world and Satan stand against the holiness and justice of God. Why? Because it means that they must stand before God some day to give an account of their lives and deeds, sins and despicable offenses, filthiness and evil.
> - The world and Satan stand against Jesus. Why? Because Jesus is the One who claimed to be the Son of God, and if He is truly the Son of God, then total allegiance is due Him. And neither the world nor Satan is willing to serve anyone other than self.

**17:14-16**

¹⁴ "I have given them your word, and the world has hated them because they are not of the world, just as I am not of the world.
¹⁵ I do not ask that you take them out of the world, but that you keep them from the evil one.
¹⁶ They are not of the world, just as I am not of the world."

Jesus cited three reasons why God needed to protect the disciples from the world and the devil:

a. **Because the world hated them (v.14).**
   The world and the devil hated the disciples of Jesus because they had the Word of God (v.14a). It is God's Word that reveals . . .
   - God's love, a sacrificial love that gives all it has, is different from the love the world wants (see Deeper Study # 1—Mt.5:44; notes—22:37-38; 22:39 for discussion)
   - God's holiness and justice and humanity's depravity, a fact that so many people reject and refuse to face
   - Christ, the Son of God Himself, who demands total allegiance and commitment to become ministers and servants of God

   In addition, the world hated the disciples because they were not of the world, even as Jesus was not of the world (v.14b). Jesus came from God, "from heaven" (see Deeper Study # 1—Jn.3:31). Jesus was not of this world, and neither are believers. Believers are born again by the Spirit of God and given the very nature of God. The world and the devil want absolutely nothing to do with a selfless and sacrificial nature, a righteous and godly nature that gives all one is and has to meet the needs of the diseased and starving and lost masses of the world (see Deeper Study # 1—Jn.3:1-15; see also Jn.1:13; 2 Co.5:17; Tit.3:5; 1 Pe.1:23; 2 Pe.1:4; 1 Jn.2:29; 4:7; 5:1).

"A new commandment I give to you, that you love one another: just as I have loved you, you also are to love one another. By this all people will know that you are my disciples, if you have love for one another." (Jn.13:34-35)

But God shows his love for us in that while we were still sinners, Christ died for us. (Ro.5:8)

By this we know love, that he laid down his life for us, and we ought to lay down our lives for the brothers [giving all we are and have]. (1 Jn.3:16)

b. Because they were needed in the world (v.15).

The disciples were needed in the world. The need was not for them to be taken out of the world; the need was for them to be kept from the evil one or from Satan (see Ep.6:10-18). The disciples were called to be ambassadors and messengers of God in the world. God's mission to save the world depended on their loyalty and faithfulness. They had to be kept and protected and covered with the armor of God.

Finally, be strong in the Lord and in the strength of his might. Put on the whole armor of God, that you may be able to stand against the schemes of the devil. (Ep.6:10-11)

Be sober-minded; be watchful. Your adversary the devil prowls around like a roaring lion, seeking someone to devour. (1 Pe.5:8)

c. Because they were now of the same nature as Jesus (v.16).

The disciples were now of the same nature as Jesus. This is the same truth stated in v.14; it is so glorious, it has to be reemphasized. Note that it is also the main reason the world and the devil attack the believer (see outline and notes—Jn.15:19-24 for more discussion).

I appeal to you therefore, brothers, by the mercies of God, to present your bodies as a living sacrifice, holy and acceptable to God, which is your spiritual worship. Do not be conformed to this world, but be transformed by the renewal of your mind, that by testing you may discern what is the will of God, what is good and acceptable and perfect. (Ro.12:1-2)

## 17:17-19

<sup>17</sup> "Sanctify them in the truth; your word is truth.
<sup>18</sup> As you sent me into the world, so I have sent them into the world.
<sup>19</sup> And for their sake I consecrate myself, that they also may be sanctified in truth."

## 5 Request 5: That God would sanctify His disciples.

Finally, Jesus prayed that God would sanctify the disciples. *Sanctify* (Gk. hagiazo) means to set apart, to make holy, to consecrate (see DEEPER STUDY # 4). How are we sanctified? *Through God's truth*, which Jesus clearly said is God's Word. God's Word refers to both the *living Word*, the full revelation of God in Jesus Christ Himself (see DEEPER STUDY # 1—Jn.14:16) and to the spoken or *written Word* (see notes—Jn.7:16-19; 14:10; 2 Ti.3:16; note 3 and DEEPER STUDY # 1, 2—2 Pe.1:19-21). The disciples needed to be set apart to God *through His truth* for two reasons. What Jesus prayed for His disciples applies to us today as well.

a. Because they were sent into the world (v.18).

The disciples were being sent into the world just as Jesus had been sent into the world. Jesus had come into the world to bring people back to God through reconciliation. The disciples had to be *set apart* to this same task.

"Go therefore and make disciples of all nations, baptizing them in the name of the Father and of the Son and of the Holy Spirit, teaching them to observe all that I have commanded you. And behold, I am with you always, to the end of the age." (Mt.28:19-20)

And he said to them, "Go into all the world and proclaim the gospel to the whole creation." (Mk.16:15)

Jesus said to them again, "Peace be with you. As the Father has sent me, even so I am sending you." (Jn.20:21)

"But you will receive power when the Holy Spirit has come upon you, and you will be my witnesses in Jerusalem and in all Judea and Samaria, and to the end of the earth." (Ac.1:8)

That is, in Christ God was reconciling the world to himself, not counting their trespasses against them, and entrusting to us the message of reconciliation. Therefore, we are ambassadors for Christ, God making his appeal through us. We implore you on behalf of Christ, be reconciled to God. (2 Co.5:19-20)

b. **Because sanctification (being set apart to God) is the way of salvation (v.19).**
Sanctification is the chosen way of salvation to reach the world. Jesus had set Himself apart to please God, and He pleased God to the ultimate degree. No matter the cost, the glory of God was to be done. Christ's perfect obedience to God was the chosen way of salvation. Being set apart to serve and worship God is what salvation is all about. This is the reason Jesus prayed for His disciples to be sanctified (see DEEPER STUDY # 1—1 Pe.1:15-16 for more discussion).

**THOUGHT 1.** Believers are sanctified through the truth, that is, through God's Word. It is through the study and practice of God's Word that we are set apart unto God. As we study God's Word, we see more and more how we are to live. As we see this, we set ourselves apart to live the way God tells us to live. The Word of God holds new instructions for the believer every day. The Word of God shows us how to be more and more conformed to the image of Christ every day. But note the crucial point: we must come to the truth, to the Word of God *every day* if we wish to be *set apart* unto God for that day.

**THOUGHT 2.** Jesus' prayer was primarily for the twelve men who were with Him, but it applies to all who would succeed them, all Christ-followers throughout the centuries. All true believers are Christ's ambassadors. We have the same responsibility as the first disciples to take the gospel to the world. If we are living faithfully for Christ, the world will hate us, just as it hated them.

Tragically, the body of Christ is divided today in so many ways. Many believers live without the joy of the Lord in their hearts. Many have compromised their personal holiness and the holiness of their churches with the evil of the world.

We ought to be powerfully moved by the prayer of Christ. May His prayer grip us anew and afresh. May it transform our lives and our churches, compelling us to be all that He prayed for His disciples to be.

## DEEPER STUDY # 4

(17:17) **Sanctify—Sanctification:** the word "sanctify" means to be set apart, to be separated (see 1 Pe.1:15-16). There are three stages of sanctification.

1. There is *initial* or *positional* sanctification. When people believe in Jesus Christ, they are immediately set apart for God permanently, once-for-all (He.3:1; see He.10:10).

2. There is *progressive* sanctification. True believers make a determined and disciplined effort to allow the Spirit of God to set them apart day by day. The Spirit of God takes them and conforms them to the image of Christ more and more. This growth takes place as long as the believer walks upon this earth (see Jn.17:17; 2 Co.3:18; Ep.5:25-26; 1 Th.5:23-24).

3. There is *eternal* sanctification. The day is coming when the believer will be perfectly set apart unto God and His service—without any sin or failure whatsoever. That day will be the great and glorious day of the believer's eternal redemption (Ep.5:27; 1 Jn.3:2).

## C. Jesus Prayed for Future Believers, 17:20–26

1. Request 1: That God know the breadth of His prayer, that He prays for all future believers as well as present believers
2. Request 2: That believers may be one
   a. The standard: As God & Christ are one
   b. The purpose: That the world may believe God sent Christ
   c. The source: God's glory[DS1]

3. Request 3: That believers may be perfected in unity[DS2]
   a. The source: Jesus within
   b. The reason: To convince the world that God sent Christ & that He loves believers
4. Request 4: That believers may be with Him in glory
   a. The reason: To behold or see His glory
   b. The assurance: God's love
5. Request 5: That believers may be filled with God's love
   a. Because unbelievers do not know God
   b. Because Christ does know God
   c. Because believers know God sent Christ
   d. Because Christ was faithful in carrying out God's purpose
      1) He declared God to men
      2) His purpose: That men might know God's love

20 "I do not ask for these only, but also for those who will believe in me through their word,

21 that they may all be one, just as you, Father, are in me, and I in you, that they also may be in us, so that the world may believe that you have sent me.

22 The glory that you have given me I have given to them, that they may be one even as we are one,

23 I in them and you in me, that they may become perfectly one, so that the world may know that you sent me and loved them even as you loved me.

24 Father, I desire that they also, whom you have given me, may be with me where I am, to see my glory that you have given me because you loved me before the foundation of the world.

25 O righteous Father, even though the world does not know you, I know you, and these know that you have sent me.

26 I made known to them your name, and I will continue to make it known, that the love with which you have loved me may be in them, and I in them."

# Division XIV

## The Revelation of Jesus, the Great Intercessor, 17:1–26

C. Jesus Prayed for Future Believers, 17:20–26

## 17:20–26
## Introduction

After praying for Himself and for His disciples, Jesus prayed for future believers, for all who would believe in Him from that moment to the end of the world. What He prayed is very precious to believers, but it is also an indictment against believers of every generation, for it points out our unwillingness to be united (see Deeper Study # 2—Jn.17:23). This is, *Jesus Prayed for Future Believers, 17:20–26*.

1. Request 1: That God know the breadth of His prayer, that He prays for all future believers as well as present believers (v.20).
2. Request 2: That believers may be one (vv.21-22).
3. Request 3: That believers may be perfected in unity (v.23).
4. Request 4: That believers may be with Him in glory (v.24).
5. Request 5: That believers may be filled with God's love (vv.25-26).

## 1 Request 1: That God know the breadth of His prayer, that He prays for all future believers as well as present believers.

17:20

$^{20}$ "I do not ask for these only, but also for those who will believe in me through their word,"

Jesus prayed for future believers, for all who would believe the message of the early disciples. This is most precious. Jesus prayed for us—for you and for me—for all of us who believe today. Just think for a moment. Who is the weakest believer on earth today? Who is the strongest? Of course only God knows, but think of the preciousness of the fact: Jesus prayed for every one of us . . .

- for the weakest as well as for the strongest
- for the diseased as well as for the healthy
- for the orphan as well as for the children of the family
- for the widow and widower as well as for the couple
- for the prisoner as well as for the free
- for the believer in the darkest jungle as well as for the believer in the limelight

No thought is more precious than the thought that Jesus prayed for us all—every one of us who believe today.

In the statement *those who will believe in Me through their word,* Jesus highlights the three essentials for people to become believers.

First, *their*—the messenger of God, the disciple of Christ, the person who proclaims the Word so that people can *believe on* the name of Jesus. There has to be a messenger to carry and proclaim the message.

> **How then will they call on him in whom they have not believed? And how are they to believe in him of whom they have never heard? And how are they to hear without someone preaching? (Ro.10:14)**

> **Therefore, we are ambassadors for Christ, God making his appeal through us. We implore you on behalf of Christ, be reconciled to God. For our sake he made him to be sin who knew no sin, so that in him we might become the righteousness of God. (2 Co.5:20-21)**

Second, *word*—their word would be God's message, God's Word. The messenger is *God's* messenger, *His* ambassador. Therefore, the Word he or she takes to the world is God's Word. Note the references to God's Word in this chapter alone.

> **"I have manifested your name to the people whom you gave me out of the world. Yours they were, and you gave them to me, and they have kept your word." (Jn.17:6)**

> **"I have given them your word, and the world has hated them because they are not of the world, just as I am not of the world." (Jn.17:14)**

> **"Sanctify them in the truth; your word is truth." (Jn.17:17)**

Third, *believe*—we must believe the Word. We are the Lord's disciples today because we believe the Word (see DEEPER STUDY # 2—Jn.2:24).

> **"Truly, truly, I say to you, whoever hears my word and believes him who sent me has eternal life. He does not come into judgment, but has passed from death to life." (Jn.5:24)**

> **"It is the Spirit who gives life; the flesh is no help at all. The words that I have spoken to you are spirit and life." (Jn.6:63)**

> **"Truly, truly, I say to you, if anyone keeps my word, he will never see death." (Jn.8:51)**

## 2 Request 2: That believers may be one.

Jesus prayed that we would all be one. This is critical, the imperative that absolutely must exist between believers. It is the central theme of Jesus' prayer (vv.11, 21, 22, 23). Believers *must be one*. Note exactly what Jesus said.

### 17:21-22

²¹ "that they may all be one, just as you, Father, are in me, and I in you, that they also may be in us, so that the world may believe that you have sent me.
²² "The glory that you have given me I have given to them, that they may be one even as we are one,"

### a. The standard: As God and Christ are one (v.21a).

The standard for our unity is the *oneness* between Jesus and His Father. Believers are to be one just as the Father and Jesus are one. The very *same kind* of unity they have is to be the unity existing between us (see DEEPER STUDY # 2—Jn.17:11 for discussion and verses of Scripture).

### b. The purpose: That the world may believe God sent Christ (v.21b).

We are to be one for a critical purpose: that the world may *believe* that the Father sent Jesus. We need to let the gravity of this statement sink in to our hearts. The eternal souls of lost people hang on our unity as believers. Grasp the truths expressed and implied by Jesus' statement:

➢ God sent Jesus (see notes—Jn.3:32-34; DEEPER STUDY # 3—3:34).

   "I know him, for I come from him, and he sent me." (Jn.7:29)

   Jesus said to them, "If God were your Father, you would love me, for I came from God and I am here. I came not of my own accord, but he sent me." (Jn.8:42; see Jn.6:38; 10:36)

➢ Jesus came that people might have life and have it more abundantly.

   "Truly, truly, I say to you, whoever hears my word and believes him who sent me has eternal life. He does not come into judgment, but has passed from death to life." (Jn.5:24)

   "The thief comes only to steal and kill and destroy. I came that they may have life and have it abundantly." (Jn.10:10)

➢ A divided witness confuses the issue and cannot stand, just as a divided house and kingdom cannot stand.

   Knowing their thoughts, he said to them, "Every kingdom divided against itself is laid waste, and no city or house divided against itself will stand." (Mt.12:25)

➢ There is only one message and one way to God, not many messages and many ways. We must be united in proclaiming that one message.

   "For God so loved the world, that he gave his only Son, that whoever believes in him should not perish but have eternal life." (Jn.3:16; see Ro.5:8; 1 Pe.2:24; 3:18)

   Jesus said to him, "I am the way, and the truth, and the life. No one comes to the Father except through me." (Jn.14:6; see 1 Ti.2:5; He.8:6; 9:5, 24; 12:24; 1 Jn.2:1)

**THOUGHT 1.** Tragically, there are many voices proclaiming so many different messages, messages of . . .

- works
- ritual and ceremony
- denominationalism
- rules and regulations
- morality
- false prophets humanism
- brotherhood
- secularism

Believers must be one; be unified, of one spirit and mind in proclaiming the central message of the gospel.

➢ There is only one central message: that God sent Jesus from heaven into the world.
➢ There is only one need of people: to believe that God did send Jesus into the world.
➢ There is only one mission: that believers be one (unified) in proclaiming the message of the glorious gospel.

   Only let your manner of life be worthy of the gospel of Christ, so that whether I come and see you or am absent, I may hear of you that you are standing firm in one spirit, with one mind striving side by side for the faith of the gospel. (Ph.1:27)

c. The source: God's glory (v.22).

The source of unity is God's glory, the very glory which Jesus Himself possessed (see Deeper Study # 1). It is the glory of God given to believers that unites believers and makes us one with Jesus and the Father and one with each other. When believers *experience* the glory of God, we become one in being, character, and purpose. Our lives are given to each other to help one another . . .
- to be the new creations God has made us
- to live as believers should, holy and righteous and pure
- to proclaim the glorious message that God has sent His Son into the world

## Deeper Study # 1

(17:22) **Glory—Unity:** this significant verse deals with the glory of the believer. Note the points made by Christ.
- ➢ God gave glory to His Son Jesus Christ.
- ➢ Jesus has given the very *same* glory to believers (see note—2 Th.2:14).
- ➢ It is the glory of God that brings unity to believers, that causes us to surround God and live and work together to please Him.

> **So we, though many, are one body in Christ, and individually members one of another. (Ro.12:5)**
>
> **Because there is one bread, we who are many are one body, for we all partake of the one bread. (1 Co.10:17)**
>
> **There is neither Jew nor Greek, there is neither slave nor free, there is no male and female, for you are all one in Christ Jesus. (Ga.3:28)**
>
> **Until we all attain to the unity of the faith and of the knowledge of the Son of God, to mature manhood, to the measure of the stature of the fullness of Christ. (Ep.4:13)**

What is the glory of God that He gave to Christ and that Christ in turn gives to believers?

| *The glory of Christ is . . .* | *The glory of the believer is . . .* |
|---|---|
| • the glory of righteousness that He secured by living a perfect life (see note—Jn.13:31-32) | • the glory of righteousness that Christ gives to the believer by faith (see notes—Jn.1:51; 13:31-32; Deeper Study # 1, 2—Ro.4:22) |
| • the glory of the cross (see notes—Jn.12:23-26; 12:27-30) | • the glory of the cross that gives to the believer both forgiveness of sins and the privilege of serving God Himself: the privilege of sacrificing all we are and have to God in order to reach a lost and desperate world (see notes—Jn.12:23-26; Deeper Study # 1—Lu.9:23; see 1 Pe.2:24) |
| • the glory of the resurrection that brought victory over death and hell (see note—Jn.13:31-32) | • the glory of the resurrection that gives the believer a new life in Christ (see Ro.6:4-5; 2 Co.5:17) |
| • the glory of the ascension and exaltation (see note—Jn.17:5-8) | • the glory of living eternally in the presence of God, being exalted to serve Him by ruling and reigning with His Son Jesus Christ forever (see Jn.14:2-3; Ro.8:16-17; Tit.2:12-13; 3:7) |

## 3 Request 3: That believers may be perfected in unity.

Jesus prayed that believers be *perfected* in unity, perfected as one body (see Deeper Study # 2—Jn.17:23). This stresses beyond question the absolute necessity that believers live in unity. The world has not been reached for Christ—millions have been lost—because believers have not been unified enough to penetrate the world with the gospel. This is the terrible indictment against believers (see Introduction). The problem is certainly not God. He is willing, and He is loving and powerful enough to use believers to reach the whole world. The problem is unquestionably believers and their lack of unity.

23 "I in them and you in me, that they may become perfectly one, so that the world may know that you sent me and loved them even as you loved me."

### a. The source: Jesus within.

Believers' source of unity is the indwelling presence of Christ within their lives. Jesus said that God is *in* Him; therefore, the presence of Christ *in the believer* means that God dwells "in" the believer. The believer actually partakes of the divine nature of God (2 Pe.1:4; see note, *Indwelling Presence*—Jn.10:37-39; 14:10; 14:18-20; 14:23-24).

> "In that day you will know that I am in my Father, and you in me, and I in you." (Jn.14:20)

> Jesus answered him, "If anyone loves me, he will keep my word, and my Father will love him, and we will come to him and make our home with him." (Jn.14:23)

> "I in them and you in me, that they may become perfectly one, so that the world may know that you sent me and loved them even as you loved me." (Jn.17:23)

> I have been crucified with Christ. It is no longer I who live, but Christ who lives in me. And the life I now live in the flesh I live by faith in the Son of God, who loved me and gave himself for me. (Ga.2:20)

> To them God chose to make known how great among the Gentiles are the riches of the glory of this mystery, which is Christ in you, the hope of glory. (Col.1:27)

> Whoever keeps his commandments abides in God, and God in him. And by this we know that he abides in us, by the Spirit whom he has given us. (1 Jn.3:24)

### b. The reason: To convince the world that God sent Christ and that He loves believers.

The purpose for a perfected unity amongst believers is that the world may *know* that God sent Jesus into the world to save it. Note that there is a difference each time Jesus prays for unity in this chapter. And each difference or point proclaims a strong message to the believer.

There is . . .
- the *unity of God's name*, of calling on God's name to keep believers from a divided world and its divisive influence (v.11)
- the *unity of God's protective power*, of calling on God's power to deliver believers from the evil of the world and the devil (v.15)
- the *unity of witness*, that the world may believe that God sent Christ (see notes—Jn.3:32-34; Deeper Study # 1—3:34). They will believe through a unified witness (v.21)
- the *unity of love*, that the world may know that God sent Christ. They will know through a unified love (v.23)

There is a world of difference between a unity of witness and a unity of love. The world may come to believe the gospel by a unified witness for Christ, but the only way the world can ever know the gospel is by a *unified love* among believers. What the world needs more than anything else is love, a great demonstration of love from a massive multitude of people. (See 1 Co.13:4-7 for the behavior and acts of love, and think about the enormous impact we could make upon the world if we really were unified in love.)

The love needed among believers is a different love from the *so-called love* of the world. The love needed is a sacrificial love that will give all it *is and has* to minister to a world that is reeling under the weight of starving, diseased, and dying masses of people (see notes, *Love*—Jn.13:33-35; 21:15-17).

"A new commandment I give to you, that you love one another: just as I have loved you, you also are to love one another. By this all people will know that you are my disciples, if you have love for one another." (Jn.13:34-35)

But God shows his love for us in that while we were still sinners, Christ died for us. (Ro.5:8)

By this we know love, that he laid down his life for us, and we ought to lay down our lives for the brothers. (1 Jn.3:16)

## DEEPER STUDY # 2

(17:23) **Perfect—Perfected** (teleioo; pronounced *tel-i-ah'-oh*): the idea of perfection is perfection of purpose. It has to do with an end, an aim, a goal, a purpose. It means fit, mature, fully grown at a particular stage of growth. For example, a fully grown child is a perfect child; he has reached the height of childhood, achieved the purpose of childhood. The word "perfect" does not mean perfection of character, that is, being without sin. It is fitness, maturity for task and purpose. It is full development, maturity of godliness (see note—Ep.4:12-16; see Ph.3:12; 1 Jn.1:8, 10).

The Bible reveals three stages of perfection.

1. *Saving* perfection. Christ's death has guaranteed forever the perfection and redemption of those set apart for God (He.10:14).

2. *Progressive* or *maturing* perfection. God reveals anything that is contrary to His purpose, and the believer is expected to correct it (Ph.3:13-15, esp. 15). The believer's holiness (2 Co.7:1) is now being perfected or made perfect (2 Co.7:1). Through God's ongoing work in his or her life, the believer is being perfected—brought to maturity—continuously (Ep.4:13; Col.4:12; Js.1:4).

3. *Redemptive* or *resurrected* perfection. The believer's purpose and aim is to "attain the resurrection of the dead. . . . [to be] perfect" (Ph.3:11-12).

The height of Christian perfection or maturity is to do good and show kindness to all people, both good and bad people. We are mature in heart when we show love to our enemies as well as to our friends (Mt.5:44-48). The love of God and of Christ are the believer's example of perfected love (see notes—Jn.13:33-35; 21:15-17).

## 4  Request 4: That believers may be with Him in glory.

17:24

Jesus prayed that believers may be with Him in glory (see notes—Jn.17:5-8; 14:1-3; *Resurrection*—Jn.14:6 for discussion). What a precious statement this is to the believer. The Lord Jesus wants us with Him. By no means does this prayer suggest that some believers will not be with Him in eternity, that some will not make it to heaven. It simply expresses the desire of our Savior's heart to spend eternity with those for whom He died. He "looked forward to the time when all His people would be in His Father's house."[1]

24 "Father, I desire that they also, whom you have given me, may be with me where I am, to see my glory that you have given me because you loved me before the foundation of the world."

> "In my Father's house are many rooms. If it were not so, would I have told you that I go to prepare a place for you? And if I go and prepare a place for you, I will come again and will take you to myself, that where I am you may be also." (Jn.14:2-3)

> For we know that if the tent that is our earthly home is destroyed, we have a building from God, a house not made with hands, eternal in the heavens. For in this tent we groan, longing to put on our heavenly dwelling. (2 Co.5:1-2)

---

1  Max Anders and Kenneth O. Gangel, eds., *Holman New Testament Commentary* (John volume), (Nashville, TN: Holman Reference, 2000). Via Wordsearch digital edition.

Because of the hope laid up for you in heaven. Of this you have heard before in the word of the truth, the gospel. (Col.1:5)

After this I looked, and behold, a great multitude that no one could number, from every nation, from all tribes and peoples and languages, standing before the throne and before the Lamb, clothed in white robes, with palm branches in their hands. (Re.7:9)

a. **The reason: To behold or see His glory.**

Jesus wanted His people to see Him in His glory. Only those who witnessed the Transfiguration saw Jesus in His fullness of glory (Mt.17:1-8; 2 Pe.1:16-18). John would later behold Christ in His glory when he received the Revelation (Re.1:9-19). But Jesus desired for all of His people to see Him *as He is* (1 Jn.3:2).

b. **The assurance: God's love.**

When we look at Jesus on Calvary, beaten, broken, and bloodied in order to accomplish His Father's will, some might question the Father's love for His Son (Is.53:1-11). But when we see Jesus exalted and glorified in heaven, we will be assured of God's love for His Son (Ph.2:5-11). Even more, we will then grasp the greatness of God's love for us, that He would subject His beloved Son to death by crucifixion for our salvation (Jn.3:16; Ro.5:8).

## 17:25-26

[25] "O righteous Father, even though the world does not know you, I know you, and these know that you have sent me.
[26] I made known to them your name, and I will continue to make it known, that the love with which you have loved me may be in them, and I in them."

## 5 Request 5: That believers may be filled with God's love.

Jesus' concluded His prayer by requesting that we may be filled with God's love. This conclusion is a striking testimony about unbelievers, about believers, and about Himself.

a. **Because unbelievers do not know God (v.25a).**

Jesus testified, first, about the world—unbelievers. The world did not know God. Jesus was the revelation of God; therefore, all who saw Jesus saw God. Yet the world rejected Him, refusing to know Him (see note, pt.3—Jn.15:19-24 for discussion). Today, the world continues with no knowledge of God. Only those who believe in Christ truly know God.

For, being ignorant of the righteousness of God, and seeking to establish their own, they did not submit to God's righteousness. (Ro.10:3)

They [men] are darkened in their understanding, alienated from the life of God because of the ignorance that is in them, due to their hardness of heart. (Ep.4:18)

Then I said, "These are only the poor; they have no sense; for they do not know the way of the Lord, the justice of their God." (Je.5:4)

But they do not know the thoughts of the Lord; they do not understand his plan, that he has gathered them as sheaves to the threshing floor. (Mi.4:12)

b. **Because Christ does know God (v.25b).**

Second, Jesus testified about His relationship with the Father. Since He is the Son of God, He knows God. He is eternal and has always existed with God (see note—Jn.17:5-8 for discussion).

"All things have been handed over to me by my Father, and no one knows the Son except the Father, and no one knows the Father except the Son and anyone to whom the Son chooses to reveal him." (Mt.11:27)

"I know him, for I come from him, and he sent me." (Jn.7:29)

"But you have not known him. I know him. If I were to say that I do not know him, I would be a liar like you, but I do know him and I keep his word." (Jn.8:55)

"Just as the Father knows me and I know the Father; and I lay down my life for the sheep." (Jn.10:15)

c. **Because believers know God sent Christ (v.25c).**
   Third, Jesus testified about believers, both those who were with Him and all who would believe down through the centuries. Believers know that God sent Christ. We know who Jesus truly is (see note, pt.2-3—Jn.17:5-8).

   > "I know him, for I come from him, and he sent me." (Jn.7:29)

   > Jesus said to them, "If God were your Father, you would love me, for I came from God and I am here. I came not of my own accord, but he sent me." (Jn.8:42)

   > "Do you say of him whom the Father consecrated and sent into the world, 'You are blaspheming,' because I said, 'I am the Son of God'?" (Jn.10:36)

   > "That they may all be one, just as you, Father, are in me, and I in you, that they also may be in us, so that the world may believe that you have sent me." (Jn.17:21)

d. **Because Christ was faithful in carrying out God's purpose (v.26).**
   Finally, Jesus testified of His faithfulness to God's will. He declared or made God known to the human race (see notes—Jn.14:6) that we might *know* the love of God and *have* the love of God dwelling "in" us (see notes—Jn.17:23).

   > "For God so loved the world, that he gave his only Son, that whoever believes in him should not perish but have eternal life." (Jn.3:16)

   > But God shows his love for us in that while we were still sinners, Christ died for us. (Ro.5:8)

   > And this is his commandment, that we believe in the name of his Son Jesus Christ and love one another, just as he has commanded us. (1 Jn.3:23)

# XV. THE REVELATION OF JESUS, THE SUFFERING SAVIOR, 18:1–19:42

## A. The Arrest of Jesus: Absolute Surrender, 18:1–11

*Mt.26:36-56; Mk.14:32-52; Lu.22:39-53*

1. **A devotion to God**
   a. Jesus left or went out to prepare Himself spiritually
   b. Jesus left or went out to prepare the scene for God's will
      1) Jesus went to a place known by Judas
      2) Judas came forth with a large force to arrest Him[DS1]

2. **A willing determination**
   a. Jesus went forward—voluntarily

   b. Jesus' courageous confession & claim

   c. Jesus' miraculous blast of revelation: "I Am"

3. **A protective or vicarious commitment**

   a. Jesus' protective love and sacrifice for His disciples
   b. Jesus' reason: To fulfill His Word

4. **An unswerving obedience**
   a. Peter's loyal but carnal zeal

   b. Jesus' iron determination to obey God's will: To drink the cup[DS2]

When Jesus had spoken these words, he went out with his disciples across the brook Kidron, where there was a garden, which he and his disciples entered.

² Now Judas, who betrayed him, also knew the place, for Jesus often met there with his disciples.
³ So Judas, having procured a band of soldiers and some officers from the chief priests and the Pharisees, went there with lanterns and torches and weapons.
⁴ Then Jesus, knowing all that would happen to him, came forward and said to them, "Whom do you seek?"
⁵ They answered him, "Jesus of Nazareth." Jesus said to them, "I am he." Judas, who betrayed him, was standing with them.
⁶ When Jesus said to them, "I am he," they drew back and fell to the ground.
⁷ So he asked them again, "Whom do you seek?" And they said, "Jesus of Nazareth."
⁸ Jesus answered, "I told you that I am he. So, if you seek me, let these men go."
⁹ This was to fulfill the word that he had spoken: "Of those whom you gave me I have lost not one."
¹⁰ Then Simon Peter, having a sword, drew it and struck the high priest's servant and cut off his right ear. (The servant's name was Malchus.)
¹¹ So Jesus said to Peter, "Put your sword into its sheath; shall I not drink the cup that the Father has given me?"

# Division XV

*The Revelation of Jesus, the Suffering Savior, 18:1-19:42*

A. The Arrest of Jesus: Absolute Surrender, 18:1-11

*Mt.26:36-56; Mk.14:32-52; Lu.22:39-53*

## 18:1-11
## Introduction

One of the most precious scenes from the life of Jesus is His praying in the Garden of Gethsemane. There, our Savior surrendered to His Father's will and to laying down His life as the sacrifice for the sins of the world.

We may all face times when obeying God's will involves suffering (1 Pe.4:19). In the Garden of Gethsemane, our Lord left us an enduring example of how we should confront those times: with determination to accomplish God's will, whatever the cost. As Jesus surrendered Himself absolutely to the Father's will, so should we. This is, *The Arrest of Jesus: Absolute Surrender*, 18:1-11.

1. A devotion to God (vv.1-3).
2. A willing determination (vv.4-6).
3. A protective or vicarious commitment (vv.7-9).
4. An unswerving obedience (vv.10-11).

(18:1-11) **Another Outline**: Absolute Surrender—Jesus Went Forth.
1. Jesus went forth devotionally (vv.1-3).
2. Jesus went forth willingly—confessing who He was (vv.4-6).
3. Jesus went forth vicariously (vv.7-9).
4. Jesus went forth purposefully—to die, to drink the cup (vv.10-11).

## 1 A devotion to God.

18:1-3

In going to the Garden of Gethsemane, Jesus displayed His devotion to God. Note the words *went out* or *forth* (Gk. exelthen, v.1) and *came* or *went forward*, or *went out* (exelthon, v.4). The idea being conveyed is *purpose*. Jesus was going forth deliberately, for a specific purpose, knowing exactly what He was doing.

**When** Jesus had spoken these words, he went out with his disciples across the brook Kidron, where there was a garden, which he and his disciples entered.

² Now Judas, who betrayed him, also knew the place, for Jesus often met there with his disciples.

³ So Judas, having procured a band of soldiers and some officers from the chief priests and the Pharisees, went there with lanterns and torches and weapons.

a. **Jesus left or went out to prepare Himself spiritually (v.1a).**

Jesus *went out* to prepare Himself spiritually. He was facing *the hour* to which God had called Him, the hour of His death (see note, Hour—Jn.2:3-5; DEEPER STUDY # 1—12:23-24). He knew that God's will was for Him to die for the sins of the world. He knew the awful separation from God that sin causes; therefore, He knew that He was to be cut off from God's presence, that God would have to forsake and turn His back on Him because of sin. He was feeling the awful pressure of God's coming judgment of sin which was to be carried out upon Him. In the flesh, Jesus wanted to flee; He wanted another way to be chosen to save the world (Mt.26:39, 42, 44). Yet He . . .

- was committed to God
- was totally *devoted* to His Father
- *must* do God's will

But to do God's will, He had to have God's help. He had to pray and seek God's face. He desperately needed God to meet His need in some special way. It was for this reason that

He headed for the garden. He was seeking to be alone with His Father, to have His Father strengthen Him for the terrible ordeal and judgment of the cross.

The point tears at the heart of the believer, for Jesus knew He was to bear the sins of the world on the cross, and the pressure was almost unbearable. Jesus could have fled; He could have turned away and insisted that the cup pass from Him. But He did not. He was totally devoted to God, so He "went out" deliberately—for the purpose of praying and seeking strength from God, for the strength to fulfill God's will. (See outline and notes—Mt.26:36-46 for discussion of the experience in the Garden of Gethsemane. John does not cover the actual agony Jesus experienced while in prayer. His purpose is simply to show the total devotion of Jesus to God's will. The other Gospels cover the Lord's unbelievable agony.)

**b. Jesus left or went out to prepare the scene for God's will (v.1b–3).**

Jesus *went out* to prepare the scene so that God's will would be done. He went to the Garden of Gethsemane, probably to the very spot where He had often prayed and spent the night when in Jerusalem (see Lu.22:39). He did not have to go there. He could have chosen some other direction to go, some other place to seek God. But He went to the place Judas knew (v.2). He was totally devoted to God, so He "went out" to set the scene for God's will to be fulfilled.

After Jesus had finished praying in the garden, Judas came with a large force to arrest Jesus (v.3; see DEEPER STUDY # 1). Jewish religious leaders accompanied the Roman soldiers who had been deployed to seize the Son of God. Matthew records a remarkable fact: Jesus knew they were coming, and He knew precisely *when* they were coming. He finished praying and called Peter, James, and John to go with Him to meet them (Mt.26:44-46).

**THOUGHT 1.** Jesus is the believer's dynamic example of devotion to God. We need to be devoted and totally committed to doing God's will. We should be *going forth* all the time . . .
- to prepare ourselves spiritually
- to prepare the scene for God's will
- to do God's will

> And after he had dismissed the crowds, he went up on the mountain by himself to pray. When evening came, he was there alone. (Mt.14:23)
>
> And rising very early in the morning, while it was still dark, he departed and went out to a desolate place, and there he prayed. (Mk.1:35)
>
> Likewise the Spirit helps us in our weakness. For we do not know what to pray for as we ought, but the Spirit himself intercedes for us with groanings too deep for words. (Ro.8:26)
>
> Evening and morning and at noon I utter my complaint and moan, and he hears my voice. (Ps.55:17)
>
> "When he calls to me, I will answer him; I will be with him in trouble; I will rescue him and honor him." (Ps.91:15)
>
> "You keep him in perfect peace whose mind is stayed on you, because he trusts in you. Trust in the LORD forever, for the LORD GOD is an everlasting rock." (Is.26:3-4)

## DEEPER STUDY # 1

(18:3) **Band, Detachment, Cohort, or Company** (speira): this was a *cohort* of soldiers. A cohort was a tenth part of a Roman legion. It usually had six hundred soldiers. On a rare occasion, the word *cohort* was used for a detachment of two hundred soldiers. The authorities also had their temple police join the force. It was a large armed force of several hundred who came out to arrest Jesus. The rumor had been that the Messiah, the promised Jewish King, had come. Apparently, the Romans felt they had to make sure there would be no uprisings when they arrested Jesus. Note an interesting fact: they brought lanterns and torches. Passover was held during the days of full moon, so there would have been plenty of natural light. Why then, were lanterns and torches needed? They were probably expecting Jesus to flee and hide in the bushes and trees and dark spots of the garden.

## 2 A willing determination.

18:1-11

If there is one point emphasized by the details of these verses, it is that Jesus—not the armed soldiers—was in control of this situation. Although Jesus had no earthly weapons, the soldiers were all taken down by the power of His Word. They did not take Jesus by force; He surrendered voluntarily to them, for He was determined to do His Father's will.

18:4-6

> ⁴ Then Jesus, knowing all that would happen to him, came forward and said to them, "Whom do you seek?"
> ⁵ They answered him, "Jesus of Nazareth." Jesus said to them, "I am he." Judas, who betrayed him, was standing with them.
> ⁶ When Jesus said to them, "I am he," they drew back and fell to the ground.

**a. Jesus went forward voluntarily (v.4).**

Jesus approached the Roman soldiers voluntarily. John specified that the Lord knew exactly what was going to happen to Him. He knew all the suffering and the pain of the judgment of God that was to fall upon Him. But He still went forward to meet the world that was rejecting Him and that was coming to arrest and kill Him. The point is, He was willing and determined to die for the sins of the world. He was voluntarily choosing to die for all people (see note, pt.2—Jn.10:17-18 for more discussion; also see Deeper Study # 2—Mt.26:37-38).

**b. Jesus' courageous confession and claim (v.5).**

Jesus did not flee from the world and its persecution. He did not try to escape or avoid being seized. Instead, He valiantly acknowledged that He was the one whom they were seeking.

- ➢ He made a courageous confession: I AM. He did not flee into the bushes or caves of the garden, fearing the persecutors. He knew God's will, and He was determined to carry out God's will.
- ➢ He made a courageous claim: I AM. This is the claim of deity. Imagine the scene. The soldiers had come out to arrest a peasant. They expected Him to flee and hide for His life. But there He was, a solitary man standing face-to-face with them, courageously proclaiming "I Am" (see Deeper Study # 1—Jn.6:20).

**THOUGHT 1.** What a dynamic example for believers! When we know the will of God, we are to do it courageously, no matter the opposition or threat.

> **Therefore, my beloved brothers, be steadfast, immovable, always abounding in the work of the Lord, knowing that in the Lord your labor is not in vain. (1 Co.15:58)**
>
> **Be watchful, stand firm in the faith, act like men, be strong. (1 Co.16:13)**
>
> **Finally, be strong in the Lord and in the strength of his might. (Ep.6:10)**
>
> **You then, my child, be strengthened by the grace that is in Christ Jesus. (2 Ti.2:1)**
>
> **Since therefore Christ suffered in the flesh, arm yourselves with the same way of thinking, for whoever has suffered in the flesh has ceased from sin, so as to live for the rest of the time in the flesh no longer for human passions but for the will of God. (1 Pe.4:1-2)**
>
> **"Be strong and courageous. Do not fear or be in dread of them, for it is the Lord your God who goes with you. He will not leave you or forsake you." (De.31:6)**

**THOUGHT 2.** Jesus' claim "I AM" is definitely the word of deity. It must have struck Judas like a lightning bolt on a cloudless day. We never know what effect a courageous confession has upon a soul. We must be faithful to our task of confessing and proclaiming Christ before a lost and hostile world.

> **I charge you in the presence of God, who gives life to all things, and of Christ Jesus, who in his testimony before Pontius Pilate made the good confession, to keep the commandment unstained and free from reproach until the appearing of our Lord Jesus Christ. (1 Ti.6:13-14)**
>
> **These all died in faith, not having received the things promised, but having seen them and greeted them from afar, and having acknowledged that they were strangers and exiles on the earth. (He.11:13)**
>
> **By this you know the Spirit of God: every spirit that confesses that Jesus Christ has come in the flesh is from God, and every spirit that does not confess Jesus is not from God. This**

is the spirit of the antichrist, which you heard was coming and now is in the world already. (1 Jn.4:2-3)

Whoever confesses that Jesus is the Son of God, God abides in him, and he in God. (1 Jn.4:15)

c. Jesus' miraculous blast of revelation: "I Am" (v.6).

A miraculous blast of revelation exploded when Jesus said, "I AM." As far as we know, there was no burst of majestic light that broke forth from Jesus. There was no supernatural manifestation or visible sign. There was only the phenomenal, powerful statement, "I AM." This is the great claim of God. When Jesus made the claim, something humanly unexplainable happened: the arresting party fell back and to the ground. Apparently, God miraculously struck them with the claim, although they did not understand. They were forcefully knocked down with the claim's . . .

- authority
- power
- presence, embodied in Jesus as He stood there

Remember that Jesus is the "I AM," the Son of God Himself. The very nature of God was embodied in Him. When He made the claim, especially in the face of such an eventful situation, there was bound to be a blast of revelation. It was as if they were slain with the sword that came out of Christ's mouth—His mighty Word (Re.19:15, 21).

**THOUGHT 1.** This is critical. People must heed the claim of Jesus Christ: the blast of revelation that He is the great "I AM." They must heed the claim while there is time. The arresting party, standing there facing Christ, still had time to confess Him. As long as a person is alive, they still have time to believe (2 Co.6:2).

"Whoever believes in him is not condemned, but whoever does not believe is condemned already, because he has not believed in the name of the only Son of God." (Jn.3:18)

"I told you that you would die in your sins, for unless you believe that I am he you will die in your sins." (Jn.8:24)

For he says, "In a favorable time I listened to you, and in a day of salvation I have helped you." Behold, now is the favorable time; behold, now is the day of salvation. (2 Co.6:2)

Take care, brothers, lest there be in any of you an evil, unbelieving heart, leading you to fall away from the living God. But exhort one another every day, as long as it is called "today," that none of you may be hardened by the deceitfulness of sin. For we have come to share in Christ, if indeed we hold our original confidence firm to the end. (He.3:12-14)

He who is often reproved, yet stiffens his neck, will suddenly be broken beyond healing. (Pr.29:1)

"The harvest is past, the summer is ended, and we are not saved." (Je.8:20)

18:7-9

⁷ So he asked them again, "Whom do you seek?" And they said, "Jesus of Nazareth."
⁸ Jesus answered, "I told you that I am he. So, if you seek me, let these men go."
⁹ This was to fulfill the word that he had spoken: "Of those whom you gave me I have lost not one."

### 3 A protective or vicarious commitment.

The disciples were in danger, but Jesus took the lead in saving them by offering Himself in their place. Christ's protective love and vicarious suffering for humanity is clearly pictured by this noble act.

a. Jesus' protective love and sacrifice for His disciples (v.8).

Jesus stepped forward in the disciples' place in order to save them from suffering and death (see DEEPER STUDY # 2—Jn.10:11). He offered to bear death alone, urging the soldiers to let His disciples go. There was no need for them to die (see Ro.5:8; 1 Pe.3:18).

b. **Jesus' reason: To fulfill His Word (v.9).**

Jesus' selfless act fulfilled His commitment to the Father. He had said that He would not lose anyone whom God had given Him (see notes—Jn.17:1-4, pt.2; 17:9-11, pt.1 for discussion). In addition, His betrayal and arrest were a fulfillment of prophecy (Ps.41:9; 109:4-13).

**THOUGHT 1.** Jesus' protection of His disciples is a picture of rich spiritual truths:

(1) It pictures the glorious security of the believer. Jesus will lose no one whom the Father has given Him. Every individual should ask God to take their life and to commit it to Christ.

> "I give them eternal life, and they will never perish, and no one will snatch them out of my hand. My Father, who has given them to me, is greater than all, and no one is able to snatch them out of the Father's hand." (Jn.10:28-29)

(2) It pictures the protection Christ has provided for all people. He has died vicariously for all, but every individual must accept His death as their own in order to be saved.

> "For God so loved the world, that he gave his only Son, that whoever believes in him should not perish but have eternal life." (Jn.3:16)

> But God shows his love for us in that while we were still sinners, Christ died for us. (Ro.5:8)

(3) It pictures the protective, vicarious commitment believers are to have to the world. We are to give ourselves—all we are and have—to meet the needs of a desperate world which reels in pain, sin, and death (see DEEPER STUDY # 1—Lu.9:23).

> And he said to all, "If anyone would come after me, let him deny himself and take up his cross daily and follow me." (Lu.9:23)

## 4 An unswerving obedience.

18:10-11

Peter thought the time had come for Jesus Christ to free Israel and establish the throne of David as the dominant nation in the world (see notes—Mt.1:1; DEEPER STUDY # 2—1:18; DEEPER STUDY # 2—3:11; notes—11:1-6; 11:2-3; DEEPER STUDY # 1—11:5; DEEPER STUDY # 2—11:6; DEEPER STUDY # 1—12:16; notes—22:42; Lu.7:21-23). Peter drew his sword and struck, slashing off the ear of Malchus, the high priest's servant (note that Peter *had* a sword). Jesus responded to Peter's rash attack by demonstrating His unswerving obedience to His Father's will.

> ¹⁰ Then Simon Peter, having a sword, drew it and struck the high priest's servant and cut off his right ear. (The servant's name was Malchus.)
> ¹¹ So Jesus said to Peter, "Put your sword into its sheath; shall I not drink the cup that the Father has given me?"

a. **Peter's loyal but carnal zeal (v.10).**

Peter's loyalty to Jesus seems admirable, but the picture painted by his behavior is carnal commitment, the kind of commitment that acts and struggles in the flesh. Peter took his stand for Jesus *in the flesh*; therefore, he failed. Eventually, he deserted Jesus. Acting in the flesh will always result in failing and deserting Jesus.

> For those who live according to the flesh set their minds on the things of the flesh, but those who live according to the Spirit set their minds on the things of the Spirit. For to set the mind on the flesh is death, but to set the mind on the Spirit is life and peace. . . . For if you live according to the flesh you will die, but if by the Spirit you put to death the deeds of the body, you will live. (Ro.8:5-6, 13)

Peter misunderstood the Lord's Word. First, Peter thought Jesus was to establish an earthly kingdom. He thought in terms of the physical and material world. Therefore, he failed to grasp the spiritual and eternal kingdom (dimension of being) proclaimed by Jesus. Second, Peter never accepted the Lord's Word. Jesus had predicted His death and forewarned the apostles, giving them extensive training for months (see notes—Mt.16:13-20, 21-28; 17:1-13; 17:22, 24-27). However, Peter refused to give up his preconceived ideas and accept what Jesus was saying. Therefore, he did not see the eternal world of the Spirit nor the eternal salvation which Jesus was securing.

b. **Jesus' iron determination to obey God's will: To drink the cup (v.11).**

Determined to obey God's will, Jesus ordered Peter to put his sword back into its sheath. Dying for the sins of the world was the bitter *cup* the Father had appointed Him to drink of; that is, it was God's will for Him (see Deeper Study # 2). Although Peter meant to fight against Christ's enemies, He was actually fighting against God's will.

> And going a little farther he fell on his face and prayed, saying, "My Father, if it be possible, let this cup pass from me; nevertheless, not as I will, but as you will." (Mt.26:39)

> "Rise, let us be going; see, my betrayer is at hand." (Mk.14:42)

> "For this reason the Father loves me, because I lay down my life that I may take it up again. No one takes it from me, but I lay it down of my own accord. I have authority to lay it down, and I have authority to take it up again. This charge I have received from my Father." (Jn.10:17-18)

> "But I do as the Father has commanded me, so that the world may know that I love the Father. Rise, let us go from here." (Jn.14:31)

## Deeper Study # 2

(18:11) **Cup:** Jesus Christ was determined not to fear nor shrink from death. This is clearly seen in Jn.10:17-18. Death for a cause is not such a great price to pay. Many people have died for causes—fearlessly and willingly. Some have faced such circumstances courageously, even *inviting* martyrdom for a cause. The Lord knew He was to die from the very beginning, and He had been preparing His disciples for His death (see note—Mt.16:13-20). However, it was not just human or physical suffering that Jesus was facing in the Garden. To suggest otherwise is totally inadequate in explaining Gethsemane. The great cup or trial Jesus was facing was separation from God (see note and Deeper Study # 2—Mt.26:37-38). This is one of the great distinctions that set Jesus apart from every other human being who has died for some cause. He was to be the sacrificial "Lamb of God" who takes away the sins of the world (Jn.1:29). He was to bear the judgment of God for the sins of the world (see note—Mt.27:46-49; see Is.53:10). Jesus Himself had already spoken of the "cup" when referring to His sacrificial death (see Deeper Study # 2—Mt.20:22-23; note—Mk.14:41-42; Deeper Study # 2—14:36; note—Jn.18:11).

Scripture speaks of the cup in several ways.

1. The cup is called the cup of the Lord's fury or wrath (Is.51:17).
2. The cup is associated with suffering and God's wrath (see Ps.11:6; Is.51:17; Lu.22:42).
3. The cup is also associated with salvation. Because Jesus drank the cup of suffering and wrath for us, we can take "the cup of salvation and call on the name of the Lord" (Ps.116:13). He bears the judgment of God for the sins of the world (Is.53:10).

## B. The Jews and Peter:
## The Cowardly Denial, 18:12-27

*Mt.26:69-75; Mk.14:53-72; Lu.22:54-62*

¹² So the band of soldiers and their captain and the officers of the Jews arrested Jesus and bound him.

¹³ First they led him to Annas, for he was the father-in-law of Caiaphas, who was high priest that year.

¹⁴ It was Caiaphas who had advised the Jews that it would be expedient that one man should die for the people.

¹⁵ Simon Peter followed Jesus, and so did another disciple. Since that disciple was known to the high priest, he entered with Jesus into the courtyard of the high priest,

¹⁶ but Peter stood outside at the door. So the other disciple, who was known to the high priest, went out and spoke to the servant girl who kept watch at the door, and brought Peter in.

¹⁷ The servant girl at the door said to Peter, "You also are not one of this man's disciples, are you?" He said, "I am not."

¹⁸ Now the servants and officers had made a charcoal fire, because it was cold, and they were standing and warming themselves. Peter also was with them, standing and warming himself.

¹⁹ The high priest then questioned Jesus about his disciples and his teaching.

²⁰ Jesus answered him, "I have spoken openly to the world. I have always taught in synagogues and in the temple, where all Jews come together. I have said nothing in secret.

²¹ "Why do you ask me? Ask those who have heard me what I said to them; they know what I said."

1. **Jesus' unjust arrest: Was taken & bound**
   a. He was led away to Annas
   b. His hour to die was rapidly approaching

2. **Peter's unnecessary denial: The denial of association**
   a. Peter and another disciple followed Jesus
      1) The other disciple knew the palace officials
      2) The other disciple arranged for Peter to enter
   b. Peter was innocently questioned by the doorkeeper
   c. Peter denied being associated with Jesus
   d. Peter made a carnal attempt to be known as one of the crowd

3. **The world's tragic denial**
   a. Jesus was asked to incriminate Himself[DS1]
      1) To prove His teaching
      2) To incriminate His followers
   b. Jesus replied forcefully
      1) His testimony was public knowledge
      2) The world knew His testimony

    c. Jesus was abused and mistreated

    d. Jesus incriminated the world

    e. Jesus was shifted about by the world

4. **Peter's cowardly denial: The denial of discipleship**
    a. He stood with the crowd, v.18
    b. He denied unequivocally that he was a disciple

5. **Peter's shattering denial: The denial of any association with Jesus**

6. **Conclusion: Jesus' Word was fulfilled**

²² When he had said these things, one of the officers standing by struck Jesus with his hand, saying, "Is that how you answer the high priest?" ²³ Jesus answered him, "If what I said is wrong, bear witness about the wrong; but if what I said is right, why do you strike me?" ²⁴ Annas then sent him bound to Caiaphas the high priest.

²⁵ Now Simon Peter was standing and warming himself. So they said to him, "You also are not one of his disciples, are you?" He denied it and said, "I am not."

²⁶ One of the servants of the high priest, a relative of the man whose ear Peter had cut off, asked, "Did I not see you in the garden with him?" ²⁷ Peter again denied it, and at once a rooster crowed.

# Division XV

## The Revelation of Jesus, the Suffering Savior, 18:1-19:42

B. The Jews and Peter: The Cowardly Denial, 18:12-27

*Mt.26:69-75; Mk.14:53-72; Lu.22:54-62*

## 18:12-27
## Introduction

This passage is a descriptive picture of cowardly denial—both the world's cowardly denial and the denial of a close disciple of the Lord's. It graphically shows what the Lord faces day by day from too many of His followers who do not stand for Him.

Our loyalty to Christ may be tested, just as Peter's was. May we humbly learn from his failure and prepare ourselves to overcome fear and threatening circumstances when our test comes. This is, *The Jews and Peter: The Cowardly Denial,* 18:12-27.
 1. Jesus' unjust arrest: Was taken and bound (vv.12-14).
 2. Peter's unnecessary denial: The denial of association (vv.15-18).
 3. The world's tragic denial (vv.19-24).
 4. Peter's cowardly denial: The denial of discipleship (v.25).
 5. Peter's shattering denial: The denial of any association with Jesus (vv.26-27).
 6. Conclusion: Jesus' Word was fulfilled (v.27).

(18:12-27) **Another Outline:** Cowardliness
 1. Cowardliness is unnecessary (vv.15-18).
 2. Cowardliness is unjust (vv.19-24).
 3. Cowardliness is worldly (v.25).

4. Cowardliness is habitual (vv.26-27).
5. Cowardliness is running back and forth (vv.18:28—19:15).

## 1 Jesus' unjust arrest: Was taken and bound.

18:12-14

After Jesus stopped Peter from resisting those sent to seize Him, the band of soldiers and Jewish leaders accomplished their unjust objective. They arrested Jesus and tied Him up, even though He had surrendered to them voluntarily (v.12).

### a. He was led away to Annas (v.13).

Jesus was led away to stand before Annas. Annas had been the High Priest but was no longer serving in this capacity. His son-in-law Caiaphas was the current High Priest (see note—Jn.11:49 for more discussion). However, as noted by John, Annas still wielded great influence. The trial before Annas was an informal trial, and the sinister plot to execute Jesus was being carried out under the shadow and secrecy of darkness.

### b. His hour to die was rapidly approaching (v.14).

Jesus' hour to die was now beginning. It had even been predicted by the world itself, by Caiaphas, the corrupt leader of the religionists (see note—Jn.11:49-53 for discussion; also see DEEPER STUDY # 1, *Hour*—Jn.12:23-24).

¹² So the band of soldiers and their captain and the officers of the Jews arrested Jesus and bound him.
¹³ First they led him to Annas, for he was the father-in-law of Caiaphas, who was high priest that year.
¹⁴ It was Caiaphas who had advised the Jews that it would be expedient that one man should die for the people.

## 2 Peter's unnecessary denial: The denial of association.

18:15-18

When Peter had pledged to lay down His life for Jesus, the Lord prophesied that Peter would deny Him three times during the same night (Jn.13:37-38). Sadly, for Peter, what Jesus predicted came to pass. Peter's first denial of Christ was the denial of association, and it was totally unnecessary. Peter's fears were unfounded, for he was in no danger. Nevertheless, Peter pretended not to be a follower of Jesus, denying any association with Him whatsoever.

### a. Peter and another disciple followed Jesus (vv.15–16).

Peter and some other disciple followed Jesus up to the gate of the high priest. The other disciple was probably John, for the account reads like an eyewitness account (see DEEPER STUDY # 1—Jn.1.39; note—Mk.14:54). This disciple knew the high priest personally. A possible explanation for this fact is that John's father, a very successful businessman, may have provided fish for the palace, making John well-known to the palace officials.[1] Therefore, he was allowed entrance into the palace and arranged for Peter to enter the palace (v.16; see DEEPER STUDY # 5—Mk.3:17). Upon entering the courtyard, Peter denied Jesus for the first time.

### b. Peter was innocently questioned by the doorkeeper (v.17a).

The doorkeeper questioned Peter about his relationship to Jesus. She knew that John was one of Jesus' disciples. Since Peter was associated with John, she naturally assumed he was also

¹⁵ Simon Peter followed Jesus, and so did another disciple. Since that disciple was known to the high priest, he entered with Jesus into the courtyard of the high priest,
¹⁶ but Peter stood outside at the door. So the other disciple, who was known to the high priest, went out and spoke to the servant girl who kept watch at the door, and brought Peter in.
¹⁷ The servant girl at the door said to Peter, "You also are not one of this man's disciples, are you?" He said, "I am not."
¹⁸ Now the servants and officers had made a charcoal fire, because it was cold, and they were standing and warming themselves. Peter also was with them, standing and warming himself.

---

1 William Barclay, *The Gospel of John* (Daily Study Bible Series), Vol. 2 (Philadelphia, PA: Westminster Press, 1960).

a disciple of Jesus. Her question appears to have been asked innocently; most likely, she had no underlying motive. She was probably either carrying on conversation or else asking Peter for some identification—simply doing her job. She seems to pose no threat or danger to Peter whatsoever.

c. **Peter denied being associated with Jesus (v.17b).**
Peter did not hesitate to answer the servant girl. He denied any association with Jesus, saying unequivocally, "I am not." Peter shamefully failed his Lord by denying any connection to Jesus and pretending not to know Him.

d. **Peter made a carnal attempt to be known as one of the crowd (v.18).**
At that point, Peter apparently separated Himself from John and attempted to blend in with the crowd. He joined the crowd, standing around with them and participating in their conversation and activities.

**THOUGHT 1.** Too many deny being associated with Christ. People see us in church or associating with other believers—innocently see us—thinking nothing about it. But when and if we are asked, we are faced with the temptation to downplay or even flatly deny any association with Christ.

**THOUGHT 2.** Too many pretend not to know Christ when out in the world . . .
- at their employment
- at their school
- at their social functions among their neighbors
- among their friends
- among strangers

We need to openly and unashamedly proclaim our relationship to the Lord Jesus Christ. Whether our fears are founded or unfounded in reality, we should not be timid about letting others know that we know Christ.

> "For whoever is ashamed of me and of my words in this adulterous and sinful generation, of him will the Son of Man also be ashamed when he comes in the glory of his Father with the holy angels." (Mark 8:38)

> For I am not ashamed of the gospel, for it is the power of God for salvation to everyone who believes, to the Jew first and also to the Greek. (Ro.1:16)

> For the Scripture says, "Everyone who believes in him will not be put to shame." (Ro.10:11)

**THOUGHT 3.** Too many try to fade into the crowd, trying to hide their faith by joining in with the crowd. Standing with and trying to blend in with the crowd will always cause a believer to deny the Lord.

> "But whoever denies me before men, I also will deny before my Father who is in heaven." (Mt.10:33)

> But in your hearts honor Christ the Lord as holy, always being prepared to make a defense to anyone who asks you for a reason for the hope that is in you; yet do it with gentleness and respect. (1 Pe.3:15)

> A false witness will not go unpunished, and he who breathes out lies will not escape. (Pr.19:5)

## 3 The world's tragic denial.

As one of Jesus' own was denying Him behind the scenes, the world itself was denying Him openly. The leaders of His own people, the Jews, were the first to try Jesus. Tragically,

**18:19-24**

¹⁹ The high priest then questioned Jesus about his disciples and his teaching.
²⁰ Jesus answered him, "I have spoken openly to the world. I have always taught in synagogues and in the temple, where all Jews come together. I have said nothing in secret.
²¹ "Why do you ask me? Ask those who have heard me what I said to them; they know what I said."
²² When he had said these things, one of the officers standing by struck Jesus with his hand, saying, "Is that how you answer the high priest?"
²³ Jesus answered him, "If what I said is wrong, bear witness about the wrong; but if what I said is right, why do you strike me?"
²⁴ Annas then sent him bound to Caiaphas the high priest.

they denied His claims to be the Son of God and God the Son; and they denied His teaching, the only words of eternal life.

### a. Jesus was asked to incriminate Himself (v.19).

Annas[2] tried to get Jesus to incriminate Himself. He questioned Christ about His disciples (trying to get Him to incriminate them) and challenged Him to prove His doctrine and His claims. How much like the world. The world will ask about Jesus' teaching, but their purpose is . . .

- not to learn His doctrine
- not to allow Him to prove His claims
- not to justify His claims
- not to secure direction and wisdom from Him

The world asks about Jesus' teaching to disprove it and to incriminate Him and His followers (see Deeper Study # 1). The world wants nothing to do with Him as the Son of God, for then the world would have to repent and subject itself to Him and the high price of following Him. If people truly acknowledge Jesus to be their Lord, they will willingly surrender their lives and everything they have to Him (see Deeper Study # 1—Lu.9:23).

> "It is the Spirit who gives life; the flesh is no help at all. The words that I have spoken to you are spirit and life." (Jn.6:63)

> "The one who rejects me and does not receive my words has a judge; the word that I have spoken will judge him on the last day." (Jn.12:48)

> "Whoever does not love me does not keep my words. And the word that you hear is not mine but the Father's who sent me." (Jn.14:24)

> Now the passage of the Scripture that he was reading was this: "Like a sheep he was led to the slaughter and like a lamb before its shearer is silent, so he opens not his mouth." (Ac.8:32)

> "Let the wicked forsake his way, and the unrighteous man his thoughts; let him return to the Lord, that he may have compassion on him, and to our God, for he will abundantly pardon." (Is.55:7)

### b. Jesus replied forcefully (vv.20-21).

Jesus' reply was forthright and forceful: His teaching and claim had been declared publicly. His testimony was public knowledge. He had done nothing in secret. His doctrine was consistent and clear. He did not have one message for the public and another message which He followed in secret. He had openly and clearly proclaimed the truth, and the world knew exactly what He had taught and claimed.

**THOUGHT 1.** The problem with the world is twofold.

(1) The world refuses to believe Jesus' claim to be the Son of God.

> "For I have come down from heaven, not to do my own will but the will of him who sent me." (Jn.6:38)

> "I know him, for I come from him, and he sent me." (Jn.7:29)

> Jesus said to them, "If God were your Father, you would love me, for I came from God and I am here. I came not of my own accord, but he sent me." (Jn.8:42)

> "Do you say of him whom the Father consecrated and sent into the world, 'You are blaspheming,' because I said, 'I am the Son of God'?" (Jn.10:36)

(2) The world seeks for some secret, symbolic meaning and doctrine in the Word of Christ.

> Jesus said to them, "If God were your Father, you would love me, for I came from God and I am here. I came not of my own accord, but he sent me. Why do you not understand what I say? It is because you cannot bear to hear my word." (Jn.8:42-43)

> "Whoever is of God hears the words of God. The reason why you do not hear them is that you are not of God." (Jn.8:47)

---

2  Annas is referred to as the high priest, even though he was not currently serving in that role. Those who had served as high priest always bore that title, even after they were out of office.

They are darkened in their understanding, alienated from the life of God because of the ignorance that is in them, due to their hardness of heart. (Ep.4:18)

And will turn away from listening to the truth and wander off into myths. (2 Ti.4:4)

Every word of God proves true; he is a shield to those who take refuge in him. Do not add to his words, lest he rebuke you and you be found a liar. (Pr.30:5-6)

But they do not know the thoughts of the LORD; they do not understand his plan, that he has gathered them as sheaves to the threshing floor. (Mi.4:12)

c. Jesus was abused and mistreated (v.22).

One of the guards reacted violently to Jesus' bold answer to the high priest. He abused Jesus, slapping Him in the face. His cruel reaction is a picture of how the world mistreats Jesus. Throughout His entire ministry, Jesus had insisted time and again that He was the Revelation of God, the Son of God Himself. (Quickly refer back to the overall outline or glance quickly over chapters 5-6, 8-12 for a feeling of how powerfully and frequently Jesus was proclaiming His deity.) Yet, the world shut its ears and reacted harshly. It wanted nothing to disturb its routine or culture. It wanted no rebuttal and no other answer given to the high priest of its own religion.

**THOUGHT 1.** The world's religion allows people to continue in their own way and do pretty much as they wish and still feel acceptable to God. Just think for a moment! How few religions—how few churches—how few priests and ministers—proclaim the true doctrine of the *Lord* Jesus. So few are willing to sacrifice their lives for the world and all they are and have in order to reach a lost, starving, and diseased world.

And he said to all, "If anyone would come after me, let him deny himself and take up his cross [die] daily and follow me." (Lu.9:23; see notes—Mt.19:21-22; 19:23-26 for more discussion)

I appeal to you therefore, brothers, by the mercies of God, to present your bodies as a living sacrifice, holy and acceptable to God, which is your spiritual worship. Do not be conformed to this world, but be transformed by the renewal of your mind, that by testing you may discern what is the will of God, what is good and acceptable and perfect. (Ro.12:1-2)

"Therefore go out from their midst, and be separate from them, says the Lord, and touch no unclean thing; then I will welcome you, and I will be a father to you, and you shall be sons and daughters to me, says the Lord Almighty." (2 Co.6:17-18)

Do not love the world or the things in the world. If anyone loves the world, the love of the Father is not in him. For all that is in the world—the desires of the flesh and the desires of the eyes and pride of life—is not from the Father but is from the world. (1 Jn.2:15-16)

d. Jesus incriminated the world (v.23).

Jesus' response incriminated—indicted, charged, condemned—the world. The world could not charge Jesus with evil. He was sinless, completely without fault. He had not lied; He had always told the truth. He was the *perfect Son of God* who had come to earth to proclaim the truth of God perfectly.

"Which one of you convicts me of sin? If I tell the truth, why do you not believe me?" (Jn.8:46; see 2 Co.5:21; He.4:15; 7:26; 1 Pe.1:19; 2:22)

However, the world stands incriminated, for the world has always rejected and mistreated the Perfect Man, the Son of God Himself. In its rejection, the world exposes itself as evil, and its most terrible evil is the rejection of the Perfect Man. (Note a critical truth: rejection of Jesus is unpardonable. The person who ultimately rejects Jesus will not be saved. A person must believe and accept the Lord Jesus Christ to be saved.)

Therefore, we are ambassadors for Christ, God making his appeal through us. We implore you on behalf of Christ, be reconciled to God. For our sake he made him to be sin who knew no sin, so that in him we might become the righteousness of God. (2 Co.5:20-21)

Knowing that you were ransomed from the futile ways inherited from your forefathers, not with perishable things such as silver or gold, but with the precious blood of Christ, like that of a lamb without blemish or spot. (1 Pe.1:18-19)

e. **Jesus was shifted about by the world (v.24).**
Jesus was shifted from one place to another. Annas shuffled Him off to Caiaphas, the current high priest. This is a picture of people seeking validation from others to disprove Jesus. Jesus (His life, teaching, claims) was cast back and forth by the hands of people who were seeking evidence to prove that He was not the Son of God.

> So that we may no longer be children, tossed to and fro by the waves and carried about by every wind of doctrine, by human cunning, by craftiness in deceitful schemes. (Ep.4:14)

> They [men] mounted up to heaven; they went down to the depths; their courage melted away in their evil plight; they reeled and staggered like drunken men and were at their wits' end. (Ps.107:26-27)

### Deeper Study # 1

(18:19) **Jesus' Jewish Trial:** demanding that Jesus incriminate Himself was against the law of Jewish justice. Under Jewish law, a defendant was not required to admit any guilt; therefore, the Jewish trial of Jesus was a mockery of justice. Several facts show this.

1. They had hastily assembled the court *at night*, but it was illegal to try cases at night. All criminals had to be tried in the day.
2. They were meeting in Annas' palace (home), not in the official court. This, too, was illegal. All cases had to be tried in court.
3. Jesus was being tried during the Passover week, but no cases were supposed to be tried during that week.
4. The leaders had not met to try Jesus, but to secretly devise charges and to condemn Him to death.

## 4 Peter's cowardly denial: The denial of discipleship.

Peter's second denial of Christ was cowardly. Not wanting to stand out from the crowd, He denied being one of Jesus' disciples.

> 25 Now Simon Peter was standing and warming himself. So they said to him, "You also are not one of his disciples, are you?" He denied it and said, "I am not."

a. **He stood with the crowd.**
After the young woman who kept the door had assumed Peter to be one of Christ's disciples, He separated himself from John and joined a crowd warming themselves around a fire, attempting to become one of them (v.18). He was still trying to blend in with the crowd when some of the people around him recognized him as one of Jesus' disciples.

b. **He denied unequivocally that he was a disciple.**
When asked about Jesus, Peter renounced the Lord again, saying, "I am not!" He denied being one of Jesus' disciples; He did not want to stand out from the world that was condemning Jesus. His terse answer implied, "I am one of you, just another man standing around and taking part in the significant events of the world" (2 Co.6:17-18).

**THOUGHT 1.** Too many believers fear, and because they fear, they lose their testimony for Christ and the opportunity to witness and win others to Christ. Too many fear . . .
- embarrassment
- ridicule
- abuse
- loss of position or worldly friends
- worldly neighbors
- business management
- loss of promotion

In many places throughout the world, believers fear consequences far more serious than these, persecutions such as imprisonment, torture, and even death. Embarrassment, ridicule, and material loss are the least of their worries. Yet they stand boldly for Christ, regardless of the cost. And their families rejoice and praise God that their loved ones were faithful to Christ, even to their death.

All who fear to stand for Christ for far lesser reasons should be terribly ashamed, and they should fall on their faces with bitter tears in repentance toward God. May we all be inspired by the example of those throughout church history—as well as of those today—who have laid down their lives for the Lord Jesus Christ.

> "For whoever is ashamed of me and of my words in this adulterous and sinful generation, of him will the Son of Man also be ashamed when he comes in the glory of his Father with the holy angels." (Mk.8:38)
>
> Therefore do not be ashamed of the testimony about our Lord, nor of me his prisoner, but share in suffering for the gospel by the power of God. (2 Ti.1:8)
>
> "Be strong and courageous. Do not fear or be in dread of them, for it is the Lord your God who goes with you. He will not leave you or forsake you." (De.31:6)

## 18:26-27a

²⁶ One of the servants of the high priest, a relative of the man whose ear Peter had cut off, asked, "Did I not see you in the garden with him?"
²⁷ Peter again denied it, and at once a rooster crowed.

## 5 Peter's shattering denial: The denial of any association with Jesus.

Peter's third denial is stunning in its level of disowning Christ. This was the most serious denial of all. One of the relatives of the man whose ear Peter had cut off claimed to have seen Him in the garden with Jesus. But Peter insisted strongly that He was not associated with Jesus. Peter denied Jesus for two very basic reasons.

First, Peter feared the people (Pr.29:25). When a quick response was called for, he was not strong and mature enough to stand for Jesus. He feared what the crowd might do to him—ridicule, abuse, arrest, and kill him—more than he feared and respected the Lord Himself. He feared that they would do to him exactly what they were doing to Jesus.

Second, Peter faltered, stumbled, and failed to die to self. He lacked love enough for Christ and others to deny himself for the sake of others.

Jesus died on the cross for the sake of the same people who stood at the foot of the cross, railing and cursing Him. He willingly died for all people that we might live. That is how much He loved. At that point in his life, Peter did not know such self-denying love. He did not know the kind of love that denies and surrenders itself for the sake of others.

**THOUGHT 1.** Peter's denial serves as a strong warning to every believer.
- Peter was a strong disciple.
- Peter knew and had trusted Jesus as the Messiah, the Son of God.
- Peter had a strong profession of loyalty to Jesus.
- Peter had just partaken of the Lord's Supper; in fact, he had just been privileged to partake of the very first Lord's Supper.
- Peter had left all to follow Jesus.
- Peter had been taught about God, and he had been taught by Jesus Himself.
- Peter had even been forewarned that the flesh was weak and that he would fail.

Yet, in spite of all these experiences and advantages, Peter still denied the Lord. If someone of Peter's devotion and stature can so easily fail, so can we.

**THOUGHT 2.** Every denial (in fact, every neglect) of Jesus downgrades the Lord's importance in a believer's life. Denial and neglect ignore just who Jesus is, the Son of God in all His power and majesty and dominion. Denial shows that we fear other people more than we fear and revere God. Neglect of Jesus shows how little we fear and reverence Him. We need to always keep in mind that the Lord will judge His people, and that it is a terrifying thing to fall into the hands of the living God (He.10:30-31).

**THOUGHT 3.** A crowd of unbelievers can put pressure on any of us. Peter was where he did not belong. He was hanging around in the midst of a worldly crowd. He belonged in one of three places: by the side of Christ; alone with God, seeking answers and understanding; or with the other apostles, rallying them in prayer for understanding and direction.

> And with many other words he bore witness and continued to exhort them, saying, "Save yourselves from this crooked generation." (Ac.2:40)
>
> And not frightened in anything by your opponents. This is a clear sign to them of their destruction, but of your salvation, and that from God. (Ph.1:28)
>
> If we endure, we will also reign with him; if we deny him, he also will deny us. (2 Ti.2:12)
>
> They profess to know God, but they deny him by their works. They are detestable, disobedient, unfit for any good work. (Tit.1:16)
>
> You therefore, beloved, knowing this beforehand, take care that you are not carried away with the error of lawless people and lose your own stability. (2 Pe.3:17)
>
> Do not enter the path of the wicked, and do not walk in the way of the evil. (Pr.4:14)

## 6 Conclusion: Jesus' Word was fulfilled.

18:27

The rooster crowed, and Jesus' word was fulfilled. Just as the Lord had predicted, Peter had tragically denied the Lord three times in one night (Jn.13:38). The ominous crow of the rooster pierced Peter to the core. Regret, failure, and shame overwhelmed him, and he wept bitter tears of remorse (see note—Mk.14:72 for discussion). But our merciful Savior would extend forgiveness to His suddenly disloyal disciple, transforming him from an utter failure to an immovable rock for Christ.

> [27] Peter again denied it, and at once a rooster crowed.

## C. The Trial Before Pilate: Indecisive Compromise, 18:28–19:15

*Mt.27:11-25; Mk.15:1-15 Lu.23:1-5, 13-25*

1. **The setting: Jesus was led into the palace or judgment hall**
   a. It was early in the morning
   b. The Jews did not enter: To avoid ritual, ceremonial uncleanness
   c. Pilate moved back and forth[DS1]
2. **Movement 1: Pilate went to Jesus' accusers—to hear their charges**
   a. The insolent charge: Jesus is a criminal who should be punished (hatred & pride)
   b. Pilate refused the case (evading responsibility)
   c. The evidence of predetermined guilt and closed hearts: They wanted Him executed—put to death[DS2]
3. **Movement 2: Pilate went to Jesus—to hear His defense**
   a. Pilate's scornful question
   b. Jesus' challenge to Pilate: A person is responsible for his own verdict
   c. Pilate's reaction: Contempt for the Jews
   d. Jesus' explanation: His kingdom is not of this world
   e. Pilate's baffled question: Is Jesus a king?
   f. Jesus' claim: He is King—to be King was the purpose for His birth[DS3]
   g. Jesus' subtle appeal: To hear His words
   h. Pilate's sincere question: What is truth?
4. **Movement 3: Pilate went back to the people—to declare Jesus' innocence**

<sup>28</sup> Then they led Jesus from the house of Caiaphas to the governor's headquarters. It was early morning. They themselves did not enter the governor's headquarters, so that they would not be defiled, but could eat the Passover. <sup>29</sup> So Pilate went outside to them and said, "What accusation do you bring against this man?" <sup>30</sup> They answered him, "If this man were not doing evil, we would not have delivered him over to you." <sup>31</sup> Pilate said to them, "Take him yourselves and judge him by your own law." The Jews said to him, "It is not lawful for us to put anyone to death." <sup>32</sup> This was to fulfill the word that Jesus had spoken to show by what kind of death he was going to die. <sup>33</sup> So Pilate entered his headquarters again and called Jesus and said to him, "Are you the King of the Jews?" <sup>34</sup> Jesus answered, "Do you say this of your own accord, or did others say it to you about me?" <sup>35</sup> Pilate answered, "Am I a Jew? Your own nation and the chief priests have delivered you over to me. What have you done?" <sup>36</sup> Jesus answered, "My kingdom is not of this world. If my kingdom were of this world, my servants would have been fighting, that I might not be delivered over to the Jews. But my kingdom is not from the world." <sup>37</sup> Then Pilate said to him, "So you are a king?" Jesus answered, "You say that I am a king. For this purpose I was born and for this purpose I have come into the world—to bear witness to the truth. Everyone who is of the truth listens to my voice." <sup>38</sup> Pilate said to him, "What is truth?" After he had said this, he went back outside to the Jews and told them, "I find no guilt in him."

³⁹ "But you have a custom that I should release one man for you at the Passover. So do you want me to release to you the King of the Jews?"
⁴⁰ They cried out again, "Not this man, but Barabbas!" Now Barabbas was a robber.

Then Pilate took Jesus and flogged him. ² And the soldiers twisted together a crown of thorns and put it on his head and arrayed him in a purple robe. ³ They came up to him, saying, "Hail, King of the Jews!" and struck him with their hands.
⁴ Pilate went out again and said to them, "See, I am bringing him out to you that you may know that I find no guilt in him."
⁵ So Jesus came out, wearing the crown of thorns and the purple robe. Pilate said to them, "Behold the man!"

⁶ When the chief priests and the officers saw him, they cried out, "Crucify him, crucify him!" Pilate said to them, "Take him yourselves and crucify him, for I find no guilt in him."
⁷ The Jews answered him, "We have a law, and according to that law he ought to die because he has made himself the Son of God."
⁸ When Pilate heard this statement, he was even more afraid.

⁹ He entered his headquarters again and said to Jesus, "Where are you from?" But Jesus gave him no answer.
¹⁰ So Pilate said to him, "You will not speak to me? Do you not know that I have authority to release you and authority to crucify you?"
¹¹ Jesus answered him, "You would have no authority over me at all unless it had been given you from above. Therefore he who delivered me over to you has the greater sin."
¹² From then on Pilate sought to release him, but the Jews cried out, "If you release this man, you are not

a. Pilate's first attempt to release Jesus: He offers a substitute

b. The mob's choice: A man of the world

5. **Movement 4: Pilate went back to Jesus—to scourge, flog Him**
   a. Savage, cruel flogging (persecution)[DS4]
   b. Crude mockery & scoffing (abused His name and person)
   c. Sham obedience (hypocrisy)

6. **Movement 5: Pilate went back to the people again—to offer a compromise**

   a. Pilate's second attempt to release Jesus by compromise: Sought the crowd's pity by presenting Jesus beaten & battered
   b. The mob's hatred (loud, harsh, mean-spirited shouting)
   c. Pilate's impossible dare for them to kill Jesus themselves: Angry, sarcastic contempt for the mob[DS5]
   d. The Jews' truthful charge[DS6]

7. **Movement 6: Pilate went back to Jesus again—to investigate the possibility of a supernatural being**
   a. Pilate's question about Jesus' origin

   b. Pilate's appeal to earthly authority: Life is in the hands of earthly authority

   c. Jesus' revelation: There is a superior, higher authority (God)
   d. Jesus' charge of guilt against Judas & the religionists

8. **Movement 7: Pilate went back to the people again—to release Jesus**
   a. Pilate tried to release Jesus a third time

b. The Jews blackmailed Pilate: He must choose between Jesus or Caesar

9. **Movement 8: Pilate went to the judgment seat before all—to give the verdict of crucifixion**

   a. Pilate's choice: His fear of Caesar was greater than his fear of Jesus

   b. The Jews' frenzied madness
   c. Pilate's bitter question
   d. The Jews' fatal choice

Caesar's friend. Everyone who makes himself a king opposes Caesar."

¹³ So when Pilate heard these words, he brought Jesus out and sat down on the judgment seat at a place called The Stone Pavement, and in Aramaic Gabbatha.
¹⁴ Now it was the day of Preparation of the Passover. It was about the sixth hour. He said to the Jews, "Behold your King!"
¹⁵ They cried out, "Away with him, away with him, crucify him!" Pilate said to them, "Shall I crucify your King?" The chief priests answered, "We have no king but Caesar."

## Division XV

*The Revelation of Jesus, the Suffering Savior, 18:1–19:42*

C. The Trial Before Pilate: Indecisive Compromise, 18:28–19:15

*Mt.27:11-25; Mk.15:1-15 Lu.23:1-5, 13-25*

# 18:28–19:15
# Introduction

The Roman trial of Jesus is a dramatic picture of indecisive compromise. The scene flows along with Pilate, moving back and forth to Jesus and to His accusers or the people. Our outline for this section should be adequate in navigating one through this lengthy passage. Therefore, the commentary section will not discuss each point. Notes and application content are added where needed (see outline and Deeper Study # 1—Mt.27:11-25; Deeper Study # 1—Mk.15:1-15; note—Lu.23:1-25 for more detailed discussion). This is, *The Trial Before Pilate; Indecisive Compromise*, 18:28—19:15.

1. The setting: Jesus was led into the palace or judgment hall (v.28).
2. Movement 1: Pilate went to Jesus' accusers—to hear their charges (vv.29-32).
3. Movement 2: Pilate went to Jesus—to hear His defense (vv.33-38).
4. Movement 3: Pilate went back to the people—to declare Jesus' innocence (vv.38-40).
5. Movement 4: Pilate went back to Jesus—to scourge, flog Him (19:1-3).
6. Movement 5: Pilate went back to the people again—to offer a compromise (vv.4-7).
7. Movement 6: Pilate went back to Jesus again—to investigate the possibility of a supernatural being (vv.8-11).
8. Movement 7: Pilate went back to the people again—to release Jesus (v.12).
9. Movement 8: Pilate went to the judgment seat before all—to give the verdict of crucifixion (vv.13-15).

18:28

²⁸ Then they led Jesus from the house of Caiaphas to the governor's headquarters. It was early morning. They themselves did not enter the governor's headquarters, so that they would not be defiled, but could eat the Passover.

## 1 The setting: Jesus was led into the palace or judgment hall.

Jesus was led into the hall of judgment. This hall was called the *Praetorium*, and it was the Roman governor's palace and headquarters. It was early morning. The Jews did not enter, for the hall was a Gentile judgment hall, and it was the Sabbath of the Passover season. To enter the judgment hall would have polluted and contaminated them ceremonially. They would have been disallowed from participating in the Passover. It was a trifling, superficial concern in light of the trial for a man's life, especially the life of God's own Son. In light of this, Pilate, the Roman governor, had to move back and forth between his palace and where the Jews were assembled (see DEEPER STUDY # 1).

**THOUGHT 1.** Too often religionists attack others, arguing over their religion and church and its plans, over ceremonies, rituals, rules, regulations, and practices. They forget the *meat* of the truth: love, joy, peace, care, understanding, and ministry (see Jn.13:33-34).

## DEEPER STUDY # 1

(18:28) **Pilate:** the Roman procurator of Judea. He was directly responsible to the Emperor in Rome for the administrative and financial management of the region. A man had to work himself up through the political and military ranks to become a procurator. Pilate was therefore an able man, experienced in the affairs of politics and government as well as the military. He held office for ten years, which shows that he was deeply trusted by the Roman government. However, the Jews despised Pilate, and Pilate despised the Jews; in particular he despised their intense practice of religion. When Pilate became procurator of Judea, he did two things that provoked the people's bitter hatred against him forever. First, on his state visits to Jerusalem, he rode into the city with the Roman standard, an eagle sitting atop a pole. All previous governors had removed the standard because of the Jews' opposition to idols. Second, Pilate launched the construction of a new water supply for Jerusalem. To finance the project, he took the money out of the temple treasury. The Jews never forgot nor forgave this act. They bitterly opposed Pilate all through his reign, and he treated them with equal contempt (see DEEPER STUDY # 1—Mk.15:1-15). On several occasions, Jewish leaders threatened to exercise their right to report Pilate to the emperor. This, of course, disturbed Pilate immensely and caused him to become even more bitter toward the Jews.

## 2 Movement 1: Pilate went to Jesus' accusers—to hear their charges.

The first movement of Pilate was to Jesus' accusers—to hear their charges (v.29). The Jewish religious leaders were insolent toward Jesus—full of contempt and arrogance. They rejected and hated Jesus, and they set themselves up as His judges. They assumed the right to judge, and they had determined that Jesus was a criminal who should be punished.

The tension between Pilate and the Jews is obvious in the religious leaders' response to Pilate. When Pilate asked them what the charges were against Jesus, they replied sharply that they would not have brought Jesus to him if Jesus were not a criminal (v.30). This response also reflected their arrogance. They felt their verdict and judgment should not be questioned.

Pilate tried to evade his responsibility. He refused to hear the case and ordered the Jewish leaders to judge Jesus themselves according to their own law. But the religionists wanted Jesus put to death, and they did not have the authority to execute Him (v.31). Note that they were mentioning death even before the trial. They had already predetermined that Jesus was guilty, and their hearts were closed to any punishment but execution. This attitude led to the fulfillment of Jesus' prophecies about His death (v.32; see DEEPER STUDY # 2).

²⁹ So Pilate went outside to them and said, "What accusation do you bring against this man?"
³⁰ They answered him, "If this man were not doing evil, we would not have delivered him over to you."
³¹ Pilate said to them, "Take him yourselves and judge him by your own law." The Jews said to him, "It is not lawful for us to put anyone to death."
³² This was to fulfill the word that Jesus had spoken to show by what kind of death he was going to die.

**THOUGHT 1.** People may reject and hate Christ; they may judge Christ not worthy to be the Lord of their lives. They may try to get rid of Christ by pushing Him away and having nothing to do with Him. But they cannot change this fact: Christ still came to love and save the world, and in the final analysis, every human being will be judged by Christ.

> "For God so loved the world, that he gave his only Son, that whoever believes in him should not perish but have eternal life." (Jn.3:16)

> "I told you that you would die in your sins, for unless you believe that I am he you will die in your sins." (Jn.8:24)

> "The one who rejects me and does not receive my words has a judge; the word that I have spoken will judge him on the last day." (Jn.12:48)

> Take care, brothers, lest there be in any of you an evil, unbelieving heart, leading you to fall away from the living God. (He.3:12)

**THOUGHT 1.** We are often called upon to take a stand for Christ. It is our duty. Yet how many of us fear ridicule, abuse, and rejection, and end up evading our responsibility? We take the same course of action Pilate took, the cowardly way out.

> Be watchful, stand firm in the faith, act like men, be strong. (1 Co.16:13)

> You then, my child, be strengthened by the grace that is in Christ Jesus. (2 Ti.2:1)

> Only let your manner of life be worthy of the gospel of Christ, so that whether I come and see you or am absent, I may hear of you that you are standing firm in one spirit, with one mind striving side by side for the faith of the gospel, and not frightened in anything by your opponents. This is a clear sign to them of their destruction, but of your salvation, and that from God. (Ph.1:27-28)

> Say to those who have an anxious heart, "Be strong; fear not! Behold, your God will come with vengeance, with the recompense of God. He will come and save you." (Is.35:4)

**THOUGHT 2.** Religionists—people who adhere strictly to their religion—reject Jesus because they do not want to hear Him; they do not want anything to do with His requirements for following Him. The only Lord they want is *themselves*.

> "For this people's heart has grown dull, and with their ears they can barely hear, and their eyes they have closed; lest they should see with their eyes and hear with their ears and understand with their heart and turn, and I would heal them." (Ac.28:27)

> You adulterous people! Do you not know that friendship with the world is enmity with God? Therefore whoever wishes to be a friend of the world makes himself an enemy of God. (Js.4:4)

## DEEPER STUDY # 2

(18:31-32) **Jesus Christ's Death:** the Jews had to force the Romans to crucify Jesus, for the Jews were not allowed to execute a criminal on the Sabbath or on feast days. From God's perspective, it had been prophesied that Christ was to be crucified, and crucifixion was the method of execution used by the Romans. Therefore, events had to be providentially shifted so there could be a Roman execution by crucifixion (see Lu.9:22-23; Jn.3:14; 8:28; 12:32).

# 3 Movement 2: Pilate went to Jesus—to hear His defense.

The second movement of Pilate was back to his palace in order to hear Jesus' defense. The Roman governor's scornful question revealed his contempt for Jesus. With a sneering tone in his voice, Pilate asked Jesus if He were the King of the Jews (v.33).

Jesus challenged Pilate to think through the issue himself (v.34). It was his responsibility to judge independently about Jesus, not to simply take the word of Jesus' accusers. In judging Jesus, every person is responsible for his or her own verdict.

Pilate's reaction reflected His contempt for the Jews (v.35). "Am I a Jew?" he snapped at Jesus, noting that the Lord's own people had brought the charges against Him.

Jesus replied that His kingdom is not of this world (v.36); that is, it is not of the physical dimension of being. It is of heaven, of the spiritual dimension of being (see DEEPER STUDY # 3—Mt.19:23-24; note—Jn.11:25-27, pt.2).

> For the kingdom of God is not a matter of eating and drinking but of righteousness and peace and joy in the Holy Spirit. (Ro.14:17)
>
> But of the Son he says, "Your throne, O God, is forever and ever, the scepter of uprightness is the scepter of your kingdom." (He.1:8)
>
> Then the seventh angel blew his trumpet, and there were loud voices in heaven, saying, "The kingdom of the world has become the kingdom of our Lord and of his Christ, and he shall reign forever and ever." (Re.11:15)

18:33-38a

³³ So Pilate entered his headquarters again and called Jesus and said to him, "Are you the King of the Jews?" ³⁴ Jesus answered, "Do you say this of your own accord, or did others say it to you about me?" ³⁵ Pilate answered, "Am I a Jew? Your own nation and the chief priests have delivered you over to me. What have you done?" ³⁶ Jesus answered, "My kingdom is not of this world. If my kingdom were of this world, my servants would have been fighting, that I might not be delivered over to the Jews. But my kingdom is not from the world." ³⁷ Then Pilate said to him, "So you are a king?" Jesus answered, "You say that I am a king. For this purpose I was born and for this purpose I have come into the world—to bear witness to the truth. Everyone who is of the truth listens to my voice." ³⁸ Pilate said to him, "What is truth?" After he had said this, he went back outside to the Jews and told them, "I find no guilt in him."

Baffled by Jesus' reply, Pilate asked the Lord directly if He were a king (v.37). Jesus acknowledged that He was a king. To be king (the King of Kings) was the purpose of His birth. However, His kingdom was not a political kingdom; it was a kingdom of truth (see DEEPER STUDY # 3). Jesus then made a subtle appeal to Pilate to believe in Him, saying that everyone who is of the truth hears His voice—heeds His words.

Seemingly sincere, Pilate proceeded to ask the age-old question, "What is truth?" (v.38a). Tragically, he didn't give Jesus the opportunity to answer. Instead, he briskly walked away, away from the One who *is* the Truth (Jn.14:6). In walking away from Jesus, Pilate was rejecting the "truth that alone could bring eternal life.[1]

**THOUGHT 1.** Every individual is personally responsible for his or her verdict about Jesus. Everyone *now* has to make a choice, for Jesus claims to be the Son of God, the only Savior of the world. We have to give our verdict: He either *is* or *is not* the King.

> He came to his own, and his own people did not receive him. But to all who did receive him, who believed in his name, he gave the right to become children of God. (Jn.1:11-12)
>
> He said to them, "But who do you say that I am?" (Mt.16:15)
>
> ... Jesus asked them a question, saying, "What do you think about the Christ? Whose son is he?" They said to him, "The son of David." (Mt.22:41-42)

**THOUGHT 2.** People usually choose to follow the person of power and fame and wealth over the person of love and morality and peace. Just take a moment and think how true this is. The immoral emphasis of films and the violent emphasis of the news alone are prime examples. Is there any wonder mankind has never known a world of love and peace and true justice? The problem is the human heart, the problem which Jesus alone can solve.

---

1 Ralph W. Harris and Stanley M. Horton, eds., *The Complete Biblical Library, New Testament (Matthew-John and Harmony)* (Tulsa, OK: Harrison House Publishers), via Wordsearch digital edition.

"But what comes out of the mouth proceeds from the heart, and this defiles a person. For out of the heart come evil thoughts, murder, adultery, sexual immorality, theft, false witness, slander." (Mt.15:18-19)

"The good person out of the good treasure of his heart produces good, and the evil person out of his evil treasure produces evil, for out of the abundance of the heart his mouth speaks." (Lu.6:45)

"I have come in my Father's name, and you do not receive me. If another comes in his own name, you will receive him. How can you believe, when you receive glory from one another and do not seek the glory that comes from the only God?" (Jn.5:43-44)

For with the heart one believes and is justified, and with the mouth one confesses and is saved. (Ro.10:10)

Keep your heart with all vigilance, for from it flow the springs of life. (Pr.4:23)

### DEEPER STUDY # 3

(18:37) **Jesus Christ's Claims:** Our Savior made several claims here.
 1. His birth was a means to an end—to be King (Mt.2:2; Jn.1:49; 1 Co.15:25).
 2. He did preexist—He came out of heaven from the very presence of God (see DEEPER STUDY # 1—Jn.1:1-5; note—1:1-2).
 3. He was the truth—absolute reality (Jn.14:6).
 4. He revealed the truth (Jn.14:9-11).
 5. He was heard by those of the truth (Jn.8:45-47).

## 18:38b-40

³⁸ Pilate said to him, "What is truth?" After he had said this, he went back outside to the Jews and told them, "I find no guilt in him.
³⁹ "But you have a custom that I should release one man for you at the Passover. So do you want me to release to you the King of the Jews?"
⁴⁰ They cried out again, "Not this man, but Barabbas!" Now Barabbas was a robber.

### 4 Movement 3: Pilate went back to the people—to declare Jesus' innocence.

Pilate's third movement was back to the people (v.38b). He wished to clear Jesus' name and to declare His innocence. Pilate hoped to satisfy the Jews' cry for blood by substituting a real criminal and revolutionary for Jesus, but the Jewish leaders were determined to murder Jesus. Therefore, they chose a man of the world—a thief—over the Man of peace, the Son of God Himself (vv.39-40).

**THOUGHT 1.** The mob's choosing of Barabbas over Jesus is a picture of people choosing other things over Jesus. People choose the path of power and fame, wealth and possessions. They reject the path of peace if it means the sacrifice of self and their belongings. Therefore, they never know peace—not personal peace or world peace. The only path to peace is to surrender to the Prince of Peace.

Therefore, since we have been justified by faith, we have peace with God through our Lord Jesus Christ. (Ro.5:1)

For he himself is our peace, who has made us both one and has broken down in his flesh the dividing wall of hostility (Ep.2:14)

And through him to reconcile to himself all things, whether on earth or in heaven, making peace by the blood of his cross. (Col.1:20)

"There is no peace," says the LORD, "for the wicked." (Is.48:22)

The way of peace they do not know, and there is no justice in their paths; they have made their roads crooked; no one who treads on them knows peace. (Is.59:8)

**THOUGHT 2.** Note how the people (the world) rejected Pilate's offer of a substitute for Jesus. God twisted the world's choice and made His Son the *substitute* for every human being, even for those who were rejecting Him in this horrible scene.

> But God shows his love for us in that while we were still sinners, Christ died for us. (Ro.5:8)
>
> For Christ also suffered once for sins, the righteous for the unrighteous, that he might bring us to God, being put to death in the flesh but made alive in the spirit. (1 Pe.3:18)

## 5 Movement 4: Pilate went back to Jesus—to scourge, flog Him.

19:1-3

Then Pilate took Jesus and flogged him. ² And the soldiers twisted together a crown of thorns and put it on his head and arrayed him in a purple robe. ³ They came up to him, saying, "Hail, King of the Jews!" and struck him with their hands.

Pilate's fourth movement was back to Jesus. In an attempt to appease the Jews, he had Jesus flogged or scourged (v.1; Lk.23:16; Ps.129:3; see DEEPER STUDY # 4). The soldiers wove a crown of thorns and slammed it into His scalp. They clothed the Savior in a purple robe—the color of royalty—and mocked Him heartlessly. They hailed Jesus as the King of the Jews while slapping His face (v.3).

This very same treatment is heaped upon Jesus by people of every generation. People persecute and attack, crudely mock and scoff at His name, His person, and His Word. They curse, abuse, ridicule, imprison, kill, and heap mistreatment upon His followers.

> "Blessed are you when others revile you and persecute you and utter all kinds of evil against you falsely on my account." (Mt.5:11)
>
> "Beware of men, for they will deliver you over to courts and flog you in their synagogues." (Mt.10:17)
>
> "Remember the word that I said to you: 'A servant is not greater than his master.' If they persecuted me, they will also persecute you. If they kept my word, they will also keep yours." (Jn.15:20)
>
> "They will put you out of the synagogues. Indeed, the hour is coming when whoever kills you will think he is offering service to God." (Jn.16:2)

Some of the people in this angry crowd had heard Jesus teach and had cheered His miracles. Some had no doubt waved palm branches and celebrated when He entered Jerusalem just a few days earlier. They are like so many today who profess to know and follow Christ; but when out in the world, they live as the world. They live hypocritical lives; their professed obedience to Christ a sham.

> And he said to them, "Well did Isaiah prophesy of you hypocrites, as it is written, 'This people honors me with their lips, but their heart is far from me.'" (Mk.7:6)
>
> They profess to know God, but they deny him by their works. They are detestable, disobedient, unfit for any good work. (Tit.1:16)

### DEEPER STUDY # 4

(19:1) **Flogging or Scourging:** Jesus was stripped and beaten with a whip. This was a savage, excruciating punishment. The whip was made of leather straps with two small balls attached to the end of each strap. The balls were made of rough lead or sharp bones or spikes so that they would cut deeply into the flesh. Jesus' hands were tied to a post above His head, and He was scourged. It was the Roman custom for the prisoner to be lashed by the presiding centurion until He was near death. (Jewish trials allowed only forty lashes; De.25:3) The criminal's back was, of course, nothing more than an unrecognizable mass of mutilated flesh.

## 6 Movement 5: Pilate went back to the people again—to offer a compromise.

**19:4-7**

⁴ Pilate went out again and said to them, "See, I am bringing him out to you that you may know that I find no guilt in him."
⁵ So Jesus came out, wearing the crown of thorns and the purple robe. Pilate said to them, "Behold the man!"
⁶ When the chief priests and the officers saw him, they cried out, "Crucify him, crucify him!" Pilate said to them, "Take him yourselves and crucify him, for I find no guilt in him."
⁷ The Jews answered him, "We have a law, and according to that law he ought to die because he has made himself the Son of God."

In Pilate's fifth movement, he shifted back again to the people. He brought out the beaten and bloodied Jesus and presented Him to the vicious throng (vv.4-5). By doing so, he was offering the Jews a compromise. He was hoping the crowd would pity Jesus when they saw Him so beaten, battered, and bloodied. He hoped the scourging would serve as a compromise and appease them. He reduced the holy Son of God to a mangled, grotesque spectacle intended to satisfy the twisted appetite of a bloodthirsty mob.

However, the savage crowd's thirst was not quenched (v.6a). Led by their chief priests and temple officials, the ferocious mob spewed out their hatred for Jesus loudly and harshly. Their cry: "Crucify Him, crucify Him!" A merciless beating was not enough for them; they wanted Jesus executed in the cruelest, most excruciating way known.

At this point, Pilate was still adamant in his refusal to kill Jesus (v.6b). He issued the mob an impossible dare, telling them to crucify Jesus themselves (see DEEPER STUDY # 5).

Pilate may not have understood Jesus, but he at least knew Jesus had committed no crimes worthy of death. Remember that this situation was as much a battle between the Roman government and the Jewish people as it was a contest for Jesus' life. Pilate's response was angry and sarcastic. It demonstrated his contempt for the crowd of Jews.

The vicious mob appealed Pilate's decision by demanding that Jesus be judged according to Jewish—rather than Roman—law. They made a truthful charge: by *their* law, Jesus deserved capital punishment, for He had blasphemed the name of the Lord by claiming to be the Son of God (see DEEPER STUDY # 6).

**THOUGHT 1.** Compromise is not the way with Jesus. Pilate needed to declare Him innocent, for He was innocent. He was not guilty of any wrongdoing. Every person needs to declare Jesus innocent, for He was completely free of sin. He was the Son of Man Himself who stands before the world as its Savior (see note—Jn.1:51).

Note the truthful charge of the Jews: "He made Himself the Son of God" (v.7). Jesus did claim to be the Son of God (see note—Jn.1:34).

"Whoever is not with me is against me, and whoever does not gather with me scatters." (Lu.11:23)

"That all may honor the Son, just as they honor the Father. Whoever does not honor the Son does not honor the Father who sent him." (Jn.5:23)

"I call heaven and earth to witness against you today, that I have set before you life and death, blessing and curse. Therefore choose life, that you and your offspring may live." (De.30:19)

### DEEPER STUDY # 5

(19:6) **The Jews and Capital Punishment:** Under the laws of the Roman conquerors,' the Jewish authorities had no right to administer capital punishment to their subjects. Only Roman figures like Pilate had such authority.

### DEEPER STUDY # 6

(19:7) **Capital Punishment:** see Le.24:16 for the Mosaic law concerning capital punishment.

## 7  Movement 6: Pilate went back to Jesus again—to investigate the possibility of a supernatural being.

18:28–19:15

When Pilate heard that Jesus had claimed to be God's Son, he was even more afraid (v.8). History tells us that Pilate was an extremely superstitious man. When Jesus claimed to be the Son of God, he thought Jesus was claiming to be the son of *a god*. The picture in his mind was that of a half-god and half-man, a god-like being that filled the popular literature and beliefs of that day. The possibility of his condemning a god struck fear in Pilate, so he went back to Jesus to investigate the possibility of a supernatural being. He questioned Jesus' origin, but Jesus did not answer him (v.9).

Pilate was angered by Jesus' silence (v.10). He appealed to his earthly authority, reminding Jesus that His life was in his hands.

Jesus answered the Roman governor with a powerful revelation: there is a superior, higher authority than human government. Pilate's authority had been given to him from above, from the God who instituted human government (v.11). Ultimately, power is not in the hands of earthly authorities. It is in the hands of God. Pilate would answer to God for how he had mistreated Jesus. However, while Pilate was guilty before God, those who had delivered Jesus to him—Judas and the Jewish religious leaders—bore the greater responsibility.

> 19:8–11
>
> ⁸ When Pilate heard this statement, he was even more afraid.
> ⁹ He entered his headquarters again and said to Jesus, "Where are you from?" But Jesus gave him no answer.
> ¹⁰ So Pilate said to him, "You will not speak to me? Do you not know that I have authority to release you and authority to crucify you?"
> ¹¹ Jesus answered him, "You would have no authority over me at all unless it had been given you from above. Therefore he who delivered me over to you has the greater sin."

> Let every person be subject to the governing authorities. For there is no authority except from God, and those that exist have been instituted by God. (Ro.13:1)

**THOUGHT 1.** Like Pilate, many today are superstitious. People must not fear (revere) the astrological charts and fortune signs and evil powers of this world. All of these things are an abomination to God. He is the only true power in the universe. What people must fear is Him who can destroy both body and soul in hell (Mt.10:28). There is only one Truth, and that is Jesus Christ Himself.

> But there was a man named Simon, who had previously practiced magic in the city and amazed the people of Samaria, saying that he himself was somebody great. They all paid attention to him, from the least to the greatest, saying, "This man is the power of God that is called Great." And they paid attention to him because for a long time he had amazed them with his magic. (Ac.8:9-11)

> But Elymas the magician (for that is the meaning of his name) opposed them, seeking to turn the proconsul away from the faith. But Saul, who was also called Paul, filled with the Holy Spirit, looked intently at him and said, "You son of the devil, you enemy of all righteousness, full of all deceit and villainy, will you not stop making crooked the straight paths of the Lord?" (Ac.13:8-10)

> "But as for the cowardly, the faithless, the detestable, as for murderers, the sexually immoral, sorcerers, idolaters, and all liars, their portion will be in the lake that burns with fire and sulfur, which is the second death." (Re.21:8)

> "There shall not be found among you anyone who burns his son or his daughter as an offering, anyone who practices divination or tells fortunes or interprets omens, or a sorcerer or a charmer or a medium or a necromancer [one who calls up the dead] or one who inquires of the dead, for whoever does these things is an abomination to the LORD. And because of these abominations the LORD your God is driving them out before you." (De.18:10-12)

> So do not listen to your prophets, your diviners, your dreamers, your fortune-tellers, or your sorcerers, who are saying to you, 'You shall not serve the king of Babylon.' (Je.27:9)

## 8 Movement 7: Pilate went back to the people again—to release Jesus.

Pilate's seventh movement was back again to the people. For the third time, he tried to release Jesus. Note that Pilate had to make a decision, choosing either Jesus or Caesar (the world). When the Jews cried out that he would not be Caesar's friend if he released Jesus, Pilate faced a serious problem: the Jews were blackmailing him. They were threatening to send a report to Caesar (see Deeper Study # 1—Jn.18:28). He was now forced to choose, and he did. Tragically, he chose the world and its way.

**19:12**

¹² From then on Pilate sought to release him, but the Jews cried out, "If you release this man, you are not Caesar's friend. Everyone who makes himself a king opposes Caesar."

> **Thought 1.** Everyone has to make a decision about Jesus. Jesus Christ is unquestionably the Son of God; therefore, we choose either Him or this world.
>
> "Whoever believes in him is not condemned, but whoever does not believe is condemned already, because he has not believed in the name of the only Son of God." (Jn.3:18)
>
> "I told you that you would die in your sins, for unless you believe that I am he you will die in your sins." (Jn.8:24)

**19:13-15**

¹³ So when Pilate heard these words, he brought Jesus out and sat down on the judgment seat at a place called The Stone Pavement, and in Aramaic Gabbatha.
¹⁴ Now it was the day of Preparation of the Passover. It was about the sixth hour. He said to the Jews, "Behold your King!"
¹⁵ They cried out, "Away with him, away with him, crucify him!" Pilate said to them, "Shall I crucify your King?" The chief priests answered, "We have no king but Caesar."

## 9 Movement 8: Pilate went to the judgment seat before all—to give the verdict of crucifixion.

Pilate's eighth movement was to the judgment seat, where he stood before all. In the end, he gave the verdict of crucifixion (v.16).

Pilate made a fatal choice. He feared Caesar more than he feared God. Note that he proclaimed the truth, saying to the Jews, "Behold your King" (v.14). But he said this in ignorance and mockery. Pilate feared . . .

- losing the people's favor
- causing problems for himself
- losing his position and security (see Deeper Study # 1—Jn.18:28)

> "I tell you, my friends, do not fear those who kill the body, and after that have nothing more that they can do. But I will warn you whom to fear: fear him who, after he has killed, has authority to cast into hell. Yes, I tell you, fear him!" (Lu.12:4-5)
>
> "'You shall not be partial in judgment. You shall hear the small and the great alike. You shall not be intimidated by anyone, for the judgment is God's. And the case that is too hard for you, you shall bring to me, and I will hear it.'" (De.1:17)
>
> The fear of man lays a snare, but whoever trusts in the Lord is safe. (Pr.29:25)
>
> "I, I am he who comforts you; who are you that you are afraid of man who dies, of the son of man who is made like grass." (Is.51:12)

The Jews' also made a fatal choice. In frenzied madness, they ferociously demanded that Jesus be crucified (v.15a). They, too, chose the world, the way of Caesar. This was a shocking choice, for God had supposedly been the God of the Jews for centuries. He was said to be the sovereign Lord of their nation (Jud.8:23; 1 S.8:7; 12:12). But now, at this very moment, they were rejecting and repudiating God as their sovereign Lord. They were choosing Caesar and the way of the world—the world's . . .

- security
- position
- power
- acceptance
- livelihood
- honor
- selfishness
- friendship
- religion

Pilate responded to their cries with the bitter question, "Shall I crucify your King?" The bloodthirsty Jews declared that their only king was Caesar—not the Son of God, their Messiah (v.15b). They had made the fatal choice.

**THOUGHT 1.** Millions today continue to make the fatal choice: the world over Jesus, unbelief over faith, death over life, turmoil over peace, despair over hope, hell over heaven.

> "But his citizens hated him and sent a delegation after him, saying, 'We do not want this man to reign over us.'" (Lu.19:14)
>
> He came to his own, and his own people did not receive him. (Jn.1:11)
>
> "The one who rejects me and does not receive my words has a judge; the word that I have spoken will judge him on the last day." (Jn.12:48)
>
> Do not love the world or the things in the world. If anyone loves the world, the love of the Father is not in him. For all that is in the world—the desires of the flesh and the desires of the eyes and pride of life—is not from the Father but is from the world. (1 Jn.2:15-16)

## D. The Crucifixion: The Major Events at the Cross, 19:16–37

*Mt.27:26-56; Mk.15:16-41; Lu.23:26-49*

1. **Event 1: Jesus bearing His cross—willingly "went out"**
   a. Pilate delivered Jesus to the soldiers
   b. Jesus went forth, bore the cross
   c. Jesus was the majestic victor, not the victim

2. **Event 2: Jesus being crucified between two sinners—the preeminent sacrifice**

3. **Event 3: The title on the cross**
   a. Pilate made an ironic announcement, Jn.18:36-37
   b. The people were indifferent to the title
   c. The religionists objected to the title
   d. Pilate sarcastically insisted the title stand

4. **Event 4: The soldiers gambling for His clothes**
   a. The insensitive men: Jesus' mother was standing by yet was not given His clothes
   b. The seamless garment: Was the same as the high priest's (mediator's) garment
   c. The fulfillment of Scripture
   d. An eyewitness verification: John saw the event

5. **Event 5: Jesus' great love for His mother**
   a. There were women at the cross

16 So he delivered him over to them to be crucified.

17 and he went out, bearing his own cross, to the place called The Place of a Skull, which in Aramaic is called Golgotha.

18 There they crucified him, and with him two others, one on either side, and Jesus between them.

19 Pilate also wrote an inscription and put it on the cross. It read, "Jesus of Nazareth, the King of the Jews."

20 Many of the Jews read this inscription, for the place where Jesus was crucified was near the city, and it was written in Aramaic, in Latin, and in Greek.

21 So the chief priests of the Jews said to Pilate, "Do not write, 'The King of the Jews,' but rather, 'This man said, I am King of the Jews.'"

22 Pilate answered, "What I have written I have written."

23 When the soldiers had crucified Jesus, they took his garments and divided them into four parts, one part for each soldier; also his tunic. But the tunic was seamless, woven in one piece from top to bottom,

24 so they said to one another, "Let us not tear it, but cast lots for it to see whose it shall be." This was to fulfill the Scripture which says, "They divided my garments among them, and for my clothing they cast lots." So the soldiers did these things,

25 but standing by the cross of Jesus were his mother and his mother's sister, Mary the wife of Clopas, and Mary Magdalene.

²⁶ When Jesus saw his mother and the disciple whom he loved standing nearby, he said to his mother, "Woman, behold, your son!"

²⁷ Then he said to the disciple, "Behold, your mother!" And from that hour the disciple took her to his own home.

²⁸ After this, Jesus, knowing that all was now finished, said (to fulfill the Scripture), "I thirst."

²⁹ A jar full of sour wine stood there, so they put a sponge full of the sour wine on a hyssop branch and held it to his mouth.

³⁰ When Jesus had received the sour wine, he said, "It is finished," and he bowed his head and gave up his spirit.

³¹ Since it was the day of Preparation, and so that the bodies would not remain on the cross on the Sabbath (for that Sabbath was a high day), the Jews asked Pilate that their legs might be broken and that they might be taken away.

³² So the soldiers came and broke the legs of the first, and of the other who had been crucified with him.

³³ But when they came to Jesus and saw that he was already dead, they did not break his legs.

³⁴ But one of the soldiers pierced his side with a spear, and at once there came out blood and water.

³⁵ He who saw it has borne witness—his testimony is true, and he knows that he is telling the truth—that you also may believe.

³⁶ For these things took place that the Scripture might be fulfilled: "Not one of his bones will be broken."

³⁷ And again another Scripture says, "They will look on him whom they have pierced."

b. Jesus saw His mother

c. Jesus demonstrated responsibility: Discharged His duty to look after His mother to John

6. **Event 6: Jesus' agonizing thirst & His deliberate effort to fulfill Scripture**
   a. Knew His purpose was achieved
   b. Was exhausted & thirsty
   c. Was given hyssop: An act recalling the Passover

7. **Event 7: Jesus' great shout of victory—salvation & reconciliation**

8. **Event 8: The spear being thrust into His side**
   a. A religious request: Concern for insignificant matters, see 18:28
   b. A brutal custom: Smashing the victim's legs to cause an earlier death
   c. A strange fact: Jesus was already dead—far sooner than most
   d. A proof of death: A soldier thrust a spear in Jesus' side—blood & water flowed out
   e. An insistence upon the accuracy of the account
      1) Purpose 1: To stir belief
      2) Purpose 2: To fulfill Scripture

# Division XV

## The Revelation of Jesus, the Suffering Savior, 18:1–19:42

### D. The Crucifixion: The Major Events at the Cross, 19:16–37

*Mt.27:26–56; Mk.15:16–41; Lu.23:26–49*

## 19:16–37
## Introduction

The most significant event in history is the crucifixion of Jesus Christ. John was an eyewitness of the crucifixion, and in this passage, he gives us his inspired account of history's darkest day. As in the previous section, the outline sufficiently conveys the details of the passage, so the commentary will not discuss each subpoint.

We are saved by Christ's death; because He died, we live. However, there is a condition. We must believe, and it is the necessity for belief that John stressed. He closed his heart-wrenching account of the Savior's crucifixion by stating his purpose for writing his testimony of what he personally witnessed that day: *"that you also may believe"* (Jn.19:35). This is, *The Crucifixion: The Major Events at the Cross,* 19:16–37.

1. Event 1: Jesus bearing His cross—willingly "went out" (vv.16–17).
2. Event 2: Jesus being crucified between two sinners—the preeminent sacrifice (v.18).
3. Event 3: The title on the cross (vv.19–22).
4. Event 4: The soldiers gambling for His clothes (vv.23–24).
5. Event 5: Jesus' great love for His mother (vv.25–27).
6. Event 6: Jesus' agonizing thirst and His deliberate effort to fulfill Scripture (vv.28–29).
7. Event 7: Jesus' great shout of victory—salvation and reconciliation (v.30).
8. Event 8: The spear being thrust into His side (vv.31–37).

(19:16–37) **Another Outline**: The Crucifixion—the Picture of Jesus Symbolized.

1. Picture 1: Jesus—the Victor (vv.16–17).
2. Picture 2: Jesus—the Preeminent Sacrifice (v.18).
3. Picture 3: Jesus—the Proclaimed King (vv.19–22).
4. Picture 4: Jesus—the High Priest, the Mediator (vv.23–24).
5. Picture 5: Jesus—the Responsible Son of Man (vv.25–27).
6. Picture 6: Jesus—the Passover Lamb (vv.28–29).
7. Picture 7: Jesus—the Triumphant Messiah (v.30).
8. Picture 8: Jesus—the Lord of the Sacraments, of the Church (vv.31–37).

### 19:16–17

¹⁶ So he delivered him over to them to be crucified.
¹⁷ and he went out, bearing his own cross, to the place called The Place of a Skull, which in Aramaic is called Golgotha.

### 1 Event 1: Jesus bearing His cross—willingly "went out."

The first event John recorded was that of Jesus bearing His cross. Note that He *willingly* "went out":

➢ Pilate delivered Him (16a).
➢ The soldiers took and led Him (v.16b).
➢ It was Jesus, however, who *bore* the cross and *went out* (v.17).

Jesus Christ was the *majestic victor*, not the victim. He was bearing the cross and going forth to Golgotha for a specific purpose—to save the world (see notes—Jn.10:17-18, pt.2; 12:27-30).

> "And as Moses lifted up the serpent in the wilderness, so must the Son of Man be lifted up, that whoever believes in him may have eternal life." (Jn.3:14-15)

> "I am the good shepherd. The good shepherd lays down his life for the sheep." (Jn.10:11)

> "Just as the Father knows me and I know the Father; and I lay down my life for the sheep." (Jn.10:15)

## 2 Event 2: Jesus being crucified between two sinners—the preeminent sacrifice.

The second event John recorded was Jesus being crucified between two sinners, two unjust thieves. This is a clear picture of two truths regarding Christ's atonement for our sins. First, it is a picture of the preeminence of His sacrifice. He was surrounded by a world of unjust people—symbolized by the two thieves—yet He was dying for them.

> He himself bore our sins in his body on the tree, that we might die to sin and live to righteousness. By his wounds you have been healed. (1 Pe.2:24)

> For Christ also suffered once for sins, the righteous for the unrighteous, that he might bring us to God, being put to death in the flesh but made alive in the spirit. (1 Pe.3:18)

[19:18]

> ¹⁸ There they crucified him, and with him two others, one on either side, and Jesus between them.

Second, it is a picture of preeminent guilt. Jesus Christ was being counted as the King of Sinners.

> For our sake he made him to be sin who knew no sin, so that in him we might become the righteousness of God. (2 Co.5:21)

> All we like sheep have gone astray; we have turned—every one—to his own way; and the LORD has laid on him the iniquity of us all. (Is.53:6)

## 3 Event 3: The title on the cross.

[19:19-22]

The third event John noted was Pilate writing the title on the cross. Pilate made an ironic announcement: He hung a sign on Jesus' cross identifying Him as "the King of the Jews" (v.19; 18:36-37).

The people read the title but were indifferent to it (v.20). It had no effect on them. There was no mass movement of sorrow and repentance, no final acceptance of Christ.

On the other hand, due to their obstinate unbelief, the religious leaders objected to the title (v.21). However, they did not demand that it be removed. In a display of spitefulness typical for them, they instead demanded that the wording be changed to read "*This man said, 'I am the King of the Jews.'*" Pilate refused to give in to their demands and curtly stated that the writing on the sign would not be changed (v.22).

Note two relevant facts:

> ¹⁹ Pilate also wrote an inscription and put it on the cross. It read, "Jesus of Nazareth, the King of the Jews."
> ²⁰ Many of the Jews read this inscription, for the place where Jesus was crucified was near the city, and it was written in Aramaic, in Latin, and in Greek.
> ²¹ So the chief priests of the Jews said to Pilate, "Do not write, 'The King of the Jews,' but rather, 'This man said, I am King of the Jews.'"
> ²² Pilate answered, "What I have written I have written."

➢ Jesus indeed claimed to be the "King of the Jews," the promised Messiah.
➢ The title "King of the Jews" mounted upon Christ's cross was written in the three great languages of the world. This providentially symbolized Christ's rightful rule as King of the Universe.

> And being found in human form, he humbled himself by becoming obedient to the point of death, even death on a cross. Therefore God has highly exalted him and bestowed on him the name that is above every name, so that at the name of Jesus every knee should bow, in heaven and on earth and under the earth, and every tongue confess that Jesus Christ is Lord, to the glory of God the Father. (Ph.2:8-11)

> To keep the commandment unstained and free from reproach until the appearing of our Lord Jesus Christ, which he will display at the proper time—he who is the blessed and only Sovereign, the King of kings and Lord of lords, who alone has immortality, who dwells in unapproachable light, whom no one has ever seen or can see. To him be honor and eternal dominion. Amen. (1 Ti.6:14-16)

## 4 Event 4: The soldiers gambling for His clothes.

19:23-24

The fourth event of the cross was the soldiers gambling for Jesus' clothes. These insensitive, worldly-minded men were void of compassion. Jesus' mother Mary was standing by the cross (v.25), yet the soldiers showed no compassion whatsoever by sharing His belongings with her. (see Ps.22:28).

²³ When the soldiers had crucified Jesus, they took his garments and divided them into four parts, one part for each soldier; also his tunic. But the tunic was seamless, woven in one piece from top to bottom,
²⁴ so they said to one another, "Let us not tear it, but cast lots for it to see whose it shall be." This was to fulfill the Scripture which says, "They divided my garments among them, and for my clothing they cast lots." So the soldiers did these things,

"For what does it profit a man to gain the whole world and forfeit his soul?" (Mk.8:36)

John notes specifically that Christ's tunic was seamless—one piece of cloth, woven from the top to the bottom (v.23). The coat or robe was identical to the robe of the high priest. It symbolized Christ, the *Mediator*, the Pontifex, which in Latin means the *bridge-builder* between God and humanity (see note—Jn.12:44; see also Ps.22:18.)

This event fulfilled Scripture (v.24; Ps.22:18). God was in charge of the cross, for it was the fulfillment of His purpose, of His great plan of salvation for mankind.

For there is one God, and there is one mediator between God and men, the man Christ Jesus, who gave himself as a ransom for all, which is the testimony given at the proper time. (1 Ti.2:5-6)

Therefore he is the mediator of a new covenant, so that those who are called may receive the promised eternal inheritance, since a death has occurred that redeems them from the transgressions committed under the first covenant. (He.9:15)

For Christ has entered, not into holy places made with hands . . . but into heaven itself, now to appear in the presence of God on our behalf. (He.9:24)

## 5 Event 5: Jesus' great love for His mother.

19:25-27

The fifth event John reported was Jesus' great love for His mother. John mentioned two touching scenes. First, he named the women at the cross (v.25). They were there at great risk. Jesus was a revolutionary in the eyes of Rome and a heretic in the eyes of the religious leaders. Therefore, any supporter of Jesus who stood at the cross ran the risk of ridicule and arrest. Nevertheless, the women stood there. Why? They loved Jesus. There is no other explanation: they simply loved Him. He had done so much for them that they were willing to stand by Him no matter the cost.

²⁵ but standing by the cross of Jesus were his mother and his mother's sister, Mary the wife of Clopas, and Mary Magdalene.
²⁶ When Jesus saw his mother and the disciple whom he loved standing nearby, he said to his mother, "Woman, behold, your son!"
²⁷ Then he said to the disciple, "Behold, your mother!" And from that hour the disciple took her to his own home.

And he said to all, "If anyone would come after me, let him deny himself and take up his cross daily and follow me." (Lu.9:23)

For the love of Christ controls us, because we have concluded this: that one has died for all, therefore all have died; and he died for all, that those who live might no longer live for themselves but for him who for their sake died and was raised. (2 Co.5:14-15)

Therefore let us go to him outside the camp and bear the reproach he endured. (He.13:13)

The second touching scene is Jesus' *care* of His mother (vv.26-27). From the cross, Jesus saw His mother standing there with John, and He demonstrated responsibility for her. He discharged His duty to look after His mother to His dear friend, John.

As Jesus suffered on the cross, His thoughts were on others, not on Himself. Every fiber of His being existed for others. Even in death, His mind and being were set on taking care of others.

➢ He was touched with the feelings of Mary's hurt and pain. In the last moments of His life on earth, He made arrangements for her care.
➢ He is touched with the feeling of our hurt and pain, so He takes care of us.

For we do not have a high priest who is unable to sympathize with our weaknesses, but one who in every respect has been tempted as we are, yet without sin. Let us then with confidence draw near to the throne of grace, that we may receive mercy and find grace to help in time of need. (He.4:15-16)

# 6 Event 6: Jesus' agonizing thirst and His deliberate effort to fulfill Scripture.

The sixth event of the cross was Jesus' agonizing thirst and deliberate effort to fulfill Scripture. Just before Jesus died, He said that He was thirsty (v.28). It had been hours since He had taken a drink of water. But Jesus did not make this statement because He was physically thirsty, even though He was exhausted, totally dehydrated, and parched. He was not complaining of thirst, not even asking for a drink. His conscious concern and purpose for saying He was thirsty was the fulfilling of Scripture (Ps.69:21) . . .

**19:28-29**

[28] After this, Jesus, knowing that all was now finished, said (to fulfill the Scripture), "I thirst."
[29] A jar full of sour wine stood there, so they put a sponge full of the sour wine on a hyssop branch and held it to his mouth.

- to show that Jesus *was truly* the Promised Messiah, the One who fulfilled Scripture
- to show that Jesus' mind was *set on* fulfilling the Scriptures of the promised Messiah
- to show that Jesus had come as the Promised Messiah to do the will of God, dying as the sacrifice for the human race. He refused to do God's will unthoughtfully, even with deadened senses and a semi-conscious mind. He had work to do in sacrificing His life for the world: He was to taste death for all people, and He would taste it in full consciousness, being as mentally alert as possible

> "This Jesus, delivered up according to the definite plan and foreknowledge of God, you crucified and killed by the hands of lawless men." (Ac.2:23)

> But we see him who for a little while was made lower than the angels, namely Jesus, crowned with glory and honor because of the suffering of death, so that by the grace of God he might taste death for everyone. (He.2:9)

> "In burnt offerings and sin offerings you have taken no pleasure. Then I said, 'Behold, I have come to do your will, O God, as it is written of me in the scroll of the book.'" . . . And by that will we have been sanctified through the offering of the body of Jesus Christ once for all. (He.10:6-7, 10)

Just as David had prophesied a thousand years earlier, they gave Jesus vinegar or sour wine to drink (v.29). They hoisted the vinegar-filled sponge on a hyssop branch, an act recalling the Passover:

> "Take a bunch of hyssop and dip it in the blood that is in the basin, and touch the lintel and the two doorposts with the blood that is in the basin. None of you shall go out of the door of his house until the morning." (Ex.12:22)

# 7 Event 7: Jesus' great shout of victory—salvation and reconciliation.

The seventh event John chronicled was Jesus' great shout of victory. Salvation and reconciliation were now possible for every human being.

**19:30**

[30] When Jesus had received the sour wine, he said, "It is finished," and he bowed his head and gave up his spirit.

Immediately before Jesus died, He cried, "It is finished." The Greek word translated *finished* (tetelestai) is the shout of victorious purpose. Jesus had completed His work, His mission, and His task. His was not the cry of a defeated martyr. It was the cry of a victorious conqueror.

Jesus then bowed His head and *gave up* (paredoken)—voluntarily released or surrendered—His spirit (Lu.23:46; Ps.31:5). It must always be remembered that Jesus *willingly* died. He willingly came to this moment of yielding and giving up His spirit unto death. Both Paul and Peter cover the Lord's work during the three days immediately following His death until the resurrection.

➢ Paul says that on the cross this happened:

> He disarmed the rulers and authorities and put them to open shame, by triumphing over them [upon the cross] in him. (Col.2:15; see also Ep.6:12)

➢ Peter says that on the cross and after death this happened:

> For Christ also suffered once for sins, the righteous for the unrighteous, that he might bring us to God, being put to death in the flesh but made alive in the spirit, in which he went and proclaimed to the spirits in prison, because they formerly did not obey, when God's patience waited

in the days of Noah, while the ark was being prepared, in which a few, that is, eight persons, were brought safely through water. (1 Pe.3:18-20; see note—1 Pe.3:18-22; DEEPER STUDY # 1—3:19-20)

➤ Paul says that after death this happened:

Therefore it says, "When he ascended on high he led a host of captives, and he gave gifts to men." (In saying, "He ascended," what does it mean but that he had also descended into the lower regions, the earth? He who descended is the one who also ascended far above all the heavens, that he might fill all things.) (Ep.4:8-10; see note—Ep.4:8-10)

## 19:31-37

## 8 Event 8: The spear being thrust into His side.

³¹ Since it was the day of Preparation, and so that the bodies would not remain on the cross on the Sabbath (for that Sabbath was a high day), the Jews asked Pilate that their legs might be broken and that they might be taken away.

³² So the soldiers came and broke the legs of the first, and of the other who had been crucified with him.

³³ But when they came to Jesus and saw that he was already dead, they did not break his legs.

³⁴ But one of the soldiers pierced his side with a spear, and at once there came out blood and water.

³⁵ He who saw it has borne witness—his testimony is true, and he knows that he is telling the truth—that you also may believe.

³⁶ For these things took place that the Scripture might be fulfilled: "Not one of his bones will be broken."

³⁷ And again another Scripture says, "They will look on him whom they have pierced."

The eighth event of the cross was that of the spear being thrust into Jesus' side. This occurred as the result of a legalistic request from the Jewish religious leaders (v.31; 18:28). The religionists' concern for trifles was somewhat shocking. Religious ceremony and ritual consumed their minds and actually became more important than a man's suffering. But not so with Christ: He was hanging there because He was concerned for mankind. He felt sympathy for human suffering, so now He had given His life for all people.

For surely it is not angels that he helps, but he helps the offspring of Abraham [the flesh of man]. Therefore he had to be made like his brothers in every respect, so that he might become a merciful and faithful high priest in the service of God, to make propitiation for the sins of the people. For because he himself has suffered when tempted, he is able to help those who are being tempted. (He.2:16-18)

The Romans granted the Jews' gruesome request (v.32). They carried out a brutal custom: smashing the victims' legs to cause an earlier death. With their legs broken, those being crucified could not raise themselves to draw a breath. Consequently, they suffocated.

But when the soldiers came to Jesus, they discovered a strange thing: He was already dead (v.33). To prove that He was dead, one of the soldiers thrust a spear into Jesus' side, and blood and water flowed out of the body of God's Son (v.34).

Christ died prematurely, much sooner than a man usually died from crucifixion. One of the reasons Rome chose crucifixion as the State's method of execution was its slow, tortuous death. By law, the criminal was to hang on the cross until he died from thirst, hunger, and exposure. Sometimes a man lingered for days under the heat of the broiling sun or the trembling cold of the winter nights. Such suffering struck fear into the hearts of the captured populace and restrained severe crime. Because Jesus died so quickly, He probably died (physically and medically speaking) from the pressure of a broken heart and of being separated from God in behalf of mankind (1 Pe.2:24; 3:18). Apparently, His heart burst, and the blood mingled with the water—the fluid of the pericardium surrounding the heart. The spear pierced the pericardium, causing the blood and water to flow. Perhaps John stressed this incident because he saw the symbol of the two ordinances pictured: baptism and the Lord's Supper.

➤ The water symbolized baptism, which is the outward picture of the washing of regeneration which Jesus was to bring.

But when the goodness and loving kindness of God our Savior appeared, he saved us, not because of works done by us in righteousness, but according to his own mercy, by the washing of regeneration and renewal of the Holy Spirit. (Tit.3:4-5)

➤ The blood symbolized the Lord's Supper, which provides a picture of the blood of Christ which cleanses us of our sins.

But if we walk in the light, as he is in the light, we have fellowship with one another, and the blood of Jesus his Son cleanses us from all sin. (1 Jn.1:7)

John closed his account of the Savior's crucifixion by insisting on its accuracy (v.35). He declared emphatically that He personally witnessed the events He described, and his testimony was impeccably true. He wanted everyone who read his account to know that he was telling the truth. Why was this stressed? John told us: he stressed his truthfulness that "you may believe" (see Deeper Study # 2—Jn.2:24).

Note another point. John suggested we are without excuse if we fail to believe. Why? Because the crucifixion and its events were a fulfillment of Scripture. (See vv.36-37; see also Ex.12:46; Nu.9:12. Psalm 34:20 predicts that not a bone of His body would be broken. See Zec.12:10, which predicts the spear. Also see Is.53, which predicts so much of the crucifixion.) This was John's second purpose for so dogmatically insisting on the accuracy of his account.

> **But these are written so that you may believe that Jesus is the Christ, the Son of God, and that by believing you may have life in his name. (Jn.20:31)**

## E. The Burial: The Conquest of Fear, 19:38-42

*Mt.27:57-66; Mk.15:42-47; Lu.23:50-56*

1. Jesus' death conquered fear in a secret disciple: Joseph of Arimathea
   a. He had feared the Jews
   b. He was now changed by Jesus' death: He boldly requested the body
2. Jesus' death conquered fear in a cowardly disciple: Nicodemus
   a. He had come to Jesus at night
   b. He was now changed: Helped in the burial
3. Jesus' death stirred open commitment
   a. They openly took the body
   b. They openly cared for the body
   c. They openly gave the best
      1) A new tomb, never before used
      2) A tomb close to Calvary
   d. They openly buried Jesus—just before the Sabbath

38 After these things Joseph of Arimathea, who was a disciple of Jesus, but secretly for fear of the Jews, asked Pilate that he might take away the body of Jesus, and Pilate gave him permission. So he came and took away his body.

39 Nicodemus also, who earlier had come to Jesus by night, came bringing a mixture of myrrh and aloes, about seventy-five pounds in weight.

40 So they took the body of Jesus and bound it in linen cloths with the spices, as is the burial custom of the Jews.

41 Now in the place where he was crucified there was a garden, and in the garden a new tomb in which no one had yet been laid.

42 So because of the Jewish day of Preparation, since the tomb was close at hand, they laid Jesus there.

## Division XV

### *The Revelation of Jesus, the Suffering Savior, 18:1-19:42*

E. The Burial: The Conquest of Fear, 19:38-42

*Mt.27:57-66; Mk.15:42-47; Lu.23:50-56*

## 19:38-42
## Introduction

Jesus' death empowers every genuine believer to conquer fear. This passage highlights the two men who claimed and buried the body of our crucified Lord. They both had believed in Jesus, but they were afraid to publicly confess their faith—like many people today. But all of that changed when they saw the Son of God selflessly lay down His life for the sins of the world.

We should read the Gospel accounts of Christ's death frequently, for if we too stay near the cross, our fears of standing for Christ will be destroyed. We will be bold witnesses for our Savior and Lord. This is, *The Burial: The Conquest of Fear,* 19:38-42.

1. Jesus' death conquered fear in a secret disciple: Joseph of Arimathea (v.38).
2. Jesus' death conquered fear in a cowardly disciple: Nicodemus (v.39).
3. Jesus' death stirred open commitment (vv.40-42).

## 1 Jesus' death conquered fear in a secret disciple: Joseph of Arimathea. 19:38-42

Watching Jesus die strengthened a secret disciple, Joseph of Arimathea, to conquer his fear of being identified with Christ. Scripture presents a revealing picture of Joseph.

19:38

### a. He had feared the Jews.

Joseph was a counselor, a senator, a member of the Sanhedrin, which was the ruling body of Israel. He was apparently...
- highly educated
- highly esteemed
- well liked
- very responsible
- capable of leadership

³⁸ After these things Joseph of Arimathea, who was a disciple of Jesus, but secretly for fear of the Jews, asked Pilate that he might take away the body of Jesus, and Pilate gave him permission. So he came and took away his body.

Scripture also reports that Joseph was a good, just (righteous), and prominent or respected man (Mk.15:43; Lk.23:50). He was a man of...
- good character
- high morals
- compassion
- justice
- decision
- truth
- law

In addition, Joseph was a man looking for the Messiah and the Kingdom of God, and he believed that Jesus was the Messiah (see notes—Lu.2:25-27; DEEPER STUDY # 3—Mt.19:23-24). He was, however, a man who feared to stand up for Jesus. John said he *secretly* followed Jesus because of his fear for the Jews. Joseph probably had met Jesus and arranged meetings with Him when the Lord had visited Jerusalem, but he feared making a public profession. His position and prestige were at stake. His peers, the other rulers, opposed Jesus. He believed in Jesus, but out of fear he kept his discipleship a secret. Note: when the vote was taken to put Jesus to death, Joseph did not agree with the decision, but it appears that he came short of standing openly for Christ (Lu.23:51).

**THOUGHT 1.** How many are as Joseph was? They are good and just people. They are believers in Christ. But they fear what their friends and fellow workers will say. They fear the loss of position, prestige, promotion, acceptance, popularity, friends, job, income, livelihood. Therefore, they do not take an open stand for Christ.

> "For whoever is ashamed of me and of my words, of him will the Son of Man be ashamed when he comes in his glory and the glory of the Father and of the holy angels." (Lu.9:26)

> "I tell you, my friends, do not fear those who kill the body, and after that have nothing more that they can do. But I will warn you whom to fear: fear him who, after he has killed, has authority to cast into hell. Yes, I tell you, fear him!" (Lu.12:4-5)

> For God gave us a spirit not of fear but of power and love and self-control. (2 Ti.1:7)

> The fear of man lays a snare, but whoever trusts in the LORD is safe. (Pr.29:25)

> "I, I am he who comforts you; who are you that you are afraid of man who dies, of the son of man who is made like grass." (Is.51:12)

### b. He was now changed by Jesus' death: He boldly requested the body.

The death of Jesus changed Joseph from a fearful man to a bold believer. When Jesus died, Joseph actually went to Pilate and asked for the Savior's body. This was a tremendous act of courage. The Romans either dumped the bodies of crucified criminals in the trash heaps or left the bodies hanging on the cross for the vultures and animals to consume. The latter served as an example of criminal punishment to the public. Joseph also braved the threat of Pilate's reaction. Pilate was fed up with the *Jesus matter*. Jesus had proven to be very bothersome to him. He could have reacted severely against Joseph.

By caring about Jesus' body, Joseph risked the disfavor and discipline of the Sanhedrin. They were the ruling body who had instigated and condemned Jesus, and Joseph was a member of the council. There was no question, he would face some harsh reaction from some of his fellow Sanhedrin members and from some of his closest friends.

The factor that turned Joseph from being a secret disciple to a bold disciple seems to be the phenomenal events surrounding the cross (the behavior and words of Jesus, the darkness, the earthquake, the torn veil). When Joseph witnessed all this, his mind connected the claims of Jesus with the Old Testament prophecies of the Messiah. Apparently Joseph saw the prophecies fulfilled in Jesus; therefore, he stepped forward, braving all risks while taking his stand for Jesus. A remarkable courage stirred by the death of Jesus!

**THOUGHT 1.** Every secret believer needs to study the cross of Christ. Really seeing the cross will turn any secret believer into a bold witness for Christ.

> For I am not ashamed of the gospel, for it is the power of God for salvation to everyone who believes, to the Jew first and also to the Greek. (Ro.1:16)
>
> But far be it from me to boast except in the cross of our Lord Jesus Christ, by which the world has been crucified to me, and I to the world. (Ga.6:14)
>
> As it is my eager expectation and hope that I will not be at all ashamed, but that with full courage now as always Christ will be honored in my body, whether by life or by death. (Ph.1:20)

**THOUGHT 2.** Joseph courageously asked to take care of the physical body of Christ. Today, the body of Christ is the church. We are to boldly step forward and take care of the church. There are times within the church when special needs demand that we be courageous and step forward to show care. In those times a fresh look at the cross will be helpful and can be used of God to stir us.

> For I decided to know nothing among you except Jesus Christ and him crucified. (1 Co.2:2)
>
> Knowing that he who raised the Lord Jesus will raise us also with Jesus and bring us with you into his presence. For it is all for your sake, so that as grace extends to more and more people it may increase thanksgiving, to the glory of God. (2 Co.4:14-15)
>
> And he died for all, that those who live might no longer live for themselves but for him who for their sake died and was raised. (2 Co.5:15)

In the end, Joseph proved that he was a man who cared deeply for Jesus. The words and acts of these two verses express care and tenderness and love and affection as well as courage and boldness. Joseph . . .

- took the body down from the cross
- wrapped the body in linen
- laid the body in a tomb wherein no person had ever been laid
- acted quickly, before the Sabbath began. Jesus died at 3 p.m. Friday afternoon (see Mk.15:33-34, 37). Friday was the day of preparation for the Sabbath. Work was forbidden on the Sabbath, so if anything was to be done with Jesus' body, it had to be done immediately. Only three hours remained for work (see note—Mk.15:42 for more discussion).

This act alone would leave no doubt about the effect of the cross on Joseph. The cross changed his life. He was no longer a secret believer; he now demonstrated a public stand for Jesus.

**THOUGHT 3.** Position, power, wealth, fame—none of these make us bold for Christ. Only true affection for Christ will make us bold, and only as we see the cross of Christ will affection for Christ be stirred.

> "And you shall love the Lord your God with all your heart and with all your soul and with all your mind and with all your strength." (Mk.12:30)
>
> We love because he first loved us. (1 Jn.4:19)
>
> "But I have this against you, that you have abandoned the love you had at first." (Re.2:4)

**THOUGHT 4.** Christ identified with the human race perfectly.
- He lived as a man, but perfectly.
- He died as a man, but perfectly (as the Ideal Man).
- He was buried as a man, but perfectly.

> Therefore he had to be made like his brothers in every respect, so that he might become a merciful and faithful high priest in the service of God, to make propitiation for the sins of the people. (He.2:17)

> And they made his grave with the wicked and with a rich man in his death, although he had done no violence, and there was no deceit in his mouth. (Is.53:9)

**THOUGHT 5.** God's own Son possessed nothing when He was on earth. Note two truths:
- Christ is the Savior of the poorest. He was born in a stable, and throughout His life He had no place of His own to lay His head (Mt.8:20; Lu.9:58). Even His tomb was a borrowed tomb.
- The rich, nonetheless, can serve Him just as Joseph of Arimathea did.

> And Jesus said to him, "Foxes have holes, and birds of the air have nests, but the Son of Man has nowhere to lay his head." (Lu.9:58)

> "Sell your possessions, and give to the needy. Provide yourselves with moneybags that do not grow old, with a treasure in the heavens that does not fail, where no thief approaches and no moth destroys." (Lu.12:33)

> "In all things I have shown you that by working hard in this way we must help the weak and remember the words of the Lord Jesus, how he himself said, 'It is more blessed to give than to receive.'" (Ac.20:35)

> For you know the grace of our Lord Jesus Christ, that though he was rich, yet for your sake he became poor, so that you by his poverty might become rich. (2 Co.8:9)

> By this we know love, that he laid down his life for us, and we ought to lay down our lives for the brothers. (1 Jn.3:16)

## 2 Jesus' death conquered fear on a cowardly disciple: Nicodemus.

Along with Joseph of Arimathea, Christ's death empowered Nicodemus to stand boldly for Christ. Most likely, Nicodemus had believed in Christ to some degree prior to His crucifixion. But up to this point, he had been afraid to be publicly identified with the Lord.

> ³⁹ Nicodemus also, who earlier had come to Jesus by night, came bringing a mixture of myrrh and aloes, about seventy-five pounds in weight.

### a. He had come to Jesus at night.

Nicodemus was the religious leader who came to Jesus in the dark of night (see note—Jn.3:1-2 for discussion of Nicodemus). He was probably the *Master Teacher*, the leading teacher of all Israel. Holding such a high position in the nation, he feared the leaders of Israel who opposed Jesus. The same fear that was in Joseph was in him: his position, authority, livelihood, and security were at stake. Consequently, he kept quiet, refusing to openly confess and take a stand for Jesus.

### b. He was now changed: he helped in the burial.

However, the cross apparently changed Nicodemus just as it had changed Joseph. Being the *Master Teacher* of Israel, Nicodemus, above everyone else, knew the prophetic Scriptures. Apparently, the events of the cross stirred him to begin making connections between the prophecies and Jesus' death. He had already been making connections between the prophecies and the words and works of Jesus. He did not fully understand, but the thoughts that were connecting Jesus and the prophecies would not leave his mind. At some point Nicodemus, although understanding little, knew at least that Jesus was the Messiah. Nicodemus had failed the Lord when He was alive, but he would not fail Jesus in His death. Perhaps not understanding the movement of his own heart toward Jesus, he boldly and courageously stepped forward to proclaim that He now believed and wanted all to know it. He walked into the stores that sold spices and bought huge amounts, the poundage fit for a king. The spices weighed about seventy pounds, an amount that only royalty could afford and use. Nicodemus wished to give the honor to his Lord that he should have given when his Lord was alive. Once proud and worldly, this man who had chosen the world over the Lord was now a broken man. Broken in heart over his Lord's death, he would now step forth in faith and love to do what he could.

While the fulfilling of Scripture throughout Christ's crucifixion was convincing, another factor undoubtedly compelled both Joseph and Nicodemus to step out of the shadows and unashamedly demonstrate their devotion to Christ: the unexplainable, illogical love the Savior displayed on the cross. Seeing Christ's willingness to submit to such a brutal execution because of His love for the world, along with the compassion He displayed for others while suffering surely stirred positive changes in these men. The immeasurable love of Christ conquered their fears, and their love for Christ burst out of their liberated spirits as they witnessed the gruesome execution of the selfless Son of God.

**THOUGHT 1.** By purchasing the spices for the Lord's body and helping in the burial of Jesus, Nicodemus took his stand for Christ. From that point on, everyone knew he loved Jesus. What a living example of courage for us as we move about the business establishments of the world!

> **But they kept silent, for on the way they had argued with one another about who was the greatest. And he sat down and called the twelve. And he said to them, "If anyone would be first, he must be last of all and servant of all." And he took a child and put him in the midst of them, and taking him in his arms, he said to them, "Whoever receives one such child in my name receives me, and whoever receives me, receives not me but him who sent me." (Mk.9:34-37)**

## 19:40-42

⁴⁰ So they took the body of Jesus and bound it in linen cloths with the spices, as is the burial custom of the Jews.
⁴¹ Now in the place where he was crucified there was a garden, and in the garden a new tomb in which no one had yet been laid.
⁴² So because of the Jewish day of Preparation, since the tomb was close at hand, they laid Jesus there.

### 3 Jesus' death stirred open commitment.

Jesus' death stirred open and unashamed commitment from these men. Both Joseph and Nicodemus had hesitated in confessing Jesus Christ openly as their Savior. Out of fear they had acted cowardly, keeping their thoughts about Jesus to themselves. But now they showed a courage and a boldness unmatched by all others. They demonstrated an open, unashamed commitment to Jesus, and they did it during a time when the apostles themselves deserted Jesus.

a. They openly took the body (v.40a).
Joseph and Nicodemus openly took the body of Jesus from the cross. In doing so, they risked the disfavor of the Sanhedrin who had instigated and condemned Jesus. Both men were opposing their fellow members of the council. There was no question that they would face a harsh reaction from some of their fellow Sanhedrin members and from some of their closest friends.

b. They openly cared for the body (v.40b).
Joseph and Nicodemus openly cared for Jesus' body. They wrapped the mangled, holy body of the Savior in linen clothes with the spices.

c. They openly gave the best (v.41).
Joseph and Nicodemus openly gave Jesus the best burial possible. They gave Him a new tomb, one never before used. Apparently it was close to Mount Calvary, the mountain where Jesus was crucified. The tomb had been bought by Joseph for his own use (Mt.27:60). This act alone would leave no question about the two men taking their stand for Jesus.

### d. They openly buried Jesus—just before the Sabbath (v.42).

Joseph and Nicodemus publicly buried Jesus just before the Sabbath (see Deeper Study # 1). This eliminated them from taking part in the great Passover Feast, and this was never done, even for the most serious reasons. Joseph and Nicodemus, by handling Jesus' body, were considered defiled for seven days for having come in contact with a corpse. Once defiled, Jewish law forbade a person from taking part in Jewish ceremonies.

Simply stated, Joseph and Nicodemus, who had been secret disciples, now stepped forward to make an unashamed commitment to Jesus. Everyone would know that they stepped forward and took care of Jesus' body. Joseph even gave his own tomb to Jesus. They were risking their positions, esteem, wealth, and even their lives by making such a pronounced commitment to the affairs of Jesus.

Note the strength of their commitment: no one from Jesus' family or from among His own disciples had stepped forward to claim the Lord's body—but these two men did.

**THOUGHT 1.** The courage demonstrated by Joseph and Nicodemus is desperately needed by all.
(1) The courage to make an unashamed commitment to Christ.
(2) The courage to risk all for Christ, even if it does cost us our position, esteem, wealth, and life.
(3) The courage to unashamedly care for the body of Christ, His church and its affairs.
(4) The courage to be an unashamed witness for Christ, no matter the cost.

> "So everyone who acknowledges me before men, I also will acknowledge before my Father who is in heaven, but whoever denies me before men, I also will deny before my Father who is in heaven." (Mt.10:32-33)
>
> "And I tell you, everyone who acknowledges me before men, the Son of Man also will acknowledge before the angels of God." (Lu.12:8)
>
> Because, if you confess with your mouth that Jesus is Lord and believe in your heart that God raised him from the dead, you will be saved. For with the heart one believes and is justified, and with the mouth one confesses and is saved. (Ro.10:9-10)
>
> If we endure, we will also reign with him; if we deny him, he also will deny us. (2 Ti.2:12)
>
> No one who denies the Son has the Father. Whoever confesses the Son has the Father also. (1 Jn.2:23)
>
> Whoever confesses that Jesus is the Son of God, God abides in him, and he in God. (1 Jn.4:15)

## Deeper Study # 1

(19:42) **Sabbath—Jesus Christ, Burial**: the need for haste in burying Jesus was urgent.

1. The Sabbath or Saturday, the day of worship for Jews, actually began at 6 p.m. on Friday. (Jewish days began at 6 p.m. and ran until 6 p.m. the next night, that is, from sundown to sundown.) Strict Jewish law said that once the Sabbath began, no work could be done, including the burial of the dead.

2. Jesus died at 3 p.m. on Friday, shortly before the Sabbath was about to begin (see Mk.15:33-34, 37). Therefore He died on the day of preparation for the Sabbath. If anything was to be done with Jesus' body, it had to be done immediately and quickly. Only three hours remained for work.

3. The Romans either dumped the bodies of crucified criminals in the trash heaps or left the bodies hanging on the cross for the vultures and animals to consume. The latter served as an example of criminal punishment to the public. If Jesus' body were not removed quickly, within these three hours, the fate of His body was set. The Romans would not care what happened to Him, and no Jew could remove Him until the Sabbath was over.

# Chapter 20

## XVI. The Revelation of Jesus, the Risen Lord, 20:1–21:25

### A. Event 1: The Great Discovery— the Empty Tomb, 20:1–10

1. **Mary's unquestioning discovery: The unsealed tomb**[DS1]
   a. She visited early
   b. She saw the stone rolled back
   c. She ran to Peter
   d. She revealed an unquestioning love: "They have taken the Lord"

2. **Peter & John's shocking discovery: The wrappings were lying undisturbed**

   a. They ran to the tomb

   b. John glanced in: Saw the linen wrappings lying undisturbed

   c. Peter entered
      1) He saw the linen wrapping lying undisturbed—as if Christ's body had evaporated
      2) He saw the head wrapping still folded

3. **John's thoughtful discovery**
   a. He saw the linen undisturbed, in its body-like fold
   b. He believed immediately
   c. He finally understood the Scripture: Until then, the disciples had not understood

Now on the first day of the week Mary Magdalene came to the tomb early, while it was still dark, and saw that the stone had been taken away from the tomb. ² So she ran and went to Simon Peter and the other disciple, the one whom Jesus loved, and said to them, "They have taken the Lord out of the tomb, and we do not know where they have laid him."

³ So Peter went out with the other disciple, and they were going toward the tomb.

⁴ Both of them were running together, but the other disciple outran Peter and reached the tomb first.

⁵ And stooping to look in, he saw the linen cloths lying there, but he did not go in.

⁶ Then Simon Peter came, following him, and went into the tomb. He saw the linen cloths lying there,

⁷ and the face cloth, which had been on Jesus' head, not lying with the linen cloths but folded up in a place by itself.

⁸ Then the other disciple, who had reached the tomb first, also went in, and he saw and believed;

⁹ for as yet they did not understand the Scripture, that he must rise from the dead.

¹⁰ Then the disciples went back to their homes.

# Division XVI

*The Revelation of Jesus, the Risen Lord, 20:1-21:25*

A. Event 1: The Great Discovery—the Empty Tomb, 20:1-10

## 20:1-10
## Introduction

In studying John's account of the resurrection, it must be remembered that John was writing an historical record. He was not interested in giving insurmountable evidence for the resurrection. His interest was twofold: (1) to give the evidence that led him to immediately understand and believe, and (2) to give enough evidence to lead anyone to immediate belief—if a person is willing to believe. He was interested in giving enough evidence to make anyone's faith viable and respectable. Having said this, John's record of Jesus' resurrection is a strong historical account of the event. To an honest, objective, and pure heart, the evidence is convincing (Lu.8:15). Note four compelling evidences of John's account.

First, the fact that morality is the point of John's Gospel eliminates any possibility of his fabricating a lie, especially a lie of such immoral proportions.

Second, the description of so many minor details, details that are so human, testifies that the phenomenal event is an event that actually took place. Such human-like details could never be built around an event whose main point was a fable. For instance, Peter and John's running and John's outrunning Peter; Mary's human response of frantic bewilderment; the young author's fearing and hesitating to enter a tomb; the author's believing without physical fact and admitting that his belief was not based on an understanding of Scripture. There are, of course, many other examples that point to the event actually taking place.

Third, the head wrapping is strong evidence for the resurrection. Only the head piece is actually said to be still in its fold. The other pieces are assumed to be still in their fold because of the phrase "not lying with the linen cloths" (v.7). Although the phrase substantially supports the assumption, it is only an assumption. The point is this: if John or any other author were fabricating a case for such a phenomenal event as the resurrection, He would state explicitly that the body wrappings along with the head wrappings were still in their fold—building evidence upon evidence.

Fourth, the changed lives of the Lord's disciples are indisputable evidence. It is psychological evidence. From seemingly *irreversible despondency* and from *being hunted down* like insurrectionist dogs, they became new creatures of enthusiasm and motivation. They were propelled by a dynamic power and bold courage. Within thirty days they were seen proclaiming a risen Christ from the very spot where their lives were being threatened. They were preaching to the very people who were seeking to arrest and execute them. Only one thing could cause them to adopt this strategy: the Lord had indeed risen, and He had implanted within them a dynamic new power never before experienced by mankind.

In discussing evidences, we must remember that God *through inspiration* has not formulated the Scripture to prove anything. God proclaims in Scripture that He *is* (exists), that He is love, and that He has shown His love supremely by sending His own Son to save a lost and dying world. What God wants from us is love and belief, love for the Lord Jesus and belief in the supreme power of a loving God. This is exactly the point of the resurrection account. We are to believe because we love even as Mary and John loved (see note 2—Mt.28:1; Jn.20:7-10; see He.11:6; 1 Jn.3:23). This is, *Event 1: The Great Discovery—the Empty Tomb,* 20:1-10.

1. Mary's unquestioning discovery: The unsealed tomb (vv.1-2).
2. Peter and John's shocking discovery: The wrappings were lying undisturbed (vv.3-7).
3. John's thoughtful discovery (vv.7-10).

## 1 Mary's unquestioning discovery: The unsealed tomb.

20:1-2

Even though Jesus was dead, Mary Magdalene was still devoted to Him. Out of love for her Lord, she went to visit His tomb immediately after the Sabbath had ended. Upon arriving, she discovered that the tomb's seal had been removed; the stone was rolled away from the door.

Now on the first day of the week Mary Magdalene came to the tomb early, while it was still dark, and saw that the stone had been taken away from the tomb.
² So she ran and went to Simon Peter and the other disciple, the one whom Jesus loved, and said to them, "They have taken the Lord out of the tomb, and we do not know where they have laid him."

**a. She visited early (v.1a).**

Mary visited the tomb early when it was still dark. Matthew actually says it was after or at the end of the sabbath, meaning between 3-6 a.m. (Mt.28:1). This reveals three significant facts.

First, Jesus arose before dawn, before the sun rose on Sunday morning. This was significant to the early Christian believers, so significant that they broke away from the common division of the week which began with the Sabbath or Saturday. They began to count their days beginning with Sunday, the day of their Lord's resurrection (see Ac.20:7; 1 Co.16:2).

Second, Jesus arose on the first day of the week, on Sunday morning. This means that He had been in the grave for three days just as He had said (Mt.12:40; 16:21; 17:23; 20:19; Mk.9:31; 10:34; Lu.9:22; 18:33; 24:7, 46). His arising from the dead was a triumph, a conquest over death. Death reigns no more. Its rule has been broken (1 Co.15:55-56; 2 Co.1:9-10; 2 Ti.1:10; He.2:9, 14-15).

Third, again—Jesus arose on the first day of the week, Sunday morning. He was in the grave on the Sabbath, unable to observe the laws governing the great season of the Passover and the Sabbath. He was dead to the law and its observances. This is symbolic of the *identification* believers gain in Christ. *In Christ's death* believers become dead to the law (see note—Ro.7:4; Mt.5:17-18).

**b. She saw the stone rolled back (v.1b).**

Mary saw the stone rolled back from the tomb (see Deeper Study # 1). This is strong evidence for the resurrection. The stone was not rolled back for the benefit of Christ, but for the witnesses to the resurrection. When Christ arose, He was in His resurrection body, the spiritual body of the spiritual dimension which has no physical bounds. He did not need the stone rolled back to leave the tomb, for material substance has no bearing on spiritual substance. However, the witnesses needed to enter the tomb to see the truth (see outline and notes—Jn.10:1-10).

**c. She ran to Peter (v.2a).**

Upon seeing that the stone had been removed, Mary ran to Peter. This is important, for it shows that Peter was still the accepted leader of Christ's followers. What a man of courageous stature and moral strength! Surely his cowardice had been broadcast and well-rumored, yet he repented and picked himself up to resume his task.

**d. She revealed an unquestioning love: "They have taken the Lord" (v.2b).**

Mary revealed an unquestioning love for Jesus. Her statement expressed both her continued devotion to Him and her continued submission to Him as her Lord. Mary is a supreme example of one who loves and believes, although she did not understand. She was one of the last to leave Jesus at the cross (see Mk.15:40, 47); one of the first to attend the tomb; and one who still called Him "Lord." Her belief was a belief of love—not a belief based merely on intellect or understanding. She knew what Jesus had done for her, and she loved Him for it. Jesus was her Lord, dead or alive (see Jn.20:13f).

> "As the Father has loved me, so have I loved you. Abide in my love." (Jn.15:9)

> Jesus said to him, "Have you believed because you have seen me? Blessed are those who have not seen and yet have believed." (Jn.20:29)

*Grace be with all who love our Lord Jesus Christ with love incorruptible. (Ep.6:24)*

*Though you have not seen him, you love him. Though you do not now see him, you believe in him and rejoice with joy that is inexpressible and filled with glory. (1 Pe.1:8)*

*Keep yourselves in the love of God, waiting for the mercy of our Lord Jesus Christ that leads to eternal life. (Jude 21)*

*"You shall love the LORD your God with all your heart and with all your soul and with all your might." (De.6:5)*

## DEEPER STUDY # 1

(20:1) **Tomb:** In Jesus' day tombs were closed by rolling a huge cartwheel-like stone in front of the entrance. They were almost impossible to remove. A deep slanting groove was hewn out of the rock at the base of the entrance for the circular stone to rest in. The stone usually weighed several tons. Such precautions were essential, because there were so many tombs ransacked in those days of widespread poverty.

The tomb was further secured by being sealed. When it was necessary to seal a tomb, the huge stone was cemented to the entrance walls or else some type of rope or binding was wrapped around the entrance stone and fastened to both sides of the tomb. Then the binding was cemented with a hardening clay or wax-like substance. In the case of some burials, usually political figures, the seal of the Emperor was also attached to the walls of the entrance. This was to strike fear of Roman retaliation against any intruder (see Mt.27:66).

In the case of Jesus' tomb, further precautions were taken by placing a patrol to guard against any foul play. This guard consisted of a *large number* of men (Mt.28:4, 11f).

## 2 Peter and John's shocking discovery: The wrappings were lying undisturbed.

20:3-7

Upon receiving the news from Mary that Jesus' body was missing, Peter and John instantly dashed to the tomb. When they arrived, they were shocked by what they discovered: the cloths that had wrapped Jesus' body were lying in the tomb undisturbed!

³ So Peter went out with the other disciple, and they were going toward the tomb.

⁴ Both of them were running together, but the other disciple outran Peter and reached the tomb first.

⁵ And stooping to look in, he saw the linen cloths lying there, but he did not go in.

⁶ Then Simon Peter came, following him, and went into the tomb. He saw the linen cloths lying there,

⁷ and the face cloth, which had been on Jesus' head, not lying with the linen cloths but folded up in a place by itself.

a. They ran to the tomb (vv.3-4).

Without delay, Peter and John "went out" to the tomb (v.3). John outran Peter and arrived at the tomb first (v.4). Imagine the mixture of emotions that surely overwhelmed these two men who were closest to Jesus. Their souls must have been flooded with a combination of panic, fear, responsibility, anxiety, and curiosity.

b. John glanced in: Saw the linen wrappings lying undisturbed (v.5).

When John arrived at the tomb, he just glanced in and noticed the linen clothes. He carefully recorded the fact that he merely stooped down to peer in; he did not actually go into the tomb.

c. Peter entered (vv.6-7).

Peter, on the other hand, actually entered the tomb (v.6). He noticed the linen cloths and the head wrapping, which was folded and set to the side (v.7). Jesus' graveclothes were lying undisturbed, as if His body had evaporated! They both knew the significance. If the body had been removed by the authorities or stolen by someone, the linen clothes would have been taken with the body or left in a disheveled mess, thrown someplace on the floor. From the description and the impact of the event upon the two disciples, neither one discussed his thoughts with the other, not while standing there at that time.

**THOUGHT 1.** Note a critical point. If a person wishes to discover the empty tomb, they must get up and "go out" to look at it (v.3). They must investigate, and then they will see. Getting up and "going out" is the only way a person can ever discover the risen Lord. Resting in the comforts and lethargy of this world will never help anybody find Jesus.

> "You search the Scriptures because you think that in them you have eternal life; and it is they that bear witness about me." (Jn.5:39)

> Now these Jews were more noble than those in Thessalonica; they received the word with all eagerness, examining the Scriptures daily to see if these things were so. (Ac.17:11)

> For he powerfully refuted the Jews in public, showing by the Scriptures that the Christ was Jesus. (Ac.18:28)

> [The gospel] which he promised beforehand through his prophets in the holy Scriptures, concerning his Son, who was descended from David according to the flesh and was declared to be the Son of God in power according to the Spirit of holiness by his resurrection from the dead, Jesus Christ our Lord. (Ro.1:2-4)

> For I delivered to you as of first importance what I also received: that Christ died for our sins in accordance with the Scriptures, that he was buried, that he was raised on the third day in accordance with the Scriptures. (1 Co.15:3-4)

> And we desire each one of you to show the same earnestness to have the full assurance of hope until the end, so that you may not be sluggish, but imitators of those who through faith and patience inherit the promises. (He.6:11-12)

## 20:7-10

⁷ and the face cloth, which had been on Jesus' head, not lying with the linen cloths but folded up in a place by itself.
⁸ Then the other disciple, who had reached the tomb first, also went in, and he saw and believed;
⁹ for as yet they did not understand the Scripture, that he must rise from the dead.
¹⁰ Then the disciples went back to their homes.

### 3 John's thoughtful discovery.

After bold Peter entered the tomb, John followed him in. What he saw provoked him to think deeply about what must have happened, and he believed that Jesus had risen from the dead.

**a. He saw the linen undisturbed, in its body-like fold (v.7).** Standing outside while Peter was inside the tomb, John's mind was apparently whirling, pondering, wondering, and thinking. Then it suddenly dawned on him: the linen clothes were lying undisturbed. The Greek word translated *folded up, rolled up,* or *folded together* (entetuligmenon) is the verb which is used for actually winding the linens around a body for burial. The Greek word is saying that the linens were still in their fold, wrapped just like they would be wrapped around a body—as if the body had just evaporated. They were not disheveled or disarranged. This amazing detail says at least four things:

➤ It would be impossible to extract a body from its wrappings and leave them in such good order.
➤ The wrappings would have been taken with the body if the body had been removed.
➤ The wrappings would have been disheveled and disarranged if thieves had ransacked the tomb.
➤ The wrappings (under any circumstances that might be conceived in removing the body) could never be placed in the exact spot on the rock slab where the body lay. Yet, this is precisely how they were lying according to the Greek text.

**b. He believed immediately (v.8).**
Pondering what the undisturbed graveclothes meant led John to believe immediately that Jesus was alive. However, John did not believe solely because of insurmountable evidence but because he loved Jesus. Seeing the linen clothes penetrated John's mind, and he remembered Jesus' prophecy that He would arise. John realized what had happened and he believed.

This is the point of this account of the linen clothes and of the way the account is recorded. This is also the point of the resurrection account. A loving God wants love—a heart full of love.

He wants a person to simply believe that God *is* (exists) and that God is a rewarder of them that love Him (He.11:6).

c. **He finally understood the Scripture: Until then, the disciples had not understood (v.9).**
Jesus had spoken of His resurrection, but the disciples had failed to understand what He meant. John's faith opened his understanding. He had not yet seen the risen Christ, but he believed that He was alive (v.29). When he believed, his mind was enlightened by the Lord and he grasped what Jesus had taught about His resurrection.

> "For God so loved the world, that he gave his only Son, that whoever believes in him should not perish but have eternal life. For God did not send his Son into the world to condemn the world, but in order that the world might be saved through him." (Jn.3:16-17)
>
> And without faith it is impossible to please him, for whoever would draw near to God must believe that he exists and that he rewards those who seek him. (He.11:6)
>
> By this we know love, that he laid down his life for us, and we ought to lay down our lives for the brothers. (1 Jn.3:16)
>
> So we have come to know and to believe the love that God has for us. God is love, and whoever abides in love abides in God, and God abides in him. (1 Jn.4:16)
>
> We love because he first loved us. (1 Jn.4:19)

## B. Event 2: The Great Recognition—Jesus Appears to Mary, 20:11-18

*Mt.28:1-15; Mk.16:1-11; Lu.24:1-49*

1. **Mary returned to the tomb**
   a. Weeping convulsively
   b. Stooping, she looked in
2. **The first startling sight: Two angels**
   a. The question of the angels: Why are you weeping?
   b. Mary's loving devotion & confession: "My Lord" has been taken
3. **The second startling sight: Jesus Himself**
   a. Mary's sense of another person—turned to see
   b. A startling question: Why weep? Who are you seeking?
   c. A false identity
      1) Because of her tears
      2) Because she faced in the wrong direction—into the grave
   d. The great recognition
4. **The third startling sight: A vision of the new commission from Jesus**
   a. Do not hold on to me
   b. Go—tell your great discovery

<sup>11</sup> But Mary stood weeping outside the tomb, and as she wept she stooped to look into the tomb.
<sup>12</sup> And she saw two angels in white, sitting where the body of Jesus had lain, one at the head and one at the feet.
<sup>13</sup> They said to her, "Woman, why are you weeping?" She said to them, "They have taken away my Lord, and I do not know where they have laid him."
<sup>14</sup> Having said this, she turned around and saw Jesus standing, but she did not know that it was Jesus.

<sup>15</sup> Jesus said to her, "Woman, why are you weeping? Whom are you seeking?" Supposing him to be the gardener, she said to him, "Sir, if you have carried him away, tell me where you have laid him, and I will take him away."
<sup>16</sup> Jesus said to her, "Mary." She turned and said to him in Aramaic, "Rabboni!" (which means Teacher).
<sup>17</sup> Jesus said to her, "Do not cling to me, for I have not yet ascended to the Father; but go to my brothers and say to them, 'I am ascending to my Father and your Father, to my God and your God.'"
<sup>18</sup> Mary Magdalene went and announced to the disciples, "I have seen the Lord"—and that he had said these things to her.

# Division XVI

## *The Revelation of Jesus, the Risen Lord, 20:1–21:25*

B. Event 2: The Great Recognition—Jesus Appears to Mary, 20:11-18

*Mt.28:1-15; Mk.16:1-11; Lu.24:1-49*

### 20:11-18
### Introduction

This thrilling passage presents one of the most precious events in history. It was our Lord's first appearance after His resurrection; He appeared to a woman who had been saved from the depths of human depravity. That woman was Mary Magdalene, one who loved Jesus with the deepest of loves because of what He had done for her. This is, *Event 2: The Great Recognition—Jesus Appears to Mary*, 20:11-18.

1. Mary returned to the tomb (v.11).
2. The first startling sight: Two angels (vv.12-13).
3. The second startling sight: Jesus Himself (vv.14-16).
4. The third startling sight: A vision of the new commission from Jesus (vv.17-18).

## 1 Mary returned to the tomb.

Mary returned to the tomb of Jesus. The exact time is not known, but she probably followed immediately behind Peter and John as they ran to the tomb. When they left the tomb (v.10), she remained behind. She was weeping convulsively. Seeing Peter and John enter the tomb gave her courage to finally stoop down and look in. What Mary began to experience would revolutionize her life. She could not ask for more.

> 11 But Mary stood weeping outside the tomb, and as she wept she stooped to look into the tomb.

**THOUGHT 1.** Two things can revolutionize any person's life.
(1) Lingering at the empty tomb of Jesus. Too many figuratively rush by His tomb, never thinking, never giving any thought to its meaning.
(2) Seeking the truth of the empty tomb, what it means to life and to the world in all its corruption and need.

## 2 The first startling sight: Two angels.

On that sacred Sunday morning in the garden, Mary witnessed three startling sights. The first was two angels posted at the head and foot of the slab where Jesus had lain (v.12; see DEEPER STUDY # 1).

> 12 And she saw two angels in white, sitting where the body of Jesus had lain, one at the head and one at the feet.
> 13 They said to her, "Woman, why are you weeping?" She said to them, "They have taken away my Lord, and I do not know where they have laid him."

a. The question of the angels: Why are you weeping (v.13a)?
The two angels were sitting right where Jesus' body had been lying. Angels are messengers of God; they are the ministering spirits of God, servants sent from heaven to carry out His will (see DEEPER STUDY # 1—He.1:4-14). On this particular occasion, they were sent to add to the spectacular significance of the resurrection and to comfort Mary in her grief. Hence, they asked her why she was weeping. They had been sent to her in particular, for they had not been in the tomb when Peter and John looked in. They were clothed in white. Matthew added (Mt.28:3) they were . . .

➢ like *lightning* (visible, quick, startling, striking, frightening, brilliant)
➢ like *snow* (white, pure, glistening)

The fact that they were dressed in white apparently symbolizes the holiness and purity of God from whose presence they had come.

> **Strive for peace with everyone, and for the holiness without which no one will see the Lord. (He.12:14)**
>
> **Since it is written, "You shall be holy, for I am holy." (1 Pe.1:16)**
>
> **Exalt the LORD our God, and worship at his holy mountain; for the LORD our God is holy! (Ps.99:9)**
>
> **And one called to another and said: "Holy, holy, holy is the LORD of hosts; the whole earth is full of his glory!" (Is.6:3)**
>
> **You who are of purer eyes than to see evil and cannot look at wrong, why do you idly look at traitors and remain silent when the wicked swallows up the man more righteous than he? (Hab.1:13)**

b. Mary's loving devotion and confession: "My Lord" has been taken (v.13b).
Mary's answer to the angels' question conveyed her love for and devotion to Jesus. She thought Jesus was dead, but nonetheless, He was still her "Lord." Mary's loving devotion and

earnest confession should touch the heart and life of every believer (see note, *Mary Magdalene*, pt.4—Jn.20:1-2 for discussion).

> "For the Father himself loves you, because you have loved me and have believed that I came from God." (Jn.16:27)

> Grace be with all who love our Lord Jesus Christ with love incorruptible. (Ep.6:24)

> Though you have not seen him, you love him. Though you do not now see him, you believe in him and rejoice with joy that is inexpressible and filled with glory. (1 Pe.1:8)

> "You shall love the LORD your God with all your heart and with all your soul and with all your might." (De.6:5)

## DEEPER STUDY # 1

(20:12) **Jesus Christ's Resurrection—Linen Clothes:** the two angels were sitting, one where the head of Jesus had lain and the other where his feet had lain. Now think about this question: how did Mary know where the feet and head had lain? There were two possible ways.

1. She was possibly one of the women who had followed Joseph of Arimathea and Nicodemus when they buried Jesus (Lu.23:55).

2. She could see the linen clothes lying in their fold just as they had been when they were wrapped around Jesus (see note—Jn.20:7-10).

### 20:14-16

¹⁴ Having said this, she turned around and saw Jesus standing, but she did not know that it was Jesus.

¹⁵ Jesus said to her, "Woman, why are you weeping? Whom are you seeking?" Supposing him to be the gardener, she said to him, "Sir, if you have carried him away, tell me where you have laid him, and I will take him away."

¹⁶ Jesus said to her, "Mary." She turned and said to him in Aramaic, "Rabboni!" (which means Teacher).

### 3 The second startling sight: Jesus Himself.

The second startling sight Mary saw that morning was the risen Lord Himself. Just imagining what Mary must have felt when she saw Jesus alive thrills the soul of every believer who genuinely loves Christ. Note four significant events.

a. **Mary's sense of another person—turned to see (v.14).**
While Mary was still speaking to the angels, she had a startling sense of another presence behind her. She immediately turned around and saw Jesus standing there, but she did not know that it was Jesus.

b. **A startling question: Why weep? Who are you seeking? (v.15a).**
The risen Lord asked His devoted follower a startling question: "Why are you weeping? Whom are you seeking?" Now note: a graveyard is where one weeps and visits a grave of a loved one.

The point is, Mary was seeking a dead Savior, a Savior who was as all other people are, frail and powerless to do anything about life and death, eternity and heaven. Her whole being was focused on a grave where her dead Savior had been lying. Mary was living as the world lives, as a stranger to God's promises, without hope, and without God in the world (Ep.2:12).

> But we do not want you to be uninformed, brothers, about those who are asleep, that you may not grieve as others do who have no hope. (1 Th.4:13)

> And my God. My soul is cast down within me; therefore I remember you from the land of Jordan and of Hermon, from Mount Mizar. (Ps.42:6)

> I sink in deep mire, where there is no foothold; I have come into deep waters, and the flood sweeps over me. (Ps.69:2)

> But when I thought how to understand this, it seemed to me a wearisome task. (Ps.73:16)

c. **A false identity (v.15b).**
Mary identified the man falsely. She thought He was the gardener and that perhaps He had removed the body for some reason. Note why she had not yet recognized Jesus:

- Mary's eyes were full of tears and her head was bowed low in the normal shyness that arises in such scenes.
- Mary was facing in the wrong direction—into the grave. She had turned back around to face where the body had been lying (v.14, see v.16).

**THOUGHT 1.** There is a message here for everyone. We need to fix our eyes upon Jesus in confronting death. Too often, we see the dead and become so wrapped up in grief that we forget the risen Lord and the great hope He gives us (Jn.3:16; 5:24; 14:2-3). There is no question about Jesus' emphasis here. This is the message He was wishing to convey to Mary. There was no need for such convulsive weeping. Weep and grieve, yes, but there is a limit. Mary could have and should have seen Him sooner.

> "Truly, truly, I say to you, whoever hears my word and believes him who sent me has eternal life. He does not come into judgment, but has passed from death to life." (Jn.5:24)

> When the perishable puts on the imperishable, and the mortal puts on immortality, then shall come to pass the saying that is written: "Death is swallowed up in victory." (1 Co.15:54)

> And [God's purpose and grace] which now has been manifested through the appearing of our Savior Christ Jesus, who abolished death and brought life and immortality to light through the gospel. (2 Ti.1:10)

> "He will wipe away every tear from their eyes, and death shall be no more, neither shall there be mourning, nor crying, nor pain anymore, for the former things have passed away." (Re.21:4)

> He will swallow up death forever; and the Lord GOD will wipe away tears from all faces, and the reproach of his people he will take away from all the earth, for the LORD has spoken. (Is.25:8)

d. The great recognition (v.16).

What a moment it was when Mary recognized Jesus! This was one of those dramatic moments that exceeds the ability of words to express. Only two words were spoken:
- "Mary"
- "Rabboni"

Note three thrilling truths. First, Mary recognized Jesus not by sight, but by His voice and the word spoken by Him. So it is with us today: we know the Lord by His Word and His Spirit.

> Then Pilate said to him, "So you are a king?" Jesus answered, "You say that I am a king. For this purpose I was born and for this purpose I have come into the world—to bear witness to the truth. Everyone who is of the truth listens to my voice." (Jn.18:37; see also Jn.17:17)

> But he who is joined to the Lord becomes one spirit with him. (1 Co.6:17)

> And who has also put his seal on us and given us his Spirit in our hearts as a guarantee. (2 Co.1:22; see 2 Co.5:5)

> For through him we both have access in one Spirit to the Father. (Ep.2:18; see Ep.1:13-14)

> By this we know that we abide in him and he in us, because he has given us of his Spirit. (1 Jn.4:13)

> "Behold, I stand at the door and knock. If anyone hears my voice and opens the door, I will come in to him and eat with him, and he with me." (Re.3:20)

Second, Mary recognized Jesus when He said her name. Jesus called Mary by name; she was one of His sheep. He knows His sheep by name, and His sheep know the sound of His voice (His Word).

> "When he has brought out all his own, he goes before them, and the sheep follow him, for they know his voice." (Jn.10:4)

> "I am the good shepherd. I know my own and my own know me." (Jn.10:14)

> "And I have other sheep that are not of this fold. I must bring them also, and they will listen to my voice. So there will be one flock, one shepherd." (Jn.10:16)

> "My sheep hear my voice, and I know them, and they follow me." (Jn.10:27)

Third, Mary called Jesus "Rabboni," not "Rabbi" (Master or Teacher). *Rabboni* (Rabbounei) was a title of greater respect and honor than just Rabbi. It was "the highest title of honors attributed," and it means "my great master."[1] Mary was acknowledging Jesus to be her supreme Teacher, the One who was due all her honor and respect, loyalty and allegiance. She was acknowledging that He was her Master and she was His humble follower (disciple).

> "Let all the house of Israel therefore know for certain that God has made him both Lord and Christ, this Jesus whom you crucified." (Ac.2:36)

> "God exalted him at his right hand as Leader and Savior, to give repentance to Israel and forgiveness of sins." (Ac.5:31)

> God is faithful, by whom you were called into the fellowship of his Son, Jesus Christ our Lord. (1 Co.1:9)

> Yet for us there is one God, the Father, from whom are all things and for whom we exist, and one Lord, Jesus Christ, through whom are all things and through whom we exist. (1 Co.8:6)

## 4 The third startling sight: A vision of the new commission from Jesus.

**20:17-18**

¹⁷ Jesus said to her, "Do not cling to me, for I have not yet ascended to the Father; but go to my brothers and say to them, 'I am ascending to my Father and your Father, to my God and your God.'"

¹⁸ Mary Magdalene went and announced to the disciples, "I have seen the Lord"—and that he had said these things to her.

The third startling sight was Mary's new commission. Apparently, Mary was so full of joy and excitement that she reached out to embrace Jesus. Immediately, Jesus gave her an unexpected command.

### a. Do not hold on to Me (v.17a).

Jesus instructed Mary to not cling to Him. *Do not cling to me* (Gk. me mou haptou) is an imperative present action. Mary wanted to delight in her love for the Lord and in the fellowship that love brought her. She was reaching out to clutch Christ's body (physically), but in doing so she was missing the point: His cross and resurrection had created a totally new relationship. He was no longer just her Rabboni, her Master. He was her Lord and God (see Jn.20:28). He was soon to ascend back to the Father, so she must not waste time clinging to Him.

### b. Go—tell your great discovery (v.17b).

Instead, Mary must run and tell of her great discovery. The Master was now her Lord and God, for He had created a new spiritual relationship with people. But His people also had a new responsibility: to tell others that He is alive, that He is the powerful Savior, that He has defeated death.

Mary obeyed Jesus immediately. She did not waver, question, or delay. She ran to the disciples and testified that Jesus was alive (v.18).

**THOUGHT 1.** Jesus' command to Mary is His command to all His people. We are to run with the message of the gospel, to tell others that He died, was buried, and rose again; and that they can be saved if they will believe in Him (1 Co.15:1-4).

> And Jesus came and said to them, "All authority in heaven and on earth has been given to me. Go therefore and make disciples of all nations, baptizing them in the name of the Father and of the Son and of the Holy Spirit, teaching them to observe all that I have commanded you. And behold, I am with you always, to the end of the age." (Mt.28:18-20)

> And he said to them, "Go into all the world and proclaim the gospel to the whole creation." (Mk.16:15)

> From now on, therefore, we regard no one according to the flesh. Even though we once regarded Christ according to the flesh, we regard him thus no longer. Therefore, if anyone is in Christ, he is a new creation. The old has passed away; behold, the new has come. (2 Co.5:16-17)

---

1 Spiros Zodhiates, ed., *The Complete Word Study Dictionary New Testament* (Chattanooga, TN: AMG Publishers, 1992), via Wordsearch digital edition.

That is, in Christ God was reconciling the world to himself, not counting their trespasses against them, and entrusting to us the message of reconciliation. Therefore, we are ambassadors for Christ, God making his appeal through us. We implore you on behalf of Christ, be reconciled to God. For our sake he made him to be sin who knew no sin, so that in him we might become the righteousness of God. (2 Co.5:19-21)

## C. Event 3: The Great Charter of the Church—
## Jesus Appears to the Disciples, 20:19-23

*Mk.16:14; Lu.24:36-49*

1. The disciples were hiding in fear: They were discussing the reports of Christ's resurrection[DS1]
2. The risen Lord suddenly appeared: His presence was very real
   a. His calm greeting: Peace
   b. His wounds: Were evidence that it was truly He
   c. His effect: Unbelievable joy when they saw Him[DS2, 3]
3. The risen Lord assigned the great commission to His disciples
4. The risen Lord breathed the Holy Spirit into the disciples
   a. The giving of the Spirit[DS4]
   b. The authority given[DS5]

¹⁹ On the evening of that day, the first day of the week, the doors being locked where the disciples were for fear of the Jews, Jesus came and stood among them and said to them, "Peace be with you."

²⁰ When he had said this, he showed them his hands and his side. Then the disciples were glad when they saw the Lord.

²¹ Jesus said to them again, "Peace be with you. As the Father has sent me, even so I am sending you."

²² And when he had said this, he breathed on them and said to them, "Receive the Holy Spirit.

²³ "If you forgive the sins of any, they are forgiven them; if you withhold forgiveness from any, it is withheld."

# Division XVI

## The Revelation of Jesus, the Risen Lord, 20:1-21:25

C. Event 3: The Great Charter of the Church—
Jesus Appears to the Disciples, 20:19-23

*Mk.16:14; Lu.24:36-49*

## 20:19-23
## Introduction

This passage reveals Jesus' first appearance to His disciples as a group after His resurrection. What would He say and talk about? What would be the topic of conversation and the subjects covered? Whatever He chose to say would be of critical importance. It is this that John focuses on: the subjects and the topics discussed when Jesus first appeared to the disciples. This is, *Event 3: The Great Charter of the Church—Jesus Appears to the Disciples, 20:19-23.*

1. The disciples were hiding in fear: They were discussing the reports of Christ's resurrection (v.19).
2. The risen Lord suddenly appeared: His presence was very real (vv.19-20).
3. The risen Lord assigned the great commission to His disciples (v.21).
4. The risen Lord breathed the Holy Spirit into the disciples (vv.22-23).

## 1 The disciples were hiding in fear: They were discussing the reports of Christ's resurrection.

The disciples were hiding for fear of the Jews. They were behind locked doors, probably in the upper room of the same house where Jesus had met with them just a few days earlier. They were afraid of the authorities who had vented so much wrath and vengeance upon their Lord. Indeed they were in imminent danger; they could be arrested and imprisoned or executed as revolutionaries, just as Jesus had been.

Note that it was Sunday, the very day that Jesus had arisen, and it was nighttime. Luke tells us there were numerous reports that Jesus had been raised from the dead (see Deeper Study # 1).

> ¹⁹ On the evening of that day, the first day of the week, the doors being locked where the disciples were for fear of the Jews, Jesus came and stood among them and said to them, "Peace be with you."

### Deeper Study # 1

(20:19) **Jesus' Resurrection—Reports:** the reports would be about the empty tomb and linen clothes discovered by Peter and John (Jn.20:6f) and the appearances to Mary Magdalene (Jn.20:14f), Peter (1 Co.15:4), the women (Mt.28:1; Mk.16:1f), and the two walking to Emmaus (Lu.24:1).

## 2 The risen Lord suddenly appeared: His presence was very real.

Remember: the doors of the room were locked. Suddenly, unexpectedly, Jesus stood before them—right in their midst. His presence was very real. His sudden appearance shook and frightened the disciples. They thought they were seeing a vision or a spirit (Lu.24:36-37). The first thing Jesus did was prove that it was really He. He did this by speaking to them and showing them His wounds (see Deeper Study # 1—Jn.21:1 for more discussion).

> ¹⁹ On the evening of that day, the first day of the week, the doors being locked where the disciples were for fear of the Jews, Jesus came and stood among them and said to them, "Peace be with you."
> ²⁰ When he had said this, he showed them his hands and his side. Then the disciples were glad when they saw the Lord.

### a. His calm greeting: Peace (v.19).

Jesus used the simple day-to-day greeting that was common among Jews, "Peace be with you." Using the greeting so familiar to the disciples would help to put them at ease. The fact that He spoke just as He had always spoken would give them some indication that it was really He and not just a vision or a spirit.

> "Peace I leave with you; my peace I give to you. Not as the world gives do I give to you. Let not your hearts be troubled, neither let them be afraid." (Jn.14:27)

> "I have said these things to you, that in me you may have peace. In the world you will have tribulation. But take heart; I have overcome the world." (Jn.16:33)

> But now in Christ Jesus you who once were far off have been brought near by the blood of Christ. For he himself is our peace, who has made us both one and has broken down in his flesh the dividing wall of hostility (Ep.2:13-14)

### b. His wounds: Were evidence that it was truly He (v.20a).

Our risen Lord proceeded to show the disciples His wounds. This must have been a dramatic and touching moment, a moment that amazed their minds. Jesus probably moved around to each of them, allowing each one to see the wounds. This convinced the disciples. They knew for sure . . .
- that they were not seeing a vision or a spirit
- that this was His body, the body of their wonderful Lord, the very same Jesus whom they had known before His crucifixion

> That which was from the beginning, which we have heard, which we have seen with our eyes, which we looked upon and have touched with our hands, concerning the word of life—the life was made manifest, and we have seen it, and testify to it and proclaim to you the eternal life, which was with the Father and was made manifest to us. (1 Jn.1:1-2)

### c. His effect: Unbelievable joy when they saw Him (v.20b).

When the disciples saw that it was indeed Jesus, unbelievable gladness burst out of them (see Deeper Study # 2; also Lu.24:41). Their spirits and attitudes were charged with joy. They were transformed from the lowest point of dejection to the highest point of triumphant conviction. They now knew what Jesus meant, that He was truly the Way to God, the Truth of God, and the Life of God (Jn.14:6).

In Him was life—His words were *literally* true. He had meant exactly what He had said (see Deeper Study # 3). They had merely spiritualized His words, twisted them to mean what they had wanted. But now they knew. They understood fully what He had meant:

➢ When He had said that He was going to die, He meant He was going to die.
➢ When He had said that He was going to arise, He meant He was going to arise.

And here He was standing before them, revealing the most glorious truth in all the universe. Mankind could now conquer sin and death and live forever. He had actually come that people may have life, and that they may have it in abundance (Jn.10:10. See Jn.10:38). They now saw and understood.

## Deeper Study # 2

(20:20) **See** (Gk. eido): means more than mere sight. It is seeing with understanding. It is the very same word used of John when he *saw and believed* (see Jn.20:8).

## Deeper Study # 3

(20:20) **Prophecies:** the disciples finally understood that Jesus had meant exactly what He was saying. When He had said that He was going to die and arise from the dead, they had spiritualized His words. But Jesus had meant exactly what He was saying: He was to literally die and arise from the dead and by such He was to usher in the Kingdom of God. Of course, this was far more meaningful than the earthly kingdom they had desired. It was the most glorious news in all the world, for people could now live beyond a few short years in an earthly kingdom; people could live in the very presence of God forever. Sin, death, and hell were now conquered.

Jesus constantly shared His death and resurrection. This fact is often overlooked. The predictions in just the Gospel of John are given here:

1. The prophecies concerning His death alone.

> "I am the good shepherd. The good shepherd lays down his life for the sheep.... just as the Father knows me and I know the Father; and I lay down my life for the sheep." (Jn.10:11, 15)

> "Now is my soul troubled. And what shall I say? 'Father, save me from this hour'? But for this purpose I have come to this hour.... Now is the judgment of this world; now will the ruler of this world be cast out. And I, when I am lifted up from the earth, will draw all people to myself." He said this to show by what kind of death he was going to die. (Jn.12:27, 31-33)

> "Little children, yet a little while I am with you. You will seek me, and just as I said to the Jews, so now I also say to you, 'Where I am going you cannot come.'" Simon Peter said to him, "Lord, where are you going?" Jesus answered him, "Where I am going you cannot follow me now, but you will follow afterward." (Jn.13:33, 36)

> "This is my commandment, that you love one another as I have loved you. Greater love has no one than this, that someone lay down his life for his friends. You are my friends if you do what I command you." (Jn.15:12-14)

"But now I am going to him who sent me, and none of you asks me, 'Where are you going?' But because I have said these things to you, sorrow has filled your heart. Nevertheless, I tell you the truth: it is to your advantage that I go away, for if I do not go away, the Helper will not come to you. But if I go, I will send him to you." (Jn.16:5–7)

"I came from the Father and have come into the world, and now I am leaving the world and going to the Father." (Jn.16:28)

"And I am no longer in the world, but they are in the world, and I am coming to you. Holy Father, keep them in your name, which you have given me, that they may be one, even as we are one. . . . But now I am coming to you, and these things I speak in the world, that they may have my joy fulfilled in themselves." (Jn.17:11, 13)

2. The prophecies concerning the resurrection alone.

"Then what if you were to see the Son of Man ascending to where he was before?" (Jn.6:62)

Jesus answered, "Even if I do bear witness about myself, my testimony is true, for I know where I came from and where I am going, but you do not know where I come from or where I am going." (Jn.8:14)

Jesus said to her, "I am the resurrection and the life. Whoever believes in me, though he die, yet shall he live, and everyone who lives and believes in me shall never die. Do you believe this?" (Jn.11:25–26)

3. The prophecies concerning both His death and resurrection.

Jesus then said, "I will be with you a little longer, and then I am going to him who sent me. You will seek me and you will not find me. Where I am you cannot come." The Jews said to one another, "Where does this man intend to go that we will not find him? Does he intend to go to the Dispersion among the Greeks and teach the Greeks? What does he mean by saying, 'You will seek me and you will not find me,' and, 'Where I am you cannot come'?" (Jn.7:33–36)

On the last day of the feast, the great day, Jesus stood up and cried out, "If anyone thirsts, let him come to me and drink. Whoever believes in me, as the Scripture has said, 'Out of his heart will flow rivers of living water.'" Now this he said about the Spirit, whom those who believed in him were to receive, for as yet the Spirit had not been given, because Jesus was not yet glorified. (Jn.7:37–39)

So he said to them again, "I am going away, and you will seek me, and you will die in your sin. Where I am going, you cannot come." So the Jews said, "Will he kill himself, since he says, 'Where I am going, you cannot come'?" He said to them, "You are from below; I am from above. You are of this world; I am not of this world. I told you that you would die in your sins, for unless you believe that I am he you will die in your sins." So they said to him, "Who are you?" Jesus said to them, "Just what I have been telling you from the beginning. I have much to say about you and much to judge, but he who sent me is true, and I declare to the world what I have heard from him." They did not understand that he had been speaking to them about the Father. So Jesus said to them, "When you have lifted up the Son of Man, then you will know that I am he, and that I do nothing on my own authority, but speak just as the Father taught me. And he who sent me is with me. He has not left me alone, for I always do the things that are pleasing to him." (Jn.8:21–29)

"For this reason the Father loves me, because I lay down my life that I may take it up again. No one takes it from me, but I lay it down of my own accord. I have authority to lay it down, and I have authority to take it up again. This charge I have received from my Father." (Jn.10:17–18)

And Jesus answered them, "The hour has come for the Son of Man to be glorified. Truly, truly, I say to you, unless a grain of wheat falls into the earth and dies, it remains alone; but if it dies, it bears much fruit." (Jn.12:23–24)

When he had gone out, Jesus said, "Now is the Son of Man glorified, and God is glorified in him. If God is glorified in him, God will also glorify him in himself, and glorify him at once." (Jn.13:31–32)

"In my Father's house are many rooms. If it were not so, would I have told you that I go to prepare a place for you? And if I go and prepare a place for you, I will come again and will take you to myself, that where I am you may be also." (Jn.14:2–3)

"Yet a little while and the world will see me no more, but you will see me. Because I live, you also will live. In that day you will know that I am in my Father, and you in me, and I in you." (Jn.14:19–20)

> "You heard me say to you, 'I am going away, and I will come to you.' If you loved me, you would have rejoiced, because I am going to the Father, for the Father is greater than I. And now I have told you before it takes place, so that when it does take place you may believe. I will no longer talk much with you, for the ruler of this world is coming. He has no claim on me." (Jn.14:28-30)
>
> "A little while, and you will see me no longer; and again a little while, and you will see me." So some of his disciples said to one another, "What is this that he says to us, 'A little while, and you will not see me, and again a little while, and you will see me'; and, 'because I am going to the Father'?" So they were saying, "What does he mean by 'a little while'? We do not know what he is talking about." Jesus knew that they wanted to ask him, so he said to them, "Is this what you are asking yourselves, what I meant by saying, 'A little while and you will not see me, and again a little while and you will see me'? Truly, truly, I say to you, you will weep and lament, but the world will rejoice. You will be sorrowful, but your sorrow will turn into joy. When a woman is giving birth, she has sorrow because her hour has come, but when she has delivered the baby, she no longer remembers the anguish, for joy that a human being has been born into the world. So also you have sorrow now, but I will see you again, and your hearts will rejoice, and no one will take your joy from you." (Jn.16:16-22)

## 20:21

<sup>21</sup> Jesus said to them again, "Peace be with you. As the Father has sent me, even so I am sending you."

## 3 The risen Lord assigned the great commission to His disciples.

After proving who He was, Jesus assigned His disciples the Great Commission. Christ linked His mission to the mission of the disciples. He was sending them just as the Father had sent Him. Every Christ-follower is sent on the very *same* mission as Christ. What is that mission?

> "For God did not send his Son into the world to condemn the world, but in order that the world might be saved through him." (Jn.3:17)

> "The thief comes only to steal and kill and destroy. I came that they may have life and have it abundantly." (Jn.10:10)

> "If anyone hears my words and does not keep them, I do not judge him; for I did not come to judge the world but to save the world." (Jn.12:47)

> Then Pilate said to him, "So you are a king?" Jesus answered, "You say that I am a king. For this purpose I was born and for this purpose I have come into the world—to bear witness to the truth. Everyone who is of the truth listens to my voice." (Jn.18:37)

The disciple is sent forth to proclaim and bear witness to the salvation of God. The disciple is the prophet and witness of the living Lord.

- ➣ Christ is the Way; the disciple *points* the Way.
- ➣ Christ is the Truth; the disciple *proclaims* the Truth.
- ➣ Christ is the Life; the disciple *shares* the Life.

The great words *sent* (apestalken) and *sending* or *send* (pempo) are two different words in Greek. The Father sending Christ is *apestalken* (indicative perfect active of *apostello*) which means first of all, *a setting apart and sending forth with delegated authority*. There are only four chapters in John where Christ does not claim to have been sent. *Pempo*, which never refers to delegated authority, is always used when Christ is sending the believer. *Pempo* always means to *dispatch under authority*.

God sent Christ and delegated *all* authority to Him (Mt.28:18). Christ delegates *no* authority to the believer. He simply dispatches messengers (Mt.28:19-20).

> There was a man sent from God, whose name was John. (Jn.1:6)

> "You did not choose me, but I chose you and appointed you that you should go and bear fruit and that your fruit should abide, so that whatever you ask the Father in my name, he may give it to you." (Jn.15:16)

> Therefore, we are ambassadors for Christ, God making his appeal through us. We implore you on behalf of Christ, be reconciled to God. For our sake he made him to be sin who knew no sin, so that in him we might become the righteousness of God. (2 Co.5:20-21)

**THOUGHT 1.** There is but one great qualification for being commissioned: receiving, possessing, and knowing the peace of Christ (see note—Jn.14:27). Unless a person has been reconciled to God *by Christ*, unless he has really made peace with God, he or she cannot represent God before the world. Every individual who has been reconciled to God—every believer—is given the assignment Jesus gave the disciples: to take the gospel to the world.

> And Jesus came and said to them, "All authority in heaven and on earth has been given to me. Go therefore and make disciples of all nations, baptizing them in the name of the Father and of the Son and of the Holy Spirit, teaching them to observe all that I have commanded you. And behold, I am with you always, to the end of the age." (Mt.28:18-20)
>
> And he said to them, "Go into all the world and proclaim the gospel to the whole creation." (Mk.16:15)
>
> "But you will receive power when the Holy Spirit has come upon you, and you will be my witnesses in Jerusalem and in all Judea and Samaria, and to the end of the earth." (Ac.1:8)

## 4 The risen Lord breathed the Holy Spirit into the disciples.

As Christ commissioned His disciples to take the gospel to the world, He gave them the power to carry out His orders. They could never accomplish their mission in their own power, nor could they go forth on their own authority.

> 22 And when he had said this, he breathed on them and said to them, "Receive the Holy Spirit.
> 23 "If you forgive the sins of any, they are forgiven them; if you withhold forgiveness from any, it is withheld."

a. **The giving of the Spirit (v.22).**

   Christ gave His apostles the Holy Spirit (see DEEPER STUDY # 4). They needed spiritual power, supernatural power, power they did not possess in themselves. The risen Lord breathed on them and commanded them to *receive* (labate, an imperative in the Greek) the Holy Spirit. It is noteworthy that the word *breathed* is the same word as *breathed* in Genesis 2:7 in the Septuagint (the ancient Greek translation of the Old Testament). Just God breathed *physical* life into Adam, the first man He created, Christ breathed *spiritual* life into those who had been born again, born spiritually, created spiritually.

   > Jesus answered, "Truly, truly, I say to you, unless one is born of water and the Spirit, he cannot enter the kingdom of God. That which is born of the flesh is flesh, and that which is born of the Spirit is spirit." (Jn.3:5-6)
   >
   > Therefore, if anyone is in Christ, he is a new creation. The old has passed away; behold, the new has come. (2 Co.5:17)
   >
   > And you were dead in the trespasses and sins (Ep.2:1)
   >
   > For we are his workmanship, created in Christ Jesus for good works, which God prepared beforehand, that we should walk in them. (Ep.2:10)

b. **The authority given (v.23).**

   Christ sent His disciples into the world with His power and also with His authority (see DEEPER STUDY # 5). Note that in Matthew's account of the Great Commission, he recorded that Christ said all authority had been given to *Him* (Mt.28:18). This was critical, for human authorities would forbid Christ's disciples to preach His message. But these disciples served a greater authority; the Son of God and God the Son was their authority. When the disciples were forced to decide whether to disobey civil authorities by continuing to preach Christ, what Jesus had said when He commissioned them no doubt compelled their decision (Ac.5:28-29).

**THOUGHT 1.** Jesus has never sent any of His followers to do His work in their own power or with their own authority. He commanded His first followers to not go forth from Jerusalem *until* God gave the Holy Spirit (Ac.1:4-5). Every servant of Christ must always be conscious of our need of God's power to do His work. If we try to do the Lord's work in our own power and strength we will surely fail.

Every servant of Christ must also be aware that we serve under the Lord's authority. We have no authority whatsoever to do ministry our way or according to how we think it should be done. In addition, when we are forced to choose between obeying God and man—whether civil authorities, church authorities, or other religious authorities—we must also choose to obey Christ, just as the apostles did. *He* is our authority. We are *His* servants, *His* ambassadors, *His* messengers. Ultimately, we answer to *Him*.

> And Jesus came and said to them, "All authority in heaven and on earth has been given to me." (Mt.28:18)

> ... And the high priest questioned them, saying, "We strictly charged you not to teach in this name, yet here you have filled Jerusalem with your teaching, and you intend to bring this man's blood upon us." But Peter and the apostles answered, "We must obey God rather than men." (Ac.5:27b-29)

> This is how one should regard us, as servants of Christ and stewards of the mysteries of God. Moreover, it is required of stewards that they be found faithful. But with me it is a very small thing that I should be judged by you or by any human court. In fact, I do not even judge myself. For I am not aware of anything against myself, but I am not thereby acquitted. It is the Lord who judges me. (1 Co.4:1-4)

> For am I now seeking the approval of man, or of God? Or am I trying to please man? If I were still trying to please man, I would not be a servant of Christ. (Ga.1:10)

> Bondservants, obey in everything those who are your earthly masters, not by way of eye-service, as people-pleasers, but with sincerity of heart, fearing the Lord. Whatever you do, work heartily, as for the Lord and not for men, knowing that from the Lord you will receive the inheritance as your reward. You are serving the Lord Christ. (Col.3:22-24)

## DEEPER STUDY # 4

(20:22) **Holy Spirit, Coming:** Jesus' breathing on the disciples was a prophetic sign of the Spirit's coming and a spiritual quickening for the disciples. It was both a symbolic and a spiritual preparation. Jesus was showing His followers that the Spirit's very special presence and power was to indwell both believers and the church as the temple of God. The Spirit, of course, was not to come until Christ's ascension (see notes—Jn.14:28-29; 16:7; DEEPER STUDY # 1—Ac.2:1-4; DEEPER STUDY # 2—8:14-17; note—10:44-48).

Note several things.

1. Christ breathed on each individual. He was symbolizing that the Holy Spirit was to indwell each believer in a very special way.

> "And I will ask the Father, and he will give you another Helper, to be with you forever, even the Spirit of truth, whom the world cannot receive, because it neither sees him nor knows him. You know him, for he dwells with you and will be in you. I will not leave you as orphans; I will come to you." (Jn.14:16-18)

> "Whoever has my commandments and keeps them, he it is who loves me. And he who loves me will be loved by my Father, and I will love him and manifest myself to him." (Jn.14:21)

> "But you will receive power when the Holy Spirit has come upon you, and you will be my witnesses in Jerusalem and in all Judea and Samaria, and to the end of the earth." (Ac.1:8)

> For you did not receive the spirit of slavery to fall back into fear, but you have received the Spirit of adoption as sons, by whom we cry, "Abba! Father!" The Spirit himself bears witness with our spirit that we are children of God, and if children, then heirs—heirs of God and fellow heirs with Christ, provided we suffer with him in order that we may also be glorified with him. (Ro.8:15-17)

> Now we have received not the spirit of the world, but the Spirit who is from God, that we might understand the things freely given us by God. (1 Co.2:12)

> Or do you not know that your body is a temple of the Holy Spirit within you, whom you have from God? You are not your own, for you were bought with a price. So glorify God in your body. (1 Co.6:19-20)

> Now to him who is able to do far more abundantly than all that we ask or think, according to the power at work within us. (Ep.3:20)

2. Christ breathed on the whole group—"on them." He was symbolizing that the Holy Spirit was to indwell the corporate body, the church as a whole in a very special way. This broader picture is further emphasized by Luke when he says there were others present with the apostles on this occasion (Lu.24:33, 49; see Deeper Study # 2—Jn.14:20; notes—1 Co.3:16; 6:19; Ep.3:6; Col.1:26-27).

> And they were all filled with the Holy Spirit and began to speak in other tongues as the Spirit gave them utterance. (Ac.2:4)
>
> Do you not know that you [the church] are God's temple and that God's Spirit dwells in you? (1 Co.3:16)

## Deeper Study # 5

(20:23) **Forgiving Sins—Authority:** this is a disputed verse; however, there are two things we can know for sure about its meaning.

- ➢ No human can forgive another person's sins.
- ➢ Believers *can proclaim* that a person's sins are forgiven *if that person receives Christ* (Jn.1:12). Believers can also proclaim that a person's sins are not forgiven if they do not receive Christ.

There is only one Mediator between God and man, the Man Christ Jesus (1 Ti.2:5-6). No other man has ever been worthy to give His life as a ransom for others. No other ransom has ever been acceptable to God. Christ Jesus alone is worthy and acceptable to die as a ransom for someone else. He alone is the Perfect Man. Therefore . . .

- only Christ can forgive and judge sins.

    > "For the Father judges no one, but has given all judgment to the Son." (Jn.5:22)
    >
    > "And he has given him authority to execute judgment, because he is the Son of Man." (Jn.5:27)
    >
    > "The one who rejects me and does not receive my words has a judge; the word that I have spoken will judge him on the last day." (Jn.12:48)
    >
    > "And when he [the Holy Spirit] comes, he will convict the world concerning sin and righteousness and judgment." (Jn.16:8)

- only representatives of Christ (believers) can say that a person is forgiven by Christ or not forgiven by Christ.

    > "I will give you the keys of the kingdom of heaven, and whatever you bind on earth shall be bound in heaven, and whatever you loose on earth shall be loosed in heaven." (Mt.16:19)
    >
    > "Truly, I say to you, whatever you bind on earth shall be bound in heaven, and whatever you loose on earth shall be loosed in heaven." (Mt.18:18)
    >
    > "If you forgive the sins of any, they are forgiven them; if you withhold forgiveness from any, it is withheld." (Jn.20:23)

## D. Event 4: The Great Conviction—Thomas' Confession, 20:24-29

| | |
|---|---|
| 1. Thomas' frustrated, reactionary spirit<br>   a. The reason: Guilt—he had forsaken & withdrawn from them<br>   b. The disciples shared the fact of Jesus' resurrection, but Thomas doubted<br>2. Thomas' false picture of Jesus<br>   a. He was just an earthly deliverer<br>   b. He was now dead<br><br>   c. Result: Persistent doubt for eight days<br>3. Thomas' confrontation with Jesus and his confession: Jesus suddenly appeared and challenged him<br>   a. The confrontation<br>      1) Jesus was aware of Thomas' unbelieving demands<br>      2) Jesus warned & called for belief<br>   b. The strong confession<br><br>4. Thomas' great lesson for all people: The person who believes without seeing will be far more blessed than those who demand proof | 24 Now Thomas, one of the twelve, called the Twin, was not with them when Jesus came. 25 So the other disciples told him, "We have seen the Lord." But he said to them, "Unless I see in his hands the mark of the nails, and place my finger into the mark of the nails, and place my hand into his side, I will never believe." 26 Eight days later, his disciples were inside again, and Thomas was with them. Although the doors were locked, Jesus came and stood among them and said, "Peace be with you." 27 Then he said to Thomas, "Put your finger here, and see my hands; and put out your hand, and place it in my side. Do not disbelieve, but believe." 28 Thomas answered him, "My Lord and my God!" 29 Jesus said to him, "Have you believed because you have seen me? Blessed are those who have not seen and yet have believed." |

# Division XVI

*The Revelation of Jesus, the Risen Lord, 20:1-21:25*

D. Event 4: The Great Conviction—Thomas' Confession, 20:24-29

## 20:24-29
## Introduction

He has gone down in history as "Doubting Thomas," but it is not entirely fair that the skeptical disciple is remembered this way. Thomas was a man of deep, selfless devotion to Christ and to souls. Church tradition and history report that he took the gospel to India, where he died as a martyr.[1] He may have been a doubter, but He did not remain a doubter. Thomas' encounter with the risen Christ transformed him from a skeptic to a sold-out servant of the Savior. His story is an excellent study on conviction and confession. This is, *Event 4: The Great Conviction—Thomas' Confession, 20:24-29*.

   1. Thomas' frustrated, reactionary spirit (vv.24-25).
   2. Thomas' false picture of Jesus (vv.25-26).
   3. Thomas' confrontation with Jesus and his confession: Jesus suddenly appeared and challenged him (vv.26-28).

---

1   Geoffrey W. Bromiley, *International Standard Bible Encyclopedia* (Grand Rapids, MI: William B. Eerdmans), via Wordsearch digital edition.

4. Thomas' great lesson for all people: The person who believes without seeing will be far more blessed than those who demand proof (v.29).

(20:24-29) **Another Outline**: Conviction—its signs, results, or reactions.
1. A frustrated reactionary spirit (v.24).
2. A false picture of Jesus (v.25).
3. A persistent doubt (v.26).
4. A critical confrontation (v.27).
5. A strong confession (v.28).
6. A great lesson for the church (v.29).

## 1 Thomas' frustrated, reactionary spirit.

20:24-25

Thomas had not been with the disciples when Jesus first appeared to them (v.24). Like so many today, he staunchly refused to believe that Jesus had actually risen from the dead. The disciples *told him* of the glorious truth (v.25). The Greek means they "kept on telling him," but Thomas became stiffnecked and obstinate in his unbelief. He even argued against their testimony, and he argued with deep intensity. He was deeply aggravated and frustrated, feeling great disappointment and guilt. The depth of his aggravation and guilt is seen in his repulsive shout, "Unless I see . . . put my finger . . . [and] put my hand into his wounds, I will not believe" (Jn.20:25).

24 Now Thomas, one of the twelve, called the Twin, was not with them when Jesus came.
25 So the other disciples told him, "We have seen the Lord." But he said to them, "Unless I see in his hands the mark of the nails, and place my finger into the mark of the nails, and place my hand into his side, I will never believe."

**a. The reason: Guilt—he had forsaken and withdrawn from them (v.24).**

What was it that frustrated Thomas so greatly and caused him to feel such intense guilt and react the way he did? Evidently . . .
- Thomas *had forsaken* the Lord, and that is enough to frustrate any person's spirit.
- Thomas had also *withdrawn* from the disciples; consequently, he was *not present* when the Lord first appeared (Jn.20:24). He missed another opportunity to be identified with Christ.

**b. The disciples shared the fact of Jesus' resurrection, but Thomas doubted (v.25a).**

As the other disciples tried repeatedly to convince Thomas of the resurrection, he became aggravated with guilt all over again. He became critical of the body of believers. It was his own fault, but as human nature so often reacts, he blamed others through his aggravated spirit. He argued against the other disciples' experience with the resurrected Lord. Having taken all he could bear, in utter frustration he shouted out, "Unless I see . . . put my finger . . . [and] put my hand into his wounds, I will not believe" (Jn.20:25). Eight more days went by before the Lord ever appeared to Thomas (Jn.20:26). Think about what he might have missed in those eight days!

**THOUGHT 1.** Persistent doubt always delays the blessings of God.

**THOUGHT 2.** Guilt, frustration, disappointment, and exclusion often result in a . . .
- haughty spirit
- reaction
- denial of facts
- fierce outburst

He said to them, "Why are you so afraid? Have you still no faith?" (Mk.4:40)

And he said to them, "O foolish ones, and slow of heart to believe all that the prophets have spoken!" (Lu.24:25)

"But my righteous one shall live by faith, and if he shrinks back, my soul has no pleasure in him." (He.10:38)

For whenever our heart condemns us, God is greater than our heart, and he knows everything. (1 Jn.3:20)

The backslider in heart will be filled with the fruit of his ways, and a good man will be filled with the fruit of his ways. (Pr.14:14)

## 20:25-26

²⁵ So the other disciples told him, "We have seen the Lord." But he said to them, "Unless I see in his hands the mark of the nails, and place my finger into the mark of the nails, and place my hand into his side, I will never believe."

²⁶ Eight days later, his disciples were inside again, and Thomas was with them. Although the doors were locked, Jesus came and stood among them and said, "Peace be with you."

## 2  Thomas' false picture of Jesus.

Thomas' doubt was caused largely by the fact that he held a false picture of Jesus. He viewed Christ through His own feelings, his own opinion, his own understanding, rather than through the truth. He could not grasp what Christ had taught the disciples about Himself because he was blinded by his own preconceptions.

a. **He was just an earthly deliverer.**

Apparently, Thomas had always thought in terms of an earthly Messiah or Savior who would make things better on this earth and in this life. When he decided to follow Jesus, he thought that an earthly kingdom was to be set up and that Christ would appoint him to be a leader in that kingdom. He saw Jesus as the promised Messiah who was to be the Son of David, that is, to come from David's line of descendants (see DEEPER STUDY # 2—Jn.1:20; note—1:23; DEEPER STUDY # 4—1:49). However, Thomas refused to see beyond the human and physical things of this world.

b. **He was now dead.**

Because of His idea of Christ, Thomas could see Jesus only as the man who was nailed to the cross and had a spear thrust into His side and was now dead (see notes—Lu.22:24-30; Jn.13:1-17—for more discussion). He refused to believe unless He personally touched Christ's body. It was not enough for Thomas to merely *see* Christ; it could be a vision, a ghost, an apparition. He had to *touch* the body of Christ—to prove for himself that Christ was real—before he would believe.

c. **Result: Persistent doubt for eight days (v.26a).**

Thomas' refusal to believe went on for over a week. For eight days, he was at odds with his companions. For eight days, he missed the joy and fellowship they shared. For eight days, he persisted in doubt, defeat, and depression—all unnecessarily.

**THOUGHT 1.** False pictures of Jesus lead to unbelief. Jesus is more than . . .
- a great teacher
- a great prophet
- a great man
- a great founder of a religion

He is even more than the greatest man who ever lived. All such beliefs—no matter how highly they esteem Jesus—are false beliefs, for they recognize Jesus only as a man. They may see Him as one of the greatest men who ever lived, but they still see Him only as a man.

**THOUGHT 2.** People prefer to see Jesus only as a man because it brings Him down to their level. It makes Him less than Lord. They believe it means . . .
- that humanity is not totally depraved, not wicked through and through; that people are not so bad that Jesus had to sacrifice His life for them
- that people can do what Jesus did, the best they can, and God will accept them
- that people do not have to follow Jesus in every little detail and teaching. Why? Because as man, they believe that Jesus was not absolutely perfect. He was wrong in some things. Where? Each person has to decide the best they can where Jesus was right and wrong. Then that person must do the best they can to follow Jesus where Jesus was right. People believe that God accepts them as long as they are "doing the best they can." (Note how this thinking allows each individual to *form* God in their own mind and after their own

likeness. They can make God as they wish God to be. They can do what they want and then say that it was allowed by God.)

Now when Jesus came into the district of Caesarea Philippi, he asked his disciples, "Who do people say that the Son of Man is?" And they said, "Some say John the Baptist, others say Elijah, and others Jeremiah or one of the prophets." (Mt.16:13-14)

"Is not this the carpenter, the son of Mary and brother of James and Joses and Judas and Simon? And are not his sisters here with us?" And they took offense at him. (Mk.6:3)

For although they knew God, they did not honor him as God or give thanks to him, but they became futile in their thinking, and their foolish hearts were darkened. Claiming to be wise, they became fools, and exchanged the glory of the immortal God for images resembling mortal man and birds and animals and creeping things. (Ro.1:21-23)

Because they [men] exchanged the truth about God for a lie and worshiped and served the creature rather than the Creator, who is blessed forever! Amen. (Ro.1:25)

## 3 Thomas' confrontation with Jesus and his confession: Jesus suddenly appeared and challenged him.

As Thomas continued to wallow in doubt and disbelief, something extraordinary happened. Jesus once again appeared unexplainably in the locked room where the disciples were assembled (v.26b). This time Thomas was there, and the risen Lord challenged the doubting disciple personally.

²⁶ Eight days later, his disciples were inside again, and Thomas was with them. Although the doors were locked, Jesus came and stood among them and said, "Peace be with you."

²⁷ Then he said to Thomas, "Put your finger here, and see my hands; and put out your hand, and place it in my side. Do not disbelieve, but believe."

²⁸ Thomas answered him, "My Lord and my God!"

### a. The confrontation (v.27).

The doors were again shut and locked (see note—Jn.20:19). Suddenly, unexpectedly, without notice, Jesus stood in the midst of the disciples. He again eased their shock by giving the normal greeting, "Peace be with you." But note what He then did: He turned immediately to confront Thomas.

Jesus revealed that He was aware of Thomas' unbelief and demands. He used the very same words that Thomas had demanded, telling the doubter specifically to touch His hands and side. Then, the loving Savior gently rebuked Thomas. He challenged Thomas to not be faithless, but to believe (v.27).

Jesus' call to believe is also a warning. Thomas had been walking down a dangerous road. The disciples had witnessed to him time and again, but he had refused each time to accept their testimony. Note exactly what Jesus said to the persistent, stiffnecked doubter:

➢ *Do not disbelieve, do not be unbelieving* or *faithfulness* (Gk. me ginou apistos): stop refusing to believe. You are running the risk of *becoming faithless* and unbelieving, beyond the point of believing. You have carried your unbelief too far. It is now time to stop the foolishness. The others have been repeatedly witnessing the truth to you. Stop the stiffnecked, obstinate unbelief. You are in danger.

"Whoever believes in him is not condemned, but whoever does not believe is condemned already, because he has not believed in the name of the only Son of God." (Jn.3:18)

Whoever believes in the Son has eternal life; whoever does not obey the Son shall not see life, but the wrath of God remains on him. (Jn.3:36)

"I told you that you would die in your sins, for unless you believe that I am he you will die in your sins." (Jn.8:24)

How shall we escape if we neglect such a great salvation? It was declared at first by the Lord, and it was attested to us by those who heard. (He.2:3)

Take care, brothers, lest there be in any of you an evil, unbelieving heart, leading you to fall away from the living God. (He.3:12)

Now I want to remind you, although you once fully knew it, that Jesus, who saved a people out of the land of Egypt, afterward destroyed those who did not believe. (Jude 5)

➤ *Believe* (see Deeper Study # 2—Jn.2:24).

"That whoever believes in him may have eternal life." (Jn.3:15)

"Truly, truly, I say to you, whoever hears my word and believes him who sent me has eternal life. He does not come into judgment, but has passed from death to life." (Jn.5:24)

Jesus said to her, "I am the resurrection and the life. Whoever believes in me, though he die, yet shall he live." (Jn.11:25)

"I have come into the world as light, so that whoever believes in me may not remain in darkness." (Jn.12:46)

But these are written so that you may believe that Jesus is the Christ, the Son of God, and that by believing you may have life in his name. (Jn.20:31)

Because, if you confess with your mouth that Jesus is Lord and believe in your heart that God raised him from the dead, you will be saved. (Ro.10:9)

**Thought 1.** Jesus knows every person's heart: their despair, doubts, fears, hope, love. He knows where and when to strike at a person's heart. However, note a crucial factor: Thomas was where Jesus could reach him. He was in the presence of believers listening to their testimony. Despite his questions, he had not shut them out.

And needed no one to bear witness about man, for he himself knew what was in man. (Jn.2:25)

And again, "The Lord knows the thoughts of the wise, that they are futile." (1 Co.3:20)

"Talk no more so very proudly, let not arrogance come from your mouth; for the Lord is a God of knowledge, and by him actions are weighed." (1 S.2:3)

"I the Lord search the heart and test the mind, to give every man according to his ways, according to the fruit of his deeds." (Je.17:10)

"He reveals deep and hidden things; he knows what is in the darkness, and the light dwells with him." (Da.2:22)

**Thought 2.** To be faithless is to be Christless. It is to be separated from Christ, without hope, and without God in the world (Ep.2:12).

### b. The strong confession (v.28).

Thomas' confession is one of the greatest in Scripture. Most likely dropping to his knees, he simply and sincerely exclaimed, "My Lord and my God!" He was now convinced of five great truths:

First, that Jesus is truly the risen Lord. All that Jesus had said was true (see Deeper Study # 3—Jn.20:20).

"Let all the house of Israel therefore know for certain that God has made him both Lord and Christ, this Jesus whom you crucified." (Ac.2:36)

"God exalted him at his right hand as Leader and Savior, to give repentance to Israel and forgiveness of sins." (Ac.5:31)

And was declared to be the Son of God in power according to the Spirit of holiness by his resurrection from the dead, Jesus Christ our Lord. (Ro.1:4)

Because, if you confess with your mouth that Jesus is Lord and believe in your heart that God raised him from the dead, you will be saved. (Ro.10:9)

Yet for us there is one God, the Father, from whom are all things and for whom we exist, and one Lord, Jesus Christ, through whom are all things and through whom we exist. (1 Co.8:6)

Second, that Jesus is both Lord and God, the Sovereign majesty of the universe (see note—Jn.1:1-2).

For in him the whole fullness of deity dwells bodily, and you have been filled in him, who is the head of all rule and authority. (Col.2:9-10)

Great indeed, we confess, is the mystery of godliness: He was manifested in the flesh, vindicated by the Spirit, seen by angels, proclaimed among the nations, believed on in the world, taken up in glory. (1 Ti.3:16)

He is the radiance of the glory of God and the exact imprint of his nature, and he upholds the universe by the word of his power. After making purification for sins, he sat down at the right hand of the Majesty on high. (He.1:3)

Third, that Jesus is the One who has come to truly reveal God, that He is the Mediator between God and humanity (see note—Jn.14:6; Deeper Study # 1—3:31; Deeper Study # 3—3:34; see 1 Ti.2:15).

Jesus said to him, "I am the way, and the truth, and the life. No one comes to the Father except through me." (Jn.14:6)

For there is one God, and there is one mediator between God and men, the man Christ Jesus. (1 Ti.2:5)

But as it is, Christ has obtained a ministry that is as much more excellent than the old as the covenant he mediates is better, since it is enacted on better promises. (He.8:6)

Therefore he is the mediator of a new covenant, so that those who are called may receive the promised eternal inheritance, since a death has occurred that redeems them from the transgressions committed under the first covenant. (He.9:15)

For Christ has entered, not into holy places made with hands, which are copies of the true things, but into heaven itself, now to appear in the presence of God on our behalf. (He.9:24)

My little children, I am writing these things to you so that you may not sin. But if anyone does sin, we have an advocate with the Father, Jesus Christ the righteous. (1 Jn.2:1)

Fourth, that Jesus accepts no half-way commitments. Jesus expected to be his Lord and his God: "*My* Lord, *my* God." Therefore, he must personally bow and worship Jesus as his Lord and his God.

For to this end Christ died and lived again, that he might be Lord both of the dead and of the living. (Ro.14:9)

Therefore God has highly exalted him and bestowed on him the name that is above every name, so that at the name of Jesus every knee should bow, in heaven and on earth and under the earth, and every tongue confess that Jesus Christ is Lord, to the glory of God the Father. (Ph.2:9-11)

And he is the head of the body, the church. He is the beginning, the firstborn from the dead, that in everything he might be preeminent. (Col.1:18)

Saying with a loud voice, "Worthy is the Lamb who was slain, to receive power and wealth and wisdom and might and honor and glory and blessing!" (Re.5:12)

Fifth, that Jesus expected an open and public confession of Him as Lord and God (Mt.10:32; Lu.12:8).

"So everyone who acknowledges me before men, I also will acknowledge before my Father who is in heaven." (Mt.10:32)

"And I tell you, everyone who acknowledges me before men, the Son of Man also will acknowledge before the angels of God." (Lu.12:8)

No one who denies the Son has the Father. Whoever confesses the Son has the Father also. (1 Jn.2:23)

Whoever confesses that Jesus is the Son of God, God abides in him, and he in God. (1 Jn.4:15)

# 4 Thomas' great lesson for all people: The person who believes without seeing will be far more blessed than those who demand proof.

²⁹ Jesus said to him, "Have you believed because you have seen me? Blessed are those who have not seen and yet have believed."

Jesus again gently rebuked Thomas by teaching him a lesson that He hoped would stay with the doubter throughout the rest of his life: those who believe without seeing will be far more blessed than those who demand proof. This lesson is for all people of all generations. Jesus wants each of us . . .

- To believe without having to see evidences and proof.

    Now faith is the assurance of things hoped for, the conviction of things not seen. (He.11:1)

- To believe because of God's tenderness and warmth.

  But God, being rich in mercy, because of the great love with which he loved us, even when we were dead in our trespasses, made us alive together with Christ—by grace you have been saved.... For by grace you have been saved through faith. And this is not your own doing; it is the gift of God, not a result of works, so that no one may boast. (Ep.2:4-5, 8-9)

- To believe because of God's love and care and because of the need and nature of the human heart.

  "For God so loved the world, that he gave his only Son, that whoever believes in him should not perish but have eternal life." (Jn.3:16)

  For all have sinned and fall short of the glory of God. (Ro.3:23)

  But God shows his love for us in that while we were still sinners, Christ died for us. (Ro.5:8)

- To believe because of our need for morality and godly character.

  But the fruit of the Spirit is love, joy, peace, patience, kindness, goodness, faithfulness, gentleness, self-control; against such things there is no law. (Ga.5:22-23; see vv.19-21)

- To believe because godly witnesses say so.

  And he said to them, "Go into all the world and proclaim the gospel to the whole creation." (Mk.16:15)

  Jesus said to them again, "Peace be with you. As the Father has sent me, even so I am sending you." (Jn.20:21)

- To believe because of the inner witness of the heart.

  They show that the work of the law is written on their hearts, while their conscience also bears witness, and their conflicting thoughts accuse or even excuse them (Ro.2:15)

- To believe because of the outer witness of nature.

  For his invisible attributes, namely, his eternal power and divine nature, have been clearly perceived, ever since the creation of the world, in the things that have been made. So they are without excuse. (Ro.1:20)

(See DEEPER STUDY # 1—Jn.2:23; DEEPER STUDY # 1, 2, 3—Mt.4:1-11 for more discussion.)

Note that Thomas ceased being obstinate and rebellious when he saw Jesus and after Jesus had rebuked him. Thomas had been at fault; he had been faithless, and his unbelief was inexcusable. The men who had proclaimed the truth to him were not liars. Neither could they all have been deceived. Up to this point, Thomas had refused to believe simply because he did not want to believe. He had acted intellectually superior and had been about to lose his soul.

The point is this: the person who believes without seeing demonstrates...
- a strength of character
- a tenderness and warmth of heart
- a sensitivity to the witness of the Holy Spirit
- an awareness to the order and beauty of all the world

Therefore, that person will be blessed with a very special joy, a joy unspeakable and full of glory.

  Though you have not seen him, you love him. Though you do not now see him, you believe in him and rejoice with joy that is inexpressible and filled with glory. (1 Pe.1:8)

**THOUGHT 1.** When people truly see what Jesus has done for Him, or when they are rebuked by the Spirit of Christ, they must cease their unbelief. They need to turn to Christ immediately, for the Lord's Spirit will not always strive with people.

  Then the LORD said, "My Spirit shall not abide in man forever, for he is flesh: his days shall be 120 years." (Ge.6:3)

  Blessed is the one who fears the LORD always, but whoever hardens his heart will fall into calamity. (Pr.28:14)

  He who is often reproved, yet stiffens his neck, will suddenly be broken beyond healing. (Pr.29:1)

### E. Event 5: The Great Purpose of the Signs (Wonderful Works) of Jesus, 20:30-31

30 Now Jesus did many other signs in the presence of the disciples, which are not written in this book;

31 but these are written so that you may believe that Jesus is the Christ, the Son of God, and that by believing you may have life in his name.

1. The great fact: Jesus did many signs
   a. In the disciples' presence
   b. Not recorded by John
2. The great purpose: To select a few signs that would lead to belief
   a. Jesus is the Christ—the Messiah
   b. Jesus is the Son of God
3. The great result: Life

# Division XVI

*The Revelation of Jesus, the Risen Lord, 20:1-21:25*

E. Event 5: The Great Purpose of the Signs (Wonderful Works) of Jesus, 20:30-31

## 20:30-31
## Introduction

Note two significant facts as an introduction to this passage. First, it is quite clear that the gospel writers did not include all that Jesus did in their gospels. In fact, they recorded very few of the signs—His wonderful, miraculous works. Contrary to what is usually thought, Jesus was apparently ministering and meeting the needs of multitudes every day—from sunrise until sundown.

Second, note the use of the word "signs." In talking about Jesus' life, the word "signs" is chosen by John. All that Jesus was and did were signs—signs demonstrating that He was the Messiah, the Son of God. In these two verses, John gives the great purpose of these signs, along with his purpose for reporting them. This is, *Event 5: The Great Purpose of the Signs (Wonderful Works) of Jesus*, 20:30-31.

1. The great fact: Jesus did many signs (v.30).
2. The great purpose: To select a few signs that would lead to belief (v.31).
3. The great result: Life (v.31).

## 1 The great fact: Jesus did many signs.

20:30

Jesus did many other signs that are not recorded in John's gospel. He performed many wonderful works. He was busy every day, actively involved either in worshiping God alone or in teaching and ministering to people. For about three years, Jesus was constantly demonstrating that He was the Messiah, the Son of God. He gave all the evidence in the world:

30 Now Jesus did many other signs in the presence of the disciples, which are not written in this book;

- ➤ acts of love and purity
- ➤ acts of righteousness and justice
- ➤ works of mercy and compassion
- ➤ works of miracles and power
- ➤ works of godliness and sovereignty
- ➤ words of truth and salvation
- ➤ words of peace and faith
- ➤ words of hope and joy
- ➤ words of morality and discipline
- ➤ words of commitment and self-denial

The point is that Jesus' life—His character and behavior, His preaching and teaching, His miracles and power—proves that He is the Messiah, the Son of God. Nobody could do the things He did unless He were the Son of God.

a. **In the disciples' presence.**

Jesus did not do the signs in secret, that is, out in a desert or off in a corner of the world. He did them out in the open, publicly. John said He did the signs in the presence of His disciples. They witnessed the signs, for Jesus saw to it that there was adequate witness and testimony. Note what John says in his epistle:

> That which was from the beginning, which we have heard, which we have seen with our eyes, which we looked upon and have touched with our hands, concerning the word of life—the life was made manifest, and we have seen it, and testify to it and proclaim to you the eternal life, which was with the Father and was made manifest to us—that which we have seen and heard we proclaim also to you, so that you too may have fellowship with us; and indeed our fellowship is with the Father and with his Son Jesus Christ. And we are writing these things so that our joy may be complete. (1 Jn.1:1-4)

b. **Not recorded by John.**

John says that he had been highly selective in the signs he had chosen to record in his gospel. There were *"many other"* signs which Jesus gave; so many in fact, "that the world itself could not contain the books that would be written" (Jn.21:25). John selected only a *few* signs to record.

**20:31**

³¹ but these are written so that you may believe that Jesus is the Christ, the Son of God, and that by believing you may have life in his name.

## 2 The great purpose: To select a few signs that would lead to belief.

John had a specific purpose in mind, so he selected specific signs that would help meet that purpose. The great purpose of John was to select a few signs that would lead people to believe (see Deeper Study # 2, *Believe*—Jn.2:24 for discussion). Every point in John's purpose is already noted and covered in John's Gospel. Referring to these notes will enhance discussion of this passage.

a. Jesus is the Christ—the Messiah (see Deeper Study # 2—Jn.1:20; note—1:23; Deeper Study # 4—1:49; notes—3:27-28; 12:12-19; 13:36-38; 20:25-28 for discussion).

b. Jesus is the Son of God (see Deeper Study # 1—Jn.1:1-5; notes—1:1-2; 1:30-31; 1:34 for discussion).

## 3 The great result: Life.

Any logical person should read the record of Jesus' wonderful works and believe that Jesus is God's Son, the Messiah, and the Savior of the World. All who do receive a great gift—*life*, eternal life, abundant life that begins now and continues forever and ever. This is the great result John hoped his gospel would achieve: that untold multitudes would have life through Jesus' name (see Deeper Study # 2—Jn.1:4; Deeper Study # 1—10:10; Deeper Study # 1—17:2-3 for discussion).

# CHAPTER 21

## F. Event 6: The Great Reality of Jesus' Resurrection Body, 21:1-14

After this Jesus revealed himself again to the disciples by the Sea of Tiberias, and he revealed himself in this way. ² Simon Peter, Thomas (called the Twin), Nathanael of Cana in Galilee, the sons of Zebedee, and two others of his disciples were together. ³ Simon Peter said to them, "I am going fishing." They said to him, "We will go with you." They went out and got into the boat, but that night they caught nothing. ⁴ Just as day was breaking, Jesus stood on the shore; yet the disciples did not know that it was Jesus. ⁵ Jesus said to them, "Children, do you have any fish?" They answered him, "No." ⁶ He said to them, "Cast the net on the right side of the boat, and you will find some." So they cast it, and now they were not able to haul it in, because of the quantity of fish. ⁷ That disciple whom Jesus loved therefore said to Peter, "It is the Lord!" When Simon Peter heard that it was the Lord, he put on his outer garment, for he was stripped for work, and threw himself into the sea. ⁸ The other disciples came in the boat, dragging the net full of fish, for they were not far from the land, but about a hundred yards off. ⁹ When they got out on land, they saw a charcoal fire in place, with fish laid out on it, and bread.

¹⁰ Jesus said to them, "Bring some of the fish that you have just caught."

¹¹ So Simon Peter went aboard and hauled the net ashore, full of large fish, 153 of them. And although there were so many, the net was not torn.

1. **Jesus appeared again**[DS1]
   a. He appeared after the proofs of the resurrection, see 20:1-31
   b. He appeared to seven disciples who were together: Hiding for fear of the authorities
   c. Peter went fishing: To meet the need for food
   d. A needed lesson—self-sufficiency is inadequate: Must know & depend on the risen Lord
2. **Jesus stood on the shore—bodily**
   a. An unexpected presence
   b. A bodily presence
3. **Jesus possessed supernatural knowledge**

   a. He used His supernatural knowledge to demonstrate His care for them

   b. He was identified by John: "The Lord"
   c. Peter accepted John's word as proof and He responded

   d. The other disciples responded and followed

4. **Jesus showed the reality of the surroundings**
   a. The land and fire
   b. The fish & bread
5. **Jesus showed that He could see, speak, hear, and feel**
   a. He instructed the disciples
   b. Peter obeyed
   c. The catch of fish was counted

6. **Jesus showed that His body was real**
   a. He invited them to eat
   b. He was known to be the Lord

   c. He served them

7. **Jesus affirmed His resurrection through this third appearance**

¹² Jesus said to them, "Come and have breakfast." Now none of the disciples dared ask him, "Who are you?" They knew it was the Lord. ¹³ Jesus came and took the bread and gave it to them, and so with the fish. ¹⁴ This was now the third time that Jesus was revealed to the disciples after he was raised from the dead.

## Division XVI

*The Revelation of Jesus, the Risen Lord, 20:1–21:25*

F. Event 6: The Great Reality of Jesus' Resurrection Body, 21:1–14

### 21:1–14
### Introduction

After Jesus' resurrection, He remained on earth for forty days until He ascended back to heaven (Ac.1:3). During this time, the risen Lord did not keep a low profile, as we would say. Jesus showed Himself publicly on a number of occasions. On one occasion, He appeared to over five hundred people at one time (1 Co.15:4-8). Jesus' many appearances proved the great reality of His resurrection body. He showed that He really did arise from the dead. Death had been conquered, and people could now live forever. In this passage, John records what happened on His third appearance to His disciples. This is, *The Great Reality of Jesus' Resurrection Body*, 21:1-14.

1. Jesus appeared again (vv.1–3).
2. Jesus stood on the shore—bodily (v.4).
3. Jesus possessed supernatural knowledge (vv.5–8).
4. Jesus showed the reality of the surroundings (v.9).
5. Jesus showed that He could see, speak, hear, and feel (vv.10–11).
6. Jesus showed that His body was real (vv.12–13).
7. Jesus affirmed His resurrection through this third appearance (v.14).

**21:1–3**

After this Jesus revealed himself again to the disciples by the Sea of Tiberias, and he revealed himself in this way.
² Simon Peter, Thomas (called the Twin), Nathanael of Cana in Galilee, the sons of Zebedee, and two others of his disciples were together.
³ Simon Peter said to them, "I am going fishing." They said to him, "We will go with you." They went out and got into the boat, but that night they caught nothing.

**1 Jesus appeared again.**

After Jesus' appearances to His disciples in the locked room where they gathered, He appeared to them again (see DEEPER STUDY # 1). John reports the details of this encounter.

a. **He appeared after the proofs of the resurrection (v.1; see 20:1-31).**

This appearance occurred after events of the previous chapter. The words *after this* or *after these things* refer to the proofs of Jesus' resurrection already recorded (Jn.20:1-31).

b. **He appeared to seven disciples who were together: Hiding for fear of the authorities (v.2).**
   Seven disciples were together. They were apparently in some home, continuing to hide for fear of the authorities (see note—Jn.20:19).

c. **Peter went fishing: To meet the need for food (v.3a).**

Peter returned to fishing. The others decided to join him, and they went out under the cover of darkness and off on some lonely strand of beach (vv.3, 9-14). In the sovereignty of God, the small band of men needed to learn a glorious lesson, so God was setting the stage for them to receive the lesson.

d. **A needed lesson—self-sufficiency is inadequate: Must know and depend on the risen Lord (v.3b).**

The disciples caught nothing, and it was in this that they were to learn the much-needed lesson: self-sufficiency is inadequate. They could no longer do anything on their own. They must know the risen Lord, and they must depend on Him. They could not provide for themselves in their own strength; they must know that the Lord is really risen, and they must learn to depend on Him.

Jesus used this experience of catching nothing to teach the disciples that He had truly risen. It was He in the resurrected body. He was truly the Risen Lord, and it was He on whom they must depend from now on.

## Deeper Study # 1

**(21:1) Jesus Christ Shows His Resurrected Body:** it is said twice in one verse that Jesus revealed or showed Himself. The purpose of these appearances was to prove that Jesus was not a spirit, vision, phantom, hallucination, or any other figment of human imagination.

He was the risen Lord—bodily. He was not someone else. His body was none other than the body of Jesus, the Carpenter from Nazareth. He had been raised from the dead—physically raised. His body was real. It was different, yes; but it was His body—perfected, no longer subject to the limitations and frailties of the physical universe and its laws. It was His body which was now transformed into a spiritual body by the power of God's Word (see Ro.1:3-4).

How did the Lord's body differ since His resurrection? Some idea can be gleaned by looking both at His resurrection body and at the glorified body promised to the believer.

1. The resurrected body of the Lord was His body, but it was radically changed. It had all the appearance of His physical body, yet it was not bound by the physical world and its material substance.
   a. It looked like the same material body, the same "flesh and bones," not some other body. It was a body that bore the marks of the nails in His hands and feet (Jn.20:20, 27). It was a body that appeared and looked like a body and that occupied space.
   b. It was a body that could travel and appear any place at will or by thought, a body unhampered by space, time, or physical substance. When He appeared, He did it suddenly, even behind locked doors (Lu.24:36; Jn.20:19).
   c. It was a body that differed enough from the earthly body that it was not clearly recognized, not at first, not until it was closely observed.
      ➣ Mary Magdalene thought He was the gardener (Jn.20:15).
      ➣ The two disciples walking toward Emmaus thought He was a traveler (Lu.24:31).
      ➣ The disciples who were fishing did not recognize Him standing on the seashore (Jn.21:4).

   However, after close observation, the Lord was recognized in all these instances. This probably indicates that our heavenly bodies will look like our earthly bodies, differing only in that they are perfected.
2. The resurrected and glorified body that is promised to the believer gives some additional insight into the kind of body Jesus now has. One of the most wonderful promises ever made to believers is given in the following verses:
   ➣ Christ will transform our lowly bodies into the likeness of His glorious body (Ph.3:21; see Mt.13:43; Ro.8:17; Col.3:4; Re.22:5).

> We will be "conformed to the image of His Son" (Ro.8:29. See 1 Co.15:49; 2 Co.3:18.)
> We will see Jesus "as He is"—in His glorified body—and we will be like Him (1 Jn.3:2).

The body of the believer is to undergo a radical change just as the Lord's body was radically changed. Several changes are promised the believer.

a. The believer will receive a spiritual body.

> It is sown a natural body [soma psuchikon]; it is raised a spiritual body [soma pneumatikon]. If there is a natural body, there is also a spiritual body. (1 Co.15:44)

Note that the *spiritual body* (soma pneumatikon) is still a body just like the *natural body* (soma psuchikon). The spiritual body still retains the qualities of the earthly body. The difference lies in its nature: it will no longer be a natural body; it will be spiritual. What does this mean? In essence, the body will be perfected and glorified: no longer subject to aging, deterioration, death, decay, pain, tears, sorrow, or crying (Re.21:4).

> So is it with the resurrection of the dead. What is sown is perishable; what is raised is imperishable. It is sown in dishonor; it is raised in glory. It is sown in weakness; it is raised in power. (1 Co.15:42-43)

Note the strong, emphatic declaration: "*There is* a natural body, and *there is* a spiritual body" (1 Co.15:44).

b. The believer will receive a body that is *not flesh and blood*. Flesh and blood are corruptible, they age, deteriorate, die, and decay.

> Jesus said, "Take away the stone." Martha, the sister of the dead man, said to him, "Lord, by this time there will be an odor, for he has been dead four days." (Jn.11:39)

> "For David, after he had served the purpose of God in his own generation, fell asleep and was laid with his fathers and saw corruption, but he whom God raised up did not see corruption." (Ac.13:36-37)

> So is it with the resurrection of the dead. What is sown is perishable; what is raised is imperishable. (1 Co.15:42)

> I tell you this, brothers: flesh and blood cannot inherit the kingdom of God, nor does the perishable inherit the imperishable. (1 Co.15:50)

> For we know that if the tent that is our earthly home is destroyed, we have a building from God, a house not made with hands, eternal in the heavens. For in this tent we groan, longing to put on our heavenly dwelling. (2 Co.5:1-2)

> All go to one place. All are from the dust, and to dust all return. (Ec.3:20)

c. The believer will receive a body that will be radically changed.

> In a moment, in the twinkling of an eye, at the last trumpet. For the trumpet will sound, and the dead will be raised imperishable, and we shall be changed. For this perishable body must put on the imperishable, and this mortal body must put on immortality. (1 Co.15:52-53)

d. The believer will be given a body that will not need reproduction for continuing the (redeemed) human race.

> "For in the resurrection they neither marry nor are given in marriage, but are like angels in heaven." (Mt.22:30)

## 21:4

⁴ Just as day was breaking, Jesus stood on the shore; yet the disciples did not know that it was Jesus.

## 2 Jesus stood on the shore—bodily.

After a long night of unsuccessful fishing, the disciples were surely glad to see morning come. As dawn broke and the sun began to rise, they saw a man standing on the shore.

a. **An unexpected presence.**

Jesus appeared suddenly and unexpectedly on the seashore. The disciples did not recognize Him, indicating that they were not expecting Him. But Jesus knew their situation. They needed food, and He came to His faithful disciples to meet their need.

### b. A bodily presence.

Christ appeared bodily; that is, His body stood there. The disciples saw a person just as they would see any other person standing on the seashore. There was no thought of a vision, hallucination, or spirit. They saw a real person on the seashore and thought nothing strange about it.

## 3 Jesus possessed supernatural knowledge.

21:5-8

Jesus asked the frustrated fishermen if they had caught any fish (v.5). He asked for their benefit—not His—for, as the omniscient God, the Lord knew they had caught nothing. And He knew something else: where the fish were.

> 5 Jesus said to them, "Children, do you have any fish?" They answered him, "No."
> 6 He said to them, "Cast the net on the right side of the boat, and you will find some." So they cast it, and now they were not able to haul it in, because of the quantity of fish.
> 7 That disciple whom Jesus loved therefore said to Peter, "It is the Lord!" When Simon Peter heard that it was the Lord, he put on his outer garment, for he was stripped for work, and threw himself into the sea.
> 8 The other disciples came in the boat, dragging the net full of fish, for they were not far from the land, but about a hundred yards off.

### a. He used His supernatural knowledge to demonstrate His care for them (v.6).

Jesus told the disciples to cast their net on the right side of the boat. He possessed supernatural knowledge; consequently, He knew where the fish were. Remember, the disciples had been commercial fishermen before their call to serve the Lord. Jesus was teaching that He, the risen Lord, was the same Lord who took care of them before the crucifixion; therefore, He would take care of them now. But there was one significant difference that they must learn. The resurrection increased His care and added much more to their salvation. He, the risen Lord, was the sovereign majesty of the universe who could use His sovereign knowledge and power to provide all things for His dear children (see Mt.6:25-34).

### b. He was identified by John: "The Lord" (v.7a).

After they did what the stranger suggested and caught more fish than they could haul in, John realized that this stranger was indeed the Lord. The miracle of knowing where the fish were, the Lord's supernatural sovereign knowledge, led John to this realization.

> "Now we know that you know all things and do not need anyone to question you; this is why we believe that you came from God." (Jn.16:30)

### c. Peter accepted John's word as proof, and He responded (v.7b).

Peter's response to Christ's presence was exactly what it should have been—exuberance and excitement. He spontaneously clothed himself fully and jumped into the lake and swam to shore.

### d. The other disciples responded and followed (v.8).

Apparently, the other disciples were not as excited as Peter was, or perhaps they were just more practical in their thinking! They followed in the boat, dragging their huge catch along.

**THOUGHT 1.** When people hear that Jesus is really alive—that He is the sovereign majesty of the universe—they should do just what these men did: rush to Him as quickly as possible.

> "God raised him [Jesus Christ] up, loosing the pangs of death, because it was not possible for him to be held by it." (Ac.2:24)
>
> Who was delivered up for our trespasses and raised for our justification. (Ro.4:25)
>
> Because, if you confess with your mouth that Jesus is Lord and believe in your heart that God raised him from the dead, you will be saved. (Ro.10:9)
>
> For since we believe that Jesus died and rose again, even so, through Jesus, God will bring with him those who have fallen asleep. (1 Th.4:14)
>
> Blessed be the God and Father of our Lord Jesus Christ! According to his great mercy, he has caused us to be born again to a living hope through the resurrection of Jesus Christ from

the dead, to an inheritance that is imperishable, undefiled, and unfading, kept in heaven for you. (1 Pe.1:3-4)

For Christ also suffered once for sins, the righteous for the unrighteous, that he might bring us to God, being put to death in the flesh but made alive in the spirit. (1 Pe.3:18)

**THOUGHT 2.** Every genuine believer experiences the supernatural care of the risen Lord. Believers knows the sovereign knowledge and care of the Lord in their daily lives (Mt.6:25-34).

**THOUGHT 3.** Peter's impetuous enthusiasm is to be admired. We should look forward to seeing Jesus with the same zeal he displayed when he realized it was Christ standing on the shore. Notice that Peter clothed himself, for he wanted to be properly covered in Jesus' presence. In like manner, we should seek to be holy, to cleanse ourselves of all filthiness of the flesh and spirit, so that, when we see Christ, we will not be ashamed.

Waiting for our blessed hope, the appearing of the glory of our great God and Savior Jesus Christ, who gave himself for us to redeem us from all lawlessness and to purify for himself a people for his own possession who are zealous for good works. (Ti.2:13-14)

Though you have not seen him, you love him. Though you do not now see him, you believe in him and rejoice with joy that is inexpressible and filled with glory. (1 Pe.1:8)

And now, little children, abide in him, so that when he appears we may have confidence and not shrink from him in shame at his coming. (1 Jn.2:28)

Beloved, we are God's children now, and what we will be has not yet appeared; but we know that when he appears we shall be like him, because we shall see him as he is. And everyone who thus hopes in him purifies himself as he is pure. Everyone who makes a practice of sinning also practices lawlessness; sin is lawlessness. (1 Jn.3:2-3)

They will see his face, and his name will be on their foreheads. (Rev.22:4)

## 21:9

⁹ When they got out on land, they saw a charcoal fire in place, with fish laid out on it, and bread.

## 4 Jesus showed the reality of the surroundings.

As further evidence of a real, physical appearance, Jesus showed the reality of the surroundings. Note the land and fire, the fish and bread. He was showing to His disciples that He was the same Jesus who had always been with them. He was not a figment of their imagination, not a vision, not even a spirit. He was in a body just like the body they had always known. And He was preparing breakfast for them! An assuring detail is that there were already fish on the fire and bread ready to be served. Truly, the Lord cares about His people and their needs.

But immediately Jesus spoke to them, saying, "Take heart; it is I. Do not be afraid." (Mt.14:27)

## 21:10-11

¹⁰ Jesus said to them, "Bring some of the fish that you have just caught."
¹¹ So Simon Peter went aboard and hauled the net ashore, full of large fish, 153 of them. And although there were so many, the net was not torn.

## 5 Jesus showed that He could see, speak, hear, and feel.

Jesus showed His disciples that He could see, speak, hear, and feel. He instructed them to gather the fish, speaking to them just as He always had (v.10). Peter obeyed and dragged the net to the shore. True to their nature as fishermen, they even counted the fish. There were 153, and they were all big ones—an impressive catch (v.11)! Jesus was heaping proof upon proof, giving the disciples indisputable evidence of His resurrection.

That which was from the beginning, which we have heard, which we have seen with our eyes, which we looked upon and have touched with our hands, concerning the word of life—the life was made manifest, and we have seen it, and testify to it and proclaim to you the eternal life, which was with the Father and was made manifest to us—that which we have seen and heard we proclaim also to you, so that you too may have fellowship with us; and indeed our fellowship is with the Father and with his Son Jesus Christ. (1 Jn.1:1-3)

## 6  Jesus showed that His body was real.

Everything Jesus did testified that His body was real. John's painstaking attention to detail reveals that Jesus wanted His disciples to have abundant evidence of His resurrection. And it shows that John wanted all who would read His Gospel to be aware of that convincing evidence.

> [12] Jesus said to them, "Come and have breakfast." Now none of the disciples dared ask him, "Who are you?" They knew it was the Lord.
> [13] Jesus came and took the bread and gave it to them, and so with the fish.

### a. He invited them to eat (v.12a).

Jesus invited the disciples to eat the meal He had prepared. Again, the point is that they must *know* it was Jesus. The risen Lord was the same Jesus who had walked and lived with them; the only difference was that He had risen from the dead in a perfected and glorified body.

### b. He was known to be the Lord (v.12b).

The disciples knew beyond question that it was the Lord. Humanly, it was not supposed to be; a dead man rising from the grave is impossible. The physical and material world knew nothing but corruption and decay, sin and death. But seated there with them was Jesus. He had risen from the dead and come back to life again. They knew that death was now conquered and that people could now live forever (Jn.20:31).

The disciples knew just what Jesus wanted them to know. They knew the great reality of His resurrection body and the great reality of His sovereign majesty and care for them in conquering death.

> "For God so loved the world, that he gave his only Son, that whoever believes in him should not perish but have eternal life." (Jn.3:16)
>
> "Truly, truly, I say to you, whoever hears my word and believes him who sent me has eternal life. He does not come into judgment, but has passed from death to life." (Jn.5:24)
>
> Jesus said to her, "I am the resurrection and the life. Whoever believes in me, though he die, yet shall he live, and everyone who lives and believes in me shall never die. Do you believe this?" (Jn.11:25-26)
>
> And which now has been manifested through the appearing of our Savior Christ Jesus, who abolished death and brought life and immortality to light through the gospel. (2 Ti.1:10)
>
> Since therefore the children share in flesh and blood, he himself likewise partook of the same things, that through death he might destroy the one who has the power of death, that is, the devil, and deliver all those who through fear of death were subject to lifelong slavery. (He.2:14-15)
>
> "He will wipe away every tear from their eyes, and death shall be no more, neither shall there be mourning, nor crying, nor pain anymore, for the former things have passed away." (Re.21:4)

### c. He served them (v.13).

Our risen Lord not only prepared breakfast for the weary disciples, He also served them. Note that this detail further establishes that Jesus had a real body. He actually picked up the bread and fish with His hands and served the food. *Took* (lambanei) may simply mean that Jesus picked up the bread, or it may indicate that He ate with them (Mt.26:26; Lk.6:4).

## 7  Jesus affirmed His resurrection through this third appearance.

The reality of Jesus' resurrection was affirmed by this third appearance to His disciples. John documented this thrilling event as one who participated in it. Remember why John was writing: to convince people to believe in Jesus as Savior and Lord.

> [14] This was now the third time that Jesus was revealed to the disciples after he was raised from the dead.

But these are written so that you may believe that Jesus is the Christ, the Son of God, and that by believing you may have life in his name. (Jn.20:31)

"For we cannot but speak of what we have seen and heard." (Ac.4:20)

"And we are witnesses to these things, and so is the Holy Spirit, whom God has given to those who obey him." (Ac.5:32)

Since we have the same spirit of faith according to what has been written, "I believed, and so I spoke," we also believe, and so we also speak. (2 Co.4:13)

### G. Event 7: The Great Question About a Disciple's Love and Devotion, 21:15-17

¹⁵ When they had finished breakfast, Jesus said to Simon Peter, "Simon, son of John, do you love me more than these?" He said to him, "Yes, Lord; you know that I love you." He said to him, "Feed my lambs."

¹⁶ He said to him a second time, "Simon, son of John, do you love me?" He said to him, "Yes, Lord; you know that I love you." He said to him, "Tend my sheep."

¹⁷ He said to him the third time, "Simon, son of John, do you love me?" Peter was grieved because he said to him the third time, "Do you love me?" and he said to him, "Lord, you know everything; you know that I love you." Jesus said to him, "Feed my sheep."

1. Jesus focused on Peter after the meal: Asked him three straightforward questions
2. Do you love me more than these?
   a. Pointed to the disciples
   b. Pointed to the fishing equipment (Peter's business)
   c. Charge 1: Feed my lambs
3. Do you love me with God's love, a sacrificial love (agapē)—love me enough to feed my people
   a. Peter's affirmation: "You know I love you" (phileō)
   b. Charge 2: Feed my sheep
4. Do you love me as a loyal brother—love me with agapē love or phileō love?
   a. The Lord's question: Do you really love me as a brother (phileō)?
   b. Peter's strong declaration: Jesus knew that he loved Him as a brother
   c. Charge 3: Feed my sheep

## Division XVI

*The Revelation of Jesus, the Risen Lord, 20:1-21:25*

G. Event 7: The Great Question About a Disciple's Love and Devotion, 21:15-17

**21:15-17**
# Introduction

This is a critical passage for the church and its ministers. It has one great lesson: love is the one basic essential for ministry. We are to serve Christ because we love Him, and, if we love Christ, we will serve Him. Without love, ministry counts for nothing in God's eyes. This passage concerns three questions asked by our Lord. This is, *Event 7: The Great Question About a Disciple's Love and Devotion*, 21:15-17.
1. Jesus focused on Peter after the meal: Asked him three straightforward questions (v.15).
2. Do you love me more than these? (v.15).
3. Do you love me with God's love, a *sacrificial love* (agapē)—love me enough to feed my people (v.16).
4. Do you love me as a loyal brother—love me with agape love or phileō love? (v.17).

(Note: this passage is best studied as a whole, comparing each question with the other two questions. Because of this, all three points are studied together and not by separate points. For this reason, the commentary does not follow the outline. The outline explains the details of Jesus' critical conversation with Peter; the commentary explains the meaning. It is also helpful to see notes, *Love*—Jn.13:33-35; 14:15.)

## 1 Jesus focused on Peter after the meal: Asked him three straightforward questions.

**21:15**

¹⁵ When they had finished breakfast, Jesus said to Simon Peter, "Simon, son of John, do you love me more than these?" He said to him, "Yes, Lord; you know that I love you." He said to him, "Feed my lambs."

The meal Jesus had prepared and served His disciples was finished. Jesus and the disciples were sitting around talking and sharing together, when Jesus focused the conversation on Peter. Keep the following four insights in mind as you study this passage:

> ➤ Jesus had already met Peter in a private session to discuss Peter's denial and to make sure he was fully restored (see 1 Co.15:4-5).
>
> ➤ Peter's leadership needed to be reinforced publicly among all the disciples. They all knew about Peter's denial.
>
> ➤ Jesus wanted to strengthen Peter to never deny Him nor fall back from his mission again.
>
> ➤ Jesus needed to teach the disciples the one basic essential for ministry. None of them, not even a charismatic leader such as Peter, could ever minister and bear godly fruit unless he *loved* the Lord and the flock of God. An individual may be the most gifted person in the world but is nothing and can do nothing of value *in God's eyes* unless they first love (see 1 Co.13:1-3). Abilities, talents, gifts, commitments, good deeds, and works simply do not qualify us before God nor make us acceptable to God. The one great thing—in fact the only thing—that makes us acceptable and that qualifies us to serve God is *love*.

These are the reasons for what Jesus now did. He turned to focus on Peter. Note: He called Peter by his full name, Simon Peter, and reminded him that he was the son of Jonas (see Jn.1:42). This did two things. It attracted everyone's attention, stressing that what was to follow was important—more important than usual. And it reminded Peter where he had come from. He was of humble beginnings, from a lowly father. All that Peter had become and would become was of God. Peter was *nothing apart from Christ* and *nothing apart from the mission he was about to receive*.

> **THOUGHT 1.** We need to know that we are nothing apart from Christ. How many persons would have more in life—more purpose, more meaning, more significance—if they would only surrender to Christ? How many have actually been called by Christ yet rejected His call; therefore, they have missed out on their purpose in life and on making their contribution to society and to the world?

## 2 Do you love me more than these?

Jesus did not ask Peter one question three times; He asked three different questions. The English wording reveals some of these differences, but the Greek text reveals them fully. In the first question, Jesus asked Peter whom he loved the most, the Lord Himself or "these." Just what is meant by "these" is not clear. Jesus could have been pointing to the disciples sitting around. If so, He meant, do you love me more than you love these men or your family? Or, Jesus could have been pointing to the fish, the nets, and the boat. If so, He was asking, do you love me more than your profession and career (see Jn.21:3)? Perhaps Scripture is unclear at this point in order to make "these" apply to anything and everything in our lives.

With the second question, Jesus asked Peter if he loved with God's love (v.16). This is seen in the Greek word for love. Jesus used one word in His question, but Peter used another in his reply. Jesus used the word *agapē*, the highest form of love, the love of God Himself. But Peter did not reply, "Yes, Lord, I *agapē* you." He said, "Yes, Lord, I *phileō* you." That is, "I love you just like a brother; I love you with a brotherly love." *Phileō* describes brotherly love, the love between two brothers. It is a love that feels affection for another.

In His third question, Christ probed the genuineness and loyalty of Peter's love (v.17). Here Jesus descended to the human level of love. This time He used *phileō*. He simply asked Peter,

"Peter, do you really love, *phileō* me—even as a brother?" And questioning the loyalty of his love grieved Peter. But Jesus assured Peter that his love would one day reach the ultimate height (v.18). Peter would be called on to demonstrate *agapē* love, the sacrificial love of God. Peter would be called on to die for Christ, to give his life for preaching the love of God to those who did not care for it and who would react violently against it.

Jesus was preparing His disciples for a new kind of love that was yet to come. Up to the time of Christ's death and ascension, the greatest love known to mankind was *phileō love*, the willingness of a person to die for a friend. But in Christ, God was showing the world a new kind of love—*agapē love*. *Agapē love* is a love so new that a new meaning had to be given to the Greek word "*agapē.*" *Agape* became the love that was willing to give and die even for an enemy. The early Christian leaders recognized this new dimension of love, so they lifted the meaning of *agapē love* up to God's love for the world. *Agapē love* is the highest level of love possible; it is the love of God, the love God had for the world that compelled Him to give His only begotten Son that we may have eternal life (Jn.3:16).

*Agape love* is Christ dying . . .
- for people who have no strength (Ro.5:6)
- for the ungodly (Ro.5:6)
- for sinners (Ro.5:8)
- for the enemies of God (Ro.5:10)

Peter and the disciples did not yet understand this. They could not because the Holy Spirit had not yet been given, and *agapē love* is shed abroad in the heart only by the Holy Spirit (Ro.5:5). It is a fruit of the Holy Spirit (Ga.5:22).

## 3 Do you love me with God's love, a sacrificial love (agapē)—love me enough to feed my people?

**16** He said to him a second time, "Simon, son of John, do you love me?" He said to him, "Yes, Lord; you know that I love you." He said to him, "Tend my sheep."

Three times Peter was commissioned to feed and tend the flock of God. If Peter really loved the Lord, then he was to be a shepherd of the flock of God. Note three truths.

First, Scripture identifies the lambs and sheep as the flock of God, that is, as the church of God. Jesus was talking about feeding His church, His disciples within the church.

> "Pay careful attention to yourselves and to all the flock, in which the Holy Spirit has made you overseers, to care for the church of God, which he obtained with his own blood." (Ac.20:28)

Notice that in this verse (Ac.20:28), the charge is to guard oneself as well as the flock of God. This is similar to what Jesus was saying to Peter: if you love me, guard yourself and be faithful; feed my lambs and sheep, my church.

Second, the flock of God is made up of both *lambs* (arnia, v.15) and *sheep* (probata, vv.16-17). Lambs are children, young converts, the handicapped or special cases, believers who need special attention. Sheep are mature believers, believers who have walked and grown in the Lord for a long time (see note, pt.5—Mt.25:31-33 for more discussion).

Third, the ministry to the flock or church is twofold. The first ministry is to *feed* (boske, vv.15, 17):

➢ To give food, teaching both the milk and meat of the Word.

> **For though by this time you ought to be teachers, you need someone to teach you again the basic principles of the oracles [Word] of God. You need milk, not solid food, for everyone who lives on milk is unskilled in the word of righteousness, since he is a child. But solid food is for the mature, for those who have their powers of discernment trained by constant practice to distinguish good from evil. (He.5:12-14)**

> **Like newborn infants, long for the pure spiritual milk, that by it you may grow up into salvation—if indeed you have tasted that the Lord is good. (1 Pe.2:2-3)**

➢ To guide into the study of the Word—showing oneself approved by God.

> Do your best to present yourself to God as one approved, a worker who has no need to be ashamed, rightly handling the word of truth. (2 Ti.2:15)

Note that the word used for *feeding* (boske) is the word used for both the lambs (v.15) and the sheep (v.17). Both the lambs and sheep are to be fed on the same Word and fed in the same way.

> "And he humbled you and let you hunger and fed you with manna, which you did not know, nor did your fathers know, that he might make you know that man does not live by bread alone, but man lives by every word that comes from the mouth of the LORD." (De.8:3; see Mt.4:4)

> "I have not departed from the commandment of his lips; I have treasured the words of his mouth more than my portion of food." (Job 23:12)

> How sweet are your words to my taste, sweeter than honey to my mouth! (Ps.119:103)

> Your words were found, and I ate them, and your words became to me a joy and the delight of my heart, for I am called by your name, O LORD, God of hosts. (Je.15:16)

The second ministry is to *tend* or *shepherd* (poimaine, v.16). Shepherding includes all the works of the ministry, everything involved in leading and caring for the sheep.

> Shepherd the flock of God that is among you, exercising oversight, not under compulsion, but willingly, as God would have you; not for shameful gain, but eagerly; not domineering over those in your charge, but being examples to the flock. (1 Pe.5:2-3)

(See note—Jn.10:2-3 for the work of a shepherd. See note—Mk.6:34.)

## 21:17

<sup>17</sup> He said to him the third time, "Simon, son of John, do you love me?" Peter was grieved because he said to him the third time, "Do you love me?" and he said to him, "Lord, you know everything; you know that I love you." Jesus said to him, "Feed my sheep."

## 4 Do you love me as a loyal brother—love me with agapē love or phileō love?

Jesus asked Peter if he loved Him with *agapē* or *phileō* love. The difference between *agapē love* and *phileō love* is as follows:

*Phileō love* is the love of tender affection, of warm and deep feelings within the heart. It is the deep and precious love of those near and dear to one's heart. It is brotherly love, a love between family members, a love that would die for its brother.

*Agapē love* is the love of the mind, of the reason, and of the will. It is a love that is born of choice; one simply chooses to love regardless of feelings. A person may insult, injure, or humiliate; but *agapē love* chooses to seek only the highest good for that person. It is sacrificial love, a love that is willing to die even for its enemies.

*Agapē love* means . . .
- sacrificial giving
- free acceptance (one freely accepts without any expectation of return)
- cherished attachment
- unselfish devotion
- personal commitment
- genuine concern
- strong loyalty
- precious tenderness

*Agapē love* was so new and so unusual that it can be said that after Christ's death a new word for love had to be created. Jesus' primary interest with Peter was, of course, that he possess *agapē love*: the love that comes from reason and will, that controls the corruptible lusts and wandering thoughts of life, that puts a willingness within a person to serve and to die for all people—even for a person's enemies. Even the enemies of God must hear the gospel and have an opportunity for salvation. However, the fact that Jesus also mentioned *phileō love* with Peter shows that God wants the love of our warm instinctive feelings as well.

*Agapē love* has at least eight characteristics:

➢ *Agapē love* is not only a love of emotions. It is a matter of the mind as well as of the heart, of the will as well as of the emotions.

> "For God so loved the world, that he gave his only Son, that whoever believes in him should not perish but have eternal life." (Jn.3:16)

For while we were still weak, at the right time Christ died for the ungodly. For one will scarcely die for a righteous person—though perhaps for a good person one would dare even to die—but God shows his love for us in that while we were still sinners, Christ died for us. (Ro.5:6-8)

In this the love of God was made manifest among us, that God sent his only Son into the world, so that we might live through him. In this is love, not that we have loved God but that he loved us and sent his Son to be the propitiation for our sins. (1 Jn.4:9-10)

➤ *Agapē love* is God's love—His very nature. It is the love that God extended toward us, in that while we were yet sinners, Christ died for us.

But God shows his love for us in that while we were still sinners, Christ died for us. . . . For if while we were enemies we were reconciled to God by the death of his Son, much more, now that we are reconciled, shall we be saved by his life. (Ro.5:8, 10)

Beloved, let us love one another, for love is from God, and whoever loves has been born of God and knows God. Anyone who does not love does not know God, because God is love. In this the love of God was made manifest among us, that God sent his only Son into the world, so that we might live through him. In this is love, not that we have loved God but that he loved us and sent his Son to be the propitiation for our sins. . . . So we have come to know and to believe the love that God has for us. God is love, and whoever abides in love abides in God, and God abides in him. (1 Jn.4:7-10, 16)

➤ *Agapē love* is a seed that can be planted in the heart only by Christ. It is a fruit of the Spirit of God.

And hope does not put us to shame, because God's love has been poured into our hearts through the Holy Spirit who has been given to us. (Ro.5:5)

But the fruit of the Spirit is love, joy, peace, patience, kindness, goodness, faithfulness. (Ga.5:22)

➤ *Agapē love* is the great love that God holds for His own dear Son.

"If you keep my commandments, you will abide in my love, just as I have kept my Father's commandments and abide in his love." (Jn.15:10)

"I made known to them your name, and I will continue to make it known, that the love with which you have loved me may be in them, and I in them." (Jn.17:26)

➤ *Agapē love* was perfectly expressed when God gave up His own Son to die for humanity.

For the love of Christ controls us, because we have concluded this: that one has died for all, therefore all have died. (2 Co.5:14)

But God, being rich in mercy, because of the great love with which he loved us. (Ep.2:4)

And to know the love of Christ that surpasses knowledge, that you may be filled with all the fullness of God. (Ep.3:19)

And walk in love, as Christ loved us and gave himself up for us, a fragrant offering and sacrifice to God. (Ep.5:2)

➤ *Agapē love* is the love which holds believers together. For three years Jesus Himself had held the apostles together. Now that He was about to leave them, what was going to keep them together and keep them at the task? One thing: the new commandment—*agapē love*. *Agapē love* is the love believers are to have for one another.

"Little children, yet a little while I am with you. You will seek me, and just as I said to the Jews, so now I also say to you, 'Where I am going you cannot come.' A new commandment I give to you, that you love one another: just as I have loved you, you also are to love one another. By this all people will know that you are my disciples, if you have love for one another." (Jn.13:33-35)

But if anyone has the world's goods and sees his brother in need, yet closes his heart against him, how does God's love abide in him? Little children, let us not love in word or talk but in deed and in truth. (1 Jn.3:17-18)

➤ *Agapē love* is the love which believers are to have for all people, whether believer or unbeliever.

Let all that you do be done in love. (1 Co.16:14)

And may the Lord make you increase and abound in love for one another and for all, as we do for you. (1 Th.3:12)

And godliness with brotherly affection, and brotherly affection with love. (2 Pe.1:7)

- *Agapē love* seeks the welfare of all.

    Let each of us please his neighbor for his good, to build him up. (Ro.15:2)

- *Agapē love* works no ill to its neighbor.

    Owe no one anything, except to love each other, for the one who loves another has fulfilled the law. For the commandments, "You shall not commit adultery, You shall not murder, You shall not steal, You shall not covet," and any other commandment, are summed up in this word: "You shall love your neighbor as yourself." Love does no wrong to a neighbor; therefore love is the fulfilling of the law. (Ro.13:8–10)

- *Agapē love* seeks opportunities to do good to all people, especially to those of the household of faith.

    So then, as we have opportunity, let us do good to everyone, and especially to those who are of the household of faith. (Ga.6:10)

    Put on then, as God's chosen ones, holy and beloved, compassionate hearts, kindness, humility, meekness, and patience, bearing with one another and, if one has a complaint against another, forgiving each other; as the Lord has forgiven you, so you also must forgive. And above all these put on love, which binds everything together in perfect harmony. (Col.3:12–14; see 1 Co.13:1f)

- *Agapē love* is proven by obedience to Christ. Doing as you wish instead of doing as God wills shows that you do not have *agapē love*.

    "If you love me, you will keep my commandments. . . . Whoever has my commandments and keeps them, he it is who loves me. And he who loves me will be loved by my Father, and I will love him and manifest myself to him." . . . Jesus answered him, "If anyone loves me, he will keep my word, and my Father will love him, and we will come to him and make our home with him." (Jn.14:15, 21, 23)

    "If you keep my commandments, you will abide in my love, just as I have kept my Father's commandments and abide in his love." (Jn.15:10)

    But whoever keeps his word, in him truly the love of God is perfected. By this we may know that we are in him. (1 Jn.2:5)

    For this is the love of God, that we keep his commandments. And his commandments are not burdensome. (1 Jn.5:3)

    And this is love, that we walk according to his commandments; this is the commandment, just as you have heard from the beginning, so that you should walk in it. (2 Jn.6)

## H. Event 8: The Great Call to Total Commitment, 21:18–25

¹⁸ "Truly, truly, I say to you, when you were young, you used to dress yourself and walk wherever you wanted, but when you are old, you will stretch out your hands, and another will dress you and carry you where you do not want to go."
¹⁹ (This he said to show by what kind of death he was to glorify God.) And after saying this he said to him, "Follow me."
²⁰ Peter turned and saw the disciple whom Jesus loved following them, the one who also had leaned back against him during the supper and had said, "Lord, who is it that is going to betray you?"
²¹ When Peter saw him, he said to Jesus, "Lord, what about this man?"
²² Jesus said to him, "If it is my will that he remain until I come, what is that to you? You follow me!"
²³ So the saying spread abroad among the brothers that this disciple was not to die; yet Jesus did not say to him that he was not to die, but, "If it is my will that he remain until I come, what is that to you?"
²⁴ This is the disciple who is bearing witness about these things, and who has written these things, and we know that his testimony is true.
²⁵ Now there are also many other things that Jesus did. Were every one of them to be written, I suppose that the world itself could not contain the books that would be written.

1. **Total commitment demands following the leadership of another (the Holy Spirit)**
    a. When young, Peter walked & did as he willed
    b. When old, another would lead Peter where he would not choose
2. **Total commitment demands the cross—death to self: "Follow me"**

3. **Total commitment demands undivided attention to one's own task**

    a. Peter questioned John's task
    b. Jesus rebuked Peter
    c. Jesus again challenged Peter to follow Him
    d. John corrected the rumor that later started because of this event

4. **Total commitment demands bearing witness to Jesus Christ**
    a. John bore witness[DS1]
    b. John's witness was true
    c. John's witness includes only a few of the things that Jesus did[DS2]

# Division XVI

*The Revelation of Jesus, the Risen Lord, 20:1–21:25*

H. Event 8: The Great Call to Total Commitment, 21:18-25

## 21:18-25
## Introduction

In this final passage of John's Gospel, he presents Jesus' life-altering call to Peter. It was a call to be totally committed to Him and the work He was appointing Peter to do, to the life He was calling Peter to lead. Christ's call to Peter is His call to all His servants, His call to each of us. This is, *Event 8: The Great Call to Total Commitment,* 21:18-25.

1. Total commitment demands following the leadership of another (the Holy Spirit) (v.18).
2. Total commitment demands the cross—death to self: "Follow me" (v.19).
3. Total commitment demands undivided attention to one's own task (vv.20-23).
4. Total commitment demands bearing witness to Jesus Christ (vv.24-25).

## 21:18

¹⁸ "Truly, truly, I say to you, when you were young, you used to dress yourself and walk wherever you wanted, but when you are old, you will stretch out your hands, and another will dress you and carry you where you do not want to go."

### 1 Total commitment demands following the leadership of another (the Holy Spirit).

Total commitment to Christ requires following the leadership of *another*. Who is meant by "another"? In this context it can mean either those who were to carry Peter to death, the Romans; or the Holy Spirit, who was to carry Peter through a life of suffering and martyrdom for the cause of Christ. Jesus seemed to be referring to the whole of Peter's life, ranging from his earlier years when he did what he wished over to his older years when he would be doing what God wished. Because of this, it seems best to understand "another" as the Holy Spirit.

Jesus was challenging Peter to serve Him, to feed His sheep (vv.15-17). He was calling Peter to total commitment, and total commitment requires following the leadership of the Holy Spirit. Christ made two points:

**a. When, young, Peter walked and did as he willed.**
When Peter was young he girded himself, dressed, and walked where he willed. Before he knew Christ, he . . .

- led his life as *he* willed
- did what *he* wanted
- went where *he* wished
- talked as *he* willed
- enjoyed the pleasures *he* desired
- chose the profession *he* wanted

When he was younger, before he ever came to know Christ, Peter was able to live and do what he wanted when he wanted. But no more. Peter could no longer live as he wished. Jesus Christ, his Savior and Lord, was now to control his life.

**b. When old, another would lead Peter where he would not choose.**
When Peter was old and mature, the Holy Spirit would dress him and carry him places he would not choose or will to go. This, of course, refers to the suffering and martyrdom Peter was to undergo for the sake of Christ.

Since Peter was accepting the call of Christ to *feed His sheep*, Peter would have to . . .

- live his life as the Spirit willed
- do what the Spirit wanted
- choose the profession the Spirit willed
- go where the Spirit wished

Jesus was saying that Peter was to be carried where he would not wish to go. He was to live a life of suffering (see his imprisonments, Ac.4:3; 5:18; 12:4). Ultimately, He would die the death of a martyr. His death would be for the cause of Christ and the glory of God. Throughout these fierce afflictions, the Holy Spirit would always be with him, carrying him through circumstances he would never choose for Himself.

Remember that Peter had a wife (see Deeper Study # 1—Mt.8:14). At the time of this event, Peter was to live some forty years or more, so he was probably a newlywed. Tradition says that Peter's wife served with him in the ministry for many years. A touching picture is given by Clement of Alexandria who reported that Peter's wife was martyred with him:

> *"On seeing his wife led to death, Peter rejoiced on account of her call and her conveyance home, and called very encouragingly and comfortingly, addressing her by name, 'Remember thou the Lord'" (Stromateis 7:6)*[1]

There is strong evidence that Peter was crucified in Rome. Tradition says he felt so unworthy to die in the same manner as his Lord that he begged to be crucified upside down.

**THOUGHT 1.** The call of Christ is not just to commitment, but to *total commitment*. Total commitment demands that we follow the leadership of the Holy Spirit.
(1) We can no longer dress and walk as we will.
(2) We are to dress and walk as the Holy Spirit wills (see notes, *Holy Spirit*—Jn.14:15–26; 16:7–15 for more discussion).

> **I appeal to you therefore, brothers, by the mercies of God, to present your bodies as a living sacrifice, holy and acceptable to God, which is your spiritual worship. Do not be conformed to this world, but be transformed by the renewal of your mind, that by testing you may discern what is the will of God, what is good and acceptable and perfect. (Ro.12:1–2)**

> **For you were bought with a price. So glorify God in your body. (1 Co.6:20)**

**THOUGHT 2.** The call of Christ involves persecution. The true believer lives a sacrificial and godly life, bearing a strong testimony and a strong witness. Such a life is rejected and opposed by most in the world.

> **And not frightened in anything by your opponents. This is a clear sign to them of their destruction, but of your salvation, and that from God. (Ph.1:28)**

> **Indeed, all who desire to live a godly life in Christ Jesus will be persecuted. (2 Ti.3:12)**

> **For to this you have been called, because Christ also suffered for you, leaving you an example, so that you might follow in his steps. (1 Pe.2:21)**

> **Beloved, do not be surprised at the fiery trial when it comes upon you to test you, as though something strange were happening to you. But rejoice insofar as you share Christ's sufferings, that you may also rejoice and be glad when his glory is revealed. If you are insulted for the name of Christ, you are blessed, because the Spirit of glory and of God rests upon you. (1 Pe.4:12–14)**

The world persecutes those who live godly; it persecutes them at work, at play, at home—wherever and whenever it pleases. The world . . .

- reproaches
- ridicules
- mocks
- bypasses
- shuns
- ignores
- attacks
- curses
- abuses
- martyrs
- murders

Christ was calling Peter to a life on the receiving end of the world's abuse, telling him that the Holy Spirit would carry him to places he would not choose. Christ tells us the same thing. Total commitment requires following the leadership of the Holy Spirit, and all who follow the Holy Spirit will suffer persecution.

**THOUGHT 3.** We are going to die, every one of us. How we die should concern us . . .
- whether we die in self: having lived in comfort, ease, plenty, pleasure, wealth, extravagance, pride, unbelief

---

1  William Barclay. *The Gospel of Matthew* (Louisville, KY: Westminster John Knox Press, 1976), Vol.1, p.313.

- whether we die for Christ: having lived a godly life, bearing testimony, witnessing, helping, giving, ministering and meeting the desperate needs of a world reeling in sin and death

  For we must all appear before the judgment seat of Christ, so that each one may receive what is due for what he has done in the body, whether good or evil. (2 Co.5:10)

  And just as it is appointed for man to die once, and after that comes judgment. (He.9:27)

## 21:19

¹⁹ (This he said to show by what kind of death he was to glorify God.) And after saying this he said to him, "Follow me."

## 2 Total commitment demands the cross—death to self: "Follow me."

After telling Peter of the difficult path that lay ahead of him, the Lord once again called Peter to follow Him. By doing so, Jesus gave Peter the opportunity to walk away, to choose another path. Peter chose to take up His cross and follow Jesus. Total commitment to Christ requires the cross, death to self. We must *follow* Christ completely, wherever the path leads (see DEEPER STUDY # 1—Lu.9:23 for discussion).

**THOUGHT 1.** The decision to follow Christ is an all or nothing decision. It is to choose a life of total commitment, wherever the path may lead. Following Christ may lead us to places we do not want to go, to do things we would rather not do. It will no doubt require some great sacrifices. For some, it may require leaving family and friends behind to go to a far-away place, even a foreign field. For some, it may require leaving a prosperous career behind to serve Christ full-time. For some, it may require the ultimate sacrifice—laying down your life for Christ.

When you answer Jesus' call to follow Him, you cannot hold anything back. There is no bargaining involved, no negotiating, no insistence on conditions. It is a total, unconditional commitment to Him.

> And he said to all, "If anyone would come after me, let him deny himself and take up his cross daily and follow me." (Lu.9:23)
>
> "If anyone comes to me and does not hate his own father and mother and wife and children and brothers and sisters, yes, and even his own life, he cannot be my disciple." (Lu.14:26)
>
> "So therefore, any one of you who does not renounce all that he has cannot be my disciple." (Lu.14:33)
>
> Again Jesus spoke to them, saying, "I am the light of the world. Whoever follows me will not walk in darkness, but will have the light of life." (Jn.8:12)
>
> "If anyone serves me, he must follow me; and where I am, there will my servant be also. If anyone serves me, the Father will honor him." (Jn.12:26)

## 21:20-23

²⁰ Peter turned and saw the disciple whom Jesus loved following them, the one who also had leaned back against him during the supper and had said, "Lord, who is it that is going to betray you?"
²¹ When Peter saw him, he said to Jesus, "Lord, what about this man?"
²² Jesus said to him, "If it is my will that he remain until I come, what is that to you? You follow me!"
²³ So the saying spread abroad among the brothers that this disciple was not to die; yet Jesus did not say to him that he was not to die, but, "If it is my will that he remain until I come, what is that to you?"

## 3 Total commitment demands undivided attention to one's own task.

Total commitment requires undivided attention to one's own task. We are not to focus on what others do or fail to do, but only on God's will for our lives.

### a. Peter questioned John's task (vv.20-21).

After hearing of his turbulent future, Peter asked Jesus what John would be doing in his ministry. Peter and John were very close. John was younger than Peter, perhaps still a teenager. Apparently, Peter had taken a very close liking to John and had taken him into his care even before Christ had come along (see Introduction section of this book where it deals with authorship). Peter's interest in John's task and future was therefore natural.

b. **Jesus rebuked Peter (v.22a).**

Jesus lovingly but firmly rebuked Peter. He told Peter that John's task was not his concern. His own task was to be his concern. Peter was not to look at another man's call and ministry and . . .
- be distracted
- wish he had that ministry
- desire another ministry
- compare their calls and ministries
- copy or conform to that ministry
- meddle

> Let no one seek his own good, but the good of his neighbor. (1 Co.10:24)

> Give no offense to Jews or to Greeks or to the church of God, just as I try to please everyone in everything I do, not seeking my own advantage, but that of many, that they may be saved. (1 Co.10:32-33)

> Do nothing from selfish ambition or conceit, but in humility count others more significant than yourselves. Let each of you look not only to his own interests, but also to the interests of others. (Ph.2:3-4)

c. **Jesus again challenged Peter to follow Him (v.22b).**

Jesus reiterated His challenge to Peter to follow Him. Christ instructed Peter to concentrate on his own call and task. He was to focus his attention, will, energy, and efforts solely on what God had *called him* to do, realizing that God knew how he could best serve and that He called Peter to that task.

**THOUGHT 1.** Our Lord's challenge to Peter is His challenge to us as well. We are not to worry about what others are doing. We are not to compare our call to theirs. God's servants are not to be preoccupied with those who serve in bigger churches or ministries, who have more money and possessions or a seemingly easier ministry. Instead, we are to concentrate on what the Lord has called us to do, on the task He has committed to us. God knows what is best for His work as well as what is best for each of us. We should trust Him, serving Him each day cheerfully, wholeheartedly, faithfully, and gratefully.

> "Pay careful attention to yourselves and to all the flock, in which the Holy Spirit has made you overseers, to care for the church of God, which he obtained with his own blood." (Ac.20:28)

> I thank him who has given me strength, Christ Jesus our Lord, because he judged me faithful, appointing me to his service. (1 Ti.1:12)

> Shepherd the flock of God that is among you, exercising oversight, not under compulsion, but willingly, as God would have you; not for shameful gain, but eagerly. (1 Pe.5:2)

> "'And I will give you shepherds after my own heart, who will feed you with knowledge and understanding.'" (Je.3:15)

> "I will set shepherds over them who will care for them, and they shall fear no more, nor be dismayed, neither shall any be missing, declares the LORD." (Je.23:4)

> "Son of man, I have made you a watchman for the house of Israel. Whenever you hear a word from my mouth, you shall give them warning from me." (Eze.3:17)

d. **John corrected the rumor that later started because of this event (v.23).**

John corrected a rumor, an error spreading throughout the church. Some had taken the words of Jesus and misconstrued them, saying that Jesus meant that John would never die. Some were saying that John would survive until Jesus' return to earth. John very simply said this was not what Jesus was saying.

**THOUGHT 1.** Note how easily the Lord's words are misunderstood unless they are taken at face value, exactly as He spoke them.

> Do your best to present yourself to God as one approved, a worker who has no need to be ashamed, rightly handling the word of truth. (2 Ti.2:15)

> But as for you, teach what accords with sound doctrine. (Tit.2:1)

## 4 Total commitment demands bearing witness to Jesus Christ.

Finally, total commitment to Christ demands bearing witness to Him and fulfilling our task on earth, just as John bore witness and fulfilled his task. As he closed his Gospel, John points out three truths about the work he had written by divine inspiration.

**21:24-25**

<sup></sup>24 This is the disciple who is bearing witness about these things, and who has written these things, and we know that his testimony is true.
<sup></sup>25 Now there are also many other things that Jesus did. Were every one of them to be written, I suppose that the world itself could not contain the books that would be written.

a. **John bore witness (v.24a).**

John bore witness to the person, life, death, and resurrection of God's Son (see Deeper Study # 1). He wrote about what He had personally seen. The Gospel of John is his witness to the world.

b. **John's witness was true (v.24b).**

John emphasized that his witness was true; he had not lied. His record was absolutely accurate in its entirety. He had not embellished, exaggerated, or misrepresented any of the information he had reported.

c. **John's witness includes only a few of the things that Jesus did (v.25).**

John did not—and could not—tell about everything Jesus did in His brief ministry on earth. In just three-and-a-half short years, Jesus did more wonderful works and taught more eternal truth than, at that time, could practically be recorded (see Deeper Study # 2). We will have to wait until we get to heaven to hear about all of our Savior's glorious words and deeds. But the ones John did write about are more than sufficient to convince any open, logical mind that Jesus is who He claimed to be: the Messiah, the Son of God, the Lamb of God who took away the sins of the world (Jn.1:29).

> But these are written so that you may believe that Jesus is the Christ, the Son of God, and that by believing you may have life in his name. (Jn.20:31)

**Thought 1.** The primary task of every believer is to bear witness to the truth: Jesus is the Christ, the Son of God who has come to give life to all people—both abundant and eternal life.

> "The thief comes only to steal and kill and destroy. I came that they may have life and have it abundantly." (Jn.10:10)

> "But you will receive power when the Holy Spirit has come upon you, and you will be my witnesses in Jerusalem and in all Judea and Samaria, and to the end of the earth." (Ac.1:8)

> And what you have heard from me in the presence of many witnesses entrust to faithful men, who will be able to teach others also. (2 Ti.2:2)

> But in your hearts honor Christ the Lord as holy, always being prepared to make a defense to anyone who asks you for a reason for the hope that is in you; yet do it with gentleness and respect. (1 Pe.3:15)

### Deeper Study # 1

(21:24) **Jesus Christ, Hope of Man:** the great witness of John (and of the other gospel writers) is:

> "For God so loved the world, that he gave his only Son, that whoever believes in him should not perish but have eternal life." (Jn.3:16)

Very simply stated, the great witness is the glorious news of the death and resurrection of Jesus Christ. The death and resurrection of Jesus Christ changes the fate of world history and the whole attitude of mankind. If the death and resurrection of Christ had never taken place...
- then of all creatures, humans would be the most miserable and hopeless
- then the life of Jesus Christ would have been the most tragic and despairing event in all history

Why? Because the most merciful and compassionate, the most giving and helpful human being in all the world was treated and killed in the most savage way. However, the death and resurrection of Jesus Christ did happen, and because it did, it has changed the whole perspective and truth of world history. Because of the death and resurrection of Jesus Christ, life and history have become purposeful. Since Christ has died and risen from the dead, people can look at the cross and get a sense, a feeling . . .

- that the punishment for sin has been paid (atonement)
- that sin can now be forgiven (forgiveness)
- that a perfect life has been sacrificed for all people (propitiation)
- that all people can now be reconciled and made one with God (reconciliation)
- that all people can now be reconciled to one another, both personally and worldwide (peace, unity, community, fellowship)
- that all people can now be declared righteous (justification)
- that all people can be made into *new creatures* before God (regeneration)
- that all people can be redeemed (redemption)
- that all people can be set apart unto God (sanctification)

## DEEPER STUDY # 2

(21:25) See note, *Jesus Christ, Works*—Jn.20:30 for discussion.

# OUTLINE AND SUBJECT INDEX

When you look up a subject and turn to the Scripture reference, you not only have the Scripture, you have *an outline and a discussion* (commentary) of the Scripture and subject.

This valuable feature of the everyWord® series becomes even more valuable once you have the complete set of books. Once you have all volumes, you will have access to each book's index, including a list of all the subjects and their Scripture references, and you will also have . . .
- An outline of *every* Scripture and subject in the Bible.
- A discussion (commentary) on every Scripture and subject.
- Every subject supported by other Scriptures or cross references.

See for yourself how the index works. Quickly glance in the sample below to the very first subject of the Index of John. It is:

**ABIDE—ABIDING**
Condition for salvation. Belief & **a**. 8:31

Turn to the reference. Glance at the Scripture and outline of the Scripture, then read the commentary. As you familiarize yourself with the OUTLINE AND SUBJECT INDEX, you will likely find it to be a useful tool in your use of the everyWord® series.

---

**ABIDE—ABIDING**
Condition for salvation. Belief & **a**. 8:31
Duty.
  To **a**. in Christ. 15:1-8
  To let the Word **a**. in us. 5:38
Proves. A person's obedience. 15:10
Results of **a**.
  Answered prayer. 15:7
  Comfort & help. 14:15-26
  Deliverance from judgment. 15:2
  Discipline and correction. 15:2-3
  Fruit. 15:5-8
Source of **a**.
  Christ. 15:1-8
  Christ's love. 15:9-11
  Holy Spirit. 14:16-17
Verses. List of. 8:31; 15:4

**ABRAHAM**
Call of. 4:22; 8:54-59
Place in Jewish history.
  Discussed. 4:22; 8:54-59
  Father of the Jews. 4:22; 8:33, 53
  Seed of. Christ. 1:23
Testimony of.
  Hoped for the Messiah. 8:56
  Rejoiced to see Jesus' day. 8:54-59
Work of. Believing. Man fails to follow his belief. 8:39-40

**ABUNDANCE—ABUNDANT** (See **LIFE; SALVATION; SPIRITUAL FOOD; SPIRITUAL SATISFACTION**)

**ACCESS**
Source. Is through Christ. 14:6

**ADAM**
Seed of. Christ. Misunderstood by Jews. 1:23

**ADOPTED—ADOPTION**
How one is **a**. By the work of Christ. 8:34-36

**ADULTERY—ADULTERERS**
Duty of the **a**. To seek forgiveness. 8:1-11
Duty of the church.
  To converse with. 4:1-42
  To forgive. 8:1-11
Is committed. In a party-like atmosphere. 8:3-6

**ADVERSARY** (See **SATAN**)

**ADVOCATE** (See **JESUS CHRIST**, Deity; Mediator; **MEDIATOR**)

**AGNOSTIC**
Duty. To be open to the truth. 4:25

**AMBASSADORS**
Chosen. By Christ to go forth. 15:16

**AMBITION—AMBITIOUS**
Evil **a**. causes.
  Self-seeking. 11:47-48; 12:10-11; 12:42-43
  The fear of losing followers. 12:10-11; 12:42-43
  The fear of losing position. 11:47-48; 12:42-43

**ANDREW, THE APOSTLE**
Brings a little boy to Jesus. 6:8-9
Discovers Jesus. The Messiah, the Christ. 1:35-42
Discussed. 6:8-9
Witnesses to his brother, Peter. 1:35-42

**ANGELS**
Appearances. In the New Testament.
  To Mary Magdalene at resurrection. 20:11; 12-13
Function toward Christ. Ascend & descend upon. 1:51

**ANGER**
Of Jesus. Over abuse of temple. 2:14-17

**ANIMAL** (See **SACRIFICE, ANIMAL**)

**ANNAS**
High priest. Discussed. 18:12-14
Tried Jesus—unofficially. 18:12-27

**ANOINT—ANOINTING**
Kinds. Day to day courtesy. 12:1-11
Of believers. Foretold. 7:37-39
Of Christ.
  By a thankful person—Mary. 12:1-11
  By the Spirit. 1:32-34

**APOSTASY** (See **DENIAL**)
Discussed. 13:18-30
Examples. Judas. A picture of **a**. 13:18-30
Traits of. 12:4-8

**APOSTLE—APOSTLES** (See **DISCIPLE**)
Call of.
  Andrew & Peter. 1:35-42
  Nathanael. 1:46-49
  Philip. 1:43-45

**APPEARANCE, OUTWARD**
Duty. To judge accurately, not by **a**. 7:24

**ARIMATHAEA, JOSEPH OF**
Buries Jesus. The conquest of fear. 19:38-42

**ASS—DONKEY**
Discussed. 12:14-15

**ASSURANCE**
Comes by.
  Being born again. Gives absolute **a**. 3:3
  Being washed. 13:6-11
  Coming to Christ. 6:37; 12:44-46
  Five things. 6:37-40
  God working all things out for good. 11:55-57
  God's keeping power. 10:27-29; 17:11-12
  God's predestination. 6:37, 39, 44-46
  Hearing Jesus' Word. 5:24; 10:27-29; 11:44-46
  Jesus' prayer. 17:9-26
  Three things. 6:40
Discussed. 6:37-40; 10:27-29; 17:9-19
Needed.
  Facing the world. 17:9-19
  Receiving eternal life. 5:24; 10:27-29
  Salvation. 10:7-10
  Securing abundant life. 10:7-10
Verses. List of. 6:39; 10:9

**ASTROLOGY**
Error of. Causes men to seek fate in stars, magic. 5:2-4

**ATHEIST—ATHEISM**
Duty. To be open to the truth. 4:25

**ATTRIBUTES** (See **GOD**, Deity; **JESUS CHRIST**, Deity)

**AUTHORITY**
Purpose. To remit & retain sins. 20:23

**BACKSLIDING** (See **APOSTASY; DENIAL**)
Described as. Denying Christ. 13:36-38; 18:15-18; 18:25-27
Warning against. Judgment will be greater. 5:13-14

**BAND**
Cohort of Roman soldiers. 18:3

**BAPTISM**
Discussed. 1:24-26
Meaning. Of water & the Spirit. 1:24-26
Of John. Reason to **b**. 1:24-26

**BARABBAS**
Criminal chosen before Christ. 18:38-40

**BARRIERS** (See **DISCRIMINATION; DIVISION; PREJUDICE**)

**BELIEVE—BELIEVING—BELIEF** (See **Faith**)
Beginning **b**. What happens. 8:31
Essential—Importance of. 3:18
  Evidences of. 4:43-45
  Only labor that pleases God. 6:29
  What believers must **b**. 17:5-8
  What one must **b**. Four things. 6:47-51
Meaning.
  Obedience. 3:36; 4:50-53; 5:5-9
  Seeing with understanding. 20:20
  To commit. 2:24
Results.
  Blessed if **b**. without demanding sight. 20:29
  Delivered from condemnation. 3:18-21
  Everlasting life. 3:16; 3:36; 6:40; 6:47-51; 11:25-26
  Great works & answered prayer. 14:12-14; 15:16
  Never die. 11:25-27
  Resurrection from the dead. 6:40
  Saves from perishing. 3:16
  To receive things of God. 15:16
  Will know the truth & be set free. 8:31-32
Source of. Jesus' Word. 4:50-53
True vs. false **b**. 2:23-24; 2:24
Verses. List of. 8:31
Why people **b**. 2:23; 4:51-53

**BELIEVER—BELIEVERS** (See **APOSTLES; DISCIPLES; MINISTERS**)
Beliefs of. (See **BELIEVE—BELIEF**)
Chosen. (See **CHOSEN**)
Christ in you. (See **INDWELLING PRESENCE**)
Denial of Christ. (See **DENIAL**)
Described as.
  A spiritual bond of friends. 15:14-15
  Sheep. 10:27-29
Duty—work.
  After being helped, healed. 5:13-14
  Described. 14:12
  To be attached to Christ. 15:1-8
  To bear witness to Christ. 21:24-25
  To do greater works than Jesus. 14:12
  To do the will & work of God. 4:31-35
  To follow the Holy Spirit. 21:18-19
  To give undivided attention to one's task. 21:20-23
  To glorify God & Christ. 11:4; 17:9-11
  To know & learn of the Father. 14:6
  To long to know the Father. How. 14:6
  To love. 13:33-35
  To obey. Not an option. 14:15
  To work before night comes. 11:7-10
Glory of.
  Chart of **b**. glory & Christ's **g**. 17:22
  Possesses **g**. of God Himself. 17:22
Life—Walk—Behavior. (See Related Subjects)
  Live in a world of religion & religionists. 16:1-6
  Objective of. Should long for the Father. 14:6
  Supreme conduct. 12:1-9
Nature. Discussed. 17:11
Relationship.
  Given to Christ by God. 17:9-11
  Know Christ by His Word or voice & Spirit. 20:14-16
  Possessed by both God & Christ. 17:9-11
  To Christ.
    As a branch. 15:1-8
    Known by **C**. Intimate knowledge. 10:14-16
    Very special. 15:9-11
  To other believers. 15:12-17
  To religionists. Persecution: a bleak picture. 16:1-6
  To the world. Persecution: a bleak picture. 15:18-27
Response to Christ. Threefold **r**. 6:66-71
Security of. (See **ASSURANCE; SECURITY**)
Traits of.
  Cp. sheep. Discussed. 10:27-29
  Hypocritical **b**. 12:4-8
  Supreme **b**. 12:3
Types of **b**.
  Discussed. 12:1-11; 15:1-8
  False **b**. (See **PROFESSION, FALSE**)
  Silent **b**. 12:42-43
Unity of. (See **UNITY**)

**BETHSAIDA**
Discussed. 1:44

**BETRAYAL**
Discussed. 13:18-30
Traits of. 12:4-8

**BIBLE** (See **SCRIPTURE; WORD OF GOD**)

**BIRTH, NEW** (See **BORN AGAIN; NEW CREATION; NEW LIFE**)

**BLESSING**
Duty. To remember & not forget **b**. 5:13-14

**BLIND—BLINDNESS** (See **SPIRITUAL BLINDNESS**)

**BLOOD** (See **JESUS CHRIST**, Blood of)

**BODY**
Identified as. The temple. By Jesus. 2:18-22

**BONDAGE, SPIRITUAL** (See **ENSLAVEMENT, SPIRITUAL**)

**BORN AGAIN** (See **NEW BIRTH**)
By the Spirit and water. 3:5
Discussed. 3:1-15

**BREAD**
Does several things for man's body. 6:33
Jesus is the **B**. of life. (See **BREAD OF LIFE; SPIRITUAL FOOD**)
Spiritual. (See **SPIRITUAL FOOD**)

**BREAD OF LIFE**
Discussed. 6:1-71
How one secures & partakes. 6:41-51
Jesus is the Bread of Life. 6:1-71
Results of partaking. 6:30-36, 41-51
Who can partake. 6:59-71

**BRIDEGROOM**
Symbol. Of Christ. 3:29-30

**BROTHER—BROTHERHOOD** (See **UNITY**)
Discussed. 15:12-17
Duty. To be a **b**. to others. 17:20-23
Failure in. What withdrawing causes. 20:24-25
Nature of. Binding force. 17:11

**BUSYBODIES** (See **GOSSIP**)

**CAIAPHAS**
High Priest. Discussed. 11:49

**CALL—CALLED**
Of disciples. (See **APOSTLE**)
Universal **c**. Jesus came to give life to the whole world. 6:33

**CANA**
Discussed. 2:1

**CAPERNAUM**
Jesus' ministry in **C**. 4:46-54

## CAPITAL PUNISHMENT
Jews not allowed the right to capital punishment. 19:7

## CARE—CARING
Duty to c. For the flock of God. 10:11-18

## CARNAL
Causes.
  Corrupt motive. 6:26-27
  Twofold. 13:36-38
Verses. List of. 6:26-27

## CENSOR—CENSORING (See JUDGING OTHERS)
Of sinners. Spirit of c. 8:3-6
Who can c. 8:7-9

## CEPHAS
Peter's name before Christ changed it. 1:42

## CHIEF PRIESTS (See HIGH PRIESTS)

## CHOSEN
By whom. Christ. 15:16
Out of the world. 15:18-19
Purpose. To go; bear fruit; receive things. 15:16
To betray Christ. 13:18

## CHRISTIAN (See BELIEVER)

## CHRISTIANITY
Accused of.
  Being a bloody religion; the worship of a "grotesque god." 6:61
Fruit of. Bearing fruit. 15:1-8
Life—Walk—Behavior.
  Contrasted with the world's life. 8:1-11

## CHURCH
Authority of. Discussed. 20:23
Cleansed—cleansing. By Christ. Supremacy over. 2:12-22
Described.
  As flock of God. 21:15-17
  As spiritual bond of friends. 15:14-15
  Body of Christ. Becomes new temple. 2:18-21
Ministry to. To feed & shepherd. 21:15-17
Mission. (See COMMISSION)
  Charter of. 20:19-23
  Christ needs the c. & the c. needs Christ. 20:21
Nature.
  Not a house of merchandise. 2:12-22
Problems. (See CARNAL; 2 Corinthians Outline)
  Being made a house of merchandise. 2:12-22
  Reveling in fellowship and not witnessing. 20:17-18
Supremacy over. By Christ. 2:12-22
Unity of. Discussed. 17:11

## CITIZENSHIP (See GOVERNMENT)

## CLEANSE—CLEANSING
Discussed. 13:6-11
How to be cleansed. By the Word. 17:17

## CLEOPHAS
Husband of Mary. 19:25

## CLOTHING (See DRESS)
Of Jesus. Gambled for. 19:23-24

## COAT
Of Jesus.
  Gambled for. 19:24
  Without seams. 19:23

## COEXISTENT
Of Christ with God. Meaning. 1:1-2

## COHORT
Meaning. A regiment of Roman soldiers. 18:3

## COLT
Discussed. 12:14-15

## COMFORTER, THE (See HOLY SPIRIT)

## COMMANDMENT—COMMANDMENTS (See OBEDIENCE)
Are demanded by J. death. 13:31-35
Jesus' c.
  Is a new c. 13:34-35
  Is onefold. 13:34-35; 15:12-17
Obeying the c.
  Is essential to abide in Christ & God. 15:10, 14-17
  Proves one's love. 14:15, 21, 24; 15:10, 14
The new c.—love. 13:31-35

## COMMISSION (See MISSION)
Described.
  As being sent. 20:21
  As being sent from the side, the heart of God. 1:6
  As proclaiming the resurrection. 20:17-18
Given by.
  Christ. 20:21
  God. 1:6
Given to. Mary Magdalene. 20:17-18
Great c. 20:19-23
Great charter of church. 20:19-23
Meaning. 1:6
Urgency of. 9:4

## COMMIT—COMMITMENT (See DEDICATION)
Essential. Love is one basic e. 21:15; 21:15-17
Meaning. 2:24

## COMMUNION (See DEVOTION)

## COMPASSION
Of Jesus.
  Groans over man's desperate plight. 11:33-36; 11:38-40
  Reaches out to man. 5:5-9
Verses. List of. 11:33-36

## COMPROMISE
Discussed. 18:28-19:15
Illust. By Pilate. 18:28-19:15

## CONDEMN—CONDEMNATION (See JUDGMENT, Condemnation)
Caused by. Unbelief. 3:18-21
Deliverance from. Discussed. 3:18
Discussed. 3:18-21
Who escapes c. 3:21

## CONFESS—CONFESSION
Duty. To c. publicly. 1:49; 19:40-42
Of Christ.
  Offends some. 6:59-71
  Why some do not c. 6:59-71

Of Thomas. Great conviction & c. 20:24-29
Source—stirred by.
  Conviction. 1:49
  Death of Jesus. 19:38-42
  Resurrection of Jesus. 20:12-13

## CONFIDENCE (See ASSURANCE—SECURITY)

## CONTENTMENT (See JOY)

## CONVERSION—CONVERTED
How a person is c. By a stirred heart.
What happens. 8:31

## CONVICTION—CONVICTS
Of Holy Spirit. Meaning. 16:8-11
Of sin. Necessary for salvation. 4:15-18
Signs of. Results, reactions. 20:24-29
Work of. The Holy Spirit. 16:8-11

## CORRUPTION
Seed of. In world. 12:31
  Physical vs. spiritual dimension. 8:23
Verses. List of. 1:14

## COURAGE—COURAGEOUS
Failure in c. (See DENY—DENIAL) 12:42-43

## COVET—COVETOUSNESS
Result. Deception, hypocrisy. Verses. List of. 12:4-8

## CREATION
Creator of. Christ. 1:1-5; 1:3
Of man.
  Discussed. 4:23
  In the image & likeness of God. 4:23
Purposes of. 4:23-24

## CRITICIZE—CRITICISM
C. the sacrifice of believers. 12:4-8
Man's c. spirit. 8:3-6
Object of c. Believers & their sacrifice. 12:4-8
Source of. Sinners. Spirit of judging others. 8:3-6

## CROSS—SELF-DENIAL
Duty. To sacrifice oneself for Christ. 12:23-26
Misunderstood. By Peter & the disciples. 13:36-38
Verses. List of. 12:23-26

## CRUCIFIXION
Described. A lingering death. 19:34

## CUP
Meaning. Symbol of Christ's suffering. 18:11

## DARKNESS
Discussed. 8:12
Deliverance of. How to get out of. 8:12
Meaning. 8:12
Nature. Loved by unbelievers. Reasons. 3:18-20
Results. Causes fear. 6:17-19
Verses. List of. 3:18-20; 11:7-10
Weakness of.
  Cannot overcome light. 1:5
  What d. does not do. Three things. 1:5

## DAVID
Choosing of. 4:22
Seed of. Messiah.

**DAVID** (*Continued*)
Promises & fulfillment. 1:45, 49
Seen as seed of David by Jews. 1:23

**DEATH—DYING**
Attitude toward.
  Fear of **d**. 6:17-19
  To be a. of hope, not despair. 20:14-16
Caused by.
  Nature. 8:23
  Sin. Penalty of. 8:21-22
  Unbelief. 8:21-22, 24
Deliverance from.
  By Christ's death. 3:14-17
  By Christ's great power. 11:1-16; 11:43-46
  Power over. Discussed. 11:38-46
  Through Jesus' return. 14:1-3
Described.
  As personal presentation to the Lord. 14:3
  As sleep. 11:13
Kinds.
  Eternal—second death. 11:25
  Physical **d**. 11:25
  Spiritual death. Dead while living. 5:24-25; 6:52-53
Meaning. Corruption—perishing. 3:16
Of believers.
  Emphasis of destination is the Father, not heaven. 14:6
  Meets Jesus at **d**. With Him immediately. 11:25-27; 14:3; 16:4-6
Preparation for persecution leading to death. How to **p**. 16:4-6
To self. (See **SELF-DENIAL**)
Verses. List of. 6:17-19

**DECEIVE—DECEPTION**
Meaning. 1:47

**DECISION** (See **JESUS CHRIST**, Responses to)
Duty—Essential.
  To be personal. Between Christ & self. 11:29
  To confess publicly. 1:49
Facts about. Spirit will not always strive with man. 7:33-34; 11:54
Responses to Christ. Three **r**. 6:66-71

**DEDICATION** (See **COMMITMENT**)
Kinds—Degrees of. Threefold. 6:66-71
Meaning. Absolute surrender. 18:1-11; 21:18-25
Proof. Feeding God's people. 21:15-17
Stirred by. The cross. 12:23-26
Why one should be **d**. God's great call. 21:18-23

**DEFILE—DEFILEMENT** (See **SIN**)

**DELIVERANCE** (See **SALVATION**)
Discussed. 14:1-3
From sin.
  Conditions. Belief & continuing. 8:34-36
  God, great forgiveness. 8:1-11
  Necessary for salvation. 4:16-18; 16:8-11
  Power to proclaim forgiveness of sin. 20:23
Misconception. Dramatic experience with God will **d**. 14:8

**DELIVERER** (See **JESUS CHRIST**)
Christ is the **d**. 6:16-21

**DEMONS** (See **EVIL SPIRITS**)

**DENARII**
Discussed. 6:7

**DENIAL**
By whom.
  Believers. Fear world, ridicule, abuse. 18:15-18
  Peter. 18:12-27
  The world & the Jews. 18:19-24
Cause of. Two **c**. 13:36-38

**DEPRAVITY** (See **MAN**, Depravity)
Cause. Illegitimate birth. 8:41-47
Discussed. 8:41-47

**DESERTION** (See **APOSTASY**; **DENIAL**)

**DESIRE** (See **LUST**)

**DESPAIR**
Caused. By death. To be conquered. 20:14-16
Result. Emptiness & prejudice. 1:46
Verses. List of. 1:46; 5:2-4

**DESPERATE**
Described. As the needy of the world. 5:5-9
Of world. Jesus reaches out to. 5:5-9

**DESTINY** (See **MAN**, Destiny)
Power of. In the hands of Jesus Christ. 5:24-25

**DESTRUCTION** (See **JUDGMENT**)

**DEVIL** (See **SATAN**)

**DEVOTION** (See **DEDICATION**)
Duty. To meditate in God's Word. Let it abide within. 5:38
Of Jesus. To God's will. 18:1-3
Purpose. To know the Father. How. 14:6

**DISCIPLES** (See **APOSTLES**; **BELIEVERS**; **MINISTERS**)
Character—Traits.
  Hypocritical; counterfeit **d**. 6:61-62; 12:4-8
  Supreme **d**. 12:3
Failure. Hiding after the death of Jesus. 20:19-23
Response to Christ. Three **r**. 6:66-71

**DISCIPLESHIP**
Eagerness of Jesus to make disciples. 1:38-39
Steps to. Illustrated by Andrew. 1:35-37

**DISCRIMINATION** (See **BARRIERS**; **DIVISION**; **PREJUDICE**)
Overcome by. Witnessing. 4:1-42

**DISHONOR**
Discussed. 4:43-45
Of Christ.
  By hometown. 4:44
  By some who were close to Him. 4:44

**DISSATISFACTION**
Cause. Sin. 4:15
Discussed. 4:15

**DISTRUST** (See **UNBELIEF**)
Nature of. Prefers not to be disturbed. 11:38-40

**DIVISION—DIVISIVENESS** (See **BARRIERS**; **DISCRIMINATION**; **PREJUDICE**)
Of world. Contrasted with unity. 17:11

**DOOR**
Title of Christ. **D**. of sheep. 10:7-10

**DOVE**
Discussed. 1:32-33

**DRAW—DRAWN**
Of God. Must draw man for salvation. Meaning. 6:44-46, 65

**EIMI**
I AM. The most basic Name of deity. Meaning. 1:1-2

**ELECT—ELECTION** (See **CHOSEN**; **PREDESTINATION**)

**ELIJAH**
Misunderstanding about. Was expected to personally return to earth. 1:20-22

**EMPTINESS**
Cause. Sin. 4:15
Discussed. 4:15

**ENDURANCE**
Duty. To continue in the love of Christ. 15:9-10
Verses. List of. 8:31

**ENSLAVEMENT, SPIRITUAL**
By sin.
  Denied. Two reasons. 8:33
  Man's **e**. by sin. 8:33-40
Verses. List of. 8:34-36

**ESCAPISM**
Peace does not come from **e**. 14:27

**ETERNAL LIFE**
Described as.
  A well of water springing up. 4:14
  God's commandment. 12:50
  Hating one's life in this world. 12:25
  Living bread. 6:35, 51, 58
  Living—never ceasing to live. 11:25-26
  Never being plucked out of Christ's hand. 10:28
  Never dying. 11:26
  Never hungering and never thirsting. 6:35
How to secure. (See **ETERNAL LIFE**, Source)
  Believing in Christ. 3:16; 5:24; 11:25; 20:31
  Believing on God who sent Christ. 5:24
  Coming to Christ. 6:35
  Eating of the bread of life—of Christ. 6:51, 58
  Hating one's life in this world. 12:25
  Hearing Christ's voice and following Him. 10:27
  Hearing God's commandment. 12:50
  Knowing God and Christ. 17:3
  Seeing the Son and believing. 6:40
  Serving Christ. 12:25-26
Meaning. 1:4; 10:10; 17:2-3
  Deliverance from death. 8:51
Results.
  Being resurrected to life. 5:28-30; 6:40; 11:23-27
  Never dying. 11:25-27
  Glorifies God and Christ. 17:1-4

Includes three great things. 6:54
Knowing the only true God and Christ. 17:2-3
Not being condemned but being saved. 3:17-21; 5:24
Not ever being plucked out of Christ's hand. 10:28
Not perishing. 3:15-16; 10:28
Transported immediately at death. Never losing consciousness. 11:25-27
Results of rejecting.
Resurrected to damnation. 5:29
Shall not see life. 3:36
Wrath of God. 3:36
Source.
Death of Christ. 3:14-15
Promised by Christ. 3:16-17; 4:14; 5:24-29; 6:35, 40, 51, 58; 10:28; 11:25-27; 12:25, 50; 17:3; 20:31
Verses. List of. 8:51; 11:25-27; 17:2-3

**EVANGELISM—EVANGELIZE**
Why **e**. Fields are ripe for harvest. 4:35

**EVIL SPIRITS**
Work of. To possess evil men. 13:27-30

**EXALT—EXALTATION** (See **JESUS CHRIST**, Exaltation of)
Duty. To **e**. Christ & not self. 3:29-30

**EXPECTATION** (See **HOPE**)

**EXPOSURE—EXPOSED**
Of sin. Known by God. 1:47-48; 2:24-25; 5:42; 13:19-20

**FAITH**
Duty. To persevere in **f**. 4:48-49
Evidence of—Proofs of.
Discussed. 4:43-45
Twofold. 4:43-45
Growth in. Martha's growth in **f**. 11:17-27
Meaning.
Commit. 2:24
Obedience. 3:36; 4:50-53; 5:5-9; 9:6-7
Stages—Kinds.
Beginning **f**. What happens. 8:31
Complaining, limited **f**. 11:21-22
Confirmed **f**. 4:53
Declared **f**. 11:25-27
Discussed. 4:46-54
Silent **f**. 12:42-43
Fundamental **f**. 11:23-24
Pessimistic; questioning; unswerving **f**. 6:1-15
Resting, unlimited **f**. 6:10-13; 11:21-22, 40
Three **k**. 11:21-27
Unlimited, resting **f**. Meaning. 11:21-22, 40
Weak **f**. Discussed. 6:7-9
Vs. works.
Discussed. 6:28-29
**F**. apart from works. 4:50

**FAITHLESSNESS**
Jesus' death reveals weak **f**. 13:36-38

**FALSE PROFESSION** (See **PROFESSION, FALSE**)

**FALSE TEACHERS** (See **TEACHERS, FALSE**)

**FAMILY**
Duty. To witness to **f**. 4:53-54
Of Christ. (See **JESUS CHRIST**, Family)

**FAVORITISM** (See **PARTIALITY, PREJUDICE**)

**FEAR, HUMAN**
Causes of. 6:17-19
Darkness. Being in the dark; spiritual blindness. 6:17-19
Men. **F**. men more than **f**. God. Reason. 19:13-15
Men. Seeking to harm. 20:19
Persecution. 20:19
Deliverance—Overcome by.
Christ's presence. 6:19-21
Discussed. 6:16-21
Results.
Causes silence—a failure to testify. 9:22
Causes unbelief. Three fears. 11:47-48

**FEAST—FEASTS**
Of Dedication. Discussed. 10:22
Of Tabernacles. Discussed. 7:37

**FEEDING OF FIVE THOUSAND**
Discussed. 6:1-15

**FELLOWSHIP** (See **BROTHERHOOD—UNITY**)
Basis—Source.
Abiding in Christ. 15:1-8
Christ. Jesus concentrates upon. 11:54
Danger—Problems.
Reveling in **f**. and not witnessing. 20:17-18
Withdrawing. What causes. 20:24-25
Described. A spiritual bond of friends. 15:14-15
Discussed. 6:56
Duty. To **f**. & be sociable. 2:1-2

**FIG TREE**
Discussed. 1:48

**FLESH**
Control of. By Christ. Christ counteracts. 1:14
Discussed. 1:14
Meaning. 1:14
Stirs a fleshy, carnal commitment. 13:36-38
Works—Shortcomings of.
Becomes focus of man. Attempts to dress up. 6:63
Profits nothing. 6:63

**FOOD, SPIRITUAL** (See **HUNGER, SPIRITUAL; SPIRITUAL FOOD**)

**FOLLOW**
Duty. To **f**. Jesus, seeking salvation & truth. 1:35-37
Meaning. 1:43

**FORGIVENESS, SPIRITUAL**
Essential—Necessity. Before service. 13:6-11
Source.
Believers given authority to remit & retain sins. 20:23

God. Man's dark sinfulness & God's great **f**. 8:1-11
Symbolized. In cleansing. 2:6-9

**FREEDOM** (See **LIBERTY**)

**FRIENDS—FRIENDSHIP** (See **BROTHERHOOD**)

**FRUIT-BEARING** (See **BELIEVER; DEDICATION**)
Discussed. 15:1-8
Facts. No **f**. apart from the vine. 15:4
Meaning. What **f**. is. Three things. 15:1-8
Purpose.
Of believers. Are chosen for **f**. 15:16
Of world. Relationship of Jesus to the people of the world. 15:1-8

**FULNESS OF TIME**
World prepared by forerunner. Three ways. 1:23

**FULNESS, SPIRITUAL** (See **HUNGER, SPIRITUAL; SATISFACTION**)
Of life. Discussed. 1:16-17
Source—Provision of.
Discussed. 6:30-36
Jesus Christ. 1:16-17; 10:9
Verses. List of. 6:34-35, 55; 10:9

**GALILEE**
Discussed. 4:43

**GIVE—GIVING**
Duty.
To **g**. what one has. Verses. List of. 6:10-13

**GLORY** (See **JESUS CHRIST**, Glory of; **GOD**, Glory of)
How to secure **g**. Death to self & service. 12:23-26
Of believer.
Chart of **g**. of Christ & of believer. 17:22
Discussed. 17:22
Of Christ. Discussed. 1:14; 12:23-26; 17:1-4
Of God. Supreme purpose of Jesus' death. 12:27-30; 17:4
Shekinah. Discussed. 1:14

**GOD**
And Christ.
Beloved Son. Verses. List of. 5:20
Dearest thing to God's heart. 3:16, 35-36; 5:20
Mutual Indwelling with **C**. 5:17-30; 8:15-16; 14:10
Revealed all His works through. 5:20
Intimate knowledge. 5:17-30; 10:14-16
One with Christ. 5:17-30; 8:15-16; 10:14-16; 14:10
Verses. List of. 5:19; 8:54-59
Existence of. Seen in Christ. 1:18; 14:9-11
Holy. Verses. List of. 20:12-13
How to know—Way to God.
Discussed. 1:18; 7:16-19
Ignorance about. Verses. List of. 4:22; 7:25-31; 8:19
Men question. 14:4-5
Only one door, Christ Himself. 10:7-8
Image of. Man created in **i**. of God. 4:23

**GOD** (Continued)
Knowledge—Omniscience.
  Knows all about men. 1:47-48; 2:24-25
  Mutual **k.** between God & Christ. 10:14-16
Love of.
  A past, proven fact. 3:16
  Cost of. What it cost God to **l.** man. 3:16
  Gave dearest thing to His heart, Own Son. 3:16
  God's great **l.** 3:16-17
  Of religious & non-religious. 3:16
  Shown in most perfect way possible. 3:16
Name—Titles.
  "My Father." Father of Christ. 1:34; 10:25, 29-30
  Savior. 4:42
Nature.
  God is True. 3:33
  Has never been seen by man. 1:18; 5:37-38; 8:19
  Invisible. 1:18; 5:37-38; 8:19
  Not distant & far off. 14:9
  Spirit. 4:23-24
Profession of. (See **PROFESSION, FALSE**)
Providence—Sovereignty.
  God overrules unbelief & uses it for good. Verses. List of. 11:55-57
Purpose. Plan for the ages. 4:22
Revealed—revelation of. Not by man, but by Christ. 1:18; 3:13, 31
Source of. Life. 5:26
Unseen. Never seen by man. Verses. List of. 5:37-38; 8:19
Will of.
  Christ came to do the **w.** of God. 6:38; 6:39, 40
  For believers. To be assured, secured. Never lost. 6:39-40
  For Christ. To have many followers. 6:39
  To save men. 4:31-35
Works of.
  Discussed. 9:4
  Draws man. 6:37-39, 44-46
  Revealed in Christ. 5:20
  To save men. 4:31-35

**GODS, FALSE** (See **IDOLATRY**)
Source. Created by man's imaginations, ideas. 8:54-59

**GOSPEL**
Duty. To be open to **g.** 4:24
Message of. Threefold. 11:28
Of John. Purpose. 20:30-31
Resistance. Response to. 6:44
Response to **g.** Hardened to. Danger of. 4:25
Writing of. Include only a few of Jesus' miracles. 20:30-31

**GOSSIP**
Prevented. By watching one's behavior around opposite sex. 4:27

**GOVERNMENT**
Official. Comes to Jesus for help. 4:46-47

**GRACE**
Meaning. 1:14, 16-17
Source. Discussed. 1:16-17

**GRATITUDE** (See **THANKFUL**)

**GREATNESS**
Condition for. How one achieves. 13:4
Demonstrated. By Jesus. Royal service. 13:1-17

**GREEKS**
Seek & approach Jesus. Four misunderstandings. 12:20-36

**GRIEF—GRIEVE—GRIEVED**
Caused by. Death. To be conquered. 20:14-16
Nature of. Often self-centered. 16:5

**GROWTH** (See **SPIRITUAL FOOD; SPIRITUAL GROWTH**)

**GUIDANCE**
By whom. Holy Spirit. 16:12-13
Promised. Discussed. 16:12-13

**GUILE—GUILELESSNESS** (See **DECEPTION**)
Meaning. 1:47

**GUILT**
Causes. Unbelief. 20:24-25

**HAPPY—HAPPINESS** (See **FULNESS, SPIRITUAL; JOY**)

**HARD—HARDNESS OF HEART**
Danger of. 4:25
Reject Christ. 5:40-41

**HARVEST**
Of souls. Ripe for reaping. 4:35

**HEALS—HEALING**
Blind man. 9:1-7
Impotent man. 5:1-16
Nobleman's son. 4:46-54
Raises the dead. Lazarus. 11:41-46

**HEART**
Duty. To be open to truth. 4:25
Troubled **h.** Deliverance from. Fivefold. 14:1-3

**HEAVEN**
Believers.
  Are not to make **h.** their object, but God. 14:6
  Are to be transported into immediately. Never lose consciousness. 11:25-27
Characteristics—Nature.
  Cannot be penetrated by man. 3:31
  Is real world, spiritual **w.** & dimension. 11:25-27
Described. As God's house. 14:1-3
Search for. Man's futile **s.** for Messiah—utopia—heaven. 8:21-24

**HERESY** (See **TEACHERS, FALSE**)

**HERITAGE**
Weakness of. Does not make one acceptable to God. 8:33

**HIGH PRIEST—CHIEF PRIESTS**
Discussed. 7:32; 11:49

**HISTORY**
Christ & **h.**
  Changed by death of Christ. 21:24
  Supreme fact of **h.**—the Incarnation. 1:10

God & **h.**
  God's plan for ages. 4:22
  Salvation came through the Jews. 4:22

**HOLD FAST** (See **ENDURANCE; PERSEVERANCE**)

**HOLY—HOLINESS**
Duty. To be holy. Verses. List of. 20:12-13
Symbolized. By white dress of angels. 20:12-13

**HOLY SPIRIT**
And Christ.
  Came upon as a dove. 1:32
  Came upon without measure. 1:32-33; 3:34; 5:32
  Given by Christ. Breathed on disciples. 20:22
  Identified the Messiah for John. 1:30-34
  Why His presence is better than having Christ with us. 16:7
Came upon—received by. Disciples. 20:22
Deity of. Discussed. 15:26-27; 16:15
Duty.
  Must follow. 21:18-19
  Must receive. Is conditional. 14:16
  Discussed. 14:15-26; 16:7-15
Dwells within believer. Verses. List of. 14:17
Fact. Will not always strive with man. 7:33-34; 11:54
Infilling. (See **HOLY SPIRIT**, Work of) 14:21-22
  Verses. List of. 14:21
Names—Titles.
  Abiding Presence of Trinity. 14:23-25
  Christ in the believer. 14:20
  Comforter. 14:16, 26; 15:26-27; 16:7
  Living Water. Meaning. 7:37-39
  Spirit of Truth. 15:26-27; 16:13
  Who He is. 14:15-26
Sins against.
  Rejected. Does not always strive with man. 7:33-34; 11:54
  Why the world cannot receive. 14:17
Source of. Christ. 7:37-39
Work of.
  Abundant life. 7:38-39
  Comfort, help. 14:16
  Convicts & convinces. Meaning. 16:8-11
  Convicts of sin, righteousness, judgment. 16:8-11
  Difference between Old & New Testament. 7:39
  Discussed. 16:7-15
  Gives life. 6:63
  Gives the gospel to the hearts of men. 6:44-46
  Gives rivers of living water. 7:37-39
  Gives special experiences, manifestations. 14:21-22
  Gives victory over world. 15:26-27
  Glorifies Jesus. 16:14-15
  Guides believers. 16:12-13
  Infills. 14:21-22
  Regenerates. 3:5-6 cp. vv.3-6
  Reveals new truth. 3:5-6
  Teaches & helps remember. 14:26

With believers & with world. 16:7-15
Witnesses to Christ. 5:32; 15:26-27

**HOME** (See **FAMILY**)

**HONESTY**
Ex. of. Nathanael. Did not deceive, bait, or mislead. 1:47

**HONOR**
Discussed. 4:44
Duty. To **h**. Christ. 4:44
Fact.
　God **h**. any man who **h**. His Son. 12:23-26
　Prophet without **h**. in own country. 4:44
　Some refuse to **h**. 4:44
Of Christ.
　By God. 8:54-59
　Discussed. 4:44
　Evidence of faith. 4:44
　Should be. 4:44; 5:22-23
　Verses. List of. 3:29-30
Of self.
　Discounted, ignored, distasteful. 8:54-59
　Results in rejecting Christ. 5:44
　Seeking **h**. for self. Verses. List of. 5:44

**HOPE**
Believer's **h**. The resurrection. 6:37-40
Duty. To persevere in **h**. seeking God's help. 4:46-47

**HOPELESS—HOPELESSNESS**
Results. Hardness, emptiness, prejudice. 1:46

**HOSANNA**
Meaning. 12:12-13

**HOUR, THE**
Meaning. Jesus' death. 12:23-24
Of man's acclaim, not Jesus' **a**. 7:6-9

**HOUSE OF GOD, THE** (See **CHURCH; TEMPLE**)

**HUMILITY**
Duty.
　Not to push oneself forward. 1:20-22
　To exalt Christ & not self. 3:29-30
　To seek the help of Christ in **h**. 4:46-47
Example. Jesus washing feet. Royal service. 13:1-17
To serve as a slave. 1:8, 27; 13:3-5

**HUNGER, SPIRITUAL**
Answer to.
　Met by man's great **h**. 6:22-29
　Verses. List of. 6:34-35, 55
Duty. To seek an answer & do something about one's **h**. 1:43-44
Satisfied by believing, not by works. 6:28-29

**HYPOCRISY—HYPOCRITE**
Discussed. Counterfeit disciples. 6:59-71
Traits of. Deception. Verses. List of. 12:4-8

**I AM**
Basic name of deity. Meaning. 6:20

**IDOLS—IDOLATRY** (See **GODS, FALSE**)

**IGNORANCE—IGNORANT**
About Christ.
　Men **i**. that Christ is the only approach to God. 4:22
　Verses. List of. 4:22
About God.
　Men do not know God. 7:25-31; 8:19
　Men **i**. in their worship of God. 4:22
　Men question God's existence. 14:4-5
　Verses. List of. 4:22; 7:25-31; 8:19

**IMAGE OF GOD**
Man created in **i**. of God. 4:23

**IMAGINATIONS, EVIL**
Creates false gods. 8:54-59
Prevented. By guarding self around opposite sex. 4:27

**INCARNATION**
Cost of. What it **c**. God to give His Son. 3:16
Discussed. 1:14-18
How. By the Word of God. Not by some grotesque method. 1:10; 6:61
Jesus Christ came out of heaven. 8:23
Proof.
　Fourfold. 1:14-18
　Of God's love. 3:17

**INDIFFERENCE** (See **HARDNESS; UNBELIEF**)

**INDWELLING PRESENCE**
Abiding. (See **ABIDE**) 15:1-8
Mutual **i**. between Christ & the believer. 6:56
Verses. List of. 6:56; 17:23
Mutual **i**. between God & Christ. 5:17-30; 8:15-16; 10:14-16; 10:37-39; 14:10; 17:10
Mutual **i**. between God, Christ, & the believer. 10:14-16; 14:18-20, 23-24
Of Christ in you. 14:18-20; 14:21, 23-24
Verses. List of. 14:20
Of the Holy Spirit. Discussed. 14:15-26; 16:7-15; 20:22-23
Verses. List of. 14:17

**INHERITANCE**
What the **i**. is. Sharing equally with Christ. 16:14-15

**INIQUITY—INIQUITIES** (See **SIN**)

**INITIATIVE**
Essential.
　To grasp opportunity. 11:7-10
　To work while day before night comes. 11:7-10

**INSIGHT** (See **SPIRITUAL SIGHT; UNDERSTANDING**)

**INTERCESSION** (See **PRAYER**)

**INVITATION**
Source.
　Extended by Jesus. He takes the initiative. 1:39-40
　God must draw man. 6:44

**ISRAEL** (See **JEWS**)
Capital punishment not allowed. 19:7
Chosen by God. Reasons. 4:22
Purpose. Why God chose. Fourfold **p**. 4:22
Religionists of Israel. (See **RELIGIONISTS**)

**JACOB**
Ladder of. Meaning. 1:51

**JAMES, THE BROTHER OF JESUS**
Confesses deity of Jesus. 1:14
Does not believe in Jesus, not at first. 7:3-5

**JESUS CHRIST** (See **INCARNATION**)
Accepted. (See **JESUS CHRIST**, Responses to)
Accused—Accusations against.
　An insurrectionist. 2:19
　A Samaritan. 8:48-50
　Of bearing false witness. 8:13
　Of being demon-possessed. 7:20-31; 8:48-50
　Of opposing religion & **r**. leaders. 7:20-24
And God. (See **GOD**, And Christ)
And the Holy Spirit. (See **HOLY SPIRIT**, And Jesus Christ)
Anointed.
　By the Holy Spirit. Full measure of the **S**. 1:32-33; 3:34
　By women. Supreme believer. 12:1-11
Approved by God. Audible voice. 12:27-30
Arrested.
　Absolute surrender. 18:1-11
　Who **a**. 11:55-57
Ascension.
　Preciousness of. To **be with** & to **know** the Father. 14:6
　Predicted. 7:33-34; 14:4-6; 20:17
　To make way for the Spirit's coming. 16:7
Authority.
　All judgment committed to. 5:22
　Five witnesses to. 5:31-39
　Jesus' astounding **a**.: Equality with God. 5:17-30
　Over life, all of life. 5:1-47
Baptism—baptized. Discussed. 1:29-34
Betrayed. Predicted. 6:70-71; 13:18-30
Birth. (See **JESUS CHRIST**, Origin)
　Divine. **b**. From & "out of" heaven. 8:23
Blood of.
　Precious. 1:29
　Repulsive to some. 6:61
Burial. In garden on Mt. Calvary. 19:40-42
Claims. (See **JESUS CHRIST**, Deity; Nature of)
　Bread of Life. 6:35, 52-53; 6:53
　Came from God. 8:42
　Deity. List of fifteen or more **c**. 10:25
　Verses. List of. 10:30-36
　Deliverer from death. 8:51-53
　Door of the sheep. 10:7-10
　Embodiment of God. 14:8-14
　Equality with God. 5:17-30
　Father is the God who men profess. 8:54-59
　Five **c**. of deity. 6:30-31
　From above—out of spiritual world, heaven. 3:31; 6:33; 7:25-31; 8:23
　Verses. List of. 3:31, 34
　God. 10:30-33

639

**JESUS CHRIST** (Continued)
- God is My Father. 1:34; 2:15-17; 5:17-18
- God never left Him alone. 8:29
- God sent Him. 3:32-34; 8:42
  - Verses. List of. 3:32-34
- God's Apostle. God's spokesman.
  - Verses. List of. 3:32-34
- Great Shepherd. Four c. 10:22-42
- I AM. 4:26; 6:20; 8:12-13, 54-59; 18:4-6
- Indwelt by God. Mutual i. with God. 8:19; 10:37-39; 14:10
- King. But not of this world. 18:33-38; 18:37
- Knows God. Intimately. 7:25-31; 8:54-59
- Knows origin & destiny. 8:14
- Life. 14:6
- Light of the world. 9:5; 11:7-10; 12:34-36
  - Meaning. 8:12
  - Proofs. 8:12-20
- Living Water. 7:37-39
- Messiah. 10:24-29; 10:25
- Misunderstandings of. Fourfold. 8:25-30; 12:20-36
- Mutual indwelling. God in Him & He in God. 8:19; 10:37-39; 14:10
- One with God, the Father. 5:17-30; 10:30-33; 14:10Verses. List of. 5:19; 8:54-59
- Out of heaven, the spiritual world. 3:31
  - Verses. List of. 3:31, 34
- Proof. Three tests. 7:16-19
- Rejected. 5:40-47
- Responses to. (See **JESUS CHRIST**, Response to)
- Resurrection & Life. 11:25-27
- Revelation of God. 8:19
- Sent by God. 3:32-34; 4:31-35; 8:42
- Shepherd of the sheep. 10:1-6, 11-21
- Sinless. 8:29, 45-47; 8:54-59
- Son of David. 1:45, 49
- Son of God. 1:34; 5:25; 10:34-36
  - Verses. List of. 1:34
- Son of Man. 1:51; 5:27; 13:31-32
  - Verses. List of. 1:51
- Source of Holy Spirit. 7:37-39
- Source of life, both abundant & eternal. 6:52-53; 7:37-39
- Spokesman for God. 3:32-34; 8:26; 14:10
  - Verses. List of. 3:32-34; 3:34; 14:6; 15:14-15
- True Vine of the world. 15:1-8
- Truth. 14:6
- Way. 14:6
- Witness is true. 8:14
- Words of God. 7:16-19; 14:10
- Works of. Are of God. 5:19-20
  - Verses. List of. 5:20
- Cleanses the temple. 2:13-16
- Concepts of.
  - Great Man only. 9:13-15
  - Man, Teacher, Prophet, Savior, etc. 9:8-41
  - Prophet. 9:16-17
  - Stages of growth in concepts. Six concepts. 9:8-41
- Compassion. (See **COMPASSION**, Of Jesus)
- Condescension. (See **JESUS CHRIST**, Humiliation)
  - From heaven to earth. 13:3-5
  - What it cost God to send Christ. 3:16
- Creator. (See **CREATION**, Creator of)
- Cross. (See **JESUS CHRIST**, Death)
  - Breaks the power of Satan. 16:11
  - Glory & power of. Another Outline. 12:20-36
  - Glory of. Discussed. 12:23-26; 17:22
  - Judged, condemned Satan. 16:11
  - Lifted up. Proves He is God. 8:28
  - Power of. 16:11
  - Repulsive & attractive. 6:61
  - What the c. does. 12:31-32; 16:11
  - Why the c. attracts man. What c. does for man. 12:32
- Death.
  - And resurrection. Predicted. 2:18-21
  - Blood of. (See **JESUS CHRIST**, Blood of)
  - Described.
    - As the Hour. 12:23-24
    - As the Lamb of God. 1:29-30
  - Destined—Determined. By God. 18:31-32
  - Doctrines of. Listed. 21:24
  - Events of. 19:16-37
    - Agonizing thirst. Promised Messiah. 19:28-29
    - Bearing cross. Went forth willingly. 19:16-17
    - Between thieves. Preeminent sacrifice. 19:18
    - Caring for His mother. Caring for others. 19:25-27
    - Gambling for His clothes. Worldly minded. 19:23-24
    - Shout of victory, salvation, reconciliation. 19:30
    - Spear thrust in His side. Symbol of baptism & Lord's Supper. 19:31-37
    - Title on cross. King, Promised Messiah. 19:19-22
  - Glory of Christ's death.
    - Great g. of person, of condescension was d. 13:3-5
    - Supreme g. was d. 12:23-30; 14:30-31; 15:9; 16:11
    - Threefold g. 13:31-32
  - Plotted. 5:16; 11:47-57
  - Predicted—Foretold. 3:14; 6:51; 7:33-34; 10:11, 17-18; 12:7-8, 31-36; 13:31-14:3; 14:30-31; 17:11
  - What disciples thought. Their interpretation. 14:8
  - Prophesied.
    - By high priest. 11:49-53
    - To be sacrificed for people. 11:49-53
  - Purpose. 4:22
    - Supreme act of obedience. 10:11, 17-18
    - Supreme reason C. died. 10:11, 17-18, 33; 12:27-30; 14:30-31; 15:9; 16:11
    - To deliver from perishing. 3:14-15
    - To give eternal life. 3:14-15
  - Repulsive to some. 6:61
  - Results.
    - A threefold glory. 13:31-32
    - Changed face & fate of history & men. 21:24
    - Judged, condemned Satan. 16:11
    - Proves He is God, the great I AM. 8:28
    - What Christ's d. does. 13:31-14:3
  - Sacrifice—sacrificial.
    - Called sacrificial Bread of God. 6:33
    - Cost to God. 3:16
    - Substitutionary. Vicarious. 1:29-30; 10:11, 17-18; 11:49-53; 18:38-40
    - Verses. List of. 11:49-53
    - Willingness. To die as God willed. 18:1-11
  - Seven pictures of. 12:20-36
  - Substitutionary. (See **JESUS CHRIST**, Death; Sacrifice)
  - Supreme act of love. 15:12-13
  - Symbolized.
    - As King of sinners. 19:18
    - By Passover Lamb. 19:28-29 (alt. outline)
    - By serpent raised up by Moses. 3:14-15
    - By the temple being destroyed & raised up. 2:18-21
    - Verses. List of. 3:16; 12:23-26
  - Voluntary—Willingness. (See **JESUS CHRIST**, Death; Sacrifice)
- Deity. (See **JESUS CHRIST**, Claims; Names—Titles)
  - Apostle of God—Sent by God. 3:32-34
    - Verses. List of. 3:32-34; 8:26-27; 14:6; 15:14-15
  - Claims to. (See **JESUS CHRIST**, Claims)
  - Coexistent with God. 1:1-2; 5:17-30
  - Eternal. 1:30-31
  - False concepts.
    - Conqueror, Provider, Indulgent Lord. 12:12-13
    - Vs. true concept. 12:12-19
  - Fullness of God. 1:16
  - God indwelling Him. (See **INDWELLING PRESENCE**)
  - God-Man. 1:14
    - Verses. List of. 10:30-33
  - Holy Spirit. Possessed the Spirit without measure. 1:32-33
  - Incarnation. (See **INCARNATION**)
  - Judgment of. Committed to Him.
    - Verses. List of. 5:22-23
  - King of the universe. 12:20-22; 19:19
  - Life. Possesses the energy of life.
    - Verses. List of. 5:26
  - Mediator. 3:17; 4:22; 10:7-8; 14:6
    - Verses. List of. 3:17; 10:7-8
  - Messenger of God. 7:16-19
    - Verses. List of. 3:32-34
  - Misunderstood. Four misunderstandings. 12:20-36
  - Mutual indwelling. In the Father & the Father in Him. 14:10
  - Mutual possession. 17:10
  - New Master. Proof. 3:22-36
  - Of God. (See **JESUS CHRIST**, Nature—Origin)
  - Omniscience. (See **JESUS CHRIST**, Knowledge) 1:47; 2:24-25

Oneness with the Father. 5:17-30; 8:16; 14:10
　Verses. List of. 5:19; 8:54-59
Predicted—Foretold. 14:1-5
Preeminence of. 1:30-31; 3:29-30
　Verses. List of. 3:29-30
Preexistence of. As God. 1:1, 30-31
Proofs.
　By works, signs. 2:23; 5:36; 10:38; 20:31-31
　Foretold. 8:12-20
　Ninefold. 5:17-30
Revelation of God. 1:50; 14:7; 14:8-11
　Verses. List of. 14:6
Savior.
　Discussed. 4:42
　False concept of. 12:12-13
Self-existent. 1:1-2; 5:26
Sinless—Perfectly obedient. 6:38; 7:18; 8:47
　Verses. List of. 6:38; 7:6-9; 7:16-19
Son of God.
　Discussed. 1:1-2; 5:25
　Verses. List of. 9:35-38
　List of references. 1:34
Son of Man. Verses. List of. 1:51
Spokesman for God. 3:32-34; 8:26-27; 14:6; 14:10
　Verses. List of. 3:32-34; 8:26-27; 14:6; 15:14-15
Teaching, doctrine was of God. 7:16-19
The Messiah. 1:35-42
The One prophesied. 1:43-45
Witness of God. 8:14
Witnesses to. Five **w**. 5:31-39
Education. Questioned by religionists. 7:11-15
Exalt—Exaltation.
　Predicted. 14:4-6
　Will be a day of universal worship. 7:6-9
Family.
　Cousin to John the Baptist. 1:30-31
　Joseph died early. 2:1-2
　Rejected Jesus. Reasons. 7:3-5
　Response by brothers. Mockery & unbelief. 7:1-9
　Tenderness shown to mother, Mary. 2:3-5; 19:25-27
Glory of—glorified.
　Chart of Christ's **g**. & believer **g**. 17:22
　Discussed. 1:14; 13:31-14:3; 17:1-8
　Eternal **g**. of. Discussed. 17:5-8
　How C. can be glorified.
　　By believers. How. 17:9-11
　　By death & service. 12:23-26
　　By the cross. Two ways. 12:23-26, 13:31-32
　Discussed. 11:4; 17:1-4
　Misunderstood. 12:23-26
Healing. (See **HEALS—HEALING**)
Hometown. Rejected. C. heart broken over. 4:44
Honor—Honored. (See **HONOR**, Of Jesus Christ)
　Verses. 3:29-30
Hour of. Meaning. His death. 2:3-5; 12:23-24
Humanity.
　Struggles with His emotions. 11:33-36
　Took on the nature of man. 1:14

Humiliation of. (See **JESUS CHRIST**, Condescension)
　Condescension. From heaven to earth. 13:3-5
　Cost to God. What it **c**. God to send Christ. 3:16
Humility of.
　Condescension from heaven to earth. 13:3-5
　Great gulf He spanned to come to earth. 13:3-5
　Washing disciples' feet. Royal service. 13:1-17
"I AM" claims. 6:20
Ignorance of. Verses. 4:22
Impact. (See **JESUS CHRIST**, Responses to)
Incarnation. (See **INCARNATION**)
Intercessor. Described. In four ways. 14:13-14
King.
　Approached as **K**. 12:20-36
　Claims to be **K**. 18:33-37
　Proclaimed as **K**. 12:12-19
　Rejected and accepted as **K**. 12:37-50
Knowledge—Omniscience.
　Intimate **k**. between **C**. & God. (See **INDWELLING PRESENCE**)
　Knows believers—intimately. 10:14-16; 11:5
　Knows every man, all about men. No one unknown. 1:47-48; 2:24-25
　Verses. 2:24-25
Life of. Picture of. Devotion—worship—mission. 8:1-2
Love of.
　Charge to believers. Continue in **l**. 15:9-10
　Discussed. 11:33-35; 13:33-35; 15:9-11; 21:15-17
　For believers. Great **l**. 13:33-35; 15:9; 15:12; 21:15-17
　For each person individually. 11:5
　His great **l**. 15:9-11
Loved. By God.
　Beloved Son. Verses. List of. 5:20
　Dearest thing to God's heart. 3:16, 35-36; 5:20
　Reasons. Threefold. 15:9
Mediator.
　By body, death, & resurrection of Lord. 2:18-21
　Claimed by Jesus. 12:44-45; 14:6
　Described. In four ways. 14:13-14
　Discussed. 12:44-46; 14:6
　Interceded for believer. 14:13-14
　Meaning. 12:44
　Only Door to God. 10:7-8; 14:6
　Reason prayer is answered. 14:13-14
　Salvation through **C**. alone. 3:17; 4:22; 10:7-8; 14:6
　Verses. List of. 3:17; 10:7-8
　Way to God. 14:6
　Worship through **C**. alone. 4:22
Message of. (See **GOSPEL**)
Ministry.
　Baptized people. 3:22-26
　To succor those rejected by family. 7:3-5
Misconception of.
　Four false concepts. 7:10-19

Good man, deceiver, unimportant. 7:11-15
Mission. (See **JESUS CHRIST**, Work of)
　To do the will of God. 4:34; 5:30; 6:38-40
　To do the works of God. 5:17; 9:4
　To give light to men. 1:4-5, 9
　To open the eyes of man. 9:1-7
　To seek & save the lost. 1:38-39, 43-44
　Urgency of. 9:4
Names—Titles.
　Apostle of God. 3:32-34
　Bread of God. 6:32
　Bread of Life. 6:33-35; 6:47-51
　Bridegroom. 3:29-30
　Christ, the Son of the Living God. 6:69
　Communicator, The great. 14:6
　Door of Sheep. 10:7-10
　Eternal. 1:1-2
　God Himself. 10:30-33
　God's Apostle. 3:32-34
　Good Shepherd. 10:11-21
　High Priest. 19:23-24
　I AM (eimi). 1:1-2; 4:26; 6:20
　Ideal man. 5:27
　Jesus of Nazareth. 1:45
　King of Israel. 1:49; 12:20-21; 18:37
　Lamb of God. Discussed. 1:29-34
　Liberator, The great. 14:6
　Life, The. Meaning. 1:4-5; 1:4; 14:6
　Light.
　　Function. Tenfold. 1:9
　　Of life. 8:1-9:41
　　Of men. 1:9-13
　　Of the world. 3:19-21; 8:12; 12:35-36; 12:46
　Living water. 4:10-14; 7:37-39
　Lord. 13:13-14
　Master. 11:28
　Messiah. (See **MESSIAH—MESSIAHSHIP**)
　　Meaning. 1:20
　　The witness of Andrew. 1:35-42
　　Thought to be Messiah. 4:25, 29
　New Master. 3:22-36
　One prophesied. 1:45
　Resurrection and life. 11:25-27
　Revelation of God. 14:7
　Shepherd of Sheep. 10:1-6; 10:11
　Son of God. List of N.T. references. 1:34; 5:25
　Son of Man.
　　Discussed. 1:51
　　List of references in John 5:27
　Spokesman, God's. 3:32-34
　Teacher. 3:2; 13:12-14
　True Bread. 6:35
　True Vine. 15:1
　Truth. 14:6
　Way to God. 14:6
　Word, The. discussed. 1:1-5, 14
Nature and Origin. (See **JESUS CHRIST**, Claims; Deity)
　Begotten—of the bosom of God. 1:14, 18; 3:16, 18
　Equal with God. 5:17-30; 5:19
　Eternal. Preexistent, coexistent, self-existent. 1:1-2, 30-31
　From above—out of heaven. 3:13, 31; 6:33; 7:17-19, 25-31; 8:14, 23
　Verses. List of. 3:31, 34

641

**JESUS CHRIST** (Continued)
Full embodiment of God. 14:8-14
Full measure of the Spirit. 3:34; 5:32
God Himself. 1:1-2; 10:33; 14:8-14
Life. Possesses the energy of life. 1:4; 5:26; 14:6; 17:3
One with God the Father. 5:17-30; 5:19; 10:30-33; 14:10
Out of heaven. 3:13
Sent by God. 3:32-34
Sinless—Perfectly obedient. 6:38; 8:45-47
Nothing in Him for Satan. 14:30-31
Verses. List of. 6:38; 7:18
Son of God. 1:34; 5:25; 10:34-36
Obedience. 10:17-18; 12:49-50
Perfectly o. to God. 6:38; 13:31-32; 15:9-11
Supreme act of o. Death on cross. 12:27-30; 14:30-31; 15:9-10, 12-13
Verses. List of. 6:38
Offends some. (See **JESUS CHRIST**, Responses to)
One with the Father. (See **JESUS CHRIST**, Claims; Deity, One with the Father) 5:17-30; 8:16; 14:10
Opinions. Divided. Prophet, Messiah, deceiver, good teacher. 7:37-53
Opposed—Opposition.
By religionists. (See **RELIGIONISTS**, Opposed Christ)
Origin. (See **JESUS CHRIST**, Nature & Origin)
Power—Omnipotence.
Confronts & conquers death. Raising Lazarus. 11:38-46
Creative p. To meet man's need for regeneration. 2:1-11
Over God's house, the temple. 2:12-22
Over man's destiny. 5:24-25
Over nature. Calming of the storm. Deliverance from fear. 6:20
To feed the multitude. Provision for human need. 6:1-15
To give life. 5:21
To resurrect men from dead. 5:28-30
Prayer life.
For future believers. 17:20-26
For Himself. 17:1-8
For His disciples. 17:9-19
High Priestly intercessory p. 17:1-26
Preexistence. (See **DEITY**, Preexistence)
Prophecy concerning.
Death & resurrection. All p. in John. 20:20
Destiny. Death, resurrection, ascension. 7:33-34
Verses & fulfillments listed. 1:45
Purpose. (See Related Subjects)
Misunderstood. 12:27-30
Sent by God. 3:32-34
Supreme p. To glorify God. 12:27-30
To be the Apostle, the Spokesman for God. 3:32-34
To be the Revelation of God. 1:1; 14:6, 8-14
To bring security. 17:11
To declare God. 1:18
To die on the cross. Supreme act of obedience. 12:27-30
To do & to fulfill God's will. 6:38

To execute judgment. 5:27
To give life abundantly. 5:26, 40; 6:37-40; 7:37-39; 10:10
To glorify God. 8:48-50
To keep man from dying & perishing. 3:16-17; 6:47-51
To save, not to judge the world. 3:17; 12:47
To serve others—sacrificially. 13:1-17
Questioned. (See **JESUS CHRIST**, Accused; Challenged)
Relationship.
To believers.
Knows believers—intimately. 10:14-16; 15:9-11
Very special. 15:9-11
To God. Intimate knowledge. 10:14-16
To people of the world. 15:1-8
Responses to. (See **UNBELIEF**)
Accepted. 1:12-13, 1:35-51
And rejected as King. 12:37-50
Believed on. 10:42; 11:45; 12:11
By authorities. Rejection—opposition. 7:32-36; 12:19
By brothers. 7:1-9
By Jews and the people. 7:10-19
By people. 7:20-31; 12:17-18
By religionists, Pharisees. (See **RELIGIONISTS**, Opposed Christ)
By pilgrims. 7:20-24
By the demon-possessed & insane: questioning, unbelief. 7:20-31
By witnesses of Lazarus' resurrection. 12:17
Divided opinions. 7:37-53
Four false concepts. 7:10-19
Four specific r. to Him. 12:1-11
Mere man—merely a good man. 7:20-31
Mockery, ridicule, unbelief. Answer to. 7:6-9
Murmuring against claims. 6:41-43
Not the same as God. 14:9
Obstinate unbelief. 11:47-57
Offended by Him. Four reasons. 6:59-71
Received by one family in particular. 11:1-3
Receiving. (See **SALVATION**)
Results of. 6:52-58
Rejected—Opposed. 1:10-11; 5:40-47; 6:36, 64-66
By religionists. (See **RELIGIONISTS**, Opposed Christ)
By world. Tragic. Reasons. 1:10-11
Nothing to do with. 7:32-36
Reasons. He is a threat to doing as one wishes. 7:32
Sought after. For help. 12:17-18
Three r. 6:66-71
Unbelief & opposition. 11:54
Resurrection.
Appearances to.
Disciples. 20:19-29
Emphasis of destination was the Father, not heaven. 14:6
Doctrines of. Listed. 21:24
Effects of.
Brings joy. 16:20-22
Changes face & fate of history & men. 21:24
Discussed. 16:16-33

Gives access into God's presence. 16:23-24
Perplexes, puzzles people. 16:16-19
Provides triumphant peace. 16:33
Reveals the nature of the Father. 16:25-27
Sevenfold. 16:16-33
Upon disciples. 20:19-20
Events of.
Angels appear to Mary Magdalene. 20:11-18
Appearance to disciples. 20:19-23; 20:24-29
Appearance to Mary Magdalene. 20:11-18
Empty tomb discovered by Mary Magdalene. 20:1-2
John discovers linen left in fold. Believes. 20:7-10
Peter & John run to empty tomb. 20:3-6
Evidence of.
Eyewitnesses. 20:19
Four e. 20:1-10
Great discovery—the empty tomb. 20:1-10
Kind of body Jesus had. 21:1
Nature of. Real presence. 21:1-14
Preciousness of. To be with & know the Father. 14:6
Predicted. 7:33-34
Proof of.
Many infallible proofs. 20:1-9
Wounds. 20:19-20
Reality of r. body. 21:1-14
The great recognition. Jesus appears to Mary Magdalene first. 20:11-18
Tomb. Discussed. 20:1
When Jesus arose. 20:1-2
Return.
Reasons. 14:1-3
Two returns for believers. Death & Second Coming. 14:1-3
Revelation—revealed. (See **REVELATION**)
As Answer to man's great hunger. 6:22-29
As Assurance & Security of bel. 6:37-40
As Authority over life. 5:1-47
As Authority over the Sabbath. 5:1-16
As Bread of Life. 6:1-71
As Coming King. 12:12-50
As Deliverer from fear. 6:16-21
As Door. 10:7, 9
As Embodiment of God. 14:8-14
As Glorified Son of Man. 12:12-50
As Great Intercessor. 17:1-26
As Great Minister. 13:1-16:33
As Light of Life. 3:19-21; 8:1-9:41; 12:35-36
As Living Water. 4:1-14
As Mediator. 14:4-7
As New Master. 3:22-36
As Object of Faith. 4:43-54
As Only Way to God. 14:4-7
As Provision for human needs. 6:1-15
As Resurrection & Life. 11:1-12:11
As Shepherd of Life. 10:1-42
As Son of God. 2:1-3:21
As Source of Spiritual Satisfaction. 6:30-36
As Suffering Savior. 18:1-19:42

As Supreme over God's house. 2:12-22
As Supreme **R**. of God. 1:1, 10; 14:6-7
As the embodiment of God. 14:8-14
Creative power. To regenerate man.
  2:1-11
God's great love. 3:16-17
Heaven. Truth. Only One who can **r**.
  heaven & truth. 3:31
Of God.
  Discussed. 1:50
  Not left in dark, groping, grasping.
    14:6-7
Of man's condemnation. 3:18-21
Reactions to. Four **r**. 12:1-11
To John the Baptist. Sign given by God.
  1:32-34
Tragedy of. Supreme **t**. 1:10-11
Witnesses to. 1:1-51
Savior.
  Discussed. 4:42
  Salvation is of **J**. 4:22
Seed of.
  Abraham. Never seen by Jews. 1:23
  Adam. Never seen by Jews. 1:23
Seeking man. (See **SEEK—SEEKING**,
  Christ **S**. Man)
Sent by God. 3:32-34; 4:31-35; 8:26-27
Shepherd.
  Contrast with false **s**. 10:16
  Great claims of. 10:22-42
  Is the door of the sheep. 10:7-10
  Of life. 10:1-42
Spokesman for God. 3:32-34; 14:10
Teaching. Is God's **t**. 7:16-17
Temple of **J**. body. Becomes **t**. of men.
  2:18-21
Trials, Legal.
  Before Caiphas, High Priest. 18:19-24
  Before Gentiles. 18:28-19:15
  Before Pilate. Indecisive compromise.
    18:28-19:15
  Charges against. 2:18; 18:19
Trials—tribulations. (See **CONDESCEN-
  SION; HUMILIATION; DEATH**, Suffer-
  ings; Related Subjects)
  One-parent family. Joseph died early.
    2:1-2
Triumphal Entry. Proclaimed as King,
  Messiah. 12:12-19
Will of. Distinct, separate from God.
  6:38
Witness of God, The. (See **DEITY**)
  By Andrew. The Messiah. 1:35-42
  By Christ. Threefold. 1:50-51
  By John the apostle.
    Five **w**. to. 5:31-39
    The Light of men. 1:9-13
    The Word. 1:1-5
    The Word made flesh. 1:14-18
  By John the Baptist.
    God became flesh. 1:15
    Special **w**. to. 1:6-8
  By Nathanael. Son of God, King of
    Israel. 1:46-49
  By Philip. One prophesied. 1:43-45
Words of.
  Of God. 7:16-19; 14:10
  Prove deity. 14:10-11; 15:15
  Rejected. 5:47; 8:37
Work of—Ministry. (See **JESUS CHRIST**,
  Mission)

Bears witness to deity. 5:19-20; 5:36;
  10:25; 14:10
Concerned with every need. 6:1-71
Judgment committed to. Reasons. 5:22
  Verses. List of. 5:22-23
Proves deity. 5:36; 14:10; 14:11;
  20:30-31
Reveals union with God. 5:20
To be light of world. Discussed. 1:9
To bring peace, joy, security. 14:27-31
To bring satisfaction. 6:30-36
To cleanse God's temple. 2:12-22
To defeat Satan. 12:31-32; 14:30;
  16:8-11
To give life. 5:21
To judge the world. 5:22
To make secure. 10:9
To open the eyes of man. 9:1-7
To quench man's thirst. 4:15
To resurrect & give life. 11:25-26
To serve and teach. 13:1-17
Was of God. Are God's works. 5:19-20
  Verses. List of. 5:20
Worship of. To be a day of universal **w**.
  7:6-9

**JEWS**
Capital punishment not allowed. 19:7
Discussed. 5:10
Errors—Mistakes of.
  Claim heritage to be children of Abra-
    ham. 8:33
  Misinterpreted God's promises. 4:22
Purposes of. Reasons chosen by God. 4:22
Rejected Jesus Christ. (See **JESUS
  CHRIST**, Responses to; **RELIGIONISTS**,
  Opposed Christ)
  Persecuted Jesus. 5:16; 7:13-15, 19
  Sought to kill Jesus. 5:16, 17-18; 7:13,
    19; 8:40, 59; 10:31-33, 39
Why Jesus came to earth as a **J**. 4:22

**JOHN THE APOSTLE**
Discovers empty tomb. Notices linen &
  believes. 20:7-10
Task of. Completed. 21:24-25
Witness to Christ.
  The Word. 1:1-5
  Word made flesh. 1:14-18

**JOHN THE BAPTIST**
A priest, but not a religionist. 1:19
Cousin to Jesus Christ. 1:30-31
Forerunner. Why **f**. necessary. 1:23
Life of. Priest, but a different kind of **p**.
  1:19
Messenger of God. 1:19-27
Witness to Christ.
  God became flesh. 1:15
  Lamb of God—Son of God. 1:29-34
  Special **w**. to. 1:6-8

**JOSEPH OF ARIMATHAEA**
Buries Jesus. Conquest of fear. 19:38

**JOY**
Discussed. 14:28-29; 15:11
Meaning. 14:28-29; 15:11
Source. 14:28-29
  Access to God. 16:23-27
  Jesus' purpose. 15:11
  Resurrection of Jesus. 16:20-22
  Salvation. Meeting Christ face-to-face.
    1:45

**JUDAS ISCARIOT**
Betrayed Christ. Predicted. 13:18-30
Traits of.
  A thief. Stole money. 12:4-8
  Sinful **t**. Threefold. 12:4-8
Was treasurer of disciples. 12:4-8

**JUDGE—JUDGING OTHERS** (See **CEN-
  SORING; CRITICISM**)
Man's condemnatory, judgmental spirit.
  8:3-6
Sins of.
  Censoring, condemning. 8:3-6
  **J**. by appearance. 7:24
Who can judge. 8:7-9

**JUDGMENT**
Committed to Christ. 5:22, 27
  Verses. List of. 5:22-23, 28-30
Conviction of. 16:8-11
Described.
  Cast away & burned. 15:4-6
  Condemnation. Jesus reveals **c**.
    3:18-21
  Separation, exclusion, shut out. 7:33-
    34; 8:21-22
How God judges.
  Allows life to perish, corrupt. 3:16
  By Christ. 5:22-23
  Judges in justice. 12:39-41
  Judicial judgment of God. 12:39-41
Of believers.
  Already paid in cross of Christ.
    12:31-32
Of unbelievers—lost.
  To be **j**. by words of Christ. Reason.
    12:47-50
Who is to be **j**.
  The believer. (See **JUDGMENT**, Of
    Believers)
  The unbeliever. (See **JUDGMENT**, Of
    Unbelievers)

**JUDICIAL BLINDNESS & REJECTION**
Law of. Discussed. 12:39-41

**JUSTIFIED—JUSTIFICATION**
How man is **j**. By cross. Discussed.
  12:32

**KEPT—KEEPING POWER OF GOD** (See
  **ASSURANCE—PREDESTINATION—
  SECURITY**)

**KIND—KINDNESS** (See **CARE—CARING;
  MINISTERING**)

**KINGDOM OF GOD**
Misunderstood. Earthly **k**. vs. spiritual.
  13:36-38

**KNOW—KNOWING—KNOWLEDGE**
Christ. (See **INDWELLING PRESENCE**)
  Intimate knowledge between **C**. &
    believers. 10:14-16; 11:5
  Intimate knowledge between **C**. &
    God. 8:55; 10:14-16
God. Intimate knowledge between **G**. &
  Christ. 10:14-16
How to **k**. God. 7:16-19; 8:31-32
Of what.
  New birth. Complete assurance, **k**.
    3:9-11
  Of Christ. Believers know **C**. by His
    Word or voice & Spirit. 20:14-16

**LABOR—LABORERS** (See **BELIEVERS; DISCIPLES; MINISTERS**)
Discussed. Subject of l. For God. 4:31-42

**LAMB OF GOD**
Discussed. 1:29-30

**LAW**
Kinds. Conditioning l. Are eight laws of c. 12:39-41
Purpose. To govern behavior & unbelief. 12:39-41
Requires two witnesses to support one's testimony. 8:17-18

**LAZARUS, THE BROTHER OF MARY & MARTHA**
And Jesus. Power over death. 11:38-46
Death of. Purposes of. 11:1-16

**LEVITES**
Discussed. 1:19

**LIBERATOR**
Jesus the l. 8:34-36; 14:6

**LIBERTY**
Believers.
  Are set free by Christ. 8:34-36
  Are set free from five things. 8:32
Source. Truth. L. from five things. 8:32

**LIFE**
Abundant l. Discussed. 10:10
Christ and l.
  Jesus' authority over l. 5:1-47
  Light of l. Meaning. 8:12-13
Defined.
  As the energy of Christ Himself. 1:4; 14:6; 17:3
  As the energy of God Himself. 1:1, 4; 17:3
Described.
  As grace. Discussed. 1:16-17
Discussed. (See Meaning)
Essential—Duty. Losing vs. gaining l. 12:25
Kinds of.
  Abundant l. Fulness of. 1:16-17; 6:55; 10:10
Eternal l. Meaning. 17:2-3
Meaning. 1:4; 10:10; 17:2-3
Verses. List of. 17:2-3
Questions of. Basic questions of l. 1:38-39
Source—Energy of l.
  Christ. 1:4; 5:21, 26, 40-41; 7:37-39; 10:10; 11:25-27; 14:6; 17:2-3
  Verses. List of. 5:26
Door to. The only d. is Christ. 10:10
Eagerness of Jesus to give l. 1:38-39
Energized, quickened by Christ. 6:58
Fulness & grace of God. Discussed. 1:16-17
God. 1:4; 5:21, 26; 17:2-3
Receiving Christ. 6:52-58
Verses. List of. 5:26
Storms of l. (See **TRIALS**)
Christ delivers from. 6:16-21

**LIGHT**
Describes.
  Believers. 12:35-36
  Christ. 8:12; 9:5; 12:34-36, 44-46
Discussed. 1:5, 9; 8:12; 12:35-36
Essential—Duty.

To become children of l. 12:36
To walk in & to believe in l. 12:34-36
False l. Men claim to be l. to mankind. 1:9
Function.
  Tenfold. 1:9
  To shine in darkness. Meaning. 1:4-5
Man and l.
  Futile search for. 8:21-24
  L. of man—Christ. 1:9-13
  Man can become child of l. 12:36
  Man claims to be the l. to mankind. 1:9
  Man does not have l. in him. 11:10
  Misunderstanding of. 8:25-30
Of life. Meaning. 8:12-13
Power of. Cannot be overcome by darkness. 1:5
Response to.
  Hated. Reasons. 3:18-21
  Rejected. 1:10-11
Revelation of.
  L. of life. 8:1-9
  L. of world. Man's need. 8:12-20
Source. Jesus Christ came to give l. to men. 1:4-5, 9
Summary of scriptural teaching. 12:35-36
Verses. List of. 1:4-5; 3:18-20
What l. does. 1:5, 9; 8:12; 12:35-36

**LIVING WATER**
Discussed. 4:1-14
Verses. List of. 4:13-14

**LOST** (See **UNBELIEVER; UNSAVED—UNRIGHTEOUS**)
Described. As of their father, the devil. 8:44
Reason. Not because of predestination, but own will. 12:37-41

**LOVE**
Acts. Is active & forceful. Not dormant. Expresses itself. 3:16
Basis. Of unity. 13:33-35; 17:23
Essential—Duty.
  Belief based upon l. 20:2, 8
  Discussed. 21:15-17
  For ministry. Absolutely e. 21:15; 21:15-17
  Meaning. 14:15, 23; 15:9, 12; 21:15-17
  Results in obedience. 14:15; 14:23
  Sacrificial l. 12:3
  To abide in Christ's l. 14:21; 15:10
  To be the mark of disciples. 13:33-35
  To l. believers. 15:17; 21:15-17
  To l. believers with the l. of Christ. 13:33-35; 15:9; 15:12
  To l. Christ.
    Basic thing God wants. 20:7-10
    Meaning. 14:15; 14:23
  Kinds of. 21:15-17
  Meaning. 21:15-17
New commandment. Meaning. 13:33-35
Of Christ (See **CHRIST**, Love of)
  For believers. 13:33-35; 15:9, 12; 21:15-17
Of God (See **GOD**, Love of)
  For Christ. 3:35; 5:20; 15:9
  Verses. List of. 5:20
  For man. Discussed. 3:16-17

Proof of. Obedience. 14:15, 21, 23-24; 15:10
Results of. Witnessing. 13:34-35; 21:15-17
Why l. Reasons for l. Is the new commandment of Christ. 13:34-35; 15:12-17

**LOYALTY** (See **COMMITMENT; DEDICATION**)
Stumbling, faltering l. 13:36-38

**LUST**
Discussed. 8:44-45
Sin of. Committed by man & Satan. 8:44-45
Verses. List of. 6:26-27

**LYING**
Discussed. 8:44-45
Sin of. Committed by man & Satan. 8:44-45

**MAN**
Creation of. (See **CREATION**)
  Discussed. 4:23
  Purpose of c. 4:23-24
Deliverance. (See **DELIVERANCE**)
  Eyes opened. Stages of. 9:8-41
  From darkness. 9:1-7
  From sin. Is conditional. 8:31-32
Depravity. (See **DEPRAVITY; MAN**, Nature; Origin; State, Present)
  A dark, carnal nature. 8:1-11, 44
  Born illegitimately. 8:41-47
  Described. As children of devil. 8:38
  Enslaved. Commits sin continually. 8:34-36
  Father of. Devil. Discussed. 8:38, 41-47
  Follows the devil. 8:38, 41-47
  Has no light in him. 3:19; 8:12
Destiny.
  Foretold by Christ. 7:33-34
  In the hands of Jesus Christ. 5:24-25
  Return to earth, to dust. 8:23
  To face God two different times. 14:3
Duty.
  To be open to truth. 4:25
  To walk in light & to believe in l. 12:34-36
Errors of.
  Claims. To be of God. To know God. 8:41-47
  Fails to do the works of Abraham: believe 8:39-40
  Focused on the material, physical world. 6:30-31
  Follows the devil. 8:38, 44
  Grasps for help in stars, magic, sorcery. 5:2-4
  Hypocritical, unbelieving. 12:4-8
  Loves not God. 5:42
  Makes no room in his heart for the Word of Christ. 8:37
  Misunderstands.
    Jesus. Tragically. 8:25-30
    M. two things. 11:37
    Light. 8:25-30
  Offended by death of Christ. 6:59-65
  Professes God, but does not know God. 8:54-59
  Rejects Christ. 5:40-47

Sin. (See **SIN**)
   Guilty of serious **s**. 8:1-11
Six **e**. 5:40-47
Hunger—Thirst of. (See **SPIRITUAL HUNGER; SEEK—SEEKING**)
6:30-36
   Deliverance. 4:15
   Described. 4:15
   Physical vs. spiritual. 4:13
   Searching for human deliverer & utopia. 6:26-29; 8:21-24
Nature. (See **MAN**, Depravity; Origin; State of, Present)
   Called branches. Attached or unattached to the vine. 15:1-8
   Cannot penetrate spiritual dimension. 8:14-16, 23, 42-43; 11:7-10
   Flesh, soul, spirit. 4:23
   Has no light in him. 11:7-10
Needs of. (See **NEED—NEEDS**)
Origin.
   Of earth. 8:23-24
   Of Satan. 8:44
   Of the physical world & the physical dimension of being. 8:23-24
   Verses. List of. 8:23-24
Relationship to Christ.
   Fails to understand **C**. 8:25-30
   Needs provided by **C**. 6:1-15; 10:9; 10:10
   Offended by Christ; view His blood as repulsive. 6:59-71
   Reactions to the revelation of **C**. Four reasons. 12:1-11
   Reject claims of **C**. Six reasons. 5:40-47
   Seeks for an earthly deliverer & utopia. 6:26-29; 8:21-24
   Unattached; attached; fruitful, etc. Vine & branches. 15:1-8
Response to Christ. (See **JESUS CHRIST**, Responses to)
   Hates & persecutes. Through the ages. Discussed. 15:18-27
   Offended by **C**. Four things. 6:59-71
   Reject.
     Do not will to come to **C**. 5:40-41
     Reason. Christ is a threat to doing as one wishes. 7:32
Spiritually dead. (See **DEATH**)
   Can hear and live now. 5:24-26
   Condemned already. 3:18-21
   Dies in sin. 8:21-24
   Misunderstands Jesus—tragically. 8:25-30
   No life apart from Jesus. 15:1-8
   Searches for utopia—in futility. 8:21-24
State of. (See **MAN**, Depravity; Nature; Origin)
   Blinded. To whom Jesus really is. 8:25-30
   Condemned. 3:18-21
   Follows & is enslaved by the devil. 8:38; 8:41-47
   Half-sincere. 6:26-29
   Hypocritical, unbelieving. 12:4-8
   In state of, condition of darkness. 11:7-10
   In state of, condition of sin. 8:34-36
   No life apart from Jesus. 15:1-8

Perishing. 3:16-17
Searching. Futile **s**. For Messiah—utopia—heaven. 6:26-29; 8:21-24
Sinful. Dark **s**. and God's great forgiveness. 8:1-11
Word & witness is unacceptable & suspicious. 5:31
Will of. (See **FREE WILL; WILL**)
Witness to self. Is suspicious. Supporting **w**. is essential. 5:31

**MANIFESTATION**
Meaning. 14:21

**MARTHA**
And Jesus. A growth in faith. 11:17-27
Family of. 12:1-2

**MARY MAGDALENE**
First to discover empty tomb. 20:1-10
First to whom Jesus appears after resurrection. 20:11-18
Given special commission by Lord after resurrection. 20:17-18

**MARY, SISTER OF MARTHA**
And Jesus. The needs of man. 11:28-37
Anointed Jesus. Picture of supreme believer. 12:3

**MATERIALISM**
Answer to. What to labor for. 6:27-29
Problem with. Focused on by man. 6:30-31

**MATURITY** (See **SPIRITUAL GROWTH**)

**MEASURE**
Law of. Whatever **m**., shall receive back. 12:39-41

**MEDIATOR** (See **JESUS CHRIST**, Mediator)

**MEDITATE—MEDITATION** (See **DEVOTION**)
Duty. To **m**. in Word of God, letting it abide within. 5:38

**MEEKNESS** (See **HUMILITY**)

**MESSIAH—MESSIAHSHIP**
Acknowledged—Proclaimed.
   As God's appointed **M**. 3:27-28
   By Andrew. 1:35-42
   By John the Baptist. 1:19-27; 3:27-28
   By Nathanael. 1:46-49
   By Peter. 6:66-69
   By Philip. 1:43-45
Claimed. (See **JESUS CHRIST**, Claims; Deity)
   Some claim to be the light of men. 1:9
   Throughout His ministry. 4:25-30; 4:39-42
Demonstrated. In Triumphal Entry. 12:12-19
False concept—Misunderstood.
   Discussed. 12:12-19
   Earthly vs. spiritual Messiah. 13:36-38
   False vs. true **c**. 12:12-19
   Four misunderstandings. 12:20-36
   Jesus as a great man. 20:25-26
Hoped for. By Abraham. 8:56
Names—Titles. Son of David. 1:23
Proof. The resurrection. 16:28
Prophecies. (See **PROPHECY**, About Christ)

Search for. 8:56
   Discussed. 6:22-29
   Man's futile **s**. for **M**. or deliverer—utopia—heaven. 8:21-24
   Reasons. 6:14-15, 22-29
Subject of. Five pictures. 4:25-30

**MESSIAH, FALSE**
Danger of. Men choose over Christ. 5:43
Men receive. 5:43

**MIND**
Duty—Essential. To give undivided attention to one's task. 21:20-23

**MINISTERS** (See **BELIEVERS; DISCIPLES**)
Authority. To remit & retain sins. 20:23
Call—Called.
   Chosen by Christ. Purposes. 15:16
   Dignity of **c**. not affected by the sins of others. 13:19-20
   Must respond in humility. 1:20-22
   Sent into world to witness. 17:17-19
   To be the messenger of God. 1:19-27
   To obscure place. 7:1-2
Commission—Mission.
   Sent and send discussed. 20:21
   Sent as Christ was sent. 20:21
   Sent by God. To do the will & work of God. 4:31-35
   Sent from God. 1:6
   To minister, to serve. 20:21
   Urgency of. 9:4
Duty. (See **MINISTRY—MINISTERING**)
   Must not pretend, seek, assume. 1:20-22
   Not to push self forward, but to be humble. Jn 1:20-22
   To be a voice only. 1:23
   To be faithful in obscure places. 7:1-2
   To be washed & cleansed. 13:6-11
   To bear witness to Jesus' death & resurrection. 21:24
   To do the will & work of God. 4:31-35
   To exalt Christ and not self. 3:29-30
   To feed & shepherd. 21:15-17
   To follow Holy Spirit. 21:18
   To give undivided attention to one's own task. 21:20-23
   To know who Jesus is. 1:20
   To labor. Fields are ripe for harvest. 4:35
   To proclaim forgiveness & judgment. 20:23
   To reach out to help others. 11:31
   To serve humbly, esteeming others. 1:8; 1:27
   To work while it is day before night comes. 11:7-10
False. (See **TEACHERS, FALSE**)

**MINISTRY—MINISTERING** (See **BELIEVERS; DISCIPLES; MINISTERS**)
Demonstration of. Royal service. 13:1-17
Dignity of. Not affected by the sin of others. 13:19-20
Discussed. 13:4-5
Duty—Work.
   To be washed & cleansed. 13:6-11
   To feed & shepherd. 21:15-17
   To **m**. as Jesus **m**. 13:12-17
   To **m**. to needy. 11:31; 13:12-14
Equipped—Resources. Love. 21:15-17

**MINISTRY—MINISTERING** (*Continued*)

Motivation for. Three things. 13:1-2
Reasons for. 13:15-17
Subject of. Labor for God. 4:31-42
Urgency of. Time limited. 9:4

**MIRACLES**
Of Jesus. Only a few included in the gospels. 20:30-31
Purpose.
  Are signs to point toward Christ. 2:23
  To lead men to believe. 2:9-10; 2:23
  To prove Jesus is the Messiah, the Son of God. 20:30-31
Rejected. By unbelievers. 12:37-41

**MISSION—MISSIONS** (See **COMMISSION**)
Described. Being sent from God. 1:6
Purpose. What it is & is not. 1:7
Source. Must be sent from the heart of God. 1:6
Urgency of. Time limited. 9:4
World-wide **m**. Christ works to enlarge the fold, to reach out. 10:14-16

**MOCKERY** (See **JESUS CHRIST**, Response. Rejected)
Of Christ. By the half-brothers of His own family. 7:3-5

**MOSES**
Symbolized—Pictured. Death of Christ. Lifting up serpent in wilderness. 3:14-15

**MOTIVE**
Kinds of. Ulterior, corrupt **m**. 12:4-8

**MURDER**
Discussed. 8:48-59
Sin of. Committed by man & Satan. 8:44-45

**MURMURING**
Against Christ & His claims. 6:41-43

**NAME**
Changed. Peter's **n**. changed by Christ. 1:42

**NATHANAEL**
Discussed. 1:46-49
Led to the Lord. 1:46-49
Witnesses to Christ: the Son of God, the King of Israel. 1:46-49

**NATION** (See **GOVERNMENT**)

**NATURE**
Discussed. Good & evil in the world. 12:31
Judgment of. Reasons. Imperfect, corruptible. 12:31
Laws governing. Eight **l**. 12:39-41

**NAZARETH**
Discussed. 1:46
Hometown of Christ. Rejected Him. Broke His heart. 4:44

**NEEDS—NECESSITIES**
Of men—Of life.
  Described as hunger. Listed. 6:32
  Five great **n**. 11:28-37
  For Light of the world. 8:12
  Met—Provided. By God. Verses. List of. 6:10-13

  No **n**. that Jesus does not want to meet. 6:1-15; 10:9-10
  Severe, desperate **n**. of life. 4:46-47
  To prepare for the Lord. 1:23
Response to. Four **r**. 6:1-15
Social vs. spiritual **n**. 2:3-5

**NEEDY, THE**
Picture of. Described. Verses. Listed. 5:2-4

**NEW BIRTH**
A confrontation with Jesus Christ. 4:30
Discussed. 3:1-15
How to secure. Facing the truth of sin. 4:16-18
Result. Changes a person's life radically. 4:30
Source. Not of man, but of God. 1:12-13

**NEW CREATION**
Of the world God's plan for the ages. 4:22

**NEW MAN** (See **NEW BIRTH**)
Result. changes a person radically. 4:30
Source.
  A confrontation with Jesus Christ. 4:30
  Drawing power of the Holy Spirit. Verses. List of. 6:44-46

**NICODEMUS**
Buries Jesus. Fear conquered by Jesus' death. 19:39
Discussed. 3:1-2
Speaks up for Christ in the Sanhedrin. 7:45-50

**NOBLEMAN**
An official in a king's court. 4:46-47

**OBEY—OBEDIENCE**
Duty. Not an option if one is a believer. 14:15, 23; 15:14-15
  Verses. List of. 15:14-15
Meaning. Faith means o. 3:36; 4:50-53; 5:5-9; 9:6-7
  Verses. List of. 4:50
Proves.
  One's faith. 4:50
  Profession, love for Christ. 14:15, 21, 23-24
Source—Stirred by. Love. 14:15, 21, 23

**OBSTINATE—OBSTINACY** (See **HEART**, Hard)

**OFFEND—OFFENDING**
What **o**. men about Christ.
  Claims of Christ. 6:61
  Cross, blood of Christ. 6:61
  Four things o. 6:59-71
  Lordship of Christ. 6:62

**OMNIPOTENCE** (See **JESUS CHRIST**, Power)

**OMNISCIENCE** (See **JESUS CHRIST**, Knowledge)

**OPPORTUNITY**
Duty. To be grasped. Timing important. 2:3-5; 11:7-10

**OPPOSE—OPPOSITION**
To Christ. (See **JESUS CHRIST**, Opposed)
His reply to those who **o**. 7:32-36

Reasons. He is a threat to doing as one wishes. 7:32

**OPTIMISM**
Faith of. But questions. 6:8-9

**ORDAINED—ORDINATION**
Purpose. To bear fruit. Threefold. 15:16
Source. By Christ. 15:16

**ORIGIN**
Of Christ (See **JESUS CHRIST**, Nature & Origin)
Of man. (See **SIN**, Nature & Origin)
Of sin. (See **SIN**, Nature & Origin)

**OUTWARD APPEARANCE** (See **APPEARANCE, OUTWARD**)
Duty. To judge accurately, not by outward appearance. 7:24

**PALM BRANCHES**
Discussed. 12:13

**PARABLE**
Vine and branches. Jesus and people. 15:1-8

**PARDON** (See **FORGIVENESS**)

**PARENTS** (See **FAMILY**)

**PARTIALITY** (See **FAVORITISM; PREJUDICE**)

**PASSIONS** (See **LUST**)

**PASSOVER**
Atmosphere. 12:12
Attendance. Two to three million. 12:12

**PASTORS** (See **MINISTERS**)

**PATIENCE** (See **ENDURANCE; PERSEVERANCE**)
Duty—Essential. To wait upon God. 11:6
Reasons. God knows the exact time, the best time to act. 11:6

**PEACE**
Discussed. 14:27
Meaning. 14:27
Source. 14:27
  Resurrection. Brings triumphant **p**. 16:33

**PENALTY**
Of sin. Is Death. 8:21-22

**PENITENCE** (See **CONFESSION; FORGIVENESS; REPENTANCE**)

**PERFECT—PERFECTED—PERFECTION**
Meaning. 17:23

**PERISH—PERISHING**
Deliverance from. By death of Christ. 3:14-15
Meaning. 3:16

**PERSECUTION—PERSECUTORS**
Answer to mockery, ridicule, sarcasm, unbelief. Given by Jesus. 7:6-9
How to overcome in **p**. 16:4-6
  Answer given by Jesus. 7:6-9
Kinds—Types of.
  Hatred. 17:14-16
  Mockery. 7:6-9
Purpose. God uses for a greater witness. Verses. List of. 11:55-57

Reasons for. Discussed. 15:19-24; 17:14-16
Response to. 16:1
By Jesus. 11:54
Warning of. True believers shall suffer. 21:18-19
Who is going to **p**.
Religionists. Discussed. 16:1-6
World. Discussed. 15:18-27
Who is to be **p**. Believers. 4:44

## PERSEVERANCE—PERSISTENCE
(See **ENDURANCE; PATIENCE; STEDFASTNESS**)
Duty.
To **p**. in faith. Essential. 4:48-49
To **p**. in hope, for God's help. 4:46-47
Example of. Government official. Stages of faith. 4:46-54
Verses. List of. 8:31

## PESSIMISM
Discussed. 6:7
Of faith. Discussed. 6:7

## PETER
Character—Life.
Cuts off the ear of an officer. 18:10-11
Great confession of. Jesus is Messiah. 6:66-69
Love is questioned by Jesus. 21:15-17
Named changed by Christ. 1:42
Conversion—Call. Led to Lord. By brother Andrew. 1:41-42
Denial of Christ.
Caused by two things. 13:36-38
Foretold. Stumbling, faltering loyalty. 13:36-38
Three **d**. Peter & the Jews. 18:12-27

## PHARISEES (See **RELIGIONISTS**)
Error—Fault of.
Condemnatory, critical spirit. 8:3-6, 33, 39, 41, 48
Put tradition before men. 9:13-34
Stumbling blocks to others. 12:42-43
Vs. Jesus.
Argue over who Jesus is. 7:45-53; 8:13, 25
Seek to arrest Jesus. 7:32
Seek to kill Jesus. 8:40, 59; 11:53
Seek to trap Jesus. 8:3-9

## PHILIP THE APOSTLE
Conversion. Led to Lord by Christ. 1:43-45
Witness of Christ. Is the One prophesied. 1:43-45

## PHYSICAL DIMENSION (See **CORRUPTION**)
Is corruptible, wasting away. (See **CORRUPTION; MAN**, Nature)
Only dimension seen & known by man. 8:14, 15-16, 23, 42-43; 11:7-10
Vs. spiritual dimension. 8:14; 8:15-16; 8:23; 8:42-43; 11:7-10

## PHYSICAL FOOD
Vs. spiritual **f**. (See **SPIRITUAL FOOD**) 4:31-35

## PILATE
Discussed. 18:28
Superstitious. 19:8-11
Trial of Jesus. Indecisive compromise. 18:28-19:15

## PITY (See **COMPASSION**)

## PLEASURE (See **WORLDLY—WORLDLINESS**)

## POWER
Meaning. 2:23
Results. Led some to believe. 2:23

## PRAY—PRAYER—PRAYING
Answers—Answered.
Why Jesus a. prayer. 14:13-14
Described. Access into God's presence. 16:23-24
How to **p**.
In name of Jesus. Meaning. 14:13-14
The prayer of great purpose. 11:41-42
Of Jesus. (See **JESUS CHRIST**, Prayer Life)
Purpose. To bear fruit. 15:16
Results—Assurance.
Answers to. Why Jesus a. prayer. 14:13-14
Source.
Love of God. Do not have to beg God to hear. 16:25-27
Resurrection of Christ. 16:23-24
When. At meals. 6:11

## PREACHING
Described. As voice crying, "Prepare." 1:23
Duty. To exalt Christ & not self. 3:29-30

## PREDESTINATION
Described. As those whom God gives to Christ. 6:37, 39, 44-46
Determined by. Eight laws. 12:39-41
Discussed. 6:37, 39, 44-46
Purpose.
That Christ will have many brothers & sisters. 6:39
To give security to the believer. 6:37, 39
Who. The chosen people of God. 15:12-17

## PREEMINENCE (See **JESUS CHRIST**, Deity)

## PREEXISTENCE
Of Christ. (See **JESUS CHRIST**, Deity; Preexistence)
Meaning. 1:1-2

## PREJUDICE (See **BARRIERS; DISCRIMINATION; DIVISION**)
Broken down—Abolished. By witnessing. 4:1-42
Disregards two things. 1:46
Example of.
Disciples toward Samaritans. 4:27
Nathanael. 1:46
Overcome. By following Jesus' example. 4:27

## PRESSURE
Cause of. Deliverance from. 4:16-18

## PRESTIGE
Fearing the loss of. 11:47-48

## PRIDE
Results.
Seeking approval & honor of men. 5:44
Verses. List of. 5:44; 8:33

## PRIEST (See **HIGH PRIEST**)

## PROBLEMS
Caused by. Trials & storms of life. 6:17-19
Deliverance from. 14:1-3
Verses. List of. 6:17-19

## PROFESSION
Kinds. Three **p**. 6:66-71

## PROFESSION, FALSE—PROFESSION ONLY
Error—Misconception.
Claim to know God, but do not really know. 8:41, 54-59
Discussed. 2:23-24
Evidence of. Not continuing. 8:31
Described. As betrayal, apostasy, counterfeit. 13:18-19
Kinds. Materialistic **p**. 6:14-15
Some claim to be the light to men. 1:9

## PROMISE—PROMISES
Of answers to prayer. (See **PRAYER**, Answers)
Purpose. To glorify God. 14:13-14
Very reason Christ chose us. 15:16
Of deliverance from death. Believe & never die. 5:24-25; 11:25-27
Of salvation. Believe & never die. 11:25-27
To laborers. Will do great works & greater than Christ. 14:12

## PROPHECY
Curiosity in. Causes distraction from duty. 13:36-38
Facts about. Not evidence of salvation. 11:51
**P**. about Christ.
List of & their fulfillments. 1:45
List of **p**. on death & resurrection in Gospel of John. 20:20
Rejected—Unbelief in. Leads to rejection of Christ. 5:45-46

## PROPHET
Honor of. Without **h**. in own country. 4:44
View of. People thought **p**. was highest call. 9:16-17

## PROVIDENCE (See **GOD**)

## PROVISION, DIVINE
Source. God. Verses. List of. 6:10-13

## PUNISHMENT (See **JUDGMENT**)

## PURE—PURITY
Of heart. Seeking 3:22-26

## PURPOSE
Of man. Why God created **m**. 4:23-24

## QUESTIONS
About Christ.
Are illogical & inconsistent. 12:37-41
Cause. Unbelief. 7:20-24; 7:25-31

## QUICKEN—QUICKENING
Meaning. Seeing & understanding the gospel as never before. 6:44-46
Source. Holy Spirit. Words of Christ. 6:63-64

## RABBONI
Meaning. 20:17-18

**RACIAL SLUR** (See **PREJUDICE**)
Not worthy of comment, attention. 8:48-50

**REAL**
Jesus, the Real. 1:9

**REAP—REAPING** (See **WITNESSING**)

**REBELLION** (See **UNBELIEF**)

**RECEPTIVE—RECEPTIVITY** (See **JESUS CHRIST**, Response to)
Duty. To be r. to Christ. 4:45

**RECOMPENSE** (See **RETALIATION**; **REVENGE**)

**RECONCILIATION**
Results. Brings peace with God. 14:27

**REGENERATION** (See **BORN AGAIN**; **NEW BIRTH**)
Discussed. 3:1-15
Meaning. 3:1-15
Result. Changes a person's life radically. 4:30
Source. Creative power of Christ. 2:3-5; 2:6-8

**REJECTION**
Of Jesus Christ. By world. 1:10-11

**REJOICING**
Meaning. 14:28-29

**RELATIONSHIPS** (See **BROTHERHOOD**)

**RELIGION**
Need. To be straightened out. 1:23
Problem.
  Dead. Tries to meet world's needs. 5:10-12
  Formal, institutional r. Discussed. 1:23

**RELIGIONISTS**
Opposed Christ. (See **JESUS CHRIST**, Response to)
  Accused Christ. Of opposing religion. Reasons. 7:20-24
  Confused over Jesus. 6:52-53
  Considered Jesus a rabble-rouser. 7:32-36
  Controlled by God. 11:55
  Deliberate, willful opposition. 5:16
  Hunted Jesus down. 11:57
  Initiated Jesus' death. 18:28-19:15
  Murmured against claims. 6:41-43
  Persecuted Jesus. 5:16
  Plotted against Jesus. 12:19
  Plotted the death of Jesus. 5:16, 17-18; 7:1-2; 8:39-40, 54-59; 10:31-33, 39
  Plotted to kill Lazarus. 12:10
  Reasons o. Christ. 5:16
Problem with—Errors.
  Can fail & fall. 7:20-24
  Confused, perplexed over Christ. 6:52-53
  Know but fail to confess. 12:42-43
  Love praise of men more than p. of God. 12:42-43
  Misinterpreted the words of Christ. 6:52-53
  Relationship to believer. Bleak r. Persecution. 16:1-6
Who they were. 5:10, 15-16

**REMEMBER**
Duty. To r. what God has done for one. 5:13-14

**REMISSION OF SIN** (See **FORGIVENESS**)

**REPENT—REPENTANCE** (See **SALVATION**; Related Subjects)
Refusal to r. A last chance given Judas. 13:21-26

**RESOURCES**
Limited r. Attitudes toward. 6:8-9, 10-13

**RESPECT** (See **HONOR**)

**REST, SPIRITUAL**
How to secure. Facing & renouncing sin. 4:16-18

**RESTORATION—RESTORING** (See **CONFESSION**; **FORGIVENESS**; **REPENTANCE**; **SALVATION**)

**RESURRECTION**
Body of. Discussed. 21:1
Comes by.
  Being drawn by God. 6:44
  Faith in Christ. 6:39-40
  Partaking of Christ. 6:54
Discussed. 5:28-30; 11:25-27; 14:3
Effects of.
  Shall usher in a just judgment. 5:28-30
Of believers. Verses. List of. 5:28-30
Stages.
  Future—at the last day. 6:39-40, 44, 54, 58
  Of just and unjust. 5:28-30
  Past. Jesus r. Lazarus. Power over death. 11:43-44
Surety of.
  Discussed. 11:25-27
  Wherever & however many places they lie. 14:3

**RETALIATION** (See **REVENGE**; **VENGEANCE**)

**REVEALED—REVELATION** (See **JESUS CHRIST**, Revelation)
Meaning. 14:21
Of Christ.
  As Answer to man's great hunger. 6:22-29
  As Bread of Life. 6:1-71
  As Deliverer from fear. 6:16-21
  As Embodiment of God. 14:8-14
  As Great Minister & His legacy. 13:1-16:33
  As Living Water. 4:1-14
  As New Master. 3:22-36
  As Object of Faith. 4:43-54
  As Provision for human needs. 6:1-15
  As Resurrection & the Life. 11:1-12:11
  As Son of God. Various r. 2:1-3:21
  As Suffering Savior. 18:1-19:42
  As Supreme r. 14:6-7
  As Way, Truth, & Life. 14:6-7
  Verses. List of. 14:6
God's great love. 3:16-17
His Creative power to meet man's need. 2:1-11
His glory. 2:11
His knowledge of all men. 2:23-25
His Supremacy over God's House. 2:12-22

Reactions to. Four r. 12:1-11
Witness to the r. of Jesus. 1:1-51
Of God.
  By Christ. Not left in dark, groping. 14:6-7
  Gave more than words. Gave a life, Christ. 12:37-41
  Is Jesus Christ. Discussed. 14:6-7
  Not distant & far off. 14:9
  Unseen. Never seen by man, but by Christ alone. 1:18; 5:37-38
  Verses. List of. 5:37-38
Other r.
  Man's condemnation. 3:18-21
  New birth. 3:1-15
  Rejected. By unbelievers. 12:37-41

**REVENGE—REVENGEFUL** (See **VENGEANCE**)
Caused by. Being hurt by the sin of a loved one. 8:3-6

**REVERENCE** (See **HONOR**, Of God; **WORSHIP**)

**REWARDS**
Described.
  Beholding Jesus' glory. 17:24
  Being honored. 12:26
  Being in glory. Verses. List of. 17:24
  Being where Jesus is. 12:26; 17:24
  Identified as. Mansions. 14:1-3
  Discussed. Six significant r. for being faithful. 4:36-38
  How to secure—Basis of. Laboring, winning souls. 4:36-38

**RIGHTEOUSNESS**
Conviction of. 16:8-11

**RULERS** (See **JESUS CHRIST**, Opposed; Response to; **RELIGIONISTS**, Opposed Christ)
Oppose Christ. Want nothing to do with Him. 7:45-53

**SABBATH—SUNDAY**
Authority over. Christ has a. over. 5:1-16; 9:14 see vv.1-41

**SACRIFICE, ANIMAL**
Vs. Christ's sacrifice. 1:29-30

**SACRIFICE, PERSONAL—SPIRITUAL** (See **DEDICATION**; **COMMITMENT**)

**SACRIFICES—SACRIFICIAL SYSTEM**
Of O.T. Sacrifices were called the sacrificial "Bread of God." Type of Christ. 6:33

**SAFETY** (See **SECURITY**)

**SALVATION—SAVED** (See **NEW BIRTH**)
Abundant life. 10:10
Conditions—How one is saved.
  By belief & continuing. 8:31-32
  By belief, not works. 6:22-29
  By doing the works of Abraham. 8:39-40
  By hearing the voice of Christ. 10:4-5
  By the stirring of hearts. 8:31
  Faith vs. works. Offends man. 6:63-65
  God's part & man's part. 6:44-46
  How one partakes of. 6:41-51
  Must be drawn to God. 6:44-46
  Must face the fact of sin. 4:16-18
  Must follow Christ. 8:12-13

Must know God. 7:16-19
Cost of. (See **JESUS CHRIST**, Death; Sacrifice)
To God. 3:16
Deliverance.
   Answer to man's great hunger. 6:22-29
   From condemnation. 3:18-21
   From darkness; light of life. 8:12-13
   From death. 5:24-25; 8:48-59
   From fear. 6:20-21
   From perishing. 3:14-16
   From what. Trouble. Fivefold deliverance. 14:1-3
   God's eternal plan. 4:22
   Man's eyes opened. 9:1-7
   Provides for human need. 6:1-15
   Stages of spiritual sight. 9:8-41
Described.
   As bread of life. 6:30-36, 47-51
   As living water. 4:10-14
   As new birth. 3:1-15
Discussed. 1:12-13; 14:1-3
Duty. To remember s. & not forget experience. 5:13-14
Errors—Misconceptions.
   Believe s. by heritage, godly parents, forefathers. 8:33
   Man rebels against being disregarded as the source of s. 6:63-64
   Spectacular, dramatic experience delivers. 14:8
Plan of. God's eternal p. 4:22
Rejection of. Is illogical. 12:37-41
Results.
   Delivered from death & given life. 5:24-25
   Delivered from perishing & given eternal life. 3:14-16
   Discussed. 6:52-58
   Eyes are opened. 9:1-7
   Given assurance. 6:37-40
   Given joy. 1:45
   Will know the truth & be set free. 8:32
Source.
   Bread of life. 6:30-36
   Christ. 3:17
      Christ alone is the Way to God. 14:4-7
      Christ alone. World feels is narrow view of s. 16:1-6
      Christ, the Light of the world. 8:12-13
      Eagerness of Christ to save. 1:38-39
   Death of Christ. 3:14-15
   Door to. Only door into God's presence is Christ Himself. Verses. List of. 10:7-8; 10:9
   God.
      Men rebel against. 6:65
      God's love. 3:16-17
   Initiative comes from Christ. 1:43-44
   Mediator of. (See **JESUS CHRIST**, Mediator)
   Of spiritual satisfaction. 6:30-36
   Salvation is of the Jews. 4:22
Stages of. 9:8-41
Universal. Jesus came to give life to all men. 6:33
Who is saved.
   The person who believes. 3:16; 5:24-25
   Who receives. 6:59-71

**SAMARIA**
Discussed. 4:4

**SAMARITANS**
Discussed. 4:4

**SANCTIFICATION**
Meaning. 17:17
Of believers. How & why. 17:17-19

**SANHEDRIN**
Discussed. 11:47

**SARCASM**
Example of. Brothers of Jesus against Him. 7:3-5

**SATAN**
Defeated—Destroyed.
   Cast out by the cross. 12:31-33; 14:30-31
   Condemned, judged by the cross. 16:11
   Had nothing in Christ. 14:30-31
   Power broken by Christ. 12:31
Described.
   As father of man. 8:38
   As father of unbelievers. 8:41-47
Discussed. 8:38, 44-45
Existence—Nature of.
   Does not act against his n. 8:44
Names—Titles.
   Evil One. 17:15
   Prince of this world. 12:31; 14:30
   The father of man. 8:44 cp. vv.42-44
   The father of sin. 8:44 cp. vv.42-44
Power of. Broken, judged by the cross. 16:11
Work—Strategy of.
   Rules world. 12:31
   To possess evil men. 13:27-30

**SATISFACTION** (See **FULNESS, SPIRITUAL**)
Involves fifteen things. 6:55
Source. Jesus Christ. Verses. List of. 10:9
Verses. List of. 6:34-35, 55

**SAVIOR**
Meaning. Discussed. 4:42
Title.
   Of Christ. 4:42
   Of God. 4:42

**SCOURGE—SCOURGING**
Discussed. 19:1
Of cords. Meaning. 2:15

**SCRIBES** (See **PHARISEES; RELIGIONISTS**)
Problem with. Condemnatory, critical spirit. 8:3-6

**SCRIPTURES** (See **WORD OF GOD**)
How to study and understand. Discussed. 12:16
Interpretation of. Understood only by the Holy Spirit. 12:16
Prophecies of. (See **PROPHECY**)
   Christ. P. of Christ & their fulfillment. 1:45
Work of—Effect. To bear witness to Christ. 5:39

**SEAL**
Believers are to set their s. to Christ. 3:33
God set His s., witness to Christ. 6:27
Meaning. 3:33

**SECURITY**
Discussed. 6:37-40; 10:9; 10:27-29
Source.
   Being washed & cleansed permanently. 13:6-11
   God's keeping power. 17:11-12; 17:14-16
   The prayer of Jesus. 17:9-19
   Twofold. 14:30-31
Verses. List of. 6:39; 10:9

**SEE—SEEING** (See **SPIRITUAL SIGHT—UNDERSTANDING**)

**SEEK—SEEKING**
Christ s. men. Goes to any limit. 1:43-44
Extends invitation; takes the initiative. 1:38-39
Men **s.** Christ.
   Half-sincere. Traits of. 12:9
   Reason men seek **C.** 12:9
   Searches for utopia, earthly messiah. 6:26-29; 8:21-24
   Some Greeks **s.** Four misunderstandings. 12:20-36
Men **s.** God. Prepares heart for receiving Christ. 4:45

**SELF-CONFIDENCE** (See **SELF-SUFFICIENCY; SELF-RIGHTEOUSNESS**)

**SELF-EXISTENCE**
Meaning. Of Christ. (See **JESUS CHRIST**, Nature, Eternal) 1:1-2

**SELF-RIGHTEOUSNESS**
Attitude—Spirit of.
   Man's critical, **s. r.** spirit. 8:3-6
   Thinking one is good enough to be acceptable to God. 8:33
Verses. List of. 8:33

**SELF-SATISFACTION**
Attitude—Spirit of. Does not want situation to be disturbed. 11:38-40

**SELF-SEEKING**
Cause. Fearing loss of position, esteem, livelihood, friends, etc. 11:47-48; 12:10-11
Discussed. 11:47-48

**SELF-SUFFICIENCY**
Results. Leads to unbelief. 5:44
Verses. List of. 8:33

**SELFISHNESS**
Results.
   Causes man to reject & oppose Christ. 11:47-48
   Causes unbelief. 11:47-48
Verses. List of. 11:47-48

**SENSATIONALISM—SPECTACULAR** (See **SIGNS**)
Seeking.
   Crowds sought Jesus for s. 12:9
   Is requested. 14:8
   Reasons. 14:8
Weakness of—Problem with. Appeals to sensations of men. 2:23

**SENSUALITY** (See **LUST**)

**SENT**
Meaning. Commissioned from God. 1:6

**SERPENT**

Symbolized—Type of. Jesus' death. Lifted up by Moses. 3:14-15

**SERVE—SERVICE** (See **MINISTRY—MINISTERING**)
Conditions—Prerequisite for s. Being washed & cleansed. 13:6-11
How to **s**. Demonstration of royal s. Washing disciples' feet. 13:1-17
Subject of. Labor for God. 4:31-42

**SHAME** (See **GUILT**)

**SHEEP**
And their Shepherd. 10:1-6
Discussed. 10:4-5
Only one door into sheepfold. Christ Himself. 10:7-8
Traits—Characteristics of. Discussed. 10:4-5, 27-29

**SHEEPFOLD**
Discussed. 10:1

**SHEKINAH GLORY**
Discussed. 1:14

**SHEPHERD**
False. Discussed. 10:1, 11-13
False vs. true s. 10:1-6, 11-18
Title of. Christ, The Good Shepherd. Four descriptions. 10:11-21
Traits—Characteristics of. Discussed. 10:2-3, 14-16

**SIGNS**
Desire for.
  Dramatic. 14:8
  Spectacular. Reasons. 12:9; 14:8
Discussed. Four Greek words. 2:23
Purpose. To prove J. is the Messiah, the Son of God. 2:23; 10:37-38; 14:11; 20:30-31
Verses. List of. 12:9
Weakness—Problem with. Not necessary for faith. 4:46-54

**SIN**
Acts—Behavior of.
  Denial. Caused by two things. 13:36-38
  Immorality. At a party-like atmosphere. 8:3-6
And suffering. Does not cause suffering. 9:1-3
Common to. Devil & man. 8:44-45
Conviction of. Necessary for salvation. 4:16-18; 16:8-11
Deliverance from. (See **DELIVERANCE**; **SALVATION**)
  Conditions. Belief & continuing. 8:31-32
  Man's **s**. and God's great forgiveness. 8:1-11
  Must be faced & renounced. 4:16-18
  Necessary for salvation. 4:16-18; 16:8-11
  Power to proclaim forgiveness for. 20:23
Exposed. 2:24-25
  Known by God. 1:47-48; 2:24-25; 5:42; 13:19-20
  Verses. List of. 5:42; 13:19-20
Origin. Satan. 8:44
Results—Penalty.
  Death. 8:21-24

Dissatisfaction. 4:15
Emptiness. 4:15
Enslaves. 8:33-40
Known by God. Knows all about s. of men. 4:16-18
Proves depravity. 8:34-36, 41-47
Secret **s**. (See **SIN**, Exposed)
Work of. Darkness. 8:3-6

**SLANDER** (See **JESUS CHRIST**, Accusations Against)

**SLEEP**
Symbol—Type. Of death. Meaning. 11:13

**SOCIAL CONCERNS**
Of mankind. Vs. spiritual **c**. 2:3-5

**SOCIAL LIFE**
Duty. To fellowship & be sociable. 2:1-2

**SON OF MAN** (See **JESUS CHRIST**, Claims, Son of Man)
Discussed. 1:51

**SORCERY** (See **SUPERSTITION**)
Error of.
  Men fear and respect supernatural forces other than God. 19:8-11
  Men seek destiny in superstition. 5:2-4
Verses. List of. 19:8-11

**SORROW** (See **GRIEF**)
Danger of. Often becomes self-centered; wallowing around in **s**. 16:5-6

**SOUL—SOULS**
And spirit. Meaning. 4:23; 4:23-24
Fact. **S**. are ripe for harvest. 4:35

**SOUL-WINNING** (See **WITNESSING**)

**SOVEREIGNTY** (See **GOD**; **JESUS CHRIST**)

**SOWING** (See **WITNESSING**)
Law of. Whatever s. shall reap. 12:39-41

**SPECTACULAR** (See **SENSATIONALISM**)

**SPIRIT**
Essential—Duty. Must worship God in s. 4:23-24
God is s. 4:23-24
Meaning. 4:23-24
Of man. Meaning. 4:23-24

**SPIRITUAL BLINDNESS**
Delivered by Christ. 9:1-7

**SPIRITUAL CONCERN**
Vs. social concern. 2:3-5

**SPIRITUAL FOOD** (See **SPIRITUAL SATISFACTION**)
Assured—Promised. To believer. 6:37
Discussed. 6:1-71
Results of partaking, eating. Discussed. 6:52-58
  Does at least four things. 6:34-35
  Gives life. Various ways. 6:33
Source.
  Believing on Christ. 6:34-35
  How one secures spiritual f. 6:41-51
Verses. List of. 6:34-35, 55
Vs. physical food. 4:31-35

**SPIRITUAL GROWTH—MATURITY**
Concern.
  Must be spiritual not physical. 4:31-35
  Must do will & work of God. 4:31-35
Source—How one **g**.
  Feasting on God day by day. 6:54
  Of spiritual satisfaction. 6:30-36
  Steps to satisfaction. 6:30-36

**SPIRITUAL HUNGER** (See **HUNGER SPIRITUAL**; **SPIRITUAL FOOD**)

**SPIRITUAL REBIRTH** (See **NEW BIRTH**; **NEW CREATION**; **NEW MAN**)

**SPIRITUAL SATISFACTION**
Assured—Promised. To believer. 6:37
Source.
  Christ, the living water. 4:13; 7:37-39
  How one secures spiritual s. 6:41-51
  Steps to satisfaction. 6:30-36

**SPIRITUAL SIGHT—SPIRITUAL UNDERSTANDING** (See **UNDERSTANDING**)
Focus is Christ & C. alone. 9:1-41
Meaning. 20:20
Promised. To those who abide in Christ. 1:38-39
Stages of. 9:8-41

**SPIRITUAL THIRST** (See **HUNGER & THIRST**; **SPIRITUAL FOOD**)

**SPIRITUAL WORLD—DIMENSION** (See **NEW BIRTH**)
Origin. Of Christ. Vs. man's origin. 8:42-43
Reality—Truth of. Unknown to man. Must be revealed. 3:13, 31; 8:14, 15-16, 19, 23, 42-43; 11:7-10
Vs. physical world, dimension. 8:14; 8:15-16; 8:23

**STARS** (See **SORCERY**; **SUPERSTITION**)
Men seek destiny in. 5:2-4

**STEWARDSHIP** (See **GIVE—GIVING**)

**STORM**
Calming of. Deliverance from fear. 6:16-21

**STRIFE** (See **DIVISION**)

**STUDY** (See **DEVOTION**; **MEDITATION**; **WORD** OF **GOD**)

**SUBSTITUTION**
Death of Christ. (See **JESUS CHRIST**, Death)

**SUFFERING**
Cause. Is not because of sin. 9:1-3; 11:4
Purpose.
  Discussed. 9:1-3; 11:4
  God's glory. 11:4
S. and sin. Discussed. 9:1-3

**SUPERSTITION** (See **SORCERY**)
Astrological charts, fortune telling. 19:8-11
Error of.
  Men fear & respect forces other than God. 19:8-11
  Men seek destiny in forces other than God. 5:2-4

**SUPPLY, DIVINE**
Source. God. Verses. List of. 6:10-13

**SURRENDER**
Absolute **s.** Arrest of Jesus. 18:1-11
Essential. Five e. 18:1-11

**SYMPATHY** (See **CARE**; **COMPASSION**; **LOVE**)

**TABERNACLES, FEAST OF** (See **FEASTS**)
7:37-39

**TEACHERS, FALSE**
Behavior—Danger of.
  Leads people to reject Christ. 11:49-53
  Leads sheep to destruction, away from life. 10:10
  Men receive own Christ. 5:43
Discussed. 10:11-13
Motive. Job, money, position, self. 10:11-13; 11:47-48

**TEMPLE**
Care—Treatment.
  Cleansed by Christ. 2:12-22
Desecrated. Ways d. 2:14
Discussed. 2:14
Nature—Described as.
  God's house. 2:15-17
  Holy Spirit. Is body of Christ & believer. 2:18-21
  Jesus' body. Becomes **t.** of men. 2:18-21
New **t.** Jesus' power to erect. 2:18-21

**TESTIMONY** (See **WITNESSING**)

**THANKFUL—THANKFULNESS—THANKSGIVING**
Duty. To give t. to God for His blessings. 5:13-14

**THIRST, SPIRITUAL**
Source of satisfaction.
  Discussed. 4:10, 13-14, 37-39
  Jesus Christ. 4:10, 13-14; 7:37-39
  Satisfied by Jesus. 7:37-39
Vs. physical. 4:13; 7:37-39

**THOMAS THE APOSTLE**
Confrontation with Christ. Great conviction & confession. 20:24-29
Questions where Jesus is going. 14:4-7

**THOUGHTS**
Evil t.
  Creates false gods. 8:54-59
  Prevented. By guarding self around opposite sex. 4:27

**TIME—TIMING** (See **OPPORTUNITY**)
Duty.
  To grasp opportunity while can. 2:3-5; 11:7-10
  To point out world's sin. 7:6-9
Facts. God knows exact, best time to act. 11:6

**TONGUE**
Duty. To be controlled. Example of disciples. 4:27

**TRANSGRESSION** (See **SIN**)

**TRIALS** (See **LIFE**, Storms of; **PROBLEMS**)
Discussed. 6:16-21
Results. Fear. 16:17-19
Verses. List of. 6:17-19

**TRINITY**
Nature. Perfect unity in Godhead. 16:14-15

**TRIUMPHAL ENTRY**
Of Christ. Proclaimed as King & Messiah. 12:12-19

**TROUBLE**
Deliverance from. 14:1-3

**TRUST** (See **BELIEVE**; **FAITH**)

**TRUTH**
Discussed. 8:32
Duty. To be open to t. 4:25
Meaning.
  Is Christ. 14:6
  Is Word of God. 8:32; 17:17-19
  True vs. false, real vs. unreal. 1:9
Power of. Liberates, sets man free. 8:32

**UNBELIEF**
Against Lord's delay. Answer to. Is coming. 7:6-9
And opposition. Of religious leaders. 11:47-57
Answer to—Deliverance from. Overcome by evidence. 20:26-29
Caused by—Reason for.
  False concepts of Jesus. 20:26
  Is not predestinated, determined by God. 12:39-41
  Loving darkness of sin. 3:18-20
  Offended by Christ. O. by four things. 6:59-71
  Rejected Lordship of Christ. 6:62
  Sixfold. 5:40-47
Discussed. 11:47-57; 12:37-41
Examples of.
  Brothers of Christ. Mock Him. 7:1-9
Faults—Problems with.
  Question Jesus' origin. Claims He is mere man. 7:20-24; 7:25-31
  Questions are illogical & inconsistent. 12:37-41
Results of.
  Five **r.** 12:39-41
  God overrules & uses for a greater witness. 11:55-57
  Guilt; frustration; disappointment. 20:24-25
  Launches eight laws of judgment into motion. 12:39-41
  What it does. 12:37-41
  What it reveals. 12:37-41
Sin. Great **s.** of. 3:18-20
Verses. List of. 5:45-46
Warning—Danger of.
  Condemned. 3:18-21
  Response of Jesus to u. Withdraws from a person. 11:47-57

**UNBELIEVER—UNBELIEVERS** (See **LOST**; **UNSAVED—UNRIGHTEOUS**)
Condemned.
  Already. Meaning. 3:18
  Picture of. 8:1-11
Destiny. Fate foretold by Christ. 7:33-34
Duty. To be open to truth. 4:25
Judgment of. 12:47-50
Life—Walk—Behavior. Can oppose, are allowed to oppose Christ. 7:33-34
Who u. are. Followers of Satan. 8:44

**UNFAITHFULNESS** (See **FAITHFULNESS**; **UNBELIEF**)

**UNITY** (See **BROTHERHOOD**; **DIVISION**)
Basis.
  A binding force. 17:11
  Christ within. 17:23
  God Himself. 17:11, 15, 17, 24
  Christ & His prayer. 17:11-12
Contrasted with the division of the world. 17:11
Discussed. 17:11, 21-22, 23
Meaning. To be one. 17:11, 20-23
Nature of.
  Threefold **n.** 17:11
  To be love. 17:23
Purpose for.
  Discussed. 17:21-22
  One body, not two. 10:14-16
Source—How to achieve.
  The great prayer of Jesus. 17:11, 20-23

**UTOPIA**
Described. As four things. 8:21
Seeking—Searching for. Man's futile search for u.—an earthly deliverer & heaven. 8:21-24
Source. Found in Christ alone. 10:7-10

**VENGEANCE** (See **RETALIATION**; **REVENGE**)
Caused by. Being hurt by the sin of a loved one. 8:3-6

**VINDICTIVE** (See **VENGEANCE**)

**VINE**
Symbol—Type. Of Jesus Christ. Relationship of Jesus to the people of the world. 15:1-8

**VINE & BRANCHES**
Parable. Relationship of Jesus to the people of the world. 15:1-8

**VISION**
Need for. To see fields of souls ready for harvest. 4:35

**VOICE**
Of Christ. Known by believers. 20:14-16

**WAITING UPON GOD**
Duty—Essential. In great crises. 11:5

**WALKING ON THE WATER**
By Jesus. 6:19-21

**WANT** (See **NEEDS—NECESSITIES**)

**WASHED—WASHING**
Discussed. 13:6-11
Spiritual w. Essential before service. 13:6-11

**WATER**
Living w.
  Discussed. 4:1-14
  Is Christ or the Holy Spirit. Discussed. 4:1-14; 7:37-39
  Verses. List of. 4:13-14
Source. Of new birth. Meaning. 3:5
Symbol—Type.
  Of Christ. 4:1-14; 7:37-39
  Of Holy Spirit. 7:37-39
Turned into wine. 2:1-11
What w. does. 7:37

## WAY, THE
Identified. As Jesus Christ. Verses. List of. 14:6

## WEAKNESS (See POWER)

## WEARY
Cause of. Deliverance from. 4:16-18
Verses. List of. 5:2-4

## WEDDING
Ceremony.
  Honored by Christ. 2:1-2
  Jewish w. Discussed. 2:1-2

## WILL (See FREE WILL)
Of Christ.
  Distinct, separate from God. 6:38
  Supreme subjection to God. 10:11; 10:17-18; 12:27-30; 14:30-31; 15:9; 16:11
Of man. (See PREDESTINATION)
  Deliberately w. to reject Christ. Reason. 5:40-41; 5:42
  Vs. predestination. Discussed. 12:39-41

## WITNESS—WITNESSING (See JESUS CHRIST, Witness to; COMMISSION; MISSION)
Challenge—Need.
  How silence fails. 12:42-43
  Impossible not to w. if truly saved. 15:26-27
  To see fields of souls ripe for harvest. 4:35
Commissioned—Commanded.
  Great C. 20:19-23
  To go as Jesus went. 20:21
  To w. to death & resurrection of Christ. 21:24
Dangers—Problems confronting w.
  How silence fails. 12:42-43
  Of a man to self. Is suspicious. 5:31
  Reveling in fellowship—not w. 20:17-18
Duty.
  To w. after conversion. 4:28-29
  To w. to home & family. 4:53-54
  To w. to neighbors & city. 4:28-29
  To w. to one's brother. 1:35-42
  To w. to one's close friend. 1:43-45
  To w. to the world. 17:17-19
How to go—Method. Proclaiming Jesus to be Messiah. 4:31-42
Purpose. Called, chosen to w. 15:16
Results.
  Strong belief seals the fact that God is true. 3:33
  To be greatly rewarded. 4:36-38
Who w.—Bears testimony. Five w. to the deity of Christ. 5:31-39

## WOMAN CAUGHT IN ADULTERY
Man's dark sinfulness & God's great forgiveness. 8:1-11

## WORD, CHRIST AS THE
Discussed. 1:1-5
Made flesh. The Incarnation. 1:14

## WORD OF GOD
Described as.
  Spirit & life. 6:63
  The truth. 17:17
  The words of Christ. 14:24
  The words of God. 14:24
Duty.
  Must allow w. to abide within. 5:38
  Must depend upon Holy Spirit to understand. Verses. List of. 12:16
  Must hear to be saved. 10:4-5
Gives a knowledge of Christ. 20:14-16
Meaning. Is truth. 17:17-19
Nature of. Truth. 17:17
Rejected—Unbelief in.
  Leads to u. in Christ. 5:45-46; 5:47; 8:37
  Seek for symbolic, mystical meaning. Verses. List of. 18:19-24
  Verses. List of. 5:45-46; 8:37
Response to.
  Man makes no room in his heart for. 8:37
  Who hears. 8:47
What the w. does.
  Cleanses. 15:3
  Is assurance & security to believer. 6:37
  Verses. List of. 10:4-5
  Sanctifies. 17:17

## WORKS
Duty.
  To do good works. 3:21
  To do greater w. than Jesus. 14:12
Need. To do the w. of God—believe on Christ. 6:29
Purpose. To lead men to believe. 2:9-11, 23
Results.
  Led some to believe. Were signs. 2:23-25
  Proves that one follows God. 3:21
Vs. faith.
  Discussed. 6:28-29
  Faith apart from w. 4:50
  Obedience and love tied together. 14:23

## WORLD
Blessed. By God. Ways b. 1:9; 1:10-11
Created—Creation. Blessed by God. How. 1:10-11
Deliverance from.
  By Holy Spirit. Convicts of sin. 16:8-11
  Victory over. 15:18-27
Described. As home of Christ. 1:10:11
History. (See HISTORY)
  God's plan for the ages. 4:22
Meaning. 15:18
Nature of.
  Corrupt. (See CORRUPTION) 12:31
  Ruled over by Satan. 12:31
  Relationship to believers. Persecutes & hates. 15:18-27; 17:14-16
Rejection. Of Christ. Difficult to understand. 1:10-11
State of—Problems with.
  Corruptible, passes away. 6:26-27
  Divisiveness. 17:11
  Focused on materialism. 6:30-31
  Guilty before God. Without excuse. 15:25
  Ignorant of God. 15:19-24
  Love of. Men fear losing w. more than God. 19:13-15
  Misunderstanding. Origin & state. 12:31-33
Vs. Christ.
  Denial of C. 18:19-24
  Judged. By cross of Christ. Discussed. 12:31-33
  Rejection of Christ. Difficult to understand. 1:10-11
  Was prepared by God for C. coming. 1:23
Vs. spiritual w. (See SPIRITUAL WORLD)

## WORLDLY—WORLDLINESS (See WORLD)
Deliverance from.
  By Holy Spirit. Convicts of sin. 16:8-11
  Time for sin to be pointed out. 7:6-9
Problem of.
  Does not satisfy or feed the heart. 6:26-27
  Opposes Christ. Reason. A threat to desires. 7:32

## WORSHIP
Discussed. 4:19-24
Duty.
  To seek God. Prepares heart for receiving Christ. 4:45
  To w. God after He has blessed. 5:13-14
  To w. in spirit & truth. 4:23-24
Evaluated by God. God knows man's heart. 1:46-49
How to w. Through Christ alone. 4:22
Nature. Is of the Jews. 4:22
Of Jesus Christ. To be a day of universal worship. 7:6-9

## WRATH
Meaning. 3:36

# LEADERSHIP MINISTRIES WORLDWIDE

Leadership Ministries Worldwide (LMW) exists to equip ministers, teachers, and lay workers in their understanding, preaching, and teaching of God's Word by publishing and distributing worldwide *The Preacher's Outline & Sermon Bible®* and related Outline Bible Resources; to reach & disciple men, women, boys, and girls for Jesus Christ.

# OUTLINE BIBLE RESOURCES

The **Outline Bible Resources** have been given to LMW for printing and distribution worldwide at/below cost, by those who remain anonymous. Our daily prayer is that each volume will lead thousands, millions, yes even billions, into a better understanding of the Holy Scriptures and a fuller knowledge of Jesus Christ the Incarnate Word, of whom the Scriptures so faithfully testify.

This material, like similar works, has come from imperfect man and is thus susceptible to human error. We are nevertheless grateful to God for both calling us and empowering us through His Holy Spirit to undertake this task. Because of His goodness and grace, *The Preacher's Outline & Sermon Bible®* New Testament and the Old Testament volumes are complete and are now being revised and expanded in the **everyWORD®** commentary series.

**In addition**, *The Minister's Personal Handbook, The Believer's Personal Handbook, The Business Leader's Personal Handbook* and other helpful **Outline Bible Resources** are available in printed form as well as on various digital platforms.

**Our Mission** is to make the Bible so understandable—its truth so clear and plain—that men and women everywhere, whether teacher or student, preacher or hearer, can grasp its message, receive Jesus Christ as Savior, and become fully-equipped disciples of Jesus Christ. It is our goal that every leader around the world, both clergy and lay, will be able to understand God's Holy Word and present God's message with more clarity, authority, and understanding—all beyond his or her own power.

God has given the strength and stamina to bring us this far. Our confidence is that as we keep our eyes on Him and remain grounded in the undeniable truths of the Word, we will continue to produce other helpful **Outline Bible Resources** for God's dear servants to use in their Bible study and discipleship.

We offer this material first to Him in whose name we labor and serve and for whose glory it has been produced and, second, to everyone everywhere who studies, preaches and teaches the Word.

**LMW (Leadership Ministries Worldwide)** publishes the world's leading outline commentary Bible series, *The Preacher's Outline & Sermon Bible®*. Our mission is to provide pastors in the global church with this and other gospel-centered resources:

*The Preacher's Outline & Sermon Bible®* - a Bible outline commentary series (44 volumes in KJV, 40 in NIV).

**The LMW app -** our Bible outline commentary digital app

**everyWORD®** - our Bible outline commentary series in ESV (call for availability)

**Handbook Series**
What the Bible Says to the Believer – The Believer's Personal Handbook
What the Bible Says to the Minister – The Minister's Personal Handbook
What the Bible Says to the Business Leader – The Business Leader's Personal Handbook
What the Bible Says about the Tabernacle
What the Bible Says about the Ten Commandments

*The Teacher's Outline & Study Bible™* - various New Testament books

Practical Illustrations
Practical Word Studies in the New Testament
Old Testament Prophets Supplement

**Study Booklets:**
Faith
Prayer
The Passion of Jesus
Wisdom

All books are available at **lmw.org**, on **amazon.com**, and at your local bookstore. *The Preacher's Outline & Sermon Bible®* is also available for sale digitally from Wordsearch, Logos, Olive Tree, Accordance and others.

Proceeds from sales, along with donations from donor partners, go to underwrite our translation and distribution projects. These projects equip pastors and leaders in the global church who have limited access to the books, resources, and training they need to prepare them to preach the Word of God clearly, plainly, and confidently.

Visit LMW's website at **lmw.org** to learn more about our mission and how you can partner with us:

**PRAY:** Please pray for the spread of the gospel and our role in it. Go to **lmw.org/stories** to join our prayer network.

**CONNECT:** LMW partners with other like-minded ministries around the world. Do you know someone who might like to connect with us? Let us know at: **info@lmw.org**

**GIVE:** The work of LMW is sustained by faithful giving. Impact the world with God's Word at **lmw.org/give.**

LMW is a 501(c)(3) ministry founded in 1992 to share God's Word, clearly explained, with pastors, bible students and Christian leaders worldwide.

lmw.org
info@lmw.org

1928 Central Ave.
Chattanooga, TN 37408

1-(800) 987-8790
(423) 855-2181

www.ingramcontent.com/pod-product-compliance
Lightning Source LLC
Chambersburg PA
CBHW080750300426
44114CB00020B/2689